Fodor's 2

ESSENTIAL
ITALY

Welcome to Italy

Italy is the kind of destination you return to over and over again. It boasts awe-inspiring art and architecture and stunning historical ruins—as well as some of the world's best food and wine. Also beckoning are sun-kissed olive groves and vineyards, and the beautiful sparkling waters of the Mediterranean Sea. As you plan your travels to Italy, please confirm that places are still open and let us know when we need to make updates by writing to us at corrections@fodors.com.

TOP REASONS TO GO

★ **Food:** Italy is a pasta lover's paradise; but don't forget the pizza and the gelato.

★ **Romance:** Whether you're strolling atmospheric Venice or sipping wine, Italy enchants.

★ **History:** The ruins of ancient Pompeii and the Leaning Tower of Pisa breathe antiquity.

★ **Art:** The big hitters—Botticelli, Michelangelo, Raphael, Caravaggio, and more.

★ **Shopping:** Few things say quality or style like "made in Italy."

★ **Stunning landscapes:** Tuscany, the Amalfi Coast, the Cinque Terre, to name just a few.

Contents

Fodor's Features

Chapter 1

EXPERIENCE ITALY

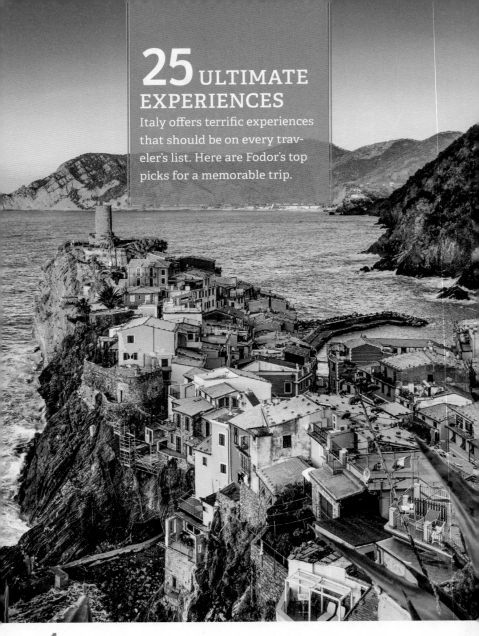

25 ULTIMATE EXPERIENCES

Italy offers terrific experiences that should be on every traveler's list. Here are Fodor's top picks for a memorable trip.

1 Hike the Cinque Terre

Walk the scenic footpaths that connect the five former fishing villages that make up the Cinque Terre; each one appears to hang off the cliffs, allowing for absolutely stunning views of the vineyards above and blue waters below. *(Ch. 10)*

2 People-Watch in Venice

Venice's Piazza San Marco (St. Mark's Square), flanked by the gorgeous Basilica di San Marco, is certainly one of the world's loveliest squares for people-watching. *(Ch. 5)*

3 Shop in Milan

In Italy's fashion capital of Milan, you'll find the highest of high-end designers in the Quadrilatero della Moda district, north of the Duomo. *(Ch. 8)*

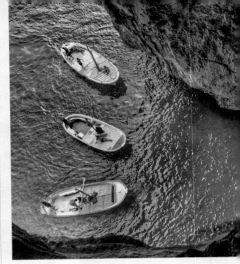

4 See Assisi's Frescoes

The peaceful medieval town of Assisi is home to enormous Basilica di San Francesco, which includes 28 frescoes showing the life of St. Francis. *(Ch. 14)*

5 Sail Away to Capri

This fabled island off the coast of Naples has long stood for glitz and glamour. It's a lovely place to escape to. *(Ch. 15)*

6 Ponder *The Last Supper*

Restoration work has returned *The Last Supper* to its original glory, so the painting is amazingly clear and luminous. *(Ch. 8)*

7 Roam a Medieval City

Perhaps Italy's best-preserved medieval city, Siena's narrow streets are fun to explore. The Piazza del Campo is one of the most beautiful squares in the country. *(Ch. 13)*

8 Discover Ravello

Wander the Amalfi Coast's refined mountaintop village and discover lush, hidden gardens, medieval fountains, and sweeping Mediterranean views. *(Ch. 15)*

9 Rent a Villa in Tuscany

One of the supreme pleasures of a visit to the countryside of Tuscany is the chance to stay in a villa—preferably one with a swimming pool and vineyard views. *(Ch. 13)*

10 Admire the Architecture

The city of Lecce is a jewel of Baroque architecture, but that is by no means its only style. Stand in Piazza Sant'Oronzo to best see and appreciate the blend. *(Ch. 16)*

11 Marvel at Mosaics

Some of the greatest Byzantine mosaics can be found in the unassuming city of Ravenna. You can view the most elaborate ones in the 5th-century Mausoleo di Galla Placidia. *(Ch. 11)*

12 Go Wine Tasting

The Barolo region produces excellent wine and is filled with hill towns and vistas. Make an appointment for a tour and tasting at one of the many wineries. *(Ch. 9)*

13 Explore Lava Fields

The largest and highest volcano in Europe, Sicily's Mount Etna, has moonlike dunes that you can walk across or view from the comfort of a cable car (the Funivia dell'Etna). *(Ch. 17)*

14 Enjoy Magical Views

Nowhere inspires as many oohs and aahs as the magnificent town of Positano, with its pastel-color houses seemingly spilling off the mountainside. *(Ch. 15)*

15 See Great Art

Florence's Galleria degli Uffizi contains the collection of art from the Medicis, including Botticelli's *Birth of Venus*, Michelangelo's *Doni Tondo*, and Caravaggio's *Bacchus*. (Ch. 12)

16 Relax by the Sea

The lovely village of Portofino hugs the coast of the Italian Riviera, with the Santa Margherita cliffs on one side and the Ligurian Sea on the other. (Ch. 10)

17 Feel Romantic

Set on the shores of beautiful Lake Como, Bellagio is often considered one of the loveliest towns in Italy. Its steep streets, lined with cobblestones, are supremely romantic. (Ch. 8)

18 Visit a Volcanic Island

Just a ferry away from Sicily's northeast coast sit the Aeolian Islands, seven volcanic islands offering dramatic scenery and wonderful snorkeling and scuba diving. (Ch. 17)

19 Hit the Slopes

The gorgeous craggy peaks of the Dolomites make the perfect place for an unforgettable ski holiday in the winter or a rejuvenating hike in the spring and summer. *(Ch. 7)*

20 Toss a Coin in Trevi Fountain

The can't-miss Trevi Fountain in Rome is a Baroque fantasy of sea beasts, seashells, and mermaids in front of a triumphal arch. *(Ch. 3)*

21 Step Back in Time

The best-preserved excavated site in the world, the commercial center of Pompeii was frozen in time when Vesuvius erupted in AD 79. *(Ch. 15)*

22 Explore a Hill Town

Wander the narrow winding streets of the walled city of San Gimignano, which is filled with 14 soaring medieval towers (originally there were more than 70). *(Ch. 13)*

23 Enjoy the Coastline

In Italy's southernmost region of Puglia, around the heel of the boot, is a wonderfully dramatic coastline, with sandstone cliffs crashing into the ocean. *(Ch. 16)*

24 Lounge on a Beach

Sardinia is justly famed for its white-sand beaches. Spend the day soaking up the sun on these beautiful strands. *(Ch. 18)*

25 Stand in Awe

Dominating Florence's skyline, the magnificent Duomo is an architectural marvel that took almost 600 years to complete. *(Ch. 12)*

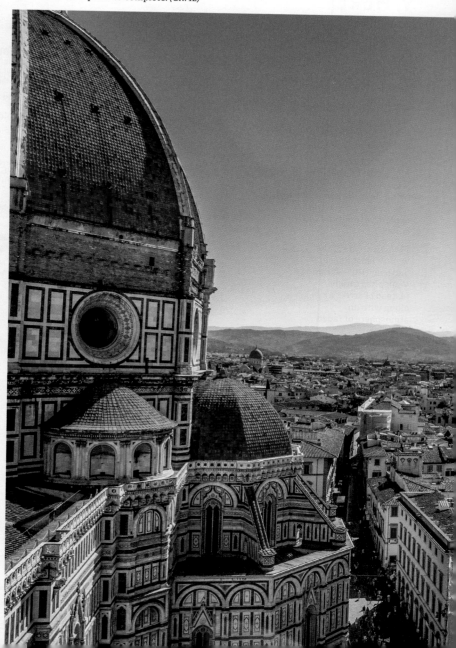

WHAT'S WHERE

1 **Rome.** Italy's capital is one of the greatest cities in Europe. It's a busy, modern metropolis where you'll encounter powerful evocations of its storied and spectacular past, from the Colosseum to St. Peter's.

2 **Side Trips from Rome.** The Eternal City is surrounded by intriguing towns and villages where you can explore without the crowds.

3 **Venice.** One of the world's most unusual—and beautiful—cities, Venice has canals instead of streets, along with an atmosphere of faded splendor.

4 **The Veneto and Friuli–Venezia Giulia.** The green plains stretching west of Venice hold three of northern Italy's most artistically significant midsize cities: Padua, Vicenza, and Verona. Farther north and east, Alpine foothills are dotted with welcoming villages and some of Italy's finest vineyards.

5 **The Dolomites.** Along Italy's northeast border, the Dolomites are the country's finest mountain playground,

Elevation	
15,577	4,748
10,825	3,300
9,840	3,000
8,860	2,700
7,875	2,400
6,900	2,100
5,900	1,800
4,920	1,500
3,940	1,200
2,920	900
1,970	600
980	300
490	150
250	75
100	30
feet	meters

with gorgeous cliffs, curiously shaped peaks, lush meadows, and crystalline lakes.

6 Milan, Lombardy, and the Lakes. The lakes of Lombardy have been attracting vacationers since the days of ancient Rome. At the center of Lombardy is Milan, Italy's second-largest city and its business capital. It's also the hub of Italian fashion and design.

7 Piedmont and the Valle d'Aosta. Here you'll find great Alpine peaks, one of the most highly esteemed food-and-wine cultures in Italy, and an elegant regional capital in Turin.

8 The Italian Riviera. Northern Italy's most attractive coastline runs along the Italian Riviera in the region of Liguria. The best beaches and temperate winter climate are west of Genoa, but the main appeal lies to the east, where fishing villages dot the seaside cliffs and coves.

9 Emilia-Romagna. Many of Italy's signature foods come from the Emilia-Romagna region. Bologna is a significant cultural center, and the mosaics of Ravenna are glittering Byzantine treasures.

WHAT'S WHERE

10 Florence. The hub of the 15th-century Renaissance, Florence is awash with artistic treasures, exceptional restaurants, and first-rate shopping, as well as a never-ending stream of tourists.

11 Tuscany. Nature outdid herself in Tuscany. The central Italian region has Florence as its principal city and many other interesting midsize towns, but the region's greatest appeal lies in the smaller towns, often perched on hilltops and not significantly altered since the Middle Ages.

12 Umbria and the Marches. A number of the smaller towns, particularly Assisi, Perugia, Spoleto, and Orvieto are fun to explore, and Umbria's Roman past is everywhere—expect to see Roman villas, aqueducts, and temples. Urbino's Ducal Palace reveals more about the Renaissance than a shelf of art history books.

13 Naples and Campania. Campania is the gateway to southern Italy. Dream away two magical weeks on

Elevation	
15,577	4,748
10,825	3,300
9,840	3,000
8,860	2,700
7,875	2,400
6,900	2,100
5,900	1,800
4,920	1,500
3,940	1,200
2,920	900
1,970	600
980	300
490	150
250	75
100	30
feet	meters

the pint-size islands of Capri and Ischia and at the fabled resorts of the Amalfi Coast. Or explore the past at the archaeological ruins of Pompeii, Herculaneum, and Paestum. Naples is a fun, chaotic metropolis.

14 Puglia, Basilicata, and Calabria. The southernmost regions of the peninsula—Puglia, Basilicata, and Calabria—are known for their laid-back medieval villages, shimmering seas, and varied landscapes. The coastline of Puglia, along the heel of Italy's boot, is popular with beachgoers, but for the most part you're off the beaten path here.

15 Sicily. The breezes are sultry and everyday life is without pretense, as witnessed in the workaday stalls of the fish markets in ports all along the Tyrrhenian and Ionian coasts, bursting with tuna, swordfish, and sardines.

16 Sardinia. The beaches here rank among the Mediterranean's finest, and ancient sites, including the Carthaginian and Roman settlements of Nora and Tharros, add to the island's distinctive character.

Italy Today

ENDURING CUISINE

The old joke goes that three-quarters of the food and wine served in Italy is good—and the rest is amazing. In some sense, that's still true, and the "good" 75% has gotten even better. Those pundits would claim that ingredients that in the past were available only to the wealthy can now be found even in the remotest parts of the country at reasonable prices. Dishes originally conceived to make the most of inferior cuts of meat or the least flavorful part of vegetables are now made with the best.

But many Italians would say that the food in Italy is getting worse. There's a proliferation of fast-food establishments, and increasing tourism has allowed many restaurants to lower their standards while raising their prices. This is true not only in Rome, but in most other tourist centers as well. The good news is Italy is home to one of the world's greatest cuisines, and its traditional favorites still put meat on bones and smiles on faces. Italian restaurateurs seem determined to make the most of the country's reputation for good food. Although quaint, family-run trattorias with checkered tablecloths, traditional dishes, and an informal atmosphere are still common if on the decline, nearly every town has a newer eatery with matching flatware, a proper wine list, and an innovative menu.

This also holds for Italian wine. Today, through investment and experimentation, Italy's winemakers are figuring out how to get the most from their gorgeous vineyards. It's fair to say that Italy now produces more types of high-quality wine from more different grape varieties than any other country in the world.

SOCCER RULES

Soccer (or, as the Italians say, *calcio*—which means "kick") stands without rival as the national sport of Italy, though some complain that big-money influence and loose financial regulations are polluting the beautiful game. That aside, Italy did win its fourth World Cup in 2006, giving the country more world titles than any other this side of Brazil. More recently, Italy won the prestigious UEFA Euro 2020 championship (though due to COVID-19 it was played in 2021). Italy's major clubs have fared better in European competition of late, but the predominance of foreign players means a smaller pool of talent to pick at national level. More games in the schedule and a dwindling fan base mean fewer people are seen at the stadium. Still, fans can't stop watching the game on television. Indeed the allure of its famed teams like Juventus, Inter, and Napoli and their *ultras* (vociferous fans) means the top league, Serie A, has a worldwide following.

AN AGING POPULATION

Italy's population is the oldest in Europe (as percentage of population)—the result of its low birth rate and one of the highest life-expectancy rates in the world. The median age of an Italian in 2022 was 48; by 2050, 34.5% of the population is forecast to be over 65.

Italy's famously stable population is now aging and set to contract according to recent estimates, putting a strain on the country's pension system and on families because elderly family members are likely to live with their children or grandchildren as retirement homes are rare. Underfunding of the public health-care system has left older Italians vulnerable.

The trend also has an impact in other areas, including politics (where older politicians are eager to promote policies aimed at older voters), the popular culture (where everything from fashion to television programming takes older consumers into consideration), and a kind of far-reaching nostalgia. Thanks to a long collective memory, it's common to hear even younger Italians celebrate or rue something that happened 50 or 60 years earlier as if it had just taken place.

THE BLACK-MARKET ECONOMY

Nobody knows how big Italy's black-market economy is, though experts all agree it's massive. The presence of the black market isn't obvious to the casual observer, but whenever a customer isn't given a printed receipt in a store or restaurant, tobacco without a tax seal is bought from a street seller, or a product or service is exchanged for another product or service, that means the transaction goes unrecorded, unreported, and untaxed. But that's all penny-ante stuff compared to what many professionals evade by neglecting to declare all they earn.

Austerity measures imposed in recent years have led to much disgruntlement among the population; now most shopkeepers insist that you take a receipt. If you don't, you could be fined, as could the shopkeeper. These measures remain in place, but the country still struggles to meet the 3% limit to its budget deficit as mandated by European Union (EU) agreements, and it is pretty certain that Italy will continue to struggle to meet it in coming years.

A GROWING PARKS SYSTEM

Italy has 25 national parks covering a total of around 1½ million hectares (5,800 square miles), or about 6% of the entire surface area of the country—more than twice as much as 25 years ago.

Part of the reason for the expansion has been a growing environmental movement in Italy, which has lobbied the government to annex undeveloped land for parks, thus protecting against development. The trend is a boon for visitors and nature lovers, who can enjoy huge expanses of unspoiled territory.

STAYING HOME IN AUGUST

Italy used to be the best example of Europe's famous August exodus, when city dwellers would spend most of the month at the seaside or in the mountains, leaving the cities nearly deserted. Today the phenomenon is less prevalent, as economic pressures have forced companies to keep operating through August.

The loss of shared vacation time for Italian workers means good things for visitors: in August there's a little more room on beaches and mountains; in addition, cities promote events for nonvacationing natives. Summers in Italy now offer a plethora of outdoor concerts and theatrical events, extended museum hours, and local festivals.

MUSEI DIFFUSI

In recent years the idea of promoting tourism away from Italy's increasingly clogged destinations has spurred the idea of *Musei Diffusi* or "Scattered Museums." COVID regulations and social-distancing measures accelerated the movement to support local communities and encourage visitors to seek out art in overlooked hilltop *borghi* (villages) instead of queuing to glimpse Botticelli's *Venus*. The trend has evolved from *Strade dei Vini* (Wine Roads) and theme itineraries: now grand collections like the Uffizi are launching curator-led online exhibition tours and dusting off artworks in storage destined for display in municipal collections.

Best Hilltop Villages in Tuscany and Umbria

ORVIETO, UMBRIA

Although medieval architectural wonders adorn Orvieto, the labyrinth of subterranean tunnels beneath the town is even more fascinating. Orvieto is also recognized for its white and red wines, its olive oils, and its culinary classics—from boar and dove to pastas and pastries.

PITIGLIANO, TUSCANY

Although most Italian villages are overflowing with impressive churches, Pitigliano may be most famous for its synagogue, drawing attention to its rich history of Jewish settlement and giving the old town its nickname of Little Jerusalem. Of course, countless churches dot the rest of this Tuscan village. There's also a smattering of museums and other historical gems like the Palazzo Orsini, a Renaissance palace built on the ruins of medieval fortresses and containing both art and archaeological museums.

SAN GIMIGNANO, TUSCANY

Most medieval towers have given way to war and erosion through the centuries, but San Gimignano retains so many that it has been dubbed the Town of Fine Towers and its historic center is a UNESCO World Heritage site. Although it's packed with immaculate examples of medieval architecture, this village is among the more tourist-minded, with contemporary events like music festivals and art exhibitions and plenty of modern conveniences and services for travelers. San Gimignano even has its own app.

VOLTERRA, TUSCANY

Twenty kilometers (12 miles) from the better-known village of San Gimignano is the less visited Volterra. Although there are some serious medieval remnants in this village, especially its narrow streets in the town center, it's much more famous for the historical periods before and after. Some of its ancient Etruscan fortification walls still surround Roman ruins, including an impressive amphitheater worth exploring (there are also remains of ancient Roman baths and a forum). The Florentine influence of the Medici family left behind some dazzling Renaissance art and architecture throughout the once bustling mercantile village. The alabaster trade remains strong today and provides beautiful souvenirs of this Tuscan treasure.

SORANO, TUSCANY

Ham it up in Sorano, where the local prosciutto is so revered that the town holds a festival for it every August. If you don't eat pork, don't worry; there are plenty of other local specialties, particularly dairy products, including sheep's milk ricotta cheese. Don't miss the Masso Leopoldina (sometimes called the Rocca Vecchia). It was once central to the defense of the town but is now a fabulous terrace that's a good place to enjoy panoramic views of Tuscany.

San Gimignano

VINCI, TUSCANY

Yes, *that* Vinci. Established in the early Middle Ages among the rolling hills of Montalbano and with Arno Valley views, Vinci's claim to fame is Leonardo da Vinci ("Leonardo from Vinci"). The town is filled with tributes to him—like the imposing wooden sculpture, *Vitruvian Man*, by Mario Ceroli; the Biblioteca Leonardiana, an archive of his manuscripts and drawings; Santa Croce, the church where he was baptized; and the Museo Leonardiano Vinci, which houses his inventions and anatomical research, including drawings, studies, and replicas, in two buildings. You can also visit the birth home of this true Renaissance man in the nearby village of Anchiano. It's accessible via a 3-km (1.8-mile) walk up the *strade verde* (a dirt path with valley views) or by car or bus.

TODI, UMBRIA

Compact and ancient Todi is a hilltop citadel town with a beautiful patch-work of architecture that includes three sturdy walls, begun by the 3rd-century-BC Etruscans followed by Roman and medieval dynasties. Starting at the café–community hub Piazza del Popolo, with an imposing 12th-century Romanesque-Gothic Duomo built upon a Roman temple, a maze of cobbled lanes and steep staircases fans out, inviting leisurely exploration. For grandstand views over roofs and the Umbrian hills beyond, climb the campanile of San Fortunato. Leafy walks abound in the Parco della Rocca, the city-wall park.

ASSISI, UMBRIA

Assisi claims history as ancient as 1000 BC and is probably best known for its most famous resident, St. Francis, whose 13th-century basilica is now a UNESCO World Heritage site, as is the entire village itself. Plenty of other impressive churches, Roman ruins, and not one but two castles top the extensive list of the town's architectural offerings. From ceramics to medieval weaponry, Assisi's artisan history is also strong. Cured meats and chocolate are popular here, so grab a snack between sword fights, and refuel on the Assisi ribbon-type pasta *stringozzi*, often served with Norcia black truffles, asparagus, or *piccante* (spicy) tomato sauce.

Best Beaches in Italy

CALA GOLORITZÉ, SARDINIA

The beach's gleaming-white limestone pebbles, limpid waters, and dramatic geological formations make it a paradisiacal summer playground. The pinnacle towering over the cove is often dotted with climbers; dozens of nearby marine caves have wonderful natural light effects; and the surrounding mountainous national park is laced with challenging trails.

TORRE GUACETO, PUGLIA

The color palate at Torre Guaceto is classic and calming: blue waters lapping chalky sands near the so-called Città Bianca (White City) of Ostuni. The beach is part of a marine reserve that extends 20 km (12 miles) along the coast and 6 km (4 miles) inland.

BAIA DEL SILENZIO, LIGURIA

Line a curvy bay with a sandy beach and warm-hued buildings, and you have Baia del Silenzio, one of Liguria's most captivating seaside amphitheaters. This very popular spot in the resort town of Sestri Levante is a fabulous place to people-watch.

CALA DEL GESSO, TUSCANY

Gorgeous Cala del Gesso is nestled in a relatively sheltered nook on southern Tuscany's Monte Argentario peninsula. Stake out a spot early in high season: the beach's shiny limestone pebbles and crystal clear turquoise waters draw sun worshippers and snorkelers aplenty.

ROCA VECCHIA, PUGLIA
A big draw at Roca Vecchia is the Grotta della Poesia (Cave of Poetry)—a natural ovoid sinkhole-pool set into limestone along the stunning Salento Coast. Swimmers like to dive in (a 16-foot drop), and scuba divers like to swim in (via an underwater sea cave).

Spiaggia di Fegina

SPIAGGIA DELLA MARINELLA, CAMPANIA
Near the town of Palinuro on the oft-overlooked Cilento Coast, stunning Spiaggia della Marinella mixes pebbles and volcanic sand against a backdrop of otherworldly rock formations.

MARASUSA, CALABRIA
The area around the lovely town of Tropea has some of Calabria's most recognizable seascapes, including those on Marasusa, where the water is a remarkable greenish-blue, the sand light-hued and ultrafine, and buildings seem to grow from the rock atop sheer cliffs.

TONNARA DI SCOPELLO, SICILY
Rustic houses, a church, medieval towers on craggy cliffs, and sea-stack rock formations make Tonnara di Scopello on the Golfo del Castellammare one of Sicily's most picturesque beaches.

SPIAGGIA DI FEGINA, LIGURIA
Hikers tackling the famous Cinque Terre often take a breather on the beautiful, pebbly Spiaggia di Fegina. If you're feeling sprightly, clamber over *faraglioni* (sea stacks) amid the waves or trek down to one end of the beach to see the 46-foot *Statua del Gigante* (Giant Statue) hewn into the rock.

SPIAGGIA NERA–CALA JANNITA, BASILICATA
Maratea is one of the Tyrrhenian coast's most alluring towns, where the fabulous Spiaggia Nera (Black Beach) has limpid waters and dramatic scenery. Spread your towel out on the dark volcanic gravel, and float amid igneous boulders.

Best Vineyard and Wine-Tasting Experiences in Tuscany

Castiglion del Bosco

ANTINORI

Antinori produces one of the best-known Super Tuscans, called Tignanello, a blend of Sangiovese with cabernet sauvignon and cabernet franc. It offers several winery/cellar tours, all of them followed by a tasting, across its different wineries in Tuscany. If you're inspired to buy a bottle (or two), the wineshop is well stocked.

AVIGNONESI

A 16th-century manor house surrounded by vineyards in Montepulciano is the setting for Avignonesi. On tours, which are followed by tastings, you'll learn about biodynamic wine making and visit the vin santo aging cellar, drying room, and barrel tunnel. Cooking classes are sometimes offered, too.

BADIA A COLTIBUONO

In Gaiole in Chianti, options at Badia a Coltibuono, which also produces olive oil, include visiting the former crypt where Chianti Classico is aged, cooking classes, or walking tours of the vineyards, about a 20-minute drive from the abbey.

Castello di Ama

BARONE RICASOLI

Situated in Gaiole in Chianti, Barone Ricasoli is Italy's oldest winery. Indeed, Bettino Ricasoli, the "Iron Baron," is said to have developed the original formula for Chianti wine in 1872. Winery experiences include a tour of Brolio castle and gardens, a cellar visit, family treasure hunts, and wineshop tastings.

CAPEZZANA

Make reservations to tour the cellars, olive oil mill, and vin santo aging cellar at Capezzana in Prato. Afterward, enjoy both wine and olive oil tastings. Cooking classes are also available, as are eight charming *agriturismo* guest rooms.

CASTELLARE DI CASTELLINA

In addition to its panoramic views, Castellare di Castellina in Castellina in Chianti is known for its sustainably produced I Sodi di S. Niccolò Super Tuscan, Chianti Classico, and vin santo dessert wine. Choose from half a dozen experiences, from traditional tours to "Wine & Bike" and a helicopter ride followed by a visit to the Renzo Piano–designed cellar of Tenuta di Rocca di Frassinello.

CASTELLO DI AMA

Visits to Gaiole in Chianti's Castello di Ama, which must be booked in advance, include tastings and tours of the property's cellars, 18th-century villas, and gardens. You can also overnight in a Villa Ricucci suite.

CASTIGLION DEL BOSCO

Castiglion del Bosco, in Montalcino, is part of a luxury Rosewood resort. Private tours, by appointment only, include visits to the cellars and vineyards plus tastings.

FONTODI

At Fontodi in Panzano, appointment-only tours highlight the winery, cellars (where some wines are aged in terra-cotta pots), and bottling process, ending with a tasting. Groups can look into staying at one of the villas here.

SALCHETO

Overlooking Montepulciano, Salcheto is a biodynamic winery that follows fully sustainable practices, including generating energy from renewable sources and purifying and recycling wastewater. The property also has a wine bar that serves food, and six farmhouse guest rooms.

Best Ancient Sites in Rome

COLOSSEUM

Perhaps the monument most symbolic of ancient Rome, the Colosseum is one of the city's most fascinating—and popular—tourist attractions. It officially opened in AD 80 with 100 days of games, including wild-animal fights and gladiatorial combat.

FORO DI TRAIANO

Trajan's Forum was the last of imperial Rome's forums—and the grandest. Comprising a basilica, two libraries, and a colonnade surrounding a piazza, it's connected to a market that once bustled with commercial activity.

PANTHEON

Built as a pagan temple, the Pantheon is Rome's best-preserved ancient site, perhaps because it was later consecrated as a church. Step inside, and you'll be amazed at its perfect proportions and the sunlight streaming in from the 30-foot-wide oculus. It's truly a wonder of ancient engineering.

ROMAN FORUM

One of the Eternal City's most emblematic sites, the Roman Forum stretches out between the Capitoline and Palatine hills. This vast area filled with crumbling columns and the ruins of temples, palaces, and shops was once the hub of the ancient world and the center of political, commercial, and religious life in the city.

CIRCUS MAXIMUS

It might be hard to imagine now, but the grassy area between the Palatine and Aventine hills was once the site of the largest hippodrome in the Roman Empire. The huge oval course was rebuilt under Julius Caesar and later enlarged by subsequent emperors. During its heyday, it hosted epic chariot races and competitions that sometimes lasted for up to 15 days.

BOCCA DELLA VERITÀ

Legend has it the mouth in this ancient stone face will bite off the hand of a liar, and tourists line up to stick their hand inside the mouth and put it to the test. (Gregory Peck's character tricks Audrey Hepburn's Princess Ann into thinking he lost a hand inside it in a scene from *Roman Holiday*.) You'll find the enigmatic face in the portico of the Church of Santa Maria in Cosmedin, near the Circus Maximus.

The Roman Forum

TEATRO MARCELLO

What looks a bit like a smaller version of the Colosseum was once ancient Rome's largest and most important theater. Julius Caesar ordered the land for the theater to be cleared, but he was murdered before it was built. It was inaugurated in AD 12 by Augustus and hosted performances of drama and song. It's kept that purpose even today, at least during the summer, when it hosts concerts.

APPIA ANTICA

Head to the southeastern edge of the city to Appia Antica Park and you can walk on the stones—which are incredibly well-preserved—that ancient Roman soldiers and citizens once trod. This thoroughfare once stretched all the way to Brindisi on the Adriatic Coast. Today, the first 16 km (10 miles) are part of a regional park, and it's a perfect spot for bike rides and picnics in the grass under the shadow of Rome's emblematic umbrella pines.

ARA PACIS AUGUSTAE

Now housed in a modern glass-and-travertine building designed by renowned American architect Richard Meier, the Ara Pacis Augustae has some of the most incredible reliefs you'll see on any ancient monument. It was commissioned to celebrate the Emperor Augustus's victories in battle and the Pax Romana, a peaceful period that followed. It's definitely worth a visit and is centrally located on the Tiber River in the Piazza di Spagna district.

TERMI DI CARACALLA

A testament to ancient Rome's bathing culture, this site on the Aventine Hill was essentially a massive spa, with saunas, baths, what would be an Olympic-size pool, and two gymnasiums for boxing, weight lifting, and wrestling.

The Best Places to Discover Volcanoes

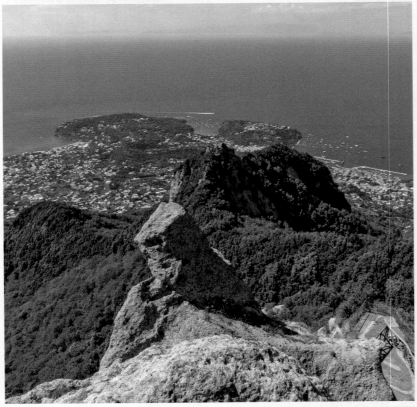

Ischia

CRATER RIM OF VESUVIUS

Peering over the edge into the 650-foot-deep crater you can glimpse and even taste the acrid, sulfuric menace of Vesuvio's steamy fumaroles. Hearts may skip a beat after the odd, unnerving earth tremor. Up here the views of the bay and the surrounding area below—Pompeii, Hercula-neum, Oplontis—hint at its immense eruptive might.

POMPEII'S PLASTER-CAST FIGURES

To get an idea of the merci-less nature of Vesuvius, visit Pompeii to see the plaster-cast ghosts of some of its AD 79 victims. Archaeologist Giuseppe Fiorelli's casts freeze the positions of the inciner-ated Pompeians: a chilling reminder of how the earth's awesome natural power can take lives in an instant.

CAMPI FLEGREI

The Campi Flegrei, or Fiery Fields, is a complex caldera volcano that some scientists now deem to be Europe's largest supervolcano.

FUMAROLES AND THERMAL SPRINGS OF ISCHIA

The island of Ischia sits within the Campi Flegrei caldera, whose gargantuan

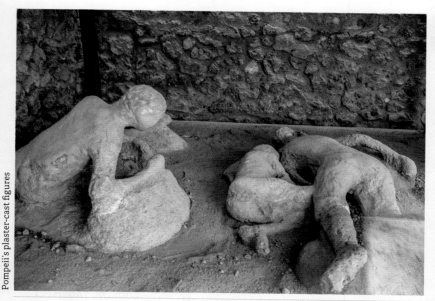

Pompeii's plaster-cast figures

magma chambers fuel the hydrothermal springs and fumaroles that soothe and heal thousands of spa-goers each day.

VILLA ROMANA

Although the Amalfi Coast is a limestone spur of the Apennines, without a fumarole or lava flow in sight, the communities some 20 km (13 miles) from Vesuvius have been shaped by volcanology. By descending into the Villa Romana ruins by the beach at Positano, you are traveling through the volcanic debris spewed by the eruption of AD 79.

SOLFATARA CRATER

In this land scarred by constant tectonic activity, there is one steamy, fumarole-fizzing, and mud-bubbling 4,000-year-old crater that has become an emblem for volcanism in this part of the world. Solfatara was a bathing curiosity on the Grand Tour and has appeared in numerous movies and music videos, including Rossellini's *Journey to Italy* and Pink Floyd's *Live at Pompeii*.

BAIA

Down at the shoreline of Baia, the sea has swallowed part of the town, and at nearby Pozzuoli, marine mollusk boreholes 20 feet up the Roman columns indicate that the sea was once much higher. These two towns attest to the shifting water levels— the rise and fall of the land surface caused by the constant emptying and filling of the magma chambers below.

HERCULANEUM

Walking down the sloping path into the Herculaneum archaeological site, you are struck by the enormity of the eruption that buried Pompeii. Scientists believe that Herculaneum was seared by a 900°F pyroclastic surge that roared down the mountain at 250 mph.

SAN SEBASTIANO

In 1944, liquid lava enveloped buildings and took off the church cupola, while walls of cooler lava crushed buildings. Today the curious can walk on those lava flows and enter modern buildings built in the 1950s and 1960s atop the lava and half-destroyed main street, Via Roma.

OSSERVATORIO VESUVIANO

Vesuvius remains the most closely monitored volcano on the planet; the research here started the science of volcanology.

Fantastic Cooking Classes in Italy

TASTE BOLOGNA (BOLOGNA, EMILIA-ROMAGNA)

Any cook worth their *sale* (salt) should spend time in Italy's foodie capital, and Taste Bologna provides a fulsome introduction to its riches. Combine their Classic Bologna Tour with the Cooking Class to get a feel for life in the market and in the kitchen.

MONTESE COOKING EXPERIENCE (SAN GIMIGNANO, TUSCANY)

Situated just outside San Gimignano, the well-loved Montese Cooking Experience is blessed with fabulous facilities, chefs, and views. The intensive four-hour Pasta Fatta in Casa session highlights not only long pastas, but also stuffed varieties.

TASTING SARDINIA: THE CENTENARIANS MEAL (CAGLIARI, SARDINIA)

The enlightening Centenarians Meal session, one of many offerings from Tasting Sardinia, takes its premise—that cooking with fresh ingredients is essential to living long and well—straight from the island's centenarians.

BUCA DI BACCO (POSITANO, CAMPANIA)

The venerable Hotel Buca di Bacco opened in the 1950s, but tucked within is the even older eponymous restaurant, established in 1916, which hosts Buca di Bacco cooking classes. You'll learn about pizza and pasta making, as well as the restaurant's signature antipasto: *gamberetti alla Clark*. The dish was created for U.S. General Mark Clark, who was stationed here at the end of World War II. When he requested a prawn cocktail, the chef combined shrimp, lettuce, and a sauce to create a version that reflected the local climate and wartime larder.

COOKING TAORMINA (TAORMINA, SICILY)

In addition to helping you hone your cooking skills, the animated young chef at Cooking Taormina explains the many exotic influences that shaped *la cucina siciliana*. The first part of the lesson stimulates the senses on a visit to Taormina's produce and fish market. Afterward, you'll use your fresh ingredients in classic Sicilian specialties.

MAMA ISA'S COOKING SCHOOL (PADUA, VENETO)

In Padua, a 30-minute drive inland from Venice, Mama Isa and family offer a tempting array of courses—from half-day introductory lessons to six-day extravaganzas—covering many of the Veneto region's culinary traditions. There are weeks' worth of classes, including bread and pasta making, vegan and vegetarian cooking, and dessert

Bari Walking Tour in Puglia

and pastry creation—even how to prepare the perfect risotto.

BARI WALKING TOUR WITH PASTA-MAKING (BARI, PUGLIA)

Deep in Bari's atmospheric *centro storico*, you'll learn about the art of making orecchiette, which is still practiced on the city's streets. The two-hour Bari Walking Tour with Pasta-Making starts with a tour of the city and its food market before heading to the chef's house to get fiddly with the dough. By the end of the session, you will have created hundreds of edible "little ears" to enjoy with a few bottles of Puglia's red Primitivo wine during the all-important tasting lunch.

ITALIANNA COOKING CLASS (ALBA, PIEDMONT)

Renowned for its rich tradition of food and wine, greatly influenced by nearby France, Piedmont is a fine destination for a foodie adventure. ItaliAnna's beginner pasta-making class, for example, is fun, flour filled, and interactive—and just one of their offerings.

SLOW COOKING CLASS (PACIANO, UMBRIA)

The family-run Slow Cooking School is based in an organic olive press, Il Fontanaro. Its most popular offering involves a tour of the mill, a rummage around the verdant market garden to select ingredients, and then a chance to get messy: mixing and kneading dough, shaping pasta, and creating the accompanying *sugo* (sauce) from scratch.

COOK WITH US IN ROME (ROMA, LAZIO)

The enthusiasm of the two Roman chefs who conduct the Cook with Us in Rome classes is contagious, making it truly fun to learn about the city's food in a morning or afternoon session.

Architectural Wonders in Venice

SAN FRANCESCO DELLA VIGNA
The harmonious combination of architectural designs by two Renaissance maestri and the tranquil neighborhood setting make this church a wonderful place to escape the crowds.

MOLINO STUCKY
This behemoth, neo-Gothic, warehouselike building, formerly a flour mill and pasta factory, on the western end of the Giudecca, certainly stands out on the Venetian skyline.

SANTA MARIA DELLA SALUTE
One of the city's most beloved and iconic churches, La Salute was built to mark the end of the 1630 plague that took almost 50,000 Venetian lives.

PONTE DI RIALTO
The iconic Ponte di Rialto was completed in 1591. Its generous arch, central portal, and Renaissance arcade make it appear so beautifully balanced that Palladio himself would surely have approved.

PUNTA DELLA DOGANA
There has been a Punta della Dogana (Sea Customs House) situated between the Grand and Giudecca Canals since the 15th century, although the building you see today was designed in the 1860s. Above the entrance tower, two Atlases lift a bronze sphere topped by the figure of Fortune.

ARSENALE
For centuries, the colossal Arsenale complex of shipyards, warehouses, and armories was Europe's largest military-industrial compound. Although many areas are still cordoned off as military zones, the southern side is open to the public during the Biennale Arte e Architettura.

JEWISH GHETTO
Originally the site of a foundry (*geto* in the local dialect), both the atmosphere and the architecture set the Jewish Ghetto apart: palazzi and *case* are taller here than elsewhere, with story upon story piled high in an effort to make the best use of limited space.

Palazzo Ducale

PALAZZO DUCALE
Adorned with a series of soaring Gothic arches topped by an ornately columned arcade, the labyrinthine Doge's Palace has a wedding-cake-like delicacy when viewed from the Piazza San Marco or the waterside Bacino di San Marco. A palace has been here since the 9th century: its present palatial pink Verona marble and Istrian limestone splendor was the vision of architect Filippo Calendario (1315–1355).

MADONNA DELL'ORTO
An alluring, redbrick Gothic church with ornate marble decoration, it was dedicated to St. Christopher, the patron saint of travelers, until a Madonna statue was found in a nearby *orto* (kitchen vegetable garden). Tintoretto's local church is where he learned his craft as a young man. Seek out the powerful *Martyrdom of St. Paul*, which captures the tension between the violent sword act of a Roman soldier and Paul's saintly calmness below rays of holy light.

CA' DA MOSTO
As you drift along the Grand Canal, you'll see palazzi far more eye-catching than the Ca' da Mosto, but none more enduring—the crumbling Byzantine-style palace has been here since the 13th century. The ground and first floors are an example of a *casa-fondaco* (a house-warehouse). A 2019–21 restoration and renovation transformed the palace into an exorbitantly luxe and pricey hotel filled with innovative design and interesting artworks.

What to Watch and Read

ITALIAN FOLKTALES BY ITALO CALVINO

In 1956 the celebrated, Cuban-born and Liguria-raised magical realist published this fabulous collection of some 200 traditional folktales from across the archipelago. The prose in the 800-page *Fiabe italiane* tome is simple yet evocative, and the stories appeal to young and old alike. They're largely fantastical morality tales involving love, loss, revenge, and adventure on the part of kings, princesses, saints, and peasants. The book is a fabulous bedtime or beach read.

AMARCORD, DIRECTED BY FEDERICO FELLINI

Amarcord ("I remember," in the Romagnol dialect) is filled with comic archetypes and dreamlike excursions inspired by Fellini's 1930s adolescence in Rimini. The rosy-cheeked protagonist, Titta, and his pals have humorous encounters with authority figures—pompous schoolteachers, frustrated fathers, cruel Fascist officials—as well as with the buxom hairdresser, Gradisca. The 1973 movie, which won the Oscar for Best Foreign Language Film, offers poignant, entertaining, and often bonkers insight into the Italian psyche, family dynamics, and interwar society. Nino Rota's wistful soundtrack adds to the feeling of nostalgia.

THE ITALIANS BY JOHN HOOPER

In this 2015 book, longtime Rome correspondent John Hooper addresses the complexities of contemporary Italy, attempting to reveal "what makes the Italian tick." Here you'll learn the lexicon needed to negotiate and understand Italian culture. Of course, food, sex, and the weather—among other things—are heartily embraced in everyday life, but there is also an *amaro* (bitter) side. Hooper illustrates how the power of the *famiglia* (family) and the *chiesa* (church) has produced a society in which *furbizia* (cunning) is rewarded and meritocracy is replaced with *raccomandazioni* (favors) to get ahead in the world.

THE LEOPARD BY GIUSEPPE TOMASI DI LAMPEDUSA

Il gattopardo, an Italian literary classic, chronicles the tumultuous, revolutionary years of the Risorgimento (1860s–early 20th century). Lampedusa was the last in a line of minor princes, and the novel, born of a lengthy depression, was published in 1958, a year after his death. Set in Sicily, the epic story of decay amid a changing society centers on the ebbing influence and power of Don Fabrizio, Prince of Salina, and his family, and hints at the emergence of the Mafia. One particularly insightful quote in the book—spoken by the prince's young nephew, Tancredi—sheds light on how Italy adapts to shifting political forces and class struggle: "For everything to stay the same, everything must change."

COSA NOSTRA BY JOHN DICKIE

Journalist and academic John Dickie packs a lot of gruesome detail into this fast-paced history of the Mafia. He traces the Cosa Nostra's origins during the Risorgimento years, its infiltration and corruption of the First Republic, and the curious and notorious role of the town of Corleone in its development. Dickie also recounts the organization's birth and rise in America, the Mafia Wars, and the recent crises and tragedies connected to Italy's corrupt political system.

THE CONFORMIST, DIRECTED BY BERNARDO BERTOLUCCI

Il conformista, Bertolucci's stylish psychological thriller set in 1930s Fascist Italy, is considered a postwar cinematic classic. As its name suggests, the 1970 film tackles the issue of conformity through the lens of the cruel, febrile political atmosphere created by Mussolini and his followers. Despite its dark themes, the movie is beautifully lit and shot, filled with vibrant colors, exquisite costuming, and atmospheric locations. It has inspired many directors of the American New Wave and beyond, including Martin Scorsese, Francis Ford Coppola, and the Coen brothers.

DELIZIA! BY JOHN DICKIE

If you think you know all there is to know about Italian food, you'll think again after reading this book. Dickie's gastronomic journey across the regions of Italy through the ages covers everything from *pastasciutta* in 12th-century Palermo to today's Slow Food movement in Turin. Carry this book with you as you travel, so you can compare your menu to, say, that for a 1529 Ferrara banquet, which featured "105 soused sea bream" and "15 large salted eels" for starters, followed by "104 roasted capon livers" and "sweet pastry tarts deep-filled with the spleens of sea bass, trout, pike and other fish." *Che delizia!*

THE GREAT BEAUTY, DIRECTED BY PAOLO SORRENTINO

Although directed by a Neapolitan, this Oscar-winning 2013 film is set in Rome and serves as a kind of contemporary *La Dolce Vita*. The lead character in *La grande bellezza*, Jep Gambardella (Toni Servillo), is an aging hedonistic journalist, who, while pining for his glory days, comes to realize the superficiality of his bourgeois lifestyle. Beset by Roman ennui after his raucous rooftop 65th-birthday bash, Jep goes in search of beauty beyond the vanity of his milieu.

THE NEAPOLITAN NOVELS

Elena Ferrante's novels (2012–15) and the HBO TV series bring multilayered postwar Naples to life, going beyond postcard beauty to portray the grim, savage reality of growing up in a rough *rione* (district). The four books explore the complexities of friendship and Italian society. With vivid depictions—mixing the palatial and the squalid—the pseudonymous author details the lifetime bond and inner lives of Elena and Lila and their interactions with a cast of characters across Italy as well as in Naples.

1992, 1993, AND 1994

The 10-episode television series *1992* and its follow-ups *1993* and *1994* (originally aired in 2015, 2017, and 2019, respectively) are political dramas that follow the intertwined lives of six people amid the tumult of early-1990s Italy. Massive cracks appear in the postwar political compromise, with the Mani Pulite (Clean Hands) investigation led by prosecutor Antonio Di Pietro initiating the fall of the First Republic. As the country is rocked by the so-called Tangentopoli (Bribesville) scandal, marketing man Stefano Accorsi sees an opportunity for an outside figure to seize power. And so up steps media tycoon Silvio Berlusconi and his populist Forza Italia party. Sound familiar?

STANLEY TUCCI: SEARCHING FOR ITALY (2021–22)

Italian-American actor Stanley Tucci goes on a culinary and cultural adventure around the Italian regions in this CNN TV production. In the first series he visits six regions, their urban centers, and fecund hinterlands. In Naples and the Amalfi Coast he visits a San Marzano tomato farm on the shadows of Vesuvius and discovers the art of mozzarella making. In Rome he samples imaginative *quinto-quarto* offal creations and Roman classics rigatoni *all'amatriciana* and *guanciale*-laden *carbonara*. Trips to Tuscany, Bologna, and Milan yield engaging encounters and mouthfuls of *bistecca alla Fiorentina*, the most sought-after Parmigiana-Reggiano cheese, and a cool hangout for an *aperitivo Milanese*. Tucci rounds off the series meeting young female vintner Arianna Occhipinti in Sicily.

Making the Most of Your Euros

TRANSPORTATION

Italy's state-sponsored train system has been given a run for its money by a private company. Sadly, the competitor (Italo) only operates major, high-speed connections (such as Rome to Naples, Florence to Venice, Milan to Bologna) and not local routes. Because of the competition, Trenitalia and Italo engage in price wars, which only plays to the consumer's advantage; depending on time of day and how far in advance you purchase the tickets, great bargains can be had.

No such good news exists for the *regionali* trains. These are trains connecting cities, highly frequented by commuters and used often by visitors who want to get to less visible towns. These trains are habitually late and almost always crowded. Patience is a virtue, and much needed when taking them, particularly during high season.

FOOD AND DRINK

Always remember, when you enter a bar, that there is almost always a two-tier pricing system: one if you stand and one if you sit. It's always cheaper to stand, but sometimes sitting is not only necessary but fun: you can relax and watch the world go by.

Italians love a good sandwich for lunch. Seek out popular sandwich shops (long lines signify that the place is worth visiting) or go to a *salumeria* (delicatessen) and have them make a sandwich for you. It will be simple—cheese and/or cold cuts with bread, no trimmings—but it will be made while you wait, fresh, delicious, and inexpensive.

SIGHTS

There are plenty of free wonderful things to see. Visit the Musei Vaticani, the Uffizi, and the Accademia in Florence (book ahead whenever possible), but don't forget that many artistic gems are found in churches, most of which can be visited with no charge (some of Caravaggio's best work can be found in various churches in Rome). Also, consider renting audio guides if you want direction to any specific place; if you find the idea of joining an organized tour daunting, most museums sell official guidebooks that can help you target what to see. Walking in *centri storici* (historic centers) is also a joy, and free. Seek out piazzas, climb towers, and look for views.

LODGING

High season in Italy runs from Easter to mid-October. If you want to have Florence practically to yourself, come in November or February (most Italian cities are very crowded during the Christmas holidays, which begin around Christmas and finish on January 6). Many hotels in cities offer bargain rates in July and August because most people are off to the beach or the mountains. Remember to factor in great heat and massive crowds, along with the money you'll save. If you decide to travel then, ensure that you have access to a pool and/or air-conditioning.

A great budget-conscious way to travel is via Airbnb (⊕ *airbnb.com*), although prices have soared in recent years, making pads in popular places pricier than many hotels. You can sleep on someone's couch, rent a private room in an apartment (sometimes with en suite bathroom), or spread out in an entire apartment or house. One of the best things about Airbnb is that many of these accommodations come with refrigerators and kitchens, which means you don't have to spend all your money eating out.

In general, whatever your lodging choice, book sooner rather than later. You'll often find better deals that way.

Chapter 2

TRAVEL SMART

Updated by
Nick Bruno

★ **CAPITAL:**
Rome

👤 **POPULATION:**
58,997,201

💬 **LANGUAGE:**
Italian

$ **CURRENCY:**
Euro

📞 **COUNTRY CODE:**
39

⚠ **EMERGENCIES:**
112

🚗 **DRIVING:**
On the right

⚡ **ELECTRICITY:**
220v/50 cycles; electrical
plugs have two round prongs

⏱ **TIME:**
6 hours ahead of New York

🌐 **WEB RESOURCES:**
www.italia.it
www.beniculturali.it

ITALY

✪ ROME

SARDINIA

MEDITERRANEAN

SICILY

SEA

Know Before You Go

A TALE OF TWO COUNTRIES

Italy as we know it is just over 160 years old, united by Giuseppe Garibaldi in 1861, and traditions and customs die hard. Differences and rivalries between the wealthier north and the more relaxed south abound, but you will need to spend time in both for the full Italian experience.

DRINK YOUR FILL

Bottled water is available everywhere but often at an inflated price. Carry a refillable bottle and fill up for free at the strategically placed water fountains in cities. In restaurants you can ask for tap water (*acqua del rubinetto*), although you may have to insist.

GO FOOTBALL CRAZY

Soccer—*calcio*—is taken very seriously in Italy, with rivalries running deep. A little knowledge of a local team's performance makes for great conversation. Just avoid wearing your Juventus shirt in Naples if you want to make new friends. To get a taste for the football fervor, its songs and excitement, visit the *stadio* of the local *squadra* (team) and join the *tifosi* (fans) on the *curve* (in the stands).

BOOK IN ADVANCE

Avoid waiting in line for hours by buying museum tickets online before your visit. Also, the earlier you buy train tickets, the less expensive they're likely to be. Trenitalia and Italo offer substantial first-come-first-served discounts on high-speed services; check their websites, and prepare to be flexible with your travel times. Discounts aren't offered on regional trains, and neither is seat reservation. Unless bought online, tickets for regional trains must be stamped before boarding.

TAKE THE BACK ROADS

So you've rented a car. Why stick to the highways? Much of Italy's beauty is along winding mountain roads or coastal secondary routes, so take your time and wander a little. Not only will you save on tolls but you'll save on fuel, too, as gas prices are generally lower than on the *autostrade*. Also, if you're renting a car between November 15 and April 15, remember to ask for snow chains (obligatory on many roads).

EAT FOR (NEARLY) NOTHING

The *aperitivo* is a staple of many areas of the north, where, for little more than the price of a drink, you can partake of a vast buffet to substitute for your evening meal. Bars vie with each other to provide the best array of pasta dishes, *pizzette*, and panini, so check out a few of them before sitting down. Look out for signs like "Aperitivo Happy Hour" and "Stuzzichini": there are bite-size snacks like *patatine* (potato chips), olives, and *grissini* (breadsticks) either served with your drink at the table, or else in a buffet-style spread replete with pasta, rice, and other dishes.

PLAN YOUR DAY

Although breakfast (*la colazione*) is generally served from 7 to 10:30, other mealtimes vary by region. In the north, lunch (*il pranzo*) is noon to 2, whereas restaurants in the south often serve it until 3. You may have difficulty finding dinner (*la cena*) in the north after 9 pm, when most southerners are just sitting down to eat (restaurants there tend not to open until 7:30). And shoppers take note: many stores close from 1 to 4:30.

LACE UP YOUR WALKING SHOES

The best—and often the only—way to see a city is on foot. Public transport works well (albeit generally better in the north), and in recent years many city and town centers have been pedestrianized. Parking costs and fines can add up (avoid ZTL or limited traffic zones), so when possible don your most comfortable shoes and prepare to pound the pavement. Fall in with a weekend afternoon *passeggiata* in smaller towns, where Italians stroll the main street.

DRINK LOCAL

Italy offers a vast array of fine wines, with each region boasting its own appellation. While you may see Chianti on a wine list in Catania, it will probably be no different to what you find at home; for a more authentic taste of the area, try a local Sicilian wine instead.

YOU GET A COFFEE IN A BAR

Coffee culture is different here. Italians take their single-shot espresso standing at a bar—where snacks and alcoholic drinks are also served, and which usually closes in the evening. Pay the cashier, then set your receipt on the counter and place your order. If you choose to sit, there is usually a surcharge, whether there is table service or not. Also, if you order a latte you'll get a glass of milk.

NEVER PASS A RESTROOM

Public restrooms in train stations usually cost €1, and bars frown on the use of theirs without making a purchase, so before you leave the hotel, restaurant, or museum, use the facilities.

DAY-TRIPPER

Lodging in tourist hot spots is at a premium during high season, but deals can be found a little farther from the action. Consider booking outside town and taking a local train or bus to see the sights—you might miss the evening atmosphere, but you'll have more to spend on lunch.

TAKE YOUR TIME

The Italian experience differs from region to region. Try to plan an itinerary that leaves time to explore each destination at leisure. Sure, quick in-and-out visits to cities will allow you to see the major sights, but rushing things means missing out on each area's unique atmosphere.

BE ITALIAN

Food is one of Italy's defining features, and locals continue to be horrified by the idea of pineapple on pizza or (heaven forbid!) ketchup on pasta. You don't need a knife to eat spaghetti (although using a spoon to help wind the pasta around a fork is allowed), and it's fine to pick your pizza up. Most restaurants set a per-person fee for *pane e coperto* (bread and cover charge), although waiters also appreciate a tip— which is standard (around 10%) in the south.

BEWARE OF SCAMS

Larger train stations are notorious for porters insisting on carrying your bags, then charging a fee, so be firm if you're not interested. Also, be careful where you store your wallet and valuables and avoid purchasing from illegal street vendors.

LOOK INTO SIGHT PASSES

Many cities and towns sell multiday passes for access to different museums and sights. These offer great savings if you plan to visit several attractions; some include deals on public transport.

LEARN THE LINGO

Most Italians have some command of English, although this isn't a fail-safe rule, particularly in the south. You can get by on hand gestures and pointing, but a *grazie* or *buongiorno* here and there can't hurt.

SPECIAL SUNDAYS FOR CULTURE

A fabulous Ministero della Cultura initiative, "Domenica al Museo," allows free entry to state-run museums, galleries, and archaeological sites throughout Italy on the first Sunday of the month. For the latest upcoming "Sunday at the Museum" details consult the list of participating institutions at ⊕ *cultura.gov.it/domenicalmuseo* and look out for the hashtag #DomenicaAl-Museo. Naturally, there are lots of crowds and families on these days.

FOOD-SHOP SAVVY

Save money on restaurant and hotel food, and pricey drinks bills, by seeking out stores to stock up. Head to the *alimentari*, the local food and general store, to buy groceries, cheese, cold cuts, and essential refreshments for hot days out, such as water in bottles. The *supermercato* has a wider selection and may stock interesting housewares and other items that make fab gifts to take home. For picnic supplies the *panificio* or *fornaio* is essential for bakery goods such as *pane* (bread) and *panini* (rolls).

Getting Here and Around

Air

Most nonstop flights between North America and Italy serve Rome's Aeroporto Internazionale Leonardo da Vinci (FCO), better known as Fiumicino, and Milan's Aeroporto Malpensa (MXP), though the airports in Venice, Pisa, and Naples also accommodate nonstop flights from the United States. Flying time to Milan or Rome is approximately 8–8½ hours from New York, 10–11 hours from Chicago, and 11½ hours from Los Angeles.

Alitalia has direct flights from London to Milan and Rome, while British Airways and smaller budget carriers provide services between Great Britain and other locations in Italy. EasyJet connects London's Gatwick and Stansted airports with a dozen or so Italian destinations. Ryanair flies from Stansted to even more airports. Since tickets are frequently sold at discounted prices, investigate the cost of flights within Italy (even one-way) where you're faced with a long, multichange train journey—a potentially time-saving alternative (although less green) way to travel.

You can take the Ferrovie dello Stato Italiane (FS) airport train or bus to Rome's Termini station or to Cadorna or Centrale in Milan; from the latter you can then catch a train to any other location in Italy. It will take about 40 minutes to get from Fiumicino to Roma Termini, less than an hour from Malpensa to Milano Centrale.

A helpful website for information (location, phone numbers, local transportation, etc.) about all the airports in Italy is ⊕ *www.italianairportguide.com*.

Bus

Italy's far-reaching regional bus network, often operated by private companies, isn't as attractive an option as in other European countries, partly due to convenient train travel. Schedules are often drawn up with commuters and students in mind and can be sketchy on weekends. But, car travel aside, regional bus companies often provide the only means of getting to out-of-the-way places. Even when this isn't the case, buses can be faster and more direct than local trains, so it's worth taking time to compare bus and train schedules. Busitalia–Sita Nord covers Tuscany, Umbria, Campania, and the Veneto. Sita Sud caters to travelers in Puglia, Basilicata, and Campania. FlixBus offers a low-cost long-distance service.

All buses, even those on long-distance routes, offer a single class of service. Cleanliness and comfort levels are high on private motor coaches, which have plenty of legroom, sizable seats, luggage storage, and usually toilets. Smoking isn't permitted on buses. Private lines usually have a ticket office in town or allow you to pay when you board.

Major Italian cities have inexpensive urban bus service. Although some city buses have ticket machines on board, generally you buy tickets from newsstands or tobacconists, while cities like Rome, Naples, and Milan allow smartphone app and Tap & Go contactless travel. Remember to get your ticket validated on board. Buses can get packed during busy travel periods, school commutes, and rush hours.

Car

Italy has an extensive network of *auto-stradas* (toll highways), complemented by equally well-maintained but free *super-stradas* (expressways). You'll need your autostrada ticket from entry to pay the toll when you exit; on some shorter auto-stradas, you pay the toll when you enter. The condition of provincial roads varies, but maintenance is generally good.

Most gas stations have self-service options. Those on autostradas are open 24 hours; others are generally open Monday through Saturday 7–7, with a break at lunchtime. Automobile Club Italiano offers 24-hour road service. To call the police in an emergency, dial ☎ 112. Auto-grill provides decent highway catering across the country.

PARKING

Curbside spaces are marked by blue lines; pay at a nearby *parcometro* machine, and leave the printed ticket on your dashboard. Fines for violations are high, and towing is common. You often need a permit to enter historic centers with a vehicle—violating this strictly enforced rule can also result in hefty fines. It's best to park in designated (preferably attended) lots; even small towns often have them just outside their historic centers.

RULES OF THE ROAD

You can rent a car with a U.S. driver's license, but Italy also requires non-Europeans to carry an International Driver's Permit (IDP), available for a nominal fee via the AAA website (⊕ www.aaa.com). Speed limits are generally 130 kph (80 mph) on autostradas, 90 kph (55 mph) on state roads, and 50 kph (30 mph) in towns; this can drop to 10 kph (6 mph) in congested areas. Exceed the speed limit by more than 60 kph (37 mph), and your license could be confiscated.

Right turns on red lights are forbidden. Headlights must be kept on outside municipalities, and you must wear seat belts. Fines for using mobile phones while driving exceed €1,500. The blood alcohol limit is 0.05% (stricter than in the United States).

 Train

The fastest trains on the Ferrovie dello Stato Italiane (FS), or Italian State Railways, are the Frecciarossa. Their privately owned competitor, Nuovo Trasporto Viaggiatori (NTV), or Italo, also runs high-speed service between all major northern cities and as far as Reggio Calabria in the south. Seat reservations are mandatory for these bullet trains, just as they are for the Eurostar and slower Intercity (IC) trains; tickets for the latter are about half the price of those for the faster trains.

You can buy your tickets at machines in the station or on ⊕ www.trenitalia. com—consider downloading the Trenitalia app. Reservations are not available on Regionale and Espresso trains, which are slower, make more stops, and are less expensive. For these trains, you must validate your ticket before boarding by punching it at a wall- or pillar-mounted yellow or green box—if you forget to do this, find a conductor immediately. Fines for attempting to ride a train without a ticket are €50–€200.

TRAIN PASSES

A rail pass can save you money on train travel. Generally, the more often you plan to travel long distances on high-speed trains, the more sense a pass makes. Keep in mind that even with a pass you still need to reserve seats on the trains that require them.

Travel Times by Train and Ferry

TO GREECE

BARI - DUBROVNIK, CROATIA

TO GREECE

Brindisi
Lecce
Taranto
Crotone
Catanzaro
Reggio Calabria
Bari
Potenza
< 5hrs 30mn >
Campobasso
Foggia
Benevento
Avellino
< 3hrs 20mn >
Sulmona
Isernia
< 4hrs 45mn >
Caserta
Salerno
< 5hrs >
NAPOLI - CATANIA 11HRS
Messina
Catania
Siracusa
Enna
< 3hrs >
NAPOLI - PALERMO 8HRS
< 3hrs 30mn >
< 1hr 15mn >
Napoli
Palermo
Agrigento
Roma
CIVITAVECCHIA - PALERMO 13HRS
Trapani
Civitavecchia
NAPOLI - OLBIA 12HRS
CIVITAVECCHIA - CAGLIARI 15HRS
OLBIA 6HRS
LIVORNO - OLBIA
CIVITAVECCHIA
CAGLIARI - PALERMO 14HRS
Olbia
< 4hrs >
Sassari
Oristano
Cagliari

KEY

○ Major train stations

National train service

Regional train service

- - - Ferry service

MODANE Border stations

<time> Eurostar (shortest) travel
time between stations.

Essentials

🍴 Dining

Italian cuisine is still largely regional, so try spaghetti *alla carbonara* (with cured pork jowl and egg yoke) in Rome, pizza in Naples, *cinghiale* (wild boar) in Tuscany, or *tartufi* (truffles) in Piedmont. Nowadays, vegetarian and gluten-free options are widely available. Still, if you have dietary restrictions, ask about ingredients; not everything is listed in menu descriptions.

The restaurants we list are the finest in each price category. Unless otherwise noted, they're open for lunch and dinner, closing one or two days a week.

MEALS
Although the distinction has blurred, *ristoranti* tend to be more elegant and expensive than trattorias or *osterie,* which serve traditional, home-style fare. Meals generally consist of an antipasto (starter) followed by a *primo* (first course), a *secondo* (main course) or *contorno* (vegetable side dish), and *dolce* (dessert). You can, of course, eat less (perhaps just a primo or secondo and a dolce). Single dishes are more the norm at an enoteca or pizzeria, and you can grab affordable snacks at bars, cafés, and spots for pizza *al taglio* (by the slice).

WINES, BEER, AND SPIRITS
The grape has been cultivated here since the time of the Etruscans, with Tuscany, Piedmont, the Veneto, Puglia, Calabria, Sicily, Le Marche, and Umbria among the renowned areas. Beer is readily available, and Italy has some excellent microbreweries, so ask about local brews. In addition, Italians are imaginative with their cocktails, so consider trying the *aperitivo della casa* (house aperitif). The legal drinking age in Italy is 18.

⇨ *Restaurant reviews throughout this guide have been shortened. For full*

information, visit Fodors.com. Restaurant prices are the average cost of a main course at dinner or, if dinner is not served, at lunch.

What It Costs in Euros			
$	$$	$$$	$$$$
AT DINNER			
under €15	€15–€24	€25–€35	over €35

➕ Health/Safety

EMERGENCIES
No matter where you are in Italy, dial ☎ *112* for all emergencies. Key words to remember for emergency situations are *aiuto* for "help" (pronounced aye-you-toh) and *pronto soccorso,* which means "first aid." When confronted with a health emergency, head straight for the Pronto Soccorso department of the nearest hospital or dial ☎ *118.* To call a Red Cross *ambulanza* (ambulance), dial ☎ *800/065510.* If you just need a doctor, ask for *un medico.* Ask the physician for *una fattura* (an invoice) to present to your insurance company for reimbursement.

HEALTH
Smoking is banned inside all public places, so sit indoors (where there's also often air-conditioning) if the smoke in outdoor seating areas bothers you.

It's always best to travel with your own trusted medications. Should you need prescription medication while in Italy, speak with a physician to ensure it's the proper kind. Aspirin (*l'aspirina*) can be purchased at any pharmacy, as can over-the-counter medicines such as ibuprofen or acetaminophen.

COVID-19

COVID-19 brought travel to a virtual standstill for most of 2020 and into 2021, but vaccinations have made travel possible and more safe. However, each destination (and each business within that destination) may have its own requirements and regulations. Consider protecting yourself by purchasing a travel insurance policy that will reimburse you for cancellation costs related to COVID-19. Not all travel insurance policies protect against pandemic-related cancellations, so always read the fine print.

Item	Average Cost
Cup of coffee	€1–€1.60
Soft drink (glass/can/bottle)	€1.80–€3.25
Glass of beer	€3.50–€7
Sandwich	€3–€5.50
2-km (1-mile) taxi ride in Rome	€9

⇨ *Hotel reviews throughout this guide have been shortened. For full information, visit Fodors.com. Hotel prices are for a standard double room in high season.*

🛏 Lodging

Many Italian lodgings, some quite luxurious, are in palazzi, villas, monasteries, and smaller historic buildings that have been restored to blend modern comforts with original atmosphere. Another option is renting a vacation property—although, in addition to budget, you should keep in mind location (street noise and neighborhood ambience in cities and towns, degree of isolation in the countryside), the availability of an elevator or the number of stairs, the utility costs, and what's supplied (furnishings, including pots and linens, as well as sundries like dish detergent).

If you're intrigued by the "locavore" movement, ask local tourism offices about *agriturismo* accommodations. Rural farm-stay properties range from luxury villas to farmhouses with basic facilities.

The lodgings we list are the cream of the crop in each price category. Properties are assigned price categories based on the rate for two people sharing a standard double room in high season, including tax and service.

What It Costs in Euros			
$	$$	$$$	$$$$
LODGING FOR TWO			
under €125	€125–€200	€201–€300	over €300

💲 Money

Of Italy's major cities—where, as in other countries, prices are higher than in the countryside—Milan is by far the most expensive. Resort areas like Capri, Portofino, and Cortina d'Ampezzo cater to wealthy vacationers and also charge top prices. Good value can be found in the scenic Trentino–Alto Adige region of the Dolomites and in Umbria and Le Marche. With a few exceptions, southern Italy and Sicily also offer bargains for those who do their homework before they leave home.

Essentials

Passport

A U.S. passport is valid for 10 years. You must apply in person if you're getting a passport for the first time; if your previous passport was lost, stolen, or damaged; or if it has expired and was issued more than 15 years ago or when you were under 16. The cost of a new passport is $165 for adults, $135 for children under 16; renewals are $130.

Tipping

In restaurants a service charge of 10%–15% may appear on your check, but it's not a given that your server will receive this; consider leaving a tip of 5%–10% (in cash) for good service. Taxi drivers also appreciate a euro or two.

In hotels, give the *portiere* (concierge) about 10% of the bill for services or €3–€5 for help with dinner reservations and such. In moderately priced hotels, leave maids about €1 per day, and tip a minimum of €1 for valet or room service. In expensive hotels, double these amounts. Guides should receive €1.50 at least per person for a half-day group tour, more if they're especially knowledgeable.

U.S. Embassy/Consulate

In addition to the embassy in Rome, the United States has consulates general in Florence, Milan, and Naples. If you're arrested or detained, ask Italian officials to notify the embassy or nearest consulate immediately. Consider participating in the U.S. Department of State's Smart Traveler Enrollment Program (STEP) (⊕ *step.state.gov/step*) to receive alerts and make it easier to locate you in an emergency.

Visa

Starting in mid-2025, entry for visa-exempt nationals from 60 countries including the U.S. and Canada will require travel authorization from ETIAS (European Travel Information and Authorization System). It is linked to your current passport and valid for three years, allowing stays up to 90 days in any 180-day period. Most applications should be approved in a few minutes via the website (⊕ *etias.com*) for a cost of €7 (free for those under 18 and over 70) but do allow at least 30 days should further evidence and an interview be required. Just note that the program's implementation has been delayed several times, so confirm in advance that ETIAS registration is required for your trip.

When to Go

High Season: June through September is expensive and busy. In August, most Italians take their own summer holidays; cities are less crowded, but many shops and restaurants close. July and August can be uncomfortably hot.

Low Season: Unless you're skiing, winter offers the least appealing weather, although it's the best time for airfare and hotel deals and to escape the crowds. Temperatures in the south can be mild.

Value Season: By late September, temperate weather and saner airfares can make for a happier trip. October is also great, but November is often rainy. March and early April weather is changeable. From late April to early May, the masses have not yet arrived.

Contacts

Air

AIRLINE SECURITY ISSUES Transportation Security Administration. (TSA). ☎ 866/289–9673 ⊕ www.tsa.gov.

AIRPORT INFORMATION Aeroporto di Bologna. (BLQ, aka Guglielmo Marconi). ⊠ 6 km (4 miles) northwest of Bologna ☎ 051/6479615 ⊕ www.bologna-airport.it. **Aeroporto di Cagliari.** (CAG, aka Elmas). ⊠ 7 km (4½ miles) from Cagliari, Via dei Trasvolatori, Elmas, Cagliari ☎ 070/211211 ⊕ www.sogaer.it. **Aeroporto di Catania.** (CTA, aka Fontanarossa). ⊠ 7 km (4½ miles) southwest of Catania ☎ 095/7239111 ⊕ www.aeroporto.catania. it. **Aeroporto di Firenze.** (FLR, aka Amerigo Vespucci or Peretola). ⊠ 6 km (4 miles) northwest of Florence ☎ 055/3061830 ⊕ www. aeroporto.firenze.it. **Aeroporto di Milan Linate.** (LIN). ⊠ 8 km (5 miles) southeast of Milan ☎ 02/232323 ⊕ www.milanolinate-airport.com. **Aeroporto di Milano Malpensa.** (MXP). ⊠ 45 km (28 miles) north of Milan ☎ 02/232323 ⊕ www.milanomalpensa-airport.com. **Aeroporto di Palermo.** (PMO, aka Falcone e Borsellino or Punta Raisi). ⊠ 32 km (19 miles) northwest of Palermo ☎ 091/7020273 ⊕ www. aeroportodipalermo.it.

Aeroporto di Pisa. (PSA, aka Aeroporto Galileo Galilei). ⊠ 2 km (1 mile) south of Pisa, 80 km (50 miles) west of Florence ☎ 050/849111 ⊕ www. pisa-airport.com. **Aeroporto di Roma Ciampino.** (CIA). ⊠ 15 km (9 miles) southwest of Rome ☎ 06/65951 ⊕ www.adr.it/web/aeroporti-di-roma-en/pax-cia-ciampino. **Aeroporto di Roma Fiumicino.** (FCO, aka Leonardo da Vinci). ⊠ 35 km (20 miles) southwest of Rome ☎ 06/65951 ⊕ www.adr.it. **Aeroporto di Venezia.** (VCE, aka Marco Polo). ⊠ 6 km (4 miles) north of Venice ☎ 041/2609260 ⊕ www. veneziaairport.it. **Aeroporto Internazionale di Napoli.** (NAP, aka Capodichino). ⊠ 5 km (3 miles) northeast of Naples ☎ 081/7896111 ⊕ www.aeroportodi-napoli.it. **Aeroporto Orio al Serio–Milan Bergamo (BGY).** ⊠ Via Orio al Serio 49/51, 24050 Grassobbio (BG) ☎ 035/8032421.

Bus

BUS ACTV Venezia. ⊠ Venice ☎ 041/041 call center ⊕ actv.avmspa. it. **ANM Napoli.** ⊠ Via G. Marino 1, Naples ☎ 800/639525 toll-free in Italy ⊕ www.anm.it. **ATAC Roma.** ☎ 06/0606 ⊕ www.atac.roma.it. **ATM Milano.** ⊠ Milan

☎ 02/48607607 ⊕ www. atm.it. **Autolinee Toscane.** ⊠ Biglietteria Firenze, Via Santa Caterina da Siena 17, Florence ☎ 800/142424 ⊕ www.at-bus.it. **Busitalia.** ⊠ Viale Fratelli Rosselli 80, Florence ☎ 075/9637001 Umbria, 800/184766 Veneto, 089/9847299 Campania ⊕ www.fsbusitalia.it. **Dolomiti Bus.** ⊠ Via Col da Ren 14, Belluno ☎ 0437/217111 ⊕ www. dolomitibus.it. **FlixBus.** ⊕ www.flixbus.com. **Marino Bus.** ☎ 080/3112335 ⊕ www.marinobus.it. **Sita Sud.** ⊠ Via S. Francesco d'Assisi 1, Putignano ☎ 080/5790111 ⊕ www. sitasudtrasporti.it.

Train

TRAIN INFORMATION FS-Trenitalia. ☎ 06/5210550 from outside Italy (English), 892021 in Italy ⊕ www. trenitalia.com. **NTV Italo.** ☎ 892020 call center ⊕ www.italotreno.it.

CONTACTS Eurail. ⊕ www. eurail.com. **Italia Rail.** ☎ 877/375–7245 in U.S., 06/97632451 in Italy ⊕ www.italiarail.com. **Rail Europe.** ⊕ www. raileurope.com. **RailPass.** ☎ 857/8585759 international, 866/7205759 toll-free from U.S. ⊕ www. railpass.com.

Helpful Italian Phrases

BASICS

Yes/no	Sí/No	see/no
Please	Per favore	pear fa-**vo**-ray
Thank you	Grazie	**grah**-tsee-ay
You're welcome	Prego	**pray**-go
I'm sorry (apology)	Mi dispiace	mee dis-pee-**atch**-ay
Excuse me, sorry	Scusi	**skoo**-zee
Good morning/ afternoon	Buongiorno	bwohn-**jor**-no
Good evening	Buona sera	**bwoh**-na **say**-ra
Good-bye	Arrivederci	a-ree-vah-**dare**-chee
Mr. (Sir)	Signore	see-**nyo**-ray
Mrs. (Ma'am)	Signora	see-**nyo**-ra
Miss	Signorina	see-nyo-**ree**-na
Pleased to meet you	Piacere	pee-ah-**chair**-ray
How are you?	Come sta?	**ko**-may-**stah**
Hello (phone)	Pronto?	**proan**-to

NUMBERS

one-half	mezzo	**mets**-zoh
one	uno	**oo**-no
two	due	**doo**-ay
three	tre	Tray
four	quattro	**kwah**-tro
five	cinque	**cheen**-kway
six	sei	Say
seven	sette	**set**-ay
eight	otto	**oh**-to
nine	nove	**no**-vay
ten	dieci	dee-**eh**-chee
eleven	undici	**oon**-dee-chee
twelve	dodici	**doh**-dee-chee
thirteen	tredici	**trey**-dee-chee
fourteen	quattordici	kwah-**tor**-dee-chee
fifteen	quindici	**kwin**-dee-chee
sixteen	sedici	**say**-dee-chee
seventeen	dicissette	dee-chah-**set**-ay
eighteen	diciotto	dee-chee-**oh**-to
nineteen	diciannove	dee-chee-ahn-**no**-vay
twenty	venti	**vain**-tee
twenty-one	ventuno	**vent**-oo-no
thirty	trenta	**train**-ta
forty	quaranta	kwa-**rahn**-ta
fifty	cinquanta	**cheen-kwahn**-ta
sixty	sessanta	seh-**sahn**-ta
seventy	settanta	seh-**tahn**-ta
eighty	ottanta	o-**tahn**-ta
ninety	novanta	no-**vahn**-ta
one hundred	cento	**chen**-to
one thousand	mille	**mee**-lay
one million	un milione	oon **mill**-oo-nay

COLORS

black	Nero	**nair**-ro
blue	Blu	bloo
brown	Marrone	ma-**rohn**-nay
green	Verde	**ver**-day
orange	Arancione	ah-rahn-**cho**-nay
red	Rosso	**rose**-so
white	Bianco	bee-**ahn**-koh
yellow	Giallo	**jaw**-low

DAYS OF THE WEEK

Sunday	Domenica	do-**meh**-nee-ka
Monday	Lunedi	loo-ne-**dee**
Tuesday	Martedi	mar-te-**dee**
Wednesday	Mercoledi	**mer**-ko-le-**dee**
Thursday	Giovedi	jo-ve-**dee**
Friday	Venerdì	ve-ner-**dee**
Saturday	Sabato	**sa**-ba-toh

MONTHS

January	Gennaio	jen-**ay**-o
February	Febbraio	feb-**rah**-yo
March	Marzo	**mart**-so
April	Aprile	a-**pril**-ay
May	Maggio	**mahd**-joe
June	Giugno	**joon**-yo
July	Luglio	**lool**-yo
August	Agosto	a-**gus**-to
September	Settembre	se-**tem**-bre
October	Ottobre	o-**toh**-bre
November	Novembre	no-**vem**-bre
December	Dicembre	di-**chem**-bre

USEFUL WORDS AND PHRASES

Do you speak English?	Parla Inglese?	**par**-la een-**glay**-zay
I don't speak Italian	Non parlo italiano	non **par**-lo ee-tal-**yah**-no
I don't understand	Non capisco	non ka-**peess**-ko
I don't know	Non lo so	non lo **so**
I understand	Capisco	ka-**peess**-ko
I'm American	Sono Americano(a)	**so**-no a-may-ree-**kah**-no(a)
I'm British	Sono inglese	**so**-no een-**glay**-zay
What's your name?	Come si chiama?	**ko**-may see kee-**ah**-ma
My name is ...	Mi chiamo...	mee kee-**ah**-mo
What time is it?	Che ore sono?	kay **o**-ray **so**-no
How?	Come?	**ko**-may
When?	Quando?	**kwan**-doe
Yesterday/today/ tomorrow	Ieri/oggi/domani	**yer**-ee/ **o**-jee/ do-**mah**-nee

This morning	Stamattina/Oggi	sta-ma-**tee**-na/ o-jee
Afternoon	Pomeriggio	po-mer-**ee**-jo
Tonight	Stasera	sta-**ser**-a
What?	Che cosa?	kay **ko**-za
What is it?	Che cos'è?	kay ko-**zey**
Why?	Perchè?	pear-**kay**
Who?	Chi?	**Kee**
Where is ...	Dov'è...	doe-**veh**
the train station?	la stazione?	la sta-tsee-**oh**-nay
the subway?	la metropolitana?	la may-tro-po-lee-**tah**-na
the bus stop?	la fermata dell'autobus?	la fer-**mah**-ta del-ow-tor-**booss**
the airport	l'aeroporto	la-er-roh-**por**-toh
the post office?	l'ufficio postale	loo-**fee**-cho po-**stah**-lay
the bank?	la banca?	la **bahn**-ka
the hotel?	l'hotel...?	lo-**tel**
the museum?	Il museo	eel moo-**zay**-o
the hospital?	l'ospedale?	lo-spay-**dah**-lay
the elevator?	l'ascensore	la-shen-**so**-ray
the restrooms?	...il bagno	eel **bahn**-yo
Here/there	Qui/là	kwee/la
Left/right	A sinistra/a destra	a see-**neess**-tra/a **des**-tra
Is it near/far?	È vicino/lontano?	ay vee-**chee**-no/ lon-**tah**-no
I'd like ...	Vorrei...	vo-**ray**
a room	una camera	oo-na **kah**-may-ra
the key	la chiave	la kee-**ah**-vay
a newspaper	un giornale	oon jore-**nah**-vay
a stamp	un francobollo	oon frahn-ko-**bo**-lo
I'd like to buy ...	Vorrei comprare...	vo-**ray** kom-**prah**-ray
a city map	una mappa della città	oo-na **mah**-pa **day**-la chee-**tah**
a road map	una carta stradale	oo-na **car**-tah stra-**dahl**-lay
a magazine	una revista	oo-na ray-**vees**-tah
envelopes	buste	**boos**-tay
writing paper	carta de lettera	**car**-tah dah **leyt**-ter-rah
a postcard	una cartolina	oo-na car-tog-**leen**-ah
a ticket	un biglietto	oon bee-**yet**-toh
How much is it?	Quanto costa?	kwahn-toe **coast**-a
It's expensive/ cheap	È caro/ economico	ay **car**-o/ ay-ko-**no**-mee-ko
A little/a lot	Poco/tanto	po-ko/**tahn**-to
More/less	Più/meno	pee-**oo**/**may**-no

Enough/too (much)	Abbastanza/ troppo	a-bas-**tahn**-sa/tro-po
I am sick	Sto male	sto **mah**-lay
Call a doctor	Chiama un dottore	kee-**ah**-mah-oondoe-**toe**-ray
Help!	Aiuto!	a-**yoo**-to
Stop!	Alt!	ahlt

DINING OUT

A bottle of ...	Una bottiglia di...	oo-na bo-**tee**-lee-ah dee
A cup of ...	Una tazza di...	oo-na **tah**-tsa dee
A glass of ...	Un bicchiere di...	oon bee-key-**air**-ay dee
Beer	La birra	la **beer**-rah
Bill/check	Il conto	eel **cone**-toe
Bread	Il pane	eel **pah**-nay
Breakfast	La prima colazione	la **pree**-ma ko-la-**tsee**-oh-nay
Butter	Il burro	eel **boor**-roh
Cocktail/aperitif	L'aperitivo	la-pay-ree-**tee**-vo
Dinner	La cena	la **chen**-a
Fixed-price menu	Menù a prezzo fisso	may-**noo** a **pret**-so **fee**-so
Fork	La forchetta	la for-**ket**-a
I am vegetarian	Sono vegetariano(a)	**so**-no vay-jay-ta-ree-**ah**-no/a
I cannot eat ...	Non posso mangiare	non **pose**-so mahn-gee-**are**-ay
I'd like to order	Vorrei ordinare	vo-**ray** or-dee-**nah**-ray
Is service included?	Il servizio è incluso?	eel ser-**vee**-tzee-o ay een-**kloo**-zo
I'm hungry/ thirsty	Ho fame/sede	oh **fah**-meh/**sehd**-ed
It's good/bad	È buono/cattivo	ay **bwo**-bo/ka-**tee**-vo
It's hot/cold	È caldo/freddo	ay **kahl**-doe/**fred**-o
Knife	Il coltello	eel kol-**tel**-o
Lunch	Il pranzo	eel **prahnt**-so
Menu	Il menu	eel may-**noo**
Napkin	Il tovagliolo	eel toe-va-lee-**oh**-lo
Pepper	Il pepe	eel **pep**-peh
Plate	Il piatto	eel pee-**aht**-toe
Please give me ...	Mi dia...	mee **dee**-a
Salt	Il sale	eel **sah**-lay
Spoon	Il cucchiaio	eel koo-kee-**ah**-yo
Tea	tè	tay
Water	acqua	**awk**-wah
Wine	vino	**vee**-noh

Great Itineraries

Northern Italy

Northern Italy is a region with high fashion, big wines, and beautiful lakes.

DAY 1: MILAN

Start off in **Milan,** Italy's capital of art, fashion, and design. Explore elegant shops around the **Duomo** and **Via Montenapoleone.** Some of Europe's great art treasures are housed in the **Brera Gallery.** The elegant **Basilica di Santa Maria presso San Satiro** is about a 20-minute walk from **Santa Maria delle Grazie,** where Leonardo's stunning *Last Supper* is housed. Spend a night at the opera in **La Scala,** Italy's most illustrious opera house.

Logistics: Central Milan is compact, with excellent public transportation.

DAY 2: BELLAGIO

Lake Como combines some of Italy's most beautiful scenery with elegant historic villas and gardens, making it truly worthy of a full-day excursion. **Bellagio** is a pretty village from which you can ferry to other points along the lake, take walking tours, hike, or just sit on a terrace watching the light play on the sapphire water and the snowcapped mountains.

Logistics: Como's San Giovanni station is just one hour by train from Milan, and Bus C10/C30 leaves hourly from here for the one-hour lakeside journey to Bellagio—you won't need a car, since most touring is on foot, by ferry, or by bus.

DAYS 3 TO 5: VERONA/ MANTUA/VICENZA

Take an early train to **Verona** (75 minutes from Milan) and settle into your hotel. Start your exploration of northern Italy's three most important art cities with Verona's ancient Roman arena, theater, and city gates; its brooding medieval palaces and castle; and its graceful bridge spanning the Adige.

The next day, make the 45-minute train trip to **Mantua,** arriving in time for lunch featuring a local specialty: *tortelli di zucca* (pumpkin-filled ravioli) served with sage butter. Check out the Mantegna frescoes in the **Palazzo Ducale,** or visit Giulio Romano's **Palazzo Te,** a 16th-century pleasure palace. Take the train back to Verona in time for dinner and, perhaps, an opera in the Roman amphitheater.

On Day 5, head to **Vicenza** (35 minutes by train) to see the palaces, villas, and public buildings of the lion of late-16th-century architecture, Andrea Palladio. Don't miss his **Teatro Olimpico** and his famous villa, **La Rotonda,** slightly out of town. If time allows, try to see the frescoes by Gianbattista and Giandomenico Tiepolo in the **Villa Valmarana ai Nani,** near La Rotonda. For lunch, try *baccalà alla vicentina,* the local salt-cod dish.

DAY 6: PADUA

Most people visit this important art and university center on a day trip out of Venice, but then they miss one of **Padua's** main attractions: the nightlife that goes on in the city's wine bars and cafés from evening until quite late. See the Giotto frescoes in the **Cappella degli Scrovegni** and the **Basilica di Sant'Antonio** before lunch, then spend a relaxing afternoon at the **Villa Pisani,** enjoying its gardens and important Tiepolo fresco.

Logistics: Trains run frequently to Padua from Verona (one hour) and Vicenza (30 minutes); you don't really have to schedule ahead.

DAY 7: VENICE

The first things you'll probably want to do in **Venice** are to take a vaporetto ride down the **Grand Canal** and see **Piazza San Marco.** After that, move on to the adjacent **Palazzo Ducale** and Sansovino's **Biblioteca Marciana,** across the piazzetta.

For lunch, take Vaporetto No. 1 to Ca' Rezzonico, and have a sandwich and a *spritz* in **Campo Santa Margherita**. From here, make your way to the **Galleria dell'Accademia** to take in its wonderful collection of Venetian paintings. In the evening, walk up the Zattere and have a drink at one of the cafés overlooking the **Canale della Giudecca**.

Logistics: Seeing the Grand Canal and Piazza San Marco in relative tranquility will be your reward for getting up at the crack of dawn (arrive at the vaporetto before 8:30 to avoid the rush) and doing a little extra planning.

DAY 8: VENICE

If the Galleria dell'Accademia has whetted your appetite for Venetian painting, start the day by visiting churches and institutions where you can see more. If your taste runs to modern art, head to the **Peggy Guggenheim Collection** and, down the street, the Pinault Collection in the refashioned **Punta della Dogana**.

In the afternoon, head for the Fondamenta Nuova station to catch a vaporetto to the outer islands: **Murano,** where you can shop for Venetian glass and visit a glass museum and workshops; **Burano,** known for lace making and colorful houses; and

Torcello, Venice's first inhabited island and home to a beautiful cathedral.

DAY 9: VENICE

Pay a visit to the **Rialto,** one of Europe's most atmospheric fish markets, where Venetians buy their fruit and vegetables as well as, of course, their fish. Note that the Rialto Market is closed on Sunday and Monday; since there is no fishing on Sunday, there can be no fresh fish available on Monday.

Have lunch in one of the excellent market-area restaurants. Then, on your last afternoon in Venice, leave time to sit with a coffee or spritz in a lively square or in a café along the **Fondamenta della Misericordia** in Cannaregio or **Campo Santa Margherita** in Dorsoduro. Alternatively, visit the Lombardo family's lyrical **Miracoli,** a short walk from the San Marco end of the Rialto Bridge, or Palladio's masterpiece, the **Redentore** church on **Giudecca**.

DAY 10: VENICE/DEPARTURE

Take one last vaporetto trip up the Grand Canal to **Piazzale Roma** and, after saying *arrivederci* to Venice, catch ATVO bus or Alilaguna boat to the airport.

Great Itineraries

Central Italy

Visit central Italy for the great art, sumptuous countryside, and outstanding food and wine.

DAY 1: FLORENCE

If you're coming in on an international flight, you'll probably settle in Florence in time for an afternoon stroll or siesta (depending on your jet-lag strategy) before dinner.

Logistics: Begin anticipating the first dinner of your trip. Look for a place near your hotel, and when you arrive, reserve a table (or have your concierge do it for you). Making a meal the focus of your first day is a great way to ease into Italian life.

DAY 2: FLORENCE

Begin at the **Uffizi Gallery,** whose extensive collection will occupy much of your morning. Next, take in the neighboring **Piazza della Signoria,** then head a few blocks north to the **Duomo** to check out Ghiberti's famous bronze doors on the **Battistero** (actually high-quality copies; the originals are in the **Museo dell'Opera del Duomo**). Climb up Brunelleschi's cathedral dome to the cupola. Spend the afternoon wandering Florence's medieval streets; or head out to **Fiesole** to see the ancient amphitheater.

Logistics: Reserve Uffizi tickets online ahead of your visit; climbs up Brunelleschi's dome must also be reserved in advance.

DAY 3: FLORENCE

Spend your morning seeing Michelangelo's *David* at the **Galleria dell'Accademia,** the **Medici Chapels,** the **Palazzo Pitti** and **Boboli Gardens,** and the churches of **Santa Maria Novella** and **Santa Croce.** If it's a clear day, spend the afternoon making your way up to **Piazzale Michelangelo** for sweeping views of the idyllic Florentine countryside. Recharge with a dinner featuring *bistecca alla fiorentina.*

Logistics: You can reach Piazzale Michelangelo by taxi or by taking Bus No. 12 or 13 from the Lungarno. Otherwise, do your best to get around on foot; Florence is a brilliant city for walking.

DAY 4: SAN GIMIGNANO

After breakfast, pick up your car and make the lazy drive from Florence to **San Gimignano.** Upon arriving in town, you'll no doubt be awed by its towers—medieval skyscrapers that provided security and served as symbols of wealth and power. After finding your way to a hotel in the old town, set out on foot to check out the city's turrets and alleyways, then enjoy a leisurely dinner.

Logistics: San Gimignano is only 57 km (35 miles) to the southwest. Consider taking a detour on the SS222 (Strada Chiantigiana) to a winery in one of the Chianti wine towns.

DAY 5: SIENA

In the morning, set out for nearby **Siena,** which is known worldwide for its Palio, a horse race involving the city's 17 *contrade* (medieval neighborhoods). You will be blown away by the precious medieval streets and memorable fan-shape **Piazza del Campo.** Don't miss the spectacular **Duomo,** the **Battistero,** and the **Spedale di Santa Maria della Scala,** an old hospital and hostel that now contains an underground archaeological museum.

Logistics: Parking can be a challenge. Look for the *stadio* (soccer stadium), where there's a parking lot that often has space.

Adriatic Sea

Ligurian Sea

Florence

San Gimignano

Arezzo

Cortona

Siena

Assisi

ELBA

Spoleto

CORSICA (FRANCE)

✪ROME

DAY 6: AREZZO/CORTONA

From Siena you'll first head to **Arezzo,** home to the **Basilica di San Francesco,** which contains important frescoes by Piero della Francesca. Check out the **Piazza Grande** along with its beautiful Romanesque church of **Santa Maria della Pieve.** Try to do all of this before lunch, after which you'll head straight to **Cortona.** Cortona is a town for walking and relaxing, not sightseeing, so enjoy yourself as you wander through the **Piazza della Repubblica** and **Piazza Signorelli,** perhaps doing a bit of shopping.

Logistics: Siena to Arezzo is 70 km (43½ miles) on the SS715 and A1 autostrada. From Arezzo to Cortona, it's just 30 km (18 miles)—take SR71.

DAY 7: ASSISI

Cross over into Umbria and see **Assisi,** the home of St. Francis that today hosts many religious pilgrims. After arrival and check-in, head straight for the **Basilica di San Francesco,** which displays the tomb of St. Francis and some unbelievable frescoes. From here, take Via San Francesco to **Piazza del Comune** and see the **Tempio di Minerva.** Break for lunch and then see **San Rufino,** the cathedral, before returning through the piazza to Corso Mazzini and **Santa Chiara.**

Logistics: From Cortona, take the SR71 to the A1 autostrada toward Perugia. After about 40 km (24 miles), take the Assisi exit (E45), and it's another 14 km (8 miles) to Assisi.

DAY 8: SPOLETO

This morning takes you to the walled city of **Spoleto,** renowned for its summer arts festival; its wonderful **Duomo;** its impressive **La Rocca** fortress; and its marvelous **Ponte delle Torri,** the 14th-century bridge that separates the town from Monteluco. Save your appetite for a serious last dinner in Italy. Try to sample black truffles, a proud product of the region, especially from mid-November to mid-March.

Logistics: The trip from Assisi to Spoleto is a pretty 47-km (29-mile) drive (SS75 to SS3) that should take less than an hour.

DAY 9: SPOLETO/DEPARTURE

It's a fair distance from Spoleto to the Florence airport, your point of departure. One alternative is to fly out of the tiny airport in Perugia. If you prefer to drive, get an early start and allow at least 2½ hours for the trip along the A1 autostrada.

Great Itineraries

Southern Italy

Come for the archaeological wonders, azure sea, and excellent Neapolitan fare.

DAY 1: NAPLES

Fly into Naples's **Aeroporto Capodichino,** a scant 5 km (3 miles) from the city. Naples is classic Italy, and many visitors end up falling in love with its alluring palazzi and spectacular pizza. If you can get over the shock of the initial cacophony and its sketchy reputation, you'll likely get hooked on its lively characters and irresistibly languid, stop-start rhythm.

Recharge with a nap and, after that, a good *caffè*—Naples has some of the world's best. You should be back on your feet in time for an evening stroll down the city's bustling shopping street, Via Toledo, to Piazza Plebiscito, before dinner and bed.

DAY 2: NAPLES

Start the day at the **Museo Archeologico Nazionale,** budgeting at least two hours for its collection, before stopping for coffee at a café in Piazza Bellini. From here, head down Via dei Tribunali, crossing Via Duomo to see Caravaggio's *The Seven Works of Mercy* at **Pio Monte della Misericordia.** Make your way back along Spaccanapoli with a brief stop at the **Cappella Sansevero** for a look at the pinnacle of Masonic sculpture. Continue on to the port and the **Castel Nuovo** and then past the **Teatro San Carlo** to the enormous **Palazzo Reale** in **Piazza Plebiscito.** Just beyond this is the **Santa Lucia** waterfront area, with the **Castel dell'Ovo.** Join the passeggiata along *lungomare* (seafront) as far as Mergellina, soaking up the atmosphere and spectacular views, and perhaps grab an aperitivo or gelato. Return to your hotel for a short rest before dinner and perhaps a night out at one of Naples's lively bars or clubs.

Logistics: This entire day is easily done on foot.

DAY 3: POMPEII/SORRENTO

After breakfast, pack your luggage, and head from Naples to **Pompeii,** one of Europe's true archaeological gems. If it's summer, be prepared for sweltering heat as you make your way through the incredible preserved ruins of a city that was devastated by the whims of **Mt. Vesuvius** nearly 2,000 years ago. You'll see the houses of noblemen and merchants, brothels, political graffiti, and more. **Sorrento,** the beginning of the fabled Amalfi Coast, is touristy, but it may well be the Italian city of your imagination: cliff hanging, cobblestone paved, and graced with an infinite variety of fishing ports and coastal views. Stop here for a relaxing dinner of fish and white wine.

Logistics: Rather than rent a car, take the Circumvesuviana, a twice-hourly train to Sorrento that stops near the ruins at Pompeii's Villa dei Misteri.

DAY 4: POSITANO/RAVELLO

Positano, your next stop, is one of Italy's most visited towns for good reason: its blue-green seas, stairs "as steep as ladders," and white Moorish-style houses are all memorable. Walk, gaze, and eat (lunch), before heading on to the less visited, yet even loftier town of **Ravello.** This aerie "closer to the sky than it is to the sea" is an Amalfi Coast dream come true. Don't miss the **Duomo, Villa Rufolo,** and **Villa Cimbrone** before settling in for dinner in the sky.

Logistics: Sorrento to Positano is a slow 15-km (9½-mile) jaunt, and then Ravello is another 26 km (16 miles) to the east, with the winding roads drawing it out for the better part of an hour. The SITA bus is your best option. Motorists should be prepared to use low gears if driving a stick shift.

DAY 5: MATERA

Those with a car will have a bit of a drive from the Amalfi Coast; leaving Campania and entering Basilicata is generally a lonely experience. Little-traveled roads, wild hills, and distant farms are the hallmarks of this province, which has perfected the art of peasant food and the deep, dark *aglianico* wines to go with it. The lengthy journey to **Matera** is worthwhile, however, to see this beautiful ancient city full of Paleolithic **Sassi** (cave-like dwellings hewn out of rock). Spend the afternoon exploring them, then enjoy a relaxing dinner at one of Matera's excellent restaurants.

Logistics: It's a long haul from Ravello to Matera—if using public transportation you may find it easier to return first to Naples—but the effort is worth it, as Basilicata's landscape is so pretty.

DAY 6: LECCE

Get an early start for your journey to the Baroque city of **Lecce,** which will mark your introduction to Puglia, the heel of Italy's boot. It's one of the country's best-kept secrets, as you'll soon find out upon checking out the spectacular church of **Santa Croce,** the ornate **Duomo,** and the harmonious **Piazza Sant'Oronzo.**

The shopping, the food, and the evening passeggiata are all great.

Logistics: It's not far from Matera to Lecce as the crow flies, but the 2½-hour trip is more involved than you might think; patience is required. Those without a car should head to Bari, then take the train south. The best driving route is via Taranto, *not* up through Bari.

DAY 7: BARI

It is a two-hour drive from Lecce to **Bari,** and many make a pit stop halfway at the beautiful hilltop town of **Ostuni.** Spend the day wandering through Bari's historic center and finish with a good fish dinner.

Logistics: Take a direct train or the coastal SS16 for 154 km (95 miles) until you hit Bari.

DAY 8: BARI/DEPARTURE

Bari's Aeroporto Karol Wojtyla is small but quite serviceable, with frequent connections through Rome and Milan.

Logistics: Bari hotels offer easy airport transfers; take advantage of them.

Great Itineraries

Venice, Florence, Rome, and Highlights in Between

Think of this itinerary as a rough draft for you to revise according to your interests and time constraints.

DAY 1: VENICE

Arrive in Venice's Marco Polo Airport, and hop on the bus to the city's main bus station. Check into your hotel, get out, and get lost along the canals for a couple of hours before dinner.

Logistics: At the main bus station, you can immediately transfer to the most delightful "bus" in the world: the vaporetto. Enjoy your first ride up the Grand Canal, and make sure you're paying attention to the *fermata* (stop) where you need to get off.

DAY 2: VENICE

If you like photography, rise before dawn to catch a vaporetto to Giudecca and walk along the long Fondamenta, observing the golden hour hues bathe Palladio's Redentore and the stunning canal views. Grab a coffee at a real Italian coffee bar before taking in the top sights, including the **Basilica di San Marco, Palazzo Ducale,** and **Galleria dell'Accademia.** Don't forget **Piazza San Marco**: the intense anticipation as you near the giant square climaxes in a stunning view of the piazza. Stop for lunch, sampling the traditional Venetian specialty *sarde in saor* (sardines in a mouthwatering sweet-and-sour preparation with onions and raisins), and check out the fish market at the foot of the **Rialto Bridge**; then see the sunset at the **Zattere** before dinner. Later, stop at a bar on the **Campo San Luca** or **Campo Santa Margherita,** where you can mingle with the students and families enjoying the open space, and toast to being free of automobiles.

Logistics: Venice is best seen on foot, with the occasional vaporetto ride. Always carry a city map: it's very easy to get totally lost here.

DAY 3: FERRARA/BOLOGNA

The ride to **Ferrara,** your first stop in Emilia-Romagna, is about 90 minutes. Visit the **Castello Estense** and **Duomo** before grabbing lunch. Wander Ferrara's cobblestone streets, then hop on the train to **Bologna** (less than an hour away). Check into your hotel, and walk around **Piazza Maggiore** before dinner, soaking up the bustle and architectural gems including the **Fontana del Nettuno.** Later check out some of Italy's best nightlife.

Logistics: The train station lies a bit outside the center of Ferrara, so you may want to take a taxi or a less expensive city bus into town.

DAY 4: BOLOGNA/FLORENCE

After breakfast, visit some of Bologna's churches and piazzas, and walk the porticoed streets admiring the city's medieval towers and tempting delis. After lunch, take the short train ride to **Florence.** You'll arrive in time for an afternoon siesta and an evening passeggiata.

DAY 5: FLORENCE

Start with the **Uffizi Gallery,** where you'll see Botticelli's *Primavera* and *Birth of Venus,* the *Madonna of the Goldfinch* by Raphael, and *Bacchus* by Caravaggio, among other works. Next, walk to **Piazza del Duomo,** site of Brunelleschi's spectacular dome, which you can climb for an equally spectacular view. After a simple trattoria lunch, either devote the afternoon to art or hike up to **Piazzale Michelangelo,** which overlooks the city. Finish the evening in style with a traditional *bistecca alla Fiorentina* (grilled T-bone steak with olive oil).

Logistics: It's best to reserve Uffizi Gallery tickets in advance; you *must* reserve in advance to climb Brunelleschi's dome.

DAY 6: LUCCA/PISA

After breakfast, board a train for a 90-minute ride to the walled medieval city of **Lucca.** Don't miss the Romanesque **Duomo** or a walk along the city's ramparts. Have lunch at a trattoria before continuing on to **Pisa** (30 minutes away) and its **Campo dei Miracoli,** where you'll spend an afternoon seeing the **Leaning Tower,** along with the **Duomo** and **Battistero.** Walk down to the banks of the Arno River and dine at one of the inexpensive local restaurants in the real city center.

Logistics: Lucca's train station is conveniently situated just outside the walled city. Although across town from the Leaning Tower, Pisa's train station isn't far from the city center.

DAY 7: ROME

Take a high-speed train bound for **Rome,** a 90-minute trip from Florence or three hours from Pisa. Although the Eternal City took millennia to build, on this whirlwind trip you'll have just two days to tour it. Make your way to your hotel and relax

for a bit before heading to the **Piazza Navona, Campo de' Fiori,** and **Trevi Fountain**—it's best in the evening—and have a stand-up aperitivo (Campari and soda is a classic) at an unpretentious local bar. For dinner, you can't go wrong at any of Rome's popular local pizzerias.

DAY 8: ROME

In the morning, head to the **Vatican Museums** to see Michelangelo's glorious frescoes at the **Sistine Chapel.** Visit **St. Peter's Basilica and Square** before heading for lunch near the Pantheon. Next, visit the magnificent **Pantheon,** and then the **Colosseum,** stopping along Via dei Fori Imperiali to check out the **Roman Forum** from above. From the Colosseum, walk or take a taxi to **Piazza di Spagna,** a good place to shop at stylish boutiques.

Logistics: Avoid lines and waits by buying tickets online.

DAY 9: ROME/DEPARTURE

Head by taxi to Termini station and catch the train to Fiumicino airport.

Logistics: For most people, the train from Termini station is preferable to a taxi ride.

Great Itineraries

Rome in 3 Days

Rome wasn't built in a day—so don't try to see it all in a day. Three days is a doable, if jam-packed, amount of time to visit the ancient city's major attractions.

Logistics: Much of the city shuts down on Sunday (including the Vatican Museums, except for the last Sunday of the month), and many restaurants and state museums are closed on Monday. To skip lines and better enjoy your experiences, reservations are a good idea at the Colosseum and the Vatican Museums; they're required for the Galleria Borghese.

DAY 1: ANCIENT ROME

Spend your first day in Rome exploring the likes of the **Roman Forum, Musei Capitolini,** and the **Colosseum.** This area is pretty compact, but you can easily spend a full morning and afternoon exploring its treasures. It's best to try and beat the crowds at the Colosseum by getting there right when it opens at 8:30 am (advance tickets help, too). A guided tour of the Forum is also a good way to make the most out of your afternoon. After your day of sightseeing, stop for a classic Roman dinner in nearby Monti.

DAY 2: THE VATICAN AND PIAZZA NAVONA

Another full day of sightseeing awaits when you make your way to the city-state known as the **Vatican.** You'll once again want to try and avoid the biggest crowds here, especially for a glimpse of the Sistine Chapel (the best way to do this is to make online reservations ahead of time). Booking a tour of the **Vatican Museums** is a good way to take full advantage of the site; most tours last two hours. Be sure to stop in and marvel at **St. Peter's Basilica,** too. Stop for lunch in nearby Prati, but after you're done with the Vatican, cross the river to **Piazza Navona.**

Spend some time exploring this glorious piazza and its sculptures, but make sure to stop by the **Pantheon** before heading to Campo de' Fiori for dinner at an outdoor restaurant. Afterward, there are plenty of nearby bars to keep you occupied.

DAY 3: PIAZZA DI SPAGNA, VILLA BORGHESE, AND TRASTEVERE

Start your morning with breakfast near the **Trevi Fountain** before doing some window-shopping up Via Condotti and along the many surrounding backstreets as you make your way to the **Spanish Steps.** Pose for some postcard-worthy photos there before heading to nearby **Villa Borghese.** If you're sick of museums, feel free to explore Rome's main park and enjoy the great views; if you're up for some more art, the **Galleria Borghese** is one of the city's best art museums. Afterward, head to trendy Trastevere for dinner, and soak up the cobblestone streets and charming medieval houses as you barhop your last night in town.

IF YOU HAVE MORE TIME

If you want to make the most of your time in the city itself, take your time exploring the many churches and cathedrals, like **Sant'Ignazio** or **San Clemente.** You can also stop by to explore gorgeous palaces, like the **Palazzo Doria Pamphilij,** and check out lesser known but just as impressive museums, like the MAXXI or the MACRO. Visiting the ancient Roman road known as the Via Appia Antica and its spooky yet mesmerizing catacombs is a great way to spend an afternoon immersed in Roman history. Make time for some shopping: early evenings are a good time to saunter around the big-label boutiques of Piazza di Spagna and historic independents of Piazza Navona. For flea market bargains check out the Mercato di Porta Portese.

On the Calendar

Winter

Carnevale. Venice earned its international reputation as the "city of Carnevale" in the 18th century, when partying would begin several months before Lent and the city seemed to be one continuous masquerade. The celebration was revived for good in the 1970s, and each year over the 15- to 17-day Carnevale period (ending on the Tuesday before Ash Wednesday), more than a half-million people attend concerts, theater and street performances, masquerade balls, historical processions, fashion shows, and contests.

If you're not planning on joining in the revelry, you'd be wise to choose another time to visit Venice. Crowds throng the streets (which become one-way, with police directing foot traffic), bridges are designated "no-stopping" zones to avoid gridlock, and prices skyrocket. ⊕ *www.carnevale.venezia.it.*

Carnevale di Acireale. With fantastical floats and entertaining parades, Acireale's carnival celebrations are known as being the best in Sicily. The exact dates depend on Easter, but events are held over the course of three weekends before the start of Lent (Ash Wednesday), when thousands of revelers pack the streets of the coastal town. ⊕ *carnevaleacireale.eu.*

Festa di Santa Lucia. The feast of Siracusa's patron, Santa Lucia, is held from December 13 to 20 at the Church of Santa Lucia alla Badia. A splendid silver statue of the saint is carried from the church to the Duomo: a torchlight procession and band music accompany the bearers, while local families watch from their balconies. ⊕ *www.basilicasantalucia.com.*

Sagra del Mandorlo in Fiore. In late February and early March, when most of the almond trees are in blossom, Agrigento hosts the Sagra del Mandorlo in Fiore, with international folk dances, a costumed parade, and the sale of marzipan and other sweet treats made from almonds. ⊕ *www.lavalledeitempli.it/mandorlo-in-fiore.*

Sant'Orso Fair. On the last weekend of January, the streets of Aosta are brightened by an arts-and-crafts market that brings artisans from all over the Valle d'Aosta. All the traditional techniques are featured: wood carving and sculpture, soapstone work, wrought iron, leather, wool, lace, and household items of all kinds. Food and wine are sold at outdoor stands and wandering minstrels enliven the whole event. ⊕ *www.fieradisantorso.it.*

Spring

Biennale di Venezia. Come springtime every two years (the even-numbered) the contemporary art world and the curious descend on Venice's Giardini pavilions, Arsenale dockside warehouses, and scattered palazzi. In odd years it's the turn of the world's leading architects to display their creations. ⊕ *www.labiennale.org.*

Festa della Madonna a Cavallo. In Scicli, Sicily, the last Saturday in May brings the festival of the town's savior, Madonna delle Milizie (Virgin Mary of Militias), celebrating the supposed moment in the 11th century when the Virgin Mary descended on horseback to rescue the Norman-ruled town from a Saracen invasion. The weekend festival includes parading a statue of the Madonna on horseback through the main piazza to intervene in a mock battle before reveling in salvation by indulging in a sweet pastry towering

On the Calendar

with whipped cream, known as a *testa di turco*. ⊕ *www.visitvigata.com*.

Festa di Sant'Efisio. On May 1, thousands of costumed villagers parade through town during Sardinia's greatest annual festival, the Festa di Sant'Efisio, named after the martyred saint who saved the city from the plague in the 17th century. The saint's statue is carried aloft through Cagliari's flower-lined streets, part of a four-day procession from Cagliari to Nora and back again (64 km [40 miles] round-trip), and is accompanied by colorful costumed groups from throughout the island in an enthusiastic celebration of traditional culture. Ask at Cagliari's tourist office about viewing the grand spectacle along the main route in Cagliari. From April on, you can find tickets at ⊕ *www.festadisantefisio.it*.

Milan Design Week. For a week in April Italy's northern powerhouse city hosts the biggest gathering of the design world. Pride of place in the calendar is the Salone di Mobile, a furniture fair like no other, staged in the cavernous Fiera Milano exhibition center and in dozens of venues across this design-mad city. ⊕ *www.salonemilano.it*.

Sagra del Pesce. The highlight of the festival of San Fortunato is held on the second Sunday of May each year in Camogli. It's a crowded, colorful, and free-to-the-public feast of freshly caught fish, cooked outside at the port in a 12-foot frying pan. ⊕ *www.camogliturismo.it*.

Scoppio del Carro (Explosion of the Cart). On Easter Sunday, Florentines and foreigners alike flock to the Piazza del Duomo to watch as the Scoppio del Carro, a monstrosity of a carriage pulled by two huge oxen decorated for the occasion, makes its way through the city center and ends

up in the piazza. Through an elaborate wiring system, an object representing a dove is sent from inside the cathedral to the baptistery across the way. The dove sets off an explosion of fireworks that come streaming from the carriage. You have to see it to believe it. ⊕ *www.visittuscany.com*.

Vinitaly. This widely attended international wine and spirits event in Verona takes place for a few days in April. Recent gatherings have attracted more than 4,000 exhibitors from two dozen countries. The festivities kick off with Opera Wine, a showcase for the top 100 Italian wines as chosen by *Wine Spectator* magazine, which takes place in the Palazzo della Gran Guardia, in Piazza Bra. ⊕ *www.vinitaly.com*.

Summer

Arena di Verona Opera Festival. During the venue's summer season (June to August), as many as 16,000 attendees sit on the original stone terraces or in modern cushioned stalls. Most of the operas presented are big and splashy, like *Aida* or *Turandot*, demanding huge choruses, and, if possible, camels, horses, or elephants. Order tickets by phone or through the arena website: if you book a spot on the cheaper terraces, be sure to take or rent a *cuscino*. ⊕ *www.arena.it*.

Estate Fiesolana. From June through August, Estate Fiesolana, a festival of theater, music, dance, and film, takes place in Fiesole's churches and in the Roman amphitheater—demonstrating that the ancient Romans knew a thing or two about acoustics. ⊕ *www.estate-fiesolana.it*.

Festa del Redentore. On the third Sunday in July, crowds cross the Canale della Giudecca by means of a pontoon bridge, built every year to commemorate the doge's annual visit to Palladio's Chiesa del Santissimo Redentore to offer thanks for the end of a 16th-century plague. The evening before, Venetians—accompanied each year by an increasing number of tourists—set up tables and chairs along the canals. As evening falls, practically the whole city takes to the streets and tables, and thousands more take to the water. Boats decorated with colored lanterns (and well provisioned with traditional Redentore meals) jockey for position to watch the grand event. Half an hour before midnight, Venice kicks off a fireworks display over the Bacino, with brilliant reflections on its waters. You'll find good viewing anywhere along the Riva degli Schiavoni; you could also try Zattere, as close to Punta Dogana as you can get, or on the Zitelle end of the Giudecca. After the fireworks, join the young folks and stay out all night, greeting the sunrise on the Lido beach, or rest up and make the procession to mass on Sunday morning. If you're on a boat, allow a couple of hours to dislodge yourself from the nautical traffic jam when the festivities break up. ⊕ *www.redentorevenezia.it.*

Festa di San Giovanni (Feast of St. John the Baptist). On June 24 Florence mostly grinds to a halt to celebrate the Festa di San Giovanni in honor of its patron saint. Many shops and bars close, and at night a fireworks display lights up the Arno and attracts thousands. ⊕ *www.visit-tuscany.com/en/ideas/june-24th-in-florence-san-giovannis-celebrations.*

Festival dei Due Mondi. Each summer Umbria hosts one of Italy's biggest arts festivals: Spoleto's Festival of the Two Worlds. Starting out as a classical music festival, it has now evolved into one of Italy's brightest gatherings of arts aficionados. Running from late June through mid-July, it features modern and classical music, theater, dance, and opera. Increasingly there are also a number of small cinema producers and their films. ⊕ *www.festivaldispoleto.com.*

Luminaria. Pisa is at its best during the Luminaria feast day, on June 16. The day honors St. Ranieri, the city's patron saint. Palaces along the Arno are lit with white lights, and there are plenty of fireworks. ⊕ *www.turismo.pisa.it/en/events.*

Ravello Festival. This festival was first staged in 1953 and partly inspired by composer Richard Wagner's declaration on setting foot in Villa Rufolo grounds: "The magical garden of Klingsor is found!" Sitting in this lofty terrace in serene Ravello, the striking Oscar Niemeyer Auditorium is the breathtaking venue for wonderful concerts. For the most uplifting musical experience secure a seat at the much-sought-after Sunrise Concert each August, where the dawning sun, divine sounds, and Amalfi Coast vistas intertwine. ⊕ *ravellofestival.info*

Taormina Film Festival. Sicily's famous festival takes place in late June and early July. ⊕ *taorminafilmfestival.com.*

Umbria Jazz Festival. Perugia is hopping for 10 days in July, when more than a million people flock to see famous names in contemporary music perform at the Umbria Jazz Festival. In recent years the stars have included Wynton Marsalis, Sting, Eric Clapton, Lady Gaga, Tony Bennett, Jeff Beck, and Elton John. There's also a shorter Umbria Jazz Winter Festival from late December to early January. ⊕ *www.umbriajazz.com.*

On the Calendar

Fall

Douja d'Or National Wine Festival. For 10 days in mid-September, Asti is host to a popular wine festival—an opportunity to see Asti and celebrate the product that made it famous. ⊕ *visit.asti.it/en/september-in-asti/douja-dor.*

Eurochocolate Festival. If you've got a sweet tooth and are visiting in fall, book early and head to Perugia for the Eurochocolate Festival. This is one of the biggest chocolate festivals in the world, with a million visitors, and is held over a week in October or November. Fill your cheeks again at Eurochocolate Spring in March. ⊕ *www.eurochocolate.com.*

Fiera Internazionale del Tartufo Bianco (International White Truffle Fair). From early October to early December, Alba hosts an internationally famous truffle fair. Merchants, chefs, and other aficionados of this pungent yet delicious fungus come from all over the world to buy and taste white truffles at the height of their season. The fourth Sunday of September sees the **Palio degli Asini**, a hilarious donkey race, a lampoon of Asti's eminently serious horse race. Tickets to watch this competition between Alba's districts, with riders dressed in medieval garb astride their stubborn beasts, can be hard to get. ■TIP→ **Hotel and restaurant reservations for October and November should be made well in advance.** ⊕ *www.fieradeltartufo.org.*

Palio di Asti. September is a month of fairs and celebrations in Asti, and this horse race that runs through the streets of town is the highlight. First mentioned in 1275, this annual event has been going strong ever since. After an elaborate procession in period costumes, nine horses and jockeys representing different sections of town vie for the honor of claiming the *palio*, a symbolic flag of victory. The race happens on a Sunday at the beginning of September each year. ⊕ *visit.asti.it.*

Sagra Musicale Umbra. Held mid-September, the Sagra Musicale Umbra celebrates sacred music in Perugia and in several towns throughout the region. ⊕ *www.perugiamusicaclassica.com.*

ROME

Updated by
Laura Itzkowitz
and Erica Firpo

⦿ **Sights**
★★★★★

🍴 **Restaurants**
★★★☆☆

🛏 **Hotels**
★★★★★

🛍 **Shopping**
★★★★☆

🍸 **Nightlife**
★★★★☆

WELCOME TO ROME

TOP REASONS TO GO

★ **The Vatican:** Although its population numbers only in the hundreds, the Vatican makes up for it with the millions who visit each year. Marvel at Michelangelo's Sistine Chapel and St. Peter's Basilica.

★ **The Colosseum:** The largest amphitheater of the Roman world was begun by Emperor Vespasian and inaugurated by his son Titus in AD 80.

★ **Piazza Navona:** You couldn't concoct a more Roman street scene: crowded café tables at street level, wrought-iron balconies above, and, at the center, Bernini's Fountain of the Four Rivers and Borromini's Sant'Agnese.

★ **Roman Forum:** This fabled labyrinth of ruins variously served as a political playground, a center of commerce, and a place where justice was dispensed during the Roman Republic and Empire.

★ **Trastevere:** This neighborhood is a maze of jumbled alleyways, traditional Roman trattorias, cobblestone streets, and medieval houses.

1 Ancient Rome with Monti and Celio. The Forum and Palatine Hill were once the hub of Western civilization.

2 The Vatican with Borgo and Prati. St. Peter's Basilica and the Sistine Chapel draw millions.

3 Piazza Navona, Campo de' Fiori, and the Jewish Ghetto. This is the heart of the historic quarter. The Ghetto still preserves the flavor of Old Rome.

4 Piazza di Spagna. Travel back to the days of the Grand Tour in this area.

5 Repubblica and the Quirinale. These areas house government offices, churches, and sights.

6 Villa Borghese and Environs. Rome's most famous park is home to the Galleria Borghese.

7 Trastevere. Rome's left bank has kept its authentic roots.

8 Aventino and Testaccio. Aventino is a posh residential area, and Testaccio is more working class.

9 Esquilino and Via Appia Antica. These neighborhoods have plenty of ancient sights and churches.

EAT LIKE A LOCAL IN ROME

A local salumeria or cured meat shop

In Rome, tradition is the dominant feature of the cuisine, with a focus on freshness and simplicity, so when Romans continue ordering the standbys, it's easy to understand why. That said, the influx of residents to the capital from other regions has yielded many variations on the staples.

ARTICHOKES

There are two well-known preparations of *carciofo*, or artichoke, in Rome. Carciofi *alla romana* are stuffed with wild mint, garlic, and pecorino, then braised in olive oil, white wine, and water. Carciofi *alla giudia* (Jewish-style) are whole artichokes, deep-fried twice, so that they open like a flower, the outer leaves crisp and golden brown, while the heart remains tender. When artichokes are in season—late winter through the spring—they're served everywhere.

BUCATINI ALL'AMATRICIANA

It might look like spaghetti with red sauce, but there's much more to *bucatini all'amatriciana*. It's a spicy, rich, and complex dish that owes its flavor to *guanciale*, or cured pork jowl, as well as tomatoes and crushed red pepper flakes. It's often served over bucatini, a hollow, spaghetti-like pasta, and topped with grated pecorino Romano.

CODA ALLA VACCINARA

Rome's largest slaughterhouse in the 1800s was in the Testaccio neighborhood, and that's where you'll find dishes like *coda alla vaccinara*, or "oxtail in the style of the cattle butcher." This dish is made from ox or veal tails stewed with tomatoes, carrots, celery, and wine, and it's usually seasoned with cinnamon. It's simmered for hours and then finished with raisins and pine nuts or bittersweet chocolate.

GELATO

Its consistency is often said to be a cross between regular American ice cream and soft-serve. The best versions of gelato are extremely flavorful, and almost always made fresh daily. When choosing a *gelateria*, watch for signs that say *gelato artigianale* (artisan- or homemade); otherwise, keep an eye out for the real deal by avoiding gelato that looks too bright or fluffy.

PIZZA

There are two kinds of Roman pizza: *al taglio* (by the slice) and *tonda* (round pizza). The former has a thicker, focac-cia-like crust and is cut into squares; these are sold by weight and generally available all day. The typical Roman pizza tonda has a very thin crust and is served almost charred. Because they're so hot, the ovens are usually fired up only in the evening, which is why Roman *pizzerie* tend to open for dinner only.

CACIO E PEPE

The name means "cheese and pepper," and this is a simple pasta dish from the *cucina povera*, or rustic cooking, tradition. It's a favorite Roman primo, usually made with *tonnarelli* (fresh egg pasta a bit thicker than spaghetti),

Artichokes

which is coated with a pecorino-cheese sauce and lots of freshly ground black pepper. Some restaurants serve the dish in an edible bowl of paper-thin baked cheese.

FRITTI

The classic Roman starter in a trattoria and especially at the pizzeria, is *fritti*: an assortment of fried treats, usually crumbed or in batter. Often, before selecting a pizza, locals will order their fritti: *filetti di baccalà* (salt cod in batter), *fiori di zucca* (zucchini flowers, usually stuffed with anchovy and mozzarella), *supplì* (rice balls stuffed with mozzarella and other ingredients), or *olive ascolane* (stuffed olives).

LA GRICIA

This dish is often referred to as a "white amatriciana" because it's precisely that: pasta (usually spaghet-ti or rigatoni) served with pecorino cheese and guanciale—thus amatrici-ana without the tomato sauce. It's a lighter alternative to carbonara in that it doesn't contain egg, and its origins date back further than the amatriciana.

Gelato

The timeless city to which all roads lead, Mamma Roma enthralls visitors today as she has since time immemorial. Here the ancient Romans made us heirs-in-law to what we call Western Civilization; where centuries later Michelangelo painted the Sistine Chapel; and where Gian Lorenzo Bernini's Baroque nymphs and naiads still dance in their marble fountains.

Today the city remains a veritable Grand Canyon of culture. Ancient Rome rubs shoulders with the medieval, the modern runs into the Renaissance, and the result is like nothing so much as an open-air museum.

But always remember: *"Quando a Roma vai, fai come vedrai"* (When in Rome, do as the Romans do). Don't feel intimidated by the press of art and culture. Instead, contemplate the grandeur from a table at a sun-drenched café on Piazza della Rotonda; let Rome's colorful life flow around you without feeling guilty because you haven't seen everything. It can't be done, anyway. There's just so much here that you'll have to come back, so be sure to throw a coin in the Trevi Fountain.

Planning

Getting Around

Although most of Rome's sights are in a relatively circumscribed area, the city is too large to be seen solely on foot. Try to avoid rush hour when taking the Metro (subway) or a bus, as public transport can

be extremely crowded. Midmorning or midday through early afternoon tends to be less busy. Otherwise, it's best to take a taxi to the area you plan to visit if it is across town. You should always expect to do a lot of walking in Rome, especially considering how little ground the subway actually covers, so plan on wearing a pair of comfortable, sturdy shoes to cushion the impact of the *sampietrini* (cobblestones). You can get free city and transit maps at municipal information booths.

METRO

Rome's integrated transportation system includes buses and trams (ATAC), the Metropolitana (the subway, or Metro), suburban trains and buses (COTRAL), and the commuter rail run by the state railway (Trenitalia). A ticket (BIT), valid for 100 minutes on any combination of buses and trams and one entrance to the Metro, costs €1.50. Tickets are sold at tobacco shops, newsstands, some coffee bars, automatic ticket machines in Metro stations, some bus stops, in machines on some buses, and at ATAC ticket booths. You can purchase individual or multiple tickets. It's always a good idea to have a few tickets handy so you don't have to hunt for a vendor when you need one. All tickets must be validated by time-stamping in the yellow meter boxes aboard buses and in Metro stations, immediately prior to boarding. Failure to validate your ticket will result in a fine of €54.90. You can now pay for fines on the ATAC website. Pay immediately, or the fine will increase to €104.90 if you pay after five days. You can also pay fines in post offices, authorized shops, or by wire transfer. Do not pay the ticket inspectors in cash; some may be equipped for payment by mobile POS.

A Roma24H ticket, or *biglietto integrato giornaliero* (integrated daily ticket), is valid for 24 hours (from the moment you stamp it) on all public transit and costs €7. You can also purchase a Roma48H (€12.50), a Roma72H (€18), and a CIS (Carta Integrata Settimanale), which is valid for one week (€24). Each option gives unlimited travel on ATAC buses, COTRAL urban bus services, trains for the Lido and Viterbo, and Metro. There's an ATAC kiosk at the bus terminal in front of Termini station. If you're going farther afield, or planning to spend more than a week in Rome, think about getting a BIRG (daily regional ticket) or a CIRS (weekly regional ticket) from the railway station. These give you unlimited travel on all state transport throughout the region of Lazio. This can take you as far as the Etruscan city of Tarquinia or medieval Viterbo.

BUS AND TRAM

Although not as fast as the Metro, bus and tram travel is more scenic. With reserved bus lanes and numerous tram lines, surface transportation is surprisingly efficient, given the volume of Roman traffic. At peak times, however, buses can be very crowded. If the distance you have to travel is not too great, walking can be a more comfortable alternative. ATAC city buses are red or gray; trams are green. Remember to board at the rear and to exit at the middle: some bus drivers may refuse to let you out the front door, leaving you to scramble through the crowd to exit the middle or rear doors. Don't forget that you must buy your ticket before boarding, and be sure to stamp it in a machine as soon as you enter. The ticket is good for a transfer and one Metro trip within the next 100 minutes. Buses and trams run 5:30 am–midnight, after which time there's an extensive network of night buses with service throughout the city.

The bus system is a bit complicated to navigate due to the number of lines, but ATAC has a website (⊕ *www.atac. roma.it*) that will help you calculate the number of stops and bus route needed, and even give you a map directing you to the appropriate stops. To navigate the site, look for the British flag in the upper right-hand corner to change the website into English. Or do as the locals do and use the Moovit app.

Addresses

In the *centro storico* (old town/historic center), most street names are posted on ceramic-like plaques on the sides of buildings, which can make them hard to see. Addresses are fairly straightforward: the street name is followed by the street number, but it's worth noting that Roman street numbering, even in the newer outskirts of town, can be erratic. Usually numbers are even on one side of the street and odd on the other, but sometimes numbers are in ascending consecutive order on one side of the street and descending order on the other side.

Etiquette

Although you may find Rome much more informal then many other European cities, Romans will nevertheless appreciate attempts to abide by local etiquette. When entering an establishment, the key words to know are: *buongiorno* (good morning), *buona sera* (good evening), and *buon pomeriggio* (good afternoon). These words can also double as a goodbye upon exit. Italians greet friends with a kiss, usually first on the right cheek, and then on the left. When you meet a new person, shake hands and say *piacere* (*pee*-ah-*chair*-ay).

Restaurants

In Rome, simple yet traditional cuisine reigns supreme. Most chefs prefer to follow the mantra of freshness over fuss, and simplicity of flavor and preparation over complex cooking techniques. Rome has been known since antiquity for its grand feasts and banquets, and dining out has always been a favorite Roman pastime. Until recently, the city's *buongustaii* (gourmands) would have been the first to tell you that Rome is distinguished more by its enthusiasm for eating out than for a multitude of world-class restaurants—but this is changing. There is an ever-growing promotion of slow-food practices, a focus on sustainably and locally sourced produce. The economic crisis forced the food industry in Rome to adopt innovative ways to maintain a clientele who were increasingly looking to dine out but wanting to spend less; the result has been the rise of "street food" restaurants, selling everything from inexpensive and novel takes on the classic *supplì* (Roman fried-rice balls) to sandwich shops that use a variety of organic ingredients.

Generally speaking, Romans like Roman food, and that's what you'll find in many of the city's trattorias and wine bars. For the most part, today's chefs cling to the traditional and excel at what has taken hundreds, sometimes thousands, of years to perfect. This is why the basic trattoria menu is more or less the same wherever you go. And it's why even the top Roman chefs feature their versions of simple trattoria classics like carbonara, sometimes in a "deconstructed"

or slightly varied way. To a great extent, Rome is still a town where the Italian equivalent of "What are you in the mood for?" still gets the answer, "Pizza or pasta."

Nevertheless, Rome is the capital of Italy, and because people move here from every corner of the Italian peninsula, there are more variations on the Italian theme in Rome than you'd find elsewhere in Italy: Sicilian, Tuscan, Pugliese, Bolognese, Marchegiano, Sardinian, and northern Italian regional cuisines are all represented. And reflecting the increasingly cosmopolitan nature of the city, you'll find a growing number of good-quality international foods here as well—particularly Japanese, Indian, and Ethiopian.

Oddly enough, though, for a nation that prides itself on *la bella figura* ("looking good"), most Romans don't fuss about music, personal space, lighting, or decor. After all, who needs flashy interior design when so much of Roman life takes place outdoors, when dining alfresco in Rome can take place in the middle of a glorious ancient site or a centuries-old piazza?

Hotels

When it comes to accommodations, Rome offers a wide selection of high-end hotels, bed-and-breakfasts, and designer boutique hotels—options that run the gamut from whimsical to luxurious. Whether you want a simple place to rest your head or a complete cache of exclusive amenities, you have plenty to choose from.

Luxury hotels are justly renowned for sybaritic comfort: postcard views over Roman rooftops, silver flatware on white linen atop a groaning breakfast-buffet table, and the fluffiest towels. But in more modest categories, very often Rome's hotels are not up to the standards of space, comfort, quiet, and service taken for granted in the United States: you'll still find places with tiny rooms, lumpy beds, and anemic air-conditioning. The good news: if you're flexible, there are happy mediums aplenty.

One thing to figure out before you arrive is which neighborhood you want to stay in. There are obvious advantages to staying in a hotel within easy walking distance of the main sights. If a picturesque location is your main concern, stay in one of the small hotels around Piazza Navona or Campo de' Fiori. If luxury is a high priority, head for Piazza di Spagna or beyond the city center, where quality/price ratios are higher and some hotels have swimming pools.

⇨ *Hotel and restaurant reviews have been shortened. For full information, visit Fodors.com. Prices in the lodging reviews are the lowest cost of a standard double room in high season. Prices in the dining reviews are the average cost of a main course at dinner, or, if dinner is not served, at lunch.*

What It Costs in Euros

	$	$$	$$$	$$$$
RESTAURANTS				
	under €15	€15–€24	€25–€35	over €35
HOTELS				
	under €125	€125–€200	€201–€300	over €300

Roman Hours

In Italy, almost nothing starts on time except for (sometimes) a theater, opera, or movie showing. Italians even joke about a "15-minute window" before actually being late somewhere. In addition, the day starts a little later than normal here, with many shops not opening until 10 am, lunch never happens before 1 pm, and dinner rarely starts before 8 pm. On Sunday, Rome virtually

shuts down, and on Monday, most state museums and exhibition halls, plus many restaurants, are closed. Daily food shop hours generally run 10 am–1 pm and 4 pm–7:30 pm or 8 pm; but other stores in the center usually observe continuous opening hours. Pharmacies tend to close for a lunch break and keep night hours (*ora rio notturno*) in rotation. As for churches, most open at 8 or 9 in the morning, close noon–3 or 4, then reopen until 6:30 or 7. St. Peter's, however, has continuous hours 7 am–7 pm (until 6 pm in the fall and winter); and the Vatican Museums are open Monday but closed Sunday (except for the last Sunday of the month).

Roma Pass

In addition to single- and multiday transit passes, a three-day Roma Pass (🎫 *€52*) covers unlimited use of buses, trams, and the Metro, plus free admission to two museums or archaeological sites of your choice and discounted entrance to others. A two-day pass is €32 and includes one museum. The pass also allows you to skip the line at the Colosseum and Castel Sant'Angelo. Purchase the pass at either of Rome's airports, at tourist information offices, or at any of the participating attractions.

Tours

Some might consider them kitsch, but guided bus tours can prove a blissfully easy way to enjoy a quick introduction to the city's top sights—if you don't feel like being on your feet all day. Sitting in a bus, with friendly tour-guide commentary (and even friendlier fellow sightseers from every country under the sun), can make for a fun experience—so give one a whirl even if you're an old Rome hand. Of course, you'll want to savor these incredible sights at your own leisure later on.

The least expensive organized sightseeing tour of Rome is the one run by **CitySightseeing Roma** (⊕ *www.city-sightseeing.it/rome*). Double-decker buses leave from Via Marsala, beside Termini station, but you can pick them up at any of their nine stopping points. A day ticket costs €30 and allows you to get off and on as often as you like. The price includes an audio guide system in six languages. The total tour takes about two hours and covers the Colosseum, Piazza Navona, St. Peter's, the Trevi Fountain, and Via Veneto. Tickets can be bought on board. Two- and three-day tickets are also available. Tours leave from Termini station every 20 minutes 9–7:30.

All operators can provide a luxury car for up to three people, a limousine for up to seven, or a minibus for up to nine, all with an English-speaking driver, but guide service is extra. Almost all operators offer "Rome by Night" tours, with or without dinner and entertainment. You can book tours through travel agents.

Visitor Information

The Department of Tourism in Rome, called Roma Capitale, staffs green information kiosks (with multilingual personnel) near important sights, as well as at Termini station and Leonardo da Vinci Airport.

When to Go

Spring and fall are the best times to visit, with mild temperatures and many sunny days. Summers are often sweltering, so come in July and August if you like, but we advise doing as the Romans do—get up and out early, seek refuge from the afternoon heat, resume activities in early evening, and stay up late to enjoy the nighttime breeze.

Most attractions are closed on major holidays. Come August, many shops and restaurants shutter as locals head out for vacation. Remember that air-conditioning is still a relatively rare phenomenon in this city, so carrying a small paper fan in your bag can work wonders. Roman winters are relatively mild, with persistent rainy spells.

Ancient Rome with Monti and Celio

Time has reduced ancient Rome to fields of silent ruins, but the powerful impact of what happened here, of the genius and power that made Rome the center of the Western world, echoes across the millennia. In this one compact area of the city, you can step back into the Rome of Cicero, Julius Caesar, and Virgil. You can walk along the streets they knew, cool off in the shade of the Colosseum that loomed over the city, and see the sculptures poised over their piazzas. Today, this part of Rome, more than any other, is a perfect example of the layering of historic eras, the overlapping of ages, of religions, of a past that is very much a part of the present.

Outside the actual ancient sites, you'll find neighborhoods like Monti and Celio, *rioni* (districts) that are just as much part of Rome's history as its ruins. These are the city's oldest neighborhoods, and today they are a charming mix of the city's past and present. Once you're done exploring ancient Rome, these are the easiest places to head for a bite to eat or some shopping.

GETTING HERE AND AROUND

The Colosseo Metro station is right across from the Colosseum and a short walk from both the Roman and the Imperial Forums, as well as the Palatine Hill. Walking from the very heart of the historic center will take about 20 minutes, much of it along the wide Via dei Fori Imperiali. The little electric Bus No. 117 from the center or No. 85 from Termini will also deliver you to the Colosseum's doorstep. Any of the following buses will take you to or near the Roman Forum: Nos. 60, 75, 85, and 170.

⊙ Sights

Arco di Costantino (*Arch of Constantine*)
RUINS | This majestic arch was erected in AD 315 to commemorate Constantine's victory over Maxentius at the Milvian Bridge. It was just before this battle, in AD 312, that Constantine—the emperor who converted Rome to Christianity—legendarily had a vision of a cross and heard the words, "In this sign thou shalt conquer." Many of the costly marble decorations for the arch were scavenged from earlier monuments, both saving money and placing Constantine in line with the great emperors of the past. It is easy to picture ranks of Roman centurions marching under the great barrel vault. ⊠ *Piazza del Colosseo, Monti* Ⓜ *Colosseo.*

Basilica di Santa Maria in Aracoeli
CHURCH | Perched atop 124 steps, on the north slope of the Capitoline Hill, Santa Maria in Aracoeli occupies the site of the temple of Juno Moneta (Admonishing Juno), which also housed the Roman mint. According to legend, it was here that the Sibyl, a prophetess, predicted to Augustus the coming of a Redeemer. Augustus responded by erecting an altar, the Ara Coeli (Altar of Heaven). This was eventually replaced by a Benedictine monastery and then by a church, which was passed in 1250 to the Franciscans, who restored and enlarged it in Romanesque-Gothic style.

Today, the Aracoeli is best known for the Santo Bambino, a much-revered olivewood figure of the Christ Child (a copy of

the 15th-century original, which was stolen in 1994). At Christmas, everyone pays homage to the "Bambinello" as children recite poems from a miniature pulpit. In true Roman style, the church interior is a historical hodgepodge, with classical columns and large marble fragments from pagan buildings, as well as a 13th-century cosmatesque pavement. The richly gilded Renaissance ceiling commemorates the naval victory at Lepanto in 1571 over the Turks. The first chapel on the right is noteworthy for Pinturicchio's frescoes of St. Bernardino of Siena (1486). ⊠ *Via del Teatro di Marcello, Piazza Venezia* ☎ *06/69763839* Ⓜ *Colosseo.*

★ The Campidoglio
PLAZA/SQUARE | Your first taste of ancient Rome should start from a point that embodies some of Rome's earliest and greatest moments: the Campidoglio. Here, on the Capitoline Hill (which towers over the traffic hub of Piazza Venezia), a meditative Edward Gibbon was inspired to write his 1764 tome, *The History of the Decline and Fall of the Roman Empire.* Of Rome's famous seven hills, the Capitoline is the smallest and the most sacred. It has always been the seat of Rome's government, and its Latin name echoes in the designation of the national and state capitol buildings of every country in the world. While there are great views of the Roman Forum from the terrace balconies to either side of the Palazzo Senatorio, the best view is from the 1st-century-BC Tabularium, now part of the Musei Capitolini. The museum café is on the Terrazza Caffarelli, with a magical view toward Trastevere and St. Peter's, and is accessible without a museum ticket. ⊠ *Piazza del Campidoglio, including the Palazzo Senatorio and the Musei Capitolini, the Palazzo Nuovo, and the Palazzo dei Conservatori, Piazza Venezia* Ⓜ *Colosseo.*

Circo Massimo (*Circus Maximus*)

RUINS | From the belvedere of the Domus Flavia on the Palatine Hill, you can see the Circus Maximus; there's also a great free view from Piazzale Ugo La Malfa on the Aventine Hill side. The giant space where 300,000 spectators once watched chariot races while the emperor looked on is ancient Rome's oldest and largest racetrack; it lies in a natural hollow between the two hills. The oval course stretches about 650 yards from end to end; on certain occasions, there were as many as 24 chariot races a day, and competitions could last for 15 days. The charioteers could amass fortunes rather like the sports stars of today. (The Portuguese Diocles is said to have totted up winnings of 35 million sestertii.)

The noise and the excitement of the crowd must have reached astonishing levels as the charioteers competed in teams, each with their own colors—the Reds, the Blues, etc. Betting also provided Rome's majority of unemployed with a potentially lucrative occupation. The central ridge was the site of two Egyptian obelisks (now in Piazza del Popolo and Piazza San Giovanni in Laterano). Picture the great chariot race scene from MGM's *Ben-Hur*, and you have an inkling of what this was like. ⊠ *Between Palatine and Aventine Hills, Aventino* ☎ *06/0608* ⬛ *€5* Ⓜ *Circo Massimo.*

★ **Colosseum** (*Colosseo*)

RUINS | The most spectacular extant edifice of ancient Rome, the Colosseum has a history that is half gore, half glory. Once able to house 50,000 spectators, it was built to impress Romans with its spectacles involving wild animals and fearsome gladiators from the farthest reaches of the empire. Senators had marble seats up front, the vestal virgins took the ringside position, the plebs sat in wooden tiers at the back, and the masses watched from the top tier. Looming over all was the amazing velarium, an ingenious system of sail-like awnings

rigged on ropes and maneuvered by sailors from the imperial fleet, who would unfurl them to protect the arena's occupants from sun or rain.

■ TIP➔ **To enter, book a combination ticket (with the Roman Forum and Palatine Hill) in advance online, though if you have a Roma Pass, you can use it.**

Tickets cost €16 plus a €2 online booking surcharge. Aim for early or late slots to minimize lines, as even the preferential lanes get busy in the middle of the day. Alternatively, you can book a tour online with a company (do your research to make sure it's reputable) that lets you skip the line. Avoid the tours sold on the spot around the Colosseum; although you can skip the lines, the tour guides tend to be dry, the tour groups huge, and the tour itself rushed. To see the arena or the underground, you must purchase a special timed-entry ticket with those features, though the arena is included if you buy the Roman Forum–Palatine complex €22 two-day Full Experience ticket. ⊠ *Piazza del Colosseo, Colosseo* ☎ *06/39967700* ⊕ *www.coopculture. it* ⬛ *Requires either the €16 24-hour ticket or the €22 Full Experience ticket (can include the arena for no additional fee, but it must be specified during the purchase)* Ⓜ *Colosseo.*

Domus Aurea (*Golden House of Nero*)

RUINS | Legend has it that Nero fiddled while Rome burned. Fancying himself a great actor and poet, he played, as it turns out, his harp to accompany his recital of "The Destruction of Troy" while gazing at the flames of Rome's catastrophic fire of AD 64. After the fire, Nero built this new palace, the extravagant Domus Aurea (Golden House)—a vast "suburban villa" that was inspired by the emperor's pleasure palace at Baia on the Bay of Naples. His new digs were huge and sumptuous, with a facade of pure gold; seawater piped into the baths; decorations of mother-of-pearl, fretted ivory, and other precious materials; and vast gardens. It was said that after completing this gigantic house, Nero exclaimed, "Now I can live like a human being!" Note that access to the site is exclusively via guided tours that use virtual reality headsets for part of the presentation. Booking ahead is essential. ✉ *Viale della Domus Aurea 1, Monti* ☎ *06/39967700 booking information* ⊕ *www.coopculture.it* ✒ *€18 including booking fee and guided visit (Mon.–Thurs. only); €23 including booking fee, guided visit, and virtual reality experience (Fri.–Sun. only)* ⚶ *Reservations essential* Ⓜ *Colosseo.*

Fori Imperiali

RUINS | A compound of five grandly conceived complexes flanked with colonnades, the Fori Imperiali contain monuments of triumph, law courts, and temples. The complexes were tacked on to the Roman Forum, from the time of Julius Caesar in the 1st century BC until Trajan in the very early 2nd century AD, to accommodate the ever-growing need for administrative buildings as well as grand monuments.

From Piazza del Colosseo, head northwest on Via dei Fori Imperiali toward Piazza Venezia. Now that the road has been closed to private traffic, it's more pleasant for pedestrians (it's closed to all traffic on Sunday). On the walls to your left, maps in marble and bronze, put up by Benito Mussolini, show the extent of the Roman Republic and Empire. The dictator's own dreams of empire led him to construct this avenue, cutting brutally through the Fori Imperiali and the medieval and Renaissance buildings that had grown upon the ruins, so that he would have a suitable venue for parades celebrating his expected military triumphs. Among the Fori Imperiali along the avenue, you can see the Foro di Cesare (Forum of Caesar) and the Foro di Augusto (Forum of Augustus). The grandest was the Foro di Traiano (Forum of Trajan), with its huge semicircular Mercati di Traiano and the Colonna Traiana (Trajan's

Column). You can walk through part of Trajan's Markets on the Via Alessandrina and visit the Museo dei Fori Imperiali, which presents the Imperial Forums and shows how they would have been used through ancient fragments, artifacts, and modern multimedia. ✉ *Via dei Fori Imperiali, Monti* ☎ *06/0608* ⊕ *www.mercatiditraiano.it* ✒ *Museum €11.50* Ⓜ *Colosseo.*

Foro di Traiano (Forum of Trajan)

RUINS | Of all the Fori Imperiali, Trajan's was the grandest and most imposing, a veritable city unto itself. Designed by architect Apollodorus of Damascus, it comprised a vast basilica, two libraries, and a colonnade laid out around the square—all at one time covered with rich marble ornamentation. Adjoining the forum were the Mercati di Traiano (Trajan's Markets), a huge, multilevel, brick complex of shops, taverns, walkways, and terraces, as well as administrative offices involved in the mammoth task of feeding the city.

The Museo dei Fori Imperiali (Imperial Forums Museum) takes advantage of the Forum's soaring vaulted spaces to showcase archaeological fragments and sculptures while presenting a video re-creation of the original complex. In addition, the series of terraced rooms offers an impressive overview of the entire forum. A pedestrian walkway, the Via Alessandrina, also allows for an excellent (and free) view of Trajan's Forum.

To build a complex of this magnitude, Apollodorus and his patrons clearly had great confidence, not to mention almost unlimited means and cheap labor at their disposal (readily provided by slaves captured in Trajan's Dacian Wars). The complex also contained two semicircular lecture halls, one at either end, which are thought to have been associated with the libraries in Trajan's Forum. The markets' architectural centerpiece is the enormous curved wall, or *exedra*, that shores up the side of the Quirinal Hill excavated by Apollodorus's gangs of laborers. Covered

Rome Metro and Suburban Railway

Tickets

A ticket (BIT) valid for 100 minutes on any combination of buses and trams and one entrance to the metro costs €1.50. Tickets are sold at newsstands, some coffee bars, ticket machines in metro stations, and ATAC and COTRAL ticket booths. Time-stamp your ticket when boarding the first vehicle, and stamp it again when boarding for the last time within 75 minutes. You stamp the ticket at Metro sliding electronic doors, and in the little yellow machines on buses and trams.

Fare fees	Price
Single fare	€1.50
Biglietto integrato giornaliero (Integrated Daily Ticket) BIG	€7
Biglietto turistico integrato (Three-Day Pass) BTI	€18
Weekly pass	€24
Monthly unlimited pass	€35

galleries and streets were constructed at various levels, following the exedra's curves and giving the complex a strikingly modern appearance.

As you enter the markets, a large, vaulted hall stands in front of you. Two stories of shops and offices rise up on either side. Head for the flight of steps at the far end that leads down to Via Biberatica. (*Bibere* is Latin for "to drink," and the shops that open onto the street are believed to have been taverns.) Then head back to the three retail and administrative tiers that line the upper levels of the great exedra and look out over the remains of the Forum. Empty and bare today, the cubicles were once ancient Rome's busiest market stalls. Though it seems to be part of the market, the Torre delle Milizie (Tower of the Militia), the tall brick tower that is a prominent feature of Rome's skyline, was actually built in the early 1200s. ✉ *Via IV Novembre 94, Monti* ☎ *06/0608* ⊕ *www.mercatiditraiano.it* 🎫 *€11.50 (€13 with exhibits)* Ⓜ *Cavour.*

★ Musei Capitolini

ART MUSEUM | Surpassed in size and richness only by the Musei Vaticani, the world's first public museum—with the greatest hits of Roman art through the ages, from the ancients to the Baroque— is housed in the Palazzo dei Conservatori and the Palazzo Nuovo, which mirror one another across Michelangelo's famous piazza. The collection was begun by Pope Sixtus IV (the man who built the Sistine Chapel) in 1473, when he donated a room of ancient statuary to the people of the city. This core of the collection includes the She Wolf, which is the symbol of Rome, and the piercing gaze of the Capitoline Brutus. Buy your ticket and enter the Palazzo dei Conservatori where, in the first courtyard, you'll see the giant head, foot, elbow, and imperially raised finger of the fabled seated statue of Constantine, which once dominated the Basilica of Maxentius in the Forum. As you walk between the two

halves of the museum, be sure to take the staircase to the Tabularium gallery and its unparalleled view over the Forum. ✉ *Piazza del Campidoglio 1, Piazza Venezia* ☎ *06/0608* ⊕ *www.museicapitolini.org* 🎫 *€11.50 (€16 with exhibitions); €13.50 with access to Centrale Montemartini; €7 audio guide* Ⓜ *Colosseo.*

★ Palatine Hill

RUINS | Just beyond the Arch of Titus, the Clivus Palatinus gently rises to the heights of the Colle Palatino (Palatine Hill)—the oldest inhabited site in Rome. Despite its location overlooking the Forum's traffic and attendant noise, the Palatine was the most coveted address for ancient Rome's rich and famous. Augustus was born on the hill, and the Houses of Livia and Augustus are today the hill's best-preserved structures, replete with fabulous frescoes. Later emperors built even bigger, and much of what we see today dates from the reign of Domitian, in the late 1st century AD. ✉ *Entrances at Piazza del Colosseo and Via di San Gregorio 30, Monti* ☎ *06/39967700* ⊕ *www.coopculture.it* 🎫 *€18 combined ticket, includes single entry to Palatine Hill–Forum site and single entry to Colosseum (if used within 24 hrs); S.U.P.E.R. ticket €22 (€24 with online reservation) includes access to the Houses of Augustus and Livia, the Palatine Museum, Aula Isiaca, Santa Maria Antiqua, and Temple of Romulus* Ⓜ *Colosseo.*

★ The Roman Forum

RUINS | Whether it's from the main entrance on Via dei Fori Imperiali or by the entrance at the Arch of Titus, descend into the extraordinary archaeological complex that is the Foro Romano and the Palatine Hill, once the very heart of the Roman world. Hundreds of years of plunder reduced the Forum to its current desolate state. But this enormous area was once Rome's pulsating hub, filled with stately and extravagant temples, palaces, and shops and crowded with

3

Sights ▼

1	Arco di Costantino	G6
2	Basilica di Santa Maria in Aracoeli	C3
3	The Campidoglio	C3
4	Circo Massimo	E8
5	Colosseum	H5
6	Domus Aurea	J4
7	Fori Imperiali	D3
8	Foro di Traiano	D2
9	Musei Capitolini	C4
10	Palatine Hill	E6
11	The Roman Forum	E4
12	San Clemente	J6
13	Santa Maria Maggiore	J2

Restaurants ▼

1	ViVi Piazza Venezia	B1

Quick Bites ▼

1	Fatamorgana Monti	I2

Hotels ▼

1	Hotel Celio	J6
2	NH Collection Roma Fori Imperiali	D1
3	Palazzo Manfredi	J5

people from all corners of the empire. What you see today are not the ruins from just one period but from a span of almost 900 years, from about 500 BC to AD 400. Nonetheless, the enduring romance of the place, with its lonely columns and great broken fragments of sculpted marble and stone, makes for a quintessential Roman experience. Lines, especially in high season, are not uncommon. Those who don't want to risk waiting in line can book their tickets online in advance, for a €2 surcharge. Choose the print-at-home option (a PDF on a smartphone works, too) and avoid the line to pick up tickets. Your ticket is valid for one entrance to the Roman Forum and the Palatine Hill, which are part of a single continuous complex. Certain sites within the Forum require a S.U.P.E.R. ticket. ✉ *Entrance at Via dei Fori Imperiali, Monti* 🕾 *06/39967700* ⊕ *www.coopculture.it* 🎫 *€18 combined ticket, includes single entry to Palatine Hill–Forum site and single entry to Colosseum (if used within 24 hrs); S.U.P.E.R. ticket €22 (€24 with online reservation) includes access to the Houses of Augustus and Livia, the Palatine Museum, Aula Isiaca, Santa Maria Antiqua, and Temple of Romulus; audio guide €5* Ⓜ *Colosseo.*

★ San Clemente

CHURCH | One of the most impressive archaeological sites in Rome, San Clemente is a historical triple-decker. A 12th-century church was built on top of a 4th-century church, which had been built over a 2nd-century pagan temple to the god Mithras and 1st-century Roman apartments. The layers were uncovered in 1857, when a curious prior, Friar Joseph Mullooly, started excavations beneath the present basilica. Today, you can descend to explore all three.

The upper church (at street level) is a gem in its own right. In the apse, a glittering 12th-century mosaic shows Jesus on a cross that turns into a living tree. Green acanthus leaves swirl and teem with small

scenes of everyday life. Early Christian symbols, including doves, vines, and fish, decorate the 4th-century marble choir screens. To the right of the sacristy (and bookshop), descend the stairs to the 4th-century church, used until 1084, when it was damaged beyond repair during a siege of the area by the Norman prince Robert Guiscard. Still intact are some vibrant 11th-century frescoes depicting stories from the life of St. Clement.

Descend an additional set of stairs to the Mithraeum, a shrine dedicated to the god Mithras. His cult spread from Persia and gained a foothold in Rome during the 2nd and 3rd centuries AD. Mithras was believed to have been born in a cave and was thus worshipped in cavernous, underground chambers, where initiates into the all-male cult would share a meal while reclining on stone couches, some visible here along with the altar block. ✉ *Via Labicana 95, Celio* 🕾 *06/7740021* ⊕ *basilicasanclemente.com/eng* 🎫 *Archaeological area €10* �-*Reservations required* Ⓜ *Colosseo.*

★ Santa Maria Maggiore

CHURCH | Despite its florid 18th-century facade, Santa Maria Maggiore is one of the city's oldest churches, built around 440 by Pope Sixtus III. One Rome's four great pilgrimage churches, it's also the city center's best example of an early Christian basilica—one of the immense, hall-like structures derived from ancient Roman civic buildings and divided into thirds by two great rows of columns marching up the nave. The other three major basilicas in Rome (San Giovanni in Laterano, St. Peter's, and St. Paul Outside the Walls) have been largely rebuilt. Paradoxically, the major reason why this church is such a striking example of early Christian design is that the same man who built the undulating exteriors circa 1740, Ferdinando Fuga, also conscientiously restored the interior, throwing out later additions and, crucially, replacing a number of the great columns.

The Cappella Sistina (Sistine Chapel), in the right-hand transept, was created by architect Domenico Fontana for Pope Sixtus V in 1585. Elaborately decorated with precious marbles "liberated" from the monuments of ancient Rome, the chapel includes a lower-level museum with some 13th-century sculptures by Arnolfo da Cambio that survived the Sack of Rome in 1527. Borgia popes Paul V and Clement VIII are buried here, as is Gian Lorenzo Bernini, under a simple engraved slab as humble as the tombs of his patrons are grand. The outside mosaic of Christ raising his hand in blessing is one of Rome's most beautiful sights, especially when lighted at night. ✉ *Piazza di Santa Maria Maggiore, Monti* ☎ *06/69886800* Ⓜ *Termini.*

🍴 Restaurants

ViVi Piazza Venezia

$$ | BISTRO | For an alternative to the heavy pastas typically found in Roman restaurants, this cheerful bistro inside Palazzo Bonaparte is a great choice. There are plenty of healthy options like excellent salads and poké bowls, as well as heartier fare such as burgers and, yes, pasta. **Known for:** fresh, healthy food; vegan and gluten-free desserts; shabby-chic design. ⑤ *Average main: €15* ✉ *Piazza Venezia 5, Piazza Venezia* ☎ *06/69228769* ⊕ *www.vivi.it* Ⓜ *Colosseo.*

☕ Coffee and Quick Bites

★ Fatamorgana Monti

$ | ICE CREAM | FAMILY | The emphasis is on all-natural ingredients at this woman-owned gelateria, which has several locations in Rome, including one near Campo de' Fiori and another in Trastevere. Flavors change often but might include favorites like stracciatella (with chocolate shavings) and hazelnut as well as more unusual flavors like matcha or carrot cake. **Known for:** all natural

ingredients; unusual flavors; gluten-free with many vegan options. ⑤ *Average main: €3* ✉ *Piazza degli Zingari 5, Monti* ☎ *06/48906955* ⊕ *www.gelateriafatamorgana.com* Ⓜ *Cavour.*

🛏 Hotels

Hotel Celio

$$ | HOTEL | At this hotel near the Colosseum, each of the small guest rooms is named after a famous Italian painter (Tiziano, Cellini, Michelangelo) and features decor that evokes the work of its namesake. **Pros:** beautiful rooftop garden; good location; comfortable beds. **Cons:** very small bathrooms; service can be iffy; breakfast not that substantial. ⑤ *Rooms from: €180* ✉ *Via dei Santissimi Quattro 35/c, Celio* ☎ *06/70495333* ⊕ *www.hotelcelio.com* ↩ *20 rooms* ⑩ *Free Breakfast* Ⓜ *Colosseo.*

NH Collection Roma Fori Imperiali

$$$$ | HOTEL | It would be hard to find a modern hotel closer to the Roman Forum—the ancient ruins are practically right outside the door. **Pros:** incredible views of ancient Rome; rooftop serves a great aperitivo and refined dinners; restaurant Oro Bistrot by renowned chef Natale Giunta. **Cons:** breakfast foods are pre-packaged; not much public space; no spa or gym. ⑤ *Rooms from: €400* ✉ *Via di Santa Eufemia 19, Monti* ☎ *06/697689911* ⊕ *www.nh-collection. com/en/hotel/nh-collection-roma-fori-imperiali* ↩ *42 rooms* ⑩ *No Meals* Ⓜ *Colosseo.*

Palazzo Manfredi

$$$$ | HOTEL | If you dream of waking up to head-on views of the Colosseum, book into this boutique hotel, which is set in a 17th-century palazzo built over the ruins of the Ludus Magnus, the gymnasium used by Roman gladiators, and offers refined luxury. **Pros:** incredible views; unparalleled location; excellent restaurant and cocktail bar. **Cons:** not all rooms have Colosseum views; some guests complain about noise; no spa. $ *Rooms from: €600* ✉ *Via Labicana 125, Colosseo* ☎ *06/77591380* ⊕ *www.palazzoman-fredi.com* ⇝ *23 rooms* ⛁ *No Meals* Ⓜ *Colosseo.*

Nightlife

★ Ai Tre Scalini

WINE BAR | An ivy-covered wine bar in the center of Monti, Rome's trendiest 'hood, Ai Tre Scalini has a warm and cozy menu of delicious antipasti and light entrées to go along with its enticing wine list. After about 8 pm, be prepared to wait—this is one extremely popular spot with locals and they don't take reservations. ✉ *Via Panisperna 251, Monti* ☎ *06/48907495* ⊕ *www.aitrescalini.org* Ⓜ *Cavour.*

★ The Court

COCKTAIL BARS | For a winning combination of creative cocktails and incredible views of the Colosseum, this bar in Palazzo Manfredi can't be beat. Bar manager Matteo "Zed" Zamberlan cut his teeth in New York's top drinking establishments, and here his creativity is on full display. The cocktails are pricey, but they come with a bounty of snacks from the hotel's acclaimed restaurant. ✉ *Via Labicana 125, Colosseo* ☎ *06/77591380* ⊕ *www.manfredihotels.com/the-court-new* Ⓜ *Colosseo.*

Shopping

★ Sacripante

CLOTHING | This tiny Monti art gallery/boutique/bar has some of the most sophisticated, retro-inspired garments in Rome. Its owner, Carlotta Cerulli, sells clothes by her mother, Wilma Silvestri, who cleverly combines vintage and contemporary fabrics for her label Le Gallinelle, creating stylish fashions with a modern edge made for everyday wear. ✉ *Via Panisperna 59, Monti* ☎ *06/48903495* ⊕ *www.facebook.com/sacripantegallery* Ⓜ *Cavour.*

The Vatican with Borgo and Prati

Climbing the steps to St. Peter's Basilica feels monumental, like a journey that has reached its climactic end. Suddenly, all is cool and dark … and you are dwarfed by the gargantuan nave and its magnificence. Above is a ceiling so high it must lead to heaven itself. Great, shining marble figures of saints frozen mid-whirl loom from niches and corners. And at the end, a throne for an unseen king whose greatness, it is implied, must mirror the greatness of his palace. For this basilica is a palace, the dazzling center of power for a king and a place of supplication for his subjects. Whether his kingdom is earthly or otherwise may lie in the eye of the beholder.

For good Catholics and sinners alike, the Vatican is an exercise in spirituality, requiring patience but delivering joy. Some come here for a transcendent glimpse of a heavenly Michelangelo fresco; others come in search of a direct connection with the divine. But what all visitors share, for a few hours, is an awe-inspiring landscape that offers a famous sight for every taste: rooms decorated by Raphael, antique sculptures like the Apollo Belvedere, famous paintings by Giotto and Bellini, and, perhaps most of all, the Sistine Chapel—for the lover of beauty, few places are as historically important as this epitome of faith and grandeur.

The Borgo and Prati are the neighborhoods immediately surrounding the Vatican, and it's worth noting that, while the Vatican may well be a priority, these neighborhoods are not the best places to choose a hotel, as they're quite far from other top sights in the city.

GETTING HERE AND AROUND

Metro stop Cipro or Ottaviano will get you within about a 10-minute walk of the entrance to the Musei Vaticani. Or, from Termini station, Bus No. 40 Express or the famously crowded No. 64 will take you to Piazza San Pietro. Both routes swing past Largo Argentina, where you can also get Bus No. 46.

A leisurely meander from the centro storico, across the exquisite Ponte Sant'Angelo, will take about a half hour.

Sights

★ Basilica di San Pietro

CHURCH | The world's largest church, built over the tomb of St. Peter, is the most imposing and breathtaking architectural achievement of the Renaissance (although much of the lavish interior dates to the Baroque period). No fewer than five of Italy's greatest artists—Bramante, Raphael, Peruzzi, Antonio da Sangallo the Younger, and Michelangelo—died while striving to erect this new St. Peter's. In 1503, Pope Julius II instructed the architect Bramante to raze all the existing buildings of the original St. Peter's, which had stood for over 1,000 years, and build a new basilica, one that would surpass even Constantine's for grandeur. It wasn't until 1626 that the new basilica was completed and consecrated. Highlights include the Loggia delle Benedizioni (Benediction Loggia), the balcony where newly elected popes are proclaimed; Michelangelo's *Pietà*; and Bernini's great bronze baldacchino, a huge, spiral-columned canopy—at 100,000 pounds, perhaps the largest bronze object in the world—as well as many other Bernini masterpieces. For views of both the dome above and the piazza below, take the elevator or stairs to the roof. Those with more stamina (and without claustrophobia) can then head up more stairs to the apex of the dome. ■ TIP→ **The basilica is free to visit, but a security check at the entrance can** create very long lines. Arrive before 8:30 or after 5:30 to minimize the wait and avoid the crowds. ⊠ *Piazza San Pietro, Vatican* ⊕ *www.vatican.va* 🎫 *Free* ⊘ *Closed during Papal General Audience (Wed. until 1 pm) and during other ceremonies in piazza* Ⓜ *Ottaviano.*

★ Cappella Sistina (*Sistine Chapel*)

ART MUSEUM | In 1508, the redoubtable Pope Julius II commissioned Michelangelo to fresco the more than 10,000 square feet of the Sistine Chapel's ceiling. The task took four years, and it's said that for many years afterward Michelangelo couldn't read anything without holding it over his head. The result, however, was the greatest artwork of the Renaissance. A pair of binoculars helps greatly, as does a small mirror—hold the mirror facing the ceiling and look down to study the reflection. More than 20 years after his work on the ceiling, Michelangelo was called on again, this time by Pope Paul III, to add to the chapel's decoration by painting the *Last Judgment* on the wall over the altar. By way of signature on this, his late great fresco, Michelangelo painted his own face on the flayed-off human skin in St. Bartholomew's hand. ■ TIP→ **The chapel is entered through the Musei Vaticani, and lines are slightly shorter after 2:30 (reservations are always advisable)—except free Sundays, which are extremely busy and when admissions close at 12:30.** ⊠ *Musei Vaticani, Vatican* ⊕ *www.museivaticani.va* 🎫 *€20 (part of the Vatican Museums)* ⊘ *Closed Sun.* Ⓜ *Ottaviano.*

Castel Sant'Angelo

CASTLE/PALACE | FAMILY | Standing between the Tiber and the Vatican, this circular castle has long been one of Rome's most distinctive landmarks. Opera lovers know it well as the setting for the final scene of Puccini's *Tosca*. Started in AD 135, the structure began as a mausoleum for the emperor Hadrian and was completed by his successor, Antoninus Pius. From the mid-6th

The Vatican with Borgo and Prati

Borgo

Sights ▼

1 Basilica di
San Pietro **C6**

2 Cappella Sistina......... **D5**

3 Castel Sant'Angelo **H5**

4 Musei Vaticani **C4**

5 Necropoli Vaticana..... **D6**

6 Piazza San Pietro **E6**

Restaurants ▼

1 Del Frate **F2**

2 Ristorante Sinatra **F2**

3 Sant'Isidoro
Pizza & Bolle **G1**

4 Taverna Angelica **F4**

Quick Bites ▼

1 Al Settimo Gelo **G1**

2 Bonci Pizzarium.......... **A3**

Hotels ▼

1 Hotel al San Pietrino.... **D1**

2 Residenza Paolo VI **D6**

century the building became a fortress, a place of refuge for popes during wars and sieges. Its name dates to AD 590, when Pope Gregory the Great, during a procession to plead for the end of a plague, saw an angel standing on the summit of the castle, sheathing his sword. Taking this as a sign that the plague was at an end, the pope built a small chapel at the top, placing a statue next to it to celebrate his vision—thus the name, Castel Sant'Angelo. Look for the Cappella di Papa Leone X (Chapel of Pope Leo X), with a facade by Michelangelo. The stairs at the far end of the courtyard lead to the open terrace for a view of the Passetto, the fortified corridor connecting Castel Sant'Angelo with the Vatican. In the *appartamento papale* (papal apartment), the Sala Paolina (Pauline Room) was decorated in the 16th century by Perino del Vaga. ✉ *Lungotevere Castello 50, Prati* ☎ *06/6819111 central line, 06/6896003 tickets* ⊕ *www. castelsantangelo.beniculturali.it* 🎫 *€13* ⊗ *Closed Mon.* Ⓜ *Lepanto.*

★ **Musei Vaticani** (*Vatican Museums*)
ART MUSEUM | Other than the pope and his papal court, the occupants of the Vatican are some of the most famous artworks in the world. Indeed, most of the Vatican Palace estimated 1,400 rooms, chapels, and galleries are given over to the Vatican Library and Museums. Beyond the glories of the Sistine Chapel, the collection is extraordinarily rich: highlights include the great antique sculptures (including the celebrated *Apollo Belvedere* in the Octagonal Courtyard and the *Belvedere Torso* in the Hall of the Muses); the Stanze di Raffaello (Raphael Rooms), with their famous gorgeous frescoes; and the Old Master paintings, such as Leonardo da Vinci's beautiful (though unfinished) *St. Jerome in the Wilderness*, some of Raphael's greatest creations, and Caravaggio's gigantic *Deposition in the Pinacoteca* ("Picture Gallery"). Guided tours start at €35, including entrance tickets, and can also

be booked online. Other offerings include a regular two-hour guided tour of the Vatican gardens. ✉ *Viale Vaticano, near intersection with Via Leone IV, Vatican* ☎ *06/69883145* ⊕ *www.museivaticani. va* 🎫 *€20* ⊗ *Closed Sun. and church holidays* Ⓜ *Cipro–Musei Vaticani or Ottaviano–San Pietro.*

Necropoli Vaticana (*Vatican Necropolis*)
CEMETERY | With advance notice you can take a 1½-hour guided tour in English of the Vatican Necropolis, under the Basilica di San Pietro, which gives a rare glimpse of early Christian Roman burial customs and a closer look at the tomb of St. Peter. Apply via the contact form online, by fax, or in person (the entrance to the office is on the left of the Bernini colonnade), specifying the number of people in the group (all must be age 15 or older), preferred language, preferred time, available dates, and your contact information in Rome. Each group will have about 12 participants. Visits are not recommended for those with mobility issues or who are claustrophobic. ✉ *Ufficio Scavi, Vatican* ☎ *06/69885318, 06/69873017 reservations* ⊕ *www.scavi.va* 🎫 *€13* ⊗ *Closed Sun. and Roman Catholic holidays* ⚠ *Reservations required* Ⓜ *Ottaviano.*

★ **Piazza San Pietro**
PLAZA/SQUARE | Mostly enclosed within high walls that recall the papacy's stormy history, the Vatican opens the spectacular arms of Bernini's colonnade to embrace the world only at St. Peter's Square, scene of the pope's public appearances and another of Bernini's masterpieces. The elliptical Piazza di San Pietro was completed in 1667 and holds about 100,000 people. It's surrounded by a pair of quadruple colonnades and is gloriously studded with 140 statues of saints and martyrs. At its center is the 85-foot-high Egyptian obelisk, which was brought to Rome by Caligula in AD 37 and moved here in 1586 by Pope Sixtus V. The Vatican post offices can be found on both sides of the square and inside the Vatican

Museums complex. ■TIP→ **The main information office is just left of the basilica as you face it.** ⊠ *Piazza di San Pietro, Vatican* ⊕ *www.vaticanstate.va* Ⓜ *Ottaviano.*

🍽 Restaurants

Del Frate

$$ | **MODERN ITALIAN** | This impressive wine bar pairs modern decor with creative cuisine and three dozen wines available by the glass. There are some fantastic seasonal specialties, but you can also get cheeses, smoked meats, and composed salads. **Known for:** shares space with one of Rome's noted wine shops; daily aperitivo with a nice selection of wines by the glass; wide selection of after-dinner drinks, including mezcal and amari (bitter cordial). ⑤ *Average main: €24* ⊠ *Via degli Scipioni 118, Prati* ☎ *06/3236437* ⊕ *www. enotecadelfrate.it* ⊙ *Closed 2 wks in Aug.* Ⓜ *Ottaviano.*

Ristorante Sinatra

$$ | **MODERN ITALIAN** | Named in homage to the Italian-American crooner, this intimate restaurant has a refined yet casual atmosphere, with wine bottles lining the walls, black-and-white photographs of jazz musicians, and vintage touches like rotary telephones. Although the menu emphasizes Italian classics, there are a few surprises, including focaccia with Spanish pata negra ham and raw shrimp in the *cacio e pepe* (pasta prepared with a pecorino-cheese sauce and black pepper). **Known for:** charming vintage setting; eclectic menu; live music. ⑤ *Average main: €18* ⊠ *Via Fabio Massimo 68, Prati* ☎ *06/3219657* ⊕ *www.ristorante-sinatra. business.site* ⊙ *Closed Sun.* Ⓜ *Lepanto.*

Sant'Isidoro Pizza & Bolle

$ | **PIZZA** | **FAMILY** | More upscale than a typical pizzeria but casual enough for a weeknight, this establishment pairs its pies with sparkling wines instead of beer. Opt for a classic pizza, or go with an innovative option, like one topped with stracciatella, raw shrimp, lemon peel, and mint. **Known for:** wide selection of sparkling wines; creative pizzas; chic modern design. ⑤ *Average main: €14* ⊠ *Via Oslavia 41, Prati* ☎ *06/89822607* ⊕ *www.pizzaebolle.it* Ⓜ *Lepanto.*

Taverna Angelica

$$$ | **MODERN ITALIAN** | The Borgo area near St. Peter's Basilica hasn't been known for culinary excellence, but Taverna Angelica was one of the first refined restaurants in this part of town. The dining room is small, which allows the chef to create a menu that's inventive without being pretentious. **Known for:** eclectic Italian dishes; high-quality cuisine; ravioli with salt cod in arrabbiata oil spiced with red chili. ⑤ *Average main: €26* ⊠ *Piazza Amerigo Capponi 6, Borgo* ☎ *06/6874514* ⊕ *www.tavernaangelica.com* ⊙ *Closed Mon.* Ⓜ *Ottaviano.*

☕ Coffee and Quick Bites

Al Settimo Gelo

$ | **ICE CREAM** | **FAMILY** | The unusual flavors of gelato scooped up here include cinnamon and ginger and fig with cardamom and walnut, but the classics also get rave reviews. Ask for a taste of the *passito* flavor, if it's available; it's inspired by the popular sweet Italian dessert wine. **Known for:** organic Sicilian lemon sorbetto; homemade whipped cream; completely gluten-free shop. ⑤ *Average main: €5* ⊠ *Via Vodice 21/a, Prati* ☎ *06/3725567* ⊕ *www.alsettimogelo.it* ⊙ *Closed Mon. and 1 wk in Aug.* Ⓜ *Lepanto.*

★ Bonci Pizzarium

$ | **PIZZA** | **FAMILY** | This tiny storefront by famed pizzaiolo Gabriele Bonci is the city's most famous place for pizza *al taglio* (by the slice). It serves more than a dozen versions, from the standard margherita to slices piled high with prosciutto and other tasty ingredients.

Continued on page 102

3

Rome THE VATICAN WITH BORGO AND PRATI

HEAVENS ABOVE:
THE SISTINE CEILING

Forming lines that are probably longer than those waiting to pass through the Pearly Gates, hordes of visitors arrive at the Sistine Chapel daily to view what may be the world's most sublime example of artistry:

Michelangelo. *The Creation of Adam*, Sistine Chapel, The Vatican, circa 1511.

Michelangelo's Sistine Ceiling. To paint this 12,000-square-foot barrel vault, it took four years, 343 frescoed figures, and a titanic battle of wits between the artist and Pope Julius II. While in its typical fashion, Hollywood focused on the element of agony, not ecstasy, involved in the saga of creation, a restoration of the ceiling, completed in 1994, and the installation of LEDs for better illumination, completed in 2018, have revolutionized our appreciation of the masterpiece of masterpieces.

By Martin Bennett

MICHELANGELO'S
MISSION IMPOSSIBLE

Designed to match the proportions of Solomon's Temple described in the Old Testament, the Sistine Chapel is named after Pope Sixtus VI, who commissioned it as a place of worship for himself and as the venue where new popes could be elected. Before Michelangelo, the barrel-vaulted ceiling was an expanse of azure fretted with golden stars. Then, in 1504, an ugly crack appeared. Bramante, the architect, managed do some patchwork using iron rods, but when signs of a fissure remained, the new Pope Julius II summoned Michelangelo to cover it with a fresco 135 feet long and 44 feet wide.

Taking in the entire span of the ceiling, the theme connecting the various scenes in this painted universe is seemingly mankind's need for redemption. The majestic panel depicting the Creation of Adam leads through the stages of the Fall and the expulsion from Eden to the tragedy of Noah found naked and mocked by his own sons. Witnessing all from the side and end walls, a chorus of ancient Prophets and Sibyls peers anxiously forward, awaiting the Redeemer who will come to save both the Jews and the Gentiles.

APOCALYPSE NOW

The sweetness and pathos of his *Pietà*, carved by Michelangelo only ten years earlier, have been left behind. The new work foretells an apocalypse, its congregation of doomed sinners facing the wrath of heaven through hanging, beheading, crucifixion, flood, and plague. Michelangelo, by nature a misanthrope, was already filled with visions of doom thanks to the fiery orations of Savonarola, whose thunderous preachments he had heard before leaving his hometown of Florence. Vasari, the 16th-century art historian, coined the word *terribilità* to describe Michelangelo's tension-ridden style, a rare case of a single word being worth a thousand pictures.

Michelangelo wound up using a condensed "Reader's Digest" version of the stories from Genesis, with the dramatis personae overseen by a punitive and terrifying God. In real life, poor Michelangelo answered to a flesh-and-blood taskmaster who was almost as vengeful: Pope Julius II. Less vicar of Christ than latter-day Caesar, he was intent on uniting Italy under the power of the Vatican and was eager to do so by any means, including riding into pitched battle. Yet this "warrior pope" considered his most formidable adversary to be Michelangelo. Applying a form of blackmail, Julius threatened to wage war on Michelangelo's Florence, to which the artist had fled after Julius canceled a commission for a grand papal tomb unless Michelangelo agreed to return to Rome and take up the task of painting the Sistine Chapel ceiling.

MICHELANGELO, SCULPTOR

A sculptor first and foremost, however, Michelangelo considered painting an inferior genre—"for rascals and sissies" as he put it. Second, there was the sheer scope of the task, leading Michelangelo to suspect he'd been set up by a rival, Bramante, chief architect of the new St. Peter's Basilica. As Michelangelo was also a master architect, he regarded this fresco commission as a Renaissance mission-impossible. Pope Julius's powerful will prevailed—and six years later the work of the Sistine Ceiling was complete. Irving Stone's famous novel *The Agony and the Ecstasy*—and the granitic 1965 film that followed—chart this epic battle between artist and pope.

THINGS ARE LOOKING UP

To better view the ceiling, bring binoculars or even just a mirror (to prevent your neck from becoming bent like Michelangelo's). Note that photos are not permitted. Admission and entry to the Sistine Chapel is only through the Musei Vaticani (Vatican Museums). To avoid crowds, visit at lunchtime or during the papal blessings and public audiences held in St. Peter's Square. Alternatively, book the Prime Experience Tour, which starts one hour before the museums open, or purchase the Extra Hours–Sistine Chapel ticket, which allows time in the chapel after the museums close.

SCHEMATIC OF THE SISTINE CEILING

PAINTING
THE BIBLE

The ceiling's biblical symbols
were ideated by three Vatican
theologians, Cardinal Alidosi,
Egidio da Viterbo, and
Giovanni Rafanelli, along with
Michelangelo. As for

the ceiling's painted framework,
this quadratura alludes to Roman
triumphal arches because Pope
Julius II was fond of mount-
ing "triumphal entries" into his
conquered cities (in imitation of
Christ's procession into
Jerusalem on Palm Sunday).

THE CENTER PANELS

Prophet turned art-critic or, perhaps doubling as ourselves, the
ideal viewer, Jonah the prophet
(painted at the altar end) gazes
up at the Creation, or Michelangelo's version of it.

1 The first of three scenes taken from the Book of Genesis: God separates Light from Darkness.

2 God creates the sun and a craterless, pre-Galilean moon, while the panel's other half offers an unprecedented rear view of the Almighty creating the vegetable world.

3 In the panel showing God separating the Waters from the Heavens, the Creator tumbles towards us as in a self-made whirlwind.

4 Pausing for breath, next admire probably Western Art's most famous image—God giving life to Adam.

5 The Creation of Eve from Adam's rib leads to the sixth panel.

6 In a sort of diptych divided by the trunk of the Tree of Knowledge of Good and Evil, Michelangelo retells the Temptation and the Fall.

7 Illustrating Man's fallen nature, the last three panels narrate, in un-chronological order, the Flood. In the first Noah offers a pre-Flood sacrifice of thanks.

8 Damaged by an explosion in 1794, next comes Michelangelo's version of Flood itself.

9 Finally, above the monumental Jonah, you can just make out the small, wretched figure of Noah, lying drunk—in pose, the shrunken anti-type of the majestic Adam five panels down the wall.

THE CREATION OF ADAM

Michelangelo's Adam was partly inspired by the Creation scenes Michelangelo had studied in the sculpted doors of Jacopo della Quercia in Bologna and Lorenzo Ghiberti's Doors of Paradise in Florence. Yet in Michelangelo's version Adam's hand hangs limp, waiting God's touch to impart the spark of life. Facing his Creation, the Creator—looking a bit like the pagan god Jupiter—is for the first time ever depicted as horizontal, mirroring the biblical "in his own likeness." Decades after its completion, a crack began to appear, amputating Adam's fingertips.

Believe it or not, the most famous fingers in Western art are the handiwork, at least in part, of one Domenico Carnevale.

Known for: Rome's best pizza al taglio; over a dozen flavors; long lines. $ *Average main: €5 ✉ Via della Meloria 43, Prati ☎ 06/39745416 ⊕ www.bonci.it ⊘ Closed Mon. Ⓜ Cipro.*

Hotels

Hotel al San Pietrino

$ | **HOTEL** | This simple budget hotel on the third floor of a 19th-century palazzo offers rock-bottom rates and is just a five-minute walk from the Vatican. **Pros:** heavenly rates near the Vatican; air-conditioning and Wi-Fi; free parking nearby. **Cons:** a couple of Metro stops from the centro storico; flat pillows and basic bedding; no bar. $ *Rooms from: €98 ✉ Via Giovanni Bettolo 43, Prati ☎ 06/3700132 ⊕ www. hotelsanpietrino.it ⇗ 11 rooms ⧖ No Meals Ⓜ Ottaviano.*

Residenza Paolo VI

$$$$ | **HOTEL** | Set in a former monastery—still an extraterritorial part of the Vatican—abutting Bernini's colonnade of St. Peter's Square, the Paolo VI (pronounced "Sesto," a reference to Pope Paul VI) is unbeatably close to St. Peter's, with comfortable and quiet guest rooms. **Pros:** direct views of St. Peter's from the rooftop terrace; quiet rooms; lovely staff and service. **Cons:** some rooms are really small; bathrooms are a tight space; far away from Rome's historical attractions. $ *Rooms from: €302 ✉ Via Paolo VI 26, Borgo ☎ 06/684870 ⊕ www.residen-zapaolovi.com ⇗ 35 rooms ⧖ Free Breakfast Ⓜ Ottaviano.*

Nightlife

Emerald's Bar

COCKTAIL BARS | This classy cocktail bar a few blocks from the Vatican makes you feel transported to a cozy salon in New York or London. In addition to some original creations, the bartenders make reliably good classics, including excellent dirty martinis. The kitchen stays open until midnight, so it's also a good spot for a late bite. ✉ *Via Crescenzio 91C, Prati ☎ 06/88654275 ⊕ www.emeraldsbar.it Ⓜ Ottaviano.*

Shopping

★ Castroni

FOOD | Opening its flagship shop near the Vatican in 1932, this gastronomic paradise has long been Rome's port of call for decadent delicacies from around the globe; there are now 13 locations throughout the city. Jonesing expats and study-abroad students pop in for local sweets, 300 types of tea, and even good old-fashioned Betty Crocker red velvet cake mix. If you need a pick-me-up, try the house-roasted espresso, which is some of the best coffee in Rome. ✉ *Via Cola di Rienzo 196/198, Prati ☎ 06/6874383 ⊕ www.castronicoladirien-zo.com Ⓜ Lepanto.*

Savelli Arte e Tradizione

SOUVENIRS | Here you'll find a fully stocked selection of religious gifts: everything from rosaries and crosses to religious artwork and Pope Francis memorabilia. Founded in 1898, this family business provides a place for pilgrims to pick up a souvenir from the Holy See and also specializes in mosaics. The store has another location at the Self-Service Restaurant in Piazza del Sant'Uffizio 6/7. It's closed on Sunday afternoon. ✉ *Via Paolo VI 27–29, Borgo ☎ 06/68307017 ⊕ savellireligious.com Ⓜ Ottaviano.*

Piazza Navona, Campo de' Fiori, and the Jewish Ghetto

Set between Via del Corso and the Tiber bend, these time-burnished districts are some of the city's most beautiful. They're filled with airy piazzas, half-hidden courtyards, and narrow streets bearing curious names. Some of Rome's most coveted residential addresses are nestled here. So, too, are the ancient Pantheon and the Renaissance square of Campo de' Fiori, but the spectacular, over-the-top Baroque monuments of the 16th and 17th centuries predominate.

The hub of the district is the queen of squares, Piazza Navona—a cityscape adorned with the most jaw-dropping fountain by Gian Lorenzo Bernini, father of the Baroque. Streets running off the square lead to many historic must-sees, including noble churches by Borromini and Caravaggio's greatest paintings at San Luigi dei Francesi. This district has been an integral part of the city since ancient times, and its position between the Vatican and Lateran palaces, both seats of papal rule, put it in the mainstream of Rome's development from the Middle Ages onward. Craftsmen, shopkeepers, and famed artists toiled in the shadow of the huge palaces built to consolidate the power of leading figures in the papal court. Artisans and artists still live here, but their numbers are diminishing as the district becomes increasingly posh and—so critics say—"Disneyfied." But three of the liveliest piazzas in Rome—Piazza Navona, Piazza della Rotonda (home to the Pantheon), and Campo de' Fiori—are lodestars in a constellation of some of the city's finest cafés, stores, and wine bars.

Although today most of Rome's Jews live outside the Ghetto, the area remains the spiritual and cultural home of Jewish Rome, and that heritage permeates its small commercial area of Judaica shops, kosher bakeries, and restaurants. The Jewish Ghetto was established by papal decree in the 16th century. It was by definition a closed community, where Roman Jews lived under lock and key until Italian unification in 1870. In 1943–44, the already small Jewish population there was decimated by deportations. Today there are a few Judaica shops and kosher groceries, bakeries, and restaurants

(especially on Via di Portico d'Ottavia), but the neighborhood mansions are now being renovated and much coveted by rich and stylish expats.

GETTING HERE AND AROUND

The Piazza Navona and Campo de' Fiori are an easy walk from the Vatican or Trastevere, or a half-hour stroll from the Spanish Steps. From Termini or the Vatican, take Bus No. 40 Express or the No. 64 to Largo Torre Argentina; then walk 10 minutes to either piazza. Bus No. 62 winds from Piazza Barberini past the Trevi Fountain to Campo de' Fiori.

From the Vatican or the Spanish Steps, it's a 30-minute walk to the Jewish Ghetto, or take the No. 40 Express or the No. 64 bus from Termini station to Largo Torre Argentina.

◉ Sights

Chiesa del Gesù

CHURCH | With an overall design by Vignola and a facade and dome by Della Porta, the first Jesuit church in Rome influenced the city's ecclesiastical architecture for more than a century. Consecrated in 1584—after the Council of Trent (1545–63) solidified the determination of the Roman Catholic Church to push back against northern Europe's Reformed Protestants—Il Gesù also became the prototype for Counter-Reformation churches throughout not only Italy but also Europe and the Americas.

Although low lighting underplays the brilliance of everything, the inside of the church drips with gold and lapis lazuli, gold and precious marbles, and gold and more gold. The interior was initially left plain to the point of austerity; when it was finally fully embellished 100 years later, no expense was spared to inspire believers with pomp and majesty. The most striking element is the ceiling, where frescoes swirl down from on high and merge with painted stucco figures at the base. The artist Baciccia achieved extraordinary effects, especially over the nave in the *Triumph of the Holy Name of Jesus.* Here, the figures representing evil who are being cast out of heaven seem to hurtle down onto the observer.

The founder of the Jesuit order himself is buried in the Chapel of St. Ignatius, in the left-hand transept. This is surely one of the most sumptuous altars in Rome, though as is typical of Baroque decoration, which is renowned for its illusions, the enormous globe of lapis lazuli that crowns the alter is really only a shell of lapis over a stucco base. Note, too, architect Carlo Fontana's heavy, bronze altar rail, which is in keeping with the surrounding opulence. ⊠ *Via degli Astalli 16, Campo de' Fiori* ☏ *06/697001* ⊕ *www. chiesadelgesu.org.*

Crypta Balbi

RUINS | The fourth component of the magnificent collections of the Museo Nazionale Romano, this museum is unusual because it represents several periods of Roman history. The crypt is part of the Balbus Theater complex (13 BC), and other parts of the complex are from the medieval period, up through the 20th century. Though the interior lacks the lingering opulence of some other Roman sites, the written explanations accompanying the well-lit exhibits are excellent, and this museum is a popular field trip for teachers and school groups. Note that recent restoration works have resulted in closures here; check for updates before visiting. ⊠ *Via delle Botteghe Oscure 31, Jewish Ghetto* ☏ *06/684851* ⊕ *museonazionaleromano.beniculturali.it/ crypta-balbi* ⊠ *€8 Crypta Balbi only; €12 includes three other Museo Nazionale Romano sites over a 1-wk period (Palazzo Altemps, Palazzo Massimo, Museo Diocleziano)* ⊗ *Closed Mon.* Ⓜ *Bus Nos. 64 and 40, Tram No. 8.*

Fontana delle Tartarughe

FOUNTAIN | FAMILY | Designed by Giacomo della Porta in 1581 and sculpted by Taddeo Landini, this fountain, set in pretty Piazza Mattei, is one of Rome's most charming. Its focal point consists of four bronze boys, each grasping a dolphin spouting water into a marble shell. Bronze turtles just out of reach of the boys' hands drink from the upper basin. The turtles were added in the 17th century by Bernini. ⊠ *Piazza Mattei, Jewish Ghetto.*

Galleria Spada

ART MUSEUM | In this neighborhood of huge, austere palaces, Palazzo Spada strikes an almost frivolous note, with its pretty ornament-encrusted courtyard and its upper stories covered with stuccoes and statues. Although the palazzo houses an impressive collection of Old Master paintings, it's most famous for its trompe-l'oeil garden gallery, a delightful example of the sort of architectural games that rich Romans of the 17th century found irresistible.

Even if you don't go into the gallery, step into the courtyard and look through the glass window of the library to the colonnaded corridor in the adjacent courtyard. You'll see—or seem to see—a statue at the end of a 26-foot-long gallery, seemingly quadrupled in depth in a sort of optical telescope that takes Renaissance's art of perspective to another level. In fact the distance is an illusion: the corridor grows progressively narrower and the columns progressively smaller as they near a statue, which is just 2 feet tall. The Baroque period is known for its special effects, and this is rightly one of the most famous. It was long thought that Borromini was responsible for the ruse; it's now known that it was designed by an Augustinian priest, Giovanni Maria da Bitonto.

Upstairs is a seignorial picture gallery with the paintings shown as they would have been, hung one over the next clear to the ceiling. Outstanding works include Brueghel's *Landscape with Windmills,* Titian's *Musician,* and Andrea del Sarto's *Visitation.* Look for the fact sheets that have descriptive notes about the objects in each room. ⊠ *Piazza Capo di Ferro 13, Campo de' Fiori* ☎ *06/6874896* ⊕ *galleri-aspada.cultura.gov.it* 🎫 *€6; free the first Sun. of the month* ⊗ *Closed Tues.*

★ Palazzo Altemps

CASTLE/PALACE | Containing some of the world's finest ancient Roman statues, Palazzo Altemps is part of the Museo Nazionale Romano. The palace's sober exterior belies a magnificence that appears as soon as you walk into the majestic courtyard, studded with statues and covered in part by a retractable awning. The restored interior hints at the Roman lifestyle of the 16th–18th centuries while showcasing the most illustrious pieces from the Museo Nazionale, including the collection of the Ludovisi noble family.

In the frescoed salons you can see the *Galata Suicida,* a poignant sculptural work portraying a barbarian warrior who chooses death for himself and his wife, rather than humiliation by the enemy. Another highlight is the large Ludovisi sarcophagus, magnificently carved from marble. In a place of honor is the *Ludovisi Throne,* which shows a goddess emerging from the sea and being helped by her acolytes. For centuries this was heralded as one of the most sublime Greek sculptures, but, today, at least one authoritative art historian considers it a colossally overrated fake. Look for the framed explanations of the exhibits that detail (in English) how and exactly where Renaissance sculptors, Bernini among them, added missing pieces to the classical works.

In the lavishly frescoed loggia stand busts of the Caesars. In the wing once occupied by early-20th-century poet Gabriele d'Annunzio (who married into the Altemps family), three rooms host the museum's Egyptian collection. ⊠ *Piazza di Sant'Apollinare 46, Piazza Navona* ☎ *06/684851* ⊕ *museoonazionaleromano.beniculturali.it* 🎫 *€8; €12 combined ticket*

includes three other Museo Nazionale Romano sites over one week (Crypta Balbi, Palazzo Massimo alle Terme, and Museo delle Terme di Diocleziano) ⊗ *Closed Mon.*

★ Palazzo Farnese

CASTLE/PALACE | Rome's most beautiful Renaissance palace is fabled for its Galleria Carracci, whose ceiling is to the Baroque age what the Sistine Chapel ceiling is to the Renaissance. The Farnese family rose to great power and wealth during the Renaissance, in part because of the favor Pope Alexander VI showed to the beautiful Giulia Farnese. The massive palace was begun when, with Alexander's aid, Giulia's brother became cardinal; it was further enlarged on his election as Pope Paul III in 1534.

The uppermost frieze decorations and main window overlooking the piazza are the work of Michelangelo, who also designed part of the courtyard, as well as the graceful arch over Via Giulia at the back. The facade on Piazza Farnese has geometrical brick configurations that have long been thought to hold some occult meaning. When looking up at the palace, try to catch a glimpse of the splendid frescoed ceilings, including the Galleria Carracci vault painted by Annibale Carracci between 1597 and 1604.

The Carracci gallery depicts the loves of the gods, a supremely pagan theme that the artist painted in a swirling style that announced the birth of the Baroque. Other opulent salons are among the largest in Rome, including the Salon of Hercules, which has an impressive replica of the ancient *Farnese Hercules.* The French Embassy, which occupies the palace, offers tours (in English) on Monday, Wednesday, and Friday; book at least a few weeks (and up to eight months) in advance through the website, and bring a photo ID. ⊠ *French Embassy, Servizio Culturale, Piazza Farnese 67, Campo de' Fiori* ☎ *06/686011* ⊕ *www.*

Piazza Navona, Campo de' Fiori, and the Jewish Ghetto

Sights ▼

1	Chiesa del Gesù	I7
2	Crypta Balbi	H7
3	Fontana delle Tartarughe	H8
4	Galleria Spada	E8
5	Palazzo Altemps	E3
6	Palazzo Farnese	D8
7	Pantheon	G5
8	Piazza Campo de' Fiori	E7
9	Piazza Navona	E5
10	Portico d'Ottavia	H9
11	San Luigi dei Francesi	F4
12	Santa Maria sopra Minerva	H5
13	Sant'Andrea della Valle	F7
14	Sant'Ivo alla Sapienza	F5
15	Sinagoga	H9
16	Via Giulia	C7

Restaurants ▼

1	Armando al Pantheon	G5
2	Ba'Ghetto	J3
3	BellaCarne	H9
4	Cul de Sac	E6
5	Da Fransceso	D5
6	Dar Filettaro a Santa Barbara	F8
7	Ditirambo	E6
8	Emma Pizzeria	G7
9	Enoteca Corsi	H6
10	Il Convivio Troiani	E3
11	Il Pagliaccio	B5
12	Il Sanlorenzo	F7
13	La Ciambella	G6
14	L'Angolo Divino	E8
15	Osteria dell'Ingegno	I4
16	Pesci Fritti	F7
17	Pierluigi	C6
18	Roscioli Salumeria con Cucina	F8

Coffee and Quick Bites ▼

1	Bar del Fico	D5
2	Gelateria Del Teatro	D4
3	Giolitti	H3
4	Pasticceria Boccione	G8
5	Sant'Eustachio il Caffè	G5

Hotels ▼

1	Albergo Santa Chiara	G6
2	Casa di Santa Brigida	D7
3	D.O.M. Hotel Roma	B6
4	Hotel Chapter Roma	G9
5	Hotel de' Ricci	C7
6	Hotel Genio	E4
7	Hotel Ponte Sisto	E9
8	The Pantheon Iconic Rome Hotel, Autograph Collection	G5

3

Rome PIAZZA NAVONA, CAMPO DE' FIORI, AND THE JEWISH GHETTO

visite-palazzofarnese.it ☎ €15 ⏱ Closed Tues., Thurs., Sat., and Sun.

★ Pantheon

RELIGIOUS BUILDING | The city's best-preserved ancient building, this former Roman temple is a marvel of architectural harmony and proportion. It was entirely rebuilt by the emperor Hadrian around AD 120 on the site of a Pantheon (from the Greek: *pan,* all, and *theon,* gods) erected in 27 BC by Augustus's right-hand man and son-in-law, Agrippa. The most striking thing about the Pantheon is not its size, immense though it is, nor even the phenomenal technical difficulties posed by so massive a construction; rather, it's the remarkable unity of the building. The diameter described by the dome is exactly equal to its height. It's the use of such simple mathematical balance that gives classical architecture its characteristic sense of proportion and its nobility. The opening at the apex of the dome, the *oculus,* is nearly 30 feet in diameter and was intended to symbolize the "all-seeing eye of the heavens." On a practical note, this means when it rains, it rains inside: look out for the drainage holes in the floor. One of the reasons the Pantheon is so well preserved is that it was consecrated as a church in AD 608. The Pantheon is also one of the city's important burial places. Its most famous tomb is that of Raphael (between the second and third chapels on the left as you enter). Mass takes place on Sunday and on religious holidays at 10:30; it's open to the public, but you are expected to arrive before the beginning and stay until the end. General access usually resumes at about 11:30. At most times (especially in high season or weekends), you should purchase tickets online in advance. ✉ Piazza della Rotonda, Piazza Navona ☎ 06/68300230 ⊕ www.museii-taliani.it ☎ €5; audio guide €8.50.

Piazza Campo de' Fiori

MARKET | FAMILY | A bustling marketplace in the morning (Monday through Saturday from 8 to 2) and a trendy meeting place the rest of the day and night, this piazza has plenty of down-to-earth charm. After lunch, it becomes a circus of bars particularly favored by study-abroad students, tourists, and young expats. Brooding over the piazza is a hooded statue of the philosopher Giordano Bruno, who was burned at the stake here in 1600 for heresy. ✉ Intersection of Via dei Baullari, Via Giubbonari, Via del Pellegrino, and Piazza della Cancelleria, Campo de' Fiori.

★ Piazza Navona

PLAZA/SQUARE | Always camera-ready, this beautiful plaza has Bernini sculptures, three gorgeous fountains, and a magnificently Baroque church (Sant'Agnese in Agone), all built atop the remains of a Roman athletics track. Pieces of the arena are still visible near the adjacent Piazza Sant'Apollinare, and the ancient spirit of entertainment lives on in the buskers and artists who populate the piazza today. The piazza took on its current look during the 17th century, after Pope Innocent X of the Pamphilj family decided to make over his family palace (now the Brazilian embassy and an ultra-luxe hotel) and its surroundings. Center stage is the Fontana dei Quattro Fiumi, created for Innocent by Bernini in 1651. Bernini's powerful figures of the four rivers represent the longest rivers of the four known continents at the time: the Nile (his head covered because the source was unknown); the Ganges; the Danube; and the Plata (the length of the Amazon was then unknown). Popular legend has it that the figure of the Plata—the figure closest to Sant'Agnese in Agone—raises his hand before his eyes because he can't bear to look upon the church's "inferior" facade designed by Francesco Borromini, Bernini's rival. It's a beautiful spot to linger over a coffee, but you can find cheaper, more authentic, and far better meals elsewhere. ✉ Piazza Navona.

Portico d'Ottavia

RUINS | Looming over the Jewish Ghetto, this huge portico, with a few surviving columns, is one of the area's most picturesque set pieces, with the church of Sant'Angelo in Pescheria built right into its ruins. Named by Augustus in honor of his sister Octavia, it was originally 390 feet wide and 433 feet long; encompassed two temples, a meeting hall, and a library; and served as a kind of grandiose entrance foyer for the adjacent Teatro di Marcello.

In the Middle Ages, the cool marble ruins of the portico became Rome's *pescheria* (fish market). A stone plaque on a pillar (it's a copy as the original is in the Musei Capitolini) states in Latin that the head of any fish surpassing the length of the plaque was to be cut off "up to the first fin" and given to the city fathers or else the vendor was to pay a fine of 10 gold florins. The heads, which were used to make fish soup, were considered a great delicacy. ✉ *Via Portico d'Ottavia 29, Jewish Ghetto* ☎ *06/0608.*

★ San Luigi dei Francesi

CHURCH | San Luigi's Contarelli Chapel (the fifth and last chapel on the left, toward the main altar) is adorned with three stunningly dramatic works by Caravaggio (1571–1610), the Baroque master of the heightened approach to light and dark. They were commissioned for the tomb of Mattheiu Cointerel in one of Rome's French churches (San Luigi is St. Louis, patron saint of France). The inevitable coin machine will light up his *Calling of Saint Matthew, Saint Matthew and the Angel,* and *Martyrdom of Saint Matthew* (seen from left to right), and Caravaggio's mastery of light takes it from there.

When painted, they caused considerable consternation among the clergy of San Luigi, who thought the artist's dramatically realistic approach was scandalously disrespectful. A first version of the altarpiece was rejected; the priests were not particularly happy with the other two, either. Time has fully vindicated Caravaggio's patron, Cardinal Francesco del Monte, who secured the commission for these works and staunchly defended them. ■ TIP→ **This church regularly enforces the rule of covered knees and shoulders, and turns away those who do not abide.** ✉ *Piazza di San Luigi dei Francesi, Piazza Navona* ☎ *06/688271* ⊕ *saintlouis-rome. net.*

★ Santa Maria sopra Minerva

CHURCH | The name of the church reveals that it was built *sopra* (over) the ruins of a temple of Minerva, the ancient goddess of wisdom. Erected in 1280 by Dominicans along severe Italian Gothic lines, it has undergone a number of more or less happy interior restorations. Certainly, as the city's major Gothic church, it provides a refreshing contrast to Baroque flamboyance. Have a €1 coin handy to illuminate the Cappella Carafa in the right transept; the small investment is worth it to better see Filippino Lippi's (1457–1504) glowing frescoes featuring a deep azure expanse of sky and musical angels hovering around the Virgin.

Under the main altar is the tomb of St. Catherine of Siena, one of Italy's patron saints and a major destination for faithful locals who drop written prayers on her final resting place. Left of the altar you'll find Michelangelo's *Risen Christ* and the tomb of the gentle artist Fra Angelico. Bernini's unusual and little-known monument to the Blessed Maria Raggi is on the fifth pier of the left-hand aisle.

In front of the church, Bernini's *Elephant and Obelisk* is perhaps the city's most charming sculpture. An inscription on the base references the church's ancient patroness, reading something to the effect that it takes a strong mind to sustain solid wisdom. ✉ *Piazza della Minerva, Piazza Navona* ☎ *06/792257* ⊕ *www.santamariasopraminerva.it.*

Sant'Andrea della Valle

CHURCH | Topped by the highest dome in Rome after St. Peter's (designed by Maderno), this imposing 17th-century church is remarkably balanced in design. Fortunately, its facade, which had turned a sooty gray from pollution, has been cleaned to a near-sparkling white. Use one of the handy mirrors to examine the early-17th-century frescoes by Domenichino in the choir vault and those by Lanfranco in the dome. One of the earliest ceilings done in full Baroque style, its upward vortex was influenced by Correggio's dome in Parma, of which Lanfranco was also a citizen. (Bring a few coins to light the paintings, which can be very dim.) The three massive paintings of St. Andrew's martyrdom are by Mattia Preti (1650–51). Richly marbled and decorated chapels flank the nave, and in such a space, Puccini set the first act of *Tosca*. ⊠ *Piazza Vidoni 6, Corso Vittorio Emanuele II, Campo de' Fiori* ☎ *06/6861339* ⊕ *santandrea.teatinos.org.*

Sant'Ivo alla Sapienza

CHURCH | This eccentric Baroque church, probably Borromini's best, has one of Rome's most delightful "domes"—a dizzying spiral said to have been inspired by a bee's stinger. The apian symbol is a reminder that the church was commissioned by the Barberini pope Urban VIII (a swarm of bees figure on the Barberini family crest), although it was completed by Alexander VII. The interior, open only for three hours on Sunday morning, is worth a look, especially if you share Borromini's taste for complex mathematical architectural idiosyncrasies. "I didn't take up architecture solely to be a copyist," he once said. Sant'Ivo is certainly the proof. ⊠ *Corso del Rinascimento 40, Piazza Navona* ⊕ *www.sivoallasapienza.eu* ⊗ *Closed Mon.–Sat., July, and Aug.*

Sinagoga

RELIGIOUS BUILDING | This synagogue has been the city's largest Jewish temple, and a Roman landmark with its distinctive aluminum dome, since its construction in 1904. The building also houses the Jewish Museum, with displays of precious ritual objects and exhibits that document the uninterrupted presence of a Jewish community in the city for nearly 22 centuries. Until the 16th century, Jews were esteemed citizens of Rome. Among them were bankers and physicians to the popes, who had themselves given permission for the construction of synagogues. But, in 1555, during the Counter-Reformation, Pope Paul IV decreed the building of the walls of the Ghetto, confining the Jews to this small flood-prone area and imposing restrictions, some of which continued to be enforced until 1870. For security reasons, entrance is via guided visit only, and tours in English are available twice a day but should be booked online ahead of time. Entrance to the synagogue is through the museum on Via Catalana. ⊠ *Lungotevere de' Cenci 15, Jewish Ghetto* ☎ *06/68400661* ⊕ *www.museoebraico.roma.it* ⊠ *€11* ⊗ *Museum closed Sat. and Jewish holidays.*

★ Via Giulia

STREET | Straight as a die and still something of a Renaissance-era diorama, Via Giulia was the first street in Rome since ancient times to be deliberately planned. It was named for Pope Julius II (of Sistine Chapel fame), who commissioned it in the early 1500s as part of a scheme to open up a grandiose approach to St. Peter's Basilica. Although the pope's plans were only partially completed, Via Giulia became an important thoroughfare in Renaissance Rome. It's still, after more than four centuries, the address of choice for Roman aristocrats, despite a recent, controversial addition: a large parking lot along one side of the street (creating it meant steamrolling through ancient and medieval ruins underneath).

A stroll around and along Via Giulia reveals elegant palaces and churches, including one, **San Eligio**, on the little side street Via di Sant'Eligio, that was designed by Raphael himself. Note also the **Palazzo Sacchetti** (✉ *Via Giulia 66*), with an imposing stone portal and an interior containing some of Rome's grandest staterooms; it remains, after 300 years, the private quarters of the Marchesi Sacchetti. The forbidding brick building that housed the **Carceri Nuove (New Prison)** (✉ *Via Giulia 52*), Rome's prison for more than two centuries, now contains the offices of the Direzione Nazionale Antimafia. Near the bridge that arches over Via Giulia's southern end is the church of **Santa Maria dell'Orazione e Morte** (Holy Mary of Prayer and Death), with stone skulls on its door. These are a symbol of a confraternity that was charged with burying the bodies of the unidentified dead found in the city streets.

Designed by Borromini and home, since 1927, to the Hungarian Academy, the **Palazzo Falconieri** (✉ *Via Giulia 1* ☎ *06/68896700*) has Borromini-designed salons and loggia that are sporadically open as part of guided tours; call for information. The falcon statues atop its belvedere are best viewed from around the block, along the Tiber embankment. Remnant of a master plan by Michelangelo, the arch over the street was meant to link massive **Palazzo Farnese,** on the east side of Via Giulia, with the building across the street and a bridge to the Villa Farnesina, directly across the river. Finally, on the right and rather green with age, dribbles that star of many a postcard, the **Fontana del Mascherone**. ✉ *Via Giulia, between Piazza dell'Oro and Piazza San Vincenzo Palloti, Campo de' Fiori.*

🍽 Restaurants

★ Armando al Pantheon
$$ | ROMAN | In the shadow of the Pantheon, this small family-run trattoria, open since 1961, delights tourists and locals alike. There's an air of authenticity to the Roman staples here, and the quality of

the ingredients and the cooking mean booking ahead through the website is a must. **Known for:** beautifully executed traditional Roman cooking; spaghetti alla gricia (with guanciale, pecorino cheese, and black pepper); reservation list that opens 30 days at a time. ⑤ *Average main: €16* ✉ *Salita dei Crescenzi 31, Piazza Navona* ⊕ *www.armandoalpantheon.it* ⊘ *Closed Sun. and Aug.*

★ Ba'Ghetto
$$ | ITALIAN | FAMILY | This well-established hot spot on the Jewish Ghetto's main promenade has pleasant indoor and outdoor seating. The kitchen is kosher (many places featuring Roman Jewish fare are not) and is known for its Judeo-Roman meat dishes mixed with Middle Eastern recipes. **Known for:** carciofi alla giudia (deep-fried artichokes) and other Roman-Jewish specialties; casual family atmosphere; tables on the pedestrianized street. ⑤ *Average main: €22* ✉ *Via del Portico d'Ottavia 57, Jewish Ghetto* ☎ *06/68892868* ⊕ *www.baghetto.com* ⊘ *Dinner Fri. and lunch Sat. are strictly for those who observe Shabbat with advance payment.*

BellaCarne
$$ | ROMAN | *Bellacarne* means "beautiful meat," and that's the focus of the menu here (though it's also what a Jewish Italian grandmother might say while pinching her grandchild's cheek). The kosher kitchen makes its own pastrami, but the setting is more fine dining than deli. **Known for:** pastrami; shabbat menu; outside seating on a lively pedestrianized street. ⑤ *Average main: €19* ✉ *Via Portico d'Ottavia 51, Jewish Ghetto* ☎ *06/6833104* ⊕ *www.bellacarne.it* ⊘ *No dinner Fri. No lunch Sat. except limited Shabbat seating that must be pre-paid.*

★ Cul de Sac
$ | WINE BAR | This popular wine bar a stone's throw from Piazza Navona is among the city's oldest and has a book-length selection of wines from Italy, France, the Americas, and elsewhere. It

offers great value and pleasant service and is a lovely spot for a light late lunch or an early dinner when most restaurants aren't open yet. **Known for:** great wine list (and wine bottle–lined interior); eclectic Italian and Mediterranean fare; relaxed atmosphere and outside tables. $ *Average main: €14* ✉ *Piazza di Pasquino 73, Piazza Navona* ☎ *06/68801094* ⊕ *www.enotecaculdesacroma.it.*

Da Francesco

$$ | **ROMAN** | **FAMILY** | For good, hearty, Roman cuisine in an area filled with mediocre touristy restaurants, head to this trattoria that's been on the scene since the late 1950s. Stick with the classics, perhaps starting off with a mixed salumi plate featuring Parma ham and buffalo mozzarella before moving on to a *primi* (first course)—the amatriciana (with tomato sauce, guanciale, and pecorino cheese) is one of the standouts. **Known for:** authentic and informal atmosphere; outside tables in summer; truffle topped pasta alla gricia. $ *Average main: €18* ✉ *Piazza del Fico 29, Piazza Navona* ☎ *06/6864009* ⊕ *www.dafrancesco.it.*

Dar Filettaro a Santa Barbara

$ | **ITALIAN** | The window reads "Filetti di Baccalà," but the official name of this small restaurant that specializes in one thing—deliciously battered and deep-fried fillets of salt cod—is Dar Filettaro a Santa Barbara. If it's in season, be sure to try the *puntarelle* (crisp chicory) tossed with garlic and anchovy dressing. **Known for:** piping hot filetti di baccalà; functional "hole-in-the-wall" interior; tables outside on the pretty square. $ *Average main: €8* ✉ *Largo dei Librari 88, Campo de' Fiori* ☎ *06/6864018* ⊕ *www.facebook.com/FilettiDiBaccala* ☉ *Closed Sun. and Aug. No lunch.*

Ditirambo

$$ | **ITALIAN** | Don't let the country-kitchen feel fool you. This little spot off of Campo de' Fiori goes a step beyond the ordinary with constantly changing offbeat takes on Italian classics. **Known for:** cozy and casual; hearty meat and pasta dishes; perfectly grilled octopus and other seafood dishes. $ *Average main: €18* ✉ *Piazza della Cancelleria 74, Campo de' Fiori* ☎ *06/6871626* ⊕ *www.ristoranteditirambo.it* ☉ *No lunch Mon. Closed Aug.*

★ Emma Pizzeria

$$$ | **ROMAN** | **FAMILY** | Smack in the middle of the city, with the freshest produce right outside its door, this pizzeria features pies made with dough by Rome's renowned family of bakers, the Rosciolis. The menu also offers a good selection of pastas, mains, and local Lazio wines. **Known for:** light, airy, and casual; thin-crust Roman pizza; tasty fritti (classic fried Roman pizzeria appetizers). $ *Average main: €25* ✉ *Via Monte della Farina 28–29, Campo de' Fiori* ☎ *06/64760475* ⊕ *www.emmapizzeria.com.*

Enoteca Corsi

$ | **ITALIAN** | Although this old-school, centro storico trattoria has been renovated, you wouldn't know it, and that's part of its charm. At lunchtime, it's often packed with a mix of civil servants from the nearby government offices, construction workers, and in-the-know tourists enjoying classic pastas, octopus salad, and *secondi* (second courses) such as roast veal with peas. **Known for:** casual atmosphere; Roman specialties; brusque but friendly service. $ *Average main: €14* ✉ *Via del Gesù 88, Piazza Navona* ☎ *06/6790821* ⊕ *www.enotecacorsi.com* ☉ *Closed Sun. and 3 wks in Aug. No dinner Sat.*

★ Il Convivio Troiani

$$$$ | **MODERN ITALIAN** | The three Troiani brothers—Angelo in the kitchen and Giuseppe and Massimo presiding over the dining room and wine cellar—have been quietly redefining the experience of Italian *alta cucina* (haute cuisine) since 1990 at this well-regarded establishment in a tiny, nondescript alley north of Piazza Navona. The service is attentive without being overbearing, and the wine list is exceptional. **Known for:** fine dining in

elegant surroundings; inventive modern Italian cooking with exotic touches; amazing wine cellar and a great somme-lier. $ *Average main: €65* ⊠ *Vicolo dei Soldati 31, Piazza Navona* ☎ *06/6869432* ⊕ *www.ilconviviotroiani.it* ⊘ *Closed Sun. and 1 wk in Aug. No lunch.*

Il Pagliaccio

$$$$ | **MODERN ITALIAN** | Some of the most innovative interpretations of fine Roman cookery can be found in this starkly chic restaurant on a backstreet between upscale Via Giulia and the Campo de' Fiori. Chef Anthony Genovese was born in France to Calabrese parents and spent time cooking in Japan and Thailand, so his dishes make use of nontraditional spices, ingredients, and preparations—garnering him a loyal following and multiple accolades. **Known for:** elaborate tasting menus; fine dining in elegant sur-roundings; discreet location. $ *Average main: €110* ⊠ *Via dei Banchi Vecchi 129a, Piazza Navona* ☎ *06/68809595* ⊕ *www. ristoranteilpagliaccio.com* ⊘ *Closed Sun., Mon., and Aug. No lunch Tues.–Fri.*

Il Sanlorenzo

$$$$ | **SEAFOOD** | A gorgeous space, with chandeliers and soaring original brick-work ceilings, is the setting for one of Rome's best seafood restaurants. Order à la carte, or if you're hungry, the eight-course tasting menu (given the quality of the fish, a relative bargain at €90), which might include cuttlefish-ink tagliatelle with mint, artichokes, and roe or shrimp from the island of Ponza with rosemary, bitter herbs, and porcini mushrooms. **Known for:** top-quality fish and seafood; spaghetti con ricci (sea urchins); elegant surroundings. $ *Average main: €70* ⊠ *Via dei Chiavari 4/5, Campo de' Fiori* ☎ *06/6865097* ⊕ *www.ilsanlorenzo.it* ⊘ *Closed 2 wks in Aug. No lunch Mon.*

La Ciambella

$$$ | **ITALIAN** | A large glass wall to the kitchen and massive skylight in the dining room hint at the contemporary leanings of this restaurant built atop the ruins of the Baths of Agrippa behind the Pantheon. The emphasis here is on high-quality ingredients and classic Italian culinary traditions interpreted for modern diners. **Known for:** elegant setting in a great location near the Pantheon; sophisticated Italian cuisine; expert wine pairings. $ *Average main: €35* ⊠ *Via dell'Arco della Ciambella 20, Piazza Navo-na* ☎ *06/6832930* ⊕ *www.la-ciambella.it* ⊘ *Closed Tues. and Wed.*

L'Angolo Divino

$ | **WINE BAR** | There's something about this cozy wine bar that makes it feel as if it's in a small traditional village instead of a bustling metropolis. The walls are lined with a tempting array of bottles from around the Italian peninsula, and the counter is stocked with cheese and salumi that can be sliced and piled on plates to order. **Known for:** excellent wine selection and advice; cozy atmosphere; late-night snacks. $ *Average main: €14* ⊠ *Via dei Balestrari 12, Campo de' Fiori* ☎ *06/6864413* ⊕ *www.angolodivino.it* ⊘ *Closed 2 wks in Aug.*

Osteria dell'Ingegno

$$ | **MODERN ITALIAN** | This casual, trendy place—vibrant with colorful paintings by local artists—is a great spot to enjoy an ancient piazza while savoring a glass of wine or a gourmet meal. The simple but innovative menu includes dishes like Roman artichokes with baccalà, beef *tagliata* (sliced grilled steak) with a red-wine reduction, and a perfectly cooked duck breast with red fruit sauce. **Known for:** a mix of traditional and inventive pastas; a great spot both for aperitifs and/or a meal; outdoor seating with views of ancient ruins. $ *Average main: €22* ⊠ *Piazza di Pietra 45, Piazza Navona* ☎ *06/6780662* ⊕ *www.osteriadellingeg-no.com* ⊘ *Closed Mon.*

Pesci Fritti

$$ | **SOUTHERN ITALIAN** | This cute jewel box of a restaurant sits on the ruins of the ancient Theatre of Pompey just behind Campo de' Fiori (note the curve of the street). Step inside, and the whitewashed walls with touches of pale sea blue will make you feel like you've escaped to the Mediterranean coast for seafood favorites. **Known for:** fried fish and seafood choices; spaghetti with clams; cozy setting. $ *Average main: €18* ✉ *Via di Grottapinta 8, Campo de' Fiori* ☎ *06/68806170* ⊕ *pescifritti.business.site* ⏾ *Closed Mon. and Aug.*

★ Pierluigi

$$$$ | SEAFOOD | This chic seafood restaurant is a fun spot on balmy summer evenings, where elegant diners sip crisp white wine at tables out on the pretty Piazza de' Ricci. The carpaccio selection is exquisite, but there is also a large selection of pastas extravagantly topped with white truffles. **Known for:** top-quality fish and seafood; tables on the pretty pedestrianized piazza; elegant atmosphere with great service. $ *Average main: €45* ✉ *Piazza de' Ricci 144, Campo de' Fiori* ☎ *06/6868717* ⊕ *www.pierluigi. it.*

★ Roscioli Salumeria con Cucina

$$ | WINE BAR | The shop in front of this wine bar will beckon you in with top-quality comestibles like hand-sliced cured ham from Italy and Spain, more than 300 cheeses, and a dizzying array of wines—but venture farther inside to try an extensive selection of unusual dishes and interesting takes on the classics. There are tables in the cozy wine cellar downstairs, but try and bag a table at the back on the ground floor (reserve well ahead; Roscioli is very popular). **Known for:** extensive wine list; arguably Rome's best spaghetti alla carbonara; unrivaled prosciutto selection. $ *Average main: €22* ✉ *Via dei Giubbonari 21, Campo de' Fiori* ☎ *06/6875287* ⊕ *www.salumeriaroscioli.com* ⏾ *Closed 1 wk in Aug.*

☕ Coffee and Quick Bites

Bar del Fico

$ | ITALIAN | FAMILY | Everyone in Rome knows Bar del Fico, located right behind Piazza Navona, so if you want to hang out with the locals, come here for a drink or something to eat at any time of day or night. In the mornings, chess players sit at tables outside under the shade of the fig tree that gives the bar its name; after sunset, the bar is packed with people sipping cocktails. **Known for:** outside tables in a pretty square; Italian-style brunch; buzzy atmosphere. $ *Average main: €12* ✉ *Piazza del Fico 26, Piazza Navona* ☎ *06/68891373* ⊕ *www.bardelfico.com.*

★ Gelateria Del Teatro

$ | ICE CREAM | FAMILY | In a window next to the entrance of this renowned gelateria, you can see the fresh fruit being used to create the day's flavors, which highlight the best of Italy—from Amalfi lemons to Alban hazelnuts. In addition to traditional options, look for interesting combinations like raspberry and sage or white chocolate with basil. **Known for:** sublime gelato; seasonal, all natural ingredients; charming location on a cobblestone street. $ *Average main: €3* ✉ *Via dei Coronari 65/66, Piazza Navona* ☎ *06/45474880* ⊕ *www.gelateriadelteatro.it.*

★ Giolitti

$ | ICE CREAM | FAMILY | Open since 1900, Giolitti near the Pantheon is Rome's old-school gelateria par excellence. Pay in advance at the register by the door; take your receipt to the counter; and choose from dozens of flavors, including chocolate, cinnamon, and pistachio. **Known for:** excellent gelato; old-school setting; wide selection of flavors. $ *Average main: €3* ✉ *Via degli Uffici del Vicario 40, Piazza Navona* ☎ *06/6991243* ⊕ *www.giolitti.it.*

Pasticceria Boccione

$ | **BAKERY** | **FAMILY** | This tiny, old-school bakery famed for its Roman-Jewish sweet specialties is easy to spot because there is always a line snaking out the door. Service is brusque, choices are few, what's available depends on the season, and when it's sold out, it's sold out.
Known for: ricotta and cherry tarts; pizza ebraica ("Jewish pizza," a dense baked sweet rich in nuts and raisins); no frills and no seats. ⑤ *Average main: €6* ✉ *Via del Portico d'Ottavia 1, Jewish Ghetto* ☎ *06/6878637* ⊘ *Closed Sat.*

Sant'Eustachio il Caffè

$ | **CAFÉ** | **FAMILY** | Frequented by tourists and government officials from the nearby Senate alike, this café is considered by many to make Rome's best coffee. Take it at the counter Roman-style—servers are hidden behind a huge espresso machine, where they vigorously mix the sugar and coffee to protect their secret method for the perfectly prepared cup (if you want yours without sugar here, ask for it *senza zucchero*). **Known for:** gran caffè (large sugared espresso); old-school Roman coffee bar vibe; 1930s interior. ⑤ *Average main: €3* ✉ *Piazza Sant'Eustachio 82, Piazza Navona* ☎ *06/68802048* ⊕ *www.caffesanteustachio.com.*

Hotels

Albergo Santa Chiara

$$$$ | **HOTEL** | Guests choose this hotel, run by members of the same family for 200 years, not only for its prime location, but also its welcoming staff, top-notch service, and comfy beds. **Pros:** near the Pantheon and Santa Maria sopra Minerva; free Wi-Fi; lovely sitting area in front, overlooking the piazza. **Cons:** some rooms are on the small side; design is a bit basic given the higher price point; street-side rooms can be noisy. ⑤ *Rooms from: €310* ✉ *Via Santa Chiara 21, Piazza Navona* ☎ *06/6872979* ⊕ *www.albergo-santachiara.com* ⇆ *96 rooms* ❶◯❶ *Free Breakfast.*

Casa di Santa Brigida

$ | **B&B/INN** | The friendly sisters of Santa Brigida oversee simple, straightforward, and centrally located accommodations in one of Rome's loveliest convents, with a rooftop terrace overlooking Palazzo Farnese. **Pros:** insider papal audience tickets; large library and sunroof; free Wi-Fi. **Cons:** weak air-conditioning; no TVs in the rooms (though there is a common TV room); payment at structure only. ⑤ *Rooms from: €50* ✉ *Piazza Farnese 96, entrance around the corner at Via Monserrato 54, Campo de' Fiori* ☎ *06/68892596* ⊕ *www.casabrigidaroma.it* ⇆ *20 rooms* ❶◯❶ *Free Breakfast.*

D.O.M Hotel Roma

$$$$ | **HOTEL** | In an old convent on Via Giulia, one of Rome's romantic ivy-covered streets, the D.O.M (Deo Optimo Maximo) is an ultrachic luxury hotel that resembles an aristocratic *casa nobile*. **Pros:** complimentary Acqua di Parma toiletries; heated towel racks; hip decor in historic setting. **Cons:** an armed guard at the anti-terrorism headquarters opposite the hotel may be off-putting for some; delicious but expensive cocktails; standard rooms are small for a five-star hotel. ⑤ *Rooms from: €550* ✉ *Via Giulia 131, Campo de' Fiori* ☎ *06/6832144* ⊕ *www.domhotelroma.com* ⇆ *18 rooms* ❶◯❶ *Free Breakfast.*

Hotel Chapter Roma

$$$$ | **HOTEL** | The edgy, of-the-moment design at this boutique hotel juxtaposes plush midcentury Italian furnishings with street art murals and industrial touches. **Pros:** trendy design; coworking space available; lively rooftop bar in summer. **Cons:** no gym; no spa; rooms below the bar can be noisy. ⑤ *Rooms from: €380* ✉ *Via di Santa Maria de' Calderari 47, Jewish Ghetto* ☎ *06/89935351* ⊕ *www.chapter-roma.com* ⇆ *47 rooms* ❶◯❶ *Free Breakfast.*

Hotel de' Ricci

$$$$ | **HOTEL** | This intimate boutique hotel from the team behind the Pierluigi restaurant is a top spot for wine lovers. **Pros:** excellent wine cellar and cigar

lounge; great location on a quiet street; perks include complimentary aperitivo and priority reservations at Pierluigi. **Cons:** there's a charge of €50 per day to bring pets; there is a weekend crowd for the brunch; no spa or gym. $ *Rooms from: €680* ⊠ *Via della Barchetta 14, Campo de' Fiori* ☎ *06/6874775* ⊕ *www.hoteldericci. com* ⊷ *8 rooms* ¡⊙¡ *No Meals.*

Hotel Genio

$$ | HOTEL | Just off the beautiful Piazza Navona, this aging but pleasant hotel has a lovely rooftop terrace that's the perfect place to enjoy a cappuccino or a glass of wine while taking in the view. **Pros:** breakfast buffet is abundant; moderate prices for the area; nice views from terrace. **Cons:** rooms facing the street can be noisy; spotty Wi-Fi; some furnishings need to be updated. $ *Rooms from: €190* ⊠ *Via Giuseppe Zanardelli 28, Piazza Navona* ☎ *06/6833781* ⊕ *www. hotelgenioroma.it* ⊷ *60 rooms* ¡⊙¡ *Free Breakfast.*

Hotel Ponte Sisto

$$$ | HOTEL | Situated in a remodeled Renaissance palazzo with one of the prettiest patio-courtyards in Rome, this hotel is a relaxing retreat close to Campo de' Fiori and Trastevere. **Pros:** rooms with views (and some with balconies and terraces); great location between Trastevere and Campo de' Fiori; beautiful courtyard garden. **Cons:** street-side rooms can be noisy; some upgraded rooms are small and not worth the price difference; a/c is controlled centrally and requires a call to the front desk to adjust. $ *Rooms from: €260* ⊠ *Via dei Pettinari 64, Campo de' Fiori* ☎ *06/6863100* ⊕ *www.hotelponte-sisto.it* ⊷ *106 rooms* ¡⊙¡ *Free Breakfast.*

The Pantheon Iconic Rome Hotel, Autograph Collection

$$$$ | HOTEL | A member of Marriott's Autograph Collection, this boutique hotel is a sleek retreat in the center of the action. **Pros:** modern design and amenities; exceptionally professional staff; Marriott Bonvoy members can redeem

points. **Cons:** some rooms lack external views; no spa or gym; design might be considered a bit cold and corporate. $ *Rooms from: €600* ⊠ *Via di Santa Chiara 4A, Piazza Navona* ☎ *06/87807070* ⊕ *www.thepantheonhotel.com* ⊷ *79 rooms* ¡⊙¡ *No Meals.*

Nightlife

Enoteca al Parlamento Achilli

WINE BAR | The proximity of this traditional *enoteca* (wine bar) to Montecitorio, the Italian Parliament building, makes it a favorite with journalists and politicos, who often stop in for a glass of wine after work. But it's the tantalizing smell of truffles from the snack counter, where a sommelier waits to organize your tasting, that will probably lure you inside. There's also a celebrated restaurant where you can book a table and enjoy a parade of elegant Italian plates. Don't forget to check out the wine shop, too. ⊠ *Via dei Prefetti 15, Piazza Navona* ☎ *06/6873446* ⊕ *achilli.restaurant.*

Il Goccetto

WINE BAR | Specializing in the vintages produced by smaller vineyards from Sicily to Venice, this historical wine bar also has a menu of Italian delicacies (meats and cheeses) that likewise represents the entire Italian peninsula. The burrata with sun-dried tomatoes is a perennial favorite. The tiny bar is well designed but is always busy and never accepts reservations. If all the seats are taken, you might be able to sip wine on the step outside while taking in the snippets of Roman life passing by. ⊠ *Via dei Banchi Vecchi 14, Campo de' Fiori* ☎ *06/99448583* ⊕ *www.ilgoccetto.com.*

Jerry Thomas Speakeasy

COCKTAIL BARS | One of just a handful of hidden bars in Rome, this intimate bar looks like a Prohibition-era haunt and serves the kind of classic cocktails you find in New York speakeasies. It's seating room only, so reservations must be made online in advance. Upon booking, you'll receive a password via email. Since it is a private club, the bar stays open late but patrons need to pay the €5 yearly membership fee once they arrive for the first time. Serious cocktail aficionados can also purchase specialty bitters and mixology tools at the Emporium across the alley from the drinks spot. ✉ *Vicolo Cellini 30, Campo de' Fiori* ☏ *340/7332980 WhatsApp only* ⊕ *www.thejerrythomasproject.it.*

The Sofa Bar Restaurant & Roof Terrace

BARS | The romantic rooftop terrace at I Sofà has a 360-degree view of the Eternal City, so it's no surprise that it's a prime spot for a late-afternoon cocktail (weather permitting). The bar takes its name from the historic stone benches carved into the wall at the entrance to the Hotel St. George. Head downstairs in the cooler months for a wide selection of craft beers on tap inside the Hotel Indigo. ✉ *Hotel Indigo Rome—St. George, Via Giulia 62, Campo de' Fiori* ☏ *06/68661846* ⊕ *www.isofadiviagiulia.com.*

Vinoteca Novecento

WINE BAR | Salami-and-cheese tasting menus and a seemingly unlimited selection of wines, Prosecco, vini santi, and grappe are highlights of this lovely (albeit tiny) enoteca with a very old-fashioned vibe. Inside, it's standing-room only; in good weather, you can sit outside at an oak barrique on a quiet cobblestone street leading to one of Rome's prettiest small squares. ✉ *Piazza delle Coppelle 47, Piazza Navona* ☏ *06/6833078.*

🎭 Performing Arts

★ Teatro Argentina

THEATER | The 18th-century Teatro Argentina evokes glamour and sophistication with its velvet upholstery, large crystal chandeliers, and beautifully dressed theatergoers, who come to see international productions of stage and dance

performances. ✉ *Largo di Torre Argentina 52, Campo de' Fiori* ☏ *06/684000314* ⊕ *www.teatrodiroma.net.*

Shopping

BEAUTY

Antica Erboristeria Romana

HEALTH & BEAUTY | Complete with hand-labeled wooden drawers holding more than 200 varieties of herbs, flowers, and tinctures, Antica Erboristeria Romana has maintained its old-world apothecary feel (it's the oldest shop of its kind in Rome, dating back to 1752). The shop stocks an impressive array of teas and herbal infusions, more than 700 essential oils, bud derivatives, and powdered extracts. ✉ *Via Torre Argentina 15, Piazza Navona* ☏ *06/6879493* ⊕ *www.anticaerboristeria-romana.it.*

CERAMICS AND DECORATIVE ARTS

★ INOR dal 1952

HOUSEWARES | For more than 50 years, INOR dal 1952 has served as a trusted friend for Romans in desperate need of an exclusive wedding gift, delicate stemware, or oh-so-perfect china place settings for a fancy Sunday lunch. Entrance is via a secluded 15th-century courtyard and up a flight of stairs. The store specializes in work handcrafted by the silversmiths of Pampaloni and Bastianelli in Florence. ✉ *Via della Stelletta 23, Piazza Navona* ☏ *06/6878579* ⊕ *www.inor.it.*

CLOTHING

★ L'Archivio di Monserrato

CLOTHING | Tailored jackets with exotic trims, dresses in eclectic prints and bold colors, and smart linen suits are some of the offerings at this airy, spacious boutique curated by Soledad Twombly (daughter-in-law of painter Cy Twombly). In addition to her original designs, look for a sophisticated mix of antique Turkish and Indian textiles, jewelry, shoes, and small housewares picked up on her travels. ⊠ *Via di Monserrato 150, Campo de' Fiori* ☎ *06/45654157* ⊕ *www.soledadtwombly.com.*

Le Tartarughe

CLOTHING | A familiar face at the city's fashion shows, designer Susanna Liso, a Rome native, mixes raw silks or cashmere and fine merino wool to create captivating, enveloping garments that sometimes feature seductive or playful elements. Both her haute-couture and ready-to-wear lines are much loved by Rome's elite. ⊠ *Via Piè di Marmo 17, Piazza Navona* ☎ *06/6792240* ⊕ *www.letartarughe.eu.*

Morgana

CLOTHING | When strolling down Via del Governo Vecchio, a street popular for funky and edgy clothing boutiques, you can't help but stop and stare at this shop's windows, where the family-run business displays some of its best hippie-chick and bridal-chic gowns, as well as Japanese Noh theater inspired coats. The highly original and highly coveted clothes are carefully crafted and hand-painted with one-of-a-kind designs. ⊠ *Via del Governo Vecchio 27, Piazza Navona* ☎ *334/7960281.*

Vestiti Usati Cinzia

CLOTHING | Vintage-clothes hunters, costume designers, and stylists alike love browsing through the racks at this fun, inviting shop, which is stocked wall-to-wall with funky 1960s and '70s apparel. There's definitely no shortage of goofy sunglasses, flower-power bell-bottoms, embroidered hippie tops, psychedelic boots, and other trippy merchandise from the days of peace and love. ⊠ *Via del Governo Vecchio 45, Piazza Navona* ☎ *06/6832945* ⊕ *cinziavestitiusati.wordpress.com.*

FOOD AND WINE

Moriondo e Gariglio

CANDY | **FAMILY** | Dating from 1850 and adhering strictly to family recipes passed on from generation to generation, this shop makes some of Rome's finest chocolate delicacies and other sweet treats. The selection of more than 80 confections includes everything from dark-chocolate truffles to marrons glacés. The chocolates shaped like every letter of the alphabet are perennial favorites, though. ⊠ *Via Piè di Marmo 21, Piazza Navona* ☎ *06/6990856* ⊕ *moriondoegariglio.com.*

JEWELRY

Massimo Maria Melis

JEWELRY & WATCHES | Drawing heavily on ancient Roman and Etruscan designs, the jewelry from former costume designer Massimo Maria Melis will carry you back in time. Working with 21-carat gold, he often incorporates antique coins in many of his exquisite bracelets and necklaces. Some of his pieces are done with an ancient technique, much loved by the Etruscans, in which tiny gold droplets are fused together to create intricately patterned designs. ⊠ *Via dell'Orso 57, Piazza Navona* ☎ *06/6869188* ⊕ *www.massimomariamelis.com.*

Quattrocolo

JEWELRY & WATCHES | Dating from 1938, this shop showcases exquisite, antique, micro-mosaic jewelry painstakingly crafted in the style perfected by the masters at the Vatican mosaic studio. The small works were beloved by cosmopolitan clientele of the Grand Tour age and offer modern-day shoppers a taste of yesteryear's grandeur. You'll also find 18th- and 19th-century cameos and beautiful engraved stones, one-of-a-kind rings from the 1960s and '70s, as well as contemporary jewelry. ⊠ *Via della Scrofa 48, Piazza Navona* ☎ *06/68801367* ⊕ *www.quattrocolo.com.*

SHOES AND ACCESSORIES

★ Chez Dede

SPECIALTY STORE | Husband-and-wife duo Andrea Ferolla and Daria Reina (he's a fashion illustrator, she's a photographer) curate a selection of clothes, bags, vintage jewelry, books, home decor, and anything else you might need in this cult favorite lifestyle-concept shop. Their signature fabric bags are designed to go from the plane straight to the beach club, and they regularly release collectible items featuring Ferolla's whimsical illustrations. ✉ *Via di Monserrato 35, Campo de' Fiori* ☎ *06/83772934* ⊕ *www.chezdede.com.*

Ibiz

LEATHER GOODS | In business since 1972, this family team creates colorful, stylish leather handbags, belts, keychains, and sandals near Piazza Campo de' Fiori. Choose from the premade collection, or order something in the color of your choice; their workshop is visible in the boutique. ✉ *Via dei Chiavari 39, Campo de' Fiori* ☎ *06/68307297* ⊕ *ibizroma.it.*

★ Maison Halaby

HANDBAGS | Lebanese designer and artist Gilbert Halaby was featured in fashion magazines like *Vogue* and created jewelry for Lady Gaga before giving up the rat race and opening his own shop, where the ethos is all about slow fashion. His boldly colored leather handbags incorporate suede, python, fringe, raffia, or jeweled handles, and his silk scarves are printed with his original watercolors, some of which are also on sale. The small, homey boutique—with a velvet sofa and lots of books, plants, and art by Halaby himself—is mainly open by appointment, but if you pass by, ring the bell, and if Gilbert is there, he might just invite you in for coffee or Campari. ✉ *Via di Monserrato 21, Campo de' Fiori* ☎ *06/96521585* ⊕ *www.facebook.com/HALABY.OFFICIAL.*

STATIONERY

★ Cartoleria Pantheon dal 1910

STATIONERY | Instead of sending a postcard home, why not send a letter written on sumptuous, handmade, Amalfi paper purchased from this shop? It also sells hand-bound leather journals in an extraordinary array of colors and sizes. There are two locations in the neighborhood.

✉ *Via della Maddalena 41, Piazza Navona* ☎ *06/6795633* ⊕ *www.cartoleriapantheon.it.*

TOYS

Al Sogno

TOYS | FAMILY | This Navona jewel, around since 1945, is crammed top to bottom with artistic, well-crafted puppets, dolls, masks, stuffed animals, and other toys for children of all ages that encourage imaginative (and low-tech) play and learning. ✉ *Piazza Navona 53, corner of Via Agonale, Piazza Navona* ☎ *06/6864198* ⊕ *www.alsogno.com.*

Piazza di Spagna

In spirit (and in fact) this section of the city is its most grandiose. The overblown Vittoriano monument, the labyrinthine treasure-chest palaces of Rome's surviving aristocracy, even the diamond-draped denizens of Via Condotti's shops—all embody the exuberant ego of a city at the center of its own universe. Here's where you'll see ladies in furs gobbling pastries at café tables and walk through a thousand snapshots as you climb the famous Spanish Steps, admired by generations from Byron to Versace. Cultural treasures abound around here: gilded 17th-century churches, glittering palazzi, and the greatest example of portraiture in Rome, Velázquez's incomparable *Innocent X* at the Galleria Doria Pamphilj. Have your camera ready—along with a coin or two—for that most beloved of Rome's landmarks, the Trevi Fountain.

GETTING HERE AND AROUND

Piazza di Spagna is a short walk from Piazza del Popolo, the Pantheon, and the Trevi Fountain. One of Rome's handiest subway stations, Spagna, is tucked just left of the steps. Buses No. 117 (from the Colosseum) and No. 119 (from Piazza del Popolo) hum through the area; the latter tootles up Via del Babuino, famed for its shopping.

Sights

⭐ Ara Pacis Augustae
(Altar of Augustan Peace)
MONUMENT | This pristine monument sits inside one of Rome's contemporary architectural landmarks: a gleaming, rectangular, glass-and-travertine structure designed by American architect Richard Meier. It overlooks the Tiber on one side and the ruins of the marble-clad Mausoleo di Augusto (Mausoleum of Augustus) on the other and is a serene, luminous oasis right in the center of Rome.

This altar itself dates from 13 BC and was commissioned to celebrate the Pax Romana, the era of peace ushered in by Augustus's military victories. When viewing it, keep in mind that the spectacular reliefs would have been painted in vibrant colors, now long gone. The reliefs on the short sides portray myths associated with Rome's founding and glory; those on the long sides display a procession of the imperial family. Although half of his body is missing, Augustus is identifiable as the first full figure at the procession's head on the south-side frieze; academics still argue over exact identifications of most of the figures. Be sure to check out the small downstairs museum, which hosts rotating exhibits on Italian culture, with themes ranging from design to film. ✉ *Lungotevere in Augusta, at the corner of Via Tomacelli, Piazza di Spagna* ☎ *06/0608* ⊕ *www.arapacis.it* 🎟 *€12, €13 when there is an exhibition* ♿ *Reservations essential for groups of 11 to 25 persons* Ⓜ *Flaminio.*

⭐ Galleria d'Arte Moderna
ART MUSEUM | Located in a former monastery, this small museum displays an impressive capsule collection of modern art, with an emphasis on Italian artists. The permanent collection is too large to be displayed at once, so exhibits rotate, displaying paintings, drawings, prints, and sculptures by the most famous names of the 19th and 20th centuries, including Giorgio de Chirico, Mario Mafai, Scipione, Gino Severini, and Giorgio Morandi. ✉ *Via Francesco Crispi 24, Piazza di Spagna* ☎ *06/0608* ⊕ *www. galleriaartemodernaroma.it* 🎟 *€9; €11.50 if there's a special exhibit* ⊙ *Closed Mon.* Ⓜ *Spagna.*

Keats-Shelley Memorial House
HISTORIC HOME | Sent to Rome in a last-ditch attempt to treat his consumptive condition, English Romantic poet John Keats—celebrated for such poems as "Ode to a Nightingale" and "Endymion"—lived in this house at the foot of the Spanish Steps. At the time, this was the heart of Rome's colorful bohemian quarter, an area favored by English expats. He took his last breath here on February 23, 1821, and is now buried in the Non-Catholic Cemetery in Testaccio. On a visit to his final home, you can see his death mask, though local authorities had all his furnishings burned after his death as a sanitary measure. You'll also find a quaint collection of memorabilia of other English literary figures of the period—Lord Byron, Percy Bysshe Shelley, Joseph Severn, and Leigh Hun—and an exhaustive library of works on the Romantics. ✉ *Piazza di Spagna 26, Piazza di Spagna* ☎ *06/6784235* ⊕ *ksh.roma.it* 🎟 *€6* ⊙ *Closed Sun.* Ⓜ *Spagna.*

Mausoleo di Augusto
MONUMENT | One of Ancient Rome's largest circular tombs, the Mausoleum of Augustus celebrates the glory of Emperor Augustus, Julius Caesar's successor. Though today's mausoleum is brick and stone, the structure was originally covered in marble and travertine, with evergreen trees planted on top, a colossal statue of the emperor at the summit, and a pair of bronze pillars inscribed with his achievements at the entrance. The mausoleum's innermost sepulchral chamber housed the ashes of several members of the Augustan dynasty, but it was subsequently raided and the urns were never found.

Between the 13th and 20th centuries, the mausoleum was a garden, an amphitheater that hosted jousting tournaments, and a concert hall, which Mussolini tore down in 1936 in a bid to restore the monument to its imperial glory. His plans were interrupted by World War II, after which the mausoleum was all but abandoned until a recent restoration reopened it to the public.

Reservations are booked online; however, it is currently closed and slated to reopen with the 2025 Jubilee Year. Check the website for up-to-date details. ⊠ *Piazza Augusto Imperatore, Piazza di Spagna* ☎ *06/0608* ⊕ *www.mausoleodiaugusto.it* ⊠ *€5* ⊘ *Closed Mon.* Ⓜ *Spagna.*

★ **Monumento a Vittorio Emanuele II, or Altare della Patria** (*Victor Emmanuel II Monument, or Altar of the Nation*)
MONUMENT | The huge white mass known as the "Vittoriano" is an inescapable landmark that has been likened to a giant wedding cake or an immense typewriter. Present-day Romans joke that you can only avoid looking at it if you are standing on it. Built to honor the unification of Italy and the nation's first king, Victor Emmanuel II, it also shelters the eternal flame at the tomb of Italy's Unknown Soldier, killed during World War I. Alas, to create this elaborate marble behemoth and the vast surrounding piazza, its architects blithely destroyed many ancient and medieval buildings and altered the slope of the Campidoglio (Capitoline Hill), which abuts it. The truly enticing feature of the Vittoriano is its rooftop terrace, which offers some of the best panoramic views of Rome. The only way up is by elevator (the entrance is located several flights of stairs up on the right as you face the monument). ⊠ *Entrances on Piazza Venezia, Piazza del Campidoglio, and Via di San Pietro in Carcere, Trevi* ☎ *06/0608* ⊕ *vive.cultura. gov.it* ⊠ *Main building free; €17 for the terrace* Ⓜ *Colosseo.*

★ **Palazzo Colonna**
CASTLE/PALACE | Rome's grandest private palace is a fusion of 17th- and 18th-century buildings that have been occupied by the Colonna family for more than 20 generations. The immense residence faces Piazza dei Santi Apostoli on one side and the Quirinale (Quirinal Hill) on the other—with a little bridge over Via della Pilotta linking to gardens on the hill—and contains an art gallery that's open to the public on Saturday morning or by guided tour on Friday morning.

The gallery is itself a setting of aristocratic grandeur; you might recognize the Sala Grande as the site where Audrey Hepburn meets the press in *Roman Holiday.* An ancient red marble *colonna* (column), which is the family's emblem, looms at one end, but the most spectacular feature is the ceiling fresco of the Battle of Lepanto painted by Giovanni Coli and Filippo Gherardi beginning in 1675. Adding to the opulence are works by Poussin, Tintoretto, and Veronese, as well as portraits of illustrious members of the family, such as Vittoria Colonna, Michelangelo's muse and longtime friend.

It's worth paying an extra fee to take the guided, English-language gallery tour, which will help you navigate through the array of madonnas, saints, goddesses, popes, and cardinals to see Annibale Carracci's lonely *Beaneater,* spoon at the ready and front teeth missing. The gallery also has a café with a pleasant terrace. ⊠ *Via della Pilotta, 17, Trevi* ☎ *06/6784350* ⊕ *www.galleriacolonna.it* ⊠ *€15 for gallery and gardens, €25 to also visit the Princess Isabelle Apartment, €30 for a guided tour on Friday* ⊘ *Closed Sun.–Thurs.* ⚲ *Friday for guided tour only* Ⓜ *Barberini.*

★ **Palazzo Doria Pamphilj**
CASTLE/PALACE | Like the Palazzo Colonna and the Galleria Borghese, this dazzling 15th-century family palace provides a fantastic glimpse of aristocratic Rome. The understated beauty of the graceful

Sights ▾

1 Ara Pacis Augustae **B3**
2 Galleria d'Arte Moderna **G4**
3 Keats-Shelley Memorial House... **E3**
4 Mausoleo di Augusto **C3**
5 Monumento a
  Vittorio Emanuele II, or
  Altare della Patria **E9**
6 Palazzo Colonna **F7**
7 Palazzo Doria Pamphilj............ **E8**
8 Sant'Ignazio **D7**
9 The Spanish Steps................. **E3**
10 Trevi Fountain **F6**

Restaurants ▾

1 Baccano............................ **E6**
2 Il Marchese **B4**
3 Matricianella....................... **C4**
4 Moma **I3**
5 Ristorante Nino **E3**
6 Settimo............................ **G2**

Coffee and Quick Bites ▾

1 Antico Caffè Greco **E3**
2 Il Gelato di San Crispino **F5**

Hotels ▾

1 Aleph Rome Hotel **H3**
2 Babuino 181 .... **C1**
3 Baglioni Hotel Regina **H2**
4 The Hassler........................ **F3**
5 Hotel de la Ville **F3**
6 Hotel Eden......................... **G2**
7 Hotel Vilòn......................... **C4**
8 Maalot Roma **E6**
9 Margutta 19 .... **D2**
10 Scalinata di Spagna............... **F3**

KEY

1 Sights
1 Restaurants
1 Quick Bites
1 Hotels

facade barely hints at the interior's opulent halls and gilded galleries, which are filled with Old Master works. The 550 paintings here include three by Caravaggio: *St. John the Baptist, Mary Magdalene,* and the breathtaking *Rest on the Flight to Egypt.* Off the eye-popping Galleria degli Specchi (Gallery of Mirrors)—a smaller version of the one at Versailles—are the famous Velázquez *Pope Innocent X,* considered by some historians to be the greatest portrait ever painted, and the Bernini bust of the same Pamphilj pope. ⊠ *Via del Corso, 305, Trevi* ☎ *06/6797323* ⊕ *www.doriapamphilj.it* ✉ *€16* ⊘ *Closed the 3rd Wed. of the month* ⚓ *Reservations required* Ⓜ *Barberini.*

★ Sant'Ignazio

CHURCH | Rome's second Jesuit church, this 17th-century landmark set on a Rococo piazza harbors some of the city's most magnificent trompe l'oeils. To get the full effect of the illusionistic ceiling by priest-artist Andrea Pozzo, stand on the small yellow disk set into the floor of the nave. The heavenly vision that seems to extend upward almost indefinitely represents the *Allegory of the Missionary Work of the Jesuits.* It's part of Pozzo's cycle of works in this church exalting the early history of the Jesuit order, whose founder was the reformer Ignatius of Loyola. The saint soars heavenward, supported by a cast of thousands, creating a jaw-dropping effect that was fully intended to rival that of the glorious ceiling by Baciccia in the nearby mother church of Il Gesù. Be sure to have coins handy for the machine that switches on the lights so you can marvel at the false dome, which is actually a flat canvas—a trompe l'oeil trick Pozzo used when the architectural budget drained dry.

Scattered around the nave are several awe-inspiring altars; their soaring columns, gold-on-gold decoration, and gilded statues are pure splendor. Splendid, too, are the occasional sacred music concerts performed by choirs from all over the world. Look for posters by the main doors, or check the website for more information. ⊠ *Piazza S. Ignazio, Trevi* ✛ *Via del Caravita 8A* ☎ *06/6794406* ⊕ *santignazio.gesuiti.it.*

★ The Spanish Steps

OTHER ATTRACTION | FAMILY | The iconic Spanish Steps (often called simply *la scalinata,* or "the staircase," by Italians) and the Piazza di Spagna from which they ascend both get their names from the Spanish Embassy to the Vatican on the piazza—even though the staircase was built with French funds in 1723. In honor of a diplomatic visit by the King of Spain, the hillside was transformed by architect Francesco de Sanctis to link the church of Trinità dei Monti at the top with the Via Condotti below. In an allusion to the church, the staircase is divided by three landings (beautifully lined with potted azaleas from mid-April to mid-May). Bookending the bottom of the steps are beloved holdovers from the 18th century, when the area was known as the "English Ghetto": the 18th-century Keats-Shelley House and Babington's Tea Rooms, both beautifully redolent of the Grand Tour era. ⊠ *Piazza di Spagna, Piazza di Spagna* Ⓜ *Spagna.*

★ Trevi Fountain

FOUNTAIN | FAMILY | Alive with rushing waters commanded by an imperious sculpture of Oceanus, the Fontana di Trevi has been all about theatrical effects from the start; it is an aquatic marvel in a city filled with them. The fountain's unique drama is largely due to its location: its vast basin is squeezed into the tight confluence of three little streets (the *tre vie,* which may give the fountain its name), with cascades emerging as if from the wall of Palazzo Poli.

Everyone knows the famous legend that if you throw a coin into the Trevi Fountain you will ensure a return trip to the Eternal City, but not everyone knows how to do it the right way. You must toss a coin with your right hand over your left shoulder, with your back to the fountain. One coin means you'll return to Rome; two, you'll return *and* fall in love; three, you'll return, find love, and marry. The fountain grosses some €600,000 a year, with every cent going to the Italian Red Cross. ⊠ *Piazza di Trevi, Trevi* Ⓜ *Barberini.*

🍴 Restaurants

Baccano
$$$ | BRASSERIE | There are plenty of options for good food at reasonable prices around the Trevi Fountain, but this Paris-inspired brasserie—open for lunch, dinner, and everything in between—is a great bet. Although it emphasizes seafood, the extensive menu has something for everyone, from salads to pasta and entrées. **Known for:** oyster bar; excellent carbonara; classic international cocktails. Ⓢ *Average main: €28* ⊠ *Via delle Muratte, 23, Trevi* ☎ *06/69941166* ⊕ *www.baccanoroma.com* Ⓜ *Barberini.*

★ Il Marchese
$$ | ITALIAN | This rustic-meets-glamorous bistro attracts locals for its flawless execution of Roman classics (many served photogenically in metal cooking pans) as well as original dishes. Its bar is known among amaro connoisseurs for having the largest selection in Rome, and the bitter liquors are the stars of the expertly crafted cocktail menu. **Known for:** beautiful design; well-executed classics; extensive selection of amaros and great cocktails. Ⓢ *Average main: €18* ⊠ *Via di Ripetta 162, Piazza di Spagna* ☎ *06/90218872* ⊕ *www.ilmarcheseroma. it* Ⓜ *Spagna.*

Matricianella
$$$ | ITALIAN | Family-owned neighborhood staple with its quintessentially Roman wooden tables and checkered tablecloths, Matricianella charms with hearty Roman dishes and a biblical wine list. Try any of the Roman pasta trifecta—amatriciana, cacio e pepe, and

carbonara—or other classics like crispy fried artichokes or saltimbocca alla romana (thin veal slices with prosciutto and sage). **Known for:** rustic charm; classic Roman dishes; extensive wine list. Ⓢ *Average main: €30* ⊠ *Via del Leone, 4, Piazza di Spagna* ☎ *06/6832100* ⊕ *www. matricianella.it* ⊗ *Closed Sun.* Ⓜ *Spagna.*

★ Moma
$$$ | MODERN ITALIAN | In front of the American embassy and a favorite of the design *trendoisie*, Michelin-starred Moma attracts well-heeled businessmen at lunch but turns into a more intimate affair for dinner. The kitchen turns out hits as it creates alta cucina (haute cuisine) made using Italian ingredients sourced from small producers. **Known for:** pasta with a twist; creative presentation; affordable fine dining. Ⓢ *Average main: €25* ⊠ *Via San Basilio 42, Piazza di Spagna* ☎ *06/42011798* ⊕ *www.ristorantemoma.it* ⊗ *Closed Sun. No lunch Sat.* Ⓜ *Barberini.*

Ristorante Nino
$$$ | ITALIAN | A favorite among international journalists and the rich and famous since the 1930s, this rustic, Tuscan-styled restaurant does not seem to have changed at all over the decades. Its menu is meat-focused with many Tuscan classics: try the *bistecca di costa all'arrabbiata*, a flavorful rib-eye steak cooked with chili and garlic. **Known for:** warm crostini spread with pâté; upscale old-school Italian vibe; ribollita (Tuscan bean soup). Ⓢ *Average main: €26* ⊠ *Via Borgognona 11, Piazza di Spagna* ☎ *06/6786752* ⊕ *ristorantenino.it* ⊗ *Closed Sun. and Aug.* Ⓜ *Spagna.*

Settimo
$$$ | ITALIAN | Crowning the Sofitel Rome Villa Borghese hotel, this chic restaurant serves fancy takes on Rome's *cucina povera* (peasant cooking) in a chic space with graphic punches of color. The terrace offers fantastic views that stretch from Villa Borghese to the dome of St. Peter's, but the interior dining room, with

its floor-to-ceiling windows and terrazzo-inspired floors, is lovely, too. **Known for:** amped-up version of classic Roman recipes; colorful, modern design; terrace with great views. ⑤ *Average main: €26* ✉ *Sofitel Rome Villa Borghese, Via Lombardia 47, Piazza di Spagna* ☎ *06/478021* ⊕ *www.settimoristorante.it* Ⓜ *Barberini.*

Coffee and Quick Bites

Antico Caffè Greco

$ | **CAFÉ** | The red-velvet chairs and marble tables of one of Rome's oldest cafés have seen the likes of Byron, Shelley, Keats, Goethe, and Casanova. Locals love basking in the more than 260 years of history held within its dark-wood walls lined with antique artwork; tourists appreciate its location amid the shopping madness of upscale Via Condotti. **Known for:** lavish historic design; perfect espresso; crystal goblets and high prices to match. ⑤ *Average main: €12* ✉ *Via dei Condotti 86, Piazza di Spagna* ☎ *06/6791700* ⊕ *anticocaffegreco.eu* Ⓜ *Spagna.*

Il Gelato di San Crispino

$ | **ICE CREAM** | **FAMILY** | Many people say this place—which is around the corner from the Trevi Fountain and had a cameo in the movie *Eat, Pray, Love*—serves the best gelato in Rome. Creative flavors like black fig, chocolate rum, Armagnac, and ginger-cinnamon all incorporate top-notch ingredients, and the shop is known for keeping its gelato hidden under metal covers to better preserve the quality. **Known for:** seasonal fruit flavors; offering only cups and no cones; wine-based gelato. ⑤ *Average main: €4* ✉ *Via della Panetteria, 42, Trevi* ☎ *06/69489518* ⊕ *www.ilgelatodisancrispino.it* Ⓜ *Barberini.*

Hotels

Aleph Rome Hotel, Curio Collection by Hilton

$$$$ | **HOTEL** | Fashionable couples tend to favor the Aleph, a former bank–turned–luxury hotel, where the motto seems to be "more marble, everywhere." The abundant facilities include two pools (one in the spa and one on the roof), a cigar lounge, a cocktail bar, and two restaurants (one on the ground floor and one on the rooftop). **Pros:** free access to the spa for hotel guests; award-winning design; terrace with small pool. **Cons:** rooms are petite for the price; rooftop views don't showcase Rome's most flattering side; buffet breakfast not included. ⑤ *Rooms from: €448* ✉ *Via San Basilio 15, Piazza di Spagna* ☎ *06/4229001* ⊕ *alephrome.com* ⇗ *80 rooms and suites* ⧂ *No Meals* Ⓜ *Barberini.*

Babuino 181

$$$ | **HOTEL** | On chic Via del Babuino, known for its high-end boutiques, jewelry stores, and antiques shops, this discreet and stylish hotel is an ideal pied-à-terre, with spacious rooms spread over two historic buildings. **Pros:** spacious suites; luxury Frette linens; iPhone docks and other handy in-room amenities. **Cons:** rooms can be a bit noisy; breakfast is nothing special; annex rooms feel removed from service staff. ⑤ *Rooms from: €261* ✉ *Via del Babuino 181, Piazza di Spagna* ☎ *06/32295295* ⊕ *www. romeluxurysuites.com/it/babuino-181* ⇗ *25 rooms* ⧂ *Free Breakfast* Ⓜ *Flaminio, Spagna.*

Baglioni Hotel Regina

$$$$ | **HOTEL** | The former home of Queen Margherita of Savoy, the Baglioni Hotel Regina, which enjoys a prime spot on the Via Veneto, is still a favorite among today's jet-setters. **Pros:** chic decor; luxury on-site spa; excellent on-site restaurant and bar. **Cons:** internal rooms overlook air-conditioning ducts; extra charge for breakfast à la carte; location isn't as prestigious as it once was. ⑤ *Rooms from: €650* ✉ *Via Veneto 72, Piazza di Spagna* ☎ *06/421111* ⊕ *www. baglionihotels.com/rome* ⇗ *117 rooms* ⧂ *No Meals* Ⓜ *Barberini.*

★ The Hassler

$$$$ | HOTEL | When it comes to million-dollar views, the best place to stay in the whole city is the Hassler, so it's no surprise many of the rich and famous (Tom Cruise, Jennifer Lopez, and the Beckhams among them) are willing to pay top dollar for a room at this exclusive hotel atop the Spanish Steps. **Pros:** prime location and panoramic views; exceptional service; sauna access included with each reservation. **Cons:** VIP rates (10% VAT not included); gym and wellness area is tiny; rooms are updated on a rolling basis, leaving some feeling dated. ⑤ *Rooms from: €1400* ✉ *Piazza Trinità dei Monti 6, Piazza di Spagna* ☎ *06/699340, 800/223–6800 in U.S.* ⊕ *www.hotelhasslerroma.com* ⌁ *87 rooms and suites* ¶⊙ *Free Breakfast* Ⓜ *Spagna.*

★ Hotel de la Ville

$$$$ | HOTEL | Occupying a prime position atop the Spanish Steps, this glamorous sister property of the beloved Hotel de Russie near the Piazza del Popolo has as a Grand Tour–inspired design featuring antiques, custom wallpaper stamped with Piranesi prints, and plenty of silk. **Pros:** must-visit rooftop bar with panoramic views; prestigious location atop the Spanish Steps; pampering spa uses signature made-in-Italy organic products. **Cons:** some rooms are a bit small for the price; service can be a bit slow at the bar; no pets allowed. ⑤ *Rooms from: €1400* ✉ *Via Sistina 69, Piazza di Spagna* ☎ *06/977931* ⊕ *www.roccofortehotels.com* ⌁ *104 rooms and suites* ¶⊙ *Free Breakfast* Ⓜ *Spagna.*

★ Hotel Eden

$$$$ | HOTEL | At what was once a favorite haunt of Ingrid Bergman, Ginger Rogers, and Fellini, dashing elegance, exquisite decor, and stunning vistas of Rome combine with true Italian hospitality. **Pros:** gorgeous rooftop terrace restaurant; tranquil spa facilities; 24-hour room service. **Cons:** breakfast not included (and very expensive, at €50); gym is standard but small; some rooms overlook an unremarkable courtyard. ⑤ *Rooms from: €1260* ✉ *Via Ludovisi 49, Piazza di Spagna* ☎ *06/478121* ⊕ *www.dorchestercollection.com/en/rome/hotel-eden* ⌁ *98 rooms and suites* ¶⊙ *No Meals* Ⓜ *Spagna.*

★ Hotel Vilòn

$$$$ | HOTEL | Set in a 16th-century mansion annexed to Palazzo Borghese and tucked behind a discreet entrance, this intimate hotel might be Rome's best-kept secret. **Pros:** gorgeous design; attentive staff; fantastic location. **Cons:** not much communal space; no spa or gym; some rooms are a bit small. ⑤ *Rooms from: €780* ✉ *Via dell'Arancio 69, Piazza di Spagna* ☎ *06/878187* ⊕ *www.hotelvilon.com* ⌁ *18 rooms and suites* ¶⊙ *Free Breakfast* Ⓜ *Spagna.*

Maalot Roma

$$$$ | HOTEL | This boutique property inside the former residence of opera composer Gaetano Donizetto aims to be a restaurant with rooms above rather than a hotel with a restaurant below. **Pros:** chic design with original art; great food at Don Pasquale restaurant; central location just steps from the Trevi Fountain. **Cons:** some rooms look directly onto the McDonald's across the street; no spa; service can be a bit slow. ⑤ *Rooms from: €750* ✉ *Via delle Murate, 78, Trevi* ☎ *06/878087* ⊕ *www.hotelmaalot.com* ⌁ *30 rooms and suites* ¶⊙ *Free Breakfast* Ⓜ *Barberini.*

Scalinata di Spagna

$$$ | B&B/INN | Perched atop the Spanish Steps, this charming boutique hotel is so popular that it's often booked far in advance. **Pros:** friendly and helpful concierge; fresh fruit in guest rooms; free Wi-Fi throughout. **Cons:** hike up the hill to the hotel; small rooms; no porter and no elevator. ⑤ *Rooms from: €257* ✉ *Piazza Trinità dei Monti 17, Piazza di Spagna* ☎ *06/45686150* ⊕ *www.hotelscalinata.com* ⌁ *30 rooms* ¶⊙ *Free Breakfast* Ⓜ *Spagna.*

Nightlife

Antica Enoteca

WINE BAR | Piazza di Spagna's historic wine bar literally corners the market on prime people-watching. Cozy up to the counter to sip a drink under the charming frescoes, or snag a coveted outdoor table. In addition to a vast selection of wine, Antica Enoteca has delectable antipasti, perfect for a snack or a light lunch, as well as a full menu of pastas and pizzas. ⊠ *Via della Croce 76/b, Piazza di Spagna* ☎ *06/6790896* ⊕ *www.anticaenoteca.com* Ⓜ *Spagna.*

Il Palazzetto Wine Bar

WINE BAR | This rooftop wine bar and restaurant wins the prize for the perfect aperitivo spot, with excellent drinks and appetizers, as well as a breathtaking view of the comings and goings on the Spanish Steps. Reach it by climbing the monumental staircase that it overlooks, or getting a lift from the elevator inside the Spagna Metro station. ⊠ *Il Palazzetto, Vicolo del Bottino 8, Piazza di Spagna* ✛ *The main entrance is a small gate at the top of the Spanish Steps* ☎ *342/1507215* ⊕ *www.hotelhasslerroma.com/en/il-palazzetto* Ⓜ *Spagna.*

Shopping

ACCESSORIES

Furla

HANDBAGS | Furla very well might be the best deal in Italian leather, selling high-quality purses and wallets at comparatively affordable prices. Be prepared to fight your way through crowds of passionate handbag lovers, all anxious to possess one of the delectable bags, wallets, or whimsical key chains in trendy sherbet hues or timeless bold color combos. ⊠ *Piazza di Spagna 22, Piazza di Spagna* ☎ *06/6797159* ⊕ *www.furla.com* Ⓜ *Spagna.*

CLOTHING

★ Brioni

CLOTHING | Founded in 1945, Brioni is hailed for its impeccably crafted menswear. Italy's best tailors create bespoke suits to exacting standards, measured to the millimeter and completely personalized from a selection of more than 5,000 spectacular fabrics. A single made-to-measure wool suit will take a minimum of 32 hours to make. The brand's prêt-à-porter line is also praised for peerless cutting and stitching. Past and present clients include Clark Gable, Barack Obama, and, of course, James Bond. ⊠ *Via Condotti 21A, Piazza di Spagna* ☎ *06/6783428* ⊕ *www.brioni.com* Ⓜ *Spagna.*

Dolce & Gabbana

CLOTHING | Dolce and Gabbana met in 1980 when both were assistants at a Milan fashion atelier, and they opened their first store in 1982. With a modern aesthetic that screams sex appeal, the brand has always thrived on excess and is known for its bold, creative designs. The Rome store has a glass ceiling above a sparkling chandelier to allow natural light to spill in, illuminating the marble floors, antique brass accents, and the latest lines for men, women, and children. ⊠ *Via Condotti 49–51, Piazza di Spagna* ☎ *06/69924999* ⊕ *www.dolcegabbana.com* Ⓜ *Spagna.*

Elena Mirò

CLOTHING | Elena Mirò is a high-end brand that offers curvy women sophisticated, beautifully feminine clothes in sizes 46 (U.S. size 12, U.K. size 14) and up. There are several locations in Rome, including one on Via Nazionale. ⊠ *Via Frattina 11, Piazza di Spagna* ☎ *06/6784367* ⊕ *www.elenamiro.com* Ⓜ *Spagna.*

Fendi

CLOTHING | Fendi has been a fixture of the Roman fashion landscape since "Mamma" Fendi first opened shop with her husband in 1925. With an eye for genius, she hired Karl Lagerfeld, whose furs and runway antics made him one of the most influential designers of the 20th century and brought international acclaim to Fendi. More recently, the atelier has gotten new life in the Italian press for its "Fendi for Fountains" campaign, which included funding the restoration of Rome's Trevi Fountain, and for moving its global headquarters to a striking Mussolini-era building known as the "square Colosseum" in the city's EUR neighborhood. The flagship store in Rome is on the ground floor of Palazzo Fendi. Upper floors contain the brand's seven private suites (the first ever Fendi hotel), and the rooftop is home to Zuma, a modern Japanese restaurant with an oh-so-cool bar that has sweeping views across the city. ⊠ *Largo Carlo Goldoni 420, Piazza di Spagna* ☎ *06/33450896* ⊕ *www.fendi. com* Ⓜ *Spagna.*

Giorgio Armani

CLOTHING | One of the most influential designers of Italian haute couture, Giorgio Armani is world-famous for dazzling evening gowns and iconic suits in clean, fluid silhouettes. The flagship store is the best place to find pieces that range from exotic runway-worthy masterpieces to more wearable collections emphasizing casual Italian elegance with just the right touch of whimsy and sexiness. ⊠ *Via dei Condotti 76, Piazza di Spagna* ☎ *06/6991460* ⊕ *www.armani.com* Ⓜ *Spagna.*

Gucci

CLOTHING | Guccio Gucci opened his first leather shop selling luggage in Florence in 1921, and, more than 100 years later, the success of the double-G trademark is unquestionable. Tom Ford joined as creative director in 1994, helping the fashion house move into a new era that refreshed the label's aesthetic with reinterpretations of old-school favorites like horsebit loafers and Jackie Kennedy scarves. Now helmed by Sabato de Sarno, Gucci remains a fashion must for virtually every A-list celebrity.

⊠ *Via Condotti 8, Piazza di Spagna* ☎ *06/6790405* ⊕ *www.gucci.com* Ⓜ *Spagna.*

★ Patrizia Pepe

CLOTHING | Patrizia Pepe first emerged on the scene in Florence in 1993 with an aesthetic that's both minimalist and bold. Jackets with oversize lapels, playful pleats, mesmerizing mesh, and the occasional feathered poof set the designs apart. Spending time in the shop of this relative newcomer to the Italian fashion scene gives you the opportunity to pick up an item or two before the brand becomes the next fast-tracked craze. ⊠ *Via Frattina 5, Piazza di Spagna* ☎ *06/6781851* ⊕ *www.patriziapepe.com* Ⓜ *Spagna.*

Prada

CLOTHING | Mario Prada founded the Italian luggage brand in 1913, but it has been his granddaughter, Miuccia, who updated the designs into the timeless investment pieces of today. You'll find the Rome store more service-oriented than the New York City branches—a roomy elevator delivers you to a series of thickly carpeted salons where a flock of discreet assistants will help you pick out dresses, shoes, lingerie, and fashion accessories. The men's store is located at Via Condotti 88/90, while the women's is down the street at 92/95. ⊠ *Via dei Condotti 88/90 and 92/95, Piazza di Spagna* ☎ *06/6790897* ⊕ *www.prada. com* Ⓜ *Spagna.*

Schostal

CLOTHING | A Piazza di Spagna fixture since 1870, this was once the go-to shop for corsets, petticoats, stockings, and bonnets. Today, it's the place to stop for essential basics that are increasingly difficult to find, like fine-quality shirts, underwear, and handkerchiefs made of wool and pure cashmere at affordable prices. ⊠ *Via della Fontanella di Borghese 29, Piazza di Spagna* ☎ *06/6791240* ⊕ *www.schostaloriginals.com* Ⓜ *Spagna.*

Valentino

CLOTHING | Valentino fills most of Piazza di Spagna, where the designer lived for decades in a lovely palazzo next to one of the multiple boutiques showcasing his eponymous designs with a romantic edginess—think studded heels or prêt-à-porter evening gowns worthy of the Oscars. Rock stars and other music lovers can also have their Valentino guitar straps personalized when they buy one at this enormous boutique. ⊠ *Piazza di Spagna 38, Piazza di Spagna* ☎ *06/94515710* ⊕ *www.valentino.com* Ⓜ *Spagna.*

Versace

CLOTHING | Versace's Rome flagship is a gem of architecture and design, with Byzantine-inspired mosaic floors, futuristic interiors with transparent walls, and merchandise that has a sexy rocker-Gothic-underground vibe. Here you'll find apparel, accessories, and home furnishings in designs every bit as flamboyant as Donatella and Allegra (Gianni's niece). ⊠ *Piazza di Spagna 12, Piazza di Spagna* ☎ *06/6784600* ⊕ *www.versace.com* Ⓜ *Spagna.*

DEPARTMENT STORES

★ La Rinascente

DEPARTMENT STORE | FAMILY | Set in a dazzling, seven-story space, Italy's best-known department store is packed topped to bottom with luxury goods, from cosmetics, handbags, and accessories to ready-to-wear designer sportswear to kitchen items and housewares. Even if you're not planning on buying anything, the basement excavations of a Roman aqueduct and the roof terrace bar with its splendid view are well worth a visit. There's also a location at Piazza Fiume. ⊠ *Via del Tritone 61, Piazza di Spagna* ☎ *02/91387388* ⊕ *www.rinascente.it* Ⓜ *Barberini.*

HEALTH & BEAUTY

Modàfferi Barber Shop

HEALTH & BEAUTY | Run by two friendly brothers, who took over the business from their father, this barbershop is preferred by actors performing at the nearby Teatro Sistina. It was founded in the 1970s and still has charmingly retro decor. They offer haircuts, beard care, manicures, pedicures, facials, and massages and have their own line of products. For extra privacy, you can request the private room. ⊠ *Via dei Cappuccini 11, Piazza di Spagna* ☎ *06/4817077* ⊕ *www.modafferibarbershop.it* Ⓜ *Barberini.*

JEWELRY

Bulgari

JEWELRY & WATCHES | Bulgari (also seen as Bvlgari) is to Rome what Tiffany is to New York and Cartier is to Paris. The jewelry giant has developed a reputation for meticulous craftsmanship melding noble metals with precious gems. In the middle of the 19th century, the great-grandfather of the current Bulgari brothers began working as a silver jeweler in his native Greece and is said to have moved to Rome with less than 1,000 lire in his pocket. This store's temple-inspired interior pays homage to the jeweler's ties to both places. ⊠ *Via dei Condotti 10, Piazza di Spagna* ☎ *06/696261* ⊕ *www.bulgari.com* Ⓜ *Spagna.*

SHOES

★ Braccialini

HANDBAGS | Founded in 1954 by Florentine stylist Carla Braccialini and her husband, Robert, this outfit makes bags that are authentic works of art in bright colors and delightful shapes, such as London black cabs or mountain chalets. The adorably quirky tote bags have picture-postcard scenes of luxury destinations made of brightly colored appliquéd leather. Be sure to check out the eccentric Temi (Theme) creature bags; the snail-shaped version made out of python skin makes a true fashion statement. There is another location on Via dei Condotti. ⊠ *Via Frattina, 117, Piazza di Spagna* ☎ *342/0338947* ⊕ *www.braccialini.it* Ⓜ *Spagna.*

Fausto Santini

SHOES | Shoe lovers with a passion for minimalist design flock to Fausto Santini to get their hands on his nerdy-chic footwear with its statement-making lines. Santini has been in business since 1970 and caters to a sophisticated, avant-garde clientele looking for elegant, classic shoes with a kick and a rainbow color palette. An outlet at Via Cavour 106, named for Fausto's father, Giacomo, sells last season's shoes at a big discount. ⊠ *Via Frattina 120, Piazza di Spagna* 🕾 *06/6784114* ⊕ *www.faustosantini.com* Ⓜ *Spagna.*

Giuseppe Zanotti

SHOES | Giuseppe Zanotti creates sought-after women's and men's shoes ranging from pencil-thin stilettos (often with a bit of sparkle or other bling) to colorful loafers to couture sneakers. The footwear here is placed on a literal pedestal so the craftsmanship can be admired from all angles. ⊠ *Piazza di Spagna, 33, Piazza di Spagna* 🕾 *06/69924220* ⊕ *www.giuseppezanotti. com* Ⓜ *Spagna.*

★ **Tod's**

SHOES | Founded in the 1920s, Tod's has grown from a small family brand into a global powerhouse so wealthy that its owner Diego Della Valle donated €20 million to the Colosseum restoration project. The shoe baron is best known for his simple, classic, understated designs done in butter-soft leather, but his light, flexible Gommini line of driving shoes with rubber-bottomed soles are popular as well. This location sells menswear and men's shoes; womenswear and women's shoes are available at another location on Via dei Condotti. ⊠ *Via della Fontanella di Borghese 56a–57, Piazza di Spagna* 🕾 *06/68210066* ⊕ *www.tods. com* Ⓜ *Spagna.*

Repubblica and the Quirinale

This sector of Rome stretches down from the 19th-century district built up around the Piazza della Repubblica—originally laid out to serve as a monumental foyer between the Termini train station and the rest of the city—and over the rest of the Quirinale. The highest of ancient Rome's famed seven hills, the Quirinale is crowned by the massive Palazzo Quirinale, home to the popes until 1870 and now Italy's presidential palace. Along the way, you can see ancient Roman sculptures, early Christian churches, and highlights from the 16th and 17th centuries, when Rome was conquered by the Baroque—and by Bernini.

Although Bernini's work feels omnipresent in much of the city center, the Renaissance-man range of his creations is particularly notable here. The artist as architect considered the church of Sant'Andrea al Quirinale one of his best; Bernini the urban designer and water worker is responsible for the muscle-bound sea god who blows his conch so provocatively in the fountain at the center of whirling Piazza Barberini. And Bernini the master gives religious passion a joltingly corporeal treatment in what is perhaps his greatest work, the *Ecstasy of St. Teresa,* in the church of Santa Maria della Vittoria.

GETTING HERE AND AROUND

Located between Termini station and the Spanish Steps, this area is about a 15-minute walk from either. Bus No. 40 will get you from Termini to the Quirinale in two stops; from the Vatican take Bus No. 64. The very central Repubblica Metro stop is on the piazza of the same name.

Sights

Capuchin Museum

CEMETERY | Devoted to teaching visitors about the Capuchin order, this museum is mainly notable for its strangely touching and beautiful crypt under the church of Santa Maria della Concezione. The bones of some 4,000 friars are arranged in odd decorative designs around the shriveled and decayed remains of their kinsmen, a macabre reminder of the impermanence of earthly life. As one sign proclaims: "What you are, we once were. What we are, you someday will be."

Upstairs in the church, the first chapel on the right contains Guido Reni's mid-17th-century *Archangel St. Michael Trampling the Devil.* The painting caused great scandal after an astute contemporary observer remarked that the face of the devil bore a surprising resemblance to Pope Innocent X, archenemy of Reni's Barberini patrons. Compare the devil with the bust of the pope that you saw in the Palazzo Doria Pamphilj and judge for yourself. ✉ *Via Veneto 27, Quirinale* ☎ *06/88803695* ⊕ *www.museoecriptaca-ppuccini.it* ✆ *€10* Ⓜ *Barberini.*

Fontana delle Api (*Fountain of the Bees*)

FOUNTAIN | The upper shell and inscription of this fountain, which is decorated with the famous heraldic bees of the Barberini family, are from a fountain that Bernini designed for Pope Urban VIII; the rest was lost when the fountain was moved to make way for a new street. The inscription caused considerable uproar when the fountain was first built in 1644. It said that the fountain had been erected in the 22nd year of the pontiff's reign, although, in fact, the 21st anniversary of Urban's election to the papacy was still some weeks away. The last numeral was hurriedly erased, but to no avail—Urban died eight days before the beginning of his 22nd year as pope. The superstitious Romans, who had regarded the inscription as a foolhardy tempting of

fate, were vindicated. ✉ *Piazza Barberini, Quirinale* Ⓜ *Barberini.*

★ MACRO

ART MUSEUM | Formerly known as Rome's Modern and Contemporary Art Gallery, and before that as the Peroni beer factory, this redesigned industrial space has brought new life to the gallery and museum scene of a city hitherto hailed for its "then," not its "now." The collection here covers Italian contemporary artists from the 1960s through today. The goal is to bring current art to the public in innovative spaces and, not incidentally, to support and recognize Rome's contemporary art scene, which labors in the shadow of the city's artistic heritage. After a few days—or millennia—of dusty marble, it's a breath of fresh air.
■ TIP→ **Check the website for occasional late-night openings and events.** ✉ *Via Nizza 138, Repubblica* ☎ *06/696271* ⊕ *www. museomacro.it* ✆ *Free* ⊘ *Closed Mon.* Ⓜ *Castro Pretorio.*

★ Palazzo Barberini/Galleria Nazionale d'Arte Antica

ART MUSEUM | One of Rome's most splendid 17th-century buildings is a Baroque landmark. The grand facade was designed by Carlo Maderno (aided by his nephew, Francesco Borromini), but when Maderno died, Borromini was passed over in favor of his great rival, Gian Lorenzo Bernini. The palazzo is now home to the Galleria Nazionale d'Arte Antica, with a collection that includes Raphael's *La Fornarina,* a luminous portrait of the artist's lover (a resident of Trastevere, she was reputedly a baker's daughter). Also noteworthy are Guido Reni's portrait of the doomed Beatrice Cenci (beheaded in Rome for patricide in 1599)—Hawthorne called it "the saddest picture ever painted" in his Rome-based novel, *The Marble Faun*—and Caravaggio's dramatic *Judith Beheading Holofernes.*

The showstopper here is the palace's Gran Salone, a vast ballroom with a ceiling painted in 1630 by the third (and too-often-neglected) master of the Roman Baroque, Pietro da Cortona. It depicts the *Glorification of Urban VIII's Reign* and has the spectacular conceit of glorifying Urban VIII as the agent of Divine Providence, escorted by a "bomber squadron" (to quote art historian Sir Michael Levey) of huge Barberini bees, the heraldic symbol of the family. ⊠ *Via delle Quattro Fontane 13, Quirinale* ☎ *06/4814591* ⊕ *www.barberinicorsini. org* ⌑ *€12, includes Galleria Corsini* ⊙ *Closed Mon.* Ⓜ *Barberini.*

★ Palazzo Massimo alle Terme

ART MUSEUM | The Museo Nazionale Romano, with items ranging from striking classical Roman paintings to marble bric-a-brac, has four locations: Palazzo Altemps, Crypta Balbi, the Museo delle Terme di Diocleziano, and this, the Palazzo Massimo alle Terme—a vast structure containing the great ancient treasures of the archaeological collection and also the coin collection. Highlights include the *Dying Niobid*, the famous bronze *Boxer at Rest*, and the *Discobolus Lancellotti*.

Among the museum's most intriguing attractions, however, are the ancient frescoes on view on the top floor. They're stunningly set up to "re-create" the look of the homes they once decorated, and their colors are remarkably preserved. You'll see stuccoes and wall paintings found in the area of the Villa Farnesina (in Trastevere), as well as those depicting a garden in bloom and an orchard alive with birds that once covered the walls of cool sunken rooms at Empress Livia's villa in Prima Porta, just outside the city. ⊠ *Largo di Villa Peretti 2, Repubblica* ☎ *06/39967700* ⊕ *www.museonazion- aleromano.beniculturali.it* ⌑ *€10, or €14 for a combined ticket including access to Crypta Balbi, Museo delle Terme di Diocleziano, and Palazzo Altemps (valid for 1 wk)* ⊙ *Closed Mon.* Ⓜ *Repubblica, Termini.*

Piazza del Quirinale

PLAZA/SQUARE | This strategic location atop the Quirinale has long been important. Indeed, it served as home of the Sabines in the 7th century BC—when they were deadly enemies of the Romans, who lived on the Campidoglio and Palatino (all of 1 km [½ mile] away). Today, it's the foreground for the presidential residence, Palazzo del Quirinale, and home to the Palazzo della Consulta, where Italy's Constitutional Court sits.

The open side of the piazza has a vista over the rooftops and domes of central Rome and St. Peter's. The Fontana di Montecavallo, or Fontana dei Dioscuri, has a statuary group of Dioscuri trying to tame two massive marble steeds that was found in the Baths of Constantine, which once occupied part of the Quirinale's summit. Unlike many ancient statues in Rome, this group survived the Dark Ages intact, becoming one of the city's great sights during the Middle Ages. The obelisk next to the figures is from the Mausoleo di Augusto (Tomb of Augustus) and was put here by Pope Pius VI in the late 18th century. ⊠ *Piazza del Quirinale, Quirinale* Ⓜ *Barberini.*

Piazza della Repubblica

PLAZA/SQUARE | Often the first view that spells "Rome" to weary travelers walking from Termini station, this round piazza was laid out in the late 1800s and follows the line of the caldarium of the vast ancient public baths, the Terme di Diocleziano. At its center, the exuberant Fontana delle Naiadi (Fountain of the Naiads) teems with voluptuous bronze ladies happily wrestling with marine monsters. The nudes weren't there when the pope unveiled the fountain in 1888— sparing him any embarrassment—but when the figures were added in 1901, they caused a scandal. It's said that the sculptor, Mario Rutelli, modeled them on the ample figures of two musical-comedy stars of the day. The colonnades now house the luxe hotel Anantara Palazzo

Repubblica and the Quirinale

Coffee and Quick Bites ▼

1 Dagnino.................. **E5**
2 La Romana dal 1947 .... **F3**
3 Mercato Centrale
   Roma **G7**
4 Pinsere................... **E4**

Hotels ▼

1 Anantara Palazzo
   Naiadi Rome Hotel...... **E6**
2 Rome Times Hotel **D7**
3 The St. Regis Rome..... **E5**

Naiadi and various shops and cafés. ⊠ *Repubblica* Ⓜ *Repubblica.*

San Carlo alle Quattro Fontane

CHURCH | Sometimes known as San Carlino because of its tiny size, this is one of Borromini's masterpieces. In a space no larger than the base of one of the piers of St. Peter's Basilica, he created a church that is an intricate exercise in geometric perfection, with a coffered dome that seems to float above the curves of the walls. Borromini's work is often bizarre, definitely intellectual, and intensely concerned with pure form. In San Carlo, he invented an original treatment of space that creates an effect of rippling movement, especially evident in the double-S curves of the facade. Characteristically, the interior decoration is subdued, in white stucco with no more than a few touches of gilding, so as not to distract from the form. Don't miss the cloister: a tiny, understated Baroque jewel, with a graceful portico and loggia above, echoing the lines of the church. ⊠ *Via del Quirinale 23, Quirinale* ☎ *06/48907729* ⊙ *Closed Sun.* Ⓜ *Barberini.*

★ Santa Maria della Vittoria

CHURCH | Designed by Carlo Maderno, this church is best known for Bernini's sumptuous Baroque decoration of the Cappella Cornaro (Cornaro Chapel, the last on the left as you face the altar), which houses his interpretation of divine love in the *Ecstasy of St. Teresa.* Bernini's masterly fusion of sculpture, light, architecture, painting, and relief is a multimedia extravaganza, with the chapel modeled as a theater, and one of the key examples of the Roman High Baroque. The members of the Cornaro family meditate on the communal vision of the great moment of divine love before them: the swooning saint's robes appear to be on fire, quivering with life, and the white marble group seems suspended in the heavens as golden rays illuminate the scene. An angel assists as Teresa abandons herself to the joys of heavenly love. To modern eyes, Bernini's representation of the saint's experience may seem more earthly than mystical. As the visiting French dignitary Charles de Brosses put it in the 18th century, "If this is divine love, I know all about it." ⊠ *Via XX Settembre 17, Largo Santa Susanna, Repubblica* ☎ *06/42740571* Ⓜ *Repubblica.*

Sant'Andrea al Quirinale

CHURCH | Designed by Bernini, this small church is one of the triumphs of the Roman Baroque period. His son wrote that Bernini considered it his best work and that he used to come here occasionally, just to sit and contemplate. Bernini's simple oval plan, a classic form in Baroque architecture, is given drama and movement by the decoration, which depicts St. Andrew's martyrdom and ascension into heaven and starts with the painting over the high altar, up past the figure of the saint above, to the angels at the base of the lantern and the dove of the Holy Spirit that awaits on high. ⊠ *Via del Quirinale 30, Quirinale* ☎ *06/4819399* ⊕ *www.santandrea. gesuiti.it* ⊙ *Closed Mon.* Ⓜ *Barberini.*

🍴 Restaurants

Il Winebar Trimani

$$$ | WINE BAR | This wine bar is run by the Trimani family of wine merchants, whose shop next door has been in business for nearly two centuries. Hot food is served at lunch and dinner in the minimalist interior, and it is also perfect for an aperitif or an early supper (it opens for evening service at 6 pm). **Known for:** warmly lit second floor for sipping; torte salate (savory tarts); 5,000 wines from around the world. ⑤ *Average main: €30* ⊠ *Via Cernaia 37/b, Repubblica* ☎ *06/4469630* ⊕ *www.trimani.com* ⊙ *Closed Sun. and 3 wks in Aug.* Ⓜ *Castro Pretorio, Repubblica.*

☕ Coffee and Quick Bites

Dagnino

$ | BAKERY | Hidden inside a covered arcade, this Sicilian pasticceria, which opened in 1955, has pastry cases filled with cannoli, cassata, cakes, and marzipan as well as savory items like sandwiches and arancini. Go for breakfast, and try the cornetto filled with ricotta and chocolate chips—this might be the only place in Rome where you can find it. **Known for:** Sicilian desserts; midcentury modern design; cornetti filled with ricotta and chocolate chips. ⑤ *Average main: €3* ✉ *Via Vittorio Emanuele Orlando 75, Repubblica* ☎ *06/4818660* ⊕ *www.dagnino.com* Ⓜ *Repubblica.*

La Romana dal 1947

$ | ICE CREAM | FAMILY | In summer, the line at this gelateria stretches out the door and around the corner. Though it's a franchise that originated in Rimini, it's loved by Romans for its rich, creamy gelato made with organic milk, fresh fruit, nuts, and chocolate. **Known for:** reasonably priced; big portions; modern decor. ⑤ *Average main: €3* ✉ *Via XX Settembre 60, Repubblica* ☎ *06/42020828* ⊕ *www.gelateriaromana.com* Ⓜ *Repubblica.*

Mercato Centrale Roma

$ | INTERNATIONAL | FAMILY | This gourmet food hall is in the last place you'd expect—Termini Station—and it's great for a quick bite even if you're not catching a train. There are stalls from some of Rome's best food purveyors, including Stefano Callegari (of *trapizzino* fame), pizzaiolo Marco Quintili, and fritti by Arcangelo Dandini. **Known for:** gourmet food hall; trapizzino (stuffed triangle-shaped pizza dough) outpost; Sicilian specialties. ⑤ *Average main: €5* ✉ *Termini Station, Via Giovanni Giolitti 36, Esquilino* ☎ *06/46202900* ⊕ *www.mercatocentrale.it* Ⓜ *Termini.*

Pinsere

$ | PIZZA | FAMILY | In Rome, you'll usually find either pizza *tonda* (round) or pizza *al taglio* (by the slice), but there's also pizza *pinsa*—an oval-shaped individual pie that's a little thicker than the classic Roman pizza. Pinsere is mostly a take-out shop, with people eating on the street for their lunch break, so it's the perfect quick meal. **Known for:** budget-friendly options; seasonal toppings; mortadella and pistachio pizzas. ⑤ *Average main: €6* ✉ *Via Flavia 98, Repubblica* ☎ *06/42020924* ⊕ *www.pinsereroma.it* ⊘ *Closed weekends and 2 wks in Aug.* Ⓜ *Castro Pretorio.*

🛏 Hotels

Anantara Palazzo Naiadi Rome Hotel

$$$$ | HOTEL | You'll experience exquisite service and pampering at this Neoclassical landmark on the Piazza della Repubblica built on the foundations of the Baths of Diocletian—it's now run by Anantara, a luxury hotel brand with roots in Thailand. **Pros:** top-notch concierge and staff; multiple romantic dining options; spa with both Asian and European-style treatments. **Cons:** food and beverages are expensive; beyond the immediate vicinity of many sights; rooms are a different style than public spaces. ⑤ *Rooms from: €750* ✉ *Piazza della Repubblica 47, Repubblica* ☎ *06/489381* ⊕ *www.anantara.com/en/palazzo-naiadi-rome* ➦ *232 rooms* ⑪ *No Meals* Ⓜ *Repubblica, Termini.*

Rome Times Hotel

$$$$ | HOTEL | This modern hotel has large, soundproofed rooms with contemporary furnishings, hardwood floors, and huge fluffy beds. **Pros:** late checkout if booked through site; free use of Samsung smartphone for calls and Internet during your stay; large bright bathrooms. **Cons:** lower floors can be noisy; rooms in the annex don't come with all the benefits of the main hotel; lighting in rooms is not optimal. ⑤ *Rooms from: €323* ✉ *Via Milano*

42, Quirinale ☎ *06/99345101* ⊕ *www.
rometimeshotel.com* ⇆ *81 rooms* �⊚I *No
Meals* Ⓜ *Repubblica.*

The St. Regis Rome

$$$$ | HOTEL | Originally opened by César
Ritz in 1894, this grande dame has a
Belle Epoque lobby filled with classic
and contemporary art, a ballroom with
painstakingly restored ceiling frescoes,
and an intimate library where you can sip
a cup of tea or something stronger. **Pros:**
houses the Roman location of international art gallery Galleria Continua; every
room comes with 24/7 butler service; the
library lounge serves a lovely afternoon
tea. **Cons:** food and drinks are pricey;
breakfast is not included; restaurant feels
more like a lounge than a proper restaurant. Ⓢ *Rooms from: €800* ⊠ *Via Vittorio
E. Orlando 3, Repubblica* ☎ *06/47091*
⊕ *www.marriott.com* ⇆ *161 rooms*
⏽⊚I *No Meals* Ⓜ *Repubblica.*

🎫 Performing Arts

★ Teatro dell'Opera

OPERA | The company at this theater, a
far younger sibling of La Scala in Milan
and La Fenice in Venice, commands an
audience during its mid-November–May
season. In the hot summer months,
it moves to the Terme di Caracalla for
an outdoor opera series. As you might
expect, the oft-preferred performance
is *Aida*, for its spectacle, which once
included real elephants. The company
has lately taken a new direction, using
projections atop the ancient ruins to
create cutting-edge sets. ⊠ *Piazza Beni-
amino Gigli 7, Repubblica* ☎ *06/481601,
06/4817003 tickets* ⊕ *www.operaroma.it*
Ⓜ *Repubblica.*

Villa Borghese and Environs

Touring Rome's artistic masterpieces
while staying clear of its hustle and
bustle can be, quite literally, a walk in
the park. Some of the city's finest sights
are tucked away in or next to green
lawns and pedestrian piazzas, offering a
breath of fresh air for weary sightseers,
especially in the Villa Borghese park.
One of Rome's largest, this park can
alleviate gallery gout by offering an oasis
in which to cool off under the ilex, oak,
and umbrella pine trees. If you feel like
a picnic, have an *alimentari* (food shop)
make you some panini before you go;
food carts within the park are overpriced.

GETTING HERE AND AROUND
The Metro stop for Piazza del Popolo
is Flaminio on Line A. The Villa Giulia,
the Galleria Nazionale d'Arte Moderna e
Contemporanea, and the Bioparco in Villa
Borghese are accessible from Via Flaminia, 1 km (½ mile) from Piazza del Popolo.
Tram No. 19 and Bus No. 3 stop at each.
Bus No. 160 and No. 628 connect Piazza
del Popolo to Piazza Venezia. Bus No. 116
goes into Villa Borghese.

👁 Sights

★ Galleria Borghese

ART MUSEUM | The luxury-loving Cardinal
Scipione Borghese had this museum
custom-built in 1612 as a showcase for
his fabulous collection of both antiquities and more "modern" works. One of
the collection's most famous works is
Canova's Neoclassical sculpture, *Pauline
Borghese as Venus Victorious*. Nearby
are three key early Baroque sculptures by
Bernini: *David, Apollo and Daphne,* and
The Rape of Persephone. You'll also find
masterpieces by Caravaggio, Raphael
(including his moving *Deposition*), Pinturicchio, Perugino, Bellini, and Rubens.
Probably the gallery's most famous

painting is Titian's allegorical *Sacred and Profane Love.* ■TIP→ **Admission to the Galleria Borghese is by reservation only. Visitors are admitted in two-hour shifts 9–5. Prime-time slots sell out days in advance, so reserve and directly (and early) through the museum's website.** ✉ *Piazzale Scipione Borghese 5, off Via Pinciana, Villa Borghese* ☎ *06/32810 reservations, 06/8413979 info* ⊕ *www.galleriaborghese.benicultur- ali.it* ✑ *€15, including €2 reservation fee; increased fee during temporary exhibi- tions* ◷ *Closed Mon.* ⚓ *Reservations essential.*

★ **MAXXI—Museo Nazionale delle Arti del XXI Secolo** (*National Museum of 21st-Century Arts*)
ART MUSEUM | Designed by the late Iraqi-British architect Zaha Hadid, this modern building plays with lots of natural light and has curving and angular lines, big open spaces, glass ceilings, and steel staircases that twist through the air—all meant to question the division between "within" and "without." The MAXXI hosts temporary exhibitions of art, architec- ture, film, and more. The permanent collection, displayed on a rotating basis, has more than 350 works from modern and contemporary artists, including Andy Warhol, Francesco Clemente, and Gerhard Richter. ✉ *Via Guido Reni 4/A, Flaminio* ☎ *06/3201954* ⊕ *www.maxxi.art* ✑ *€15* ◷ *Closed Mon.* Ⓜ *Flaminio, then Tram No. 2 to Apollodoro.*

★ **Piazza del Popolo**
PLAZA/SQUARE | **FAMILY** | With its obelisk and twin churches, this immense square marks what was, for centuries, Rome's northern entrance, where all roads from the north converged and where visitors, many of them pilgrims, got their first impression of the Eternal City. The desire to make this entrance to Rome some- thing special was a pet project of popes and their architects for more than three centuries. Although it was once crowded with fashionable carriages, the piazza today is a pedestrian zone. At election

time, it's the scene of huge political rallies, and on New Year's Eve, Rome stages a mammoth alfresco party here. ✉ *Piazza del Popolo* Ⓜ *Flaminio.*

★ **Santa Maria del Popolo**
CHURCH | Standing inconspicuously in a corner of the vast Piazza del Popolo, this church often goes unnoticed, but the treasures inside make it a must for art lovers. Bramante enlarged the apse, which was rebuilt in the 15th century on the site of a much older place of worship. Inside, in the first chapel on the right, you'll see some frescoes by Pinturicchio from the mid-15th century; the adjacent Cybo Chapel is a 17th-century exercise in decorative marble.

Raphael designed the famous Chigi Chapel, the second on the left, with vault mosaics—showing God the Father in Benediction—as well as statues of Jonah and Elijah. More than a century later, Bernini added the oval medallions on the tombs and the statues of Daniel and Habakkuk. Finally, the Cerasi Chapel, to the left of the high altar, holds two Caravaggios: *The Crucifixion of St. Peter* and *The Conversion of St. Paul.* Exuding drama and realism, both are key early Baroque works that show how "modern" 17th-century art can appear. Compare their style with the much more restrained and classically "pure" *Assumption of the Virgin* by Annibale Carracci, which hangs over the altar of the chapel. ✉ *Piazza del Popolo 12, near Porta del Popolo, Piazza del Popolo* ☎ *06/3610836* ⊕ *www.agos- tiniani.it* Ⓜ *Flaminio.*

★ **Villa Borghese**
CITY PARK | **FAMILY** | Rome's Central Park, the Villa Borghese was originally laid out as a recreational garden in the early 17th century by Cardinal Scipione Borghese. The word "villa" was used to mean suburban estate, of the type developed by the ancient Romans and adopted by Renaissance nobles. Today's gardens cover a much smaller area—by 1630, the perimeter wall was almost 5 km

KEY
- **1** Sights
- **1** Restaurants
- **1** Quick Bites
- **1** Hotels

Parioli

Via Francesco Siacci

Viale Liegi

Via di Villa Sacchetti

Via Ulisse Aldrovandi

V. delle Tre Madonne

Via Ulisse Aldrovandi

Via A. Bertoloni

Viale G. Rossini

Via Emilio de Cavalieri

Via Guido d'Arezzo

Via Vincenzo Bellini

Via Luigi Boccherini

Via N. Porpora

Via Salaria

Giardino Zoologico

Bioparco

Via del Giardino Zoologico

Via Mercadante

Via C. Monteverdi

Via Giovanni Paisiello

Via Donizetti

Via Mercadante

Via Simeto

Giardino dell Lago

Via P. Raimondi

Parco dei Daini

Via Po

Via Basento

Via Adda

Viale dell'Uccelliera

Via J. Peri

Via G. Alfieri

Villa Albani

V.le Pietro Canonica

V.le dei Cavalli Marini

V.le dei Pupazzi

Via Pinciana

Via Salaria

Villa Borghese

Via Isonzo

Via Tevere

Via Veneto

Piazzale d. Canestre

V.le W. Goethe

V.le del Museo Borghese

Via Po

Via Aniene

Via Salaria

V. le S. Paolo de Brasile

Via Campania

Galoppatoio

Corso d'Italia

Via Piemonte

Via Sardegna

Via Puglie

V. Liguria

V. Sicilia

Via Piave

Via P.ta Pinciana

Via Vitt. Veneto

Via Lazio

Villa Borghese and Environs

(3 miles) long. At the end of the 18th century, Scottish painter Jacob More remodeled the gardens into the English style popular at the time. In addition to the gloriously restored Galleria Borghese, the highlights of the park are Piazza di Siena, a graceful amphitheater, and the botanical garden on Via Canonica, where there is a pretty little lake as well as the neoclassical faux–Temple of Aesculapius, the Biopark zoo, Rome's own replica of London's Globe Theatre, and the Villa Giulia museum.

The Carlo Bilotti Museum (⊕ www.museocarlobilotti.it) is particularly attractive for Giorgio de Chirico fans, and there is more modern art in the nearby Galleria Nazionale d'Arte Moderna e Contemporanea. The 63-seat children's movie theater, Cinema dei Piccoli, shows films for adults in the evening. There's also Casa del Cinema, where film buffs can screen films or sit at the sleek, cherry-red, indoor-outdoor café (you can find a schedule of events at ⊕ www.casadelcinema.it). ⊠ Main entrances at Porta Pinciana, the Pincio, Piazzale Flaminio (Piazza del Popolo), Viale delle Belle Arti, and Via Mercadante, Villa Borghese Ⓜ Flaminio.

🍴 Restaurants

Acquolina
$$$$ | **MODERN ITALIAN** | This two-Michelin-starred restaurant turns out delicious and high-quality seafood dishes that surprise and evoke a sensory experience. Tortelli are served with cheese, black pepper, eel, and onion, and all the dishes are artfully presented. **Known for:** elaborate tasting menus; spaghetti with langoustines; sophisticated desserts. Ⓢ Average main: €200 ⊠ The First Arte, Via del Vantaggio 14, Piazza del Popolo ☎ 06/3201590 ⊕ www.acquolinaristorante.it ☉ Closed Sun. and Mon. ☞ Tasting menus only Ⓜ Flaminio.

Al Ceppo
$$$ | **ITALIAN** | The well-heeled, the business-minded, and those with refined palates frequent this outpost of tranquility. The owners hail from Le Marche, the region northeast of Rome that encompasses inland mountains and the Adriatic coastline, so dishes from their native region feature alongside seafood and meats ready to be grilled. **Known for:** grilled meat and fish; authentic Le Marche cuisine; excellent wine list. Ⓢ Average main: €30 ⊠ Via Panama 2, Villa Borghese ☎ 06/8419696 ⊕ www.ristorantealceppo.it ☉ No lunch Mon. Closed 3 wks in Aug.

★ La Pergola
$$$$ | **MODERN ITALIAN** | Dinner here is a truly spectacular and romantic event, with incomparable views across the city matched by a stellar dining experience that includes top-notch service as well as sublimely inventive fare. The difficulty comes in choosing from among Michelin-starred chef Heinz Beck's *alta cucina* (high cuisine) specialties. **Known for:** fagotelli La Pergola stuffed with pecorino, eggs, and cream with guanciale and zucchini; award-winning wine list; weekend reservations that book up three months in advance. Ⓢ Average main: €75 ⊠ Rome Cavalieri, A Waldorf Astoria Resort, Via Alberto Cadlolo 101, Monte Mario ☎ 06/35092152 ⊕ www.romecavalieri.com ☉ Closed Sun. and Mon., 3 wks in Aug., and 3 wks in Jan. No lunch 🎩 Jacket required.

☕ Coffee and Quick Bites

Canova
$$ | **ITALIAN | FAMILY** | Esteemed director Federico Fellini, who lived around the corner on Via Margutta, used to come here all the time and even had an office in the back. His drawings and black-and-white stills from his films remain on display in the hallway that leads to the interior dining room, but the best place to sit for people-watching with a coffee, light

lunch, or aperitivo is on the terrace out front. **Known for:** great people-watching; sandwiches and other light fare; Fellini's old hangout. ⑤ *Average main: €15* ✉ *Piazza del Popolo 16, Piazza del Popolo* ☎ *06/3612231* ⊕ *www.canovapiazzadel-popolo.it* Ⓜ *Flaminio.*

Hotels

The First Arte

$$$$ | **HOTEL** | Set in a 19th-century Neo-classical palace, this cozy boutique hotel was remodeled to feature high-tech, elegant guest rooms while keeping the core structure, including unique windows and tall ceilings, intact. **Pros:** fitness room with Technogym equipment; staff that is eager to please; more than 200 works of art on display from Galleria Mucciaccia. **Cons:** some rooms can be dark; rooftop bar can get quite crowded; no spa. ⑤ *Rooms from: €500* ✉ *Via del Vantaggio 14, Piazza del Popolo* ☎ *06/45617070* ⊕ *www.pavil-ionshotels.com/rome/thefirstarte* ⤳ *29 rooms* ⦿ *Free Breakfast* Ⓜ *Flaminio.*

★ Hotel de Russie

$$$$ | **HOTEL** | Occupying a 19th-century hotel that once hosted royalty, Picasso, and Cocteau, the Hotel de Russie is now the first choice in Rome for government bigwigs and Hollywood high rollers seeking ultimate luxury in a secluded retreat. **Pros:** big potential for celebrity sightings; well-equipped gym and world-class spa; excellent Stravinskij cocktail bar has outdoor tables on the Piazzetta Valadier. **Cons:** faster Internet comes at a fee; breakfast not included; very expensive. ⑤ *Rooms from: €1700* ✉ *Via del Babu-ino 9, Piazza del Popolo* ☎ *06/328881* ⊕ *www.roccofortehotels.com* ⤳ *120 rooms* ⦿ *No Meals* Ⓜ *Flaminio.*

The Hoxton, Rome

$$ | **HOTEL** | British brand The Hoxton's first foray into Italy is a design lover's dream filled with 1970s-inspired bespoke furniture, art tomes, and plants that transform the large lobby into intimate seating nooks perfect for socializing and coworking. **Pros:** stylish design; friendly staff; great food and drinks. **Cons:** far from main sights, with the closest Metro stop a mile away; rooms have little storage space for clothes; no gym or spa. ⑤ *Rooms from: €189* ✉ *Largo Benedetto Marcello 220, Parioli* ☎ *06/94502700* ⊕ *www.thehoxton.com/rome* ⤳ *192 rooms* ⦿ *No Meals.*

Rome Cavalieri, A Waldorf Astoria Hotel

$$$$ | **RESORT** | **FAMILY** | Set in a quiet residential neighborhood amid 15 acres of lush Mediterranean parkland, the Rome Cavalieri is a true hilltop oasis with magnificent views as well as three outdoor pools, one indoor pool, and a palatial spa. **Pros:** famed art collection, including a Tiepolo triptych from 1725; complimentary shuttle to city center; impressive on-site restaurant. **Cons:** you definitely pay for the luxury of staying here—everything is expensive; outside the city center; not all rooms have great views. ⑤ *Rooms from: €420* ✉ *Via Alberto Cadlolo 101, Monte Mario* ☎ *06/3509* ⊕ *www.romecavalieri.com* ⤳ *370 rooms* ⦿ *No Meals.*

Nightlife

★ Stravinskij Bar at the Hotel de Russie

COCKTAIL BARS | The Stravinskij Bar, in the Hotel de Russie, is the best place to sample la dolce vita. Celebrities, blue bloods, and VIPs hang out in the gorgeous Piazzetta Valadier where mixed drinks and cocktails are well above par. There are also healthy smoothies and bites if you need to refuel. ✉ *Hotel de Russie, Via del Babuino 9, Piazza del Popolo* ☎ *06/3288874* ⊕ *www.roccoforte-hotels.com* Ⓜ *Flaminio.*

Performing Arts

★ Auditorium Parco della Musica

CONCERTS | Architect Renzo Piano conceived and constructed the Auditorium Parco della Musica, a futuristic complex made up of three enormous, pod-shaped concert halls, which have hosted some of the world's greatest music acts. The Sala Santa Cecilia is a massive hall for grand orchestra and choral concerts; the Sala Sinopoli is more intimately scaled for smaller troupes; and the Sala Petrassi was designed for alternative events. All three are arrayed around the Cavea (amphitheater), a vast outdoor Greco-Roman-style theater. The Auditorium also hosts seasonal festivals, including the Rome Film Fest. ⊠ *Viale Pietro de Coubertin 30, Flaminio* ☏ *06/80241281* ⊕ *www.auditorium.com* Ⓜ *Flaminio, then Tram No. 2 to Apollodoro.*

Teatro Olimpico

THEATER | Part of Rome's theater circuit, the 1930s-era Teatro Olimpico is one of the main venues for cabaret, contemporary dance companies, visiting international ballet companies, and touring Broadway shows. ⊠ *Piazza Gentile da Fabriano 17, Flaminio* ☏ *349/2378200* ⊕ *www.teatroolimpico.it* Ⓜ *Flaminio, then Tram 2 to Mancini.*

Shopping

★ Il Marmoraro

SPECIALTY STORE | This tiny shop is a holdout of Via Margutta's days as a street full of artists and artisans. Sandro Fiorentino's father opened the shop in 1969 (he carved plaques like the one that marks Federico Fellini's house up the street), and Sandro still engraves the marble by hand. The shop is packed full of plaques, many with clever phrases, which make a great souvenir. Sandro will also engrave a message of your choice upon request. ⊠ *Via Margutta 53B, Piazza del Popolo* ☏ *335/6593612* Ⓜ *Spagna.*

Trastevere

Across the Tiber from the Jewish Ghetto is Trastevere (literally "across the Tiber"), long cherished as Rome's Greenwich Village and now subject to rampant gentrification. In spite of this, Trastevere remains about the most tightly knit community in the city, the Trasteverini proudly proclaiming their descent from the ancient Romans. Ancient bridges—the Ponte Fabricio and the Ponte Cestio—link Trastevere and the Ghetto to Isola Tiberina (Tiber Island), a diminutive sandbar and one of Rome's most picturesque sights.

GETTING HERE AND AROUND

From the Vatican or Spanish Steps, expect a 30- to 40-minute walk to reach Trastevere. From Termini station, take Bus No. 40 Express or No. 64 to Largo di Torre Argentina, where you can switch to Tram No. 8 to get to Trastevere. If you don't feel like climbing the steep Gianicolo, take Bus No. 115 from Largo dei Fiorentini, then enjoy the walk down to the northern reaches of Trastevere or explore the leafy residential area of Monteverde Vecchio on the other side of the hill.

◉ Sights

Isola Tiberina (*Tiber Island*)

ISLAND | **FAMILY** | It's easy to overlook this tiny island in the Tiber, but you shouldn't. In terms of history and sheer loveliness, charming Isola Tiberina—shaped like a boat about to set sail—gets high marks. Cross onto the island via Ponte Fabricio, Rome's oldest remaining bridge, constructed in 62 BC. On the north side of the island crumbles the romantic ruin of the Ponte Rotto (Broken Bridge), which dates from 179 BC. Descend the steps to the lovely river embankment to see a Roman relief of the intertwined-snakes symbol of Aesculapius, the great god of healing.

In imperial times, Romans sheathed the entire island with marble to make it look like Aesculapius's ship, replete with a towering obelisk as a mast. Amazingly, a fragment of the ancient sculpted ship's prow still exists. You can marvel at it on the downstream end of the embankment. Today, medicine still reigns here. The island is home to the hospital of Fatebenefratelli (literally, "Do good, brothers"). Nearby is San Bartolomeo, built at the end of the 10th century by the Holy Roman Emperor Otto III and restored in the 18th century.

During summer, the island hosts an outdoor cinema while its rim is dotted with white tented bars and pop-up eateries. ⊠ Trastevere ✛ Isola Tiberina can be accessed by Ponte Fabricio or Ponte Cestio.

Palazzo Corsini

ART MUSEUM | A brooding example of Baroque style, the palace (once home to Queen Christina of Sweden) is across the road from the Villa Farnesina and houses part of the 16th- and 17th-century sections of the collection of the Galleria Nazionale d'Arte Antica. Among the star paintings in this manageably sized collection are Rubens's St. Sebastian Healed by Angels and Caravaggio's St. John the Baptist. Stop in if only to climb the 17th-century stone staircase, itself a drama of architectural shadows and sculptural voids. Behind, but separate from, the palazzo is the University of Rome's Orto Botanico, home to 3,500 species of plants, with various greenhouses around a stairway/fountain with 11 jets. ⊠ Via della Lungara 10, Trastevere ☎ 06/68802323 Galleria Corsini, 06/32810 Galleria Corsini tickets, 06/49917107 Orto Botanico ⊕ www.barberinicorsini.org ⊠ €12 Galleria Corsini, including entrance to Palazzo Barberini within 20 days; €5 Orto Botanico ⊗ Closed Mon.

★ Santa Cecilia in Trastevere

CHURCH | This basilica commemorates the aristocratic St. Cecilia, patron saint of musicians. One of ancient Rome's most celebrated early Christian martyrs, she was most likely put to death by the Emperor Diocletian just before the year AD 300. After an abortive attempt to suffocate her in the baths of her own house (a favorite means of quietly disposing

of aristocrats in Roman days), she was brought before the executioner. But not even three blows of the executioner's sword could dispatch the young girl. She lingered for several days, converting others to the Christian cause, before finally dying. In 1595, her body was exhumed—it was said to look as fresh as if she still breathed—and the heart-wrenching sculpture by eyewitness Stefano Maderno that lies below the main altar was, he insisted, exactly how she looked.

Time your visit in the morning to enter the cloistered convent to see what remains of Pietro Cavallini's Last Judgment, dating from 1293. It's the only major fresco in existence known to have been painted by Cavallini, a contemporary of Giotto. To visit the frescoes, ring the bell of the convent to the left of the church entrance between 10 am and 12 pm. ⊠ Piazza di Santa Cecilia 22, Trastevere ☎ 06/45492739 ⊕ www.bene-dettinesantacecilia.it ⊠ Frescoes €2.50, underground €2.50 ⊗ Access to frescoes closed in the afternoon.

★ Santa Maria in Trastevere

CHURCH | Built during the 4th century and rebuilt in the 12th century, this is one of Rome's oldest and grandest churches. It is also the earliest foundation of any Roman church to be dedicated to the Virgin Mary. The 18th-century portico draws attention to the facade's 800-year-old mosaics, which represent the parable of the Wise and Foolish Virgins. They enhance the whole piazza, especially at night, when the church front and bell tower are illuminated.

With a nave framed by a processional of two rows of gigantic columns (22 in total) taken from the ancient Baths of Caracalla, and an apse studded with gilded mosaics, the interior conjures the splendor of ancient Rome. Overhead is Domenichino's gilded ceiling (1617). The church's most important mosaics, Pietro Cavallini's six panels of the Life of the Virgin, cover the semicircular apse. Note

Trastevere

Sights ▼	**Restaurants** ▼	**Coffee and Quick Bites** ▼	**Hotels** ▼
1 Isola Tiberina............ **H3**	1 Antico Arco............. **B4**	1 Biscottificio Innocenti................. **H4**	1 Casa di Santa Francesca Romana a Ponte Rotto............. **H4**
2 Palazzo Corsini......... **D1**	2 Da Enzo al 29.......... **I4**	2 Suppli Roma............. **F5**	2 Hotel Santa Maria...... **E3**
3 Santa Cecilia in Trastevere **H5**	3 Da Lucia **D3**		3 Hotel Trastevere **E4**
4 Santa Maria in Trastevere **E3**	4 Pizzeria Ai Marmi....... **G4**		4 Relais Le Clarisse....... **F5**
5 Villa Farnesina **D1**			

the building labeled "Taberna Meritoria" just under the figure of the Virgin in the Nativity scene, with a stream of oil flowing from it; it recalls the legend that a fountain of oil appeared on this spot, prophesying the birth of Christ. Off the piazza's northern side is a street called Via delle Fonte dell'Olio in honor of this miracle. ⊠ *Piazza Santa Maria in Trastevere, Trastevere* ☎ *06/5814802* ⊕ *www.santamariaintrastevere.it.*

★ Villa Farnesina

CASTLE/PALACE | Money was no object to the extravagant Agostino Chigi, a banker from Siena who financed many papal projects. His munificence is evident in this elegant villa, built for him in about 1511. Agostino entertained the popes and princes of 16th-century Rome, impressing his guests at riverside suppers by having his servants clear the table by casting the precious silver and gold dinnerware into the Tiber (indeed, nets were unfurled a foot or two beneath the water's surface to retrieve the valuable ware).

In the magnificent Loggia of Psyche on the ground floor, Giulio Romano and others created the frescoes from Raphael's designs. Raphael's lovely *Galatea* is in the adjacent room. On the floor above you can see the trompe-l'oeil effects in the aptly named Hall of Perspectives by Peruzzi. Agostino Chigi's bedroom, next door, was frescoed by Il Sodoma with the *Wedding of Alexander and Roxanne*, which is considered to be the artist's best work. The palace also houses the Gabinetto Nazionale delle Stampe, a treasure trove of old prints and drawings. ⊠ *Via della Lungara 230, Trastevere* ☎ *06/68027268* ⊕ *www.villafarnesina.it* 💳 *€12* ⊘ *Closed Sun.*

🍴 Restaurants

★ Antico Arco

$$$ | **MODERN ITALIAN** | Founded by three friends with a passion for wine and fine food, Antico Arco attracts diners from Rome and beyond with its refined culinary inventiveness. The location on top of the Janiculum Hill makes for a charming setting, and inside, the dining rooms are plush, modern spaces, with whitewashed brick walls, dark floors, and black velvet chairs. **Known for:** changing seasonal menu; molten chocolate soufflé cake; extensive wine cellar. 💲 *Average main: €35* ⊠ *Piazzale Aurelio 7, Trastevere* ☎ *06/5815274* ⊕ *anticoarco.it* ⊘ *Closed Tues.*

★ Da Enzo al 29

$ | **ROMAN** | In the quieter part of Trastevere, the family-run Da Enzo is everything you would imagine a classic Roman trattoria to be. There are just a few tables, but diners from around the world line up to eat here—a testament to the quality of the food. **Known for:** cacio e pepe (pasta with pecorino-cheese sauce and black pepper), carbonara, and other Roman classics; boisterous, authentic atmosphere; small space with long waits. 💲 *Average main: €14* ⊠ *Via dei Vascellari 29, Trastevere* ☎ *06/5812260* ⊕ *www.daenzoal29.com* ⊘ *Closed Sun. and 2 wks in Aug.*

Da Lucia

$ | **ROMAN** | **FAMILY** | There's no shortage of old-school trattorias in Trastevere, but this one has a strong following. Both locals and expats enjoy the brusque but "authentic" service and the hearty Roman fare; snag a table outside in warm weather for the true Roman experience of cobblestone-terrace dining. **Known for:** bombolotti (a tubular pasta) all'amatriciana; homemade gnocchi; involtini (beef rolls). 💲 *Average main: €14* ⊠ *Vicolo del Mattonato 2, Trastevere* ☎ *06/5803601* ⊘ *Closed Mon.–Wed. and Aug.*

Pizzeria Ai Marmi

$ | **PIZZA** | **FAMILY** | This place is packed pretty much every night with diners munching on crisp pizzas that come out of the wood-burning ovens at top speed. It's best not to go during peak dining hours, so go early or late if you don't want to wait. **Known for:** excellent wood-oven pizzas; fried starters such as supplì (breaded fried rice balls); open until midnight for a late-night bite. $ *Average main: €13* ✉ *Viale Trastevere 53, Trastevere* ☎ *06/5800919* ⊕ *www.facebook.com/aimarmi* ⊗ *Closed Wed. and 3 wks in Aug. No lunch.*

☕ Coffee and Quick Bites

★ Biscottificio Innocenti

$ | **ITALIAN** | **FAMILY** | The scent of cookies wafts out into the street as you approach this family-run bakery, where a small team makes sweet treats the old-school way in a massive oven bought in the 1960s. There are dozens of varieties of baked goods, mostly sweet but some savory. **Known for:** old-school family-run bakery; dozens of varieties of baked goods; brutti ma buoni ("ugly but good") hazelnut cookies. $ *Average main: €3* ✉ *Via della Luce 21, Trastevere* ☎ *06/5803926* ⊕ *www.facebook.com/BiscottificioInnocenti* ⊗ *Closed Sun. and 2 wks in Aug.*

Supplì Roma

$ | **ROMAN** | **FAMILY** | Trastevere's best supplì (Roman-style rice croquettes) have been served at this hole-in-the-wall takeout spot since 1979. At lunchtime, the line spills out onto the street with locals who've come for the namesake treats, as well as fried baccalà fillets and stuffed zucchini flowers. **Known for:** old-fashioned baked pizza with spicy marinara sauce; gnocchi on Thursday (the traditional day for it in Rome); classic fried risotto ball with ragù or cacio e pepe. $ *Average main: €6* ✉ *Via di San Francesco a Ripa 137, Trastevere* ☎ *06/5897110* ⊕ *www.suppliroma.it* ⊗ *Closed Sun. and 2 wks in Aug.*

Hotels

Casa di Santa Francesca Romana a Ponte Rotto

$$ | **HOTEL** | In the heart of Trastevere but tucked away from the hustle and bustle of the medieval quarter, this comfortable, affordable hotel in a former monastery is centered on a lovely green courtyard and still has a chapel off the corridor. **Pros:** rates can't be beat; triple rooms for small groups; free breakfast. **Cons:** a bit far from Metro, but there are tram and bus stops nearby; few amenities besides TV room and reading room; main door locks at midnight, requiring guests to ring the bell. $ *Rooms from: €140* ✉ *Via dei Vascellari 61, Trastevere* ☎ *06/5812125* ⊕ *www.sfromana.it* ⤴ *37 rooms* ⦿ *Free Breakfast.*

Hotel Santa Maria

$$$ | **HOTEL** | A Trastevere treasure with a pedigree going back four centuries, this ivy-covered, mansard-roofed, rosy-brick-red, erstwhile Renaissance-era convent—just steps away from the glorious Santa Maria in Trastevere church and a few blocks from the Tiber—has sweet and simple guest rooms: a mix of brick walls, "cotto" tile floors, oak furniture, and matching bedspreads and curtains. **Pros:** a quaint and pretty oasis in a central location; spacious rooms for groups; lovely rooftop terrace with views across the city. **Cons:** tricky to find; not the best value for money; church bells may wake light sleepers. $ *Rooms from: €250* ✉ *Vicolo del Piede 2, Trastevere* ☎ *06/5894626* ⊕ *www.hotelsantamariatrastevere.it* ⤴ *20 rooms* ⦿ *Free Breakfast.*

Hotel Trastevere

$$ | **HOTEL** | This hotel captures the villagelike charm of the Trastevere district and offers basic, clean, comfortable rooms. **Pros:** good rates for location; convenient to tram and bus; friendly staff. **Cons:** rooms are a little worn around the edges; few amenities; standard rooms

are quite small. $ *Rooms from: €180* ✉ *Via Luciano Manara 24/a, Trastevere* ☎ *06/5814713* ⊕ *www.hoteltrastevere. net* ↩ *14 rooms* ⦿ *Free Breakfast.*

Relais Le Clarisse

$$ | **B&B/INN** | Set within the former cloister grounds of the Santa Chiara order, with beautiful gardens, Le Clarisse makes you feel like a personal guest at a friend's villa, thanks to the comfortable size of the guest rooms and personalized service. **Pros:** spacious rooms with comfy beds; high-tech showers/tubs with good water pressure; complimentary high-speed Wi-Fi. **Cons:** this part of Trastevere can be noisy at night; check when booking as you may be put in neighboring building; no restaurant or bar. $ *Rooms from: €200* ✉ *Via Cardinale Merry del Val 20, Trastevere* ☎ *06/58334437* ⊕ *www. leclarissetrastevere.com* ↩ *17 rooms* ⦿ *Free Breakfast.*

 ## Nightlife

★ Freni e Frizioni

COCKTAIL BARS | This hipster hangout is great for a sunset aperitivo or for late-night socializing. Though the vibe is artsy and laid-back, the bartenders take their cocktails seriously—and have the awards to prove it. In warmer weather, the crowd overflows into the large terrazza overlooking the Tiber and the side streets of Trastevere. ✉ *Via del Politeama 4, Trastevere* ☎ *06/45497499* ⊕ *www. freniefrizioni.com.*

 ## Shopping

BOOKSTORES

Almost Corner Bookshop

BOOKS | Bursting at the seams with not an inch of space left on its shelves, this tiny little bookshop is a favorite meeting point for English speakers in Trastevere. Irish owner Dermot O'Connell goes out of his way to find what you're looking for, and if he doesn't have it in stock he'll make a special order for you. The shop carries everything from popular best sellers to translated Italian classics, as well as lots of good books about Rome. ✉ *Via del Moro 45, Trastevere* ☎ *06/5836942* ⊕ *www.facebook.com/ AlmostCornerBookshop.*

MARKETS

Porta Portese

MARKET | **FAMILY** | One of the biggest flea markets in Italy welcomes shoppers in droves every Sunday from 7 am to 2 pm. Treasure seekers and bargain hunters love scrounging around the hundreds of tents for new and vintage clothing and accessories, antique furniture, used books, and other odds 'n' ends. Bring your haggling skills, and cash (preferably small bills—it'll work in your favor when driving a bargain); many stallholders don't accept credit cards, and the nearest ATM is a hike. ✉ *Via Portuense and adjacent streets between Porta Portese and Via Ettore Rolli, Trastevere.*

Aventino and Testaccio

The Aventino district is somewhat rarefied, where some houses still have their own bell towers and private gardens are called "parks," without exaggeration. Like the emperors of old on the Palatine, the fortunate residents here look out over the Circus Maximus and the river, winding its way far below. Testaccio is perhaps the world's only district built on broken pots: the hill of the same name was born from discarded pottery used to store oil, wine, and other goods loaded from nearby Ripa, when Rome had a port and the Tiber was once a mighty river to an empire. It's quiet during the day, but on Saturday buzzes with the loud music from rows of discos and clubs.

Sights

★ Centrale Montemartini

ART MUSEUM | A decommissioned early-20th-century power plant is now this intriguing exhibition space for the overflow of ancient art from the Musei Capitolini collection. Getting here is half the fun. A 15-minute walk from the heart of Testaccio will lead you past walls covered in street art to the urban district of Ostiense. Head southwest and saunter under the train tracks passing buildings adorned with four-story-high murals until you reach the often-uncrowded Centrale Montemartini, where Roman sculptures and mosaics are set amid industrial machinery and pipes.

Unusually, the collection is organized by the area in which the ancient pieces were found. Highlights include the former boiler room filled with ancient marble statues that once decorated Rome's private villas, such as the beautiful *Esquiline Venus*, as well as a large mosaic of a hunting scene. ■TIP→ **A purchase of the Capitolini Card will allow entry into Musei Capitolini and Centrale Montemartini.** ⊠ *Via Ostiense, 106, Testaccio* ☎ *06/0608* ⊕ *www.centralemontemartini.org* 🎟 *€11.50; admission included with the purchase of the Capitolini Card (€14.50)* 🕐 *Closed Mon.* Ⓜ *Garbatella.*

★ Gran Priorato di Roma dell'Ordine di Malta

RELIGIOUS BUILDING | **FAMILY** | Although the line to peek through the keyhole of a nondescript green door in the Gran Priorato, the walled compound of the Knights of Malta, sometimes snakes around Piazza dei Cavalieri di Malta, the enchanting view is worth the wait. Far across the city, you'll see the dome of St. Peter's Basilica flawlessly framed by the keyhole and tidily trimmed hedges that lie just beyond the locked door. The priory and the square are the work of Giovanni Battista Piranesi, an 18th-century engraver who is more famous for etching Roman

views than for orchestrating them, but he fancied himself a bit of an architect and did not disappoint.

Founded in the Holy Land during the Crusades, the Knights of Malta is the world's oldest and most exclusive order of chivalry. The knights amassed huge tracts of land in the Middle East and were based on the Mediterranean island of Malta from 1530 until 1798, when Napoléon expelled them. In 1834, they established themselves in Rome, where ministering to the sick became their raison d'être. ■TIP→ **Private, guided tours of the Gran Priorato are usually offered on Friday morning, but you must prebook by email.** ⊠ *Via Santa Sabina and Via Porta Lavernale, Aventino* ⊕ *www.ordinedimaltaitalia.org/gran-priorato-di-roma* ✉ *visitorscentre@orderofmalta.int* 🎟 *From €5 per person (min. of 10 people), plus the cost of the required guide, €80 in Italian, €100 in any other language. If a group has already formed, then anyone may join for the regular entry fee* 🕐 *Villa closed Jul., Aug., and Dec.* ♿ *Reservations required* Ⓜ *Circo Massimo; Tram No. 3.*

★ Santa Maria in Cosmedin

CHURCH | **FAMILY** | One of Rome's oldest churches—built in the 6th century and restored in the late 19th century—is on the Piazza della Bocca della Verità, originally the location of the Forum Boarium, ancient Rome's cattle market and later the site of public executions. Although the church has a haunting interior and contains the flower-crowned skull of St. Valentine, who is celebrated every February 14th, it plays second fiddle to the renowned artifact installed out in its portico.

The Bocca della Verità (Mouth of Truth) is in reality nothing more than an ancient drain cover, unearthed during the Middle Ages. Legend has it, however, that the teeth will clamp down on a liar's hand if they dare to tell a fib while holding their fingers up to the fearsome mouth. Hordes of tourists line up to take the test

Sights ▼

1 Centrale Montemartini.............. **E8**
2 Gran Priorato di Roma
 dell'Ordine di Malta................ **E3**
3 Santa Maria in Cosmedin.......... **F2**
4 Terme di Caracalla................. **H4**

Restaurants ▼

1 Checchino dal 1887................ **D5**
2 Flavio al Velavevodetto **D5**
3 La Torricella **C5**
4 Marigold **E6**
5 Porto Fluviale...................... **E7**

Coffee and Quick Bites ▼

1 Trapizzino **D4**

Hotels ▼

1 Hotel San Anselmo **E4**

3

Rome AVENTINO AND TESTACCIO

KEY

1 Sights
1 Restaurants
1 Quick Bites
1 Hotels

0 — 1,000 feet

0 — 300 m

every day (kids especially get a kick out of it). ✉ *Piazza della Bocca della Verità 18, Aventino* ☎ *06/6787759* ⊕ *www.cosmedin.org* Ⓜ *Circo Massimo.*

Terme di Caracalla (*Baths of Caracalla*)
RUINS | FAMILY | The Terme di Caracalla are some of Rome's most massive—yet least visited—ruins. Begun in AD 206 by the emperor Septimius Severus and completed by his son, Caracalla, the 28-acre complex could accommodate 1,600 bathers at a time. Along with an Olympic-size swimming pool and baths, the complex also had two gyms, a library, and gardens. The impressive baths depended on slave labor, particularly the unseen stokers who toiled in subterranean rooms to keep the fires roaring in order to heat the water.

Rather than a simple dip in a tub, Romans turned "bathing" into one of the most lavish leisure activities imaginable. A bath began in the sudatoria, a series of small rooms resembling saunas, which then led to the caldarium, a circular room that was humid rather than simply hot. Here a strigil, or scraper, was used to get the dirt off the skin. Next stop: the warm(-ish) tepidarium, which helped start the cool-down process. Finally, it ended with a splash around the frigidarium, a chilly swimming pool.

Although some black-and-white mosaic fragments remain, most of the opulent mosaics, frescoes, and sculptures have found their way into Rome's museums. Nevertheless, the towering walls and sheer size of the ruins give one of the best glimpses into ancient Rome's ambitions. A new portable video guide allows a glimpse of the past grandeur, with images and audio that describes how the ruins appeared centuries ago. If you're here in summer, don't miss the chance to catch an open-air opera or ballet in the baths, put on by the Teatro dell'Opera di Roma. ✉ *Viale delle Terme di Caracalla 52, Aventino* ☎ *06/39967702* ⊕ *www.coopculture.it* 🎟 *€8 (includes Villa dei Quintili and Tomba di Cecilia Metella);* *€17 includes video guide* ⊙ *Closed Mon.* Ⓜ *Circo Massimo.*

Restaurants

Checchino dal 1887
$$$ | ROMAN | Literally carved into the side of a hill made up of ancient shards of amphorae, this upscale, family-run establishment has an exceptional wine cellar and stellar contemporary cocktails that incorporate traditional local ingredients. One of the first restaurants to open near Testaccio's (now long-closed) slaughterhouse, it still serves classic offal dishes—though the white-jacketed waiters are happy to suggest other options. **Known for:** old-school Roman cooking; old-school Roman waiters; coda alla vaccinara (Roman-style oxtail). ⑤ *Average main: €25* ✉ *Via di Monte Testaccio 30, Testaccio* ☎ *06/5743816* ⊕ *www.checchino-dal-1887.com* ⊙ *Closed Mon. and Tues., Aug., and 2 wks in Jan.* Ⓜ *Piramide.*

★ Flavio al Velavevodetto
$$ | ROMAN | It's everything you're looking for in a true Roman eating experience: authentic, in a historic setting, and filled with Italians eating good food at good prices. In this very *romani di Roma* (Rome of the Romans) neighborhood, surrounded by discos and bars, you can enjoy classic local dishes, from vegetable antipasto to cacio e pepe (said to be the best version in the city) and lamb chops. **Known for:** authentic Roman atmosphere and food; outdoor covered terrace in summer; polpette di bollito (fried breaded meatballs). ⑤ *Average main: €16* ✉ *Via di Monte Testaccio 97, Testaccio* ☎ *06/5744194* ⊕ *www.ristorantevelavevodetto.it* Ⓜ *Piramide.*

La Torricella
$$ | SEAFOOD | FAMILY | This family-run institution has been serving seafood in the working-class Testaccio neighborhood for more than 40 years, and if you visit

the local market early enough you might spot the owner selecting the freshest fish, which mainly arrives from Gaeta, south of Rome. The menu changes every day, but look for house specialties like *paccheri* (a very large, tubular pasta) with *totani* (baby calamari), pasta with *telline* (small clams), or the wondrously simple spaghetti with lobster. **Known for:** fresh, local seafood; relaxed but refined setting with outdoor seating; polpette di pesce al sugo (fish balls in tomato sauce). ⑤ *Average main: €18* ⊠ *Via Evangelista Torricelli 2/12, Testaccio* ☎ *06/5746311* ⊕ *www.la-torricella.com* ⏱ *Closed Mon.* Ⓜ *Piramide.*

★ Marigold

$ | **SCANDINAVIAN** | Run by a Danish-Italian duo, this hip restaurant has a Scandinavian-meets-Roman design and menu. It draws a young, international crowd who come for the sourdough, cinnamon buns, and veggie-forward dishes. **Known for:** sourdough breads and other baked goods; specialty coffee; minimalist Italian design. ⑤ *Average main: €13* ⊠ *Via Giovanni da Empoli, 37, Testaccio* ☎ *06/87725679* ⊕ *marigoldroma.com* ⏱ *Closed Mon. and Tues., 3 wks in Aug., and 2 wks in Dec. No dinner* Ⓜ *Ostiense.*

Porto Fluviale

$ | **ITALIAN** | Set in a structure so massive that it takes up the better part of a block on a street that's gone from gritty clubland to popular nightspot, Porto Fluviale is a bar, café, pizzeria, lunch buffet, and lively evening restaurant with a sprawling design that honors the area's industrial past. The menu is all-encompassing, too, with dishes that highlight cuisine from all over Italy. **Known for:** good cocktails; pizza from wood-burning oven; cicheti (Venetian-style tapas). ⑤ *Average main: €13* ⊠ *Via del Porto Fluviale 22, Testaccio* ☎ *06/5743199* ⊕ *www.portofluviale.com* Ⓜ *Piramide.*

Coffee and Quick Bites

Trapizzino

$ | **ROMAN** | **FAMILY** | Stefano Callegari is one of Rome's most famous pizza makers, but at Trapizzino he's doing something a bit different. The name of the restaurant is derived from the Italian words for sandwich (*tramezzino*) and pizza, and the result is something like an upscale pizza pocket, stuffed on the spot with local specialties like chicken alla cacciatore, or *trippa* (tripe), or roast pumpkin, pecorino, and almonds. **Known for:** casual setting, with seating available next door; eggplant parmigiana and meatball sandwiches; Italian craft beer. ⑤ *Average main: €5* ⊠ *Via Giovanni Branca 88, Testaccio* ☎ *06/43419624* ⊕ *www.trapizzino.it* ⏱ *Closed 1 wk in Aug.* Ⓜ *Piramide.*

Hotels

Hotel San Anselmo

$$$ | **HOTEL** | Set in a *molto* charming garden atop the Aventine Hill, this refurbished 19th-century villa is a romantic retreat. **Pros:** free Wi-Fi; historic building with artful interior; garden where you can enjoy breakfast. **Cons:** some rooms are quite small; limited public transportation; no full restaurant. ⑤ *Rooms from: €220* ⊠ *Piazza San Anselmo 2, Aventino* ☎ *06/570057* ⊕ *www.aventinohotels.com/sananselmo* ⇆ *34 rooms* ⑩ *Free Breakfast* Ⓜ *Circo Massimo.*

♈ Nightlife

★ Tram Depot

COCKTAIL BARS | A coffee stand by day and cocktail bar by night, this outdoor establishment began life as a city tram car back in 1903. Now the historic carriage has been converted to a kiosk permanently stationed on a park corner with retro tables and garden seating. A trendy crowd descends at sunset for an evening spritz, and seats are at a premium until the wee hours of the morning.

Since it is entirely outside, Tram Depot is mainly open in the warmer months of the year (April through November); but weather permitting, the kiosk stays open on the weekends year round. ✉ *Via Marmorata 13, Testaccio* ☎ *380/6455154* ⊕ *www.facebook.com/TramDepotOfficial* Ⓜ *Piramide.*

Shopping

★ Volpetti

FOOD | A Roman institution for 50 years, Volpetti sells excellent cured meats and salami from its buzzing deli counter. The food selection also includes genuine buffalo-milk mozzarella, fresh pasta, Roman pecorino, olive oils, balsamic vinegars, and fresh bread. The rich aromas and flavors are captivating from the moment you enter the store—pull up a high stool and order a sampling platter with a glass of wine. It's also a great place for assembling gift baskets, and offers worldwide shipping. ✉ *Via Marmorata 47, Testaccio* ☎ *375/5130898* ⊕ *www.volpetti.com* Ⓜ *Piramide.*

Esquilino and Via Appia Antica

Esquilino, covering Rome's most sprawling hill—the Esquiline—lies at the edge of the tourist maps, near the Termini station. Today, culturally diverse inhabitants of different nationalities live and work in the area. It's not the cobblestone-street atmosphere that most think of when they think of Rome. Far south lies catacomb country—the haunts of the fabled underground graves of Rome's earliest Christians, arrayed to either side of the Queen of Roads, the Via Appia Antica (Appian Way). Strewn with classical ruins and dotted with grazing sheep, the road stirs images of chariots and legionnaires returning from imperial conquests. It was completed in 312 BC by Appius Claudius,

who laid it out to connect Rome with settlements in the south, in the direction of Naples. Though time and vandals have taken their toll on the ancient relics along the road, the catacombs remain to cast their spirit-warm spell. Today, the dark, gloomy catacombs contrast strongly with the Appia Antica's fresh air, verdant meadows, and evocative classical ruins.

GETTING HERE AND AROUND

The Esquilino Hill can be reached via the Vittorio Emanuele subway station, one stop from Termini station. Bus No. 150F runs from Piazza del Popolo to Esquilino.

The initial stretch of the Via Appia Antica is not pedestrian-friendly—there is fast, heavy traffic and no sidewalk all the way from Porta San Sebastiano to the Catacombe di San Callisto. To reach the catacombs, take Bus No. 218 from San Giovanni in Laterano. Alternatively, take Metro Line A to Colli Albani and then Bus No. 660 to the Tomba di Cecilia Metella.

◉ Sights

Catacombe di San Callisto (*Catacombs of St. Calixtus*)

CEMETERY | Burial place of several very early popes, this is Rome's oldest and best-preserved underground cemetery. One of the (English-speaking) friars who acts as custodian of the catacomb will guide you through its crypts and galleries, some adorned with early Christian frescoes. Watch out for wrong turns: this catacomb is five stories deep! ∎**TIP→ This site has a large parking area and is favored by big groups; it can get busy.** ✉ *Via Appia Antica 110, Via Appia Antica* ☎ *06/5130151* ⊕ *www.catacombe-sancallisto.it* 🎫 *€10* 🕙 *Closed Wed. and mid-Jan.–Feb.*

★ Catacombe di San Sebastiano
(*Catacombs of St. Sebastian*)
CEMETERY | The 4th-century church at this site was named after the saint who was buried in its catacomb, which burrows underground on four different levels. This

Sights ▼

1 Catacombe
di San
Callisto **B4**

2 Catacombe
di San
Sebastiano . **B4**

3 Mausoleo
di Cecilia
Metella **B5**

4 Parco degli
Acquedotti.. **D5**

5 Porta
Maggiore ... **B2**

Restaurants ▼

1 Eufrosino
Osteria **C3**

2 L'
Archeologia . **B4**

**Coffee and
Quick Bites** ▼

1 Panella **A1**

KEY

1 Sights

1 Restaurants

1 Quick Bites

---

was the only early Christian cemetery to remain accessible during the Middle Ages, and it was from here that the term "catacomb" is derived—it's in a spot where the road dips into a hollow, known to the Romans as a *catacumba* (Greek for "near the hollow"). ✉ *Via Appia Antica 136, Via Appia Antica* ☎ *06/7850350* ⊕ *www. catacombe.org* 🎟 *€10* ⊘ *Closed Dec.*

Mausoleo di Cecilia Metella

CEMETERY | For centuries, sightseers have flocked to this famous landmark, one of the most complete surviving tombs of ancient Rome. One of the many round mausoleums that once lined the Appian Way, this tomb is a smaller version of the Mausoleum of Augustus, but impressive nonetheless. It was the burial place of a Roman noblewoman: the wife of the son of Crassus, who was one of Julius Caesar's rivals and known as the richest man

in the Roman Empire (infamously entering the English language as "crass").

The original decoration includes a frieze of bulls' skulls near the top. The travertine stone walls were made higher, and the medieval-style crenellations were added when the tomb was transformed into a fortress by the Caetani family in the 14th century. An adjacent chamber houses a small museum with exhibits on the area's geological phases. Entrance to this site also includes access to the splendid Villa dei Quintili. ✉ *Via Appia Antica 161, Via Appia Antica* ☎ *06/7886254* ⊕ *www. parcoarcheologicoappiaantica.it* 🎟 *€8, includes all the sites in the Parco dell'Appia Antica (Villa dei Quintili, Antiquarium di Lucrezia Romana, Complesso di Capo di Bove, Tombe della Via Latina, and the Villa dei Setti Bassi)* ⊘ *Closed Mon.*

158

★ Parco degli Acquedotti

CITY PARK | **FAMILY** | This massive park, technically part of the Parco dell'Appia Antica, was named for the six remaining aqueducts that formed part of the famously elaborate system that carried water to ancient Rome. The park has some serious film cred: it was featured in the opening scene of *La Dolce Vita* and in a rather memorable scene depicting some avant-garde performance art in *La Grande Bellezza*. On weekends, it's a popular place for locals to picnic, exercise, and generally enjoy a day out with their kids or dogs. ⊠ *Via Lemonia 221, Via Appia Antica* ⊕ *www.parcodegliacquedotti.it* ⊠ *Free* Ⓜ *Giulio Agricola, Subaugusta.*

Porta Maggiore *(Great Gate)*

RUINS | The massive, 1st-century-AD arch was built as part of the original Aqua Claudia and then incorporated into the walls hurriedly erected in the late 3rd century as Rome's fortunes began to decline. The great arch of the aqueduct subsequently became a *porta* (city gate) and gives an idea of the grand scale of ancient Roman public works. On the Piazzale Labicano side, to the east, is the curious Baker's Tomb, erected in the 1st century BC by a prosperous baker (predating both the aqueduct and the city walls); it's shaped like an oven to signal the deceased's trade. The site is now in the middle of a public transport node and is close to Rome's first tram depot (going back to 1889). ⊠ *Piazza di Porta Maggiore, Esquilino* Ⓜ *Tram No. 5, 14, or 19.*

🍴 Restaurants

Eufrosino Osteria

$ | **ITALIAN** | **FAMILY** | At this welcoming osteria run by three young owners, wood-paneled walls, terrazzo floors, and green pendant lamps evoke 1970s nostalgia. The menu adheres to the Roman tradition, with homestyle dishes like chicken cacciatora, squid with peas, and the quartet of Roman pastas. **Known for:**

old school Roman dishes; slow-food principles; neighboring pizzeria. Ⓢ *Average main: €14* ⊠ *Via di Tor Pignattara, 188, Via Appia Antica* ☎ *348/5883932* ⊕ *www. facebook.com/EufrosinoRoma* ⊗ *Closed Mon. and Tues. No lunch weekdays* Ⓜ *Malatesta, Porta Furba.*

L'Archeologia

$$$ | **ITALIAN** | In this circa-1804 farmhouse you can dine beside the fireplace in cool weather or in the garden under age-old vines in summer. Specialties include risotto with blue cheese and chestnuts, rack of lamb with Jerusalem artichoke, and fresh seafood. **Known for:** ancient wine cellar La Cantina; hand-painted frescoes; romantic setting. Ⓢ *Average main: €28* ⊠ *Via Appia Antica 139, Via Appia Antica* ☎ *06/7880494* ⊕ *www.larcheologia.it* ⊗ *Closed Tues. No lunch weekdays.*

☕ Coffee and Quick Bites

Panella

$ | **BAKERY** | **FAMILY** | Opened in 1929, this bakery sells both sweet and savory items, including more than 70 types of bread. Line up for the pizza *al taglio* (by the slice) at lunchtime, or sit down at one of the outdoor tables for a cappuccino and cornetto or an aperitivo replete with mini sandwiches made on homemade buns. **Known for:** one of Rome's best bakeries; crostata, tartlets, and other sweet treats; espresso with zabaione. Ⓢ *Average main: €10* ⊠ *Via Merulana 54, Esquilino* ☎ *06/4872435* ⊕ *www.panellaroma.com* Ⓜ *Vittorio Emanuele.*

Chapter 4

SIDE TRIPS
FROM ROME

4

Updated by
Natalie Kennedy

👁 Sights	🍴 Restaurants	🛏 Hotels	🛍 Shopping	🍸 Nightlife
★★★★☆	★★★☆☆	★☆☆☆☆	★☆☆☆☆	★☆☆☆☆

WELCOME TO SIDE TRIPS FROM ROME

TOP REASONS TO GO

★ **Ostia Antica:** This excavated ancient Roman port city is brimming with ruins, mosaics, and structures, which convey a picture of everyday life in the empire.

★ **Tivoli's Villa d'Este:** Hundreds of fountains cascading and shooting skyward (one even plays music on organ pipes) will delight you at this spectacular garden.

★ **Castelli Romani:** Enjoy a raucous Roman lunch and an escape to the ancient hilltop wine towns on the city's doorstep.

★ **Viterbo:** This town may be modern, but it has a Gothic papal palace, a Romanesque cathedral, and the magical medieval quarter of San Pellegrino. It's also the gateway to the *terme* (hot springs) closest to Rome.

★ **Bizarre and beautiful gardens:** The 16th-century proto-Disneyland Parco dei Mostri (Monster Park) is famed for its fantastic sculptures; the stately Villa Lante, a few miles away, is a postcard-perfect Renaissance garden of swirling, manicured hedges.

1 Viterbo. The capital of Tuscia and a 13th-century time capsule with papal connections.

2 Bagnaia. The site of a 16th-century cardinal's summer home with an elaborate garden.

3 Caprarola. A hilltop village that is home to the huge Palazzo Farnese.

4 Bomarzo. The town with the eccentric Monster Park forest.

5 Ostia Antica. An ancient Roman port, now an archaeological site.

6 Tivoli. A fitting setting for the regal Villa Adriana and the unforgettable Villa d'Este, a park filled with gorgeous fountains.

7 Palestrina. Originally an ancient pagan sanctuary and home to the father of musical counterpoint.

8 Frascati. A historic getaway amid the Alban Hills and famed for its wine.

9 Castel Gandolfo. A lakeside town otherwise known as the pope's summer retreat.

10 Ariccia. Home to the grand Palazzo Chigi.

11 Nemi. A pretty hamlet, with an eagle's-nest perch above a volcanic lake.

Less well known than neighboring Tuscany, Lazio, the region that encompasses Rome, is often bypassed by foreign visitors. This is a pity, since the area, which stretches from the Apennine Mountains to the Mediterranean, has dozens of fascinating towns and villages, as well as scenic lakes, enchanting gardens, national parks, and forests.

A trip outside Rome introduces you to a more intimate aspect of Italy, where local customs and feast days are still enthusiastically observed, and local gastronomic specialties take precedence on restaurant menus. Despite proximity to the capital and the increased commuter traffic congestion of today, each of the towns here has managed to preserve its unique character.

Ostia Antica, ancient Rome's seaport, is one of the region's top attractions—it rivals Pompeii in the quality of its preservation, and it easily outshines the Roman Forum thanks to its beautiful setting. Emperors, cardinals, and popes have long escaped to verdant retreats in Tivoli, Viterbo, and the Alban Hills, and their amazing villas, palaces, and gardens add to nature's allure.

So if the nonstop Vespa traffic and long lines at the Colosseum start to wear on you, do as the Romans do: spend a day out of town. There's plenty to explore and experience.

MAJOR REGIONS

Tuscia. Tuscia (the modern name for the Etruscan domain of Etruria) is a region of dramatic beauty punctuated by deep, rocky gorges and thickly forested hills, with dappled light falling on wooded paths. This has been a preferred locale for the retreats of wealthy Romans for ages, a place where they could build grand villas and indulge their sometimes-eccentric gardening tastes.

The provincial capital, Viterbo, which overshadowed Rome as a center of papal power for a time during the Middle Ages, lies in the heart of Tuscia. The farmland east of Viterbo conceals small quarries of the dark, volcanic *peperino* stone, which shows up in the walls of many buildings here. Lake Bolsena lies in an extinct volcano, and the sulfur springs still bubbling up in the modern spas were once used by the ancient Romans. Bagnaia and Caprarola are home to palaces and gardens; the garden statuary at Bomarzo is in a league of its own—somewhere between the beautiful and the bizarre.

Although the ideal way to explore this region is by car, from Rome you can reach Viterbo by train and then get to Bagnaia by local bus. If you opt to travel by train or bus, however, check schedules carefully; you may have to allow for an overnight if you want to do a round of the region's sights.

Tivoli and Palestrina. Tivoli is a five-star draw, its main attractions being its two villas. There's an ancient one in which Hadrian reproduced the most beautiful monuments in the then-known world, and a Renaissance one, in which Cardinal Ippolito d'Este created a water-filled wonderland. Unfortunately, the Via Tiburtina from Rome to Tivoli passes through miles of industrial areas with chaotic traffic, so whether you are driving or taking the bus, follow the A24 motorway to avoid it. Or take the train, which offers a slightly more scenic journey.

You'll know you're close to Tivoli when you see vast quarries of travertine marble and smell the sulfurous vapors of the little spa, Bagni di Tivoli. Both sites are outdoors and entail walking. With a car, you can continue your loop through the mountains east of Rome, taking in the ancient pagan sanctuary at Palestrina, with its ancient Roman treasures housed in a museum that is spectacularly set on the slopes of Mt. Ginestro.

The Castelli Romani. These *castelli* aren't really castles, as their name would seem to imply. Rather, they're little towns on the slopes of the Alban Hills just to the southeast of Rome. And the Alban Hills aren't really hills, but extinct volcanoes. There were castles here in the Middle Ages, however, when each of these towns, fiefs of rival Roman lords, had its own fortress to defend it.

Some centuries later, the area was given over to villas and retreats, notably the pope's summer residence at Castel Gandolfo and the 17th- and 18th-century villas that transformed Frascati into the Beverly Hills of Rome. Arrayed around the rim of an extinct volcano that encloses two crater lakes, the string of picturesque towns of the Castelli Romani are surrounded by vineyards, olive groves, and chestnut woods—no wonder overheated Romans have always loved to escape here.

In addition to their lovely natural settings, the Castelli have also been renowned for their wine since the ancient Roman times. In the narrow, medieval alleyways of the oldest parts of the various villages, you can still find old-fashioned taverns where the locals sit on wooden benches, quaffing the golden nectar straight from the barrel.

Traveling around the countryside, you can also pop into some of the local vineyards for tastings. Exclusive local gastronomic specialties include the bread of Genzano, baked in traditional wood-fired ovens; the *porchetta* (roast suckling pig) of Ariccia; and the *pupazza* biscuits of Frascati, shaped like women or mermaids with three or more breasts (an allusion to ancient fertility goddesses).

Each town has its own feasts and saints' days, celebrated with costumed processions and colorful events. Some are quite spectacular, like the annual Marino Wine Festival in October, when the town's fountains flow with wine; or the Flower Festival of Genzano in June, when an entire street is carpeted with millions of flower petals, arranged in elaborate patterns.

Planning

Getting Here and Around

There's reliable public transit from Rome to Ostia Antica, Frascati, Tivoli, and Viterbo. Castel Gandolfo is also reachable by train—so long as you don't mind a short uphill walk from the station. COTRAL is the regional bus company outside of Rome, but timetables can be limited. For other destinations, having a car is a big advantage—going by bus or Trenitalia can add hours to your trip, and the routes and schedules are often puzzling.

CONTACTS COTRAL. ⊠ *Via Bernardino Alimena 105* ☎ *800/174471* ⊕ *www. cotralspa.it.* **Trenitalia.** (*Italian National Railway System*) ☎ *199/892021, 06/3000* ⊕ *www.trenitalia.com.*

Making the Most of Your Time

Ostia Antica is in many ways an ideal day trip from Rome: it's fascinating, it's not far from the city, it's reachable by public transit, and it takes about half a day to do. Villa d'Este and Villa Adriana in Tivoli also make for a manageable, though fuller, day trip. There's so much to see at these two sights alone, but also be sure to visit Tivoli's picturesque gorge, which is strikingly crowned by an ancient Roman temple to Vesta (which is now a part of the incomparable outdoor terrace at the famed Sibilla restaurant). Other destinations can be visited in a day, but you'll get more out of them if you stay the night.

One classic five-day itinerary that takes in the area's grand villas, ancient ruins, and pretty villages begins with Ostia Antica, the excavated port town of ancient Rome. You can then head north to explore Viterbo's medieval streets on Day 2. On Day 3, take in the hot springs or the gardens of Bomarzo, Bagnaia, and Caprarola. For Day 4, head to Tivoli's delights. Then, on Day 5, take a relaxing trip to the Castelli Romani, where Frascati wine is produced. Admire the sparkling volcanic lakes, visit quiet museums, find a spot at a family-run local restaurant, and explore the narrow streets of these small hill towns.

Hotels

Former aristocratic villas with frescoed ceilings, *agriturismi* farmhouses, luxury spas at natural hotsprings, and cozy bed-and-breakfasts in the village center are just a few of the lodging options here. You won't find much in the way of major chain hotels, though.

Restaurants

You certainly won't go hungry while exploring the Roman countryside. Whether you choose a five-star establishment or a simple eatery, you can be sure of a fresh, clean tablecloth and friendly, attentive service. Odds are that the ingredients will come from the farmer down the road, and the owner will be in the kitchen, personally preparing the time-honored dishes that have made Italian cuisine so celebrated around the world.

⇨ *Hotel and restaurant reviews have been shortened. For full information, visit Fodors.com. Prices in the lodging reviews are the lowest cost of a standard double room in high season. Prices in the dining reviews are the average cost of a main course at dinner, or, if dinner is not served, at lunch.*

What It Costs in Euros			
$	$$	$$$	$$$$
HOTELS			
under €125	€125–€200	€201–€300	over €300
RESTAURANTS			
under €15	€15–€24	€25–€35	over €35

Visitor Information

City information kiosks, around Rome's main squares and at tourist sights, can give you information about the Castelli Romani, Ostia Antica, and Tivoli. The Tuscia area is served by the central tourist office in Viterbo.

CONTACT Visit Lazio. ⊕ *www.visitlazio. com.*

Viterbo

104 km (64 miles) northwest of Rome.

Viterbo is a regional commercial center, and much of the modern city is loud and industrial. But the city's charming medieval core still sits within 12th-century walls and reflects a time when it became the seat of the papal court.

Old buildings and their characteristic exterior staircases made of peperino, the deep-gray local stone, are contrasted here and there with the golden tufa rock of walls and towers. Window boxes are bright with geraniums. Artisan shops and bottegas still operate in settings that have remained practically unchanged over the centuries. The Papal Palace and the cathedral, which sit at the heart of the oldest part of the city, enhance the effect.

Viterbo is also a spa center. Just outside town are renowned natural hot springs that have been frequented by popes and mere mortals alike since the Middle Ages.

GETTING HERE AND AROUND

Direct train service from Rome's Stazione Trastevere takes one hour and 40 minutes. Note that many commuters live in towns along the line, so stops can be more frequent, and travel times longer, during peak transit times. Viturbo's *centro storico* (historic center) is a short walk from the train station.

By car, take either the old Roman consular road, the Via Cassia, which passes near Caprarola, or, the faster A1 toll highway to the Orte exit and then the 204 highway, with a detour to Bomarzo. On good days, the drive is just over an hour and 30 minutes but the trip can take a couple of hours or more, depending on traffic.

VISITOR INFORMATION
CONTACT Viterbo Tourism Office.
⊠ *Piazza Martiri D'Ungheria, Viterbo* ☎ *0761/226427* ⊕ *www.promotuscia.it.*

Sights

Cattedrale di San Lorenzo
CHURCH | Viterbo's Romanesque cathedral was built over the ruins of the ancient Roman Temple of Hercules. During World War II, the roof and the vault of the central nave were destroyed, and you can still see the mark the shrapnel left on the columns closest to the pulpit. Subsequently, the church was rebuilt to reflect its medieval design, and it still has many original details, including a beautiful Cosmati floor that dates from the 13th century.

Three popes are buried here, including Pope Alexander IV (1254–61), whose body was hidden so well by the canons, out of fear that it would be desecrated, that it has never been found. The adjoining Museo del Colle del Duomo has a collection of 18th-century reliquaries, Etruscan sarcophagi, and a painting of the Crucifixion that has been attributed to Michelangelo. The ticket to the museum also grants you entrance to the Palazzo Papale, located on the same square. ⊠ *Piazza San Lorenzo, Viterbo* ☎ *320/7911328* ⊕ *www.archeoares.it* 🎟 *€10, includes tour of Cattedrale di San Lorenzo, Palazzo dei Papi, and Museo del Colle del Duomo* ☉ *Closed Tues. during Mar.–Nov.*

Palazzo dei Papi (*Papal Palace*)
CASTLE/PALACE | This Gothic palace was built in the 13th century as a residence for popes looking to get away from the

city. At the time, Rome was notoriously ridden with malaria and the plague, not to mention rampaging factions of rival barons. In 1271 the palace was the scene of a novel type of rebellion. A conclave held that year to elect a new pope dragged on for months. The people of Viterbo were exasperated by the delay, especially as custom decreed that they had to provide for the cardinals' board and lodging for the duration of the conclave. To speed up the deliberations, the townspeople tore the roof off the great hall where the cardinals were meeting, and put them on bread and water. A new pope—Gregory X—was elected in short order.

Today, you can visit the great hall, step out on the pretty loggia, and admire the original frescoes in the small adjoining room. ■TIP→ **An audio guided tour is free with the purchase of a ticket and lasts 45 minutes, starting from Museo del Colle del Duomo.** ⊠ *Piazza San Lorenzo, Viterbo* ☎ *393/0916060* ⊕ *www.archeoares.it* 🎟 *€10, includes tour of Cattedrale di San Lorenzo, Palazzo dei Papi, and Museo del Colle del Duomo* ☉ *Closed Tues. during Mar.–Nov.*

San Pellegrino
HISTORIC DISTRICT | One of the best-preserved medieval districts in Italy, San Pellegrino has charming vistas of arches, vaults, towers, exterior staircases, worn wooden doors on great iron hinges, and tiny hanging gardens. You pass many antiques shops and craft workshops, as well as numerous restaurants, as you explore the little squares and byways. The Fontana Grande in the piazza of the same name is the largest and most extravagant of Viterbo's Gothic fountains. ⊠ *Via San Pellegrino, near Palazzo dei Papi and Cattedrale di San Lorenzo, Viterbo.*

★ Terme dei Papi
HOT SPRING | Viterbo has been a spa town for centuries, and this excellent complex just a few miles outside the town walls continues the tradition, providing health and beauty treatments with an Etruscan

twist: try a facial with local volcanic mud or a steam bath in an ancient cave. The main draw, however, is the 21,000-square-foot outdoor limestone pool, into which Viterbo's famous 59°C (138°F) mineral water pours—and gives a jolt with its sulfurous odor.

You can rent floats and deck chairs, but you'll need your own bathrobe and towel unless you're staying the night at the spa hotel. Day passes tend to sell out but can be booked online up to five days ahead of your visit. ⊠ *Strada Bagni 12, 5 km (3 miles) west of town center, Viterbo* ☎ *0761/3501* ⊕ *termedeipapi.it* ⊠ *Pool €18 weekdays, €25 weekends, €30 on holidays* ☙ *Closed Tues.*

Restaurants

★ Osteria del Vecchio Orologio

$ | **ITALIAN** | Tucked on a side street off the medieval Piazza delle Erbe, the Osteria del Vecchio Orologio offers top-quality Tuscia specialties like wild boar ragu and local lake fish in a warm and informal atmosphere. Overflow seating for this popular eatery can be found at the cozy wine bar two doors down. **Known for:** cute, cupboard-lined walls; local ingredients; extensive wine list. ⑤ *Average main: €14* ⊠ *Via Orologio Vecchio 25, Viterbo* ☎ *335/337754* ⊕ *www.alvecchioorologio.it* ☙ *Closed Tues. No lunch Mon. or Wed.–Fri.*

Taverna Etrusca

$$ | **ITALIAN** | **FAMILY** | Located between the heart of San Pellegrino and Porta Romana, this friendly trattoria is known for its excellent home cooking and pizza. Be sure to admire the Etruscan-inspired decorations and check out the dessert—all the gelato is made on-site. **Known for:** homemade pasta alla viterbese (spicy red sauce with fennel); tagliolini (ribbon pasta) with lemon; great gelato. ⑤ *Average main: €15* ⊠ *Via Annio 8, Viterbo* ☎ *347/8516619* ⊕ *www.tavernaetrusca.it* ☙ *Closed Sun.*

Tre Re

$$ | **ITALIAN** | Viterbo's oldest restaurant—and one of the most ancient in Italy—has been operating in the centro storico since 1622. The small, wood-paneled dining room, chummily packed with tables, was a favorite haunt of movie director Federico Fellini and, before that, of British and American soldiers during World War II. **Known for:** traditional local dishes; roasted suckling pig; locals touch the historic Tre Re (Three Kings) sign for luck. ⑤ *Average main: €15* ⊠ *Via Macel Gattesco 3, Viterbo* ☎ *0761/304619* ⊕ *www.ristorante-trere.com* ☙ *Closed Thurs.*

Hotels

Palazzo Ubertini Urban Suites

$$ | **HOTEL** | Set in a historic building on the edge of Viterbo's medieval district, Palazzo Ubertini has converted the stately space into ten bright, modern rooms with small kitchenettes. **Pros:** welcome box with local food products for self-catering breakfast; elegant modern design; options for self check-in and check-out. **Cons:** no on-site restaurant; reception only open 8 am–8 pm; location in limited traffic zone complicates parking. ⑤ *Rooms from: €170* ⊠ *Via Chigi, 7, Viterbo* ☎ *07/611871137* ⊕ *www.palazzoubertini.eu* ⇆ *10 rooms* ⟡ *No Meals.*

Bagnaia

5 km (3 miles) east of Viterbo.

The tranquil village of Bagnaia is the site of the 16th-century cardinal Alessandro Montalto's summer retreat, which is quite an extravaganza.

GETTING HERE AND AROUND

Local buses run here from nearby Viterbo. By train, the stop here is 10 minutes beyond that for Viterbo stop—few local trains actually do stop, though, so check beforehand. If you prefer to drive, take the A1 to the exit for Orte and follow signs for Bagnaia. There is free parking across the bridge from the main square, but competition for a spot can be high on the weekends.

Sights

Villa Lante

CASTLE/PALACE | FAMILY | The main draw of the sweet but underwhelming village of Bagnaia is the hillside garden and park that surround the two small, identical residences. They were both built in the 16th century but by different owners and more than 30 years apart. The first belonged to Cardinal Gianfrancesco Gambara. Cardinal Alessandro Montalto built the second and commissioned the virtuoso architect Giacomo Barozzi (circa 1507–73)—who was known as Vignola and who later worked with Michelangelo on St. Peter's—to design a stunning garden filled with grottoes, fountains, and immaculately manicured hedges.

An adjacent untamed park contrasts with the symmetry of the formal gardens, where the lowest terrace has a centerpiece fountain fed by water channeled down the hillside. On another terrace, water runs through a groove carved in the long stone table where the cardinal entertained his friends, chilling wine in the running water. It's just one of the whimsical water features that were devised for the cardinal. ⊠ *Via Jacopo Barozzi 71, Bagnaia* ☎ *07/61288008* ⊕ *direzioneregionalemuseilazio.cultura.gov.it* 🖅 *€8* 𝄇 *Closed Mon.*

Caprarola

21 km (13 miles) southeast of Bagnaia, 19 km (12 miles) southeast of Viterbo.

The wealthy and powerful Farnese family took over this sleepy village in the 1500s and had the architect Vignola design a huge palace and gardens to rival the great residences of Rome. Farnese also rearranged the little town of Caprarola to enhance the palazzo's setting, which sits on top of a hill overlooking the town.

GETTING HERE AND AROUND
Caprarola is served by COTRAL bus, leaving from Rome's Saxa Rubra Station on the Roma Nord suburban railway line. By car from the city, take the Via Cassia to Civita Castellana, and follow the fork towards Ronciglione then onto to Caprarola.

Sights

★ Palazzo Farnese

CASTLE/PALACE | When Cardinal Alessandro Farnese, Pope Paul III's grandson, retired to Caprarola, he intended to build a residence that would reflect the family's grandeur. In 1559, he entrusted the task to the leading architect Giacomo Barozzi da Vignola, who came up with some innovative ideas. A magnificent spiral staircase, lavishly decorated with allegorical figures, mythical landscapes, and grotesques by Antonio Tempesta, connected the main entrance with the cardinal's apartments on the main floor. The staircase was gently inclined, with very deep but low steps, so that the cardinal could ride his horse right up to his bedchamber.

A tour of the five-sided palatial villa includes the Hall of Farnese Triumphs, the Hercules Room, and the Antechamber of the Council of Trent, all painted by the Zuccari brothers. Of special interest is the Hall of the Maps, with the ceiling depicting the zodiac and the walls frescoed with maps of the world as known to 16th-century cartographers. The palace is surrounded by a formal, two-tiered Renaissance garden. ⊠ *Piazza Farnese 1, Caprarola* ☎ *0761/646052* ⊕ *direzioneregionalemuseilazio.cultura.gov.it* 🖅 *€10, includes garden; free the first Sun. of the month* 𝄇 *Closed Mon.*

🍴 Restaurants

Antica Trattoria del Borgo

$$ | ROMAN | FAMILY | Visitors to Caprarola's landmark Palazzo Farnese often round out the experience with a hearty meal at this celebrated trattoria. There's a cozy, familial atmosphere inside, and when the weather permits, a pleasant seating area outside. **Known for:** local salumi (cured) and grilled meat; chestnut flour pasta; homemade desserts. ⓢ *Average main: €20 ⊠ Via Borgo Vecchio 107, Caprarola ☎ 0761/645252 ⊕ www.anticatrattoriadelborgo.it ⊗ Closed Mon. No dinner Sun., Tues., or Wed.*

Bomarzo

15 km (9 miles) northeast of Viterbo.

Once a fief of the powerful Orsini family, Bomarzo is home to the Parco dei Mostri, the town's main attraction, which was created in the nearby woodlands to amuse and astound the Orsinis' guests. In the village center, the 16th-century Palazzo Orsini is now the seat of the town council. Inside, there is a princely hall, frescoed by Pietro da Cortona, the famous Italian Baroque fresco painter and architect.

GETTING HERE AND AROUND

Bomarzo is easily reached by car from the A1 autostrada. If you want to go there directly, carry on to the Attigliano exit. Parco dei Monstri is some 6 km (4 miles) from that point. Alternatively, come out at Orte and branch off at Casalone on the Viterbo road. A COTRAL bus also travels here four times a day from Viterbo and takes about half an hour.

👁 Sights

Parco dei Mostri (*Monster Park*)

GARDEN | FAMILY | This eerie fantasy, originally known as the Village of Marvels, or the Sacred Wood, was created in 1552 by Prince Vicino Orsini, with the aid of the famous artist Pirro Ligorio. The surreal park is populated with weird and fantastic sculptures of mythical creatures intended to astonish illustrious guests. The works, carved in outcroppings of mossy stone in shady groves and woodland, include giant tortoises and griffins and an ogre's head with an enormous gaping mouth and a table with chairs set inside. Children love it, and there are photo ops galore. The park has a self-service café (open Sunday only, in winter) and a gift shop. ⊠ *Localita Giardino, 1½ km (1 mile) west of Bomarzo, Bomarzo ☎ 0761/924029 ⊕ www.sacrobosco.eu ☑ €13; €8 children (4–13 years).*

🍴 Restaurants

Trattoria Quattro e Quattro 8

$ | ITALIAN | FAMILY | The name of this cozy trattoria between Bomarzo's Sacro Bosco and the historic center is a reference to its eight tables—four upstairs and four downstairs. The small family-run restaurant serves up lunches of traditional pastas and simple main courses with friendly and speedy efficiency. **Known for:** lombrichelli (local long pasta); coveted outdoor tables in good weather; beef with porcini mushrooms. ⓢ *Average main: €12 ⊠ Via Madonna della Valle, 9, Bomarzo ☎ 334/7871945 ⊕ www. facebook.com/pasticceriadolcissima ⊗ Closed Mon. No dinner.*

Ostia Antica

30 km (19 miles) southwest of Rome.

Founded around the 4th century BC, Ostia served as Rome's port city for several centuries until the Tiber changed course, leaving the town high and dry. What has been excavated here is a remarkably intact Roman town. A visit to the excavations takes two to three hours, including 20 minutes for the museum. Good walking shoes are essential, and, on hot days, arrive when the gates open or late in the afternoon, so you can tour during the coolest times of the day.

Inside the site, there's a coffee bar with snacks and a bookshop, but the best idea is to plan to have lunch outside the archaeological area, in the town's compact medieval quarter.

GETTING HERE AND AROUND

The best way to get to Ostia Antica is by train. The Ostia Lido train leaves every 15 minutes from the Porta San Paolo station adjacent to Rome's Piramide station on Metro B, stopping off at Ostia Antica en route; the trip takes 35 minutes. By car, take the Via del Mare that leads off from Rome's EUR district. Be prepared for heavy traffic, especially at peak hours, on weekends, and in summer.

Sights

Castello di Giulio II

CASTLE/PALACE | FAMILY | The distinctive castle, easily spotted as you come off the footbridge from the train station and part of the medieval *borgo* (old town), was built in 1483 by the future Pope Julius II when he was the cardinal bishop of Ostia. The structure's triangular form is unusual for military architecture, but it was strategically placed for defense when the Tiber River still flowed below its walls. After crossing a drawbridge to gain access the castle's interior, you'll find a small exhibit of historical sketches on the second floor. ⊠ *Piazza della Rocca 13, Ostia Antica* ⊕ *www.ostiaantica. beniculturali.it* ⏢ *€6* ⊙ *Closed Mon.*

★ Scavi di Ostia Antica (*Ostia Antica Excavations*)

RUINS | FAMILY | At its peak, the ancient port town at this site was home to a cosmopolitan population of rich businessmen, wily merchants, sailors, slaves, and their respective families. Great warehouses were built here in the 2nd century AD to handle goods that passed through, notably huge shipments of grain from Africa. Indeed, the port did so much

business that it necessitated the construction of *insulae* (apartment buildings) to provide housing for the city's growing population.

The increasing importance of nearby Portus and the inexorable decline of the Roman Empire eventually led to the port's abandonment. In addition, the coastline retreated over the millennia, and a 16th-century flood diverted the course of the Tiber. Tidal mud and windblown sand buried the ancient port town until the 19th century, when it was extensively excavated.

You can wander through the massive archaeological site and explore its curious corners, mosaic floors, fallen columns, and huge Roman amphitheater. There's also an on-site cafeteria. ■TIP→ **The recently excavated ports of Tiberius and Claudius are nearby and included in the ticket.** ⊠ *Viale dei Romagnoli 717, Ostia Antica* ☎ *06/56358099* ⊕ *www.ostiantica.beniculturali.it* ⏢ *€18, valid for 8 consecutive days; free 1st Sun. of month* ⊙ *Closed Mon.*

🍴 Restaurants

Arianna al Borghetto

$$ | ROMAN | FAMILY | A short walk from the excavations—tucked away in the charming walled medieval borgo of Ostia Antica next to the Castello di Giulio II—this cozy trattoria is an ideal spot to restore your energy with some seasonal dishes and Roman specialties. On warm days, request an outdoor table. **Known for:** traditional carbonara; seasonal artichokes; charming outdoor seating. ⑤ *Average main: €15* ⊠ *Via del Forno 11, Ostia Antica* ☎ *06/56352956* ⊕ *www.facebook.com/alborghetto.ostia* ⊙ *Closed Mon. No dinner Sun.*

Pizzeria Clementina

$$ | PIZZA | FAMILY | A 10-minute drive from Ostia Antica in Fiumicino, modern Rome's fishing port, Pizzeria Clementina is set on a seaside promenade

with views of bobbing boats. The fried appetizers and the pizzas are made using ingredients sourced from the hills around the city or from the daily catches brought in by local fishermen. **Known for:** supplì (fried risotto balls) with braised oxtail; savory cornetto with smoked provola and roasted mushrooms; porchetta-topped pizza. $ *Average main: €18* ⊠ *Via della Torre Clementina, 158, Fiumicino* ☎ *328/8181651* ⊕ *www.pizzeriaclementina.it* ⊗ *Closed Mon. No lunch Tues.–Sat.*

Tivoli

36 km (22 miles) northeast of Rome.

In ancient times, anyone who was anyone had a villa in Tivoli, including Crassus, Trajan, Hadrian, Horace, and Catullus. The town fell into obscurity, however in the medieval era until the Renaissance, when popes and cardinals returned and built villas showy enough to rival those of their extravagant predecessors.

Nowadays Tivoli is small but vibrant, with winding streets and views over the surrounding countryside. The deep Aniene River gorge, which runs through the center of town, is crossed by a romantically sited bridge over cascading waterfalls. Two jewels of ancient Roman architecture also crown its cliffs—the round Temple of Vesta (or the Sybil, the prophetess credited with predicting the birth of Christ) and the ruins of the rectangular temple of the hero-god Tibur, the mythical founder of the city. These can be viewed across the gorge from the Villa Gregoriana Park, named for Pope Gregory XVI, who saved Tivoli from chronic water damage by diverting the river through a tunnel, weakening its flow. An unexpected side effect was the creation of the Grande Cascata (Grand Cascade), a waterfall formed by the huge jet of water that shoots picturesquely into the valley below.

You may also want to set your sights on the Antico Ristorante Sibilla, set up against the Temple of Vesta. From its dining terrace you can take in one of the most remarkable and romantic landscape views in Italy.

GETTING HERE AND AROUND

Unless you have nerves of steel, it's best to skip the drive to Tivoli. Hundreds of businesses line the Via Tiburtina from Rome, and bottleneck traffic is nearly constant. You can avoid some of the congestion by taking the Roma–L'Aquila toll road. Luckily, there are abundant public transport options (although not having a car makes visiting Hadrian's Villa slightly less convenient).

Buses leave every 15 minutes from the Ponte Mammolo stop on Metro B; the ride takes an hour. Regional Trenitalia trains from both Termini and Tiburtina stations will have you in Tivoli in about an hour—or a swift 30 minutes if you plan ahead and catch one of the few express trains each day. Villa d'Este is in the town center, and there is a bus service from Tivoli's main square to Hadrian's Villa.

VISITOR INFORMATION

CONTACT PIT (Punto Informativo Turistico). (*Tivoli Tourist Office*) ⊠ *Piazzale Nazioni Unite, Tivoli* ☎ *0774/313536* ⊕ *www. visittivoli.eu.*

 ## ⊙ Sights

★ **Villa Adriana** (*Hadrian's Villa*)
RUINS | Set below the ancient settlement of Tibur, this astonishingly grand 2nd-century villa was an exclusive retreat, where the marvels of the classical world were reproduced for a ruler's pleasure. Hadrian, who succeeded Trajan as emperor in AD 117, was a man of genius and intellectual curiosity, fascinated by the accomplishments of the Hellenistic world. From AD 125 to 134, architects, laborers, and artists worked on his dreamy villa, re-creating some of the monuments and sights that the emperor had seen on his travels in Egypt, Asia Minor, and Greece.

During the Middle Ages, the site was sacked by barbarians and Romans alike, and many of the statues and architectural features ended up in the Vatican Museums. Nonetheless, the colossal remains are impressive: the ruins rise in a garden setting of green lawns framed with oleanders, pines, and cypresses. Not surprisingly, Villa Adriana is a UNESCO World Heritage site, and it's one that has not yielded up all its secrets. Archaeologists recently discovered the site of the Temple of Isis, complete with several sculptures, including one of the falcon-headed god Horus. ■TIP→ A visit to the villa, which sits outside town, takes at least two hours (carry water on hot days); maps dispensed at the ticket office will help you get your bearings. ✉ *Largo Margherite Yourcenar 1, 6 km (4 miles) southwest of Tivoli, Tivoli* ☎ *0774/39967200* ⊕ *www.coopculture.it/en/poi/hadrians-villa* ⤳ *€12; free 1st Sun. of month.*

★ Villa d'Este

GARDEN | FAMILY | One of Italy's UNESCO World Heritage sites, Villa d'Este was created by Cardinal Ippolito d'Este in the 16th century. This villa in the center of Tivoli was the most amazing pleasure garden of its day, and it still stuns modern visitors with its beauty. Cardinal d'Este (1509–72), a devotee of the Renaissance celebration of human ingenuity over nature, was inspired by the excavation of nearby Villa Adriana. He paid architect Pirro Ligorrio an astronomical sum to create an extraordinary garden filled with nymphs and grottoes. In addition, the Aniene River was diverted to water the garden and feed the several hundred fountains that cascade, shoot skyward, imitate birdsong, and simulate rain. Note especially the musical Fontana dell'Organo, whose water dances to an organ tune every two hours starting at 10:30 am.

Romantics will love the night tour of the gardens and floodlit fountains that takes place on Friday and Saturday in summer. ■TIP→ **Allow at least an hour for a visit, which involves steep inclines and many stairs. There are vending machines for refreshments by the bookshop.** ✉ *Piazza Trento 5, Tivoli* ☎ *0774/39967900* ⊕ *www.coopculture.it/en/poi/villa-deste* ⤳ *€15; free 1st Sun. of month Oct.–Mar.*

🍴 Restaurants

★ Antico Ristorante Sibilla

$$ | ITALIAN | Founded as a hotel and restaurant in 1720 and set beside the striking Roman Temple of Vesta and the Sanctuary of the Sybil, this establishment has an idyllic, wisteria-draped terrace overlooking the deep gorge of the Aniene River, with a thundering waterfall in the background. Standards are high, and the trip to Tivoli is worth it even if you do nothing more than order a lunch of upscale versions of local dishes and take in the spectacular view. **Known for:** beautiful terrace with a superb view; salt-baked fish; homemade pasta with seasonal ingredients. ⑤ *Average main: €20* ✉ *Via della Sibilla 50, Tivoli* ☎ *0774/335281* ⊕ *www.ristorantesibilla.com* ⊘ *Closed Mon.*

🛏 Hotels

Torre Sant'Antonio

$ | B&B/INN | Set inside a tower that dates from the 1300s, this small but cozy hotel offers two private rooms on the edge of the historic center. **Pros:** historic setting; modern interior design; easy walk to most major sites. **Cons:** limited parking nearby; old windowpanes let in some street noise; no 24-hour front desk. ⑤ *Rooms from: €90* ✉ *Vicolo Sant'Antonio 35, Tivoli* ☎ *347/8037983* ⊕ *www.torresantantonio-tivoli.it* ⤳ *2 rooms* ○ *No Meals.*

Palestrina

27 km (17 miles) southeast of Tivoli, 37 km (23 miles) east of Rome.

Except to students of ancient history and music lovers, Palestrina is little known outside Italy. Romans, however, flock to the small hillside town filled with sherbet-colored houses in summer, when its famed breezes offer a refreshing break from the hot city. In addition to the relatively cooler weather, the town is known for its most famous native son, Giovanni Pierluigi da Palestrina, born here in 1525, and considered the master of counterpoint and polyphony. He composed 105 Masses, as well as madrigals, Magnificats, and motets. There is a small museum dedicated to his life and work in the town center.

Ancient Praeneste (modern Palestrina) flourished much earlier than Rome. It was the site of the Temple of Fortuna Primigenia, which dates from the 2nd century BC and was one of the largest, richest, most frequented temple complexes in all antiquity—people came from far and wide to consult its famous oracle. In modern times no one had any idea of the extent of the complex until World War II bombings exposed ancient foundations built upon huge artificial terraces, which stretch from the upper part of the town as far downhill as its central duomo.

GETTING HERE AND AROUND

COTRAL buses leave from the Anagnina terminal on Rome's Metro A as well as from the Tiburtina railway station. Alternatively, you can take a train to Zagarolo, where a COTRAL bus takes you on to Palestrina. The total trip takes 45 minutes. By car, take the A1 (Autostrada del Sole) to the San Cesareo exit and follow the signs to Palestrina. The drive takes about an hour.

Sights

Palazzo Barberini

HISTORY MUSEUM | FAMILY | A bomb blast during World War II exposed the remains of the immense Temple of Fortune that covered the entire hillside under present-day Palestrina. Large arches and terraces are now visible, and you can walk or take a local bus up to the imposing Palazzo Barberini, which crowns the highest point and was built in the 17th century along the semicircular lines of the original Roman temple.

The palace now contains the Museo Nazionale Archeologico di Palestrina, with items found on the site that date from throughout the classical period, including Etruscan bronzes, pottery, and terra-cotta statuary as well as Roman artifacts. In addition, a model of the temple as it was in ancient times helps you appreciate its original immensity. The museum highlight, however, is a massive, incredibly preserved, 1st-century BC mosaic that colorfully details a Nile River scene, complete with ancient Egyptian boats, waving palm trees, and animals. ⊠ *Piazza della Cortina 1, Palestrina* ☎ *06/9538100* ⊕ *direzioneregionalemuseilazio.cultura. gov.it* 🎫 *€7.*

🍴 Restaurants

Il Piscarello

$$ | ITALIAN | FAMILY | Tucked away in a garden at the bottom of a steep side road, this elegant restaurant comes as a bit of a surprise. The menu has both seafood and meat dishes (some topped with white and black truffles), and the pasta can be made gluten-free if you call at least one day ahead of time. **Known for:** truffle-topped dishes; excellent service; outdoor seating in summer. ⑤ *Average main: €20* ⊠ *Via delle Pratarine 2, Palestrina* ☎ *06/9574326* ⊕ *www.ristoranteilpiscarello.it* ⊘ *Closed Mon. No lunch Tues.–Thurs. No dinner Sun.*

Frascati

20 km (12 miles) south of Rome.

Frascati is one of the easiest villages of the Castelli Romani to get to from central Rome, as well as one of the most enjoyable to navigate. After climbing the stairs from the train station or driving uphill to the entrance of the town, stroll through Frascati's lively old center. Via Battisti, leads away from the looming Villa Aldobrandini and into Piazza San Pietro with its imposing gray-and-white cathedral. Inside is the cenotaph of Prince Charles Edward, last of the Scottish Stuart dynasty, who tried unsuccessfully to regain the British Crown and died an exile in Rome in 1788.

A little arcade beside the monumental fountain at the back of the piazza leads into Market Square. Here, the smell of fresh baking will entice you into the Purificato family bakery to see the traditional honey-flavored pupazza biscuits, modeled on pagan fertility symbols.

Take your pick from the cafés and trattorias fronting the central Piazzale Marconi, or do as the locals do: buy fruit from the market gallery at Piazza del Mercato, then get a huge slice of porchetta from one of the stalls, a hunk of *casareccio* bread, and a few *ciambelline frascatane* (ring-shaped cookies made with wine), and take your picnic to any one of the nearby *cantine* (homey wine bars) to settle in for some sips of tasty, inexpensive vino. Or continue on to nearby Grottaferrata to take in its one-of-a-kind abbey.

GETTING HERE AND AROUND

An hourly train along a single-track line through vineyards and olive groves takes you to Frascati from Rome's central Stazione Termini. The trip takes 45 minutes. By car, take the Via Tuscolano, which branches off the Appia Nuova road just after the Archbasilica St. John Lateran in Rome, and drive straight up.

VISITOR INFORMATION

CONTACT Frascati Point (Tourism Office). ✉ *Piazza G. Marconi 5, Frascati* ☎ *06/94184406* ⊕ *www.comune.frascati. rm.it.*

◉ Sights

Abbey of San Nilo Grottaferrata

CHURCH | In Grottaferrata, a busy village a couple of miles from Frascati, the main attraction is a walled citadel founded by St. Nilo, who brought his group of Basilian monks here in 1004, when he was 90. The order is unique in that it's Roman Catholic but observes Greek Orthodox rites. It is the last surviving Byzantine-Greek monastery in Italy, and has a distinctive blend of art and architecture.

The fortified abbey with its soaring bell tower, considered a masterpiece of martial architecture, was restructured in the 15th century by Antonio da Sangallo for the future Pope Julius II. The abbey church, inside the second courtyard, has glittering Byzantine mosaics and a revered icon of Mary with child set into a marble tabernacle designed by Bernini. The Farnese chapel, leading from the right nave, contains a series of frescoes by Domenichino.

If you make arrangements in advance, you can visit the library, which is one of the oldest in Italy. The abbey also has a famous laboratory for the restoration of antique books and manuscripts, where Leonardo's *Codex Atlanticus* was restored in 1962 and more than a thousand precious volumes were saved after the disastrous Florence flood in 1966. ✉ *Corso del Popolo 128, Grottaferrata* ☎ *06/9459309* ⊕ *www.abbaziasannilo. org* 🎟 *Free.*

★ Poggio Le Volpi

WINERY | Lazio's wines may not be as famous as those of Tuscany or Piedmont, but this award-winning family-run winery is leading the way for the region. The family's wine-making roots stretch back to 1920, but it was third-generation winemaker Felice Mergè who turned the winery into a destination with two restaurants: the casual Epos bistro and the fine-dining Barrique, where a tasting menu is served in the barrel aging room. Tours are available by appointment only, which means the best way to experience this place is to book a table at one of the restaurants and request a tour. ⊠ *Via Fontana Candida 3/C, Monte Porzio Catone* ☎ *06/9426980* ⊕ *www.poggiolevolpi. com* ⊟ *Tours available by appointment* ⊘ *Closed Mon.*

Villa Falconieri

HISTORIC HOME | In the mid-1500s, Bishop Alessandro Rufini of Melfi constructed a stunning country retreat on the site of an earlier Roman villa in the hills outside the city. Pope Paul III soon played a hand in enlarging the villa, as a part of his broader plan to enhance the village of Frascati. The villa was eventually purchased by the Falconieri family in 1628, who gave their name to the estate, and commissioned an extension by Borromini—though the extent of the famed architect's contributions are debatable. What is certain is that the Falconieri family built a legacy-worthy library that hosted intellectuals and writers from around Europe, and established a tradition of offering 20 annual scholarships to promising young art students. The villa is now home to the Academy *Vivarium Novum,* a humanities institute based on the educational tradition of Renaissance schools, that opens its doors to its fresco-filled campus every Sunday with guided tours (in Italian) from 10 am–12 pm. Reserve a spot by emailing ✑ *visite@vivariumnovum.net.* ⊠ *Viale Borromini, 5, Frascati* ☎ *06/6689034* ⊕ *www.vivariumnovum. net* ⊘ *Closed Mon.–Sat.*

Restaurants

Antica Fontana

$$ | ROMAN | Across the road from the Abbey of San Nilo is one of Grottaferrata's most esteemed restaurants, which has been run by the Consoli family since 1989. The decor is rustic but stylish, with plants hanging from the ceiling and rows of polished antique copper pans and molds decorating the walls. **Known for:** homemade pizza with excellent dough; fettuccine with porcini; pleasant outdoor terrace. ⑤ *Average main: €22* ⊠ *Via Domenichino 24, Grottaferrata* ☎ *347/4044492* ⊕ *www.facebook.com/ ristoranteanticafontana* ⊘ *Closed Mon.*

★ Cacciani

$$ | ITALIAN | The Cacciani family has been running this stylish restaurant in the heart of Frascati old town since 1922, when it was a popular hangout for the likes of Clark Gable and Gina Lollobrigida. Perched high on a rise overlooking the town and the Roman plain, there are spectacular views from the Cacciani terrace, but you can also keep an eye on the gorgeous food being prepared in the open kitchen. **Known for:** tonnarelli cacio e pepe prepared at the table; great views; elegant local wines. ⑤ *Average main: €22* ⊠ *Via Armando Diaz 13, Frascati* ☎ *06/9420378* ⊕ *www.cacciani.it* ⊘ *Closed Mon. No dinner Sun.*

Il Grottino Frascati

$$ | ITALIAN | This former wine cellar just beyond Frascati's market square is now a cheerful trattoria serving hearty portions of traditional Roman dishes and pizza. In summer you can sit under an awning outside and enjoy the sweeping view over the plain toward Rome. **Known for:** pasta alla gricia (with pecorino cheese, black pepper, and guanciale); casual atmosphere; extensive wine list. ⑤ *Average main: €15* ⊠ *Viale Regina Margherita 41–43, Frascati* ☎ *06/9416873* ⊕ *www. facebook.com/IlGrottinoDiAlfredo.*

★ **Osteria del Fico Vecchio**

$$ | ITALIAN | Only a couple of miles outside Frascati, this 16th-century coaching inn has a tastefully renovated dining room and an old fig tree (its namesake) that shades a charming, table-filled garden. Long known for its excellent cooking, which was beloved by Italian director Federico Fellini, the classic restaurant still prepares typical Roman dishes, among them *pollo al diavolo* (spicy braised chicken) and *abbacchio allo scottadito* (sizzling grilled lamb). **Known for:** pretty garden for outdoor dining; classic cacio e pepe; grilled meats. $ *Average main: €20 ⊠ Via Anagnina 257, Grottaferrata ☎ 06/9459261 ⊕ www.alfico.it ⊗ No lunch Thurs.*

 Hotels

★ **Park Hotel Villa Grazioli**

$ | HOTEL | One of the region's most famous residences, this patrician villa halfway between Frascati and Grottaferrata is now a first-class hotel with frescoed halls and salons—though the guest rooms are admittedly less ornate and standard-issue. **Pros:** incredible frescoes in the main building; elegant atmosphere; wonderful views of the countryside. **Cons:** situated at the end of a long, narrow lane; not all rooms are in the main building; rather basic breakfast. $ *Rooms from: €120 ⊠ Via Umberto Pavoni 19, Grottaferrata ⊕ Narrow turnoff from the SP216 road going from Grottaferrata roundabout to Frascati ☎ 06/945400 ⊕ www.villa-grazioli.it ➤ 62 rooms ⊙ Free Breakfast.*

Castel Gandolfo

8 km (5 miles) southwest of Frascati, 25 km (15 miles) south of Rome.

This scenic little town has been the preferred summer retreat of popes for centuries. It was the Barberini Pope Urban VIII who first headed here, eager to escape the malarial miasmas that afflicted summertime Rome. before long, the city's princely families also set up country estates around here.

The 17th-century Villa Pontificia has a superb position overlooking Lake Albano and amid one of Italy's most gorgeous gardens. Fortunately, these treasures are now open to the public as papal audiences are no longer held in the Castel Gandolfo villa. There's a fountain on the little square in front of the palace by Bernini, who also designed the nearby Church of San Tommaso da Villanova, which has works by Pietro da Cortona.

The village has a number of whimsical craft workshops and traditional food purveyors, in addition to the souvenir shops on the square. On the horizon, the silver astronomical dome belonging to the Specola Vaticana observatory—one of the first in Europe and where the scientific Pope Gregory XIII indulged his interest in stargazing—is visible for miles around.

GETTING HERE AND AROUND
There's hourly train service for Castel Gandolfo from Termini Station (Rome–Albano line), and buses leave frequently from the Anagnina terminal of Metro A. The trip takes about 40 minutes, and the village is reachable by a 10-minute uphill walk from the station.

By car, take Via Appia from San Giovanni in Rome and follow it straight to Albano, where you branch off for Castel Gandolfo (which takes about 45 minutes, depending on traffic).

VISITOR INFORMATION
CONTACT PIT Tourist Office Castel Gandolfo. ⊠ *Via Massimo D'Azeglio, Castel Gandolfo ⊕ A green kiosk on your right as you walk up the road, just outside the town walls ⊕ www.comune.castelgandolfo.rm.it.*

Sights

Lakeside Lido

BEACH | FAMILY | This waterside promenade—down a steep incline from the pretty town—is lined with restaurants, ice-cream parlors, and cafés and is a favorite spot for Roman families to relax on summer days. No motorized craft are allowed on the lake, but you can rent paddleboats and kayaks. In summer, you can also take a short guided boat trip to learn about the geology and history of the lake, which lies at the bottom of an extinct volcanic crater. The deep sapphire waters are full of swans, herons, and other birds, and there is a nature trail along the wooded end of the shore for those who want to get away from the crowds.

Deck chairs are available for rent on the small beach, and you can stop for a plate of freshly prepared pasta or a gigantic Roman sandwich at one of the little snack bars under the oak and alder trees. There's also a small permanent fairground for children, and local vendors often set up temporary shops selling crafts, toys, and snacks on the warmer weekends. ⊠ *Lake Albano, Castel Gandolfo* ⊠ *Free.*

Palazzo Apostolico di Castel Gandolfo

CASTLE/PALACE | For centuries, the Apostolic Palace of Castel Gandolfo was the summer retreat of popes, who kept the papal villa and extensive grounds completely private. Luckily for tourists, Pope Francis decided that he was too busy to use it and had it opened to the public. Inside you can view the Gallery of Pontifical Portraits, ceremonial garments, and the imposing papal throne in the Sala degli Svizzeri. The private area of the palace with the pope's bedchamber, his library, study, and offices are also open to visitors. ⊠ *Piazza della Libertà, Castel Gandolfo* ☎ *06/69863111* ⊕ *www.museivaticani.va* ⊠ *€12 including pontifical gardens* ⊙ *Closed Mon.–Thurs. and on Catholic holidays.*

Pontifical Gardens Villa Barberini

GARDEN | FAMILY | In 2016, Pope Francis opened the 136-acre pontifical estate and its glorious gardens to the public, which includes the archaeological remains of the palace of the Roman Emperor Domitian (dating from the 1st century AD) and the home farm, which supplies the Vatican with fresh dairy products and eggs. ⊠ *Via Massimo D'Azeglio (entrance gate), Castel Gandolfo* ⊕ *www.museivaticani. va* ⊠ *€12 with pontifical palace* ⊙ *Closed Mon.–Thurs.* ⊜ *Reservations required.*

🍴 Restaurants

Antico Ristorante Pagnanelli

$$$ | ITALIAN | One of the most refined restaurants in the Castelli Romani has been in the same family since 1882. Its dining room windows open onto a breathtaking view across Lake Albano to the conical peak of Monte Cavo. **Known for:** homemade gnocchetti with clams and black truffles; elegant and cozy interior with an open fire in winter; impeccable wine list and famed wine museum in basement. ⑤ *Average main: €30* ⊠ *Via Gramsci 4, Castel Gandolfo* ☎ *06/9360004* ⊕ *www.pagnanelli.it.*

Bucci

$$$ | ITALIAN | Situated in the heart of the village of Castel Gandolfo, Bucci occupies a splendid position overlooking Lake Albano far below with an outdoor terrace shaded by a grape pergola. Food has traditional roots but offers a modern twist, ranging from lasagna with crispy *guanciale* (Roman bacon) to spicy stewed calamari. **Known for:** contemporary Italian menu; vine-covered terrace; chilled local wine. ⑤ *Average main: €28* ⊠ *Via De' Zecchini 31, Castel Gandolfo* ☎ *06/9323334* ⊕ *ristorantebucci.it* ⊙ *Closed mid-Jan.–Feb.*

🛏 Hotels

Hotel Castelgandolfo

$$ | **HOTEL** | Overlooking the volcanic crater of Lake Albano and a minute's walk from the Apostolic Palace, this intimate hotel in the heart of Castel Gandolfo is a romantic retreat. **Pros:** convenient location; ideal for romantics; full breakfast buffet. **Cons:** some rooms only have street views; small, narrow balconies; no designated parking. $ *Rooms from: €140 ⊠ Via De' Zecchini 27, Castel Gandolfo* ☏ *06/9360521* ⊕ *www.hotelcastelgandolfo.com* ⌁ *18 rooms* ⦿ *Free Breakfast.*

Ariccia

8 km (5 miles) southwest of Castel Gandolfo, 26 km (17 miles) south of Rome.

Ariccia is a gem of Baroque town planning. When Fabio Chigi, scion of the superwealthy banking family, became Pope Alexander VII, he commissioned Gian Lorenzo Bernini to redesign his country estate and make it worthy of his new station. Bernini restructured not only the existing 16th-century palace, but also the town gates, the main square—with its graceful loggias and twin fountains—and the round church of Santa Maria dell'Assunzione (with a dome said to be modeled on the Pantheon). The rest of the village was coiled around the apse of the church down into the valley below.

Ariccia's splendid heritage was largely forgotten in the 20th century, and yet it was once one of the highlights of every artist's and writer's Grand Tour. Corot, Ibsen, Turner, Longfellow, and Hans Christian Andersen all stayed here. Today's village visitors are drawn by both the artistic landmarks and celebrated local culinary traditions.

GETTING HERE AND AROUND

For Ariccia, take the COTRAL bus from the Anagnina terminal of Metro A. Buses on the Albano–Genzano–Velletri line stop under the monumental bridge that spans the Ariccia Valley, where an elevator whisks you up to the main town square. If you take a train or COTRAL bus to Albano Laziale, you can proceed by local bus to Ariccia or continue on foot through the first town and over the bridge (it's just under 1½ km [1 mile]). If you're driving, follow the Via Appia Nuova to Albano and carry on to Ariccia.

👁 Sights

★ Palazzo Chigi

CASTLE/PALACE | This is a true rarity: a Baroque residence whose original furniture, paintings, drapes, and decorations are largely intact. The Italian film director Luchino Visconti used the villa, which sits just at the end of Ariccia's famous bridge, for most of the interior scenes in his 1963 film *The Leopard.* The rooms of the *piano nobile* (main floor)—which, unlike Rome's Palazzo Chigi, are open to the public, but only on guided tours—contain intricately carved pieces of 17th-century furniture, as well as textiles and costumes from the 16th to the 20th century.

The Room of Beauties is lined with paintings of the loveliest ladies of the day, and the Nuns' Room showcases portraits of 10 Chigi sisters, all of whom took the veil. You can get a close look (with a guide) at Le Stanze del Cardinale (Cardinal's Rooms), the suites occupied by the pleasure-loving Cardinal Flavio Chigi. ⊠ *Piazza di Corte 14, Ariccia* ☏ *06/9330053* ⊕ *www.palazzochigiariccia.it* ⌁ *€15 guided visit to piano nobile, Cardinal's Rooms, and Baroque Museum; €12 for self-visit* 🕐 *Palazzo closed Mon. Park closed Oct.–Mar.*

The monumental bridge connects Ariccia to Albano and offers beautiful views of Palazzo Chigi and Santa Maria Assunta.

Santa Maria Assunta in Cielo
(*Church of the Assumption*)

CHURCH | Directly across from Palazzo Chigi is the Church of the Assumption, with its distinctive blue dome and round shape designed by none other than Gian Lorenzo Bernini. The artistic architect had his best students execute most of the work of building and decorating the Pantheon-inspired church, creating porticoes outside and an elaborately plastered cupola inside, which steals the show in the otherwise simple interior. ⊠ *Piazza di Corte, Ariccia* ☏ *06/9330637* ⏱ *Closed noon–4 daily.*

🍴 Restaurants

A visit to Ariccia isn't complete without tasting the local gastronomic specialty: porchetta, a delicious whole-roasted pig stuffed with herbs, that goes well with the local Romanella wine. The shops on the central Piazza di Corte will make up a sandwich for you, or you can do what the Romans do: head for one of the *fraschetta* (a casual, boisterous countryside restaurant) wine cellars, which also serve cheese, cold cuts, pickled vegetables, olives, and the occasional plate of pasta.

Pass Palazzo Chigi and turn left under the arch to find several establishments in a long row on the other side of the street. Take your pick and ask for a seat on a wooden bench at a trestle table covered with simple white paper; be ready to make friends and maybe join in a sing-along.

L'Aricciarola

$ | **ITALIAN** | **FAMILY** | This fraschetta around the corner from Palazzo Chigi is great for people-watching, which you can do while enjoying a platter of cold cuts and assorted cheeses, washed down with a carafe of local Castelli wine. Order your own appetizers and slices of porchetta at the counter near the door, snag a table on the patio, flag down a waiter if you want to order a hot dish like pasta, and then settle into the rustic setting surrounded by Roman families who've abandoned the city for the day to enjoy the local food. **Known for:** classic porchetta; local cold cuts; very casual and friendly atmosphere. $ *Average main: €12* ⊠ *Via Borgo S. Rocco 9, Ariccia* ☎ *06/9334103* ⊕ *www.facebook.com/osterialaricciarola* ⊙ *Closed Mon. and 2 wks in Jan.*

Nemi

8 km (5 miles) east of Ariccia, 34 km (21 miles) south of Rome.

A bronze statue of Diana the Huntress greets you at the entrance to Nemi, the smallest and prettiest village of the Castelli Romani. Perched on a spur of rock 600 feet above the little oval-shaped lake of the same name, which is formed from a volcanic crater, the town has an eagle's-nest view over the rolling Roman countryside as far as the coast, some 18 km (11 miles) away.

The main street, Corso Vittorio Emanuele, takes you to the quaint Piazza Umberto I, lined with flower-box homes and outdoor cafés serving desserts made with the town's famous tiny wild strawberries which are harvested from the woodlands that line the crater bowl around the lake.

GETTING HERE AND AROUND

Nemi is hard to reach without a car. COTRAL buses from the Anagnina station on Metro A go to the town of Genzano, where a local bus travels to Nemi every two hours. If the times aren't convenient, you can sometimes find a taxi or simply walk the 5 km (3 miles) around Lake Nemi.

By car, take the panoramic route known as the Via dei Laghi (Road of the Lakes). Follow the Appia Nuova from St. John Lateran and branch off on the well-signposted route after Ciampino airport. Follow the Via dei Laghi toward Velletri until you see signs for Nemi. ■TIP→ **Only residents can drive through the village, so be sure to park at the entrance to the town.**

◉ Sights

Museo delle Navi Romane
(*Roman Ship Museum*)
HISTORY MUSEUM | FAMILY | In the 1930s, the Italian government drained Nemi's lake to recover two magnificent ceremonial ships, loaded with sculptures, bronzes, and art treasures, that were submerged for 2,000 years. The Museo delle Navi Romane, on the lakeshore below the town of Nemi, was built to house the ships, but they were destroyed in a fire during World War II. Inside are scale models, finds from the Bronze Age Diana sanctuary and the area nearby, and an excellent video exhibit explaining the history of the ships. There's also a colossal statue of the infamous and extravagant Roman emperor Caligula, who had the massive barges built; the Italian police once snatched the marble sculpture back from tomb robbers just as they were about to smuggle it out of the country. ⊠ *Via del Tempio di Diana 13, Nemi* ☎ *06/9398040* ⊕ *direzioneregionalemuseilazio.cultura. gov.it* ☞ *€5* ⊙ *Closed Mon.*

◉ Restaurants

★ La Fiocina
$$ | **ITALIAN** | Set on the tranquil shores of Lake Nemi, next to the Roman Ship Museum, La Fiocina has been serving local specialties, including lake fish and homemade gnocchi with porcini mushrooms, for more than 50 years. The interior is elegant and welcoming, with a roaring fireplace on cooler days; in warmer months, you can dine on the terrace overlooking the lake. **Known for:** coregone lake fish; garden terrace with lake views; wild Nemi strawberries. $ *Average main: €18* ⊠ *Via delle Navi di Tiberio 9, Nemi* ☎ *06/9391120* ⊕ *ristorantelafiocin.wixsite.com/lafiocina* ⊙ *Closed Mon. and Tues.*

La Specchio di Diana

$$ | **ITALIAN** | Halfway down the main street on the left is the town's most historic inn (where Byron stayed when visiting the area) with a wine bar and café at street level and a full restaurant on the second floor. ■ TIP→ **It also has several small apartments and rooms available to rent by the night in the village center.**

Known for: polenta al sugo di lepre (hare sauce); spectacular lake views; desserts topped with local Nemi strawberries.

⑤ *Average main: €16* ✉ *Corso Vittorio Emanuele 13, Nemi* ☎ *06/9368714* ⊕ *www.specchiodidiana.it.*

Chapter 5

VENICE

Updated by
Liz Humphreys
and Erla Zwingle

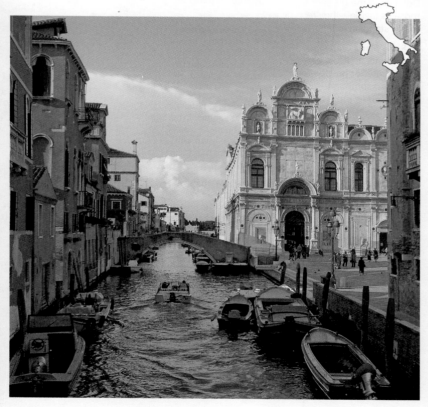

⊙ Sights	🍴 Restaurants	🛏 Hotels	🛍 Shopping	🍸 Nightlife
★★★★★	★★★★☆	★★★★★	★★★☆☆	★★☆☆☆

WELCOME TO VENICE

TOP REASONS TO GO

★ **Cruising the Grand Canal:** The beauty of its palaces, enhanced by the play of light on the water, make a trip down Venice's "Main Street" unforgettable.

★ **Basilica di San Marco:** Don't miss the gorgeous mosaics inside—they're worth standing in line for.

★ **Santa Maria Gloriosa dei Frari:** Its austere, cavernous interior houses Titian's *Assumption*—one of the world's most beautiful altarpieces—plus several other spectacular art treasures.

★ **Gallerie dell'Accademia:** Legendary masterpieces of Venetian painting will overwhelm you in this fabled museum.

★ **Sipping wine and snacking at a bacaro:** For a sample of tasty local snacks and excellent Veneto wines in a uniquely Venetian setting, head for one of the city's many wine bars.

1 San Marco. The neighborhood at the center of Venice is filled with fashion boutiques, art galleries, and grand hotels.

2 Dorsoduro. This graceful residential area is home to renowned art galleries; the Campo Santa Margherita is a lively student hangout.

3 San Polo and Santa Croce. These bustling *sestieri* (districts) have all sorts of shops, several major churches, and the Rialto fish and produce markets.

4 Cannaregio. This sestiere has some of the sunniest open-air canalside walks in town; the Jewish Ghetto has a fascinating history.

5 Castello. With its gardens, park, and narrow, winding walkways, it's the sestiere least influenced by Venice's tourist culture.

6 San Giorgio Maggiore and Giudecca. San Giorgio is graced with its magnificent namesake church, and Giudecca has wonderful views of Venice.

7 Islands of the Lagoon. Each island in Venice's northern lagoon has its own allure.

185

EATING AND DRINKING WELL IN VENICE

Pescheria (fish market)

The catchword in Venetian restaurants is "fish." How do you learn about the catch of the day? A visit to the Rialto's *pescheria* (fish market) is more instructive than any book, and when you're dining at a well-regarded restaurant, ask for a recommendation.

Traditionally, fish is served with a bit of salt, maybe some chopped parsley, and a drizzle of olive oil—no lemon; lemon masks the flavor. Ask for an entire wild-caught fish; it's much more expensive than its farmed cousin but certainly worth it. Antipasto may be prosciutto *di San Daniele* (from the Veneto region) or *sarde in saor* (fresh panfried sardines marinated with onions, raisins, and pine nuts). Risotto, cooked with shellfish or veggies, is a great first course. Pasta? Enjoy it with seafood: this is *not* the place to order spaghetti with tomato sauce. Other pillars of regional cooking include *pasta e fagioli* (thick bean soup with pasta); polenta, often with *fegato alla veneziana* (liver with onion); and that dessert invented in the Veneto, tiramisu.

GOING BACARO

You can sample regional wines and scrumptious *cicheti* (small snacks) in *bacari* (wine bars), a great Venetian tradition. Crostini and *polpette* (meat, fish, or vegetable croquettes) are popular cicheti, as are small sandwiches, seafood salads, *baccalà mantecato* (creamy, whipped salt cod), and toothpick-speared items like roasted peppers, marinated artichokes, and mozzarella balls.

SEAFOOD

Granseola (crab), *moeche* (tiny, locally caught soft-shell crabs), sweet *canoce* (mantis shrimp), *capelunghe* (razor clams), calamari, and *seppie* or *seppioline* (cuttlefish) are all prominently featured, as well as *rombo* (turbot), *branzino* (sea bass), *San Pietro* (John Dory), *sogliola* (sole), *orate* (gilthead bream), and *triglia* (mullet). Trademark dishes include sarde in saor, *frittura mista* (tempura-like fried fish and vegetables), and baccalà mantecato.

RISOTTO, PASTA, POLENTA

As a first course, Venetians favor the creamy rice dish risotto *all'onda* ("undulating," as opposed to firm), prepared with vegetables or shellfish. When pasta is served, it's generally accompanied by seafood sauces, too: *pasticcio di pesce* is lasagna-type pasta baked with fish, and *bigoli* is a strictly local whole-wheat pasta shaped like thick spaghetti, usually served *in salsa* (an anchovy-onion sauce with a dash of cinnamon), or with *nero di seppia* (cuttlefish-ink sauce). Pasta e fagioli is another classic first course, and polenta is a staple—served creamy or fried in wedges, generally as an accompaniment to stews or *seppie in nero* (cuttlefish in black ink).

Linguine with clam sauce

VEGETABLES

The larger islands of the lagoon are known for their legendary vegetables, such as the Sant'Erasmo *castraure*, sinfully expensive but heavenly tiny white artichokes that appear for a few days in spring. Spring treats include the fat white asparagus from neighboring Bassano or Verona, and artichoke bottoms (*fondi*), usually sautéed with olive oil, parsley, and garlic. From December to March the prized local radicchio *di Treviso* is grilled and frequently served with a bit of melted Taleggio cheese from Lombardy. Fall brings small wild mushrooms called *chiodini* and *zucca di Mantova,* a yellow squash with a gray-green rind used in soups, puddings, and ravioli stuffing.

SWEETS

Tiramisu lovers will have ample opportunity to sample this creamy delight made from ladyfingers soaked in espresso and rum or brandy and covered with mascarpone cream and cinnamon. Gelato, *sgroppino* (prosecco, vodka, and lemon sorbet), and *semifreddo* (soft homemade ice cream) are other sweets frequently seen on Venetian menus, as are almond cakes and dry cookies served with dessert wine. Try *focaccia veneziana,* a sweet raised cake made in the late fall and winter.

Tiramisu

Venice is often called La Serenissima, or "the most serene," a reference to the majesty, wisdom, and power of this city that was for centuries a leader in trade between Europe and Asia and a major center of European culture. Built on water by people who saw the sea as defender and ally, and who constantly invested in its splendor with magnificent architectural projects, Venice is a city unlike any other.

No matter how often you've seen it in photos and films, the real thing is more dreamlike than you could ever imagine. Its most notable landmarks, the Basilica di San Marco and the Palazzo Ducale, are exotic mixes of Byzantine, Romanesque, Gothic, and Renaissance styles, reflecting Venice's ties with the rest of Italy and with Constantinople to the east. Shimmering sunlight and silvery mist soften every perspective here; it's easy to understand how the city became renowned in the Renaissance for its artists' use of color. It's full of secrets, inexpressibly romantic, and frequently given over to pure, sensuous enjoyment.

You'll see Venetians going about their daily affairs in vaporetti, in the *campi* (squares), and along the *calli* (narrow streets). Despite their many challenges (including more frequent flooding and overcrowding), they are proud of their city and its history and are still quite helpful to those who show proper respect for Venice and its way of life.

Planning

Getting Oriented

Venice proper is quite compact, and you should be able to walk across it in a couple of hours, even counting a few minutes for getting lost. Vaporetti will save wear and tear on tired feet but won't always save you much time.

Venice is divided into six sestieri: Cannaregio, Castello, Dorsoduro, San Marco, San Polo, and Santa Croce. More sedate outer islands float around them—San Giorgio Maggiore and Giudecca just to the south; beyond them the Lido, the barrier island; and to the north, Murano, Burano, and Torcello.

Getting Here and Around

AIR

CONTACT Aeroporto Marco Polo.
☎ 041/2609260 ⊕ www.veniceairport.it.

LAND TRANSFERS
CONTACT ATVO. ☎ 0421/5944 ⊕ www.atvo.it.

WATER TRANSFERS
From Marco Polo terminal, it's a mostly covered seven-minute walk to the dock where boats depart for Venice's historic center. The ride is in a closed boat so you won't get much of a view; plus, it's more expensive and generally slower than the bus to Piazzale Roma (unless your hotel is near a boat station).

CONTACT Alilaguna. ☎ 041/2401701 ⊕ www.alilaguna.it.

CAR
Venice is at the end of the SR11, just off the east–west A4 autostrada. There are no cars in Venice; if possible, return your rental when you arrive.

A warning: don't be waylaid by illegal touts, often wearing fake uniforms, who try to flag you down and offer to arrange parking and hotels; use one of the established garages, mainly clustered at Piazzale Roma. Consider reserving a space in advance. The **Autorimessa Comunale** (☎ 041/2722394 ⊕ avm.avmspa.it) costs €30 for 24 hours with online reservations. **Garage San Marco** (☎ 041/5232213 ⊕ parclick.it) costs €18 from 5 pm to 5 am, and €45 for 24 hours with online reservations. For brief stays, opt for **Parcheggio Sant'Andrea** (☎ 041/2722384 ⊕ avm.avmspa.it), where up to two hours costs €7. On its own island, **Isola del Tronchetto** (☎ 041/5207555 ⊕ www.tronchettoparking.it) charges €25 for 24 hours. Watch for signs coming over the bridge—you turn right just before Piazzale Roma.

Many hotels and the casino have guest discounts with the San Marco or Tronchetto garages. A perfectly convenient alternative is to park in Mestre, on the mainland, and take a train (10 minutes, €1.40) or bus into Venice. The garage across from the station and the Bus 2 stop costs €22 for up to 24 hours.

PUBLIC TRANSPORTATION
WATER BUSES
CONTACT ACTV. ☎ 041/041 call center ⊕ actv.avmspa.it.

WATER TAXIS
A *motoscafo* isn't cheap: you'll spend about €70 for a short trip in town, €90 to the Lido, and €100 or more per hour to visit the outer islands. It is strongly suggested to book through the **Consorzio Motoscafi Venezia** (☎ 041/2406712 ⊕ www.motoscafivenezia.com) to avoid an argument with your driver over prices. A water taxi can carry up to 10 passengers, with an additional charge of €10 per person for more than four people, so if you're traveling in a group, it may not be that much more expensive than a vaporetto.

TRAIN
Venice has rail connections with many major cities in Italy and Europe. Note that Venice's train station is **Venezia Santa Lucia,** not to be confused with Venezia Mestre, which is the mainland stop prior to arriving in the historic center. Some trains don't continue beyond the Mestre station; in such cases you can catch the next Venice-bound train. Get a ticket on the Trenitalia app or a paper ticket from the kiosk on the platform and validate it (in the yellow time-stamp machine) to avoid a fine.

Making the Most of Your Time

The hordes of tourists here are legendary, especially in spring and fall but during other seasons, too—there's really no "off-season" in Venice. Unfortunately, tales of impassable tourist-packed streets and endless queues to get into the Basilica di San Marco are not exaggerated. A little bit of planning, however, will help you avoid the worst of the crowds.

Most tourists do little more than take the vaporetto down the Grand Canal to Piazza San Marco, see the piazza and the basilica, and walk up to the Rialto and back to the station. You'll want to visit these areas, too, but do so in the early morning, before most tourists have finished their breakfast cappuccinos. Because many tourists are other Italians who come for a weekend outing, you can further decrease your competition for Venice's pleasures by choosing to visit the city on weekdays.

Away from San Marco and the Rialto, the streets and quays of Venice's beautiful medieval and Renaissance residential districts receive only a moderate amount of traffic. Besides the Grand Canal and the Piazza San Marco, and perhaps Torcello, the other historically and artistically important sites are seldom overcrowded. Even on weekends you probably won't have to queue up for the Gallerie dell'Accademia.

Restaurants

Dining options in Venice range from ultra-high-end establishments, where jackets are required, to very casual eateries. Once staunchly traditional, many restaurants have revamped their dining rooms and their menus, creating dishes that blend classic elements with ingredients and methods less common to the region. Mid- and upper-range restaurants often offer innovative options as well as mainstays.

Unfortunately, Venice also has its share of overpriced, mediocre eateries. Restaurants catering to tourists have little motivation to maintain quality since most diners are one-time patrons. You

are better off at a restaurant frequented by locals, who are interested in the food, not the views. Avoid places with cajoling waiters outside, as well as those that don't display their prices or have showy tourist menus translated into a dozen languages. For the same €15–€20 you'd spend at such places, you could do better at a bacaro making a meal of cicheti.

Hotels

Venetian magic lingers when you retire for the night, whether you're staying in a grand hotel or budget *locanda* (inn). Hotels usually occupy very old buildings, often without elevators or lounge areas. It's not at all unusual for each room to be different, even on the same floor: windows overlooking charming canals and bleak alleyways are both common. Venice is one of the most popular destinations on Earth—so book your lodging as far in advance as possible.

In terms of location, the area in and around San Marco is the most crowded and expensive. Still convenient but more tranquil areas include Dorsoduro, Santa Croce, and Cannaregio (though the area around the train station can be hectic), or even Castello in the area beyond the Pietà church. Also take into consideration the proximity of a vaporetto stop, especially if you have heavy baggage. Regardless of where you stay, it's essential that you have detailed directions to your hotel: note not only its street address but also its sestiere as well as a nearby landmark or two. Even if you arrive by water taxi, you may still have a bit of a walk.

⇨ *Hotel and restaurant reviews have been shortened. For full information, visit Fodors.com. Prices in the lodging reviews are the lowest cost of a standard double room in high season. Prices in the dining reviews are the average cost of a main course at dinner, or, if dinner is not served, at lunch.*

What It Costs in Euros

	$	$$	$$$	$$$$
RESTAURANTS				
	under €15	€15–€24	€25–€35	over €35
HOTELS				
	under €125	€125–€200	€201–€300	over €300

Nightlife

Nightlife offerings in Venice are, even by rather sedate standards, fairly tame. Most bars must close by midnight, especially those that offer outdoor seating. Piazza San Marco is a popular meeting place in nice weather, when the cafés stay open relatively late and all seem to compete to offer the best live music. The younger crowd, Venetians and visitors alike, tend to gravitate toward the area around the Ponte di Rialto, with Campi San Bartolomeo and San Luca on one side and Campo Rialto Nuovo on the other. Especially popular with university students and young people from the mainland are the bars around Campo Santa Margherita.

Passes and Discounts

Avoid lines and hassle with the online **Venezia Unica City Pass** (⊕ www.veneziaunica.it). This all-in-one pass can be used for public transportation and entry to museums, churches, and other attractions; you only pay for the services you wish to add. You'll receive an email with the pass, which you can show for entry at sights, though you'll still need to physically collect your transportation pass at an ACTV automatic ticket machine or ticket point located around the city.

Fifteen of Venice's most significant churches covered by the Venezia Unica City Pass are part of the **Chorus Foundation** umbrella group (☏ 041/2750462

⊕ www.chorusvenezia.org), which coordinates their administration, hours, and admission fees. Churches in this group are open to visitors all day except Sunday morning. Single church entry costs €3; you have a year to visit all 15 with the €12 Chorus Pass, which you can get at any participating church or online.

The Museum Pass (€40) from **Musei Civici** (☏ 041/2405211 ⊕ www.visitmuve.it/en/tickets) includes single entry to 11 Venice city museums for six months.

Performing Arts

Visit ⊕ www.agendavenezia.org for a preview of musical, artistic, and sporting events. Venezia News (VENews), available at newsstands, has similar information but also includes in-depth articles about noteworthy events. The tourist office publishes a handy, free quarterly Calendar in Italian and English, listing daily events and current museum and venue hours. Venezia da Vivere (⊕ www.veneziadavivere.com/en) is a seasonal guide listing cool cultural happenings and places. And don't ignore the posters you see plastered on the walls as you walk— often they contain the most up-to-date information you can find.

⇨ For more information on festivals in Venice, see On the Calendar in Travel Smart.

CARNEVALE
Although Carnevale has traditionally been associated with the time leading up to the Roman Catholic period of Lent, it originally started out as a principally secular annual period of partying and feasting to celebrate Venice's victory over Ulrich II, Patriarch of Aquileia, in 1162. To commemorate the annual tribute Ulrich was forced to pay, a bull and 12 pigs were slaughtered in Piazza San Marco each year on the day before Lent. Since then, the city has marked the days preceding Quaresima (Lent) with abundant feasting

and wild celebrations. The word *car-nevale* is derived from the words *carne* (meat) and *levare* (to remove), as eating meat was restricted during Lent. The use of masks for Carnevale was first mentioned in 1268, and its direct association with Lent was not made until the end of the 13th century.

Venice earned its international reputation as the "city of Carnevale" in the 18th century, when partying would begin several months before Lent and the city seemed to be one continuous masquerade. During this time, income from tourists became a major source of funds in La Serenissima's coffers. With the Republic's fall in 1797, Carnevale was prohibited by the French and the Austrians. From Italian reunification in 1866 until the fall of Fascism in the 1940s, the event was alternately allowed or banned, depending on the government's stance.

It was revived for good in the 1970s, when residents began taking to the calli and campi in their own impromptu celebrations. It didn't take long for the tourist industry to embrace Carnevale as a means to stimulate business in low season. And their faith is well placed: each year over the 10- to 12-day Carnevale period (ending on the Tuesday before Ash Wednesday), more than a half-million people attend concerts, theater and street performances, masquerade balls, historical processions, fashion shows, and contests. Stop by any tourist office (☎ *041/2424* ⊕ *www.veneziaunica.it*) for information, but be aware it can be mobbed. If you're not planning on joining in the revelry, you'd be wise to choose another time to visit Venice. Crowds throng the streets (which become one-way, with police directing foot traffic), bridges are designated "no-stopping" zones to avoid gridlock, and prices skyrocket.

Shopping

Alluring shops abound in Venice. You'll find countless vendors of such trademark wares as glass, lace, and high-end textiles. The authenticity of some goods can be suspect, but they're often pleasing to the eye, regardless of origin. You will also find interesting craft and art studios with high-quality, one-of-a-kind articles. Antiques, especially antique Venetian glass, are almost invariably cheaper outside of Venice, because Venetians are ready to pay high prices for their own heritage.

The San Marco area is full of shops and couture boutiques, such as Armani, Missoni, Valentino, Fendi, and Versace. Leading from Piazza San Marco, you'll find some of Venice's busiest shopping streets—Le Mercerie, the Frezzeria, Calle dei Fabbri, and Calle Larga XXII Marzo. Other good shopping areas surround Calle del Teatro and Campi San Salvador, Manin, San Fantin, and San Bartolomeo. You can find somewhat less expensive, more varied, and more imaginative shops between the Ponte di Rialto and San Polo and in Santa Croce, and art galleries in Dorsoduro from the Salute to the Accademia. Regular store hours are usually 9 to 12:30 and 3:30 or 4 to 7:30; some stores close Saturday afternoon or Monday morning.

Tours

Venice has a variety of tours with expert guides; just be sure to choose a guide that's authorized if you book a private tour. Some excursions also include a boat tour as a portion of a longer walking tour. And, of course, a gondola ride is always an excellent way to take in the sights of the city.

GONDOLA RIDES

The best location to hire a gondola depends on your preference. For a waterside view of Grand Canal palaces, board a boat at one of the main gondola stations, such as Santa Maria del Giglio or San Toma. For a quieter experience, start your tour from a peaceful *fondamenta* (quay) in Cannaregio or Castello, like the Fondamenta S. Severo. The price of a 40-minute ride is €80 for up to six passengers, increasing to €100 between 7 pm and 8 am. Every 20 minutes extra is an additional €40. ■TIP→ **Agree with your gondolier on price and duration of the ride beforehand to avoid confusion and unexpected costs.**

PRIVATE TOURS

A Guide in Venice

GUIDED TOURS | This popular company offers a wide variety of innovative, entertaining, and informative themed tours—including master artisan, art, and architecture tours—for private groups of up to eight people. Guided tours generally last two to three hours, with a fee of €90 per hour, which does not include admissions or transportation fees. ☎ *0348/5927974* ⊕ *www.aguideinvenice.com.*

See Venice

GUIDED TOURS | Luisella Romeo is a delightful guide capable of bringing to life even the most convoluted aspects of Venice's art and history. She can customize tours depending on guests' areas of interest, including Murano and glass art, music in Venice, and photography tours. ☎ *0349/0848303* ⊕ *www.seevenice.it.*

Walks Inside Venice

GUIDED TOURS | For a host of particularly creative group and private tours—from history to art to gastronomy—check out Walks Inside Venice. The maximum group size is six, and tour guides include people with advanced university degrees and published authors. ☎ *0347/2530560, 0335/5229714* ⊕ *www.walksinsidevenice.com.*

Visitor Information

The multilingual staff of the Venice tourism office (☎ *041/2424* ⊕ *www.veneziaunica.it*) can provide directions and up-to-the-minute information. Branches can be found at Marco Polo Airport; the Venezia Santa Lucia train station; Garage Comunale, on Piazzale Roma; and at Piazza San Marco near Museo Correr at the southwest corner. The train station branch is open daily 8 am–6:30 pm; other branches have similar hours.

San Marco

Extending from Piazza San Marco (St. Mark's Square) to the Ponte di Rialto, this sestiere is the historical and commercial heart of Venice. Restaurants in its eponymous square—the only one in Venice given full stature as a "piazza" and, hence, often referred to simply as "the Piazza"—heave with tourists, but enjoying an *aperitivo* (pre-dinner drink) here is an unforgettable experience.

This sestiere is also graced with some of Venice's loveliest churches, best-endowed museums, and finest hotels (often with Grand Canal views). In addition, it's the city's main shopping district. Some of the famous Venetian glass producers from Murano have boutiques in San Marco, as do many Italian designers. Its mazes of streets are also lined with shops that sell elegantly wrought jewelry among other items.

TIMING

You can easily spend several days seeing the historical and artistic monuments in and around Piazza San Marco alone, but at a bare minimum, plan on at least an hour for the basilica and its wonderful mosaics. Add on another half hour if you want to see its Pala d'Oro, Galleria, and Museo di San Marco. You'll want at least an hour to appreciate the Palazzo Ducale. Leave another hour for the Museo

Correr, through which you also enter the archaeological museum and the Libreria Sansoviniana. If you choose to simply take in the piazza itself from a café table at an establishment with an orchestra, keep in mind there will be an additional charge for the music.

⊙ Sights

★ Basilica di San Marco
(*St. Mark's Basilica*)
CHURCH | The Basilica di San Marco is not only the religious center of a great city, but also an expression of the political, intellectual, and economic aspiration and accomplishments of a place that, for centuries, was at the forefront of European culture. It is a monument not just to the glory of God, but also to the glory of Venice. The basilica was the doges' personal chapel, linking its religious function to the political life of the city, and was endowed with all the riches the Republic's admirals and merchants could carry off from the Orient (as the Byzantine Empire was then known), earning it the nickname "Chiesa d'Oro" (Golden Church). The glory of the basilica is, of course, its medieval mosaic work; about 30% of the mosaics survive in something close to their original form. The earliest date from the late 12th century, but the great majority date from the 13th century. A 4th- or 5th-century treasure—the Cotton Genesis, the earliest illustrated Bible—was brought from Constantinople and supplied the designs for the exquisite mosaics of the Creation and the stories of Abraham, Joseph, and Moses that adorn the narthex (entrance hall). Remember that this is a sacred place: guards may deny admission to people in shorts, sleeveless dresses, and tank tops. ⊠ *Piazza San Marco, San Marco 328, San Marco* ☎ *041/2708311* ⊕ *www.basilicasanmarco.it* ⊲ *Standard tickets: Basilica €3, Pala d'Oro €5, museum and*

Loggia dei Cavalli €7, bell tower €10. Skip-the-line tickets: Basilica €6, Pala d'Oro €12, museum and Loggia dei Cavalli €15, full ticket (Basilica, museum, Loggia dei Cavalli) €20, bell tower €12 ⊘ *Basilica and Pala d'Oro closed for tourist visits (church services only) Sun. till 2 pm* Ⓜ *Vaporetto: Zaccaria, Vallaresso.*

Campanile di San Marco
(*St. Mark's Bell Tower*)
VIEWPOINT | Construction of Venice's famous brick bell tower (325 feet tall, plus the angel) began in the 9th century; it took on its present form in 1514. During the 15th century, the tower was used as a place of punishment: immoral clerics were suspended in wooden cages from the tower, some forced to subsist on bread and water for as long as a year; others were left to starve. In 1902, the tower unexpectedly collapsed, taking with it Jacopo Sansovino's marble loggia (1537–49) at its base. The largest original bell, called the Marangona, survived. The crushed loggia was promptly reconstructed, and the new tower, rebuilt to the old plan, reopened in 1912. On a clear day the stunning view includes the Lido, the lagoon, and the mainland as far as the Alps, but strangely enough, none of the myriad canals that snake through the city. ⊠ *Piazza San Marco, San Marco* ☎ *041/2708311* ⊕ *www.basilicasanmarco.it* ⊲ *€10, skip-the-line tickets €12* Ⓜ *Vaporetto: San Zaccaria, Vallaresso.*

★ Museo Correr
HISTORY MUSEUM | This museum of Venetian art and history contains an impressive sculpture collection by Antonio Canova and important paintings by Giovanni Bellini, Vittore Carpaccio (Carpaccio's famous painting of the Venetian courtesans is here), and other major local painters in the Neoclassical Rooms and Picture Gallery. The museum's highlights are the 20 sumptuously decorated and meticulously restored Royal Rooms,

Continued on page 202

CRUISING THE GRAND CANAL

THE BEST INTRODUCTION TO VENICE IS A TRIP DOWN MAIN STREET

Venice's Grand Canal is one of the world's great thoroughfares. It winds its way from Piazzale Roma to Piazza San Marco, passing 200 palazzi built from the 13th to the 18th centuries by Venice's richest and most powerful families. There's a theatrical quality to a boat ride on the canal: it's as if each pink- or gold-tinted façade is trying to steal your attention from its rival across the way.

In medieval and Renaissance cities, wars and sieges required defense to be an element of design; but in rich, impregnable Venice, you could safely show off what you had. But more than being simply an item of conspicuous consumption, a Venetian's palazzo was an embodiment of his person—not only his wealth, but also his erudition and taste.

The easiest and cheapest way to see the Grand Canal is to take the Line 1 vaporetto (water bus) from Piazalle Roma to San Marco. The ride takes about 35 minutes. Invest in a day ticket and you can spend the better part of a day hopping on and off at the vaporetto's many stops, visiting the sights along the banks. Keep your eyes open for the highlights listed here; some have fuller descriptions later in this chapter.

Traditional gondola rowing down
the Grand Canal

FROM PIAZZALE ROMA TO RIALTO

Palazzo Labia
Tiepolo's masterpiece, the cycle of Antony and Cleopatra, graces the grand ballroom in this palazzo. The Labia family, infamous for their ostentation, commissioned the frescos to celebrate a marriage and had Tiepolo use the face of the family matriarch, Maria Labia, for that of Cleopatra. Luckily, Maria Labia was known not only for her money, but also for her intelligence and her beauty.

Santa Maria di Nazareth

Ponte di Scalzi

R. DI BIASIO

FERROVIA

SANTA CROCE

Stazione Ferrovia Santa Lucia

Ponte di Calatrava

After you pass the Ferrovia, the baroque church immediately to your left is the baroque **Santa Maria di Nazareth**, called the Chiesa degli Scalzi (Church of the Barefoot).

After passing beneath the Ponte di Scalzi, ahead to the left, where the Canale di Cannaregio meets the Grand Canal, you'll spy **Palazzo Labia**, an elaborate 18th-century palace built for the social-climbing Labia family. Known for their ostentation even in this city

where modesty was seldom a virtue, the Labias chose a location that required three façades instead of the usual one.

A bit farther down, across the canal, is the 13th-century **Fondaco dei Turchi**, an elegant residence that served as a combination commercial center and ghetto for the Turkish community. Try not to see the side towers and the crenellations; they were added during a 19th-century restoration.

Beyond it is the obelisk-topped **Ca' Belloni-Battagia**, designed for the Belloni family by star architect Longhena. Look for the family crest he added prominently on the façade.

On the opposite bank is architect Mauro Codussi's magnificent **Palazzo Vendramin-Calergi**, designed just before 1500. Codussi ingeniously married the fortress-like Renaissance style of the Florentine Alberti's Palazzo Rucellai to the lacy delicacy of the Venetian Gothic, creating the prototype of the Venetian Renaissance palazzo. The palazzo is now Venice's casino.

Palazzo Vendramin-Calergi

Venice's first Renaissance palazzo. Immediately recognized as a masterpiece, it was so highly regarded that later, when its subsequent owners, the Calergi, were convicted of murder and their palace was to be torn down as punishment, the main building was spared.

Ca' d'Oro

Inspired by stories of Nero's Domus Aurea (Golden House) in Rome, the first owner had parts of the façade gilded with 20,000 sheets of gold leaf. The gold has long worn away, but the Ca' D'Oro is still Venice's most beautiful Gothic palazzo.

GHETTO

S. MARCUOLA

Ca' Belloni-Battagia

S. STAE

Ca' da Mosto

Venice's oldest surviving palazzo gives you an idea of Marco Polo's Venice. More than any other Byzantine palazzo in town, it maintains its original 13th-century appearance.

Ca' Pesaro

Fondaco dei Turchi

Depositi del Megio

San Stae Church

SAN POLO

Ca' Corner della Regina

CA' D'ORO

Pescheria

Stop by in the morning to see the incredible variety of fish for sale. Produce stalls fill the adjacent fondamenta. Butchers and cheesemongers occupy the surrounding shops.

Rialto Mercato

Fondaco dei Tedeschi

Ca' dei Camerlenghi

RIALTO

SAN MARCO

The whimsically baroque church of **San Stae** on the right bank is distinguished by a host of marble saints on its façade.

Farther along the bank is one of Longhena's Baroque masterpieces, **Ca' Pesaro**. It is now the Museum of Modern Art.

Next up on the left is **Ca' d'Oro** (1421-1438), the canal's most spendid example of Venetian Gothic domestic design. Across from this palazzo is the loggia of the neo-Gothic **pescheria**, Venice's fish market.

Slightly farther down, on the bank opposite from the vegetable market, is the early 13th-century **Ca' da Mosto**, the oldest building on the Grand Canal. The upper two floors are later additions, but the ground floor and piano nobile give you a good idea of a rich merchant's house during the time of Marco Polo.

As you approach the Rialto Bridge, to the left, just before the bridge, is the

Fondaco dei Tedeschi. German merchants kept warehouses, offices, and residences here; its façade was originally frescoed by Titian and Giorgione.

FROM RIALTO TO THE PONTE DELL' ACCADEMIA

SAN POLO

Ponte di Rialto

RIALTO

Ca' Foscari
The canal's most imposing Gothic masterpiece, Ca' Foscari was built to blot out the memory of a traitor to the Republic.

Palazzo Barzizza

Ca' Loredan

S. SILVESTRO

Ca' Farsetti

Ca' Grimani

Palazzo Pisani Moretta

S. ANGELO

TOMA

Ca' Garzoni

Ca' Balbi

Palazzo Grassi

Ca' Rezzonico

SAN MARCO

REZZONICO

ACCADEMIA

Gallerie dell'Accademia

DORSODURO

The shop-lined **Ponte di Rialto** was built in stone after former wooden bridges had burned or collapsed. As you pass under the bridge, on your left stands star architect Sansovino's Palazzo Dolfin Manin. The white stone–clad Renaissance palace was built at huge expense and over the objections of its conservative neighbors.

A bit farther down stand **Ca' Loredan** and **Ca' Farsetti**, 13th-century Byzantine palaces that today make up Venice's city hall.

Along the same side is the **Ca' Grimani**, by the Veronese architect Sanmichele. Legend has it that the palazzo's oversized windows were demanded by the young Grimani's fiancée, who insisted that he build her a palazzo on the Canale Grande with windows larger than the portal of her own house.

At the Sant'Angelo landing, the vaporetto passes close to Codussi's **Ca' Corner-Spinelli**. Back on the right bank, in a lovely salmon color, is the graceful **Palazzo Pisani Moretta**, built in the mid-15th century and typical of the Venetian Gothic palazzo of the generation after the Ca' D'Oro.

A bit farther down the right bank, crowned by obelisks, is **Ca' Balbi**. Niccolò Balbi built this elegant palazzo in order to upstage his former landlord, who had insulted him in public. Farther down the right bank, where the Canale makes a sharp turn, is the imposing **Ca' Foscari**. Doge Francesco Foscari tore down an earlier palazzo on this spot and built this splendid palazzo to erase memory of the traitorous former owner. It is now the seat of the University of Venice.

Continuing down the right bank you'll find Longhena's **Ca' Rezzonico**, a magnificent baroque palace. Opposite stands the Grand Canal's youngest palace, Giorgio Massari's **Palazzo Grassi**, commissioned in 1749. It houses part of the François Pinot contemporary art collection.

Near the canal's fourth bridge, is the former church and monastery complex that houses the world-renowned **Gallerie dell'Accademia**, the world's largest and most distinguished collection of Venetian art.

ARCHITECTURAL STYLES ALONG THE GRAND CANAL

BYZANTINE: 13th century
Distinguishing characteristics: high, rounded arches, relief panels, multicolored marble.

Examples: Fondaco dei Turchi, Ca' Loredan, Ca' Farsetti, Ca' da Mosto

GOTHIC: 14th and 15th centuries
Distinguishing characteristics: pointed arches, high ceilings, and many windows.

Examples: Ca' d'Oro, Ca' Foscari, Palazzo Pisani Moretta, Ca' Barbaro (and, off the canal, Palazzo Ducale)

RENAISSANCE: 16th century
Distinguishing characteristics: classically influenced emphasis on harmony and motifs taken from classical antiquity.

Examples: Palazzo Vendramin-Calergi, Ca' Grimani, Ca' Corner-Spinelli, Ca' dei Camerlenghi, Ca' Balbi, Palazzo Corner della Ca' Granda, Palazzo Dolfin Manin, and, off the canal, Libreria, Sansoviniana on Piazza San Marco

BAROQUE: 17th century
Distinguishing characteristics: Renaissance order wedded with a more dynamic style, achieved through curving lines and complex decoration.

Examples: churches of Santa Maria di Nazareth, San Stae, and Santa Maris della Salute; Ca' Belloni Battaglia, Ca' Pesaro, Ca' Rezzonico

FROM THE PONTE DELL'ACCADEMIA TO SAN ZACCARIA

Ca' Barbaro
John Singer Sargent, Henry James, and Cole Porter are among the guests who have stayed at Ca' Barbaro. It was a center for elegant British and American society during the turn of the 20th century.

Santa Maria Della Salute
Baldessare Longhena was only 26 when he designed this church, which was to become one of Venice's major landmarks. Its rotunda form and dynamic Baroque decoration predate iconic Baroque churches in other Italian cities.

S A N   M A R C O

Ponte dell' Accademia

ACCADEMIA

Ca' Pisani-Gritti

Palazzo Corner della Ca' Granda

Casetta Rossa

S. M. DEL GIGLIO

D O R S O D U R O

Ca' Barbarigo

SALUTE

Palazzo Salviati

S. Maria della Salute

Palazzo Venier dei Leoni
Eccentric art dealer Peggy Guggenheim's personal collection of modern art is here. At the Grand Canal entrance to the palazzo stands Marino Marini's sexually explicit equestrian sculpture, the Angel of the Citadel. Numerous entertaining stories have been spun around the statue and Ms. Guggenheim's overtly libertine ways.

Ca' Dario
Graceful and elegant Ca' Dario is reputed to carry a curse. Almost all its owners since the 15th century have met violent deaths or committed suicide. It was, nevertheless, a center for elegant French society at the turn of the 20th century.

Down from the Accademia bridge, on the left bank next door to the fake Gothic Ca' Franchetti, is the beautiful **Ca' Barbaro**, designed by Giovanni Bon, who was also at work about that time on the Ca' D'Oro.

Farther along on the left bank Sansovino's first work in Venice, the **Palazzo Corner della Ca' Granda**, begun in 1533, still shows the influence of his Roman Renaissance contemporaries, Bramante and Giulio Romano. It faces the uncompleted **Palazzo Venier dei Leoni**, which holds the Peggy Guggenheim Collection, a good cross-section of the visual arts from 1940 to 1960.

Ca' Dario a bit farther down, was originally a Gothic palazzo, but in 1487 it was given an early Renaissance multicolored marble façade.

At this point on the canal the cupola of **Santa Maria della Salute** dominates the scene. The commission for the design of the church to celebrate the Virgin's rescuing Venice

from the disastrous plague of 1630, was given to the 26-year-old Longhena. The young architect stressed the new and inventive aspects of his design, likening the rotunda shape to a crown for the Virgin.

Basilica di S. Marco

Palazzo Ducale

S. ZACCARIA

PIAZZA SAN MARCO

VALLARESSO

Palazzo Dandolo a San Moise

Punta della Dogana

The Grand Canal is 2½ miles long, has an average depth of 9 feet, and is 76 yards wide at its broadest point and 40 yards at its narrowest.

SAN GIORGI MAGGIORE

Across from the Salute, enjoying the magnificent view across the canal, are a string of luxury hotels whose historic façades have either been radically modified or are modern neo-Gothic fantasies. The main interest here is the rather unimposing Hotel Monaco e Gran Canal, the former Palazzo Dandolo a San Moise, which contains Europe's first casino, the famous ridotto, founded in 1638. It was a stomping ground of Casanova, and was closed by the Republic in 1774 because too much money was being lost to foreigners.

At the **Punta della Dogana** on the tip of Dorsoduro, Japanese architect Tadao Ando, using Zen-inspired concepts of space, has transformed a 17th–century customs house into a museum for contemporary art. It is a fitting coda to the theme of Venice as living center for international artistic creativity, as set by Calatrava's bridge at the beginning of the Grand Canal.

At the Vallaresso vaporetto stop you've left the Grand Canal, but stay on board for a view of the **Palazzo Ducale**, with **Basilica di San Marco** behind it, then disembark at San Zaccaria.

Let's Get Lost

Getting around Venice presents some unusual problems: the city's layout has few straight lines; house numbering seems nonsensical; and the six sestieri of San Marco, Cannaregio, Castello, Dorsoduro, Santa Croce, and San Polo all duplicate each other's street names. What's more, addresses in Venice are given by sestiere rather than street, making them of limited help in getting around. Venetians commonly give directions by pinpointing a major landmark, such as a church, and telling you where to go from there.

The numerous vaporetto lines can be bewildering, too, and often the only option for getting where you want to go is to walk. Yellow signs, posted on many busy corners, point toward the major landmarks—San Marco, Rialto, Accademia, and so forth—but don't count on finding such markers once you're deep into residential neighborhoods. Even buying a good map at a newsstand—the kind showing all street names and vaporetto routes—won't necessarily keep you from getting lost. To make matters worse, map apps on smart phones, for some reason, give frequently erroneous results for Venice.

Fortunately, as long as you maintain your patience, getting lost in Venice can be a pleasure. For one thing, being lost is a sign that you've escaped the tourist throngs. And although you might not find the Titian masterpiece you'd set out to see, you could wind up coming across an ageless *bacaro* (a traditional wine bar) or a quirky shop that turns out to be the highlight of your afternoon. Opportunities for such serendipity abound. Keep in mind that the city is self-contained: sooner or later, perhaps with the help of a patient native, you can rest assured you'll regain your bearings.

home to three ruling dynasties from the 19th century to 1920, and where Sissi, the empress of Austria, once stayed; English visits take place at 10:30 am and 3:30 pm daily and can be booked online. Several rooms also convey the city's proud naval history through highly descriptive paintings and numerous maritime objects, including ships' cannons and some surprisingly large iron mast-top navigation lights. ✉ *Piazza San Marco 52, Ala Napoleonica, opposite Basilica, San Marco* ☎ *041/2405211* ⊕ *correr.visitmuve.it* ✉ *Royal Rooms Itinerary Ticket €14, including Museo Correr, Museo Archeologico, and Biblioteca Nazionale Marciana. Museums of San Marco Pass €30 (€25 when booked online at least 30 days in advance), includes Museo Correr, Museo Archeologico, Biblioteca* *Nazionale Marciana, and Palazzo Ducale. Museum Pass €41, includes all four museums plus seven civic museums. Royal Rooms tour only €5 with Museums of San Marco Pass or Museum Pass* Ⓜ *Vaporetto: San Zaccaria, Vallaresso.*

★ **Palazzo Ducale** (*Doge's Palace*)
CASTLE/PALACE | Rising majestically above Piazzetta San Marco, this Gothic fantasia of pink-and-white marble—the doges' residence from the 10th century and the central administrative center of the Venetian Republic—is a majestic expression of Venetian prosperity and power. Upon entering, you'll find yourself in an immense courtyard with some of the first evidence of Venice's Renaissance architecture, including Antonio Rizzo's 15th-century Scala dei Giganti (Stairway

of the Giants). The palace's sumptuous chambers have walls and ceilings
covered with works by Venice's greatest
artists. In the Anticollegio you'll find *The
Rape of Europa* by Veronese and Tintoretto's *Bacchus and Ariadne Crowned by
Venus*. The ceiling of the Sala del Senato
(Senate Chamber), featuring *The Triumph
of Venice* by Tintoretto, is magnificent,
but it's dwarfed by his masterpiece
Paradise in the Sala del Maggiore Consiglio (Great Council Hall), the world's
largest oil painting. The popular Secret
Itineraries tour lets you visit the doge's
private apartments and hidden passageways. ⊠ *Piazza San Marco 1, San Marco*
☎ *041/42730892 tickets* ⊕ *palazzoducale.
visitmuve.it* ✉ *Museums of San Marco
Pass €30 (€25 when booked online
at least 30 days in advance), includes
Museo Correr, Museo Archeologico, Biblioteca Nazionale Marciana, and Palazzo
Ducale. Museum Pass €41, includes all
four museums plus seven civic museums. Secret Itineraries or Doge's Hidden
Treasures tour €32* Ⓜ *Vaporetto: San
Zaccaria, Vallaresso.*

★ Palazzo Grassi

ART MUSEUM | Built between 1748 and
1772 by Giorgio Massari for a Bolognese
family, this palace is one of the last of
the great noble residences on the Grand
Canal. Once owned by auto magnate
Gianni Agnelli, it was bought by French
businessman François Pinault in 2005 to
showcase his highly esteemed collection
of modern and contemporary art (which
has now grown so large that Pinault
rented the Punta della Dogana, at the
entryway to the Grand Canal, for his
newest acquisitions). Pinault brought in
Japanese architect Tadao Ando to remod-
el the Grassi's interior. Check online for
a schedule of temporary art exhibitions.
⊠ *Campo San Samuele 3231, San Marco*
☎ *041/2401308* ⊕ *www.palazzograssi.
it* ✉ *€15, includes Punta della Dogana*
☉ *Closed Tues.* Ⓜ *Vaporetto: San Samuele, Sant'Angelo.*

★ Piazza San Marco (*St. Mark's Square*)

PLAZA/SQUARE | **FAMILY** | One of the world's
most beautiful squares, Piazza San
Marco (St. Mark's Square) is the spiritual
and artistic heart of Venice, a vast open
space bordered by an orderly procession
of arcades marching toward the fairy-tale
cupolas and marble lacework of the Basilica di San Marco. From midmorning on, it
is generally packed with tourists. (If Venetians have business in the piazza, they try
to conduct it in the early morning, before
the crowds swell.) At night the piazza can
be magical, especially in winter, when
mists swirl around the lampposts and the
campanile.

Facing the basilica, on your left, the
long, arcaded building is the Procuratie
Vecchie, renovated to its present form
in 1514 as offices and residences for the
powerful procurators, or magistrates.

On your right is the Procuratie Nuove,
built half a century later in a more
imposing, classical style. It was originally
planned by Venice's great Renaissance
architect Jacopo Sansovino (1486–1570),
to carry on the look of his Libreria Sansoviniana (Sansovinian Library), but he
died before construction on the Nuove
had begun. Vincenzo Scamozzi (circa
1552–1616), a pupil of Andrea Palladio
(1508–80), completed the design and
construction. Still later, the Procuratie
Nuove was modified by architect Bal-
dassare Longhena (1598–1682), one of
Venice's Baroque masters.

When Napoléon (1769–1821) entered
Venice with his troops in 1797, he
expressed his admiration for the piazza
and promptly gave orders to alter it. His
architects demolished a church with a
Sansovino facade in order to build the
Ala Napoleonica (Napoleonic Wing), or
Fabbrica Nuova (New Building), which
linked the two 16th-century procuratie
and effectively enclosed the piazza.

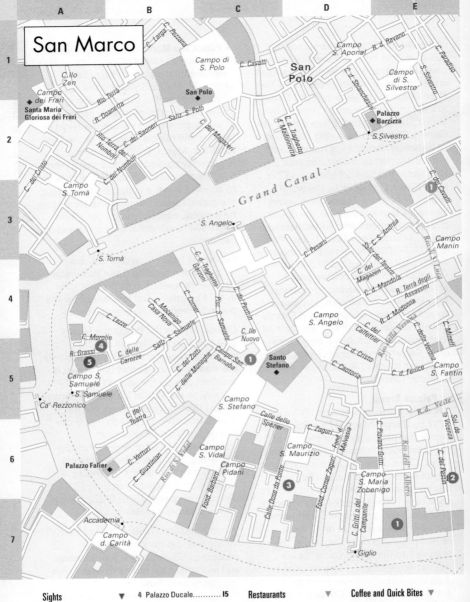

San Marco

Sights ▼

1 Basilica di San Marco.............. **I4**
2 Campanile di San Marco.............. **H5**
3 Museo Correr **G5**
4 Palazzo Ducale........... **I5**
5 Palazzo Grassi **A5**
6 Piazza San Marco **H5**
7 Ponte di Rialto........... **G1**

Restaurants ▼

1 Enoteca al Volto......... **E3**
2 Harry's Bar **G6**
3 Ristorante Quadri....... **H4**

Coffee and Quick Bites ▼

1 Bar all'Angolo............ **C5**
2 Caffè Florian.............. **H5**
3 Gelatoteca Suso **H1**
4 Gran Caffè Quadri **H4**

Hotels ▼

1 The Gritti Palace, a
  Luxury Collection
  Hotel, Venice **E7**

2 Hotel Flora **E6**

3 Novecento
  Boutique Hotel **D6**

4 Palazzina Grassi **A5**

5 The St. Regis
  Venice **F7**

KEY

❶ Sights

❶ Restaurants

❶ Quick Bites

❶ Hotels

Taking a Gondola Ride

Riding a gondola along the canals is an iconic Venetian experience—and one that's still very much worth doing, despite the expense. It's not hard to find a gondolier, donned in traditional striped garb, beckoning from the helm of a docked boat to take you on a relaxing ride along the city's waterways. Venture away from the busy area around the Grand Canal and look for a boat on one of the smaller, quieter waterways so you can nestle into the plushly upholstered seats and float by Venice's legendary facades without being distracted by the crowds. Go in the morning to watch the city come to life, in the late afternoon when the colors of the buildings are especially vibrant, or at sunset for maximum romance. Boats sit six people, and signs posted on the red-and-white striped poles throughout the city list the standard rates for a 30-minute gondola ride (€80 during the day, €100 after 7 pm; 20-minute increments can be added for an additional fee).

Piazzetta San Marco is the "little square" leading from Piazza San Marco to the waters of Bacino San Marco (St. Mark's Basin); its *molo* (landing) once served as the grand entrance to the Republic. Two imposing columns tower above the waterfront. One is topped by the winged lion, a traditional emblem of St. Mark that became the symbol of Venice itself; the other supports St. Theodore, the city's first patron, along with his dragon. (A third column fell off its barge and ended up in the bacino before it could be placed alongside the others.) Although the columns are a glorious vision today, the Republic traditionally executed convicts here—and some superstitious Venetians still avoid walking between them. ⊠ *Piazza San Marco, San Marco* Ⓜ *Vaporetto: San Zaccaria, Vallaresso.*

★ **Ponte di Rialto** (*Rialto Bridge*)
BRIDGE | FAMILY | The competition to design a stone bridge across the Grand Canal attracted the best architects of the late 16th century, including Michelangelo, Palladio, and Sansovino, but the job went to the less famous (if appropriately named) Antonio da Ponte (1512–95). His pragmatic design, completed in 1591, featured shop space and was high enough for galleys to pass beneath. Putting practicality and economy over aesthetic considerations—unlike the classical plans proposed by his more famous contemporaries—da Ponte's bridge essentially followed the design of its wooden predecessor. But it kept decoration and cost to a minimum at a time when the Republic's coffers were low, due to continual wars against the Turks and competition brought about by the Spanish and Portuguese opening of oceanic trade routes. Along the railing you'll enjoy one of the city's most famous views: the Grand Canal vibrant with boat traffic. ⊠ *San Marco* Ⓜ *Vaporetto: Rialto.*

🍴 Restaurants

Enoteca al Volto
$$ | VENETIAN | A short walk from the Ponte di Rialto, this bar has been around since 1936, and the satisfying cicheti and *primi* have a lot to do with its staying power. Grab a table out front, or take refuge in one of the two small, dark rooms with a ceiling plastered with wine labels that provide a classic backdrop for simple fare, including a delicious risotto that is served daily from noon, plus a solid wine

list of both Italian and foreign vintages. **Known for:** great local and international wine selection; tasty and inexpensive cicheti; fantastic main courses, including risotto and pasta with seafood. $ *Average main: €17* ✉ *Calle Cavalli, San Marco 4081, San Marco* ☎ *041/5228945* ⊕ *enotecaalvolto.com* Ⓜ *Vaporetto: Rialto.*

★ Harry's Bar

$$$$ | VENETIAN | For those who can afford it, lunch or dinner at Harry's Bar is as much a part of a visit to Venice as a walk across Piazza San Marco or a vaporetto ride down the Grand Canal. Inside, the suave, subdued beige-on-white decor is unchanged from the 1930s, and the classic Venetian fare is carefully and excellently prepared. **Known for:** being the birthplace of the Bellini cocktail; see-and-be-seen atmosphere; signature crepes flambées and famous Cipriani chocolate cake. $ *Average main: €70* ✉ *Calle Vallaresso, San Marco 1323, San Marco* ☎ *041/5285777* ⊕ *www.cipriani.com* Ⓜ *Vaporetto: Vallaresso.*

★ Ristorante Quadri

$$$$ | VENETIAN | Although the lavish interior has been updated by designer Philippe Starck, this restaurant above the famed café of the same name is still steeped in Venetian ambience and history (it was where Turkish coffee was introduced to the city in the 1700s). When the Alajmo family (of the celebrated Le Calandre near Padua) took over, they put their accomplished sous-chef from Padua in charge of the kitchen, resulting in the addition of dishes—best sampled with a tasting menu—that are complex and sophisticated, with a wonderful wine list to match. **Known for:** sophisticated and modern Italian cuisine; seasonal tasting menus; revitalized designer decor. $ *Average main: €170* ✉ *Piazza San Marco 121, San Marco* ☎ *041/5222105* ⊕ *alajmo.it* ⊘ *Closed Mon., Tues., and 3 wks in Jan. No lunch Wed.–Fri.* Ⓜ *Vaporetto: Giardinetti, Vallaresso.*

☕ Coffee and Quick Bites

Bar all'Angolo

$ | CAFÉ | This corner of Campo Santo Stefano is a pleasant place to sit and watch the Venetian world go by. The café staff are in constant motion, so you'll receive your coffee, spritz, panino (a sandwich warmed on a griddle), or *tramezzino* (sandwich on untoasted white bread, usually with a mayonnaise-based filling) in short order; consume it at your leisure at one of the outdoor tables, at the bar, or at the tables in the back. **Known for:** simple yet satisfying fare, like tramezzini and panini; tasty homemade desserts, including tiramisu and cakes; good people-watching. $ *Average main: €12* ✉ *Campo Santo Stefano, San Marco 3464, just in front of Santo Stefano church, San Marco* ☎ *041/5220710* ⊘ *Closed Sun. and Jan.* Ⓜ *Vaporetto: Sant'Angelo.*

★ Caffè Florian

$$ | CAFÉ | Florian is not only Italy's first café (1720), but also one of its most beautiful, with glittering, neo-Baroque decor and 19th-century wall panels depicting Venetian heroes. The coffee, drinks, and snacks are good, but most people come for the atmosphere and history: this was the only café to serve women during the 18th century; it was frequented by artistic notables like Wagner, Goethe, Goldoni, Lord Byron, Marcel Proust, and Charles Dickens; and it was the birthplace of the international art exhibition that became the Venice Biennale. **Known for:** prime location on St. Mark's Square; beautiful, historic interior; hot chocolate, coffee, and quick nibbles. $ *Average main: €18* ✉ *Piazza San Marco 57, San Marco* ☎ *041/5205641* ⊕ *caffeflorian.com* ⊘ *Closed early Jan.* Ⓜ *Vaporetto: Giardinetti, Vallaresso.*

★ Gelatoteca Suso

$ | ICE CREAM | FAMILY | Try this fun shop for gelato that's out of the ordinary: think walnut cream with caramelized fig, or vanilla with rum raisins and Malaga wine; sorbets and milk shakes are also on offer. There's a second location on Salizada S Giovanni Grisostomo, in Cannaregio. **Known for:** unusual flavors; vegan ice cream options; convenient location on way to Rialto Bridge. Ⓢ *Average main: €5* ✉ *Sotoportego de la Bissa, San Marco 5453, San Marco* ☎ *041/3084136* ⊕ *suso. gelatoteca.it* Ⓜ *Vaporetto: Rialto.*

★ Gran Caffè Quadri

$$ | **CAFÉ** | Come for breakfast, a predinner aperitivo, or anything in between at this always lively historic coffeehouse—opened in 1775 and taken over by the famous culinary Alajmo family in 2011—in the center of the action on Piazza San Marco. Choose from a wide selection of pastries at breakfast (though the cappuccino and brioche combo is always a classic), pizzas at lunch, and tramezzini and cicheti all day long. **Known for:** extensive (though pricey) aperitivo; celebrity owners; prime people-watching. Ⓢ *Average main: €20* ✉ *Piazza San Marco 121, San Marco* ☎ *041/5222105* ⊕ *alajmo.it* Ⓜ *Vaporetto: Giardinetti, Vallaresso.*

Hotels

★ The Gritti Palace, a Luxury Collection Hotel, Venice

$$$$ | **HOTEL** | With handblown chandeliers, sumptuous textiles, and sweeping canal views, this grande dame (whose history dates from 1525, when it was built as the residence of the prominent Gritti family) represents aristocratic Venetian living at its best. **Pros:** truly historical property; Grand Canal location; classic Venetian experience. **Cons:** major splurge; some find service a tad snooty; few spa amenities. Ⓢ *Rooms from: €1568* ✉ *Campo Santa Maria del Giglio 2467, San Marco* ☎ *041/794611* ⊕ *www. thegrittipalace.com* ⮠ *82 rooms* †○† *No Meals* Ⓜ *Vaporetto: Giglio.*

Hotel Flora

$$$ | **HOTEL** | The elegant and refined facade announces a charming, and reasonably priced, place to stay; the hospitable staff, the tastefully decorated rooms, and the lovely garden, where guests can breakfast or drink, do not disappoint. **Pros:** central location; peaceful hidden garden; excellent breakfast. **Cons:** some rooms can be on the small side; no water views; old-fashioned lobby doesn't invite hanging out. Ⓢ *Rooms from: €250* ✉ *Calle Bergamaschi, San Marco 2283/A, just off Calle Larga XXII Marzo, San Marco* ☎ *041/5205844* ⊕ *www.hotelflora.it* ⮠ *40 rooms* †○† *Free Breakfast* Ⓜ *Vaporetto: Vallaresso.*

★ Novecento Boutique Hotel

$$$ | **HOTEL** | A stylish yet intimate retreat tucked away on a quiet *calle* (street) midway between Piazza San Marco and the Accademia Bridge offers exquisite rooms tastefully decorated with original furnishings and tapestries from the Mediterranean and Far East. **Pros:** intimate, romantic atmosphere; unique design sensibility; complimentary afternoon tea. **Cons:** most rooms only have showers, not tubs; no elevator; some rooms can be noisy. Ⓢ *Rooms from: €259* ✉ *Calle del Dose, San Marco 2683/84, off Campo San Maurizio, San Marco* ☎ *041/2413765* ⊕ *www.novecento.biz* ⮠ *9 rooms* †○† *Free Breakfast* Ⓜ *Vaporetto: Santa Maria del Giglio.*

Palazzina Grassi

$$$$ | **HOTEL** | The only hotel in Italy outfitted by famed French designer Philippe Starck boasts a clubby atmosphere, over-the-top contemporary rooms lined with Murano glass, and so-close-you-can-touch-them Grand Canal views. **Pros:** fun, modern take on Venetian design; next door to Palazzo Grassi art space and walking distance to St. Mark's; friendly, helpful service. **Cons:** food in restaurant not up to par; bathrooms smaller than they should be; can be loud when parties are in full swing. Ⓢ *Rooms*

from: €436 ⊠ Ramo Grassi, San Marco
☎ 041/5284644 ⊕ www.palazzinagrassi.
com ↪ 26 rooms ⦿ Free Breakfast
Ⓜ Vaporetto: San Samuele.

★ The St. Regis Venice

$$$$ | HOTEL | Whimsical design details
evoking the Venetian landscape abound
in this elegant, contemporary hotel
constructed from five historic palazzi
with phenomenal views onto the Grand
Canal. **Pros:** wonderful central location;
terraces with unbeatable views; St. Regis
butler service for all guests. **Cons:** sleek
modern style not for fans of Venetian
opulence; standard rooms on the small
side; few spa amenities (no pool or
saunas). Ⓢ Rooms from: €1053 ⊠ San
Marco 2159, San Marco ☎ 041/2400001
⊕ www.marriott.com ↪ 169 rooms
⦿ No Meals Ⓜ Vaporetto: Vallaresso.

Nightlife

Bacarando in Corte dell'Orso

WINE BAR | It is easy to see why this place
is popular with the locals, offering fairly
priced cocktails, a reasonable assortment
of cicheti, and a good selection of Italian
wine, but the warm ambience, friendly
staff, and occasional live jazz are the main
draws. The kitchen stays open until late.
⊠ Corte Dell'Orso, San Marco 5495, San
Marco ✛ Tucked away in alley across
from Church of San Giovanni Grisostomo
☎ 041/5238280 ⊕ www.bacarando.com
Ⓜ Vaporetto: Rialto.

Bacaro Jazz

BARS | This Venetian-style dive bar has
strong cocktails, a jazz soundtrack, and
hundreds of bras hanging from the
ceiling. The lively daily happy hour is a
great time to visit. ⊠ San Marco 5546,
San Marco ☎ 041/5285249 ⊕ bacarojazz.
it Ⓜ Vaporetto: Rialto.

★ Bar Longhi

BARS | The Gritti Palace is home to one
of the most exclusive watering holes
in town (though thankfully open to the
public), lined with 18th-century paintings

and Murano chandeliers. You can also
enjoy your cocktail on the patio with
prime views onto the Grand Canal.
⊠ The Gritti Palace, Campo Santa Maria
del Giglio, San Marco 2467, San Marco
☎ 041/794611 ⊕ www.thegrittipalace.
com Ⓜ Vaporetto: Giglio.

🛍 Shopping

★ Al Duca d'Aosta

CLOTHING | The most stylish of Venetians
and visitors alike come here for women's
and men's designer labels for every taste.
Brands include Burberry, Fendi, Givenchy,
Lanvin, Loewe, Moncler, and many
others; be prepared to be wowed. ⊠ San
Marco 284, San Marco ☎ 041/5220733
⊕ www.alducadaosta.com Ⓜ Vaporetto:
San Marco, Zaccaria.

★ Atelier Segalin di Daniela Ghezzo

SHOES | This artist turned master shoe-
maker produces one-of-a-kind creations
from exotic leathers. Though the shoes
start at €650 and usually take at least
six weeks to finish, you'll truly feel like
you're wearing a masterpiece. ⊠ Calle
dei Fuseri, San Marco 4365, San Marco
☎ 041/5222115 ⊕ www.danielaghezzo.it
Ⓜ Vaporetto: Rialto.

★ Friulane Dittura

SHOES | Run by a second-generation
shoemaker, this shop is one of the only
places left in the city still producing
Venice's iconic friulane slippers, invented
in the 19th century and hand-stitched
from velvet and rubber. The shoes are
still worn by gondoliers today. ⊠ Calle
Fiubera, San Marco 943, San Marco
☎ 041/5231163 ⊕ www.facebook.com/
friulanedittura Ⓜ Vaporetto: San Marco.

★ Giuliana Longo

HATS & GLOVES | A hat shop that's been
around since 1901 offers an assortment
of Venetian and gondolier straw hats,
Panama hats from Ecuador, caps and
berets, and some select scarves of silk
and fine wool; there's even a special corner dedicated to accessories for antique

Venetian Art Glass

The glass of Murano is Venice's number one product, and you'll be confronted by mind-boggling displays of traditional and contemporary glassware—much of it kitsch and not made in Venice. Traditional Venetian glass is hot blown glass, not lead crystal; it comes in myriad forms that range from the classic ornate goblets and chandeliers, to beads, vases, sculpture, and more. Beware of paying "Venetian" prices for glass made elsewhere. A piece claiming to be made in Murano may guarantee its origin, but not its value or quality; the prestigious Venetian glassmakers—like Venini, Seguso, Salviati, and others—sign their pieces, but never use a "made in Murano" label. To make a smart purchase, take your time and be selective. You can learn a great deal without sales pressure at the Museo del Vetro (⊕ *museovetro.visitmuve.it*) on Murano; unfortunately, you'll likely find the least attractive glass where public demonstrations are offered. Although prices in Venice and on Murano are comparable, shops in Venice with wares from various glassworks may charge slightly less.

■TIP→ A "free" taxi to Murano always comes with sales pressure. Take the vaporetto included in your transit pass, and, if you prefer, a private guide who specializes in the subject but has no affinity to any specific furnace.

cars. ⊠ *Calle del Lovo, San Marco 4813, San Marco* ☎ *041/5226454* ⊕ *www.giulianalongo.com* Ⓜ *Vaporetto: San Marco.*

★ Jesurum Venezia 1870

FABRICS | A great deal of so-called Burano Venetian lace is now machine-made in China—and there really is a difference. Unless you have some experience, you're best off going to a trusted place. Jesurum has been the major producer of handmade Venetian lace since 1870. Its lace is, of course, all modern production, but if you want an antique piece, the people at Jesurum can point you in the right direction. ⊠ *Calle Veste, San Marco 2024, San Marco* ☎ *041/5238969* ⊕ *www.jesurum.it* Ⓜ *Vaporetto: Vallaresso.*

★ MuranoVitrum

GLASSWARE | You'll find Murano-made glassworks, including glasses, vases, chandeliers, mirrors, and sculptures, in this friendly family-owned shop. ⊠ *San Marco 1229, San Marco* ☎ *041/5206358* ⊕ *www.muranovitrum.com* Ⓜ *Vaporetto: Vallaresso.*

T Fondaco dei Tedeschi

DEPARTMENT STORE | This 15th-century Renaissance commercial center served as Venice's main post office for many years, but was remodeled and returned to its historical roots as a luxury department store. Here you can find a large assortment of high-end jewelry, clothing, and other luxury items. Plus, fabulous views can be had from the rooftop terrace—book a free 15-minute visit online; reservations open 21 days before the visit date. ⊠ *Calle Fondaco dei Tedeschi, near San Marco end of Ponte di Rialto, San Marco* ☎ *041/3142000* ⊕ *www.dfs.com* Ⓜ *Vaporetto: Rialto.*

Dorsoduro

The sestiere Dorsoduro (named for its "hard back" solid clay foundation) is across the Grand Canal to the south of San Marco. It is a place of meandering canals, the city's finest art museums, monumental churches, and *scuole* (Renaissance civic institutions) filled with works by Titian, Veronese, and Tiepolo, and a promenade called the Zattere, where on sunny days you'll swear half the city is out for *passeggiata* (a stroll). The eastern tip of the peninsula, the Punta della Dogana, is capped by the dome of Santa Maria della Salute and was once the city's customs point; the old customs house is now a museum of contemporary art.

TIMING

You can easily spend a full day in the neighborhood. Devote at least a half hour to admiring the Titians in the imposing and monumental Santa Maria della Salute, and another half hour to the wonderful Veroneses in the peaceful, serene church of San Sebastiano. The Gallerie dell'Accademia demands a few hours, but if time is short an audio guide can help you cover the highlights in about an hour. Ca' Rezzonico deserves at least an hour, as does the Peggy Guggenheim Collection.

 Sights

★ Ca' Rezzonico

HISTORY MUSEUM | Designed by Baldassare Longhena in the 17th century, this gigantic palace was completed nearly 100 years later by Giorgio Massari and became the last home of English poet Robert Browning (1812–89). Stand on the bridge by the Grand Canal entrance to spot the plaque with Browning's poetic excerpt, "Open my heart and you will see graved inside of it, Italy ...," on the left side of the palace. The spectacular centerpiece is the eye-popping Grand Ballroom, which has hosted some of the grandest parties in the city's history, from its 18th-century heyday to the 1969 Bal Fantastica (a Save Venice charity event that attracted every notable of the day, from Elizabeth Taylor to Aristotle Onassis). Today the upper floors of the Ca' Rezzonico are home to the especially delightful Museo del Settecento (Museum of Venice in the 1700s). Its main floor

successfully retains the appearance of a magnificent Venetian palazzo. ⊠ *Fondamenta Rezzonico, Dorsoduro 3136, Dorsoduro* ☎ *041/2410100* ⊕ *carezzonico. visitmuve.it* 🎟 *€10 (free with Museum Pass)* ⊘ *Closed Mon.–Wed.* Ⓜ *Vaporetto: Ca' Rezzonico.*

Campo Santa Margherita

PLAZA/SQUARE | Lined with cafés and restaurants generally filled with students from the two nearby universities, Campo Santa Margherita also has produce vendors and benches where you can sit and take in the bustling local life of the campo. Also close to Ca' Rezzonico and the Scuola Grande dei Carmini, and only a 10-minute walk from the Gallerie dell'Accademia, the square is the center of Dorsoduro social life. It takes its name from the church to one side, closed since the early 19th century and now used as an auditorium. On weekend evenings, especially in the summer, it attracts hordes of students, even from the mainland. ⊠ *Campo Santa Margherita, Dorsoduro* Ⓜ *Vaporetto: Zattere, Ca' Rezzonico.*

★ Gallerie dell'Accademia

ART MUSEUM | The greatest collection of Venetian paintings in the world hangs in these galleries founded by Napoléon in 1807 on the site of a religious complex he had suppressed. The galleries were carefully and subtly restructured between 1945 and 1959 by the renowned Venetian architect Carlo Scarpa. Highlights include works by Jacopo Bellini, the father of the Venetian Renaissance, as well as the richly colored paintings of his more accomplished son Giovanni; *The Tempest* by Giorgione, a revolutionary work that has intrigued viewers and critics for centuries; *Feast in the House of Levi,* which got Veronese summoned to the Inquisition; and several of Tintoretto's finest works. Don't miss the views of 15th- and 16th-century Venice by Carpaccio and Gentile Bellini, Giovanni's brother—you'll recognize many places you've seen on

Sights ▼

1	Ca' Rezzonico **D4**
2	Campo Santa Margherita.......... **C4**
3	Gallerie dell'Accademia **E6**
4	Gesuati................................. **D7**
5	Peggy Guggenheim Collection... **G6**
6	Punta della Dogana **I6**
7	San Sebastiano **A5**
8	Santa Maria della Salute **H6**
9	Scuola Grande dei Carmini....... **B4**

Restaurants ▼

1	Estro Vino e Cucina................. **C2**
2	Impronta **D3**
3	La Bitta............................... **C5**
4	Osteria alla Bifora **B4**
5	Osteria Enoteca ai Artisti **C5**

Coffee and Quick Bites ▼

1	Caffè Bar Ai Artisti **C5**
2	Cantine del Vino già Schiavi...... **D6**
3	Imagina Cafè **D3**
4	Osteria al Squero **D7**
5	Pasticceria Tonolo.................. **C3**

Hotels ▼

1	Ca Maria Adele **H7**
2	Hotel American Dinesen........... **F7**
3	Il Palazzo Experimental **B6**
4	La Calcina **E7**
5	Locanda Ca' Zose................... **G6**
6	Palazzo Stern....................... **D5**
7	Pensione Accademia Villa Maravege.................... **D5**

your walks. Booking tickets in advance isn't essential but does free you from having to stand in line, as you choose the time you want to come when you book. ✉ *Campo de la Carità, Dorsoduro 1050, Campo della Carità just off Accademia Bridge, Dorsoduro* ☎ *041/5222247, 041/5243354 reservations when calling from outside Italy* ⊕ *www.gallerieaccademia.it/en* ⌨ *€12; subject to increases for special exhibitions* Ⓜ *Vaporetto: Accademia, Zattere.*

Gesuati (*Church of Santa Maria del Rosario*)
CHURCH | After the Dominicans took over the church of Santa Maria della Visitazione from the suppressed order of Gesuati laymen in 1668, Giorgio Massari, the last of the great Venetian Baroque architects, was commissioned to build this structure between 1726 and 1735. It has an important Gianbattista Tiepolo (1696–1770) illusionistic ceiling and several other of his works, plus those of his contemporaries Giambattista Piazzetta (1683–1754) and Sebastiano Ricci (1659–1734). Outside on the right-hand wall above a small staircase is a bronze door decorated with a series of panels showing scenes from the life of Jesus by noted Venetian sculptor Francesco Scarpabolla. ✉ *Fondamenta Zattere ai Gesuati, Dorsoduro* ☎ *041/2750462, 041/5205921 church office* ⊕ *www. chorusvenezia.org* ⌨ *€3 (free with Chorus Pass)* ☉ *Closed Sun.* Ⓜ *Vaporetto: Zattere.*

Peggy Guggenheim Collection
ART MUSEUM | FAMILY | Housed in the incomplete but nevertheless charming Palazzo Venier dei Leoni, this choice selection of 20th-century painting and sculpture represents the taste and extraordinary style of the late heiress Peggy Guggenheim. Through wealth, social connections, and a sharp eye for artistic trends, Guggenheim (1898–1979) became an important art dealer and collector from the 1930s through the

1950s, and her personal collection here includes works by Picasso, Kandinsky, Pollock, Motherwell, and Ernst (her onetime husband). The museum serves beverages, snacks, and light meals in its refreshingly shady and artistically sophisticated garden. ✉ *Fondamenta Venier dei Leoni, Dorsoduro 701–704, Dorsoduro* ☎ *041/2405411* ⊕ *www.guggenheim-venice.it* ⌨ *€16* ☉ *Closed Tues.* Ⓜ *Vaporetto: Accademia, Salute.*

★ **Punta della Dogana**
ART MUSEUM | Funded by the billionaire who owns a major share in Christie's Auction House, the François Pinault Foundation commissioned Japanese architect Tadao Ando to redesign this fabled customs house—sitting at the *punta,* or point of land, at the San Marco end of the Grand Canal—now home to a changing roster of works from Pinault's renowned collection of contemporary art. The streaming light, polished surfaces, and clean lines of Ando's design contrast beautifully with the massive columns, sturdy beams, and brick of the original Dogana. Even if you aren't into contemporary art, a visit is worthwhile just to see Ando's amazing architectural transformation. Be sure to walk down to the punta for a magnificent view of the Venetian basin. Check online for a schedule of temporary exhibitions. ✉ *Punta della Dogana, Dorsoduro* ☎ *041/2401308* ⊕ *www.pinaultcollection.com/palazzograssi/en* ⌨ *€15 with Palazzo Grassi* ☉ *Closed Tues.* Ⓜ *Vaporetto: Salute.*

★ **San Sebastiano**
CHURCH | Paolo Veronese (1528–88), though still in his twenties, was already the official painter of the Republic when he began the ceiling oil panels and wall frescoes at San Sebastiano in 1555. For decades he continued to embellish the church with very beautiful illusionistic scenes. The cycles of scenes in San Sebastiano are considered to be his supreme accomplishment. His three oil paintings in the center of the ceiling

depict scenes from the life of Esther, a rare theme in Venice. Veronese is buried beneath his bust near the organ. ⊠ *Campazzo San Sebastiano, Dorsoduro* ☎ *041/2750462* ⊕ *www.chorusvenezia.org* ⍰ *€3 (free with Chorus Pass)* ⊘ *Closed Sun.* Ⓜ *Vaporetto: San Basilio.*

★ Santa Maria della Salute
CHURCH | The most iconic landmark of the Grand Canal, La Salute (as this church is commonly called) is best viewed from the Riva degli Schiavoni at sunset or from the Accademia Bridge by moonlight. Baldassare Longhena (later Venice's most important Baroque architect) won a competition in 1631 to design a shrine honoring the Virgin Mary for saving Venice from a plague that over two years (1629–30) killed 47,000 residents, or one-third of the city's population. Outside, this ornate white Istrian stone octagon is topped by a colossal cupola with snail-like ornamental buttresses. Check the website for information on guided tours. ⊠ *Punta della Dogana, Dorsoduro* ☎ *041/2743928* ⊕ *basilicasalutevenezia.it* ⍰ *Church free, sacristy €6, sacristy and art gallery €12, balustrade of the prophets €5, dome €8* Ⓜ *Vaporetto: Salute.*

Scuola Grande dei Carmini
HISTORIC SIGHT | When the order of Santa Maria del Carmelo commissioned Baldassare Longhena to finish the work on the Scuola Grande dei Carmini in the 1670s, their confraternity was one of the largest and wealthiest in Venice. Little expense was spared in the stuccoed ceilings and carved wooden paneling, and the artwork is remarkable. The paintings by Gianbattista Tiepolo that adorn the Baroque ceiling of the **Sala Capitolare** (Chapter House) are particularly alluring. In what many consider his best work, the artist's nine canvases vividly transform some rather conventional religious themes into dynamic displays of color and movement. ⊠ *Campo dei Carmini, Dorsoduro 2617, Dorsoduro* ☎ *041/5289420* ⊕ *www.scuolagrandecarmini.it* ⍰ *€7* Ⓜ *Vaporetto: Ca' Rezzonico.*

🍽 Restaurants

★ Estro Vino e Cucina
$$$ | MODERN ITALIAN | Wine lovers shouldn't miss this cozy and compact gastro-bistro run by the Spezzamonte brothers, which offers wine from more than 700 vineyards along with modern takes on classic Venetian dishes, such as *scampi in saor* (marinated langoustines) and grilled local amberjack. If you can't choose, let the helpful servers suggest the perfect vino to pair with your à la carte dishes or tasting menu. **Known for:** extensive natural wine list; ambitious local cuisine; vibrant atmosphere. $ *Average main: €28* ⊠ *Crosera San Pantalon, Dorsoduro 3778, Dorsoduro* ☎ *041/4764914* ⊕ *www.estrovenezia.com* ⊘ *Closed Tues.* Ⓜ *Vaporetto: San Tomà, Piazzale Roma.*

Impronta
$$$ | VENETIAN | This sleek café is a favorite lunchtime haunt for professors from the nearby university and local businesspeople, when you can easily have a beautifully prepared *primo* (first course) or *secondo* (second course), plus a glass of wine, for a reasonable price; there's also a good selection of sandwiches and salads. Unlike most local eateries, this spot is open from breakfast through late dinner, and you can dine well in the evening on imaginative pasta, seafood, and meat dishes. **Known for:** imaginative dishes; contemporary decor; all-day dining. $ *Average main: €25* ⊠ *Dorsoduro 3815, Calle Crosera by Calle San Pantalon, Dorsoduro* ☎ *041/2750386* ⊕ *improntarestaurantvenice.com/en/* ⊘ *Closed Sun. and 2 wks in Aug.* Ⓜ *Vaporetto: San Tomà, Piazzale Roma.*

★ La Bitta
$$ | NORTHERN ITALIAN | For a break from all the fish and seafood options in Venice, this is your place; the meat- and veggie-focused menu (inspired by the cuisine of the Venetian mainland) presents a new temptation at every course,

and market availability keeps the dishes changing almost every day. The home-made desserts are all luscious (it's been said that La Bitta serves the best panna cotta in town), and you can trust the owner's selections from her excellent wine and grappa lists, which tend to favor small local producers. **Known for:** meat dishes (no seafood); seasonally inspired menus; friendly and efficient service. ⑤ *Average main: €23* ✉ *Calle Lunga San Barnaba, Dorsoduro 2753/A, Dorsoduro* ☎ *041/5230531* ⊕ *facebook.com/labittavenezia* ▬ *No credit cards* ⊘ *Closed weekends. No lunch* Ⓜ *Vaporetto: Ca' Rezzonico, Zattere.*

★ Osteria alla Bifora

$$ | VENETIAN | A beautiful and atmospheric bacaro, Alla Bifora has such ample, satisfying fare that most Venetians consider it a full-fledged restaurant. Offerings include overflowing trays of cold, sliced meats and cheeses; various preparations of *baccalà* (cod); and Venetian classics, such as *polpette* (croquettes), and marinated anchovies. **Known for:** good selection of regional wines by the glass; seppie in nero con polenta (cuttlefish in ink with polenta); warm and friendly owners. ⑤ *Average main: €18* ✉ *Campo Santa Margherita, Dorsoduro 2930, Dorsoduro* ☎ *041/5236119* ⊘ *Closed Jan. and Aug.* Ⓜ *Vaporetto: Ca' Rezzonico.*

★ Osteria Enoteca ai Artisti

$$$ | VENETIAN | Pop into this canal-side restaurant at lunch for a satisfying primo or come for dinner to sample fine and fresh offerings; the candlelit tables that line the *fondamenta* (quay) suggest romance, and the service is friendly and welcoming. The posted menu—with choices like tagliatelle with porcini mushrooms and tiger prawns, or a filleted John Dory with tomatoes and pine nuts—changes daily (spot the date at the top) and seasonally. **Known for:** delicious pasta and seafood offerings; superlative tiramisu; truly helpful service. ⑤ *Average main: €25* ✉ *Fondamenta della Toletta, Dorsoduro 1169a, Dorsoduro* ☎ *041/5238944* ⊕ *www.enotecaartisti. com* ⊘ *Closed Sun. and Mon.* Ⓜ *Vaporetto: Ca' Rezzonico, Zattere.*

☕ Coffee and Quick Bites

Caffè Bar Ai Artisti

$ | CAFÉ | Caffè Ai Artisti gives locals, students, and travelers alike good reason to pause and refuel. The location is central, pleasant, and sunny—perfect for people-watching and taking a break before the next destination—and the hours are long. **Known for:** relaxing with a coffee; evening Aperol spritz or wine; chilling with the locals. ⑤ *Average main: €8* ✉ *Campo San Barnaba, Dorsoduro 2771, Dorsoduro* ☎ *393/9680135* Ⓜ *Vaporetto: Ca' Rezzonico.*

★ Cantine del Vino già Schiavi

$ | WINE BAR | A mainstay for anyone living or working in the area, this beautiful, family-run, 19th-century bacaro across from the *squero* (gondola boatyard) of San Trovaso has original furnishings and one of the city's best wine cellars, and the walls are covered floor to ceiling with bottles for purchase. The cicheti (small snacks) here are some of the most inventive—and freshest—in Venice (feel free to compliment the signora, who makes them up to twice a day); everything's eaten standing up, as there's no seating. **Known for:** excellent quality cicheti; plenty of wine choices; boisterous local atmosphere. ⑤ *Average main: €8* ✉ *Fondamenta Nani, Dorsoduro 992, Dorsoduro* ☎ *041/5230034* ⊕ *www.cantinaschiavi. com* ⊘ *Closed Sun. and 3 wks in Aug.* Ⓜ *Vaporetto: Accademia, Zattere.*

Imagina Cafè

$ | ITALIAN | This friendly café and art gallery, located between Campo Santa Margherita and Campo San Barnaba, is a great place to stop for a spritz, or even for a light lunch or dinner. The highlights are the freshly made salads, but their panini and *tramezzini* (triangle-shaped

Italian sandwich) are also among the best in the area. **Known for:** tasty sandwiches and salads; good wines and cocktails; pleasant outdoor seating. $ *Average main: €10* ⊠ *Rio Terà Canal, Dorsoduro 3126, Dorsoduro* ☎ *041/2410625* ⊕ *www.imaginacafe.it* Ⓜ *Vaporetto: Ca' Rezzonico.*

Osteria al Squero

$$ | ITALIAN | It wasn't long after this lovely little wine bar (not a restaurant) appeared across from Squero San Trovaso that it became a neighborhood—and citywide— favorite. The Venetian owner has created a personal vision of what a good bar should offer: a variety of sumptuous cicheti, panini, and cheeses to be accompanied by just the right regional wines (ask for his recommendation). **Known for:** tasty cicheti; good veggie options; pretty canal views. $ *Average main: €20* ⊠ *Fondamenta Nani, Dorsoduro 943/944, Dorsoduro* ☎ *041/2960479* ⊕ *osteriaalsquero.wordpress.com* ⊘ *Closed Sun.* Ⓜ *Vaporetto: Zattere, Accademia.*

Pasticceria Tonolo

$ | BAKERY | One of Venice's premier confectioneries has been in operation since 1886. During Carnevale it's still one of the best places in town for *frittelle*, or fried doughnuts (traditional raisin or cream-filled), and at Christmas and Easter, this is where Venetians order their focaccia veneziana, the traditional raised cake— well in advance. **Known for:** arguably the best pastries in Venice; excellent coffee; can't-miss doughnuts. $ *Average main: €5* ⊠ *Calle San Pantalon, Dorsoduro 3764, Dorsoduro* ☎ *041/5237209* ⊕ *pasticceria-tonolo-venezia.business.site* ⊘ *Closed Mon.* Ⓜ *Vaporetto: San Tomà, Ca' Rezzonico.*

 Hotels

⭐ **Ca Maria Adele**

$$$$ | HOTEL | One of the city's most intimate and elegant getaways blends terrazzo floors, dramatic Murano chandeliers, and antique-style furnishings with contemporary touches, particularly in the African-wood reception area and breakfast room. **Pros:** quiet and romantic; imaginative decor; tranquil yet convenient spot near Santa Maria della Salute. **Cons:** no elevator and lots of stairs; bathrooms on the small side; no restaurant (just breakfast room). $ *Rooms from: €419* ⊠ *Campo Santa Maria della Salute, Dorsoduro 111, Dorsoduro* ☎ *041/5203078* ⊕ *www.camariaadele.it* ⊘ *Closed 3 wks in Jan.* 🛏 *12 rooms* ⓘ◯⫯ *Free Breakfast* Ⓜ *Vaporetto: Salute.*

Hotel American Dinesen

$$$ | HOTEL | If you're in Venice to see art, you can't beat the location of this hotel, where all the spacious rooms have brocade fabrics and Venetian-style lacquered furniture. **Pros:** near Gallerie dell'Accademia and Peggy Guggenheim Collection; on a bright, quiet, exceptionally picturesque canal; some rooms have canal-view terraces. **Cons:** canal-view rooms are more expensive; style could be too understated for those expecting Venetian opulence; bathrooms can feel cramped. $ *Rooms from: €221* ⊠ *Fondamenta Bragadin, Dorsoduro 628, Dorsoduro* ☎ *041/5204733* ⊕ *www.hotelamerican.it* 🛏 *34 rooms* ⓘ◯⫯ *No Meals* Ⓜ *Vaporetto: Accademia, Salute, Zattere.*

Il Palazzo Experimental

$$$ | HOTEL | Of-the-moment Parisian designer Dorothée Meilichzon composed the striped pastel color palette at this hip boutique hotel—the first Experimental Group property in Italy—hidden inside a Renaissance palazzo facing the Giudecca Canal. **Pros:** fun, whimsical decor; quiet location away from the Venice crowds; trendy cocktail bar on-site. **Cons:** not all rooms have water views; little storage space in bathrooms; no gym. $ *Rooms from: €279* ⊠ *Fondamenta Zattere Al Ponte Lungo, Dorsoduro 1411, Dorsoduro* ☎ *041/0980200* ⊕ *www.palazzoexperimental.com* 🛏 *32 rooms* ⓘ◯⫯ *No Meals* Ⓜ *Vaporetto: Zattere, San Basilio.*

La Calcina

$$ | HOTEL | Many notables (including Victorian-era art critic John Ruskin) have stayed at this hotel, though they might not recognize it after its series of upscale renovations; it has an enviable location along the sunny Zattere, as well as comfy rooms and apartments with parquet floors, original 19th-century furniture, and firm beds. **Pros:** panoramic views from some rooms; quiet, peaceful atmosphere; well-regarded restaurant with terrace over the Giudecca Canal. **Cons:** not for travelers who prefer ultramodern surroundings; no elevator; most rooms on the small side. $ *Rooms from: €149* ✉ *Zattere ai Gesuati, Dorsoduro 780, Dorsoduro* ☎ *041/5206466* ⊕ *www.lacalcina.com* ↗ *25 rooms* ⦿ *Free Breakfast* Ⓜ *Vaporetto: Zattere, Accademia.*

Locanda Ca' Zose

$$ | HOTEL | The idea that the Campanati sisters named the 15 rooms in their renovated 17th-century locanda after the stars and constellations of the highest magnitude in the Northern Hemisphere says something about how personally this place is run. **Pros:** quiet but convenient location; canal views; efficient, personal service. **Cons:** no outdoor garden or terrace; no Wi-Fi in rooms (but free in lounge, as is computer use); unimpressive breakfast. $ *Rooms from: €127* ✉ *Calle Barbaro, Dorsoduro 193/B, Dorsoduro* ☎ *041/5226635* ⊕ *www.hotelcazose.com* ↗ *15 rooms* ⦿ *No Meals* Ⓜ *Vaporetto: Salute.*

★ Palazzo Stern

$$$ | HOTEL | This opulently refurbished neo-Gothic palazzo features marble-column arches, terrazzo floors, frescoed ceilings, mosaics, and a charming carved staircase, and some rooms have tufted walls and parquet flooring. **Pros:** excellent hotel service; lovely views from many rooms; modern renovation retains historic ambience. **Cons:** standard rooms don't have views; Grand Canal–facing rooms can be a bit noisy; no restaurant, gym, or spa. $ *Rooms from: €280* ✉ *Calle del Traghetto, Dorsoduro 2792/A, Dorsoduro* ☎ *041/2770869* ⊕ *www.palazzostern.it* ↗ *24 rooms* ⦿ *No Meals* Ⓜ *Vaporetto: Ca' Rezzonico.*

Pensione Accademia Villa Maravege

$$ | HOTEL | Behind iron gates in one of the busiest parts of the city is this renowned Gothic-style villa with gardens and charmingly decorated accommodations with Venetian-style antique reproductions and fine tapestry. **Pros:** a unique villa in the heart of Venice; two gardens where guests can breakfast, drink, and relax; complimentary drinks and snacks at the bar. **Cons:** no guest rooms have Grand Canal views; bathrooms can be on the small side; no restaurant. $ *Rooms from: €185* ✉ *Fondamenta Bollani, Dorsoduro 1058, Dorsoduro* ☎ *041/5210188* ⊕ *www.pensioneaccademia.it* ↗ *27 rooms* ⦿ *Free Breakfast* Ⓜ *Vaporetto: Accademia.*

Nightlife

Al Chioschetto

BARS | Although this popular place consists only of a kiosk set up to serve some outdoor tables, it is located on the Zattere and thus provides a wonderful view of the Giudecca Canal. It's a handy meet-up spot for locals, especially students from the nearby university, and a useful stop-off for tourists in nice weather for a spritz or a panino. Keep in mind, though, that "the kiosk" exists for quick refreshments and not for lingering. The view and the sunshine (and especially the sunset) are the main draw; the food and drink, while acceptable, are not exceptional. ✉ *Fondamenta delle Zattere al Ponte Lungo, Dorsoduro 1406/A, Dorsoduro* ☎ *348/3968466* Ⓜ *Vaporetto: San Basilio, Zattere.*

⭐ **Il Caffè Rosso** (*Bar Rosso*)
BARS | The sign above the door simply says "CAFFÈ," but it has long since been called "Bar Rosso" for its bright-red exterior. The ideal people-watching spot on one of the busiest campos, it has far more tables outside than inside. A favorite with students and faculty from the nearby university, it's a good place to start the day with coffee and croissant, or later to enjoy a drink. ⊠ *Campo Santa Margherita, Dorsoduro 2963, Dorsoduro* ☎ *041/5287998* ⊕ *www.facebook.com/cafferosso.venezia* Ⓜ *Vaporetto: Ca' Rezzonico, Piazzale Roma, San Tomà.*

Orange
BARS | Modern, hip, and complemented by an internal garden, this welcoming bar anchors the south end of Campo Santa Margherita, the liveliest campo in Venice. You can have *piadine* (thin flatbread) sandwiches, salads, and drinks while watching soccer games on a massive screen inside, or sit at the tables facing the campo. Despite being close to the university, Orange is frequented primarily by young working people from the mainland and tourists. Open till 2 am every night. ⊠ *Campo Santa Margherita, Dorsoduro 3054/A, Dorsoduro* ☎ *041/5234740* ⊕ *facebook.com/orangevenezia* Ⓜ *Vaporetto: Ca' Rezzonico, Piazzale Roma.*

🛍 Shopping

Il Grifone
HANDBAGS | Of Venice's few remaining artisan leather shops, Il Grifone is the standout with respect to quality, tradition, and the guarantee of an exquisite product. For more than 30 years, Antonio Peressin has been making bags, purses, belts, and smaller leather items that have a wide following because of his precision and attention to detail. His goods remain reasonably and accessibly priced. ⊠ *Fondamenta del Gafaro, Dorsoduro 3516, Dorsoduro* ☎ *041/5229452, 329/3948907* ⊕ *www.ilgrifonevenezia.it* Ⓜ *Vaporetto: Piazzale Roma.*

Marina e Susanna Sent
JEWELRY & WATCHES | The beautiful and elegant glass jewelry of Marina and Susanna Sent has been featured in *Vogue.* Look also for vases and other exceptional design pieces. Other locations are on the Fondamenta Serenella on Murano and in San Polo under the Sotoportego dei Oresi at Rialto. ⊠ *Campo San Vio, Dorsoduro 669, Dorsoduro* ☎ *041/5208136* ⊕ *www.marinaesusannasent.com* Ⓜ *Vaporetto: Salute, Accademia, Zattere.*

San Polo and Santa Croce

The two smallest of Venice's six sestieri, San Polo and Santa Croce, were named after their main churches, although the Chiesa di Santa Croce was demolished in 1810. The city's most famous bridge, the Ponte di Rialto, unites San Marco (east) with San Polo (west). The Rialto takes its name from Rivoaltus, the high ground on which it was built. You'll find some of Venice's most lauded restaurants here, and shops abound in the area surrounding the Ponte di Rialto. On the San Marco side you'll find fashion, on the San Polo side, food.

TIMING
To do the area justice requires at least half a day. If you want to take part in the food shopping, come early to beat the crowds. Campo San Giacomo dell'Orio, west of the main thoroughfare that takes you from the Ponte di Rialto to Santa Maria Gloriosa dei Frari, is a peaceful place for a drink and a rest. The museums of Ca' Pesaro are a time commitment—you'll want at least two hours to see them both.

San Polo and Santa Croce

Sights

Ca' Pesaro

ART MUSEUM | Baldassare Longhena's grand Baroque palace, begun in 1676, is the beautifully restored home of two impressive collections. The Galleria Internazionale d'Arte Moderna has works by 19th- and 20th-century artists, such as Klimt, Kandinsky, Matisse, and Miró. It also has a collection of representative works from the Venice Biennale that amounts to a panorama of 20th-century art. The pride of the Museo Orientale is its collection of Japanese art—and especially armor and weapons—of the Edo period (1603–1868). It also has a small but striking collection of Chinese and Indonesian porcelains and musical instruments. ⊠ *Fondamenta Pesaro, Santa Croce 2076, Santa Croce* ☎ *041/721127 Galleria* ⊕ *capesaro.visitmuve.it* ☎ *€14, includes both museums (free with Museum Pass)* ⊙ *Closed Mon.* Ⓜ *Vaporetto: San Stae.*

Campo San Polo

PLAZA/SQUARE | Only Piazza San Marco is larger than this square, and the echo of children's voices bouncing off the surrounding palaces makes the space seem even bigger. Campo San Polo once hosted bullfights, fairs, military parades, and packed markets, and now comes especially alive on winter days when a temporary ice-skating rink is installed. In the summer, an outdoor cinema is set up with 1,300 seats.

The Chiesa di San Polo has been restored so many times that little remains of the original 9th-century church, and the 19th-century alterations were so costly that, sadly, the friars sold off many great paintings to pay bills. Although Gianbattista Tiepolo is represented here, his work is outdone by 16 paintings by his son Giandomenico (1727–1804), including the *Stations of the Cross* in the oratory to the left of the entrance. The younger Tiepolo also created a series of expressive and theatrical renderings of the saints. Look for altarpieces by Tintoretto and Veronese that managed to escape auction.

San Polo's bell tower (begun 1362), across the street from the entrance to the church, remained unchanged over the centuries—don't miss the two lions, playing with a disembodied human head and a serpent, on the wall just above the tower's doorway. Tradition has it that the head refers to that of Marino Faliero, the doge executed for treason in 1355. ⊠ *Campo San Polo, San Polo* ☎ *041/2750462* ⊕ *www.chorusvenezia. org* ☎ *Chiesa di San Polo €3 (free with Chorus Pass)* ⊙ *Closed Sun.* Ⓜ *Vaporetto: San Silvestro, San Tomà.*

San Giacomo de l'Orio

PLAZA/SQUARE | Theories abound on this lovely square's unusual name; one hypothesis is that there was once a laurel tree here and the Venetian dialect has thoroughly transformed the word (*lauro* in Italian). In any case, today's trees lend it shade and character. Add benches and a fountain (with a drinking bowl for dogs), and the pleasant, oddly shaped campo becomes a welcoming place for friendly conversation and neighborhood kids at play. The church of San Giacomo dall'Orio (another common spelling) was founded in the 9th century on an island still populated (the legend goes) by wolves. The current church dates from 1225. ⊠ *Campo San Giacomo dall'Orio, Santa Croce* ☎ *041/2750462* ⊕ *www.chorusvenezia. org* ☎ *Church €3.50 (free with Chorus Pass)* ⊙ *Church closed Sun.* Ⓜ *Vaporetto: San Stae, Riva de Biasio.*

San Giovanni Elemosinario

CHURCH | Storefronts make up the facade, and market guilds—poulterers, messengers, and fodder merchants—built the altars at this church intimately bound to the Rialto markets. The original church was completely destroyed by a fire in 1514 and rebuilt in 1531 by Scarpagnino, who had also worked on the Scuola di San Rocco. During a more recent restoration, workers stumbled upon a frescoed cupola by Pordenone (1484–1539) that had been painted over centuries earlier. Don't miss Titian's *St. John the Almsgiver* and Pordenone's *Sts. Catherine, Sebastian, and Roch*. It is open for services conducted according to the Orthodox Romanian rite. ⊠ *Rialto Ruga Vecchia San Giovanni, San Polo 479, San Polo* ☎ *041/2750462, 328/6911239* ⊕ *www.chorusvenezia.org* ✉ *€3.50 (free with Chorus Pass)* ⊘ *Closed weekdays* Ⓜ *Vaporetto: San Silvestro, Rialto Mercato.*

San Stae

CHURCH | The church of San Stae—the Venetian name for Sant' Eustachio (St. Eustace)—was reconstructed in 1687 by Giovanni Grassi and given a new facade in 1707 by Domenico Rossi. Renowned Venetian painters and sculptors of the early 18th century decorated this church around 1717 with the legacy left by Doge Alvise II Mocenigo, who's buried in the center aisle. San Stae affords a good opportunity to see the early works of Gianbattista Tiepolo, Sebastiano Ricci, and Giovanni Battista Piazzetta, as well as those of the previous generation of Venetian painters, with whom they had studied. ⊠ *Campo San Stae, Santa Croce* ☎ *041/2750462* ⊕ *www.chorusvenezia. org* ✉ *€3.50 (free with Chorus Pass)* ⊘ *Closed Fri.–Tues.* Ⓜ *Vaporetto: San Stae.*

★ Santa Maria Gloriosa dei Frari

CHURCH | Completed in 1442, this immense Gothic church of russet-color brick, known locally as "I Frari," is famous for its array of spectacular Venetian paintings and historic tombs. In the sacristy, see Giovanni Bellini's 1488 triptych *Madonna and Child with Saints*. The Corner Chapel is graced by Bartolomeo Vivarini's altarpiece *St. Mark Enthroned* and *Saints John the Baptist, Jerome, Peter, and Nicholas*. In the first south chapel of the chorus, there is a fine sculpture of St. John the Baptist by

Donatello, dated 1438, with a psychological intensity rare for early Renaissance sculpture. Titian's renowned *Assumption*, unveiled in 1518, is at the far end of the nave, above the altar. ⊠ *Campo dei Frari, San Polo* ☎ *041/2728630* ⊕ *www. basilicadeifrari.it* ✉ *€5 (free with Chorus Pass)* ⊘ *Closed Sun. morning* Ⓜ *Vaporetto: San Tomà.*

★ Scuola Grande di San Rocco

ART MUSEUM | This elegant example of Venetian Renaissance architecture was built between 1516 and 1549 for the essentially secular charitable confraternity bearing the saint's name. The Venetian *scuole* were organizations that sometimes had loose religious affiliations, through which the artisan class could exercise some influence upon civic life. San Rocco was a protector against the plague, and his scuola was one of the city's most magnificent. While the building is bold and dramatic outside, its contents are even more stunning—a series of more than 60 paintings by Tintoretto. *Moses Striking Water from the Rock, The Brazen Serpent*, and *The Fall of Manna* represent three afflictions—thirst, disease, and hunger—that San Rocco sought to relieve. ⊠ *Campo San Rocco, San Polo 3054, San Polo* ☎ *041/5234864* ⊕ *www.scuolagrandesanrocco.it* ✉ *€10* Ⓜ *Vaporetto: San Tomà, Piazzale Roma.*

🍴 Restaurants

Al Nono Risorto

$$ | VENETIAN | FAMILY | This friendly trattoria popular with the locals is only a short walk from the Rialto markets. The pizza—not a Venetian specialty, generally speaking—is pretty good here, but the star attractions are the generous appetizers and excellent shellfish pastas. (The "reborn nono" refers to a small lagoon sea snail, a Venetian favorite.) In good weather, you can enjoy your meal in the pergola-covered courtyard (do reserve if you want to snag a table there). **Known for:** traditional starters and pastas; quite

tasty pizzas; pretty outdoor garden seating. $ *Average main: €16* ✉ *Sotoportego de Siora Bettina, Santa Croce 2338, Santa Croce* ☎ *041/5241169* ⊕ *alnonorisortovenezia.com* ⊘ *Closed Jan.* Ⓜ *Vaporetto: Rialto Mercato, San Stae.*

★ Al Paradiso

$$$ | MODERN ITALIAN | In a small dining room made warm and cozy by its pleasing and unpretentious decor, proprietor Giordano makes all diners feel like honored guests. Unlike many elegant restaurants, Al Paradiso serves generous portions, and many of the delicious antipasti and primi are quite satisfying; you may want to follow the traditional Italian way of ordering and wait until you've finished your antipasto or your primo before you order your secondo. **Known for:** large appetizer and pasta portions; tasty meat and fish mains; central location near the Ponte di Rialto. $ *Average main: €26* ✉ *Calle del Paradiso, San Polo 767, San Polo* ☎ *041/5234910* ⊕ *www.ristorantealparadiso.com* ⊘ *Closed 3 wks Jan. and Feb.* Ⓜ *Vaporetto: San Silvestro.*

Alla Madonna

$$ | VENETIAN | "The Madonna" used to be world-famous as *the* classic Venetian trattoria, but in recent decades has settled into middle age. Owned and operated by the Rado family since 1954, this Venetian institution looks like one, with wood beams, stained-glass windows, and a panoply of paintings on white walls. **Known for:** freshly prepared seafood; traditional Venetian cuisine; old-time atmosphere. $ *Average main: €18* ✉ *Calle della Madonna, San Polo 594, San Polo* ☎ *041/5223824* ⊕ *www.ristoranteallamadonna.com* ⊘ *Closed Wed. and Jan.* Ⓜ *Vaporetto: San Silvestro, Rialto Mercato.*

Antica Besseta

$$$ | VENETIAN | Tucked away in a quiet corner of Santa Croce, with a few tables under an ivy shelter, the Antica Besseta dates from the 19th century, and it retains some of its old feel. The menu focuses on vegetables and fish, according to what's at the market, with some pasta and meat dishes, too. **Known for:** classic Italian pastas, like spaghetti con vongole (with clams); simple menu of fish and meat choices; charming old-fashioned feel. $ *Average main: €30* ✉ *Salizzada de Ca' Zusto, Santa Croce 1395, Santa Croce* ☎ *041/721687* ⊕ *www.anticabesseta.it* ⊘ *Closed Tues.* Ⓜ *Vaporetto: Riva de Biasio.*

★ Antiche Carampane

$$$ | SEAFOOD | Judging by its rather modest and unremarkable appearance, you wouldn't guess that Piera Bortoluzzi Librai's trattoria is among the finest fish restaurants in the city both because of the quality of the ingredients and because of the chef's creative magic. You can choose from a selection of classic dishes with a modern and creative touch. **Known for:** superlative fish and seafood; modernized Venetian dishes; popular with visitors and locals (so book ahead). $ *Average main: €30* ✉ *Rio Terà delle Carampane, San Polo 1911, San Polo* ☎ *041/5240165* ⊕ *www.antichecarampane.com/en/* ⊘ *Closed Sun. and Mon., 10 days in Jan., and 3 wks July–Aug.* Ⓜ *Vaporetto: San Silvestro.*

La Zucca

$$$ | NORTHERN ITALIAN | Simple place settings, wood lattice walls, and a mélange of languages make La Zucca (The Pumpkin) feel much like a typical, somewhat sophisticated vegetarian restaurant that you could find in any European city. What makes La Zucca special is simply great cooking and the use of fresh, local ingredients—many of which, like the particularly sweet zucca itself, aren't normally found outside northern Italy. **Known for:** seasonal vegetarian-focused dishes; homestyle Italian cooking; flan di zucca (pumpkin pudding). $ *Average main: €30* ✉ *Calle del Tentor, at Ponte del Megio, Santa Croce 1762, Santa Croce* ☎ *041/5241570* ⊕ *www.lazucca.it* ⊘ *Closed Sun.* Ⓜ *Vaporetto: San Stae.*

★ Ristorante Osteria Da Fiore

$$$$ | VENETIAN | The understated atmosphere, simple decor, and quiet elegance featured alongside Da Fiore's modern take on traditional Venetian cuisine certainly merit its international reputation. With such beautifully prepared cuisine, you would expect the kitchen to be run by a chef with a household name; however, the kitchen is headed by owner Maurizio Martin's wife, Mara, who learned to cook from her grandmother. **Known for:** sophisticated traditional Venetian dishes; delicious tasting menus; reservations required. $ Average main: €54 ⊠ Calle del Scaleter, San Polo 2202, San Polo ☎ 349/5522629 booking via WhatsApp, 041/721308 ⊕ www.ristorantedafiore.com ☉ Closed 3 wks in Jan. and Sun. Ⓜ Vaporetto: San Tomà, San Silvestro.

Coffee and Quick Bites

All'Arco

$ | WINE BAR | Just because it's noon and you only have enough time between sights for a sandwich doesn't mean that it can't be a satisfying, even an exceptional, one. There's no menu at All'Arco, but a scan of what's behind the glass counter is all you need; order what entices you, or have Roberto or Matteo (father and son) suggest a cicheto or panino. **Known for:** top-notch cicheti; platters of meats and cheeses; friendly and helpful service. $ Average main: €10 ⊠ Calle Arco, San Polo 436, San Polo ☎ 041/5205666 ☉ Closed Wed. Ⓜ Vaporetto: Rialto Mercato, San Silvestro.

Caffè dei Frari

$ | CAFÉ | Just over the bridge in front of the Frari church is this old-fashioned place where you'll find an assortment of sandwiches and snacks, but it is the atmosphere, and not the food, that is the main attraction. Established in 1870, it's one of the last Venetian tearooms with its original decor, and while prices are a bit higher than in cafés in nearby Campo Santa Margherita, the vibe and the friendly "retro" atmosphere make the added cost worthwhile. **Known for:** lovely historic setting; well-made cocktails; quality cicheti. $ Average main: €10 ⊠ Fondamenta dei Frari, San Polo 2564, San Polo ☎ 347/8293158, 041/4767305 ☉ Closed Sun. and Mon. No dinner Ⓜ Vaporetto: San Tomà.

Cantina Do Mori

$ | WINE BAR | This is the original bacaro, in business continually since 1462; cramped but warm and cozy under hanging antique copper pots, it has served generations of workers from the Rialto markets. In addition to young local whites and reds, the well-stocked cellar offers reserve labels, many available by the glass; between sips you can choose to munch the wide range of cicheti on offer, or a few tiny well-stuffed tramezzini, appropriately called francobolli (postage stamps). **Known for:** good choice of wines by the glass; fine selection of cicheti and sandwiches; delicious baccalà mantecato, with or without garlic and parsley. $ Average main: €12 ⊠ Calle dei Do Mori, San Polo 429, San Polo ☎ 041/5225401 ☉ Closed Sun. Ⓜ Vaporetto: Rialto Mercato.

Hotels

★ Hotel al Ponte Mocenigo

$$ | HOTEL | At this hotel—once home to the Santa Croce branch of the Mocenigo family, which counts a few doges in its lineage—a columned courtyard welcomes you, and guest room decor nods to the building's history, with canopied beds, striped damask fabrics, lustrous terrazzo flooring, and gilt-accented furnishings. **Pros:** fantastic value; friendly and helpful staff; enchanting courtyard (the perfect spot for an aperitivo). **Cons:** beds are on the hard side; standard rooms are small; rooms in the annex can be noisy. $ Rooms from: €140 ⊠ Salizzada San Stae, Santa Croce 1985, Santa Croce ☎ 348/3020942, 041/5244797

⊕ *www.alpontemocenigo.com* ⟿ *11 rooms* ⦿❘ *Free Breakfast* Ⓜ *Vaporetto: San Stae.*

La Villeggiatura

$$ | **HOTEL** | If eclectic Venetian charm is what you seek, this luminous residence near the Rialto has it: each of the individually decorated guest rooms has its own theater-theme wall painting by a local artist. **Pros:** relaxed atmosphere and friendly, personalized service; meticulously maintained; well located near markets, artistic monuments, and restaurants. **Cons:** no elevator and lots of stairs; no view to speak of, despite the climb; no restaurant (though breakfast is served). Ⓢ *Rooms from: €140* ✉ *Calle dei Botteri, San Polo 1569, San Polo* ☎ *338/8531264, 041/5244673* ⊕ *www.lavilleggiatura.it* ⟿ *6 rooms* ⦿❘ *Free Breakfast* Ⓜ *Vaporetto: Rialto Mercato.*

★ Oltre il Giardino

$$$$ | **HOTEL** | Behind a brick wall, just over the bridge from the Frari church, this palazzo named "Beyond the Garden" is hard to find but well worth the effort: a sheltered location, large canal-side garden, and individually decorated guest rooms make it feel like a country house. **Pros:** peaceful, gracious, and convenient setting; glorious walled garden; friendly owners happy to share their Venice tips. **Cons:** a beautiful, though not particularly Venetian, ambience; rooms book up quickly; no in-house restaurant (though breakfast served). Ⓢ *Rooms from: €330* ✉ *Fondamenta Contarini, San Polo 2542, San Polo* ☎ *331/5460266 WhatsApp, 041/2750015* ⊕ *www.oltreilgiardino-venezia.com* ⊙ *Closed Jan.* ⟿ *6 rooms* ⦿❘ *Free Breakfast* Ⓜ *Vaporetto: San Tomà.*

▼ Nightlife

★ Il Mercante

COCKTAIL BARS | When the clock strikes 6 pm, historic Caffè dei Frari transforms into this lively craft cocktail bar that will dazzle your inner adventurer. Relax on a velvet sofa while savoring remarkably inventive drinks paired with flavorful small bites. Each pairing has a distinctive name; "Amatriciana" is composed of vodka, dry vermouth, and black tea, served with Parmesan foam, pineapple gel, and balsamic vinegar (billed as "strong, smoky, tasty"). ✉ *Fondamenta dei Frari, San Polo 2564, San Polo* ☎ *347/8293158 mobile* ⊕ *www.ilmercantevenezia.com* Ⓜ *Vaporetto: San Tomà.*

Naranzaria

BARS | At the friendliest of the several bar-restaurants that line the Erbaria, near the Rialto markets, enjoy a cocktail outside, along the Canal Grande, or at a cozy table inside the renovated 16th-century warehouse. Although the food is acceptable, the ambience is really the main attraction. The kitchen closes at 11, and occasionally there is live music (usually jazz, Latin, or rock) on Sunday evening. On summer evenings, especially the weekend, the market area draws crowds of young people from Venice, the lagoon islands, and the mainland. ✉ *Sotoportego del Bancogiro, L'Erbaria, San Polo 130, San Polo* ☎ *041/7241035* ⊕ *www.naranzaria.it* Ⓜ *Vaporetto: Rialto Mercato.*

Shopping

Gilberto Penzo

CRAFTS | **FAMILY** | The gondola and lagoon boat expert in Venice creates scale models of a wide variety of Venetian boats in his nearby *laboratorio* (workshop). (If the retail shop is closed, a sign posted on the door will explain how to find Signor Penzo.) When he's not busy sawing and sanding, Mr. Penzo writes historical and technical books about traditional Venetian boats, including the gondola. Here you'll also find gondola model kits, as well as some forcole (Venetian rowing oarlocks). ✉ *Calle Seconda dei Saoneri, San Polo 2681, San Polo* ☎ *041/5246139* ⊕ *www.veniceboats.com* Ⓜ *Vaporetto: San Tomà.*

★ Il Tabarro San Marco di Monica Daniele

SPECIALTY STORE | This petite shop is the best place in town to find traditional Venetian wool capes, known as *tabarro*, and classic hats, such as the Ezra Pound (soft fedora), the *tricorno* (three-cornered hat), and the *cilindro* (top hat). ⊠ *Calle del Scaleter, San Polo 2235, San Polo* ☎ *041/5246242* ⊕ *www.monicadaniele.com* Ⓜ *Vaporetto: San Stae, San Silvestro.*

Laberintho

JEWELRY & WATCHES | A tiny bottega near Campo San Polo is run by a team of young goldsmiths and jewelry designers specializing in inlaid stones. The work on display in their shop is exceptional, and they also create customized pieces. ⊠ *Calle del Scaleter, San Polo 2236, San Polo* ☎ *041/710017* ⊕ *www.laberintho.com* Ⓜ *Vaporetto: San Stae, San Silvestro.*

Cannaregio

Seen from above, this part of town seems like a wide field plowed by several long, straight canals linked by perpendicular streets—not typical of Venice, where the shape of the islands usually defines the shape of the canals. Cannaregio's main thoroughfare, the Strada Nova (New Street, converted from a canal in 1871), is the longest street in Venice; it runs parallel to the Grand Canal.

TIMING

Although it's more residential and less sight-rich than other Venice neighborhoods, you'll still need several hours here to explore the Ca' d'Oro palace and Madonna dell'Orto and Santa Maria dei Miracoli churches, and to wander the Jewish Ghetto. Cannaregio is a great place to spend a morning before taking the vaporetto to Murano and Burano, which departs from the Fondamente Nove stop.

Sights

Ca' d'Oro

HISTORY MUSEUM | One of the classic postcard sights of Venice, this exquisite Venetian Gothic palace was once literally a "Golden House," when its marble tracery and ornaments were embellished with gold. It was created by Giovanni and Bartolomeo Bon between 1428 and 1430 for the patrician Marino Contarini, who had read about the Roman emperor Nero's golden house in Rome, the Domus Aurea, and wished to imitate it as a present to his wife. Her family owned the land and the Byzantine *fondaco* (palace–trading house) previously standing on it; you can still see the round Byzantine arches incorporated into the Gothic building's entry porch. ⊠ *Calle Ca' d'Oro, Cannaregio 3933, Cannaregio* ☎ *041/5200345* ⊕ *www.cadoro.org* ⌣ *€8.50* Ⓜ *Vaporetto: Ca' d'Oro.*

Casino di Venezia—Palazzo Vendramin-Calergi

CASINO | Hallowed as the site of Richard Wagner's death and today Venice's most glamorous casino, this magnificent edifice found its fame centuries earlier: Venetian star architect Mauro Codussi (1440–1504) essentially invented Venetian Renaissance architecture with this design. Built for the Loredan family around 1500, Codussi's palace married the fortresslike design of the Florentine Alberti's Palazzo Rucellai with the lightness and delicacy of the Venetian Gothic. Note how Codussi beautifully exploits the flickering light of Venetian waterways to play across the building's facade and to pour in through the generous windows. Consult the website to book a guided tour of the small Museo Wagner upstairs, where an archive, events, and concerts may interest Wagnerians.

Venice has always prized the beauty of this palace. In 1652 its owners were convicted of a rather gruesome murder, and the punishment would have involved, as was customary, the demolition of their palace. The murderers were banned from the Republic, but the palace, in view of its beauty and historical importance, was spared. Only a newly added wing was torn down. ⊠ *Cannaregio 2040, Cannaregio* ☎ *041/5297111* ⊕ *www.casinovenezia.it* 🎫 *Casino ticket €50: includes €20 playing credit, vaporetto ticket, parking, and a drink; free for visitors staying at a Venice hotel (with prior written confirmation from the hotel, by 6 pm that day)* Ⓜ *Vaporetto: San Marcuola.*

★ Gesuiti (*Chiesa di Santa Maria Assunta*)

CHURCH | The interior walls of this early-18th-century church (1715–30) resemble brocade drapery, and only touching them will convince skeptics that rather than embroidered cloth, the green-and-white walls are inlaid marble. This trompe-l'oeil decor is typical of the late Baroque's fascination with optical illusion. Toward the end of his life, Titian tended to paint scenes of suffering and sorrow in a nocturnal ambience. A dramatic example of this is on display above the first altar to the left: Titian's daring *Martyrdom of St. Lawrence* (1578), taken from an earlier church that stood on this site. Tintoretto's *Assumption* (1555), originally commissioned for the destroyed Crociferi church, demands reverence. The Crociferi's surviving oratory, or prayer hall (Oratorio dei Crociferi), located across from the church, features some of Palma Giovane's best work, painted between 1583 and 1591. The oratory can be visited only by advance reservation by phone. ⊠ *Campo dei Gesuiti, Cannaregio* ☎ *041/5231610 Gesuiti, 041/3096605 oratory* ⊕ *www.gioiellinascostidivenezia.it* 🎫 *Gesuiti €2; Oratorio dei Crociferi €8* ⚓ *Reservations needed to visit oratory* Ⓜ *Vaporetto: Fondamente Nove.*

★ Jewish Ghetto

HISTORIC DISTRICT | The very first Jewish Ghetto in Europe also contains the continent's highest density of Renaissance-era synagogues, and visiting them on a guided tour is interesting not only culturally but also aesthetically. In 1516, the Venetian Senate voted to confine Jews to an island in Cannaregio, whose gates were locked at night and whose canals were patrolled. In the 16th century, the community grew with refugees from the Inquisition. Although the gates were pulled down after Napoléon's 1797 arrival, the Ghetto was reinstated during the Austrian occupation. Full freedom wasn't realized until 1866 with the founding of the Italian state. Many Jews fled Italy after Mussolini's 1938 racial laws, but of the remainder, all but eight were killed by the Nazis. You can visit some of the historic buildings of the Ghetto on guided tours, which run in English every hour from 10 am to 5 pm (starting 9 am on Fridays) every day except Saturday. ⊠ *Campo del Ghetto Nuovo, Cannaregio* ☎ *055/2989815* ⊕ *www.ghettovenezia. com* 🎫 *€15 for guided tour* ⊗ *No guided tours on Sat. or Jewish holidays.*

★ Madonna dell'Orto

CHURCH | Though built toward the middle of the 14th century, this church takes its character from its beautiful late-Gothic facade, added between 1460 and 1464; it's one of the most beautiful Gothic churches in Venice. Tintoretto lived nearby, and this, his parish church, contains some of his most powerful work. Lining the chancel are two huge (45 feet by 20 feet) canvases, *Adoration of the Golden Calf* and *Last Judgment.* In glowing contrast to this awesome spectacle is Tintoretto's *Presentation of the Virgin at the Temple* and the simple chapel where he and his children, Marietta and Domenico, are buried. Paintings by Domenico, Cima da Conegliano, Palma Giovane, Palma Vecchio, and Titian also hang in the church. A chapel displays a photographic reproduction of a precious *Madonna and Child* by Giovanni Bellini. The original was stolen one night in 1993. Don't miss the beautifully austere, late-Gothic cloister (1460), which you enter through the

small door to the right of the church; it is frequently used for exhibitions but may be open at other times as well. ✉ *Campo della Madonna dell'Orto, Cannaregio* ☎ *041/719933* 🎫 *€3* ⊘ *Closed Sun.* Ⓜ *Vaporetto: Orto.*

Museo Ebraico (*Jewish Museum*)
SYNAGOGUE | The "dispersed museum" comprises three of the Ghetto's five synagogues (the 16th-century Tedesca, Canton, and Italiana) plus a compact, well-arranged museum that highlights centuries of Venetian Jewish culture. Among the artifacts on display are splendid silver Hanukkah lamps and Torahs, beautifully decorated wedding contracts handwritten in Hebrew, and an important library. The recently created and wonderful Giardino Segreto della Scuola Spagnola, a secret garden with rich plant life and a sukkah, is also open to the public occasionally. Tours of the Ghetto and its synagogues in Italian and English leave from the museum hourly. ✉ *Campo del Ghetto Nuovo, Cannaregio 2902/B, Cannaregio* ☎ *055/2989815* 🎫 *€15 guided tour* ⊘ *Closed Sat.* Ⓜ *Vaporetto: San Marcuola, Guglie.*

★ **Santa Maria dei Miracoli**
CHURCH | Tiny yet harmoniously proportioned, this Renaissance gem, built between 1481 and 1489, is sheathed in marble and decorated inside with exquisite marble reliefs. Architect Pietro Lombardo (circa 1435–1515) miraculously compressed the building to fit its lot, then created the illusion of greater size by varying the color of the exterior, adding extra pilasters on the building's canal side, and offsetting the arcade windows to make the arches appear deeper. The church was built to house *I Miracoli*, an image of the Virgin Mary by Niccolò di Pietro (1394–1440) that is said to have performed miracles—look for it on the high altar. ✉ *Campo Santa Maria Nova, Cannaregio* ☎ *041/2750462* ⊕ *www.chorusvenezia.org* 🎫 *€3.50 (free with Chorus*

Pass) ⊘ *Closed Sun., open for service only* Ⓜ *Vaporetto: Rialto.*

🍴 Restaurants

★ **Algiubagiò**
$$$ | ITALIAN | Established in 1950, this restaurant along the quiet, northern outlier of Fondamente Nove has grandstand views of the San Michele island and various menus showcasing seasonal fish, meat, and pasta dishes. The friendly staff also serve ice cream, drinks, and sandwiches, making its modern bar, chic dining rooms, and lagoon-side platform restful environs to pause any time of day. **Known for:** airy respite for lunch or a snack; romantic spot for dinner; innovative dishes like spaghetti alla spirulina. Ⓢ *Average main: €35* ✉ *Fondamente Nove, Cannaregio 5039, Cannaregio* ☎ *041/5236084* ⊕ *www.algiubagio.net* ⊘ *Closed Tues.* Ⓜ *Vaporetto: Fondamente Nove.*

Da'a Marisa
$$ | ITALIAN | This is the most famous restaurant in Venice for the city's working class; if you can get a table for lunch, you'll eat, without any choice, what Marisa prepares for her local clientele—generally, big portions of excellent pasta followed by a hearty roast meat course (frequently game, more infrequently fish), for an inexpensive fixed price. Dinner is more expensive, and you may have some choice, but not much; for the authentic "Marisa experience," go for lunch. **Known for:** Venetian classics like baccalà mantecato; limited menu choices and cramped inside; genuine local atmosphere and gruff service. Ⓢ *Average main: €18* ✉ *Fondamenta di San Giobbe 652B, Cannaregio* ☎ *041/720211* ⊕ *trattoria-daa-marisa.business.site* ⊘ *No dinner Sun., Mon., and Wed.*

Enoteca Do Colonne
$ | WINE BAR | Venetians from the neighborhood frequent this friendly bacaro, not just for a glass of very drinkable wine,

Cannaregio

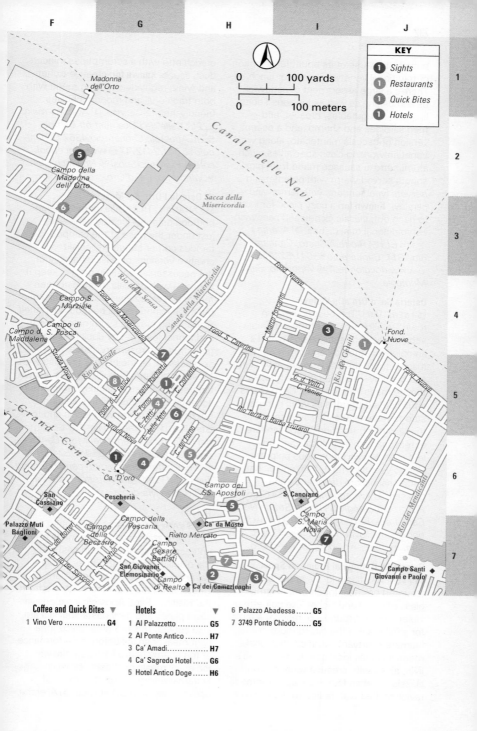

but also because of its bountiful selection of traditional Venetian cicheti for lunch. There's a large assortment of sandwiches and panini, as well as luscious tidbits like grilled vegetables, breaded and fried sardines and shrimp, and a decent version of baccalà mantecato, along with Venetian working-class specialties, such as *musetto* (a sausage made from pigs' snouts served warm with polenta) and *nervetti* (veal tendons with lemon and parsley). **Known for:** a cozy place for locals to hang out; classic cicheti and sandwiches; traditional offal dishes. Ⓢ *Average main: €13* ⌧ *Rio Terà Cristo, Cannaregio 1814, Cannaregio* ☎ *041/5240453* ⊕ *www.docolonne.it* Ⓜ *Vaporetto: San Marcuola.*

Osteria Ca' d'Oro alla Vedova

$$ | VENETIAN | "The best *polpette* in town," you'll hear fans of the venerable Vedova say, and that explains why it's an obligatory stop on any *giro d'ombra* (bacaro tour); the polpette are always hot and crunchy—and also gluten-free, as they're made with polenta. Ca' d'Oro is a full-fledged trattoria as well, but make sure to reserve ahead: it's no secret to those seeking traditional Venetian fare at reasonable prices, locals and travelers alike. **Known for:** famous polpette; classic Venetian meat, fish, and cicheti; traditional bacaro decor and wine glasses. Ⓢ *Average main: €18* ⌧ *Calle del Pistor, Cannaregio 3912, off Strada Nova, Cannaregio* ☎ *041/5285324* ⊕ *www.facebook.com/allavedova* ⊙ *Closed Thurs. and Sun. morning* Ⓜ *Vaporetto: Ca' d'Oro.*

Osteria La Bottega ai Promessi Sposi

$$ | VENETIAN | Join locals at the *banco* (counter) premeal for an *ombra* (small glass of wine) and cicheti like polpette or violet eggplant rounds, or reserve a table for a full meal in the dining room or the intimate courtyard. A varied, seasonal menu includes local standards like calf's liver, along with creative variations on classic Venetian fare, such as homemade ravioli stuffed with radicchio di Treviso or

orecchiette with a scrumptious minced-duck sauce. **Known for:** creative cicheti and wine; regularly changing menu with both traditional and modern choices; friendly, helpful service. Ⓢ *Average main: €22* ⌧ *Calle de l'Oca, just off Campo Santi Apostoli, Cannaregio 4367, Cannaregio* ☎ *041/2412747* ⊕ *www.facebook.com/AiPromessiSposi* ⊙ *No lunch Mon.* Ⓜ *Vaporetto: Ca' d'Oro.*

★ Osteria l'Orto dei Mori

$$$ | ITALIAN | This small, popular neighborhood osteria—located canal-side, just under the nose of the campo's famous corner statue—specializes in creative versions of classic Italian (but not necessarily Venetian) dishes; keep it Venetian with baccala mantecato then *fegato alla veneziana* (liver with onions) or push the experimental boat out with their Sicilian king prawns swimming in curry and fennel followed by duck breast with grapefruit and rosemary sauce. Don't skip dessert, as their boozy tiramisu with Moscato di Pantelleria wins raves. **Known for:** traditional Italian dishes with modern accents; choice local wine selection; buzzing atmosphere with locals and tourists alike. Ⓢ *Average main: €27* ⌧ *Campo dei Mori, Fondamenta dei Mori, Cannaregio 3386, Cannaregio* ☎ *041/5243677* ⊕ *www.osteriaortodeimori.com* ⊙ *Closed Tues. and Wed.* Ⓜ *Vaporetto: Orto, Ca' d'Oro, San Marcuola.*

Tiziano

$ | ITALIAN | A fine variety of excellent *tramezzini* (sandwiches made of untoasted white bread triangles) lines the display cases at this busy *tavola calda* (roughly the Italian equivalent of a cafeteria) on the main thoroughfare from the Rialto to Santi Apostoli; inexpensive salad plates and daily pasta specials are also served. This is a great place for a light meal or snack before a performance at the nearby Teatro Malibran. **Known for:** quick meals or snacks, especially tramezzini; noisy spot; efficient (if occasionally grumpy) service. Ⓢ *Average* main: €10 ✉ Salizada San Giovanni Crisostomo, Cannaregio 5747, Cannaregio ☎ 041/5235544 ⊕ bartiziano.business. site Ⓜ Vaporetto: Rialto.

★ Vini da Gigio

$$$ | VENETIAN | A brother-sister team run this refined trattoria, where you're made to feel as if you've been personally invited to lunch or dinner. Indulge, perhaps, in spaghetti with clams and cod roe or arugula-stuffed ravioli, seafood risotto made to order for two, or sesame-encrusted tuna. Just note, though, that it's the meat dishes that steal the show: the steak with red-pepper sauce and fegato alla veneziana are among the best in town. **Known for:** superb meat dishes like fegato alla veneziana; one of the city's best wine cellars; helpful and professional service. $ Average main: €26 ✉ Fondamenta San Felice, Cannaregio 3628/A, Cannaregio ☎ 041/5285140 ⊕ www.vinidagigio.com ☉ Closed Mon., Tues., and 2 wks in Aug. Ⓜ Vaporetto: Ca' d'Oro.

☕ Coffee and Quick Bites

★ Vino Vero

$ | WINE BAR | Swing by this pint-sized wine bar for cicheti and crostini that are just a bit different and fresher than what you'll find elsewhere, along with a fine selection of natural wines. Though there's not much space inside, try to snag one of the coveted seats by the canal, which becomes a buzzy evening spot at aperitivo time. **Known for:** large selection of both Italian and international natural wines; delectable small bites; pretty canal-side seating. $ Average main: €14 ✉ Fondamenta de la Misericordia, Cannaregio 2497, Cannaregio ☎ 041/2750044 ⊕ vinovero.wine ☉ No lunch Mon. Ⓜ Vaporetto: Madonna dell'Orto, Ca' d'Oro.

 ## Hotels

Al Palazzetto

$$ | B&B/INN | FAMILY | Understated Venetian decor, original exposed-beam ceilings and terrazzo flooring, and large rooms suitable for families or small groups are hallmarks of this intimate, family-owned guesthouse. **Pros:** authentic 18th-century palace; clean and quiet; good value for Venice. **Cons:** old-fashioned decor; not many amenities; a bit rough around the edges. $ Rooms from: €159 ✉ Calle delle Vele, Cannaregio 4057, Cannaregio ☎ 041/2750897 ⊕ www.guesthouse.it ⇱ 5 rooms ⓘ Free Breakfast Ⓜ Vaporetto: Ca' d'Oro.

★ Al Ponte Antico

$$$$ | HOTEL | The intimate upstairs terrace of this hospitable 16th-century palace inn is a perfect spot to survey the nearby Rialto scene while enjoying evening aperitivi and their fabulous homemade breakfasts. **Pros:** unique upper-level terrace overlooks Grand Canal; Peruch family-run warmth and attentive service; Matteo and Barbara's made-to-order omelets and Venetian pastries. **Cons:** in one of the busiest areas of the city (although not particularly noisy); beds a little hard for some; books up quickly. $ Rooms from: €360 ✉ Calle dell'Aseo, Cannaregio 5768, Cannaregio ☎ 041/2411944 ⊕ www.alponteantico.com ⇱ 9 rooms ⓘ Free Breakfast Ⓜ Vaporetto: Rialto.

Ca' Amadi

$$$ | HOTEL | A historic 13th-century palazzo near the Rialto markets is a welcome retreat on a tranquil corte (court), and individually decorated rooms have tufted walls and views of a lively canal or a quiet courtyard. **Pros:** classic Venetian style; some canal-view rooms; handy for sightseeing. **Cons:** rooms vary a lot in size and quality; no restaurant (simple continental breakfast served, though); reception staff not always helpful or available. $ Rooms from: €220 ✉ Corte Amadi, Cannaregio 5815, Cannaregio ☎ 041/5285210

⊕ *www.caamadi.it* ↵ *6 rooms* ⦿ *Free Breakfast* Ⓜ *Vaporetto: Rialto.*

Ca' Sagredo Hotel

$$$$ | **HOTEL** | This expansive palace has been the Sagredo family residence since the mid-1600s and has the decor to prove it: a massive staircase has Longhi wall panels soaring above it; large common areas are adorned with original art by Tiepolo, Longhi, and Ricci; and a traditional Venetian style dominates guest rooms, many of which have canal views and some of which have original art and architectural elements. **Pros:** canal views from some rooms; some of the city's best-preserved interiors; rooftop terrace and indoor bar. **Cons:** impersonal, formal atmosphere; heat in rooms controlled by front desk; no coffee- or tea-making facilities in rooms. ⑤ *Rooms from: €468* ⊠ *Campo Santa Sofia, Cannaregio 4198/99, Cannaregio* ☎ *041/2413111* ⊕ *www.casagredohotel.com* ↵ *42 rooms* ⦿ *No Meals* Ⓜ *Vaporetto: Ca' d'Oro.*

Hotel Antico Doge

$$$ | **HOTEL** | Once the home of Marino Faliero, a 14th-century doge who was executed for treason, this palazzo has been attentively "modernized" in elegant 18th-century Venetian style: all rooms are adorned with brocades, damask-tufted walls, gilt mirrors, and parquet floors—even the breakfast room has a stuccoed ceiling and Murano chandelier. **Pros:** romantic, atmospheric decor; convenient to the Rialto and beyond; some rooms have whirlpool tubs. **Cons:** no outdoor garden or terrace; no elevator; area outside hotel is very busy and noisy. ⑤ *Rooms from: €255* ⊠ *Campo Santi Apostoli, Cannaregio 5643, Cannaregio* ☎ *041/7799990* ⊕ *www.anticodoge.com* ↵ *20 rooms* ⦿ *No Meals* Ⓜ *Vaporetto: Ca' d'Oro, Rialto.*

Palazzo Abadessa

$$$ | **HOTEL** | At this atmospheric late-16th-century palazzo, you can experience warm hospitality, a lush private garden, and unusually spacious guest rooms well appointed with antique-style furniture, frescoed or stuccoed ceilings, and silk fabrics. **Pros:** enormous walled garden, a rare and delightful treat in crowded Venice; unique and richly decorated guest rooms; superb guest service. **Cons:** many of the bathrooms need a refurb; no restaurant (buffet breakfast served); poor soundproofing. ⑤ *Rooms from: €292* ⊠ *Calle Priuli, Cannaregio 4011, off Strada Nova, Cannaregio* ☎ *041/2413784* ⊕ *www.abadessa.com* ⊘ *Closed last 2 wks in Jan.* ↵ *15 rooms* ⦿ *Free Breakfast* Ⓜ *Vaporetto: Ca' d'Oro.*

3749 Ponte Chiodo

$$ | **B&B/INN** | Spending time at this charming guesthouse secreted away down narrow Calle Racheta near the Ca' d'Oro vaporetto stop is like staying with a friend: service is warm and helpful, with lots of suggestions for dining and sightseeing. **Pros:** highly attentive service; relaxed atmosphere; pretty private garden. **Cons:** bathroom decor dated; no restaurant, though breakfast is served in the garden; not for those looking for large-hotel amenities (no spa or gym). ⑤ *Rooms from: €170* ⊠ *Calle Racheta, Cannaregio 3749, Cannaregio* ☎ *041/2413935, 348/2473520 mobile* ⊕ *www.pontechiodo.it* ↵ *6 rooms* ⦿ *Free Breakfast* Ⓜ *Vaporetto: Ca' d'Oro.*

ⓨ Nightlife

El Sbarlefo

WINE BAR | The odd name is Venetian for "smirk," although you'll be hard-pressed to find one at this cheery, familiar bacaro with a wine selection as ample as the cicheti on offer. The spread of delectables ranges from classic polpette of meat and tuna to tomino cheese rounds to speck and robiola rolls, and the selection of wines is equally intriguing. There's often live jazz and blues on Friday and Saturday nights. El Sbarlefo has a second location in Dorsoduro, in the calle just behind the church of San Pantalon. ⊠ *Salizada del*

Pistor, off Campo Santi Apostoli, Cannaregio 4556/C, Cannaregio ☎ 041/5246650 Ⓜ Vaporetto: Ca' d'Oro.

TiME Social Bar

COCKTAIL BARS | The seasonal cocktails at this charming mixology bar, many of which use fruit and homemade bitters, win rave reviews from visitors and locals alike. There are also small nibbles on offer if hunger strikes. ✉ Rio Terà Farsetti, Cannaregio 1414, Cannaregio ☎ 338/3636951 mobile ⊕ www.facebook.com/venicecocktail Ⓜ Vaporetto: San Marcuola Casino.

Un Mondo di Vino

WINE BAR | Recharge with some wine or a cicheto or two—meat, fish, and vegetarian choices are on offer—at this cozy, friendly spot near the Miracoli church. Numerous wines are available by the glass, and the helpful servers are often happy to crack open a bottle for sampling if there's something you fancy. ✉ Salizzada San Cancian, Cannaregio ☎ 041/5211093 ⊕ www.bacarounmondodivino.it Ⓜ Vaporetto: Rialto, Ca' d'Oro.

🛍 Shopping

★ Gianni Basso Stampatore

STATIONERY | Beloved of artists and celebrities, this traditional printer run by amiable Gianni and his son creates handmade business cards, stationery, and invitations using vintage letterpress machinery. You can choose from the selection on offer or have your own custom designed and shipped to you at home. Ask Gianni about the history of the place and his loyal global clientele, and he'll likely regale you with tales and a tour of his lovingly curated museum-workshop. Don't touch the antique equipment, though. ✉ Calle del Fumo, Cannaregio 5306, Cannaregio ☎ 041/5234681 Ⓜ Vaporetto: Fondamente Nove.

★ Vittorio Constantini

ANTIQUES & COLLECTIBLES | FAMILY | This glass artist's workshop features unusual, intricate pieces inspired by nature—birds, butterflies, beetles, and other insects—appreciated by adults and children alike. ✉ Calle del Fumo, Cannaregio 5311, Cannaregio ☎ 041/5222265 ⊕ www.vittoriocostantini.com Ⓜ Vaporetto: Fondamente Nove.

Castello

Castello, Venice's largest sestiere, includes all of the land from east of Piazza San Marco to the city's easternmost tip. Its name probably comes from a fortress that once stood on one of the eastern islands. Not every well-off Venetian family could find a spot or afford to build a palazzo on the Grand Canal. Many who couldn't instead settled in western Castello, taking advantage of its proximity to the Rialto and San Marco, and built the noble palazzi that today distinguish this area from the fisher's enclave in the more easterly streets of the sestiere. During the days of the Republic, eastern Castello was the primary neighborhood for workers in the shipbuilding Arsenale located in its midst and now home to the Venice Biennale. Foodies flock here for some of the city's most creative modern Italian cuisine.

TIMING

Unless you're here during the Biennale—in which case, you'll be spending at least a full day or two at the Arsenale—you can check out the neighborhood's three gorgeous churches (San Francesco della Vigna, Santi Giovanni e Paolo, and San Zaccaria), as well as the lovely rooms in the Scuola di San Giorgio degli Schiavoni (if it's open, which it isn't always), in half a day.

Sights

Arsenale

MILITARY SIGHT | Visible from the street, the Porta Magna (1460), an impressive Renaissance gateway designed by Antonio Gambello, was the first classical structure to be built in Venice. It is guarded by four lions—war booty of Francesco Morosini, who took the Peloponnese from the Turks in 1687. The Arsenale is said to have been founded in 1104 on twin islands. The immense facility that evolved—it was the largest industrial complex in Europe built prior to the Industrial Revolution—was given the old Venetian dialect name *arzanà*, borrowed from the Arabic *darsina'a,* meaning "workshop." At the height of its activity, in the early 16th century, it employed as many as 16,000 *arsenalotti,* workers who were among the most respected shipbuilders in the world. The Arsenale developed a type of pre–Industrial Revolution assembly line, which allowed it to build ships with astounding speed and efficiency. The Arsenale's efficiency was confirmed time and again—whether building 100 ships in 60 days to battle the Turks in Cyprus (1597) or completing one perfectly armed warship, start to finish, while King Henry III of France attended a banquet. ⊠ *Campo de la Tana 2169, Castello* Ⓜ *Vaporetto: Arsenale.*

★ San Francesco della Vigna

CHURCH | Although this church contains some interesting and beautiful paintings and sculptures, it's the architecture that makes it worth the hike through a lively, middle-class residential neighborhood. The Franciscan church was enlarged and rebuilt by Jacopo Sansovino in 1534, giving it the first Renaissance interior in Venice; its proportions are said to reflect the mystic significance of the numbers three and seven dictated by Renaissance neo-Platonic numerology. The soaring but harmonious facade was added in 1562 by Palladio. The church represents a unique combination of the work of the two great stars of 16th-century Veneto architecture. The complex contains three cloisters that house vegetable plots and the city's oldest vineyard. ⊠ *Campo di San Francesco della Vigna, Castello* ☏ *041/5206102* ⊕ *www.facebook.com/sanfrancescodellavignavenezia* Ⓜ *Vaporetto: Celestia.*

★ San Zaccaria

CHURCH | More a museum than a church, San Zaccaria has a striking Renaissance facade, with central and upper portions representing some of Mauro Codussi's best work. The lower portion of the facade and the interior were designed by Antonio Gambello. The original structure of the church was 14th-century Gothic, with its facade completed in 1515, some years after Codussi's death in 1504, and it retains the proportions of the rest of the essentially Gothic structure. Inside is one of the great treasures of Venice, Giovanni Bellini's celebrated altarpiece, *La Sacra Conversazione,* easily recognizable in the left nave. Completed in 1505, when the artist was 75, it shows Bellini's ability to incorporate the aesthetics of the High Renaissance into his work. ⊠ *Campo San Zaccaria, 4693 Castello, Castello* ☏ *041/5221257* ⊕ *chorusvenezia.org* ☜ *Church free, chapels and crypt €3.50 (free with Chorus Pass)* ⊘ *Closed Sun. morning* Ⓜ *Vaporetto: San Zaccaria.*

★ Santi Giovanni e Paolo

CHURCH | This gorgeous Italian Gothic church of the Dominican order, consecrated in 1430, looms over one of the most picturesque squares in Venice: the Campo Giovanni e Paolo, centered around the magnificent 15th-century equestrian statue of Bartolomeo Colleoni by the Florentine Andrea Verrocchio. Bartolomeo Bon's portal, combining Gothic and classical elements, was added between 1458 and 1462, using columns salvaged from Torcello. The 15th-century Murano stained-glass window near the side entrance is breathtaking for its beautiful colors and figures. ⊠ *Campo dei Santi Giovanni e Paolo, Castello*

✉ 041/5235913 ⊕ www.santigiovannie-paolo.it ✆ €3.50 ⊘ Closed weekends Ⓜ Vaporetto: Fondamente Nove, Rialto.

★ Scuola di San Giorgio degli Schiavoni (Scuola Dalmata)

HISTORIC SIGHT | Founded in 1451 by the Dalmatian community, this small scuola, or confraternity, was, and still is, a social and cultural center for migrants from what is now Croatia. It contains one of Italy's most beautiful rooms, harmoniously decorated between 1502 and 1507 by Vittore Carpaccio. Although Carpaccio generally painted legendary and religious figures against backgrounds of contemporary Venetian architecture, here is perhaps one of the first instances of "Orientalism" in Western painting. ■**TIP→ Opening hours are quite flexible. Since this is a must-see site, book in advance so you won't be disappointed.** ✉ Calle dei Furlani, Castello 3259/A, Castello ☎ 041/5228828 ⊕ www.scuoladalmatavenezia.com ✆ €6 Ⓜ Vaporetto: Arsenale, San Zaccaria.

🍴 Restaurants

Al Covo

$$$ | **VENETIAN** | For years, Diane and Cesare Benelli's Al Covo has set the standard of excellence for traditional, refined Venetian cuisine; the Benellis are dedicated to providing their guests with the freshest, highest-quality fish from the Adriatic, and vegetables, when at all possible, from the islands of the Venetian Lagoon and the fields of the adjacent Veneto region. Although their cuisine could be correctly termed "classic Venetian," it always offers surprises, like the juicy crispness of their legendary fritto misto (fried mixed seafood and vegetables)—reliant upon an unconventional secret ingredient in the batter—or the heady aroma of their fresh anchovies marinated in wild fennel, an herb somewhat foreign to Veneto.

Known for: sophisticated Venetian flavors; top-notch local ingredients; Diane's chocolate cake for dessert. $ Average main: €31 ✉ Campiello Pescaria, Castello 3968, Castello ☎ 041/5223812 ⊕ www.ristorantealcovo.com ⊘ Closed Tues. and Wed., 3 wks in Jan., and 10 days in Aug. Ⓜ Vaporetto: Arsenale.

★ Alle Testiere

$$$ | **VENETIAN** | The name is a reference to the old headboards that adorn the walls of this tiny, informal restaurant, but the food (not the decor) is undoubtedly the focus. Local foodies consider this one of the most refined eateries in the city thanks to chef Bruno Gavagnin's gently creative take on classic Venetian fish dishes; the chef's artistry seldom draws attention to itself but simply reveals new dimensions of familiar fare, creating dishes that stand out for their lightness and balance. **Known for:** daily changing fish offerings, based on what's fresh at the market; excellent pasta with seafood; wonderful wine selection. $ Average main: €29 ✉ Calle del Mondo Novo, Castello 5801, Castello ☎ 041/5227220 ⊕ www.osterialletestiere.it ⊘ Closed Sun. and Mon., 3 wks in Jan. and Feb., and 4 wks in July and Aug.

★ Corte Sconta

$$$ | **SEAFOOD** | The heaping seafood antipasti alone is reason enough to visit this classic seafood-focused eatery close to the Biennale—think tuna and swordfish carpaccio, spider crab, clams, crab pâté, and a variety of fish. But you'll also want to stay for the excellent mains, particularly soft-shell crab, mixed grilled fish, and spaghetti vongole, plus the lovely courtyard setting. **Known for:** some of the best seafood in town; charming atmosphere with outdoor seating; service with a sense of humor. $ Average main: €28 ✉ Calle del Pestrin, Castello 3886, Castello ☎ 041/5227024 ⊕ www.cortescontavenezia.com ⊘ Closed Sun. and Mon. Ⓜ Vaporetto: Arsenale.

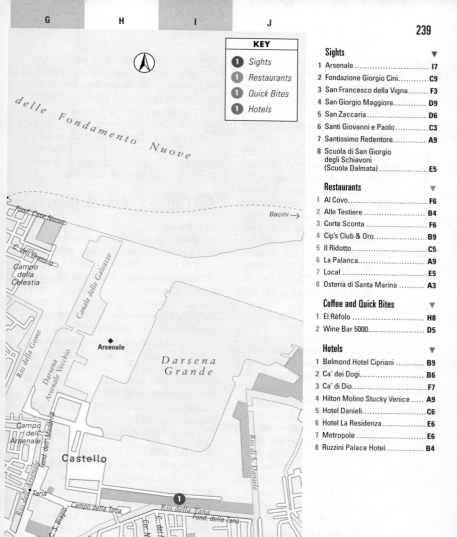

KEY

- 1 Sights
- 1 Restaurants
- 1 Quick Bites
- 1 Hotels

Sights ▼

1 Arsenale **I7**
2 Fondazione Giorgio Cini........... **C9**
3 San Francesco della Vigna........ **F3**
4 San Giorgio Maggiore............. **D9**
5 San Zaccaria...................... **D6**
6 Santi Giovanni e Paolo............ **C3**
7 Santissimo Redentore............. **A9**
8 Scuola di San Giorgio
   degli Schiavoni
   (Scuola Dalmata) **E5**

Restaurants ▼

1 Al Covo........................... **F6**
2 Alle Testiere **B4**
3 Corte Sconta **F6**
4 Cip's Club & Oro.................. **B9**
5 Il Ridotto **C5**
6 La Palanca........................ **A9**
7 Local **E5**
8 Osteria di Santa Marina **A3**

Coffee and Quick Bites ▼

1 El Rèfolo **H8**
2 Wine Bar 5000.................... **D5**

Hotels ▼

1 Belmond Hotel Cipriani **B9**
2 Ca' dei Dogi...................... **B6**
3 Ca' di Dio........................ **F7**
4 Hilton Molino Stucky Venice **A9**
5 Hotel Danieli...................... **C6**
6 Hotel La Residenza **E6**
7 Metropole **E6**
8 Ruzzini Palace Hotel............. **B4**

Il Ridotto

$$$$ | MODERN ITALIAN | Longtime restaurateur Gianni Bonaccorsi has established an eatery where he can pamper a limited number of lucky patrons with his imaginative cuisine and impeccable taste in wine. *Ridotto* means "small, private place," which this very much is, evoking an atmosphere of secrecy and intimacy; the innovative menus tend toward lighter but wonderfully tasty versions of classic dishes. **Known for:** some of the most creative cuisine in Venice; excellent five- or seven-course tasting menus; extensive wine recommendations. $ *Average main: €40* ⊠ *Campo SS. Filippo e Giacomo, Castello 4509, Castello* ☎ *041/5208280* ⊕ *www.ilridotto.com* ⊗ *Closed Wed. No lunch Tues. and Thurs.* Ⓜ *Vaporetto: San Zaccaria.*

Local

$$$$ | VENETIAN | In a simple yet charming setting with beamed ceilings and terrazzo floors, a sister and brother team oversee their "new Venetian cuisine," where local ingredients are used to prepare reinvented traditional dishes, often with Japanese influences. It's tasting-menu only, with seven or nine courses (or a less expensive four-course option at weekday lunch), and wine pairings from their extensive list are a recommended treat. **Known for:** tiramigiù dessert: coffee, marsala, and mascarpone; ingredients from Italian producers and daily catch; highly attentive staff. $ *Average main: €150* ⊠ *Salizzada dei Greci, Castello 3303, Castello* ☎ *041/2411128* ⊕ *www.ristorantelocal.com* ⊗ *Closed Tues. and Wed. No lunch Sun. and Thurs.* Ⓜ *Vaporetto: San Zaccaria.*

Osteria di Santa Marina

$$$$ | VENETIAN | The candlelit tables on this romantic campo are inviting enough, but it's the intimate restaurant's imaginative kitchen that's likely to win you over; you can order consistently excellent pasta, fish, or meat dishes à la carte or opt for one of the rewarding tasting menus. The wine list is ample and well thought out, and the service is gracious, warm, and professional. **Known for:** innovative and artfully presented modern Venetian food; charming setting; wonderful wine pairings. $ *Average main: €33* ⊠ *Campo Santa Marina, Castello 5911, Castello* ☎ *041/5285239* ⊕ *www.osteriadisantamarina.com* ⊗ *Closed Sun. and 2 wks in Aug. No lunch Mon.* Ⓜ *Vaporetto: Rialto.*

☕ Coffee and Quick Bites

★ El Rèfolo

$$ | WINE BAR | At this contemporary cantina and hip hangout in a very Venetian neighborhood, the owner pairs enthusiastically chosen wines and artisanal beers with select meat, savory cheese, pasta dishes, and seasonal vegetable combos. With outside-only seating (not particularly comfortable), it's more appropriate for an aperitivo and a light meal. **Known for:** good selection of wine and beer; filling panini, meat and cheese plates; boisterous atmosphere outside in nice weather. $ *Average main: €16* ⊠ *Via Garibaldi, Castello 1580, Castello* ☎ *320/3267536 mobile* ⊕ *www.facebook.com/elrefolo/* ⊗ *Closed Mon.* Ⓜ *Vaporetto: Arsenale.*

Wine Bar 5000

$ | WINE BAR | Nibble on a selection of cicheti or a cheese or meat plate at this cozy wine bar on Campo San Severo, near the Basilica dei Frari. You can either dine inside the brick-walled, Murano glass–chandeliered space, or watch the gondolas sail by at a table outdoors next to the quiet adjacent Severno canal. **Known for:** large wine list, including biodynamic options; lovely outdoor seating area; small but well-prepared choice of cicheti and salads. $ *Average main: €13* ⊠ *Campo San Severo, Castello 5000, Castello* ☎ *041/3097891* ⊕ *winebar5000.it* ⊗ *Closed Wed.* Ⓜ *Vaporetto: San Zaccaria.*

Hotels

Ca' dei Dogi

$$$ | HOTEL | A quiet courtyard secluded from the San Marco melee offers an island of calm in six guest rooms and two apartments (some with private terraces overlooking the Doge's Palace, one with a Jacuzzi), which are individually decorated with contemporary furnishings and accessories. **Pros:** amazing location close to Doge's Palace and Piazza San Marco; balconies with wonderful views; traditional Italian restaurant on-site. **Cons:** rooms are on the small side; no elevator and lots of stairs; bathrooms can feel cramped. $ *Rooms from: €250 ⊠ Corte Santa Scolastica, Castello 4242, Castello ☎ 041/2413751 ⊕ www.cadeidogi. it ⊗ Closed 3 wks in Dec. ⌁ 6 rooms* ⦿ *Free Breakfast* Ⓜ *Vaporetto: San Zaccaria.*

Ca' di Dio

$$$$ | HOTEL | Housed in a palace dating from 1272, with interiors updated by of-the-moment architect Patricia Urquiola, this deluxe hotel offers rooms with views of San Giorgio Maggiore island, two restaurants, and two internal courtyards, all within striking distance of the Venice Biennale grounds. **Pros:** most guest rooms are suites; convenient to the Biennale; on-site gym and spa. **Cons:** staff can be a tad aloof; not for fans of traditional design; a walk from traditional Venetian sights. $ *Rooms from: €593 ⊠ Riva Ca' di Dio, Castello 5866, Castello ☎ 041/0980238 ⊕ vretreats.com/en/ ca-di-dio ⌁ 66 rooms* ⦿ *Free Breakfast* Ⓜ *Vaporetto: Arsenale.*

★ Hotel Danieli

$$$$ | HOTEL | One of the city's most famous lodgings—built in the 14th century and run as a hotel since 1822—lives up to its reputation: the chance to explore the wonderful, highly detailed lobby is itself a reason to book an overnight stay, plus the views along the lagoon are fantastic, the rooms gorgeous, and the food fabulous. **Pros:** historical and inviting lobby; amazing rooftop views; tasty cocktails at Bar Dandolo. **Cons:** lots of American tourists; some rooms feel dated; service can be indifferent. $ *Rooms from: €1200 ⊠ Riva degli Schiavoni, Castello 4196, Castello ☎ 041/5226480 ⊕ hoteldanieli.com ⌁ 210 rooms* ⦿ *No Meals* Ⓜ *Vaporetto: San Zaccaria.*

Hotel La Residenza

$$$ | HOTEL | Set in a quiet campo, this renovated 15th-century Gothic-Byzantine palazzo has simple but spacious rooms and lovely public spaces filled with chandeliers, 18th-century paintings, and period reproduction furnishings. **Pros:** lavish salon and breakfast room; quiet residential area, steps from Riva degli Schiavoni and 10 minutes from Piazza San Marco; affordable rates. **Cons:** no elevator; basic, dated guest room decor; average breakfast. $ *Rooms from: €245 ⊠ Campo Bandiera e Moro, Castello 3608, Castello ☎ 041/5285315 ⊕ www. venicelaresidenza.com ⌁ 15 rooms* ⦿ *No Meals* Ⓜ *Vaporetto: Arsenale.*

Metropole

$$$$ | HOTEL | Atmosphere prevails in this labyrinth of opulent, intimate spaces featuring classic Venetian decor combined with Eastern influences: common areas and guest rooms are filled with an assortment of antiques and curiosities. **Pros:** hotel harkens back to the gracious Venice of a bygone era; suites have private roof terraces with water views; gorgeous Oriental Bar & Bistrot. **Cons:** one of the most densely touristed locations in the city; some standard rooms and bathrooms are small; quirky, eccentric collections on display not for everyone. $ *Rooms from: €520 ⊠ Riva degli Schiavoni, Castello 4149, Castello ☎ 041/5205044 ⊕ www. hotelmetropole.com ⌁ 67 rooms* ⦿ *Free Breakfast* Ⓜ *Vaporetto: San Zaccaria.*

Ruzzini Palace Hotel

$$$ | HOTEL | Renaissance- and Baroque-style common areas are soaring spaces with Venetian terrazzo flooring, frescoed

and exposed-beam ceilings, and Murano chandeliers; guest rooms tastefully mix historical style with contemporary furnishings and appointments. **Pros:** a luminous, aristocratic ambience; located on a lively Venetian campo not frequented by tourists; cheaper rates for standard rooms often available. **Cons:** plain bathrooms; relatively far from a vaporetto stop; no restaurant on-site. $ *Rooms from: €260* ✉ *Campo Santa Maria Formosa, Castello 5866, Castello* ☎ *041/2410447* ⊕ *www.ruzzinipalace.com* ⇌ *28 rooms* ❑ *No Meals* Ⓜ *Vaporetto: San Zaccaria, Rialto.*

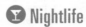 Nightlife

Bar Dandolo
COCKTAIL BARS | Even if you're not staying at Hotel Danieli, it's worth a stop to marvel at its bar's over-the-top decor—replete with ornate ceilings, stained glass, marble columns, and chandeliers—inside a 14th-century palace. Though pricey, it's a highly atmospheric place to sample their signature Vesper martini or another cocktail of your choice, usually accompanied by live piano music. ✉ *Hotel Danieli, Riva degli Schiavoni, Castello 4196, Castello* ☎ *041/5226480* ⊕ *www.hoteldanieli.com* Ⓜ *Vaporetto: San Zaccaria.*

Zanzibar
BARS | This kiosk bar is very popular on warm summer evenings with Venetians and tourists drinking spritz and nibbling popcorn. It's all about the location under the soaring church of Santa Maria Formosa, which makes it an atmospheric place for people-watching; plus, if you like a boogie, they stage occasional music (mainly reggae and dub) nights, and carnival events. Although there's food, it's mostly limited to conventional Venetian sandwiches and commercial ice cream. ✉ *Campo Santa Maria Formosa, Castello 5840, Castello* ☎ *345/2885654* ⊕ *www.facebook.com/zanzibar5840* Ⓜ *Vaporetto: San Zaccaria.*

Shopping

Kalimala
LEATHER GOODS | This shop should not be missed if you are looking for soft leather bags that are a perfect match for almost any outfit, handmade leather shoes, or quality belts. ✉ *Salizzada San Lio, Castello 5387, Castello* ☎ *041/5283596* ⊕ *kalimala.net* Ⓜ *Vaporetto: Rialto.*

★ Papier Mache—Laboratorio di Artigianato Artistico
SPECIALTY STORE | **FAMILY** | If you're looking for an authentic Venetian mask, this is the place to go. Owner Stefano and his talented team of artists create exquisite handmade masks that can be custom ordered if you don't see what you want, as well as shipped worldwide. ✉ *Calle Lunga Santa Maria Formosa, Castello 5174/B, Venice* ☎ *041/5229995* ⊕ *www.papiermache.it* Ⓜ *Vaporetto: Ospedale.*

San Giorgio Maggiore and Giudecca

Beckoning travelers across St. Mark's Basin is the island of San Giorgio Maggiore, separated by a small channel from Giudecca. A tall brick campanile on that distant bank nicely complements the Campanile of San Marco. Beneath it looms the stately dome of one of Venice's greatest churches, San Giorgio Maggiore, the creation of Andrea Palladio. To the west, on Giudecca, is Palladio's other masterpiece, the church of the Santissimo Redentore.

You can reach San Giorgio Maggiore via Vaporetto Line 2 from San Zaccaria. The next three stops on the line take you to Giudecca. The island's past may be shrouded in mystery, but despite recent gentrification by artists and well-to-do bohemians, it's still down-to-earth and one of the city's few remaining primarily working-class neighborhoods.

Did You Know?

The nobility in Venice used to be extremely competitive about their gondolas, decorating them in flamboyant colors and over-the-top ornaments. A law in the 16th century put an end to that. Today, all gondolas in Venice must be painted boring black, though they are allowed three flourishes: a curly tail, a pair of seahorses, and a multi-pronged prow.

Interestingly, you find that most Venetians don't even consider the Giudecchini Venetians at all.

TIMING

A half day should be plenty of time to visit the area. Allow about a half hour to see each of the churches and an hour or two to look around Giudecca.

◉ Sights

★ Fondazione Giorgio Cini (*Cini Foundation*)

SPECIALTY MUSEUM | Adjacent to San Giorgio Maggiore is a complex that now houses the Cini Foundation, established in 1951 as a cultural center dedicated to humanist research. It contains a beautiful cloister designed by Palladio in 1560, his refectory, a library designed by Longhena, and various archives. In a woodland area you can wander amid 10 "Vatican Chapels" created for the 2018 Architecture Biennale by renowned architects, including Norman Foster. Another stunning feature is the Borges Labyrinth, a 1-km (½-mile) path through a boxwood hedge that allows visitors to take a 45-minute contemplative walk. It was designed by Randoll Coate and inspired by the Jorge Luis Borges short story "The Garden of Forking Paths." An evocative audio guide, composed by Antonio Fresa and performed by Teatro La Fenice's orchestra, may accompany your pensive stroll. Guided tours are given daily (except Wednesday), and reservations are required. ⊠ *Isola di San Giorgio Maggiore, San Giorgio Maggiore* ☎ *366/4202181* ⊕ *www.visitcini.com* ⊠ *€15 for Tour 1 (Foundation buildings), Tour 2 (Borges Labyrinth) €24, Tour 3 (The Vatican Chapels and woods) €25; €22 for two tours combined; €28 for three tours combined* ۩ *Closed Wed.* ⚓ *Reservations required* Ⓜ *Vaporetto: San Giorgio.*

★ San Giorgio Maggiore

CHURCH | There's been a church on this island since the 8th century. Today's refreshingly airy and simply decorated church of brick and white marble was begun in 1566 by Palladio and displays his architectural hallmarks of mathematical harmony and classical influence. *The Last Supper* and the *Gathering of Manna,* two of Tintoretto's later works, line the chancel. To the right of the entrance hangs *The Adoration of the Shepherds* by Jacopo Bassano. Book ahead for a tour of the private rooms to view Carpaccio's *St. George and the Dragon* (1516) and what is considered to be Tintoretto's final work, *The Entombment of Christ* (1594). The campanile (bell tower) dates from 1791. ■TIP→ **Take an elevator to the top of the campanile for unparalleled 360-degree views of the lagoon, islands, and Venice itself.** ⊠ *Isola di San Giorgio Maggiore, San Giorgio Maggiore* ☎ *041/5227827* ⊕ *www.abbaziasangiorgio.it* ⚓ *Church free, campanile €6* Ⓜ *Vaporetto: San Giorgio.*

Santissimo Redentore

CHURCH | After a plague in 1576 claimed some 50,000 people—nearly one-third of the city's population (including Titian)—Andrea Palladio was asked to design a commemorative church. Giudecca's Capuchin friars offered land and their services, provided the building's design was in keeping with the simplicity of their hermitage. Consecrated in 1592, after Palladio's death, the Redentore (considered Palladio's supreme achievement in ecclesiastical design) is dominated by a dome and a pair of slim, almost minaretlike bell towers. Its deceptively simple, stately facade leads to a bright, airy interior. There aren't any paintings or sculptures of note, but the harmony and elegance of the interior makes a visit worthwhile. ⊠ *Fondamenta San Giacomo, Giudecca* ☎ *041/5231415* ⊕ *www.chorusvenezia.org* ⚓ *€3.50 (free with Chorus Pass)* ۩ *Closed Sun.* Ⓜ *Vaporetto: Redentore.*

Restaurants

Cip's Club & Oro

$$$$ | VENETIAN | Located on the water's edge, looking out at the Venice skyline, the Belmond Cipriani's exclusive outdoor-indoor Cip's Club bar and Oro restaurant is best known for its breathtaking views, but the exquisite and very pricey tasting menu (from €250) of Venetian classics and extensive wine list certainly don't play second fiddle. Taking the complimentary 10-minute boat ride to and from San Marco also adds to the thoroughly James Bond sense of drama and romance. **Known for:** sublime Venice vistas with a Bellini; sophisticated service; relaxing lunch destination. $ *Average main: €60* ✉ *Belmond Hotel Cipriani, Giudecca 10, Giudecca* ☎ *041/240801* ⊕ *www.belmond.com* Ⓜ *Vaporetto: Zitelle.*

★ La Palanca

$$ | ITALIAN | It's all about the views at this classic, informal wine bar–restaurant, where tables perched on the water's edge are often filled with chatty patrons, particularly at lunchtime. The homemade pasta and fish dishes are highly recommended, and although they don't really serve dinner, a filling selection of *cicheti* is offered in the evening. **Known for:** sea bass ravioli, grilled seafood, and baccalà; good, affordable wine list; superlative views. $ *Average main: €19* ✉ *Isola della Giudecca 448, Giudecca* ☎ *041/5287719* ⊕ *www.facebook.com/lapalancagiudecca* Ⓧ *Closed Sun.* Ⓜ *Vaporetto: Palanca.*

Hotels

★ Belmond Hotel Cipriani

$$$$ | HOTEL | With amazing service, wonderful rooms, fab restaurants, and a large pool and spa—all just a five-minute boat ride from Piazza San Marco (the hotel water shuttle leaves every 15 minutes, 24 hours a day)—the Cipriani is Venetian luxe at its best. **Pros:** old-world charm meets modern luxury; Olympic-size heated saltwater pool; Michelin-starred restaurant. **Cons:** very expensive; may be too quiet for some; gym not open 24 hours. $ *Rooms from: €1850* ✉ *Giudecca 10, Giudecca* ☎ *041/240801* ⊕ *www.belmond.com* Ⓧ *Closed mid-Nov.–early Apr.* ⤴ *96 rooms* ⦿ *Free Breakfast* Ⓜ *Vaporetto: Zitelle.*

Hilton Molino Stucky Venice

$$$$ | HOTEL | FAMILY | Wooden beams and iron columns are some of the original details still visible in this redbrick former flour mill–turned-hotel, which also features sublime views across the lagoon to Venice, particularly from the lively rooftop bar. **Pros:** extremely helpful staff; shuttle boat to San Marco; ample breakfast buffet. **Cons:** can hear noise from other rooms; hotel itself a bit confusing to navigate; food offerings on the pricey side. $ *Rooms from: €401* ✉ *Giudecca 810, Giudecca* ☎ *041/2723311* ⊕ *www.hilton.com/en/hotels/vcehihi-hilton-molino-stucky-venice* ⤴ *379 rooms* ⦿ *No Meals* Ⓜ *Vaporetto: Palanca.*

Nightlife

Skyline Rooftop Bar

COCKTAIL BARS | For arguably the best views of Venice anywhere, visit this buzzy eighth-floor hotel cocktail bar. There are regular DJ and live music events during the summer months. Their cocktails, such as their signature gin martini The Gentlemen (€22), are not cheap. ✉ *Hilton Molino Stucky Venice, Giudecca 810, Giudecca* ☎ *041/2723316* ⊕ *www.skylinebarvenice.it* Ⓜ *Vaporetto: Palanca.*

Shopping

Fortuny Tessuti Artistici

FABRICS | The original Fortuny textile factory, built on former convent grounds, has been converted into a showroom. Prices are over-the-top, but it's worth a trip to see the extraordinary colors and textures of their hand-printed silks and velvets. Call in advance to arrange a tour

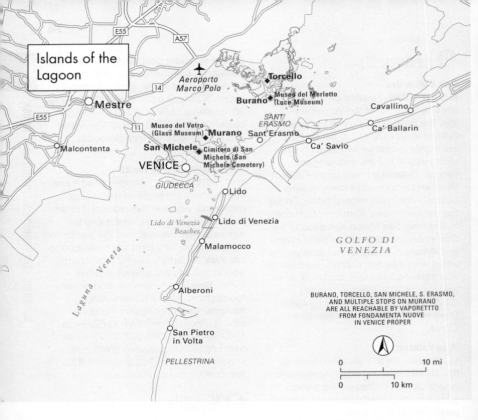

Mestre

Malcontenta

E55

E55

A57

14

11

Aeroporto Marco Polo

Torcello

Burano

Museo del Merletto (Lace Museum)

Cavallino

Ca' Ballarin

Museo del Vetro (Glass Museum)

Murano

Sant'Erasmo

SANT' ERASMO

Ca' Savio

San Michele

Cimitero di San Michele (San Michele Cemetery)

VENICE

GIUDECCA

Lido

Lido di Venezia Beaches

Lido di Venezia

GOLFO DI VENEZIA

Malamocco

Laguna Veneta

Alberoni

San Pietro in Volta

PELLESTRINA

BURANO, TORCELLO, SAN MICHELE, S. ERASMO, AND MULTIPLE STOPS ON MURANO ARE ALL REACHABLE BY VAPORETTTO FROM FONDAMENTA NUOVE IN VENICE PROPER

0   10 mi

0   10 km

of the buildings and gorgeous gardens. ✉ *Fondamenta San Biagio, Giudecca 805, Giudecca* ☎ *041/5287697* ⊕ *fortuny.com* Ⓜ *Vaporetto: Palanca.*

Islands of the Lagoon

The perfect vacation from your Venetian vacation is an escape to Murano, Burano, and sleepy Torcello, the islands of the northern lagoon, or to the Lido, Venice's barrier island that forms the southern border of the Venetian Lagoon. Torcello is legendary for its beauty and breathing room, and makes a wonderful destination for a picnic (be sure to pack a lunch). Burano, which has a long history of lace production, is an island of fishing traditions and houses painted in a riot of colors—blue, yellow, pink, ocher, and dark red. Murano is renowned

for its glass, and you can tour a glass factory here, but be warned that you will be pressured to buy. San Michele, a vaporetto stop on the way to Murano, is the cemetery island of Venice, the resting place of many international artists who have chosen to spend eternity in this beautiful city. Finally, the Lido, which protects Venice from the waters of the Adriatic, forms the beach of Venice, and is home to a series of elegant bathing establishments.

TIMING

Hitting all the sights on all the islands takes a busy, full day. If you limit yourself to Murano and San Michele, you can easily explore for an ample half day; the same goes for Burano and Torcello. In summer the express Vaporetto Line 7 will take you to Murano from San Zaccaria (the Jolanda landing) in 25 minutes;

Line 3 will take you from Piazzale Roma to Murano via the Canale di Cannaregio in 21 minutes; otherwise, local Line 4.1 makes a 45-minute trip from San Zaccaria every 20 minutes, circling the east end of Venice, stopping at Fondamente Nove and San Michele on the way. To see glassblowing, get off at Colonna; the Museo stop will put you near the Museo del Vetro.

Line 12 goes from Fondamente Nove direct to Murano and Burano every 30 minutes (from there, Torcello is a five-minute ferry ride on Line 9); the full trip takes 45 minutes each way. To get to Burano and Torcello from Murano, pick up Line 12 at the Faro stop (Murano's lighthouse). Line 1 runs from San Marco to the Lido in about 20 minutes.

Sights

★ Cimitero di San Michele (San Michele Cemetery)

CEMETERY | It's no surprise that serenity prevails on San Michele in Venice's northern lagoon. The city's island cemetery is surrounded by ocher brick walls and laced with cypress-lined pathways amid plots filled with thousands of graves; there's also a modern extension completed by British architect David Chipperfield in 2017. Among those who have made this distinctive island their final resting place are such international arts and science luminaries as Igor Stravinsky, Sergei Diaghilev, Ezra Pound, and the Austrian mathematician Christian Doppler (of the Doppler effect). You're welcome to explore the grounds if you dress respectfully and adhere to a solemn code of conduct. Photography and picnicking are not permitted. ⊠ *Isola di San Michele, San Michele* ☎ *041/7292841* ⊕ *www.comune.venezia.it/it/content/ cimitero-smichele* ⌴ *Free* Ⓜ *Vaporetto: San Michele.*

Museo del Merletto (Lace Museum)

HISTORY MUSEUM | FAMILY | Home to the Burano Lace School from 1872 to 1970, the palace of Podestà of Torcello now houses a museum dedicated to the craft for which this island is known. Detailed explanations of the manufacturing process and Burano's distinctive history as a lace-making capital provide insight into displays that showcase everything from black Venetian Carnival capes to fingerless, elbow-length "mitten gloves" fashionable in 17th-century France. Portraits of Venice's aristocracy as well as embroidered silk and brocade gowns with lace embellishments provide greater societal context on the historical use of lace in European fashion. You can also watch interesting lace-making demonstrations. ⊠ *Piazza Galuppi 187, Burano* ☎ *041/730034* ⊕ *museomerletto. visitmuve.it* ⌴ *€5, Island Museums Ticket €12 (also includes Murano Glass Museum), free with Museum Pass* ⊗ *Closed Mon.* Ⓜ *Vaporetto: Burano.*

★ Museo del Vetro (Glass Museum)

ART MUSEUM | FAMILY | This compact yet informative museum displays glass items dating from the 3rd century to today. You'll learn all about techniques introduced through the ages (many of which are still in use), including 15th-century gold-leaf decoration, 16th-century filigree work that incorporated thin bands of white or colored glass into the crystal, and the 18th-century origins of Murano's iconic chandeliers. A visit here will help you to understand the provenance of the glass you'll see for sale—and may be tempted to buy—in shops around the island. ⊠ *Fondamenta Marco Giustinian 8, Murano* ☎ *041/739586 office, 041/2434914 tickets* ⊕ *museovetro. visitmuve.it* ⌴ *€10; Island Museums Ticket €12 (also includes Burano Lace Museum); free with Museum Pass* Ⓜ *Vaporetto: Murano Museo.*

Beaches

Lido di Venezia Beaches

BEACH | FAMILY | Most hotels on the Lido have access to charming beach clubs with cabanas, striped umbrellas, and chaise longues—all of which are often available for nonguests to use for a fee. On either end of the long barrier island, the public beaches offer a more rustic but still delightful setting for nature lovers to dig their toes in the sand. **Amenities:** food and drink; lifeguards; showers; toilets. **Best for:** swimming; walking. ⊠ *Lido di Venezia, Lido* ☎ *041/8627117* ⊕ *www.visitlido.it* Ⓜ *Vaporetto: Lido.*

Restaurants

Acquastanca

$$$ | VENETIAN | Grab a seat among locals at this charming, intimate eatery—the perfect place to pop in for a lunchtime *primo* or to embark on a romantic evening. The name, referring to the tranquility of the lagoon at the turn of the tide, reflects this restaurant's approach to food and service, and you'll find such tempting seafood-based dishes as gnocchi with scallops and zucchini and curried scampi with black rice; tasteful decor sets the mood with exposed brick, iron and glass accents, and charming fish sculptures. **Known for:** light and fresh traditional food; focus on seafood dishes; relaxing atmosphere. Ⓢ *Average main: €28* ⊠ *Fondamenta Manin 48, Murano* ☎ *041/3195125* ⊕ *www.acquastanca. it* ⊘ *Closed Sun. No dinner Tues.–Thurs. and Sat.* Ⓜ *Vaporetto: Murano Colonna, Murano Faro.*

Busa alla Torre da Lele

$$$ | VENETIAN | If you're shopping for glass on Murano and want to sample some first-rate home cooking for lunch, you can't do better than stopping in this unpretentious trattoria in the island's central square. Friendly waiters will bring you ample portions of pasta, with freshly made seafood-based sauces, and a substantial variety of carefully grilled or baked fish. **Known for:** tasty local fish and seafood; reliable lunch stop in Murano; outdoor dining on a square. Ⓢ *Average main: €27* ⊠ *Campo Santo Stefano 3, Murano* ☎ *041/739662* ⊘ *No dinner* Ⓜ *Vaporetto: Murano Colonna.*

Locanda Cipriani Restaurant

$$$ | VENETIAN | A nearly legendary restaurant—Hemingway came here often to eat, drink, and brood under the veranda's greenery—established by a nephew of Giuseppe Cipriani (the founder of Harry's Bar), this inn profits from its idyllic location on the island of Torcello. The food is not exceptional, especially considering the high prices, but dining here is more about getting lost in Venetian magic; the menu features pastas and lots of seafood. **Known for:** wonderful historic atmosphere; traditional Venetian cuisine, with a focus on seafood; a peaceful lunch choice when you want to get away from Venice. Ⓢ *Average main: €33* ⊠ *Piazza Santa Fosca 29, Torcello* ☎ *041/730150* ⊕ *www.locandacipriani.com* ⊘ *Closed Tues. and early Jan.–mid-Feb. No dinner Sun.–Thurs.* Ⓜ *Vaporetto: Torcello.*

Trattoria Al Gatto Nero

$$$ | SEAFOOD | Since 1965, Al Gatto Nero has offered the best fish on Burano; no matter what you order, though, you'll savor the pride the owner and his family have in their lagoon, their island, and the quality of their *cucina* (maybe even more so when enjoying it on the picturesque fondamenta). The fish is top quality and couldn't get any fresher; all pastas and desserts are made in-house; the fritto misto is outstanding for its lightness and variety of fish; risotto alla Buranella features gò (short for ghiozzo fish), a Burano *cucina povera* ("kitchen of the poor") standard that had almost disappeared from local menus until Anthony Bourdain introduced it to travelers. **Known for:** the freshest fish and seafood around; risotto Burano style, using local ghiozzi fish; tagliolini (thin spaghetti) with spider crab.

⑤ *Average main: €33* ✉ *Fondamenta della Giudecca 88, Burano* ☎ *041/730120* ⊕ *www.gattonero.com* ◷ *Closed Mon., 1 wk in July, and 3 wks in Nov. No dinner Sun., Wed., and Thurs.* Ⓜ *Vaporetto: Burano.*

⭐ Venissa

$$$$ | **MODERN ITALIAN** | Stroll across the bridge from Burano to the islet of Mazzorbo to see some of the Venetian islands' only working vineyards, amid which sits this charming restaurant where seasonal dishes incorporate vegetables, herbs, and flowers fresh from the garden and fish fresh from the lagoon, served in seven- or 10-course tasting menus (there's also a more casual osteria). To accompany your meal, pick out a local wine like the Dorona di Venezia, made with the island's native grape. **Known for:** creative, sometimes avant-garde dishes; relaxed setting with tables overlooking the vines; perfect wine pairings. ⑤ *Average main: €160* ✉ *Fondamenta Santa Caterina 3, Mazzorbo* ☎ *041/5272281* ⊕ *www.venissa. it* ◷ *Closed Wed. in Sept.; Tues. and Wed. the rest of the year; 10 days in late Nov.; and early Jan.–Feb.* Ⓜ *Vaporetto: Mazzorbo.*

Hotels

Hotel Excelsior Venice Lido Resort

$$$$ | **HOTEL** | **FAMILY** | Built in 1908, this grand hotel with Moorish decor has old-fashioned charm and loads of amenities—from a private beach with white cabanas and a seasonal bar and restaurant to a swimming pool, gym, and tennis courts (though, oddly, no spa). **Pros:** lovely beachfront location; convenient water shuttle every 30 minutes to and from Venice proper; friendly, welcoming staff. **Cons:** could do with a refresh; restaurants on the expensive side; can get very busy in summer and around the Venice Film Festival. ⑤ *Rooms from: €540* ✉ *Lungomare Marconi 41, Lido* ☎ *041/5260201* ⊕ *www.*

hotelexcelsiorvenezia.com ⤴ *196 rooms* ⑪⃝ *Free Breakfast* Ⓜ *Vaporetto: Lido.*

⭐ Hyatt Centric Murano Venice

$$ | **HOTEL** | Befitting its location on Murano, this well-situated hotel is in a former glassmaking factory and has vitreous works of art throughout; it also has spacious, contemporary guest rooms with dark-wood floors and brown-and-cream color schemes. **Pros:** excellent breakfast buffet; vaporetto stop right outside the hotel; free airport transfers; easy walk to restaurants and shops. **Cons:** most rooms have no views; gym is basic; extra charge for using sauna and steam room. ⑤ *Rooms from: €193* ✉ *Riva Longa 49, Murano* ☎ *041/2731234* ⊕ *www.hyatt. com/hyatt-centric/vcect-hyatt-centric-murano-venice* ⤴ *119 rooms* ⑪⃝ *No Meals* Ⓜ *Vaporetto: Murano Museo.*

⭐ JW Marriott Venice Resort & Spa

$$$$ | **RESORT** | Once you get a taste of the resort's lush gardens, fabulous spa, and fantastic pools—all set on an exclusive island called Isole Delle Rose, a 20-minute boat ride from Venice—you may find yourself quickly settling in to la dolce vita. **Pros:** relaxed vibe; spacious rooms; loads of amenities. **Cons:** getting to and from Venice can feel like a hassle; not much Venetian style in rooms; extra charge for spa. ⑤ *Rooms from: €641* ✉ *Isola delle Rose, Laguna di San Marco, Venezia Succursale 12, Venice* ☎ *041/8521300* ⊕ *www.jwvenice.com* ◷ *Closed mid-Nov.–Feb.* ⤴ *266 rooms* ⑪⃝ *Free Breakfast.*

Shopping

⭐ Davide Penso

JEWELRY & WATCHES | This Venice-born, Murano-based artist makes gorgeous glass necklaces, earrings, and bracelets using the lampwork technique, where he shapes colored glass rods over a flame. ✉ *Fondamenta Riva Longa 48, Murano* ☎ *041/739819* ⊕ *www.davidepenso.info* Ⓜ *Vaporetto: Museo Murano.*

★ Emilia Burano

FABRICS | This is not your grandmother's lace—these fourth-generation lace makers have updated their designs to produce exquisite bed linens, lampshades, and other items. ⊠ *Piazza Galuppi 205, Burano* ☎ *041/9345738* ⊕ *emiliaburano.it* Ⓜ *Vaporetto: Burano.*

★ MaMa Salvadore Murano

GLASSWARE | To see more of glassmaking's artistic side, visit this gallery-shop that highlights works from international contemporary glass artists. ⊠ *Fondamenta da Mula 148, Murano* ☎ *331/6224359 mobile* ⊕ *www.facebook.com/mamamurano* Ⓜ *Vaporetto: Murano.*

★ Salviati

GLASSWARE | One of the oldest and most prestigious Italian glassmakers (founded in 1859), Salviati partners with renowned international designers, including Tom Dixon, to create beautiful contemporary pieces. ⊠ *Fondamenta Radi 16, Murano* ☎ *041/5274085* ⊕ *www.salviati.com* Ⓜ *Vaporetto: Murano Museo, Murano Navagero.*

★ Simone Cenedese

GLASSWARE | This talented second-generation glass master produces intricately designed and often whimsical glass chandeliers and sculptures. ⊠ *Calle Bertolini 6, Murano* ☎ *041/5274455* ⊕ *simonecenedese.it* Ⓜ *Vaporetto: Murano Faro, Murano Colonna.*

Chapter 6

THE VENETO AND FRIULI–VENEZIA GIULIA

Updated by
Nick Bruno

● Sights	⑪ Restaurants	🏩 Hotels	● Shopping	☻ Nightlife
★★★★☆	★★★★★	★★★★☆	★★☆☆☆	★☆☆☆☆

WELCOME TO THE VENETO AND FRIULI–VENEZIA GIULIA.

TOP REASONS TO GO

★ **Giotto's frescoes in the Cappella degli Scrovegni:** In this Padua chapel, Giotto's expressive and innovative frescoes foreshadowed the Renaissance.

★ **Villa Barbaro in Maser:** Master architect Palladio's graceful creation meets Veronese's splendid frescoes in a one-time-only collaboration.

★ **Opera in Verona's ancient arena:** The performances may not be top-notch, but even serious opera fans can't resist the spectacle of these shows.

★ **Roman and early Christian ruins at Aquileia:** Aquileia's beautiful ruins offer a glimpse of the transition from pagan to Christian Rome and are almost entirely free of tourists.

★ **The wine roads north of Treviso:** A series of routes takes you through beautiful hillsides to some of Italy's finest wines.

1 Padua. An old university city brimming with art and history, Padua is most noted for Giotto's Cappella degli Scrovegni frescoes.

2 Verona. One of the best preserved and most beautiful cities in Italy.

3 Vicenza. This elegant art city bears the signature of the great 16th-century architect Andrea Palladio.

4 Marostica. A small hilltop-citadel town renowned for a biennial human-scale chess game.

5 Asolo. The "City of a Hundred Horizons" is in the wine-producing hills.

6 Treviso. This town with beguiling canals has more than a touch of Venetian style.

7 Udine. This city has medieval and Renaissance splendors, including works by Tiepolo.

8 Cividale del Friuli. The Natisone River and ravine and the Julian Alps provide a ravishing backdrop to this town.

9 Aquileia. This was a pivotal port town in Augustus's Rome.

10 Trieste. This port city has Belle Époque cafés and palaces.

EATING AND DRINKING WELL IN THE VENETO AND FRIULI–VENEZIA GIULIA

Baked sea bream

With the decisive seasonal changes of the Venetian Arc, it's little wonder that many restaurants shun printed menus. Elements from field and forest define much of the region's cuisine, including white asparagus, herbs, chestnuts, radicchio, and wild mushrooms.

Restaurants of the Venetian Arc tend to cling to tradition, not only in the food they serve, but also when they serve it. From 2:30 in the afternoon until about 7:30 in the evening most places are closed (though you can pick up a snack at a bar during these hours), and on Sunday afternoon restaurants are packed with Italian families and friends indulging in the weekly ritual of lunching out.

Meals are still sacred for most Italians, so don't be surprised if you get disapproving looks as you gobble down a sandwich or a slice of pizza while seated on the church steps or a park bench. (In many places it's actually illegal to do so.)

THE BEST IN BEANS

Pasta e fagioli (a thick bean soup with pasta, served slightly warm or at room temperature) is made all over Italy. Folks in the Veneto, though, take special pride in their version, made from particularly fine beans grown around the village of Lamon, near Belluno. *Il fagiolo di Lamon* derives from the *Borlotto di Vigevano* bean and was first introduced by a monk in the 1500s via the Spanish court's colonial links to Mexico and Guatemela.

FISH

The catch of the day is always a good bet, whether it's sweet and succulent Adriatic shellfish, sea bream, bass, or John Dory, or freshwater fish from Lake Garda, near Verona. A staple in the Veneto is *baccalà*: this is dried salt cod, which, alongside *stoccafisso*, air-dried cod, was introduced to Italy during the Renaissance by northern European traders. Dried cod is soaked in water or milk and then prepared in a different way in each city. In Vicenza, baccalà *alla vicentina* confusingly uses stoccafisso, which is cooked with onions, milk, and cheese, and is generally served with polenta.

MEAT

In the Veneto, traditional dishes feature offal as much as the prime cuts. Beef (including veal), pork, rabbit, horse, and donkey meat are standard, while goose, duck, and guinea fowl are common poultry options. In Friuli–Venezia Giulia, menus show the influence of Austria-Hungary: you may find deer and hare on the menu, as well as Eastern European–style goulash. One unusual treat served throughout the Veneto is *nervetti*—cubes of gelatin from a calf's knee prepared with onions, parsley, olive oil, and lemon.

Radicchio

Creamed salted cod

PASTA, RISOTTO, POLENTA

For *primi* (first courses), the Veneto dines on *bigoli* (thick whole-wheat pasta), generally served with an anchovy-onion sauce delicately flavored with cinnamon, or creamy risotto flavored with vegetables or shellfish. Polenta is everywhere, whether it's a stiff porridge topped with Gorgonzola, or a stew, or a patty grilled and served alongside meat or fish.

RADICCHIO DI TREVISO

In fall and winter be sure to try the radicchio di Treviso, a red endive grown near that town but popular all over the region. Cultivation is very labor-intensive, so it can be expensive. It's best in a veal or chicken stew, in a risotto, or just grilled or baked with a drizzle of olive oil and perhaps a little Taleggio cheese from neighboring Lombardy.

WINE

The Veneto produces more D.O.C. (Denominazione di Origine Controllata) wines than any other region in Italy. Amarone, the region's crowning achievement, is a robust, full-bodied red. The best of the whites are Soave, prosecco, and *pinot bianco* (pinot blanc). In Friuli–Venezia Giulia, local wines include *friulano*, a dry, lively white made from the sauvignon vert grape, and *picolit*, a dessert wine.

The arc around Venice—stretching from Verona to Trieste, encompassing the Veneto and Friuli–Venezia Giulia regions—is indisputably one of the most culturally rich areas in Italy, an intellectual and spiritual feast of architecture, painting, and sculpture. Since the 16th century, the art, architecture, and way of life here have all reflected Venetian splendor.

It wasn't always this way. Back in the Middle Ages, Padua and Verona were independent cities that developed substantial cultural traditions of their own, leaving behind many artistic treasures. And even while it was under Venice's political domination, 16th-century Vicenza contributed more to the cultural heritage of La Serenissima than it took from her—in large part because of its master architect, Andrea Palladio.

This region is primarily flat, green farmland. As you move inland, though, you encounter low hills, which swell and rise in a succession of plateaus and high meadows, culminating in the snowcapped Dolomite Alps. Much of the pleasure of exploring here comes from discovering the variations on the Venetian theme that give a unique character to each of the towns. Some, such as Verona, Treviso, and Udine, have a solid medieval look at their heart. Padua, with its narrow arcaded streets, tree-lined canals, and large student population, is romantic and youthful. Vicenza, ennobled by the architecture of Palladio, is elegant and wealthy. Udine, in Friuli–Venezia

Giulia, is genteel yet rustic, an intricately sculpted city that's home to the first important frescoes by Gianbattista Tiepolo. In Trieste, once the main port of the Austro-Hungarian Empire, you can find survivors of those days in its Viennese-inspired coffeehouses and *buffets*—hole-in-the-wall eateries serving sausages and other pork dishes.

Unlike the western regions of northern Italy, the Veneto and Friuli–Venezia Giulia were slow to move from an agricultural to an industrial economy, and even now the region depends upon small- and medium-size businesses, many of which are still family-run. The area, therefore, has attracted far fewer migrants from elsewhere in Italy and thus maintained its cultural identity; local dialects, for example, may have all but died out in places like Milan and Turin, but they still thrive in the Veneto and Friuli–Venezia Giulia. Even when residents speak standard Italian, it is frequently laced with local words and pronounced with a distinctive nasal-sounding musicality.

MAJOR REGIONS

The Veneto. Influenced by the city of Venice on the marshy Adriatic coast, the Veneto is a prosperous region dotted by fortified cities with captivating history and undulating vineyards. Padua's alluring architecture, art, and canal network may reflect the Venetian influence as the closest terra firma dominion, but its ancient, pioneering university—famed for its humanist alumni—creates a beguiling buzz of cycling students, food markets, and commerce. With the cooling Dolomite Alpine waters of the Adige River snaking through its medieval, Roman, and Venetian heart, Verona combines splendor with intimacy. Perfectly formed and wealthy Vicenza is where the peerless Palladio put his harmonious architectural plans into bricks, mortar, and gleaming marble. Heading north toward the snowcapped Dolomites, Marostica draws visitors moved by commanding views and an biannual human-scale game of chess on a colossal board. Set amid verdant hills, Asolo dines out on its 19th-century heyday as an idyllic village muse for artists and poets. Moated and medieval Treviso retains a thriving and tranquil air in arcaded streets and leafy canals.

Friuli–Venezia Giulia. Heading northeast of the Veneto, the atmosphere of the Friuli–Venezia Giulia region derives from its fascinating mix of Italian, Slavic, and Central European influences. Sitting atop foothills below the Carnic Alps, the university city of Udine mixes semirural provincial charms with the grandeur of Venetian architecture and the rococo riches of 18th-century artist Gianbattista Tiepolo. A short hop east and set amid scenic wooded valleys, Cividale del Friuli brims with Roman, Celtic, and Lombard archaeological artifacts. Following the Natisone River down to tranquil Aquileia, you'll hear echoes of ancient Rome in this erstwhile port and spot signs of early Christianity in its mosaics. Bordering Slovenia, the strategic Adriatic port city of Trieste mixes Eastern, Central, and Western European cultures, giving it a liminal atmosphere of nostalgia and intrigue, beloved by writers and artists.

Planning

When to Go

The towns and services of the Veneto and Friuli–Venezia Giulia are generally busy all year, with all but a few attractions accessible to visitors. Summer months are generally very humid but dry and hot. The most precipitation and fog fall between November and March, although these months can be rewarding for city sightseeing and immersion in local culture and seasonal food. Toward the foothills of the Dolomites, there are cooler summers and snowfall in winter, while the northeast Adriatic corner around the Gulf of Trieste can have year-round breezy days from eastern winds.

Getting Here and Around

BUS

There are interurban and interregional connections throughout the Veneto and Friuli–Venezia Giulia, handled by nearly a dozen private bus lines. To figure out which line will get you where, the best strategy is to seek assistance from local tourist offices.

CAR

Padua, Vicenza, and Verona are on the highway (and train line) between Venice and Milan. Seeing them without a car isn't a problem; in fact, having a car can even complicate matters. The cities sometimes limit automobile access, permitting cars only with plates ending in an even number on even days, odd on odd, or prohibiting them altogether on weekends. There's no central source for information about these sporadic traffic restrictions; the best strategy is to check with your hotel before arrival for an update. You will need a car to get the most out of the hill country that makes up much of the Venetian Arc, and it will be particularly useful for visiting Aquileia, a rather interesting archaeological site with limited public transportation.

The two main access roads to the Venetian Arc from southern Italy are both linked to the A1 (Autostrada del Sole), which connects Bologna, Florence, and Rome. They are the A13, which ends in Padua, and the A22, which passes through Verona running north–south. Linking the region from east to west is the A4, the primary route from Milan to Trieste, skirting Verona, Padua, and Venice along the way. The distance from Verona to Trieste via the A4 is 263 km (163 miles; 2½ hours), with one break in the autostrada near Venice/Mestre. Branches link the A4 with Treviso (A27) and Udine (A23).

TRAIN

Trains on the main routes from the south stop twice hourly in Verona, Padua, and Venice. From northern Italy and the rest of Europe, trains usually enter via Milan or through Porta Nuova in Verona. Treviso and Udine both lie on the main line from Venice to Tarvisio. Unfortunately, there are no daytime express trains between Venice and Tarvisio, only the slower inter-regional and regional service with at least two changes. There is now a regional three-hour through-train service between Trieste and the neighboring Slovenian capital Ljubljana (Lubiana in Italian). To the west of Venice, the main line running across the north of Italy stops at Padua (30 minutes from Venice), Vicenza (1 hour), and Verona (1½ hours); to the east is Trieste (2 hours). Local trains link Vicenza to Treviso (1 hour) and Udine to Trieste (1 hour).

Be sure to take Regionale Veloce (fast regional) trains whenever possible; a local "milk run" or Regionale that stops in every village along the way can take considerably longer. The fastest trains are the Frecce, but reservations are mandatory and fares are much higher than on regional services.

TRAIN CONTACT Trenitalia. ☎ *892021* ⊕ *www.trenitalia.com.*

Planning Your Time

Lined up in a row west of Venice are Padua, Vicenza, and Verona—three prosperous small cities that are worth at least one day each on a northern Italy itinerary. Verona has the most grandeur and most varied attractions, as well as the widest selection of hotels and restaurants. It's probably the best choice for a base in the area, even though it also draws the most tourists. The hills north of Venice make for good driving, with appealing villages set in a visitor-friendly wine country.

East of the Veneto, the region of Friuli–Venezia Giulia is off the main tourist circuit. You probably won't go here on a first trip to Italy, but by your second or third visit you may be drawn by its caves and castles, its battle-worn hills, and its mix of Italian and Central European culture. The port city of Trieste, famous for its elegant cafés, has a quiet character that some people find dull but others find alluring.

Note that several of the most interesting and important sights in the Venetian Arc require reservations or are open only at limited times, so plan ahead. For instance, reservations are now required 24 hours in advance to see the Giotto frescoes in Padua's Cappella degli Scrovegni. On the outskirts of Vicenza, the Villa della Rotonda, one of Palladio's masterpieces, is not open in winter and has very limited hours when it is open. Another important Palladian conception, Villa di Maser or Villa Barbaro, also has limited hours.

Restaurants

Although the Veneto is not considered one of Italy's major culinary destinations, the region offers many opportunities for exciting gastronomic adventures. The fish offerings are among the most varied and freshest in Italy (and possibly Europe), and the vegetables from the islands in the Venetian lagoon are considered a national treasure. Carnivores are spoiled for choice here with donkey and horse on many menus, from donkey ragù with bigoli pasta to lean equine preparations like *sfilacci di cavallo* (dry shredded horsemeat), carpaccio, and more hearty *pastissada de caval* (stew). Take a break from pasta and try the area's wonderful, creamy risottos and hearty polenta.

Hotels

Rates tend to be higher in Padua and Verona; in Verona especially, seasonal rates vary widely and soar during trade fairs and the opera season. There are fewer good lodging choices in Vicenza, perhaps because overnighters are drawn to the better restaurant scenes in Verona and Padua. *Agriturismo* (farm stay) information is available at tourist offices and sometimes on their websites. Ask about weekend discounts, often available at hotels catering to business clients. Substantial savings can sometimes be had by booking through reservation services on the Internet.

⇨ *Hotel and restaurant reviews have been shortened. For full information, visit Fodors.com. Prices in the hotel reviews are the lowest cost of a standard double room in high season. Prices in the dining reviews are the average cost of a main course at dinner, or, if dinner is not served, at lunch.*

What It Costs in Euros

	$	$$	$$$	$$$$
RESTAURANTS	under €15	€15–€24	€25–€35	over €35
HOTELS	under €125	€125–€200	€201–€300	over €300

Padua

42 km (25 miles) west of Venice.

A romantic warren of arcaded streets, Padua has long been one of the major cultural centers of northern Italy. It has first-rate artistic monuments and, along with Bologna, is one of the few cities in the country where you can catch a glimpse of student life.

Its university, founded in 1222 and Italy's second oldest, attracted such cultural icons as Dante (1265–1321), Petrarch (1304–74), and Galileo Galilei (1564–1642), thus earning the city the sobriquet *La Dotta* (The Learned). Padua's Basilica di Sant'Antonio, begun around 1238, attracts droves of pilgrims, especially on his feast day, June 13. Three great artists—Giotto (1266–1337), Donatello (circa 1386–1466), and Mantegna (1431–1506)—left significant works in Padua, with Giotto's Scrovegni Chapel being one of the best-known, and most meticulously preserved, works of art in the country. Today, a cycle-happy student body—some 60,000 strong—flavors every aspect of local culture. Don't be surprised if you spot a *laurea* (graduation) ceremony marked by laurel leaves, mocking lullabies, and X-rated caricatures.

GETTING HERE AND AROUND

The train trip between Venice and Padua is short, and regular bus service originates from Venice's Piazzale Roma. By car from Venice, Padua is on the Autostrada Torino–Trieste A4/E70. Take the

San Carlo exit and follow Via Guido Reni to Via Tiziano Aspetti into town. Regular bus service connects Venice's Marco Polo airport with downtown Padua.

Padua is a walker's and cyclist's city, with an excellent tram and bus network. If you arrive by car, leave your vehicle in one of the parking lots on the outskirts or at your hotel. Unlimited bus and tram service is included with the Urbs Picta Card (€28 or €35, valid for 48 or 72 hours), which allows entry to all the city's eight principal sights. It's available at tourist information offices and at some museums and hotels. Join the cycling throngs by hiring a bike or e-bike with Forever Bike (⊕ www.foreverbike. com ☎ 049/8717574).

VISITOR INFORMATION
CONTACT Padua Tourism Office. ⊠ Padova Railway Station, Piazzale Stazione, Padua ☎ 049/5207415 ⊕ www.turismopadova.it.

Sights

Abano Terme
HOT SPRING | A very popular hot-springs spa town about 12 km (7 miles) southwest of Padua, Abano Terme lies at the foot of the Euganean Hills among hand-tilled vineyards. If a bit of pampering sounds better than traipsing through yet another church or castle, indulge yourself with a soak, a massage, or mud treatments, which are especially recommended for joint aches. A good-value day pass (€35) is available at Hotel Antiche Terme Ariston Molino Buja for access to their thermal pools (⊕ aristonmolino. it). ⊠ Abano Terme ✛ Take Padua West exit off A4, or Terme Euganee exit off A13 ☎ 049/8669061 ⊕ www.abano.it; aristonmolino.it.

★ Basilica di Sant'Antonio
(Basilica del Santo)
CHURCH | Thousands of faithful make the pilgrimage here each year to pray at the tomb of St. Anthony, while others come to admire works by the 15th-century Florentine master Donatello. His equestrian statue (1453) of the condottiere Erasmo da Narni, known as Gattamelata, in front of the church is one of the great masterpieces of Italian Renaissance sculpture. The huge church, which combines elements of Byzantine, Romanesque, and Gothic styles, was probably begun around 1238, seven years after the death of the Portuguese-born saint. The Cappella del Santo (housing the tomb of the saint) dates from the 16th century. ⊠ Piazza del Santo, Padua ☎ 049/8225652 ⊕ www.basilicadelsanto. it ⊠ Basilica free, museum complex €7 ☉ Museum complex closed Mon.

Burchiello Excursion, Brenta Canal
BODY OF WATER | During the 16th century the Brenta was transformed into a mainland version of Venice's Grand Canal with the building of nearly 50 waterside villas. Back then, boating parties viewed them from burchielli—beautiful river barges. Today the Burchiello excursion boat makes full- and half-day tours along the Brenta in season, departing from Padua and Venice; tickets can also be bought at travel agencies. You visit three houses, including the Villas Pisani and Foscari, with a lunchtime break in Oriago (€25 or €29 extra). There is also the option to rent or bring your own bike to explore partly on wheels as part of a trip. Note that most houses are on the left side coming from Venice, or the right from Padua. ⊠ Via Porciglia 34, Padua ☎ 049/8760233 ⊕ www.ilburchiello.it ⊠ €79 half day, €129 full day; lunch extra ☉ Closed Mon. and Nov.–Feb.

★ Cappella degli Scrovegni
(The Arena Chapel)
CHURCH | The emotional intensity and naturalism of the frescoes illustrating the lives of Mary and Jesus in this world-famous chapel broke new ground in Western art. Enrico Scrovegni commissioned these frescoes to atone for the sins of his deceased father, Reginaldo, the usurer condemned to the Seventh Circle

of the Inferno in Dante's *Divine Comedy.* Giotto and his assistants worked on the frescoes from 1303 to 1305, arranging them in tiers to be read from left to right. To preserve the artwork, doors are opened only every 15 minutes. ⊠ *Piazza Eremitani 8, Padua* ☎ *049/2010020 reservations* ⊕ *www.cappelladegliscrovegni.it* 🎫 *€16, includes Musei Civici and Palazzo Zuckermann.*

Chiesa degli Eremitani

CHURCH | This 13th-century church houses substantial fragments of Andrea Mantegna's frescoes (1448–50), which were damaged by Allied bombing in World War II. Despite their fragmentary condition, Mantegna's still beautiful and historically important depictions of the martyrdom of St. James and St. Christopher show the young artist's mastery of extremely complex problems of perspective. ⊠ *Piazza Eremitani, Padua* ☎ *049/8756410.*

Montegrotto Terme

HOT SPRING | At this spa town about 13 km (8 miles) southwest of Padua, you can luxuriate in thermal mineral pools. Montegrotto Terme has several hotels whose treatments vary from simple massage and thermal and mud baths to hydrokinetic therapy. Scuba enthusiasts head here for the world's deepest indoor pool, Y-40 Deep Joy. The verdant hills of the nearby Parco dei Colli Euganei provide opportunities for walking, cycling, and other outdoor pursuits. The nearest railway stop, on the Bologna–Padua line, is Terme Euganee–Montegrotto. Taxis are available outside the station. ⊠ *Montegrotto Terme ✛ Terme Euganee exit off A13* ☎ *049/8928311* ⊕ *www.visitabanomontegrotto.com.*

★ Musei Civici degli Eremitani
(*Civic Museum*)

SPECIALTY MUSEUM | Usually visited along with the neighboring Cappella degli Scrovegni, this former monastery houses a rich array of exhibits and has wonderful cloister gardens with a mix of ancient architectural fragments and modern sculpture. The Pinacoteca displays works of medieval and modern masters, including some by Tintoretto, Veronese, and Tiepolo. Standouts are the *Giotto Crucifix,* which once hung in the Cappella degli Scrovegni, and the *Portrait of a Young Senator,* by Giovanni Bellini (1430–1516). ⊠ *Piazza Eremitani 8, Padua* ☎ *049/8204551* ⊕ *www.padovanet.it* 🎫 *€11, €16 with Scrovegni Chapel and Palazzo Zuckermann; Urbs Picta Card* ⊘ *Closed Mon.*

Orto Botanico (*Botanical Garden*)

GARDEN | The Venetian Republic ordered the creation of Padua's botanical garden in 1545 to supply the university with medicinal plants, and it retains its original layout. You can stroll the arboretum—still part of the university—and wander through hothouses and beds of plants that were introduced to Italy in this late-Renaissance garden. A St. Peter's palm, planted in 1585, inspired Goethe to write his 1790 essay, "The Metamorphosis of Plants." ⊠ *Via Orto Botanico 15, Padua* ☎ *049/8273939* ⊕ *www.ortobotanicopd.it* 🎫 *€10* ⊘ *Closed Mon.*

★ Palazzo del Bo

CASTLE/PALACE | The University of Padua, founded in 1222, centers on this predominantly 16th-century palazzo with an 18th-century facade. It's named after the Osteria del Bo (*bo* means "ox"), an inn that once stood on the site. It's worth a visit to see the perfectly proportioned anatomy theater (1594), the beautiful Old Courtyard, and a hall with a lectern used by Galileo. You can enter only as part of a guided tour; weekend/public holiday tours allow access to other parts of the university including the gorgeous 1930–40s interiors by Milanese architect-designer Gio Ponti; most guides speak English, but it is worth checking ahead by phone. ⊠ *Via 8 Febbraio, Padua* ☎ *049/8275111 university switchboard, 049/8273939* ⊕ *www.unipd.it* 🎫 *Historical tour €8; €15 extended "Gio Ponti" tour weekends and public holidays.*

Padua

KEY

- ● Sights
- ● Restaurants
- ● Quick Bites
- ● Hotels

The Venetian Arc, Past and Present

Long before Venetians made their presence felt on the mainland in the 15th century, Ezzelino III da Romano (1194–1259) laid claim to Verona, Padua, and the surrounding lands and towns. He was the first of a series of brutal and aggressive rulers who dominated the cities of the region until the rise of Venetian rule. Because of Ezzelino's cruel and violent nature, Dante consigned his soul to Hell.

After Ezzelino was ousted, powerful families such as Padua's Carrara and Verona's della Scala (Scaligeri) vied throughout the 14th century to dominate these territories. Venetian rule ushered in a time of relative peace, when noble families from the lagoon and the mainland commissioned Palladio and other accomplished architects to design their palazzi and villas. This rich classical legacy, superimposed upon medieval castles and fortifications, is central to the identities of present-day Padua, Vicenza, and Verona.

The region remained under Venetian control until the Napoleonic invasion and the fall of the Venetian Republic in 1797. The Council of Vienna ceded it, along with Lombardy, to Austria in 1815. The region revolted against Austrian rule and joined the Italian Republic in 1866.

Friuli–Venezia Giulia has been marched through, fought over, hymned by patriots, and romanticized by writers that include James Joyce, Rainer Maria Rilke, Pier Paolo Passolini, and Jan Morris. The region has seen Fascists and Communists, Romans, Hapsburgs, and Huns. It survived by forging sheltering alliances—Udine beneath the wings of San Marco (1420), Trieste choosing Duke Leopold of Austria (1382) over Venetian domination.

Some of World War I's fiercest fighting took place in Friuli–Venezia Giulia, where memorials and cemeteries commemorate hundreds of thousands who died before Italian troops arrived in 1918 and liberated Trieste from Austrian rule. Trieste, along with the whole of Venezia Giulia, was annexed to Italy in 1920. During World War II the Germans occupied the area and placed Trieste in an administrative zone along with parts of Slovenia. The only Nazi extermination camp on Italian soil, the Risiera di San Sabba, was in a suburb of Trieste. After the war, during a period of Cold War dispute, Trieste was governed by an allied military administration; it was officially reannexed to Italy in 1954, when Italy ceded the Istrian peninsula to the south to Yugoslavia. These arrangements were not finally ratified by Italy and Yugoslavia until 1975.

Palazzo della Ragione

CASTLE/PALACE | Also known as Il Salone, the spectacular arcaded reception hall in Padua's original law courts is as notable for its grandeur—it's 85 feet high—as for its colorful setting, surrounded by shops, cafés, and open-air fruit and vegetable markets. Nicolò Miretto and Stefano da Ferrara, working from 1425 to 1440, painted the frescoes after Giotto's plan, which was destroyed by a fire in 1420. The stunning space hosts art shows, and an enormous wooden horse, crafted for a public tournament in 1466, commands pride of place. It is patterned after the famous equestrian statue by Donatello in front of the Basilica di Sant'Antonio, and may, in fact, have been designed by Donatello himself in the last year of his life. ⊠ *Piazza della Ragione, Padua* ☎ *049/8205006* ⊕ *padovacultura.pado-vanet.it* ⊠ *€8 (free with Urbs Picta Card)* ⊙ *Closed Mon.*

Piazza dei Signori

PLAZA/SQUARE | Some fine examples of 15th- and 16th-century buildings line this square. On the west side, the **Palazzo del Capitanio** (facade constructed 1598–1605) has an impressive **Torre dell'Orologio**, with an astronomical clock dating from 1344 and a portal made by Falconetto in 1532 in the form of a Roman triumphal arch. The 12th-century **Battistero del Duomo** (Cathedral Baptistry), with frescoes by Giusto de' Menabuoi (1374–78), is a few steps away. ⊠ *Piazza dei Signori, Padua* ☎ *049/656914* ⊕ *www.battisteropadova.it* ⊠ *Battistero €12 (free with Urbs Picta Card).*

Villa Pisani

CASTLE/PALACE | FAMILY | Extensive grounds with rare trees, ornamental fountains, and garden follies surround this extraordinary palace in Stra, 13 km (8 miles) southeast of Padua. Built in 1721 for the Venetian doge Alvise Pisani, it recalls Versailles more than a Veneto villa. This was one of the last and grandest of many stately residences constructed along the Brenta River from the 16th to 18th centuries by wealthy Venetians. Gianbattista Tiepolo's (1696–1770) spectacular fresco on the ballroom ceiling, *The Apotheosis of the Pisani Family* (1761), alone is worth the visit. For a relaxing afternoon, explore the gorgeous park and maze. ⊠ *Via Doge Pisani 7, Stra* ☎ *049/502074* ⊕ *villapisani.beniculturali.it* ⊠ *€12, €6 park only* ⊙ *Closed Mon.*

🍴 Restaurants

★ Enoteca dei Tadi

$$ | ITALIAN | In this cozy and atmospheric cross between a wine bar and a restaurant, you can put together a fabulous, inexpensive dinner from various classic dishes from all over Italy. Portions are small, but prices are reasonable—just follow the local custom and order a selection, perhaps starting with fresh *burrata* (mozzarella's creamier cousin) with tomatoes, or a selection of prosciutti or salami. **Known for:** several kinds of lasagna; intimate and rustic setting; bountiful wine and grappa list. ⑤ *Average main: €22* ⊠ *Via dei Tadi 16, Padua* ☎ *338/4083434 mobile* ⊕ *www.enotecadeitadi.it* ⊙ *Closed Mon. No dinner Sun.*

L'Anfora

$$ | WINE BAR | This mix between a traditional *bacaro* (wine bar) and an osteria is a local institution, opened in 1922. Stand at the bar with a cross section of Padovano society, from construction workers to professors, and peruse the reasonably priced menu of simple *casalinga* (home-cooked dishes), plus salads and a selection of cheeses. **Known for:** atmospheric art-filled osteria with wood interior; no-nonsense traditional Veneto food; hearty pasta dishes like pasta con fagioli. ⑤ *Average main: €17* ⊠ *Via Soncin 13, Padua* ☎ *049/656629* ⊕ *osteria-lanfora.eatbu.com* ⊙ *Closed Sun. (except in Dec.).*

Le Calandre

$$$$ | MODERN ITALIAN | Traditional Veneto recipes are given a highly sophisticated and creative treatment here, and the whole theatrical tasting-menu experience and gorgeous table settings can seem by turns revelatory or overblown at this high-profile place. Owner-chef Massimiliano Alajmo's creative, miniscule-portion dishes, passion for design (bespoke lighting, carved wooden tables, and quirky plates), and first-class wine list make this an option for a pricey celebratory meal. **Known for:** theatrical, sensory dining experience; playful (or to some, pretentious) touches; reservations essential. ⑤ *Average main: €200* ⊠ *Via Liguria 1, Sarmeola* ✛ *7 km (4 miles) west of Padua* ☎ *049/630303* ⊕ *www.calandre.com* ⊙ *Closed Sun. and Mon. No lunch Tues.*

Osteria dal Capo

$$ | **VENETIAN** | Located in the heart of what used to be Padua's Jewish ghetto, this friendly trattoria serves almost exclusively traditional Veneto dishes, and it does so with refinement and care. Everything from the well-crafted dishes to the unfussy ship's dining cabin–like decor and elegant plates reflect decades of Padovano hospitality. **Known for:** intimate and understated dining at decent prices; meaty-sauced pasta dishes; limited tables mean reservations essential. $ *Average main: €19* ⊠ *Via degli Obizzi 2, Padua* ☎ *049/663105* ⊕ *www.osteriadalcapo.it* ⊘ *Closed Sun. No lunch Mon.*

☕ Coffee and Quick Bites

Bar Romeo

$ | **NORTHERN ITALIAN** | Deep in the atmospheric Sotto Salone market, this busy bar does a fab selection of filled *tramezzini* (triangular sandwiches), panini, and other snacks. It's a great place to hear the local dialect and mingle with the market workers and shoppers any time of day; grab a breakfast coffee and brioche, a glass of Falanghina, or a bit later—after 11 am perhaps—an apertivo with snacks. **Known for:** good-value sandwiches; friendly staff and Padovano vibe; superb selection of wine by the glass. $ *Average main: €6* ⊠ *26 Sotto Salone, Padua* ☎ *340/5560611 mobile.*

Hotels

Al Fagiano

$ | **HOTEL** | The refreshingly funky surroundings in this self-styled art hotel include sponge-painted walls, brush-painted chandeliers, and views of the spires and cupolas of the Basilica di Sant'Antonio. **Pros:** great for art lovers or those after a unique ambience; relaxed, quirky, homey atmosphere; convenient location. **Cons:** not all rooms have views; some find the way-out-there (some risqué) art a bit much; lots of stairs.

$ *Rooms from: €120* ⊠ *Via Locatelli 45, Padua* ☎ *049/8750073* ⊕ *www.alfagiano. com* ⇆ *40 rooms* ❖❖ *No Meals.*

Albergo Verdi

$ | **HOTEL** | One of the best-situated hotels in the city provides understated modern rooms and public areas that tend toward the minimalist without being severe, while the intimate breakfast room with mid-century Eames Eiffel chairs and adjoining terrace is a tranquil place to start the day. **Pros:** excellent location close to Piazza dei Signori; bountiful breakfast selection; 24-hour bar service. **Cons:** student noise in piazza-facing rooms; few views; steep stairs and small elevator. $ *Rooms from: €120* ⊠ *Via Dondi dell'Orologio 7, Padua* ☎ *049/8364163* ⊕ *www.albergoverdipadova.it* ⇆ *14 rooms* ❖❖ *Free Breakfast.*

Palazzo Mantua Benavides

$$$ | **HOTEL** | Housed within a 16th-century palace, where renowned Florentine architect Bartolomeo Ammannati carved colossal statuary, the four spacious suites and three apartments with kitchenettes here offer a wonderful atmospheric alternative to regular hotel accommodation. **Pros:** near the Scrovegni and Musei Eremitani; verdant grounds; palatial surroundings. **Cons:** lack of hotel services and amenities; pricey €25 parking; no in-room safes. $ *Rooms from: €280* ⊠ *Piazza Eremitani 18, Padua* ☎ *380/8932289* ⊕ *palazzomantuabenavides.com* ⇆ *7 suites* ❖❖ *Free Breakfast.*

��️ Nightlife

CAFÉS AND WINE BARS
★ Caffè Pedrocchi

WINE BAR | No visit to Padua is complete without taking time to sit in this historic café and iconic Padovano venue, patronized by luminaries like the French novelist Stendhal in 1831. Nearly 200 years later, it remains central to the city's social life. The café was built in the Egyptian Revival style, and it's now famed for its innovative aperitivi and signature mint coffee. The accomplished, innovative restaurant serves breakfast, lunch, and dinner. The grand salons and terrace provide a backdrop for the occasional jazz, swing, and cover bands. ⊠ *Piazzetta Pedrocchi, Padua* ☎ *049/8781231* ⊕ *www.caffepedrocchi.it.*

Shopping

★ Mercato Sotto il Salone

FOOD | Under the Salone there's an impressive food market where shops sell choice salami and cured meats, local cheeses, wines, coffee, and tea. With the adjacent Piazza delle Erbe fruit and vegetable market, you can pick up all the makings of a fine picnic. On weekends and public holidays, the buzzy piazza is often filled with a cornucopia of street food options, as well as wine and beer stalls, many run by the makers themselves. ⊠ *Piazza della Ragione, Padua* ⊕ *mercatosottoilsalone.it.*

Zotti Antiquariato

ANTIQUES & COLLECTIBLES | Owned by antiques dealer Pietro Maria Zotti—who has worked for more than 40 years in the trade—this always-changing shop has fascinating finds from Venetian artworks to stylish mid-century furniture, plus lots of smaller, more affordable items, including books, prints, jewelry, militaria, and coins. ⊠ *Selciato San Nicolò 5, Padua* ☎ *338/2930830 mobile* ⊕ *www.antichitazotti.com.*

Activities

LoVivo Tours

CULTURAL TOURS | A local tour operator offers a wealth of interesting tours and experiences that won't break the bank, covering Padua's cultural and UNESCO sites, a tour of the Riviera di Brenta villas, the area's intriguing garden labyrinths (including a lavender maze), and various excursions (including hiking and bike adventures) in the Euganean Hills. ⊠ *Via*

Cocktail Hour on Padua's Piazzas

One of Padua's greatest traditions is the outdoor en masse consumption of aperitifs: a spritz mixing Aperol or Campari with soda water and wine, prosecco (sparkling wine), or wine. It all happens in Piazza delle Erbe and Piazza delle Frutta. Several bars there provide drinks in plastic cups, so you can take them outside and mingle among the crowds. The ritual, practiced primarily by students, begins at 6 or so, at which hour you can also pick up a snack from one of the outdoor vendors.

A. Vespucci 17, Abano Terme, Padua ☎ *049/2969340* ⊕ *www.lovivo.it* From €40.

Verona

114 km (71 miles) west of Venice, 60 km (37 miles) west of Vicenza.

On the banks of the fast-flowing River Adige, enchanting Verona has timeless monuments, a picturesque town center, and a romantic reputation as the setting of Shakespeare's *Romeo and Juliet.* With its lively Venetian air and proximity to Lake Garda, it attracts hordes of tourists, especially Germans and Austrians. Tourism peaks during summer's renowned season of open-air opera in the arena and during spring's Vinitaly, one of the world's most important wine expos. For five days you can sample the wines of more than 3,000 wineries from dozens of countries.

Verona grew to power and prosperity within the Roman Empire as a result of its key commercial and military position in northern Italy. With its Roman arena, theater, and city gates, it has the most significant monuments of Roman antiquity north of Rome. After the fall of the empire, the city continued to flourish under the guidance of barbarian kings, such as Theodoric, Alboin, Pepin, and Berenger I, reaching its cultural and artistic peak in the 13th and 14th centuries under the della Scala (Scaligero) dynasty. (Look for the *scala*, or ladder, emblem all over town.) In 1404 Verona traded its independence for security and placed itself under the control of Venice. (The other recurring architectural motif is the lion of St. Mark, a symbol of Venetian rule.)

If you're going to visit more than one or two sights, it's worth purchasing a Verona Card, available at museums, churches, and tobacconists for €20 (for 24 hours) or €25 (48 hours). It buys a single admission to most of the city's significant museums and churches, plus you can ride free on city buses. If you're mostly interested in churches, an €8 cumulative ticket is sold at Verona's major houses of worship and gains you entry to the Duomo, San Fermo Maggiore, San Zeno Maggiore, and Sant'Anastasia. Note that Verona's churches strictly enforce their dress code: no sleeveless shirts, shorts, or short skirts.

GETTING HERE AND AROUND
Verona is midway between Venice and Milan. Several trains per hour depart from any point on the Milan–Venice line. By car, from Venice, take the Autostrada Trieste–Torino A4/E70 to the SS12 and follow it north into town.

VISITOR INFORMATION
CONTACT Verona Tourism Office (IAT Verona). ✉ *Palazzo Barbieri, Via Leoncino 61, Piazza Bra, Verona* ☎ *045/8068680* ⊕ *www.veronatouristoffice.it/en.*

Sights

In addition to ancient Verona's famous Roman theater and arena, two of its city gates (Porta dei Leoni and Porta dei Borsari) and a beautiful triumphal arch (Arco dei Gavi) have survived. These graceful and elegant portals provide an idea of the high aesthetic standards of their time. Look, too, beyond the main sights of the Città Antica (historic center): take time to wander the streets, and be sure not to miss out on the many leafy stretches of the riverside Lungadige. Away from the crowds there's a wealth of varied architecture from ancient Rome to the Fascist era to the contemporary, as well as tranquil spots for feeding the ducks.

Arche Scaligere
TOMB | On a little square off Piazza dei Signori are the fantastically sculpted Gothic tombs of the della Scala family, who ruled Verona during the late Middle Ages. The 19th-century English traveler and critic John Ruskin described the tombs as graceful places where people who have fallen asleep live. The tomb of Cangrande I (1291–1329) hangs over the portal of the adjacent church and is the work of the Maestro di Sant'Anastasia. The tomb of Mastino II, begun in 1345, has an elaborate baldachin, originally painted and gilded, and is surrounded by an iron grillwork fence and topped by an equestrian statue. The latest and most elaborate tomb is that of Cansignorio (1375), the work principally of Bonino da Campione. The major tombs are all visible from the street. ✉ *Via Arche Scaligere, Verona.*

Arco dei Gavi
RUINS | This stunning structure is simpler and less imposing, but also more graceful, than the triumphal arches in Rome. Built in the 1st century by the architect Lucius Vitruvius Cerdo to celebrate the accomplishments of the patrician Gavia family, it was highly esteemed by several Renaissance architects, including Palladio. ✉ *Corso Cavour, Verona.*

Verona

KEY
- ● Sights
- ● Restaurants
- ● Quick Bites
- ● Hotels

Sights ▶

1	Arche Scaligere	G2
2	Arco dei Gavi	D3
3	Arena di Verona	E3
4	Castelvecchio	D3
5	Duomo	F1
6	Funicular of Castel San Pietro	G1
7	Loggia del Consiglio	F2
8	Museo Archeologico and Teatro Romano	G1
9	Palazzo degli Scaligeri	F2
10	Palazzo della Ragione and Torre dei Lamberti	F2
11	Piazza delle Erbe	F2
12	Porta dei Borsari	E2
13	Porta dei Leoni	G3
14	San Zeno Maggiore	B2
15	Sant'Anastasia	G1

Restaurants ▶

1	Antica Osteria al Duomo	F1
2	Il Desco	G2

Quick Bites ▶

1	Caffè Borsari	F2

Hotels ▶

1	Escalus Luxury Suites	E3
2	Gabbio d'Oro	F2
3	Hotel Accademia	F3
4	Hotel Indigo Verona – Grand Hotel Des Arts	E3

Arena di Verona

RUINS | FAMILY | Only Rome's Colosseum and Capua's arena would dwarf this amphitheater, built for gymnastic competitions, choreographed sacrificial rites, and games involving hunts, fights, battles, and wild animals. Although four arches are all that remain of the arena's outer arcade, the main structure is complete and dates from AD 30. In summer, you can join up to 16,000 for spectacular opera productions and pop or rock concerts (extra costs for these events). ■TIP→ **The opera's the main thing here: when there is no opera performance, you can still enter the interior, but the arena is less impressive inside than the Colosseum or other Roman amphitheaters.** ✉ *Piazza Bra 5, Verona* ☎ *045/8003204 visit, 045/8005151 performance tickets* ⊕ *www.arena.it* 🎫 *€10 (free with VeronaCard); €11 includes entrance to nearby Museo Lapidario Maffeiano.*

★ Castelvecchio

CASTLE/PALACE | This crenellated, russet brick building with massive walls, towers, turrets, and a vast courtyard was built for Cangrande II della Scala in 1354 and presides over a street lined with attractive old buildings and palaces of the nobility. Only by going inside the Museo di Castelvecchio can you really appreciate this massive castle complex with its vaulted halls. You also get a look at a significant collection of Venetian and Veneto art, medieval weapons, and jewelry. The interior of the castle was restored and redesigned as a museum between 1958 and 1975 by Carlo Scarpa, one of Italy's most accomplished architects. ■TIP→ **Behind the castle is the fortified Ponte Scaligero (1355), which spans the River Adige and is a fab spot for taking photos.** ✉ *Corso Castelvecchio 2, Verona* ☎ *045/7110129* ⊕ *museodicastelvecchio.comune.verona.it* 🎫 *€6 (free with VeronaCard)* ⊘ *Closed Mon.*

Duomo

CHURCH | The present church dedicated to Santa Maria Assunta was begun in the 12th century in the Romanesque style; there are paleo-Christian remains under the Sant' Elena and Canons' cloister, while later additions are mostly Gothic. On pilasters guarding the main entrance are 12th-century carvings thought to represent Oliver and Roland, two of Charlemagne's knights and heroes of several medieval epic poems. Inside, Titian's *Assumption* (1530) graces the first chapel on the left. ✉ *Via Duomo, Verona* ☎ *045/592813* ⊕ *www.chieseverona.it* 🎫 *€4 (€8 Church Cumulative Ticket or free with VeronaCard).*

★ Funicular of Castel San Pietro

VIEWPOINT | Opened in 2017, this funicular ride ascends 500 feet from near the Teatro Romano up to a panoramic terrace in just 90 seconds, affording fabulous Veronese views. For the adventurous, there's scope for long walks around the parkland paths and quiet lanes crisscrossing the elevated city walls. ✉ *Via Fontanelle S. Stefano, Verona* ☎ *342/8966695 mobile* ⊕ *www.funicolarediverona.it* 🎫 *€3 round-trip, €2 one-way.*

Loggia del Consiglio

GOVERNMENT BUILDING | This graceful structure on the north flank of Piazza dei Signori was finished in 1492 and built to house city council meetings. Although the city was already under Venetian rule, Verona still had a certain degree of autonomy, which was expressed by the splendor of the loggia. Very strangely for a Renaissance building of this quality, its architect remains unknown, but it's the finest surviving example of late-15th-century architecture in Verona. The building is not open to the public, but the exterior is worth a visit. ✉ *Piazza dei Signori, Verona.*

Museo Archeologico and Teatro Romano

HISTORY MUSEUM | The archaeological holdings of this museum in a 15th-century former monastery consist largely of the donated collections of Veronese citizens proud of their city's classical past. You'll find few blockbusters here, but there are some noteworthy pieces (especially among the bronzes), and it is interesting to see what cultured Veronese collected between the 17th and 19th centuries. The museum complex includes the Teatro Romano, Verona's 1st-century theater, which is open to visitors and an atmospheric music venue. ⊠ *Rigaste del Redentore 2, Verona* ☎ *045/7110129* ⊕ *museoarcheologico.comune.verona.it* 🔌 *€4.50 (free with VeronaCard)* ۞ *Closed Mon.*

Palazzo degli Scaligeri (*Palazzo di Cangrande*)

CASTLE/PALACE | The della Scala family ruled Verona from this stronghold built (over Roman ruins) at the end of the 13th century and then inhabited by Cangrande I. At that time Verona controlled the mainland Veneto from Treviso and Lombardy to Mantua and Brescia, hence the building's alternative name as a seat of Domini di Terraferma (Venetian administration): Palazzo del Podestà. The portal facing Piazza dei Signori was added in 1533 by the accomplished Renaissance architect Michele Sanmicheli. You have to admire the palazzo from the outside, as it's not open to the public. ⊠ *Piazza dei Signori, Verona.*

★ Palazzo della Ragione and Torre dei Lamberti

VIEWPOINT | An elegant 15th-century pink-marble staircase leads up from the *mercato vecchio* (old market) courtyard to the magistrates' chambers in this 12th-century palace, built at the intersection of the main streets of the ancient Roman city. The interior now houses exhibitions and the 1,600-strong artwork collection of the **Galleria d'Arte Moderna Achille Forti,** including the alluring Meditazione (1851) by Francesco Hayez. You can get the highest view in town from atop the attached 270-foot-high Romanesque Torre dei Lamberti. About 50 years after a lightning strike in 1403 knocked its top off, it was rebuilt and extended to its current height. ⊠ *Piazza dei Signori, Verona* ☎ *045/9273027* ⊕ *torredeilamberti.it; gam.comune. verona.it* 🔌 *€4 gallery only; €6 tower only (both free with VeronaCard)* ۞ *Gallery closed Mon.* ۩ *Book the tower visit in advance by phone.*

Piazza delle Erbe

PLAZA/SQUARE | Frescoed buildings surround this medieval square, where a busy Roman forum once stood; during the week it's still bustling, as vendors sell produce and trinkets, much as they have been doing for generations. Eyes are drawn to the often sun-sparkling Madonna Verona fountain (1368) and its Roman statue (the body is from AD 380, with medieval additions). ⊠ *Piazza delle Erbe, Verona.*

★ Porta dei Borsari

RUINS | As its elegant decoration suggests, this is the main entrance to ancient Verona—dating, in its present state, from the 1st century. It's at the beginning of the narrow, pedestrianized Corso Porta Borsari, now a smart shopping street leading to Piazza delle Erbe. ⊠ *Corso Porta Borsari, Verona.*

Porta dei Leoni

RUINS | The oldest of Verona's elegant and graceful Roman portals, the Porta dei Leoni (on Via Leoni, just a short walk from Piazza delle Erbe) dates from the 1st century BC, but its original earth-and-brick structure was sheathed in local marble during the early imperial era. It has become the focus of a campaign against violence—there are often flowers and messages by the monument—in memory of the murder of a young Veronese here in 2009. ⊠ *Via Leoni, Verona.*

⭑ San Zeno Maggiore

CHURCH | One of Italy's finest Roman-esque churches is filled with treasures, including a rose window by the 13th-century sculptor Brioloto that represents a wheel of fortune, with six of the spokes formed by statues depicting the rising and falling fortunes of mankind. The 12th-century porch is the work of Maestro Niccolò; it's flanked by marble reliefs by Niccolò and Maestro Guglielmo depicting scenes from the Old and New Testaments and from the legend of Theodoric. The bronze doors date from the 11th and 12th centuries; some were probably imported from Saxony, and some are from Veronese workshops. They combine allegorical representations with scenes from the lives of saints.

Inside, look for the 12th-century statue of San Zeno to the left of the main altar. In modern times it has been dubbed the "Laughing San Zeno" because of a misinterpretation of its conventional Romanesque grin. A famous *Madonna and Saints* triptych by Andrea Mantegna (1431–1506) hangs over the main altar, and a peaceful cloister (1120–38) lies to the left of the nave. The detached bell tower was finished in 1173. ⊠ *Piazza San Zeno, Verona* ☎ *045/592813* ⊕ *www.chieseverona.it* 🎫 *€4 (€8 Church Cumulative Ticket or free with VeronaCard).*

Sant'Anastasia

CHURCH | Verona's largest church, begun in 1290 but only consecrated in 1471, is a fine example of Gothic brickwork and has a grand doorway with elaborately carved biblical scenes. The main reason for visiting this church, however, is *St. George and the Princess* (dated 1434, but perhaps earlier) by Pisanello (1377–1455). It's above the Pellegrini Chapel off the main altar. As you come in, look also for the *gobbi* (hunchbacks) supporting the holy-water basins. ⊠ *Piazza Sant'Anastasia, Verona* ☎ *045/592813* ⊕ *www.chieseverona.it* 🎫 *€4 (€8 Church Cumulative Ticket or free with VeronaCard).*

🍴 Restaurants

⭑ Antica Osteria al Duomo

$$ | NORTHERN ITALIAN | This side-street eatery, lined with old wood paneling and decked out with musical instruments, serves traditional Veronese classics, like bigoli (thick whole-wheat spaghetti) with donkey ragù and *pastissada con polenta* (horsemeat stew with polenta). Don't be deterred by the unconventional meats—they're tender and delicious, and this is probably the best place in town to sample them. **Known for:** blackboard menu, bar, and wooden interiors; occasional live music; rustic courtyard. ⑤ *Average main: €20* ⊠ *Via Duomo 7/A, Verona* ☎ *045/8004505* ⊗ *Closed Sun. except in Dec. and during wine fair.*

⭑ Il Desco

$$$$ | MODERN ITALIAN | Opened in 1981 by Elia Rizzo, the nationally renowned fine-dining Desco cuisine is now crafted by talented son Matteo. True to Italian and Rizzo culinary traditions, he preserves natural flavors through careful ingredient selection, adding daring combinations inspired by stints in kitchens around the world. **Known for:** inventive, colorful plates of food; elegant, arty surroundings fit for a modern opera; pricey three- or five-course tasting menus. ⑤ *Average main: €115* ⊠ *Via Dietro San Sebastiano 7, Verona* ☎ *045/595358* ⊕ *www.ristoranteildesco.it* ⊗ *Closed Sun. and Mon. (open for dinner Mon. in July, Aug., and Dec.).*

☕ Coffee and Quick Bites

⭑ Caffè Borsari

$ | NORTHERN ITALIAN | This bustling café-bar is famed for its excellent creamy coffee and freshly made brioche—it's cheek by jowl *al banco* (at the counter/bar), with Veronese patrons spilling outside. The narrow space with star-vaulted ceiling on the charming Corso Borsari cobbles is packed with coffee- and tea-making pots and cups, as are its walls with colorful gifts and oddities according to the time of year. **Known for:** indulgent hot chocolate; selection of coffee, tea, candies, and chocolates for gift giving; famed for their schiuma (froth) creations. $ *Average main: €4 ⊠ Corso Portoni Borsari 15, Verona ☎ 045/8031313 ⊕ facebook.com/ caffeborsari.*

Hotels

Book hotels months in advance for spring's Vinitaly, usually in early April, and for opera season. Verona hotels are also very busy during the January, May, and September gold fairs in neighboring Vicenza. Hotels jack up prices considerably at all these times.

Escalus Luxury Suites
$$$$ | HOTEL | FAMILY | Near the Arena and Verona's marble-paved main shopping street, Via Mazzini, these suites and mini-apartments offer contemporary minimalist style in muted colors; the larger ones have handy kitchenettes, and all have swank bathrooms. **Pros:** chic location near sights and shopping; family-friendly Glamour Deluxe Suite with balcony; large showers. **Cons:** checkout is before 11 am; constant passeggiata hum from Via Mazzini; minimalist decor not to everyone's taste. $ *Rooms from: €315 ⊠ Vicolo Tre Marchetti 12, Verona ☎ 045/8036754 ⊕ www.escalusverona. com ⤳ 6 suites ⦿ Free Breakfast.*

Gabbia d'Oro
$$$$ | HOTEL | Occupying a historic building off Piazza delle Erbe in the ancient heart of Verona, this hotel is a romantic fantasia of ornamentation, rich fabrics, and period-style furniture. **Pros:** central location; great breakfast; romantic atmosphere. **Cons:** some very small rooms, especially considering the price; small bathrooms; some guests may find the decor overly ornate, even stuffy. $ *Rooms from: €364 ⊠ Corso Porta Borsari 4/a, Verona ☎ 045/8003060*

⊕ *www.hotelgabbiadoro.it ⤳ 27 rooms* ⦿ *Free Breakfast.*

Hotel Accademia
$$$ | HOTEL | The Palladian facade of columns and arches here hint at the well-proportioned interior layout: expect an elegant contemporary take on Art Deco in public spaces and immaculate if impersonal traditional-style decor in guest rooms. **Pros:** central location; good fitness room; rooftop solarium. **Cons:** expensive parking; some may find the decor lacking; service and breakfast under-par. $ *Rooms from: €281 ⊠ Via Scala 12, Verona ☎ 045/596222 ⊕ www. hotelaccademiaverona.it ⤳ 96 rooms* ⦿ *Free Breakfast.*

Hotel Indigo Verona – Grand Hotel Des Arts
$$$ | HOTEL | Handily placed near both the Arena and train station, the art-inspired Indigo is a handsome 1920s Stile Liberty palazzo with stylish design touches and a sophisticated loungy feel throughout. **Pros:** good parking and transport links; cool bar and courtyard; warm customer service. **Cons:** on busy Corso Porta Nuova; limited breakfast choice; dated room decor. $ *Rooms from: €245 ⊠ Corso Porta Nuova 105, Verona ☎ 0800/9880220 ⊕ www.ihg.com/hotelindigo ⤳ 62 rooms* ⦿ *Free Breakfast.*

⊙ Performing Arts

★ Arena di Verona Opera Festival
OPERA | Milan's La Scala and Naples's San Carlo offer performances more likely to attract serious opera fans, but neither offers a greater spectacle than the Arena di Verona. During the venue's summer season (June to August), as many as 16,000 attendees sit on the original stone terraces or in modern cushioned stalls. Most of the operas presented are big and splashy, like *Aida* or *Turandot*, demanding huge choruses, lots of color and movement, and, if possible, camels, horses, or elephants. Order tickets by phone or through the arena website. If

you book a spot on the cheaper terraces, be sure to take or rent a cushion—four hours on a 2,000-year-old stone bench can be an ordeal. ⊠ *Box office, Via Dietro Anfiteatro 6/b, Verona* ☎ *045/8005151* ⊕ *www.arena.it* 🎫 *From €35 (for general admission).*

Vinitaly
FESTIVALS | This widely attended international wine and spirits event takes place in Verona over four days in April. ⊠ *Fiera di Verona, Viale del Lavoro 8, Verona* ☎ *045/8298111* ⊕ *www.vinitaly.com.*

 Shopping

BOOKS AND PRINTS
Libreria del Novecento
BOOKS | All bibliophiles should make a beeline to this small bookshop with its fascinating selection of secondhand volumes spanning many subjects. Have a rummage to unearth paperbacks with alluringly designed covers, collectibles, first editions, and intriguing art books. They also have a selection of overpriced vinyl records and CDs. ⊠ *Via Santa Maria in Chiavica 3/A, Verona* ☎ *045/8008108* ⊕ *www.libreriadelnovecento.it.*

Museo Conte–Antica Tipografia
ART GALLERY | Look out for the striking Fascism-era signage typography above the door—TIPOGRAFIA—and enter Verona's oldest printing press, opened in 1750 and run by the Conte family since the '30s. Marvel at the well-oiled working machinery, tools, and rows of printing blocks before perusing their striking, colorful prints and stationery. Since 2000 it's become a nonprofit cultural association. Call in advance as opening hours are sporadic. ⊠ *Via Santa Maria in Chiavica 3, Verona* ☎ *045/8003392* ⊕ *facebook.com/ museoconteveronaassociazioneculturale.*

FOOD AND WINE
De Rossi
FOOD | Opened in 1947, De Rossi is a Veronese institution producing oven-hot bread, cakes, pastries, biscotti, and other specialties like fresh pasta. ⊠ *Corso Porta Borsari 3, Verona* ☎ *045/8002489* ⊕ *www.derossi.it.*

 Activities

★ Adige Rafting
RAFTING | FAMILY | Briefed by expert guides and issued with paddles and life jackets, the adventurous can set off on a *gommone* (dinghy) from the Chievo (eastern) area of town and navigate the cool waters of the Adige, finishing up at the picnic area of Boschetto. Along the 8-km (5-mile) stretch of river there are wonderful water-level views of Verona's architectural and natural riches. The trip takes around three hours, with two hours spent on the water, including a fun race along the way. ⊠ *Centro Sportivo Bottagisio, Via del Perloso 14/A, Verona* ☎ *347/8892498 mobile* ⊕ *adigerafting. it* 🎫 *€25.*

Vicenza

74 km (46 miles) west of Venice, 43 km (27 miles) west of Padua.

A visit to Vicenza is a must for any student or fan of architecture. This elegant, prosperous city bears the distinctive signature of the 16th-century architect Andrea Palladio, whose name has been given to the "Palladian" style of architecture. He emphasized the principles of order and harmony using the classical style of architecture established by Renaissance architects, such as Brunelleschi, Alberti, and Sansovino. He used these principles and classical motifs not only for public buildings but also for private dwellings. His elegant villas and palaces were influential in propagating classical architecture in Europe, especially Britain, and later in America—most notably at Thomas Jefferson's Monticello.

In the mid-16th century Palladio was commissioned to rebuild much of

Vicenza, which had been greatly damaged during wars waged against Venice by the League of Cambrai (1505), an alliance of the papacy, France, the Holy Roman Empire, and several neighboring city-states. He made his name with the renovation of the basilica, begun in 1549 in the heart of Vicenza, and then embarked on a series of lordly buildings, all of which adhere to the same classicism and principles of harmony.

GETTING HERE AND AROUND

Vicenza is midway between Padua and Verona; several trains leave from Venice every hour. By car, take the Autostrada Brescia–Padova/Torino–Trieste A4/E70 to SP247 North directly into Vicenza.

VISITOR INFORMATION

CONTACT Vicenza Tourism Office. ✉ Piazza Giacomo Matteotti 12, Vicenza ☎ 0444/320854 ⊕ www.vicenzae.org.

👁 Sights

Museo Civico di Palazzo Chiericati

CASTLE/PALACE | This imposing Palladian palazzo (1550) would be worthy of a visit even if it didn't house Vicenza's Museo Civico. Because of the ample space surrounding the building, Palladio combined elements of an urban palazzo with those he used in his country villas. The museum's important Venetian holdings include significant paintings by Cima, Tiepolo, Piazzetta, and Tintoretto, but its main attraction is an extensive collection of rarely found works by painters from the Vicenza area, among them Jacopo Bassano (1515–92) and the eccentric and innovative Francesco Maffei (1605–60), whose work foreshadowed important currents of Venetian painting of subsequent generations. An audio guide QR code (€5) via your smartphone or tablet is available at the entrance. ⊠ *Piazza Matteotti, Vicenza* ☎ *0444/222811* ⊕ *www.museicivicivicenza.it* ☒ *€7; €20 Vicenza Card, includes Palazzo Barbaran da Porto and Teatro Olimpico, plus others* ⊙ *Closed Mon.*

Palazzo Barbaran da Porto (Palladio Museum)

CASTLE/PALACE | Palladio executed this beautiful city palace for the Vicentine noble Montano Barbarano between 1570 and 1575. The noble patron, however, did not make things easy for Palladio; the architect had to incorporate at least two preexisting medieval houses, with irregularly shaped rooms, into his classical, harmonious plan. It also had to support the great hall of the *piano nobile* (moving floor) above the fragile walls of the original medieval structure. The wondrous palazzo is one of Palladio's most harmonious constructions; the viewer has little indication that this is actually a transformation of a medieval structure. The palazzo also contains a museum dedicated to Palladio and is the seat of a center for Palladian studies. ⊠ *Contrà Porti 11, Vicenza* ☎ *0444/323014* ⊕ *www. palladiomuseum.org* ☒ *€8; €20 Vicenza Card, includes Palazzo Chiericati and Teatro Olimpico, plus others* ⊙ *Closed Mon. and Tues.*

Piazza dei Signori

PLAZA/SQUARE | At the heart of Vicenza, this square contains the Palazzo della Ragione (1549), the project with which Palladio made his name by successfully modernizing a medieval building, grafting a graceful two-story exterior loggia onto the existing Gothic structure. Commonly known as Palladio's basilica, the palazzo served as a courthouse and public meeting hall (the original Roman meaning of the term "basilica") and is now open only when it houses exhibits. The main point of interest, though, is the loggia, is visible from the piazza. Take a look also at the Loggia del Capitaniato, opposite, which

Palladio designed but never completed. ⊠ *Piazza dei Signori, Vicenza.*

Santa Corona

CHURCH | An exceptionally fine *Baptism of Christ* (1502), a work of Giovanni Bellini's maturity, hangs over the altar on the left, just in front of the transept of this church. Santa Corona also houses the elegantly simple Valmarana chapel, designed by Palladio. Ask about the free audio guide via QR code for smartphone/ tablet at the entrance. ⊠ *Contrà S. Corona, Vicenza* ☎ *0444/320854* ⊕ *www. museicivicivicenza.it* ☒ *€3 (free with Vicenza Card)* ⊙ *Closed Mon.*

★ Teatro Olimpico

PERFORMANCE VENUE | Palladio's last, perhaps most spectacular work was begun in 1580 and completed in 1585, after his death, by Vincenzo Scamozzi (1552–1616). Based closely on the model of ancient Roman theaters, it represents an important development in theater and stage design and is noteworthy for its acoustics and the cunning use of perspective in Scamozzi's permanent backdrop. The anterooms are frescoed with images of important figures in Venetian history. One of the few Renaissance theaters still standing, it can be visited (with guided tours) during the day and is used for concerts, operas, and other performances. ⊠ *Ticket office, Piazza Matteotti 12, Vicenza* ☎ *0444/964380* ⊕ *www.teatrolimpicovicenza.it* ☒ *€11; €20 Vicenza Card, includes Palazzo Barbaran da Porto and Palazzo Chiericati, plus others* ⊙ *Closed Mon.*

★ Villa La Rotonda (*Villa Almerico Capra*)

HISTORIC HOME | Commissioned in 1556 as a suburban residence for Paolo Almerico, this beautiful Palladian villa is the purest expression of Palladio's architectural theory and aesthetic. More a villa-temple than a residence, it contradicts the rational utilitarianism of Renaissance architecture and demonstrates the priority Palladio gave to the architectural symbolism of celestial harmony over practical considerations. A visit to view the interior can be difficult to schedule—the villa remains privately owned, and visiting hours are limited to the weekend—but this is a worthwhile stop, if only to see how Palladio's harmonious arrangement of smallish interconnected rooms around a central domed space paid little attention to the practicalities of living. The interior decoration, mainly later baroque stuccowork, contains some allegorical frescoes in the cupola by Palladio's contemporary, Alessandro Maganza.

Even without a peek inside, experiencing the exterior and the grounds is a must for any visit to Vicenza. The villa is a 20-minute walk from town or a cab (€13) or bus ride (No. 8) from Vicenza's Piazza Roma. Private tours are by appointment; see the website for the latest visiting details. ⊠ Via della Rotonda, Vicenza ☏ 0444/321793 ⊕ www.villalarotonda.it ☋ €15 with guided tour ⊙ Interior closed Mon.–Thurs. late Mar.–late Nov.

★ Villa Valmarana ai Nani

HISTORIC HOME | Inside this 17th- to 18th-century country house, named for the statues of dwarfs adorning the garden, is a series of frescoes executed in 1757 by Gianbattista Tiepolo depicting scenes from classical mythology, the *Iliad*, Tasso's *Jerusalem Delivered*, and Ariosto's *Orlando furioso* (The Frenzy of Orlando). They include his *Sacrifice of Iphigenia*, a major masterpiece of 18th-century painting. The neighboring *foresteria* (guesthouse) is also part of the museum; it contains frescoes showing 18th-century life at its most charming and scenes of chinoiserie popular in the 18th century, by Tiepolo's son Giandomenico (1727–1804). The garden dwarfs are probably taken from designs by Giandomenico. You can reach the villa on foot by following the same path that leads to Palladio's Villa La Rotonda. ⊠ Via dei Nani 2/8, Vicenza ☏ 0444/321803 ⊕ www.villavalmarana.com ☋ €12.

🍴 Restaurants

★ Osteria Il Cursore

$$ | NORTHERN ITALIAN | This cozy 19th-century *locale storico* (historic hostelry) is steeped in Vicentina atmosphere, from the bar serving local wines and *sopressa* (premium salami) to the intimate dark-wood restaurant serving hearty classics. Grab a table out back for a sit-down meal of robust dishes like bigoli (thick, egg-enriched spaghetti) with duck, spaghetti with baccalà (cod), and, in spring, *risi e bisi* (rice with peas). **Known for:** great-value pasta; buzzy atmosphere, especially on Vicenza soccer-match days; quality wine and cold cuts. $ *Average main:* €16 ⊠ Stradella Pozzetto 10, Vicenza ☏ 0444/323504 ⊕ www.osteriacursore.it ⊙ Closed Tues.

Ponte delle Bele

$$ | NORTHERN ITALIAN | Many of Vicenza's wealthier residents spend at least part of the summer in the Alps to escape the heat, and the dishes of this popular and friendly trattoria reflect the hearty influences of neighboring Alpine areas of the Trentino and Tyrol on local cuisine. The house specialty, *stinco di maiale al forno* (roast pork shank), is wonderfully fragrant, with herbs and aromatic vegetables and roast potatoes. **Known for:** hearty Vicentina classics, including baccalà served with polenta; unfussy, relaxed atmosphere and kitschy Alpine decor; mountain cheeses and cold cuts. $ *Average main:* €15 ⊠ Contrà Ponte delle Bele 5, Vicenza ☏ 0444/320647 ⊕ www.pontedellebele.it ⊙ Closed Sun. and 2 wks in Aug.

Righetti

$ | ITALIAN | Vicentini of all generations gravitate to this popular self-service cafeteria for classic dishes that don't put a dent in your wallet. Expect hearty helpings of fare such as *orzo e fagioli* (barley and bean soup) and baccalà alla vicentina (stockfish Vicenza style). **Known for:** classic dishes; very popular, especially for lunch; entertaining local atmosphere. $ Average main: €12 ⊠ Piazza Duomo 3, Vicenza ☎ 0444/543135 ⊕ www. selfrighetti.it ⊘ Closed weekends and 1 wk in Jan. and Aug.

Coffee and Quick Bites

Pasticceria Sorarù

$ | NORTHERN ITALIAN | Nestled under the porticoes of Piazzetta Palladio, the historic Pasticceria Sorarù occupies the former Cafeteria Palladio (1870) and is an ever-reliable spot for the freshest breakfast brioche with cappuccino, and a cornucopia of pastry delights. Inside, you can lean on the handsome old wooden counter and sample a pastry or three while admiring the glass jars filled with colorful candies. **Known for:** traditional Vicentino pastries and gelato; zaèti (polenta and raisin) biscuits and famous plum cake; seating under the porticoes. $ Average main: €5 ⊠ Piazzetta Andrea Palladio 17, Vicenza ☎ 0444/320915 ⊕ www.facebook.com/pasticceriasoraru.

🛏 Hotels

During annual gold fairs in January and September, it may be quite difficult to find lodging. If you're coming then, be sure to reserve well in advance and expect to pay higher rates.

Due Mori

$ | HOTEL | The public areas and guest rooms at one of the oldest (1883) hotels in the city, just off Piazza dei Signori, are filled with turn-of-the-20th-century antiques, and regulars favor the place because the high ceilings in the main building make it feel light and airy. **Pros:** traditionally furnished rooms in central location; rate same year-round; free Wi-Fi. **Cons:** no a/c, whirring ceiling fans instead; basic breakfast; no TVs in rooms. $ Rooms from: €100 ⊠ Contrà Do Rode 24, Vicenza ☎ 0444/321886 ⊕ www. albergoduemori.it ⊘ Closed 2 wks in

early Aug. and 2 wks in late Dec. 🛏 30 rooms ⊚ No Meals.

★ Hotel Campo Marzio

$$ | HOTEL | Rooms at this comfortable full-service hotel—a five-minute walk from the train station and right in front of the city walls—are ample in size, with a mix of contemporary and traditional accents. **Pros:** great location; free bike hire; set back from the street, so it's quiet and bright. **Cons:** breakfast room a tad uninspiring; businesslike exterior; no in-room tea- or coffeemaking facilities. $ Rooms from: €150 ⊠ Viale Roma 21, Vicenza ☎ 0444/5457000 ⊕ www. hotelcampomarzio.com 🛏 36 rooms ⊚ Free Breakfast.

🏃 Activities

Palladian Routes

CULTURAL TOURS | FAMILY | Based in the handsome Palazzo Valmarana Braga, this company offers a wealth of tours around the province of Vicenza. Their one-day Vicenza Landscapes and Spirit of Palladio tour is among their most popular e-bike jaunts. Visit their office to pick up your bike and accessories with GPS, and be guided by a narration app via smartphone around gorgeous landscapes, three villas, and the verdant shores of Lago di Fimon. ⊠ Palazzo Valmarana Braga, Corso Fogazzaro 16, Vicenza ☎ 0444/1270212 ⊕ www.palladianroutes.com 🎫 From €38 for e-bike hire; from €59 for an e-bike tour.

Marostica

26 km (16 miles) northeast of Vicenza, 93 km (58 miles) northwest of Venice.

From the 14th-century Castello Inferiore, where the town council still meets, an ancient stone wall snakes up the hill to enclose the Castello Superiore, which has commanding views. Marostica's most celebrated feature is the

Treviso and
the Hillside Towns

checkerboard-like square made with colored stone, Piazza Castello. The big annual event here, held in September in even-number years, is the Partita a Scacchi, a human-scale chess game.

GETTING HERE AND AROUND

There's no train station in Marostica. The closest rail connection is Bassano del Grappa, about 8 km (5 miles) away. There are regular bus connections from Vicenza's main station on STV Bus No. E05; the trip takes about 45 minutes. By car, take the SS248 northeast from Vicenza, or southwest from Bassano.

VISITOR INFORMATION

CONTACT Associazione Pro Marostica. ✉ *Piazza Castello 1, Marostica* ☎ *0424/72127* ⊕ *www.marosticascacchi.it.*

👁 Sights

Castello di Marostica

CASTLE/PALACE | FAMILY | Sitting on the summit of Monte Pauso, the origins of fortifications here stretch back to the turn of the first millennium, and a guided tour of the castle delves into its bloody history, and the lives and tastes of its former residents. The fairy-tale-like castle form makes it a fine backdrop to the giant chess game staged outside the impressive drawbridge and crenellated, pitted walls. Legend has it that the moat was the watery, muddy realm of an Egyptian crocodile brought here by the town's most famous son, the physician and botanist Prospero Alpini (1553–1617). The atmospheric interiors house collections of court clothing including those of the Venetian Podestà, arms and armature, and a fresco attributed to Mantegna

(1454–57). The Sale Espostive stages exhibitions and cultural events, and has a curious sculpture of doge Foscari kneeling before the lion of San Marco. ⊠ *Via Cansignorio della Scala 4, Marostica* ☎ *0424/72127* ⊕ *www.marosticascacchi. it* ⊠ *Free* ☞ *Book a guided tour by phone or online.*

 Restaurants

★ Osteria Madonnetta

$ | VENETIAN | Opened in 1904, this ever-reliable osteria serves hearty traditional *cucina veneta* in wonderfully homey, rustic surroundings. Take a seat under the dark wooden beams or in the leafy courtyard, and let the friendly staff guide you through a menu, dominated by meat dishes and seasonal soups, that has barely changed in decades. **Known for:** baccalà alla vicentina; sweet, grappa-infused zaeti biscuits; quirky, history-filled decor including a chess-theme fireplace. ⑤ *Average main: €14* ⊠ *Via Vajenti 21, Marostica* ☎ *0424/75859* ⊕ *www.osteriamadonnetta.it* ⊗ *Closed Thurs.*

 Hotels

Due Mori

$ | B&B/INN | Although this inn dates from the 18th century, the interior is minimalist and clean-lined—Rooms 7, 8, 11, and 12 redress the balance with picture-perfect views of the town's upper castle, while other windows look out onto the city walls or olive-tree-filled terraces. **Pros:** only hotel within the city walls; travel transfers and bikes available; great views of castle from some rooms. **Cons:** limited breakfast choice; noise from Corso Mazzini–facing rooms; bland decoration. ⑤ *Rooms from: €107* ⊠ *Corso Mazzini 73, Marostica* ☎ *0424/471777* ⊕ *www.duemori.com* ⤳ *12 rooms* ⑩ *Free Breakfast.*

 Performing Arts

Partita a Scacchi

THEATER | FAMILY | A human-scale chess game known as the Partita a Scacchi is acted out by players in medieval costume on the second weekend in September in even-number years. The game dates from 1454 and originated as a peaceful way of settling a love dispute for the hand of the daughter of the lord of Marostica Castle. The orders are still given in the local Veneto dialect. A game is presented on Friday and weekend evenings as well as Sunday afternoon. If you book an evening show and do not have a hotel reservation in Marostica, be sure you have a way of getting back afterward. Buses do not run late in the evening, and taxis, if you can find one, may hike up their rates. Tickets go on sale in February; the tourist office can help with bookings. ⊠ *Piazza Castello 1, Marostica* ☎ *0424/72127* ⊕ *www. marosticascacchi.it* ⊠ *From €46 for an atmospheric 9 pm game.*

Asolo

27 km (17 miles) east of Marostica.

Once considered the most romantic and charming of Veneto towns, the hamlet of Asolo has unfortunately lost much of its appeal, now that it's given over completely to tourism and vacation houses, with almost no local population. It does still make a nice stop for lunch after a visit to the Palladian villa at Maser, but try to avoid it on weekends and holidays, when the crowds pour in.

Through the centuries, Veneto aristocrats built elegant villas on the hillside, and in the 19th century Asolo became the idyllic haunt of musicians, poets, and painters. Back then it was one of Italy's most perfectly situated villages, with views across miles of hilly countryside; now it bears some of the scars of modern development.

Asolo hosts a modest antiques market on the second Sunday of every month.

GETTING HERE AND AROUND

There's no train station in Asolo; the closest one is in Montebelluna, 12 km (7½ miles) away. Bus connections are infrequent, and buses are not coordinated with trains, making it about a 2½-hour trip from Venice via public transportation. The best option is to drive.

By car from Treviso, take Via Feltrina and continue onto Via Padre Agostino Gemelli (SR348). Follow SR348 about 16 km (10 miles), then turn left on SP667, which you follow for almost 4 km (2½ miles). At the roundabout, take the first exit, Via Monte Grappa (SP248), and follow it for 6½ km (4 miles) to Via Loredan, where you turn right and then left onto Via Biordo Vecchio. Asolo is less than 7 km (4½ miles) away from the Palladian Villa Barbaro at Maser.

VISITOR INFORMATION

CONTACT Asolo IAT Tourism Office. ⊠ Piazza Maggiore 73 (aka Piazza Garibaldi), Asolo ☎ 0423/529046 ⊕ www.asolo.it.

 Sights

★ **Museo Canova** (*Gypsoteca*)
ART MUSEUM | The most significant cultural monument in the Asolo area is this museum dedicated to the work of the Italian neoclassical sculptor Antonio Canova (1757–1822), whose sculptures are featured in many major European and North American cultural institutions. Set up shortly after the sculptor's death in his hometown, the village of Possagno, the museum houses most of the original plaster casts, models, and drawings made by the artist in preparation for his marble sculptures. In 1957 the Museo Canova was extended by the Italian architect Carlo Scarpa. ⊠ Via Canova 74, 13½ km (8¼ miles) northwest of Asolo, Possagno ☎ 0423/544323 ⊕ www.museocanova.it ⊠ €10 ☉ Closed Mon.

Museo Civico, Torre Civica, and La Rocca
HISTORY MUSEUM | In the Piazza Maggiore, the frescoed 15th-century Loggia del Capitano contains the Museo Civico, which displays a collection of eccentric memorabilia—the Italian actress Eleonora Duse's correspondence, the poet Robert Browning's spinet, and portraits of the noble Caterina Cornaro (1454–1510). There is also access to the nearby medieval tower, Torre Civica, partially rebuilt after an earthquake in 1685. It affords great views just above its handsome 18th-century clock, designed by Bartolomeo Ferracina, the genius engineer behind clocks in Venice's Piazza San Marco and Sant'Antonio da Padova. Temporary exhibitions are also staged in the tower, along with guided tours. Those after a woodland stroll should head up to the 1,000-foot Monte Ricco medieval hilltop fortress La Rocca—the views are fabulous but the structure itself is sometimes off-limits. ⊠ Piazza Maggiore, Asolo ☎ 0423/952313 ⊕ www.museoasolo.it ⊠ €5 Museo Civico; €3 Torre Civica; €3 La Rocca; €9 combined ticket ☉ Closed weekdays.

★ **Tempio Canoviano**
MONUMENT | One of the most impressive and historically significant neoclassical buildings in Italy, the Tempio Canoviano, a church, was designed by Canova in 1819 and finished in 1830, incorporating motifs from the rotunda of the Roman Pantheon and the pronaos of the Parthenon. The church contains several works by Canova, including his tomb, along with paintings by Luca Giordano, Palma il Giovane, and Il Pordenone. A series of staircases gives access to the cupola roof and wonderful countryside views. ⊠ Piazza Canova, Possagno ⊹ 16 km (10 miles) north of Asolo ☎ 0423/544323 ⊕ www.tempiocanoviano.it ⊠ Free; cupola €2.50 ☉ Closed Mon.

Tomba Brion
MONUMENT | One of the major monuments of contemporary Italian architecture, the Brion family tomb was

designed and built by the architect Carlo Scarpa (1906–78) between 1970 and 1972. Combining Western rationalism with Eastern spirituality, Scarpa avoids the gloom and bombast of conventional commemorative monuments, creating, in his words, a secluded Eden. ⊠ *SP6 (Via Castellana), about 7 km (4½ miles) south of Asolo, near village of San Vito di Altivole, Asolo* ⊕ *fondoambiente.it/luoghi/ memoriale-brion* ⊑ *Guided tours €10* ⊘ *Closed Nov.–Feb.*

 Restaurants

Al Bacaro

$$ | ITALIAN | At this rustic, wood-rich family-style osteria, it's worth giving the robust local specialties, such as tripe, snails, or stewed game, a go—many of them served with polenta. Less adventurous diners can go for other homey options, such as goulash, polenta with cheese and mushrooms, or one of Bacaro's open-face sandwiches, generously topped with fresh salami, speck, or other cold cuts. **Known for:** good, meaty country fare; crammed with local artifacts and patrons' hand-scribbled witticisms; seasonal vegetables and meat. $ *Average main: €17* ⊠ *Via Browning 165, Asolo* ☎ *0423/55150* ⊕ *www.albacaroanticaosteria.it* ⊘ *Closed Wed. No dinner Mon. and Tues. No lunch Fri.*

★ Locanda Baggio

$$ | ITALIAN | A fabulous garden setting and warm yet unfussy country-style dining rooms elevate this family-run restaurant, renowned for Nino Baggio's elegant creative take on traditional cuisine. This is the finest restaurant in Asolo, and the prix-fixe menu (you can also order à la carte) delivers one of the best-value top-quality dining options in the Veneto. **Known for:** inventive, tasty food; white truffles and other seasonal specialties; warm hospitality. $ *Average main: €24* ⊠ *Via Bassane 1, Asolo* ☎ *0423/529648* ⊕ *www.locandabaggio.it* ⊘ *Closed Mon. No dinner Sun. No lunch Tues.*

 Hotels

★ Albergo Al Sole

$$$ | HOTEL | This elegant pink-washed hotel in a 16th-century building overlooks the main square and has wide views over picturesque Asolo or its leafy hinterland. **Pros:** central location with beautiful views; free bike hire; shuttle service to the surrounding area. **Cons:** huge rate increase in the high season; standard rooms have less interesting views than more expensive ones; expensive drinks and hidden extras. $ *Rooms from: €270* ⊠ *Via Collegio 33, Asolo* ☎ *0423/951332* ⊕ *www.albergoalsole.com* ⊘ *Closed early Jan.–late Feb.* ↩ *23 rooms* ⊙⧟ *Free Breakfast.*

Hotel Asolo

$ | HOTEL | FAMILY | This tastefully modernized 18th-century farmhouse just outside Asolo retains exposed stone, brick, and wooden joists creating a calming rural ambience in its spacious public areas, simply furnished rooms, and handsome guesthouse. **Pros:** verdant grounds; free parking; excellent service. **Cons:** a longish stroll to Asolo itself; some road traffic noise; simple room furnishings might not be for everyone. $ *Rooms from: €100* ⊠ *Via Castellana 9, Asolo* ☎ *0423/952963* ⊕ *www.hotel-asolo.com* ↩ *32 rooms* ⊙⧟ *Free Breakfast.*

Villa Cipriani

$$$ | HOTEL | From its 19th-century furnishings to a 21st-century spa and a romantic garden, this luxurious 16th-century villa turned hotel strives for opulence. **Pros:** incomparable views, including from the terrace; truly elegant grounds; spa services and outdoor panoramic pool. **Cons:** small bathrooms; exorbitant parking fees; rooms in the annex are very small. $ *Rooms from: €293* ⊠ *Via Canova 298, Asolo* ☎ *0423/523411* ⊕ *www.villacipriani.it* ⊘ *Closed Jan.–early Mar.* ↩ *29 rooms* ⊙⧟ *Free Breakfast.*

Treviso

37 km (23 miles) southeast of Asolo, 30 km (19 miles) north of Venice.

Treviso has been dubbed "Little Venice" because of its meandering, moss-bank canals. They can't really compare with Venice's spectacular waterways, but Treviso's historic center, with its medieval arcaded streets, does have a great deal of charm. Treviso is a fine place to stop for a few hours on the way from Venice to the wine country in the north or to the Palladian villas in the hinterland.

Allied bombing on Good Friday in 1944 destroyed half the city—it was bombed by mistake after a report that Hitler would be in Tarvisio, on the Austrian border, was misread. Despite this, Treviso managed to preserve what remained of its old town's narrow streets while introducing modernity far more gently than in many other parts of Italy. These days it's one of the wealthiest small cities in the country, with fashionable shops and boutiques at every turn in the busy city center.

GETTING HERE AND AROUND

Treviso is 30 minutes by train from Venice; there are frequent daily departures. By car from Venice, pick up the SS13 (Via Terraglio) in Mestre and follow it all the way to Treviso; the trip takes about 45 minutes.

VISITOR INFORMATION

CONTACT Treviso IAT Tourism Office.
☒ *Piazza Borsa 4, Treviso* ☏ *0422/595780* ⊕ *www.visittreviso.it.*

Sights

Conegliano

TOWN | This attractive town, with Venetian-style villas and arcaded streets, lies 23 km (14 miles) north of Treviso in wine-producing country and is known for its sparkling white wine, prosecco.

Its other claim to fame is its connection with Gianbattista Cima—called Cima di Conegliano. Along with Giovanni Bellini, Cima is one of the greatest painters of the early Venetian Renaissance, and the town's elegant 14th-century Duomo houses an altarpiece he painted in 1492. The front of the Duomo is formed by the frescoed late-medieval facade and Gothic arcade of the Scuola dei Battuti. If you stop in town, be sure to taste the prosecco, sold in local wine bars and shops. There is regular train service from Treviso. ☒ *Conegliano* ☏ *0438/4131* ⊕ *www.visitconegliano.it.*

Duomo

CHURCH | The Cattedrale San Pietro Apostolo, or Duomo, was given a 19th-century neoclassical makeover but retains the Renaissance splendor of the Malchiostro Chapel, with an *Annunciation* by Titian (1520) and Pordenone's (1484–1539) *Adoration of the Magi* frescoes. The crypt has 12th-century columns. Bring a handful of coins for the coin-operated lights that illuminate the artwork. To the left of the Duomo is the Romanesque Battistero di San Giovanni (11th–12th centuries), which is probably quite similar in style to the medieval Duomo; it's open only for special exhibitions. ☒ *Piazza del Duomo, Treviso* ☏ *0422/545720* ⊕ *www.diocesitv.it.*

La Pescheria

HISTORIC DISTRICT | A short walk east of Piazza dei Signori is the *pescheria* (fish market; opened in 1856), set on an island on Cagnan Grande, one of the small canals that flow through town. The picturesque, leafy setting here is completed by the surrounding handsome medieval buildings, including Ca' dei Carraresi, Ca' Brittoni, and the former convent of the Monache Camaldolesi. Seek out two beguiling female statues close to Trevisani hearts around these parts: *La Sirenetta* or Little Mermaid emerges from the Cagnan Grande; and on Vicolo Podestà, Fontana Delle Tette's serene-looking signorina spouts water—and on special occasions, *vino rosso* and *vino bianco*—from her breasts. ⊠ *Vicolo Podestà, Treviso.*

Piazza dei Signori

PLAZA/SQUARE | The center of medieval Treviso, this Piazza dei Signori remains the town's social hub, with outdoor cafés and some impressive public buildings. The most important of these, the Palazzo dei Trecento (1185–1268), was the seat of the city government, composed of the Council of 300, during the Middle Ages. It was rebuilt after bombing in 1944. Step inside to view its beautiful loggia, the Salone, replete with impressive wooden roof trusses and elaborate frescoed walls. ⊠ *Piazza dei Signori, Treviso.*

Quartiere Latino

HISTORIC DISTRICT | While strolling the city, take in this handsomely restored district between Riviera Garibaldi and Piazza Santa Maria Battuti. It's the site of university buildings, upscale apartments, and restaurants and shops. ⊠ *Treviso.*

San Nicolò

CHURCH | The most important church in Treviso, this huge Venetian Gothic structure from the early 14th century has an ornate vaulted ceiling and frescoes (circa 1350) of saints by Tommaso da Modena (circa 1325–79) on the columns. The depiction of St. Agnes on the north side is particularly interesting, combining the naturalism initiated a few decades earlier by Giotto with the grace and elegance of Gothic abstraction. Also worth examining are Tommaso's realistic portraits of 40 Dominican friars, found in the Sala del Capitolo of the seminary next door. They include the earliest known painting of a subject wearing eyeglasses, an Italian invention (circa 1280–1300). ⊠ *Seminario Vescovile, Via San Nicolò, Treviso* ☎ *0422/548626* ⊕ *www.sannicolotreviso. it* ⊘ *Closed Sun. morning except to worshippers.*

★ Villa Barbaro (Villa di Maser)

NOTABLE BUILDING | At the Villa Barbaro (1554) near the town of Maser, you can see the exquisite results of a onetime collaboration between two of the greatest artists of their age: Palladio was the architect, and Paolo Veronese did the interiors. You can easily spend a couple of hours here, so set aside time for lingering in the gorgeous grounds, admiring the honey-hue exterior and ornate statuary, including the dreamlike nymphaeum and pool. A visit is particularly immersive because the superb condition of the grounds and interior creates an uncanny atmosphere: nowhere else in the Veneto do you get such a vivid feeling for the combination of grandeur and leisure with a tangible whiff of a working farm.

Villa Barbaro, a short drive from Asolo, is most accessible by private car; the closest train station is Montebelluna. Buses leave for Maser from the bus station at Treviso, Montebelluna, or Bassano di Grappa. The bus will leave you at a stop about 1½ km (1 mile) from Maser. Hours can vary, so check the website. ⊠ *Via Cornuda 7, Maser, Treviso* ☎ *0432/923004* ⊕ *www.villadimaser. it* ⊠ *€9* ⊘ *Closed Mon., Apr.–Oct., and weekdays Nov.–Mar.*

Restaurants

All'Antico Portico

$$ | **ITALIAN** | **FAMILY** | This little old brick trattoria on a beguiling piazza with views of the Santa Maria Maggiore church is a favorite among locals and tourists, who flock to its cozy wood-trimmed interior. The menu changes daily but always features well-executed versions of simple local dishes, from risottos and pastas to a variety of seafood and meat dishes. **Known for:** set under the 15th-century porticoes; homemade pasta and white truffle; mamma's baccalà alla veneziana recipe. ⑤ *Average main: €22* ⊠ *Piazza Santa Maria Maggiore 18, Treviso*

Traveling the Wine Roads

You'd be hard-pressed to find a more stimulating and varied wine region than northeastern Italy. From the Valpolicella, Bardolino, and Soave produced near Verona to the superlative whites of the Collio Goriziano region, wines from the Veneto and Friuli–Venezia Giulia earn more Denominazione di Origine Controllata (DOC) seals for uniqueness and quality than those of any other area of Italy.

You can travel on foot, by car, or by bicycle over hillsides covered with *cantine* (vineyards), each field nurturing subtly different grape varieties. Be advised that Italy has become more stringent about its driving regulations; designated drivers can help avoid the risk of fines, embarrassment, or worse.

In the stretch of country north of Treviso, you can follow designated wine roads—tours that blend a beautiful rural setting with the delights of the grape. Authorized wineshops, where you can stop and sample, are marked with a sign showing a triangular arrangement of red and yellow grapes. There are three routes to choose from, and you can do them all comfortably over the course of a day or two.

Montello and Asolo Hills

This route provides a good balance of vineyards and nonwine sights. It winds from Nervesa della Battaglia, 18 km (10 miles) north of Treviso, past two prime destinations in the area, the village of Asolo and the Villa Barbaro at Maser. Asolo produces good prosecco, while Montello, a hill near Nervesa, favors merlot and cabernet. Both areas also yield pinot noir and chardonnay.

Piave River

The circular route follows the Piave River and runs through orchards, woods, and hills. Among the area's gems are the dessert wines Torchiato di Fregona and Refrontolo Passito, both made according to traditional methods.

Raboso del Piave, renowned since Roman times, ages well and complements local dishes such as beans and pasta or goose stuffed with chestnuts. Other reds include merlot and cabernet sauvignon.

Prosecco

La Strada del Prosecco (Prosecco Road) runs for 47 km (29 miles) between Valdobbiadene and Conegliano, home of Italy's first wine institute, winding between knobby hills covered in grapevines. These hang in festoons on row after row of pergolas to create a thick mantle of green.

Turn off the main route to explore the narrower country lanes. They meander past numerous family wineries where you can taste and buy the wines. It's well worth setting aside time to explore the most scenic southern stretches: between Renfrontolo and Col San Martino there's the ancient San Vigilio church and the celebrated Follador winery, while the Cartizze hills afford breathtaking views. Spring is an excellent time to visit, with no fewer than 15 local wine festivals held between March and early June.

☎ 0422/545259 ⊕ www.anticoportico.it ⊘ Closed Tues. No dinner Mon.

Beccherie

$$$$ | ITALIAN | Adventurous foodies with deep pockets should book a table in this stylish blue-and-wood-accented dining room, located behind Treviso's Palazzo dei Trecento old meat market, for an experience that marries Trevigiano culinary traditions with contemporary elegance. It was here back in the late '60s that the famous dessert tiramisu was invented and the Beccherie, opened in 1939, still makes it to the original, featherlight recipe. **Known for:** inventive, beautifully presented food; contemporary design and tasting menus; special tiramisu. ⑤ Average main: €38 ⊠ Piazza Ancilotto 10, Treviso ☎ 0422/540871 ⊕ www.lebeccherie.it ⊘ Closed Tues.

Il Basilisco

$$ | ITALIAN | Gastronomically adventurous diners who visit this quirky restaurant filled with stylish mid-century furnishings will find cucina povera (peasant food) given an inventive twist. The chef is a passionate slow-food champion, so expect local and seasonal meat and vegetables, as well as excellent seafood and an extensive wine list from Italy and farther afield. **Known for:** inventive use of quinto quarto (offal); vibrant contemporary decor and design; homemade pasta, cured meats, and antipasti. ⑤ Average main: €20 ⊠ Via Bison 34, Treviso ☎ 0422/541822 ⊕ www.ristorantebasilisco.com ⊘ Closed Sun. No lunch Mon.

Odeon alla Colonna

$$ | NORTHERN ITALIAN | Dine in the atmospheric arcaded canal-side vicolo on Odeon's superb-value pasta, meat, and seafood dishes, or amid the columns in the high-ceilinged salone. As befits the intriguing historic setting and interiors, the menu showcases traditional Trevisano ingredients with the occasional flavorsome twist. **Known for:** take-away dried pasta, risotto, and so on from their deli counter; light lunches, heaped salads,

and homemade pasta dishes; special tasting menus and cultural gatherings. ⑤ Average main: €18 ⊠ Vicolo Rinaldi 3, Treviso ☎ 0422/541012 ⊕ www.odeonlacolonna.it.

Toni del Spin

$$ | ITALIAN | Wood paneled and with a 1930s-style interior, this bustling trattoria has a wholesome menu based on local Veneto cooking. The "spin" in the restaurant's name refers to the spine of the baccalà, one of several justly famous specialties (served without the titular spine); also try the sopa coada, a pigeon-and-bread soup. **Known for:** Veneto specialties and great wine choices; idiosyncratic, sometimes brusque service; terrazza dining in warmer months. ⑤ Average main: €17 ⊠ Via Inferiore 7, Treviso ☎ 393/9863597 mobile ⊕ www.ristorantetonidelspin.com ⊘ Closed 3 wks in July and Aug. No lunch Mon.

Coffee and Quick Bites

Caffetteria Broli

$ | NORTHERN ITALIAN | This central coffee bar serves lots of different espressi and cappuccini—topped with chocolate and cream and other enhancements—as well as a cornucopia of great-value tramezzini (finger sandwiches), piadine (Italian flatbread wraps), and panini. Pop in most times of the day (closes at 7:30 pm; 1 pm Sunday) for a selection of classic pasta primi and secondi, as well as healthy juices and vegan options. **Known for:** brioche and other pastries topped with fruit; insalatoni (heaped salads); vegan selection. ⑤ Average main: €8 ⊠ Vicolo Broli 8/10, Treviso ☎ 0422/582225.

Hotels

Hotel San Nicolò

$$ | HOTEL | Comfort combines with warm hospitality and distinctive decor—public areas are elegant with choice antiques, while each guest room is themed after a global city—at this well-run central hotel

in a handsome palazzo near Chiesa di San Nicolò. **Pros:** individual character in each guest room; warm, family-run customer service; low-season deals. **Cons:** road noise in some rooms; some rooms on the small size; no elevator. ⑤ *Rooms from: €180* ⊠ *Via Risorgimento 54, Treviso* ☎ *0422/590114* ⊕ *www.relais-sannicolo.com* ⟳ *10 rooms* ⦿ *Free Breakfast.*

Udine

127 km (79 miles) northeast of Venice.

The main reason for devoting some time to Udine is to see works by Gianbattista Tiepolo (1696–1770), one of the greatest European painters of the 18th century. Distributed in several palaces and churches around town, this is the largest assembly of his art outside Venice. In fact, Udine calls itself "la città di Tiepolo."

The largest city on the Friuli side of the region, Udine has a provincial, genteel-meets-rustic atmosphere with oodles of charm. The city sometimes seems completely unaffected by tourism, and things are still done the way they were decades ago. In the medieval and Renaissance historical center of town, you'll find unevenly spaced streets with appealing wine bars and open-air cafés. Friulani are proud of their culture, with many restaurants featuring local cuisine, and street signs and announcements written in both Italian and Friulano (Furlan), which, although it is classified as a dialect, is really a separate language from Italian.

Commanding a view from the Alpine foothills to the Adriatic Sea, Udine stands on a mound that, according to legend, was erected so Attila the Hun could watch the burning of Aquileia, an important Roman center to the south. Although the legend is unlikely (Attila burned Aquileia about 500 years before the first historical mention of Udine), the view from Udine's castle across

the alluvial plane down to the sea is impressive. In the Middle Ages Udine flourished, thanks to its favorable trade location and the right granted by the local patriarch to hold regular markets.

GETTING HERE AND AROUND

There's frequent train service from both Venice and Trieste; the trip takes about two hours from Venice, and a little over an hour from Trieste. By car from Venice, take the SR11 to the E55 and head east. Take the E55 (it eventually becomes the Autostrada Alpe Adria) to SS13 (Viale Venezia) east into Udine. Driving from Trieste, take the SS202 to the E70, which becomes the A4. Turn onto the E55 north, which is the same road you would take coming from Venice. Driving times are 1½ to 2 hours from Venice and 1 hour from Trieste.

VISITOR INFORMATION

The tourist office and website (⊕ *www.turismofvg.it*) sells the FVG (Friuli Venezia Giulia) Card, which includes admission to most museums in Udine and other important sites in the region. Its price ranges from €30 (for 48 hours) up to €40 (for one week).

CONTACT Udine IAT Tourism Office. ⊠ *Piazza I Maggio 7, Udine* ☎ *0432/295972* ⊕ *www.turismofvg.it.*

 Sights

⭐ Castello and Musei Civici

CASTLE/PALACE | The hilltop castle (construction began in 1517) has panoramic views extending to Monte Nero (7,360 feet) in neighboring Slovenia, but head inside to see Udine's civic museums of art and archaeology, with myriad collections that can detain you for hours. On the ground floor are the Museo del Risorgimento (tracing the history of Italian unification) and Museo Archeologico; the third floor is the Museo della Fotografia, with fascinating 19th- and 20th-century images of the Friuli. Particularly worthwhile is the national and regional art collection in the Galleria d'Arte Antica, which has canvases by Venetians Vittore Carpaccio (circa 1460–1525) and Gianbattista Tiepolo, the recently restored (2020) *Il San Francesco Riceve le Stimmate* (St. Francis Receiving the Stigmata) by Caravaggio, and carefully selected works by lesser-known but still interesting Veneto and Friuli artists. ■ TIP➜ **The museum's small collection of drawings includes several by Tiepolo; some find his drawings even more moving than his paintings.** ⊠ *Via Lionello 1, Udine* ☎ *0432/1272591* ⊕ *www.civicimuseiudine.it* ⌨ *€8, €10 Unico ticket also includes Casa Cavazzini and Museo Etnografico del Friuli, €15 Unico Musei tickets also includes Museo Diocesano (free with FVG Card)* ⦿ *Closed Mon.*

Duomo

CHURCH | A few steps from the Piazza della Libertà is Udine's 1335 Duomo, with some significant works by Tiepolo. Its Cappella del Santissimo has important early frescoes by Tiepolo, and the Cappella della Trinità has a Tiepolo altarpiece. There is also a beautiful late Tiepolo *Resurrection* (1751) in an altar by the sculptor Giuseppe Toretti. Ask the Duomo's attendant to let you into the adjacent Chiesa della Purità to see more important late paintings by Tiepolo. The Museo del Duomo, housed in two 14th century chapels and baptistery, contains sculptures (including a fine funereal marble sarcophagus), paintings, textiles, and devotional jewels. ⊠ *Piazza del Duomo 1, Udine* ☎ *0432/505302* ⊕ *www.cattedraleudine.it* ⌨ *Free* ⦿ *Museum closed Tues.*

★ Museo d'Arte Moderna e Contemporanea–Casa Cavazzini

ART GALLERY | Udine's fine civic collection of modern and contemporary art is housed in the handsome and part-modernized 16th-century Casa Cavazzini, which retains some ornate apartment interiors. The first and second floors display the permanent collection: first-floor highlights include bold sculptural works by the three Udinese brothers Dino, Mirko, and Afro Basaldella, with a backdrop of 14th-century frescoes discovered during the 2012 refurbishing. There are also fine works by Giorgio Morandi, Renato Guttuso, and Carlo Carrà. Up a floor is the Collezione Astaldi, spanning the 1920s through the 1960s, and Collezione FRIAM, with '60s and '70s works. Worth seeking out are Giorgio de Chirico's *I Gladiatori* (1931) and pieces by 20th-century American icons Willem de Kooning, Roy Lichtenstein, and Sol LeWitt. Entry to themed temporary exhibitions costs extra. ⊠ *Via Cavour 14, Udine* ☎ *0432/1273772* ⊕ *www.civicimuseiudine.it* ⌨ *€5 (€12 temporary shows), €10 Unico ticket also includes Castello and Museo Etnografico del Friuli, €15 Unico Musei tickets also includes Museo Diocesano (free with FVG Card)* ⦿ *Closed Mon.*

★ Museo Diocesano e Gallerie del Tiepolo

CASTLE/PALACE | The handsome Palazzo Patriarcale o Arcivescovile contains several rooms of frescoes by the young Gianbattista Tiepolo, painted from 1726 to 1732, which comprise the most important collection of early works by Italy's most brilliant 18th-century painter. The Galleria del Tiepolo (1727) contains superlative Tiepolo frescoes depicting the stories of Abraham, Isaac, and Jacob. The *Judgment of Solomon* (1729) graces the Pink Room. There are also beautiful and important Tiepolo frescoes in the staircase, throne room, and palatine chapel of this palazzo. Even in these early works we can see the Venetian master's skill in creating an illusion of depth, not only through linear perspective, but also through subtle gradations in the intensity of the colors, with the stronger colors coming forward and the paler ones receding into space. Tiepolo was one of the first artists to use this method of representing space and depth, which reflected the scientific discoveries of perception and optics in the 17th century.

The Museo Diocesano here features sculptures from Friuli churches from the 13th through 18th centuries; and don't miss the magnificent library, the Biblioteca Arcivescovile Delfiniana. ⊠ *Piazza Patriarcato 1, Udine* ☎ *0432/25003* ⊕ *www.musdioc-tiepolo.it* ☜ *€8, includes Museo Diocesano; €15 Unico Musei ticket bundles Museo Diocesano with Musei Civici (free with FVG Card)* ⊘ *Closed Tues.*

Piazza della Libertà

PLAZA/SQUARE | Udine was conquered by the Venetians in 1420, so there is a distinctly Venetian stamp on the architecture of the historic center, most noticeably here, in the large main square. The Loggia del Leonello, begun in 1428, dominates the square and houses the municipal government. Its similarity to the facade of Venice's Palazzo Ducale (finished in 1424) is clear, but there is no evidence that it is an imitation of that palace. It's more likely a product of the same architectural fashion. Opposite stands the Renaissance Porticato di San Giovanni (1533–35) and the Torre dell'Orologio, a 1527 clock tower with naked *mori* (Moors), who strike the hours on the top. ⊠ *Piazza della Libertà, Udine.*

🍽 Restaurants

★ Hostaria alla Tavernetta

$$ | FRIULIAN | The trusty Hostaria (open since 1954) has rustic fireside dining downstairs and more elegantly decorated rooms upstairs, where there's also an intimate terrace under the Duomo. It's a great place for sampling regional specialties such as *orzotto* (barley prepared like risotto), delicious *cjalzòns* or *cjarsons* (ravioli from the Carnia), and seasonal meat dishes, accompanied by a fabulous wine list. **Known for:** rustic yet sophisticated atmosphere; Friulian ingredients and traditions; superb local Collio wine, grappa, and regional selections. ⑤ *Average main: €24* ⊠ *Via di Prampero 2, Udine*

☎ *0432/501066* ⊕ *www.allatavernetta. com* ⊘ *Closed Sun. and Mon.*

★ Vitello d'Oro

$$$ | ITALIAN | Udine's very chic landmark restaurant is the one reserved most by locals for special occasions, and the menu features the freshest meat and fish in sophisticated dishes served with moodily lit culinary stagecraft. You might start with an antipasto of assorted raw shellfish, including the impossibly sweet Adriatic scampi, followed by the fresh fish of the day. **Known for:** seafood served raw and cooked; large terrace popular in summer; multicourse tasting menu. ⑤ *Average main: €28* ⊠ *Via Valvason 4, Udine* ☎ *0432/508982* ⊕ *www.vitellodoro.com* ⊘ *Closed Tues. No lunch Wed. and Thurs.*

☕ Coffee and Quick Bites

★ Grosmi Caffè

$ | NORTHERN ITALIAN | Under the porticoes of gorgeous Piazza Matteoti, with its vibrant student and dialect-speaking locals, Grosmi is a reliable choice for excellent coffee, pastries, and people-watching. Although the brioche filled with chocolate, custard, or fruit jam are staples, some opt for a small cake or macaroon to accompany their caffeine fix. **Known for:** selection of imported blends; tables on the piazza; brioche, pastries, and cakes. ⑤ *Average main: €5* ⊠ *Piazza Giacomo Matteotti 9, Udine* ☎ *0432/506411* ⊕ *biquadrocaffe.it.*

🛏 Hotels

Hotel Clocchiatti Next

$ | HOTEL | You have two smart and contrasting choices here: the 19th-century villa, with canopy beds and Alpine-style wood ceilings and paneling; and the "Next Wing," with rich colors and spare furnishings in starkly angular rooms. **Pros:** stylish, individually decorated rooms; excellent breakfast for €10 extra; a tranquil Zen-garden haven. **Cons:** 10-minute drive from town center; small bathrooms; some rooms need a refresh. $ *Rooms from: €116* ✉ *Via Cividale 29, Udine* ☎ *0432/505047* ⊕ *www.hotelclocchiatti.it* ➥ *27 rooms* ❏| *No Meals.*

Hotel Ristorante Allegria

$$ | **HOTEL** | Renovation of this 15th-century building took a decidedly minimalist approach: the breakfast room, lounges, and guest rooms feature plenty of light wood, mood lighting, and sleek, angular design. **Pros:** well-appointed, neutral-hue rooms; easy access, secure garage; easy walking distance to the center. **Cons:** rooms may be too minimalist for some; fee for parking; a/c can be unreliable. $ *Rooms from: €145* ✉ *Via Grazzano 18, Udine* ☎ *0432/201116* ⊕ *www.hotelallegria.it* ➥ *21 rooms* ❏| *Free Breakfast.*

🏃 Activities

L'Ippovia del Cormor

BIKING | L'Ippovia del Cormor is a 26-km (16-mile) path that allows walkers, runners, cyclists, and horseback riders to immerse themselves in the rural hamlets north of Udine, including Tricesimo, Colloredo di Monte Albano, Cassacco, and Treppo Grande. The path rises and ends at Buja, where the source of the River Cormor bubbles with numerous streams, including the Rio Gelato, and is surrounded by the mountain peaks. Contact Cussigh Bike for suitably robust wheels to hire. ✉ *Via del Lavoro, Feletto Umberto-Tavagnacco, Udine* ☎ *0432/688268 Cussigh Bike* ⊕ *www.cussighbike.it.*

Cividale del Friuli

17 km (11 miles) east of Udine, 144 km (89 miles) northeast of Venice.

Cividale is the most important place for taking in the impressive and beautiful art of the Lombards, a Germanic people who entered Italy in 568 and who ruled parts of Italy until the late 8th century. The city was founded in AD 53 by Julius Caesar, then commander of Roman legions in the area. Here you can also find Celtic, Roman, and medieval Jewish ruins alongside Venetian Gothic buildings, including the Palazzo Comunale. Strolling through the part of the city that now occupies the former Gastaldia, the Lombard ducal palace, gives you spectacular views of the medieval city and the river.

GETTING HERE AND AROUND
There's hourly train service from Udine. Since the Udine–Cividale train line isn't part of the Italian national rail system, you have to buy the tickets from the electronic machines, the MPL tobacconist, or the newsstand Edicola 103 within the Udine station. You can't buy a ticket through to Cividale from another city.

By car from Udine, take Via Cividale, which turns into SS54; follow SS54 into Cividale.

VISITOR INFORMATION
CONTACT Informacittà office. ⊠ *Palazzo de Nordis, Piazza Duomo 5, Cividale del Friuli* ☎ *0432/710460* ⊕ *www.cividale.com.*

 Sights

Duomo
CHURCH | Cividale's Renaissance Duomo is largely the work of Pietro Lombardo, principal architect of Venice's famous Santa Maria dei Miracoli. The interior was restructured in the 18th century by another prominent Venetian architect, Giorgio Massari. The church contains a magnificent 12th-century silver gilt altarpiece. ⊠ *Piazza Duomo, Cividale del Friuli* ☎ *0432/731144* ⊕ *www.duomo-cividale.it.*

Museo Archeologico
HISTORY MUSEUM | Trace the area's history here and learn about the importance of Cividale and Udine in the period following the collapse of the Roman Empire. The collection includes Roman mosaics and epigraphs as well as weapons and exquisite jewelry from 6th-century Lombard warriors, who swept through much of what is now Italy. ⊠ *Piazza Duomo 13, Cividale del Friuli* ☎ *0432/700700* ⊕ *www.museoarcheologicocividale. beniculturali.it* ☞ *€4; €9 combined ticket, includes Museo Archeologico and Museo Cristiano e Tesoro del Duomo (free with FVG Card).*

Museo Cristiano e Tesoro del Duomo
SPECIALTY MUSEUM | Entered via a courtyard to the right of the Duomo, this museum contains two interesting, important, and surprisingly beautiful monuments of Lombard art: the Altar of Duke Ratchis (737–744) and the Baptistry of Patriarch Callisto (731–776). Both were found under the floor of the present Duomo in the early 20th century. The museum also has two fine paintings by Veronese, one by Il Pordenone, and a small collection of medieval and Renaissance vestments. ⊠ *Via Candotti 1, Cividale del Friuli* ☎ *0432/730403* ⊕ *www.mucris.com* ☞ *€4; €9 combined ticket, includes Museo Archeologico and Museo Cristiano e Tesoro del Duomo (free with FVG Card)* ⊘ *Closed Mon. and Tues.*

Palazzo de Nordis: Galleria d'Arte De Martiis
ART GALLERY | Opened in 2020 and housed in a magnificent historic palazzo, originally dating from the 15th century, the Gallery showcases the De Martiis family's exquisite collection of 20th-century art. Among the figurative works is a saucy Toulouse-Lautrec, and there are eye-popping impressionist masterpieces

by Karel Appel and Victor Vasarely.

■ TIP→ **For tourist info visit the ground-floor Sportello Informacittà.** ⊠ *Piazza Duomo 5, Cividale del Friuli* ☏ *0432/710357* ⊕ *palazzodenordis.it* 🎫 *€8; free with FVG Card.*

★ **Tempietto Longobardo** (*Lombard Church*)

CHURCH | Seeing the beautiful and historically important Tempietto Longobardo from the 8th century is more than enough reason to visit Cividale. Now inside the 16th-century Monastery of Santa Maria in Valle, the Tempietto was originally the chapel of the ducal palace, known as the Gastaldia. The west wall is the best-preserved example of the art and architecture of the Lombards, a Germanic people who entered Italy in 568. It has an archway with an exquisitely rendered vine motif, guarded by an 8th-century procession of female figures, showing the Lombard interpretation of classical forms that resembles the style of the much earlier Byzantine mosaics in Ravenna, a town that had passed briefly to Lombard rule in 737. The post-Lombard frescoes decorating the vaults and the east wall date from the 13th and 14th centuries, and the fine carved wooden stalls also date from the 14th century. ⊠ *Via Monastero Maggiore, Cividale del Friuli* ☏ *0432/700867* ⊕ *www.tempietto-longobardo.it* 🎫 *€4; €9 combined ticket, includes Museo Archeologico and Museo Cristiano e Tesoro del Duomo (free with FVG Card).*

 Restaurants

Alla Speranza

$$$ | **NORTHERN ITALIAN** | This well-thought-of osteria-trattoria lands the freshest seafood and creates exquisite, beautifully presented plates; the chefs constantly delight with new things to try such as homemade spirulina grissini, unusual flavor combos, and vibrant garnishes. Dine in the rustic yet refined dining room with its exposed stone, wooden beams, and coved ceilings, or outside on the gorgeous terrace with piazza views. **Known for:** fresh seafood with colorful flowers, herbs, and crunchy garnishes; innovative desserts and aperitivi; superb wine list. ⑤ *Average main: €27* ⊠ *Piazza Foro Giulio Cesare 15, Cividale del Friuli* ☏ *0432/731131* ⊕ *www.allasperanza.net* ⊘ *Closed Mon. No lunch Tues.–Thurs.*

 Hotels

B&B dai Toscans

$ | **B&B/INN** | In a central location, this 15th-century palazzo, once home to the dukes of Tuscany, is now a charming and romantic bed-and-breakfast with parquet flooring throughout, a pleasant if unremarkable breakfast room, and large guest rooms furnished in antique style. **Pros:** large, well-appointed rooms; triples for families; no- or low-fee nearby parking. **Cons:** some noise from the street and the cathedral bells; quirky decor not to everyone's taste; can be a struggle hauling luggage in this pedestrianized area. ⑤ *Rooms from: €95* ⊠ *Corso Mazzini 15/1, Cividale del Friuli* ☏ *3490/765288 mobile* ⊕ *daitoscans.it* ⇥ *5 rooms* 🍴 *Free Breakfast.*

Aquileia

123 km (77 miles) east of Venice, 42 km (25 miles) south of Udine.

This sleepy little town is refreshingly free of the tourists that you might expect at such a culturally historic place. In the time of Emperor Augustus, it was Italy's fourth-most-important city (after Rome, Milan, and Capua), as well as the principal northern Adriatic port of Italy and the beginning of Roman routes north. Aquileia's Roman and early Christian remains offer an image of the transition from pagan to Christian Rome.

GETTING HERE AND AROUND

Getting to Aquileia by public transportation is difficult but not impossible. There's frequent train service from Venice and Trieste to Cervignano di Friuli, which is 8 km (5 miles) away from Aquileia by taxi (about €25) or infrequent bus service. (Ask the newsstand attendant or the railroad ticket teller for assistance.) By car from Venice or Trieste, take Autostrada A4 (Venezia–Trieste) to the Palmanova exit and continue 17 km (11 miles) to Aquileia. From Udine, take Autostrada A23 to the Palmanova exit.

VISITOR INFORMATION

CONTACT Aquileia Infopoint. ⊠ *Via Giulia Augusta 11, Aquileia* ☏ *0431/919491* ⊕ *www.turismofvg.it.*

 Sights

Aquileia Archaeological Site

RUINS | Roman remains of the forum, houses, cemetery, and port are surrounded by cypresses here, and the little stream was once an important waterway extending to Grado. Unfortunately, many of the excavations of Roman Aquileia could not be left exposed, because of the extremely high water table under the site, and had to be reburied after archaeological studies had been conducted; nevertheless, what remains aboveground, along with the monuments in the archaeological museum, gives an idea of the grandeur of this ancient city. The area is well signposted. ⊠ *Near basilica, Aquileia* ☎ *Free.*

★ La Basilica di Aquileia

CHURCH | The highlight of the Basilica complex is the spectacular 3rd- to 4th-century mosaic covering the entire floor of the basilica and the adjacent crypt, which make up one of the most important early Christian monuments. Theodore, the basilica's first bishop, built two parallel basilicas (now the north and the south halls) on the site of a Gnostic chapel in the 4th century. These were joined by a third hall, forming a "U." The complex later accumulated the Romanesque portico and Gothic bell tower. The mosaic floor of the basilica is the remains of the floor of Theodore's south hall.

In his north hall, Theodore retained much of the floor of the earlier Gnostic chapel, whose mosaics represent the ascent of the soul, through the realm of the planets and constellations, to God, who is represented as a ram. (The ram, at the head of the zodiac, is the Gnostic generative force.) This integration of Gnosticism into a Christian church is interesting, since Gnosticism had been branded a heresy by early church fathers.

The 4th-century mosaics of the Südalle (the south hall is the present-day nave) represent the story of Jonah as prefiguring the salvation offered by the Church. Down a flight of steps, the Cripta degli Affreschi contains 12th-century frescoes.

In Piazza Capitolo, the Domus and Palazzo Episcopale's newest discoveries reveal fascinating layers of the city's history, with beautiful geometric mosaics and frescoes, and original walls. ⊠ *Piazza Capitolo 1, Aquileia* ☎ *0431/919719* ⊕ *www.fondazioneaquileia.it* ☎ *€5 Cripta degli Affreschi with Cripta Scavi; €2 campanile; €10 whole complex; all sites free with FGV card* ☉ *Campanile closed Oct.–Mar.*

Museo Archeologico

SPECIALTY MUSEUM | The museum's wealth of material from Roman times includes portrait busts from the Republican era, semiprecious gems, amber—including preserved flies—and goldwork, and a fine glass collection. Beautiful pre-Christian mosaics are from the floors of Roman houses and palaces. ⊠ *Via Roma 1, Aquileia* ☎ *0431/91016* ⊕ *www.museoarcheologicoaquileia.beniculturali.it* ☎ *€9 (free with FGV card)* ☉ *Closed Mon.*

Trieste

163 km (101 miles) east of Venice, 77 miles (48 km) east of Aquileia.

Trieste is Italy's only truly cosmopolitan city. In a country—perhaps even in a continent—where the amalgamation of cultures has frequently proved difficult, Trieste stands out as one of the few authentic melting pots. Not only do Italian, Slavic, and Central European cultures meet here, they actually merge to create a unique Triestino culture. To discover this culture, visiting Trieste's coffeehouses, local eateries, and piazzas is probably more important than visiting its churches and museums, interesting though they are.

Trieste is built along a fringe of coastline where the rugged Karst Plateau tumbles abruptly into the beautiful Adriatic. The city's history, the sea, and its inhabitants are shaped by the power of the fierce northerly to northeasterly wind, the bora. It was the only port of the Austro-Hungarian Empire and, therefore, a major industrial and financial center. In the early years of the 20th century, Trieste and its surroundings also became famous by their association with some of the most important names of Italian literature, such as Italo Svevo, and Irish and German writers. James Joyce drew inspiration from the city's multiethnic population, and Rainer Maria Rilke was inspired by the coast to the west.

The city has lost its importance as a port and a center of finance, but perhaps because of its multicultural nature, at the juncture of Latin, Slavic, and Germanic Europe, it's never fully lost its role as an intellectual center. In recent years the city has become a center for science and technology. The streets hold a mix of monumental neoclassical and art nouveau architecture, built by the Austrians

during Trieste's days of glory, granting an air of melancholy stateliness to a city that lives as much in the past as the present.

Italian revolutionaries of the 1800s rallied their battle cry around Trieste, because of what they believed was foreign occupation of their motherland. After World War II the sliver of land including Trieste and a small part of Istria became an independent, neutral state that was officially recognized in a 1947 peace treaty. Although it was actually occupied by British and American troops for its nine years of existence, the Free Territory of Trieste issued its own currency and stamps. In 1954 a Memorandum of Understanding was signed in London, giving civil administration of Trieste to Italy.

GETTING HERE AND AROUND

Trains to Trieste depart regularly from Venice, Udine, and other major Italian cities. By car, it's the eastern terminus of the Autostrada Torino–Trieste (E70). The city is served by Trieste–Friuli Venezia Giulia Airport, which receives flights from major Italian airports and some European cities. The airport is 33 km (20½ miles) from the city; transfers into Trieste are by taxi or APT coach G51.

VISITOR INFORMATION

CONTACT Trieste Infopoint. ⊠ *Piazza Unità d'Italia 4, Trieste* ☎ *040/3478312, 335/7429440 mobile* ⊕ *www.discover-trieste.it.*

Sights

Castello di Duino

CASTLE/PALACE | This 14th-century castle, the property of the Princes of Thurn and Taxis, contains a collection of antique furnishings and an amazing Palladian circular staircase, but the main attractions are the surrounding gardens and the spectacular views. In 1912 Rainer Maria Rilke wrote much of his masterpiece, the *Duino Elegies,* here. The easy path along the seacoast from the castle toward Trieste has gorgeous views that rival those of the Amalfi Coast and the Cinque Terre. For more spectacular cliff-top views, visit the ruins of the nearby 11th-century Castelvecchio. ⊠ *Frazione Duino 32, 12 km (7½ miles) from Trieste, Duino ⊹ Take Bus No. 44 or 51 from Trieste train station to Duino* ☎ *040/208120* ⊕ *www. castellodiduino.it* ⊠ *€11; €13.50 Castello di Duino and Castello Vecchio* ⊙ *Closed Tues.; closed weekdays Nov.–mid-Mar., except a few special days (contact for latest).*

Castello di San Giusto

CASTLE/PALACE | This hilltop castle, built between 1470 and 1630, was constructed on the ruins of the Roman town of Tergeste. Given the excellent view, it's no surprise that 15th-century Venetians turned the castle into a shipping observation point; the structure was further enlarged by Trieste's subsequent rulers, the Hapsburgs. The castle also contains the Civic Museum, which has a collection of furnishings, tapestries, and weaponry, as well as Roman artifacts in the atmospheric Lapidario Tergestino. ⊠ *Piazza della Cattedrale 3, Trieste* ☎ *040/309362* ⊕ *www.castellodisangiustotrieste.it* ⊠ *€5 includes all complex museums* ⊙ *Closed Mon. Oct.–Mar.*

Cattedrale di San Giusto

CHURCH | Dating from the 14th century and occupying the site of an ancient Roman forum, the cathedral contains remnants of at least three previous buildings, the earliest a hall dating from the 5th century. A section of the original floor mosaic still remains, incorporated into the floor of the present church. In the 9th and 11th centuries two adjacent churches were built—the Church of the Assumption and the Church of San Giusto. The beautiful apse mosaics of these churches, done in the 12th and 13th centuries by a Venetian artist, still remain in the apses of the side aisles of the present church. The mosaics in the main apse

date from 1932. In the 14th century the two churches were joined and a Romanesque-Gothic facade was attached, ornamented with fragments of Roman monuments taken from the forum. The jambs of the main doorway derive from Roman funereal stelae. ⊠ *Piazza della Cattedrale 2, Trieste* ☎ *040/2600892* ⊕ *www.sangiustomartire.it.*

★ LETS Museum Literature Trieste

ART MUSEUM | Opened in 2024, Trieste's newest museum brings together various collections exploring multifarious facets of the written word and the lives of literary figures who have become synonymous with the city. Sections include the introductory "History Kiosk," a wonderful space dedicated to cinematic adaptations, and immersive exhibitions dedicated to James Joyce, Italo Svevo, and poet Umberto Saba. If you fancy a leaf through 1,000 books, there's the "Writers' Bookstore," and listening stations allow visitors to enjoy audiobooks while gazing through picture windows with city views. ⊠ *Palazzo Biserini, Piazza Hortis 4, Trieste* ☎ *040/3478312* ⊕ *lets.trieste.it.*

★ Miramare

CASTLE/PALACE | FAMILY | A 19th-century castle on the Gulf of Trieste, this is nothing less than a major expression of the culture of the decaying Austrian Hapsburg monarchy: nowhere else— not even in Vienna—can you savor the decadent opulence of the last years of the empire. Maximilian of Hapsburg, brother of Emperor Franz Josef and the retired commander of the Austrian Navy, built the seafront extravaganza between 1856 and 1860, complete with a throne room under a wooden ceiling shaped like a ship's keel. The rooms are generally furnished with copies of medieval, Renaissance, and French period furniture, and the walls are covered in red damask. In 1864 Maximilian became emperor of Mexico at the initiative of Napoléon III. He was executed three years later by a Mexican firing squad.

During the last years of the Hapsburg reign, Miramare became one of the favorite residences of Franz Josef's wife, the Empress Elizabeth (Sissi). The castle was later owned by Duke Amedeo of Aosta. Changing exhibitions in the revamped Sala Progetti showcase the impressive museum archive. Tours in English are available by reservation. Surrounding the castle is a gorgeous 54-acre park. To get here from central Trieste, take Bus No. 36 from Piazza Oberdan; it runs every half hour. ⌖ *Viale Miramare, off SS14, Trieste* ✛ *7 km (4½ miles) northwest of Trieste* ☎ *040/224143* ⊕ *miramare.cultura.gov.it* ☞ *€12, with guided tour €20.*

Museo d'Antichità J. J. Winckelmann

HISTORY MUSEUM | On the hill near the Castello, this eclectic collection showcases statues from the Roman theater, mosaics, and a wealth of artifacts from Egypt, Greece, and Rome. There's also an assortment of glass and manuscripts. The Orto Lapidario (Lapidary Garden) has classical statuary, pottery, and a small Corinthian temple. The collection was renamed in 2018 after the pioneering art historian and Hellenist J. J. Winckelmann, who was murdered in Trieste in 1768. ⌖ *Via Cattedrale 1, Trieste* ☎ *040/310500* ⊕ *museoantichitawinckelmann.it* ☞ *Free* ⊗ *Closed Mon.*

★ Museo Revoltella–Galleria d'Arte Moderna

ART MUSEUM | Housed in three magnificent buildings and partly remodeled by influential Italian architect Carlo Scarpa, the Revoltella provides a stimulating survey of 19th- and 20th-century art and decoration. Building on the bequeathment of the grand palazzo and art of Triestino collector-industrialist Pasquale Revoltella (1795–1869), the institution has continued to add important artworks from the Venice Biennale by the likes of Carrà, Mascherini, Morandi, de Chirico, Manzù, Fontana, and Burri. In contrast, a gorgeous cochlear staircase connects the three floors of the museum: its history and 1850–60 cityscapes are on the ground floor; 19th-century classical statuary, portraits, and historic scenes take up the first; while the third preserves opulent *saloni.* ⌖ *Via Diaz 27, Trieste* ☎ *040/6754350* ⊕ *museorevoltella.it* ☞ *€7* ⊗ *Closed Tues.*

Piazza Unità d'Italia

PLAZA/SQUARE | The imposing square, ringed by grandiose facades, was set out as a plaza open to the sea, like Venice's Piazza San Marco, in the late Middle Ages. It underwent countless changes through the centuries, and its present size and architecture are essentially products of late-19th- and early-20th-century Austria. It was given its current name in 1955, when Trieste was finally given to Italy. On the inland side of the piazza, note the facade of the **Palazzo Comunale** (Town Hall), designed by the Triestino architect Giuseppe Bruni in 1875. It was from this building's balcony in 1938 that Mussolini proclaimed the infamous racial laws, depriving Italian Jews of most of their rights. The sidewalk cafés on this vast seaside piazza are popular meeting places in the summer months. ⌖ *Piazza Unità d'Italia, Trieste.*

Risiera di San Sabba

HISTORIC SIGHT | In September 1943 the Nazi occupation established Italy's only concentration camp in this rice-processing factory outside Trieste. In April 1944 a crematorium was put into operation. The Nazis destroyed much of the evidence of their atrocities before their retreat, but a good deal of the horror of the place is still perceivable in the reconstructed museum (1975). The site, an Italian national monument since 1965, receives more than 100,000 visitors per year. ⌖ *Via Giovanni Palatucci 5, Trieste* ✛ *Take municipal Bus No. 8 or 10; off the Autostrada A4, take exit Valmaura/Stadio/Cimitero* ☎ *040/826202* ⊕ *www.risierasansabba.it* ☞ *Free.*

San Silvestro

CHURCH | This small Romanesque gem, dating from the 9th to the 12th centuries, is the oldest church in Trieste that's still in use and in approximately its original form. Its interior walls have some fragmentary remains of Romanesque frescoes. The church was deconsecrated under the secularizing reforms of the Austrian emperor Josef II in 1785 and was later sold to the Swiss Evangelical community; it then became, and is still, the Reformed Evangelical and Waldensian Church of Trieste. ⊠ *Piazza San Silvestro 1, Trieste* ☎ *040/632770* ⊕ *triestevangelica.org* ⊠ *Free.*

Teatro Romano

RUINS | The ruins of this 1st-century amphitheater, opposite the city's *questura* (police station), were discovered during 1938 demolition work. Its crumbling and partly grassy steps can be viewed from the street, while its statues are now displayed at the Museo Civico. The space is used for summer plays and concerts. ⊠ *Via del Teatro Romano, Trieste.*

🍴 Restaurants

Al Bagatto

$$$ | SEAFOOD | At this warm and sophisticated seafood place, going strong since 1966 near Piazza Unità d'Italia, you'll find exquisite dishes that honor the traditions of the Mancussi family. Although now run by the Leonardi family, Roberto Mancussi's culinary ethos remains: integrating nouvelle ingredients without overshadowing the freshness of whatever local fish he bought in the market that morning. **Known for:** freshest seafood beautifully prepared; more than 300 wine labels and spirits; novel culinary experience. ⑤ *Average main: €31* ⊠ *Via Luigi Cadorna 7, Trieste* ☎ *040/301771* ⊕ *www. albagatto.it* ⊗ *Closed Sun. No lunch Mon.*

Buffet da Siora Rosa

$$ | NORTHERN ITALIAN | FAMILY | Serving delicious and generous portions of traditional Triestino buffet fare, such as boiled pork and sausages with savory sauerkraut, Siora Rosa is a bit more comfortable than many buffets. In addition to ample seating in the simple dining room, there are tables outside for when the weather is good. **Known for:** well-loved Trieste institution (opened 1921); chatty locals speaking in dialect; meat dishes galore. ⑤ *Average main: €19* ⊠ *Piazza Hortis 3, Trieste* ☎ *040/301460* ⊕ *www.facebook.com/buffetdasiorarosa* ⊗ *Closed Sun. and Mon.*

★ Suban

$$$ | NORTHERN ITALIAN | An easy trip just outside town, this landmark trattoria—serving Triestino food with Slovene, Hungarian, and Austrian accents—has been in business since 1865. Sit by the dining room fire or relax on a huge terrace with a pergola, watching the sun set as you tuck into rich soups and roasts spiced with rosemary, thyme, and sweet paprika. **Known for:** meat dishes with Mitteleuropean influences; jota carsolina (a rich soup of cabbage, potatoes, and beans); warm hospitality. ⑤ *Average main: €25* ⊠ *Via Comici 2, Trieste* ⊹ *Take Bus No. 35 from Piazza Oberdan* ☎ *040/54368* ⊕ *www.suban.it* ⊗ *Closed Tues. and 2 wks in early Jan.*

★ Trattoria Nerodiseppia

$$ | NORTHERN ITALIAN | For over a decade the Cusma family have been serving Triestini regulars beautifully crafted seafood, alongside a few seasonal meat and vegetarian dishes. Dining in warm, modern interiors under the arches of a refurbished storehouse, choose from Giulio's exquisite but small seafood plates like fish carpaccio, spaghetti *con bottarga e tonno* (cured fish roe and tuna), and fritto misto (fried seafood medley). **Known for:** compact, seasonal menu; Friuli, Carso DOC, and Croatian wines; especially fab seafood starters, mains, and desserts. ⑤ *Average main: €23* ⊠ *Via Luigi Cadorna 23, Trieste* ☎ *040/301377* ⊕ *trattorianerodiseppia.com* ⊗ *Closed Sun. and Mon.*

☕ Coffee and Quick Bites

Da Pepi

$ | **NORTHERN ITALIAN** | A Triestino institution, this is the oldest and most esteemed of the many "buffet" restaurants serving pork and sausages around town, with a wood-paneled interior and seating outside. It specializes in *bollito di maiale,* a dish of boiled pork and pork sausages accompanied by delicately flavored sauerkraut, mustard, and grated horseradish. **Known for:** porky platter La Caldaia Da Pepi; panino porzina (pork shoulder with mustard and kren [horseradish]); good for a snack on the hoof. $ *Average main: €14* ⊠ *Via Cassa di Risparmio 3, Trieste* ☎ *040/366858* ⊕ *www.buffetdapepi.it* ⊘ *Closed Sun. and last 2 wks in July.*

Hotels

★ Duchi d'Aosta

$$$$ | **HOTEL** | Bang smack in regal Piazza Unità d'Italia, this grande dame of a hotel is beautifully furnished in Venetian Renaissance style, with dark-wood antiques, rich carpets, and plush fabrics. **Pros:** lots of charm paired with modern convenience; outstanding indoor pool and spa on grand scale; excellent breakfast. **Cons:** rooms overlooking the piazza can be very expensive; restaurant overpriced; expensive and inconvenient parking. $ *Rooms from: €320* ⊠ *Piazza Unità d'Italia 2/1, Trieste* ☎ *040/7600011* ⊕ *duchidaosta.com* ⊃ *55 rooms* ⦿ *Free Breakfast.*

★ Hotel Riviera & Maximilian's

$$$ | **HOTEL** | Set on gorgeous, verdant grounds with stunning sea views, this cliff-top hotel—a villa with a modern annex—offers a mix of traditional and minimalist rooms, many with private balconies. **Pros:** superb views of the Golfo di Trieste; area for swimming in sea; Exentia spa facilities. **Cons:** far from town; rooms on the small side; set on a busy road. $ *Rooms from: €235* ⊠ *Strada Costiera 22, Trieste* ⊹ *7 km (4½ miles) north of Trieste* ☎ *040/224551* ⊕ *www.hotelrivieraemaximilian.com* ⊃ *67 rooms* ⦿ *Free Breakfast.*

★ L'Albero Nascosto Hotel Residence

$$$ | **B&B/INN** | There's plenty of architectural character mixed with contemporary, artsy warmth in the guest rooms of this central, 18th-century building, while the nearby annex offers four spacious apartments. **Pros:** very central; spacious and simple but tasteful rooms; friendly, knowledgeable hosts. **Cons:** no elevator; street noise can be a problem (if noise sensitive, ask for a room in the back); tricky parking nearby. $ *Rooms from: €210* ⊠ *Via Felice Venezian 18, Trieste* ☎ *040/300188* ⊕ *www.alberonascosto.it* ⊃ *10 rooms* ⦿ *Free Breakfast.*

Victoria Hotel Letterario

$$ | **HOTEL** | The former home of James Joyce is a real gem of a hotel—with stylish, unfussy traditional decor and a just-out-of-town location that's convenient for both local sightseeing and trips into the Karst mountains. **Pros:** large, pleasant, light-filled rooms; excellent two-bedroom apartments for longer stays; wellness center and spa. **Cons:** parking fee; a bit removed and a stroll into town; some rooms suffer from traffic noise. $ *Rooms from: €171* ⊠ *Alfredo Oriani 2, Trieste* ☎ *040/362415* ⊕ *www.hotelvictoriatrieste.com* ⊃ *44 rooms* ⦿ *No Meals.*

❢ Nightlife

Trieste is justly famous for its coffee. The elegant civility of Trieste plays out beautifully in a café culture combining the refinement of Vienna with the passion of Italy. In Trieste, as elsewhere in Italy, ask for a caffè and you'll get a thimbleful of high-octane espresso. Your cappuccino here will come in the Viennese fashion, with a dollop of whipped cream. Many cafés are part of a *torrefazione* (roasting shop), so you can sample a cup and then buy beans to take with you.

★ Antico Caffè San Marco

GATHERING PLACE | Few cafés in Italy can rival Antico Caffè San Marco for its historic and cultured atmosphere. Founded in 1914, it was largely destroyed in World War I and rebuilt in the 1920s, then restored several more times, but some of the original art nouveau interior remains. It became a meeting place for local intellectuals and was the haunt of the Triestino writers Italo Svevo and Umberto Saba: the wonderful bookshop hosts literary events. It remains open until 11:45 pm on Friday and Saturday, and light meals are available. ✉ *Via Battisti 18, Trieste* ☎ *040/2035357* ⊕ *www.caffesanmarco.com.*

Caffè degli Specchi

GATHERING PLACE | For a great view of the great piazza, you can't do better than this café, whose many mirrors make for engaging people-watching. Originally opened in 1839, it was taken over by the British navy after World War II, and Triestini were not allowed in unless accompanied by someone British. Because of its location, the café—which stays open late—is heavily frequented by tourists. It's now owned by the Segafredo Zanetti coffee company, and some feel it has lost its local character. ✉ *Piazza Unità d'Italia 7, Trieste* ☎ *040/661973* ⊕ *www.caffespecchi.it.*

Caffè Tommaseo

GATHERING PLACE | Founded in 1830, this classic café is a comfortable place to linger, especially on weekend evenings and at lunchtime on Sunday, when there's live music. Although you can still have just a coffee, Tommaseo has evolved into a restaurant, with an extensive menu. It's open nightly until 10:30. ✉ *Piazza Tommaseo 4/C, Trieste* ☎ *040/362666* ⊕ *www.caffetommaseo.it.*

Performing Arts

Teatro Verdi

OPERA | Trieste's main opera house, built under Austrian rule in 1801, is of interest to aficionados of fine architecture as well as music lovers. Gian Antonio Selva, the architect of Venice's Teatro La Fenice, designed the interior, and Matteo Pertsch, responsible for Milan's Teatro alla Scala, designed the facade. You'll have to attend a performance to view Teatro Verdi's interior; guided tours aren't conducted for individuals. ■ **TIP→ Opera season runs from October through May, with a brief operetta festival in July and August.** ✉ *Piazza Verdi 1, Trieste* ☎ *040/6722298* ⊕ *www.teatroverdi-trieste.com.*

Shopping

Katastrofa

ANTIQUES & COLLECTIBLES | Head to this bonkers emporium for an entertaining and eye-popping perusal of 20th-century antiques and ephemera, from vintage stereo equipment and funky furniture to quirky artworks and designer handbags. ✉ *Via Armando Diaz 4, Trieste* ☎ *338/2272351 mobile* ⊕ *www.facebook.com/KatastrofaTrieste.*

Rigatteria

ANTIQUES & COLLECTIBLES | Opened in 1981, the fascinating Rigatteria is crammed with antiques, paintings, and a cornucopia of printed matter, including books, newspapers, and magazines, many documenting Triestina life over the decades. ✉ *Via Malcanton 12, Trieste* ☎ *040/630866* ⊕ *www.rigatteria.com.*

Chapter 7

THE DOLOMITES

Updated by
Liz Humphreys

⊙ Sights	🍴 Restaurants	🛏 Hotels	🛍 Shopping	🍸 Nightlife
★★★★☆	★★★★☆	★★★★☆	★☆☆☆☆	★★☆☆☆

WELCOME TO THE DOLOMITES

TOP REASONS TO GO

★ **Driving in the Dolomites:** Your Fiat rental will think it's a Ferrari on a gorgeous drive through the heart of the Dolomites.

★ **Hiking:** No matter your fitness level, there's an unforgettable walk in store for you here.

★ **Skiing:** The Dolomites are renowned as one of Europe's top locations for winter sports, and will cohost the 2026 Winter Olympics along with Milan.

★ **Museo Archeologico dell'Alto Adige, Bolzano:** The impossibly well-preserved body of the iceman Ötzi, the star attraction at this museum, provokes countless questions about what life was like 5,000 years ago.

★ **Trento:** A graceful fusion of Austrian and Italian styles, this breezy frescoed town is famed for its imposing castle.

1 Trento. Piazza del Duomo is a highlight.

2 Rovereto. Enjoy the medieval center.

3 Madonna di Campiglio. A favorite for skiers and hikers.

4 Bolzano (Bozen). High-gabled houses are hallmarks.

5 Bormio. History, ski trails, and spa treatments.

6 Merano (Meran). Come here for the thermal waters.

7 Naturno (Naturns). Known for its hiking trails and castle museum.

8 Caldaro (Kaltern). The Strada del Vino runs through this wine town.

9 Bressanone (Brixen). The castle is a big draw.

10 Brunico (Bruneck). Don't miss the medieval quarter.

11 Misurina. The Three Peaks views are lovely.

12 Canazei. Come for the hiking and skiing.

13 Ortisei (St. Ulrich). Woodcarving workshops dot this town.

14 Corvara. Known for skiing and fine hotels.

15 Cortina d'Ampezzo. This ski resort has lots of summer activities.

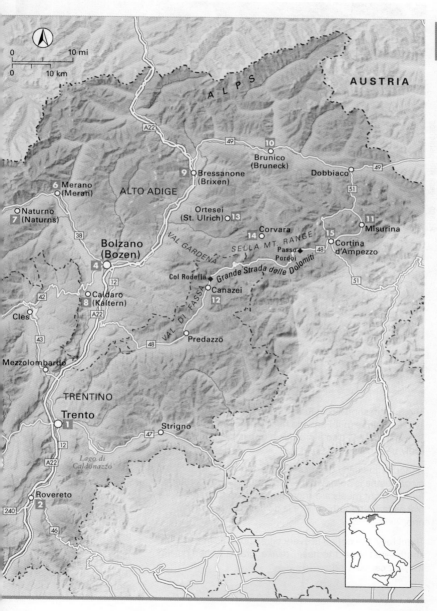

0   10 mi
0   10 km

A L P S

AUSTRIA

A22

49

10 Brunico
(Bruneck)

Dobbiaco

9 Bressanone
(Brixen)

49

51

6 Merano
(Meran)

ALTO ADIGE

7 Naturno
(Naturns)

Ortesei
(St. Ulrich) **13**

11 Misurina

38

Corvara

14

SELLA MT. RANGE

15

Cortina
d'Ampezzo

VAL GARDENA

Bolzano
(Bozen)

Passo
Pordoi

48

4

12

Col Rodella Grande Strada delle Dolomiti

8 Caldaro
(Kaltern)

Canazei

12

51

42

A22

VAL DI FASSA

Cles

43

48

Predazzo

Mezzolombardo

TRENTINO

Trento **1**

Strigno

47

12

Lago di
Caldonazzo

A22

Rovereto

2

240

46

EATING AND DRINKING WELL IN THE DOLOMITES

Asiago cheese with pistachios

Everything in Alto Adige (and, to a lesser extent, Trentino) has more than a tinge of the Teutonic—and food is no exception. The rich and creamy cuisine here, including fondue, polenta, and barley soup, reflects the Alpine climate and Austrian and Swiss influences.

The quintessential restaurant is the wood-paneled Tyrolean *stube* (pub) serving hearty meat-and-dumpling fare, and there's also a profusion of pastry shops and lively beer halls.

Although the early dining schedule you'll find in Germany or Austria is somewhat tempered here, your options for late-night meals are more limited than they are in places farther south, where la dolce vita has a firmer grip.

Thankfully, the coffee is every bit as good as in parts south—just expect to hear "*danke, grazie*" when paying for your cappuccino.

BEST OF THE WURST

Not to be missed are the outdoor wurst carts. After placing your order you'll get a sheet of wax paper, followed by a dollop of mustard, a kaiser roll, and your chosen sausage. You can sometimes make your selection by pointing to whatever picture is most appealing; if not, pass on the familiar-sounding Frankfurter and try the local Merane. Carts can reliably be found in Bolzano (try Piazza delle Erbe, or in front of the archaeological museum) and Merano (Piazza del Grano, or along the river).

POLENTA AND DUMPLINGS

Polenta is a staple in the region, in both creamy and firm renditions, often topped with cheese or mushrooms (or both). Dumplings also appear on many menus; the most distinctive to the region are *canederli* (also known as Knödel) made from seasoned bread in many variations, and served either in broth or with a sauce. Other dumplings to look for are the dense *strangolapreti* (literally, "priest-chokers") and *gnocchi di ricotta alla zucca* (ricotta and pumpkin dumplings).

Polenta with porcini mushrooms

CHEESE

Every isolated mountain valley in Trentino–Alto Adige seems to make its own variety of cheese, and the local specialty is often simply called *nostrano* (ours). The best known of them are the mild Asiago and *fontal,* as well as the more pungent *puzzone di Moena* (literally, "stinkpot"). Also try the *schiz*: fresh cheese that's sliced and fried in butter.

PASTRIES AND BAKED GOODS

Bakeries turn out a wide selection of crusty dark rolls and caraway-studded rye breads—maybe not typical Italian bread, but full of flavor. Pastries here are reminiscent of what you'd find in Vienna. Apple strudel is everywhere, and for good reason: the best apples

Apple strudel

in Italy are grown here. There are other exceptional fruits as well, including pears, plums, and grapes, which make their way into baked goods.

ALIMENTARI

If you're planning a picnic or getting provisions for a hike, you'll be well served by the fine *alimentari* (food shops) of Trentino and Alto Adige. They stock a bounty of regional specialties, including cheeses, pickles, salami, and smoked meats. These are good places to pick up a sample of *speck tirolese*, the salt-cured, cold-smoked deboned ham hock usually cut in paper-thin slices like prosciutto (though proud speck producers often bristle at the comparison).

WINE

Although Trentino and Alto Adige aren't as esteemed for their wines as many other Italian regions, they produce a wide variety of crisp, dry, and aromatic whites—Kerner, Müller-Thurgau, and Traminer, to name a few—not surprisingly, more like what you'd expect from German vineyards than Italian. Among the reds, look for *lagrein* and the native *teroldego,* a fruity, spicy variety produced only in the tiny valley north of Trento. The Trento D.O.C. appellation yields a marvelous sparkling wine in a class with Champagne.

The Dolomites, those inimitable craggy peaks Le Corbusier called "the most beautiful work of architecture ever seen," are never so arresting as at dusk, when the last rays of sun create a pink hue that languishes into purple—a magnificent transformation locals call the *enrosadira*. You can certainly enjoy this glow from a distance, but the Dolomites are such an appealing year-round destination precisely because of the many ways to get into the mountains themselves. And once there, in short order your perspective—like the peaks around you—will take on a rosy hue.

The Dolomites are strange, rocky pinnacles that jut straight up like chimneys; they are, in fact, the otherworldly pinnacles that Leonardo depicted in the background of his *Mona Lisa*. In spite of this incredible beauty, the vast mountainous domain of northeastern Italy has remained relatively undeveloped. Below the peaks, rivers meander through valleys dotted with peaceful villages, while pristine lakes are protected by picture-book castles. In the most secluded Dolomite vales, unique cultures have flourished: the Ladin language, an offshoot of Latin still spoken in the Val Gardena and Val di Fassa, owes its unlikely survival to centuries of topographic isolation.

The more accessible parts of Trentino–Alto Adige, on the other hand, have a history of near-constant intermingling of cultures. The region's Adige and Isarco Valleys make up the main access route between Italy and Central Europe, and as a result, the language, cuisine, and architecture are a blend of north and south. The province of Trentino is largely Italian-speaking, but Alto Adige is predominantly Germanic: until World War I the area was Austria's Südtirol. As you move north toward the famed Brenner Pass—through the prosperous valley towns of Rovereto, Trento, and Bolzano—the Teutonic influence is increasingly dominant; by the time you reach Bressanone, it's hard to believe you're in Italy at all.

MAJOR REGIONS

Trentino. Until the end of World War I, the Trentino–Alto Adige/Südtirol region was part of Austria-Hungary. Although today the province of Trentino remains unmistakably Italian, Germanic influences are palpable in its architecture, cuisine, culture, and language. Visitors are drawn by the historical sites and cosmopolitan nature of Trento, while numerous year-round mountain resorts, like the fashionable Madonna di Campiglio, can be found in the wings of this butterfly-shape region. Culture-hounds will want to visit Rovereto, a town just south of Trento known for its fine contemporary art museum.

Bolzano. With castles and steeples topping the landscape, this quiet city at the confluence of the Isarco (Eisack) and Talvera Rivers has retained its provincial appeal. Proximity to fabulous skiing and mountain climbing—not to mention the world's oldest preserved human body—make it a very worthwhile destination. And its streets are immaculate: after Milan, residents here have the highest per capita earnings of any city in Italy.

The Western Dolomites. The Parco Nazionale dello Stelvio extends through western Trentino and the Altoatesino area of Alto Adige and beyond into eastern Lombardy. It's named for the famed Stelvio, Europe's highest road pass and site of the highest battle fought during World War I (also to ski slopes where the 2026 Winter Olympics downhill skiing competitions will take place). Even if you don't want to ski its trails or indulge in one of its renowned spa treatments, the well-preserved town of Bormio still merits a visit for its history and character.

Alto Adige. In the province of Alto Adige (Südtirol/South Tyrol), Germanic and Italian culture balance harmoniously, as do medieval and modern influences, with ancient castles regularly hosting contemporary art exhibitions. Prosperous valley towns, such as the famed spa center of Merano, the medieval town of Bressanone, and the wine village of Caldaro, entice those seeking both relaxation and the finer pleasures.

The Heart of the Dolomites. This area between Bolzano and the mountain resort Cortina d'Ampezzo—home to many 2026 Winter Olympics events—is dominated by two major valleys, Val di Fassa and Val Gardena. Both share the spectacular panorama of the Sella mountain range. Along the scenic Grande Strada delle Dolomiti (Great Dolomites Road), you'll find Canazei, Ortisei, and Corvara, resort towns with skiing and hiking galore. The Tre Cime (Three Peaks), the best-known symbol of the Dolomites, are visible from the lakeside town of Misurina and worth a gander if not a hike.

Planning

Getting Here and Around

BUS

Regular bus service connects larger cities to the south (Verona, Venice, and Milan) with valley towns in Trentino–Alto Adige (Rovereto, Trento, Bolzano, and Merano). You'll need to change to less frequent local buses to reach resorts and smaller villages in the mountains beyond.

If you're equipped with current schedules and don't mind adapting your schedules to theirs, it's possible to visit even the remotest villages by bus. ATVO, Cortina-Express, and FlixBus provide year-round service to Cortina from Venice airport and Mestre train station daily. FlixBus also connects Venice directly with Bolzano and Trento. DolomitiBus covers the eastern Dolomites, including a number of small towns. SAD provides service from Bolzano and Bressanone. Trentino Trasporti offers buses within Trento and Rovereto. Südtirolmobil provides further information on local services.

BUS CONTACTS ATVO. ☎ *0421/5944* ⊕ *www.atvo.it.* **CortinaExpress.** ☎ *0436/867350* ⊕ *www.cortinaexpress. it.* **DolomitiBus.** ☎ *0437/217111* ⊕ *www. dolomitibus.it.* **FlixBus.** ☎ *0294/759208 within italy* ⊕ *www.flixbus.com.* **SAD.** ✉ *Bolzano* ☎ *0471/450111* ⊕ *www.sad. it.* **südtirolmobil.** ☎ *0471/220880* ⊕ *www. suedtirolmobil.info.* **Trentino Trasporti.** ☎ *0461/821000* ⊕ *www.trentinotrasporti. it.*

CAR

Driving is easily the most convenient way to travel in the Dolomites; it can be difficult to reach the ski areas (or any town outside of Rovereto, Trento, Bolzano, or Merano) without a car. Driving is also the most exhilarating way to get around, as you rise from broad valleys into mountains with narrow, winding roads straight out of a sports-car ad. The most important route in the region is the A22 autostrada, the main north–south highway linking Italy with Central Europe by way of the Brenner Pass. It connects Innsbruck with Bressanone, Bolzano, Trento, and Rovereto, and near Verona joins the A4, which runs east–west across northern Italy, from Trieste to Turin. By car, Trento is 3 hours from Milan and 2½ hours from Venice. Bolzano is another 45-minute drive to the north, with Munich 4 hours farther on.

Caution is essential (tap your horn in advance of hairpin turns), as are chains in winter, when roads are often covered in snow. Sudden closures are common, especially on high mountain passes, and can occur as early as September and as late as May. Even under the best conditions, expect to negotiate mountain roads at speeds no greater than 50 kph (30 mph).

TRAIN

The rail line following the course of the Isarco and Adige Valleys—from Munich and Innsbruck, through the Brenner Pass, and southward past Bressanone, Bolzano, Trento, and Rovereto en route to Verona—is well trafficked, making trains

a viable option for travel between these towns. Eurocity trains on the Dortmund–Venice and Munich–Innsbruck–Rome routes stop at these stations, and you can connect with other Italian lines at Verona. Although branch lines from Trento and Bolzano do extend into some of the smaller valleys (including hourly service between Bolzano and Merano), most mountain attractions are beyond the reach of trains.

TRAIN CONTACTS Italo. ☎ *892020 call center* ⊕ *www.italotreno.it.* **Trenitalia.** ☎ *892021 within Italy* ⊕ *www.trenitalia. com.*

Making the Most of Your Time

For a brief stay, your best choice for a base is vibrant Bolzano, where you can get a sense of the region's contrasts— Italian and German, medieval and modern. After a day or two in town, venture an hour south to history-laden Trento, north to the lovely spa town of Merano, or southwest to Caldaro and its Strada di Vino; all are viable day trips from Bolzano, and Trento and Merano make good places to spend the night as well.

If you have more time, you'll want to get up into the mountains, which are the region's main attraction. The trip on the Grande Strada delle Dolomiti through the Heart of the Dolomites from Bolzano to Cortina d'Ampezzo is one of Italy's most spectacular drives. Summer or winter, this is a great destination for mountain sports, with scores of trails for world-class hiking and skiing.

Be sure to look into the Südtirol Museumobil Card when planning your visit. Besides entry to 90 museums, the card allows you free use of the regional train system from Brennero to Trento, and the use of all public buses in Alto Adige (Südtirol/South Tyrol). The card is available for three days (€55) or seven days (€65). The Museumobil Card can be purchased at train stations, tourist offices, and some museums (⊕ *www.suedtirolmobil.info*). The Brixen Card (free with paid lodging in Bressanone) offers free transportation throughout Trentino and Alto Adige (Südtirol/South Tyrol) and entrance to nearly 90 museums, plus free gondola rides and discounts at partner venues. See ⊕ *www.brixen.org* for a list of participating hotels and bed-and-breakfasts.

Detailed information about *vie ferrate* (mountain paths with steel cables and fixed anchors and ladders) in the eastern Dolomites can be found at ⊕ *www. dolomiti.org*. Capable tour organizers include the Scuola di Alpinismo (Mountaineering School) in Madonna di Campiglio (☎ *0465/442634* ⊕ *www. guidealpinecampiglio.it*) and in Cortina d'Ampezzo (☎ *0436/868505* ⊕ *www. guidecortina.com*).

Restaurants

When dining out in the Dolomites, it's evident you are in a region of Italy that was once part of Austria-Hungary. Although you can still find traditional Italian pasta and pizza, there's a considerable amount of Austro-Germanic flair. Sausages, spaetzle, meats, cheeses, and polenta—foods that will sustain the body through a long day of skiing or hiking—can be found on nearly every menu, although you'll also find more contemporary restaurants using seasonal ingredients in a lighter style. Many restaurants either raise their own crops and livestock or have a direct relationship with their farmers and providers.

Hotels

Classic Dolomite lodging includes restored castles, chalets, and stately 19th-century hotels. The small villages that pepper the Dolomites often have

scores of flower-bedecked inns, many of them inexpensive. Hotel information offices at train stations and tourist offices can help if you've arrived without reservations. The Bolzano train station has a 24-hour hotel service, and tourist offices will give you a list of all the hotels in the area, arranged by location, stars, and price. Hotels at ski resorts cater to longer stays at full or half board. Many Italians come to the Dolomites every winter for their Settimana Bianca (White Week), and if you care to join them you should book ski vacations as packages well in advance. Most rural accommodations close from early November to mid- or late December, as well as for two months or so after Easter. The majority of *rifugi* (mountain huts) on hiking trails are operated by the Club Alpino Italiano (⊕ *www.cai.it*). Contact information for both CAI-run and private rifugi is available from local tourist offices; most useful are those in Madonna di Campiglio (⊕ *www. campigliodolomiti.it*), Cortina d'Ampezzo (⊕ *www.dolomiti.org*), Val di Fassa (⊕ *www.fassa.com*), and Val Gardena (⊕ *www.val-gardena.com*).

⇨ *Hotel and restaurant reviews have been shortened. For full information, visit Fodors.com. Prices in the hotel reviews are the lowest cost of a standard double room in high season. Prices in the dining reviews are the average cost of a main course at dinner, or, if dinner is not served, at lunch.*

What It Costs in Euros			
$	$$	$$$	$$$$
RESTAURANTS			
under €15	€15–€24	€25–€35	over €35
HOTELS			
under €125	€125–€200	€201–€300	over €300

Trento

58 km (36 miles) south of Bolzano.

Trento is a prosperous, cosmopolitan university town that retains an architectural charm befitting its historical importance. It was here, from 1545 to 1563, that the structure of the Catholic Church was redefined at the Council of Trent, the starting point of the Counter-Reformation, which brought half of Europe back to Catholicism. Today, the word *consiglio* (council) appears everywhere in Trento—in hotel, restaurant, and street names, and even on wine labels. The Piazza del Duomo remains splendid, and its enormous medieval palazzo dominates the city landscape in virtually its original form.

The 24-hour Trentino Card (⊕ *www.trento.info/en/trentino-guest-card*) is given free (via email or text) to hotel guests, and grants free or discounted admission to museums as well as all public transportation. Non–hotel guests can make use of the 48-hour Museum Pass (€22), which allows unlimited access to all museums and castles in Trento and Rovereto as well as free public transportation in Trentino. It can be bought online (⊕ *www.trento.info/en/museum-pass*), at tourist offices, or at participating museums, and can even be converted into a three-month card for no extra charge.

GETTING HERE AND AROUND

The A22 autostrada is the main highway to Trento. From the north, take the Trento Nord exit; from the south, take the Trento Sud exit. There are signs directing you to the city center. Trento is easily accessible from Venice (2½ hours) and Verona (just over an hour), and is only 4½ hours from Munich. The city center is pedestrian-friendly, or you can use the transit options in conjunction with the Trentino Card for discounts on the city buses.

TOURS

Guided Tours of Trento

GUIDED TOURS | FAMILY | Two-hour guided tours of Trento's city center depart from the tourist office on Saturday at 10 am, in Italian and English. Reserve your place on the tour by 2 pm the day before by email or online. ⊠ *Piazza Dante 24, Trento* ☎ *0461/216000* ⊕ *www.trento.info/en* ☞ *€10, €8 with Trento Card.*

VISITOR INFORMATION

CONTACT Trento Tourism Office. ⊠ *Piazza Dante 24, Trento* ☎ *0461/216000* ⊕ *www.trento.info/en.*

Sights

Belvedere di Sardagna

VIEWPOINT | FAMILY | Take the Funivia Trento–Sardagna cable car up to the Belvedere di Sardagna, a lookout point 1,200 feet above medieval Trento. ■**TIP→ This is open year-round but can close due to inclement weather.** ⊠ *Via Monte Grappa 1, Trento* ☎ *0461/031000* ⊕ *www.trentinotrasporti.it* ☞ *€5 round-trip.*

★ **Castello del Buonconsiglio** (*Castle of Good Counsel*)

CASTLE/PALACE | FAMILY | The position and size of this stronghold of the prince-bishops made it easier to defend than the Palazzo Pretorio. Look for the evolution of architectural styles: the medieval fortifications of the Castelvecchio section (on the far left) were built in the 13th century; the fancier Renaissance Magno Palazzo section (on the far right) wasn't completed until 300 years later. The 13th-century **Torre dell'Aquila** (Eagle's Tower) is home to the castle's artistic highlight, a 15th-century *ciclo dei mesi* (cycle of the months). The four-wall fresco is full of charming and detailed scenes of medieval life in both court and countryside. ⊠ *Via Bernardo Clesio 5, Trento* ☎ *0461/233770* ⊕ *www.buonconsiglio.it* ☞ *€10; Torre Aquila €2.50* ⊗ *Closed Mon.* ⚎ *Timed visits must be booked online in advance.*

Trentino and the Western Dolomites

Duomo (*Cattedrale di San Vigilio*)

CHURCH | This massive Romanesque church, also known as the Cathedral of San Vigilio (St. Vigilius), forms the southern edge of the Piazza del Duomo. Locals refer to this square as the city's *salotto* (sitting room), as in fine weather it's always filled with students and residents drinking coffee, sipping an aperitif, or reading the newspaper. The Baroque Fontana del Nettuno presides over it all. When skies are clear, pause here to savor the view of the mountaintops enveloping the city.

Within the Duomo, unusual arcaded stone stairways border the austere nave. Ahead is the *baldacchino* (altar canopy), a copy of Bernini's masterpiece in St. Peter's in Rome. To the left of the altar is a mournful 16th-century crucifixion, flanked by the Virgin Mary and John the Apostle. This crucifix, by German artist Sisto Frey, was a focal point of the Council of Trent: each decree agreed on during the two decades of deliberations was solemnly read out in front of it. Stairs on the left side of the altar lead down to the 4th-century Paleo-Christian burial vault (Early Christian Basilica). Outside, check out the bronze scale model of the city on the south side of the cathedral, then walk around to the back to see an exquisite display of 14th-century stone-mason artistry, from the small porch to the intriguing knotted columns on the graceful apse. ✉ *Piazza del Duomo, Trento* ☎ *0461/231293* ⊕ *www.cattedralesan-vigilio.it* ⭐ *Free. Early Christian Basilica €3* ⊗ *Early Christian Basilica closed Sun. morning and Tues.*

★ **MUSE – Museo delle Scienze di Trento**
(*Science Museum of Trento*)
SCIENCE MUSEUM | FAMILY | Extending over
six floors, in a 41,000-foot space, this
interactive science museum, designed
by Renzo Piano, encourages families of
all ages to explore science and nature. As
befits the region, mountain imagery plays
a big part in the displays and is used to
investigate the Dolomites' history and
even life on Earth. There's also a sensory
experience room for younger kids up
to five years old. ⊠ *Corso del Lavoro e
della Scienza 3, Trento* ☎ *0461/270311*
⊕ *www.muse.it* 🎫 *€12* ⊘ *Closed Mon.*

Museo Diocesano Tridentino

HISTORY MUSEUM | Located inside the
Palazzo Pretorio, the Museo Diocesano
Tridentino is where you can see paintings
and other objects that come from the
treasury of the adjoining Cathedral of
San Vigilio. This includes many carved
wood altars and statues; an 11th-century
sacramentary, or book of services; the
seating plan of the prelates during the
Council of Trent; and early-16th-century
tapestries by Pieter van Aelst (1502–56),
the Belgian artist who carried out Raphael's 15th-century designs for the Vatican
tapestries. The palazzo itself was built in
the 13th century and designed to seem
like a wing of the Duomo; it became the
fortified residence of the prince-bishops,
who enjoyed considerable power and
autonomy within the medieval hierarchy. The remarkable palazzo has lost
none of its original splendor. Accessible
through the museum, a subterranean
archaeological area beneath the adjacent
cathedral reveals remnants of the Early
Christian Basilica of San Vigilio. ⊠ *Piazza
del Duomo 18, Trento* ☎ *0461/234419*
⊕ *www.museodiocesanotridentino.it*
🎫 *€7, includes entrance to Early Christian
Basilica* ⊘ *Closed Tues.* ⚲ *Recommended to purchase tickets online in advance.*

**Tridentum — Spazio Archeologico Sotterra-
neo del Sas** (*S.A.S.S.*)
RUINS | FAMILY | The ancient Roman
city of Tridentum lies beneath much of
Trento's city center. Centuries of Adige
River flooding buried ruins that only
recently have been unearthed on public
and private land. Beneath this piazza lies
the largest of the archaeological sites,
which reveals some marvels of Roman
technology, such as underfloor heating
and subterranean sewers complete
with manhole covers. The Romans
also used lead pipes for four centuries
before recognizing it was hazardous to
health. ⊠ *Piazza Cesare Battisti, Trento*
☎ *0461/230171* ⊕ *www.cultura.trentino.it*
🎫 *€2.50* ⊘ *Closed Mon.*

Via Belenzani

STREET | Locals refer to this street as
Trento's outdoor gallery because of the
frescoed facades of the hallmark Renaissance palazzi. It's an easy 50-yard walk
up the lane behind the church of Santa
Maria Maggiore. ⊠ *Via Belenzani, Trento.*

🍴 Restaurants

★ Locanda Margon

$$$$ | MODERN ITALIAN | Inside an elegant
country house perched atop a steep hill
and set amongst the vineyards, about
a 10-minute drive south of Trento's
center, talented chef Edoardo Fumagalli
creates thoroughly modern cuisine that
pairs perfectly with the Lunelli family's
sparkling Ferrari wines. Choose from
three tasting menus, which feature local
ingredients such as Garda lemons, ricotta
from the surrounding farm, and Dolomite
trout roe; for lighter appetites, the more
casual bistro next door offers á la carte
dishes. **Known for:** panoramic vineyard
vistas; liberal use of ingredients from
the surrounding area; beautifully plated
dishes. ⑤ *Average main: €145* ⊠ *Via
Margone di Ravina 15, Trento* ✛ *5½ km
(3½ miles) south of Trento city center*
☎ *0461/349401* ⊕ *locandamargon.it*
⊘ *Closed Tues. No dinner Mon.*

Osteria a Le Due Spade

$$ | NORTHERN ITALIAN | What started out as a Tyrolean tavern around the time of the Council of Trent is today an intimate restaurant that adeptly serves superb innovative dishes, using both local and international ingredients. The menu changes throughout the year and offers a choice of a four-course meat, fish, or vegetarian menu (dishes are also available á la carte); decadent additions of fois gras and cheese are also possible. **Known for:** creative fine dining; knowledgeable, welcoming staff; cozy wood-paneled interior. ⑤ *Average main: €23* ⊠ *Via Rizzi 11, Trento* ☎ *0461/234343* ⊕ *www.leduespade. com* ⊗ *Closed Sun. No lunch Mon.*

Ristorante Al Vò

$ | NORTHERN ITALIAN | Trento's oldest trattoria (it's the descendant of a 14th-century tavern) remains one of its most popular lunch spots. Locals crowd into a simple, modern dining room to enjoy regional specialties like gnocchi with vegetables and *baccalà* (salt cod); an impressive (and inexpensive) selection of local wines is available. **Known for:** Trento's oldest eatery; knowledgeable, welcoming staff; fine selection of wines. ⑤ *Average main: €12* ⊠ *Vicolo del Vò 11, Trento* ☎ *0461/985374* ⊕ *www.ristorantealvo.it* ⊗ *Closed Sun. No dinner.*

Scrigno del Duomo

$$ | NORTHERN ITALIAN | More than 30 wines by the glass, accompanied by an excellent selection of local cheeses, are served in this chic eatery, which has outside seating in the piazza. Salads and regional specialties are prepared in the open kitchen by gourmet chefs; the downstairs room features *graffito* (graffiti) murals from local artist Luigi Senesi, while the Roman wall running under the Duomo is also in clear view. **Known for:** traditional food and local wine; fine views of the cathedral; local art and history. ⑤ *Average main: €22* ⊠ *Piazza del Duomo 29, Trento* ☎ *0461/220030* ⊕ *www. scrignodelduomo.com.*

Coffee and Quick Bites

Antica Birreria Pedavena

$ | NORTHERN ITALIAN | FAMILY | Come for the beer—several varieties are brewed in-house and served in this charismatic beer hall—and stay for the meals that include wursts, meat and cheese platters, pizzas, and huge salads. Smaller wood-paneled dining rooms and a summer terrace allow for more peaceful dining. **Known for:** fine selection of brewed-in-house beers; typical Bavarian meats; enormous beer hall. ⑤ *Average main: €14* ⊠ *Piazza di Fiera 13, Trento* ☎ *0461/986255* ⊕ *www.birreriapedavena. com* ⊗ *Closed Tues.*

Hotels

Accademia Hotel Trento

$$ | HOTEL | Stylish, contemporary bedrooms with comfortable beds and handsome lithographs occupy an ancient, character-filled house close to the railway station and Piazza del Duomo. **Pros:** central location; plentiful breakfast buffet; helpful staff. **Cons:** Internet can be iffy; no wellness area (though one room has its own whirlpool tub and sauna); rather basic decor. ⑤ *Rooms from: €141* ⊠ *Vicolo Colico 4, Trento* ☎ *0461/233600* ⊕ *www.accademiahotel.it* ⊗ *Closed 1 wk at Christmas* ⇆ *40 rooms* ⦿ *Free Breakfast.*

Castel Pergine

$$$ | B&B/INN | FAMILY | The stone and brick chambers, prison cells, and chapels in this labyrinthine 13th-century castle (occupied by Trento's prince-bishops in the 16th century) today contain spare, rustic guest rooms with carved-wood trim, lace curtains, and heavy wooden beds—some of them canopied. **Pros:** romantic setting; great restaurant; authentic castle experience. **Cons:** simple accommodations; need a car to get around; bathrooms are very small. ⑤ *Rooms from: €214* ⊠ *Via al Castello 10, Pergine Valsugana* ✛ *11 km (7 miles) east* of Trento ☎ 0461/531158 ⊕ www.castel-pergine.it ⊘ Closed Nov.–Mar. Restaurant closed Wed., bistro closed Tues. ↩ 20 rooms ⦿ No Meals.

Grand Hotel Trento
$$ | HOTEL | This contemporary, rounded facade stands out among the ancient palazzi nearby, but inside you'll find a handsome marble-paved lobby, rich drapery in the restaurant, and ample rooms with clubby wood-trimmed furniture. **Pros:** near train station; professional service; wellness center. **Cons:** busy neighborhood; dated decor; basic bathroom amenities. ⑤ Rooms from: €155 ⊠ Piazza Dante 20, Trento ☎ 0461/271000 ⊕ www.grandhoteltrento.com ↩ 136 rooms ⦿ Free Breakfast.

 Performing Arts

★ **I Suoni delle Dolomiti** (The Sounds of the Dolomites)
FESTIVALS | FAMILY | Held from mid-August to mid-September high in the hills of Trentino, this series of free concerts offers the chance to enjoy chamber music performances amid grassy meadows and mountain views. ⊠ Trento ☎ 0461/219300 ⊕ www.visittrentino.info/en/isuonidelledolomiti ⩾ Free, except for certain concerts.

 Shopping

Enoteca del Corso
FOOD | A bit outside the town center, this atmospheric shop is laden with wines, sweets, and other local products. ⊠ Corso 3 Novembre 64, Trento ☎ 0461/916424.

Lunelli Specialità Trento
FOOD | This specialty food shop boasts an impressive array of sauces, as well as wines, grappas, and liqueurs. A picnic can be handily assembled from a huge assortment of local salamis and cheeses. ⊠ Via Mazzini 46, Trento ☎ 0461/238053 ⊕ www.lunellitrento.it.

Rovereto

24 km (15 miles) south of Trento, 75 km (47 miles) south of Bolzano.

A 15th-century Venetian castle dominates Rovereto's compact medieval centro storico (historic center), with one of Italy's finest contemporary art museums just steps away. ■TIP→ **The Trento Museum Pass also includes entry to sites here in Rovereto.**

GETTING HERE AND AROUND
By car from Trento, take the A22/E45 for 28 km (17 miles) to Rovereto. Frequent trains run from Trento to Rovereto; the journey takes about 13 minutes.

VISITOR INFORMATION
CONTACT Rovereto Tourism Office. ⊠ Corso Rosmini 21, Rovereto ☎ 0464/430363 ⊕ www.visitrovereto.it.

 Sights

Mart Rovereto (Museo di Arte Moderna e Contemporanea di Trento e Rovereto)
ART MUSEUM | Most of the 20,000 works of contemporary and modern art in this collection are from the 20th century. Rotating exhibitions and special events throughout the year highlight still more contemporary art. ⊠ Corso Bettini 43, Rovereto ☎ 0464/438887 ⊕ www.mart.tn.it ⩾ €15 ⊘ Closed Mon.

Museo Storico Italiano della Guerra (Italian Historical War Museum)
HISTORY MUSEUM | This museum was founded after World War I to commemorate the conflict—and to warn against repeating its atrocities. An authoritative exhibition of military artifacts is displayed in the medieval castle perched above Rovereto; the views alone warrant a visit. From May through October you can also see a collection of artillery from the Great War housed in a former air-raid shelter. ⊠ Via Castelbarco 7, Rovereto ☎ 0464/438100 ⊕ www.museodellaguerra.it ⩾ €11 ⊘ Closed Mon.

Hotels

Hotel Rovereto

$ | **HOTEL** | The Zani family runs this modern, centrally located hotel, which has welcoming public spaces, warm-color guest rooms, and one of the city's most appealing restaurants. **Pros:** excellent restaurant; unbeatable location; distinctive decor. **Cons:** some rooms are on the small side; small parking area; design choices, like sinks in some rooms, not to everyone's taste. ⓢ *Rooms from: €119* ✉ *Corso Rosmini 82/D, Rovereto* ☎ *0464/435222* ⊕ *www.hotelrovereto.it* ⏱ *Restaurant closed Sun. No lunch* ⤳ *49 rooms* ❑ *No Meals.*

Madonna di Campiglio

80 km (50 miles) northwest of Trento, 100 km (62 miles) southwest of Bolzano.

The winter resort of Madonna di Campiglio vies with Cortina d'Ampezzo as the most fashionable place for Italians to ski and be seen in the Dolomites. Madonna's popularity is well deserved, with 62 lifts connecting 156 km (97 miles) of well-groomed ski runs and equally good lodging and trekking facilities. The resort itself is a modest 5,000 feet above sea level, but the downhill runs, summer hiking paths, and mountain-biking trails venture high up into the surrounding peaks (including Pietra Grande at 9,700 feet).

GETTING HERE AND AROUND

By car from Trento, take the SS45 toward Vezzano. After Vezzano, continue to the SS237 until Ragoli, and turn onto the SP34. Follow the SP34 for 6 km (4 miles), and turn onto the SS239 for another 23 km (15 miles) until you arrive at Madonna di Campiglio. The more convenient railway station is at Trento; then you can ride the Trentino Trasporti bus for 2½ hours from Trento (four times daily) or take the

FlySki Shuttle during ski season (€19 one-way, €29 round-trip).

VISITOR INFORMATION

CONTACT Madonna di Campiglio Tourism Office. ✉ *Via Pradalago 4, Madonna di Campiglio* ☎ *0465/447501* ⊕ *www.campigliodolomiti.it.*

 Sights

Campo Carlo Magno

VIEWPOINT | The stunning pass at Campo Carlo Magno (5,500 feet) is 3 km (2 miles) north of Madonna di Campiglio. This is where Charlemagne is said to have stopped in AD 800 on his way to Rome to be crowned emperor. You, too, can stop here to gaze upon the whole of northern Italy. If you continue north, take the descent with caution—in the space of a mile or so, hairpin turns and switchbacks deliver you down more than 2,000 feet. ✉ *3 km (2 miles) north of Madonna di Campiglio, Madonna di Campiglio.*

 Restaurants

Cascina Zeledria

$$ | **NORTHERN ITALIAN** | Although most of Madonna's visitors dine at resort hotels, Italians consider an on-mountain meal in a remote, rustic refuge like this one to be an indispensable part of a proper ski week. You can drive or hike up in summer months, but in winter, you ski, snowshoe, or are collected by a Sno-Cat and ferried 10 minutes up the slopes; once there, you'll sit down to grill your own meats and vegetables over stone griddles. **Known for:** authentic experience in a rural mountain setting; house specialty mushrooms and polenta; local wine. ⓢ *Average main: €24* ✉ *Località Zeledria, Madonna di Campiglio* ☎ *0465/440303* ⊕ *www.zeledria.it* ⏱ *Closed May–mid-June and mid-Sept.–Nov.*

Ferrari Spazio Bollicine Nabucco

$$$ | WINE BAR | Although it has a stylish black-and-white color scheme, this restaurant/wine bar nevertheless has the feel of a rustic, intimate chalet. Settle into pleasant surroundings for an après-ski aperitif or a light meal made with local ingredients and paired with the sparkling wines of Ferrari, a well-known Trentino vintner. **Known for:** predinner cocktails; intimate atmosphere; central location. $ *Average main: €30* ✉ *Piazza Righi B3, Madonna di Campiglio* ☎ *0465/440756* ⊕ *www.ferraritrento.com* ⊘ *Closed May–Nov.*

 ## Hotels

Hotel Casa del Campo

$$$ | HOTEL | Just yards from both the downhill slopes and the *ski-fon-do* (cross-country skiing) paths, this charming, Tyrolean-style hotel has an on-site restaurant as well as spacious guest rooms, complete with orthopedic mattresses, soaking tubs, regional wood-and-fabric decor, and tremendous views. **Pros:** good-size rooms; great location for outdoor activities year-round; sheltered parking. **Cons:** dated furnishings; small TVs; thin pillows. $ *Rooms from: €216* ✉ *Passo Campo Carlo Magno, Madonna di Campiglio* ☎ *0465/443130* ⊕ *www.casadelcampo.it* ⤴ *15 rooms* ⦿ *Free Breakfast.*

★ Lefay Resort & SPA Dolomiti

$$$$ | RESORT | FAMILY | Blending beautifully into the mountain landscape, this deluxe lodging just south of Madonna di Campiglio features one of the largest and most impressive spas in the Alps. **Pros:** exceptional breakfast offerings; wonderful spa facilities; gorgeous architectural design. **Cons:** high prices on food and drinks; electric fireplaces in the rooms aren't as charming as real ones (though more sustainable); pools could be more heated in colder seasons. $ *Rooms from: €490* ✉ *Via Alpe di Grual 16, Pinzolo* ✛ *13 km (8 miles) south of Madonna di Campiglio* ☎ *0465/768800* ⊕ *dolomiti.lefayresorts.com* ⤴ *88 rooms* ⦿ *Free Breakfast.*

Savoia Palace Hotel

$$ | HOTEL | At Madonna's most traditional lodging, guest rooms and lounges are full of carved-wood and mountain-style furnishings, and two fireplaces blaze away in the bar, where you can relax while recalling the day's exploits on the ski slopes. **Pros:** central location in town; warm atmosphere; nice, though small, spa. **Cons:** old-fashioned decor; faces a busy street; can be noisy. $ *Rooms from: €148* ✉ *Viale Dolomiti di Brenta 18, Madonna di Campiglio* ☎ *0465/441004* ⊕ *www.savoiapalace.it* ⊘ *Closed mid-Apr.–June and mid-Sept.–Nov.* ⤴ *60 rooms* ⦿ *Free Breakfast.*

TH Madonna di Campiglio Golf Hotel

$$ | HOTEL | FAMILY | You need to make your way north to the Campo Carlo Magno Pass to reach this grand hotel, the former summer residence of Hapsburg emperor Franz Josef, replete with verandas, Persian rugs, and bay windows. **Pros:** attractive indoor pool; elegant rooms; kids' club for children ages 3–11. **Cons:** long walk into town; food not up to par; rooms can be noisy. $ *Rooms from: €197* ✉ *Via Cima Tosa 3, Madonna di Campiglio* ☎ *0465/441003, 049/2956411 reservations* ⊕ *www.thcampiglio.it* ⊘ *Closed Apr.–June and Sept.–early Dec.* ⤴ *109 rooms* ⦿ *Free Breakfast.*

 ## Activities

GOLF

Madonna di Campiglio Golf Club

GOLF | The 9-hole Madonna di Campiglio course is one of the highest in Europe, at 5,400 feet. It's only open mid-June through late September. ✉ *Via Cima Tosa 16, near Golf Hotel, Madonna di Campiglio* ☎ *0465/440622* ⊕ *www.golfcampiglio.it* ⌧ *€50; €75 mid-July–late Aug.* ⅃ *9 holes, 6090 yards, par 70.*

HIKING AND CLIMBING

The Madonna di Campiglio tourism office has maps of a dozen trails leading to waterfalls, lakes, and stupefying views.

Monte Spinale (*Spinale Peak*)
HIKING & WALKING | FAMILY | The cable car to 6,900-foot-high Monte Spinale offers magnificent views of the Brenta Dolomites in winter; it also runs during peak summer season and leads to many hikes at the vista. Alternatively, you can opt for an intermediate-level hike from town to the top, which takes around two hours to complete. ⊠ *Off Via Monte Spinale, Madonna di Campiglio* ☎ *0465/447744* ⊕ *www.ski.it* 🚡 *Cable car €10 round-trip.*

SKIING

⭐ **Campiglio Dolomiti di Brenta Val di Sole Val Rendena Skiarea**
SKIING & SNOWBOARDING | FAMILY | Miles of interconnecting ski runs—some of the best in the Dolomites—are linked by the cable cars and lifts of Campiglio Dolomiti di Brenta Val di Sole Val Rendena Skiarea. Advanced skiers will like the extremely difficult terrain found on certain mountain faces, and intermediate and beginner skiers will find many runs at their levels, all accessible from town. There are also plenty of off-piste opportunities. Passes can be purchased online or at the main *funivia* (cable car) in town, and multiday passes are available. ⊠ *Via Presanella 12, Madonna di Campiglio* ☎ *0465/447744* ⊕ *www.ski.it* 🚡 *Passes from €41 per day.*

Bolzano (Bozen)

32 km (19 miles) south of Merano, 50 km (31 miles) north of Trento.

Bolzano (Bozen), capital of the autonomous province of Alto Adige, is tucked among craggy peaks in a Dolomite valley 77 km (48 miles) from the Brenner Pass and Austria. Tyrolean culture dominates Bolzano's language, food, architecture, and people. It's hard to remember that

you're in Italy when walking the city's colorful cobblestone streets and visiting its lantern-lighted cafés, where you may enjoy sauerkraut and a beer among a lively crowd of German speakers. That said, the fine Italian espresso and the boutiques will help to remind you where you are. The long, narrow arcades of Via dei Portici house shops that specialize in Tyrolean crafts and clothing, as well as many Italian designers.

The Bolzano Bozen Guestcard, free of charge at participating accommodations, grants free entry to more than 90 museums in Bolzano and Alto Adige, as well as free transport throughout the region.

GETTING HERE AND AROUND

By car from Trento, take the A22 for 60 km (37 miles) to Bolzano Sud. The train station is just steps away from Piazza Walther and has regular service from Italy and Munich (four hours). The SASA bus can help you connect between Bolzano and other parts of the region. There is an airport in Bolzano, but its connections are not as convenient as the larger airports serving Venice, Verona, and Munich.

VISITOR INFORMATION

CONTACT Bolzano Tourism Office. ⊠ *Via Alto Adige 60, Bolzano* ☎ *0471/307000* ⊕ *www.bolzano-bozen.it.*

Sights

Assumption of Our Lady Cathedral (*Duomo*)
CHURCH | A lacy spire looks down on the mosaic-like roof tiles of the city's Gothic cathedral, built between the 12th and 14th centuries. Inside are 14th- and 15th-century frescoes and an intricately carved stone pulpit dating from 1514. Outside, don't miss the Porta del Vino (Wine Gate) on the northeast side facing the square; decorative carvings of grapes and harvest workers attest to the long-standing importance of wine to this region. ⊠ *Piazza della Parrocchia 27, Bolzano* ☎ *0471/978676* ⊕ *dompfarre. bz.it* 🚡 *Free.*

Sights ▼

1 Assumption of Our Lady
 Cathedral **C4**
2 Castel Roncolo **C1**
3 Messner Mountain
 Museum Firmian **A5**
4 Museo Archeologico
 dell'Alto Adige **B3**
5 Passeggiata del
 Guncina **A2**
6 Piazza delle Erbe **C3**
7 Piazza Walther **D3**
8 Renon (Ritten)
 Plateau **E3**

Restaurants ▼

1 Batzen Häusl **D2**
2 Hopfen & Co. **C3**
3 Ristorante
 Cavallino Bianco **D2**
4 Wirthaus Vögele **C3**

Coffee and Quick Bites ▼

1 Vögelino **D3**

Hotels ▼

1 Castel Hörtenberg **E2**
2 Hotel Bad Schörgau **C1**
3 Hotel Greif **D3**
4 Parkhotel Laurin **D4**
5 Schloss Hotel Korb **A5**

Castel Roncolo (*Schloss Runkelstein*)
CASTLE/PALACE | FAMILY | Green hills and farmhouses north of town surround this meticulously kept castle (also called Runkelstein Castle, or Schloss Runkelstein in German) with a tiled roof. It was built in 1237, destroyed half a century later, and then rebuilt soon thereafter. The world's largest cycle of secular medieval frescoes, beautifully preserved, is inside. A tavern in the courtyard serves excellent local food and wines. To get here from Piazza Walther, take Bus No. 12 or 14; there's also a free shuttle bus that runs from June to October and late November to early January. Alternatively, it's a 45-minute walk from Piazza delle Erbe: head north along Via Francescani, continue through Piazza Madonna, connecting to Via Castel Roncolo. If you drive or take the bus, be advised that you'll still have a 5- to 10-minute walk up to the castle. ⊠ *Via San Antonio 15, Bolzano* ☎ *0471/329808 castle* ⊕ *www.runkelstein.info* ▧ *€10* ⊗ *Closed Mon.*

★ **Messner Mountain Museum Firmian**
ART MUSEUM | FAMILY | Perched on a peak overlooking Bolzano, the 10th-century Castle Sigmundskron is home to one of six mountain museums established by Reinhold Messner—the first climber to conquer Everest solo and the first to reach its summit without oxygen. The Tibetan tradition of *kora*, a circular pilgrimage around a sacred site, is an inspiration for the museum, where visitors contemplate the relationship between human and mountain, guided by images and objects Messner collected during his adventures. The museum is 3 km (2 miles) southwest of Bolzano, just off the Appiano exit on the highway to Merano. ⊠ *Sigmundskron Castle 53, Sigmundskronerstrasse, Bolzano* ☎ *0471/631264* ⊕ *www.messner-mountain-museum.it* ▧ *€15* ⊗ *Closed Thurs. and mid-Nov.–mid-Mar.*

★ **Museo Archeologico dell'Alto Adige**
HISTORY MUSEUM | FAMILY | This museum has gained international fame for Ötzi, its 5,300-year-old iceman, discovered in 1991 and the world's oldest naturally preserved body. In 1998 Italy acquired it from Austria after it was determined that the body lay 100 yards inside Italian territory. The iceman's leathery remains are displayed in a freezer vault, preserved along with his longbow, ax, and clothing. The rest of the museum relies on models and artifacts from nearby archaeological sites, and exhibitions change regularly. An English audio guide leads you not only through Ötzi's Copper Age, but also into the preceding Mesolithic and Neolithic eras, and the Bronze and Iron Ages that followed. ⊠ *Via Museo 43, Bolzano* ☎ *0471/320100* ⊕ *www.iceman.it* ▧ *€13* ⊗ *Closed Mon. Jan.–June and Sept.–Nov.* ⌖ *Online reservations recommended up to 3 days in advance.*

Passeggiata del Guncina
PROMENADE | FAMILY | An 8-km (5-mile) botanical promenade dating from 1892 ends with a panoramic view of Bolzano. Recent updates include signposting for various species of plants and trees, as well as benches and picnic tables. You can choose to return to town along the same path, or you can walk along the River Fago and end up back in the center of Bolzano. ⊠ *Entrance near Vecchia Parrocchiale di Gries, across river and up Corsa Libertà, Bolzano* ▧ *Free.*

Piazza delle Erbe
PLAZA/SQUARE | A bronze statue of Neptune, which dates from 1745, presides over this square's bountiful fruit and vegetable market. Stalls spill over with colorful displays of local produce; bakeries and grocery stores showcase hot breads, pastries, cheeses, and delicatessen meats—a complete picnic. Try the speck tirolese (cured and lightly smoked ham from Tyrol, Austria) and the apple strudel. ⊠ *Piazza delle Erbe, Bolzano* ▧ *Free.*

Piazza Walther

PLAZA/SQUARE | This pedestrians-only square is Bolzano's heart; in warmer weather it serves as an open-air living room where locals and tourists can be found at all hours sipping a drink (such as a glass of chilled Riesling). The piazza's namesake was the 12th-century German wandering minstrel Walther von der Vogelweide, whose songs lampooned the papacy and praised the Holy Roman Emperor. In the center of the piazza stands Heinrich Natter's white-marble, neo-Romanesque *Monument to Walther*, built in 1889. ⊠ *Piazza Walther, Bolzano* 🎟 *Free.*

★ Renon (Ritten) Plateau

NATURE SIGHT | **FAMILY** | The earth pyramids of Renon Plateau are a bizarre geological formation where erosion has left a forest of tall, thin, needlelike spires of rock, each topped with a boulder. To get here, take the Soprabolzano cable car from Via Renon, about 300 yards left of the Bolzano train station. At the top, switch to the electric train that takes you to the plateau, which is in Collalbo, just above Bolzano. The cable car takes about 12 minutes and the train takes around 18 minutes. The final 30-minute hike along gentle Trail No. 24 is free. ⊠ *Via Renon, Collalbo* 🕾 *0471/356100* ⊕ *www.ritten. com* 🎟 *Cable car €10 round-trip, electric train €6 round-trip.*

Restaurants

Batzen Häusl

$$ | **ECLECTIC** | Locals hold animated conversations over pints of beer in this modern take on a traditional stube. Tasty South Tyrolean specialties include *bierspeckknodeln* (homemade beer bacon dumplings) and *bauerngröstl* (beef, onion, and potato fry-up), and there's also a wide menu of salads, pastas, and burgers. **Known for:** convivial atmosphere; home-brewed beer on tap; late-night dining. ⑤ *Average main: €16* ⊠ *Via Andreas Hofer 30, Bolzano* 🕾 *0471/050950* ⊕ *www.batzen.it.*

Hopfen & Co.

$$ | **NORTHERN ITALIAN** | Fried white *würstel* (sausage), sauerkraut, and grilled ribs complement the excellent home-brewed Austrian-style pilsner and wheat beer at this bustling pub-restaurant. Hopfen & Co. attracts Bolzano's students, young professionals, and tourists alike. **Known for:** home-brewed beer; bustling atmosphere; traditional pub environment. ⑤ *Average main: €17* ⊠ *Piazza delle Erbe, Obstplatz 17, Bolzano* 🕾 *0471/300788* ⊕ *www.boznerbier.it.*

Ristorante Cavallino Bianco

$$ | **NORTHERN ITALIAN** | A spacious, comfortable dining room near Via dei Portici is a dependable favorite with locals and visitors alike. A wide selection of Italian and German dishes are served to large tables of families enjoying their meals together. **Known for:** generations of cooking; crowded, friendly atmosphere; local dishes, such as canederli in brodo (bread dumplings in broth). ⑤ *Average main: €16* ⊠ *Via Bottai 6, Bolzano* 🕾 *0471/973267* ⊕ *www.weissesroessl.org* ⊗ *Closed Sun. No dinner Sat.*

★ Wirtshaus Vögele

$$ | **NORTHERN ITALIAN** | Ask locals where they like to dine out, and odds are they'll tell you Vögele, one of the area's oldest inns, where the menu features Tyrolean standards such as *canederli* (bread dumplings) with speck and venison. The classic wood-paneled dining room on the ground level is often packed, but don't despair—the restaurant has two additional floors. **Known for:** friendly vibe; late dining; local dishes. ⑤ *Average main: €22* ⊠ *Goethestr 3, Bolzano* 🕾 *0471/973938* ⊕ *www.voegele.it* ⊗ *Closed Sun. No dinner Sat.*

Coffee and Quick Bites

★ Vögelino

$ | **ITALIAN** | The more casual little sister to long-standing favorite Vögele serves coffee and croissants for breakfast, plus all manner of focaccia, ice cream and cake, and aperitivo (think *stuzzichini*, or savory Italian snacks, and Aperol spritz) all day long. The prime spot on bustling Piazza Walther is perfect for people-watching while catching some rays. **Known for:** focaccia of the day; fine selection of wine and cocktails; pleasant central location. ⓢ *Average main: €12* ⊠ *Piazza Walther 2, Bolzano* ☎ *0338/8485646* ⊕ *www.voegelino.com* ☾ *Closed Sun. No dinner.*

Hotels

Castel Hörtenberg

\$\$\$\$ | **HOTEL** | The modern and the ancient contrast beautifully in the contemporary interiors of this renovated palace, only about a 10-minute walk from lively Piazza Walther, but in a quiet neighborhood that seems a world away. **Pros:** relaxing spa area with outdoor pool; lovely stone-walled restaurant in the old dungeon; large-size guest rooms. **Cons:** modern interior design a bit generic; no coffee- or tea-making facilities in the guest rooms; service can be standoffish at times. ⓢ *Rooms from: €428* ⊠ *Via Monte Tondo 4, Bolzano* ☎ *0471/1800355* ⊕ *www.castel-hoertenberg.com* ➳ *24 rooms* ✶○✶ *Free Breakfast.*

★ Hotel Bad Schörgau

\$\$\$ | **HOTEL** | You'll get a warm welcome at this charming family-run hotel in the Sarentino Valley, which has incorporated natural materials into the design and an innovative philosophy into the menus, including a substantial cellar of natural wines. **Pros:** peaceful, relaxing surroundings; delicious cuisine and wines; large, out-of-the-ordinary spa area. **Cons:** some rooms are carpeted; not much else around the immediate area; beds on the hard side. ⓢ *Rooms from: €286* ⊠ *Via Ronco 24, Sarentino* ✛ *17 km (11 miles) north of Bolzano* ☎ *0471/623048* ⊕ *www.bad-schoergau.com* ☾ *Closed Mar.–late Apr. and June* ➳ *22 rooms* ✶○✶ *Free Breakfast.*

★ Hotel Greif

\$\$\$ | **HOTEL** | Individually designed guest rooms in a centuries-old Bolzano landmark feature modern furnishings with clean lines, as well as contemporary art paired with 19th-century paintings and sketches. **Pros:** elegant decor; helpful staff; central location. **Cons:** rooms vary in size; some rooms have small windows; no on-site spa. ⓢ *Rooms from: €288* ⊠ *Piazza Walther 1, Bolzano* ☎ *0471/318000* ⊕ *www.greif.it* ➳ *33 rooms* ✶○✶ *Free Breakfast.*

Parkhotel Laurin

\$\$\$ | **HOTEL** | An exercise in Art Nouveau opulence, presiding over a large park in the middle of town, this elegant hotel features art-filled guest rooms, handsome public spaces, and an exceptional restaurant. **Pros:** convenient location; excellent restaurant; high standard of service. **Cons:** rooms facing park can be noisy; can be packed with business groups; decor a bit old-fashioned. ⓢ *Rooms from: €286* ⊠ *Via Laurin 4, Bolzano* ☎ *0471/311000* ⊕ *www.laurin.it* ➳ *100 rooms* ✶○✶ *Free Breakfast.*

Schloss Hotel Korb

\$\$\$ | **B&B/INN** | This romantic 13th-century castle with crenellations and a massive tower is perched in a park amid vine-covered hills, viewed from some of the cozy guest rooms through Romanesque arched windows. **Pros:** romantic setting; charming traditional furnishings; very nice indoor and outdoor pools. **Cons:** not all rooms are in the castle; need a car to get around; a/c cannot be adjusted. ⓢ *Rooms from: €290* ⊠ *Via Castel d'Appiano 5, Missiano* ☎ *0471/636000* ⊕ *www.schloss-hotel-korb.com* ☾ *Closed mid-Nov.–Mar.* ➳ *49 rooms* ✶○✶ *Free Breakfast.*

Nightlife

Grifoncino

COCKTAIL BARS | The Hotel Greif's sleek, modern cocktail bar (where the actual bar is made out of empty bottles) serves the best libations in town. The drinks menu betrays a particular fondness for gin, but the staff also excel at making cocktails tailored to your preferences. In the summer months, the bar transfers to the hotel's rooftop. ⊠ *Via della Rena 28, Bolzano* ☎ *0471/318000* ⊕ *www.greif.it.*

Parkhotel Laurin Bar

BARS | The Laurin Bar hosts jazz combos on Friday between October and May and a jazz pianist every Saturday evening. In summer, the bar moves outside to the pretty garden, where a DJ spins tunes on Thursday night. ⊠ *Via Laurin 4, Bolzano* ☎ *0471/311000* ⊕ *www.laurin.it.*

Shopping

CRAFTS

Artigiani Atesini

CRAFTS | This is the largest store for locally made handcrafted goods. ⊠ *Via Portici 39, Bolzano* ☎ *0471/978590* ⊕ *www.facebook.com/suedtiroler.werkstaetten.*

MARKETS

Christkindlmarkt (*Christmas market*)

MARKET | FAMILY | From the end of November to the first week after New Year's there's a traditional Christkindlmarkt in Piazza Walther, with stalls selling all kinds of Christmas decorations and local handcrafted goods. ⊠ *Piazza Walther, Bolzano* ⊕ *www.mercatinodinatalebz.it.*

Piazza della Vittoria

MARKET | A weekly flea market takes place Saturday morning in Piazza della Vittoria. ⊠ *Piazza della Vittoria, Bolzano.*

Activities

BIKING

Südtirol Rad Bici Alto Adige

BIKING | FAMILY | If you're in decent shape, one great way to see some of the surrounding castles, lakes, and forested valleys of the Dolomites is by bike. Südtirol Rad can help with bike rentals from mid-April till early November. ⊠ *Via Renon 45, Bolzano* ☎ *0473/201500*

⊕ *www.suedtirol-rad.com* 🚲 *Bike rental from €25 per day.*

Bormio

97 km (60 miles) northwest of Madonna di Campiglio, 100 km (62 miles) southwest of Merano.

At the foot of Stelvio Pass, Bormio is the most famous ski resort on the western side of the Dolomites, with 50 km (31 miles) of long pistes and a nearly 6,000-foot vertical drop; the 2026 Winter Olympics men's downhill skiing competition will take place here. In summer its cool temperatures and clean air entice Italians away from cities on the humid Lombard plain. This dual-season popularity supports the plentiful shops, restaurants, and hotels in town. Bormio has been known for the therapeutic qualities of its waters since the Roman era, and there are numerous spas.

GETTING HERE AND AROUND

Take the SS239 North toward Dimaro. Turn onto the SS42 and follow it for 41 km (25 miles). Turn right onto Via Roma, and, after 2 km (1 mile), turn right onto Via Valtellina for 24 km (15 miles), and then turn right at SP78. Merge onto the SS38, and follow it to Bormio. In the summertime, you can choose to turn off the SS42 at Ponte di Legno, onto the SS300, and follow it to the end in Bormio. This takes you through Stelvio National Park. The nearest railway is in Tirano, which is half an hour away by bus. Tirano is serviced by Trenitalia and Italo, as well as the UNESCO World Heritage–designated Rhaetian Railway (Bernina Express).

VISITOR INFORMATION

CONTACT Bormio Tourism Office. ⊠ *Via Roma 131/B, Bormio* ☎ *0342/903300* ⊕ *www.bormio.eu.*

👁 Sights

Parco Nazionale dello Stelvio

NATIONAL PARK | FAMILY | The Alps' (and Italy's) biggest national park is spread over 1,350 square km (520 square miles) and four provinces. Opened in 1935 to preserve flora and protect fauna, today it has more than 1,200 types of plants, 600 different mushrooms, and more than 160 species of animals, including the chamois, ibex, and roe deer. There are many entrances to the park and five visitor centers. ◼ **TIP→ Bormio makes a good base for exploring—the closest entrance to town is the year-round gateway at Torre Alberti.** ✉ *Via Roma 131, Bormio* ☎ *0473/830430* ⊕ *www.parconazion-ale-stelvio.it* 🎟 *Free.*

🍴 Restaurants

Ristorante Kuerc

$$ | NORTHERN ITALIAN | FAMILY | This building was for centuries where justice was publicly served to accused witches, among others. Today, it's a great place to enjoy bewitching specialties like bresaola with rocket salad and Parmesan or *pizzoccheri* (buckwheat pasta) with garlic and winter vegetables. **Known for:** interesting history; pleasant location; innovative gourmet dishes. ⑤ *Average main: €24* ✉ *Piazza Cavour 8, Bormio* ☎ *0342/910787* ⊕ *www.ristorantekuerc.it* 🕑 *Closed Tues.*

🛏 Hotels

La Genzianella

$$ | HOTEL | FAMILY | Unpretentious Alpine chic meets contemporary decor, with warm pine, ceramics, rich textiles, and wood-beamed ceilings—and all but one of the guest rooms have balconies. **Pros:** great for bikers; handy to slopes and town; excellent on-site restaurant. **Cons:** no pool; some beds are two twins pushed together; rooms can be compact. ⑤ *Rooms from: €195* ✉ *Via Zandilla 6, Bormio* ☎ *0342/904485* ⊕ *www.*genzianella.com 🕑 *Closed mid-Apr.– mid-May and late Sept.–mid-Dec.* ⤶ *39 rooms* ⊙ *Free Breakfast.*

🏃 Activities

SKIING

★ Bormio Ski

SKIING & SNOWBOARDING | FAMILY | You can buy a ski pass and pick up a trail map at the base of the funivia (cable car), in the center of town (or buy the pass in advance online), before connecting to the Bormio 2000 station (6,600 feet) on Vallecetta, the main resort mountain. From there, you can ski down intermediate trails (the majority of Bormio's runs), use the extensive lift network to explore secondary ski areas, or get another funivia up to the Bormio 3000 station at Cima Bianca (9,800 feet) for more challenging terrain (the Stelvio slope will be the site of the men's downhill races in the 2026 Winter Olympics). The cable car also runs July to mid-September, when it is used by mountain bikers to reach long trails through breathtaking Alpine terrain; less ambitious visitors can wander around and then ride the cable car back down. ✉ *Via Battaglion Morbegno 25, Bormio* ☎ *0342/901451* ⊕ *www.bormioski.eu* 🎟 *Ski pass from €53 for 1 day. Cable car Bormio–Bormio 2000 €17 round-trip; cable car Bormio 2000–Bormio 3000 €17 round-trip; cable car Bormio–Cima Bianca €22 round-trip.*

SPAS

Bormio Terme

SPA | FAMILY | From outdoor swimming pools to private baths, there are plenty of ways for the entire family to enjoy the healing qualities of the thermal waters. General admission gets you a full day in the pools, saunas, and Turkish baths. Spa and beauty treatments are also available; book ahead to avoid disappointment. You do not need to pay for the pools if you are only enjoying spa treatments. ✉ *Via Stelvio 14, Bormio* ☎ *0342/901325* ⊕ *www.bormioterme.it* 🎟 *Entrance fee from €22, massages from €40, facials from €54.*

QC Terme Bagni Vecchi (*Old Baths*)
SPA | Ancient Roman baths predate the thermal springs, caves, and waterfalls that are now known as the Bagni Vecchi. Leonardo da Vinci soaked here in 1493, and today you can also take the waters, as well as book massages and treatments. The spa complex includes thermal baths, saunas, aromatherapy, and a salt grotto. Bagni Vecchi only accepts those aged 14 or older. ⊠ *Via Bagni Nuovi 7, Molina* ☎ *0289/747201* ⊕ *www.qcterme. com* ⬛ *Admission fee from €44, massages from €49, facials from €49.*

Merano (Meran)

29 km (18 miles) north of Bolzano, 16 km (10 miles) east of Naturno.

The second-largest town in Alto Adige, Merano (Meran) was once the capital of the Austrian region of Tyrol. When the town and surrounding area were ceded to Italy as part of the 1919 Treaty of Versailles, Innsbruck became Tyrol's capital. Merano continued to be known as a spa town, attracting European nobility for its therapeutic waters and its "grape cure," which consists simply of eating the grapes grown on the surrounding hillsides. Sheltered by mountains, Merano has an unusually mild climate, with summer temperatures rarely exceeding 80°F (27°C) and winters that usually stay above freezing, despite the skiing within easy reach. Along the narrow streets of Merano's old town, houses have little towers and huge wooden doors, and the pointed arches of the Gothic cathedral sit next to neoclassical and Art Nouveau buildings. Merano serves as a good respite from mountain adventures, or from the bustle of nearby Trento and Bolzano.

GETTING HERE AND AROUND
By car from Bolzano, take the SP165 to the SP117 toward Merano (29 km [18 miles]). There is regular service by Trenitalia to the train station in Merano from many points in Italy.

VISITOR INFORMATION
CONTACT Merano Tourism Office. ⊠ *Corso Libertà 45, Merano* ☎ *0473/272000* ⊕ *www.merano-suedtirol.it.*

◉ Sights

★ Castel Trauttmansdorff
GARDEN | FAMILY | This Gothic castle was restored in the 19th century and now serves as a museum that celebrates more than 250 years of tourism in South Tyrol. But the real draw is the expansive garden, where exotic flora is organized by country of origin. The castle is about 2 km (1 mile) southeast of town on the Sentiero di Sissi; you can walk in about 45 minutes from the center of Merano on Sissi's Path, or take Bus No. 4 or 1B from the Merano train station. ⊠ *Via Valentino 51/a, Merano* ☎ *0473/255600* ⊕ *www.trauttmansdorff.it* ⬛ *€16* ⊘ *Closed mid-Nov.–late Mar.*

Chiesa di San Nicolò (*Duomo*)
CHURCH | The 14th-century Gothic cathedral, with a crenellated facade and an ornate campanile, sits in the heart of the old town. The Capella di Santa Barbara, just behind the Duomo, is an octagonal church containing a 15th-century pietà. ◼ TIP→ **Mass is held in German only.** ⊠ *Piazza del Duomo, Merano* ☎ *0473/230174* ⊕ *www.stadtpfarre-meran.it* ⬛ *Free.*

Museo Agricolo di Brunnenburg
HISTORY MUSEUM | FAMILY | Overlooking the town, atop Mt. Tappeinerweg, is Castel Fontana, which was the home of poet Ezra Pound from 1958 to 1964. Still in the Pound family, the castle now houses the Museo Agricolo di Brunnenburg, devoted to Tyrolean country life. Among its exhibits are a smithy and a room with Pound memorabilia. ⊠ *Ezra Pound Strada 3, Tirolo* ✛ *Take Bus No. 3, which departs every hr on the hr from Merano to Dorf Tirol (20 mins)* ☎ *339/1803086 mobile*

⊕ *www.brunnenburg.net* ⌑ *€8* ⊘ *Closed Fri. and Sat., and early Nov.–late Mar.*

★ Promenades

PROMENADE | FAMILY | A stroll along one of Merano's well-marked, impossibly pleasant promenades may yield even better relaxation than time in its famous spa. Passeggiata Tappeiner (Tappeiner's Promenade) is a 3-km (2-mile) path with panoramic views from the hills north of the Duomo and diverse botanical pleasures along the way. Passeggiata d'Estate (Summer Promenade) runs along the shaded south bank of the Passirio River, and the Passeggiata d'Inverno (Winter Promenade), on the exposed north bank, provides more warmth and the Wandelhalle—a sunny area decorated with idyllic paintings of surrounding villages. The popular Austrian empress Sissi (Elisabeth of Wittelsbach, 1837–98) put Merano on the map as a spa destination; a trail named in her honor, the Sentiero di Sissi (Sissi's Walk), follows a path from Castel Trauttmansdorff to the heart of Merano. ⊠ *Merano.*

🍴 Restaurants

★ Prezioso

$$$$ | MODERN ITALIAN | South Tyrol native Egon Heiss uses ingredients from Castel Fragsburg's gardens as well as produce from nearby organic farms, and meat and fish from area producers, to create his beautiful versions of hyperlocal dishes. Delicious items on Prezioso's five-course tasting menus may include potato dumplings with Alpine cheese, Alpine salmon, and lamb from the Funes Valley—traditional cuisine elevated by modern preparations and artful presentations. **Known for:** refined local cuisine; organic ingredients; mountainside setting. ⑤ *Average main: €185* ⊠ *Castel Fragsburg, Via Fragsburg 3, Merano* ✛ *8½ km (5 miles) southeast of Merano* ☎ *0473/244071* ⊕ *www.fragsburg.com* ⊘ *Closed Sun., Mon., and mid-Nov.–mid-Apr. No lunch.*

Saxifraga

$$ | ITALIAN | To reach this charming eatery, which occupies an enviable position overlooking Merano and the peaks enveloping the town, climb the stairs behind the Duomo or hike up along the Passeggiata Tappeiner. The kitchen serves well-prepared dumplings, pasta, and other local specialties—just don't leave without trying the homemade breads. **Known for:** charcuterie and cheeses; delicious desserts; beautiful views. ⑤ *Average main: €20* ⊠ *Via Monte San Zeno 33, Passeggiata Tappeiner (Tappeiner's Promenade), Merano* ☎ *0473/239249* ⊕ *www.saxifraga.it* ⊘ *Closed Tues. and Nov.–Mar. No dinner Oct. and Apr.–mid-May.*

★ Sissi

$$$$ | NORTHERN ITALIAN | The sterile surroundings of this restaurant, a short walk from Via dei Portici, belie its culinary delights—namely, rustic regional dishes reenergized and prepared with precision. Three-, five-, and seven-course tasting menus change according to the chef's whim and the season, but they usually include a modernized *vitello tonnato* (veal with tuna sauce), delightful homemade pasta and dumplings, and decadent meat dishes such as veal stewed in Lagrein, the area's renowned red wine; vegetarian options are also available. **Known for:** varied tasting menu; fantastic wine list; highly polished service. ⑤ *Average main: €39* ⊠ *Via Galilei 44, Merano* ☎ *0473/231062* ⊕ *sissi.andreafenoglio.com* ⊘ *Closed Mon. and late Jan.–mid-Mar. No lunch Tues.*

☕ Coffee and Quick Bites

Vinothek Relax

$$ | NORTHERN ITALIAN | If you have difficulty choosing from the long list of tasty pizzas here, ask the friendly English-speaking staff for help with the menu. You're unlikely to find a better selection of wine, or a more pleasant environment for sampling; you can also buy bottles of the locally produced vintages to take home. **Known for:** large choice of wines; top-notch pizzas and local cuisine; helpful service. $ *Average main: €15* ✉ *Via Cavour 31, opposite Palace Hotel, Merano* ☎ *0473/236735* ⊕ *www.weine-relax.it* ⊘ *Closed Thurs., Sun., and 2 wks in Feb. and Mar.*

Hotels

★ Castel Fragsburg

$$$$ | HOTEL | For a taste of old-school Italian glamour just outside of Merano, you can't do better than this elegant Relais & Chateaux property high up in the mountains, set amid 4 acres of gardens and featuring a Michelin-starred restaurant and spa that both use products sourced from the land. **Pros:** beautiful landscape; wonderful spa concept; discreet, courteous service. **Cons:** drive up to hotel not for faint of heart; not a lot of indoor common space for relaxing; classic decor not to everyone's taste. $ *Rooms from: €576* ✉ *Via Fragsburg 3, Merano* ⊹ *8½ km (5 miles) southeast of Merano* ☎ *0473/244071* ⊕ *www.fragsburg.com* ⊘ *Closed mid-Nov.–mid-Apr.* ⇌ *20 rooms* ❌ *Free Breakfast.*

★ Hotel Terme Merano

$$$$ | HOTEL | If you're in Merano to pamper yourself, you can't do much better than the Hotel Terme: as its name suggests, it's connected to the expansive Terme Merano (a stay here includes free, unlimited access via a "bathrobe tunnel"), and it also has the rooftop Sky Spa with indoor and outdoor pools and saunas. **Pros:** delicious breakfast offerings; well-equipped gym; very central location. **Cons:** rooms on the plain side; accommodations above bar can be noisy; staff can be unfriendly at times. $ *Rooms from: €394* ✉ *Piazza Terme 1, Merano* ☎ *0473/259000* ⊕ *www.hoteltermemerano.it* ⇌ *139 rooms* ❌ *Free Breakfast.*

★ Miramonti Boutique Hotel

$$$$ | HOTEL | FAMILY | Perched up in the hills 4,035 feet above Merano, this striking Alpine hotel takes full advantage of its superlative views with floor-to-ceiling windows in the guest rooms, a panoramic restaurant, and an infinity pool. **Pros:** second-to-none mountain views; tasty and well-presented food at breakfast and dinner; kids' play area and dedicated splash time in the pool. **Cons:** no air-conditioning in rooms; three-night minimum stay; spa not open till noon and forest sauna till 2 pm. $ *Rooms from: €473* ✉ *Via San Caterina 14* ⊹ *12 km (7½ miles) southeast of Merano* ☎ *0473/279335* ⊕ *www.hotel-miramonti.com* ⊘ *Closed mid-Mar.–late Apr.* ⇌ *44 rooms* ❌ *Free Breakfast.*

Shopping

Via dei Portici (*Laubengasse*)

NEIGHBORHOOD | Merano's narrow, arcaded main shopping street runs west from the cathedral. Here you can find regional products—wood carvings, Tyrolean-style clothing, embroidery, cheeses, salami, and fruit schnapps—alongside standard clothing-boutique stock. ✉ *Via dei Portici, Merano.*

🏃 Activities

BIKING
Sissi Tours

BIKING | Merano makes for a scenic place to explore by bike, and Sissi Tours offers guided day trips that include e-bike rental and helmet. Tours are usually held in German, so ask in advance if English is preferred. ✉ *Viale Europa, Merano* ☎ *0473/424344* ⊕ *www.sissitours.it* ⛋ *Full-day guided bike tour €104.*

SPAS
★ Terme Merano

SPA | FAMILY | This sprawling spa complex has 25 pools (15 indoor pools open year-round and 10 outdoor pools open from mid-May to mid-September) and

Stumbling on Ötzi

It was at the Similaun rifugio in September 1991 that a German couple arrived talking of a dead body they'd discovered near a "curious pickax." The couple, underestimating the age of the corpse by about 5,300 years, thought it was a matter for the police. This was to be the world's introduction to Ötzi, the oldest mummy ever found. World-famous mountaineers Reinhold Messner and Hans Kammerlander happened to be passing through the same rifugio during a climbing tour, and a few days later they were on the scene, freeing the iceman from the ice, and Ötzi's remarkable story was underway.

Today, you can see Ötzi on display, along with his longbow, ax, and clothes, at Bolzano's Museo Archeologico dell'Alto Adige, where he continues to be preserved at freezing temperatures.

six saunas (with an indoor "snow room" available for cooling down). Along with the family-friendly options for bathing, personalized services for grown-ups include traditional cures using local products, such as grape-based applications and hay baths. ⊠ *Piazza Terme 9, Merano* ☎ *0473/252000* ⊕ *www.termemerano. it* ☒ *From €17 for 2 hrs in thermal baths; from €26 for 2 hrs in thermal baths and saunas; from €37 for full day's use of baths and saunas. Massages and facials from €72.*

Naturno (Naturns)

44 km (27 miles) northwest of Bolzano, 61 km (38 miles) east of Passo dello Stelvio.

As the name suggests, Naturno is a great location for a nature-based vacation; you can access a number of hiking trails to explore the area by foot. City planners have redesigned the town, reducing traffic and making the town more pedestrian-friendly. The locals take great pride in their produce; the fresh fruit, wine, and cheeses of this area are alone worth the drive.

GETTING HERE AND AROUND

By car from Bolzano, take the SS42 to the SS38 toward Merano. Naturno is 15 km (9 miles) past Merano. The town is very pedestrian-friendly, so talk to your hotel about where to leave your car, or head straight to a parking garage. Naturno is easily accessible by train from Bolzano or Merano.

VISITOR INFORMATION

CONTACT Naturno Tourism Office. ⊠ *Via Municipio 1, Naturno* ☎ *0473/666077* ⊕ *www.merano-suedtirol.it.*

Sights

Bräustüberl Forst (*FORST Brewery*)
BREWERY | The source of the full-flavor beer served throughout the region is the striking FORST Brewery, on the road connecting Naturno and Merano. Tours can be arranged if you call ahead, but you can also just turn up between late May and September to sample the product line. In high season, cross a flower-lined covered wooden bridge to reach the delightful beer garden (Braugarten Forst), which then becomes a festive Christmas forest from December to early January. ⊠ *Via Venosta 10, Lagundo* ☎ *0473/221887* ⊕ *www.forst.it* ☒ *Free* ☉ *Beer garden closed late Sept.–late Apr.*

Did You Know?

There are three different hiking areas in Naturno: in the valley, wide easy paths traverse apple orchards and meadows; on the slopes of the Sonnenberg, trails run along ancient irrigation channels; the most popular hiking trail around Naturno is the Merano High Mountain Trail, a long-distance tour between mountain huts.

★ Messner Mountain Museum Juval
(*Castel Juval*)

ART MUSEUM | FAMILY | Since 1983 this 13th-century castle in the hills above the hamlet of Stava has been the summer home of the South Tyrolese climber and polar adventurer Reinhold Messner—the first climber to conquer Everest solo. Part of the castle has been turned into one of six in Messner's chain of mountain museums, where visitors can view his collection of Tibetan art and masks from around the world. You can download an app to use as a self-guided tour. It's a 10-minute shuttle ride from the parking lot below, plus a 15-minute walk up to the castle, or a 60- to 90-minute hike on local trails; wear sturdy shoes, even if you take the shuttle, as the paths are uneven. ✉ *Juval 3, Castelbello* ☎ *0471/631264* ⊕ *www.messner-mountain-museum. it* ⊒ *€14, shuttle bus €8 round-trip* ⊗ *Closed Wed. and early Nov.–late Mar.*

St. Prokulus Kirchlein (*St. Proculus Church*)

CHURCH | Frescoes here are some of the oldest in the German-speaking world, dating from the 8th century. A small, modern museum offers multimedia installations (in Italian or German only) presenting four epochs in the region's history: ancient, medieval, Gothic, and the era of the Great Plague of 1636 (which claimed a quarter of Naturno's population, some of whom are buried in the church's cemetery). There are leaflets and other information in English on request. ✉ *Via San Procolo 1/a, Naturno* ☎ *348/673139 mobile* ⊕ *www.prokulus. org* ⊒ *€6* ⊗ *Closed Mon., Wed., weekends, and Nov.–mid-Mar.*

Caldaro (Kaltern)

15 km (9 miles) south of Bolzano.

This vineyard village, with clear views of castles high up in the surrounding mountains, represents the centuries of division that forged the unique character of the area. Caldaro architecture is famous for the way it blends Italian Renaissance elements of balance and harmony with the soaring windows and peaked arches of the Germanic Gothic tradition—the church of Santa Caterina, on the main square, is a good example. The warmest bathing lake in the Alps is just 4 km (2½ miles) away.

GETTING HERE AND AROUND
By car from Bolzano, follow the SS42 south toward Caldaro. This road is famously known as the Strada del Vino (Wine Road), and you will pass several vineyards along the way. If you head straight to the Wine Museum in Caldaro, you can pick up maps and plan a route through the vineyards based on specific tastes.

VISITOR INFORMATION
CONTACT Caldaro Tourism Office. ✉ *Marktplatz 8, Caldaro* ☎ *0471/963169* ⊕ *www. kaltern.com.*

◉ Sights

★ Elena Walch
WINERY | This sustainably farmed 148-acre property produces some of the region's most renowned wines, in particular Gewürztraminer and Pinot Nero. It's overseen by Elena herself along with her daughters Julia and Karoline. Stop by their gorgeous Castel Ringberg site for a short vineyard hike (May through mid-October, by reservation), or have lunch at their Ostaria al Castello, which has panoramic views over the vines and down to Lake Caldaro. You can also do tastings in their historical cellar at a second vineyard site closer to Tramin (from May through August); the wine shop and bistro there are open daily year-round. ✉ *Castel Ringberg, San Giuseppe al Lago 1, Caldaro* ☎ *0471/860172* ⊕ *www.elenawalch.com* ⊒ *€25 for 2-hr vineyard tour with wine tasting* ⊗ *Castel Ringberg wine shop and osteria closed mid-Oct.–Apr.*

Alto Adige and The Heart of the Dolomites

★ South Tyrolean Wine Museum

SPECIALTY MUSEUM | Head here to learn how local wine has historically been made, stored, served, and worshipped, through a series of entertaining exhibits. ✉ *Via dell'Oro 1, near main square, Caldaro* ☎ *0471/963168* ⊕ *www.museo-del-vino.it* 🎟 *€6* ◷ *Closed Sun., Mon., and mid-Nov.–Mar.*

🍴 Restaurants

★ Alois Lageder Paradeis

$$ | NORTHERN ITALIAN | Just off of the Strada del Vino (Wine Road), this charming eatery and wine bar lets you indulge in seasonal dishes while sampling some of the biodynamic wines produced by one of the Trentino area's most well-known vintners. When the weather's nice, dining in the pretty courtyard among lemon trees, with mountaintops visible just behind, really lives up to the "paradise" name. **Known for:** gorgeous garden-like setting; organic ingredients, including produce from their veggie garden; chance to sample older vintages for a great price. ⑤ *Average main: €22* ✉ *Via Casòn Hirschprunn 1, Margrè* ☎ *0471/809580* ⊕ *en.paradeis-aloislageder.eu* ◷ *Closed Sun. No dinner.*

Bressanone (Brixen)

42 km (25 miles) northeast of Bolzano.

Bressanone is an important artistic center and was the seat of prince-bishops for centuries. Like their counterparts in Trento, these medieval administrators had the delicate task of serving two masters—the pope (the ultimate spiritual authority) and the Holy Roman Emperor (the civil and military power), who were virtually at war throughout the Middle Ages. Bressanone's prince-bishops became experts at tact and diplomacy.

The BrixenCard offers free transportation throughout Alto Adige (Südtirol/South Tyrol) and grants entry to almost 90 museums, plus free guided tours and discounts at partner venues; it's free to guests of local hotels.

GETTING HERE AND AROUND

Driving from Bolzano, follow the SS12 northeast 42 km (26 miles) to Bressanone. Trains run from Bolzano, as does Sudtirol bus no. 350.

VISITOR INFORMATION

CONTACT Bressanone Tourism Office.
⊠ *Regensburger Allee 9, Bressanone* ☎ *0472/275252* ⊕ *www.brixen.org.*

Sights

Abbazia di Novacella

CHURCH | This Augustinian abbey founded in 1142 has been producing wine for at least nine centuries and is most famous for the delicate stone-fruit character of its dry white Sylvaner. As you wander the delightful grounds, note the progression of Romanesque, Gothic, and Baroque building styles. Guided tours of the abbey, in various languages, depart daily except Sunday. Guided tours of the vineyard are also available, in English, by reservation. ⊠ *Via Abbazia 1, Varna* ✛ *3 km (2 miles) north of Bressanone* ☎ *0472/836189* ⊕ *www.kloster-neustift. it* 🖾 *Abbey visit €17; wine tastings with vineyard tour €25* ☉ *Closed Sun.*

Duomo di Bressanone

CHURCH | The imposing town cathedral was built in the 13th century but acquired a Baroque facade 500 years later; its 14th-century cloister is decorated with medieval frescoes. ⊠ *Piazza Duomo 1, Bressanone* ☎ *0472/834034* ⊕ *www. bz-bx.net* 🖾 *Free.*

🍴 Restaurants

Fink

$$ | NORTHERN ITALIAN | This warm, wood-paneled upstairs dining room is under the arcades of the pedestrians-only town center; unlike most other restaurants in the region, Fink serves food all day long, with no break between lunch and dinner, just a slightly shortened menu. In addition to hearty Tyrolean specialties, such as dumplings and *gröstl* (meat, onion, and potato fry-up), there are affordable daily set meals. **Known for:** using regional and seasonal products; bustling atmosphere; central location. ⑤ *Average main: €24* ⊠ *Kleine Lauben 4, Bressanone* ☎ *0472/834883* ⊕ *www. fink1896.it* ☉ *Closed Sun. and Mon.*

★ Restaurant Apostelstube

$$$$ | ITALIAN | In a pretty Art Deco setting inside Hotel Elephant, wunderkind chef Mathias Bachmann whips up beautifully presented and creative Italian cuisine with an Asian flair in his nightly six-course tasting menus. Dishes change with the seasons, but if they're on the menu, don't miss the nori tartlet with asparagus or Hokkaido Wagyu with miso and black applesauce. **Known for:** using seasonal products; thoughtful wine pairings; elegant atmosphere. ⑤ *Average main: €135* ⊠ *Hotel Elephant, Via Rio Bianco 4, Bressanone* ☎ *0472/832750* ⊕ *www. hotelelephant.com* ☉ *Closed Mon.– Thurs. No lunch.*

Hotels

★ Forestis

$$$$ | HOTEL | It's all about the views at this minimalistic yet quietly luxurious retreat (for guests age 14 and over) high up in the mountains at 1,800 meters (5,900 feet), reached by winding roads through the pretty forest—rooms in the main building exude cozy mountain chalet vibes, while those in the Tower have a more polished feel along with astounding Alpine views in the suites and

Hiking the Dolomites

In 2009 UNESCO (the United Nations Educational, Scientific, and Cultural Organization) added the Dolomites to its list of natural heritage sites. The dramatic terrain, inspiring vistas, and impossibly pleasant climate are complemented by excellent facilities for enjoying the mountains.

Picking a Trail

The Dolomites have a well-maintained network of trails for hiking and rock climbing. As long as you're in reasonably good shape, the number of appealing hiking options can be overwhelming. Trails are well marked and designated by grades of difficulty: T for tourist path, H for hiking path, EE for expert hikers, and EEA for equipped expert hikers. On any of these paths you're likely to see carpets of mountain flowers between clutches of dense evergreens, with chamois and roe deer milling about.

If you're just out for a day in the mountains, you can leave the details of your walk open until you're actually on the spot; local tourist offices (especially those in Cortina and Madonna) can help you choose the right route based on trail conditions, weather, and desired exertion level.

Traveling the Vie Ferrate

If you're looking for an adventure somewhere between hiking and climbing, consider a guided trip along the vie ferrate, or "iron paths" (⊕ www.ferrate365.it). These routes offer fixed climbing aids (steps, ladders, bridges, safety cables) left by Alpine divisions of the Italian and Austro-Hungarian armies and later converted for recreational use. Previous experience is generally not required, but vertigo-inducing heights do demand a strong stomach.

Bedding Down

One of the pleasures of an overnight adventure in the Dolomites is staying at a rifugio, one of the refuges that dot the mountainsides, often in remote locations. There are hundreds of them, and they range in comfort from spartan to posh. Most fall somewhere in between—they're cozy mountain lodges with dormitory-style accommodations. Pillows and blankets are provided (there's no need to carry a sleeping bag), but you have to supply your own sheet. Bathrooms are usually shared, with cold showers. Reservations are a must, especially in August, although Italian law requires rifugi to accept travelers for the night if there's insufficient time to reach other accommodations before dark.

Eating Well

Food is as much a draw at rifugi as location. The rustic dishes, such as salami, dumplings, and hearty stews, are all excellent—an impressive feat, made all the more remarkable when you consider that supplies often have to arrive by helicopter. Your bed for the night, with breakfast and dinner included, may cost from €55 to €80 per person. Snacks and packed lunches are available for purchase, but many opt to sit down for the midday meal. Multilingual stories are swapped, food and wine shared, and new adventures launched.

penthouses, two of which boast their own fireplace, sauna, and outdoor pool. **Pros:** unbeatable vistas from all guest rooms; delicious food at breakfast and dinner; all-inclusive minibar drinks and snacks. **Cons:** quite expensive; sometimes overrun by influencers; Alpine roads to the hotel challenging for some. $ *Rooms from: €745* ✉ *Palmschoss 22, Bressanone* ✛ *20 km (12 miles) southeast of Brixen* ☎ *0472/521008* ⊕ *www. forestis.it* ⊘ *Closed Apr.–late May* ⤴ *62 rooms* ⦿ *Free Breakfast.*

★ Hotel Elephant

$$$ | HOTEL | At this recently renovated cozy inn—more than 500 years old and still one of the region's best—each room is unique, and many are filled with antiques and paintings. **Pros:** lovely ambience; good restaurants; lavish breakfast. **Cons:** rooms vary in size; soundproofing in rooms could be better; some bathrooms are small. $ *Rooms from: €222* ✉ *Via Rio Bianco 4, Bressanone* ☎ *0472/832750* ⊕ *www.hotelelephant. com* ⤴ *44 rooms* ⦿ *Free Breakfast.*

Brunico (Bruneck)

33 km (20 miles) east of Bressanone, 65 km (40 miles) northwest of Cortina d'Ampezzo.

Located in the heart of the Val Pusteria, this quiet and quaint town is divided by the Rienza River. The modern part of Brunico is on one side of the river, and on the other is the medieval quarter, nestled below a 13th-century bishop's castle.

GETTING HERE AND AROUND

From Bressanone follow the E66 east for 30 km (19 miles) to Brunico. If driving from Cortina d'Ampezzo, take the SR51 to Toblach and continue to the SS49 toward Brunico. There are bus (SAD) and train (Trenitalia) connections available at Bolzano.

VISITOR INFORMATION

CONTACT Brunico Tourism Office. ✉ *Piazza Municipio 7, Brunico* ☎ *0474/555722* ⊕ *www.bruneck.com.*

⊙ Sights

★ Lumen Museum

ART MUSEUM | Take a cable car to the top of Kronplatz to reach this 19,375-square-foot museum dedicated to mountain photography (actually, you have your choice of eight different cable cars, two from the town of Brunico). Once inside, you'll find pictures from Alpine photography's early days all the way to the present, taken by photographers from mountainous regions throughout the world and displayed across four floors. Lumen also houses AlpiNN, a casual restaurant from critically acclaimed chef Norbert Niederkofler of St. Hubertus fame. Note that the museum can be difficult to access in winter if you're not a skier; it's down a slight, rather terrifying incline from the top of the mountain. Be aware that the museum closes at 4 pm (last admission at 3:30), so that you won't miss the last cable car back down. ✉ *Kronplatz–Plan de Corones Mountain Station, Brunico* ✛ *Take a cable car up to Kronplatz* ☎ *0474/431090* ⊕ *www.lumenmuseum. it* 🎟 *€17* ⊘ *Closed mid-Apr.–May and mid-Oct.–Nov.*

★ Messner Mountain Museum Corones

SPECIALTY MUSEUM | **FAMILY** | High atop the Mountain Station Kronplatz–Plan de Corones, almost 7,500 feet above Brunico, the newest museum from mountaineer Reinhold Messner displays climbing equipment and other Alpine paraphernalia from the 1800s until now. It also examines all facets of mountaineering through painting, sculpture, and other media. Equally interesting is the museum's Zaha Hadid–designed concrete building: its sloped roof makes it seem like a miniature mountain, and its outdoor lookout point affords magnificent vistas. Note that the museum closes at

The craggy peaks around Canazei are particularly stunning at sunset.

4 pm (last admission at 3:30), so that you won't miss the last cable car back down. ⊠ *Kronplatz–Plan de Corones Mountain Station, Brunico* ⊹ *Take a cable car up to Kronplatz* ☎ *0474/501350* ⊕ *www.messner-mountain-museum.it* 🎫 *€14* 🕐 *Closed mid-Apr.–May and early–late Nov.*

★ Messner Mountain Museum Ripa

SPECIALTY MUSEUM | FAMILY | This fascinating, comprehensive museum within the 13th-century Bruneck Castle looks at the lives of mountain-dwelling people from Europe, Asia, Africa, and South America through artifacts, tools, statues, paintings, living spaces, and more. Part of the experience is reaching the castle itself: it's a 15-minute hike up to it on a path accessed just off Brunico's pedestrian area. ⊠ *Schlossweg 2, Brunico* ☎ *0474/410220* ⊕ *www.messner-mountain-museum.it* 🎫 *€14* 🕐 *Closed Tues., late Apr.–mid-May, and early Nov.–early Dec.*

South Tyrolean Folklore Museum

MUSEUM VILLAGE | FAMILY | A re-creation of a medieval rural village, including farmhouses, craft workshops, and bread bakers, is built around a 300-year-old mansion. The wood-carving displays are especially interesting. ⊠ *Herzog-Diet-Strada 24, Brunico* ☎ *0474/552087* ⊕ *www.volkskundemuseum.it* 🎫 *€9* 🕐 *Closed Mon. and Nov.–mid-Apr.*

🍴 Restaurants

★ Oberraut

$$ | ITALIAN | Drive up into the hills about 12 minutes northeast of Brunico to reach this charming chalet-style family-run eatery, which has an expansive terrace with great views overlooking the mountains. Hearty dishes use local ingredients—including meat from their farm, vegetables from their gardens and greenhouses, and grain from their own mill—and the delightful servers are happy to recommend seasonal specialties.

Known for: Alpine vistas; deer and beef dishes; zero-kilometer philosophy. ⑤ *Average main: €22* ✉ *Via Ameto 1, Brunico* ☎ *0474/559977* ⊕ *oberraut.it* ⊙ *Closed Thurs.*

🛏 Hotels

Das Majestic Hotel & Spa

$$$ | HOTEL | FAMILY | Right in front of the Plan de Corones chairlift, this is a great base for a skiing or hiking vacation, with bus service to the ski slopes and a spa and pools on-site to unwind after a big day out. **Pros:** convenient for skiers and hikers; nice indoor and outdoor pools; spacious rooms. **Cons:** meal portions are a little small; no covered parking; far from town center. ⑤ *Rooms from: €298* ✉ *Via Im Gelände 20, Brunico* ☎ *0474/410993* ⊕ *www.hotel-majestic.it* ⊙ *Closed mid-Apr.–mid-May* ⟿ *60 rooms* ⏍ *Free Breakfast.*

★ Falkensteiner Hotel Kronplatz

$$$$ | HOTEL | FAMILY | This family-friendly ultramodern hotel near the Plan de Corones chairlift, made up of four sleek connected houses designed by Italian architect Matteo Thun, offers spacious rooms and an expansive spa. **Pros:** eager-to-help staff; extravagant breakfast buffet; wonderful spa area. **Cons:** can hear traffic noise in some rooms; service can be distracted at times; not all rooms have mountain views. ⑤ *Rooms from: €408* ✉ *Via Funivia 1/c, Brunico* ☎ *0474/862400* ⊕ *www.falkensteiner.com* ⊙ *Closed Apr.–mid-May* ⟿ *97 rooms* ⏍ *All-Inclusive.*

Hotel Post

$$ | HOTEL | This homey hotel housed in a former post office dating from the 1880s is the most central, appealing lodging choice in town. **Pros:** professional staff; central location; parking on-site. **Cons:** modern decor lacks historical charm; simple breakfast; small spa. ⑤ *Rooms from: €172* ✉ *Via Bastioni 9, Brunico* ☎ *0474/834001* ⊕ *www.hotelpost-bruneck.com* ⟿ *39 rooms* ⏍ *No Meals.*

Misurina

115 km (71 miles) east of Bolzano.

Nestled on the shores of Lake Misurina, among the Dolomites, Misurina's high altitude, low air humidity, and total absence of dust mites and air pollution has some saying that the "Pearl of the Dolomites" has some of the purest air in the world. The town itself is rather small, but it's a perfect base to explore Lake Misurina and the Tre Cime of Lavaredo. The surrounding mountains are rich in history and artifacts from the First World War and earlier conflicts. Along some of the hikes and vie ferrate (mountain paths with steel cables and fixed anchors and ladders), you can explore caves and trenches complete with informational placards giving details about troop positions and fighting.

GETTING HERE AND AROUND

From Brunico, drive southeast on the SS49/E66 to Dobbiaco. Turn right onto SS51 and drive for 13 km (8 miles). Turn left onto SP49 in the direction of Auronzo. Arrive at Lago di Misurina in 6 km (4 miles).

VISITOR INFORMATION

CONTACT Misurina Tourism Office. ✉ *Via Monte Piana 2, Misurina* ☎ *0435/39016* ⊕ *auronzomisurina.it.*

Sights

★ Tre Cime di Lavaredo

MOUNTAIN | FAMILY | Without a doubt, the Three Peaks—Cima Piccola (9,373 feet), Cima Grande (9,839 feet), and Cima Ovest (9,753 feet)—are the symbols of the Dolomite UNESCO World Heritage site. From the town of Misurina, only two of the Tre Cime are visible. In order to get up close and personal, drive or take a bus along the dedicated toll road (usually open June through October; car parking €30). Once at the top, follow Footpath 101 from Rifugio Auronzo to

Forcella Laveredo (easy) for about an hour. There are many other footpaths and vie ferrate which allow you to climb the cime and access the base. Rifugi offer hot meals without a reservation, as well as dorm-style lodging, which is best reserved in advance. ⊠ *Parco Naturale Tre Cime, Auronzo di Cadore* ☎ *0435/99603* ⊕ *www.drei-zinnen.info.*

🍽 Restaurants

Malga Rin Bianco

$$$ | **NORTHERN ITALIAN** | **FAMILY** | For fresh, properly cooked regional food, this *malga* (Alpine hut) with great mountain views can't be beat—just make a reservation, especially in winter, when you must be transported over on a snowmobile by day and a shuttle at night (in summer, you can drive all the way). Salamis and cheeses are made on-site, and the bar serves both commercial and homemade grappas, many of which are brewed with local herbs; also try some *capriolo* (mountain goat stew), polenta, *skitz* (grilled cheese that doesn't melt), or fresh local mushrooms. **Known for:** scenic mountain location; local food; great views. ⑤ *Average main: €26* ⊠ *Via Monte Piana 35, Strada Tre Cime, Misurina* ☎ *0320/5699375* ⊕ *www.rinbianco.com* ⊘ *Closed 1 month after Easter, and Nov.*

🛏 Hotels

Chalet Lago Antorno

$$ | **B&B/INN** | **FAMILY** | Located in a quiet, panoramic spot, this chalet is ideal for exploring the mountains or simply relaxing amid the beauty of the Alps. **Pros:** family-run; typical decor and regional flavor; idyllic mountain setting. **Cons:** away from town center; minimum night stays in peak season; some rooms are small. ⑤ *Rooms from: €157* ⊠ *Località Lago Misurina, Misurina* ☎ *0320/9625700* ⊕ *www.lagoantorno.it* ⊘ *Closed late Oct.–late Dec.* ⤴ *10 rooms* ⎮⊙⎮ *Free Breakfast.*

Grand Hotel Misurina

$$ | **HOTEL** | **FAMILY** | On the shores of beautiful Lake Misurina and just a few kilometers from renowned winter resort Cortina d'Ampezzo, this grand hotel has simply furnished rooms that range from standard fare to full apartments. **Pros:** located in town center; perfect for large groups; shuttle to ski areas. **Cons:** rooms have simple furnishings; dated decor; extra charge and limited time slots for the spa. ⑤ *Rooms from: €163* ⊠ *Via Monte Piana 21, Misurina* ☎ *0435/39191* ⊕ *www.grandhotelmisurina.com* ⊘ *Closed Apr.–mid-May and early Oct.–late Dec.* ⤴ *125 rooms* ⎮⊙⎮ *Free Breakfast.*

Activities

BIKING

Cycling enthusiasts flock to the Dolomites for the challenging mountain terrain, and much of the region is used by Olympic athletes to train. In addition, several important cycling races (such as the Giro di Italia) take place in this area. Some of the descents along gravelly roads set off a rush of adrenaline, while others follow paved roads and bike paths. The Auronzo-Misurina Cycle Track provides about 32 km (20 miles) of bicycle path between the two towns.

SKIING

Two major ski lifts service the area: the Col de Varda lift in Misurina, and the Monte Agudo lift in Auronzo di Cadore (about a 30-minute drive from Misurina), which takes you from Taiarezze (2,952 feet) to Rifugio Monte Agudo (5,160 feet). The views from Auronzo differ from Misurina in that all Tre Cime are visible. Restaurants and maps are available at the top.

Col de Varda

SKIING & SNOWBOARDING | **FAMILY** | The major ski lift servicing the area from Misurina climbs to Col de Varda, with a summit of 6,909 feet. Rifugio Col de

Varda, at the top, has a bar and restaurant, as well as rooms to rent. In the summer, the area is an excellent starting point for great hiking and biking excursions. At any time of the year, the views of Lake Misurina, Mt. Cristallo, the Sesto Dolomites, and the Cadini, Sorapiss, and Tofane massifs are breathtaking. ⊠ *Misurina* ☎ *0435/39013* ⊕ *www.auronzomisurina.it* ⌕ *€13 round-trip.*

Monte Cristallo

SKIING & SNOWBOARDING | Some of the most impressive views (and steepest slopes) are on Monte Cristallo. ⊠ *Misurina* ☎ *0436/861035* ⊕ *faloriacristallo.it* ⌕ *From €68 for 1-day pass.*

Canazei

45 km (28 miles) southwest of Misurina.

Of the year-round resort towns in the Val di Fassa, Canazei is the most popular. The mountains around this small town are threaded with hiking trails and ski slopes set amid large clutches of conifers.

GETTING HERE AND AROUND

Bus service from Bolzano and Bressanone (the nearest train stations) is infrequent, and schedules are often interrupted or canceled. By car from the A22 autostrada, take the Bolzano Nord exit onto the SS241. Cross the Passo Costalunga into the Val di Fassa. From the town of Vigo, follow signs for Canazei.

VISITOR INFORMATION

CONTACT Canazei Tourism Office. ⊠ *Piazza G. Marconi 5, Canazei* ☎ *0462/609500* ⊕ *www.fassa.com.*

Sights

★ Col Rodella

VIEWPOINT | **FAMILY** | An excursion from Campitello di Fassa, about 4 km (2½ miles) west of Canazei, to the vantage point at Col Rodella has unmissable

views. A cable car rises some 3,000 feet to a full-circle vista of the Heart of the Dolomites, including the Sasso Lungo and the rest of the Sella range. ⊠ *Localita' Ischia 1, Canazei* ☎ *0462/608811* ⊕ *www.valdifassalift.it* ⌕ *Col Rodella cable car €25 round-trip.*

Passo Pordoi

MOUNTAIN | **FAMILY** | At 7,346 feet, Passo Pordoi is the highest surface-road pass in the Dolomites. It connects Arabba, in Val Cordevole (Province of Belluno), with Canazei, in Val di Fossa (Province of Trento). Views from the top include the Sassolungo and Sella group of mountains, and even the Marmolada Glacier. There are several hotels and a ski school located at the pass, as well as some souvenir shops, restaurants, and snack carts. While the hotels are not glamorous, some do offer half-board packages at reasonable rates. The road up to the pass from Canazei has a few scenic and picnic pull-offs, plus 28 hairpin turns.

Skiing is available year-round. The most popular winter skiing areas are Belvedere and Sella Ronda, and much of the area is part of the Dolomiti Superski package. Even if the road for the pass is closed, many of the cable cars in neighboring valley towns will be running to various summits.

From Passo Pordoi you can get a cable car (May through October) to the Sass Pordoi, often called the Terrazza delle Dolomiti (Terrace of the Dolomites). At more than 9,100 feet, it offers myriad hiking trails and vie ferrate with varying degrees of difficulty (none of which are easy), leading to rifugi and the region's other peaks and passes. ⊠ *Strada del Pordoi, Canazei* ☎ *0462/608811* ⊕ *www.valdifassalift.it* ⌕ *Sass Pordoi cable car €27 round-trip.*

Hotels

Alla Rosa

$$ | HOTEL | Ask for a room with a balcony: the view of the imposing Dolomites is the real attraction in accommodations that pleasantly blend rustic and contemporary furnishings. **Pros:** in the center of town; great views; plentiful breakfast buffet. **Cons:** bathrooms could use an update; busy neighborhood; no restaurant for lunch or dinner. ⑤ *Rooms from: €146* ✉ *Strada del Faure 18, Canazei* ☎ *0462/601107* ⊕ *www.hotelallarosa.com* 🛏 *49 rooms* ⦿ *Free Breakfast.*

Ortisei (St. Ulrich)

28 km (17 miles) northwest of Canazei.

Ortisei (St. Ulrich), the jewel in the crown of Val Gardena's resorts, is a hub of activity in both summer and winter; there are hundreds of miles of hiking trails and accessible ski slopes. Ortisei has been a family-friendly mountain vacation destination since the 1930s. The most famous cable car in the area, the Alpe di Siusi, operates in summer and winter. As the largest village in the Val Gardena, Ortisei makes a picturesque and practical base for exploring much of the heart of the Dolomites.

For centuries Ortisei has also been famous for the expertise of its wood carvers, and there are still numerous workshops. Apart from making religious sculptures—particularly the wayside calvaries you come upon everywhere in the Dolomites—Ortisei's carvers were long known for producing wooden dolls, horses, and other toys. As itinerant peddlers, they traveled every spring on foot with their loaded packs as far as Paris, London, and St. Petersburg. Shops in town still sell woodcrafts.

GETTING HERE AND AROUND

By car from Bolzano, take the SS12 to the SS242 in the direction of Ortisei. From Canazei, follow the SS242 north to Ortisei. Free bus service is available from participating accommodations on the Val Gardena network from Bolzano and Bressanone and other points around the region. The Gardena Card gives unlimited use of all the lifts (18) of the region for one price.

VISITOR INFORMATION

CONTACT Ortisei Tourist Office. ✉ *Via Rezia 1, Ortisei* ☎ *0471/777600* ⊕ *www. valgardena.it.*

Sights

Alpe di Siusi Cable Car

TRANSPORTATION | FAMILY | First opened in 1935, the cable car from Ortisei to Alpe di Siusi climbs more than 6,100 feet to the widest plateau in Europe. There are more than 57 square km (22 square miles) of Alpine pastures lined with summertime hiking trails. In the winter, 20 ski lifts and cross-country ski paths keep active visitors happy. There is a restaurant at the top of the Mt. Seuc ski lift, or you can pick up a map at the tourist office in Ortisei listing the mountain huts and restaurants that can be reached on foot. Opening days and times depend on the season and daily weather conditions; check the website or call ahead to avoid disappointment. ✉ *Setil Strada 9, Ortisei* ☎ *0471/797897* ⊕ *www.funiviaortisei.eu* 💶 *€29 round-trip* ⊗ *Closed early Nov.– early Dec. and early Apr.–mid-May.*

Museo della Val Gardena

ART MUSEUM | FAMILY | Fine historic and contemporary examples of local woodworking are on display here, as well as a retrospective on the life of local film director Luis Trenker. ✉ *Via Rezia 83, Ortisei* ☎ *0471/797554* ⊕ *www. museumgherdeina.it* 💶 *€8* ⊗ *Closed late Mar.–mid-May and mid-Oct.–early Dec.; closed Sat.–Wed. early Dec.–late Mar.*

(except Dec. 26–Jan. 7), Sun.–Fri. July and Aug., and weekends mid-May–June, and Sept.–mid-Oct.

 Hotels

Cavallino Bianco Family Spa Grand Hotel
$$$$ | RESORT | FAMILY | With delicate wooden balconies and an eye-catching wooden gable, the pink Cavallino Bianco (Little White Horse) looks like a gigantic dollhouse, and it is, in fact, marketed toward families. **Pros:** excellent family facilities; cheerful rooms; laundry facilities. **Cons:** in the busy town center; public areas a bit dated; very expensive. ⑤ *Rooms from: €653 ⊠ Via Rezia 22, Ortisei ☎ 0471/783333 ⊕ www.cavallino-bianco.com ⊘ Closed mid-Apr.–mid-May ➠ 104 rooms � ⌑ All-Inclusive.*

Hotel Grones
$$$$ | HOTEL | FAMILY | The attention to detail at this family-run hotel, located just a few minutes' walk from the ski slopes or downtown, makes it a great base for a mountain vacation. **Pros:** friendly staff; shuttle service to ski stations; spa with nice indoor pool. **Cons:** it's an uphill walk from town; pool and whirlpool not quite warm enough; bed linens/bath towels could be higher quality. ⑤ *Rooms from: €322 ⊠ Via Stufan 110, Ortisei ☎ 0471/797040 ⊕ www.hotelgrones.com ⊘ Closed Apr., May, and early Oct.–early Dec. ➠ 23 rooms ⌑ Free Breakfast.*

 Activities

SKIING
With almost 600 km (370 miles) of accessible downhill slopes and more than 90 km (56 miles) of cross-country skiing trails, Ortisei is one of the most popular ski resorts in the Dolomites. Prices are good, and facilities are among the most modern in the region. In warmer weather, the slopes surrounding Ortisei are a popular hiking destination, as well as a playground for vehicular mountain adventures like biking, rafting, and paragliding.

Sella Ronda
SKIING & SNOWBOARDING | FAMILY | An immensely popular ski route, the Sella Ronda relies on well-placed chairlifts to connect 26 km (16 miles) of downhill skiing around the colossal Sella massif, passing through several towns along the way. You can ski the loop, which requires intermediate ability and a full day's effort, either clockwise or counterclockwise. Going with a guide is recommended. ⊠ *Ortisei, Ortisei ☎ 0471/777777 ⊕ www.val-gardena.com ➠ From €67 for 1-day pass.*

Corvara

29 km (18 miles) east of Ortesei (St. Ulrich).

Corvara is the main town of the Alta Badia, known for its prime skiing and hiking location in the middle of the Sella Ronda. The first chairlift in Italy opened here in 1946, and today there are two cable cars—the Col Alto and the Boè—along with 11 chairlifts, making Corvara a convenient base for an active holiday in winter or summer. Corvara is also the start of the First World War Ski Tour, a 79-km (49-mile) route around Col di Lana that takes you past wartime relics like trenches and forts. The town itself is pleasant and walkable, with a smattering of restaurants, bars, and ski rental and sporting goods stores.

GETTING HERE AND AROUND
To get to Corvara from Bolzano, take the A22 north to Bressanone/Pusteral. Turn right on the SS244, and take it all the way to Corvara. From Ortisei, take the SS242 to the SS243 into Corvara. Buses arrive many times daily from Bolzano and Bressanone.

VISITOR INFORMATION
CONTACTS Corvara Tourist Office. ⊠ *Strada Col Alt 36, Corvara ☎ 0471/836176 ⊕ www.altabadia.org.*

Sights

Boè Cable Car

TRANSPORTATION | FAMILY | This cable car takes hikers and skiers from Corvara up Piz Boè, the highest mountain of the Sella group, at 10,341 feet. Once at the first station, you can hike the Sella Ronda, ski back down, or ride a chairlift farther up to the Vallon Peak for more challenging skiing or hiking in the warmer months. Paragliding is also popular from the Vallon area. ⊠ *Strada Burjé 10, Corvara* ☎ *0471/836073* ⊕ *www.moviment. it/en/boe-ski-lift-corvara.php* 🎫 *€21.10 round-trip.*

Col Alto Cable Car

TRANSPORTATION | FAMILY | The site of Italy's first chairlift in 1946 now has modern yellow eight-seater cable cars that ascend to a height of 6,562 feet. From there you have access to ski lifts that take you all over the Alta Badia region and, in summer, to trails that include a 10-km (6-mile) route to the Rifugio Pralongià. You can rent skis and snowboards at the Ski Service Colalto, located at the bottom of the lift. ⊠ *Strada Col Alt 36, Corvara* ☎ *0471/836073* ⊕ *www. moviment.it/en/col-alt-ski-lift-corvara.php* 🎫 *€15.20 round-trip.*

Restaurants

La Stüa de Michil

$$$$ | ITALIAN | You'll feel like you're dining in a traditional Alto Adige hut at the Perla hotel's critically acclaimed restaurant, which features wood-beamed ceilings. Menu items are complex, modern takes on regional cuisine: even a simple veal dish might be served with reserve Alpine cheese and black truffle. **Known for:** romantic atmosphere; interesting wine pairings (not all Italian); daring ingredient combinations. ⑤ *Average main: €180* ⊠ *Strada Col Alt 105, Corvara* ☎ *0471/831000* ⊕ *www.lastuademichil.it* ⊘ *Closed Apr.–mid-June, and late Sept.– early Dec. No lunch.*

★ Ristorante Rifugio Col Alt

$$ | ECLECTIC | From town, take the Col Alt cable car—or a snowcat (by reservation only) for dinner on Wednesday and Friday—to this surprisingly modern restaurant with amazing panoramas from 6,562 feet. The wide-ranging menu features everything from salads to hearty fried potatoes, eggs, and bacon (perfect after a morning of skiing), and the interesting wine list is heavy on natural producers, since the affable owner is a fan and often has local winemakers in for tastings. **Known for:** unbeatable vistas; an enormous terrace; memorable wines at affordable prices. ⑤ *Average main: €22* ⊠ *Monte Cabinovia, Strada Col Alt 1, Corvara* ⊹ *Take Col Alt cable car* ☎ *0471/836324* ⊕ *rifugiocolalt.it* ⊘ *Closed mid-Apr.–mid-June and mid-Sept.–early Dec.*

Hotels

Ciasa Salares

$$$ | HOTEL | FAMILY | This refined, amenities-filled hotel has a distinctly Germanic vibe and lots of mountain atmosphere—from its outdoor hot tub and sauna to its simple guest rooms, with light-wood paneling, white accents, and balconies, to its underground fondue room–wine cellar (24,000 bottles with a focus on biodynamic producers). **Pros:** a number of top-notch dining choices; lovely spa; more affordable than comparable hotels. **Cons:** some rooms feel a bit cramped; service can be standoffish; not ski-in, ski-out. ⑤ *Rooms from: €247* ⊠ *Strada Prè de Vì 31, Località Armentarola, 10 km (6 miles) east of Corvara, San Cassiano* ☎ *0471/849445* ⊕ *www.ciasasalares. it* ⊘ *Closed Apr.–mid-June* 🛏 *50 rooms* ﺊ *Free Breakfast.*

★ La Perla

$$$$ | HOTEL | Best described as "Alpine country chic," this luxe yet rustic family-run hotel has spacious wood-latticed rooms with mountain-view balconies, a spa, lots of cozy sitting areas, and a much-lauded restaurant. **Pros:** ski-in, ski-out; convenient location next to both the mountains and town; extremely friendly service. **Cons:** rooms can be hot; expensive drinks; ski room could use a refresh. ⑤ *Rooms from: €767* ✉ *Strada Col Alt 105, Corvara* ☎ *0471/831000* ⊕ *www.laperlacorvara.it* ⊘ *Closed Apr.–early June and late Sept.–early Dec.* ⇱ *50 rooms* ⦿ *All-Inclusive.*

Activities

HIKING

Corvara offers hikes for all levels, including the popular Col Alt Pralongià hike—an easy, level hike that passes through pasture lands—as well as a number of walks in the Puez-Odle nature reserve. Hikers looking for more challenging, steeper routes should start at the top of the Boè cable car.

SKIING

Alta Badia

SKIING & SNOWBOARDING | The Alta Badia ski area, which includes 53 ski lifts and 130 km (80 miles) of slopes, is cheaper and more Austrian in character than the more famous ski destinations in this region. Groomed trails for cross-country skiing (usually loops marked off by the kilometer) accommodate differing degrees of ability. Inquire at the local tourist office. ✉ *Alta Badia, Corvara* ☎ *0471/836176 Corvara tourism office* ⊕ *www.altabadia.org* ⇱ *€67 day pass.*

Cortina d'Ampezzo

38 km (24 miles) east of Corvara.

The archetypal Dolomite resort, Cortina d'Ampezzo entices those seeking both relaxation and adventure, and will host the 2026 Winter Olympics along with Milan. The town is the western gateway to the Strade Grande delle Dolomiti and actually crowns the northern Veneto region and an area known as Cadore in the northernmost part of the province of Belluno. Like Alto Adige to the west, Cadore (birthplace of the Venetian Renaissance painter Titian) was on the Alpine front during World War I, and was the scene of many battles that have been commemorated in refuges and museums. Cortina remains, for many, Italy's most idyllic incarnation of an Alpine ski town.

GETTING HERE AND AROUND

To drive to Cortina d'Ampezzo from Trento or Bolzano, take the A22 autostrada north to Bressanone/Pustertal. Turn right on the SS49/E66, then right on to the SS51 and follow it into Cortina. The Südtirolmobil site provides itineraries for train and bus arrivals from around the region. The town itself is pedestrian-friendly and has local bus service to area ski slopes. Beware of taxis, as the rates are very high—and the fare may begin from the taxi's point of origin, not necessarily where you get in the vehicle.

VISITOR INFORMATION

CONTACT Cortina d'Ampezzo Tourism Office. ✉ *Corso Italia 81, Cortina d'Ampezzo* ☎ *0436/869086* ⊕ *www.dolomiti.org.*

⊙ Sights

Surrounded by mountains and dense forests, the "Queen of the Dolomites" is in a lush meadow 4,000 feet above sea level. The town hugs the slopes beside a fast-moving stream, and a public park extends along one bank. Higher in the valley, luxury hotels and the villas of the rich are identifiable by their attempts to hide behind stands of firs and spruces. The bustling center of Cortina d'Ampezzo has little nostalgia, despite its alpine appearance, with its tone set by shops and cafés as chic as their well-dressed patrons. Unlike neighboring resorts that have a strong Germanic flavor, Cortina d'Ampezzo is unapologetically Italian and distinctly fashionable.

Restaurants

La Tavernetta

$$ | **NORTHERN ITALIAN** | These Tirolean-style wood-paneled dining rooms near the Olympic ice-skating rink are a Cortina institution. Join the local clientele in sampling terrific pizza along with house specialties such as pork cheek in Barolo sauce. **Known for:** typical dishes; nice wine selection; house-made desserts. ⑤ *Average main: €24* ✉ *Via Castello 53, Cortina d'Ampezzo* ☎ *0436/868102* ⊗ *Closed Mon.*

Ristorante Lago Pianozes di Alberti Massimo

$$$ | **NORTHERN ITALIAN** | The owner of this small, endearing establishment—just outside Cortina and beside picturesque Lago Pianozes—is friendly and knowledgeable, not only about the food and wine but also about the region. The menu varies according to the seasons, always incorporating local recipes—seating is limited, though, so reservations are recommended. **Known for:** delightful location; local dishes; friendly staff. ⑤ *Average main: €28* ✉ *Campo di Sotto Pianozes 1, Cortina d'Ampezzo* ☎ *366/3591737* ⊕ *www.facebook.com/lago.pianozes* ⊗ *Closed Mon. and early May–late June.*

★ SanBrite

$$$$ | **MODERN ITALIAN** | Most of the ingredients, including fabulous handmade cheeses and butter, used at this charming Michelin-starred organic dairy-turned-eatery (whose name means "healthy pasture") come from the family farm, Agriturismo El Brite de Larieto, perched 1,800 meters (5,900 feet) above the sea. Out of this local bounty, chef Riccardo Gaspari and his wife Ludovica craft impressive and highly personal dishes you'll find nowhere else in the Dolomites, such as the signature spaghetti with mountain pine oil and scent of the forest ice cream. **Known for:** farm-to-table cuisine; six-course tasting menu (plus à la carte dishes); stunning mountain views. ⑤ *Average main: €50* ✉ *Via Alverà, Cortina d'Ampezzo* ☎ *0436/863882* ⊕ *www.sanbrite.it* ⊗ *Closed Wed., May–early June, and Nov.*

Hotels

Hotel Corona

$$$ | **HOTEL** | Modern art adorns the small but comfortable pine-paneled rooms at this inviting lodge, once owned by noted ski instructor Luciano Rimoldi; ski slopes and the town center are a 10-minute walk away. **Pros:** quiet location; friendly staff; ski shuttle stops out front. **Cons:** small rooms; outside the town center; dated decor. ⑤ *Rooms from: €220* ✉ *Via Val di Sotto 12, Cortina d'Ampezzo* ☎ *0436/3251* ⊕ *www.hotelcorona.dolomiti.com* ⊗ *Closed Apr.–May and mid-Sept.–Nov.* ⇱ *44 rooms* ❏ *Free Breakfast.*

Hotel De la Poste

$$$ | **HOTEL** | Loyal skiers return year after year to this old-school mountain retreat, where each unique room has antiques in characteristic Dolomite style (almost all have wooden balconies) and the main terrace bar is one of Cortina's social centers. **Pros:** professional service; charging stations for electric cars; lively atmosphere. **Cons:** no pool or spa; dated furnishings; street noise can be an issue. ⑤ *Rooms from: €221* ✉ *Piazza Roma 14, Cortina d'Ampezzo* ☎ *0436/4271* ⊕ *www.delaposte.it* ⊗ *Closed Apr.–late May and mid-Oct.–early Dec.* ⇱ *72 rooms* ❏ *Free Breakfast.*

Hotel de Len

$$$$ | **HOTEL** | At this mountain-chic inn in the center of Cortina, from the same owners as Puglia's famed Borgo Egnazia resort, sustainable materials and chill vibes add up to the most modern boutique hotel in town. **Pros:** convenient, central location; very friendly staff; lovely spa area with great views. **Cons:** parking costs extra; restaurant food could be

better; only first hour free at spa, then must pay to use. $ *Rooms from: €499* ✉ *Via Cesare Battisti 66, Cortina d'Ampezzo* ☎ *0436/4246* ⊕ *hoteldelen.it* ⤴ *22 rooms* ᵀᴼᵀ *Free Breakfast.*

⚡ Activities

HIKING AND CLIMBING
Cortina has more than 400 km (249 miles) of hiking routes, ranging from forests to Alpine lakes, including the popular Lake Sorapis, famous for its amazing blue colors. Hiking information is available from the excellent local tourism office.

★ Cima Tofana
HIKING & WALKING | FAMILY | Cima Tofana is home to the Dolomites' third highest peak, Tofana di Mezzo, at 3,244 meters (10,643 feet). In the summer months, you can access a 360-degree panoramic terrace with phenomenal views, along with hiking trails and vie ferrate. Adventurous types can opt for the moderately difficult 15-minute hike up to the top of Tofana di Mezzo. Reach Cima Tofana by taking three cable cars: from Cortina to Col Dursciè up to Ra Valles and then on to Cima Tofana. ✉ *Cortina d'Ampezzo* ☎ *0436/5052* ⊕ *www.freccianelcielo.com* ✉ *€60–€70 round-trip for cable cars from Cortina to Cima Tofana* ⊙ *Closed early Apr.–early June and late Sept.–early Dec.*

Gruppo Guide Alpine Cortina Scuola di Alpinismo (*Mountaineering School*)
HIKING & WALKING | This group organizes climbing trips and trekking adventures. ✉ *Corso Italia 69/a, Cortina d'Ampezzo* ☎ *0436/868505* ⊕ *www.guidecortina. com* ✉ *Guided climbing trips from €330 per person.*

SKIING
Cortina offers ski options—with many long and picturesque runs—for all levels of skier in its three main ski areas: Cinque Torre (Lagazuoi and Faloria), Cristallo, and Tofana. Along with gondolas

directly from the center of town, efficient ski-bus service connects Cortina with the high-speed chairlifts and gondolas that ascend in all directions from the valley.

★ Cinque Torri – Lagazuoi
SKIING & SNOWBOARDING | FAMILY | The Cinque (5) Torri – Lagazuoi ski area includes 16 slopes of low and medium difficulty, including the 8.5-km (5.3-mile) Armenterola run, with panoramic views of the Fannes-Sennes-Prags Nature Park. From the Tofana ski area, take the Cortina Skyline gondola to reach the Cinque Torri slopes. ✉ *Between Giau Pass and Falzarego Pass, Cortina d'Ampezzo* ☎ *0436/871178* ⊕ *5torri.it* ✉ *Cortina Skyline cable car: €18 one-way, €23 round-trip* ⊙ *Closed mid-Apr.–June and mid-Sept.–late Dec.*

Cortina d'Ampezzo Ski Pass
SKIING & SNOWBOARDING | FAMILY | If you only want to ski in and around Cortina, this ski pass that includes 120 km (74 miles) of slopes in the Cortina d'Ampezzo, San Vito di Cadore, Auronzo, and Misurina resorts could be your best bet. You can buy the pass at ticket offices next to ski lifts throughout the area. ✉ *Via Marconi 15, Cortina d'Ampezzo* ☎ *0436/862171* ⊕ *skipasscortina.com* ✉ *€67 for 1 day.*

Dolomiti Superski Pass
SKIING & SNOWBOARDING | FAMILY | The Dolomiti Superski Pass provides access to the surrounding Dolomites, with 450 lifts and gondolas serving 1,200 km (750 miles) of trails. There's also a Dolomiti Supersummer Pass, good from mid-May to mid-November. Buy the passes at the ticket office next to the bus station and at other outlets in the Dolomites. ✉ *Via Marconi 15, Cortina d'Ampezzo* ☎ *0471/795397* ⊕ *www.dolomitisuperski.com* ✉ *Superski: from €68 for 1 day, lower rates for longer durations. Supersummer: €62 for 1 day.*

Faloria – Cristallo

SKIING & SNOWBOARDING | FAMILY | The Faloria – Cristallo ski area includes seven ski lifts and 15 slopes, ranging from beginner blue trails to advanced black trails. The Faloria gondola runs from the center of town up to Monte Faloria. ⊠ *Via Ria de Zeta 10, Cortina d'Ampezzo* ☎ *0436/5889* ⊕ *www.faloriacristallo.it* 🚟 *Cable car: €25 round-trip.*

Passo Falzarego

SKIING & SNOWBOARDING | The topography of the Passo Falzarego ski area, 16 km (10 miles) east of town, is dramatic. From here, a cable car takes you to one of the highest points in the Dolomites (Rifugio Lagazuoi)—where, on a clear day, you'll experience some of the best views. It's also easy to see why this was such a deadly area for soldiers in the Great War. Hiking is uneven in places, and there are vie ferrate that require the use of helmets and flashlights; other paths lead to tunnels that don't require helmets. You can reach Passo Falzarego from Cortina by transferring from the Freccia nel Cielo cable car to the Cortina Skyline cable car, or by taking a car or bus. ⊠ *Between Lagazuoi and Col Gallina opposite Sass de Stria, Cortina d'Ampezzo* ☎ *0436/867301 cable car ticket office* ⊕ *lagazuoi.it* 🚟 *Lagazuoi cable car: €26 round-trip late Dec.–early Apr.; €26.50 round-trip June, July, and Sept.–late Oct.; €29 round-trip Aug.* ☉ *Lagazuoi cable car closed early Apr.–May and late Oct.–late Dec.*

★ Tofana

SKIING & SNOWBOARDING | FAMILY | The Tofana ski area—home to past Alpine Ski World Cups and Alpine World Ski Championships, and the site of the Alpine Skiing event at the 2026 Winter Olympics, on the challenging Olympia delle Tofane slope—has 11 ski lifts and 37 slopes, with six black (advanced) slopes, 12 red (intermediate) slopes, and 19 blue (beginner) slopes. The Freccia del Cielo gondola runs from the center of Cortina up to Col Durscié at 1,778 meters (5,883 feet), where a second cable car ascends to Ra Valles at 2,470 meters (8,104 feet). At each stop, you'll find restaurants, slopes, and, of course, great vistas. From Tofana (at the Son dei Prade stop), the Cortina Skyline gondola lets you access more slopes at the Cinque Torri ski area (at the Bai de Dones stop). ⊠ *Via dello Stadio 12, Cortina d'Ampezzo* ☎ *0436/5052* ⊕ *www.freccianelcielo.com* 🚟 *Cable car: €20 round-trip from Cortina to Col Durscié; €33 round-trip in winter and €30 in summer from Cortina to Ra Valles* ☉ *Closed early Apr.–mid-June and late Sept.–mid-Dec.*

Chapter 8

MILAN, LOMBARDY, AND THE LAKES

8

Updated by
Elizabeth Shemaria

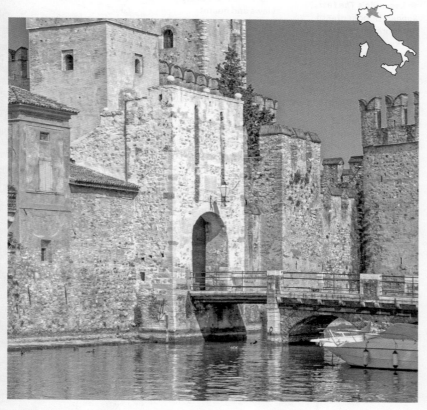

☉ Sights	🍴 Restaurants	🛏 Hotels	🛍 Shopping	🍸 Nightlife
★★★★☆	★★★★☆	★★★★☆	★★★★★	★★★☆☆

WELCOME TO
MILAN, LOMBARDY, AND THE LAKES

TOP REASONS TO GO

★ **Lake Como:** Ferries crisscross the waters, taking you from picture-book villages to stately villas to Edenic gardens—all against the backdrop of the snowcapped Alps.

★ **Leonardo's *The Last Supper*:** Behold one of the world's most famous works of art for yourself.

★ **The sky's no limit:** A funicular ride in Bergamo whisks you up to the magnificent medieval city.

★ **Milan alla moda:** As you window-shop the afternoon away in Milan's Quadrilatero della Moda district, catch a glimpse of fashion's latest trends.

★ **A night at La Scala:** What the Louvre is to art, Milan's La Scala is to the world of opera.

★ **Lake Garda and Lake Maggiore:** The former is great for outdoors enthusiasts; the latter has plentiful islands to explore.

★ **Cremona's violins:** If you are in the market for a violin, you'll find the world's best here in more than 150 shops.

1 Milan. The international fashion capital.

2 Bergamo. A charming medieval quarter.

3 Cremona. The birthplace of the violin.

4 Mantua. The Palazzo Ducale is a must.

5 Lake Iseo and Franciacorta. Lovely views and quaint restaurants.

6 Sirmione. A bustling spa town.

7 Riva del Garda. Stroll, sunbathe, or windsurf.

8 Gargnano. Don't miss the pleasant beach.

9 Gardone Riviera. A lovely town set against the Alps.

10 Bellagio. The belle of Lake Como.

11 Tremezzo. Explore two 18th-century villas.

12 Cernobbio. Villa d'Este hotel commands pride of place.

13 Como. A former silk town, with an urban vibe.

14 Stresa and the Isole Borromee. Grand hotels abound here.

15 Verbania. Gorgeous gardens and villas.

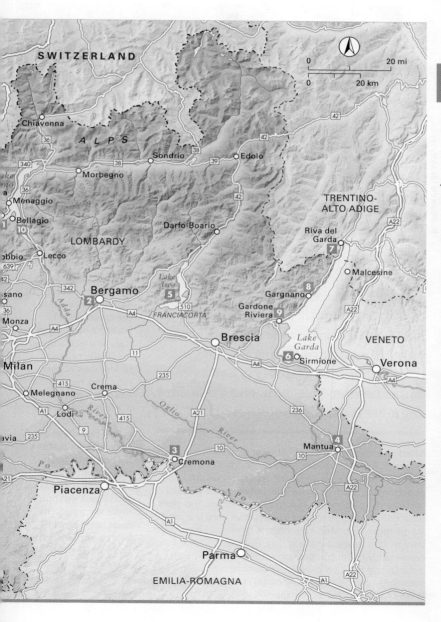

EATING WELL IN MILAN, LOMBARDY, AND THE LAKES

Rice from the Lombardy region

Lombardy may well offer Italy's most varied, rich, and refined cuisine. Local cooking is influenced by the neighboring regions of the north; foreign conquerors have left their mark; and today, business visitors, industrious immigrants, and well-traveled Milanese are likely to find more authentic ethnic cuisine in Milan than in any other Italian city.

Milan runs counter to many established Italian dining customs. A "real" traditional Milanese meal is a rarity; instead, Milan offers a variety of tastes, prices, and opportunities, from expense-account elegance in fancy restaurants to abundant *aperitivo*-hour nibbles. The city's cosmopolitan nature means trends arrive here first, and things move fast. Meals are not the drawn-out pastime they tend to be elsewhere in Italy. But the food is still consistently good: competition among restaurants is fierce and the local clientele is demanding, which means you can be reasonably certain that if a place looks promising, it won't disappoint.

THE COTOLETTA QUESTION

Everyone has an opinion on *cotoletta*, the breaded veal cutlet known across Italy as *una Milanese*. It's clearly related to Austria's Wiener schnitzel, but did the Austrians introduce it when they seized Milan, or did they take it home when they left? Some think it's best with fresh tomato and arugula on top; others find this sacrilege. Two things unite all camps: the meat must be well beaten until it's thin, and it must never leave a grease spot after it's fried.

REGIONAL SPECIALTIES

Ask an Italian what Lombards eat, and you're likely to hear *cotoletta, càsoeûla,* and *risotto giallo*—all dishes that reinforce Lombardy's status as the crossroads of Italy. *Cotoletta alla Milanese* may very well have Austrian roots. *Càsoeûla* is a cabbage-and-pork stew that resembles French cassoulet, though some say it has Spanish origins. *Risotto giallo* (also known as *risotto Milanese*) is colorful and perfumed with exotic saffron.

Veal Milanese

BUTTER AND CHEESE

Geography and a strong agricultural tradition mean that animal products are more common here than in southern Italy; butter and cream, for example, take the place of olive oil. One rare point of agreement about cotoletta is that it's cooked in butter, and the first and last steps of risotto making—toasting the rice, then letting it "repose" before serving—use ample amounts of butter. And the second-most-famous name in Italian cheese (after Parmesan) is likely Gorgonzola, named for a town near Milan; the best now comes from Novara.

RISOTTO

Rice is Lombardy's answer to pasta, and the region is the center of Italian (and European) rice production. From Milan's risotto giallo with its saffron tint, to Mantua's risotto with pumpkin or sausage, there's no end to the variety. Canonical risotto should be *all'onda,* flowing off the spoon like a wave. In keeping with the Italian tradition of wasting nothing, yesterday's risotto is flattened in a pan and fried in butter to produce *riso al salto,* which at its best has a crispy crust and a tender middle.

PANETTONE

Panettone, a tall, fluffy yeast bread, is flavored with candied fruit. Invented in Milan, it graces nearly every table during the Christmas holiday. Consumption begins on December 7, Milan's patron saint's day, and goes until supplies run out at January's end.

WINE

The Franciacorta region around Brescia makes highly regarded sparkling wines, often called the "Champagne of Italy" since they're produced using the same labor-intensive method. The Valtellina area to the northeast of Milan produces two notable reds from the *nebbiolo* grape: Valtellina Superiore and the intense dessert wine Sforzato di Valtellina. Lake breezes yield crisp, smooth whites from the shores of Lake Garda.

Panettone

8

Milan, Lombardy, and the Lakes   EATING WELL IN MILAN, LOMBARDY, AND THE LAKES

Lombardy is one of Italy's most dynamic regions, offering everything from world-class ski slopes to summer lake resorts, and Milan is the pulse of the nation—commercial, fashionable, and forward-looking. The Renaissance cities of the Po Plain—Cremona and Mantua—offer the romantic Italy visitors dream about, embracing their past by preserving national treasures while keeping an eye on the present.

Topping any list of the region's attractions are the glacial lakes at the very feet of the Alps, praised as the closest thing to paradise by writers throughout the ages, from Virgil to Hemingway.

Millions of travelers have concurred: for sheer beauty, the lakes of northern Italy—Como, Maggiore, Garda, Iseo, and Orta—have few equals. Along their shores are 18th- and 19th-century villas, exotic formal gardens, sleepy villages, and dozens of Belle Époque–era resorts that were once Europe's most fashionable and that still retain a powerful allure.

Milan can be disappointingly modern and congested—a little too much like the place you've come to Italy to escape—but its historic buildings and art collections in many ways rival those of Florence and Rome. And if you love to shop, Milan is one of the world's great fashion centers, offering experiences and goods for every taste.

MAJOR REGIONS

Milan. Long the country's capital of commerce, finance, fashion, and media, Milan is also Italy's transport hub, with the biggest international airport.

The Po Plain, Lake Garda, and Lake Iseo. Italy's wealthiest, most populous region is home not only to Milan but also to nearby medieval towns that once rivaled Milan in power. Bergamo, set against the Bergamese Alps, is a modern town connected by funicular to its lovely ancient counterpart, and Cremona is renowned for its incomparable violin-making tradition.

An hour's drive from Milan, sleepy Lake Iseo merits a stop for waterfront eateries amid picture-postcard settings. Lake Garda is the region's biggest and, by most accounts, cleanest lake. Places of note include the port town Gargnano (known for its association with Mussolini) and quaint 19th-century Gardone Riviera.

Lakes Como and Maggiore. Palatial villas, rose-laden belvederes, and majestic Alpine vistas are among the treasures of Lake Como—Europe's deepest lake. Many travelers head directly to boats for Bellagio and the *centro di lago*, the beautiful center region of the lake's three branches. Lake Maggiore has a unique geographical position: its mountainous western shore is in Piedmont, its lower eastern shore is in Lombardy, and its northern tip is in Switzerland.

Planning

Getting Here and Around

AIR

The region's main international gateway airport is Aeroporto Malpensa (⊕ *www. milanomalpensa-airport.com*), 48 km (30 miles) northwest of Milan. Some international and domestic flights also fly into more central Aeroporto Linate (⊕ *www. milanolinate-airport.com*), 7 km (4 miles) east of Milan, while European low-cost carriers like Ryanair use Aeroporto Milano Bergamo Orio al Serio, 55 km (34 miles) northeast of Milan and 5 km (3 miles) south of Bergamo.

BOAT

Frequent daily ferry and hydrofoil services link the lakeside towns and villages. Residents take them to get to work and school, while visitors use them for exploring the area. There are also special round-trip excursions, some with (optional) dining service on board.

CONTACT Navigazione Laghi.
🕾 *800/551801 in Italy* ⊕ *www.navigazionelaghi.it.*

BUS

Bus service isn't the best way to travel between cities here because trains are faster, cheaper, and more convenient. There's regular bus service for reaching and traveling between the small towns

on the lakes. It's less convenient than going by boat or by car, and it's used primarily by locals (particularly schoolchildren), but sightseers can use it as well. The bus service around Lake Garda serves mostly towns on the western shore.

CONTACTS Arriva Italia. 🕾 *035/289000 call center* ⊕ *www.arriva.it.* **Autostradale.** 🕾 *02/30089000* ⊕ *www.autostradale.it.*

CAR

Getting almost anywhere by car is a snap, as several major highways intersect at Milan, all connected by the *tangenziale,* the city's ring road. The A4 autostrada runs west to Turin and east to Venice; the A1 leads south to Bologna, Florence, and Rome; the A7 angles southwest down to Genoa. The A8 goes northwest toward Lake Maggiore, and the A9 runs north past Lake Como and into Switzerland's southernmost tip.

To get around the lakes themselves by car, you have to follow secondary roads. The SP572 follows the southern and western shores of Lake Garda, the SS45bis edges the northernmost section of the western shore, and the SR249 runs along the eastern shore. Around Lake Como, follow the SS340 along the western shore, the SS36 on the eastern shore, and the SP583 on the lower arms. The SS33 and SS34 trace the western shore of Lake Maggiore. The SP469 runs on the western side of Lake Iseo, while the SP510 borders the east. Although the roads around the lakes can be beautiful, they're full of harrowing twists and turns, making for a slow, challenging drive— often with an Italian speed racer on your tail.

CONTACT ACI (Automobile Club d'Italia). 🕾 *803/116* ⊕ *www.aci.it.*

TRAIN

Milan's majestic Central Station (Milano Centrale), 3 km (2 miles) northwest of the Duomo, has frequent service within the region to Como, Bergamo, Brescia,

Sirmione, Cremona, and Mantua. There are plenty of signs to help you get around, but its sheer size requires considerable amounts of walking and patience, so allow for some extra time here.

Tickets bought without a reservation need to be validated by stamping them in yellow machines on the train platforms, or, for tickets purchased online, by following directions in your email confirmation. Tickets with reservations don't require validation. When in doubt, validate—it can't hurt. For general information on trains and schedules, as well as online ticket purchases, visit the website of the Italian national railway, Trenitalia, also known as Ferrovie dello Stato (FS).

CONTACT Trenitalia. ✉ *Milan* ☎ *892021 in Italy* ⊕ *www.trenitalia.com.*

Making the Most of Your Time

Italy's commercial hub isn't usually at the top of the list for visiting tourists, but Milan is the nation's most modern city, with its own sophisticated appeal: its fashionable shops rival those of New York and Paris, its soccer teams are Italy's answer to the Yankees and the Mets, its opera performances set the standard for the world, and its art treasures are well worth the visit.

The biggest draw in the region, though, is the Lake District. Throughout history, the magnificently beautiful lakes of Como, Garda, Maggiore, Iseo, and Orta have attracted their fair share of well-known faces—from Winston Churchill and Russian royalty to George Clooney and Madonna. Each lake town has its own history and distinct character. If you have limited time, visit the lake you think best suits your style, but if you have time to spare, make the rounds to two or three to get a sense of their contrasts.

Restaurants

You'll find lots of traditional northern Italian restaurants in this region, and can pretty much count on menus divided into pasta, fish, and meat options. As in the rest of Italy, it's common for dishes to feature seasonal and local ingredients. Meal prices in Milan tend to be higher than in the rest of the region (and quite high for European cities in general), though this is also where you'll see examples of the latest food trends and more adventurous choices on the menus.

Hotels

Given that this is the wealthiest part of Italy, most hotels here cater to a clientele willing to pay for extra comfort. Outside Milan, many are converted villas with well-landscaped grounds. Most of the famous lake resorts are expensive; many smaller lakeside hotels are more reasonably priced. Local tourism offices throughout the region are an excellent source of information about affordable lodging.

Please note that the time for "high season" can vary here—in the lakes it's the height of summer, not surprisingly, but in Milan it depends on what fairs and exhibitions are being staged. Prices in almost all hotels can go up dramatically during Salone, the furniture and design fair in early April. Fashion, travel, and tech fairs also draw big crowds throughout the year, raising prices. In contrast to other cities in Italy, however, you can often find discounts on weekends. The lakes, including Maggiore and Garda, have little to offer except quiet from November to March, when most gardens, hotels, and restaurants are closed.

⇨ *Hotel and restaurant reviews have been shortened. For full information, visit Fodors.com. Prices in the hotel reviews* are the lowest cost of a standard double room in high season. Prices in the dining reviews are the average cost of a main course at dinner, or, if dinner is not served, at lunch.

What It Costs in Euros

	$	$$	$$$	$$$$
HOTELS				
	under €125	€125–€200	€201–€300	over €300
RESTAURANTS				
	under €15	€15–€24	€25–€35	over €35

Milan

Rome may be bigger and wield political power, but Milan and the affluent north are what really make the country go. Leonardo da Vinci's *The Last Supper* and other great works of art are here, as well as a spectacular Gothic Duomo, the finest of its kind.

And yet, Milan hasn't won the battle for hearts and minds when it comes to tourism. Most visitors prefer Tuscany's hills and Venice's canals to Milan's hectic efficiency and wealthy indifference. But its secrets reveal themselves slowly to those who look. A side street conceals a garden complete with flamingos (Giardini Invernizzi, on Via dei Cappuccini, just off Corso Venezia; closed to the public, but you can still catch a glimpse), and a renowned 20th-century-art collection hides modestly behind an unspectacular facade a block from Corso Buenos Aires (the Casa-Museo Boschi di Stefano).

Virtually every invader in European history—Gaul, Roman, Goth, Lombard, and Frank—as well as a long series of rulers from France, Spain, and Austria, took a turn at ruling the city. After being completely sacked by the Goths in AD 539 and by the Holy Roman Empire under Frederick Barbarossa in 1157, Milan became one of the first independent city-states of the Renaissance. Its heyday of self-rule proved comparatively brief. From 1277 until 1500 it was ruled first by the Visconti and then the Sforza dynasties. These families were known, justly or not, for a peculiarly aristocratic mixture of refinement, classical learning, and cruelty; much of the surviving grandeur of Gothic and Renaissance art and architecture is their doing. Be on the lookout in your wanderings for the Visconti family emblem—a viper, its jaws straining wide, devouring a child.

GETTING HERE AND AROUND

The city center is compact and walkable; trolleys and trams make it even more accessible, and the efficient Metropolitana (subway) and buses provide access to locations farther afield. Driving in Milan is difficult and parking a real pain, so a car is a liability. In addition, drivers within the second ring of streets (the *bastioni*) must pay a daily congestion charge on weekdays between 7:30 am and 7:30 pm (until 6 pm on Thursday). You can pay the charge at news vendors, tobacconists, Banca Intesa Sanpaolo ATMs, or with the EasyPark app (⊕ www.easyparkitalia.it); parking meters and parking garages in the area also include it in the cost. There is also a public bike sharing system called BikeMi (⊕ www.bikemi.com).

BICYCLE
CONTACT BikeMi. ☎ 02/48607607 ⊕ www.bikemi.com.

PUBLIC TRANSPORTATION
A standard public transit ticket within the central zones of Milan costs €2.20 and is valid for a 90-minute trip on a subway, bus, or tram. An all-inclusive subway, bus, and tram pass costs €7.60 for 24 hours or €15.50 for three consecutive days. Another option is a Carnet (€19.50), good for 10 tram, bus, or subway rides. Individual tickets and passes can be purchased from news vendors, tobacconists, at ticket machines at all subway

stops, at ticket offices at the Duomo and other subway stops, and on your phone via the ATM Milano app. You can also pay for a subway ride using a contactless credit card at the turnstile to avoid ticket purchasing lines.

Once you have your ticket, either stamp it or insert it into the slots in station turnstiles or on poles inside trolleys and buses. (Electronic tickets won't function if they become bent or demagnetized. If you have a problem, contact a station manager, who can usually issue a new ticket.) Trains run from 6 am to 12:30 am.

CONTACTS ATM. (*Azienda Trasporti Milanesi*) ☎ *02/48607607* ⊕ *www.atm. it/en*. **Radiobus.** ☎ *02/48034803* ⊕ *www. atm.it/en*.

TAXI

Taxi fares in Milan are higher than in American cities; a short ride can run about €15 during rush hour or fashion week. You can get a taxi at a stand with an orange "Taxi" sign, or by calling one of the taxi companies. Most also have apps you can download to order taxis from your phone; some let you text or use WhatsApp to hail a cab. Dispatchers may speak some English; they'll ask for the phone number you're calling from, and they'll tell you the number of your taxi and how long it'll take to arrive. If you're in a restaurant or bar, ask the staff to call a cab for you.

CONTACTS 026969. ☎ *02/6969* ⊕ *www.026969.it*. **Taxi028585.** ☎ *02/8585* ⊕ *www.milanoradiotaxi.it*. **Taxiblu.** ☎ *02/4040* ⊕ *www.taxiblu.it*.

TOURS
CONTACT City Sightseeing Milano. ☎ *02/867131* ⊕ *www.city-sightseeing.it/ en/milan*.

VISITOR INFORMATION
CONTACT Milan Tourism Office. ⊠ *Piazza del Duomo 14, next to Palazzo Reale, Duomo* ☎ *02/88455555* ⊕ *www.yesmilano.it*.

Duomo

Milan's main streets radiate out from the massive Duomo, a late-Gothic cathedral begun in 1386. Heading north is the handsome Galleria Vittorio Emanuele II, an enclosed shopping arcade that opens at one end to the world-famous opera house known as La Scala. Via Manzoni leads northeast from La Scala to the Quadrilatero della Moda, or fashion district. Heading northeast from the Duomo is the pedestrian-only street Corso Vittorio Emanuele II. Northwest of the Duomo is Via Dante, at the top of which is the imposing outline of the Castello Sforzesco.

Sights

Battistero Paleocristiano/Baptistry of San Giovanni alle Fonti
ARCHAEOLOGICAL SITE | More specifically known as the Baptistry of San Giovanni alle Fonti, this 4th-century baptistry is one of two that lie beneath the Duomo. Although opinion remains divided, it is widely believed to be where Ambrose, Milan's first bishop and patron saint, baptized Augustine. Tickets also include a visit to the Duomo and its museum. ⊠ *Piazza del Duomo, Duomo* ✛ *Enter through Duomo* ☎ *02/72023375* ⊕ *www.duomomilano.it* 🎟 *€12, including admission to Duomo and museum; €25, including Duomo, museum, and roof with elevator, valid for 72 hrs* Ⓜ *Duomo*.

★ Duomo
CHURCH | There is no denying that for sheer size and complexity, the Duomo is unrivaled in Italy. It is the second-largest church in the country—the largest being St. Peter's in Rome. This intricate Gothic structure has been fascinating and exasperating visitors and conquerors alike since it was begun by Gian Galeazzo Visconti III (1351–1402), first duke of Milan, in 1386. Consecrated in the 15th or 16th century, it was not completed until just

before the coronation of Napoléon as king of Italy in 1809.

The building is adorned with 135 marble spires and 2,245 marble statues. The Duomo's most famous sculpture is the gruesome but anatomically instructive figure of *San Bartolomeo* (St. Bartholomew), who was flayed alive. As you enter the apse to admire those splendid windows, glance at the sacristy doors to the right and left of the altar. The lunette on the right dates from 1393 and was decorated by Hans von Fernach. ⊠ *Piazza del Duomo, Duomo* ☎ 02/72023375 ⊕ *www.duomomilano.it* 🕿 *Cathedral and museum €10; cathedral, museum, and archaeological area €12; stairs to roof €20; elevator €25* Ⓜ *Duomo*.

★ Galleria Vittorio Emanuele II

STORE/MALL | This spectacular late-19th-century Belle Époque tunnel is essentially one of the planet's earliest and most select shopping malls, with upscale tenants that include Gucci and Prada. This is the city's heart, midway between the Duomo and La Scala. It teems with life, which makes for great people-watching from the tables that spill out from bars and restaurants, where you can enjoy an overpriced coffee. Books, clothing, food, hats, and jewelry are all for sale. Known as Milan's "parlor," the Galleria is often viewed as a barometer of the city's well-being. ⊠ *Piazza del Duomo, Duomo* Ⓜ *Duomo*.

Milano Osservatorio—Fondazione Prada

SPECIALTY MUSEUM | This contemporary photography and visual languages exhibition space, developed in partnership with Fondazione Prada, is spread over two floors in the Galleria Vittorio Emanuele II. Exhibitions, which rotate several times a year, explore the cultural and social implications of expression. The space itself, bombed after World War II and then fully restored, is worth visiting just for the unique view of the Galleria dome through the large windows. You can reach the gallery via the elevator next to the Prada store. ⊠ *Galleria Vittorio Emanuele II, Piazza del Duomo, Duomo* ☎ 02/56662611 ⊕ *www.fondazioneprada. org/visit/milano-osservatorio* 🕿 *€10; €15, including Fondazione Prada* ☉ *Closed Tues.* Ⓜ *Duomo*.

Museo del Novecento

ART MUSEUM | Ascend a Guggenheim-esque spiral walkway to reach the modern works at this petite yet dense collection of Italian contemporary art, adjacent to the Duomo. The museum highlights 20th-century Italian artists, including a strong showing of Futurists, like Boccioni and Severini, and sculptures from Marini, along with a smattering of works by other European artists, including Picasso, Braque, and Matisse. ⊠ *Via Marconi 1, Duomo* ☎ 02/88444061 ⊕ *www.muse-odelnovecento.org* 🕿 *€5 (free every 1st and 3rd Tues. of month after 2)* ☉ *Closed Mon.* Ⓜ *Duomo*.

★ Palazzo Reale

ART MUSEUM | Elaborately decorated with painted ceilings and grand staircases, this former royal palace close to the Duomo is almost worth a visit in itself; however, it also functions as one of Milan's major art galleries, with a focus on modern artists. Exhibitions have highlighted works by Picasso, Chagall, Warhol, Pollock, and Kandinsky. Check the website before you visit to see what's on; purchase tickets online in advance to save time in the queues, which are often long and chaotic. ⊠ *Piazza del Duomo 12, Duomo* ☎ 02/88445181 ⊕ *www.palazzorealemi-lano.it* 🕿 *Varies by exhibition* ☉ *Closed Mon.* Ⓜ *Duomo*.

Pinacoteca Ambrosiana

ART MUSEUM | Cardinal Federico Borromeo, one of Milan's native saints, founded this picture gallery in 1618 with the addition of his personal art collection to a bequest of books to Italy's first public library. The core works of the collection include such treasures as Caravaggio's *Basket of Fruit,* Raphael's monumental preparatory drawing (known

Sights ▼

1. Battistero Paleocristiano/ Baptistry of San Giovanni alle Fonti **H5**
2. Duomo **H5**
3. Galleria Vittorio Emanuele II....................... **G4**
4. Milano Osservatorio— Fondazione Prada **G4**
5. Museo del Novecento **G6**
6. Palazzo Reale **H7**
7. Pinacoteca Ambrosiana.......... **D6**
8. Santa Maria Presso San Satiro **E7**

Restaurants ▼

1. Da Giacomo Arengario........... **G6**
2. La Vecchia Latteria................ **E7**
3. Piz **D7**

Coffee and Quick Bites ▼

1. Camparino in Galleria **G5**
2. Piccolo Peck **E6**

Hotels ▼

1. Hotel Gran Duca di York........ **C6**
2. Hotel Spadari al Duomo........... **E6**
3. Maison Milano | UNA Esperienze **F6**
4. Park Hyatt Milan.................... **F4**
5. Room Mate Giulia.................. **F5**

as a "cartoon") for *The School of Athens,* which hangs in the Vatican, and Leonardo da Vinci's *Portrait of a Musician.* The highlight for many is Leonardo's *Codex Atlanticus,* which features thousands of his sketches and drawings. ⊠ *Piazza Pio XI 2, Duomo* ☎ *02/806921* ⊕ *www. ambrosiana.it/en* ✑ *€16.50* ⊘ *Closed Wed.* Ⓜ *Duomo.*

Santa Maria Presso San Satiro

CHURCH | Just a few steps from the Duomo, this architectural gem was first built in 876 and later perfected by Bramante (1444–1514), demonstrating his command of proportion and perspective—hallmarks of Renaissance architecture. Bramante tricks the eye with a famous optical illusion that makes a small interior seem extraordinarily spacious and airy, while accommodating a beloved 13th-century fresco. ⊠ *Via Torino 17–19, Duomo* ☎ *02/874683* Ⓜ *Duomo; Tram No. 2, 3, 4, 12, 14, 19, 20, 24, or 27.*

🍴 Restaurants

Da Giacomo Arengario

$$$$ | **ITALIAN** | Join businesspeople, ladies who lunch, and in-the-know travelers at this elegant restaurant atop the Museo del Novecento and with a glorious Duomo view (be sure to request a window table, though, or risk being relegated to a viewless back room). To complement the vistas, choose from a selection of well-prepared seafood, pasta, and meat courses for lunch and dinner; the servers are happy to recommend pairings from the extensive wine list. **Known for:** amazing Duomo views from tables by the windows; contemporary Milanese dishes; wine pairings. ⑤ *Average main: €38* ⊠ *Via Marconi 1, Duomo* ☎ *02/72093814* ⊕ *giacomomilano.com/en* Ⓜ *Duomo.*

La Vecchia Latteria

$$ | **VEGETARIAN** | In its two small dining rooms, this family-owned lunch spot serves an impressive amount of vegetarian cuisine. Nestled on a small street just steps away from the Duomo, it offers an array of freshly prepared seasonal selections from a daily-changing menu; try the *misto forno* (mixed plate), which offers a taste of several different small dishes. **Known for:** Italian-focused vegetarian cuisine; varied menu; retro '50s atmosphere. ⑤ *Average main: €15* ⊠ *6 Via dell'Unione, Duomo* ☎ *02/874401* ⊕ *www.facebook.com/la.vecchia.latteria* ⊘ *Closed Sun. No dinner* ☞ *Reservations suggested* Ⓜ *Duomo or Missori.*

★ Piz

$ | **PIZZA** | Fun, lively, and full of locals, this casual and inexpensive pizzeria on a side street near the Duomo has just four kinds of thin-crust pizza on the menu—luckily, all are excellent. Choose from *margherita, bianca* (white, with no tomato), marinara (with no mozzarella), and the pizza of the day; although you'll inevitably need to wait, you'll likely get a free glass of prosecco and a slice of pizza while you do. **Known for:** pizzas with seasonal toppings; free before- and after-dinner drinks; bustling vibe. ⑤ *Average main: €11* ⊠ *Via Torino 34, Duomo* ☎ *02/72096413* ⊕ *www.facebook.com/pizmilano* Ⓜ *Duomo; Tram No. 2, 3, or 14.*

☕ Coffee and Quick Bites

Camparino in Galleria

$$$ | **EUROPEAN** | One thing has remained constant in the Galleria: the Camparino, whose inlaid counter, mosaics, and wrought-iron fixtures have been welcoming tired shoppers since 1867. Small plates to be enjoyed with a Campari aperitif are served in pretty Bar di Passo downstairs, while a more extensive range of Campari cocktails paired with food for aperitivo or dinner is available in elegant Sala Spiritello upstairs. **Known for:** contemporary versions of Campari cocktails; high-end aperitivo; prime people-watching. ⑤ *Average main: €30* ⊠ *Galleria Vittorio Emanuele, Piazza del*

Duomo 21, Duomo ☎ 02/86464435 ⊕ www.camparino.com Ⓜ Duomo.

Piccolo Peck

$$ | SANDWICHES | The café at this foodie paradise near the Duomo features Italian specialty foods such as excellent cheeses, charcuterie, vegetables in olive oil, seafood, and sandwiches. It also reinterprets classic dishes like Russian salad and pâté, which can be washed down with a fine selection of wines by the glass or a bottle from its cellar of global labels. **Known for:** wide bakery selection, including classic brioche; delicious Italian treats from the famed Peck deli; casual atmosphere. $ *Average main: €20* ✉ *Via Spadari 9, Duomo* ☎ *02/8023161* ⊕ *www.peck.it/en/restaurants/piccolo-peck* Ⓜ *Tram No. 2, 12, 14, 16, or 19.*

 Hotels

Hotel Gran Duca di York

$$$ | HOTEL | The spare but classically elegant and efficient rooms at this hotel are arranged around a courtyard—four have private terraces—and offer good value for pricey Milan. **Pros:** central location; friendly staff; good breakfast. **Cons:** limited amenities (no restaurant or gym); many rooms on the small side; showers can be tiny. $ *Rooms from: €240* ✉ *Via Moneta 1, Duomo* ☎ *02/874863* ⊕ *www.ducadiyork.com* ⤳ *33 rooms* ⓘⓞⓘ *Free Breakfast* Ⓜ *Cordusio or Duomo; Tram No. 2, 12, 14, 16, or 27.*

Hotel Spadari al Duomo

$$$ | HOTEL | That this chic city-center inn is owned by an architect's family comes through in details like the custom-designed furniture and paintings by young Milanese artists in the stylish guest rooms. **Pros:** good breakfast; central location; attentive staff. **Cons:** some rooms on the small side; street noise can be a problem; no restaurant. $ *Rooms from: €299* ✉ *Via Spadari 11, Duomo* ☎ *02/72002371* ⊕ *www.spadarihotel.com* ⤳ *40 rooms* ⓘⓞⓘ *Free*

Breakfast Ⓜ Duomo; Tram No. 2, 3, 12, 14, 16, 24, or 27.

Maison Milano | UNA Esperienze

$$$ | HOTEL | Inside this faithfully restored palazzo dating from the early 1900s, spaciousness is accentuated with soft white interiors, muted fabrics and marble, and contemporary lines. **Pros:** the warmth of a residence and the luxury of a design hotel; lovely bathrooms; friendly staff. **Cons:** breakfast not included; not much of a lobby; no restaurant or bar. $ *Rooms from: €264* ✉ *Via Mazzini 4, Duomo* ☎ *02/69826949* ⊕ *www.gruppouna.it/esperienze/maison-milano* ⤳ *27 rooms* ⓘⓞⓘ *No Meals* Ⓜ *Duomo; Tram No. 2, 3, 12, 14, 16, 24, or 27.*

★ Park Hyatt Milan

$$$$ | HOTEL | Extensive use of warm travertine stone and modern art creates a sophisticated yet inviting backdrop at the Park Hyatt, where spacious, opulent guest rooms have walk-in closets and bathrooms with double sinks, glass-enclosed rain showers, and separate soaking tubs. **Pros:** central location; contemporary decor and amenities; excellent restaurant. **Cons:** not particularly intimate; very expensive; some rooms showing a little wear. $ *Rooms from: €1,250* ✉ *Via Tommaso Grossi 1, Duomo* ☎ *02/88211234* ⊕ *www.hyatt.com/en-US/hotel/italy/park-hyatt-milan/milph* ⤳ *106 rooms* ⓘⓞⓘ *No Meals* Ⓜ *Duomo; Tram No. 1.*

★ Room Mate Giulia

$$$$ | HOTEL | For hip, design-focused lodging with a friendly feel and prime location right next to the Galleria and around the corner from the Duomo, you can't do much better than the city's outpost from Spanish hotel chain Room Mate. **Pros:** amazing location; fresh, appealing design; spa. **Cons:** expensive breakfast and room a bit cramped; gym on the small side; busy location means some noise in rooms. $ *Rooms from: €328* ✉ *Via Silvio Pellico 4, Duomo* ☎ *02/80888900* ⊕ *www.room-matehotels.com/en/giulia* ⤳ *85 rooms* ⓘⓞⓘ *No Meals* Ⓜ *Duomo; Tram No. 1.*

Nightlife

Bar STRAF

BARS | This architecturally stimulating but dimly lit place has such artistic features as recycled fiberglass panels and vintage 1970s furnishings. The music is an eclectic mix of chill-out tunes during the daytime, with more upbeat and vibrant tracks pepping it up at night. Located on a quiet side street near the Duomo, STRAF, inside the hotel of the same name, draws a young and lively, if tourist-heavy, crowd. ⊠ *Via San Raffaele 3, Duomo* ☎ *02/805081* ⊕ *www.straf.it/bar* Ⓜ *Duomo.*

🎭 Performing Arts

★ Teatro alla Scala

OPERA | You need know nothing of opera to sense that La Scala is closer to a cathedral than a concert hall. Hearing opera sung in this magical setting is an unparalleled experience: it is, after all, where Verdi established his reputation and where Maria Callas sang her way into opera lore. It stands as a symbol—both for the performer who dreams of singing here and for the opera buff—and its notoriously demanding audiences are apt to jeer performers who do not measure up. At the Museo Teatrale alla Scala you can admire an extensive collection of librettos, paintings of the famous names of Italian opera, posters, costumes, antique instruments, and design sketches for the theater. ⊠ *Piazza della Scala, Largo Ghiringhelli 1, Duomo* ☎ *02/72003744 theater, 02/88797473 museum* ⊕ *www.teatroalascala.org* 🎫 *Museum €12* Ⓜ *Duomo or Cordusio; Tram No. 1.*

🛍 Shopping

Borsalino

HATS & GLOVES | The kingpin of milliners, Borsalino has managed to stay trendy since it opened in 1857. ⊠ *Galleria Vittorio Emanuele II 92, Duomo* ☎ *02/89015436* ⊕ *www.borsalino.com* Ⓜ *Duomo; Tram No. 1.*

Gucci

CLOTHING | This Florence-born brand attracts lots of fashion-forward tourists in hot pursuit of its monogrammed bags, shoes, and accessories. ⊠ *Galleria Vittorio Emanuele II, Duomo* ☎ *02/8597991* ⊕ *www.gucci.com* Ⓜ *Duomo; Tram No. 1.*

La Rinascente

DEPARTMENT STORE | The flagship location of this always bustling and very central department store—adjacent to both the Duomo and the Galleria Vittorio Emanuele II—carries a wide range of Italian and international brands (both high-end and casual) for men, women, and children. There's also a fine selection of beauty and home products. ⊠ *Piazza Duomo, Duomo* ☎ *02/91387388* ⊕ *www.rinascente.it* Ⓜ *Duomo; Tram No. 1, 2, 12, 14, 16, or 27.*

Castello

This 15th-century castle is home to crypts, battlements, tunnels, and an interesting array of museums.

👁 Sights

Castello Sforzesco

HISTORIC SIGHT | Wandering the grounds of this tranquil castle and park near the center of Milan is a great respite from the often-hectic city, and the interesting museums inside are an added bonus. Highlights include the Sala delle Asse, a frescoed room attributed to Leonardo da Vinci (1452–1519), and Michelangelo's unfinished *Rondanini Pietà*, believed to be his last work. The *pinacoteca* (picture gallery) features 230 paintings from medieval times to the 18th century, and the Museo dei Mobili e delle Sculture Lignee (Furniture Museum) includes a delightful collection of Renaissance treasure chests. ⊠ *Piazza Castello, Castello* ☎ *02/88463700* ⊕ *www.milanocastello.*

it *Castle free, museums €5 (free every 1st and 3rd Tues. of month after 2, and 1st Sun. of month)* ⊘ *Museums closed Mon.* Ⓜ *Cadorna, Lanza, or Cairoli; Tram No. 1, 2, 4, 12, 14, or 19; Bus No. 18, 37, 50, 58, 61, or 94.*

🎭 Performing Arts

Teatro Dal Verme
CONCERTS | Frequent classical, rock, and jazz concerts by international artists are staged here from October to May. ✉ *Via San Giovanni sul Muro 2, Castello* ☎ *02/87905* ⊕ *www.ipomeriggi.it* Ⓜ *Cairoli; Tram No. 1 or 4.*

Sempione

Just beyond the Sforzesco Castle grounds is a large park that holds an aquarium, the Triennale museum, and the Torre Branca.

◉ Sights

Parco Sempione
CITY PARK | FAMILY | Originally the gardens and parade grounds of the Castello Sforzesco, this open space was reorganized during the Napoleonic era, when the arena on its northeast side was constructed, and then turned into a park during the building boom at the end of the 19th century. It is still the lungs of the city's fashionable western neighborhoods, and the **Aquarium** still attracts Milan's schoolchildren. The park became a bit of a design showcase in 1933 with the construction of the Triennale. ✉ *Piazza Sempione, Sempione* ⊕ *www.yesmilano.it/en/see-and-do/itineraries/explore-parco-sempione* ▣ *Free* Ⓜ *Cairoli, Lanza or Cadorna; Tram No. 1, 2, 4, 12, 14, 19, or 27; Bus No. 43, 57, 61, 70, or 94.*

Torre Branca
VIEWPOINT | It is worth visiting Parco Sempione just to see the Torre Branca. Designed by architect Gio Ponti

(1891–1979), who was behind so many of the projects that made Milan the design capital that it is, this steel tower rises 330 feet over the Triennale. Take the elevator to get a nice view of the city, then have a drink at the glitzy Justme Milano Restaurant and Club at its base. ✉ *Parco Sempione, Sempione* ☎ *02/6847122* ⊕ *www.museobranca.it/torre-branca* ▣ *€6* ⊘ *Closed Mon., Tues., and Thurs., and mid-May–mid-Nov.* Ⓜ *Cadorna; Tram No. 1; Bus No. 61.*

Triennale Design Museum
ART MUSEUM | In addition to honoring Italy's design talent, the Triennale also offers a regular series of exhibitions on design from around the world. A spectacular bridge entrance leads to a permanent collection, an exhibition space, and a stylish café and rooftop restaurant with expansive views. The Triennale also manages the fascinating museum-studio of designer Achille Castiglioni, in nearby Piazza Castello (hour-long guided tours are available Tuesday through Friday at 10, 11, and noon, and one Saturday a month ▣ *€15*. Call or email in advance to book: ☎ *02/8053606* ✐ *info@achillecastiglioni.it*). ✉ *Via Alemagna 6, Sempione* ☎ *02/72434244* ⊕ *www.triennale.org* ▣ *From €15* ⊘ *Closed Mon.* Ⓜ *Cadorna; Bus No. 61.*

Brera

To the north of the Duomo lie the winding streets of this elegant neighborhood, once the city's bohemian quarter.

◉ Sights

★ Pinacoteca di Brera (*Brera Art Gallery*)
ART MUSEUM | The collection here is star-studded even by Italian standards. Highlights include the somber *Cristo Morto* (Dead Christ) by Mantegna, which dominates Room VI with its sparse palette of umber and its foreshortened perspective, Raphael's (1483–1520)

Sposalizio della Vergine (Marriage of the Virgin), and *La Vergine con il Bambino e Santi (Madonna with Child and Saints)*, by Piero della Francesca (1420–92), an altarpiece commissioned by Federico da Montefeltro (shown kneeling, in full armor, before the Virgin). ⊠ *Via Brera 28, Brera* ☎ *02/72105141* ⊕ *www.pinaco-tecabrera.org* ⊿ *€15* ⊘ *Closed Mon.* Ⓜ *Montenapoleone or Lanza; Tram No. 1, 4, 12, 14, or 27; Bus No. 61.*

⊗ Restaurants

★ Cittamani

$$$ | **MODERN INDIAN** | Celebrity chef Ritu Dalmia runs well-regarded Italian restaurants in India, so it's no surprise that her restaurant in Milan offers a mash-up of modern Indian food with Italian and international ingredients; even the decor, with shelves of pottery and terrazzo floors, is a cultural combo. Look for unexpected flavors and a mix of small plates, more substantial mains, and utterly delicious fusion desserts. **Known for:** Indian food quite different from the norm; nontraditional naans; sleek contemporary setting. Ⓢ *Average main: €25* ⊠ *Piazza Mirabello 5, Brera* ☎ *02/38240935* ⊕ *www.cittam-ani.com* ⊘ *Closed Sun. No lunch Sat.* Ⓜ *Moscova or Turati; Bus No. 43 or 94.*

Fioraio Bianchi Caffè

$$$ | **MODERN ITALIAN** | A French-style bistro in the heart of Milan, Fioraio Bianchi Caffè was opened more than 40 years ago by Raimondo Bianchi, a great lover of flowers; in fact, eating at this restaurant is a bit like dining in a Parisian boutique with floral decor. Despite the French atmosphere, the dishes have Italian flair and ensure a classy, inventive meal. **Known for:** charming, flower-filled, shabby-chic setting; creative Italian-style bistro food; great spot for morning coffee and pastries. Ⓢ *Average main: €28* ⊠ *Via Montebello 7, Brera* ☎ *02/29014390* ⊕ *www.fioraiobianchicaffe.it* ⊘ *Closed Sun. and 3 wks in Aug.* Ⓜ *Turati.*

☕ Coffee and Quick Bites

N'Ombra de Vin

$$ | **WINE BAR** | This enoteca serves wine by the glass and, in addition to the plates of *salumi* (Italian cold cuts) and cheese nibbles, has light food and not-so-light desserts. It's a great place for people-watching on Via San Marco, while indoors offers a more dimly lit, romantic setting; check out the impressive vaulted basement, where bottled wines and spirits are sold. **Known for:** atmospheric setting in an Augustinian refectory; Italian and French wines; solid tapas dishes. Ⓢ *Average main: €18* ⊠ *Via S. Marco 2, Brera* ☎ *02/6599650* ⊕ *www.nom-bradevin.it* Ⓜ *Lanza, Turati, or Montenapoleone; Tram No. 1, 2, 4, 12, or 14.*

▭ Hotels

Bulgari Hotel Milano

$$$$ | **HOTEL** | Housed in an 18th-century palazzo on a quiet street a short stroll from Brera and Montenapoleone shopping, the Bulgari offers up chic yet restrained rooms, an enormous garden, and a celebrity-chef-helmed restaurant. **Pros:** excellent spa, with heated pool, sauna, and Jacuzzi; trendy and fashionable guests; convenient location for sightseeing. **Cons:** rooms are a bit bland; service not quite up to par; extremely expensive. Ⓢ *Rooms from: €1650* ⊠ *Via Privata Fratelli Gabba 7/b, Brera* ☎ *02/8058051* ⊕ *www.bulgarihotels.com/en_US/milan* ⊄ *61 rooms* ⦿*No Meals* Ⓜ *Montenapoleone.*

☉ Nightlife

Il Bar at Bulgari Hotel Milano

BARS | Having drinks or a light lunch at the Bulgari Hotel bar (Il Bar or The Bar) lets you step off the asphalt and into one of the city's most impressive private urban gardens—even indoors you seem to be outside, separated from the elements by a towering wall of glass. The Bar is a great place to run into international hotel guests and jet-setting Milanese, and the staff mix up a wide range of traditional and novel drinks—including the Bulgari Cocktail with gin, Aperol, and orange, pineapple, and lime juices. ✉ *Via Privata Fratelli Gabba 7/b, Brera* ☎ *02/8058051* ⊕ *www.bulgarihotels.com/en_US/milan/bar-and-restaurant/il-bar* Ⓜ *Montenapoleone; Tram No. 1.*

👜 Shopping

With its narrow streets and outdoor cafés, Brera is one of Milan's most charming neighborhoods. Wander through it to find smaller shops with some appealing offerings from lesser-known names that cater to the well-heeled taste of this upscale area. The densest concentration is along Via Brera, Via Solferino, and Corso Garibaldi.

Mercato di Via S. Marco

MARKET | The Monday- and Thursday-morning markets here cater to the wealthy residents of the central Brera neighborhood. In addition to food stands where you can get cheese, roast chicken, and dried beans and fruits, there are several clothing and shoe stalls that are important stops for some of Milan's most elegant women. ✉ *Via San Marco, near Via Castelfidardo, Brera* Ⓜ *Lanza; Tram No. 2, 4, 12, or 14.*

Sant'Ambrogio

If the part of the city to the north of the Duomo is dominated by shopping, Sant'Ambrogio and other parts to the south are known for art. The most famous piece is *Il Cenacolo*—known in English as *The Last Supper.* If you have time for nothing else, make sure you see this masterpiece, which is housed in the refectory of Santa Maria delle Grazie. Reservations are required to see it, and you should make yours at least three weeks before you depart for Italy, so you can plan the rest of your time in Milan.

👁 Sights

Basilica di Sant'Ambrogio (*Basilica of St. Ambrose*)

CHURCH | Milan's bishop, St. Ambrose (one of the original Doctors of the Catholic Church), consecrated this church in AD 387. St. Ambroeus, as he is known in Milanese dialect, is the city's patron saint, and his remains—dressed in elegant religious robes, a miter, and gloves—can be viewed inside a glass case in the crypt below the altar. Until the construction of the more imposing Duomo, this was Milan's most important church. Much restored and reworked over the centuries (the gold-and-gem-encrusted altar dates from the 9th century), Sant'Ambrogio still preserves its Romanesque characteristics, including 5th-century mosaics. The church is often closed for weddings on Saturdays. ✉ *Piazza Sant'Ambrogio 15, Sant'Ambrogio* ☎ *02/86450895* ⊕ *www.basilicasantambrogio.it* Ⓜ *Sant'Ambrogio; Bus No. 50, 58, or 94.*

Chiesa di San Maurizio al Monastero Maggiore

CHURCH | Next to the Museo Civico Archeologico, you'll find this little gem of a church, constructed starting in 1503 and decorated almost completely with magnificent 16th-century frescoes. The modest exterior belies the treasures inside, including a concealed back room once used by nuns that includes a fascinating fresco of Noah loading the ark with animals, including two unicorns. ✉ *Corso Magenta 15, Sant'Ambrogio* ☎ *02/88445208* ⊕ *www.museoarcheologicomilano.it/oltre-il-museo/la-chiesa-s.-maurizio-al-monastero-maggiore* ⊙ *Closed Mon.* Ⓜ *Cadorna or Cairoli; Tram No. 16 or 27; Bus No. 50, 58, or 94.*

Castello, Sempione,
Brera, Sant'Ambrogio,
Fiera and San Siro

★ **The Last Supper/Il Cenacolo/Santa Maria delle Grazie**

HISTORIC SIGHT | Leonardo da Vinci's *The Last Supper,* housed in this church and former Dominican monastery, has had an almost unbelievable history of bad luck and neglect. Its near destruction in an American bombing raid in August 1943 was only the latest chapter in a series of misadventures, including—if one 19th-century source is to be believed—being whitewashed over by monks. After years of restorers patiently shifting from one square centimeter to another, Leonardo's masterpiece is free of centuries of retouching, grime, and dust. Astonishing clarity and luminosity have been regained, helped by lighting, and a timed entry system where small groups are ushered into climate-controlled rooms with automatic glass doors, to prevent humidity.

Despite Leonardo's carefully preserved preparatory sketches, in which the apostles are clearly labeled by name, there still remains some small debate about a few identities in the final arrangement. There can be no mistaking Judas, however—small and dark, isolated from the terrible confusion that has taken the hearts of the others. Reservations are required to view the work. Viewings are in 15-minute timed-entry slots, and visitors must arrive 30 minutes before. Reservations can be made online. Reserve at least three weeks ahead if you want a Saturday slot, two weeks for a weekday slot. Some city bus tours include a visit in their regular circuit, which may be a good option. ⊠ *Piazza Santa Maria delle Grazie 2, off Corso Magenta, Sant'Ambrogio* ☎ *02/92800360 reservations, 02/4676111 church* ⊕ *www.cenacolovinciano.net* 🎟 *Last Supper €15* ⊘ *Closed Mon.* Ⓜ *Cadorna or Conciliazione; Tram No. 18.*

Museo Civico Archeologico (*Municipal Archaeological Museum*)

HISTORY MUSEUM | Appropriately situated in the heart of Roman Milan, this museum housed in a former monastery displays everyday utensils, jewelry, silver plate, and several fine examples of mosaic pavement from Mediolanum, the ancient Roman name for Milan. The museum opens into a garden that is flanked by the square tower of the Roman circus and the polygonal Ansperto tower, adorned with frescoes dating to the end of the 13th and 14th centuries that portray St. Francis and other saints receiving the stigmata. ⊠ *Corso Magenta 15, Sant'Ambrogio* ☎ *02/88445208* ⊕ *www.museoarcheologicomilano.it* 🎟 *€5 (free every 1st and 3rd Tues. of month after 2, and 1st Sun. of month)* ⊘ *Closed Mon.* Ⓜ *Cadorna or Cairoli; Tram No. 16 or 27; Bus No. 50, 58, or 94.*

Museo Nazionale della Scienza e Tecnologia Leonardo da Vinci (*National Museum of Science and Technology*)

SCIENCE MUSEUM | FAMILY | This converted cloister is best known for the collection of models based on Leonardo da Vinci's sketches. One of the most visited rooms features interactive, moving models of the famous *vita aerea* (aerial screw) and *ala battente* (beating wing), thought to be forerunners of the modern helicopter and airplane, respectively. The museum also houses a varied collection of industrial artifacts, including trains, and several reconstructed workshops, including a watchmaker's, a lute maker's, and an antique pharmacy. ⊠ *Via San Vittore 21, Sant'Ambrogio* ☎ *02/02485551* ⊕ *www. museoscienza.org* 🎟 *€10, €20 including tour of submarine* ⊘ *Closed Mon.* Ⓜ *Sant'Ambrogio; Bus No. 50, 58, or 94.*

🍴 Restaurants

DaDa in Taverna

$$$ | MODERN ITALIAN | This wood-paneled taverna near the stock exchange, within a house from the 14th century, was transformed into a contemporary restaurant and cocktail bar; it's the perfect spot to enjoy a mix of both traditional and more innovative fare. Pastas, classic *risotto alla*

Milanese (creamy saffron risotto) and robust *secondi* (main courses) of meat and fish are available at dinner. **Known for:** inventive dishes; fantastic wine and cocktail selection; historical setting with a bright and modern edge. $ *Average main: €26* ⊠ *Via Morigi 8, Sant'Ambrogio* ☎ *02/36755232* ⊕ *www.dadaintaverna. com* ⊘ *Closed Sun.* Ⓜ *Cairoli or Cordusio; Tram 1, 2, 4, 12, 14, 16, or 27.*

Hotels

Antica Locanda Leonardo

$$$ | HOTEL | A feeling of relaxation prevails in this 19th-century building, and the neighborhood—the church that houses *The Last Supper* is a block away—is one of Milan's most desired and historic. **Pros:** very quiet and homey; breakfast is ample; friendly, helpful staff. **Cons:** more like a bed-and-breakfast than a hotel; old-fashioned decor; breakfast is an extra fee. $ *Rooms from: €203* ⊠ *Corso Magenta 78, Sant'Ambrogio* ☎ *02/48014197* ⊕ *www.anticalocandaleonardo.com* ⊘ *Closed 1st wk in Jan. and 3 wks in Aug.* ⇌ *24 rooms* ⦿⧠ *No Meals* Ⓜ *Conciliazione, Sant'Ambrogio, or Cadorna; Tram No. 1, 16, 19, or 27.*

Fiera and San Siro

Fiera is a quiet suburb northwest of the city center. Neighboring San Siro is home to Stadio Meazza (commonly known as San Siro Stadium), where AC and Inter Milan play their home matches.

Activities

San Siro Stadium (Stadio Meazza)

SOCCER | FAMILY | AC Milan and Inter Milan, two of the oldest teams in Europe, vie for the heart of soccer-mad Lombardy. They share the use of San Siro Stadium (Stadio Meazza) during their August–May season. With more than 60,000 of the 80,000 seats appropriated by season-ticket holders and another couple of thousand allocated to visiting fans, tickets to Sunday games can be difficult to come by. Buy advance AC Milan tickets at ⊕ *www.acmilan.com*, at the Casa Milan ticket office at Via Aldo Rossi 8, or at VivaTicket sales points. They're also sold at the stadium booth on match days. Inter tickets are available at ⊕ *www.inter.it*. Tours are also available (⊕ *www.sansirostadium.com/en/museum-tour*). ⊠ *Piazzale Angelo Moratti, San Siro* ☎ *02/48798201* ⊕ *www.sansirostadium.com* Ⓜ *San Siro Stadio; Tram No. 16; Bus No. 49.*

Quadrilatero

Via Manzoni, which lies northeast of La Scala, leads to Milan's Quadrilatero della Moda, or fashion district.

Sights

Museo Bagatti Valsecchi

HISTORIC HOME | Glimpse the lives of 19th-century Milanese aristocrats in a visit to this lovely historic house museum, once the home of two brothers, Barons Fausto and Giuseppe Bagatti. Family members inhabited the house until 1974; it opened to the public as a museum in 1984. The house is decorated with the brothers' fascinating collection of 15th- and 16th-century Renaissance art, furnishings, and objects, including armor, musical instruments, and textiles. The detailed audio guide included with admission provides a thorough insight into the history of the artworks and intriguing stories of the family itself. ⊠ *Via Gesu 5, Quadrilatero* ☎ *02/76006132* ⊕ *www. museobagattivalsecchi.org* ☐ *€12* ⊘ *Closed Mon. and Tues.* Ⓜ *Montenapoleone; Tram No. 1.*

Museo Poldi-Pezzoli

ART MUSEUM | This exceptional museum, opened in 1881, was once a private residence and collection, and contains not only pedigreed paintings but also porcelain, textiles, and a cabinet with scenes from Dante's life. The gem is undoubtedly *Portrait of a Lady* by Piero del Pollaiolo (1431–98), one of the city's most prized treasures and the source of the museum's logo. The collection also includes masterpieces by Botticelli (1445–1510), Andrea Mantegna (1431–1506), Giovanni Bellini (1430–1516), and Fra Filippo Lippi (1406–69). ⊠ *Via Manzoni 12, Quadrilatero* ☎ *02/794889* ⊕ *www.museopoldipezzoli.it* 💰 *€14* 🕐 *Closed Tues.* Ⓜ *Montenapoleone or Duomo; Tram No. 1.*

🍴 Restaurants

Don Carlos

$$$$ | ITALIAN | One of the few restaurants open after La Scala lets out, Don Carlos, in the Grand Hotel et de Milan, is nothing like its indecisive operatic namesake (whose betrothed was stolen by his father). Flavors are bold, presentation is precise and full of flair, service is attentive, and the walls are blanketed with sketches of the theater. **Known for:** veal Milanese; homemade pasta; late-night hours. 💲 *Average main: €39* ⊠ *Grand Hotel et de Milan, Via Manzoni 29, Quadrilatero* ☎ *02/72314640* ⊕ *www. ristorantedoncarlos.it/en* 🕐 *No lunch* Ⓜ *Montenapoleone; Tram No. 1 or 2.*

★ Seta

$$$$ | MODERN ITALIAN | Modern Italian cuisine made using interesting ingredients is the draw at this restaurant with sophisticated brown-and-turquoise decor in Milan's Mandarin Oriental Hotel. The best way to experience the intricate dishes is through the seven-course tasting menu; for a less expensive option, opt for the three-course "carte blanche" lunch menu. **Known for:** ultracreative dishes; wonderful Italo-centric wine list; top-notch service. 💲 *Average main: €160* ⊠ *Via Andegari 9, Quadrilatero* ☎ *02/87318897* ⊕ *www.mandarinoriental.com/milan/la-scala/fine-dining/restaurants/italian-cuisine/seta* 🕐 *Closed Sun.*

and Mon.,1st wk of Jan., and 3 wks in Aug. Ⓜ *Montenapoleone; Tram No. 1.*

🛏 Hotels

★ Armani Hotel Milano

$$$$ | HOTEL | This minimalist boutique hotel looks like it has been plucked from the pages of a sleek magazine, and it should: it was designed by fashion icon Giorgio Armani to evoke the same sculptural, streamlined aesthetic—and tailored comfort—as his signature clothing. **Pros:** complimentary (except for alcohol) minibar; lovely spa area and 24-hour gym; great location near major shopping streets. **Cons:** breakfast (only included in some rates) not up to par; some noise issues from neighboring rooms; a few signs of wear and tear. 💲 *Rooms from: €1180* ⊠ *Via Manzoni 31, Quadrilatero* ☎ *02/88838888* ⊕ *www.armanihotelmilano.com* 🔌 *95 rooms* ❍ *No Meals* Ⓜ *Montenapoleone.*

Four Seasons Hotel Milano

$$$$ | HOTEL | Built in the 15th century as a convent, with a colonnaded cloister, this sophisticated retreat certainly exudes a feeling that is anything but urban. **Pros:** quiet, elegant setting that feels removed from noisy central Milan; friendly and helpful staff; large rooms. **Cons:** decor is a bit old-fashioned; breakfast isn't included in the rate; expensive. 💲 *Rooms from: €1345* ⊠ *Via Gesù 6–8, Quadrilatero* ☎ *02/77088* ⊕ *www.fourseasons.com/milan* 🔌 *118 rooms* ❍ *No Meals* Ⓜ *Montenapoleone; Tram No. 1.*

Grand Hotel et de Milan

$$$$ | HOTEL | Only blocks from La Scala, you'll find everything you would expect from a traditionally elegant European hotel, where tapestries and persimmon velvet enliven a 19th-century look without sacrificing dignity and luxury. **Pros:** traditional and elegant; great location off Milan's main shopping streets; staff go above and beyond to meet guest needs. **Cons:** gilt decor may not suit

Sights ▼

1 Museo Bagatti
  Valsecchi **C3**
2 Museo Poldi-Pezzoli.... **B4**

Restaurants ▼

1 Don Carlos................ **C3**
2 Seta **B3**

Hotels ▼

1 Armani Hotel Milano **C3**
2 Four Seasons Hotel
  Milano................... **D3**
3 Grand Hotel et
  de Milan **C3**
4 Hotel Senato **D2**
5 Mandarin Oriental,
  Milan **B3**

those who like more modern design; no spa; some small rooms. $ *Rooms from: €751* ✉ *Via Manzoni 29, Quadrilatero* ☎ *02/723141* ⊕ *www.grandhoteletdemilan.it* ⤸ *72 rooms, 23 suites* 1⊙1 *No Meals* Ⓜ *Montenapoleone.*

Hotel Senato
$$$$ | HOTEL | The central courtyard of this boutique hotel near Milan's fashion district is covered in a layer of water, a cheeky nod to the Naviglio Grande canal that once ran in front of the 19th-century palace, which now has a sleek, minimalist design and artsy touches like brass ginkgo biloba–leaf lamps, serpentine mosaic floor patterns, and flowers and music selected by curators. **Pros:** cool designer touches; lovely breakfast buffet with local products; convenient location. **Cons:** some rooms on the small side; noise can be an issue; basic gym facilities. $ *Rooms from: €360* ✉ *Via Senato 22, Quadrilatero* ☎ *02/781236* ⊕ *www.senatohotelmilano.it* ⤸ *43 rooms* 1⊙1 *Free Breakfast* Ⓜ *Turati or Palestro; Tram No. 1; Bus No. 61 or 94.*

★ Mandarin Oriental, Milan
$$$$ | HOTEL | FAMILY | A sense of refined luxury pervades the guest rooms and public spaces of this sophisticated hotel, located just off the main Via Montenapoleone shopping street; from the elegant bedrooms with supercomfortable beds and oversize bathrooms with underfloor heating to the highly rated restaurant and one of the largest spas in Milan (9,700 square feet), you'll be taken care of here. **Pros:** wonderful and attentive service; tranquil spa and 24-hour fitness center; top restaurant on-site. **Cons:** very expensive; only some rooms have views; can be difficult to find. $ *Rooms from: €1203* ✉ *Via Andegari 9, Quadrilatero* ☎ *02/87318888* ⊕ *www.mandarinoriental.com* ⤸ *70 rooms, 34 suites* 1⊙1 *No Meals* Ⓜ *Montenapoleone; Tram No. 1.*

 Nightlife

Armani/Bamboo Bar
BARS | With high ceilings, louvered windows, and expansive views of the city's rooftops, this modern architectural marvel is a great spot to enjoy a relaxing cup of tea or a predinner aperitivo. ✉ *Via Manzoni 31, Quadrilatero* ☎ *02/88838703* ⊕ *www.armanihotels.com/it/hotels/armani-hotel-milano/dining* Ⓜ *Montenapoleone; Tram No. 1.*

 Shopping

Armani Megastore
SPECIALTY STORE | Armani Junior, Emporio Armani, Armani Fiori (flowers), Armani Dolci (chocolate), and Armani Libri (books) are all under this monumental store's roof. ✉ *Via Manzoni 31, Quadrilatero* ☎ *02/62312600* ⊕ *www.armani.com* Ⓜ *Montenapoleone; Tram No. 1.*

★ DMAG Outlet
CLOTHING | This store has some of the best prices in the area for luxury items, such as Prada, Gucci, Lanvin, and Cavalli. DMAG has two other locations, at Via Forcella 13 and Via Bigli 4. ✉ *Via Manzoni 44, Quadrilatero* ☎ *02/36514365* ⊕ *www.dmag.eu* Ⓜ *Montenapoleone; Tram No. 1.*

★ Dolce & Gabbana
CLOTHING | This fabulous duo has created an empire based on sultry designs for men and women. The gorgeous three-story flagship store features clothing for both, plus accessories. ✉ *Via della Spiga 3, Quadrilatero* ☎ *02/77884555* ⊕ *www.dolcegabbana.it* Ⓜ *San Babila; Tram No. 61 or 94.*

Missoni
CLOTHING | Famous for their kaleidoscope-pattern knits, this family-run brand sells whimsical designs for men and women. ✉ *Via Pietro Verri 5, Quadrilatero* ☎ *02/87046300* ⊕ *www.missoni.com* Ⓜ *Montenapoleone or San Babila; Tram No. 1.*

Miu Miu

CLOTHING | Prada's more upbeat, youthful brand has a wide offering of boldly printed women's fashions and accessories. ⊠ *Via Sant'Andrea 21, Quadrilatero* ☎ *02/76001799* ⊕ *www.miumiu.com* Ⓜ *Montenapoleone, San Babila, or Palestro; Tram No. 1.*

Prada

CLOTHING | Founded in Milan in 1913 selling steamer trunks and handbags, Prada has several locations throughout the city. Its store on Via Montenapoleone showcase its women's collection. ⊠ *Via Montenapoleone 8, Quadrilatero* ☎ *02/7771771* ⊕ *www.prada.com* Ⓜ *Montenapoleone, San Babila, or Palestro; Tram No. 1.*

Roberto Cavalli

CLOTHING | Famous for his wild-animal prints, Roberto Cavalli creates sexy designs for men and women. ⊠ *Via Montenapoleone 6, Quadrilatero* ☎ *02/7630771* ⊕ *www.robertocavalli.com* Ⓜ *San Babila.*

Salvatore Ferragamo Donna

LEATHER GOODS | This Florence-based brand is a leader in leather goods and accessories, and carries designs for women in this store. ⊠ *Via Montenapoleone 3, Quadrilatero* ☎ *02/76000054* ⊕ *www.ferragamo.com* Ⓜ *San Babila.*

Salvatore Ferragamo Uomo

LEATHER GOODS | Ferragamo's men's accessories, leather goods, and ties are a staple for Milan's male fashion set. ⊠ *Via Montenapoleone 20/4, Quadrilatero* ☎ *02/76006660* ⊕ *www.ferragamo.com* Ⓜ *Montenapoleone; Tram No. 1.*

Tod's

LEATHER GOODS | This leather-goods leader sells luxury handbags as well as a variety of shoes for men and women. It also offers men's and women's clothing. ⊠ *Via Montenapoleone 13, Quadrilatero* ☎ *02/76002423* ⊕ *www.tods.com* Ⓜ *Montenapoleone, San Babila, or Palestro; Tram No. 1.*

Valentino

CLOTHING | Even after the departure of its founding father, Valentino Garavani, this fashion brand still flourishes. ⊠ *Via Montenapoleone 20, Quadrilatero* ☎ *02/76006182* ⊕ *www.valentino.com* Ⓜ *Montenapoleone; Tram No. 1.*

Versace

CLOTHING | Run by flamboyant Donatella Versace and known for its rock-and-roll styling, the first store of this fashion house opened on Via della Spiga in 1978, not far from its current location in the Quadrilatero della Moda shopping district. ⊠ *Via Monte Napoleone 11, Quadrilatero* ☎ *02/76008528* ⊕ *www.versace.com* Ⓜ *San Babila or Montenapoleone.*

Porta Garibaldi

This stylish, upscale, and buzzing district is home to the emblematic 10 Corso Como concept store and the colorful and lively Piazza Gae Aulenti, which is a study in Milan's modern architecture, including the 757-foot UniCredit Tower. New construction, stylish restaurants, and urban parks provide a modern break from historical sightseeing.

◉ Sights

ADI Design Museum Compasso d'Oro

SPECIALTY MUSEUM | More than 350 of the most renowned Italian industrial design objects are showcased in this former Enel electricity plant. The items in the permanent collection were selected during biennial judging for Compasso d'Oro (Golden Compass) awards from 1954 until today. Some of the exhibits are grouped by category, like cars (1960 Abarth-Fiat Monza Zagato, 1959 Fiat 500, and 2014 Ferrari F12berlinetta) and coffeemakers (Alessi's 9090 from 1979 and Napoletana from 1981). ⊠ *Piazza Compasso d'Oro, 1, Garibaldi* ☎ *02/36693790* ⊕ *www.adidesignmuseum.org* 🎟 *€15* 🕙 *Closed Fri.* ☞ *Tickets may be* purchased online, or at the museum with a credit card or mobile wallet (no cash accepted) Ⓜ Garibaldi.

Piazza Gae Aulenti
PEDESTRIAN MALL | Welcome to the modern era. The piazza named for the famed Italian female architect is a stroll into the future of architectural design. Here you'll find Italy's tallest skyscraper (the 757-foot mirrored and spired UniCredit Tower), IBM Studios (a curved and wood-slatted innovation lab), a Tesla dealership, and an LED tree surrounded by reflective pools. Linger through a botanical garden, *Biblioteca degli Alberi* (library of trees), and join locals picnicking when the weather cooperates. ✉ *Piazza Gae Aulenti, Garibaldi* Ⓜ *Garibaldi.*

🍴 Restaurants

★ Ceresio 7 Pools & Restaurant
$$$$ | CONTEMPORARY | Book well in advance for one of Milan's most fashionable eateries, where the tables are lacquered red and modern artwork crowds the walls—exactly what you'd expect from the twin brothers, Dean and Dan Caten, behind the fashion label Dsquared2. The food cred matches the scene—with fresh, creative, sophisticated pastas and other dishes. **Known for:** luxe ingredients like lobster, king crab, and truffles; place for seeing and being seen; swimming pools and terrace views. Ⓢ *Average main: €39* ✉ *Via Ceresio 7, Garibaldi* ☎ *02/31039221* ⊕ *www.ceresio7.com* Ⓜ *Garibaldi; Tram No. 2, 4, 12, or 14; Bus No. 37 or 190.*

Ratanà
$$$ | MODERN ITALIAN | Chef Cesare Battisti infuses the Milanese dishes of his childhood with a contemporary twist at this lively restaurant. Its two patios face a park with skyline views, and its dining room is decorated with vintage items (like an Olivetti typewriter and Scandalli accordion). **Known for:** meat- and fish-focused menu with contemporary

and traditional dishes; setting in a former historical house; more than 500 wines. Ⓢ *Average main: €28* ✉ *Via Gaetano de Castillia 28, Garibaldi* ☎ *02/87128855* ⊕ *www.ratana.it* ⊙ *Closed 2 wks in Aug. and 2 wks in Dec.* Ⓜ *Gioia.*

☕ Coffee and Quick Bites

Zàini
$ | DESSERTS | The Zàini family opened its chocolate factory here in 1913, on a side street off Corso Como. Today, its black-and-white marble-tile-floored and chandelier-lit café is a stop for coffee paired with a Zàini classic like Emilia (dark chocolate named after the family's nanny) or Boero (cherry cordial); or dozens of cakes and other sweets. **Known for:** decadent hot chocolate; artfully wrapped chocolate gifts; elegant breakfast spot. Ⓢ *Average main: €10* ✉ *Via Carlo de Cristoforis 5, Garibaldi* ☎ *02/694914449* ⊕ *www.zainimilano.com* Ⓜ *Garibaldi.*

🛏 Hotels

Hotel VIU Milan
$$$$ | HOTEL | A short walk from trendy Corso Como and the historic Cimitero Monumentale, this sleek business-focused hotel features vertical gardens outside and contemporary Italian-designed furnishings within—but its true pièce de résistance is an inviting rooftop pool with panoramic views. **Pros:** stylish modern decor; spacious bathrooms; high-quality food. **Cons:** out-of-the-way location for central Milan; hotel has a signature scent, which may bother perfume-averse guests; rooftop terrace sometimes not useable due to events. Ⓢ *Rooms from: €315* ✉ *Via Aristotile Fioravanti 6, Garibaldi* ☎ *02/80010910* ⊕ *www.hotelviumilan.com* ⌕ *124 rooms* ❚⚬❚ *No Meals* Ⓜ *Monumentale; Tram No. 10, 12, or 14.*

Porta Garibaldi and Repubblica

KEY
- 1 Sights
- 1 Restaurants
- 1 Quick Bites
- 1 Hotels

✿ Nightlife

★ Blue Note

LIVE MUSIC | The famous New York night-club's Milan outpost features regular performances by some of the most famous names in jazz, as well as blues and rock concerts. Dinner is also available. ✉ *Via Borsieri 37, Garibaldi* ☎ *02/69016888* ⊕ *www.bluenotemilano.com* Ⓜ *Isola; Tram No. 7, 31, or 33.*

🛍 Shopping

★ 10 Corso Como

SPECIALTY STORE | A shrine to Milan's creative fashion sense, the concept store 10 Corso Como was founded by the former fashion editor and publisher Carla Sozzani. The clothing and design establishment also includes a restaurant-café, gallery, bookstore, and small hotel. ✉ *Corso Como 10, Corso Como* ☎ *02/29002674* ⊕ *www.10corsocomo. com* Ⓜ *Porta Garibaldi.*

Repubblica

Some of the city's best hotels can be found around the Piazza della Repubblica.

🍴 Restaurants

Mercato Centrale

$ | **FOOD HALL** | Without traveling across the city, you can try the creations of some of the most well-known food purveyors in Milan. Follow neon signs with sketches of the type of food on offer to pick from standbys such as *risotto* from Sergio Barzetti and fish from Pescheria Pedol at Milan's version of the concept food hall that's also in Florence, Rome, and Turin. **Known for:** late-night dining; wide variety of Italian street food; high quality for affordable prices. ⑤ *Average main: €10* ✉ *Via Giovanni Battista Sammartini 2, Repubblica* ☎ *02/37928400* ⊕ *www.mercatocentrale.it/milano* Ⓜ *Central Station; Tram No. 5, 9, or 10.*

☕ Coffee and Quick Bites

★ Pavè

$ | **BAKERY** | Your main problem at Pavè will be deciding what to order among rows of cakes, tarts, classic Italian brioches (with sweet fillings like cream and jam), and other pastries. When everything is this drool-worthy, your best strategy is to come with friends and share your favorites. **Known for:** chocolate and fruit-filled tarts; vegan pastries; sandwiches and crostini on homemade bread. ⑤ *Average main: €10* ✉ *Via Felice Casati 27, Repubblica* ☎ *02/37905491* ⊕ *www. pavemilano.com* Ⓜ *Repubblica.*

🛏 Hotels

Hotel Principe di Savoia Milano

$$$$ | **HOTEL** | Milan's grande dame has all the exquisite trappings of a traditional luxury hotel: lavish mirrors, drapes, and carpets; limousine services; and some of the city's largest guest rooms, outfitted with eclectic fin de siècle furnishings. **Pros:** substantial health club–spa; close to Central Station; shuttle to Duomo and shopping district. **Cons:** located in a not-very-attractive neighborhood; not near major sites; breakfast and other meals overly expensive; showing a bit of wear and tear. ⑤ *Rooms from: €545* ✉ *Piazza della Repubblica 17, Repubblica* ☎ *02/91387010* ⊕ *www.dorchestercollection.com/en/milan/hotel-principe-di-savoia* ⇥ *301 rooms* ⑩ *No Meals* Ⓜ *Repubblica; Tram No. 1, 9, or 33.*

ME Milan Il Duca

$$$$ | **HOTEL** | This outpost of the Spanish hotel brand ME by Meliá has a lively party atmosphere, with rousing music playing in the lobby, a design-conscious vibe, and a happening rooftop bar with panoramic city views. **Pros:** great rooftop bar; spacious rooms; young, vibrant atmosphere. **Cons:** no spa; may feel overdesigned to some; can be noisy. ⑤ *Rooms from: €486* ✉ *Piazza della Repubblica 13, Repubblica* ☎ *02/84220108* ⊕ *www.*

melia.com/it/hotels/italia/milano/me-mi-lan-il-duca ⟿ *132 rooms* �’❘ *No Meals* Ⓜ *Repubblica; Tram No. 1, 5, 9, 10, or 33.*

Westin Palace

$$$$ | **HOTEL** | Don't be fooled by the functional exterior of one of Milan's premier business addresses: inside, rooms have a contemporary look with soothing gray walls and marble bathrooms. **Pros:** full-service hotel with extensive amenities; renovated rooms in both modern and more traditional styles; good-size gym open 24/7. **Cons:** lacking in local character; not in the most central or attractive location; Wi-Fi can be spotty in some rooms. ⑤ *Rooms from: €352* ✉ *Piazza della Repubblica 20, Repubblica* ☎ *02/63361* ⊕ *www.marriott.com/hotels/travel/milwi-the-westin-palace-milan* ⟿ *231 rooms* ❘❍❘ *No Meals* Ⓜ *Repubblica; Tram No. 1, 5, 9, or 33.*

Nightlife

Radio Rooftop Bar

COCKTAIL BARS | Some of Milan's most beautiful people congregate for an Aperol spritz and a selection of international tapas on this terrace with panoramic views of the city. Located at the top of the ME Milan Il Duca, the bar has heat lamps to keep visitors here even in cooler weather. ✉ *Piazza della Repubblica 13, Repubblica* ☎ *02/84220108* ⊕ *www.melia.com/en/hotels/italy/milan/me-mi-lan-il-duca/restaurants/radio-rooftop-bar* Ⓜ *Repubblica; Tram No. 1, 5, 9, 10, or 33.*

Cinque Giornate

Located just east of the city center, Cinque Giornate marks the location of the Five Days revolt against Austrian rule in Milan.

🍴 Restaurants

Da Giacomo

$$$$ | **ITALIAN** | The fashion and publishing crowds, as well as international bankers and businesspeople, favor this Milanese-Ligurian restaurant. The emphasis is on fish, and with its tile floor and bank of fresh seafood, the place has a refined neighborhood-bistro style. **Known for:** sophisticated dining; specialty gnocchetti alla Giacomo (with seafood and tomato); extensive wines, cocktails, and after-dinner drinks. ⑤ *Average main: €40* ✉ *Via P. Sottocorno 6, Cinque Giornate* ⊹ *Entrance in Via Cellini* ☎ *02/76023313* ⊕ *www.giacomomilano.com* Ⓜ *Tram No. 9, 12, 23, or 27; Bus No. 60 or 73.*

☕ Coffee and Quick Bites

De Santis

$ | **SANDWICHES** | Whether you want to grab a quick sandwich or linger with a glass of wine, since 1964, De Santis is the spot if you're hungry any time of day. There's a selection of traditional sandwiches like Gianmarco with prosciutto, basil, tomato, and soft cow's milk cheese, and the Doralice with mortadella, fontina, and tomato. **Known for:** inventive sandwich fillings; late-night quick meals and drinks; sandwiches made-to-order. ⑤ *Average main: €12* ✉ *Via Cesare Battisti 19, Cinque Giornate* ☎ *02/92862257* ⊕ *www.paninidesantis.it* ⊗ *Closed Sun.*

Palestro

Nestled just below the Giardini Pubblici Indro Montanelli park, Palestro is filled with galleries, museums, and historical landmarks.

● Sights

GAM: Galleria d'Arte Moderna/Villa Reale
ART MUSEUM | One of the city's most beautiful buildings is an outstanding example of neoclassical architecture, built between 1790 and 1796. After it was donated to Napoléon, who lived here briefly with Empress Josephine, it became known as the Villa Reale. The collection consists of works donated by prominent Milanese art collectors. It emphasizes 18th- and 19th-century Italian works, but also has a smattering of 20th-century Italian pieces. ⊠ *Via Palestro 16, Palestro* ☎ *02/88445947* ⊕ *www. gam-milano.com* ⛟ *€5 (free every 1st and 3rd Tues. of month after 2 pm)* ⊘ *Closed Mon.* Ⓜ *Palestro or Turati; Tram No. 1 or 2; Bus No. 94 or 61.*

Villa Necchi Campiglio
HISTORIC HOME | In 1932, architect Piero Portaluppi designed this sprawling estate in an Art Deco style, with inspiration coming from the decadent cruise ships of the 1920s. Once owned by the Necchi Campiglio industrial family, the tasteful and elegant three-level home and garden—which sits on Via Mozart, one of Milan's most exclusive streets—is a reminder of the refined, modern culture of the nouveaux riches who accrued financial power in Milan during that era. There is also a café on the grounds that is open 10 am–6 pm. ∎TIP→ **An audio tour is included with the entrance fee, and can be listened to on a mobile device. Tours in English are available on Saturday at 11:30 am and 2:30 pm with advanced booking.** ⊠ *Via Mozart 14, Palestro* ☎ *02/76340121* ⊕ *www.fondoambiente.it/villa-nec-chi-campiglio-eng* ⛟ *€15 (€22 for guided visit); garden-only €4* ⊘ *Closed Mon. and Tues.* Ⓜ *Palestro, San Babila, or Montenapoleone; Bus No. 54, 61, or 94.*

Porta Venezia

This district is home to parks and gardens, museums, galleries, and one end of the famed Corso Buenos Aires shopping street.

● Sights

Fondazione Luigi Rovati
ART MUSEUM | This isn't your typical Etruscan history museum. A seven-year project led by the Luigi Rovati foundation transformed two levels of a palazzo commissioned by the Prince of Piombino in 1871 into a stone-carved contemporary museum where ancient artifacts stand alongside those from the 20th century and beyond. Digital installations translate Etruscan into English and Italian on some of the objects, while an immersive moving floor map shows the civilization's major cities before its Roman conquest. A rotating display of contemporary exhibits along with permanent works on the main floor continues the play of ancient and modern, such as with Andy Warhol's interpretation of an Etruscan scene in the same room as archaeological finds. Giardino Padiglione, and its adjoining Andrea Aprea Bistrot, is an ideal spot for an afternoon aperitif or coffee. ⊠ *Corso Venezia 52, Porta Venezia* ☎ *02/38273001* ⊕ *www.fondazioneluigiro-vati.org* ⛟ *€16* ⊘ *Closed Mon. and Tues.* Ⓜ *Porta Venezia; Tram No. 9.*

Giardini Pubblici Indro Montanelli
(*Public Gardens Indro Montanelli*)
GARDEN | FAMILY | Giuseppe Piermarini, architect of La Scala, laid out these gardens across Via Palestro from the Villa Reale in 1770. Designed as public pleasure gardens, today they are still popular with families who live in the city center. Generations of Milanese have taken a ride on the miniature train and merry-go-round. The park also contains a small planetarium and the Museo Civico di Storia Naturale (Municipal Natural History Museum). ⊠ *Corso Venezia 55, Porta Venezia*

Cinque Giornate, Palestro, Porta Venezia, and Buenos Aires

☎ 02/88463337 ⊕ www.comune.milano.
it/aree-tematiche/verde/verde-pubblico/
parchi-cittadini/giardini-indro-montanelli
🔎 Gardens free, museum €5 (free every
1st and 3rd Tues. of month after 2 pm and
1st Sun. of month) ⊙ Museum closed
Mon. Ⓜ Palestro; Tram No. 9, 29, or 30.

🍽 Restaurants

Joia
$$$$ | VEGETARIAN | At this hushed,
haute-cuisine vegetarian haven near
Piazza della Repubblica, delicious dishes—all without eggs and many without
flour—are served in a minimalist beige
room that puts the focus solely on the
artistry of the food. Vegetarians, who
often get short shrift in Italy, will marvel
at the variety of culinary offerings made
from many organic and biodynamic
ingredients. **Known for:** imaginative
presentations; ever-changing menu; well-
thought-out wine selection. ⑤ Average
main: €60 ⊠ Via Panfilo Castaldi 18, Porta
Venezia ☎ 02/29522124 ⊕ www.joia.it/en
⊙ Closed Sun. and Mon., 2 wks in Aug.,
and Dec. 24–Jan. 6 Ⓜ Repubblica or Porta
Venezia; Tram No. 1, 5, 9, or 33.

LùBar
$$ | SICILIAN | Dining at LùBar, which was
started by three children of Milan fashion
designer Luisa Beccaria and which is
tucked into the side of the Galleria d'Arte
Moderna, feels like eating inside a green-
house—only with fashionable people
among the trees and plants. The cozy,
chic environs lend themselves perfectly
to nibbling on small plates of modern
Sicilian food—for lunch, an afternoon
snack, or a light dinner—many served on
Caltagirone ceramics straight from Sicily.
Known for: Sicilian street food like arancini
and polpette (meatballs); LùBar Spritz
made with Amara, a Sicilian blood orange
amaro; charming, relaxed atmosphere.
⑤ Average main: €21 ⊠ Via Palestro 16,
Porta Venezia ☎ 02/83527769 ⊕ www.
lubar.it Ⓜ Palestro or Turati; Tram No. 1 or
2; Bus No. 94 or 61.

☕ Coffee and Quick Bites

Égalité
$ | FRENCH | The 15 different types of daily
breads along with tarts, croissants, and
a decadent selection of other desserts
have a French influence at this bakery
with robin's-egg blue sidewalk tables and
chairs and a viewing window into the
bakers behind the scenes of it all. Grab
an easy breakfast, lunch, or aperitif as
you soak up the aroma of fresh-baked
baguettes. **Known for:** bread made with
Moulin Céard French flour; aperitif
dishes with cheeses, meats, pickles,
and jams; hearty sandwiches. ⑤ Average
main: €12 ⊠ Via Melzo 22, Porta Venezia
☎ 02/91763465 ⊕ www.egalitemilano.it.

Buenos Aires

This street in northeastern Milan is one
of the busiest in the city and has more
than 350 stores and outlets to choose
from.

◉ Sights

Casa-Museo Boschi di Stefano (Boschi di
Stefano House and Museum)
HISTORIC HOME | To most people, Italian
art means Renaissance art, but the 20th
century in Italy was also a time of artistic
achievement. An apartment on the second
floor of a stunning Art Deco building
designed by Milan architect Portaluppi
houses this collection, which was donated
to the city of Milan in 2003 and is a tribute
to the enlightened private collectors who
replaced popes and nobles as Italian
patrons. The walls are lined with the works
of postwar greats, such as Fontana, de
Chirico, and Morandi. Along with the art,
the museum holds distinctive postwar
furniture, sculptures, and stunning Murano
glass chandeliers. ⊠ Via Jan 15, Buenos
Aires ☎ 02/88464748 ⊕ www.casamuseo-
boschidistefano.it 🔎 Free ⊙ Closed Mon.
Ⓜ Lima; Tram No. 33; Bus No. 60.

💬 Coffee and Quick Bites

★ Marghe

$ | NEAPOLITAN | At Marghe, crafting Neapolitan-style pizza is art—as the line of people outside the restaurant each night suggests. Book in advance to grab a table in the rustic and lively dining room with exposed concrete walls, floral-tiled floors, and pendant lights, where pizzas are delivered quickly and piping hot. **Known for:** ingredients from Naples and the Amalfi Coast; local atmosphere; delicious pizza. $ *Average main: €12* ✉ *Via Plinio 6, Buenos Aires* ☎ *02/2047117* ⊕ *www.marghepizza.com* Ⓜ *Lima.*

Porta Romana

Porta Romana is a hip and vibrant neighborhood.

👁 Sights

★ Fondazione Prada

ART MUSEUM | New structures of metal and glass and revamped buildings once part of a distillery from the 1910s now contain this museum's roughly 205,000 square feet. The modern art showcased here is not for the faint of heart. Permanent pieces, such as *Haunted House,* featuring works by Louise Bourgeois and Robert Gober, are avant-garde and challenging, and temporary exhibitions highlight cutting-edge Italian and international artists. Don't hesitate to ask one of the helpful, knowledgeable staffers for guidance navigating the expansive grounds, which can be confusing. And don't miss the Wes Anderson–designed café, Bar Luce, for a drink or snack, or the restaurant Torre for an aperitivo or a full meal with panoramic views from on high. The Fondazione is a hike from the city center; expect a 10-minute walk from the metro station to the galleries. ✉ *Largo Isarco 2, Porta Romana* ☎ *02/56662611* ⊕ *www.fondazioneprada.*

Formula 1 Racing

Italian Grand Prix. Italy's Formula 1 fans are passionate and huge numbers converge in September for the Italian Grand Prix, held 15 km (9 miles) northeast of Milan in Monza. The racetrack was built in 1922 within the Parco di Monza. Check the website for dates, as well as for special category races, like classic cars and motorcycles. Visitors are allowed to zoom around the track on certain days—guided by a professional driver, of course. ✉ *Monza Eni Circuit, Via Vedano 5, Parco di Monza, Monza* ☎ *24821 in Italy* ⊕ *www.monzanet.it.*

org 🎫 *€15 for full visit admission, which includes a ticket to Milano Osservatorio* 🕐 *Closed Tues.* Ⓜ *Lodi TIBB; Tram No. 24; Bus No. 65.*

🍴 Restaurants

Pastamadre

$$ | MODERN ITALIAN | Mobiles and natural-wood lanterns decorate this cozy restaurant where house-made pasta is the main event. Start with crusty sourdough bread and small dishes of seasonal salads, vegetables, and fish served on plates crafted in a Milan ceramics studio. **Known for:** pasta made in-house; intimate setting; vegetarian options. $ *Average main: €17* ✉ *Via Bernardino Corio 8, Porta Romana* ☎ *02/55190020* ⊕ *www.pastamadremilano.it* 🕐 *Closed Sun. and Mon.* Ⓜ *Porta Romana.*

U Barba

$$ | LIGURIAN | Simple, fresh, authentic Ligurian specialties will take you back to lazy summer days on the Italian Riviera—even during Milan's gray winters. Such coastal classics as *trofie al pesto*

(an egg-free pasta served with pesto) and *bagnun di acciughe* (anchovy soup), coupled with a basket of warm focaccia or a side of *farinata* (a chickpea pancake) reign supreme in this Milan favorite. **Known for:** fresh pasta, also available to take home; charming setting with vintage furniture; seasonal changing menu. $ *Average main: €20* ⊠ *Via Pier Candido Decembrio 33, Porta Romana* ☎ *02/45487032* ⊕ *www.ubarba. it* ⊘ *Closed Mon. No lunch weekdays* Ⓜ *Lodi TIBB; Tram No. 16; Bus No. 90.*

☕ Coffee and Quick Bites

Marlà

$ | **BAKERY** | Whether you stop for a cappuccino and one of their gigantic brioche (similar to a croissant) filled with jam, cream, or an unconventional salted-caramel for breakfast, an afternoon break with a selection of minicakes, or to eat a quick sandwich, any craving can be satisfied at Marlà—the acronym for the first names of the two owners, Marco Battaglia and Lavinia Franco. Keep in mind that you may not have room for dinner if you stop by this sea green–and-white modern café in the afternoon. **Known for:** mini cheesecakes and tiramisu; specialty desserts from Tuscany, Lombardy, and Sicily; wide selection of breakfast pastries. $ *Average main: €10* ⊠ *Corso Lodi 15, Porta Romana* ☎ *02/36536410* ⊕ *www.marlapasticceria.it* ⊘ *Closed Mon.* Ⓜ *Porta Romana.*

Ticinese

This boho district is also home to the Basilica di San Lorenzo Maggiore and the Basilica di Sant'Eustorgio.

⊙ Sights

San Lorenzo Maggiore alle Colonne

CHURCH | Sixteen ancient Roman columns line the front of this sanctuary; remnants of 4th-century Paleo-Christian mosaics survive in the Cappella di Sant'Aquilino (Chapel of St. Aquilinus). ⊠ *Corso di Porta Ticinese 35, Ticinese* ☎ *02/89404129* ⊕ *www.sanlorenzomaggiore.com* ⊠ *Mosaics €2* Ⓜ *Missori.*

Restaurants

★ [bu:r] di Eugenio Boer

$$$$ | **MODERN ITALIAN** | Named after the phonetic spelling of the Dutch-Italian chef's last name, this innovative, high-concept restaurant, whose quiet dining rooms are done up in gray and gold, offers a choice of interesting tasting menus and à la carte options. Boer's contemporary Italian food is beautifully presented and full of complex flavors, and the well-matched wines lean toward the natural. **Known for:** personalized cuisine; traditional dishes with an ultramodern spin; helpful and well-informed service. $ *Average main: €105* ⊠ *Via Mercalli 22, Ticinese* ☎ *02/62065383* ⊕ *www.restaurantboer.com* ⊘ *Closed Mon. and Tues. No lunch weekdays* Ⓜ *Crocetta; Tram No. 15; Bus No. 94.*

Hotels

★ Aethos Milan

$$$ | **HOTEL** | The decor in this eclectic, extremely hip hotel at the foot of the lively Corso di Porta Ticinese and by the Navigli canals features sports memorabilia from golf, horseback riding, boxing, and others. **Pros:** contemporary flair; interesting location near many restaurants and bars; very friendly staff. **Cons:** lacking some of the amenities of large hotels; about a half-hour hike from the Duomo and central attractions; bar noise can be heard in some rooms. $ *Rooms from: €244* ⊠ *Piazza XXIV Maggio 8, Porta Ticinese* ☎ *02/89415901* ⊕ *www. aethoshotels.com/milan* ⤳ *32 rooms* ⑪ *No Meals* Ⓜ *Tram No. 3 or 9.*

Porta Romana,
Ticinese, Navigli,
and Tortona

KEY

- 1 Sights
- 1 Restaurants
- 1 Quick Bites
- 1 Hotels

Sights ▼	Restaurants ▼	Coffee and Quick Bites ▼	Hotels ▼
1 Armani/Silos............ **B3**	1 Al Fresco................ **A3**	1 Marià...................... **E4**	1 Aethos Milan............. **C3**
2 Fondazione Prada **E4**	2 [bu:r] di Eugenio Boer ... **E3**		2 Hotel Magna Pars
3 MUDEC (Museo delle	3 142...................... **B3**		Suites Milano **B3**
Culture) **A3**	4 Pastamadre **E4**		
4 Navigli District **B4**	5 U Barba **E4**		
5 San Lorenzo Maggiore			
alle Colonne **D2**			

Navigli

One of the oldest neighborhoods in the city, Navigli is a quiet, artistic hub during the weekdays and a lively hot spot on nights and weekends.

Sights

★ Navigli District

HISTORIC DISTRICT | In medieval times, a network of *navigli,* or canals, crisscrossed the city. Almost all have been covered over, but two—Naviglio Grande and Naviglio Pavese—are still navigable. The area's chock-full of boutiques, art galleries, cafés, bars, and restaurants, and at night the Navigli serves up a scene about as close as you will get to southern Italian–style street life in Milan. On weekend nights, it is difficult to walk among the youthful crowds thronging the narrow streets along the canals. Check out the antiques fair on the last Sunday of the month from 9 to 6. ■ TIP➔ **During the summer months, be sure to put on some mosquito repellent.** ⊠ *South of Corso Porta Ticinese, Navigli* ☎ *02/89409971* ⊕ *www.navigliogrande.mi.it/eventi* Ⓜ *Porta Genova; Tram No. 2, 3, 9, 14, 15, 29, or 30.*

Restaurants

142

$$ | MODERN ITALIAN | From day to night, step into the chic living room of 142 for whatever you are craving. Drink coffee and eat a homemade brioche at a bar decorated in crown caps or eat lunch or dinner at tables with a hand-painted Pollock flourish, while browsing a selection of art books. **Known for:** playful plating and setting; all day and late-night dining; seafood dishes with flair. ⑤ *Average main: €24* ⊠ *Corso Cristoforo Colombo 6, Navigli* ☎ *02/47758490* ⊕ *www.142. restaurant* ۩ *Closed Mon. No dinner Sun.* Ⓜ *Porto Genova: Tram No. 2, 9, 10, or 14.*

Nightlife

Rita

BARS | Though it's a bit difficult to find, on a side street in the popular aperitivo haunt of Navigli, the expertly mixed cocktails, well-prepared snacks, and excellent playlist make this classic worth the hunt. It also serves burgers, sandwiches, and more substantial plates for dinner. ⊠ *Via Angelo Fumagalli 1, Navigli* ☎ *02/8372865* ⊕ *www.ritacocktails.com* Ⓜ *Porta Genova; Tram No. 2.*

★ Ugo Bar

BARS | Flanked by a long bar and tables lit by candles, and featuring floral wallpaper and eclectic framed paintings of animals, this bar has a moody living-room vibe. It's a charming place for a drink, if you can squeeze past the crowds. There is also a handful of outdoor tables for prime people-watching. ⊠ *Via Corsico 12, Navigli* ☎ *02/39811337* ⊕ *www.instagram.com/ ugococktailbar* Ⓜ *Porta Genova; Tram No. 9 or 10.*

Performing Arts

Auditorium di Milano Fondazione Cariplo

CONCERTS | This modern hall, known for its excellent acoustics, is home to the Orchestra Sinfonica di Milano (Symphonic Orchestra) and Coro Sinfonico di Milano Giuseppe Verdi (Symphonic Choir). The season, which runs from September to June, includes many top international performers and rotating guest conductors. ⊠ *Largo Gustav Mahler, at Corso San Gottardo, Navigli* ☎ *02/83389401* ⊕ *www.sinfonicadimilano.org* Ⓜ *Tram No. 3 or 15; Bus No. 59 or 91.*

🛍 Shopping

Antonioli

CLOTHING | Antonioli raises the bar for Milan's top trendsetters. Uniting the most cutting-edge looks of each season, it is among the fashion-forward concept

Did You Know?

The oldest canal in Milan, the Naviglio Grande was built between 1177 and 1257. It's more than 50 km (31 miles) long and was primarily used for transporting goods. Today, the area around the canal is hopping with charming boutiques, galleries, cafés, and restaurants. Take a boat tour down the waterway and take in the neighborhood.

stores in the city. Aside from Italian brands like Valentino, it also stocks a competitive international array of designers, like Ann Demeulemeester, Rick Owens, Givenchy, Maison Margiela, and Vetements. ⊠ *Via Pasquale Paoli 1, Navigli* ☎ *02/36564834* ⊕ *www.antonioli. eu* Ⓜ *Porta Genova; Tram No. 2.*

Tortona

Tortona's former factories, warehouses, and workshops are now a creative hub packed with shops, studios, and the MUDEC, a museum with modern and contemporary art and special exhibitions.

Sights

Armani/Silos

SPECIALTY MUSEUM | About 600 pieces, from about 1980 to the present, by famed Milanese fashion designer Giorgio Armani are displayed on four floors of this airy 48,000-square-foot museum, housed in a 1950s building that was formerly a Nestlé cereal storage facility. The collection includes many of Armani's famous suits and clothes worn to the Oscars and other celebrity-studded events. A digital archive lets you explore Armani's full body of work, and a café lets you stop for a restorative espresso. Temporary exhibitions explore photography, architecture, and other themes related to design. ⊠ *Via Bergognone 40, Tortona* ☎ *02/91630010* ⊕ *www.armanisilos.com* ⊠ *€12* ⊗ *Closed Mon. and Tues.* Ⓜ *Sant'Agostino or Porta Genova; Tram No. 2 or 14; Bus No. 68 or 90/91.*

MUDEC (Museo delle Culture)

ART MUSEUM | Home to a permanent collection of ethnographic displays as well as temporary exhibitions of big-name artists such as Basquiat and Miró, MUDEC is in the vibrant Zona Tortona area of the city. British architect David Chipperfield designed the soaring space in a former factory. The permanent collection includes art, objects, and documents from Africa, Asia, and the Americas. Book in advance for the most popular temporary exhibits. There's also a highly rated restaurant, Enrico Bartolini Mudec, as well as a more casual bistro. ⊠ *Via Tortona 56, Tortona* ☎ *02/54917* ⊕ *www. mudec.it* ⊠ *Permanent collection free, special exhibitions from €12* ⊗ *Closed Mon. until 2:30 pm* Ⓜ *Sant'Agostino or Porta Genova; Tram No. 2 or 14; Bus No. 68 or 90/91.*

Restaurants

Al Fresco

$$$ | **MODERN ITALIAN** | In Italian, *al fresco* means open-air, and when the weather cooperates you can dine in the candlelit garden of this restaurant converted from a former factory. The string lights and wooden tables create a romantic setting, while indoors, a greenhouse with terra-cotta floors is decorated with seasonal floral arrangements, chandeliers, and pendant lights to add to the 19th-century charm. **Known for:** extensive menu and many vegetarian options; fish and tempura courses; garden setting. Ⓢ *Average main: €25* ⊠ *Via Savona 50, Tortona* ☎ *02/49533630* ⊕ *www.alfrescomilano.it* Ⓜ *Porto Genova.*

🛏 Hotels

Hotel Magna Pars Suites Milano

$$$$ | **HOTEL** | This ultrastylish all-suites boutique hotel in a former perfume factory has Italian-designed furnishings; paintings by local Brera Academy artists; and sleek, white accommodations—each with its own signature scent (such as fruity, woodsy, or floral) and all overlooking one of two tranquil courtyards. **Pros:** modern, design-y feel; attentive service; wonderful food at the attached restaurant. **Cons:** spa on the small side; a bit of a trek to central attractions; perfumed rooms not for everyone. Ⓢ *Rooms from: €432* ⊠ *Via Forcella 6, Tortona*

☎ 02/8338371 ⊕ www.magnapars.it
↪ 60 suites ⫯⦿⫯ Free Breakfast Ⓜ Porta
Genova; Tram No. 2, 9, or 19.

Bergamo

52 km (32 miles) northeast of Milan.

If you're driving from Milan to Lake
Garda, the perfect deviation from your
autostrada journey is the lovely medieval town of Bergamo, which is also a
wonderful side trip by train from Milan.
With direct service from Milan, you'll be
whisked from the restless pace of city
life to the medieval grandeur of Bergamo
Alta in less than an hour.

GETTING HERE AND AROUND
Bergamo is along the A4 autostrada. By
car from Milan, take the A51 out of the
city to pick up the A4; the drive is 52 km
(32 miles) and takes about 45 minutes.
By train, Bergamo is about one hour from
Milan and 1½ hours from Desenzano del
Garda-Sirmione station.

VISITOR INFORMATION
CONTACT Bergamo Tourism Office. ✉ *Torre
del Gombito, Via Gombito 13, Bergamo
Alta, Bergamo* ☎ *035/242226* ⊕ *www.
visitbergamo.net.*

◉ Sights

Accademia Carrara
ART MUSEUM | Bergamo is home to an art
collection that's surprisingly rewarding
given its size and remote location. Many
of the Venetian masters are represented—Mantegna, Bellini, Carpaccio (circa
1460–1525/26), Tiepolo (1727–1804),
Francesco Guardi (1712–93), and Can-
aletto (1697–1768), as well as Botticelli (1445–1510). ✉ *Piazza Carrara 82,
Bergamo Bassa, Bergamo* ☎ *035/234396
weekdays, 035/4122097 weekends*
⊕ *www.lacarrara.it* ⛰ *€15.*

Campanone
CLOCK | The massive 13th-century Torre
Civica (Civic Tower), known as the Cam-
panone, offers a great view of the two
cities. Climb the stairs or take an elevator
to the top of the tower, where the bells
ring every half hour and then 100 times
each night at 10 to commemorate the
closure of the city gates during Venetian
rule. ✉ *Piazza Vecchia, Bergamo Alta,
Bergamo* ☎ *035/247116* ⊕ *www.muse-
odellestorie.bergamo.it/luogo/campanone*
⛰ *€5* ⊙ *Closed Mon.*

Cappella Colleoni
CHURCH | Bergamo's **Duomo** and **Battistero**
are the most substantial buildings in
Piazza Duomo. But the most impressive structure is the Cappella Colleoni,
which boasts a kaleidoscope of marble
decoration and golden accents. ✉ *Piazza Duomo, Bergamo Alta, Bergamo*
☎ *035/210061* ⊙ *Closed Mon.*

Restaurants

★ Al Donizetti
$$ | **NORTHERN ITALIAN** | Find a table in the
back of this central, cheerful restaurant
before choosing local cured meats and
cheeses to accompany your wine. A few
versions of polenta, daily pastas, and
other heartier dishes are also available;
just save room for the desserts, which
go well with the sweet wines. **Known for:**
beef tartare; 900-bottle wine selection
with many by the glass; chocolate
desserts. Ⓢ *Average main: €20* ✉ *Via
Gombito 17/a, Bergamo Alta, Bergamo*
☎ *035/242661* ⊙ *Closed Tues.*

Da Ornella
$$ | **NORTHERN ITALIAN** | The vaulted
ceilings of this popular trattoria on the
upper town's main street are marked
with ancient graffiti, created by (patiently)
holding candles to the stone overhead.
The house specialties are simple but
tasty: polenta *taragna* (with buckwheat
flour) cooked with butter and cheese
and served with rabbit, chicken, or sliced

The medieval town of Bergamo at sunrise is a stunning sight.

mushrooms with oil, garlic, and parsley. **Known for:** local salame; historical setting; casoncelli (meat-filled pasta from Lombardy) dell'Ornella. $ *Average main: €20* ⊠ *Via Gombito 15, Bergamo Alta, Bergamo* ☎ *035/232736* ⊘ *Closed Thurs.*

Vineria Cozzi

$$$ | **WINE BAR** | The wine list at this romantic but informal *vineria* (wine bar) is exceptional—both by the glass and by the bottle—and there's also an array of flavorful foods, from snacks to sumptuous full-course meals typical of the region. The atmosphere is warm and charming, harking back more than 150 years to when the spot was first established in Bergamo as a lively meeting place. **Known for:** quirky historical decorations; cellar with more than 300 wines; polenta dishes as starters and mains. $ *Average main: €27* ⊠ *Via B. Colleoni 22, Bergamo Alta, Bergamo* ☎ *035/238836* ⊕ *www.vineriacozzi.it* ⊘ *Closed Wed.*

Coffee and Quick Bites

La Marianna

$ | **ICE CREAM** | **FAMILY** | *Stracciatella* gelato—a creamy combination of milk, egg yolks, vanilla, sugar, and dark chocolate shavings—is Italy's answer to chocolate-chip ice cream. While you'll see the flavor in gelaterie across Italy, one pastry shop, and city, Bergamo, claims it as its own. **Known for:** outdoor courtyard away from the crowds of Città Alta; decorated seasonal cookies and cakes; upscale gelateria atmosphere. $ *Average main: €10* ⊠ *Largo Colle Aperto 4, Bergamo* ☎ *035/237027* ⊕ *www.lamarianna.it.*

Hotels

Mercure Bergamo Centro Palazzo Dolci

$ | **HOTEL** | Set in a restored 19th-century palazzo, this Bergamo Basso hotel has modern comforts and a friendly, efficient staff, making it a good choice for both business and leisure travelers. **Pros:** convenient to train station, airport, and some shopping; good value; bountiful breakfast buffet. **Cons:** basic rooms; no parking on-site; no restaurant. $ *Rooms from: €124* ⊠ *Viale Papa Giovanni XXIII 100, Bergamo Bassa, Bergamo* ☎ *035/227411* ⊕ *mercurebergamocentropalazzodolci. com-hotel.com* ↝ *92 rooms* ⦿| *No Meals.*

Relais San Vigilio

$$$$ | **HOTEL** | Brothers Gigi and Paolo Zani transformed a castle and soldiers' barracks dating from the Middle Ages into a retreat just above the Città Alta. **Pros:** lovely views and spacious garden with many sitting areas; quiet location away from the crowds; hotel layout in two buildings offers extra privacy among rooms. **Cons:** some bathrooms are small; 10-minute walk or quick funicular ride to Città Alta; expensive on-site parking in small garage with narrow driveway. $ *Rooms from: €324* ⊠ *Via al Castello 7/9, Bergamo* ☎ *035/2650987* ⊕ *www. relaissanvigilio.it* ↝ *9 rooms* ⦿| *Free Breakfast.*

Cremona

100 km (62 miles) southeast of Milan.

Cremona is a classical-music lover's dream. With violin shops on nearly every block along its crooked old streets, it is where the world's best violins are crafted. Andrea Amati (1510–80) invented the modern instrument here in the 16th century. Though cognoscenti continue to revere the Amati name, it was an apprentice of Amati's nephew for whom the fates had reserved wide and lasting fame. In a career that spanned an incredible 68 years, Antonio Stradivari (1644–1737) made more than 1,200 instruments—including violas, cellos, harps, guitars, and mandolins, in addition to his fabled violins. They remain among the most coveted, most expensive stringed instruments in the world.

Cremona's other claim to fame is *torrone* (nougat), which is said to have been

created here in honor of the marriage of Bianca Maria Visconti and Francesco Sforza, which took place in October 1441. The new confection, originally prepared by heating almonds, egg whites, and honey over low heat, and shaped and named after the city's tower, was created in symbolic celebration. The annual Festa del Torrone is held in the main piazza over the third or fourth week of November.

GETTING HERE AND AROUND

By car from Milan, start out on the A1 autostrada and switch to the A21 at Piacenza; the drive is about 100 km (62 miles) and takes about 1½ hours. By train, Cremona is about an hour from Milan and 1½ hours from Desenzano, near Sirmione on Lake Garda.

VISITOR INFORMATION

CONTACT Cremona Tourism Office. ⊠ *Piazza del Comune 5, Cremona* ☎ *0372/407081* ⊕ *www.turismocremona. it.*

 Sights

Duomo

CHURCH | Cremona's Romanesque Duomo was consecrated in 1190. It's an impressive structure in a breathtaking piazza, and certainly one of the most beautiful churches in Italy. Here you can find the *Story of the Virgin Mary and the Passion of Christ,* the central fresco of an extraordinary cycle commissioned in 1514 and featuring the work of local artists, including Boccaccio Boccaccino, Giovanni Francesco Bembo, and Altobello Melone. ⊠ *Piazza del Comune, Cremona* ☎ *0373/495082* ⊕ *www.cattedraledicre- mona.it.*

★ Museo del Violino

SPECIALTY MUSEUM | At this lovely and informative museum dedicated to all things violin, even those not already enamored by the instrument will find something to appreciate. Historic violins made in Cremona by masters, including Stradivari, are presented as works of art;

The Po Plain,
Lake Garda,
and Lake Iseo

be sure to get the audio guide included with admission to listen to recordings as you stroll. An audio chamber lets you hear a musical performance in "3D audio"—and if you're lucky, there will be a live concert going on at the innovative on-site auditorium, where the seats wrap around the stage and musicians for an immersive experience. ⊠ *Palazzo dell'Arte, Piazza Marconi 5, Cremona* ☏ *0372/801801, 0372/080809 tickets* ⊕ *www.museodelviolino.org* 🎟 *€12* ⊗ *Closed Mon.*

Piazza del Comune

PLAZA/SQUARE | The Duomo, tower, baptistery, and Palazzo Communale (city hall) surround this distinctive and harmonious square: the combination of old brick, rose- and cream-color marble, terra-cotta, and old copper roofs brings Romanesque, Gothic, and Renaissance together with unusual success. ⊠ *Piazza del Comune, Cremona.*

Piazza Roma 1

PLAZA/SQUARE | Legendary violin maker Antonio Stradivari lived, worked, and died near the verdant square at Piazza Roma 1 (not open to the public). According to local lore, Stradivari kept each instrument in his bedroom for a month before varnishing it, imparting part of his soul before sealing and sending it out into the world. In the center of the park is a copy of Stradivari's tombstone, while the original is in the Violin Museum. ⊠ *Piazza Roma 1, Cremona.*

Torrazzo (*Big Tower*)

CLOCK | Dominating Piazza del Comune is perhaps the tallest campanile in Italy, visible for a considerable distance across the Po Plain. The tower's astronomical clock is the 1583 original. Climb the 500-plus steps to the top for amazing views; along the way, you can stop at the Museo Verticale for informative displays on astronomy and ancient methods of measuring time. ⊠ *Piazza del Comune, Cremona* ☏ *0372/495082* ⊕ *www.museoverticale. it* 🎟 *€10 with baptistery* ⊗ *Closed Mon.*

🍴 Restaurants

La Sosta

$$ | NORTHERN ITALIAN | This osteria looks to the 16th century for culinary inspiration, with excellent homemade salami and a popular primo—*marubini Cremonesi ai tre brodi* (stuffed meat ravioli in broth)—made according to time-tested recipes. Order the tiramisu and an accompanying dessert wine for a perfect finish. **Known for:** cheese tasting menu; Cremonese sausage and veal osso buco; extensive wine cellar with dessert wines. ⑤ *Average main: €24* ⊠ *Via Sicardo 9, Cremona* ☏ *0372/456656* ⊕ *www.osterialasosta.it* ⊗ *Closed Mon. and 3 wks in Aug. No dinner Sun.*

☕ Coffee and Quick Bites

⭐ Pasticceria Duomo

$ | CAFÉ | This portal to the past opened in 1883 and still serves up such handmade local delights as *pan torrone* (a loaf cake made with chunks of nougat) and *torta cremona* (a cake made with almond flour and filled with Amarena cherries). A relaxing stop between visiting museums, it's the perfect place to have a cappuccino. **Known for:** torrone (nougat) in many shapes and sizes; old-world charm; seasonal decorated cakes and pastries. ⑤ *Average main: €10* ⊠ *Via Boccaccino 6, Cremona* ☏ *0372/22273.*

🛏 Hotels

Delle Arti Design Hotel

$$ | HOTEL | With modern interiors and eclectic but comfortable designer furniture, this aptly named hotel makes a nice counterpoint to the historical surroundings of Cremona. **Pros:** convenient central location; friendly staff; good breakfast options. **Cons:** small bathrooms; hallways can be a little dark; starting to show its age. ⑤ *Rooms from: €157* ⊠ *Via Bonomelli 8, Cremona* ☏ *0372/23131* ⊕ *www.dellearti. com* 🛏 *33 rooms* 🍴 *Free Breakfast.*

Hotel Impero
$$ | HOTEL | Just a few minutes' walk from the Duomo and the Museo del Violino, this comfortable hotel with functional yet pleasant rooms (the best of which overlook the piazza) is well equipped to satisfy both leisure and business travelers. **Pros:** central location; highly professional staff; spacious rooms. **Cons:** rooms are a little bland and outdated; outside noise can be a problem, especially on weekends; breakfast is basic. $ *Rooms from: €127* ⊠ *Piazza della Pace 21, Cremona* ☎ *0372/413013* ⊕ *www.hotelimpero.cr.it* ⟿ *51 rooms* ⦿ *Free Breakfast.*

Shopping

Sperlari
FOOD | Sperlari and parent company Fieschi have grown into a confectionery empire, but it all started at this handsome shop, which has been selling Cremona's famous nougat and its best *mostarda* (a spicy-sweet condiment made of candied fruit in a syrup with mustard mixed in) since 1836. While shopping for these items—as well as teas, marmalades, and other Italian delights—be sure to check out the historical product display at the back of the store. ⊠ *Via Solferino 25, Cremona* ☎ *0372/22346* ⊕ *www. sperlari1836.com.*

Mantua

192 km (119 miles) southeast of Milan.

Mantua (Mantova in Italian) stands tallest among the ancient walled cities of the Po Plain; it may not be flashy or dramatic, but its beauty is subtle and deep, hiding a rich trove of artistic, architectural, and cultural gems beneath its slightly somber facade. Its fortifications are circled on three sides by the passing Mincio River, which long provided Mantua with protection, fish, and a steady stream of river tolls on its meandering way from Lake Garda to the Po.

GETTING HERE AND AROUND
Mantua is 5 km (3 miles) west of the A22 autostrada. The drive from Milan, following the A4 to the A22, takes a little more than two hours. The drive from Cremona, along the SP10, is 1¼ hours. Most trains arrive in just under two hours from Milan, depending on the type of service, and in about 1½ hours from Desenzano, near Sirmione on Lake Garda, via Verona.

VISITOR INFORMATION
CONTACT Mantua Tourism Office. ⊠ *Piazza Sordello 23, Mantua* ☎ *0376/288208* ⊕ *www.turismo.mantova.it.*

Sights

Be sure to pick up a Mantova Sabbioneta Card (☎ *0376/230339* ⊕ *www.mantovacard.it*) at the tourism office, Palazzo Ducale, or Palazzo Te. It costs €25 and entitles you to visit 17 museums and monuments (with a €5.50 supplement to visit Camera degli Sposi) and also includes access to city buses, including Sabbioneta.

★ Palazzo Ducale
CASTLE/PALACE | The 500-room palace that dominates the Mantua skyline was built for the Gonzaga family, though much of the art within the castle was sold or stolen as the dynasty waned in power and prestige. A glimpse of past grandeur can still be spotted as you enter the palace, turn immediately left, and walk up a steep hallway, arriving in Camera degli Sposi (literally, the "Wedded Couple's Room") where Duke Ludovico and his wife held court. Reservations are recommended, either by phone or online (⊕ *www.ducalemantova.org*). ⊠ *Piazza Sordello 40, Mantua* ☎ *041/2411897* ⊕ *www.mantovaducale.beniculturali.it* 🎫 *€9, €15 including Camera degli Sposi (€5.50 with Mantova Sabbioneta Card)* ⊗ *Closed Mon.*

★ Palazzo Te

CASTLE/PALACE | One of the greatest of all Renaissance palaces, built between 1525 and 1535 by Federico II Gonzaga, is the Mannerist masterpiece of artist-architect Giulio Romano. Two highlights are the Camera di Amore e Psiche (Room of Cupid and Psyche), which depicts a wedding set among lounging nymphs, and the gasp-inducing Camera dei Giganti (Room of the Giants) that shows Jupiter expelling the Titans from Mount Olympus. The scale of the latter is overwhelming; the floor-to-ceiling work completely envelops the viewer. Note the etched graffiti from as far back as the 17th century to the left as you enter the room. ⊠ *Viale Te 13, Mantua* ☎ *0376/323266* ⊕ *www.centropalazzote. it* ☎ *€15* ☉ *Closed Tues.*

Sant'Andrea

CHURCH | Mantegna's tomb is in the first chapel to the left in this basilica, most of which was built in 1472. The current structure, a masterwork by the architect Alberti, is the third built on this spot to house the relic of the Precious Blood: the crypt holds two reliquaries containing earth believed to be soaked in the blood of Christ, brought to Mantua by Longinus, the soldier who pierced his side. They are displayed only on Good Friday. ⊠ *Piazza di Mantegna 1, Mantua* ☎ *0376/320220* ⊕ *www.parrocchiasantanselmomantova.it.*

🍴 Restaurants

Ambasciata

$$$$ | **NORTHERN ITALIAN** | Heralded as one of Italy's classic gourmet restaurants, Ambasciata (Italian for "embassy") emphasizes elegance in tiny Quistello, 20 km (12 miles) southeast of Mantua. Those who are willing to make the trek (and pay the bill) can order à la carte or opt for the tasting menu (from €80) with an ever-changing array of traditionally inspired creations, such as the famed *tortelli di zucca* (pumpkin tortelli with pumpkin cream and Parmigiano-Reggiano), or mains like guinea fowl with mostarda, and roast pigeon with 25-year reserve balsamic vinegar. **Known for:** intricate cuisine coupled with classics; whimsical setting; attentive service. ⑤ *Average main: €80* ⊠ *Piazzetta Ambasciatori del Gusto 1, Quistello* ☎ *0376/619169* ⊕ *www.ristorantelambasciata.eu* ☉ *Closed Mon. and Tues.*

☕ Coffee and Quick Bites

Freddi

$ | **BAKERY** | The Freddi family's history in Piazza Cavallotti began more than 100 years ago. On the edge of the historical center of town, it's still where locals queue to buy Mantua's traditional pastas and pastries—don't miss *sbrisolona* (meaning "crumbs" in Italian), a hybrid cookie and pie that you'll see sold everywhere with varying levels of quality. **Known for:** Mantuan almond sweets; friendly local spot; location between the train station and major sites. ⑤ *Average main: €10* ⊠ *Piazza Cavallotti 7, Mantua* ☎ *0376/321418* ⊕ *www.panificiofreddi.it* ☉ *Closed Sun.*

🛏 Hotels

Casa Poli

$$ | **HOTEL** | **FAMILY** | A refreshing minimalist influence, attention to detail, and creative touches (like the room number projected onto the hall floor) create a welcoming ambience with contemporary flair. **Pros:** attentive staff; tasteful and modern; families welcome. **Cons:** although convenient, not in the absolute center of the city; some traffic noise in front-facing rooms; no on-site restaurant. ⑤ *Rooms from: €146* ⊠ *Corso Garibaldi 32, Mantua* ☎ *0376/288170* ⊕ *www. hotelcasapoli.it* ⇄ *27 rooms* ⦿ *Free Breakfast.*

Lake Iseo and Franciacorta

108 km (67 miles) northeast of Milan.

The lesser known of Lombardy's lakes, Iseo is a haven for cyclists and sailors around Monte Isola. With 117 cellars and more than 7,783 acres of vineyards across 124 miles, for wine lovers, Franciacorta is a region not to be missed.

GETTING HERE AND AROUND

Frequent trains make the hour-long trip from Milano Centrale to Brescia. From there, hourly trains run to the town of Iseo (about half an hour) and then up Lake Iseo's eastern shore. You'll need a car to reach the western side or the Franciacorta wine region just south of the lake.

To drive from Milan or Bergamo, take the A4/E64; exit at Rovato on SP51 in the direction of Iseo. The trip takes about one hour and 20 minutes from Milan and 30 minutes from Bergamo. Ferries run from Sulzano, Sale Marasino, Iseo, and Tavernola Bergamasca to Monte Isola.

VISITOR INFORMATION

CONTACT Lake Iseo and Franciacorta Tourism Office. ⊠ *Lungolago Marconi 2/c, Iseo* ☎ *030/980209* ⊕ *www.visitlakeiseo.info.*

◉ Sights

Ca' del Bosco

WINERY | Modern sculptures adorn the grounds of this respected Franciacorta winery (one of the largest in the region). Enjoyable hour-long cellar tours conclude with a 30-minute tasting; information about tour availability can be requested online. ⊠ *Via Albano Zanella 13, Erbusco* ☎ *030/7766111* ⊕ *www.cadelbosco.com* ⌷ *Tours and tastings from €75.*

★ Monte Isola

ISLAND | The largest island within any European lake, Monte Isola allows no cars (except authorized vehicles), making it the

perfect place for leisurely walks and bike rides. The main towns are Siviano, with medieval mansions; Peschiera Maraglio, an old fishing village with 16th-century homes and the Church of St. Michele; and Carzano, with the 18th-century San Giovanni Battista church. Walk around the water and stop at the many restaurants and gelaterie, or, for more exercise, trek uphill to admire the views back to the shore. Frequent ferries from Sulzano stop at Peschiera Maraglio, and ferries from Sale Marasino arrive at Carzano; there are less frequent ferries from Iseo and Tavernola Bergamasca. ⊠ *Monte Isola* ☎ *030/9825088* ⊕ *www.visitmonteisola.it.*

🍴 Restaurants

★ Due Colombe Ristorante Al Borgo Antico

$$$$ | **NORTHERN ITALIAN** | Visitors to Lake Iseo would do well to follow the locals' lead by sampling the delightful cooking at this cozy restaurant just south of the lake. The elegant dining area, with wood-beam ceilings and stone walls, is juxtaposed with the thoroughly modern menu, which offers a selection of "classic" and "creative" dishes. **Known for:** Franciacorta sauces; countryside setting; more than 900 wines to select from. ⑤ *Average main: €40* ⊠ *Via Foresti 13, Borgonato* ☎ *030/9828227* ⊕ *www.duecolombe.com* ⊘ *Closed Mon.–Wed. No dinner Sun. No lunch Thurs.*

☕ Coffee and Quick Bites

Fabio Nazzari

$ | **BAKERY** | Watch Fabio Nazzari at work in this pastry lab and chocolate shop off Iseo's Piazza Garibaldi. When you do, you'll see why locals fill sleek black tables, both inside and outside in the piazza, to pair coffee with French-inspired sweets along with Italian dessert classics. **Known for:** breakfast spot with a dozen filled croissant flavors; delicately decorated mini cakes; exotic fruit ingredients. ⑤ *Average* *main:* €10 ⊠ *Piazza Garibaldi 15, Iseo* ☎ *030/9821756* ⊕ *www.nazzari-iseo.it.*

Hotels

★ L'Albereta

$$$$ | RESORT | Set in an early-20th-century villa amid Franciacorta's hilly vineyards, this Relais & Chateaux property is a true sanctuary, with an enormous spa, a botanical garden, and vast, sculpture-filled grounds to explore. **Pros:** cozy, calm, and luxurious atmosphere; excellent on-site restaurants; beautiful surroundings. **Cons:** rooms quite varied in terms of size and level of renovation; not all rooms have Lake Iseo views; breakfast not included. ⑤ *Rooms from: €477* ⊠ *Via Vittorio Emanuele 23, Erbusco* ☎ *030/7760550* ⊕ *www.albereta.it* ⇌ *57 rooms* ⦿⦿ *No Meals.*

Sensole

$ | HOTEL | The tranquility and flavors of Lake Iseo permeate through this relaxed retreat in the tiny village Sensole on car-free Monte Isola—nine simple rooms in a 19th-century palazzo have black and white contemporary decor and the best have sweeping lake views; or soak up the panorama from the top-floor terrace. **Pros:** affordable prices for the area; serene location; superb on-site restaurant and bistro. **Cons:** bathroom design is a bit outdated; not all rooms have lake views; only reachable by ferry, with less frequent service to Sensole in the off-season. ⑤ *Rooms from: €100* ⊠ *Sensole 10, Monte Isola* ☎ *030/6091762* ⊕ *www.sensole.it* ⦿ *Closed Jan. 8–early Feb.* ⇌ *9 rooms* ⦿⦿ *No Meals.*

Sirmione

138 km (86 miles) east of Milan.

Dramatically rising out of Lake Garda is the enchanting town of Sirmione. *"Paene insularum, Sirmio, insularumque ocelle,"* wrote Catullus in a homecoming poem: "It is the jewel of both peninsulas and islands." The forbidding Castello Scaligero stands guard behind the small bridge connecting Sirmione to the mainland; beyond, cobbled streets wind their way through medieval arches past lush gardens, stunning lake views, and gawking crowds. Originally a Roman resort town, Sirmione served under the dukes of Verona and later Venice as Garda's main point of defense. It has now reclaimed its original function, and is often overcrowded with visitors. Cars aren't allowed into town, and there's extremely limited parking just outside the center. If arriving by car, the best option on weekends and during high season is a 30-minute walk or short bus ride to the historical center from the large parking lot on Via Ederle at the traffic circle at the start of the road into Sirmione.

GETTING HERE AND AROUND

The town of Sirmione, at the south end of the lake, is 10 km (6 miles) from Desenzano, which has regular train service; it's about one hour and 20 minutes by train from Milan and 25 minutes from Verona. The A4 autostrada passes to the south of the lake, and the A22 runs north–south about 10 km (6 miles) from the eastern shore.

VISITOR INFORMATION

CONTACT Sirmione Tourism Office. ⊠ *Viale Marconi 8, Sirmione* ☎ *349/7285327 mobile* ⊕ *www.visitsirmione.com.*

Sights

Bardolino

TOWN | This small town—one of the most popular summer resorts on the lake—is 32 km (20 miles) north of Sirmione along Lake Garda's eastern shore, at the wider end. It's most famous for its red wine, which is light, dry, and often slightly sparkling; the Festa dell'Uva e del Vino (Grape and Wine Festival), held here in early October, is a great excuse to indulge in the local product. Bardolino has two handsome Romanesque churches, both near the center: San Severo, from the 11th century, and San Zeno, from the 9th. ⊠ *Bardolino* ☎ *045/7210087 tourist office* ⊕ *www.visitbardolino.it.*

Castello Scaligero di Sirmione

CASTLE/PALACE | As hereditary rulers of Verona for more than a century before they lost control of the city in 1402, the Della Scala counted Garda among their possessions. It was they who built this lakeside redoubt, along with almost all the other castles on the lake. You can go inside to take in a lake view from the tower, or you can swim at the nearby beach. ⊠ *Piazza Castello 34, Sirmione* ☎ *030/916468* ⊕ *www.beniculturali.it/ luogo/castello-scaligero-di-sirmione* 🔳 *€7.*

Grotte di Catullo (*Grottoes of Catullus*)

RUINS | Locals will almost certainly tell you that these romantic lakeside ruins were once the site of the villa of Catullus (87–54 BC), one of the greatest pleasure-seeking poets of all time. Modern-day archaeology, however, does not concur, and there is some consensus that this was the site of two villas of slightly different periods, dating from about the 1st century AD. But never mind—the view through the cypresses and olive trees is lovely, and even if Catullus didn't have a villa here, he is closely associated with the area and undoubtedly did have a villa nearby. The ruins are at the top of the isthmus and are poorly signposted: walk through the historic center and past the various villas to the top of the spit; the entrance is on the right. A small museum offers a brief overview of the ruins (on the far wall). ⊠ *Piazzale Orti Manara, Sirmione* ☎ *030/916157* ⊕ *www.grottedicatullo. beniculturali.it* 🔳 *€9.*

🍴 Restaurants

La Rucola 2.0

$$$$ | MODERN ITALIAN | Next to the castle and tucked into three charming rooms, this elegant, intimate restaurant is considered by many to be Sirmione's finest. Its creative tasting menus feature an appealing mix of fish (from the lake or the sea), meat, and vegetarian dishes, all accompanied by a good choice of wines. **Known for:** tasting menus; open kitchen; fantastic wine list. ⑤ *Average main: €103* ⊠ *Vicolo Strentelle 3, Sirmione* ☎ *030/916326* ⊕ *www.ristorantelarucola. it* ⊘ *Closed Sun. No lunch Mon.; Oct. 5– May 31 closed Thurs. and no lunch Fri.*

Ristorante Al Pescatore

$$ | SEAFOOD | Freshwater fish is the specialty at this simple, popular restaurant in Sirmione's historic center. Try the grilled trout with a bottle of local white, and then settle your meal with a walk in the nearby park. **Known for:** grilled fresh fish from the lake; extensive variety of pasta and seafood; inexpensive meals. ⑤ *Average main: €22* ⊠ *Via Giovanni Piana 20/22, Sirmione* ☎ *030/916216* ⊕ *www. ristorantealpescatore.com* ⊘ *Closed Thurs.*

🛏 Hotels

Hotel Sirmione e Promessi Sposi

$$$ | HOTEL | A homey feel with comfortable beds and upholstered furnishings with matching drapery, along with a luxurious thermal spa, keeps many guests returning year after year. **Pros:** next to the lake and near Castello; beautiful grounds; nice spa area. **Cons:** not all rooms have lake views; hotel could use a refresh; service can be indifferent. ⑤ *Rooms from: €230* ⊠ *Piazza Castello 19, Sirmione* ☎ *030/916331, 030/9904922 booking* ⊕ *www.termedisirmione.com* 🛏 *102 rooms* ⑩ *Free Breakfast.*

★ Palace Hotel Villa Cortine

$$$$ | HOTEL | This former private villa in a secluded park is known for its bucolic lakeside setting, charming decor of the older rooms, and accommodating staff. **Pros:** an opulent experience; lovely pool area; beautiful grounds. **Cons:** noise heard in some rooms; no spa at hotel but thermal baths a short walk away; no gym. $ *Rooms from: €516* ⊠ *Viale C. Gennari 2, Sirmione* ☎ *030/9905890* ⊕ *www.hotelvillacortine.com* ⊗ *Closed mid-Oct.–Apr.* ⤴ *54 rooms* ⦿ *Free Breakfast.*

Riva del Garda

180 km (112 miles) northeast of Milan.

Riva del Garda is set on the northern tip of Lake Garda, against a dramatic backdrop of jagged cliffs and miles of beaches. The old city, surrounding a pretty harbor, was built up during the 15th century, when it was a strategic outpost of the Venetian Republic.

GETTING HERE AND AROUND

Riva del Garda is along Lake Garda's scenic SS45bis. By car from Milan, head to the A35 from SP14. The drive is 167 km (103 miles) and takes approximately three hours.

VISITOR INFORMATION

CONTACT Riva del Garda Tourism Office.
⊠ *Largo Medaglie d'Oro al Valor Militare 5, Riva del Garda* ☎ *0464/554444* ⊕ *www.gardatrentino.it.*

Sights

Piazza III Novembre

PLAZA/SQUARE | This lakeside piazza, the heart of Riva del Garda, is surrounded by medieval palazzi. Standing there and looking out over the lake, you can understand why Riva del Garda has become a windsurfing destination: air currents ensure good breezes on even the most sultry midsummer days. ⊠ *Piazza III Novembre, Riva del Garda* ☎ *0464/554444* ⊕ *www.gardatrentino.it.*

Torre Apponale

VIEWPOINT | Predating the Venetian period by three centuries, this sturdy tower looms above the medieval residences of the main square; its crenellations recall its defensive purpose. You can climb the 165 steps to see the view from the top. ⊠ *Piazza III Novembre, Riva del Garda* ☎ *0464/573869* ⊕ *www.gardatrentino. it* ⊞ *€2.*

Restaurants

Peter Brunel

$$$$ | MODERN EUROPEAN | Walk through a Japanese garden off a country road east of Riva del Garda to enter multiple-Michelin-star-awarded chef Peter Brunel's light-filled, turquoise velvet-chaired restaurant. Each of the dozen sleek white tables are decorated with a unique sculpture, and jazz music sets the tone. **Known for:** dishes inspired by the chef's travels and Northern Italian roots; chic lounge areas to enjoy before and after meal drinks; impeccable service and presentation. $ *Average main: €130* ⊠ *Vina Linfano 47, Arco* ☎ *0464/076705* ⊕ *www.peterbrunel.com* ⊗ *Closed Sun., Mon., Feb., and 2 wks in Nov.*

Ristorante Castel Toblino

$$$ | NORTHERN ITALIAN | A lovely stop for a drink or a romantic dinner, this 16th-century castle is right on a lake in Sarche, about 20 km (12 miles) north of Riva toward Trento. Dishes highlight seasonal local ingredients, including mountain cheeses, salmon, trout, duck, and deer. **Known for:** castle setting; fish tasting menu; wine list featuring Trentino varieties. $ *Average main: €30* ⊠ *Localita' Castel Toblino 1, Sarche* ☎ *0461/864036* ⊕ *www.casteltoblino.com* ⊗ *Closed mid-Oct.–late Mar.*

☕ Coffee and Quick Bites

★ Eta Beta

$ | ICE CREAM | FAMILY | Matteo Mutti's gelato flavors have personality—like cheesecake with red pepper, rosemary, and pineapple, which might sound strange, but leaves a delightful impression on your taste buds. Other standouts are "Anni '90," inspired by Mutti's favorite tastes of the '90s—sour cherry and chocolate chip—and "Disaronno," swirled with a Lombardy liquor that is infused from apricot pits. **Known for:** gelato flavors that you won't find elsewhere; fun atmosphere; wide selection of cones, sundaes, and sizes. ⑤ *Average main: €5* ⊠ *Via Disciplini 14, Riva del Garda* ☎ *0464/554614* ⊕ *www.facebook.com/gelateriaetabeta* ⊘ *Closed Nov.–Mar.*

🛏 Hotels

Du Lac et du Parc Grand Resort

$$$ | RESORT | FAMILY | Highly personalized service and well-appointed guest rooms (including bungalows perfect for families) are among the hallmarks of Riva's largest resort; another is the beautifully manicured 17-acre garden with more than 200 species of plants. **Pros:** lush, expansive grounds with two swimming pools, plus kids' pool; pampering and indulgent staff; lovely spa area. **Cons:** not that cozy; no beach of its own; can hear noise in some rooms. ⑤ *Rooms from: €246* ⊠ *Viale Rovereto 44, Riva del Garda* ☎ *0464/566600* ⊕ *www.dulacetduparc.com* ⊘ *Closed mid-Nov.–late Mar.* ⤳ *163 rooms* ¶⊘*l Free Breakfast.*

Hotel Sole Relax & Panorama

$$ | HOTEL | A 15th-century palazzo in the center of town is the setting for this classic, comfortable, and relatively affordable hotel, where front rooms have terraces with breathtaking lake views and the rooftop terrace is a perfect retreat from summer's crowded beaches. **Pros:** prime location on the lake; modern hotel conveniences; comfortable beds. **Cons:** sometimes taken over by tour groups; not for those looking for ultracontemporary design; food gets mixed reviews. ⑤ *Rooms from: €136* ⊠ *Piazza III Novembre 35, Riva del Garda* ☎ *0464/552686, 0464/557809 reservations* ⊕ *www.hotelsoleriva.it* ⊘ *Closed Nov.– Dec. 21 and early Jan.–Mar.* ⤳ *80 rooms* ¶⊘l *Free Breakfast.*

Lido Palace

$$$$ | HOTEL | In a 19th-century lakeside palace, Riva's most chic hotel has a high-end spa; sleek public spaces with turquoise mod couches and classic floor-to-ceiling windows; and contemporary guest rooms, where slate floors and brown-and-gray color schemes are offset by crisp white linens. **Pros:** friendly service; gorgeous spa and pools; top-notch food. **Cons:** not all rooms have lake views or balconies; on the pricey side; coffee- or tea-making facilities in room only on request. ⑤ *Rooms from: €620* ⊠ *Viale Carducci 10, Riva del Garda* ☎ *0464/021899* ⊕ *www.lido-palace.it* ⊘ *Closed mid-Jan.–late Mar.* ⤳ *44 rooms* ¶⊘l *Free Breakfast.*

★ Luise

$$ | HOTEL | FAMILY | Outdoor perks here include a big garden, a large swimming pool, and free bikes to explore paths around the lake; interior draws include unique design touches—such as the lobby's collection of vintage luggage labels—and spacious rooms, all with comfy beds and a playful vibe and some with a whirlpool tub and a balcony. **Pros:** pleasant service; reasonably priced for the area; great for kids. **Cons:** some rooms can be noisy; 10-minute walk to center of Riva; no gym. ⑤ *Rooms from: €159* ⊠ *Viale Rovereto 9, Riva del Garda* ☎ *0464/550858* ⊕ *www.hotelluise.com* ⊘ *Closed mid-Nov.–late Mar.* ⤳ *68 rooms* ¶⊘l *Free Breakfast.*

Gargnano

30 km (19 miles) southwest of Riva del Garda, 144 km (89 miles) northeast of Milan.

This small port town was an important Franciscan center in the 13th century. Today, it comes alive in the summer, when German tourists, many of whom have villas here, crowd the small pebble beach. An Austrian flotilla bombarded the town in 1866, and some of the houses still bear marks of cannon fire. Mussolini owned two houses in Gargnano: one is the luxury hotel Villa Feltrinelli.

GETTING HERE AND AROUND
Gargnano is about a 30-minute drive south of Riva del Garda along the SS45bis.

VISITOR INFORMATION
CONTACT Gargnano Tourism Office. ⊠ *Via Roma 45, Gargnano* ☎ *0365/042100* ⊕ *www.thisisgargnano.it.*

 Restaurants

La Tortuga
$$$$ | **NORTHERN ITALIAN** | This trattoria is more sophisticated than it first appears: not only does it serve local dishes with novel twists, but it also has an extensive wine cellar. *Capesante scottate con salse ai diversi sapori* (seared scallops with different sauces) and *palette di piccoli campioni di lago e di mare* (mixed lake and sea fish) are worthy introductions to regional delights. **Known for:** fish and meat tasting menu; extensive cheese selection; delightful service. $ *Average main: €46* ⊠ *Via XXIV Maggio 5, Gargnano* ☎ *0365/71251* ⊕ *www.ristorantela-tortuga.it* ♾ *Closed Tues. and Dec.–Mar. No lunch.*

 Hotels

Garni Bartabel
$ | **B&B/INN** | The small rooms at this cozy main-street inn—where breakfast is served on an elegant lake-view terrace—have attractive Venetian-style furnishings and pastel color schemes. **Pros:** attractive lake views; a bargain for this area; delicious breakfast. **Cons:** few luxuries; not all rooms have lake views or terraces; can hear road noise. $ *Rooms from: €104* ⊠ *Via Roma 39, Gargnano* ☎ *0365/71300* ⊕ *www.hotelbartabel.it* ♾ *Closed Nov.– Mar.* ⌐ *11 rooms* ⦿| *Free Breakfast.*

Lefay Resort & Spa Lago di Garda
$$$$ | **RESORT** | The first thing you'll notice about this elegant resort in the hills above Gargnano are the stupendous lake and mountain views; the second thing will be its enormous spa, which is so filled with amenities (heated indoor-outdoor pool, saunas, well-equipped lake-view gym, extensive treatment menu) that you might just want to stay all day—and some guests do. **Pros:** fabulously relaxing spa; lovely location; delicious breakfast buffet. **Cons:** village of Gargnano is down a steep and twisty road; restaurant not up to standards of rest of hotel; prices for food and drink excessively high. $ *Rooms from: €590* ⊠ *Via Angelo Feltrinelli 136, Gargnano* ☎ *0365/241800* ⊕ *lagodigarda.lefayre-sorts.com/it* ♾ *Closed early Jan.–early Feb.* ⌐ *93 rooms* ⦿| *Free Breakfast.*

Villa Feltrinelli
$$$$ | **HOTEL** | This 1892 Art Nouveau villa hotel, named for the Italian publishing family who once vacationed here, has attracted the likes of Winston Churchill, D.H. Lawrence, and Benito Mussolini to its private lake-view gardens; extensive library; sumptuous and palatial rooms (as befits the final bill); and overall opulent interior of fresco ceilings, wood paneling, and antique ceramics. **Pros:** first-class luxury hotel; like stepping into a bygone era; amazing service including laundry

and valet services, and in-room bar. **Cons:** one of the most expensive hotels on the lake (or elsewhere); no gym; some find the attitude a bit arrogant. $ *Rooms from: €1800* ✉ *Via Rimembranza 38/40, Gargnano* ☎ *0365/798000* ⊕ *www.villafeltrinelli.com* ⊙ *Closed mid-Oct.–mid-Apr.* ⤳ *20 suites* ⦿ *Free Breakfast.*

Gardone Riviera

12 km (7 miles) southwest of Gargnano, 124 km (77 miles) northeast of Milan.

Now pleasantly faded, this once-fashionable 19th-century resort is best known these days for the hilltop estate of the poet Gabriele D'Annunzio, made as an elaborate memorial to himself. The middle-European appearance of its towers and palaces helps set this lakeside town apart from the rest of Italy. With the Italian Alps in the background and crystalline lake views in the summer, it's a gorgeous, albeit underappreciated, destination.

GETTING HERE AND AROUND
Gardone Riviera is about 22 km (13 miles) east of Brescia and 126 km (77 miles) east of Milan. By car from Milan, head for the A35 autostrada from SP14.

VISITOR INFORMATION
CONTACT Gardone Riviera Tourism.
✉ *Corso Repubblica 1, Gardone Riviera* ☎ *348/8954214 mobile* ⊕ *www.rivieradelgarda.com.*

◉ Sights

★ Heller Garden
GARDEN | This 2½-acre garden is a place to get lost while navigating stepping stones over lily ponds, climbing rock formations, and walking across wooden bridges. The treasures to be found are nearly 100 different Alpine, subtropical, and Mediterranean plant species and 30 modern art installations by the likes of Roy Lichtenstein, Joan Miró, and Auguste Rodin. A former vineyard, Heller Garden was first cultivated in 1903 by Austrian dentist and botanist Arthur Hruska, and bought in 1988 by artist Andrè Heller (although he is no longer the owner). ✉ *Via Roma 2, Gardone Riviera* ☎ *0366/410877* ⊕ *www.hellergarden.com* ⊠ *€12* ⊙ *Closed Nov.–Feb.*

Il Vittoriale
HISTORIC HOME | The estate of the larger-than-life Gabriele D'Annunzio (1863–1938)—one of Italy's major modern poets, and later war hero and supporter of Mussolini—is filled with the trappings of his conquests in art, love, and war. His eccentric house crammed with quirky memorabilia can only be seen during a 35-minute guided tour (available in English), and the extensive gardens are definitely worth a stroll, particularly to see the curious full-size warship's prow. There's also an imposing mausoleum, made of white marble, along with three museums showcasing personal items from D'Annunzio's exploits, including one devoted to his cars. ✉ *Via Vittoriale 12, Gardone Riviera* ☎ *0365/296511* ⊕ *www.vittoriale.it* ⊠ *€18 park, 3 museums, and guided tour of house; €15 park and 3 museums; €12 park and 2 museums* ⊙ *House closed Mon. and Tues. Nov.–Jan. and Mon. in Feb.*

Salò Market (Mercato Di Salò)
MARKET | Four kilometers (2½ miles) south of Gardone Riviera is the enchanting lakeside town of Salò, which history buffs may recognize as the capital of the ill-fated Social Republic, set up in 1943 by the Germans after they liberated Mussolini from the Gran Sasso. Every Saturday morning an enormous market is held in the Piazza Mario Pedrazzi, with bargains on household goods, clothing, food, and other items. In August or September a vendor often sells locally foraged *tartufi neri* (black truffles) at affordable prices. ✉ *Piazza Mario Pedrazzi, Salò.*

Restaurants

★ Ristorante Lido 84

$$$$ | **MODERN ITALIAN** | Dining in this bright, airy space feels like enjoying a meal in a fabulous friend's modern lake cottage—if the friend had floor-to-ceiling windows overlooking Lake Garda and a top-notch chef on hand. For an adventure in flavors from across the country, choose from two tasting menus and complement your meal with Italian or international wines in four- or five-glass pairings. **Known for:** unusual ingredients from all across Italy; rose cake with zabaglione; exquisite lake setting. ⑤ *Average main: €60* ✉ *Corso Zanardelli 196, Gardone Riviera* ☎ *0365/20019* ⊕ *www.ristorantelido84.com* ⊗ *Closed Tues., Wed., and early Jan.–mid-Feb.*

🛏 Hotels

★ Grand Hotel Fasano

$$$$ | **RESORT** | Used as a hunting lodge in the 19th century, the Fasano has matured into a seasonal hotel with high standards, opulent rooms, and many amenities—including an Aveda Destination Spa and a well-regarded restaurant, Il Fagiano, in addition to three more casual eateries (one a short walk away). **Pros:** exquisitely stylish rooms; relaxing surroundings; gorgeous spa. **Cons:** not all rooms have lake views; staff can seem indifferent; food gets mixed reviews. ⑤ *Rooms from: €414* ✉ *Corso Zanardelli 190, Gardone Riviera* ☎ *0365/290220* ⊕ *www.ghf.it* ⊗ *Closed Nov.–Mar.* ⇆ *79 rooms* ⦿ *Free Breakfast.*

Villa del Sogno

$$$$ | **HOTEL** | A narrow winding road takes you from town to this imposing villa, now a luxurious hotel retreat thanks to its valley and lake views and its peaceful grounds, which have an outdoor pool and a tennis court. **Pros:** endless amenities; individually decorated rooms; expansive terrace overlooking the lake. **Cons:** food gets mixed reviews; remote location; staff can be indifferent. ⑤ *Rooms from: €419* ✉ *Via Zanardelli 107, Gardone Riviera* ☎ *0365/290181* ⊕ *www.villadelsogno.it* ⊗ *Closed Nov.–mid-Apr.* ⇆ *38 rooms* ⦿ *Free Breakfast.*

Villa Fiordaliso

$$$ | **HOTEL** | A fine restaurant and five tastefully furnished guest rooms are housed in the pink-and-white lakeside villa given to Benito Mussolini's mistress, Claretta Petacci, by Il Duce himself—indeed, the expensive Claretta Suite is probably where they conducted their affair. **Pros:** combines cinematic charm with the intimacy of a B&B; amazing setting on the lake; elaborate breakfast spread. **Cons:** short on amenities (no spa or pool); can sometimes be noisy; may be too small for some people. ⑤ *Rooms from: €300* ✉ *Corso Zanardelli 150, Gardone Riviera* ☎ *0365/20158* ⊕ *www.villafiordaliso.it* ⊗ *Closed mid.-Oct.–mid-Mar.* ⇆ *5 rooms* ⦿ *Free Breakfast.*

Bellagio

30 km (19 miles) northeast of Como, 56 km (35 miles) northwest of Bergamo.

Sometimes called the prettiest town in Europe, Bellagio always seems perfectly adorned, with geraniums ablaze in every window and bougainvilleas veiling its staircases, or *montées*. At dusk Bellagio's nightspots—including the wharf, where an orchestra may be serenading dancers under the stars—beckon you to come and make merry. It's an impossibly enchanting location, one that inspired the French composer Gabriel Fauré to call Bellagio "a diamond contrasting brilliantly with the sapphires of the three lakes in which it is set."

GETTING HERE AND AROUND
Boats can take you from here to Tremezzo, where Napoléon's worst Italian enemy, Count Sommariva, resided at Villa Carlotta; and a bit farther south of Tremezzo, to Villa del Balbianello via

Lakes Como and Maggiore

Lenno. Check timetables at ⊕ *www.navigazionelaghi.it*.

VISITOR INFORMATION

CONTACT Bellagio Tourism Office. ⊠ *Piazza della Chiesa 14, Bellagio* ☎ *031/951555* ⊕ *www.bellagiolakecomo.com*.

Sights

Villa Melzi

GARDEN | The famous gardens of the Villa Melzi were once a favorite picnic spot for Franz Liszt, who advised author Louis de Ronchaud in 1837, "When you write the story of two happy lovers, place them on the shores of Lake Como. I do not know of any land so conspicuously blessed by heaven." The gardens are open to the public, and though you can't get into the 19th-century villa, don't miss the lavish Empire-style family chapel. The Melzi were Napoléon's greatest allies in Italy (the family has passed down the name "Josephine" to the present day). ⊠ *Lungo Lario Manzoni, Bellagio* ☎ *031/950318* ⊕ *www.giardinidivillamelzi.it* 🎟 *€10* ⊙ *Closed Nov.–late Mar.*

Villa Monastero

GARDEN | By ferry from Bellagio it's a quick trip across the lake to Varenna. The principal sight here is the spellbinding garden of the Villa Monastero, which, as its name suggests, was originally a monastery. There's also a house museum where you can admire 18th-century furnishings, as well as an international science and convention center. ⊠ *Viale Giovanni Polvani 4, Varenna* ☎ *0341/295450* ⊕ *www.villamonastero.eu* 🎟 *Garden €10, garden and house €13* ⊙ *Check the website for updated seasonal hours.*

Villa Serbelloni Garden

GARDEN | This property of the Rockefeller Foundation has celebrated gardens on the site of Pliny the Elder's villa, overlooking Bellagio. There are only two 1½-hour-long guided visits per day, at 11 am and 3:30 pm, with a maximum of 60 people each, and in May they tend to be booked by whole groups. Book in advance on the website and arrive early at the starting point at the Bellagio tourist office in the medieval tower in St. Giacomo Square. The garden also closes due to bad weather. ⊠ *Piazza della Chiesa 14, Bellagio* 🕾 *031/951555* ⊕ *www.bellagiolakecomo.com/en/bellagio-lake-como-italy/POI-points-of-interest/villa-serbelloni-garden* 🎫 *€10* ⊗ *Closed Mon. and early Nov.–mid-Mar.*

 Restaurants

★ Ristorante La Punta

$$$ | ITALIAN | When tourist-heavy Bellagio starts to wear you down, seek respite at this charming restaurant located on the town's very northernmost point, a scenic 10-minute walk from the center, with amazing lake views of Varenna to the north and Tremezzo to the west. As you might expect, the menu is heavy on lake fish; although the dishes aren't innovative, they're fresh and well prepared, and the view makes the experience even better. **Known for:** superfresh fish; superlative Lake Como views; friendly service. ⑤ *Average main: €27* ⊠ *Via Eugenio Vitali 19, Bellagio* 🕾 *031/951888* ⊕ *www.ristorantelapunta.it* ⊗ *Closed Nov.–Mar.*

 Hotels

Du Lac

$$$ | HOTEL | Most of the modern, inviting guest rooms at this comfortable, good-value old hotel—owned by an Anglo-Italian family and right in the center of Bellagio's action—have lake and mountain views, and the rooftop terrace garden is a perfect spot for drinks or dozing.

Pros: pleasant terrace garden; fabulous buffet breakfast; friendly service. **Cons:** beds too hard for some; some of the decor could use a refresh; the boat dock right in front of the hotel can be noisy. ⑤ *Rooms from: €260* ⊠ *Piazza Mazzini 32, Bellagio* 🕾 *031/950320* ⊕ *www.bellagiohoteldulac.com* ⊗ *Closed Nov.–Mar.* 🛏 *42 rooms* 🍽 *Free Breakfast.*

★ Grand Hotel Villa Serbelloni

$$$$ | HOTEL | The 19th-century luxury at this grand lake hotel—originally designed to cradle nobility and still a refined haven for the discreetly wealthy—has not so much faded as mellowed: guest rooms remain immaculate and plush; public areas are still awash with gilt ornamentation and marble; and breakfast is served in a ballroom. **Pros:** old-world grandeur; lovely gardens; great pools. **Cons:** could use some sprucing up; staff helpfulness varies widely; expensive food and drink. ⑤ *Rooms from: €810* ⊠ *Via T. Olivielli 1, Bellagio* 🕾 *031/950216* ⊕ *www.villaserbelloni.com* ⊗ *Closed Nov.–early Apr.* 🛏 *94 rooms* 🍽 *Free Breakfast.*

Hotel Belvedere

$$$$ | HOTEL | FAMILY | In Italian, *belvedere* means "beautiful view," and it's an apt name for this enchanting spot, where the modern rooms have classic touches such as antique furniture, decorative tiles, and marble bathrooms. **Pros:** attention to detail; great views; has a spa and a lovely pool. **Cons:** a climb from the waterfront; must request a lake-view balcony room in advance; fewer on-site amenities than other similarly priced hotels. ⑤ *Rooms from: €732* ⊠ *Via Valassina 31, Bellagio* 🕾 *031/950410* ⊕ *www.belvederebellagio.com* ⊗ *Closed Nov.–Mar.* 🛏 *63 rooms* 🍽 *Free Breakfast.*

Hotel Florence

$$ | HOTEL | Most of the large and comfortable rooms in this 1880s villa across from the ferry stop are furnished with interesting antiques and have splendid views of the lake. **Pros:** central location; appealing public spaces; lovely bar with outdoor lake-facing seating. **Cons:** location may feel too central if you're looking to get away from it all; some baths only have handheld showers; hotel could use an update. ⑤ *Rooms from: €170* ✉ *Piazza Mazzini 46, Bellagio* ☎ *031/950342* ⊕ *www.hotelflorencebellagio.it* ⊘ *Closed mid-Oct.–Apr.* ⇌ *30 rooms* ⦿ *Free Breakfast.*

Tremezzo

34 km (21 miles) north of Cernobbio, 79 km (49 miles) north of Milan.

The dreamy lakeside town of Tremezzo is close to two outstanding and magical villas, as well as sprawling gardens and one of the lake's grandest hotels.

GETTING HERE AND AROUND
Tremezzo is along the SS340. By car from Milan, the drive is 79 km (48 miles) following the A8 autostrada and takes about 90 minutes.

VISITOR INFORMATION
CONTACT Tremezzo Tourist Office.
✉ *Via Statale Regina 3, Tremezzo* ☎ *0344/40493* ⊕ *www.tremezzinatourism.com.*

Sights

Villa Carlotta
GARDEN | If you're lucky enough to visit Tremezzo in late spring or early summer, you will find the magnificent Villa Carlotta a riot of color, with more than 14 acres of azaleas and dozens of varieties of rhododendrons in full bloom. The height of the blossoms is late April to early May. The villa was built between 1690 and 1743 for the luxury-loving marquis Giorgio Clerici. The garden's collection is remarkable, particularly considering the difficulties of transporting delicate plants before the age of aircraft. Palms, banana trees, cacti, eucalyptus, a sequoia, orchids, and camellias are among the more than 500 species.

The villa's interior is worth a visit, particularly if you have a taste for the romantic sculptures of Antonio Canova (1757–1822). The best known is his *Cupid and Psyche*, which depicts the lovers locked in an odd but graceful embrace, with the young god above and behind, his wings extended, while Psyche awaits a kiss that will never come. The villa can be reached by boat from Bellagio and Como. ✉ *Via Regina 2, Tremezzo* ☎ *0344/40405* ⊕ *www.villacarlotta.it* ⊠ *€15* ⊘ *Closed early Nov.–Mar.*

★ Villa del Balbianello
HISTORIC HOME | The relentlessly picturesque Balbianello may be the most magical house in all of Italy; you probably know it from cameos in the movies *Casino Royale* and *Star Wars Episode II: Attack of the Clones*. It sits on its own little promontory, Il Dosso d'Avedo, around the bend from the tiny fishing village of Ossuccio. The villa is composed of loggias, terraces, and *palazzini* (tiny palaces), all spilling down verdant slopes to the shore, where you'll find an old Franciscan church, a magnificent stone staircase, and a statue of San Carlo Borromeo blessing the waters.

The villa is usually reached from Como and Bellagio by boat, which leaves you at the village of Lenno. From there, marked signs lead you to the villa—it's either accessible by foot via a 20-minute walk or a more challenging 45-minute hike. ✉ *Via Guido Monzino 1, Lenno* ⊹ *5 km (3 miles) southwest of Tremezzo* ☎ *0344/56110* ⊕ *www.fondoambiente.it/ luoghi/villa-del-balbianello* ⊠ *€24 villa and gardens, includes 1-hr guided tour; €13 gardens only* ⊘ *Check the website for seasonal and special event closures.*

◉ Coffee and Quick Bites

Cantina Follie
$ | **WINE BAR** | This cantina's leafy patio is reached by hiking up the stairs into the neighborhood above Tremezzo. There's a collection of more than 300 wines to sample along with *tagliere* (cutting

boards) of local cheeses, preserved meats, and vegetarian and vegan options. **Known for:** shady setting away from the main street; cheese and wine pairings; local products. ⑤ *Average main: €14* ⊠ *Via Alessandro Volta 14, Tremezzo* ☎ *0344/42311* ⊕ *www.cantinafollie.it* ⊘ *Closed Tues. and Dec.–Feb.*

Hotels

★ Grand Hotel Tremezzo

$$$$ | **RESORT** | Creature comforts in this turn-of-the-20th-century building—one of the top grand hotels on the lake—include a lush park, three heated swimming pools (one of them floats on pontoons on the lake), a small private beach, and sumptuous guest rooms where old-world style meets modern amenities. **Pros:** lakeside location with beautiful views; attractive spa; gracious service. **Cons:** not well situated if you're looking for shopping or nightlife; very expensive; somewhat busy road between hotel and lake. ⑤ *Rooms from: €1600* ⊠ *Via Regina 8, Tremezzo* ☎ *0344/42491* ⊕ *www. grandhoteltremezzo.com* ⊘ *Closed mid-Nov.–early Apr.* ⊶ *90 rooms* ⑩ *Free Breakfast.*

Hotel Rusall

$$ | **B&B/INN** | Amid a large garden on the hillside above Tremezzo, this hotel offers small, private, comfortably simple rooms; a pool with a nice view; and a popular restaurant that serves tasty Italian classics. **Pros:** lovely walks into town and in the countryside; more intimate than grander lake hotels; good on-site restaurant and half-board rates. **Cons:** takes some effort to reach and walk to town; rooms are fairly basic; air-conditioning can be an issue in rooms and common areas. ⑤ *Rooms from: €140* ⊠ *Via San Martino 2, Tremezzo* ☎ *0344/40408* ⊕ *www.rusallhotel.com* ⊘ *Closed Jan.–mid-March* ⊶ *23 rooms* ⑩ *Free Breakfast.*

Cernobbio

5 km (3 miles) north of Como, 53 km (33 miles) north of Milan.

The legendary resort of Villa d'Este is reason enough to visit this jewel on the lake, but the town itself is worth a stroll. The place still has a neighborhood feel to it, especially on summer evenings and weekends, when the piazza is full of families and couples strolling.

GETTING HERE AND AROUND
Cernobbio is on the SS340, 6 km (4 miles) north of the city of Como; from Milan take the A9 and follow signs for Como. The drive is 53 km (33 miles) and takes about one hour.

VISITOR INFORMATION
CONTACT Cernobbio Tourism Office.
⊠ *Largo Alfredo Campanini 1, Cernobbio* ☎ *347/8818532* ⊕ *www.mylakecomo.co/ en/cernobbio.*

Sights

Villa Bernasconi

HISTORIC HOME | Art Nouveau details, such as intricately-carved floral balconies and tile work, are enough to make you get out of the car for a closer look at this villa on the main road from Como to Cernobbio. The turreted two-story former home of textile tycoon Davide Bernasconi was built on the grounds of his company's silk mills at the turn of the century and is now an interactive museum. Among the rooms with original wood-inlay ceilings, decorative stained glass, and marble mosaic floors, are audio installations that recount the history of Bernasconi's empire and the Lake Como area's silk industry. Temporary exhibits highlight contemporary Italian artists and fashion design. ⊠ *Largo Campanini 2, Cernobbio* ☎ *031/3347209* ⊕ *www.villabernasconi. eu* ⬜ *€8* ⊘ *Closed Tues.–Thurs.* ⬚ *Reservations recommended.*

🍴 Restaurants

Il Gatto Nero

$$$ | **NORTHERN ITALIAN** | Reservations are a must for this longtime favorite in the hills above Cernobbio. The lake view is splendid, and specialties include home-made pastas and fish dishes with a dash of international flair. **Known for:** classic cotoletta alla Milanese; high-end wine selection; lovely terrace. ⑤ *Average main: €34* ⊠ *Via Monte Santo 69, Cernobbio* ☏ *031/512042* ⊕ *www.ristorantegat-tonero.it* ⊘ *Closed Mon.* ☞ *Credit card required for reservations; €30/person no-show fee for missed reservations or late cancellations.*

Il Giardino

$$ | **NORTHERN ITALIAN** | "The Garden" has an expansive patio that's a shady respite from the summer sun. Though mainly known for its pizza, the restaurant also has an extensive menu of fish and meat dishes. **Known for:** extensive outdoor seating; tasty pizza; fun vibe. ⑤ *Average main: €19* ⊠ *Via Regina 73, Cernobbio* ☏ *031/511154* ⊕ *www.giardinocernobbio. com* ⊘ *Closed Wed. Nov.–Feb. No lunch Thurs.*

Lido di Cernobbio

$$$ | **ITALIAN** | Right next to the Cernobbio ferry stop, this pretty restaurant offers a nice selection of local wines and, whenever possible, uses local ingredients in its pizza, pasta, fish, and meat dishes. Though the modern gray interior is pleasant, try for a table on the terrace, and note that, in season, you can rent a sun bed and use the pools (one for adults and one for kids) before or after your meal. **Known for:** lovely lake scenery; solid Italian dishes; family-friendly atmosphere. ⑤ *Average main: €25* ⊠ *Piazza Risorg-imento 5, Cernobbio* ☏ *031/4446437* ⊕ *www.lidodicernobbio.com* ⊘ *Closed Wed. and Nov.–Mar.*

★ Materia

$$$$ | **MODERN ITALIAN** | This aesthetically simple bistro-style restaurant, spruced up with modern art, draws a mainly local crowd for some of the most inventive food creations and presentation in the Como region. The imaginative vegeta-ble-focused cuisine makes good use of local ingredients, and the frequently changing surprise five- or seven-course tasting menus are a particular delight, especially when paired with the mostly natural wines on offer. **Known for:** use of organic herbs and vegetables from their greenhouse; vegetarian tasting menu; Italian and international wines from small producers. ⑤ *Average main: €40* ⊠ *Via Cinque Giornate 32, Cernobbio* ☏ *031/2075548* ⊕ *www.ristorantemate-ria.it* ⊘ *Closed Mon. No lunch Tues.*

☕ Coffee and Quick Bites

Anagramma

$ | **ITALIAN** | Communal garden tables and atrium seating in a space that's also Cernobbio's tourist info point make for a pleasant stop for a coffee and pastry, light lunch, or aperitif. Baked goods, such as apple and *frangipane* (almond cream) cake and sourdough bread for sand-wiches and tagliere plates (with local cheese, salumi, and lake fish), are made daily in-house. **Known for:** relaxed garden setting; house-made breakfast pastries and bread; convenient stop on the way to other lake towns. ⑤ *Average main: €10* ⊠ *Largo Alfredo Campanini 1, Cernobbio* ☏ *031/4446483* ⊘ *Closed Mon.*

🛏 Hotels

Passalacqua

$$$$ | **RESORT** | Count Andrea Lucini Passa-lacqua hosted artists and politicians at this 5-acre lakefront villa in Moltrasio, just north of Cernobbio, until the count's death in 1890; today the Bellini Suite (a 2,700-square-foot suite with an opulent

music room reserved for Vincenzo Bellini while he composed operas) and 23 others, have restored frescoes, Murano glass chandeliers, and luxurious soaking tubs. **Pros:** luxurious and quiet retreat; in-room extras such as Dyson hair tools and Aqua Como products; highly attentive staff. **Cons:** not all rooms have lake views; a bit difficult to find off a side road; food and drinks are very expensive. ⑤ *Rooms from: €1500* ⊠ *Via Besana 59, Moltrasio* ☎ *031/44311* ⊕ *www.passalacqua.it/en* ⊗ *Closed Feb.–late Mar.* ⊲⊃ *24 suites* ⊖⊙⊖ *Free Breakfast.*

★ Villa d'Este

$$$$ | RESORT | Europe's rich and famous have long favored this hotel, one of Italy's grandest, where rooms are done in Empire style; a broad veranda sweeps out to the lakefront; a swimming pool extends above the water; a restaurant offers top-notch views and cuisine; there are four private villas; and pavilions, miniature forts, and other follies ensure whimsical garden walks. **Pros:** fine service; amazing grounds; excellent restaurant. **Cons:** may feel too formal for some; not all rooms have lake views; all this grandness comes with a hefty price tag. ⑤ *Rooms from: €1283* ⊠ *Via Regina 40, Cernobbio* ☎ *031/3481* ⊕ *www. villadeste.com* ⊗ *Closed mid-Nov.–mid-Mar.* ⊲⊃ *152 rooms, 4 private villas* ⊖⊙⊖ *Free Breakfast.*

Como

5 km (3 miles) south of Cernobbio, 30 km (19 miles) southwest of Bellagio, 50 km (31 miles) north of Milan.

Como commands the south shore of the lake. In its center, elegant cobblestone pedestrian streets wind their way past parks and bustling cafés. However, it's only partly a resort: the city also has an industrial heritage, deeply rooted in the production of textiles, particularly silk and the silk trade. If traveling by car, leave

it at the edge of the town center in the well-lit underground parking facility right on the lake.

GETTING HERE AND AROUND

Como is easily reachable by regional trains from Milan from Porta Garibaldi, Cadorna, and Milano Centrale stations, and the ride is about one hour. If driving from Milan, take the A9 and follow signs for Como; the journey is 50 km (31 miles) and takes about one hour.

VISITOR INFORMATION

CONTACT Como Tourism Office. ⊠ *Via Albertolli 7, Como* ☎ *031/4493068, 031/269712* ⊕ *www.visitcomo.eu/en.*

◉ Sights

Duomo

CHURCH | The splendid 15th-century Renaissance-Gothic Duomo was begun in 1396. The facade was added in 1455, and the transepts were completed in the mid-18th century. The dome was designed by Filippo Juvarra (1678–1736), chief architect of many of the sumptuous palaces of the royal house of Savoy. The facade has statues of two of Como's most famous sons, Pliny the Elder and Pliny the Younger, whose writings are among the most important documents from antiquity. Inside, the works of art include Luini's *Holy Conversation,* a fresco cycle by Morazzone, and the *Marriage of the Virgin Mary* by Ferrari. ⊠ *Piazza del Duomo, Como* ☎ *031/3312275* ⊕ *www. cattedraledicomo.it.*

Museo della Seta *(Silk Museum)*

SPECIALTY MUSEUM | From silkworm litters to textile finishing machinery to temporary exhibitions, this small but complete collection preserves the history of a manufacturing region that continues to supply a large proportion of Europe's silk. The friendly staffers will give you an overview of the museum; they are also happy to provide brochures and information about local retail shops. The location isn't well marked: follow the textile school's driveway around to the low-rise concrete building on the left, and take the shallow ramp down to the entrance. ⊠ *Via Castelnuovo 9, Como* ☎ *031/303180* ⊕ *www. museosetacomo.com* 🖃 *€10* ⊗ *Closed Mon.*

San Fedele

CHURCH | At the heart of Como's medieval quarter, the city's first cathedral is well worth a peek. The apse walls and ceiling are completely frescoed, as are the ceilings above the altar. ⊠ *Piazza San Fedele, Como* ☎ *031/3868316* ⊕ *www.parrocchiasanfedelecomo.it.*

🍴 Restaurants

★ Feel Como

$$$$ | MODERN ITALIAN | Your palate will travel from the lakes (eel with leek) to the countryside (juniper risotto) to the mountains (tripe), all from the comfort of your table, at this cozy stone-arched eatery tucked into Como's commercial district. Expect creative takes on Italian cuisine, like deconstructed ravioli, using both local and more exotic ingredients, best sampled with a tasting menu. **Known for:** witty variations on local cuisine; gorgeous platings; extensive wine list. $ *Average main: €65* ⊠ *Via Generale Armando Diaz 54, Como* ☎ *0334/7264545* ⊕ *www. feelcomo.com* ⊗ *Closed Mon. and Tues. No lunch Wed.–Fri.*

Rivenoteca

$$$ | NORTHERN ITALIAN | A former 17th-century convent is now a lively enoteca run by Alberto and Catia Rivetti, offering more than 600 wines, as well as spirits and beers—all from northern Italy. Old and new merge in this warm and friendly spot with sage and rose walls, an original decorative ceiling, and a hallway with an automatic dispenser with more than 30 wines available on demand—get up from your seat to taste as many wines as you'd like using a prepaid card. **Known for:** local wines and spirits, including from the owners' winery; dispenser for wines

"on demand" in three sizes, or by the bottle; entirely Lombard-focused cuisine. $ *Average main: €33* ⊠ *Via A. Diaz 56, Como* ☎ *035/225283* ⊕ *www.rivenoteca. it* ⊗ *Closed Sun. No lunch Mon.–Thurs.*

🛏 Hotels

★ Il Sereno Lago di Como

$$$$ | RESORT | Throughout this, the first European outpost of the luxe Il Sereno Hotel in St. Barths, you'll find floor-to-ceiling lake-view windows and an understated retro-mod aesthetic, with a muted palette of browns and grays complementing a panoply of wood, stone, leather, and copper accents. **Pros:** cool modern design; hushed elegance throughout; fabulous views. **Cons:** extremely expensive; not for lovers of historical villas; can be difficult to find. $ *Rooms from: €2240* ⊠ *Via Torrazza 10, Torno* ☎ *031/5477800* ⊕ *www.ilsereno.com* ⊗ *Closed Nov.– mid-Mar.* ↝ *40 suites* ⏐⊙⏐ *Free Breakfast.*

Mandarin Oriental, Lago di Como

$$$$ | HOTEL | The nine 19th-century villas that comprise this Lake Como outpost of the extravagant Mandarin chain have been thoroughly updated for the 21st century, offering a quiet setting (just north of the busy town of Como) and luxurious amenities that include a 14,000-square-foot spa and a swimming pool that "floats" above the lake. **Pros:** amazingly peaceful setting; fabulous wellness facilities; complimentary minibar. **Cons:** location a bit isolated from other towns; food not up to par; service can be haphazard. $ *Rooms from: €1300* ⊠ *Via E. Caronti 69, Blevio* ☎ *031/32511* ⊕ *www.mandarinoriental.com/lake-como/ blevio/luxury-hotel* ⊗ *Closed mid-Nov.– mid-Mar.* ↝ *75 rooms* ⏐⊙⏐ *Free Breakfast.*

Posta Design Hotel

$$ | HOTEL | Just a block from the lake, on downtown Como's pedestrian-only Piazza Volta, this boutique hotel has a minimalist modern interior that's in perfect keeping with its exterior—the 1931 building that

houses it was designed by Rationalist architect Giuseppe Terragni. **Pros:** central location; comfortable rooms; friendly service. **Cons:** rooms on lower floors can be noisy; sparse amenities (no minibars in rooms, no breakfast, no gym); Internet must be logged into each time. $ *Rooms from: €175* ✉ *Via Garibaldi 2, Como* ☎ *031/2769011* ⊕ *www.postadesignhotel.com* ➔ *14 rooms* ⊙ *No Meals.*

Activities

Lake Como has lots of ways to stay active and outdoors, from windsurfing at the lake's northern end, to boating, sailing, and Jet Skiing at Como and Cernobbio. The lake is also quite swimmable in summer. For hikers there are lovely paths all around the lake. For an easy trek, take the funicular up to Brunate, and walk along the mountain to the lighthouse for a stunning view of the lake.

Stresa and the Isole Borromee

80 km (50 miles) northwest of Milan.

One of the better known resorts on the western shore, Stresa is a tourist town, which provided Hemingway with one of the settings in *A Farewell to Arms.* It has capitalized on its central lakeside position, though the luxurious elegance that distinguished its heyday has faded; grand hotels are still grand, but traffic now encroaches on their parks and gardens.

The best way to escape to yesteryear is to head for the Isole Borromee (Borromean Islands) in Lake Maggiore. Boats to the three islands depart from the dock at Stresa's Piazza Marconi, as well as from Piazzale Lido at the northern end of the promenade. There's also a boat from Verbania; check locally for the seasonal schedule. Although you can hire a private boat, it's cheaper and just as convenient

to use the regular service. Make sure you buy a ticket allowing you to visit all the islands—Bella, Superiore dei Pescatori, and Madre. The islands take their name from the Borromeo family, which has owned them since the 12th century.

GETTING HERE AND AROUND

Trains run regularly from Milan to the town of Stresa on Lake Maggiore; the trip takes 1–1½ hours, depending on the type of train. By car from Milan to Stresa, take the A8 autostrada to the A8dir, and from the A8dir take the A26; the drive is about 1¼ hours.

VISITOR INFORMATION

CONTACT Stresa & Isole Borromee Tourism Office. ✉ *Piazza Marconi 16, Stresa* ☎ *0323/933478* ⊕ *www.isoleborromee.it.*

Sights

Isola Bella (*Beautiful Island*)

ISLAND | The most famous of the three Isole Borromee (Borromean Islands), is named after Isabella, whose husband, Carlo III Borromeo (1538–84), built the palace and terraced gardens here for her as a wedding present. Before Count Carlo began his project, the island was rocky and almost devoid of vegetation; the soil for the garden had to be transported from the mainland. For a splendid view of the lake, wander up the 10 terraces of Teatro Massimo. In the gardens, white peacocks roam among the scented shrubs. Visit Palazzo Borromeo to see the rooms where famous guests—including Napoléon and Mussolini—stayed in 18th-century splendor. ✉ *Isola Bella* ☎ *0323/933478* ⊕ *www.isoleborromee. it* ✆ *Garden and palace €21 online (€22 at the ticket office)* ⊙ *Closed early Nov.–mid-Mar.*

★ **Isola Madre** (*Mother Island*)

GARDEN | All of this Borromean island is a botanical garden, with a season that stretches from late March to late October due to the climatic protection of the mighty Alps and the tepid waters of

Lake Maggiore. The cacti and palm trees here, so far north and so near the border with Switzerland, are a beautiful surprise. Two special times to visit are April, for the camellias, and May, for azaleas and rhododendrons. Also on the island is a 16th-century palazzo, where the Borromeo family still lives for part of the year. ⊠ *Isola Madre* ☎ *0323/933479* ⊕ *www. isoleborromee.it* 🎫 *€18 online; €19 at the ticket office (palace and garden)* ☉ *Closed early Nov.–mid Mar.*

Isola Superiore dei Pescatori (*Island of the Fishermen*)

ISLAND | Stop for lunch at the smallest Borromean island, less than 100 yards wide and only about ½ km (¼ mile) long. It's an ideal place to visit before, after, or in between touring the other two islands. Of the 10 or so restaurants on this island the two worth visiting are Ristorante Il Verbano (☎ *0323/31226*) and Ristorante Belvedere (☎ *0323/32292*). The island with little lanes strung with fishing nets and dotted with shrines to the Madonna is a crowded place filled with souvenir stands and shops in high season. ⊠ *Isola dei Pescatori.*

🍴 Restaurants

★ Ristorante Lastresa

$$ | NORTHERN ITALIAN | The nondescript exterior of this buzzy eatery off one of Stresa's main streets belies its chic, stylish interior. Dishes made with seasonal ingredients dominate the menu, but, no matter the season, you'll find local lake fish, both marinated and panfried, as well as a solid list of wines from throughout the region and across Italy. **Known for:** locals' favorite; friendly, knowledgeable waitstaff; Piedmont dessert sampler. ⑤ *Average main: €23* ⊠ *Via Principessa Margherita 22, Stresa* ☎ *0323/33240* ⊕ *www.ristorantelastresa.it* ☉ *Closed Tues. and Sept.–Mar. No lunch Mon.*

Trattoria due Piccioni

$$ | MODERN ITALIAN | In a town with an overabundance of touristy pizza and pasta places, this unassumingly modern family-run bistro raises the bar. Although the shabby-chic decor and friendly service entice, the real draw is the short but smart menu of creative Italian dishes and vegetarian options. **Known for:** inventive local cuisine; intriguing desserts; attentive service. ⑤ *Average main: €18* ⊠ *Via P. Tommaso 61, Stresa* ☎ *0323/934556* ⊕ *www.facebook.com/duepiccioni* ☉ *Closed Wed.*

☕ Coffee and Quick Bites

Pasticceria Marcolini

$ | BAKERY | Margheritine cookies were first baked in Stresa for Margherita of Savoy in 1857 while she was still a princess. Named for the first queen of Italy as well as for their shape like a daisy (*margherita* in Italian), the biscuits' recipe includes cooked egg yolk and an abundant supply of powdered sugar, making them crumble effortlessly in your mouth. **Known for:** locals' spot for breakfast and special occasions; gift boxes to take cookies home; sweets made following traditional Stresa recipes. ⑤ *Average main: €10* ⊠ *Via Vincenzo de Vit 14, Stresa* ☎ *0323/30364* ⊕ *www.facebook.com/ pasticceriamarcolini* ☉ *Closed Tues.*

🛏 Hotels

★ Grand Hotel des Iles Borromees

$$$ | HOTEL | This palatial, Liberty-style hotel has catered to a demanding European clientele since 1863, and although its spacious salons and guest rooms still have lavish turn-of-the-last-century furnishings, there are signs of modernity, including a redesigned bar (Hemingway Bar), low-calorie and gluten-free options at the restaurant, and extensive wellness treatments. **Pros:** bygone-era grace and style plus modern amenities; sumptuous rooms, particularly the fabulous

Hemingway Suite; nice pool and spa selection. **Cons:** bathrooms could use a refresh; decor may be over the top for some; Internet can be on the slow side. ⑤ *Rooms from: €250* ✉ *Corso Umberto I 67, Stresa* ☏ *0323/938938* ⊕ *www. borromees.com* ⊗ *Closed Dec. and Jan.* ⇥ *179 rooms* ⦿ *Free Breakfast.*

Verbania

16 km (10 miles) north of Stresa, 102 km (63 miles) northwest of Milan.

The quaint town of Verbania is across the Gulf of Pallanza from its more touristy neighbor, Stresa. It is known for the Villa Taranto, which has magnificent botanical gardens. With its majestic gardens and greenery, Verbania is often called the Garden of Lake Maggiore.

GETTING HERE AND AROUND
By car from Milan take the A8 to Lago Maggiore, traveling 102 km (63 miles); Verbania is on SS34 and the drive takes about one hour and 45 minutes.

VISITOR INFORMATION
CONTACT Verbania Tourism. ✉ *Corso Zanitello 6/8, Lungolago di Pallanza, Verbania* ☏ *0323/503249* ⊕ *www.verbania-turismo.it.*

Sights

Santa Caterina del Sasso Ballaro
CHURCH | Near the town of Laveno, this beautiful lakeside hermitage was constructed in the 12th century by a local merchant to express his gratitude for having been saved from the wrath of a storm. Seemingly carved out of its supporting cliff, it's particularly striking as you approach it by boat, although, after docking, you'll need to climb 80 steps. Alternatively, park in the lot above and walk down a 268-step staircase; there's an elevator, though it's not as scenic. ✉ *Via Santa Caterina 13, Leggiuno* ☏ *0332/647014* ⊕ *www.eremosantacaterina.it* ⦿ *€5.*

Villa Taranto
GARDEN | **FAMILY** | The Villa Taranto was acquired in 1931 by Scottish captain Neil McEachern, who helped make the magnificent gardens here what they are today, adding terraces, waterfalls, more than 3,000 plant species from all over the world—including 300 varieties of dahlias—and broad meadows sloping gently to the lake. While the gardens can be visited, the villa itself is not open to the public. ✉ *Via Vittorio Veneto 111, Verbania* ☏ *0323/556667* ⊕ *www.villataranto.it* ⦿ *€13* ⊗ *Closed early Nov.–early Mar.*

Hotels

Il Chiostro
$ | **HOTEL** | Using space formed from a 17th-century monastery merged with an adjoining 19th-century textile factory, this hotel offers plain, functional rooms, some overlooking a lovely garden. **Pros:** friendly, efficient staff; lovely breakfast; affordable for the area. **Cons:** rooms are fairly plain; limited amenities; small bathrooms. ⑤ *Rooms from: €90* ✉ *Via Fratelli Cervi 14, Verbania* ☏ *0323/404077* ⊕ *www. chiostrovb.it* ⇥ *100 rooms* ⦿ *Free Breakfast.*

Chapter 9

PIEDMONT AND THE VALLE D'AOSTA

Updated by
Liz Humphreys

👁 Sights	🍴 Restaurants	🛏 Hotels	🛍 Shopping	🍸 Nightlife
★★★☆☆	★★★★★	★★★★☆	★★☆☆☆	★☆☆☆☆

WELCOME TO PIEDMONT AND THE VALLE D'AOSTA

TOP REASONS TO GO

★ **Sacra di San Michele:** Explore one of the country's most spectacularly situated religious monuments.

★ **Castello di Fénis:** This castle transports you back in time to the Middle Ages.

★ **Monte Bianco:** A cable-car ride over a snowcapped mountain will take your breath away.

★ **Turin's Museo Egizio:** A surprising treasure— one of the world's richest collections of Ancient Egyptian art outside Cairo, Egypt.

★ **Regal wines:** Some of Italy's most revered reds— led by Barolo, the "king of wines"—come from the hills of southern Piedmont.

★ **Turin's Galleria Sabauda:** Witness to the regal splendor of the reigning House of Savoy, this museum is famed for its spectacular collection of Old Masters.

1 Turin. Neoclassical piazzas and Baroque palazzi have been restored in grand style.

2 Asti. Home of its namesake *spumante,* a sweet sparkling wine.

3 Alba. A city that's renowned for its truffles and mushrooms.

4 The Barolo Region. Birthplace of the celebrated nebbiolo grape.

5 Gavi. This town boasts charming streets and famed white wine.

6 Bard. A strategic medieval town with an impressive fortress.

7 Breuil-Cervinia/The Matterhorn. This skier's paradise straddles the Swiss border.

8 Castello di Fénis. Castello di Fénis is embellished with many towers.

9 Aosta. This is one of Italy's most livable cities.

10 Courmayeur/Monte Bianco. A cozy mountain town, popular with skiers.

11 Venaria Reale. An expansive 16th-century Savoy palace.

12 Rivoli. This charming town is a highlight.

13 Sacra di San Michele. This 11th-century abbey once controlled 176 European churches.

EATING AND DRINKING WELL IN PIEDMONT AND THE VALLE D'AOSTA

Selection of grissini (bread sticks)

In Piedmont and the Valle d'Aosta you can find rustic specialties from farmhouse hearths, fine cuisine with a French accent, and everything in between. The Piedmontese take their food and wine very seriously.

There's a significant concentration of upscale restaurants in Piedmont, with refined cuisine designed to showcase the region's fine wines. Wine-oriented menus are prevalent both in cities and in the country, where even simply named trattorias may offer a *menu di degustazione* (a multicourse tasting menu that highlights the chef's specialties) accompanied by wine pairings.

In Turin the ritual of the *aperitivo* (aperitif) has been finely tuned, and most cafés from the early evening onward provide lavish buffets that are included in the price of a cocktail—a respectable substitute for dinner if you're traveling on a limited budget. As a result, restaurants in Turin tend to fill only after 9 pm.

GREAT GRISSINI

Throughout the region—and especially in Turin—you'll find that most meals are accompanied by *grissini* (bread sticks). When they are freshly made and hand-rolled, these renditions are a far cry from the thin and dry, plastic-wrapped versions available elsewhere. Grissini were invented in Turin in the 17th century to ease the digestive problems of little Prince Vittorio Amedeo II (1675–1730). Napoléon called them *petits batons* and was supposedly addicted to them.

TRUFFLES

The *tartufo* (truffle) is a peculiar delicacy—a gnarly clump of fungus that grows wild in forests a few inches underground. It's hunted down using truffle-sniffing dogs. The payoff is a powerful, perfume flavor that makes gourmets swoon and for which they are willing to pay a small fortune. Although truffles are more abundant farther south in Umbria, the most coveted ones are the *tartufi bianchi* (white truffles) from Alba in Piedmont. A thin shaving of truffle often tops pasta dishes; they're also used to flavor soups and other dishes.

White truffles

POLENTA AND PASTA

The area's best-known dish is probably polenta, creamy cornmeal served with *carbonada* (a meat stew), melted cheese, or wild mushrooms. *Agnolotti*—crescent-shape pasta stuffed with meat filling—is another specialty, often served with the pan juices of roast veal.

CHEESE

In keeping with their northern character, Piedmont and the Valle d'Aosta are both known for *fonduta,* a version of fondue made with melted cheese, eggs, and sometimes grated truffles. Fontina and ham also often deck out the ubiquitous French-style crepes *alla valdostana,* served casserole-style.

Agnolotti (meat-filled pasta)

MEAT

The locally raised beef of Piedmont is some of Italy's most highly prized; it's often braised or stewed with the region's hearty red wine. In winter, *bollito misto* (various meats, boiled and served with a rich sauce) shows up on many menus, and fritto misto, a combination of fried meats and vegetables, is another specialty.

DESSERTS AND SWEETS

Although desserts here are less sweet than in some other Italian regions, treats like *panna cotta* (a puddinglike cooked cream), *torta di nocciole* (hazelnut torte), and *bonet* (a pudding made with hazelnuts, cocoa, milk, and macaroons) are delights. Turin is renowned for its delicate pastries and fine chocolates—especially for *gianduiotti,* made with hazelnuts.

WINE

Piedmont is one of Italy's most important wine regions, producing full-bodied reds, such as Barolo, Barbaresco, freisa, barbera, and the lighter dolcetto. Asti Spumante, a sweet sparkling wine, comes from the region, as does the white wine Gavi, from the southeast. The Valle d'Aosta is famous for brandies made from fruits or herbs.

Northwest Italy's Piedmont and Valle d'Aosta regions come with a large dose of mountain splendor, culinary achievement, and scenic beauty. Two of Europe's most famous peaks, Monte Bianco (Mont Blanc) and Monte Cervino (the Matterhorn), straddle the Valle d'Aosta's borders with France and Switzerland, and the region draws skiers and hikers from all over.

To the south, the mist-shrouded lowlands are home to Turin, a city that may not have the artistic treasures of Rome or the cutting-edge style of Milan but has developed a sense of urban sophistication that makes it a pleasure to visit. The fourth-largest city in the country, it was once overlooked on tourist itineraries as a mere industrial center (Fiat is based here), but the 2006 Winter Olympic Games put Turin on many tourists' map.

Farther south, vineyards carpet the rolling hills of the Langhe, Monferrato, and Gavi regions, where Barolo, Barbaresco, Asti Spumante, and Gavi wines—some of Italy's finest—are produced. It's here, as well, that the prized white truffle of Alba is found and celebrated during an autumn fair.

Piedmont has the longest border with France of any region, and the fact of its having been ruled by the French Savoy for centuries is revealed in a Gallic influence in all walks of life—especially in food and architecture. Turin's mansard roofs and porticoed avenues can make a walk through its streets feel like a stroll down a Parisian boulevard.

MAJOR REGIONS

Southeast of Turin. In the hilly, wooded Monferrato area, and farther south in the Langhe near Alba and in the Gavi region, the landscape is a patchwork of vineyards and dark woods, dotted with hill towns and castles like medieval Castello di Fénis. This area produces some of Italy's most famous red wines, as well as sparkling whites like Asti Spumante and the dry white Gavi.

The Valle d'Aosta. In this region near the French–Swiss border, the unspoiled beauty of the Alps' highest peaks, the Matterhorn and Mont Blanc, competes with the magnificent scenery of Italy's oldest national park, Gran Paradiso. Luckily, the region is so small that you don't have to choose. The main Aosta Valley, largely on an east–west axis, is hemmed in by high mountains. Pont St. Martin, north of Ivrea, is the beginning of bilingual (Italian and French) territory.

West of Turin and beyond. As you head west from Turin into the *colline* ("little hills"), castles and medieval fortifications begin to appear and the Alps come into better view. In this region lie the story-book medieval town of Rivoli; 12th-century abbeys like Sacra di San Michele; a 16th-century Savoy hunting lodge, Venaria Reale; and, farther west in the mountains, the ski resort of Sestriere, one of the venues used during the 2006 Winter Games.

Planning

Getting Here and Around

BUS

Turin's main bus station is in Corso Bolzano, near the Porta Susa train station. There's also a major bus station at Aosta, across the street from the train station.

CONTACTS Arriva Italia. ⊠ *Turin* ☎ *035/289000* ⊕ *torino.arriva.it.* **Flix Bus.** ☎ *029/4759208* ⊕ *www.flixbus.com.* **GTT.** ⊠ *Turin* ☎ *800/019152 toll-free in Italy* ⊕ *www.gtt.to.it/cms.*

CAR

Like any mountainous region, the Italian Alps can be tricky to navigate by car. Roads that look like highways on the map can be narrow and twisting, with steep slopes and cliff-side drops. Generally, roads are well maintained, but the distance covered by all of those curves tends to take longer than you might expect, so it's best to figure in extra time for getting around. This is especially true in winter, when weather conditions can slow traffic and close roads. Check with local tourist offices or, in a pinch, with the police to make sure roads are passable and safe.

For travel across the French, Swiss, and Italian borders in Piedmont and the Valle d'Aosta, only a few routes are usable year-round: the 12-km (7-mile) Mont Blanc tunnel connecting Chamonix with Courmayeur; the Colle del Gran San Bernardo/Col du Grand-Saint-Bernard (connecting Martigny to Aosta on Swiss highway E27 and Italian highway SS27, with 6 km [4 miles] of tunnel); and the Traforo del Fréjus (between Modane and Susa, with 13 km [8 miles] of tunnel). Other passes become increasingly unreliable between November and April.

TRAIN

Turin is on the main Paris–Rome TGV express line and is also connected with Milan, 60 minutes away on the fast train. The fastest (Frecciarossa) trains cover the 667-km (414-mile) trip to Rome in just over four hours; other trains take between five and seven hours.

Services to the larger cities east of Turin are part of the extensive and reliable train network of the Lombard Plain. In the mountains to the west of the region's capital, however, train service begins to peter out in favor of bus connections; information about train-bus mountain services can be obtained from train stations and tourist information offices, or by contacting Trenitalia, the Italian national train service, or Italo, the privately owned high-speed train company.

CONTACTS Italo. ☎ *892020* ⊕ *www.italotreno.it.* **Trenitalia.** ☎ *892021 toll-free in Italy* ⊕ *www.trenitalia.com.*

Making the Most of Your Time

Turin needs at least two or three days to visit properly. If you have extra time, visit one of the magnificent palaces built by the Savoy family. They surround Turin in the so-called *corona di delizie* (crown of delights) and make for an easy day trip.

Plan on several days to visit the Langhe and Monferrato areas. The towns of Alba and Asti should not be missed, but neither should the smaller wine towns that dot the rolling hills of both regions. You may also want to add a day or two to relax and visit wineries in the Gavi region. You'll need your own car in all these areas, but the rewards are great views, great food, and great wine. If coming in September and October, when there are festivals in both Alba and Asti, make sure to book your trip well in advance.

Unless you are planning on a skiing or hiking holiday, the Valle d'Aosta requires less time to visit. The emphasis here is on the natural beauty of the mountains, but if you are driving between France and Italy, the region certainly merits a one- or two-night stopover, in either Courmayeur or Aosta; be sure not to miss Castello di Fénis and the Forte di Bard on your way.

Restaurants

In this region's restaurants you'll taste a difference between the mountain and the city, but the hearty peasant fare served in tiny stone villages and the French-accented delicacies of the plain are both eminently satisfying.

Hotels

High standards and good service are characteristic of Turin's better hotels, and the same is true at top mountain resorts. Hotels in Turin and other major towns are generally geared to business travelers; make sure to ask whether lower weekend rates or special deals for two- or three-night stays are available.

Summer vacationers and winter skiers keep occupancy rates and prices high at resorts during peak seasons. Many mountain hotels require guests to pay for either half or full board and insist on a stay of several nights; some have off-season rates that can reduce the cost by a full price category. If you're planning to ski, ask about packages that give you a discount on lift tickets.

⇨ *Hotel and restaurant reviews have been shortened. For full information, visit Fodors.com. Prices in the hotel reviews are the lowest cost of a standard double room in high season. Prices in the dining reviews are the average cost of a main course at dinner, or, if dinner is not served, at lunch.*

What It Costs in Euros			
$	$$	$$$	$$$$
RESTAURANTS			
under €15	€15–€24	€25–€35	over €35
HOTELS			
under €125	€125–€200	€201–€300	over €300

Turin

128 km (80 miles) west of Milan.

Turin (Torino, in Italian) is roughly in the center of Piedmont–Valle d'Aosta; it's on the Po River, on the edge of the Po Plain, which stretches east all the way to the Adriatic. Turin's flatness and wide, angular, tree-lined boulevards are a far cry from Italian *metropoli* to the south; the region's decidedly northern European bent is quite evident in its nerve center. Aside from its role as northwest Italy's major industrial, cultural, intellectual, and administrative hub, Turin also has a reputation as Italy's capital of black magic and the supernatural. This distinction is enhanced by the presence of Turin's most famous and controversial relic, the Sacra Sindone (Shroud of Turin), still believed by many Catholics to be Christ's burial shroud. (For its part, the Vatican has not taken an official position on its authenticity.)

GETTING HERE AND AROUND

Turin is well served by the Italian autostrada system and can be reached easily by car from all directions: from Milan on the A4 (two hours); from Bologna (four hours) and Florence (five hours) on the A1 and A21; from Genoa on the A6 (two hours). Bus service to and from other major Italian cities is also plentiful, and Turin can be reached by fast train service from Paris in less than six hours. Fast train service also connects the city with Milan, Genoa, Bologna, Venice, Florence, and Rome.

VISITOR INFORMATION

The city's tourist office organizes group and personal guided tours. It also provides maps and details about a wide range of thematic self-guided walks through town. The Torino+Piemonte Card, which provides discounts on transportation and museum entrances for one-, two-, three-, or five-day visits, can be purchased here.

CONTACT Turin Tourist Information Center. ⊠ *Piazza Castello, at Via Garibaldi, Turin* 🕾 *011/535181* ⊕ *www.turismotorino.org.*

 ## Sights

DOWNTOWN TURIN

Many of Turin's major sights are clustered around Piazza Castello, and others are on or just off the portico-lined Via Roma, one of the city's main thoroughfares, which leads 1 km (½ mile) from Piazza Castello south to Piazza Carlo Felice, a landscaped park in front of the train station. First opened in 1615, Via Roma was largely rebuilt in the 1930s, during the Mussolini era.

Duomo di San Giovanni

CHURCH | The most impressive part of Turin's 15th-century cathedral is the Cappella della Sacra Sindone (Chapel of the Holy Shroud), where the famous relic is housed in a sealed casket. The Sacra Sindone is a 12-foot-long sheet of linen, thought by millions to be the burial shroud of Christ, bearing the light imprint of his crucified body. The shroud first made an appearance around the middle of the 15th century, when it

was presented to Ludovico of Savoy in Chambéry. In 1578 it was brought to Turin by another member of the Savoy royal family, Duke Emanuele Filiberto.

It was only in the 1990s that the Catholic Church began allowing rigorous scientific study of the shroud. Not surprisingly, the results have been hazy. On one hand, three separate university teams—in Switzerland, Britain, and the United States—have concluded, as a result of carbon-14 analysis, that the cloth dates from between 1260 and 1390. On the other hand, they are unable to explain how medieval forgers could have created the shroud's image. Either way, the shroud continues to be revered as a holy relic, exhibited to the public on very rare occasions. ⊠ *Piazza San Giovanni, Centro* 🕾 *011/4361540* ⊕ *www.facebook.com/ parrocchiaduomotorino* 🎟 *Free.*

Galleria Civica d'Arte Moderna e Contemporanea (GAM)

ART MUSEUM | In 1863 Turin was the first Italian city to begin a public collection devoted to contemporary art. Housed in a modern building on the edge of downtown, a permanent display of more than 600 paintings, sculptures, and installation pieces (from a collection of more than 45,000 works of art) provides an exceptional glimpse of how Italian contemporary art has evolved since the late 1800s. The Futurist, Pop, neo-Dada, and Arte Povera movements are particularly well represented, and the gallery has a fine video and art film collection. ⊠ *Via Magenta 31, Centro* 🕾 *011/5211788* ⊕ *www.gamtorino.it* 🎟 *€10* 🕘 *Closed Mon.*

★ Galleria Sabauda (*Savoy Gallery*)

ART MUSEUM | Housed in the restored Manica Nuova (new wing) of the Palazzo Reale, the gallery displays some of the most important paintings from the vast collections of the house of Savoy. The collection is particularly rich in Dutch and Flemish paintings: note the *Stigmate di San Francesco* (*St. Francis Receiving the*

416

Turin

Sights ▼

1 Duomo di San Giovanni **B2**
2 Galleria Civica d'Arte Moderna e Comtemporanea (GAM).. **A5**
3 Galleria Sabauda **B2**
4 Mole Antonelliana **C3**
5 Museo d'Arte Orientale.... **A2**
6 Museo dell' Automobile... **A9**
7 Museo di Antichità **B2**
8 Museo Egizio **B3**
9 Palazzo Carignano... **B3**
10 Palazzo Madama **B3**
11 Palazzo Reale **B2**
12 Parco del Valentino.... **B7**
13 Piazza San Carlo.... **B4**
14 Pinacoteca Agnelli....... **A9**
15 Sassi-Superga Cog Train.... **D2**

Restaurants ▼

1 Al Garamond... **B4**
2 Casa Vicina... **A9**
3 Consorzio ... **A3**
4 Da Mauro .. **B4**
5 Del Cambio. **B3**
6 Vintage 1997.......... **A3**

Quick Bites ▼

1 Al Bicerin ... **A1**
2 Il Mercato Centrale Torino........ **B1**

Hotels ▼

1 Best Western Hotel Genio.. **A5**
2 Grand Hotel Sitea......... **B4**
3 Hotel Victoria Torino........ **B4**

TO DOCKS DORA

Via Vitt. Andres

Via Cigliano

C. Giulio

C. Cesana

Via Cordieramo

Via XI Febbraio

Via Finochietto

Via Palas

Lungo Dora Firenze

Via Foggia

Corso Palatino

Lungo Dora Napoli

Via Messina

Via Regina

Corso Verona

Corso Vercelli

Via Cattania

Via Calgliari

Sottopasso Repubblica

Via Giulia

Via S. Chiara

Via S. Domenico

Via Sant'Agostino

Via Monte di Pietà

Via S. Tommaso

Via Bertolatti

Quadrilatero
Pza. della Repubblica
Porta Palatina

Pza. San Giovanni

Via Tasso

C. Verde

Via Garibaldi

Via Barbaroux

Via Pietro Micca

Via XX Settembre

Palazzo di Città

Teatro Romano

Piazzetta Reale

Corso Regina Margherita

Dora Riparia

Via Bligny

Corso San Maurizio

Via C. Battis

Via Santa Giulia di Barolo

Via degli Artisti

Via Ferrari

Via Sant'Ottavio

Via Giuseppe Verdi

Via Montebello

TO SUPERGA

Via Giulia di Barolo

Via Vanchiglia

Via Rossini

Via Po

Via Bava

Via Pescatore

Via della Rocca

Corso San Maurizio Macchiavelli

Piazza Castello

Pza. Carlo Alberto

Via Principe Amedeo

Piazza Carlo Emanuele II

Piazza Vittorio Veneto

Murazzi

Via Maria Vittoria

Via Giovanni Giolitti

Via Cavour

Via GiBennardi

Via Bonafous

Via Carlo Alberto

Via Principe Amedeo

Via Roero

Via Plana

Via Vanchiglia

Ponte Vittorio Emanuele I

Piazza San Carlo

Piazza Carlo Felice

Via Roma

Via Lagrange

Via dell'Arsenale

Via S. Francesco da Paola

Aiuola C. Balbo

Piazza Bodoni

Piazza Cavour

Lungo Po A. Diaz

Corso Cairoli

Corso Moncalieri

Train Station

Corso Vittorio Emanuele II

Via B. Galliari

Via S. Pio V

Via Accademia Albertina

Via S. Massimo

Via Frat. Calandra

Via della Rocca

Via Bogino

Ponte Umberto

Corso Moncalieri

Via Berthollet

Piazza Mad. Cristina

Via Nizza

Via S. Pellico

Via Baretti

Via Lombroso

Corso del Fiume

Via Madama Cristiana

Via G. Gozzano

Via Principe Tommaso

Via C. Marconi

Via Valperga

Via Bidone

Via Ormea

Corso Massimo D'Azeglio

Viale Virgilio

Po

Corso Giovanni Lanza

Corso Giovanni Lanza

Parco del Valentino

Corso Moncalieri

Viale Settimio Severo

Via S. Q. D. Morgari

Via Saluzzo

Via O. Cantone

C. Raffaello

Palazzo Torino Esposizioni

Via V. Monti

TO LINGOTTO

Corso Dante

Ponte Princ. Isabella

KEY

1 *Sights*
1 *Restaurants*
1 *Quick Bites*
1 *Hotels*

0   500 meters
0   500 yards

A   B   C   D

Stigmata) by Jan van Eyck (1395–1441), in which the saint receives the marks of Christ's wounds while a companion cringes beside him. ⊠ *Piazetta Reale 1, Centro* ☏ *011/19560449* ⊕ *museireali. beniculturali.it* ⚏ *€15, includes the Royal Museums (Palazzo Reale, Armeria Reale, Cappella della Sindone, Museo di Antichità, Giardini Reali, and Biblioteca Reale)* ⊘ *Closed Mon.*

★ Mole Antonelliana

NOTABLE BUILDING | **FAMILY** | You can't miss the unusual square dome and thin, elaborate spire of this Turin landmark above the city's rooftops. This odd structure, built between 1863 and 1889, was intended to be a synagogue, but costs escalated and eventually it was bought by the city; it now houses the Museo Nazionale del Cinema (National Cinema Museum), a worthy sight for film buffs. At scheduled times on weekends, you can walk all the way up to the top of the dome, a journey not for the faint of heart (and not permitted for children under age six). ⊠ *Via Montebello 20, Centro* ☏ *011/8138563* ⊕ *www.museocinema.it* ⚏ *Museum €12, elevator to panoramic terrace €9, combination ticket €17, walking by foot to dome €10* ⊘ *Closed Tues.*

Museo d'Arte Orientale (*Asian Art Museum*)

ART MUSEUM | Housed in the magnificently renovated 17th-century Palazzo Mazzonis, this is a beautifully displayed collection of Southeast Asian, Chinese, Japanese, Himalayan, and Islamic art, including sculptures, paintings, and ceramics. Highlights include a towering 13th-century wooden statue of the Japanese temple guardian Kongo Rikishi and a sumptuous assortment of Islamic manuscripts. ⊠ *Via San Domenico 11, Centro* ☏ *011/443693* ⊕ *www.maotorino. it* ⚏ *€10* ⊘ *Closed Mon.*

Museo di Antichità

HISTORY MUSEUM | A small but fascinating collection of artifacts found at archaeological sites in and around Turin is displayed here. A spiral ramp winds down through the subterranean museum, and as in a real archaeological site, the deeper you go, the older the objects on display. A life-size silver bust of the Roman emperor Lucius Verus (AD 161–169) is one of the masterpieces of the collection. ⊠ *Via XX Settembre 88, Centro* ☏ *011/19560449* ⊕ *museireali. beniculturali.it* ⚏ *€15, includes the Royal Museums (Galleria Sabauda, Palazzo Reale, Armeria Reale, Cappella della Sindone, Giardini Reali, and Biblioteca Reale)* ⊘ *Closed Mon.*

★ Museo Egizio

HISTORY MUSEUM | **FAMILY** | The Egyptian Museum's superb collection includes statues of pharaohs and mummies and entire frescoes taken from royal tombs. The striking sculpture gallery, designed by the Oscar-winning production designer Dante Ferretti, is a veritable who's who of ancient Egypt. Look for the magnificent 13th-century-BC statue of Ramses II and the fascinating Tomb of Kha. The latter was found intact with furniture, supplies of food and clothing, and writing instruments. ⊠ *Via Accademia delle Scienze 6, Centro* ☏ *011/4406903* ⊕ *www.museoegizio.it* ⚏ *€18* ⊘ *Closed Mon. afternoon.*

Palazzo Carignano

HISTORY MUSEUM | Half of this building is the Baroque triumph of Guarino Guarini, the priest and architect who designed many of Turin's most noteworthy buildings. Built between 1679 and 1685, his redbrick palace later played an important role in the creation of the modern-day nation. Vittorio Emanuele II of Savoy (1820–78), the first king of a united Italy, was born here, and, after a 19th-century neoclassical extension, Italy's first parliament met here between 1860 and 1865. The palace now houses the Museo del Risorgimento, a museum honoring the 19th-century movement for Italian unity. ⊠ *Via Accademia delle Scienze 5, Centro* ✛ *Entrance at Piazza Carlo Alberto 8*

☎ 011/5621147 ⊕ www.museorisorgi-
mentotorino.it 🎫 €10 ۞ Closed Mon.

Palazzo Madama

HISTORY MUSEUM | In the center of Piazza
Castello, this castle was named for the
Savoy queen Maria Cristina, who made it
her home in the 17th century. The building incorporates the remains of a Roman
gate with late-medieval and Renaissance additions, and the monumental
Baroque facade and grand entrance
staircase were added by Filippo Juvarra
(1678–1736). The palace now houses
the Museo Civico d'Arte Antica, whose
collections comprise more than 30,000
items dating from the Middle Ages to the
Baroque era. ⊠ Piazza Castello 10, Centro
☎ 011/5211788 ⊕ www.palazzomadama-
torino.it 🎫 Staircase and courtyard free,
museum €10 ۞ Closed Tues.

★ Palazzo Reale

CASTLE/PALACE | FAMILY | This 17th-century
palace, a former Savoy royal residence, is
an imposing work of brick, stone, and marble that stands on the site of one of Turin's
ancient Roman city gates. In contrast to its
sober exterior, the two main floors of the
palace's interior are swathed in luxurious
rococo trappings, including tapestries and
gilt ceilings. The gardens were laid out in
the late 17th century by André Le Nôtre,
landscape designer at Versailles, and the
Armeria Reale (Royal Armory) wing holds
a collection of arms and armor. ⊠ Piazzetta
Reale 1, Centro ☎ 011/4361455 ⊕ musei-
reali.beniculturali.it 🎫 €15, includes the
Royal Museums (Galleria Sabauda, Armeria
Reale, Cappella della Sindone, Museo di
Antichità, Giardini Reali, and Biblioteca
Reale) ۞ Closed Mon.

Piazza San Carlo

PLAZA/SQUARE | Surrounded by shops,
arcades, fashionable cafés, and elegant
Baroque palaces, this is one of the most
beautiful squares in Turin. In the center
stands a statue of Duke Emanuele
Filiberto of Savoy, the victor at the battle
of San Quintino, in 1557. The melee
heralded the peaceful resurgence of Turin

under the Savoy after years of bloody
dynastic fighting. The fine bronze statue
erected in the 19th century is one of
Turin's symbols. At the southern end of
the square, framing the continuation of
Via Roma, are the twin Baroque churches
of San Carlo and Santa Cristina. ⊠ Piazza
San Carlo, Centro.

ALONG THE PO

The Po River is narrow and unprepos-
sessing here in Turin, only a hint of the
broad waterway that it becomes as it
flows eastward toward the Adriatic. It's
flanked, however, by formidable edifices,
a park, and a lovely pedestrian path.

★ Museo dell'Automobile

SPECIALTY MUSEUM | FAMILY | No visit
to this motor city would be complete
without a pilgrimage to see the perfectly
preserved Bugattis, Ferraris, and Isotta
Fraschinis at this museum. Here you can
get an idea of the importance of Fiat—
and cars in general—to Turin's economy.
There's a collection of antique cars from
as early as 1896, and displays show how
the city has changed over the years as
a result of the auto industry. ⊠ Corso
Unità d'Italia 40, Millefonti ☎ 011/677666
⊕ www.museoauto.com 🎫 €15 ۞ Closed
Mon. after 2 pm.

Parco del Valentino

CITY PARK | FAMILY | This pleasant riverside
park is a great place to stroll, bike, or
jog. Originally the grounds of a relatively
simple hunting lodge, the park owes its
present arrangement to Madama Maria
Cristina of France, who received the land
and lodge as a wedding present after her
marriage to Vittorio Amedeo I of Savoy.
The building, now home to the University
of Turin's Faculty of Architecture, is not
open to the public. However, you can
visit the Orto Botanico di Torino (Botanical Garden of Turin) just north of the
castle. ⊠ Viale Mattioli 25, San Salvario
☎ 011/6705980 botanical gardens ⊕ www.
ortobotanico.unito.it 🎫 Botanical gardens
€5 ۞ Botanical gardens closed weekdays
except for holidays, and early Nov.–Mar.

★ Pinacoteca Agnelli

ART MUSEUM | This gallery was opened by Gianni Agnelli (1921–2003), the head of Fiat and patriarch of one of Italy's most powerful families, just four months before his death. There are four magnificent scenes of Venice by Canaletto (1697–1768); two splendid views of Dresden by Canaletto's nephew, Bernardo Bellotto (1720–80); and several works by Manet (1832–83), Renoir (1841–1919), Matisse (1869–1954), and Picasso (1881–1973). ✉ *Via Nizza 230, Lingotto* ☎ *011/0925011* ⊕ *www.pinacoteca-agnelli.it* ✆ *€10* ⊘ *Closed Mon.*

Sassi-Superga Cog Train

TRAIN/TRAIN STATION | **FAMILY** | The 18-minute ride from Sassi up the Superga hill is a real treat on a clear day. The view of the Alps is magnificent at the hilltop **Parco Naturale Collina Torinese,** a tranquil retreat from the bustle of the city. If you feel like a little exercise, you can walk back down to Sassi (about two hours) on one of the well-marked wooded trails that start from the upper station. Other circular trails lead through the park and back to Superga. Note that a bus replaces the train on Wednesday, although the ride up the hill is still just as lovely. ✉ *Piazza G. Modena, Sassi* ☎ *800/019152* ⊕ *www.gtt.to.it* ✆ *€4 one-way and €6 round-trip on weekdays, €6 one-way and €9 round-trip on weekends.*

 Restaurants

★ Al Garamond

$$$ | **PIEDMONTESE** | The well-spaced tables and the ancient brick vaulting in this small, bright space set the stage for game, meat, fish, and seafood dishes served with creative flair. The level of service is very high, even by demanding Turin standards. **Known for:** chef's table experience; mix of traditional and inventive dishes; merging Sicilian and Piedmontese cuisine. ⑤ *Average main: €28* ✉ *Via G. Pomba 14, Centro* ☎ *011/8122781* ⊕ *www.algaramond.it*

⊘ *Closed Sun., Aug., and Jan. 7–14. No lunch Mon., Tues., and Sat.*

★ Casa Vicina

$$$$ | **PIEDMONTESE** | Tucked away on the third floor of the Green Pea sustainable retail venture (next to Eataly Lingotto), one of Turin's top destinations for fine dining is run by the fourth generation of the Vicina family, with Claudio and wife Anna leading the kitchen and Stefano managing the front of house. Excellent-quality traditional Piedmontese dishes are served with creative style, and the wine list is an encyclopedia, featuring not only the top Barolo producers but also many other small but notable wineries. **Known for:** fresh agnolotti pasta; fixed-price tasting and gastronomic menus; layered bagna càuda served in a martini glass. ⑤ *Average main: €47* ✉ *Via Ermanno Fenoglietti 20/b, 3rd fl. of Green Pea, Lingotto* ☎ *011/6640140* ⊕ *www.casavicina.com* ⊘ *Closed Sun. and Mon.*

Consorzio

$$ | **PIEDMONTESE** | Extremely popular for lunch during the week, this lively and informal osteria is in Turin's business district. The service is relaxed, the decor is low-key, the menu highlights organic meats and vegetables from Piedmont, and there's a good selection of natural wines. **Known for:** wide selection of cheeses from across Europe; Piedmont dishes like agnolotti gobbi (stuffed pasta); creative presentation. ⑤ *Average main: €20* ✉ *Via Monte di Pietà 23, Centro* ☎ *011/2767661* ⊕ *ristoranteconsorzio.it* ⊘ *Closed Sun. and Mon.*

Da Mauro

$$ | **TUSCAN** | After a flux of Tuscan migrants moved to Turin in the '60s, Da Mauro was one of the first restaurants to cater to their tastes, mixing Tuscan dishes into the largely Piedmontese menu. Service is brisk and efficient for a local crowd at lunch and dinner—it's not the place to come for a slow-paced meal. **Known for:** fresh pasta dishes like agnolotti al ragù; affordable, daily-changing menu; Tuscan specialties. $ *Average main: €16* ✉ *Via Maria Vittoria 21, Centro* ☎ *0349/1513068* ⊕ *www.facebook.com/ristorantedamauro* ⊘ *Closed Mon.*

★ Del Cambio

$$$$ | PIEDMONTESE | Set in a palace dating from 1757, this is one of Europe's most beautiful and historic restaurants, with decorative moldings, mirrors, and hanging lamps contrasted with ultramodern takes on Piedmontese cuisine from young Michelin-starred chef Matteo Baronetto. Order an inventive signature dish such as the Piedmontese salad, with around 24 artfully composed ingredients, and an expertly prepared meat or fish dish, or opt for the six- or seven-course tasting menu to sample more of the chef's innovative cooking. **Known for:** beautifully presented plates; elegant atmosphere; well-selected wine pairings. $ *Average main: €65* ✉ *Piazza Carignano 2, Centro* ☎ *011/546690* ⊕ *delcambio.it* ⊘ *Closed Mon. No dinner Sun. No lunch Tues.–Thurs.*

★ Vintage 1997

$$$ | NORTHERN ITALIAN | The first floor of an elegant town house in the center of Turin makes a fitting location for this sophisticated restaurant. There's an excellent wine list with regional, national, and international vintages well-represented, and tasting menus, including a feast that covers the full range of the restaurant's cuisine and desserts. **Known for:** Piedmontese roasted veal; selection of rare cheeses; tasting menus from three to 10 courses. $ *Average main: €32* ✉ *Piazza Solferino 16/h, Centro* ☎ *011/535948* ⊕ *www.vintage1997.com* ⊘ *Closed Sun. No lunch Sat.*

☕ Coffee and Quick Bites

★ Al Bicerin

$ | CAFÉ | FAMILY | A chocolate lover's pilgrimage to Turin inevitably leads to this café where Nietzsche, Puccini, Dumas, and the political reformer Cavour have all sipped. If you order the house specialty, *bicerin* (a hot drink with layers of chocolate, coffee, and cream), or a flavored *zabaioni* (warm eggnog), and browse the collection of chocolate goodies including chocolate-flavored pasta, you'll understand why. **Known for:** elegant presentation; traditional Gianduiotto chocolates; wide assortment of creative sweet drinks. $ *Average main: €6* ✉ *Piazza della Consolata 5, Centro* ☎ *011/4369325* ⊕ *bicerin.it* ⊘ *Closed Wed. and Aug.*

★ Il Mercato Centrale Torino

$ | INTERNATIONAL | FAMILY | When you're not in the mood for an Italian-style lunch or dinner (read: leisurely), head to the Mercato Centrale for a selection of foods—from more than 20 food stands—like fresh pasta, fish, roast meats, pizza, and fried dishes; more international options including ramen and Peruvian plates; and a good choice of cocktails, wines, and beer. But don't fill up on the mains, as you'll also find a delightful selection of baked goods and, of course, gelato, for a sweet finish. **Known for:** lively crowds; late-night hours (open Sunday–Thursday till 11 pm, and Friday and Saturday till midnight); wide selection of dishes. $ *Average main: €12* ✉ *Piazza della Repubblica 25, Centro* ☎ *011/0898040* ⊕ *www.mercatocentrale.com/turin.*

Hotels

Best Western Hotel Genio

$$ | HOTEL | Although they're just steps away from the main train station, these spacious and tastefully decorated rooms are a quiet haven from the bustle of the city. **Pros:** convenient location; abundant breakfast; good-sized rooms and bathrooms. **Cons:** street noise in some rooms; claustrophobic elevators; hotel interiors a bit worn. $ *Rooms from: €148* ✉ *Corso Vittorio Emanuele II 47, Centro* ☎ *011/6505771* ⊕ *www.hotelgenio.it* ⤴ *113 rooms* ❍ *No Meals.*

★ Grand Hotel Sitea

$$ | HOTEL | One of the city's finest hotels, the Sitea is in the historic center and decorated in a warm classical style; the common areas and guest rooms are elegant, spacious, and comfortable. **Pros:** central location; well-appointed rooms; large bathrooms. **Cons:** air-conditioning and street noise can be loud in some rooms; carpets are a little worn; bathrooms could use a refresh. $ *Rooms from: €171 ⊠ Via Carlo Alberto 35, Centro* ☎ *011/5170171* ⊕ *www.grandhotelsitea.it* ↘ *120 rooms* ❦❦ *No Meals.*

Hotel Victoria Torino

$$ | HOTEL | Style, attention to detail, and comfort are hallmarks of this retreat that's furnished like a refined English home. **Pros:** tranquil location in the center of town; good spa facilities; wonderful breakfast. **Cons:** standard rooms are small; no on-site restaurant; no gym. $ *Rooms from: €178 ⊠ Via Nino Costa 4, Centro* ☎ *011/5611909* ⊕ *www.hotelvictoria-torino.com* ↘ *106 rooms* ❦❦ *Free Breakfast.*

❦ Nightlife

Caffè Elena

BARS | This café/bar is a trendy place for an aperitif or for a drink before going out to a show or dancing. It's in the large piazza at the end of Via Po. ⊠ *Piazza Vittorio Veneto 5, Centro* ☎ *329/5767414 mobile* ⊕ *www.caffeelena.it.*

Pastis

GATHERING PLACE | The Quadrilatero Romano, which roughly corresponds to the grid pattern of Roman Turin near Piazza della Repubblica, is a hopping area filled with nightclubs and international restaurants. Places open and close with startling frequency here, but Pastis has shown considerable staying power. ☒ *Piazza Emanuele Filiberto 9/b, Centro* ☎ *011/5211085* ⊕ *pastistorino.com.*

🎭 Performing Arts

MUSIC

⭐ Lingotto Musica

MUSIC | Classical music concerts are held at this theater designed by Renzo Piano in the renovated Lingotto building; internationally famous conductors and orchestras are frequent guests. ☒ *Via Nizza 280, Lingotto* ☎ *333/9382545 ticket office* ⊕ *www.lingottomusica.it.*

OPERA

⭐ Teatro Regio

OPERA | Premieres at the Teatro Regio, one of Italy's leading opera houses, sell out well in advance. You can buy tickets for most performances at the box office or on the website, where discounts are often offered on the day of the performance. The season runs from October through July. ☒ *Piazza Castello 215, Centro* ☎ *011/8815241* ⊕ *www.teatroregio.torino.it.*

🛍 Shopping

CHOCOLATE

⭐ Peyrano

CHOCOLATE | FAMILY | The most famous of all Turin chocolates is the wedge-shape gianduiotto, flavored with hazelnuts and first concocted in 1867. The tradition has been continued at this family-run shop, where more than 80 types of chocolates and other sweets are made. ☒ *Corso Moncalieri 47, Centro* ☎ *011/6602202* ⊕ *www.peyrano.com.*

⭐ Stratta

CHOCOLATE | FAMILY | In business since 1836, this famed shop sells confectionery of all kinds—not just the chocolates in the lavish window displays but also fancy cookies, rum-laced fudges, and magnificent cakes. ☒ *Piazza San Carlo 191, Centro* ☎ *011/547920* ⊕ *www.stratta1836.it.*

MARKETS

Balon Flea Market

MARKET | Go to this famous market for bargains on secondhand books, antiques, and clothing. There is good browsing to be had among the stands, which spill out of Borgo Dora onto the surrounding side streets. During the second weekend of every month, the market extends its hours into Sunday, becoming the so-called Gran Balon. (Be aware, however, that the market is also famous for its pickpockets.) ☒ *Via Borgo Dora, Centro* ☎ *011/4369741* ⊕ *www.balon.it.*

⭐ Mercato di Porta Palazzo

MARKET | For food lovers, people-watchers, or anyone interested in the lively local scene, the immensely popular market in this huge square to the north of town is not to be missed. Outdoors, the keepers of hundreds of vegetable stands vie with one another to create the most appetizing displays. Indoors, the meat vendors provide an equally tantalizing array of local products, while the fishmongers proudly display the fresh catch of the day. ☒ *Piazza della Repubblica, Centro* ☎ *011/5216242* ⊕ *scopriportapalazzo.com.*

SPECIALTY FOOD AND DELIS

⭐ Borgiattino

FOOD | Specialty food stores and delicatessens abound in central Turin, but for a truly spectacular array of cheeses and other delicacies, this should be your first stop. ☒ *Corso Vinzaglio 29, Centro* ☎ *011/5629075* ⊕ *www.borgiattino.com.*

⭐ Eataly Turin Lingotto

FOOD | FAMILY | Now with branches in Milan, Florence, Bologna, New York, and Tokyo, the original home of Eataly is probably Turin's most famous food emporium. In addition to the market, there are kitchenware and cookbook stores, plus a wine bar and several different

Hit the Slopes

Skiing is the major sport in both Piedmont and the Valle d'Aosta. Excellent facilities abound at resort towns such as Courmayeur and Breuil-Cervinia. The so-called Via Lattea (Milky Way)—six skiing areas near Sestriere with 400 km (almost 250 miles) of linked runs and 90 ski lifts—provides practically unlimited skiing. Lift tickets, running around €47 for a day's pass, are a good deal compared to those at major U.S. resorts.

To Italian skiers, a weeklong holiday on the slopes is known as a *settimana*

bianca (white week). Ski resort hotels in Piedmont and the Valle d'Aosta encourage these getaways by offering six- and seven-day packages, and though they're designed with the domestic market in mind, you can get a bargain by taking advantage of them. The packages usually (though not always) include half or full board.

You should have your passport with you if you plan a day trip into Switzerland—although the odds are that you won't be asked to show it.

---

counters and restaurants serving pizza, haute cuisine (Giù da Guido, a branch of the Michelin-starred restaurant Guido da Costigliole), and lots more in between. ✉ *Via Ermanno Fenoglietti 14, Lingotto* ☎ *020/9997900* ⊕ *www.eataly.net.*

Asti

60 km (37 miles) southeast of Turin.

Asti is best known outside Italy for its wines—excellent reds as well as the famous sparkling white spumante. In the 12th century Asti began to develop as a republic, at a time when other Italian cities were also flexing their economic and military muscles. It flourished in the following century, when the inhabitants began erecting lofty towers for its defense. In the center of Asti some of these remain, among them the 13th-century Torre Comentina and the well-preserved Torre Troyana. The 18th-century church of Santa Caterina has incorporated one of Asti's medieval towers, the Torre Romana (itself built on an ancient Roman base), as its bell tower.

GETTING HERE AND AROUND
Asti is less than an hour away from Turin by car on the A21 autostrada. Train service from Turin to Asti is frequent and fast, and Itabus service directly connects the two towns.

VISITOR INFORMATION
CONTACT Asti Tourism Office. ✉ *Piazza Alfieri 34, Asti* ☎ *0141/530357* ⊕ *visit. asti.it.*

Sights

Collegiata di San Secondo
CHURCH | This Gothic church is dedicated to Asti's patron saint, believed by some to have been decapitated by the Emperor Hadrian on this very spot. San Secondo is also the patron of the city's favorite folklore and sporting event, the annual Palio di Asti, a colorful medieval-style horse race that's similar to Siena's. It's held each year on a Sunday in early September in the vast Campo del Palio to the south of the church. ✉ *Piazza San Secondo, south of Corso Vittorio Alfieri, Asti* ☎ *0141/399339* ⊕ *www.comune. asti.it* 🎫 *Free.*

Duomo (*Cattedrale di Santa Maria Assunta*)

CHURCH | Dedicated to the Assumption of the Virgin, the Duomo is an object lesson in Italian Gothic architecture. Completed in the early 14th century, it is decorated so as to emphasize geometry and verticality: pointed arches and narrow vaults are completely covered with frescoes that direct your gaze upward. The porch on the south side of the cathedral facing the square was built in 1470; it represents the Gothic style at its most florid and excessive. ⊠ *Piazza Cattedrale, Via San Giovanni 8, Asti* ☎ *0141/399489* ⊕ *www.diocesiasti.it* ⊡ *Free.*

 Restaurants

★ **Il Cavallo Scosso**

$$$ | MODERN ITALIAN | In a contemporary villa built entirely of wood on the outskirts of Asti, chef Enrico Pivieri uses a mix of local and international ingredients to create new takes on traditional dishes with a global flair. The Shaken Horse is especially strong in seafood—rare for meat-heavy Piedmont—with such creative plates as gnocchi with cuttlefish ink in miso broth with smoked sardines and fried Sicilian anchovies with *giardiniera* (pickled vegetables in vinegar). **Known for:** modern interpretations of meat and seafood dishes; beef tartare marinated with citrus fruits, seared scampi, and beetroot; choice of three tasting menus. ⑤ *Average main: €28* ⊠ *Via Al Duca 23/d, Asti* ☎ *0141/211435* ⊕ *www.ilcavalloscosso.it.*

L'Angolo del Beato

$$ | PIEDMONTESE | At this Asti institution, in a building that dates to the 12th century (as you'll see from the exposed brick walls and original wood-beamed ceiling), you'll find that regional specialties are the main attractions. There's also an extensive list of several hundred Piedmont wines. **Known for:** tonno di coniglio (rabbit marinated in olive oil and garlic) antipasto; roasted meats; risotto

with barbera wine. ⑤ *Average main: €18* ⊠ *Vicolo Cavalleri 2, Asti* ☎ *0141/531668* ⊕ *www.angolodelbeato.it* ⊘ *Closed Sun., 1st wk of Jan., and 10 days in Aug.*

 Hotels

★ **Relais Sant'Uffizio**

$$$ | HOTEL | FAMILY | You may be surprised to learn that this now delightfully peaceful and elegant retreat—with a luxurious spa and swimming pool, surrounded by vineyards and rolling hills—was once home to the Inquisition in the 16th century. **Pros:** tranquil and beautiful location; excellent spa and exercise facilities; good value for the amenities. **Cons:** a bit isolated; a number of rooms are a walk from the main building; soundproofing could be better in some rooms. ⑤ *Rooms from: €220* ⊠ *Strada Sant Uffizio 1, Cioccaro di Penango, Asti* ⊹ *20 km (12 miles) north of Asti* ☎ *0141/916292* ⊕ *www.relaissantuffizio.com* ⊲ *41 rooms* ⊙ *Free Breakfast.*

Alba

30 km (18 miles) southwest of Asti.

This small town has a gracious atmosphere and a compact core, studded with medieval towers and Gothic buildings. In addition to being a wine center for the region, Alba is known as the "City of the White Truffle" for delicious little tubers that cost as much as €2,200 a pound. For picking out your truffle and having a few wisps shaved on top of your food, expect to shell out an extra €16 or so—definitely worth doing for a second-to-none foodie experience.

For the true truffle experience, visit during the annual Fiera Internazionale Tartufo Bianco D'Alba (International Alba White Truffle Fair ⊕ *www.fieradeltartufo.org*) mid-October to mid-December for a truffle market, cooking shows, food with truffles, wine tasting, and even educational games for kids.

GETTING HERE AND AROUND

By car from Turin follow the A6 autostrada south to Marene and then head east on the A33, which connects Asti and Alba. GTT offers frequent bus service between Alba and Turin—the journey takes approximately 1½ hours. Direct trains run to Alba from Turin's Lingotto station; the trip takes about an hour.

VISITOR INFORMATION

CONTACT Alba Tourism Office. ⊠ *Piazza Risorgimento 2, Alba* ☎ *0173/35833* ⊕ *www.visitlmr.it.*

◉ Sights

★ Castello di Neive

WINERY | This family-run, 160-acre wine estate produces wine from seven vineyards in the Langhe region. Barbaresco is their star wine, and they also make fine barbera and dolcetto. Visitor tours, by appointment only, include a look inside their 18th-century castle, including the wine cellars, as well as a tasting of three wines. ⊠ *Piazzetta Demaria 1, Neive* ☎ *329/2125171 mobile* ⊕ *www.castellodineive.it* 🎫 *Tour and tasting from €10* 🕐 *Closed Tues.* ⚠ *Reservations required.*

Restaurants

★ Guido da Costigliole

$$$$ | **NORTHERN ITALIAN** | Inside atmospheric stone-walled ancient cellars, the latest incarnation of Guido—which began in 1961 in Costigliole d'Asti—is now managed by the son of the original owners. It serves excellent preparations of traditional dishes best sampled with one of the three tasting menus (including one vegan option), along with superlative pairings of wine from the surrounding regions. **Known for:** agnolotti pasta filled with meat; wonderful wine list; gelato of the moment. 🟡 *Average main: €50* ⊠ *Relais San Maurizio, Località San Maurizio 59, Santa Stefano Belbo* ✛ *22 km (14 miles) east of Alba* ☎ *0141/844455* ⊕ *www.guidodacostigliole.it* 🕐 *Closed Sun. No lunch.*

Lalibera

$$ | **PIEDMONTESE** | Modern and subdued, this small spot on a quiet backstreet is conducive to a leisurely meal while trying a huge selection of Barolo wines. On the menu you'll find Piedmontese starters, pastas, and a variety of tasty meat dishes, and there's also a superb selection of local cheeses. **Known for:** tajarin pasta al ragù; Piedmontese wines and cheeses; locally sourced meat and produce. 🟡 *Average main: €20* ⊠ *Via Elvio Pertinace 24/a, Alba* ☎ *0173/293155* ⊕ *www.lalibera.com* 🕐 *Closed Sun. and Mon., 3 wks in Aug., and late Dec.–mid-Jan.*

★ L'Inedito Vigin Mudest

$$ | **PIEDMONTESE** | Delicious regional specialties with tartufo-focused and fixed-price tasting menus are served at this bustling family-run restaurant in the center of Alba. Seasonal recipes emphasize local vegetables, nuts (particularly hazelnuts), and meats like rabbit and venison. **Known for:** agnolotti del plin (stuffed ravioli) with truffles; fresh tajarin (tagliolini with egg dough); braised beef marinated in Barolo. 🟡 *Average main: €18* ⊠ *Via Vernazza 11, Alba* ☎ *0173/441701* ⊕ *www.lineditoviginmudest.it* 🕐 *Closed Wed.*

Osteria dell'Arco

$$ | **PIEDMONTESE** | Delicious, hearty dishes using local ingredients are served here in a lovely setting with wine bottles lining the walls. In addition to lots of game meats, you'll find a nice selection of seafood dishes with a hint of Liguria. **Known for:** house-made pastas; Slow Food movement cooking; meat and fish crudos. 🟡 *Average main: €16* ⊠ *Piazza Savona 5, Alba* ☎ *0173/363974* ⊕ *www.osteriadellarco.it* 🕐 *Closed Sun. Dec.–Sept.*

Vincafè

$$ | **WINE BAR** | This excellent *enoteca*, with a contemporary casual atmosphere, has a whole range of Piedmont specialties to pair with local wines. You'll find more than 60 labels, as well as grappas and liqueurs, on the menu. **Known for:**

Langhe wine pairings; Piedmontese crudos; late-night dining. ⑤ *Average main: €16* ⊠ *Via Emanuele 12, Alba* ☎ *0173/364603* ⊕ *www.vincafe.com.*

Hotels

★ Locanda del Pilone

$$ | B&B/INN | It would be hard to imagine a more commanding position for these simply but tastefully decorated accommodations and the Michelin-starred restaurant above Alba. **Pros:** spectacular location with a 360-degree view; excellent restaurant; abundant breakfast. **Cons:** while not far from Alba, you do need a car to get around; parking can be challenging; rooms near common areas can be noisy. ⑤ *Rooms from: €195* ⊠ *Località Madonna di Como 34, Alba* ☎ *0173/366616* ⊕ *www.locandadelpilone. com* ⊙ *Closed Jan.–mid-Apr.* ⤴ *6 rooms* ⦿ *Free Breakfast.*

★ Relais San Maurizio

$$$$ | HOTEL | FAMILY | The first luxury hotel in Piedmont, opened in 2002 inside a 17th-century monastery, is still one of the most extravagant places to stay in the region, with a 10,764-square-foot spa, an outdoor swimming pool, tennis courts, and a Michelin-star restaurant. **Pros:** ultra-relaxing spa area with unique treatments; wonderful dining options; elegant, old-fashioned charm. **Cons:** breakfast choices could be more extensive; bathrooms could use an update; some rooms on the small side. ⑤ *Rooms from: €566* ⊠ *Località San Maurizio 39* ✛ *22 km (14 miles) east of Alba* ☎ *0141/841900* ⊕ *www.relaissanmaurizio.it* ⤴ *36 rooms* ⦿ *Free Breakfast.*

★ Villa La Madonna

$$$$ | HOTEL | This art-filled boutique hotel (one of the two sister-owners is a photographer) surrounded by vineyards exudes a sense of casual luxury and a modern design aesthetic, from the

sitting room with an open fireplace to the lively outdoor pool with retro snack bar. **Pros:** cozy, comfortable feel; all rooms have outdoor spaces; delicious food at the in-house eatery. **Cons:** some rooms rather small; no TVs or phones in rooms; minimum-night stays in some seasons. ⑤ *Rooms from: €345* ⊠ *Regione Madonna 21, Monastero Bormida* ✛ *45 km (28 miles) southeast of Alba* ☎ *348/8366141 mobile* ⊕ *villalamadonna.com* ⊙ *Closed mid-Nov.–late Mar.* ⤴ *18 rooms* ⦿ *Free Breakfast.*

The Barolo Region

17 km (11 miles) southwest of Alba, 72 km (45 miles) southeast of Turin.

The Langhe district produces some of the top wines in Italy (Barolo and Barbaresco), along with the less-famous but well-regarded dolcetto (from Dogliani) and arneis and nebbiolo (from Roero). Try to schedule a day trip to one or several of the wine estates here.

GETTING HERE AND AROUND
The easiest way to reach Barolo and its wineries is to drive from Alba.

Sights

Marchesi di Barolo

WINERY | Right in the town of Barolo, this wine estate makes an easy, if touristy, option for getting to know the local wines. In the estate's user-friendly enoteca you can taste wine, buy some of the thousands of bottles from vintages going way back, and look at display bottles, including an 1859 Barolo. Marchesi di Barolo's *cantine* (wine cellars), at ⊠ *Via Roma 1,* are open daily; book tours and tastings in advance online. ⊠ *Via Roma 1, Barolo* ☎ *0173/564419* ⊕ *marchesibarolo. com* ⤴ *From €35 for tour and tasting* ⤴ *Reservations essential.*

Rocche dei Manzoni

WINERY | A good, accessible example of the new school of Barolo wine making (small oak barrels, blended wines) is this estate, about 6 km (4 miles) south of Barolo. Rocche dei Manzoni's reds include Barolo, dolcetto, Langhe Rosso, and barbera. Visits take about two hours and include a guided tour of the wine cellar plus a tasting of three wines; reserve in advance online. ⊠ *Località Manzoni Soprani 3, Monforte d'Alba* ☎ *0173/78421* ⊕ *www.barolobig.com* ☞ *From €30 for tour and tasting* ⊘ *Closed Dec. 23–Jan. 8; week of Aug. 12; and weekends in Jan.–mid-Mar. and mid-June–Aug.* ⚲ *Reservations required.*

WiMu—Il Museo del Vino a Barolo

SPECIALTY MUSEUM | FAMILY | Spread over three floors of the Barolo Castle, this quirky wine museum looks at the emotions behind the region's top tipple. The entertaining interactive exhibits explore such themes as the moon in harmony, the geometry of life, and the history of wine, through films, displays, and art—just don't expect a glass of Barolo at the end. ⊠ *Castello Comunale Falletti, Piazza Falletti, Barolo* ☎ *0173/386697* ⊕ *www. wimubarolo.it* ☞ *€9* ⊘ *Closed Feb., and weekdays from mid- to late Jan.*

Restaurants

★ Massimo Camia

$$$$ | PIEDMONTESE | Chef Massimo Camia's restaurant is in an elegant and modern space, with views of the Barolo vineyards that surround the Damilano winery; the service is impeccable and the food is divine. The restaurant is outside the town of La Morra, a 20-minute drive to the southwest of Alba. **Known for:** inventive meat, seafood, and game dishes; extensive cheese menu; amuse-bouches and wine pairings. ⑤ *Average main: €38* ⊠ *SP122 (Alba–Barolo), La Morra* ☎ *0173/56355* ⊕ *www.massimocamia.it* ⊘ *Closed Tues. and Wed.*

Hotels

Casa di Langa

$$$$ | HOTEL | Billed as the first sustainable luxury hotel in Barolo, Casa di Langa uses local materials in its architecture, organic ingredients in its restaurant, and recycled water to irrigate the 104 acres of vineyards and land on its property. **Pros:** fabulous outdoor heated pool; convenient location for Barolo area wine tasting; tasty restaurant food. **Cons:** not all rooms have views; service not up to par; decor rather on the plain side. ⑤ *Rooms from: €506* ⊠ *Località Talloria 1* ☎ *0173/520520* ⊕ *www.casadilanga.com* ⇥ *39 rooms* ⦿❘ *Free Breakfast.*

Gavi

117 km (73 miles) east of Barolo, 100 km (62 miles) southeast of Turin.

This pretty medieval town nestled in the hills of southeastern Piedmont—and very close to the Ligurian border, only about 50 km (30 miles) north of Genoa—is all about the wine: specifically, the cortese grape used to make Gavi, one of Italy's best-known white wines. Since the town of Gavi is less touristed than Piedmont's other wine areas, you can spend a relaxing day or two wandering its charming streets and taking a countryside drive to admire the lovely vineyard scenery.

GETTING HERE AND AROUND

From Barolo, take the A33 autostrada north past Asti and then head east on the E70. Near Tortona, take the A7 south and exit onto the SP161. It's about an hour and a half from Barolo to Gavi by car, and around the same distance from Turin. It's possible to take a combination of buses and trains between Barolo and Gavi (switching in Alba and Turin), but not recommended unless you have lots of time and patience.

Valle d'Aosta

👁 Sights

⭐ Forte di Gavi

MILITARY SIGHT | FAMILY | The origins of
this imposing military fortress perched
on a rocky hilltop above Gavi are rather
murky, but it's thought to have first been
built atop the ruins of a 10th-century
castle before being enlarged between
the 16th and 18th centuries. The fortress
was used as a military prison during
both world wars, and today you can
take a 45-minute tour to learn about its
history as well as tour the courtyards,
guards' towers, and other rooms; call or
email ✎ *drm-pie.gavi@beniculturali.it* at
least one day in advance for a reservation—and also to check opening times,
as they can be erratic. Even if you don't
see the inside of the fort, the area around
it offers stunning views of the town of
Gavi and the Alto Monferrato hills below.

✉ *Via al Forte 14, Gavi* ☎ *0143/643554*
🎫 *€5; free 1st Sun. of month Oct.–Mar.*

🍽 Restaurants

⭐ Cantine del Gavi

$$$$ | PIEDMONTESE | FAMILY | Inside an
enchanting 18th-century palace with
arched ceilings, this zero-kilometer
restaurant uses products only from the
surrounding area, including vegetables,
herbs, and edible flowers from its own
gardens, in its weekly changing seven-course tasting menus. In the warmer
months, don't miss dining amongst the
roses in the romantic courtyard, where a
smaller three-course menu with cocktail of the day is also offered. **Known for:**
risotto al Gavi, which changes by season;
wonderful wine selection, with a focus on
Piedmont and France; lovely garden setting. $ *Average main: €65* ✉ *Via Goffredo*

Mameli 69, Gavi ☎ 0143/642458 ⊕ www.
ristorantecantinedelgavi.it ⊘ Closed
Mon.–Wed. No lunch Thurs. and Fri.

 Hotels

★ Locanda La Raia

$$$$ | HOTEL | Atop a hill surrounded
by vineyards, this modernized country
house–turned–cozy inn offers all the
comforts needed for a relaxing stay—
large-sized guest rooms with comfy beds,
a tasty restaurant focused on farm-fresh
ingredients, and an inviting indoor/outdoor
pool. **Pros:** wonderfully relaxing environment; spectacular views; delicious food
and wines. **Cons:** can hear some noise
from street and other rooms; must book
in advance to use spa; air-conditioning can
be loud. ⑤ *Rooms from: €383* ✉ *Località Lomellina 26, Gavi ☎ 0143/642860*
⊕ *www.la-raia.it ⊘ Closed mid-Nov.–late
Mar.* ⇌ *12 rooms* ⦙⦙ *Free Breakfast.*

★ Nordelaia

$$$$ | HOTEL | A stay at this charming,
rural-chic hotel surrounded by vineyards
is like visiting a stylish friend's country
home—one with impeccably good taste
in design and cuisine. **Pros:** luxe yet
homey atmosphere; gorgeous environs;
friendly service. **Cons:** terrace pool is
unheated; a little out of the way from
Piedmont's main wine region; prices
on the high side. ⑤ *Rooms from: €392*
✉ *Via Piazze 14–16, Cremolino ✛ 28 km
(17 miles) west of Gavi ☎ 0143/038045*
⊕ *nordelaia.com ⊘ Closed mid-Jan.–mid-
Mar.* ⇌ *12 rooms* ⦙⦙ *Free Breakfast.*

Bard

65 km (40 miles) north of Turin.

This small medieval town clings to a
rocky crag that almost completely blocks
the entrance to the Valle d'Aosta from
Piedmont. Recognized for its strategic
importance since prehistoric times, the
location was first fully fortified by the

Romans, and then by the Ostrogoths
in the 6th century. As befits its military
heritage, the village is rather gray and
somber, but the magnificent fortress that
sits atop it makes a visit well worthwhile.

GETTING HERE AND AROUND
Bard is just off the A5 autostrada, which
runs north from Turin into the Valle d'Aosta—by car the trip takes about an hour.
There are trains about every two hours
from Turin and more regular service to
and from Aosta. Traveling to Bard by bus
is not a viable option.

 Sights

★ Forte di Bard

SPECIALTY MUSEUM | FAMILY | A few
minutes beyond the French-speaking
village of Pont St. Martin, you pass through
the narrow Gorge de Bard to reach the
fortress that has stood guarding the valley
entrance for more than eight centuries. It
now houses five museums: Museo delle
Alpi, dedicated to the history and culture
of the Valle d'Aosta region; Le Prigioni,
an interactive walk through the former
prisons; Museo delli Fortificazioni, which
looks at defense techniques (fortifications)
over the centuries; Museo delle Frontiere,
which examines the political, economic,
and cultural meaning of borders; and a children's museum, Le Alpi dei Ragazzi. ✉ *Via
Vittorio Emanuele II, Bard ☎ 0125/833811*
⊕ *www.fortedibard.it* ☞ *€8 for 1 museum,
€12 for 2 museums, €24 for all museums*
⊘ *Closed Mon. mid-Sept.–late July.*

Breuil-Cervinia/
The Matterhorn

*50 km (30 miles) north of Bard, 116 km
(72 miles) north of Turin.*

Sitting in a huge natural basin at the foot
of the Matterhorn, this town, once a high
Alpine pasture, grew to become one of
Europe's most famous ski areas when

a road connecting it to the Valle d'Aosta was completed in 1934. It bustles in the winter and has become a popular spot for hikers in the summer, but it's sleepy for much of the rest of the year.

GETTING HERE AND AROUND
From Aosta take the A5 autostrada and then the SR46 (1 hour); from Turin take the A5 and then the SR46 (90 minutes). Arriva Italia has regular bus service from Turin and Milan. Breuil-Cervinia isn't on a train line.

Sights

★ **Matterhorn** (*Monte Cervino in Italian; Mont Cervin in French*)
MOUNTAIN | FAMILY | The famous peak straddles the border between Italy and Switzerland, and all sightseeing and skiing facilities are operated jointly. Splendid views of the peak can be seen from Plateau Rosa, which can be reached by cable car from the center of Breuil-Cervinia. The cable car gives access to climbing and off-trail skiing on ridges that were once inaccessible. The Matterhorn Glacier Ride II cable car from Cervinia directly to Zermatt opened in summer 2023. This hour-long ride is the highest border crossing in the Alps. ⊠ *Breuil-Cervinia* ☎ *0166/944311* ⊕ *www.cervinia. it* ⛟ *From Breuil-Cervinia to Plateau Rosa: €35 one-way, €55 round-trip. From Breuil-Cervinia to Zermatt: €127 one-way, €194 round-trip.*

Hotels

★ **Hermitage**
$$$$ | RESORT | The entryway's marble relief of St. Theodolus reminds you that this was once a hermitage, but asceticism has given way to comfort and elegance—a fire is always glowing in the enormous hearth, the dining room is candlelit, the bright bedrooms have balconies, and the suites have antique fireplaces and 18th-century furnishings. **Pros:** superlative staff; refined atmosphere;

Road to Gaul

Between Bard and the town of Donnas, 5 km (3 miles) south along the SS26, you can walk a short but fascinating stretch of a 1st-century Roman consular road that passed this way en route to France. Still showing the deeply worn tracks left by the passage of cart and chariot wheels, this section includes an archway carved through solid rock (used during the Middle Ages as the Donnas city gate) and a milestone ("XXXVI," counting 36 Roman miles from Aosta).

frequent shuttle service into town and to ski lifts. **Cons:** located 2 km (1 mile) from the town center; books up quickly; expensive for the area. ⑤ *Rooms from: €473* ⊠ *Via Piolet 1, Località Chapellette, Breuil-Cervinia* ☎ *0166/948998* ⊕ *www. hotelhermitage.com* ⊙ *Closed mid-Apr.–mid-June and Sept.–late Nov.* ⛟ *47 rooms* ◎ *Free Breakfast.*

Les Neiges d'Antan
$$$$ | B&B/INN | In an evergreen forest at Perrères, just outside Cervinia, this family-run inn is quiet and cozy, with three big fireplaces and a nice view of the Matterhorn. **Pros:** secluded and beautiful setting; wonderful restaurant; well-designed spa facilities. **Cons:** 5 km (3 miles) outside Breuil-Cervinia (a car is essential); entrance and lobby areas are showing some wear; no elevator. ⑤ *Rooms from: €446* ⊠ *Frazione Cret de Perrères 10, Breuil-Cervinia* ☎ *0166/948775* ⊕ *lesneigesdantan.it* ⊙ *Closed Oct.* ⛟ *24 rooms* ◎ *All-Inclusive.*

🏃 Activities

CLIMBING
Serious climbers can make the ascent of the Matterhorn from Breuil-Cervinia after registering with the local mountaineering

The mighty Matterhorn straddles Switzerland and Italy and has one of the highest summits in Europe.

officials at the tourist office. This ascent is for experienced climbers only. Less demanding hikes follow the lower slopes of the Marmore river valley, south of town.

Società Guide Alpine del Cervino
SNOW SPORTS | FAMILY | The Society's guides are available to accompany you on treks and also lead skiing, snow-shoeing, ice-climbing, and rock-climbing excursions. ✉ *Via Circonvallazione 2, Breuil-Cervinia* ☎ *0166/948169* ⊕ *www. guidedelcervino.com* ✉ *Ski touring, ice climbing, and rock climbing from €400 per person per day; group snowshoeing from €30 per person for 2 hrs; private snowshoeing from €120 per person for 2 hrs.*

SKIING
More than 70 lifts and a few hundred miles of ski runs, ranging from beginner to expert, make Breuil-Cervinia Val-tournenche one of the best and most popular resort areas in Italy. Because the slopes border a glacier, there's skiing year-round.

Castello di Fénis

34 km (21 miles) northwest of Bard, 104 km (65 miles) north of Turin.

The tiny town of Fénis owes its origins to the presence of the medieval castle that once provided shelter for the local peasants who lived nearby. Today, the population of the town is less than 2,000, most either farmers or part of the tourist industry.

GETTING HERE AND AROUND
To reach the castle by car, take the Nus exit from the A5 autostrada. Arriva Italia buses provide infrequent service between Aosta and Fénis. It's about a 10-minute train ride from Aosta to the train station in Nus, a 2-km (1-mile) walk from the castle.

Sights

⭐ **Castello di Fénis**
CASTLE/PALACE | FAMILY | The best-pre-served medieval fortress in Valle d'Aosta,

this many-turreted castle was built in the mid-14th century. The 15th-century court-yard surrounded by wooden balconies is elegantly decorated with well-preserved frescoes. Inside you can see the kitchen, with an enormous fireplace that provided central heat in winter; the armory; and the spacious, well-lighted rooms used by the lord and lady of the manor. ⊠ Località Chez-Sapin 1, Fénis ☏ 0165/764263 ⊕ valledaostaheritage. com ⊠ €11 ⊙ Closed Mon. Sept.–June (except holidays).

Aosta

12 km (7 miles) west of Castello di Fénis, 113 km (70 miles) north of Turin.

Aosta stands at the junction of two of the important trade routes that connect France and Italy, the valleys of the Rhône and the Isère. Its significance as a trading post was recognized by the Romans, who built a garrison here in the 1st century BC, and the present-day layout of the streets is the clearest example you'll find of Roman urban planning in Italy. Well-preserved Roman walls form a perfect rectangle around the center, and the regular pattern of streets reflects its role as a military stronghold. Although its gray-stone buildings and slate roofing give the town a rather cold feeling, Aosta has appeared on several lists as one of the most livable towns in Italy.

GETTING HERE AND AROUND
Aosta is off the A5 autostrada and can easily be reached by car or bus from Milan and Turin. Arriva Italia buses regularly travel to and from Milan, Turin, and Chamonix in France. Train service is also available from Turin (two hours) and from Milan (three hours), but you'll have to transfer.

VISITOR INFORMATION
CONTACT Aosta Tourism Office. ⊠ Piazza Porta Praetoria 3, Aosta ☏ 0165/236627 ⊕ www.lovevda.it.

Sights

Arco di Augusto
HISTORIC SIGHT | At the eastern entrance to town, and commanding a fine view over Aosta and the mountains, stands the Arco di Augusto (Arch of Augustus), built in 25 BC to mark Rome's victory over the Celtic Salassi tribe. (The sloping roof was added in 1716 in an attempt to keep rain from seeping between the stones.) ⊠ Piazza Arco d'Augusto, Aosta ⊠ Free.

Cattedrale di Santa Maria Assunta (Aosta Cathedral)
CHURCH | Aosta's cathedral dates from the 10th century, but all that remains from that period are the bell towers. The decoration inside is primarily Gothic, but the main attraction of the cathedral predates that era by 1,000 years: among the many ornate objects housed in the treasury museum is a carved ivory diptych from AD 406 portraying the Roman emperor Honorius. You can also see frescoes dating from the 11th century above the Gothic vaults. The treasury and frescoes can only be visited on weekends between 3 and 5:30 pm, or with advance reservation on weekdays (except Wednesdays) also from 3 to 5:30 pm. ⊠ Piazza Papa Giovanni XXIII, Aosta ☏ 0165/40251 ⊕ cattedraleaosta.it ⊠ Duomo free, treasury museum €4, frescoes and treasury museum €5.

Restaurants

Trattoria Praetoria
$$ | NORTHERN ITALIAN | Just outside the Porta Pretoria, this simple and unpretentious restaurant serves hearty local dishes, including homemade pastas and desserts. They're also well-known for their tasty gluten-free recipes. **Known for:** polenta with a variety of sauces and accompaniments; apple tart with vanilla sauce; savory crepes. ⑤ Average main: €24 ⊠ Via Sant'Anselmo 9, Aosta

☎ *0165/35473* ⊕ *www.trattoriapraetoria.it*
🕓 *Closed Thurs. No dinner Wed.*

⭐ Vecchio Ristoro

$$$$ | **NORTHERN ITALIAN** | Chef Filippo Oggioni took over this traditional restaurant in 2019, adding freshness and creative versions of regional recipes and decadent desserts, available à la carte or as five- or seven-course tasting menus, including a five-course vegetarian option. The elegant, intimate spaces of this converted mill are furnished with antiques, and a traditional ceramic stove provides additional warmth in cool weather. **Known for:** regional tasting menus; wonderful wine pairings; game dishes. ⑤ *Average main: €50* ✉ *Via Tourneuve 4, Aosta* ☎ *0165/33238* ⊕ *ristorantevecchioristoro. it* 🕓 *Closed Sun. and Mon.*

Hotels

⭐ Hotel Milleluci

$$$ | **B&B/INN** | At this small and inviting family-run hotel overlooking Aosta, guest rooms are bright and charmingly decorated; some have balconies and all have splendid views of the city and mountains. **Pros:** panoramic views; great spa amenities; cozy and traditionally decorated rooms. **Cons:** 1 km (½ mile) north of town, so a car is needed to get around; no a/c; small bathrooms. ⑤ *Rooms from: €220* ✉ *Località Porossan Roppoz 15, Aosta* ☎ *0165/235278* ⊕ *www.hotelmilleluci.com* 🛏 *28 rooms* ⑩ *Free Breakfast.*

Courmayeur/ Monte Bianco

35 km (22 miles) northwest of Aosta, 150 km (93 miles) northwest of Turin.

The main attraction of Courmayeur is a knock-'em-dead view of Europe's highest peak, Monte Bianco. The celebrities and the wealthy who come here these days are following a tradition that dates back to the late 17th century, when Courmayeur's natural springs first began to attract visitors. The spectacle of the Alps gradually surpassed the springs as the biggest draw: the Alpine letters of the English poet Percy Bysshe Shelley were almost advertisements for the region. Since 1965, when the Mont Blanc Tunnel opened, ever-increasing numbers of travelers have passed through the area, and it's now hugely popular with both skiers in winter and hikers during the summer. Planners have managed to keep some restrictions on wholesale development within the town, and its angled rooftops and immaculate cobblestone streets maintain a cozy feeling.

GETTING HERE AND AROUND

Courmayeur is on the A5 autostrada and can easily be reached by car from both Turin and Milan by way of Aosta. There is FlixBus service from Milan and Arriva Italia buses run regularly from both Turin and Milan. Train service isn't available.

VISITOR INFORMATION

CONTACT Courmayeur Tourism Office. ✉ *Piazzale Monte Bianco 15, Courmayeur* ☎ *0165/842060* ⊕ *www.lovevda.it.*

Sights

⭐ Monte Bianco (*Mont Blanc*)

MOUNTAIN | Monte Bianco's attraction is not so much its shape, which is much less distinctive than that of the Matterhorn, as its expanse and the awesome vistas from the top. You can reach the summit via a cable car that ascends from Entrèves, just below the Mont Blanc Tunnel. In summer, if so inclined, you can then switch cable cars and descend into Chamonix, in France. In winter you can ski parts of the route off-piste. The Funivia Entrèves whisks you up first to the Pavillon du Mont Fréty in just four minutes—a starting point for many beautiful hikes—and then in six minutes to the spectacular viewing platform at Punta Helbronner (more than 11,000 feet), which is also the border post with France.

The next stage up (in summer only) is on the Télépherique de l'Aiguille du Midi, as you pass into French territory. The trip is particularly impressive; you dangle over a huge glacial snowfield (more than 2,000 feet below) and make your way slowly to the viewing station above Chamonix. It's one of the most dramatic rides in Europe. From this point you're looking down into France, and if you change cable cars at the Aiguille du Midi station, you can make your way down into Chamonix itself. ⊠ SS26, Courmayeur ☎ 0165/89196 in Courmayeur, 0450/532275 in Chamonix ⊕ www.montebianco.com ☜ €24 round-trip to Pavillon du Mont Fréty, €56 round-trip to Punta Helbronner, €35 round-trip to Aiguille du Midi, €38 round-trip to Chamonix ⊗ Closed Nov., May, and depending on weather conditions and demand.

Parco Nazionale del Gran Paradiso

NATIONAL PARK | FAMILY | Cogne, 52 km (32 miles) southeast of Courmayeur, is the gateway to this huge park, which was once the domain of King Vittorio Emanuele II (1820–78). Bequeathed to the nation after World War I, it is one of Europe's most rugged and unspoiled wilderness areas, with wildlife and many plant species protected by law. The park is one of the few places in Europe where you can see the ibex (a mountain goat with horns up to 3 feet long) and the chamois (a small antelope). The park, which is 703 square km (271 square miles), is open free of charge throughout the year; there's an information office in Cogne. ■TIP➔ **Try to visit in May, when spring flowers are in bloom and most of the meadows are clear of snow.** ⊠ Villaggio Cogne 81, Cogne ☎ 011/8606233 ⊕ www.pngp.it ☜ Free.

Hotels

Auberge de la Maison

$$$$ | HOTEL | Most guest rooms here have balconies with spectacular views of Monte Bianco, and the plush fabrics, wood-burning stoves, and Alpine prints on the walls give the feeling of a cozy country inn. **Pros:** secluded location in the center of Entrèves; hotel spa; charming decor. **Cons:** minimum stay in high seasons (summer and winter); not all standard rooms have views of Monte Bianco; spa and pool can be crowded and loud in high season. ⑤ Rooms from: €397 ⊠ Via Passerin d'Entrèves 16, Courmayeur ☎ 0165/869811 ⊕ www.aubergemaison.it ⊗ Closed Apr.–early June and Nov. ➬ 33 rooms �“⦁❙ Free Breakfast.

Grand Hotel Royal e Golf

$$$ | HOTEL | With wide terraces and wood paneling, this longtime landmark in the center of Courmayeur is one of the most elegant spots in town, and the cheery guest rooms have plenty of amenities. **Pros:** central location on main traffic-free street; panoramic views; lovely spa and outdoor heated pool. **Cons:** dated rooms could use an update; service can be standoffish at times; no air-conditioning and rooms sometimes on the warm side. ⑤ Rooms from: €298 ⊠ Via Roma 87, Courmayeur ☎ 0165/831611 ⊕ www.hotelroyalegolf.com ⊗ Closed Easter–mid-June and mid-Sept.–Nov. ➬ 70 rooms ❙❙ Free Breakfast.

Hotel Croux

$$$ | HOTEL | FAMILY | Half the guest rooms at this bright and comfortable hotel have balconies, the other half have great views of the mountains, and all have contemporary furnishings. **Pros:** central location; delicious breakfast with local products; free shuttle to ski lifts. **Cons:** rooms are simple; on a busy road; no coffee or tea in the rooms. ⑤ Rooms from: €220 ⊠ Via

Croux 8, Courmayeur ☎ 0165/846735 ⊕ www.hotelcroux.it ⊙ Closed mid-Apr.–mid-June, Oct., and Nov. ⇆ 28 rooms ⦿ Free Breakfast.

★ Villa Novecento Romantic Hotel
$$$ | HOTEL | Run with friendly charm and efficiency, the Novecento is a peaceful haven with the style of a comfortable mountain lodge, complete with a log fire in winter, traditional fabrics, wooden furnishings, and early-19th-century prints. **Pros:** frequent shuttle to the slopes and town; good restaurant and excellent breakfast; away from the main tourist area. **Cons:** parking is limited; some guests find the beds uncomfortable; no air-conditioning. Ⓢ Rooms from: €205 ✉ Viale Monte Bianco 64, Courmayeur ☎ 0165/1825622 ⊕ www.villanovecento. it ⊙ Closed mid-Apr.–May and mid-Oct.–late Nov. ⇆ 22 rooms ⦿ Free Breakfast.

Activities

SKIING
Courmayeur Mont Blanc
SNOW SPORTS | Courmayeur pales in comparison to its French neighbor, Chamonix, in both the quality and the number of its ski runs. But with good natural snow cover, the trails and vistas are spectacular. A huge gondola leads from the center of Courmayeur to Plan Chécrouit, where other gondolas and lifts lead to the slopes. The skiing around Monte Bianco is particularly good, and the off-piste options are among the best in Europe. The routes from Cresta d'Arp (the local peak) to Dolonne, and from La Palud into France, should be done with a guide. Contact the Courmayeur tourist office for complete information about lift tickets, ski runs, and weather conditions. ✉ Strada Dolonne La Villette 1, Courmayeur ☎ 0165/841612 ⊕ www.courmayeur-montblanc.it ⛷ 1-day ski pass €65.

Società delle Guide Alpine
(Alpine Guide Society)
SKIING & SNOWBOARDING | The society provides Alpine guide services year-round. ✉ Strada Villair 2, Courmayeur ☎ 0165/842064 ⊕ www.guidecourma-yeur.com ⛷ Guides from €95 for 1 day.

Venaria Reale

10 km (6 miles) northwest of Turin.

This immense palace was built in the 16th century as a hunting lodge.

GETTING HERE AND AROUND
Starting in Turin, from the north side of Piazza della Repubblica, take Bus No. 11 to reach Venaria; the trip takes approximately 60 minutes. By car, follow Corso Regina Margherita to the A55 autostrada. Head north and leave the highway at the Venaria exit, following signs for the Venaria Reale.

Sights

★ Reggia di Venaria Reale
CASTLE/PALACE | FAMILY | Extensive Italianate gardens surround this magnificent 16th-century UNESCO-protected hunting lodge built for Carlo Emanuele II of Savoy. Inside, its Great Gallery is worthy of Versailles, and the attached chapel (Capella di Sant'Uberto) and stables were designed in the 1720s by Sicilian architect Filippo Juvarra. The Theatre of History and Magnificence houses a fascinating historical exhibition that tells the story of the House of Savoy. The upper floors are reserved for changing exhibitions. ✉ Piazza della Repubblica 4, Venaria Reale ☎ 011/4992333 ⊕ www. lavenaria.it ⛷ €20 ⊙ Closed Mon.

Rivoli

16 km (10 miles) southwest of Venaria, 13 km (8 miles) west of Turin.

The Savoy court was based in Rivoli in the Middle Ages, and the town retains several remnants from that richly dramatic period.

GETTING HERE AND AROUND
GTT buses and trams regularly link central Turin with Rivoli; the journey takes just over one hour. By car, follow Corso Francia from central Turin all the way to Rivoli; unless there's a lot of traffic, the trip should take a half hour.

◉ Sights

Casa del Conte Verde (*House of the Green Count*)
HISTORIC HOME | The richly decorated House of the Green Count, in the oldest part of Rivoli, attests to the wealth and importance of its onetime owner, Amedeo VI of Savoy (1334–83). Legend has it that the count attended tournaments dressed all in green, hence the name. Inside, a small gallery occasionally hosts temporary exhibitions, which may increase the entrance fee. ✉ *Via Fratelli Piol 8, Rivoli* ☎ *011/9563020* ⊕ *www. comune.rivoli.to.it* ⊠ *€5 (varies with exhibitions)* ⊘ *Closed Mon. and Tues., and Wed.–Fri. until 4 pm.*

★ Castello di Rivoli Museo d'Arte Contemporanea (*Castle of Rivoli Museum of Contemporary Art*)
ART MUSEUM | The Baroque castle of Rivoli now houses a fascinating museum of contemporary art. The building was begun in the 17th century and then redesigned, but never finished, by architect Filippo Juvarra in the 18th century; it was finally converted into a museum in the late 20th century by the minimalist Turin architect Andrea Bruno. ✉ *Piazzale Mafalda di Savoia, Rivoli* ☎ *011/9565222* ⊕ *www.castellodirivoli.org* ⊠ *€10 (varies for temporary exhibitions)* ⊘ *Closed Mon. and Tues.*

Sacra di San Michele

26 km (17 miles) west of Rivoli, 43 km (27 miles) west of Turin.

Perhaps best known as inspiration for the setting of Umberto Eco's novel *The Name of the Rose,* this abbey was built on Monte Pirchiriano in the 11th century so it would stand out: it occupies the most prominent location for miles around, hanging over a 3,280-foot bluff.

GETTING HERE AND AROUND
From Turin, take the train to Avigliana and then a 14-km (9-mile) taxi ride or uphill hike from the station. By car take the Avigliana Est exit from the A32 autostrada (Torino–Bardonecchia).

◉ Sights

★ Sacra di San Michele
CHURCH | To reach the church—built between 983 and 987 AD, and which inspired Umberto Eco to write *The Name of the Rose*—you must climb 150 steps from the Porta dello Zodiaco, a splendid Romanesque doorway decorated with the signs of the zodiac. On the left side of the interior are 16th-century frescoes representing New Testament themes; on the right are depictions of the founding of the church. ✉ *Via Sacra di San Michele 14, Sant'Ambrogio di Torino* ☎ *011/939130* ⊕ *www.sacradisanmichele.com* ⊠ *€8.*

Chapter 10

THE ITALIAN RIVIERA

Updated by
Elizabeth Shemaria

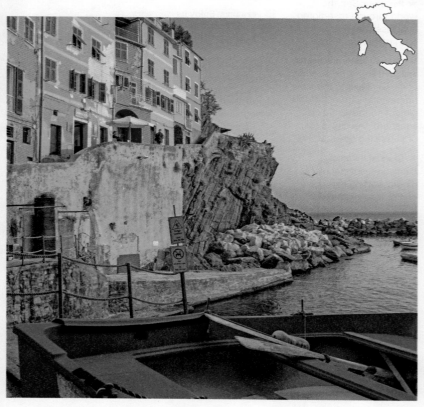

⊙ **Sights**
★★★☆☆

🍴 **Restaurants**
★★★★☆

🛏 **Hotels**
★★★★☆

⊙ **Shopping**
★☆☆☆☆

🍸 **Nightlife**
★☆☆☆☆

WELCOME TO THE ITALIAN RIVIERA

TOP REASONS TO GO

★ **The Cinque Terre:** Hike the famous Cinque Terre trails past gravity-defying vineyards, colorful rock-perched villages, and the deep blue Mediterranean Sea.

★ **Portofino:** See the world through rose-tinted sunglasses at this glamorous little harbor village.

★ **Genoa's historical center and port:** From the palaces of Via Garibaldi to the labyrinthine backstreets of the old city to the world-class aquarium, the city is full of surprising delights.

★ **Giardini Botanici Hanbury:** A spectacular natural setting harbors one of Italy's largest, most exotic botanical gardens, near Bordighera.

★ **Pesto:** The basil-rich sauce was invented in Liguria, and it's never been equaled elsewhere.

1 **Riomaggiore.** The first of the Cinque Terre villages has a small harbor and coastal views.

2 **Manarola.** Terraced vineyards, olive trees, and pastel houses fill the town.

3 **Corniglia.** Climb (365 steps) to the most remote Cinque Terre town.

4 **Vernazza.** Enjoy its lively piazza and a postcard-worthy port view.

5 **Monterosso al Mare.** Come here for festivals, beaches, clear water, and plentiful accommodations.

6 **Lerici.** White-sand beaches, hiking trails, and seaside cafés are memorable.

7 **La Spezia.** This busy port city has outdoor markets and palm-lined streets.

8 **Portovenere.** Quaint passageways and a castle distinguish the port town.

9 **Levanto.** This makes an ideal base for diving, surfing, hiking, and day trips around Liguria.

10 **Sestri Levante.** The small seaside village is framed by two bays.

PIEMONTE

FRANCE

Pieve di Teco

Imperia

Taggia

Ventimiglia

San Remo

Giardini Botanici Hanbury

Bordighera

Monte Carlo

MONACO

11 **Santa Margherita Ligure.** Palm trees, attractive hotels, and a yacht-filled marina add appeal.

12 **Portofino.** This vacation spot for the rich and famous has a castle, cliff-side gardens, and fancy boutiques.

EATING AND DRINKING WELL IN THE ITALIAN RIVIERA

Vegetable-topped focaccia bread

Ligurian cuisine might surprise you. As you'd expect, given the long coastline, it employs all sorts of seafood, but its real claim to fame is the exemplary use of vegetables and herbs.

Basil is practically revered in Genoa—the word is derived from the Greek *basileus,* meaning "king"—and the city is considered the birthplace of pesto, the basil-rich pasta sauce. This and other herbs (laurel, fennel, and marjoram) are cultivated, but also grow wild on the sun-kissed hillsides. Naturally, seafood plays a prominent role on the menu, appearing in soups, salads, and pasta dishes. Vegetables—particularly artichokes, eggplant, and zucchini—are abundant, and usually prepared with liberal amounts of olive oil and garlic.

Like much of Italy, Liguria has a wide range of eating establishments from cafeteria-like *tavole calde* to family-run trattorias to sophisticated *ristoranti.* Lunch is served between 12:30 and 2:30 and dinner between 7:30 and 11. Also popular, especially in Genoa, are *enoteche* (wine bars), which serve simply prepared light meals late into the night.

FABULOUS FOCACCIA

When you're hankering for a snack, turn to bakeries and small eateries serving focaccia. The flatbread is more dense and flavorful here than what's sold as focaccia in American restaurants—it's the region's answer to pizza, usually eaten on the go. It comes simply salted and drizzled with olive oil; flavored with rosemary and olives; covered with cheese or anchovies; and even *ripiena* (stuffed), usually with cheese or vegetables and herbs.

ANTIPASTI

Seafood antipasti are served in abundance at most Ligurian restaurants. Typical dishes include marinated anchovies from Monterosso, *cozze ripiene* (mussel shells stuffed with minced mussel meat, prosciutto, Parmesan, herbs, and bread crumbs), and *soppressata di polpo* (flattened octopus in olive oil and lemon sauce).

PASTA

Liguria's classic sauce is pesto, made from basil, garlic, olive oil, pine nuts, and hard cheese. It's usually served with *trenette* (similar to spaghetti) or the slightly sweet *testaroli* (a flat pasta made from chestnut flour). You can also find *pansotti* (triangular pockets filled with a cheese mixture), and *trofie* (short twists) with *salsa di noci*, a rich sauce of garlic, walnuts, and cream that, as with pesto, is ideally pounded with mortar and pestle. Spaghetti *allo scoglio* has an olive oil, tomato, and white-wine-based sauce containing an assortment of local *frutti di mare* (seafood) like shrimp, clams, mussels, and cuttlefish.

FISH AND MEAT

Fish is the best bet for a second course: the classic preparation is a whole grilled or baked whitefish—branzino and *orata* (dorado) are good

Trofie pasta with tomato sauce

choices—served *alla Ligure,* with olives, potatoes, tomatoes, Ligurian spices, and a drizzle of olive oil. A popular meat dish is *cima alla Genovese*, a veal roll stuffed with a mixture of eggs and vegetables, served as a cold cut.

PANIGACCI

One of the real treats of the region is *panigacci*. Small, terra-cotta dishes known as *testine* are placed in a wood-burning oven or fire to heat at the highest of temperatures. Then balls of dough are laid in the dishes, which are stacked one on top of the other in order to flatten and cook the dough. Panigacci are usually served with *stracchino* cheese, pesto or nut sauce, and cold cuts.

WINE

Local vineyards produce mostly light and refreshing whites, such as *pigato* from the Ponente and *vermentino* from the Levante, although both light reds and appealing *rosato* (Italian rosé) are on the rise. Rossese di Dolceacqua, from near the French border, is considered the best red wine the region has to offer, but for a more robust accompaniment to meats, opt for the full-bodied reds of the neighboring Piedmont region. For a post-dinner or dessert wine, try the *sciacchetrà,* made exclusively in the Cinque Terre.

Cheese-filled pansotti pasta

Nestled between the south of France and the Tuscan border lies the region of Liguria, with verdant mountains to the north and east, and the sapphire-blue Mediterranean to the south and west. In between is a land of lush vegetation, medieval hilltop hamlets, panoramic vistas, colorful seaside villages, pristine beaches, and one of Italy's most underrated cities, Genoa.

There is plenty to do—from hiking and biking, to water sports and fishing, to eating (very) well—and plenty to see, including some of Italy's most aesthetically pleasing architecture. It's also easy to just enjoy la dolce vita along this coast, better known as the Italian Riviera.

The Italian Riviera oozes charm and irresistible allure, with many seaside resort towns and colorful villages that stake intermittent claim to the rocky shores of the Ligurian Sea and seem like the long-lost cousins of newer seaside paradises found elsewhere. It has been a haven for artists, writers, celebrities, and royalty since the 1800s, and continues to fascinate visitors throughout the year due to its mild climate. Here the grandest palazzi share space with frescoed, angular *terratetti* (tall, skinny houses). The rustic and elegant, the provincial and chic, the small-town and cosmopolitan all collide here in a sun-drenched blend that defines the Italian side of the Riviera. There are chic resort towns such as San Remo and Portofino, the unique beauty and outdoor adventures of the Cinque Terre, numerous quaint seaside and

hilltop villages to explore, plus the history and architectural charm of Genoa. Mellowed by balmy breezes blowing in from the sea, travelers bask in the sun, explore the picturesque fishing villages, and pamper themselves at the resorts that dot this ruggedly beautiful landscape.

MAJOR REGIONS

Cinque Terre. The beautiful Cinque Terre is the heart of the Italian Riviera. In their rugged simplicity, the five old fishing towns of Monterosso al Mare, Vernazza, Corniglia, Manarola, and Riomaggiore seem to mock the glitzy neighboring resorts. With a blue sea in the foreground, multicolor buildings emerge almost seamlessly from cliffs, and rocky mountains rise precipitously to vineyards and olive groves. The terrain is so steep that for centuries, footpaths were the only way to get around. Since its 1997 UNESCO World Heritage designation, the Cinque Terre has become one of Italy's most popular destinations. Eastward from Genoa to Lerici (encompassing the Cinque Terre and a naval port, La Spezia) stretches the Riviera di Levante (Riviera of the Rising Sun). It has a raw, unpolished feel, and its rugged coastline is dotted with colorful fishing villages like Camogli, Portovenere, and Sestri Levante. It also has one of Europe's well-known playgrounds for the rich and famous, the inlet of Portofino, and nearby Santa Margherita Ligure is popular with well-to-do Italians. From this area's twisting roads, the hills plummet sharply to the sea. Beaches tend to be rocky, yet there are some lovely sandy stretches in Lerici, Monterosso al Mare, Levanto, and Paraggi (near Portofino).

Genoa. The seaside city of Genoa (Genova in Italian), birthplace of Christopher Columbus, has a long history as a major trading station, and in the Middle Ages and the Renaissance, Genoa became a wealthy, prestigious commercial center. Its bankers, merchants, and princes adorned their city with palaces, churches, and impressive art collections. Today Genoa is a cultural center worth a look. Nearby Nervi is a stately resort town.

The Riviera di Ponente. West of Genoa, the Riviera di Ponente (Riviera of the Setting Sun) covers the narrow strip of northwest Liguria from Genoa to the French border. The sapphire Mediterranean Sea to one side and the verdant foothills of the Alps on the other allow for temperate weather, which is why it's also called the Riviera dei Fiori (Riviera of the Flowers). Once filled with seaside villages and elegant homes, this area struggles to balance natural beauty with resort development, as in glitzy San Remo. Highly populated resorts and some overly industrialized areas are jammed into the thin stretch of white-sand and pebble beaches. There are still several worthwhile villages, like Finale Ligure, Albegna, and Bordighera, along the sea and hinterland. Bordighera is near Giardini Botanici Hanbury, one of Italy's most beautiful groupings of gardens. The Riviera di Levante may retain more of its natural beauty, but the Ponente remains popular with visitors looking for sunshine, nightlife, and relaxation.

Planning

When to Go

The Italian Riviera is extremely seasonal, apart from Genoa, a city with year-round cultural attractions. The region has a typical Mediterranean climate with warm summers and rainy winters, making high season (Easter and June–August in particular) the best time to visit, though it can be really crowded as well as lively. From April to October, the area bustles with shops, cafés, clubs, and restaurants that stay open late. The rest of the year, the majority of resorts close down, and you'll be hard-pressed to find accommodations or restaurants open.

Getting Here and Around

BUS

Generally speaking, buses are a difficult way to come and go in Liguria. Although there are local buses that run between some villages along the Riviera Ponente and Riviera Levante, it's not an extensive network and can be a challenge to navigate.

CONTACT AMT. ☎ 848/000030 charge for calling, 010/5582414 ⊕ www.amt. genova.it.

CAR

With the freedom of a car, you could drive from one end of the Riviera to the other on the autostrada in about three hours. Two good roads run parallel to each other along the coast of Liguria. Closer to shore and passing through all the towns and villages is the SS1, or Via Aurelia, which was laid out by the ancient Romans and has excellent views at almost every turn. It gets very crowded in July and August. More direct and higher up than SS1 are autostradas A10, west of Genoa, and A12, to the south—engineering wonders with literally hundreds of long tunnels and towering viaducts. These routes save time on weekends, in summer, and on days when festivals slow traffic in some resorts to a standstill.

TRAIN

Train travel on the national railway, Ferrovie dello Stato, is by far the most convenient mode of transportation throughout the region. It takes 3½ hours for an express train to cover the entire Ligurian coast. Local trains take upward of five hours or more to get from one end of the coast to the other, stopping in or near all the towns along the way. For schedules, check ⊕ *www.trenitalia.com/en.html.*

Planning Your Time

Your first decision, particularly given limited time, is between the two Rivieras. The Riviera di Levante (east of Genoa) is more rustic and has a more distinct personality, with the unique Cinque Terre, ritzy Portofino, and the panoramic Gulf of Poets. The Riviera di Ponente (west of Genoa) is a classic European resort experience with some white-sand beaches and more nightlife and accommodation choices—similar to, but not as glamorous as, the French Riviera across the border.

In either case, your second decision is whether to visit Genoa. Despite its rough exterior and (diminishing) reputation as a seamy port town, Genoa's artistic and cultural treasures are significant—you won't find anything remotely comparable elsewhere in the region. Unless your goal is to avoid urban life entirely, consider a night or two in the city.

Hiking

Walking Liguria's extensive network of trails while taking in the gorgeous views is a major outdoor activity and regional attraction. The mild climate and laid-back state of mind can lull you into underestimating just how strenuous such walks can be. Wear good shoes, use sunscreen, and carry plenty of water—you'll be glad you did. Trail maps are available from tourist information offices, or upon entry to the Cinque Terre National Park.

On the Portofino promontory, the relatively easy walk to the Abbazia di San Fruttuoso is popular, and there's a more challenging hike from Ruta to the top of Monte Portofino and back down to Camogli. From Genoa, you can take the Zecca–Righi funicular up to Righi and walk along the ring of fortresses that used to defend the city.

Walking tours can introduce you to lesser-known aspects of the region. For the Cinque Terre and the rest of the Province of La Spezia, Cinqueterre Experience (✉ *Viale Amendola 172, La Spezia* ☎ *333/2909560, mobile* ⊕ *www.cinqueterrexperience.com*) is a good source for English-speaking and other foreign-language guides. A day tour (lasting from 1½ hours to a full day) is €350 (not including tips; this price is for a group of up to 20 people. Tours with no hiking are also offered (maximum 35 people) at the same price.

Restaurants

While fine dining can be found in Liguria, you are more likely to enjoy a casual atmosphere, often with an amazing sea view. Expect both the decor and dishes to be simple but flavorful; fish and seafood are highlights here.

Hotels

Liguria's lodging may be a step behind more developed areas like Positano and Taormina, so be sure to reserve its better accommodations (and the relatively limited options in the Cinque Terre) far in advance. Lodging tends to be pricey in high season, particularly June to August.

⇨ *Hotel and restaurant reviews have been shortened. For full information, visit Fodors.com. Prices in the lodging reviews are the lowest cost of a standard double room in high season. Prices in the dining reviews are the average cost of a main course at dinner, or, if dinner is not served, at lunch.*

What It Costs in Euros

	$	$$	$$$	$$$$
RESTAURANTS				
	under €15	€15–€24	€25–€35	over €35
HOTELS				
	under €125	€125–€200	€201–€300	over €300

Riomaggiore

17 km (11 miles) southwest of La Spezia, 101 km (60 miles) southeast of Genoa.

At the eastern end of the Cinque Terre, Riomaggiore is built into a river gorge (hence the name, which means "major river") and is easily accessible from La Spezia by train or car. The landscape is terraced and steep—be prepared for many stairs!—and leads to a small harbor, protected by large slabs of alabaster and marble that serve as tanning beds for sunbathers. The harbor is also the site of several outdoor cafés with fine views. According to legend, the settlement of Riomaggiore dates as far back as the 8th century, when Greek religious refugees came here to escape persecution by the Byzantine emperor.

The village is divided into two parts. If you arrive by train, you will have to pass through a tunnel that flanks the train tracks to reach the historic side of town. To avoid the crowds and get a great view of the Cinque Terre coast, walk straight uphill as soon as you exit the station. This winding road takes you over the hill to the 14th-century **church of St. John the Baptist,** toward the medieval town center and the Genovese-style tower houses that dot the village. Follow Via Roma (the Old Town's main street) downhill, pass under the train tracks, and you'll arrive in the charming fishermen's port. Lined with traditional fishing boats and small trattorias, this is a lovely spot for a romantic lunch or dinner. Unfortunately, Riomaggiore doesn't have as much old-world charm as its sister villages; its easy accessibility has brought traffic and more construction here than elsewhere in the Cinque Terre.

GETTING HERE AND AROUND
The enormous parking problems presented by these cliff-dwelling villages have been mitigated somewhat by a large, covered parking structure at La Spezia Centrale station, which costs around €2.50 per hour in summer. It's clean and secure (you cannot enter without a ticket code to open the door), and it's open 24/7. This is a good backup solution for those with cars, although others may choose to take a day trip from Pisa or Lucca and rely on bus and train services. Arrive early, as it can fill up by midmorning, especially in high season.

VISITOR INFORMATION
CONTACT Riomaggiore Welcome Center.
✉ *Riomaggiore train station, Piazza Rio Finale, Riomaggiore* ☎ *0187/760091* ⊕ *www.parconazionale5terre.it.*

Accessing Cinque Terre Trails

When to Go

The ideal times to visit the Cinque Terre are September and May, when the weather is mild and the summer tourist season isn't in full swing (June through August can be unbearably hot and crowded).

Getting Here and Around

Between mid-March and mid-October there is a local train between La Spezia and Levanto that stops at each of the Cinque Terre villages and runs every 30 minutes. Tickets for each leg of the journey (around €5) are available at all five train stations. In Corniglia, the only one of the Cinque Terre that isn't at sea level, a shuttle service (€7.50) is provided for those who don't wish to climb (or descend) the 300-plus steps that link the train station with the cliff-top town.

The Explora 5 Terre shuttle-bus operates a daily service between La Spezia and the villages; a day ticket costs €18.50.

Along the Cinque Terre coast two ferry lines operate. From June to September, Golfo Paradiso runs from Genoa and Camogli to Monterosso al Mare (a round-trip ticket costs €45). Other tours are also available. From late March to October, the smaller but more frequent Golfo dei Poeti

stops at each village from Lerici (east of Riomaggiore) to Monterosso, with the exception of Corniglia, two to five times a day (a round-trip ticket costs €28–€41); you can also purchase one-way tickets.

Admission

Entrance tickets for using the trails are available at ticket booths located at the start of each section of Trail No. 2, and at information offices in the Levanto, Monterosso, Vernazza, Corniglia, Manarola, Riomaggiore, and La Spezia train stations. A one-day Cinque Terre Card costs €7.50, which includes a trail map and an information leaflet; a two-day pass is €14.50.

The Cinque Terre Carta Treno, which allows access to the park plus unlimited daily use of the regional train between La Spezia, the five villages, and Levanto just north of Monterosso, varies in cost, with higher prices during holidays and summer. Rates are €19.50–€32.50 for a one-day pass, €34–€59 for a two-day pass, and €46.50–€78.50 for a three-day pass.

For More Information

⊕ www.cinqueterre.com; www.lecinqueterre.org; www.parconazionale-5terre.it; www.explora5terre.it; www.golfoparadiso.it; www.navigazionegolfodeipoeti.it.

👁 Sights

Riomaggiore

TOWN | This village at the eastern end of the Cinque Terre is built into a river gorge (hence the name, which means "major river"). It has a tiny harbor protected by large slabs of alabaster and marble, which serve as tanning beds for sunbathers as well as being the site of several outdoor cafés with fine views. According to legend, the settlement of Riomaggiore dates as far back as the 8th century, when Greek religious refugees came here to escape persecution by the Byzantine emperor. ⊠ Riomaggiore ☎ 0187/920633 ⊕ www.parconazionale-5terre.it.

Continued on page 450

HIKING THE CINQUE TERRE

FIVE REMOTE VILLAGES MAKE ONE MUST-SEE DESTINATION

"Charming" and "breathtaking" are adjectives that get a workout when you're traveling in Italy, but it's rare that both apply to a single location. The Cinque Terre is such a place, and this combination of characteristics goes a long way toward explaining its tremendous appeal.

The area is made up of five tiny villages (Cinque Terre literally means "Five Lands") clinging to the cliffs along a gorgeous stretch of the Ligurian coast. The terrain is so steep that for centuries footpaths were the only way to get from place to place. It just so happens that these paths provide beautiful views of the rocky coast tumbling into the sea, as well as access to secluded beaches and grottoes.

Backpackers "discovered" the Cinque Terre in the 1970s, and its popularity has been growing ever since. Despite summer crowds, much of the original appeal is intact. Each town has maintained its own distinct charm, and views from the trails in between are as breathtaking as ever.

Monterosso   Corniglia   Terracing around Corniglia

HIKING THE CINQUE TERRE

Mount Malpertuso ▲

Mount Castello ▲

Monterosso—Vernazza Trail
The most demanding portion of the trail. Often narrow, with significant climbs and descents, particularly near Vernazza. Your labors are rewarded with the Trail No. 2's best views.

Le Stalle

Trail No 8a

Mount Gaginara ▲

38

(Red Trail)

Drignana

Vernazza—Corniglia Trail
Ups and downs interspersed with olive groves and terraced vineyards.

370

Madonna di Soviore

Trail No 1

Santuario del Reggio
1hr

1hr 30min

51

Trail No 8

Santuario Bernardino
1hr

Trail No 89

S. Bernardo
Trail No 8

Trail No 7

3 km/2 mi—1 hr 30 min

Trail No 2 (Blue Trail)
3 km/2 mi—2 hrs

Guvano Beach

Vernazza

Palma Pt

del Frate Island

Molinara Pt

0   1 mi

0   1 km

Monterosso al Mare

FERRY TO LEVANTO

Monterosso
The most resortlike of the villages, with the largest beach.

Vernazza
Pretty and visitor-friendly. The best spot for lingering in a café and watching waves crash against the shore.

THE CLASSIC HIKE

Hiking is the most popular way to experience the Cinque Terre, and Trail No. 2, the Sentiero Azzurro (Blue Trail), is the most traveled path. To cover the entire trail is a full day: it's approximately 13 km (8 miles) in length, takes you to all five villages, and requires about five hours, not including stops, to complete. The best approach is to start at the eastern-most town of Riomaggiore and warm up your legs on the easiest segment of the trail. As you work your way west, the hike gets progressively more demanding. Between Corniglia and Manarola take the ferry (which provides its own beautiful views) or the inland train running between the towns instead.

Manarola

Along Lovers' Lane

Via dell'Amore

Corniglia— Manarola Trail
This section of the trail is currently closed.

Manarola—Riomaggiore Trail
Known as the Via dell'Amore (Lovers' Lane). A wide, paved, flat path with fine views.

KEY

.... Major footpaths

------------ Sanctuary footpaths

.... Connecting footpaths

45min — Hiking times

☩ Sanctuaries

Corniglia
Perched on a cliff 500 feet above the sea, reached by a switchback path (or by shuttle bus).

Manarola
The most photogenic of the villages, best seen from the cemetery a few minutes up the path toward Corniglia.

Riomaggiore
Cliff-clinging buildings are almost as striking as those in Manarola. Stairs to the left of the train station entrance cross over the tracks and lead to the trailhead.

BEYOND TRAIL NO.2

Trail No. 2 is just one of a network of trails crisscrossing the hills. If you're a dedicated hiker, spend a few nights and try some of the other routes. Trail No. 1, the Sentiero Rosso (Red Trail), climbs from Portovenere (east of Riomaggiore) and returns to the sea at Levanto (west of Monterosso al Mare). To hike its length takes from 9 to 12 hours; the ridge-top trail provides spectacular views from high above the villages, each of which can be reached via a steep path. Other shorter trails go from the villages up into the hills, some leading to religious sanctuaries. Trail No. 9, for example, starts from the old section of Monterosso and ends at the Madonna di Soviore Sanctuary.

Hiking the Cinque Terre

Though often described as relaxing and easy, the Cinque Terre also have several hiking options if you wish to exert yourself a little. Many people do not realize just how demanding parts of these trails can be—it's best to come prepared. We recommend bringing a Cinque Terre Card and cash (smaller shops, eateries, and the park entrances may not accept credit cards).

When all trails are completely open, a hike through the villages takes about four to five hours; add time for exploring each village and taking a lunch break—it's an all-day, if not two-day, trek. We recommend an early start, especially in summer when midday temperatures can rise to 90°F. Note that only Sentiero Azzurro (Trail No. 2) requires the Cinque Terre Card. The other 20-plus trails in the area are free. All trails are well marked with a red-and-white sign. Trails from village to village get progressively steeper from south (Riomaggiore) to north (Monterosso). If you're a day-tripper with a car, use the underground lot at La Spezia Centrale train station (€2.50 per hour in summer) and take the train to Riomaggiore (6–8 minutes).

Our Favorites

Other trails to consider include **Monterosso to Santuario Madonna di Soviore**, a fairly strenuous but rewarding 1½ hours up to a lovely 8th-century sanctuary. There is also a restaurant and a priceless view. **Riomaggiore to Montenero and Portovenere** is one hour up to the sanctuary and another three hours to Portovenere, passing through some gorgeous, less-traveled terrain. **Manarola to Volastra to Corniglia** runs high above the main trail and through vineyards and lesser-known villages. **Monterosso to Levanto** is a good 2½-hour hike, passing over Punta Mesco with glorious views of the Cinque Terre to the south, Corsica to the west, and the Alps to the north.

Each town has something that passes for a beach (usually with lots of pebbles or slabs of terraced rock), but there is only one option for both sand and decent swimming—in Monterosso, just across from the train station. It's equipped with chairs, umbrellas, and snack bars.

Precautions

If you're hitting the trails, carry water with you, wear sturdy shoes (hiking boots are best), and have a hat and sunscreen handy. Note that the lesser-used trails aren't as well maintained as Trail No. 2. If you're undertaking the full Trail No. 1 hike, bring something to snack on as well as your water bottle. Note that currently the Via dell'Amore and the portion of Trail No. 2 between Manarola and Corniglia are closed indefinitely due to landslides.

■TIP→ Check weather reports, especially in late fall and winter; thunderstorms can make shelterless trails slippery and dangerous. Rain in October and November can cause landslides and close trails altogether.

Manarola

16 km (10 miles) southwest of La Spezia,
117 km (73 miles) southeast of Genoa.

The enchanting pastel houses of Manarola spill down a steep hill overlooking a spectacular turquoise swimming cove and a bustling harbor. The whole town is built on black rock. Above the town, ancient terraces still protect abundant vineyards and olive trees. This village is the center of wine and olive oil production in the region, and its streets are lined with shops selling local products.

Surrounded by steep terraced vineyards, Manarola's one road tumbles from the Chiesa di San Lorenzo (14th century) high above the village, down to the rocky port. Since the Cinque Terre wine cooperative is located in Groppo, a hamlet overlooking the village (reachable by foot or by the green park bus; ask at park offices for schedules), the vineyards are accessible. If you'd like to snap a shot of the most famous view of the town, you can walk from the port area to the cemetery above. Along the way you'll pass the town's playground, bathrooms, and a tap with clean drinking water.

GETTING HERE AND AROUND

Though it's possible to drive and park (in a lot above town, which means walking down), it's much easier to arrive by often overly crowded train. Trains run from La Spezia or Levanto; both are very short journeys and cost around €5.

VISITOR INFORMATION

CONTACT Manarola Welcome Center.
⊠ *Manarola train station, Via dell'Amore, Manarola* ☎ *0187/760511* ⊕ *www.parconazionale5terre.it.*

Sights

Manarola

TOWN | Enchanting pastel houses spill down a steep hill overlooking a spectacular turquoise swimming cove and a bustling harbor. The whole town is built on black rock. Above the town, ancient terraces still protect abundant vineyards and olive trees. This village is the center of the wine and olive oil production of the region, and its streets are lined with shops selling local products. ⊠ *Manarola* ☎ *0187/760511* ⊕ *www.parconazionale-5terre.it.*

Hotels

★ La Torretta

$$$$ | **HOTEL** | One of the Cinque Terre's few "boutique" hotels is in a 17th-century tower that sits high on the hill above the rainbow-hue village of Manarola, with truly lovely views of the terraced vineyards, colorful village homes, and the Mediterranean sea; inside, decor is chic, sleek, and antiques-bedecked. **Pros:** no-smoking policy; free luggage transfer; stellar staff. **Cons:** steep walk up to the hotel; some rooms are small; books up quickly. ⑤ *Rooms from: €350* ⊠ *Vico Volto 20, Cinque Terre, Manarola* ☎ *0187/920327* ⊕ *www.torrettas.com* ⊙ *Closed Nov.–Mar.* ⊷ *15 rooms* ⦿ *No Meals.*

Corniglia

27 km (17 miles) northwest of La Spezia,
100 km (60 miles) southeast of Genoa.

The buildings, narrow lanes, and stairways of Corniglia are strung together amid vineyards high on the cliffs. On a clear day, views of the entire coastal strip are excellent, from Elba in the south to the Italian Alps in the north. The high perch and lack of harbor make this farming community the most remote and therefore least crowded of the Cinque Terre. In fact, the 365 steps that lead up from the train station to the town center dissuade many tourists from making the hike to the village. You can also take the green park bus, but they run infrequently and are usually packed with tired hikers.

Corniglia is built along one road edged with small shops, bars, gelaterias, and restaurants. Midway along Via Fieschi is the Largo Taragio, the main square and heart of the village. Shaded by leafy trees and umbrellas, this is a lovely spot for a mid-hike gelato break.

GETTING HERE AND AROUND

This town has very limited parking and it's much simpler to take the train from either La Spezia or Levanto.

VISITOR INFORMATION

CONTACT Corniglia Welcome Center.
⊠ *Corniglia train station, Via alla Stazione, Corniglia* ☏ *0187/1857573* ⊕ *www. parconazionale5terre.it.*

Sights

Corniglia

TOWN | Stone buildings, narrow lanes, and stairways are strung together amid vineyards high on the cliffs; on a clear day views of the entire coastal strip are excellent. The high perch and lack of harbor make this farming community the most remote of the Cinque Terre. ⊠ *Corniglia* ☏ *0187/812523* ⊕ *www.parconazionale-5terre.it.*

San Pietro

CHURCH | On a pretty pastel square sits the 14th-century church of San Pietro. The rose window of marble imported from Carrara is impressive, particularly considering the work required to get it here. ⊠ *Via Fieschi 19, Corniglia* 🎫 *Free.*

Vernazza

27 km (17 miles) west of La Spezia, 96 km (59 miles) southeast of Genoa.

With its narrow streets and small squares, Vernazza is arguably the most charming of the Cinque Terre towns, and usually the most crowded. Historically, it was the most important of them and—since Vernazza was the only one fortunate enough to have a natural port—the wealthiest, as evidenced by the elaborate arcades, loggias, and marble work lining Via Roma and Piazza Marconi.

The village's pink slate-roof houses and colorful squares contrast with the remains of the medieval fort and castle, including two towers, in the old town. The Romans first inhabited this rocky spit of land in the 1st century. Today, Vernazza has a fairly lively social scene. Piazza Marconi looks out across Vernazza's small sandy beach to the sea, toward Monterosso. The numerous restaurants and bars crowd their tables and umbrellas on the outskirts of the piazza, creating a patchwork of sights and sounds that form one of the most unique and beautiful places in the world.

GETTING HERE AND AROUND

Driving to Vernazza is complicated, and it's much easier to take a short train ride from either La Spezia or Levanto. Trains run frequently.

VISITOR INFORMATION

CONTACT Vernazza Welcome Center. ⊠ *Vernazza train station, Via Roma 51, Vernazza* ☏ *0187/028316* ⊕ *www.parconazionale-5terre.it.*

Sights

If Mass is not going on (a cord blocks the entrance if it is), take a peek into the church of St. Margaret of Antioch, where little has changed since its enlargement in the 1600s. This 14th-century edifice has simple interiors but truly breathtaking views toward the sea—a stark contrast to the other more elaborate churches of the Cinque Terre.

On the other side of the piazza, stairs lead to a lookout fortress and cylindrical watchtower, built in the 11th century as protection against pirate attacks. For a small fee you can climb to the top of the tower for a spectacular view of the coastline.

Vernazza

TOWN | With narrow streets and small squares, the village that many consider to be the most charming of the five towns has the best access to the sea—a geographic reality that made the village wealthier than its neighbors, as evidenced by the elaborate arcades, loggias, and marble work. The village's pink, slate-roof houses and colorful squares contrast with the remains of the medieval fort and castle, including two towers, in the old town. The Romans first inhabited this rocky spit of land in the 1st century. Today, Vernazza has a fairly lively social scene. It's a great place to refuel with a hearty seafood lunch or linger in a café between links of the seaside hike. ⊠ *Vernazza* ☎ *0187/028316* ⊕ *www. parconazionale5terre.it.*

 Restaurants

Gambero Rosso

$$$ | **LIGURIAN** | Relax on Vernazza's main square at this fine trattoria looking out onto the church of Santa Maria d'Antiochi. Enjoy such delectable dishes as shrimp salad, vegetable torte, and *risotto alla ciccio* (with squid, prawns, and mussels). **Known for:** piazza view; fresh seafood; pesto. $ *Average main: €33* ⊠ *Piazza Marconi 7, Vernazza* ☎ *0187/812265* ⊕ *www.ristorantegamberorosso.net* ⊘ *Closed Thurs. and Nov.–late Mar.*

★ **Ristorante Belforte**

$$ | **LIGURIAN** | High above the sea in one of Vernazza's remaining medieval stone towers is this unique spot serving

delicious Cinque Terre cuisine such as branzino *sotto sale* (cooked under salt), *tagliolini al nero di seppia con gamberi* (fresh pasta with squid ink sauce and prawns), and *polpo di scoglio alla griglia* (grilled octopus). The setting is magnificent, so try for an outdoor table. **Known for:** incredible views; grilled octopus; lively atmosphere. $ *Average main: €20* ⊠ *Via Guidoni 42, Vernazza* ☎ *0187/812222* ⊕ *www.ristorantebelforte.it* ⊘ *Closed Tues. and Nov.–late Mar.*

 Hotels

La Malà

$ | **B&B/INN** | A cut above other lodging options in the Cinque Terre, these small guest rooms are equipped with flat-screen TVs, air-conditioning, marble showers, and comfortable bedding and have views of the sea or the port, which can also be enjoyed at their most bewitching from a shared terrace literally suspended over the Mediterranean. **Pros:** clean, fresh-feeling rooms; views; helpful, attentive staff. **Cons:** some stairs are involved; books up quickly; child-friendly (either a pro or a con). $ *Rooms from: €110* ⊠ *Via San Giovanni Battista 29, Vernazza* ☎ *334/2875718 mobile* ⊕ *www.lamala.it* ⊘ *Closed early Jan.–late Feb.* ⤹ *4 rooms* ⦿ *Free Breakfast.*

Monterosso al Mare

32 km (20 miles) northwest of La Spezia, 89 km (55 miles) southeast of Genoa.

It's the combined draw of beautiful beaches, rugged cliffs, crystal clear turquoise waters, and plentiful small hotels and restaurants that has made Monterosso al Mare the largest of the Cinque Terre villages (population 1,800) and also the busiest in midsummer.

And Monterosso has festivals enough to match its size. They start with the Lemon Festival in May. Then, on the second

Sunday after Pentecost, comes the Flower Festival of Corpus Christi: during the afternoon, the streets and alleyways of the historic center are decorated with thousands of colorful flower petals, set in beautiful designs, over which an evening procession passes. Finally, the Salted Anchovy and Olive Oil Festival takes place each year during the second weekend of September.

GETTING HERE AND AROUND

The largest of the "Five Lands," it's possible to drive and park nearby, but it's best to take the train either from La Spezia or Levanto.

VISITOR INFORMATION

CONTACT Monterosso al Mare Welcome Center. ⊠ *Monterosso al Mare train station, Via Fegina 40, Monterosso al Mare* ☎ *0187/817059* ⊕ *www.parconazionale-5terre.it.*

 Sights

Heading west from the train station, you pass through a tunnel and exit into the *centro storico* (historic center) of the village.

Monterosso al Mare

TOWN | Nestled into the wide valley that leads to the sea, Monterosso is built above numerous streams, which have been covered to make up the village's main streets. Via Buranco, the oldest street in Monterosso, leads to the most characteristic piazza of the village, Piazza Matteotti. Locals pass through here daily to shop at the supermarket and butcher. This piazza also contains the oldest and most typical wineshop in the village, Enoteca da Eliseo—stop here between 6 pm and midnight to share tables with fellow tourists and locals over a bottle of wine. There's also the Chiesa di San Francesco, built in the 12th century and an excellent example of the Ligurian Gothic style. Its distinctive black stripes and marble rose window make it one of the most photographed sites in the Cinque Terre.

Fegina, the newer side of the village (and site of the train station), has relatively modern homes ranging from the Liberty style (Art Nouveau) to the early 1970s. At the far eastern end of town, you'll run into a private sailing club sheltered by a vast rock carved with an impressive statue of Neptune. From here, you can reach the challenging trail to Levanto (a great 2½-hour hike). This trail has the added bonus of a five-minute detour to the ruins of a 14th-century monastery. The expansive view from this vantage point allowed the monks who were housed here to easily scan the waters for enemy ships that might invade the villages and alert residents to coming danger. Have your camera ready for this Cinerama-like vista.

The local outdoor market is held on Thursday and attracts crowds of tourists and villagers from along the coast to shop for everything from pots, pans, and underwear to fruits, vegetables, and fish. Often a few stands sell local art and crafts, as well as olive oil and wine. ⊠ *Monterosso al Mare* ☎ *0187/817059* ⊕ *www.parconazionale5terre.it.*

Restaurants

★ Enoteca Internazionale

$ | WINE BAR | Located on the main street, this bar offers a large selection of wines, both local and from farther afield, plus delicious light fare; its umbrella-covered patio is a welcoming spot to recuperate after a day of hiking. The bar's certified sommeliers are forthcoming with helpful suggestions on pairing local wines with their tasty bruschette. **Known for:** extensive local wine list; patio dining; helpful staff. ⑤ *Average main: €13* ⊠ *Via Roma 62, Monterosso al Mare* ☎ *0187/817278* ⊕ *www.enotecainternazionale.com* ⊙ *Closed Jan. and Feb.*

★ Miky

$$$ | SEAFOOD | This is arguably the best restaurant in Monterosso, specializing in tasty, fresh seafood dishes like grilled calamari and monkfish ravioli. If their *catalana* (poached lobster and shrimp with sliced raw fennel and carrot) happens to be on the menu, know that it's a winner. **Known for:** sunny seaside setting; fresh seafood; fine dining. $ *Average main: €28 ⊠ Via Fegina 104, Monterosso al Mare ☎ 0187/817608 ⊕ www.ristorante-miky.it ⊘ Closed Tues. and Nov.–Mar.*

 Hotels

Bellambra

$$$$ | **B&B/INN** | Modern rooms with charm and comfort in the heart of the old town make this place a terrific base for exploring the Cinque Terre. **Pros:** an apartment for up to six people; spacious rooms and bathrooms; central location. **Cons:** can be a bit noisy; no elevator with steep, narrow stairs; books up quickly. $ *Rooms from: €369 ⊠ Via Roma 64, Monterosso al Mare ☎ 392/0121912 mobile ⊕ www.bellambra5terre.com ⌁ 4 rooms ⦿ No Meals.*

★ Il Giardino Incantato

$$ | **B&B/INN** | With wood-beam ceilings and stone walls, the stylishly restored and updated rooms in this 16th-century house in the historic center of Monterosso ooze comfort and old-world charm. **Pros:** spacious rooms; gorgeous garden; excellent hosts. **Cons:** no views; no under-14s or pets; there are only four rooms so books up quickly. $ *Rooms from: €200 ⊠ Via Mazzini 18, Monterosso al Mare ☎ 0187/818315 ⊕ www.ilgiardinoincantato.net ⊘ Closed Nov.–Mar. ⌁ 4 rooms ⦿ Free Breakfast.*

Porto Roca

$$$ | **HOTEL** | Far from the madding crowds, Porto Roca is perched on the famous terraced cliffs right over the main beach, with large balconies to savor panoramic views of the magnificent sea. **Pros:** unobstructed sea views; tranquil location; shuttle bus into town (though walking there is eminently possible). **Cons:** two- or three-night minimum stay

in high season; back-facing rooms can be a bit dark; somewhat removed from town. $ *Rooms from: €210 ⊠ Via Corone 1, Monterosso al Mare ☎ 0187/817502 ⊕ www.portoroca.it ⊘ Closed early Nov.–early Apr. ⌁ 43 rooms ⦿ Free Breakfast.*

Lerici

106 km (66 miles) southeast of Genoa, 65 km (40 miles) west of Lucca.

Lerici, part of the Riviera di Levante, is on the spectacular Bay of La Spezia, otherwise known as the Gulf of Poets, and is famous for its natural beauty. Near Liguria's border with Tuscany, this picturesque village dates back to medieval times when, under the rule of Pisa, it fought cross-bay battles with the Genovese town of Portovenere, as well as with local pirates. The town is set on a magnificent coastline of gray cliffs jutting down into a crystal clear sea and surrounded by a national park that is like an unframed painting of pine forests, olive trees, and tiny colorful hamlets. The waterfront piazza is filled with trompe-l'oeil frescoed buildings, and seaside cafés line a charming little harbor that holds sailboats and *gozzi*, the typical small fishing boats of the area.

Several white-sand beaches and bathing establishments dot the 2-km (1-mile) walk along the bay from the village center to nearby San Terenzo. From the village, you can also reach some beautiful hiking trails that head southeast to both seaside and hilltop villages like Fiascherino, Tellaro, and Montemarcello.

GETTING HERE AND AROUND

By car, Lerici is less than a 10-minute drive west from the A12, with plenty of signage indicating the way. There's a large parking lot (fee) about a 10-minute walk along the seaside promenade from the center. By train, the closest station is either Sarzana (10-minute drive) or La Spezia Centrale (20-minute drive) on the main north–south line between Genoa and Pisa.

Cinque Terre and Riviera di Levante

VISITOR INFORMATION
CONTACT Lerici Tourism Office. ⊠ *Info-point, Via S. Biaggini 552 (next to Hotel Florida), Lerici* ☎ *0187/960700* ⊕ *www.stlerici.it.*

⊙ Sights

Castello di Lerici

CASTLE/PALACE | The promontory is dominated by this 13th-century Pisan castle, which now houses temporary art exhibitions and is a superb location for weddings as it overlooks the entire Gulf of Poets. ⊠ *Piazza S. Giorgio 1, Lerici* ☎ *0187/967840* ⊕ *www.stlerici.it/castello-di-lerici* ⊠ *€6* ☉ *Closed Mon. Oct.–May.*

🍴 Restaurants

Bontà Nascoste

$$$ | **ITALIAN** | In the local dialect, *bontà nascoste* means "hidden goodness," a reference to its back-alleyway location and consistently delicious dishes, which include fresh pasta, local fish, and a handful of meat choices. There are only six tables (and a couple more outside in summer), so reserve ahead. **Known for:** inventive seafood dishes; cozy atmosphere; crudo. ⑤ *Average main: €26* ⊠ *Via Cavour 52, Lerici* ☎ *0187/965500* ⊕ *www.bontanascoste.it* ☉ *No lunch Mon. and Wed.*

★ Gianni D'Amato

$$$ | **LIGURIAN** | Perched amid the clustered old houses in seaside Tellaro, 4 km (2½ miles) southeast of Lerici, this small, unpretentious family-run restaurant with

wooden tables and plenty of windows has become a foodie destination. The imaginative seafood-focused menu changes often, and the pretty building also houses a small inn (Locanda Miranda) with seven charming and comfortable rooms. **Known for:** locally sourced fish; cozy dining room; savory gelato and tiramisu. ⓢ *Average main: €32 ⊠ Via Fiascherino 92, Tellaro* ☎ *0187/964012* ⊕ *www.giannidamato.it* ⊘ *Closed Mon. and Nov.*

 ## Hotels

★ Doria Park

$$ | HOTEL | FAMILY | Its location—set amid hills of olive trees yet steps from the village center—makes this hotel with bright rooms and contemporary furnishings one of the best places to stay in Lerici. **Pros:** sea views; comfortable beds; free parking and convenient location near town and the beach. **Cons:** stairs, narrow paths, and elevator are not equipped for people with mobility issues; expensive restaurant; three-night minimum stay in summer. ⓢ *Rooms from: €164 ⊠ Via Carpanini 9, Lerici* ☎ *0187/967124* ⊕ *www. doriaparkhotel.it* ⇌ *44 rooms* ⦿⦿ *Free Breakfast.*

Florida

$$$ | HOTEL | FAMILY | Prepare to relax at this family-run seaside establishment, where one pleasure is lounging on one of the deck chairs on the hotel's rooftop solarium and enjoying its sea views. **Pros:** beachfront location; bay views from most rooms; abundant breakfast. **Cons:** a bit generic in character; can be noisy; small beds in some rooms. ⓢ *Rooms from: €209 ⊠ Lungomare Biaggini 35, Lerici* ☎ *0187/967332* ⊕ *www.hotelflorida. it* ⊘ *Closed late Dec.–early Jan.* ⇌ *40 rooms* ⦿⦿ *Free Breakfast.*

La Spezia

11 km (7 miles) northwest of Lerici, 103 km (64 miles) southeast of Genoa.

La Spezia is sometimes thought of as nothing but a large, industrialized naval port en route to the Cinque Terre and Portovenere; it does possess some charm, however, and it also gives you a look at a less tourist-focused part of the Riviera. Its palm-lined promenade, fertile citrus parks, renovated Liberty-style palazzi, and colorful balcony-lined streets make parts of La Spezia surprisingly beautiful. Monday through Saturday morning, you can stroll through the fresh fish, produce, and local cheese stalls at the outdoor market on Piazza Cavour, and on Friday take part in the busy flea market on Via Garibaldi. There's also modern Porto Mirabello, with a pool club, shops, and several restaurants that overlook the fleet of superyachts.

GETTING HERE AND AROUND

By car, take the exit for La Spezia off the A12. La Spezia Centrale train station is on the main north–south railway line between Genoa and Pisa.

VISITOR INFORMATION

CONTACT La Spezia Tourism Office. ⊠ *Museo Civico, Via del Prione 243, La Spezia* ☎ *0187/026152* ⊕ *www.visitspezia.it.*

 ## Sights

Castello di San Giorgio

CASTLE/PALACE | FAMILY | The remains of this massive 13th-century castle, atop a small hill above the modern town, now house a small museum dedicated to local archaeology. ⊠ *Via XXVII Marzo, La Spezia* ☎ *0187/751142* ⊕ *museodelcastello. museilaspezia.it* ⓣ *€6* ⊘ *Closed Mon.*

Restaurants

La Pia Centenaria

$ | **PIZZA** | Considered an institution, this white-walled, simply decorated pizzeria dates back to 1887. It gets quite busy at lunchtime, with locals inside or, in summer, on the patio munching happily on *farinata* (a chickpea pancake and a Ligurian delicacy) and thick-crust pizza served hot out of the wood-burning oven. **Known for:** affordable lunch menu; traditional Ligurian recipes; variety of pizza toppings. ⑤ *Average main: €6* ✉ *Via Magenta 12, La Spezia* ☎ *0187/739999* ⊕ *www.lapia.it* ◷ *Closed Sun.*

Portovenere

12 km (7 miles) south of La Spezia, 114 km (70 miles) southeast of Genoa.

The colorful facades and pedestrian-only *calata* (promenade) make Portovenere the quintessential Ligurian seaside village; it's often called the "sixth town" of the Cinque Terre—but with half the crowds. As a UNESCO World Heritage site, Portovenere is lined with tall, thin *terratetto* houses (town houses), which date from as far back as the 11th century and which were connected in a wall-like formation to protect against attacks by Pisans and local pirates. Its tiny *carruggi* (alleylike passageways) lead to an array of charming shops, homes, and gardens, and eventually to the village's impressive Castle Doria, high on the olive-tree-covered hill. To the west, standing guard over the Mediterranean, is the picturesque medieval Chiesa di San Pietro, once the site of a temple to Venus (Venere in Italian), from which Portovenere gets its name. Nearby, in a rocky area leading to the sea, is Byron's Cave, one of the poet's favorite spots for swimming out into the sea.

GETTING HERE AND AROUND

By car from the port city of La Spezia, follow the signs for Portovenere. It's about a 20-minute winding drive along the sea through small fishing villages. From La Spezia train station you can hire a taxi for about €30. By bus from Via Garibaldi in La Spezia (a 10-minute walk from the train station) it takes about 30 minutes.

VISITOR INFORMATION

CONTACT Portovenere Tourist Office.
✉ *Piazza Bastreri 7, Portovenere* ☎ *0187/790691* ⊕ *www.portovenere. com.*

Sights

Grotto Arpaia

CAVE | Near the entrance to the huge, strange Grotto Arpaia, at the base of the sea-swept cliff, is a plaque recounting the strength and courage of Lord Byron (1788–1824) as he swam across the gulf to the village of San Terenzo, near Lerici, to visit his friend Shelley (1792–1822). The poet is said to have written his lengthy narrative poem *Childe Harold's Pilgrimage* in Portovenere. ✉ *SP530 92, Portovenere.*

★ San Pietro

CHURCH | With its black-and-white-striped exterior, this 13th-century Gothic church is a spectacular landmark recognizable from far out at sea and upon entering the village. It is built on the site of an ancient pagan shrine, on a formidable solid mass of rock above the Grotto Arpaia. There's a fantastic view of the Cinque Terre coastline from the church's front porch. ✉ *Piazza Lazzaro Spallanzani, Portovenere* ☎ *0187/790684* ⊕ *www.parrocchiaporto-venere.org.*

10

🍴 Restaurants

Bacicio

$ | WINE BAR | This enoteca and antipasto bar is popular with locals and tourists looking for typical regional dishes, fresh fish, and a lengthy wine list. The owner designed the entire place, right down to the tables and chairs made from anchors and old boats. **Known for:** anchovies cooked many ways; fresh fish crostini; generous portions at reasonable prices. ⑤ *Average main: €14* ✉ *Via Cappellini 17, Portovenere* ☎ *0187/793031* ⊘ *Closed Thurs. in summer, evenings in winter.*

⭐ Il Timone

$$ | LIGURIAN | FAMILY | Find some of the best food in Portovenere at this airy, affordable, and casual portside restaurant. The menu is typical "Ligure," ranging from meat to pasta with seafood, and also offers *farinata* (fried pancake), focaccia, and pizza. **Known for:** comfortable patio in summer; all-inclusive tasting menus; Ligurian farinata and pizza. ⑤ *Average main: €17* ✉ *Via Olivo 29, Portovenere* ☎ *0187/914595* ⊕ *www.pizzeriailtimone.it* ⊘ *Closed Tues. and mid-Jan.–Feb. No lunch Mon. and Wed.–Fri.*

Locanda Lorena

$$$ | LIGURIAN | Across the small bay of Portovenere lies the rugged island of Palmaria, where there are only a few restaurants (making for high prices), including this place with lovely seafront views and headliners like fresh pasta and local fish. To get here, take the restaurant's free Riva boat from the Portovenere jetty. **Known for:** quaint seaside setting; catch-of-the-day specials; incredible Portovenere views. ⑤ *Average main: €28* ✉ *Palmaria Island, Portovenere* ☎ *0187/792370* ⊕ *www.locandalorena.com* ⊘ *Closed Nov.*

🛏 Hotels

Grand Hotel Portovenere

$$$$ | HOTEL | This 13th-century Franciscan monastery turned elegant hotel incorporates modern enhancements while retaining the structure's impressive rose facade, arches, and frescoes. **Pros:** excellent location and views; comfortable beds and mostly spacious rooms; shuttle service to a private beach. **Cons:** some rooms are small; some room amenities are limited, no in-room tea or coffeemaker; expensive restaurant and bar. ⑤ *Rooms from: €409* ✉ *Via Giuseppe Garibaldi 5, Portovenere* ☎ *0187/777751* ⊕ *www.portoveneregrand.com* ⊘ *Closed Nov.–late Mar.* 🛏 *46 rooms* ⦿ *Free Breakfast.*

Hotel Belvedere

$$ | HOTEL | True to its name (which means "nice view"), the best rooms in this sunny Liberty-style building face the bay of Portovenere, with lovely vistas of Palmaria Island and the Gulf of Poets. **Pros:** sea views from the terrace and some rooms; family rooms available; good value for the location despite plain decor. **Cons:** modernization required; limited parking; rooms facing the street are noisy. ⑤ *Rooms from: €160* ✉ *Via Giuseppe Garibaldi 26, Portovenere* ☎ *0187/790608* ⊕ *www.belvedereportovenere.it* ⊘ *Closed Nov.–Mar.* 🛏 *17 rooms* ⦿ *Free Breakfast.*

Levanto

47 km (29 miles) northwest of Portovenere, 60 km (36 miles) southeast of Genoa.

Nestled at the end of a valley of pine forests, olive groves, vineyards, and medieval villages lies this sunny seaside town, an alternative and usually less expensive base for exploring the Cinque Terre and the Riviera di Levante.

By car, take the Carodanno/Levanto exit off the A12 for 25 minutes to the town center. By train, Levanto is on the main north–south railway, one stop north of Monterosso.

VISITOR INFORMATION
CONTACT Levanto Tourism Office. ☒ *Piazza Cavour 1, Levanto* ☎ *0187/808125* ⊕ *www.visitlevanto.it.*

Sights

Levanto
TOWN | With its long sandy beach, colorful old quarter, and breathtakingly beautiful hiking paths, Levanto has become a haven not only for sun worshippers but also for divers, surfers, and hikers. The path between Levanto and Monterosso al Mare, about a 2½-mile hike, is freely accessible. This is also an ideal starting point for day trips by train or boat to many interesting places along the Riviera, such as Portovenere, Lerici, Tellaro, and Fiascherino, in the direction of La Spezia; and Portofino, Santa Margherita, Camogli, and Sestri Levante, in the direction of Genoa. ☒ *Levanto* ☎ *0187/808125* ⊕ *www.visitlevanto.it.*

Sestri Levante

37 km (22 miles) northwest of Levanto, 28 km (17 miles) southeast of Santa Margherita Ligure.

Halfway between the Cinque Terre and Portofino lies this lovely seaside resort. The old village is on a peninsula with the beautiful Baia del Silenzio on one side and the Baia delle Favole and promenade on the other. The Baia delle Favole (*favole* means "fairy tales") was named in honor of the Danish author Hans Christian Andersen, who visited Sestri for a short time.

By car, it is a five-minute drive off the A12. The Sestri Levante train station is on the main north–south train line between Genoa and Pisa; it's just a five-minute walk to the beach and old village.

VISITOR INFORMATION
CONTACT Sestri Levante Tourist Office. ☒ *Corso Colombo 50, Sestri Levante* ☎ *0185/478530* ⊕ *www.sestri-levante. net.*

Beaches

Baia del Silenzio
BEACH | The Bay of Silence is a sandy cove east of the pedestrian-only street in the old town, with pastel-color bars and restaurants edging the sand and bobbing boats dotting the horizon. It's a picture-postcard public beach and an idyllic setting for a dip in the Mediterranean, frequented mostly by locals and some visiting crowds in summer. You can also take a short walk up to the Convento dei Cappuccini, a church dedicated to the Virgin Mary. The monastery was built at the end of the 17th century and offers a spectacular panoramic view. **Amenities**: food and drink. **Best for**: solitude, walking. ☒ *Baia del Silenzio, Sestri Levante* ☎ *0185/478530* ⊕ *www.sestri-levante.net.*

Restaurants

Cantina del Polpo
$$$ | **LIGURIAN** | This cozy former cantina with wood paneling, a fireplace, and local maritime memorabilia serves some of the best dishes in town. Using the bounty of the two bays that frame the village, its chefs create inventive tasting menus and standout mains, which, in addition to expertly seasoned fish, include homemade pastas and gnocchi. **Known for:** friendly staff; creative seafood-focused tasting menus at affordable prices; hard-to-find regional wines. ⑤ *Average main: €25* ☒ *Via Camillo Benso Cavour 2, Sestri Levante* ☎ *0185/485296* ⊕ *www.*

cantinadelpolpo.it ⊗ Closed Wed. and mid-Feb.–mid-Mar.

Hotels

Grand Hotel dei Castelli

$$$$ | B&B/INN | You can see the Baia delle Favole from this castle-turned-hotel on a promontory, and you just might feel you've been transported to a fairy tale here. **Pros:** grand setting with spectacular views of the two bays; beautiful grounds; private inlet. **Cons:** some rooms and public areas have a dated feel; steep walk (or slow elevator) down to the beach; guests are charged for private beach access. ⑤ Rooms from: €300 ⊠ Via Penisola di Levante 26, Sestri Levante ☎ 0185/487020 ⊕ www.hoteldeicastelli.it/en ⊗ Closed Nov.–mid-Mar. ⇆ 50 rooms ¶⊙¶ Free Breakfast.

Santa Margherita Ligure

31 km (19 miles) southeast of Genoa.

A beautiful old resort town favored by well-to-do Italians, Santa Margherita Ligure has everything a Riviera playground should have—plenty of palm trees and attractive hotels, cafés, and a marina packed with yachts. Some of the older buildings have trompe-l'oeil frescoed exteriors that are typical of this part of the Riviera. For many people, this pleasant, convenient base represents the perfect balance on the Italian Riviera: more spacious than the Cinque Terre; less glitzy than San Remo; more relaxing than Genoa and environs; and ideally situated for day trips, such as an excursion to Portofino.

GETTING HERE AND AROUND

By car, take the Rapallo exit off the A12 and follow the signs, about a 10-minute drive. The Santa Margherita Ligure train station is on the main north–south line between Genoa and Pisa.

VISITOR INFORMATION

CONTACT Santa Margherita Ligure Tourism Office. ⊠ Piazza Vittorio Veneto, Santa Margherita Ligure ☎ 0185/287485 ⊕ www.comunesml.it.

Restaurants

Oca Bianca

$$ | EUROPEAN | In a departure from the local norm, meat dishes, not seafood, are the specialty on the menu at Oca Bianca. Choices include tasty pastas as well as mouthwatering preparations of beef, lamb, pork, and octopus. **Known for:** lively outdoor seating in summer; multiple steak preparations; classic sauces for meat dishes. ⑤ Average main: €24 ⊠ Via XXV Aprile 21, Santa Margherita Ligure ☎ 0185/288411 ⊕ www.ristoranteocabianca.it ⊗ Closed Mon. No lunch Tues.–Sat.

★ U Giancu

$$ | LIGURIAN | Although the walls of Fausto Oneto's restaurant are covered in original cartoons, and a playground is the main feature of the outdoor seating area, this chef-owner is completely serious about his cooking, which follows the seasons. His own garden provides the freshest possible vegetables, the wine list (ask to visit the cantina) is excellent, and there are lively morning Ligurian cooking lessons. **Known for:** lamb dishes; creative and playful setting; vegetables fresh from the restaurant's garden. ⑤ Average main: €20 ⊠ Via San Massimo 78, Località San Massimo ☎ 0185/261212 ⊕ www.ugiancu.it ⊗ Closed Wed. and Nov. No lunch Mon.–Sat.

Hotels

Grand Hotel Miramare

$$$$ | RESORT | Classic Riviera elegance prevails at this palatial hotel overlooking the bay, where antique furniture and crystal chandeliers fill the high-ceiling rooms. **Pros:** top-notch service close to the beach; wellness and fitness centers; well-maintained rooms and marble

bathrooms. **Cons:** traffic in summer from the road in front of the hotel; sea access is down the grand entrance staircase and across a busy street; beach is run by different managment than the hotel. $ *Rooms from: €820* ⊠ *Via Milite Ignoto 30, Santa Margherita Ligure* ☏ *0185/287013* ⊕ *www.grandhotelmiramare.it* ⊘ *Closed Nov.–late Mar.* ⊷ *72 rooms* ⏐⊙⏐ *Free Breakfast.*

Hotel Continental

$$$$ | **HOTEL** | A stately seaside mansion surrounded by a lush garden shaded by tall palms and a pine trees offers stylish accommodations done in a blend of classic furnishings, mostly inspired by the 19th century. **Pros:** lovely location; private beach; panoramic views from some rooms and the dining area. **Cons:** rooms in the annex need to be refurbished; beach access included in room rates, but lounge chairs and cabanas are extra; located off a road that gets busy in high season. $ *Rooms from: €445* ⊠ *Via Pagana 8, Santa Margherita Ligure* ☏ *0185/286512* ⊕ *www.hotel-continental.it* ⊘ *Closed Jan.–mid-Mar.* ⊷ *68 rooms* ⏐⊙⏐ *Free Breakfast.*

Hotel Jolanda

$$$ | **HOTEL** | They may not have sea views, but the stylish, comfortable rooms here are decorated in a classic style, and some have large balconies. **Pros:** reasonable rates in a high-price area; outdoor areas for dining and relaxing; spa and massage options. **Cons:** no sea view; street noise can be intrusive; some rooms and indoor common areas feel cramped. $ *Rooms from: €252* ⊠ *Via Luisito Costa 6, Santa Margherita Ligure* ☏ *0185/287512* ⊕ *www.hoteljolanda.it* ⊘ *Closed mid-Oct.–Dec.* ⊷ *45 rooms* ⏐⊙⏐ *Free Breakfast.*

Santa Margherita Palace & Spa

$$$ | **HOTEL** | Just a short walk from the old town, this well-kept and well-equipped hotel offers modern rooms with contemporary furnishings and spa and gym facilities. **Pros:** handy central location; helpful staff; modern bathrooms (some rooms have Jacuzzis). **Cons:** the neighborhood is less charming than the old town and seaside; no beach access; expensive breakfast. $ *Rooms from: €256* ⊠ *Via Roma 9, Santa Margherita Ligure* ☏ *0185/287139* ⊕ *www.santamargheritapalace.com* ⊘ *Closed Nov.–Mar.* ⊷ *53 rooms* ⏐⊙⏐ *No Meals.*

Portofino

5 km (3 miles) southeast of Santa Margherita Ligure, 36 km (22 miles) east of Genoa.

One of the most photographed villages along the coast, with a decidedly romantic and highly affluent aura, Portofino has long been a popular destination for the rich and famous. Once an ancient Roman colony and taken by the Republic of Genoa in 1229, it has also been ruled by the French, English, Spanish, and Austrians, as well as by marauding bands of 16th-century pirates. Elite British tourists first flocked to the lush harbor in the mid-1800s. Some of Europe's wealthiest drop anchor in Portofino in summer, but they stay out of sight by day, appearing in the evening after buses and boats have carried off the day-trippers.

There's not actually much to *do* in Portofino other than stroll around the wee harbor, see the castle, walk to Punta del Capo, browse at the pricey boutiques, and sip a coffee while people-watching. However, weaving through picture-perfect cliff-side gardens and gazing at yachts framed by the sapphire Ligurian Sea and the cliffs of Santa Margherita can make for quite a relaxing afternoon. There are also several tame, photo-friendly hikes into the hills to nearby villages.

Unless you're traveling on a deluxe budget, you may want to stay in Camogli or Santa Margherita Ligure rather than at one of Portofino's few very expensive hotels. Restaurants and cafés are also pricey: don't expect to have a beer here for much under €10.

GETTING HERE AND AROUND

By car, exit at Rapallo off the A12 and follow the blue signs (about a 20-minute drive mostly along the coast). Trying to reach Portofino by bus or car on the single narrow road can be a nightmare in summer and on holiday weekends.

The nearest train station is Santa Margherita Ligure. No trains go directly to Portofino: you must stop at Santa Margherita, then take public Bus No. 782 from there (€5). Alternatively, you can take a boat from Santa Margherita.

Portofino can be reached from Santa Margherita on foot: it's about a 60-minute walk along the sea, but be aware that many parts of the narrow road have no sidewalk.

VISITOR INFORMATION

CONTACT Portofino Tourism Office. ⊠ *Via Roma 35, Portofino* ☎ *0185/215037* ⊕ *www.comune.portofino.genova.it.*

Sights

Abbazia di San Fruttuoso (*Abbey of San Fruttuoso*)

CHURCH | A medieval stronghold built by the Benedictines of Monte Cassino protects a minuscule fishing village that can be reached only on foot or by water—a 20-minute boat ride from Portofino and also reachable from Camogli, Santa Margherita Ligure, and Rapallo. The restored abbey is now the property of a national conservation fund (FAI) and occasionally hosts temporary exhibitions; it also contains the tombs of some illustrious members of the Doria family. Plan on spending a few hours enjoying the abbey and grounds, and perhaps lunching at one of the modest beachfront trattorias nearby (open only in summer). Boatloads of visitors can make this place very crowded very fast; you might appreciate it most off-season. ⊠ *Portofino* ✈ *15-min*

boat ride or 2-hr walk northwest of Portofino* ☎ *0185/772703* ⊕ *www.fondoambiente.it* ☜ *€9* ⊘ *Closed Mon. Nov.–Feb.* ⚲ *Reservations essential.*

San Giorgio

CHURCH | This small church, sitting on a ridge above Portofino, is said to contain the relics of its namesake, brought back from the Holy Land by the Crusaders. Portofino enthusiastically celebrates St. George's Day every April 23. ⊠ *Above harbor, Salita San Giorgio, Portofino* ☜ *Free.*

Beaches

Paraggi

BEACH | The only sand beach near Portofino is at Paraggi, a cove on the road between Santa Margherita Ligure and Portofino. The bus will stop here on request. **Amenities:** food and drink. **Best for:** swimming, walking. ⊠ *Via Strada Provinciale, Portofino.*

Punta Portofino

VIEWPOINT | Pristine views can be had from the deteriorating *faro* (lighthouse) at Punta Portofino, a 15-minute walk along the point that begins at the southern end of the port. Along the seaside path you can see numerous impressive, sprawling private residences behind high iron gates. **Amenities:** none. **Best for:** walking. ⊠ *Viale Rainusso 1, Portofino.*

🍴 Restaurants

Ristorante Puny

$$$ | LIGURIAN | If you want to be in the middle of everything and dine well, and don't mind spending a small fortune, then you'll want (and need) a reservation at this waterfront restaurant in Portofino. Quite simply, it's *the* place to be seen while dining on baked fish and homemade pasta dishes. **Known for:** pappardelle al portofino (with tomato and pesto sauce); baked mini octopus; dining right on the port. ⑤ *Average main:*

€32 ⊠ Piazza Martiri dell'Olivetta 4–5, on harbor, Portofino ☎ 0185/269037 ⊕ www. punyportofino.com ⊘ Closed Thurs. and Dec.–Feb.

Coffee and Quick Bites

Canale

$ | BAKERY | If the staggering prices at virtually all of Portofino's cafés and restaurants are enough to ruin your appetite, join the long line outside this family-run bakery where you will find more affordable eats. At this takeaway spot, the focaccia is baked on-site, along with all kinds of sandwiches and other refreshments. **Known for:** takeout only; one of few budget options in Portofino; delicious pastries. ⑤ *Average main: €10 ⊠ Via Roma 30, Portofino ☎ 0185/269248 ⊕ www.panificiocanale.it ⊘ Closed Wed. and Nov.*

🛏 Hotels

Belmond Hotel Splendido

$$$$ | HOTEL | FAMILY | This 1920s luxury hotel oozes charm, taste, and lovely scenery, with a particular attention to color—from the coordinated floral linens in corals and gold in the guest rooms to the fresh flowers in the reception rooms, the two restaurants, and on the large terrace. **Pros:** rooms have garden or sea views; lovely manicured grounds; attentive staff. **Cons:** be prepared to spend upward of €100 for a simple lunch for two; pool and other common areas can be noisy because of the kid-friendly atmosphere; location makes it a hike to get to the center of Portofino. ⑤ *Rooms from: €2650 ⊠ Viale Baratta 16, Portofino ☎ 0185/267801 ⊕ www.belmond. com/hotel-splendido-portofino ⊘ Closed Oct.–early June ⇴ 67 rooms ⑩ Free Breakfast.*

Eight Hotel Portofino

$$$$ | HOTEL | At this intimate hotel, comfortable and soothingly designed guest rooms—some with canopy beds, pastel walls, and ultramodern bathrooms—are spread across two small 19th-century town houses on a quiet backstreet. **Pros:** walking distance to the harbor and village; private garden; comfortable beds and a choice of pillows. **Cons:** some lower-level rooms don't receive much light; no sea views; some rooms are small. ⑤ *Rooms from: €935 ⊠ Via Del Fondaco 11, Portofino ☎ 0185/26991 ⊕ portofino. eighthotels.it ⊘ Closed Oct.–Easter ⇴ 18 rooms ⑩ Free Breakfast.*

Activities

HIKING

If you have the stamina, you can hike to the Abbazia di San Fruttuoso from Portofino. It's a steep climb at first, and the walk takes about ½ hours one-way. If you're extremely ambitious and want to make a day of it, you can hike another 2½ hours all the way to Camogli. Much more modest hikes from Portofino include a one-hour uphill walk to Cappelletta delle Gave, a bit inland in the hills, from where you can continue downhill to Santa Margherita Ligure (another 1½ hours); there is also a gently undulating paved trail leading to the beach at Paraggi (½ hour). Finally, there's a 2½-hour hike from Portofino that heads farther inland to Ruta, through Olmi and Pietre Strette. The trails are well marked, and maps are available at the tourist information offices in Rapallo, Santa Margherita Ligure, Portofino, and Camogli.

Camogli

15 km (9 miles) northwest of Portofino, 20 km (12 miles) southeast of Genoa.

Camogli, at the edge of the large promontory and nature reserve known as the Portofino Peninsula, has always been a town of sailors. By the 19th century it was leasing its ships throughout the continent. Today, multicolor houses, staircases with incredible sea views, and a massive 17th-century seawall mark this appealing harbor community, which is perhaps as beautiful as Portofino but without the glamour. When exploring on foot, don't miss the antiquated second harbor, reached through a narrow archway at the northern end of the first one.

GETTING HERE AND AROUND

By car, exit the A12 at Recco and follow the signs. There are several parking lots (fee) near the village center. Camogli is on the main north–south railway line between Genoa and La Spezia.

VISITOR INFORMATION

CONTACT Camogli Tourism Office. ⊠ *Via XX Settembre 33, Camogli* ☎ *0185/771066* ⊕ *www.welcomecamogli.it.*

Sights

Ruta

TRAIL | The footpaths that leave from Ruta, 4 km (2½ miles) east of Camogli, thread through rugged terrain and contain a multitude of plant species. Weary hikers are sustained by stunning views of the Riviera di Levante from various vantage points along the way. ⊠ *Camogli.*

San Rocco, San Nicolò, and Punta Chiappa

TOWN | From Camogli, you can reach these hamlets along the western coast of the peninsula either on foot or by boat. They're more natural and less fashionable than those facing south on the eastern coast. In the small Romanesque church at San Nicolò, sailors who survived dangerous voyages came to offer thanks. ⊠ *Camogli.*

Restaurants

Vento Ariel

$$ | **SEAFOOD** | This friendly restaurant serves some of the best seafood in town on the covered terrace or the indoor patio with wicker chairs, where you can watch the bustling activity in the old port. Only the freshest catches are presented; try the "Bagnun" anchovy soup or any of the pastas. **Known for:** outdoor seating with views; fresh seafood; relaxed atmosphere. ⑤ *Average main: €18* ⊠ *Calata Porticciolo 1, Camogli* ☎ *0185/771080* ⊕ *www.ventoariel.it* ⊙ *Closed Wed., 10 days in Dec., and weekdays Jan.–mid-Feb. in bad weather.*

Coffee and Quick Bites

Revello

$ | **LIGURIAN** | You'll know this focacceria and pasticceria by the line out the door, as you walk along the beach before entering the archway to the old port. This tiny spot—where you can see focaccia being baked through a window into its kitchen—specializes in Liguria's favorite bread, *farinata* or chickpea flatbread (baked late afternoons from October to March) and several flavors of *camogliesi* (rum-filled is the original), a sweet that the shop's owner, Giacomo, invented in 1970. **Known for:** camogliesi sweets; wide variety of focaccia flavors; no seating, so take your treats away. ⑤ *Average main: €5* ⊠ *Via Giuseppe Garibaldi 183, Camogli* ☎ *0185/770777* ⊕ *www.revellocamogli. com* ⊙ *Closed 3 wks in Jan. and 2 wks in mid-Sept.*

🛏 Hotels

Cenobio dei Dogi

$$$ | **HOTEL** | Perched majestically above Camogli's beaches, the former summer palace of Genoa's doges features many guest rooms with expansive balconies and commanding vistas of the city's port. **Pros:** location and setting are wonderful; pool and gardens; direct access to private beach. **Cons:** books quickly in high season; plain decor in some rooms; neighborhood is less charming than the old town. ⑤ *Rooms from: €259* ⊠ *Via Nicolò Cuneo 34, Camogli* ☎ *0185/7241* ⊕ *www.cenobio.it* ⤙ *103 rooms* ⑩ *Free Breakfast.*

★ Locanda I Tre Merli

$$ | B&B/INN | In a typical Ligurian terratetto on the old port, this charming *locanda,* or inn, is reminiscent of old-world voyages but with the amenities to make it a comfortable and relaxing stop for today's traveler. **Pros:** friendly staff; quaint port location and views; small spa with whirlpool tub and Turkish bath. **Cons:** can be a bit noisy in the summer months; located right on the port, so you have to park a distance away; narrow corridors. Ⓢ *Rooms from: €135* ⊠ *Via Scalo 5, Camogli* ☎ *0185/776752* ⊕ *www. locandaitremerli.com* ⇩ *5 rooms* �◉ *No Meals.*

Villa Rosmarino

$$$$ | B&B/INN | A beautiful Ligurian villa in the Camogli hills offers chic, contemporary, and comfortable accommodations along with well-manicured gardens and outdoor sitting areas, arbors, and a welcoming pool. **Pros:** stylish modern decor; lovely garden with pool; excellent breakfast. **Cons:** some rooms are small and have minimal storage; the hike uphill is not ideal in summer months; parking can be challenging. Ⓢ *Rooms from: €301* ⊠ *Via Figari 38, Camogli* ☎ *0185/771580* ⊕ *www.villarosmarino.com* ☉ *Closed Nov.–Feb.* ⇩ *6 rooms* ◉ *Free Breakfast.*

Genoa

20 km (12 miles) northwest of Camogli, 144 km (89 miles) south of Milan.

Genoa (Genova in Italian) was the birthplace of Christopher Columbus, but the city's proud history predates the famous explorer by hundreds of years. Genoa was already an important trading station by the 3rd century BC, when the Romans conquered Liguria. The Middle Ages and the Renaissance saw it rise to become a jumping-off place for the Crusaders, a commercial center of tremendous wealth and prestige, and a strategic bone of international contention. A network of fortresses defending the city connected by a wall second only in length to the Great Wall of China was constructed in the hills above, and Genoa's bankers, merchants, and princes adorned the city with palaces, churches, and impressive art collections.

Crammed into a thin crescent of land between sea and mountains, Genoa expanded up rather than out, taking on the form of a multilayer wedding cake, with churches, streets, and entire residential neighborhoods built on others' rooftops. Public elevators and funiculars are as common as buses and trains.

With its impressive palaces and museums, one of the largest medieval city centers in Europe, and an elaborate network of ancient hilltop fortresses, Genoa may be just the dose of culture you're looking for. Europe's biggest boat show, the annual Salone Nautico Internazionale, is held here. Fine restaurants are abundant, and classical dance and music are richly represented. The Teatro Carlo Felice is the local opera venue, and it's where the internationally renowned annual Niccolò Paganini Violin Contest takes place.

If you're planning to do much sightseeing, consider investing in a Genova Museum Card (€15), which allows entry to all 28 of the city-administered museums as well as all AMT transport services within a 24-hour period. Buy one at most of the museums included in the package or online at ⊕ *www.museidigenova.it/en/museum-card.* More information on this and other tourist passes are available from the tourist office in Via Garibaldi.

GETTING HERE AND AROUND

By car, take the Genoa Ovest exit off the A12 and take the upper bridge (*sopraelevata*) to the second exit, Genova Centro–Piazza Corvetto. Be forewarned: driving in Genoa is harrowing and best avoided whenever possible. If you want to see the city on a day trip, go by train; regular service operates to and from Genoa's two main stations, Principe and Brignole. If you're staying in the city, park in a garage or by valet and travel by foot and taxi throughout your stay.

The best way by far to get around Genoa is on foot, with the occasional assistance of public transportation. Many of the more interesting districts are either entirely closed to traffic, have roads so narrow that no car could fit, or are, even at the best of times, blocked by gridlock. Although it might seem a daunting task, exploring the city is made simple by its geography. The historical center of Genoa occupies a relatively narrow strip of land running between the mountains and the sea. You can easily visit the most important monuments in one or two days. The main bus station in Genoa is at Piazza Principe. Local buses operated by the municipal transport company, AMT, serve the steep valleys that run to some of the towns along the western coast. Tickets may be bought at local bus stations or at newsstands. (You must have a ticket before you board.) This company also operates the funicular railways and the elevators that service the steeper sections of the city.

CONTACTS AMT. ⊠ *Palazzo Ducale, Molo* ☎ *848/000030, 010/5582414* ⊕ *www. amt.genova.it.* **Stazione Principe.** ⊠ *Piazza del Principe, San Teodoro* ⊕ *www.trenitalia.com.*

VISITOR INFORMATION
CONTACT Genoa Tourism Office. ⊠ *Via Garibaldi 12/r, Maddalena* ☎ *010/5572903* ⊕ *www.visitgenoa.it.*

◉ Sights

THE MEDIEVAL CORE AND POINTS ABOVE

The medieval center of Genoa, threaded with tiny streets flanked by 11th-century portals, is roughly the area between the port and Piazza de Ferrari. This mazelike pedestrian zone is officially called the Caruggi District, but the Genovese, in their matter-of-fact way, simply refer to the area as the place of the *vicoli* (alleys). In this warren of narrow cobbled streets extending north from Piazza Caricamento, the city's oldest churches sit among tiny shops selling antique furniture, coffee, cheese, rifles, wine, gilt picture frames, camping gear, and even live fish. The 500-year-old apartment buildings lean so precariously that penthouse balconies nearly touch those across the street, blocking what little sunlight would have shone through to the cobblestones. Wealthy Genovese built their homes in this quarter in the 16th century, and prosperous guilds—such as the goldsmiths for whom Vico degli Indoratori and Via degli Orefici were named—set up shop here.

Castelletto
VIEWPOINT | To reach this charming neighborhood high above the city center, you take one of Genoa's historical municipal elevators that whisk you skyward from Piazza del Portello, at the end of Galleria Garibaldi, for a spectacular view of the old city. ⊠ *Piazza del Portello, Castelletto* 🚋 *Free.*

Cimitero Monumentale di Staglieno
CEMETERY | One of the most famous of Genovese landmarks is this bizarrely beautiful cemetery; its fanciful marble and bronze sculptures sprawl haphazardly across a hillside on the outskirts of town. A pantheon holds indoor tombs and some remarkable works like an 1878 *Eve* by Villa. Don't miss Rovelli's 1896 **Tomba Raggio,** which shoots Gothic spires out of the hillside forest. The cemetery began operation in 1851 and has been lauded by such visitors as Mark Twain and Evelyn Waugh. It covers a good deal of ground (allow at least half a day to explore). Take Bus Nos. 13 or 14 from the Stazione Genova Brignole, Bus No. 34 from Stazione Principe, or a taxi. ⊠ *Piazzale Resasco 2, Genoa* ☎ *010/5576470* ⊕ *www.staglieno.comune. genova.it* 🚋 *Free (€5 guided tours).*

Genoa

Sights ▼

Restaurants ▼

Coffee and Quick Bites ▼

Hotels ▼

Ferrovia Genova–Casella

TRAIN/TRAIN STATION | FAMILY | The Genova–Casella Railroad is a good way to get a sense of the rugged landscape around Genoa; the train departs about every 90 minutes, and a bus supplements some routes. In operation since 1929, it runs from Piazza Manin in Genoa (follow Via Montaldo from the center of town, or take Bus No. 34 or 36 to the piazza) through the beautiful countryside above the city, arriving in the rural hill town Casella. The tiny train traverses precarious switchbacks that afford sweeping views of the Ligurian hills. In Casella Paese (the last stop) you can hike, eat lunch, or check out the view and ride back. Canova (two stops from the end of the line) is the start of two possible hikes: a two-hour (one-way) trek to a small sanctuary, Santuario della Vittoria, and a grueling four-hour hike to the hill town of Creto. Another worthwhile stop is Sant'Olcese Tullo, where you can take a half-hour (one-way) walk through the Sentiero Botanico di Ciaé, a botanical garden and forest refuge with a tiny medieval castle. ⊠ *Genoa* ☎ *010/5582414* ⊕ *www.ferroviagenovacasella.it* ☜ *€3 one-way.*

Galleria Nazionale di Palazzo Spinola

ART MUSEUM | Housed in the richly adorned Palazzo Spinola north of Piazza Soziglia, this beautiful museum contains masterpieces by Luca Giordano and Guido Reni. The *Ecce Homo*, by Antonello da Messina (1430–79), is a hauntingly beautiful painting, of historical interest because it was the Sicilian Antonello who first brought Flemish oil paints and techniques to Italy from his sojourns in the Low Countries. Or so some contend. ⊠ *Piazza Pellicceria 1, Genoa* ☎ *010/2705300* ⊕ *www.palazzospinola. beniculturali.it* ☜ *€10 with Palazzo Reale* ⊙ *Closed Sun. and Mon. (except 1st and 3rd Sun. of month; free entry 1st Sun.).*

Granarolo Funicular

TRANSPORTATION | FAMILY | Take a cog railway up the steeply rising terrain to another part of the city's fortified walls. It takes 15 minutes to hoist you from Stazione Principe to Porta Granarolo, 1,000 feet above, where the sweeping view gives you a sense of Genoa's size. The funicular departs about every 30 minutes. ⊠ *Piazza del Principe, San Teodoro* ☎ *010/5582414* ⊕ *www.amt.genova.it* ☜ *€2 (ticket valid 110 minutes).*

Museo d'Arte Orientale Chiossone

ART MUSEUM | One of Europe's most noteworthy collections of Japanese, Chinese, and Thai objects is housed in galleries in the Villetta di Negro park on the hillside above Piazza Portello. There's also a fine view of the city from the museum's terrace. ⊠ *Piazzale Mazzini 4, Maddalena* ☎ *010/5577950* ⊕ *www.museidigenova. it/en/oriental-museum-e-chiossone* ☜ *€5* ⊙ *Closed Mon.*

Palazzo Bianco

CASTLE/PALACE | It's difficult to miss the splendid white facade of this town palace and museum as you walk down Via Garibaldi (also known as Strada Nuova), one of Genoa's most important streets. The building houses a fine collection of 16th- and 17th-century art, with the Spanish and Flemish schools well represented. There's also a textiles collection. ⊠ *Via Garibaldi 11, Genoa* ☎ *010/5572193* ⊕ *www.museidigenova.it* ☜ *€9, includes Palazzo Rosso and Palazzo Tursi* ⊙ *Closed Mon.*

★ Palazzo Reale

CASTLE/PALACE | Lavish rococo rooms provide sumptuous display space for paintings, sculptures, tapestries, and Asian ceramics. The 17th-century palace—also known as Palazzo Balbi Durazzo—was built by the Balbi family, enormously wealthy Genovese merchants. Its regal pretensions were not lost on the Savoy, who bought the palace and turned it into a royal residence in the early 19th century. The gallery of mirrors and the ballroom on the upper floor are particularly decadent. ■TIP→ **The formal gardens provide a welcome respite from the bustle of the city, as well as great views of the harbor.** ⊠ *Via Balbi 10, Pré* ☎ *010/2710236* ◻ *€10 with Galleria Nazionale di Palazzo Spinola* ☉ *Closed Sun. and Mon. (except 1st Sun. of month when it's free entry).*

Palazzo Rosso

CASTLE/PALACE | This 17th-century Baroque palace, named for the red stone used in its construction, now contains, apart from a number of lavishly frescoed suites, works by Veronese, Guido Reni, and Sir Anthony van Dyck. ⊠ *Via Garibaldi 18, Genoa* ☎ *010/5572193* ⊕ *www. museidigenova.it* ◻ *€9, includes Palazzo Bianco and Palazzo Tursi* ☉ *Closed Mon.*

Palazzo Tursi

GOVERNMENT BUILDING | In the 16th century, wealthy resident Nicolò Grimaldi had a palace built of pink stone quarried in the region, and today it has been reincarnated as Genoa's Palazzo Municipale (Municipal Building). Most of the goings-on inside are the stuff of local politics and weddings, but you can visit the richly decorated Sale Paganiniane (Paganini rooms), where the famous Guarnerius violin belonging to Niccolò Paganini (1782–1840) is typically displayed, and the gardens that connect the palace with the neighboring Palazzo Bianco. There is also a collection of five centuries worth of coins, as well as ceramics that were used in homes and pharmacies. ⊠ *Via Garibaldi 9, Maddalena* ☎ *010/5572193* ⊕ *www.museidigenova.it* ◻ *€9, includes Palazzo Bianco and Palazzo Rosso* ☉ *Closed Mon.*

Zecca-Righi Funicular

OTHER ATTRACTION | A seven-stop commuter funicular begins just off of Piazza della Nunziata and ends at a high lookout on the fortified gates in the 17th-century city walls. Ringed around the circumference of the city are a number of huge fortresses; this gate was part of the city's system of defenses. From Righi you can undertake scenic all-day hikes from one fortress to the next. ⊠ *Piazza della Nunziata, Genoa* ☎ *010/5582414* ⊕ *www.amt. genova.it* ◻ *€2 (ticket valid 110 minutes).*

SOUTHERN DISTRICTS AND THE AQUARIUM

Inhabited since the 6th century BC, the oldest section of Genoa lies on a hill to the southwest of the Caruggi district. Today, apart from a section of 9th-century wall near Porta Soprana, there's little to show that an imposing castle once stood here. Though the neighborhood is quite run-down, some of Genoa's oldest churches make it a worthwhile excursion. Heading down the hill, you can stroll along the harbor. Once squalid and unsafe, the port was given a complete overhaul during Genoa's preparations for the Columbus quincentennial celebrations of 1992, and additional restorations in 2003 and 2004 revitalized the waterfront. You can easily reach the port on foot by following Via San Lorenzo downhill from Genoa's cathedral, Via delle Fontane from Piazza della Nunziata, or any of the narrow vicoli that lead down from Via Balbi and Via Pré.

Acquario di Genova

AQUARIUM | FAMILY | Europe's biggest aquarium is a must for children. Fifty tanks of marine species, including sea turtles, dolphins, seals, eels, penguins, jellyfish, and sharks, share space with educational displays, touch pools, and re-creations of marine ecosystems, among them a tank of coral from the Indian Ocean and a wall that replicates a forest in Madagascar. The Aquarium Village complex (additional cost) includes two biospheres with tropical plants and birds, as well as a virtual reality room. ■TIP→ **Buy tickets online in advance for the lowest prices.** If arriving by car, take the Genova Ovest exit from the autostrada. ⊠ *Ponte Spinola, Genoa* ☎ *010/23451* ⊕ *www.acquariodigenova.it* ◻ *From €22.*

Childhood Home of Christopher Columbus

HISTORIC HOME | The ivy-covered remains of this fabled medieval house—just a very small portion of it—stand in the gardens below the Porta Soprana. A small collection of objects and reproductions relating to the life and travels of Columbus are on display inside. Just outside the house, take a minute to admire the charming remains of the *chiostro di Sant'Andrea*, a medieval cloister dating from the 13th century. ⊠ *Piazza Dante, Molo* ☎ *331/2605009 mobile* ⊕ *www.museidigenova.it* ☞ *€3* ⊘ *Closed Mon.*

Galata Museo del Mare

SPECIALTY MUSEUM | FAMILY | Devoted to the city's seafaring history, this museum is probably the best way, at least on dry land, to get an idea of the changing shape of Genoa's busy port. Highlighting the displays is a full-size replica of a 17th-century Genovese galleon. ⊠ *Calata de Mari 1, Genoa* ☎ *010/2533555* ⊕ *www.galatamuseodelmare.it* ☞ *€17* ⊘ *Closed Mon. Nov.–Feb.*

The Harbor

OTHER ATTRACTION | A boat tour (with Consorzio Liguria Via Mare, for example) gives you a good perspective on the layout of the harbor, which dates to Roman times. The Genoa inlet, the largest along the Italian Riviera, was also used by the Phoenicians and Greeks as a harbor and a staging area from which they could penetrate inland to form settlements and to trade. The port is guarded by the Diga Foranea, a striking 5-km-long (3-mile-long) wall built into the ocean. The Lanterna, a lighthouse more than 360 feet tall, was built in 1544; it's one of Italy's oldest lighthouses and a traditional emblem of Genoa. ⊠ *Porto Vecchio.*

Il Bigo

VIEWPOINT | FAMILY | Designed by world-renowned architect Renzo Piano, this spiderlike white structure was erected in 1992 to celebrate the Columbus quincentenary. You can take its **Ascensore Panoramico Bigo** (Bigo Panoramic Elevator) up 650 feet for a 360-degree view of the harbor, city, and sea. In winter there's an ice-skating rink next to the elevator, in an area covered by sail-like awnings. Check the website for seasonal opening hours. ⊠ *Ponte Spinola, Genoa* ☎ *010/23451* ⊕ *www.acquariodigenova.it/bigo-panoramic* ☞ *Elevator €5* ⊘ *Closed Mon. morning and weekdays Nov.–Feb.*

MOG

MARKET | A bustling place, this produce, fish, and meat market in a former church cloister has added a second-floor bar, restaurant, and cooking school. Experience the sensory overload of colorful everyday Genovese life while watching the merchants and buyers banter over prices on the ground floor, and then head upstairs for a drink, a cooking lesson, or to try authentic Ligurian cuisine. ⊠ *Via XX Settembre 75/r, Portoria* ☎ *010/8973000* ⊕ *www.moggenova.it.*

Museo di Sant'Agostino

ART MUSEUM | Damaged during World War II, the 13th-century Gothic church of Sant'Agostino now houses a museum displaying pieces of medieval architecture, sculptures, and frescoes. Highlights of the collection are the enigmatic fragments of a tomb sculpture by Giovanni Pisano (circa 1250–1315). Surviving from the original construction are the fine campanile with a Moorish inlaid marble design and two well-preserved cloisters (one of which is the only triangular cloister in Europe). ⊠ *Piazza Sarzano 35/r, Genoa* ☎ *010/5576753* ⊕ *www.museidigenova.it/en/museum-st-augustine* ☞ *€5* ⊘ *Closed Mon.* ☞ *At the time of this writing, the museum was closed for renovation; check for current opening times before visiting.*

Palazzo Ducale

ART GALLERY | This palace was built in the 16th century over a medieval hall, and its facade was rebuilt in the late 18th century and later restored. It now houses temporary exhibitions upstairs and a couple of cocktail bars and restaurants on the ground floor. The amazingly large courtyard (which is free) is worth strolling through. ⊠ *Piazza Matteotti 9, Portoria* ☎ *010/8171600* ⊕ *www.palazzoducale. genova.it* ⌁ *Tickets from €11* ⊘ *Closed Mon.*

Porta Soprana
NOTABLE BUILDING | A striking 12th-century twin-tower structure, this medieval gateway stands on the spot where a road from ancient Rome entered the city. It is just steps uphill from Christopher Columbus's boyhood home. ⊠ *Piazza Dante, Molo.*

San Lorenzo
CHURCH | Contrasting black and white marble, so common in Liguria, embellishes the cathedral at the heart of medieval Genoa, inside and out. Consecrated in 1118, the church honors St. Lawrence, who passed through the city on his way to Rome in the 3rd century. For hundreds of years the building was used for state purposes, such as civic elections, as well as religious. Note the 13th-century Gothic portal, the fascinating twisted barbershop columns, and the 15th- to 17th-century frescoes inside. The last campanile dates from the early 16th century. The Museo del Tesoro di San Lorenzo (San Lorenzo Treasury Museum) inside has some stunning pieces from medieval goldsmiths and silversmiths, work for which medieval Genoa was renowned. ⊠ *Piazza San Lorenzo, Genoa* ☎ *010/2700295 museum, 010/27001 cathedral office* ⊕ *www.chiesadigenova. it/cattedrale, www.museidigenova.it* ⌁ *Cathedral free, museum €5* ⊘ *Museum closed Sun.*

San Matteo
CHURCH | This typically Genovese black-and-white-striped church dates from the 12th century; its crypt contains the tomb of Andrea Doria (1466–1560), the Genovese admiral who maintained the independence of his native city. The well-preserved Piazza San Matteo was, for 500 years, the seat of the Doria

family, which ruled Genoa and much of Liguria from the 16th to the 18th century. The square is bounded by 13th- to 15th-century houses decorated with portals and loggias. ⊠ *Piazza San Matteo, Maddalena* ☎ *010/2474361* ⊕ *www.parrocchiasanmatteo.org* ⌁ *Free* ⊘ *Closed Mon.*

Santa Maria di Castello
CHURCH | One of Genoa's most significant churches, this early Christian structure was rebuilt in the 12th century and finally completed in 1513. You can view some fine artwork in the attached museum and in the cloisters, where a wall displays a superb *Annunciation* by the German Justus da Ravensburg. Volunteers may be on hand to guide you around (not during religious services). ⊠ *Salita di Santa Maria di Castello 15, Genoa* ☎ *376/1865764 mobile* ⊕ *www.santamariadicastello.it* ⌁ *Free.*

🍴 Restaurants

Gaia
$ | LIGURIAN | For a truly Genovese experience, this unassuming restaurant, located in the basement of an old palazzo in the heart of the centro storico between Strada Nuova and the port, is just the place. You'll find some of the best, most authentic food in the city, with a focus on fish, meat dishes, and, of course, pesto. **Known for:** cozy, old-world atmosphere; stuffed anchovies; Genovese dishes. ⑤ *Average main: €14* ⊠ *Vico dell'Argento 13/r, Maddalena* ☎ *010/2461629* ⊘ *Closed Sun.*

I Cuochi
$$ | LIGURIAN | This cozy bistro-style restaurant is popular with locals and visitors alike for its refined, almost elegant menu of primarily seafood dishes, with a few pastas and meats. The decor is Art Nouveau with exposed brick walls and small, square tables. **Known for:** artistically presented seafood and desserts; romantic setting; contemporary Ligurian dishes.

The Art of the Pesto Pestle

You may have known Genoa primarily for its salami or its brash explorer, but the city's most direct effect on your life away from Italy may be through its cultivation of one of the world's best pasta sauces. The sublime blend of basil, extra-virgin olive oil, garlic, pine nuts, and grated pecorino and Parmigiano-Reggiano cheeses that forms *pesto alla Genovese* is one of Italy's crowning culinary achievements, a concoction that the late Italian food writer Marcella Hazan called "the most seductive of all sauces for pasta." Ligurian pesto is served usually over spaghetti, gnocchi, lasagna, or—most authentically—trenette (a flat, spaghetti-like pasta) or trofie (short, doughy pasta

twists), typically mixed with boiled potatoes and green beans. Pesto is also occasionally used to flavor minestrone. Sometimes it appears in other tasty guises (like focaccia).

The small-leaf basil grown in the region's sunny seaside hills is considered by many to be the best in the world, and pesto sauce was invented primarily as a showcase for that singular flavor. The simplicity and rawness of pesto is one of its virtues, as cooking (or even heating) basil ruins its delicate flavor. In fact, pesto aficionados refuse even to subject the basil leaves to an electric blender; Genovese (and other) foodies insist that true pesto can be made only with mortar and pestle.

$ *Average main: €20* ⊠ *Vico del Fieno 18/r, Maddalena* ☎ *010/2476170* ⊘ *Closed Sun. No lunch weekdays.*

Il Genovese

$ | **LIGURIAN** | At this bright and friendly trattoria with a maritime theme, you can dine on some of the city's best pesto and Ligurian dishes in a casual, comfortable setting. The staff are knowledgeable about the region's specialties and the wines on the always interesting menu, and even if you don't order a pesto dish, taste some with bread before your meal. **Known for:** award-winning pesto; local atmosphere near Brignole station; good value for the price. $ *Average main: €14* ⊠ *Via Galata 35/r, Brignole* ☎ *010/8692937* ⊕ *www.ilgenovese.com* ⊘ *Closed Sun.*

La Locanda in Centro

$$ | **LIGURIAN** | There's a warm and welcoming atmosphere at this osteria near Brignole station. Despite the young, enthusiastic staff, it has a reassuringly old-fashioned character, with a setting of chandeliers, bare brick walls, and shelves of wine bottles. **Known for:** great service; quality, unusual meat dishes; traditional setting. $ *Average main: €18* ⊠ *Via Domenico Fiasella 70/r, Brignole* ☎ *010/8693922* ⊕ *www.lalocandaincentro.com* ⊘ *Closed Sun. No lunch Sat.*

Pesciolino

$$ | **SEAFOOD** | With its slightly quirky but quality cuisine, attentive staff, moderate prices, and central position near Via Roma, this place ticks all the boxes for a satisfying lunchtime or evening meal-stop. The accent is firmly on seafood, often with an unusual twist, evident in such dishes as lobster salad, fish soup, and roast octopus. **Known for:** quirky seafood dishes; attentive service; good and affordable wine list. $ *Average main: €19* ⊠ *Best Western City Hotel, Piazzetta S. Sebastiano, Genoa* ☎ *010/5532131* ⊕ *www.locandapesciolino.it* ⊘ *No lunch Sun.*

Spin Ristorante-Enoteca

$$ | LIGURIAN | Dishes are created specifically to complement wines at this casually elegant enoteca with dark wood tables and bottle-lined walls in the heart of the modern town. The Ligurian menu varies daily, but the real draws are the excellent antipasti and the vast wine list, which includes many organic selections. **Known for:** wines take precedence; elegant setting in an otherwise brash part of town; delicious antipasti. $ Average main: €18 ⊠ Via C. Barabino 120/r, Foce ☎ 010/594513 ⊕ www.spinristorante-enoteca.com ⊘ Closed Sun.

Coffee and Quick Bites

I Canovacci

$ | ITALIAN | There's a steady crowd of regulars at this modern and homey lunch spot and dry goods store on a typical vicolo. The reasonably priced, good-value daily menu follows the seasons, with generous portions of fish and pasta, sandwiches, vegetables, and homemade desserts. **Known for:** efficient and friendly staff; seasonal ingredients, some of which are also sold in its grocery store; vegetarian options. $ Average main: €12 ⊠ Via dei Macelli di Soziglia 60, Genoa ☎ 010/0985417 ⊘ Closed Sun. No dinner.

La Moucca

$ | BURGER | Just a few steps from Porta Soprana and the Childhood Home of Christopher Columbus, this place makes a handy stop for a snack and a sightseeing pause. On street level is a straightforward café (with some seating upstairs, too) offering sandwiches, pastries, and ice cream, while in the basement (accessed by a separate door) you'll find a cavernous hall where succulent hamburgers and other hot snacks are the main draw. **Known for:** delicious burgers; great beers; lively atmosphere. $ Average main: €8 ⊠ Piazza Dante 31/r, Molo ☎ 010/0017695 ⊕ www.lamoucca.com.

Hotels

★ B&B Hotel Genova

$ | B&B/INN | FAMILY | This simple and utterly charming inn is a stone's throw away from the main train station (Piazza Principe), and is handily located near most sights. **Pros:** location; charming staff; great value. **Cons:** might be too close to the train station for some; books up quickly; no on-site garage. $ Rooms from: €86 ⊠ Piazza Acquaverde 1, Genoa ☎ 010/4030343 ⊕ www.hotelbb.com ⊐ 108 rooms ⦿ No Meals.

★ Grand Hotel Savoia

$$$ | HOTEL | As you enter this 1890s-vintage hotel above Piazza Acquaverde, you'll be transported from the modern city to a more glamorous era, thanks to details such as the original marble floors and lush gilt and richly colored velvet furniture in common areas. **Pros:** convenient location near Stazione Principe; rooftop restaurant and bar; comfortable rooms with luxury amenities. **Cons:** Principe station area not the best in the city; rooms on lower floors face next-door buildings; spa on the small side. $ Rooms from: €219 ⊠ Via Arsenale di Terra 5, Genoa ☎ 010/27721 ⊕ www.grandhotelsavoiagenova.it ⊐ 117 rooms ⦿ No Meals.

Hotel Bristol Palace

$$ | HOTEL | One of Europe's gracious 19th-century grand hotels, the Bristol Palace guards its reputation for courtesy, service, and elegance, offering mostly spacious, handsomely furnished, high-ceilinged guest rooms and lovely public spaces. **Pros:** outdoor terrace is lovely in summer months; in the heart of the shopping district; beautiful period details in some rooms. **Cons:** on a busy street that can be noisy; parking is a bit expensive; some standard rooms are small. $ Rooms from: €200 ⊠ Via XX Settembre 35, Portoria ☎ 010/592541 ⊕ www.hotelbristolpalace.it ⊐ 133 rooms ⦿ Free Breakfast.

Hotel Palazzo Grillo

$$$ | HOTEL | Formerly the Grillo family palace, this sumptuously comfortable boutique hotel integrates architectural details from the 1500s to the 1700s—like an original marble entryway and staircase, frescoed ceilings, and frieze details in some rooms—with clean-lined modern luxury. **Pros:** comfortable rooms with large bathrooms and high-end mattresses; great character and charm; terrace with cathedral views. **Cons:** can be hard to find; understated modern décor not to everyone's taste; parking is a little distant. $ *Rooms from: €220* ✉ *Piazza delle Vigne 4, Maddalena* ☎ *010/2477356* ⊕ *www.hotelpalazzogrillo.it* ⊗ *Closed Jan.–mid-Feb.* ⇌ *25 rooms* ⦿ *No Meals.*

Nightlife

Groove

PUB | An extensive collection of beers, bare brick walls hung with rock posters, and cheerful staff give this place buried in Genoa's vicoli (alleys) a good-time feel. A menu of burgers (with vegan options), hot dogs, and salads will quell any hunger pangs, too. It stays open till midnight or later. ✉ *Via ai Quattro Canti di S. Francesco 32/r, Maddalena* ☎ *320/4293658 mobile* ⊕ *www.grooveburger.it.*

Performing Arts

Teatro Carlo Felice

OPERA | The World War II–ravaged opera house in Genoa's modern center, Piazza de Ferrari, was rebuilt and reopened in 1991 to host the fine Genovese opera company; its massive tower has been the subject of much criticism. Lavish productions of old favorites and occasional world premieres are staged throughout the year. ✉ *Piazza de Ferrari, Passo Eugenio Montale 4, Portoria* ☎ *010/5381433* ⊕ *www.operacarlofelicegenova.it.*

Shopping

Liguria is famous for fine lace, silver-and-gold filigree work, and ceramics. Also look for bargains in velvet, macramé, olive wood, and marble. Genoa is the best spot to find all these specialties. In the heart of the medieval quarter, Via Soziglia is lined with shops selling handicrafts and tempting foods. Via XX Settembre and Via Roma are famous for their exclusive shops. High-end shops line Via Luccoli. The best shopping area for trendy-but-inexpensive Italian clothing is near San Siro, on Via San Luca.

CLOTHING AND LEATHER GOODS

Pescetto

CLOTHING | Look for designer clothes, perfumes, and fancy gifts like high-end soaps and silk scarves at Pescetto. ✉ *Via Scurreria 8, Molo* ☎ *010/2473433* ⊕ *www.pescetto.it.*

JEWELRY

Luigi Codevilla

JEWELRY & WATCHES | Established in 1830, Codevilla is known as one of the best jewelers in the city. They sell top-of-the-line watches and custom jewelry. ✉ *Via Roma 83/r, Maddalena* ☎ *010/8938278* ⊕ *www.luigicodevilla.it.*

WINES

Vinoteca Sola

WINE/SPIRITS | The owner of this shop specializes in discovering the best wines from across Italy. During the fall you can taste the latest wines, and all year you can purchase your favorites and have them shipped home. You can even buy futures for vintages to come. ✉ *Piazza Colombo 13–15/r, near Stazione Brignole, Brignole* ☎ *010/561329* ⊕ *www.vinotecasola.it.*

Riviera di
Ponente

Busalla

Mondovi

PIEMONTE

Millesimo

LIGURIA

A26

Pegli

Arenzano

Genoa
see detail
map

Nervi

Savona

Spotorno

Bardineto

Noli
Finale
Ligure

Borghetto
Santo Spirito

Albenga

Tende

Pieve di
Teco

LIGURIAN SEA

Cervo

FRANCE

Bussana
Vecchia

Taggia

Imperia

RIVIERA DI PONENTE

TO CORSICA

Ventimiglia

San Remo

Monte
Carlo

Giardini
Botanici
Hanbury

Bordighera

MONACO

TO
BARCELONA

TO
CORSICA

0   20 mi

0   20 km

Nervi

11 km (7 miles) east of Genoa.

The identity of this stately late-19th-century resort, famous for its 1½-km-long (1-mile-long) seaside Passeggiata Anita Garibaldi, its palm-lined roads, and its 300 acres of parks rich in orange trees, is given away only by the sign on the sleepy train station. Although Nervi is technically part of Genoa, its peace and quiet are as different from the city's hustle and bustle as its clear blue water is from the crowded port. From the centrally located train station, walk east along the seaside promenade to reach the beaches, a cliffside restaurant, and the 2,000 varieties of rose in the public Parco Villa Grimaldi, all the while enjoying one of the most breathtaking views on the Riviera. Nervi and the road between it and Genoa are known for their nightlife in summer.

GETTING HERE

By car, exit the A12 at Genova Nervi and follow the "Centro" signs. The Nervi train station is on the main north–south line, and you can also take the commuter trains from Genova Principe and Brignole.

⊙ Sights

GAM (Galleria d'Arte Moderna di Genova)

ART MUSEUM | Beautifully situated in a 16th-century villa (with a garden and great views), this collection houses a vast amount of paintings, sculptures, and drawings from the very recent past. The artists are largely not household names, but a visit here is well worth it (as are their contemporary exhibitions). ⊠ *Villa Saluzzo Serra, Via Capolungo 3, Nervi*

☎ 010/5576976 ⊕ www.museigenova.it ⬚ €6 ⊙ Closed Mon.

Wolfsoniana

ART MUSEUM | The private collection of businessman Mitchell Wolfson Jr. has turned into an eclectic museum displaying his whims and caprices. ⊠ Via Serra Gropallo 4, Nervi ☎ 010/5575595 ⊕ www.wolfsoniana.it ⬚ €5 ⊙ Closed Mon.

Finale Ligure

72 km (44 miles) southwest of Genoa.

Lovely Finale Ligure is actually made up of three small villages—Finalmarina, Finalpia, and Finalborgo—and makes a wonderful base for exploring the Riviera di Ponente. The former two have fine sandy beaches and a mix of traditional and modern resort amenities. Finalborgo, less than 1 km (½ mile) inland, is a medieval walled village, beautifully preserved and now containing characterful shops and restaurants. The surrounding countryside is pierced by deep, narrow valleys and caves; the limestone outcroppings provide the warm pinkish stone found in many buildings in Genoa. Rare reptiles lurk among the exotic flora.

GETTING HERE AND AROUND

By car, take the Finale Ligure exit off the A10 and follow the "Centro" signs. Finale Ligure is on the main train line between Genoa and France.

VISITOR INFORMATION

CONTACT Finale Ligure Tourism Office. ⊠ Via San Pietro 14, FInalmarina, Finale Ligure ☎ 019/681019 ⊕ www.visitfinaleligure.it.

Sights

Noli

TOWN | Just 9 km (5½ miles) northeast of Finale Ligure, the ruins of a castle loom benevolently over Noli, a tiny medieval gem. It's hard to imagine that this charming seaside village was—like Genoa, Venice, Pisa, and Amalfi—a prosperous maritime republic in the Middle Ages. Let yourself get lost among its labyrinth of cobblestone streets filled with shops and cafés or enjoy a day in the sun on its lovely stretch of beach. If you don't have a car, get a bus for Noli at Spotorno, where local trains stop. ⊠ Noli ⊕ www.nolitourism.it.

Restaurants

Ai Torchi

$$$ | **LIGURIAN** | This restored 5th-century olive oil mill is now a chic restaurant in the historical center of Finalborgo. The high prices are justified by excellent seafood and meat dishes as well as the pampering setting of clean white, arched and vaulted rooms that foster an air of space and tranquility. **Known for:** traditional Ligurian cuisine with a contemporary twist; delicious fresh fish and vegetables; airy and modern dining area. ⑤ Average main: €30 ⊠ Via dell'Annunziata 12, Finale Ligure ☎ 019/690531 ⊕ www.aitorchi.it ⊙ Closed Tues., Wed., and mid-Jan.–mid-Feb. No lunch.

Hotels

Ca de' Tobia

$$$ | **B&B/INN** | This lovely little guesthouse on the seafront promenade of Noli is stylishly done with wood floors, splashes of bright colors, and modern decor. **Pros:** modern furniture and bathrooms; easy beach access; great breakfast and aperitivo. **Cons:** street noise; parking can be a challenge; more expensive than many comparable hotels in town. ⑤ Rooms from: €220 ⊠ Via Aurelia 35, Noli ☎ 019/7485845 ⊕ www.cadetobia.it ⊙ Closed 2 wks in Nov. ➦ 6 rooms ⑩ Free Breakfast.

Punta Est

$$$ | **HOTEL** | **FAMILY** | The grand former home of a musician and composer, this 18th-century villa perched on a fragrant hillside above white-sand beaches has

since had a wing added, creating a wonderful retreat from the crowds at the water's edge. **Pros:** dining on the terrace with views; close to the beach; relaxing pool and gardens. **Cons:** some rooms are a bit outdated; a busy road must be crossed to walk to or from the sea; some noisy rooms because of their proximity to the terrace. ⑤ *Rooms from: €260* ✉ *Via Aurelia 1, Finale Ligure* ☎ *019/600611* ⊕ *www.puntaest.com* ☉ *Closed mid-Oct.–mid-May* ⬎ *36 rooms* ⦿ *Free Breakfast.*

San Remo

146 km (90 miles) southwest of Genoa.

Once the crown jewel of the Riviera di Ponente, San Remo is still the area's largest resort, lined with polished hotels, exotic gardens, and seaside promenades. Renowned for its VIP crowd, glittering casino, annual music festival, and romantic setting, San Remo maintains remnants of its glamorous past from the late 19th century to World War II, but it also suffers from the same epidemic of overbuilding that has changed so much of the Ponente for the worse. Still, it continues to be a lively town, even in the off-season.

The Mercato dei Fiori, Italy's most important wholesale flower market, is held here in a market hall between Piazza Colombo and Corso Garibaldi, though it's open to dealers only. More than 20,000 tons of carnations, roses, mimosa flowers, and innumerable other kinds of cut flowers are dispatched from here each year. As the center of northern Italy's flower-growing industry, the town is surrounded by hills where verdant terraces are now blanketed with plastic to form immense greenhouses.

GETTING HERE AND AROUND
By car, take the San Remo exit off the A10 and follow the "Centro" signs. San Remo is on the main train line between Genoa and France.

VISITOR INFORMATION
CONTACT San Remo Tourism Office. ✉ *Corso Garibaldi 1, San Remo* ☎ *0184/580500* ⊕ *www.lamialiguria.it/localita/sanremo.*

◉ Sights

Bussana Vecchia
TOWN | In the hills where flowers are cultivated for export, this self-consciously picturesque former ghost town is a flourishing artists' colony. The town was largely destroyed by an earthquake in 1877, when the inhabitants packed up and left en masse. For almost a century the houses, church, and crumbling bell tower were empty shells, overgrown by weeds and wildflowers. Since the 1960s, painters, sculptors, artisans, and bric-a-brac dealers have restored the dwellings as houses and studios. You need a car to visit the town. ✉ *8 km (5 miles) east of San Remo, San Remo* ⊕ *www.bussanavecchia.it.*

La Pigna (*The Pinecone*)
NEIGHBORHOOD | San Remo's steep and labyrinthine old town climbs upward to Piazza Castello, which offers a splendid view of the town and sea below. Some lovely old palazzi and squares have been restored, and the neighborhood gives you a sense of what it was like to live in San Remo centuries ago. ✉ *Old Town, San Remo.*

San Remo Casinò
CASINO | In addition to gaming, this lovely 1905 Art Nouveau landmark offers two restaurants, bars, and a theater that hosts concerts. Admission is free, but if you want to try your luck at the gaming tables, bets begin at around €10, depending on the time of day or night. ■**TIP**➜ **In the upstairs rooms, dress is elegant ("smart casual"), with jacket and tie requested**

Did You Know?

The gorgeous Hanbury
Botanic Gardens were
completely devastated
in World War II. In 1960,
Lady Hanbury sold the
property to the State
of Italy and in 1987, the
University of Genoa
began restoration. Today
it's considered one of the
most beautiful gardens
in Italy.

at the French gaming tables. ⊠ *Corso degli Inglesi 18, San Remo* ☎ *0184/5951* ⊕ *www.casinosanremo.it* ▨ *Free.*

Restaurants

Trattoria Piccolo Mondo

$$ | **LIGURIAN** | Vintage wooden furniture and peach-colored walls evoke the homey charm of this small family-run trattoria in a pedestrians-only alley. A faithful clientele keeps the kitchen busy, so get here early to grab a table and order Ligurian specialties—fresh pasta, pesto, and vegetable and seafood dishes. **Known for:** warm and friendly service; reasonable prices; polpo e patate (stewed octopus with potatoes). ⑤ *Average main: €17* ⊠ *Via Piave 7, San Remo* ☎ *0184/509012* ⊘ *Closed Sun. and 2 wks in June and July. No dinner Mon.*

Hotels

Hotel Paradiso

$$$ | **HOTEL** | There's an air of seclusion and a respite from hectic San Remo in these bright, well-equipped rooms—some with balconies and sea views—that face a quiet, palm-fringed garden and pool. **Pros:** nice pool and private beach; on-site restaurant and bar; secluded yet near town. **Cons:** steep walk up some stairs and a hill from seafront; paid parking with restricted space; some rooms are small and dated. ⑤ *Rooms from: €244* ⊠ *Via Roccasterone 12, San Remo* ☎ *0184/571211* ⊕ *www.paradisohotel.it* ⊘ *Closed early Nov.–late Dec.* ↵ *41 rooms* ⑩ *Free Breakfast.*

Royal Hotel Sanremo

$$$$ | **HOTEL** | With its heated seawater swimming pool in a tropical garden and guest rooms (some with sea views) with an attention to traditional design and modern amenities, this is considered one of Liguria's most luxurious resorts. **Pros:** the glamour of yesteryear with high-end amenities; excellent service; relaxing pool open April through October. **Cons:**

expensive on-site meals and beverages; some bathrooms could be updated; pool area can be crowded in high season. ⑤ *Rooms from: €340* ⊠ *Corso Imperatrice 80, San Remo* ☎ *0184/5391* ⊕ *www.royalhotelsanremo.com* ⊘ *Closed early Nov.–early Feb.* ↵ *126 rooms* ⑩ *Free Breakfast.*

Bordighera

12 km (7 miles) southwest of San Remo, 155 km (96 miles) southwest of Genoa.

Bordighera is an attractive seaside resort with panoramas (on a clear day) from Genoa to Monte Carlo. A large English colony settled here in the second half of the 19th century and is still very much in evidence today; you regularly find people drinking afternoon tea in the cafés, and streets are named after Queen Victoria and Shakespeare.

GETTING HERE AND AROUND

By car, take the Bordighera exit off the A10 and follow the signs for "Centro," about a 10-minute drive. Bordighera is on the main railway line between Genoa and France.

VISITOR INFORMATION

CONTACT Bordighera Tourism Office. ⊠ *Via Vittorio Emanuele 172, Bordighera* ☎ *0184/262882* ⊕ *www.visitbordighera.it.*

Sights

★ Giardini Botanici Hanbury

GARDEN | Mortola Inferiore is the site of the world-famous Hanbury Botanical Gardens, one of the largest and most beautiful in Italy. Planned and planted in 1867 by a wealthy English merchant, Sir Thomas Hanbury, and his botanist brother, Daniel, the terraced gardens contain species from five continents, including many palms and succulents. ⊠ *Corso Montecarlo 43, Località Mortola Inferiore, Ventimiglia* ☎ *0184/229507* ⊕ *www.giardinihanbury.com* ▨ *€10* ⊘ *Closed Mon. Nov.–Feb.*

Lungomare Argentina

PROMENADE | Running parallel to the ocean, Lungomare Argentina is a pleasant 1½-km (1-mile) promenade, which begins at the western end of the town and provides good views westward to the French Côte d'Azur. Most Thursday mornings it's also the site of a bustling outdoor market. ⊠ *Bordighera.*

Restaurants

Buga Buga

$$ | ITALIAN | There's usually a crowd of locals congregated at this lively bar and restaurant, often accompanied by their dogs and children. In the morning, tasty brioches start off the festivities and segue neatly into lunch. **Known for:** good wines by the glass accompanied by lovely snacks; opens early, closes late; pavement seating. ⑤ *Average main: €22* ⊠ *Corso Italia 13, Bordighera* ☎ *0184/998001* ⊕ *www.ristorantebuga-buga.com.*

Magiargè

$$ | LIGURIAN | A mix of great charm and great food make this small, bustling osteria in the historic center an absolute dining delight. Dishes are Ligurian with a focus on local fish, and the list of local wines, including organic selections, is excellent. **Known for:** cozy dining room with curved archways; salt cod with chickpea polenta; multicourse set menus of Ligurian specialties. ⑤ *Average main: €21* ⊠ *Via Dritta 2, Bordighera* ☎ *0184/262946* ⊕ *www.facebook.com/ magiargebordighera* ⊙ *Closed Mon. and Tues.*

Hotels

★ Hotel Villa Elisa

$$$ | HOTEL | On a street filled with beautiful old villas, this Victorian-era former private residence has a relaxed and friendly atmosphere, beautiful gardens, a spa, and well-appointed rooms (some with balconies). **Pros:** gregarious staff; old-world charm; an amazing breakfast buffet. **Cons:** the spa costs extra outside of specified hours; books up quickly; somewhat removed from the center of things. ⑤ *Rooms from: €210* ⊠ *Via Romana 70, Bordighera* ☎ *0184/261313* ⊕ *www.villaelisa.com* ⊙ *Closed Nov.– Feb.* ⇨ *30 rooms* ¶○¶ *Free Breakfast.*

EMILIA–ROMAGNA

Updated by
Nick Bruno

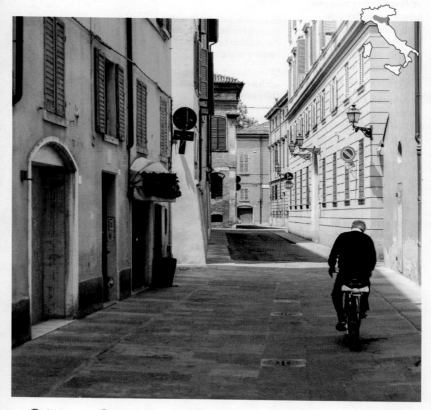

👁 Sights	🍴 Restaurants	🛏 Hotels	💼 Shopping	🍸 Nightlife
★★★★☆	★★★★★	★★★★☆	★★☆☆☆	★★☆☆☆

WELCOME TO EMILIA–ROMAGNA

TOP REASONS TO GO

★ **The signature food of Emilia:** This region's food—prosciutto crudo, Parmesan cheese, balsamic vinegar, and above all, pasta—makes the trip to Italy worthwhile.

★ **Mosaics that take your breath away:** The intricate tiles in Ravenna's Mausoleo di Galla Placidia, in brilliantly well-preserved colors, depict vivid portraits and pastoral scenes.

★ **Arguably Europe's oldest wine bar:** Nicolaus Copernicus tippled here while studying at Ferrara's university in the early 1500s—Enoteca al Brindisi, in the historic center, has been pouring wine since 1435.

★ **The nightlife of Bologna:** This red-roof city has had a lively student culture since the university—Europe's oldest—was founded in the late 11th century.

★ **The medieval castles of San Marino:** Its three castles dramatically perch on a rock more than 3,000 feet above the flat landscape of Romagna.

1 Piacenza. With its majestic piazzas, fine cathedral, and palatial museum, this town at Emilia's northwestern end makes a fitting introduction to the region.

2 Busseto. Opera aficionados visit to pay homage to one of Italy's greatest composers, Giuseppe Verdi.

3 Parma. Internationally known for its foodstuffs, Parma also boasts a battery of sights.

4 Modena. Endowed with a compact, beautifully preserved city center and a magnificent cathedral, this town repays a leisurely wander.

5 Bologna. Emilia's principal cultural and intellectual center is famed for its arcaded sidewalks, medieval towers, and sublime restaurants.

6 Ferrara. This prosperous, tidy town north of Bologna has a rich medieval past and distinctive cuisine.

7 Imola. There is plenty more to this place than its famous Formula One racetrack, including an attractive city center.

8 Faenza. This handsome settlement has bequeathed its name to the majolica ceramics, or *faience*, for which it is best known.

9 Rimini. A beach resort on the Adriatic coast, Rimini has noteworthy Roman and Renaissance monuments.

10 San Marino. Officially an independent republic, this quirky enclave is a tourist hot spot.

11 Ravenna. The main attractions of this well-preserved Romagna city are its mosaics—glittering treasures left from Byzantine rule.

EATING AND DRINKING WELL IN EMILIA-ROMAGNA

Homemade tortellini

Italians rarely agree about anything, but many concede that some of the country's finest foods originated in Emilia-Romagna. Tortellini, fettuccine, Parmesan cheese, prosciutto crudo, and balsamic vinegar are just a few of the Italian delicacies born here.

One of the beauties of Emilia-Romagna is that its exceptional food can be had without breaking the bank. Many trattorias serve up classic dishes, mastered over the centuries, at reasonable prices. Cutting-edge restaurants and wine bars are often more expensive; their inventive menus are full of *fantasia*—reinterpretations of the classics. For the budget-conscious, Bologna, a university town, has great places for cheap eats.

Between meals, you can sustain yourself with the region's famous sandwich, the *piadina*. It's made with pitalike thin bread, usually filled with prosciutto or mortadella, cheese, and vegetables, then put under the grill and served hot, with the cheese oozing at the sides. These addictive sandwiches can be savored at sit-down places or ordered to go.

THE REAL RAGÙ

Emilia-Romagna's signature dish is *tagliatelle al ragù* (flat noodles with meat sauce), which inspired the "spaghetti Bolognese" eaten outside Italy. This *primo* (first course) is on every menu, and no two versions are the same. The sauce starts in a sauté pan with finely diced carrots, onions, and celery. Purists add nothing but minced beef, but some use *guanciale* (pork cheek), sausage, veal, or chicken. Broth is added, and sometimes wine, milk, or cream.

PORK PRODUCTS

It's not just mortadella and cured pork products like prosciutto crudo and *culatello* that Emilia-Romagnans go crazy for—they're wild about the whole hog. You'll frequently find *cotechino* and *zampone*, both *secondi* (second courses), on menus. Cotechino is a savory, thick, fresh sausage served with lentils on New Year's Eve (the combination is said to augur well for the new year) and with mashed potatoes year-round. Zampone, a stuffed pig's foot, is redolent of garlic and deliciously fatty.

Pumpkin-stuffed tortelli

BOLLITO MISTO

The name means "mixed boil," and they do it exceptionally well in this part of Italy. According to Emilia-Romagnans, *bollito misto* was invented here, although other Italians—especially those from Milan, Verona, and Piedmont—might dispute this claim. Chicken, beef, tongue, and zampone are tossed into a stockpot and boiled; they're then removed from the broth and served with a fragrant *salsa verde* (green sauce), made with parsley and spiced with anchovies, garlic, and capers. This simple yet rich dish is usually served with mashed potatoes on the side, and savvy diners will mix some of the piquant salsa verde into the potatoes as well.

STUFFED PASTA

Among the many Emilian variations on stuffed pasta, tortellini are the smallest. *Tortelli* and *cappellacci* are larger pasta "pillows," about the size of a brussels sprout, but with the same basic form as tortellini. They're often filled with pumpkin or spinach and cheese. *Tortelloni* are, in theory, even bigger, although their size varies. Stuffed pastas are generally served simply, with melted butter, sage, and Parmigiano-Reggiano cheese or, in the case of tortellini, *in brodo* (in beef, chicken, or capon broth or some combination thereof), which brings out the subtle richness of the filling.

WINES

Emilia-Romagna's wines accompany the region's fine food rather than vying with it for accolades. The best-known is *Lambrusco,* a sparkling red produced on the Po Plain that has some admirers and many detractors. It's praised for its tartness and condemned for the same; it does, however, pair brilliantly with the local fare. The region's best wines include Sangiovese di Romagna (somewhat similar to Chianti), from the Romagnan hills, and Barbera from the Colli Piacentini and Apennine foothills. Castelluccio, Bonzara, Zerbina, Leone Conti, and Tre Monti are among the region's top producers.

Cotechino sausage

Gourmets the world over claim that Emilia-Romagna's greatest contribution to humankind has been gastronomic. Birthplace of fettuccine, tortellini, lasagna, prosciutto, balsamic vinegar, and Parmigiano-Reggiano cheese, the region has a spectacular culinary tradition.

But there are many reasons to come here aside from the desire to be well fed: Parma's Correggio paintings, Giuseppe Verdi's villa at Sant'Agata, the medieval splendor of Bologna's palaces, Ferrara's medieval alleys, and, perhaps foremost, the Byzantine beauty of mosaic-rich Ravenna—glittering as brightly today as it did 1,500 years ago.

As you travel through Emilia, the western half of the region, you'll encounter the sprawling plants of Italy's industrial food giants, like Barilla and Fini, standing side by side with the fading villas and farmhouses. Bologna, the principal city of Emilia, is a busy cultural and, increasingly, business center, less visited but in many ways just as engaging as the country's more famous tourist destinations.

The historic border between Emilia to the west and Romagna to the east lies near the fortified town of Dozza. Emilia is flat, but just east of the Romagnan border the landscape gets hillier and more sparsely settled. Finally, it flattens again into the low-lying marshland of the Po Delta, which meets the Adriatic Sea. Each fall, in both Romagna and Emilia, the trademark fog rolls in off the Adriatic to hang over the flatlands in winter, coloring the region with a spooky, gray glow.

MAJOR REGIONS

Emilia. The westernmost part of the region, Emilia, is richly redolent of the history and culture of northern Italy. The Via Emilia, an ancient Roman road, runs through Emilia's heart in a straight shot from medieval Piacenza, southeast of Milan, through Bologna and ultimately to Romagna and the Adriatic Coast. On the way you encounter many of Italy's cultural riches—notably the culinary and artistic treasures of Parma and Modena. Northeast of Bologna, explore the mist-shrouded tangle of streets in Ferrara's charismatic old town.

Romagna. The mostly rural Romagna has rolling hills dotted with handsome farmhouses, giving way at its eastern end to the lively resorts and sandy beaches of the Adriatic coast. Imola, most famed for its Formula One racetrack, is traditionally regarded as the western gateway to Romagna. From here it's a short hop to Faenza, home to dozens of shops selling its well-known ceramics. Most visitors to Romagna make a beeline for Ravenna, the site of shimmering Byzantine mosaics, and the mini-state of San Marino, to the south, is a curiosity worth a brief detour for its castles.

Planning

When to Go

Extending along the valley of the River Po, Emilia-Romagna's predominantly flat and featureless landscape is subject to hot summers and cold, foggy winters. It's humid year-round, so rain is always a possibility and fairly common during the winter months. Tourism is mainly cultural in the region and thus isn't particularly subject to seasonal variations, though you can expect to see some resorts along the Romagna coast close in winter, particularly around Rimini.

Getting Here and Around

CAR

Driving is the best way to get around Emilia-Romagna. Roads are wide, flat, and well marked; distances are short; and beautiful farmhouses and small villages offer undemanding detours.

A car is particularly useful for visiting the spa towns of Romagna, which aren't well connected by train. Historic centers are off-limits to cars, but they're also quite walkable, so you may just want to park your car and get around on foot once you arrive.

Entering Emilia-Romagna by car is as easy as it gets. Coming in from the northwest on the Autostrada del Sole (A1), you'll first hit Piacenza, a mere 45-minute drive southeast of Milan. On the other side of the region, Venice is about an hour from Ferrara by car on the A13.

Bologna is on the autostrada, so driving between cities is a breeze, though take special care if you're coming from Florence, as the road is winding and the drivers speed. The Via Emilia (SS9), one of the oldest roads in the world, runs through the heart of the region.

Although less scenic, the A1 autostrada, which runs parallel to the Via Emilia from Bologna, can get you where you're going about twice as fast. From Bologna, the A13 runs north to Ferrara, and the A14 takes you east to Ravenna. Much of the historic center of Bologna is closed off to cars daily from 7 am to 8 pm—look out for ZTL (Zona Traffico Limitato) road signs.

TRAIN

When it comes to public transportation in the region, trains are better than buses—they're fairly efficient and quite frequent, and most stations aren't too far from the center of town. The railroad track follows the Via Emilia (SS9). In Emilia it generally takes 30–60 minutes to get from one major city to the next. To reach Ferrara or Ravenna, you typically have to change to a local train at Bologna. Ferrara is a half hour north of Bologna on the train, and Ravenna is just over an hour east.

Bologna is an important rail hub for northern Italy and has frequent, fast service to Milan, Florence, Rome, and Venice. The routes from Bologna to the south usually go through Florence, about 40 minutes away on a high-speed train. The high-speed Frecciarossa train service cuts the time from Milan to Bologna to only one hour. On the northeastern edge of the region, Venice is 1½ hours east of Ferrara by train. Check the website of the state railway, the **Trenitalia** (aka Ferrovie dello Stato or FS ⊕ *www.trenitalia.com*), for information, or stop in a travel agency, as many sell train tickets (without a markup) and agents often speak English. **Italo** (⊕ *www.italotreno.it/en*), a privately owned high-speed train line, competes with the state-sponsored service. Italo's Milan–Rome line makes stops in Reggio Emilia, Bologna, and Florence; the Venice–Naples line stops in Padua, Bologna, Florence, and Rome. Some of these also stop at secondary stations.

Planning Your Time

Plan on spending at least two days in Bologna, the region's cultural and historical capital. You shouldn't miss Parma, with its stunning food and graceful public spaces. Also plan on visiting Ferrara, a misty, mysterious medieval city. If you have time, go to Ravenna for its memorable Byzantine mosaics and Modena for its harmonious architecture and famous balsamic vinegar.

If you have only a few days in the region, it's virtually impossible to do all five of those cities justice. If you're a dedicated gourmand (or *buona forchetta,* as Italians say), move from Bologna west along the Via Emilia (SS9) to Modena and Parma. If you're more interested in architecture, art, and history, choose the eastern route, heading north on the A13 to Ferrara and then southeast on the SS16 to Ravenna.

If you have more time, you won't have to make such tough choices. You can start in neighboring Lombardy and Milan, go east, and finish on the Adriatic—or vice versa.

Restaurants

Dining options range from mom-and-pop-style informal trattorias to three-star Michelin restaurants. Food in Emilia-Romagna is not for the faint of heart (or those on diets): it is rich, creamy, and cheesy. Local wines pair remarkably well with this sumptuous fare. You may want to rethink Lambrusco, as it marries well with just about everything on the menu.

Hotels

Emilia-Romagna has a reputation for demonstrating a level of efficiency uncommon in most of Italy. Even the smallest hotels are usually well run, with high standards of quality and service.

Bologna is very much a businessperson's city, and many hotels here cater to the business traveler, but there are smaller, more intimate hotels as well. It's smart to book in advance—the region hosts many fairs and conventions that can fill up hotels even during low season.

⇨ *Hotel and restaurant reviews have been shortened. For full information, visit Fodors.com. Prices in the hotel reviews are the lowest cost of a standard double room in high season. Prices in the dining reviews are the average cost of a main course at dinner, or, if dinner is not served, at lunch.*

What It Costs in Euros			
$	$$	$$$	$$$$
RESTAURANTS			
under €15	€15–€24	€25–€35	over €35
HOTELS			
under €125	€125–€200	€201–€300	over €300

Piacenza

67 km (42 miles) southeast of Milan, 150 km (93 miles) northwest of Bologna.

Piacenza has always been associated with industry and commerce. Its position on the Po River has made it an important inland port since the Etruscans, and then the Romans, had thriving settlements here. As you approach the city today, you could be forgiven for thinking that it holds little of interest. Piacenza is surrounded by ugly industrial suburbs (with particularly unlovely concrete factories and a power station), but if you forge ahead you'll discover a well-preserved medieval center and an unusually clean city. Its prosperity is evident in the great shopping along Corso Vittorio Emanuele II. Among its cultural highlights is the annual jazz festival each spring.

Emilia-Romagna Through the Ages

Ancient History. Emilia-Romagna owes its beginnings to a road. In 187 BC the Romans built the Via Aemilia—a long road running northwest from the Adriatic port of Rimini to the central garrison town of Piacenza—and it was along this central spine that the primary towns of the region developed.

Despite the unifying factor of what came to be known as the Via Emilia, this section of Italy has had a fragmented history. Its eastern part, roughly the area from Faenza to the coast (known as Romagna), looked first to the Byzantine east and then to Rome for art, political power, and, some say, national character. The western part, from Bologna to Piacenza (Emilia), looked more to the north with its practice of self-government and dissent.

Bologna was founded by the Etruscans and eventually came under the influence of the Roman Empire. The Romans established a garrison here, renaming the old Etruscan settlement Bononia. It was after the fall of Rome that the region began its fragmentation. Romagna, centered in Ravenna, was ruled from Constantinople. Ravenna eventually became the capital of the empire in the west in the 5th century, passing to papal control in the 8th century. Even today, the city is filled with reminders of two centuries of Byzantine rule.

Family Ties. The other cities of the region, from the Middle Ages on, became the fiefdoms of important noble families—the Este in Ferrara and Modena, the Pallavicini in Piacenza, and the Bentivoglio in Bologna. Today all these cities bear the marks of their noble patrons. When in the 16th century the papacy managed to exert its power over the entire area, some of these cities were divided among the papal families—hence the stamp of the Farnese family on Parma and Piacenza.

A Leftward Tilt. Emilia-Romagna (and Bologna, in particular) has an established and hearty tradition of rebellion and dissent. The Italian socialist movement was born in this region, as was Benito Mussolini. In keeping with the political climate of his home region, he was a firebrand socialist during the early part of his career. Despite having Mussolini as a native son, Emilia-Romagna didn't take to Fascism: it was here that the anti-Fascist resistance was born, and during World War II the region suffered terribly at the hands of the Fascists and the Nazis.

GETTING HERE AND AROUND

Regional trains run often from Milan to Piacenza and take a little less than an hour, and Frecciarossa trains make it from Milan to Bologna in an hour. Services from Bologna to Piacenza take about 1½ hours and closer to 2 hours on some regional trains. Both have frequent service. Piacenza is easily accessible by car via the A1, either from Milan or from Bologna. If you're coming from Milan, take the Piacenza Nord exit; from Bologna, the Piacenza Est exit.

VISITOR INFORMATION

CONTACT Piacenza Tourism Office. ✉ *Piazza Cavalli 7, Piacenza* ☎ *0523/492001* ⊕ *visitpiacenza.it/iat/iat-r-piacenza.*

0   20 mi

0   20 km

⊙ Sights

Duomo

CHURCH | Attached like a sinister balcony to the bell tower of Piacenza's 12th-century Duomo is a *gabbia* (iron cage), where miscreants were incarcerated naked and subjected to the scorn of the crowd in the marketplace below. Inside the cathedral, less evocative but equally impressive medieval stonework decorates the pillars and the crypt, and there are extravagant frescoes in the dome of the cupola begun by Morazzone (1573–1626). Guercino (1591–1666) completed them upon Morazzone's death. If you're feeling strong, you can climb the spiral staircase to the cupola for a closer view. Nearby at Via Prevostura 7, Kronos Museum displays the cathedral's collection of religious artworks, reliquaries, textiles and medieval manuscripts. ⊠ *Piazza*

Duomo 33, Piacenza ☎ *0523/044542* ⊕ *www.cattedralepiacenza.it* 🎫 *Free; cupola €10; Kronos Museum €6; combined ticket €12* ⊙ *Cupola and Kronos closed Mon.*

Musei di Palazzo Farnese

ART MUSEUM | The eclectic city-owned museum of Piacenzan art and antiquities is housed in the vast Palazzo Farnese, a monumental palace began in 1558, but never completed as planned. The highlight of the museum's collection is the tiny 2nd-century-BC Etruscan Fegato di Piacenza, a bronze tablet shaped like a *fegato* (liver), marked with the symbols of the gods of good and ill fortune. The collection also contains Botticelli's beautiful *Madonna and Child with St. John the Baptist*. The museum's eclectic collections include not only artworks and sculpture but also archaeological, armory, carriages, glass and ceramics, and Risorgimento artifacts. ⊠ *Piazza Cittadella 29, Piacenza* ☎ *0523/492658* ⊕ *www.palazzofarnese.piacenza.it* ⊠ *€10* ⊗ *Closed Mon.*

Piazza dei Cavalli (*Square of the Horses*)
PLAZA/SQUARE | The hub of the city is the Piazza dei Cavalli, with the flamboyant equestrian statues from which the piazza takes its name. These are depictions of Ranuccio Farnese (1569–1622) and, on the left, his father, Alessandro (1545–92). The latter was a beloved ruler, enlightened and fair; Ranuccio, his successor, less so. Both statues are the work of Francesco Mochi, a master Baroque sculptor. Dominating the square is the massive 13th-century Palazzo Pubblico, also known as Il Gotico. This two-tone, marble-and-brick, turreted and crenellated building was the seat of town government before Piacenza fell under the iron fists of the ruling Pallavicini and Farnese families. ⊠ *Piazza dei Cavalli, Piacenza.*

Busseto

30 km (19 miles) southeast of Piacenza, 25 km (16 miles) south of Cremona in Lombardy.

Sleepy Busseto's greatest claim to fame is local son Giuseppe Verdi (1813–1901), who was born in nearby Le Roncole, and his "Casa Natale" (birthplace) is now a museum and shrine to the maestro. Busseto sits in the middle of cultivated countryside, and was known since Carolingian times as Buxetum. In 1533 it attracted the attention of Hapsburg emperor Charles V, who became lord of the city. Now it attracts opera lovers who wish to walk in the grand maestro's footsteps—by hearing one of his works at the local theater or exploring the places he frequented. At time of press, Verdi's former residences, villas Verdi and Pallavicino, remained closed to the public due to legal issues.

GETTING HERE AND AROUND

If you're coming by car from Parma, drive along the A1/E35 and follow signs for the A15 in the direction of Milan/La Spezia. Choose the exit in the direction of Fidenza/Salsomaggiore Terme, following signs to the SP12, which connects to the SS9W. At Fidenza, take the SS588 heading north, which will take you into Busseto. If you're without a car, you'll have to take a bus from Piacenza or Parma, as there's no train service.

VISITOR INFORMATION

CONTACT Busseto Tourism Office. ⊠ *Piazza G. Verdi 10, Busseto* ☎ *0524/92487* ⊕ *www.bussetolive.com.*

◉ Sights

Casa Natale di Giuseppe Verdi

HISTORY MUSEUM | An engaging audioguide itinerary for each of the eight modestly furnished rooms of Verdi's birthplace evokes the atmosphere of his family life here, shared with his seamstress mother and *osteria* (tavern)-running father. Despite Verdi's worldwide success and fame he never forgot his origins. In 1863 he wrote: "Sono stato, sono e sarò sempre un paesano delle Roncole: "I was, am, and always will be a Roncole peasant." ⊠ *Via della Processione 1, Roncole Verdi, Busseto* ☎ *0524/801331* ⊕ *www.bussetolive.com/ it/poi/casa-natale-giuseppe-verdi* ⊠ *€5* ⊗ *Closed Mon.*

Teatro Verdi

HISTORIC SIGHT | In the center of Busseto is the lovely Teatro Verdi, dedicated, as you might expect, to the works of the hamlet's famous son. Guided tours (in both English and Italian) of the well-preserved, ornate, 19th-century-style theater are offered every half hour. Check with the Busseto tourist office for the performance schedule. ⊠ *Piazza G. Verdi 10, Busseto* ☎ *0524/92487* ⊕ *www.bussetolive.com* ⊠ *Tours €5* ⊗ *Closed Mon.*

Parma

40 km (25 miles) southeast of Busseto, 97 km (60 miles) northwest of Bologna.

Parma stands on the banks of a tributary of the Po River. Despite damage during World War II, much of the stately historic center seems untouched by modern times. This is a prosperous city, and it shows in its well-dressed residents, clean streets, and immaculate piazzas.

Bursting with gustatory delights, Parma draws crowds for its sublime cured pork product, *prosciutto crudo di Parma* (known locally simply as "prosciutto crudo"). The pale-yellow Parmigiano-Reggiano cheese produced here and in nearby Reggio Emilia is the original—and best—of a class known around the world as Parmesan.

GETTING HERE AND AROUND

Train service, via Frecciabianca, Intercity, and Regionale trains, runs frequently from Milan and Bologna. It takes around 1¼ hours from Milan and slightly less than an hour on fast trains from Bologna. By car, Parma is just off the A1 autostrada, halfway between Bologna and Piacenza.

VISITOR INFORMATION

CONTACT Parma Welcome Tourism Office. ✉ *Piazza Garibaldi 1, Parma* ☎ *0521/218889* ⊕ *www.parmawelcome. it.*

Sights

Battistero di San Giovanni Battista
(*Baptistery*)

CHURCH | Baptisms still happen in this baptistery designed by Benedetto Antelami between 1196 and 1216. It has a simple Pink Verona–marble Romanesque exterior and an uplifting Gothic interior. The doors are richly decorated with figures, animals, and flowers, and inside, the building has stucco figures (probably carved by Antelami) showing the months

and seasons, and a vibrantly decorated cupola. Early-14th-century frescoes depicting scenes from the life of Christ grace the walls. ✉ *Piazza del Duomo, Parma* ☎ *0521/208699* ⊕ *www.piazzaduomoparma.com* ⌖ *€12 combined with Museo Diocesano.*

★ Camera di San Paolo

HISTORIC SIGHT | This was the reception room for the erudite abbess Giovanna da Piacenza, who hired Correggio in 1519 to provide its decoration: mythological scenes are depicted in glorious frescoes of the *Triumphs of the Goddess Diana,* the *Three Graces,* and the *Three Fates.* ✉ *Via Melloni 3, off Strada Garibaldi, near Piazza Pilotta, Parma* ☎ *0521/287195* ⌖ *€8* ⊘ *Closed Tues. and Wed.*

Duomo

CHURCH | The magnificent 12th-century cathedral has two vigilant stone lions standing guard beside the main door; inside is some notable art in styles from medieval to Mannerist. The arch of the entrance is decorated with a delicate frieze of figures representing the months of the year, a motif repeated inside the baptistery. Some of the church's original artwork still survives, notably the simple yet evocative *Descent from the Cross,* a carving in the right transept by Benedetto Antelami (active 1178–1230), whose masterwork is this cathedral's baptistery. It's an odd juxtaposition to turn from his austere work to the exuberant fresco in the dome, the *Assumption of the Virgin* by Antonio Allegri, better known to us as Correggio (1494–1534). The fresco was not well received when it was unveiled in 1530. "A mess of frogs' legs," the bishop of Parma is said to have called it. Today Correggio is acclaimed as one of the leading masters of Mannerist painting. ■ TIP→ **The fresco is best viewed when the sun is strong, as this building is not particularly well lit.** ✉ *Piazza del Duomo, Parma* ☎ *0521/208699* ⊕ *www.piazzaduomoparma.com.*

Museo del Parmigiano Reggiano

SPECIALTY MUSEUM | FAMILY | The trademark crumbly cheese is the focus of this museum, which is part of the collective known as Musei del Cibo whose goal is to showcase the region's most famous foods. There's a video that demonstrates the process of making Parmigiano-Reggiano and exhibits that explore the history of the cheese. Tastings are also offered, and cheese is available to purchase. ⊠ Corte Castellazzi, Via Volta 5 ✛ 28 km (17 miles) northwest of Parma ☎ 340/1939057 mobile ⊕ www.museidelcibo.it ☜ €5; €12 Musei del Cibo card for all the food museums ⊘ Closed weekdays (open by appointment), and Dec.–Feb.

Museo del Prosciutto di Parma

SPECIALTY MUSEUM | FAMILY | Part of the collective known as Musei del Cibo, which works to showcase the region's most famous foods, this museum offers an in-depth look at Italy's most famous cured pork product. It offers tastings, a bit of history on prosciutto, and a tour through the process of making it. A gift shop ensures that you can take some of this marvelous product home. ⊠ Via Bocchialini 7, Parma ✛ Langhirano, 22 km (13 miles) from Parma ☎ 340/1939057 mobile ⊕ www.museidelcibo.it ☜ €5; €12 Musei del Cibo card for all the food museums ⊘ Closed weekdays (open by appointment only) and Dec. 9–Feb. 28.

Piazza del Duomo

PLAZA/SQUARE | FAMILY | The impressive cobblestone piazza scene contains the cathedral and the Battistero, plus the Palazzo del Vescovado (Bishop's Palace). Behind the Duomo is the Baroque church of San Giovanni Evangelista. ⊠ Piazza del Duomo, Parma.

Piazza Garibaldi

PLAZA/SQUARE | FAMILY | This piazza is the heart of Parma, where people gather to pass the time of day, start their passeggiata (constitutional), or simply hang out; the square and nearby Piazza del Duomo make up one of the loveliest historic centers in Italy. Strada Cavour, leading off the piazza, is Parma's prime shopping street. It's also crammed with wine bars teeming with locals, so it's a perfect place to stop for a snack or light lunch or a drink. ⊠ Piazza Garibaldi, Parma.

★ Pilotta Museums

ART GALLERY | With one ticket, you can visit the Pilotta museums. The Galleria Nazionale contains masterpieces by Correggio, Leonardo da Vinci, and Bronzino. The Baroque Teatro Farnese, built in 1617–18, is made entirely of wood—though largely destroyed in a 1944 Allied bombing raid, it's been flawlessly restored. In the Archeological Museum see Etruscan, Roman, and Egyptian artifacts; the Palatina Library houses more than 500 religious manuscripts; and the Bodoniano museum covers printmaking. ⊠ Piazza della Pilotta 15 ☎ 0521/233617 ⊕ www.complessopilotta.it ☜ €18 ⊘ Closed Mon.

San Giovanni Evangelista

CHURCH | Beyond the elaborate Baroque facade of San Giovanni Evangelista, the Renaissance interior reveals several works by Correggio: St. John the Evangelist (in the lunette above the door in the left transept) is considered among his finest. Also in this church are works by Parmigianino (1503–40), a contemporary of Correggio's. ⊠ Piazzale San Giovanni 1, Piazza del Duomo, Parma ☎ 0521/1651508 ⊕ www.monasterosangiovanni.com.

Santa Maria della Steccata

CHURCH | Dating from the 16th century, this delightful church has one of Parma's most recognizable domes. In the dome's large arch there's a wonderful decorative fresco by Francesco Mazzola, better known as Parmigianino. He took so long to complete it that his patrons briefly imprisoned him for breach of contract. ⊠ Piazza Steccata 9, off Via Dante near Piazza Garibaldi, Parma ☎ 0521/380500 ⊕ www.diocesi.parma.it.

🍽 Restaurants

La Filoma

$$ | **EMILIAN** | The dining room here evokes the turn of the 19th century with its high ceilings, chandeliers, and damask drapes. The food shines, from the classic *anolini in brodo di manzo e cappone* (a local variation on tortellini in brodo) to the exquisite roast veal stuffed with prosciutto and Parmigiano-Reggiano. **Known for:** regional specialties that don't break the bank; Parmigiana di melanzane (eggplant Parm) and other vegetarian options; excellent wine list. $ *Average main:* €23 ⊠ *Borgo XX Marzo 15, Parma* ☎ *0521/206181* ⊕ *www.ristorantelafiloma.it* ⊘ *Closed Wed. and 10 days in July.*

★ La Forchetta

$$$ | **ITALIAN** | Sicily-born Parma transplant Angelo Cammarata makes magic in his small eatery on the ground floor of a 16th-century palazzo, where the menu teems with Parma classics as well as modern takes on Sicilian dishes. Creatures from the sea play a starring role—from a selection of raw seafood starters to *spaghettone di sarde* (sardines) and catch of the day *al forno* (baked). **Known for:** cozy interior; great choice of quality fish dishes; lip-smacking cannoli. $ *Average main:* €25 ⊠ *Borgo San Biagio 6d, Parma* ☎ *0521/208812* ⊕ *laforchettaparma.it* ⊘ *Closed Tues. No dinner Sun.*

La Greppia

$$ | **EMILIAN** | Little-known by tourists but popular with locals in the know, this small and select restaurant just down the street from Palazzo della Pilotta in the historic center offers up traditional Parmesan cooking with stylistic flourishes. The chef has a nice touch with classics like *anolini ripieni di stracotto in brodo di cappone* (dumplings stuffed with stewed meat in a capon stock) but also prepares innovative dishes. **Known for:** impeccable service; good gluten-free choices; superb antipasti and desserts. $ *Average main:* €19 ⊠ *Strada Garibaldi*

39, Parma ☎ *0521/233686* ⊕ *facebook.com/lagreppiaparma.*

Ristorante Parizzi

$$ | **EMILIAN** | Chef-owner Marco Parizzi is the third-generation cook in this elegant restaurant, originally his grandfather's *salumeria* (delicatessen), where he now serves a mix of Parmense classics and contemporary creations. The *anolini alla parmigiana in brodo di manzo e gallina* (pasta with Parmigiano-Reggiano in broth) is a more typical dish, while the *faraona in crosta di frutta secca* (guinea fowl cooked with dried fruits and mushroom sauce) is a flight of fancy. **Known for:** special menu with white truffles from Alba in autumn; inventive tasting menus; affordable, well-curated wine list. $ *Average main:* €24 ⊠ *Strada della Repubblica 71, Parma* ☎ *0521/285952* ⊕ *www.ristoranteparizzi.it* ⊘ *Closed Mon., Aug., and Jan. 8–15.*

☕ Coffee and Quick Bites

★ Tabarro

$ | **EMILIAN** | Convivial, lively, and full of locals, this favorite little wine bar on one of Parma's main drags has a couple of keg tables outside, a few stools on the ground floor, and several more small tables upstairs. The menu is based largely on cheese and pork products (equine as well: people in this part of the world like to eat horse) and is designed to pair with, and accentuate, the fine wines on offer. **Known for:** international wine list; delicious crostini; the ebullient hosts. $ *Average main:* €14 ⊠ *Strada Farini 5/b* ☎ *0521/200223* ⊕ *www.tabarro.net* ⊘ *No lunch weekdays.*

🛏 Hotels

★ Palazzo dalla Rosa Prati

$$ | **HOTEL** | Marchese Vittorio dalla Rosa Prati has converted part of his family's 15th-century palace on Piazza del Duomo into luxurious, self-catering accommodations, and those with connecting rooms

are ideal for families. **Pros:** spacious, well-appointed rooms with small kitchenettes; historical setting; apartments perfect for families or friends traveling together. **Cons:** meager breakfast; parking can sometimes be a problem; books up quickly. ⑤ *Rooms from: €150* ⊠ *Strada al Duomo 7, Parma* ☎ *0521/386429* ⊕ *www.palazzodallarosaprati.it* ⌁ *19 rooms* ❏❍❏ *No Meals.*

Parizzi Suites and Studio

$ | **B&B/INN** | A 17th-century palace has been refurbished with 21st-century amenities to provide a lovely place to rest one's head: the suites are under the same management as the Parizzi restaurant (it's a shared entrance), so you can just glide downstairs for a marvelous meal. **Pros:** central location; great staff; breakfast served in rooms. **Cons:** no parking; some parts need a refurb; somewhat removed from the center of things. ⑤ *Rooms from: €100* ⊠ *Strada della Repubblica 71, Parma* ☎ *0521/207032* ⊕ *www.parizzisuite.com* ⌁ *13 suites* ❏❍❏ *No Meals.*

Modena

56 km (35 miles) southeast of Parma, 38 km (24 miles) northwest of Bologna.

Modena is famous for local products: Maserati, Ferrari, and opera star Luciano Pavarotti, born near here and buried in his family plot in Montale Rangone in 2007. However, it's Modena's heavenly scented balsamic vinegar, aged up to 40 years, that's probably its greatest achievement. The town has become another Emilian food mecca, with terrific restaurants and *salumerie* (delicatessens) at every turn.

GETTING HERE AND AROUND

Modena, on the Bologna–Milan line, is easily accessible by train, and it's an easy walk from the station to the *centro storico*. The Intercity connection from Florence takes about 90 minutes. By car, Modena is just off the A1 autostrada.

TOURS

Consorzio Produttori Aceto Balsamico Tradizionale di Modena

FOOD AND DRINK TOURS | Connoisseurs of balsamic vinegar can arrange visits to local producers through the Consorzio. It's best to contact the organization via its website to obtain a list of producers offering tours. ⊠ *Strada Vaciglio Sud 1085/1, Modena* ☎ *059/395633* ⊕ *www.balsamico.it* ⌁ *Free.*

VISITOR INFORMATION

CONTACT Modena Tourism Office. ⊠ *Piazza Grande 14, Modena* ☎ *059/2032660* ⊕ *www.visitmodena.it.*

◉ Sights

Duomo

CHURCH | Begun by the architect Lanfredo in 1099 and consecrated in 1184, the 12th-century Romanesque cathedral has medieval sculptures depicting scenes from Genesis on the facade, but walk around to the Piazza Grande side as well to see the building's marvelous arcading. It's a rare example of a cathedral having more than one principal view. The interior, completely clad in brick, imparts a sober and beautiful feel. An elaborate gallery has scenes of the Passion of Christ carved by Anselmo da Campione and his assistants circa 1160–80. The tomb of San Geminiano is in the crypt. The white-marble bell tower is known as **La Torre Ghirlandina** (the Little Garland Tower) because of its distinctive weather vane. ⊠ *Piazza Grande, Modena* ☎ *059/216078* ⊕ *www.duomodimodena.it.*

★ Galleria Estense

ART MUSEUM | Modena's principal museum, housed in the Palazzo dei Musei and located just a short walk from the Duomo, has an impressive collection assembled in the mid-17th century by Francesco d'Este (1610–58), Duke of Modena. The Galleria Estense is named in his honor and contains masterpieces by Bernini, Correggio, El

Greco, Tintoretto, Velázquez, Veronese, and Salvator Rosa among others. The Biblioteca Estense here is a huge collection of illuminated manuscripts, of which the best known is the beautifully illustrated *Bible of Borso d'Este* (1455–61). ⊠ *Largo Porta Sant'Agostino 337, Modena* 🕾 *059/4395711* ⊕ *www.gallerie-estensi. beniculturali.it* 🎫 *€8* ⊗ *Closed Mon.*

★ **Mercato Storico Albinelli**

MARKET | FAMILY | Locals and visitors flock to this fruit, vegetable, meat, and fish market with good reason. Ingredients are of the finest and of the freshest, and visually the place is a glorious sight to behold. A restaurant inside (outside seating when the weather agrees) serves much of what comes from the market. It's been around in this current incarnation since 1931, and it's pretty easy to see why. ⊠ *Via Luigi Albinelli 13, Modena* ⊕ *mercatoalbinelli.it* ⊗ *Closed Sun.*

Museo Enzo Ferrari

SPECIALTY MUSEUM | The home of the much revered founder of the Ferrari automobile marque, Enzo Ferrari, has been imaginatively enlarged and converted into a museum dedicated to his life and work. Besides the various trophies and engines on display, visitors can view an absorbing video that tells the Ferrari story and see the restored workshop belonging to Enzo's father, Alfredo, and, in a futuristic pavilion built alongside, a grand array of contemporary and vintage cars. ■TIP→ **A joint ticket is available with the Museo Ferrari in Maranello.** ⊠ *Via Paolo Ferrari 85, Modena* 🕾 *059/4397979* ⊕ *www.ferrari.com* 🎫 *€27, combination ticket with Museo Ferrari in Maranello €38.*

Museo Ferrari Maranello

SPECIALTY MUSEUM | This museum has become a pilgrimage site for auto enthusiasts. It takes you through the illustrious history of Ferrari, from early 1951 models to the present—the legendary F50 and cars driven by Michael Schumacher in

Formula One victories being highlights. You can also take a look at the glamorous life of founder Enzo Ferrari (a re-creation of his office is on-site) and get a glance at the production process. ⊠ *Via Dino Ferrari 43, Maranello* ⊕ *In Maranello, 17 km (11 miles) south of Modena* 🕾 *0536/949713* ⊕ *www.ferrari.com* 🎫 *€27, combination ticket with Museo Enzo Ferrari in Modena €38.*

🍴 Restaurants

Aldina

$$ | EMILIAN | On the second floor of a building across from the covered market, steps from the Piazza Grande, this simple, typical trattoria is in the very nerve center of the city. Here you'll find exemplary preparations of the region's crown jewels: tortellini in brodo, tagliatelle al ragù, and roasted meats. **Known for:** inexpensive regional food loved by locals; authentically old-fashioned character; tortellini in brodo. ⑤ *Average main: €17* ⊠ *Via Albinelli 40, Modena* 🕾 *059/236106* ⊕ *www.trattoriaaldina.it* ▤ *No credit cards* ⊗ *Closed Sun. in Aug. No dinner Mon.–Thurs.*

★ **Danilo**

$$ | EMILIAN | Honest cooking doesn't get much better than this: host Danilo has been at the helm for decades and oversees his restaurant with a keen eye and great spirit. The food here is local, terrific, and unpretentious. **Known for:** il filetto all'aceto balsamico (beef fillet with a sumptuous balsamic sauce); well-priced wine list; attentive and courteous staff. ⑤ *Average main: €18* ⊠ *Via Coltellini 31, Modena* 🕾 *059/216691* ⊕ *www.ristorantedadanilomodena.it* ⊗ *Closed Sun.*

Hosteria Giusti

$$$ | EMILIAN | In the back room of the Salumeria Giusti, established in 1605 and reportedly the world's oldest deli, you'll find just four tables in a room tastefully

Continued on page 504

ONE TASTE AT A TIME

4 towns, dozens of foods, and a mouthful of flavors you'll never forget

Imagine biting into the silkiest prosciutto in the world or the most delectable homemade tortellini you've ever tasted. In Emilia, Italy's most famous food region, you'll discover simple tastes that exceed all expectations. Beginning in Parma and moving eastward to Bologna, you'll find the epicenters of such world-renowned culinary treats as *prosciutto crudo*, Parmigiano-Reggiano, *aceto balsamico*, and tortellini. The secret to this region is not the discovery of new and exotic delicacies, but rather the rediscovery of foods you thought you already knew—in much better versions than you've ever tasted before.

TASTE 1 | PROSCIUTTO CRUDO

From Piacenza to the Adriatic, ham is the king of meats in Emilia-Romagna, but nowhere is this truer than in **Parma.**

Parma is the world's capital of *prosciutto crudo*, raw cured ham (*crudo* for short). Ask for *crudo di Parma* to signal its local provenance; many other regions also make their own crudo.

Quality testing

CRUDO LANGUAGE
It's easy to get confused with the terminology. Crudo is the product that Americans simply call "prosciutto" or the Brits might call "Parma ham." *Prosciutto* in Italian, however, is a more general term that means any kind of ham, including *prosciutto cotto*, or simply *cotto*, which means "cooked ham." Cotto is an excellent product and frequent pizza topping that's closer to (but much better than) what Americans would put in a deli sandwich.

Greasing the ham

Crudo is traditionally eaten in one of three ways: in a dry sandwich (*panino*); by itself as an appetizer, often with shaved butter on top; or as part of an appetizer or snack platter of assorted *salumi* (cured meats).

WHAT TO LOOK FOR
For the best crudo di Parma, look for slices, always cut to order, that are razor thin and have a light, rosy red color (not dark red). Don't be shy about going into a simple *salumeria* (a purveyor of cured meats) and ordering crudo by the pound. You can enjoy it straight out of the package on a park bench—and why not?

Fire branding

BEST SPOT FOR A SAMPLE
You can't go wrong with any of Parma's famed salumerie, but **Salumeria Garibaldi** is one of the town's oldest and most reliable. You'll find not only spectacular prosciutto crudo, but also delectable cheeses, wines, porcini mushrooms, and more.

Quality trademark

LEARN MORE
For more information on crudo di Parma, contact the **Consorzio del Prosciutto di Parma** through the tourist office, or stop by the famous store, **La Prosciutteria**.

A cut above

TASTE 2 | PARMIGIANO-REGGIANO

From Parma, it's only a half-hour trip east to **Reggio Emilia**, the birthplace of the crumbly and renowned Parmigiano-Reggiano cheese. Reggio (not to be confused with Reggio di Calabria in the south) is a charming little Emilian town that has been the center of production for this legendary cheese for more than 70 years.

Warming milk in copper cauldrons

SAY CHEESE

Grana is the generic Italian term for hard, aged, full-flavored cheese that can be grated. Certain varieties of Pecorino Romano, for example, or Grana Padano, also fall under this term, but Parmigiano-Reggiano, aged for as long as four years, is the foremost example.

Breaking up the curds

NOT JUST FOR GRATING

In Italy, Parmigiano-Reggiano is not only grated onto pasta, but also often served by itself in chunks, either as an appetizer—perhaps accompanied by local salumi—or even for dessert, when it might be drizzled with honey or Modena's balsamic vinegar.

MEET THE MAKERS

If you're a cheese enthusiast, you shouldn't miss the chance to take a free two-hour guided tour of a Parmigiano-Reggiano–producing farm. You'll witness the entire process and get to meet the cheesemakers. Tours can be booked online (⊕ *www.parmigianoreggiano.com*) via the **Consorzio del Formaggio Parmigiano-Reggiano** in Reggio Emilio.

Placing cheese in molds

BEST SPOT FOR A SAMPLE

The production of Parmigiano-Reggiano is heavily controlled by the Consorzio del Formaggio, so you can buy the cheese at any store or supermarket in the region and be virtually guaranteed equal quality and price. For a more distinctive shopping experience, however, try buying Parmigiano-Reggiano at the street market on Reggio's central square. The market takes place on Tuesday and Friday from 8 am to 1 pm year-round. You can pick up a small piece to eat while you're in Italy, or have larger pieces shrink-wrapped to take home.

Aging cheese wheels

Parmigiano-Reggiano

TASTE 3 | ACETO BALSAMICO DI MODENA

Tasting tradizionale vinegar

Modena is home to *Aceto Balsamico Tradizionale di Modena*, a kind of balsamic vinegar unparalleled anywhere else on Earth. The balsamic vinegar you've probably tried—even the pricier versions sold at specialty stores—may be good on salads, but it bears only a fleeting resemblance to the real thing.

HOW IS IT MADE?

The *tradizionale* vinegar that passes strict government standards is made with Trebbiano grape must, which is cooked over an open fire, reduced, and fermented from 12 to 25 or more years in a series of specially made wooden casks. As the vinegar becomes more concentrated, so much liquid evaporates that it takes more than 6 gallons of must to produce one quart of vinegar 12 years later. The result is an intense and syrupy concoction best enjoyed sparingly on grilled meats, strawberries, or Parmigiano-Reggiano cheese. The vinegar has such a complexity of flavor that some even drink it as an after-dinner liqueur.

Wooden casks for fermenting

BEST SPOT FOR A SAMPLE

The **Consorzio Produttori Antiche Acetaie** offers tours and tastings by reservation only. The main objective of the consortium is to monitor the quality of the authentic balsamic vinegar, made by only a few licensed restaurants and small producers.

The consortium also limits production, keeping prices sky high. Expect to pay €60 for a 100-ml (3.4 oz) bottle of tradizionale, which is generally aged 12 to 15 years, or €90 and up for the older tradizionale extra vecchio variety, which is aged 25 years.

But perhaps the best place to sample this vinegar, in its various stages and permutations, is in situ—that is, in any one of Modena's remarkable restaurants. You can have a simple trattoria meal at **Ermes**, whose recipes rely heavily on that liquid gold. Or you can splurge at **Osteria Francescana**, where three-starred Michelin chef Massimo Bottura works miracles with local ingredients.

OTHER TASTES OF EMILIA

■ **Cotechino:** a sausage made from pork and lard, a specialty of Modena

■ **Culatello de Zibello:** raw cured ham produced along the banks of the Po River, and cured and aged for more than 11 months

■ **Mortadella:** soft, smoked sausage made with beef, pork, cubes of pork fat, and seasonings, a specialty of Bologna

■ **Ragù:** a sauce made from minced pork and beef, simmered in milk, onions, carrots, and tomatoes

■ **Salama da sugo:** salty, oily sausage aged and then cooked, a specialty of Ferrara

■ **Tortelli and cappellacci:** pasta pillows with the same basic form as tortellini, but stuffed with cheese and vegetables

TASTE 4 | TORTELLINI

The venerable city of **Bologna** is called "the Fat" for a reason: this is the birthplace of tortellini, not to mention other specialties such as mortadella and ragù. Despite the city's new reputation for chic nightclubs and flashy boutiques, much of the food remains as it ever was.

Simple beginnings

You'll find the many Emilian variations on stuffed pasta all over the region, but they're perhaps at their best in Bologna, especially the native tortellini.

INSPIRED BY THE GODS
According to one legend, tortellini was inspired by the navel of Venus, goddess of love. As the story goes, Venus and some other gods stopped at a local inn for the night. A nosy chef went to their room to catch a glimpse of Venus. Peering through the keyhole, he saw her lying only partially covered on the bed. He was so inspired after seeing her perfect navel that he created a stuffed pasta, tortellini, in its image.

Stretching the dough

ON THE MENU
Tortellini is usually filled with beef (sometimes cheese), and is served two ways: *asciutta* is "dry," meaning it is served with a sauce such as ragù, or perhaps just with butter and Parmigiano. *Tortellini in brodo* is immersed in a lovely, savory beef broth.

Adding the filling

Tortellini alla panna contains a meat filling and is sauced with cream. Aficionados, however, argue frequently about what to stuff into these little bundles, and no two cooks do it the same. Some purists insist that only beef will do; others mix it up with sausages, mortadella, spices, and cheese (usually Parmigiano).

BEST SPOT TO BUY
Don't miss **Tamburini**, Bologna's best specialty food shop, where aromas of Emilia-Romagna's famous specialties waft out through the room and into the streets.

Shaping each piece

Tortellini di Bologna

done with antique furnishings. You'll also find some of the best food in Emilia-Romagna—perfectly executed takes on traditional dishes such as *gnocco fritto* (fried dough) stuffed with pancetta or prosciutto, and *anolini in brodo di Cappone* (pasta in possibly the most fragrant broth in the world). **Known for:** gnocco fritto with prosciutto; cozy setting; popular and pricey. $ *Average main: €28* ✉ *Via Farini 75 and Vicolo Squallore 46, Modena* ☎ *059/222533* ⊕ *www.hosteriagiusti. it* ⊘ *Closed Sun., Mon., Aug., Dec., and early Jan. No dinner.*

★ Mon Café

$$ | ECLECTIC | Locals love this lively café because it does just about everything and does it well, beginning at 7 in the morning with excellent coffee and tasty breakfast pastries and ending long after dark with *aperitivi* (aperitifs), cocktails, and dinner. The fairly limited menu includes Italian tapas and starters and mains with vegetarian and fish options. **Known for:** fresh fruit cocktails; excellent breakfasts and service; atmospheric interior. $ *Average main: €20* ✉ *Corso Canalchiaro 128, Modena* ☎ *059/223257* ⊕ *mon-cafe.it* ⊘ *Closed Mon. No dinner Sun.*

Osteria Francescana

$$$$ | EMILIAN | Chef-proprietor Massimo Bottura has done stints with Adrià and Ducasse, takes inspiration from music and literature, and pours all these influences into creating some of the fanciest plates in all of Italy while remaining true to his Modenese roots. The restaurant contains only 12 tables and it's possible to order à la carte; for the full haute cuisine experience opt for the seasonal tasting menu with the accompanying wine pairing (€535). **Known for:** a reverential atmosphere; eye-wateringly pricey tasting menu; reservations required months in advance. $ *Average main: €110* ✉ *Via Stella 22, Modena* ☎ *059/223912* ⊕ *www.osteriafrancescana.it* ⊘ *Closed Sun., Mon., and 2 wks in Aug.*

Coffee and Quick Bites

Archer

$$ | ITALIAN | Bibliophile proprietor (she named her establishment after a Henry James heroine) Marina Bersani presides over this sleek wine bar. High ceilings provide plenty of places to store her vast collection of unique wines, and the short-but-sweet menu offers lots of traditional classics like *affettati misti* (sliced, cured pork products), as well as cheese plates. **Known for:** unique wines; crostini for snacking; outdoor seating. $ *Average main: €15* ✉ *Via Cesare Battisti 54, Modena* ☎ *059/237656* ⊕ *www. archermodena.it* ⊘ *Closed Mon. and 3 wks in Aug.*

Hotels

Hotel Rua Frati 48 in San Francesco

$$$$ | HOTEL | Set in a Renaissance palazzo in central Modena, this luxurious bolthole combines modern and antique furnishings, and has a selection of spacious room and suites (the Royal has a beautiful frescoed ceiling) with smart marble bathrooms. **Pros:** excellent restaurant and bountiful breakfast; mini-spa, gym, and fitness center; exceptional service. **Cons:** pricey; may lack character for some; the standard Deluxe decor uninspiring. $ *Rooms from: €449* ✉ *Rua dei Frati Minori 48, Modena* ☎ *059/7474411* ⊕ *ruafrati48.com* ⇆ *30 rooms* ⦿ *Free Breakfast.*

Phi Hotel Canalgrande

$$ | HOTEL | In a calm location within easy walking distance of Modena's main tourist attractions, this hotel housed in an old palazzo has plenty of old-world character in the form of antique paintings, fancy plasterwork, and trompe l'oeil in the public rooms. **Pros:** great central position; spacious gardens; secure garage parking. **Cons:** dated in parts; service is sometimes poor; inadequate soundproofing in some rooms. $ *Rooms from: €140* ✉ *Corso Canalgrande 6, Modena*

☎ 059/217160 ⊕ www.hotelcanalgran-demodena.com ⟿ 67 rooms ۩ Free Breakfast.

★ Quartopiano

$$ | B&B/INN | Proprietor Antonio di Resta shows his impeccable sense of style and love of all things French in a lovely little bed-and-breakfast just a few steps from the Duomo. **Pros:** intimate setup in the heart of town; lovely bath products and fluffy towels; owner provides helpful local advice. **Cons:** with only two rooms, it books up quickly; space a bit cramped; breakfast in a separate establishment. ⑤ Rooms from: €160 ⊠ Via Bonacorsa 27, Modena ☎ 348/0189112 mobile ⊕ www.bbquartopiano.it ⟿ 2 rooms ۩ Free Breakfast.

Bologna

117 km (72 miles) north of Florence in Tuscany, 57 km (35 miles) southeast of Modena.

Bologna, a city rich with cultural jewels, has long been one of the best-kept secrets in northern Italy. Tourists in the know bask in the shadow of its leaning medieval towers and devour the city's wonderful food.

The charm of the centro storico, with its red-arcaded passageways and sidewalks, can be attributed to wise city counselors who, at the beginning of the 13th century, decreed that roads couldn't be built without *portici* (porticoes). Were these counselors to return to town eight centuries later, they'd marvel at how little has changed.

Bologna, with a population of about 392,000, has a university-town vibe—and it feels young and lively in a way that many other Italian cities don't.

GETTING HERE AND AROUND

Frequent train service from Florence to Bologna makes getting here easy. The Italo and Frecciarossa and Frecciargento (high-speed trains) run several times an hour and take just under 40 minutes. Otherwise, you're left with the *regionale* (regional) trains, which putter along and get you to Bologna in around 1¾ hours. The historic center is an interesting and relatively effortless walk from the station—though it takes about 20 minutes.

If you're driving from Florence, take the A1, exiting onto the A14, and then get on the RA1 to Exit 7–Bologna Centrale. The trip takes about an hour. From Milan, take the A1, exiting to the A14 as you near the city; from there, take the A13 and exit at Bologna; then follow the RA1 to Exit 7–Bologna Centrale. The trip takes just under three hours.

VISITOR INFORMATION

Bologna Welcome card (from €25) offers free and discounted entry to many sights, including the Musei Civici for up to 15 days. The Welcome Card Plus (€40) includes extras such as guided tours with Discover Bologna, the City Red Bus, and San Luca Express mini tourist train to the Sanctuary of San Luca (⊕ www.bolognawelcome.com/en/information/bologna-welcome-card-eng).

CONTACT Bologna Tourism Offices. ⊠ Piazza Maggiore 1/e, Bologna ☎ 051/6583111 ⊕ www.bolognawelcome.com.

⊙ Sights

Basilica di San Petronio

CHURCH | Construction on this vast cathedral began in 1390, and the work still isn't finished more than 600 years later. Above the center of the door is a Madonna and Child flanked by Saints Ambrose and Petronius, the city's patrons. Michelangelo, Giulio Romano, and Andrea Palladio (among others), submitted designs for the facade, which were all eventually rejected. The Bolognesi had planned an even bigger church but had to tone down construction when the university seat was established next door in 1561. The most important art in the church is in the

Bologna

Sights ▼

1 Basilica di
San Petronio C3
2 Fontana del Nettuno..... C3
3 Le Due Torri.............. C3
4 MAMbo and
Museo Morandi......... B1
5 Museo Internazionale
e Biblioteca della
Musica di Bologna D4
6 Palazzo Comunale B3
7 Palazzo del Podestà.... C3
8 Palazzo Re Enzo.......... C3
9 Pinacoteca Nazionale... E2
10 San Domenico C4
11 Santo Stefano D4
12 Santuario Madonna
di San Luca.............. A5
13 Torre dell'Orologio
(Clock Tower)........... B3
14 Università di Bologna ... E2

Restaurants ▼

1 Da Cesari B4
2 Ristorante I Portici....... C1
3 Trattoria
Caffè del Rosso C2
4 Trattoria di Via Serra C1
5 Trattoria Gianni
a la Vecia Bulagna....... C3

Coffee and Quick Bites ▼

1 Mercato di Mezzo C3
2 Sfoglia Rina.............. C3
3 Tamburini C3

Hotels ▼

1 Art Hotel Orologio B3
2 Grand Hotel
Majestic già Baglioni.... C3
3 Hotel Corona D'Oro...... C3

fourth chapel on the left: these frescoes by Giovanni di Modena date to 1410–15. ⊠ *Piazza Galvani 5, Piazza Maggiore* ☎ *051/231415* ⊕ *www.basilicadisanpetronio.org* 🎫 *Free* 🕑 *Museo di San Petronio closed Mon.*

Fontana del Nettuno

FOUNTAIN | Sculptor Giambologna's elaborate 1563–66 Baroque fountain and monument to Neptune occupying Piazza Nettuno has been aptly nicknamed "Il Gigante" (The Giant). Its exuberantly sensual mermaids and undraped god of the sea drew fire when it was constructed—but not enough, apparently, to dissuade the populace from using the fountain as a public washing stall for centuries. ⊠ *Piazza del Nettuno, next to Palazzo Re Enzo, Piazza Maggiore.*

Le Due Torri

NOTABLE BUILDING | FAMILY | Two landmark medieval towers, mentioned by Dante in *The Inferno*, stand side by side in the compact Piazza di Porta Ravegnana. Once, every family of importance had a tower as a symbol of prestige and power (and as a potential fortress). Now only 24 remain out of nearly 100 that once presided over the city. Torre Garisenda (late 11th century), which tilts 4 degrees (Pisa's leans 3.9), was shortened to 157 feet in the 1300s. Torre degli Asinelli (1119) is 318 feet tall and leans 7½ feet; both towers and the piazza are currently closed to visitors while the tottering Torre Garisenda is being carefully monitored. ⊠ *Piazza di Porta Ravegnana, East of Piazza Maggiore* ☎ *051/6583111* ⊕ *www.duetorribologna.com.*

★ MAMbo and Museo Morandi

ART MUSEUM | The museum—the name stands for Museo d'Arte Moderna di Bologna, or Bologna's Museum of Modern Art—houses a permanent collection of modern art. All of this is set within the sleek minimalist structure built in 1915 as the Forno del Pane, a large bakery. Seek out the powerful Arte e Ideologia section for Guttuso's *Funerali di Togliatti* (1972),

a charged symbol of pride and pain for many Bolognesi and Italiani. The work of Bologna's celebrated abstract painter Giorgio Morandi (1890–64), known for his muted still life paintings of domestic objects and landscapes, can be viewed at the Museo Morandi here. The fab bookshop and MAMbo Cafè complete the complex. ⊠ *Via Don Minzoni 14, Bologna* ☎ *051/6496611* ⊕ *www.mambo-bologna.org* 🎫 *€6 permanent collection; €6 temporary shows* 🕑 *Closed Mon.*

Museo Internazionale e Biblioteca della Musica di Bologna

SPECIALTY MUSEUM | The music museum in the spectacular Palazzo Aldini-Sanguineti, with its 17th- and 18th-century frescoes, offers among its exhibits a 1606 harpsichord and a collection of beautiful music manuscripts dating from the 1500s. ⊠ *Strada Maggiore 34, University area* ☎ *051/2757711* ⊕ *www.museibologna.it/musica* 🎫 *€5* 🕑 *Closed Mon.*

Palazzo Comunale

GOVERNMENT BUILDING | When Bologna was an independent city-state, this huge palace dating from the 13th to 15th century was the seat of government—a function it still serves today in a building that is a mélange of styles. Over the door is a statue of Bologna-born Pope Gregory XIII (reigned 1572–85), most famous for reorganizing the calendar. The Collezioni Comunali d'Arte museum exhibits medieval paintings as well as some Renaissance works by Luca Signorelli (circa 1445–1523) and Tintoretto (1518–94). ⊠ *Piazza Maggiore 6, Piazza Maggiore* ☎ *051/2193998 Collezioni Comunali d'Arte, 051/2194400 Sala Borsa* ⊕ *www.museibologna.it* 🎫 *Collezioni Comunali d'Arte €6; Sala Borsa free* 🕑 *Collezioni Comunali d'Arte closed Mon.; Sala Borsa closed Sun.*

Palazzo del Podestà

NOTABLE BUILDING | This classic Renaissance palace facing the Basilica di San Petronio was erected from 1484–94, and attached to it is the soaring Torre dell'Arengo. The bells in the tower have rung whenever the city has celebrated, mourned, or called its citizens to arms. It may not be open to the public, but head under the palazzo's atmospheric vaulted arches to experience the resonant magic of the Voltone del Podestà: whisper into the right-angled brick walls below a saintly statue to communicate with a pal opposite. ⊠ *Piazza Maggiore 1, Piazza Maggiore.*

Palazzo Re Enzo

CASTLE/PALACE | Built in 1244, this palace became home to King Enzo of Sardinia, who was imprisoned here in 1249 after he was captured during the fierce battle of Fossalta. He died here 23 years later. The palace has other macabre associations as well: common criminals received last rites in the tiny courtyard chapel before being executed in Piazza Maggiore. The colonnaded courtyard is worth a peek, and its two grand *saloni* (salons) are used for events including concerts. ⊠ *Piazza del Nettuno 1/c, Piazza Maggiore* ☎ *051/6583192* ⊕ *www.palazzoreenzo.com.*

Pinacoteca Nazionale

ART GALLERY | Bologna's principal art gallery contains many works by the immortals of Italian painting; its prize possession is the *Ecstasy of St. Cecilia* by Raphael (1483–1520). There's also a beautiful polyptych by Giotto (1267–1337), as well as *Madonna with Child and Saints Margaret, Jerome, and Petronius* (altarpiece of St. Margaret) by Parmigianino (1503–40); note the rapt eye contact between St. Margaret and the Christ child. ⊠ *Via delle Belle Arti 56, University area* ☎ *051/4209411* ⊒ *€8* ⊘ *Closed Mon.*

San Domenico

CHURCH | The tomb of St. Dominic, who died here in 1221, is called the Arca di San Domenico and is found in this church in the sixth chapel on the right. Many artists participated in its decoration, notably Niccolò di Bari, who was so proud of his 15th-century contribution that he changed his name to Niccolò dell'Arca to recall this famous work. The young Michelangelo (1475–1564) carved the angel on the right and the image of San Petronio. In the right transept of the church is a tablet marking the last resting place of hapless King Enzo, the Sardinian ruler imprisoned in the Palazzo Re Enzo. The attached museum contains religious relics. ⊠ *Piazza San Domenico 13, off Via Garibaldi, South of Piazza Maggiore* ☎ *051/6400411* ⊕ *www.sandomenicobologna.it.*

★ Santo Stefano

CHURCH | This splendid and unusual basilica contains between four and seven connected churches (authorities differ). A 4th-century temple dedicated to Isis originally occupied this site, but much of what you see was erected between the 10th and 12th centuries. Just outside the church, which probably dates from the 5th century (with later alterations), is the Cortile di Pilato (Pilate's Courtyard), named for the basin in the center. Despite the fact that the basin was probably crafted around the 8th century, legend has it that Pontius Pilate washed his hands in it after condemning Christ. ⊠ *Piazza Santo Stefano, Via Santo Stefano 24, University area* ☎ *051/4983423* ⊕ *www.santostefanobologna.it* ⊘ *Closed during services.*

★ Santuario Madonna di San Luca

CHURCH | With panoramic views and grandiose Baroque architecture atop the forested Colle della Guardia hill some 5 km (3 miles) southwest of Piazza Maggiore, the 1765-consecrated Sanctuary of San Luca church is a symbol of Bologna. For a bona fide Bolognese pilgrimage climb the 950-foot hill on foot from Porta Saragozza protected by the 666 arches (alluding to the Madonna-crushed devil) and 15 chapels of the world's longest portico (3.9 km/2.4 miles). The final ceremonial section (completed in 1721) begins at the monumental Arco del

Meloncello which echoes the orange-hued architecture of the basilica itself. Visitors can ascend a further 110 steps into the cupola for 180-degree views as part of the new San Luca Sky Experience. For a less strenuous route to the sanctuary hop on the No. 20 bus then the 58 minibus (from Villa Spada), or the San Luca Express *trenino* (mini tourist train; €13 return) from the city center. To avoid the crowds set out early morning. ⊠ *Via di San Luca 36, Beyond the City Center* ☎ *051/6142339* ⊕ *www.santuariodisanluca.it; www.succedesoloabologna. it/san-luca-sky-experience-en* ⊠ *San Luca Sky Experience €5; free plus San Luca Express with Bologna Welcome Card.*

Torre dell'Orologio (Clock Tower)

CLOCK | For a spectacular view of Piazza Maggiore and the Bolognesi hills from two terraces, as well as a look at how Bologna's oldest clock keeps the city punctual, climb the Torre dell'Orologio, or d'Arccursio tower. Opened to the public in 2021, it was built in 1249 as University of Bologna law professor Accursio da Bagnolo's monumental timepiece for his home in the piazza. The clock mechanism you'll see dates from 1773, as found on the horologist's inscription "Rinaldo Gandofli Accademic Clementi Fece 1773," among the clock's movement, gears, and swinging pendulum. ⊠ *Piazza Maggiore 6, Bologna* ☎ *051/6583111* ⊕ *www.bolognawelcome.com* ⊠ *€10* ⌕ *Reservations required.*

★ Università di Bologna

COLLEGE | Take a stroll through the streets of the university area: a jumble of buildings, some dating as far back as the 15th century and most to the 17th and 18th. The neighborhood, as befits a college town, is full of bookshops, coffee bars, and inexpensive restaurants. Political slogans and sentiments are scrawled on walls all around the university and tend to be ferociously leftist, sometimes juvenile, and often entertaining. Among the 15 university museums, the most interesting is the Museo di Palazzo Poggi, which displays scientific instruments plus paleontological and botanical artifacts. ⊠ *Via Zamboni 33, University area* ☎ *051/2099610 museum* ⊕ *sma.unibo. it/it/il-sistema-museale/museo-di-palazzo-poggi* ⊠ *€7 museum* ⊙ *Closed Mon.*

🍴 Restaurants

★ Da Cesari

$$ | EMILIAN | Host Paolino Cesari has been presiding over his eatery since 1962, and he and his staff go out of their way to make you feel at home. The food's terrific, and if you love pork products, try anything on the menu with *mora romagnola*: Paolino has direct contact with the people who raise this breed that nearly became extinct (he calls it "my pig"). **Known for:** pork dishes like flavorful salame; wine list with lots of local bottles; traditional setting. ⑤ *Average main: €22* ⊠ *Via de' Carbonesi 8, South of Piazza Maggiore* ☎ *051/237710* ⊕ *www. da-cesari.it* ⊙ *Closed Sun., Aug., and 1 wk in Jan.*

Ristorante I Portici

$$$$ | EMILIAN | The frescoed ceiling, parquet flooring, and live classical music are clues that this sophisticated restaurant (part of the hotel of the same name) occupies a former theater and *café-chantant*, or musical venue, from the late 19th century. It's the perfect setting for an evening of fine dining featuring mainly Emilian-inspired dishes with modern touches and the vision of chef Nicola Annunziata. **Known for:** sumptuous surroundings in a former theater; sophisticated culinary offerings; refined and attentive service. ⑤ *Average main: €45* ⊠ *Via dell'Indipendenza 69, North of Piazza Maggiore* ☎ *051/42185* ⊕ *www. iporticihotel.com* ⊙ *Closed Sun. and Mon. No lunch Tues.–Thurs.*

510

Trattoria Caffè del Rosso

$ | EMILIAN | Here, in the mirrored interior, a mostly young crowd chows down on classic regional fare at affordable prices. Nimble staff bearing multiple plates sashay neatly between the closely spaced tables delivering such standards as tortellini in brodo and *cotoletta alla Bolognese* (veal with Parmigiano-Reggiano and prosciutto). **Known for:** student haunt with great-value regional food; affordable wine list; fun atmosphere. ⑤ *Average main: €14* ⊠ *Via Augusto Righi 30, University area* ☎ *051/236730* ⊘ *No dinner Sun.*

Trattoria di Via Serra

$$ | EMILIAN | At this simple trattoria off the main tourist circuit, much care has been taken with the decor: the rooms, overseen by host Flavio, are small and intimate, and the wooden walls painted a creamy whitish gray. Chef Tommaso gives equal care to the menu and deftly turns out Bolognese classics, as well as dishes with a modern twist—among the antipasti, his *tosone fresco avvolto nella pancetta* incorporates Parmigiano-Reggiano, unsmoked bacon, and greens. **Known for:** all locally sourced ingredients; modern riffs on classic dishes; convivial atmosphere. ⑤ *Average main: €19* ⊠ *Via Serra 9/b, Beyond the City Center* ☎ *051/6312330* ⊕ *www.trattoriadiviaserra.it* ⊘ *Closed Sun. and Mon. No dinner Tues. and Aug.*

★ Trattoria Gianni a la Vecia Bulagna

$$ | EMILIAN | At the bottom of an alley off Piazza Maggiore, this unassuming place—known to locals as simply "Da Gianni"—is all about hearty traditional food. The usual starters are on hand—including a tasty tortellini in brodo—in addition to daily specials; bollito misto (mixed boiled meat) is a fine option here, and the *cotechino con puré di patate* (pork sausage with mashed potatoes) is elevated to sublimity by the accompanying salsa verde. **Known for:** tortellini in brodo; efficient and friendly service; busy local spot. ⑤ *Average main: €21*

⊠ *Via Clavature 18, Piazza Maggiore* ☎ *051/229434* ⊕ *www.trattoria-gianni.it* ⊘ *Closed Mon. and 1 wk in early Jan. No dinner Sun.*

☕ Coffee and Quick Bites

Mercato di Mezzo

$ | ITALIAN | FAMILY | This former fruit and vegetable market, established in medieval times and transformed into a covered market after unification, has now morphed into a fancy gourmet food hall. Various outlets offer quality Bologna classics plus some innovations, including tortellini, gnocchi and tortelloni at DeGusto Coop; focaccia from Bologna Food Company; panini, pasta, and cold cuts at L'Antica Bottega; and fried fish and quirky fish hamburgers at Pescheria del Pavaglione. **Known for:** its pork and cheese products; buzzy Bolognesi atmosphere; great wines by the glass. ⑤ *Average main: €14* ⊠ *Via Clavature 12, Piazza Maggiore* ☎ *379/1855172 mobile* ⊕ *www.facebook.com/mercatodimezzobologna* ⊘ *Closed Mon.*

Sfoglia Rina

$ | ITALIAN | FAMILY | The *pastaio* (pasta-maker) tradition in this bright honeycomb tiled pasta shop and casual restaurant—which often has a line around the block—started in 1963 in a town about 9½ km (6 miles) southwest of Bologna. There, Rina De Franceschi rolled *sfoglia* (dough) following family recipes. **Known for:** fresh pasta in many varieties; weekly vegetarian-friendly specials; affordable and wide-ranging menu. ⑤ *Average main: €13* ⊠ *Via Castiglione 5/b, Bologna* ☎ *051/9911710* ⊕ *www.sfogliarina.it.*

Tamburini

$ | WINE BAR | Two small rooms inside plus kegs and bar stools outside make up this lively, packed little spot. The overwhelming plate of *affettati misti* is crammed with top-quality local cured meats and succulent cheeses, and the adjacent salumeria offers many wonderful items to take away. **Known for:** cheese and cured meat plates; abundant portions; lively atmosphere with a vast wine selection. $ *Average main: €12* ⊠ *Via Caprarie 1, Piazza Maggiore* ☎ *051/234726* ⊕ *www.tamburini.com.*

🛏 Hotels

★ Art Hotel Orologio
$$ | HOTEL | FAMILY | The location of this stylish and welcoming family-run hotel can't be beat: it's right around the corner from Piazza Maggiore on a quiet piazza. **Pros:** central location; family-friendly rooms; fresh and bountiful breakfast. **Cons:** some street noise; pet-friendly environment may not appeal to allergy sufferers; limited facilities. $ *Rooms from: €184* ⊠ *Via IV Novembre 10, Piazza Maggiore* ☎ *051/7457411* ⊕ *www.art-hotel-orologio.com* ↵ *34 rooms* ⏅ *Free Breakfast.*

Grand Hotel Majestic già Baglioni
$$$$ | HOTEL | From the marble lobby to the luxury rooftop-terrace suites, Bologna's oldest and grandest hotel, set in an 18th-century palazzo impresses with its classical aristocratic French decor and top-notch food. **Pros:** central location; spa and gym; sophisticated Carracci restaurant dining. **Cons:** poor soundproofing and street noise in some rooms; breakfast could be better; service may feel aloof to some. $ *Rooms from: €495* ⊠ *Via dell'Indipendenza 8, Piazza Maggiore* ☎ *051/225445* ⊕ *grandhotelmajestic. duetorrihotels.com* ↵ *106 rooms* ⏅ *Free Breakfast.*

Hotel Corona D'Oro
$$$$ | HOTEL | Elegance and historic charm are the keynotes of this converted medieval palazzo once belonging to the powerful Azzoguidi family, just a short stroll from Piazza Maggiore and all the main attractions. **Pros:** helpful, friendly staff; spacious and silent rooms; historic character. **Cons:** steps on some floors are not ideal for anyone with mobility

issues; housekeeping efficiency is patchy; some rooms are small. $ *Rooms from: €395* ⊠ *Via Oberdan 12, Bologna* ☎ *051/7457611* ⊕ *www.hco.it* ↵ *40 rooms* ⏅ *Free Breakfast.*

🍸 Nightlife

BARS
Caffè Rubik
BARS | Get a taster for Bologna's student life at this quirky joint run by Alessio, Edoardo, and a friendly troupe in an historic *tabaccheria*-bar premises. Take at pew inside by day or night amid an eclectic decor of old cassettes, artworks, and an ever-diverse soundtrack, or outside under the porticoes; choose from a menu of classic cocktails, beers, wine, and their beloved *amari* (Italian digestifs with a twist) plus juices, caffè, pastries, and toasted sandwiches. ⊠ *Via Marsala 31/d, North of Piazza Maggiore* ☎ *051/0140660* ⊕ *www.cafferubik.com.*

Le Stanze
BARS | At Le Stanze you can sip an aperitivo or a late-night drink amid a young and noisy clientele. The incredibly grand decor includes 17th-century frescoes in what was once the private chapel of the Palazzo Bentivoglio. The adjoining restaurant offers a small selection of Bologna favorites. ⊠ *Via del Borgo di San Pietro 1, University area* ☎ *051/228767* ⊕ *www. lestanzecafe.it.*

★ Osteria del Sole
WINE BAR | Although "osteria" in an establishment's name suggests that food will be served, such is not the case here. This place is all about drinking wine; the entrance door has warnings such as "He who doesn't drink will please stay outside." It's been around since 1465, and locals pack in, bearing food from outside to accompany the wine. ⊠ *Vicolo Ranocchi 1/d, Piazza Maggiore* ☎ *347/9680171 mobile* ⊕ *www.osteriadelsole.it.*

MUSIC VENUES

Bravo Caffè

LIVE MUSIC | Rub shoulders with artsy celebs, locals, and visitors who dine while listening to intimate jazz, funk, rock, and pop artists from Italy and beyond. It can be a special, intimate place to see legends like Luca Carboni, Tullio de Piscopo, Nicola Conte, Suzanne Vega, Lisa Stansfield, Billy Cobham, and Roy Ayers. ✉ *Via Mascarella 1 Bologna, North of Piazza Maggiore* ☎ *051/266112* ⊕ *www.bravocaffe.it.*

★ Cantina Bentivoglio

LIVE MUSIC | Since 1987, this historic venue has hosted jazz and other musical *maestri*, such as Chet Baker, Max, Roach, Herbie Hancock, and Caetano Veloso. You can enjoy light and more substantial meals here as well. ✉ *Via Mascarella 4/b, University area* ☎ *051/265416* ⊕ *www.cantinabentivoglio.it.*

 Performing Arts

MUSIC AND OPERA

Teatro Comunale

MUSIC | This 18th-century theater presents concerts by Italian and international orchestras throughout the year, but the highly acclaimed opera performances from January to July and October to December are the main attraction. Reserve seats for those performances well in advance. ✉ *Largo Respighi 1, University area* ☎ *051/529019* ⊕ *www.tcbo.it* 🎫 *From €10 for balcony tickets.*

 Shopping

CLOTHING

Castel Guelfo The Style Outlets

OUTLET | If you don't feel like paying Galleria Cavour prices, this mall is about 20 minutes outside Bologna. It includes more than 50 stores, among them brands such as Calvin Klein Jeans, Puma, and Swarovski. ✉ *Via del Commercio 4/2, Loc. Poggio Piccolo* ✛ *Take the A14 toward Imola, Castel San Pietro Terme exit; 980 feet after tollbooth, turn right onto Via San Carlo* ☎ *0542/670765* ⊕ *castel-guelfo.thestyleoutlets.it/en.*

Galleria Cavour

MALL | Opened in 1959, the upscale Galleria houses many of the fashion giants, including Armani, Gucci, Saint Laurent, and Tod's. ✉ *Via Luigi Carlo Farini, South of Piazza Maggiore* ☎ *051/226889* ⊕ *galleriacavour.it.*

WINE AND FOOD

Bologna is a good place to buy wine. Several shops have a bewilderingly large selection—to go straight to the top, ask the managers which wines have won the prestigious Tre Bicchieri (Three Glasses) award from Gambero Rosso's wine bible, *Vini d'Italia.*

La Baita Vecchia Malga

FOOD | Fresh tagliolini, tortellini, and other Bolognese pasta delicacies are sold here, along with sublime food to eat at small tables here or take away. The cheese counter is laden with superlative local specimens. ✉ *Via Pescherie Vecchie 3/a, Piazza Maggiore* ☎ *051/223940* ⊕ *www.vecchiamalganegozi.com.*

Paolo Atti & Figli

FOOD | This place has been producing some of Bologna's finest pastas, cakes, and other delicacies since 1868. There's a second branch at Via Drapperie 6. ✉ *Via Caprarie 7, Piazza Maggiore* ☎ *051/220425* ⊕ *www.paoloatti.com.*

★ Roccati

CANDY | Sculptural works of chocolate, as well as basic bonbons and simpler sweets, have been crafted here since 1909. ✉ *Via Clavature 17/a, Piazza Maggiore* ☎ *051/261964* ⊕ *www.roccaticioccolato.com.*

Ferrara

*47 km (29 miles) northeast of Bologna,
74 km (46 miles) northwest of Ravenna.*

When the legendary Ferrarese filmmaker Michelangelo Antonioni called his beloved hometown "a city that you can see only partly, while the rest disappears to be imagined," perhaps he was referring to the low-lying mist that rolls in off the Adriatic each winter and shrouds Ferrara's winding knot of medieval alleyways, turreted palaces, and ancient wine bars—once frequented by the likes of Copernicus—in a ghostly fog. But perhaps Antonioni was also suggesting that Ferrara's striking beauty often conceals a dark and tortured past.

Today you're likely to be charmed by Ferrara's prosperous air and meticulous cleanliness, its excellent restaurants and chic bars (for coffee and any other liquid refreshment), and its lively wine-bar scene. You'll find aficionados gathering outside any of the wine bars near the Duomo even on the foggiest of weeknights. Although Ferrara is a UNESCO World Heritage site, the city draws amazingly few tourists—which only adds to its appeal.

GETTING HERE AND AROUND

Train service is frequent from Bologna (usually three trains per hour) and takes either a half hour or 50 minutes, depending on which train type you take. It's around 35 minutes from Florence to Bologna, and then about a half hour from Bologna to Ferrara. The walk from the station is easy (about 20 minutes) and not particularly interesting. You can also take Bus No. 1, No. 6, or No. 9 from the station to the center; buy your ticket at the newsagent inside and remember to stamp your ticket upon boarding the bus.

If you're driving from Bologna, take the RA1 out of town, then the A13 in the direction of Padua, exiting at Ferrara Nord. Follow the SP19 directly into the center of town. The trip should take about 45 minutes.

VISITOR INFORMATION

CONTACT Ferrara Tourism Office. ✉ *Castello Estense, Piazza Castello, Ferrara* ☎ *0532/419190* ⊕ *www.ferrarainfo.com.*

Sights

Casa Romei

CASTLE/PALACE | Built by the wealthy banker Giovanni Romei (1402–83), this vast structure with a graceful courtyard ranks among Ferrara's loveliest Renaissance palaces. Mid-15th-century frescoes adorn rooms on the ground floor; the piano nobile contains detached frescoes from local churches as well as lesser-known Renaissance sculptures. The Sala delle Sibille has a very large 15th-century fireplace and beautiful coffered wood ceilings. ✉ *Via Savonarola 30, Ferrara* ☎ *0532/234130* ⊕ *www.ferrarraterraeacqua.it* 🎫 *€5.*

★ Castello Estense

CASTLE/PALACE | The former seat of Este power, this massive castle dominates the center of town, a suitable symbol for the ruling family: cold and menacing on the outside, lavishly decorated within. The public rooms are grand, but deep in the bowels of the castle are dungeons where enemies of the state were held in wretched conditions. The prisons of Don Giulio, Ugo, and Parisina have some fascinating features, like 15th-century graffiti. Lovers Ugo and Parisina (stepmother and stepson) were beheaded in 1425 because Ugo's father, Niccolò III, didn't like the fact that his son was cavorting with his stepmother.

The castle was established as a fortress in 1385, but work on its luxurious ducal quarters continued into the 16th century. Representative of Este grandeur are the Sala dei Giochi, painted with athletic scenes, and the Sala dell'Aurora, decorated to show the times of the day. The terraces of the castle and the hanging garden have fine views of the town and countryside. You can traverse the castle's drawbridge and wander through many of its arcaded passages whenever the castle gates are open. ⊠ *Piazza Castello, Ferrara* ☎ *0532/419180* ⊕ *www.castelloestense.it* 🖾 *€12* ☉ *Closed Tues.*

Duomo

CHURCH | The magnificent Gothic cathedral, a few steps from the Castello Estense, has a three-tier facade of slender arches and beautiful sculptures over the central door. Work began in 1135 and took more than 100 years to complete. The interior was completely remodeled in the 17th century. On Palm Sunday 2024, the Duomo reopened having undergone major restoration after the 2012 earthquake; the extensive works uncovered ornately sculpted capitals hidden behind plaster for more than three centuries. ⊠ *Piazza della Cattedrale, Ferrara* ☎ *0532/207449* ⊕ *www.cattedralediferrara.it.*

Museo della Cattedrale

ART MUSEUM | Some of the original decorations of the town's main church, the former church, and the cloister of San Romano reside in the Museo della Cattedrale, across the piazza from the Duomo. Inside you'll find 22 codices commissioned between 1477 and 1535; early-13th-century sculptures by the Maestro dei Mesi; a mammoth oil on canvas by Cosmè Tura from 1469; and an exquisite Jacopo della Quercia, the *Madonna della Melagrana*. Although this last work dates from 1403 to 1408, the playful expression on the Christ child seems very 21st century. ⊠ *Via San Romano 1, Ferrara* ☎ *0532/244949* ⊕ *www.ferrarainfo.com* 🖾 *€6* ☉ *Closed Mon.*

Museo Nazionale dell'Ebraismo Italiano e della Shoah (*Museum of Italian Judaism and the Shoah*)

SPECIALTY MUSEUM | The collection of ornate religious objects and multimedia installations at this museum (commonly known as MEIS) bears witness to the long history of the city's Jewish community. This history had its high points—1492, for example, when Ercole I invited the Jews to come over from Spain—and its lows, notably 1627, when Jews were enclosed within the ghetto, where they were forced to live until the advent of a united Italy in 1860. The triangular warren of narrow cobbled streets that made up the ghetto originally extended as far as Corso Giovecca (originally Corso Giudecca, or Ghetto Street). When it was enclosed, the neighborhood was restricted to the area between Via Scienze, Via Contrari, and Via di San Romano. The museum is located about a 15-minute walk from the former Jewish ghetto. Guided tours may be booked in advance by emailing or calling the museum. ⊠ *Via Piangipane 81, Ferrara* ☎ *0532/1912039* ⊕ *meis.museum* 🖾 *€10* ☉ *Closed Mon.*

Palazzo dei Diamanti (*Palace of Diamonds*)

ART MUSEUM | Named for the 8,500 small pink-and-white marble pyramids (or "diamonds") that stud its facade, this building was designed to be viewed in perspective—both faces at once—from diagonally across the street. Work began in the 1490s and finished around 1504. Inside the palazzo is the Pinacoteca Nazionale which houses 13th- to 17th-century Ferrarese painting, plus temporary shows. ⊠ *Corso Ercole I d'Este 21, Ferrara* ☎ *0532/244949* ⊕ *www.palazzodiamanti.it* 🖾 *€15.*

★ Palazzo Schifanoia

HISTORIC SIGHT | The oldest, most characteristic area of Ferrara is south of the Duomo, stretching between the Corso Giovecca and the city's ramparts. Here various members of the Este family built pleasure palaces, the best known of which is the Palazzo Schifanoia (*schifanoia* means "carefree" or, literally, "fleeing boredom"). Begun in the late 14th century, the palace was remodeled between 1464 and 1469. Inside is Museo Schifanoia, with its lavish interior—particularly the Salone dei Mesi, which contains an extravagant series of frescoes showing the months of the year and their mythological attributes. ⊠ *Via Scandiana 23, Ferrara* ☎ *0532/244949* ⊕ *www. ferrarainfo.com* ⊠ *€12* ⊗ *Closed Mon.*

Via delle Volte

STREET | One of the best-preserved medieval streets in Europe, the Via delle Volte clearly evokes Ferrara's past. The series of ancient *volte* (arches) along the narrow cobblestone alley once joined the merchants' houses on the south side of the street to their warehouses on the north side. The street ran parallel to the banks of the Po River, which was home to Ferrara's busy port. ⊠ *Via delle Volte, Ferrara.*

🍴 Restaurants

⭐ Enoteca al Brindisi

$ | **WINE BAR** | Ferrara is a city of wine bars, beginning with this one (allegedly Europe's oldest), which opened in 1435—Copernicus drank here while a student in the late 1400s, and the place still has an undergraduate aura. The twentysomething staff pours well-chosen wines by the glass, and they serve *cappellacci di zucca* (pasta stuffed with squash) with two different sauces (ragù or butter and sage). **Known for:** set menus at great prices; characterful interior; full of locals, students, and visitors. **$** *Average main: €12* ⊠ *Via Adelardi 11, Ferrara* ☎ *0532/473744* ⊕ *www.albrindisi.net* ⊗ *Closed Mon. and 1 wk in late Jan.*

⭐ L'Oca Giuliva

$$ | **EMILIAN** | Food, service, and ambience harmonize blissfully at this casual but elegant restaurant inside a 12th-century building. The chef shows a deft hand with area specialties and shines with the fish dishes. **Known for:** creative antipasti and seafood dishes; cappellacci di zucca (pumpkin-stuffed pasta); Ferrarese, meat

and seafood tasting menus. **$** *Average main: €20* ⊠ *Via Boccacanale di Santo Stefano 38/40, Ferrara* ☎ *0532/207628* ⊕ *www.ristorantelocagiuliva.it* ⊗ *Closed Tues. No lunch Thurs.*

Molto Più Che Centrale

$$ | **EMILIAN** | A winning combination of traditional and innovative dishes is the big draw at this colorful, contemporary restaurant with splashy modern art spread over two floors. Young chef Giacomo Garutti delivers Ferrarese classics like *salamina da sugo con purè* (salami atop creamy mashed potatoes) alongside fried and grilled seafood, and innovations like cappellacci pasta filled with pumpkin, orange, and ginger. There's a good wine list, too. **Known for:** local dishes with modern flourishes; upbeat, contemporary setting; attentive waitstaff. **$** *Average main: €19* ⊠ *Via Boccaleone 8, Ferrara* ☎ *0532/1880070* ⊕ *www.moltopiu-checentrale.it* ⊗ *Closed Thurs.*

⭐ Quel Fantastico Giovedì

$$ | **EMILIAN** | Locals and other cognoscenti frequent this sleek eatery just minutes away from Piazza del Duomo, where chef Gabriele Romagnoli uses prime local ingredients to create gustatory sensations on a menu that changes daily. Fish and seafood figure prominently among his dishes, such as with a *gratinato* (similar to a French au gratin) with seafood. **Known for:** seasonal menu; notable fish and seafood dishes; excellent service. **$** *Average main: €19* ⊠ *Via Castelnuovo 9, Ferrara* ☎ *0532/760570* ⊗ *Closed Wed.*

🛏 Hotels

⭐ Locanda Borgonuovo

$ | **B&B/INN** | In the early 18th century this lodging began life as a convent (later suppressed by Napoléon), but now it's a delightful city-center bed-and-breakfast, popular with performers at the city's Teatro Comunale. **Pros:** phenomenal breakfast featuring local foods and terrific cakes made in-house; bicycles can be borrowed for free; knowledgeable local advice. **Cons:** steep stairs to reception area and rooms; must reserve far in advance as this place books quickly; decor may be a bit over-fussy for some. $ *Rooms from: €100* ⊠ *Via Cairoli 29, Ferrara* ☎ *0532/211100* ⊕ *www.borgonuovo.com* ⇥ *5 rooms* ⊚ *Free Breakfast.*

Imola

82 km (51 miles) south of Ferrara, 42 km (26 miles) southeast of Bologna.

Affluent Imola, with its wide and stately avenues, lies on the border between Emilia and Romagna. It was populated as early as the Bronze Age, came under Roman rule, and was eventually annexed to the Papal States in 1504. Imola is best known for its Formula One auto-racing tradition: the San Marino Grand Prix was held here every spring from 1981 until 2006. Auto racing as a serious sport in Imola dates to 1953, when, with the support of Enzo Ferrari, the racetrack just outside the city center was inaugurated. The venue sometimes returns to the Formula One calendar, but you'll more likely find yourself in Imola shopping for its well-known ceramics or sampling the cuisine at the town's world-famous restaurant, San Domenico.

GETTING HERE AND AROUND

Local trains from Bologna run often and take 20–30 minutes. If you're driving from Bologna, take the RA1 to the A14 (following signs for Ancona). Take the exit for Imola. If you're coming from Milan, you can catch the Frecciarossa to Bologna (a little over an hour), and then transfer to the local train.

VISITOR INFORMATION

CONTACT IAT Imola Tourism Office. ✉ *Galleria del Centro Cittadino, Via Emilia 135, Imola* ☎ *0542/602207* ⊕ *www.visitareimola.it.*

Restaurants

★ San Domenico

$$$$ | MODERN ITALIAN | Year after year this restaurant defends its position as one of Italy's most refined dining destinations, and heads of state, celebrities, and lovers of fine food venture here to savor chef Valentino Marcattilii's wondrous creations. Typical of these is his memorable *uovo in raviolo San Domenico,* in which a large raviolo is stuffed with a raw egg yolk—it cooks only a little, then spills out and mixes with Parmigiano-Reggiano, butter, and black truffles (depending on the season). **Known for:** creative destination dining worth the price; raviolo filled with egg yolk; impeccable service. ⑤ *Average main: €65* ✉ *Via G. Sacchi 1, Imola* ☎ *0542/29000* ⊕ *www.sandomenico.it* ⊙ *Closed Mon. No dinner Sun. Closed Sun. and Mon. June–Aug. No lunch Sat. June–Aug.*

Faenza

16 km (10 miles) southeast of Imola, 49 km (30 miles) southeast of Bologna.

In the Middle Ages, Faenza was the crossroads between Emilia-Romagna and Tuscany, and the 15th century saw many Florentine artists working in town. In 1509, when the Papal States took control, Faenza became something of a backwater. It did, however, continue its 12th-century tradition of making top-quality glazed earthenware. In the 16th century local artists created a color called *bianchi di Faenza* (Faenza white), which was widely imitated and wildly desired all over Europe. The Frenchified *faience,* referring to the color and technique, soon entered the lexicon, where it remains to this day. In the central Piazza del Popolo, dozens of shops sell local ceramics.

GETTING HERE AND AROUND

Trains run frequently from Bologna to Faenza, making the trip in 25–45 minutes. There's also sporadic service from Florence, a beautiful ride of under two hours. The walk to the centro storico, though easy, isn't especially interesting.

By car it takes about an hour from Bologna. Follow the SP253 to the RA1, at which point pick up on the A14/E45 heading in the direction of Ancona. Exit and take the SP8 into Faenza.

VISITOR INFORMATION

CONTACT Pro Loco IAT Faenza Tourism Office. ✉ *Voltone della Molinella 2, Faenza* ☎ *0546/25231* ⊕ *www.prolocofaenza.it.*

◉ Sights

Museo Internazionale delle Ceramiche

ART MUSEUM | One of the largest ceramics museums in the world has a well-labeled, well-lit collection, with objects from the Renaissance among its highlights. Although the emphasis is clearly on local work, the rest of Italy and the globe are also represented. Don't miss the 20th- and 21st-century galleries, which prove that decorative arts often surpass their practical limitations and become genuinely sculptural. ✉ *Viale Baccarini 19, Faenza* ☎ *0546/697311* ⊕ *www.micfaenza.org* ◻ *€12* ⊙ *Closed Mon.*

Restaurants

Marianaza

$$ | ITALIAN | A large open-hearth fireplace dominates this rustic trattoria, and wonderful aromas of grilled meats and garlic greet you as you walk in. Marianaza successfully showcases the best of *la cucina romagnola* (the cuisine of Romagna): the extraordinary primi are mostly made with fresh pasta—tagliatelle or *garganelli* (egg-based and tubular)—while secondi rely heavily on the grill. **Known for:** good-value grilled meats; fresh pasta; Romagna specialties. $ *Average main: €19* ✉ *Via Torricelli 21, Faenza* ☎ *0546/681461* ⊕ *www.marianaza.com* ☾ *Closed Sun. and Wed.*

Rimini

70 km (43½ miles) southeast of Faenza, 52 km (32 miles) southeast of Ravenna, 121 km (75 miles) southeast of Bologna.

Rimini is one of the most popular summer resorts on the Adriatic Coast and one of the most popular in Italy. July and August are the most crowded, packed with people who don't mind crammed beaches and not-terribly-blue water. In the off-season (October through March), Rimini is a cold, windy fishing port with few places open. Any time of year, one of Rimini's least touristy areas is the port; rambling down the Via Sinistra del Porto or Via Destra del Porto past all the fishing boats, you're far from the crush of sunbathers.

The town stands at the junction of two great Roman consular roads, the Via Emilia and the Via Flaminia. In Roman times it was an important port, making it a strategic and commercial center. From the 13th century onward, Rimini was controlled by the Malatesta family, an unpredictable clan equally capable of grand gestures and savage deeds.

GETTING HERE AND AROUND

Trains run hourly from Ravenna to Rimini and take about an hour. By car from Ravenna, take the SS16/E55, then follow the SS3bis/E45/E55 in the direction of Roma/Ancona. Follow directions for Ancona Nord, then follow signs for Ancona. Take the A14/E55 to the Rimini Nord exit, then the SP136 to the SS16, and follow signs for the center of town. Alternatively, take the coastal road, SS16, which hugs the shoreline much of the way, passing through Cervia. Though only 52 km (32 miles), this scenic route is naturally slower (beware of fog in winter). The coast north of Rimini is lined with dozens of small resort towns, but only one really has any charm—the seaport of Cesenatico—the others are mini-Riminis, and in summer the narrow road is hopelessly clogged with traffic.

There's frequent train service (usually three or four trains per hour) from Bologna to Rimini. It takes one to two hours, depending on which train you choose. By car from Bologna, take the SP253 out of town, pick up the RA1, and then enter the A14 heading toward Ancona. Get off at the Rimini Nord exit and follow the SP136 to the SS16 to the center of town.

VISITOR INFORMATION

CONTACT Rimini Tourism Office. ✉ *Piazzale Federico Fellini 3, Rimini* ☎ *0541/53399* ⊕ *www.riminiturismo.it.*

Sights

Arco d'Augusto

HISTORIC SIGHT | Rimini's oldest monument is the Arco d'Augusto, now stranded in the middle of a square just inside the city ramparts. It was erected in 27 BC, making it among the oldest surviving ancient Roman arches. ✉ *Largo Giulio Cesare at Corso d'Augusto, Rimini.*

★ Museo Fellini

ART MUSEUM | The life and magical cinematic oeuvre of Rimini's favorite 20th-century son, the celebrated film director Federico Fellini, is explored in depth at this wonderfully atmospheric and suitably dreamlike museum, opened in 2021. Spread over three sites—Castel Sismondo, Palazzo del Fulgor, and Piazza Malatesta—and through multimedia, sculpture, iconic film props, costumes, playful installations, and archive material, the exhibits chart the maestro's formative and Italian cinema's golden years. Fellini's artistic friends and collaborators are center-stage, too: screens project clips of Giulietta Masina in *La Strada* (1956) and Marcello Mastroianni in *La Dolce Vita*

(1960), the evocative music of Nino Rota scores enliven every corner, and there's a Fellini-esque sculpture of a reposing Anita Ekberg. Palazzo del Fulgor, and the cinema immortalized in Fellini's semi-autobiographical love letter to Rimini, *Amarcord* (1973), has a changing program of Fellini's filmography. ⊠ *Castel Sismondo, Piazza Malatesta, Rimini* ☎ *0541/793781* ⊕ *www.fellinimuseum.it* ⊠ *€10* ◯ *Closed Mon.*

Tempio Malatestiano

CHURCH | The Malatesta family constructed the Tempio Malatestiano, also called the Basilica Cattedrale, with a masterful facade by Leon Battista Alberti (1404–72). Inside, the chapel to the right of the high altar contains a wonderful (if faded) fresco by Piero della Francesca (1420–92) depicting Sigismondo Malatesta kneeling before a saint. The two greyhounds in the right corner are significantly less faded than the rest. ⊠ *Via IV Novembre 35, Rimini* ☎ *0541/51130* ⊕ *www.diocesi. rimini.it* ⊠ *Free.*

 Restaurants

La Marianna

$$ | ITALIAN | It's all about fish at this welcoming spot, and aside from vegetable side dishes and dessert there's little on the menu that wasn't recently swimming (or lurking) in the sea. Locals flock here, and with good reason—the food is excellent, and the prices are reasonable. **Known for:** locally caught seafood across all courses; lively outdoor dining; reasonable prices. ⓢ *Average main: €17* ⊠ *Viale Tiberio 19, Rimini* ☎ *0541/22530* ⊕ *www. trattorialamarianna.it.*

 Hotels

Grand Hotel Rimini

$$$$ | HOTEL | FAMILY | This 1908 extravaganza, made famous by Federico Fellini in his film *Amarcord*, is grander than ever with ongoing restorations that keep the place completely current while maintaining its Belle Époque charm. **Pros:** sumptuous buffet breakfast that starts early (7 am) and ends late (11 am); Fellini's beloved Terrazza; amenities including everything from a spa and a private beach to programs for children in summer. **Cons:** 1 km (½ mile) from Rimini's historic center; sea view rooms cost more; books up quickly in July and August. ⓢ *Rooms from: €310* ⊠ *Parco Federico Fellini, Rimini* ☎ *0541/56000* ⊕ *www.grandhotelrimini.com* ⌐ *172 rooms* ❍ *Free Breakfast.*

San Marino

20 km (12½ miles) southwest of Rimini, 139 km (86 miles) southeast of Bologna.

The world's smallest and oldest republic, as San Marino dubs itself, is surrounded entirely by Italy. It consists of three ancient castles perched on sheer cliffs rising implausibly out of the flatlands of Romagna, and a tangled knot of cobblestone streets below that are lined with tourist boutiques, cheesy hotels and restaurants, and gun shops. A visit here is justified, however, by the sweeping views from the castle of the countryside. The 3,300-foot-plus precipices will make jaws drop and acrophobes quiver.

Visiting San Marino in winter (off-season) increases the appeal of the experience, as tourist establishments shut down and you more or less have the castles to yourself. In August every inch of walkway on the rock is mobbed with sightseers. Don't worry about changing money, showing passports, and the like (although the tourist office in Piazza Garibaldi will stamp your passport for €5). San Marino is, for all practical purposes, Italy—except, that is, for its majestic perch, its lax gun laws, and its high national voter turnout rate.

GETTING HERE AND AROUND

To get to San Marino by car, take highway SS72 west from Rimini. From Borgo Maggiore, at the base of the rock, a cable car will whisk you up to the town. Alternatively, you can drive up the winding road; public parking is available. There is a regular bus service to and from Rimini train station, with service sometime every hour throughout the year (less frequent service on Sunday); a one-way ticket from Rimini to San Marino costs €6. The trip takes about 50 minutes.

VISITOR INFORMATION

CONTACT San Marino Tourism Office.
⊠ Piazza Garibaldi, San Marino
☎ 0549/882914 ⊕ www.visitsanmarino.com.

◉ Sights

Piazza della Libertà

PLAZA/SQUARE | One must-see is the Piazza della Libertà, where the Palazzo Pubblico is guarded by soldiers in green uniforms. As you'll notice by peering into the shops along the old town's winding streets, the republic is famous for crossbows and other items (think fireworks or firearms) that are illegal almost everywhere else. ⊠ Piazza della Libertà, San Marino.

Tre Castelli

CASTLE/PALACE | San Marino's headline attractions are its Tre Castelli—medieval architectural wonders that appear on every coat of arms in the city—and some spectacular views. Starting in the center of town, walk a few hundred yards past the trinket shops, along a paved cliff-top ridge, from the 10th-century Rocca della Guaita to the 13th-century Rocca della Cesta (containing a museum of ancient weapons; worthwhile mostly for the views from its terraces and turrets) and finally to the 14th-century Rocca Montale (closed to the public), the most remote of the castles. Every step of the way affords spectacular views of Romagna

and the Adriatic—it's said that on a clear day you can see Croatia. The walk makes for a good day's exercise but is by no means arduous. Even if you arrive after visiting hours, it's supremely rewarding. ⊠ San Marino ☎ 0549/991369 ⊕ www.cultura.sm ⊠ La Torre Guaita and La Torre Cesta €9.

Ravenna

80 km (50 miles) northwest of San Marino, 93 km (58 miles) southeast of Ferrara.

A small, quiet, and well-heeled city, Ravenna has brick palaces, cobblestone streets, magnificent monuments, and spectacular Byzantine mosaics. The high point in its civic history occurred in the 5th century, when Pope Honorious moved his court here from Rome. Gothic kings Odoacer and Theodoric ruled the city until it was conquered by the Byzantines in AD 540. Ravenna later fell under the sway of Venice, and then, inevitably, the Papal States.

Because Ravenna spent much of its past looking east, its greatest art treasures show that Byzantine influence. Churches and tombs with the most unassuming exteriors contain within them walls covered with sumptuous mosaics. These beautifully preserved Byzantine mosaics put great emphasis on nature, which you can see in the delicate rendering of sky, earth, and animals. Outside Ravenna, the town of Classe hides even more mosaic gems.

GETTING HERE AND AROUND

By car from Bologna, take the SP253 to the RA1, and then follow signs for the A14/E45 in the direction of Ancona. From here, follow signs for Ravenna, taking the A14dir Ancona–Milano–Ravenna exit. Follow signs for the SS16/E55 to the center of Ravenna. From Ferrara the drive is more convoluted, but also more interesting. Take the SS16 to the RA8 in the direction of Porto Garibaldi, taking the Roma/Ravenna exit. Follow the SS309/E55 to the SS309dir/E55, taking the SS253 Bologna/Ancona exit. Follow the SS16/E55 into the center of Ravenna.

By train, there are one or two direct services hourly from Bologna, taking 70 minutes.

VISITOR INFORMATION

CONTACT Ravenna Tourism Office. ✉ *Piazza San Francesco 7, Ravenna* ☎ *0544/35755* ⊕ *www.turismo.ra.it.*

Sights

★ Basilica di San Vitale

CHURCH | The octagonal church of San Vitale was built in AD 547, after the Byzantines conquered the city, and its interior shows a strong Byzantine influence. The area behind the altar contains the most famous works, depicting Emperor Justinian and his retinue on one wall, and his wife, Empress Theodora, with her retinue, on the opposite one. Notice how the mosaics seamlessly wrap around the columns and curved arches on the upper sides of the altar area. ■TIP→ **School groups can sometimes swamp the site from March through mid-June.** ✉ *Via San Vitale, off Via Salara, Ravenna* ☎ *0544/541688* ⊕ *www.ravennamosaici.it* 🎟 *€11 combination ticket, includes other diocesan monuments.*

Battistero Neoniano

CHURCH | Next door to Ravenna's 18th-century cathedral, this baptistery has one of the town's most important mosaics. It dates from the beginning of the 5th century AD, with work continuing through the century. In keeping with the building's role, the great mosaic in the dome shows the baptism of Christ, and beneath are the Apostles. The lowest register of mosaics contains Christian symbols, the Throne of God, and the Cross. Note the naked figure kneeling next to Christ—he is the personification of the River Jordan. ✉ *Piazza Duomo, Ravenna* ☎ *0544/541688* ⊕ *www.ravennamosaici.it* 🎟 *€11 combination ticket, includes other diocesan monuments (€2 supplement for Baptistery and Mausoleum)* ♿ *Reservations essential.*

Classis Ravenna – Museo della Città e del Territorio

SPECIALTY MUSEUM | FAMILY | In Classe, a short distance outside Ravenna, this museum dazzlingly illustrates the history of Ravenna and its environs from the pre-Roman era to the Lombard conquest in AD 751. The museum occupies a refurbished sugar refinery, and with the help of multimedia presentations and panels in Italian and English, it chronicles the Roman, Ostrogoth, and Byzantine periods. Displays include bronze statuettes, stone sculptures, glassware, and mosaic fragments. A separate room summarizes the building's more recent history. It's an easy walk from Sant'Apollinare in Classe. ■TIP→ **To get here from Ravenna, take Bus No. 4 from the station or the local train to Classe, or use the cycle path from the city center.** ✉ *Via Classense 29, off SS71, Classe* ☎ *0544/473717* ⊕ *www.classisravenna.it* 🎟 *€8* ⊘ *Closed Mon.*

Domus dei Tappeti di Pietra (House of the Stone Carpets)

RUINS | This archaeological site with lovely mosaics was uncovered in 1993 during digging for an underground parking garage near the 18th-century church of Santa Eufemia. Ten feet below ground level lie the remains of a Byzantine palace dating from the 5th and 6th centuries AD. Its beautiful and well-preserved network of floor mosaics displays elaborately designed patterns, creating the effect of luxurious carpets. ✉ *Via Barbiani 16, Ravenna* ✛ *Enter through Sant'Eufemia church* ☎ *0544/473678* ⊕ *www.domusdeitappetidipietra.it* 🎟 *€6* ⊘ *Closed Mon.*

Sights ▼

1 Basilica di San Vitale... **B2**
2 Battistero Neoniano.... **B4**
3 Classis Ravenna –
  Museo della Città e del
  Territorio **E5**
4 Domus dei Tappeti
  di Pietra **A2**
5 MAR-Museo Nazionale
  di Ravenna.............. **B2**
6 Mausoleo di Galla
  Placidia **B1**
7 Sant'Apollinare in
  Classe **E5**
8 Sant'Apollinare
  Nuovo **E4**
9 Tomba di Dante **D4**

Restaurants ▼

1 Ca' de Vèn **C4**
2 Osteria del
  Tempo Perso **B2**

Hotels ▼

1 Albergo Cappello **C3**
2 Hotel Sant'Andrea **A3**
3 Palazzo Bezzi **E4**

MAR-Museo Nazionale di Ravenna

(*National Museum of Ravenna*)
SPECIALTY MUSEUM | Next to the Church
of San Vitale and housed in a former
Benedictine monastery, the museum
contains artifacts from ancient Rome,
Byzantine fabrics and carvings, and pieces of early Christian art. The collection is
well displayed and artfully lighted. In the
first cloister are marvelous Roman tomb
slabs from excavations nearby; upstairs,
you can see a reconstructed 18th-century
pharmacy. ⊠ *Via San Vitale 17, Ravenna* ☎ *0544/213902* ⊕ *ravennantica.it/
en/national-museum-of-ravenna* ⊠ *€6*
⊘ *Closed Mon.*

★ Mausoleo di Galla Placidia

CHURCH | The little tomb and the great
church stand side by side, but the tomb
predates the Basilica di San Vitale by
at least 100 years: these two adjacent
sights are decorated with the best-
known, most elaborate mosaics in
Ravenna. Galla Placidia was the sister
of the Roman emperor Honorius, who
moved the imperial capital to Ravenna in
AD 402. This mid-5th-century mausoleum
is her memorial.

The simple redbrick exterior only serves
to enhance by contrast the richness of the
interior mosaics, in deep midnight blue
and glittering gold. The tiny central dome
is decorated with symbols of Christ, the
evangelists, and striking gold stars. Eight
of the Apostles are represented in groups
of two on the four inner walls of the
dome; the other four appear singly on the
walls of the two transepts. There are three
sarcophagi in the tomb, none of which are
believed to actually contain the remains
of Galla Placidia. ■ TIP→ Visit early or late
in the day to avoid the school groups that
can sometimes swamp the Mausoleo from
March through mid-June. ⊠ *Via San Vitale
17, off Via Salara, Ravenna* ☎ *0544/541688*
⊕ *www.ravennamosaici.it* ⊠ *€11 combination ticket, includes other diocesan
monuments (€2 supplement for mausoleum and baptistery).*

Sant'Apollinare in Classe

CHURCH | This church about 5 km (3 miles)
southeast of Ravenna is landlocked now,
but when it was built, it stood in the
center of the busy shipping port known
to the ancient Romans as Classis. The
arch above and the area around the high
altar are rich with mosaics. Those on the
arch, older than the ones behind it, are
considered superior. They show Christ in
Judgment and the 12 lambs of Christianity leaving the cities of Jerusalem
and Bethlehem. In the apse is the figure
of Sant'Apollinare himself, a bishop of
Ravenna, and above him is a magnificent
Transfiguration against blazing green
grass, animals in odd perspective, and
flowers. ⊠ *Via Romea Sud 224, off SS71,
Classe* ☎ *0544/527308* ⊕ *info.raven-
nantica.it* ⊠ *€5 or €10 including Classis
Ravenna museum* ⊘ *Closed Mon.*

Sant'Apollinare Nuovo

CHURCH | The mosaics displayed in this
church date from the early 6th century,
making them slightly older than those
in San Vitale. Since the left side of the
church was reserved for women, it's
only fitting that the mosaics on that wall
depict 22 virgins offering crowns to the
Virgin Mary. On the right wall, 26 men
carry the crowns of martyrdom; they
approach Christ, surrounded by angels.
⊠ *Via Roma 53, at Via Guaccimanni,
Ravenna* ☎ *0544/541688* ⊕ *www.raven-
namosaici.it* ⊠ *€11 combination ticket,
includes other diocesan monuments.*

Tomba di Dante

TOMB | Exiled from his native Florence,
the author of *The Divine Comedy* died
here in 1321, and Dante's tomb is in a
small neoclassical building next door
to the large church of St. Francis. The
Florentines have been trying to reclaim
their famous son for hundreds of years,
but the Ravennans refuse to give him
up, arguing that since Florence did
not welcome Dante in life, it does not
deserve him in death. Perhaps as pen-
ance, every September the Florentine

11

Emilia-Romagna RAVENNA

government sends olive oil that's used to fuel the light hanging in the chapel's center. ⊠ *Via Dante Alighieri 9, Ravenna* ☎ *0544/215676* ⊕ *vivadante.it* ⎘ *€5* ⊘ *Closed Mon.*

🍴 Restaurants

Ca' de Vèn

$$ | ITALIAN | These buildings, joined by a glass-ceilinged courtyard, date from the 15th century, so the setting itself is reason enough to come; that the food is so good makes a visit here all the more satisfying. At lunchtime Ca' de Vèn teems with locals tucking in to *piadine* (a typical Romagnolo flatbread) stuffed or topped with various ingredients, and the grilled dishes—including *tagliata di pollo* (sliced chicken breast tossed with arugula and set atop exquisitely roasted potatoes)— are among the highlights. **Known for:** grilled meats; weekly menu of Romagnolo specialties; majestic, high-ceilinged lively setting. ⑤ *Average main: €18* ⊠ *Via Corrado Ricci 24, Ravenna* ☎ *0544/30163* ⊕ *www.cadeven.it* ⊘ *Closed Mon.*

★ Osteria del Tempo Perso

$$ | ITALIAN | A couple of jazz-, rock-, and food-loving friends joined forces to open this smart little restaurant in the center. The interior's warm terra-cotta-sponged walls give off an orange glow, and wine bottles line the walls, interspersed with photographs of musical greats—but the food is what counts. **Known for:** terrific seafood dishes; fine wine list; homemade pastas. ⑤ *Average main: €22* ⊠ *Via Gamba 12, Ravenna* ☎ *0544/215393* ⊕ *www.osteriadeltempoperso.it* ⊘ *No lunch weekdays.*

🛏 Hotels

Albergo Cappello

$$ | HOTEL | Originally opened in the late 19th century and restored a century later, this small, charming place exhibits a Venetian influence, with Murano chandeliers hanging from the high coffered wood ceilings in common rooms. **Pros:** good location in historic area and near sights; accommodating staff; wine bar and good restaurant. **Cons:** patchy air-conditioning; parking sometimes hard to find; occasional street noise in some rooms. ⑤ *Rooms from: €149* ⊠ *Via IV Novembre 41, Ravenna* ☎ *0544/219813* ⊕ *www.albergocappello.it* ⤿ *7 rooms* ⦿ *Free Breakfast.*

Hotel Sant'Andrea

$$ | B&B/INN | FAMILY | For a quiet and welcoming lodging on a residential street a stone's throw from the Basilica di San Vitale, look no further—it even has a delightful garden. **Pros:** quiet neighborhood; good-size guest rooms and family suites, some with terraces; cheery and helpful staff. **Cons:** can get a little noisy; reception closes at 9 pm; few facilities. ⑤ *Rooms from: €133* ⊠ *Via Carlo Cattaneo 33, Ravenna* ☎ *0544/215564* ⊕ *www.santandreahotel.com* ⤿ *12 rooms* ⦿ *Free Breakfast.*

Palazzo Bezzi

$$ | HOTEL | Set in a historic, central palazzo, Bezzi is the best bet in town for reliable, friendly customer service, and a comfortable stay amid modern surroundings, a quiet garden, and panoramic rooftop solarium. **Pros:** central yet quiet location; small spa and gym; reliable service, cleanliness, and maintenance. **Cons:** pricey garage parking; no bar or restaurant; some may find the decor soulless. ⑤ *Rooms from: €169* ⊠ *Via di Roma 45, Ravenna* ☎ *0544/36926* ⊕ *palazzobezzi.it* ⤿ *32 rooms* ⦿ *Free Breakfast.*

Chapter 12

FLORENCE

Updated by
Elizabeth Shemaria

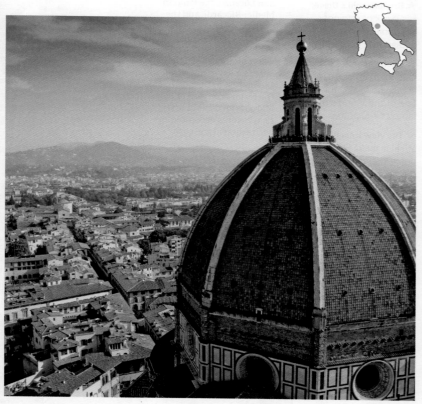

⊙ Sights	🍴 Restaurants	🛏 Hotels	🛍 Shopping	🍸 Nightlife
★★★★★	★★★★★	★★★★★	★★★★★	★★★★☆

WELCOME TO FLORENCE

TOP REASONS TO GO

★ **Galleria degli Uffizi:** Italian Renaissance art doesn't get much better than the contents of this vast collection bequeathed in 1737 by the last Medici, Anna Maria Luisa.

★ **Brunelleschi's Dome:** His work of engineering genius is the city's undisputed centerpiece.

★ **Michelangelo's *David*:** One look, up close, and you'll know why this is one of the world's most famous sculptures.

★ **The view from Piazzale Michelangelo:** From this perch the city is laid out before you. The colors at sunset heighten the experience.

★ **Piazza Santa Croce:** After you've had your fill of Renaissance masterpieces, idle here and watch the world go by.

1 Around the Duomo. You're in the heart of Florence here. Among the numerous highlights are the city's greatest museum (the Uffizi) and arguably its most impressive square (Piazza della Signoria).

2 San Lorenzo. The complex of the basilica of San Lorenzo, the Palazzo Medici-Riccardi, and the Galleria dell'Accademia bears the imprints of the Medici and of Michelangelo, culminating in the latter's masterful statue *David*. Just to the north, the former convent of San Marco is an oasis of artistic treasures decorated with ethereal frescoes.

3 Santa Maria Novella. This part of town includes the train station, 16th-century palaces, and the city's swankest shopping street, Via Tornabuoni.

4 Santa Croce. The district centers on its namesake basilica, which is filled with the tombs of Renaissance (and other) luminaries. The area is also known for its leather shops.

5 The Oltrarno. Across the Arno you encounter the massive Palazzo Pitti and the narrow streets and alleys of the hip Santo Spirito neighborhood.

EATING AND DRINKING WELL IN FLORENCE

A well-stocked local wine shop

In Florence, simply prepared meats, grilled or roasted, are the culinary stars, usually paired with seasonal vegetables like artichokes or porcini. *Bistecca* (steak) is popular here, but there's plenty more that tastes great on the grill.

Traditionalists go for their gustatory pleasures in *trattorie* (casual restaurants) and *osterie* (down-home restaurants), places where decor is unimportant and place mats are mere paper. Culinary innovation comes slowly in this town, though some cutting-edge restaurants have been appearing.

By American standards, Florentines eat late: 1:30 or 2 pm is typical for lunch and 9 pm for dinner is considered early. Consuming a *primo* (first course), *secondo* (second course), and *dolce* (dessert) is largely a thing of the past. For lunch, many Florentines simply grab a panino and a glass of wine at a bar. Those opting for a simple trattoria lunch often order a plate of pasta and dessert.

STALE AND STELLAR

Stale bread is the basis for three classic Florentine primi: *pappa al pomodoro, ribollita,* and *panzanella.* Pappa is made with either fresh or canned tomatoes and that stale bread. Ribollita is a vegetable soup with *cavolo nero* (Tuscan kale) and cannellini beans, thickened with bread. Panzanella is reconstituted Tuscan bread combined with tomatoes, cucumber, and basil. These dishes are all enhanced with a generous application of fragrant Tuscan olive oil.

A CLASSIC ANTIPASTO: CROSTINI DI FEGATINI

This beloved dish consists of a chicken-liver spread, presented warm or at room temperature, on toasted, garlic-rubbed bread. It can be served smooth, like a pâté, or in a chunkier, more rustic version. It's made by sautéing chicken livers with finely diced carrot and onion, enlivened with the addition of wine, broth, or Marsala reductions, and mashed anchovies and capers.

Bistecca alla Fiorentina

A CLASSIC SECONDO: BISTECCA ALLA FIORENTINA

The town's culinary pride and joy is a thick slab of beef, resembling a T-bone steak, from large white oxen called Chianina. The meat's slapped on the grill, seared on both sides, and served rare, sometimes with a pinch of salt.

A CLASSIC CONTORNO: CANNELLINI BEANS

Simply boiled, beans provide the perfect accompaniment to bistecca. The small white ones are best when they go straight from the garden into the pot. They should be anointed with a generous dose of Tuscan olive oil; the combination is oddly felicitous, and it goes a long way toward explaining why Tuscans are referred to as *mangiafagioli* (bean eaters) by other Italians.

A CLASSIC DOLCE: BISCOTTI DI PRATO

These are sometimes the only dessert on offer. *Biscotti* means twice-cooked (or, in this case, twice-baked). They are hard almond cookies that soften considerably when dipped languidly into *vin santo* ("holy wine"), a sweet dessert wine, or into a simple *caffè*.

A CLASSIC WINE: CHIANTI CLASSICO

This blend from the region just south of Florence relies mainly on the local, hardy Sangiovese grape; it's aged for at least one year before hitting the market. (*Riserve*—reserve—is aged at least an additional six months.)

Chianti is usually the libation of choice for Florentines. Traditionalists opt for the younger, fruitier (and usually less expensive) versions often served in straw flasks. You can sample Chianti Classico all over town and buy it in local supermarkets.

Biscotti

Its magical combination of beauty and history has drawn people to Florence for centuries, and then it draws them back again. It offers myriad moments of personal illumination before its palazzi, its churches, and its art museums, as well as in interaction with the people you meet there.

Florence has captivated visitors for ages now, probably ever since the powerful Medici family first staged jousts and later lavish pageants to celebrate their weddings. Its mostly sober beauty continued to attract people from all over Europe intent on taking in the achievements of the past on their Grand Tour of Europe. Sometimes this heady combination of art and beauty has proven overwhelming, as it did for French author and diplomat Stendhal in 1817, whose visit to the church of Santa Croce occasioned palpitations and a fainting spell.

Today, however, visitors are more often overwhelmed by the press of their own numbers intent on taking it all in before moving on to the next stop on their tightly scheduled tours. Florence has always been visitor-friendly—the historical center of the city can be crossed on foot in less than half an hour, and the picturesque surrounding hills are a short bus ride away. But the flood of tourists has made the natives more reticent. A visitor is more likely to bump into or to exchange views with other visitors than with native Florentines, all busy catering to tourists' needs. Few Florentines, these days, can afford to live in the center. Even the university has pulled some buildings out to a suburb.

By day, the city is overrun with busloads of day-trippers; come evening by droves of U.S. study-abroad students intent on immersion in the native *aperitivo* (pre-dinner drink) culture. Where have all the Italians gone, you wonder? Fear not, they still come out on Sundays to walk in family groups along the major shopping streets, school groups still pack museums, and they still hold parades in Renaissance costume to mark various historical or religious occasions. Caffè culture still thrives. All this will be revealed to the attentive visitor who sees past the crowds and takes the time to look around the corner onto a quieter street, piazza, or neighborhood.

When the sun sets over the Arno and, as Mark Twain described it, "overwhelms Florence with tides of color that make all the sharp lines dim and faint and turn the solid city to a city of dreams," it's hard not to fall under the city's spell.

Planning

Getting Here and Around

AIR

To get into the city center from the airport by car, take the autostrada A11. The T2 tram will take you directly to and from the airport and the center of town. Buy tickets at machines outside the tram stops.

CONTACTS Aeroporto A. Vespucci. ⊠ *10 km (6 miles) northwest of Florence, Florence* ☎ *055/30615* ⊕ *www.aeroporto. firenze.it.* **Aeroporto Galileo Galilei.** ⊠ *12 km (7 miles) south of Pisa and 80 km (50 miles) west of Florence, Florence* ☎ *050/849300* ⊕ *www.pisa-airport.com.*

BIKE AND MOPED

Brave souls (cycling in Florence is difficult at best) may rent bicycles at easy-to-spot locations at Fortezza da Basso, the Stazione Centrale di Santa Maria Novella, and Piazza Pitti. Otherwise, try **Alinari** (⊠ *Via San Zanobi 40/r, San Marco* ☎ *055/280500* ⊕ *www.alinarirental. com*). You'll be up against hordes of tourists and those pesky *motorini* (mopeds). (For a safer ride, try Le Cascine, a former Medici hunting ground turned into a large public park with paved pathways.) The historic center can be circumnavigated via bike paths lining the *viali*, the ring road surrounding the area. If you want to go native, rent a noisy Vespa (Italian for "wasp") or other make of motorcycle or *motorino*. Try **Vespa Hangar** (⊠ *Via degli Avelli 2* ☎ *351/5494122 mobile*).

BUS

Florence's flat, compact city center is made for walking, but when your feet get weary you can use the efficient bus system, which includes the small electric buses making the rounds in the center. Buses also climb to Piazzale Michelangelo and San Miniato south of the Arno.

Autolinee Toscana (⊕ *www.at-bus.it*) has updated schedules on its website. Tickets should be bought in advance from tobacco shops, newsstands, automatic ticket machines near main stops, online, or using a mobile app. Paper tickets must be validated in the machine immediately upon boarding. You may also buy tickets on the bus, but the cost is approximately double.

You have several ticket options, all valid for one or more rides on all lines. A €1.70 ticket purchased in advance is good for one hour from the time it is first validated. A Carnet of multiple tickets—each valid for 70 minutes—costs €6 (four) or €15.50 (10). A weekly pass costs €14.70.

Autolinee Toscana also provides service to Siena and San Gimignano. Long-distance **FlixBus** (⊕ *www.global.flixbus.com*) provides inexpensive service between Florence and other cities in Italy and Europe.

CAR

Florence is connected to the north and south of Italy by the Autostrada del Sole (A1). It takes about 1½ hours of driving on scenic roads to get to Bologna (although heavy truck traffic over the Apennines often makes for slower going), about 3 hours to Rome, and 3–3½ hours to Milan. The Tyrrhenian Coast is an hour west on the A11.

An automobile in Florence is a major liability. If your itinerary includes parts of Italy where you'll want a car (such as Tuscany), pick the vehicle up on your way out of town.

TAXI

Taxis usually wait at stands throughout the city (in front of the train station and in Piazza della Repubblica, for example). You can also call radio dispatch (☎ *055/4390, 055/4242*) for one to pick you up wherever you are.

The meter starts at €3.30 if you get a taxi at a stand or €5.50 if you call for one. Extra charges apply at night, on Sunday, and for luggage. Women out on the town after midnight are entitled to a 10% discount on the fare; you must, however, request it or call radio dispatch (☎ 055/4378557).

TRAIN

Florence is on the principal Italian train route between most European capitals and Rome, and within Italy it is served frequently from Milan, Venice, and Rome by Intercity (IC) and nonstop Eurostar trains. Avoid trains that stop only at the Campo di Marte or Rifredi station, which are not convenient to the city center.

CONTACT Stazione Centrale di Santa Maria Novella. ✉ *Piazza della Stazione, Santa Maria Novella* ☎ *89 20 21 Trenitalia in Italy (fee for call)* ⊕ *www.trenitalia.com.*

Making the Most of Your Time

With some planning, you can see Florence's most famous sights in a couple of days. Start off at the city's most awe-inspiring architectural wonder, the **Duomo,** climbing to the top of the dome if you have the stamina (and are not claustrophobic: it gets a little tight going up and coming back down). On the same piazza, check out Ghiberti's bronze doors at the **Battistero.** (They're actually high-quality copies; the Museo dell'Opera del Duomo has the originals.) Set aside the afternoon for the **Galleria degli Uffizi,** making sure to reserve tickets in advance.

On Day 2, visit Michelangelo's *David* in the **Galleria dell'Accademia**—reserve tickets here, too. Linger in **Piazza della Signoria,** Florence's central square, where a copy of *David* stands in the spot the original occupied for centuries, then head east a couple of blocks to **Santa Croce,** the city's most artistically rich church.

Double back and walk across Florence's landmark bridge, the **Ponte Vecchio.**

Do all that, and you'll have seen some great art, but you've just scratched the surface. If you have more time, put the **Bargello,** the **Museo di San Marco,** and the **Cappelle Medicee** at the top of your list. When you're ready for an art break, stroll through the **Boboli Gardens** or explore Florence's lively shopping scene, from the food stalls of the **Mercato Centrale** to the chic boutiques of the **Via Tornabuoni.**

HOURS

Florence's sights keep tricky hours. Some are closed Wednesday, some Monday, some every other Monday. Quite a few shut their doors each day (or on most days) by 2 in the afternoon. Things get even more confusing on weekends. Make it a general rule to check the hours closely for any place you're planning to visit; if it's someplace you have your heart set on seeing, it's worthwhile to call to confirm.

Here's a selection of major sights that might not be open when you'd expect (⇨ *consult the Sights listings within this chapter for full details).* And be aware that, as always, hours can and do change. Also note that on the first Sunday of the month, all state museums are free. That means that the Accademia and the Uffizi, among others, do not accept reservations. Unless you are a glutton for punishment (i.e., large crowds), these museums are best avoided on that day.

The **Accademia** and the **Uffizi** are both closed Monday. Note, too, that on the first Sunday of the month, all state museums, including these two, are free and do not accept reservations.

The **Bargello** is closed on Tuesday and the second and fourth Sunday of the month. Otherwise, it's open from 8:15 am until 1:50 pm (until 6:50 pm on Saturday).

The **Battistero** is open daily 8:30 am to 7:30 pm.

The **Cappelle Medicee** are closed Tuesday. Otherwise, it's open from 8:15 am to 6:50 pm.

The **Duomo** is closed on Sunday and open from 10:15 am to 6:45 pm the rest of the week.

Museo di San Marco closes at 1:50 pm—except for alternating Sundays and Mondays, when it's closed entirely.

Palazzo Medici-Riccardi is closed Wednesday.

RESERVATIONS

At most times of day a line of people snakes around the Uffizi. They're waiting to buy tickets, and you don't want to be one of them. Instead, Instead, book online (⊕ *www.uffizi.it*) or call ahead (☎ *055/294883*) for a reservation.

Go to the museum's reservation door (door 3) 10 minutes before the appointed hour (at least 30 minutes before in high season), give the clerk your reservation number, or show your digital ticket, pick up your paper ticket, and go inside. You'll pay €4 for this privilege, but it's money well spent. Money-saving combo tickets are available as well.

You'll also want to book in advance for Galleria dell'Accademia (⊕ *www. galleriaaccademiafirenze.it*), where lines rival those of the Uffizi. Reservations can also be made for the Palazzo Pitti, the Bargello, and several other sights, but they usually aren't needed—although, lately, in summer, lines can be long at Palazzo Pitti. An alternative strategy is to check with your hotel—many will handle reservations.

Restaurants

Florence's popularity with tourists means that, unfortunately, there's a higher percentage of mediocre restaurants here than you'll find in most Italian towns (Venice, perhaps, might win that prize). Some restaurant owners cut corners and let standards slip, knowing that a customer today is unlikely to return tomorrow, regardless of the quality of the meal. So, if you're looking to eat well, it pays to do some research, starting with the recommendations here. Dining hours start at around 1 for lunch and 8 for dinner. Many of Florence's restaurants are small, so reservations are a must. You can sample such specialties as creamy fegatini (a chicken-liver spread) and ribollita (minestrone thickened with bread and beans and swirled with extra-virgin olive oil) in a bustling, convivial trattoria, where you share long wooden tables set with paper place mats, or in an upscale *ristorante* with linen tablecloths and napkins.

Hotels

Florence is equipped with hotels for all budgets; for instance, you can find both budget and luxury hotels in the *centro storico* (historic center) and along the Arno. Florence has so many famous landmarks that it's not hard to find lodging with a panoramic view. The equivalent of the genteel *pensioni* of yesteryear can still be found, though they are now officially classified as "hotels." Generally small and intimate, they often have a quaint appeal that usually doesn't preclude modern plumbing. Florence's importance not only as a tourist city but also as a convention center and the site of the Pitti fashion collections guarantees a variety of accommodations.

The high demand also means that, except in winter, reservations are a must.

⇨ *Hotel and restaurant reviews have been shortened. For full information, visit Fodors.com. Prices in the hotel reviews are the lowest cost of a standard double room in high season. Prices in the dining reviews are the average cost of a main course at dinner, or, if dinner is not served, at lunch.*

12

Florence PLANNING

What It Costs in Euros			
$	$$	$$$	$$$$
RESTAURANTS			
under €15	€15–€24	€25–€35	over €35
HOTELS			
under €125	€125–€200	€201–€300	over €300

Shopping

Window-shopping in Florence is like visiting an enormous contemporary-art gallery. Many of today's greatest Italian artists are fashion designers, and most keep shops in Florence. Discerning shoppers may find bargains in the street markets.

■ TIP→ **Do not buy any knockoff goods from any of the hawkers plying their fake Prada (or any other high-end designer) on the streets. It's illegal, and fines are astronomical if the police happen to catch you. (You pay the fine, not the vendor.)**

Shops are generally open 9–1 and 3:30–7:30, and are closed Sunday and Monday mornings most of the year. Summer (June to September) hours are usually 9–1 and 4–8, and some shops close Saturday afternoon instead of Monday morning. When looking for addresses, you'll see two color-coded numbering systems on each street. The red numbers are commercial addresses and are indicated, for example, as "31/r." The blue or black numbers are residential addresses. Most shops take major credit cards and ship purchases, but because of possible delays it's wise to take your purchases with you.

SHOPPING DISTRICTS

Florence's most fashionable shops are concentrated in the center of town. The fanciest designer shops are mainly on **Via Tornabuoni** and **Via della Vigna Nuova.** The city's largest concentrations of antiques shops are on **Borgo Ognissanti** and the Oltrarno's **Via Maggio.** The **Ponte Vecchio** houses reputable but very expensive jewelry shops, as it has since the 16th century. The area near **Santa Croce** is the heart of the leather merchants' district.

Tours

Alone-in-the-Duomo VIP Tour

SPECIAL-INTEREST TOURS | FAMILY | Partnering with international companies such as Walks and Devour Tours, City Experiences (⊕ www.cityexperiences.com) is able to offer unique, once-in-a-lifetime tours. On the 1.75-hour Alone-in-the-Duomo experience, for instance, you not only get after-hours access to the cathedral, but you also climb up to the dome, visit private terraces, and watch as the official Key Master locks up for the night—all while accompanied by knowledgeable guides. ☎ 800/459–8105 City Experiences Main U.S. Contact Center, 888/683–8670 City Experiences Walks (Toll-Free in U.S.), 068/5960143 City Experiences Walks (in Italy) ⊕ www.takewalks.com/florence-tours ⌨ From $136.

Visitor Information

The Florence tourist office (☎ 039/055000 ⊕ www.feelflorence.it), has branches at the airport, just outside Piazza Santa Croce, across the street from Stazione di Santa Maria Novella (the main train station), and at the Bigallo in Piazza del Duomo. The offices are generally open from 9 am until 7 pm (2 pm on Sunday and holidays). The multilingual staff will answer questions, give you directions, and provide information on the latest performing-arts happenings and other events. The website also provides information in English.

Around the Duomo

The heart of Florence, stretching from the Piazza del Duomo south to the Arno, is as dense with artistic treasures as any place in the world. Its churches, medieval towers, Renaissance palaces, and world-class museums and galleries contain some of the most outstanding achievements of Western art.

Much of the centro storico is closed to automobile traffic, but you still must dodge mopeds, cyclists, and masses of fellow tourists as you walk the narrow streets, especially in the area bounded by the Duomo, Piazza della Signoria, Galleria degli Uffizi, and the Ponte Vecchio. Via dei Calzaiuoli, between Piazza del Duomo and Piazza della Signoria, is the city's favorite passeggiata.

Sights

★ Bargello
ART MUSEUM | This building started out in the Middle Ages as the headquarters for the *capitano del popolo* (captain of the people) during the Middle Ages and was later a prison. It now contains the Museo Nazionale, which has one of Italy's finest collections of Renaissance sculpture. The remarkable masterpieces by Michelangelo (1475–1564), Donatello (circa 1386–1466), and Benvenuto Cellini (1500–71) are distributed amid an eclectic collection of arms, ceramics, and miniature bronzes, among other things. ⊠ *Via del Proconsolo 4, Bargello* ☎ *055/0649440* ⊕ *www.bargellomusei. beniculturali.it* ⊑ *€10* ⊘ *Closed Tues. and 2nd and 4th Sun. of the month.*

★ Battistero (*Baptistery*)
RELIGIOUS BUILDING | The octagonal Baptistery is one of the supreme monuments of the Italian Romanesque style and one of Florence's oldest structures. The round Romanesque arches on the exterior date from the 11th century, and the interior dome mosaics from the beginning of the mid-13th century are justly renowned, but they could never outshine the building's famed bronze Renaissance doors decorated with panels crafted by Lorenzo Ghiberti. Michelangelo declared them so beautiful that they could serve as the Gates of Paradise. ⊠ *Piazza del Duomo, Duomo* ☎ *055/2645789* ⊕ *www. duomo.firenze.it* ⊑ *Admission is via one of 3 combo tickets, each valid for 3 days: €30 Brunelleschi Pass (with Campanile, Cupola of the Duomo, Museo dell'Opera del Duomo, and Santa Reparata Basilica Cripta); €20 Giotto Pass (with Campanile, Museo dell'Opera, and Cripta); €15 Ghiberti Pass (with Museo dell'Opera and Cripta).*

Campanile
NOTABLE BUILDING | **FAMILY** | The Gothic bell tower designed by Giotto (circa 1266–1337) is a soaring structure of multicolor marble originally decorated with sculptures by Donatello and reliefs by Giotto, Andrea Pisano, and others (which are now in the Museo dell'Opera del Duomo). A climb of 414 steps rewards you with a close-up of Brunelleschi's cupola on the Duomo next door and a sweeping view of the city. ⊠ *Piazza del Duomo, Duomo* ☎ *055/2645789* ⊕ *www. duomo.firenze.it* ⊑ *Admission is via one of 2 combo tickets, each valid for 3 days: €30 Brunelleschi Pass (with Battistero, Cupola of the Duomo, Museo dell'Opera del Duomo, and Santa Reparata Basilica Cripta); €20 for Giotto Pass (with Battistero, Museo dell'Opera, and Cripta).*

★ Duomo (*Cattedrale di Santa Maria del Fiore*)
CHURCH | In 1296, Arnolfo di Cambio was commissioned to build "the loftiest, most sumptuous edifice human invention could devise" in the Romanesque style. The immense Duomo was not completed until 1436, the year it was consecrated. The imposing facade dates only from the 19th century; its neo-Gothic style somewhat complements Giotto's genuine Gothic 14th-century campanile.

Around the Duomo

The real glory of the Duomo, however, is Filippo Brunelleschi's dome, presiding over the cathedral with a dignity and grace that few domes to this day can match.

Brunelleschi's cupola was one of the great engineering breakthroughs of all time: most of Europe's later domes, including that of St. Peter's in Rome, were built employing Brunelleschi's methods, and today the Duomo has come to symbolize Florence in the same way that the Eiffel Tower symbolizes Paris. The interior is a fine example of Florentine Gothic, though much of the cathedral's best-known art has been moved to the nearby Museo dell'Opera del Duomo. ⊠ *Piazza del Duomo, Duomo* ☎ *055/2645789* ⊕ *www.duomo.firenze.it* ⛪ *Church is free. Admission to the cupola is via the €30 Brunelleschi Pass, a 3-day combo ticket that also includes the Battistero, Campanile, Museo dell'Opera del Duomo, and Santa Reparata Basilica Cripta* ⊙ *Closed Sun.* ⚠ *Timed-entry reservations required for the cupola.*

★ **Galleria degli Uffizi**
ART MUSEUM | The Medici installed their art collections at Europe's first modern museum, open to the public (at first only by request) since 1591. Among the highlights are Paolo Uccello's *Battle of San Romano*; the *Madonna and Child with Two Angels* by Fra Filippo Lippi; *Birth of Venus* and *Primavera* by Sandro Botticelli; the portraits of the Renaissance duke Federico da Montefeltro and his wife Battista Sforza by Piero della Francesca; the *Madonna of the Goldfinch* by Raphael; Michelangelo's *Doni Tondo*; the *Venus of Urbino* by Titian; and the splendid *Bacchus* by Caravaggio. Late in the afternoon is the least crowded time to visit. For a €4 fee, advance tickets (recommended) can be reserved by phone, online, or, once in Florence, at the Uffizi's reservation booths (⊠ *Uffizi presale*

booth, Piazza Pitti ☎ *055/294883*), at least one day in advance of your visit. ⊠ *Piazzale degli Uffizi 6, Piazza della Signoria* ☎ *055/294883* ⊕ *www.uffizi.it* 💶 *From €12* ⊙ *Closed Mon.* ⌖ *Entrance fee doubles during high season.*

Mercato Nuovo (*New Market*)
MARKET | FAMILY | The open-air loggia, built in 1551, teems with souvenir stands, but the real attraction is a copy of Pietro Tacca's bronze *Porcellino* (which translates as "little pig" despite the fact the animal is, in fact, a wild boar). The sculpture is Florence's equivalent of the Trevi Fountain: put a coin in his mouth, and if it falls through the grate below (according to one interpretation), it means you'll return to Florence someday. What you're seeing is a copy of a copy: Tacca's original version, in the Museo Bardini, is actually a copy of an ancient Greek work. ⊠ *Via Por Santa Maria at Via Porta Rossa, Piazza della Repubblica* ☎ *339/3271143 mobile* ⊕ *www.mercatodelporcellino.it.*

★ **Museo dell'Opera del Duomo**
(*Cathedral Museum*)
ART MUSEUM | A seven-year restoration, completed in 2015, gave Florence one of its most modern, up-to-date museums. The exhibition space was doubled, and the old facade of the cathedral, torn down in the 1580s, was re-created with a 1:1 relationship to the real thing. Both sets of Ghiberti's doors adorn the same room. Michelangelo's *Pietà* finally has the space it deserves, as does Donatello's *Mary Magdalene.* ⊠ *Piazza del Duomo 9, Duomo* ☎ *055/2302885* ⊕ *www.duomo.firenze.it* 💶 *Admission is via one of 3 combo tickets, each valid for 3 days: €30 Brunelleschi Pass (with Battistero, Campanile, Cupola of the Duomo, and Santa Reparata Basilica Cripta); €20 Giotto Pass (with Battistero, Campanile, and Cripta); €15 Ghiberti Pass (with Battistero and Cripta)* ⊙ *Closed 1st Tues. of month.*

Continued on page 545

Florence Through the Ages

Guelph vs. Ghibelline. Although Florence can lay claim to a modest importance in the ancient world, it didn't come into its own until the Middle Ages. In the early 1200s, the city, like most of the rest of Italy, was rent by civic unrest. Two factions, the Guelphs and the Ghibellines, competed for power. The Guelphs supported the papacy, and the Ghibellines supported the Holy Roman Empire. Bloody battles—most notably one at Montaperti in 1260—tore Florence and other Italian cities apart. By the end of the 13th century, the Guelphs ruled securely, and the Ghibellines had been vanquished. This didn't end civic strife, however: the Guelphs split into the Whites and the Blacks for reasons still debated by historians. Dante, author of *The Divine Comedy*, was banished from Florence in 1301 because he was a White.

The Guilded Age. Local merchants had organized themselves into guilds by some time beginning in the 12th century. In 1250, they proclaimed themselves the *primo popolo* (literally, "first people"), making a landmark attempt at elective, republican rule. Though the episode lasted only 10 years, it constituted a breakthrough in Western history. Such a daring stance by the merchant class was a by-product of Florence's emergence as an economic powerhouse. Florentines were papal bankers; they instituted the system of international letters of credit, and the gold florin became the international standard of currency. With this economic strength came a building boom. Sculptors such as Ghiberti and Donatello decorated the

new churches; painters such as Giotto and Masaccio frescoed their walls.

Mighty Medici. Though ostensibly a republic, Florence was blessed (or cursed) with one very powerful family, the Medici, who came to prominence in 1434 and were initially the de facto rulers and then the absolute rulers of Florence for several hundred years. It was under patriarch Cosimo il Vecchio (1389–1464) that the Medici's position in Florence was securely established. Florence's golden age occurred during the reign of his grandson Lorenzo de' Medici (1449–92). Lorenzo was not only an astute politician but also a highly educated man and a great patron of the arts. Called "Il Magnifico" (the Magnificent), he gathered around him poets, artists, philosophers, architects, and musicians.

Lorenzo's son Piero (1471–1503) proved inept at handling the city's affairs. He was run out of town in 1494, and Florence briefly enjoyed its status as a republic while dominated by the Dominican friar Girolamo Savonarola (1452–98). After a decade of internal unrest, the republic fell and the Medici returned to power, but Florence never regained its former prestige. By the 1530s most of the major artistic talent had left the city—Michelangelo, for one, had settled in Rome. The now-ineffectual Medici, eventually attaining the title of grand dukes, remained nominally in power until the line died out in 1737, after which time Florence passed from the Austrians to the French and back again until the unification of Italy (1865–70), when it briefly became the capital under King Vittorio Emanuele II.

THE DUOMO

FLORENCE'S BIGGEST MASTERPIECE

For all its monumental art and architecture, Florence has one undisputed centerpiece: the Cathedral of Santa Maria del Fiore, better known as the Duomo. Its cupola dominates the skyline, presiding over the city's rooftops like a red hen over her brood. Little wonder that when Florentines feel homesick, they say they have "*nostalgia del cupolone.*"

The Duomo's construction began in 1296, following the design of Arnolfo di Cambio, Florence's greatest architect of the time. By modern standards, construction was slow and haphazard—it continued through the 14th and into the 15th century, with some dozen architects having a hand in the project.

In 1366, Neri di Fioravante created a model for the hugely ambitious cupola: it was to be the largest dome in the world, surpassing Rome's Pantheon. But when the time finally came to build the dome in 1418, no one was sure how—or even if—it could be done. Florence was faced with a 143 foot hole in the roof of its cathedral, and one of the greatest challenges in the history of architecture.

Fortunately, local genius Filippo Brunelleschi was just the man for the job. Brunelleschi won the 1418 competition to design the dome, and for the next 18 years he oversaw its construction. The enormity of his achievement can hardly be overstated. Working on such a large scale (the dome weighs 37,000 tons and uses 4 million bricks) required him to invent hoists and cranes that were engineering marvels. A "dome within a dome" design and a novel herringbone bricklaying pattern were just two of the innovations used to establish structural integrity. Perhaps most remarkably, he executed the construction without a supporting wooden framework, which had previously been thought indispensable.

Brunelleschi designed the lantern atop the dome, but he died soon after its first stone was laid in 1446; it wouldn't be completed until 1461. Another 400 years passed before the Duomo received its facade, a 19th-century neo-Gothic creation.

DUOMO TIMELINE

1296 Work begins, following design by Arnolfo di Cambio.

1302 Arnolfo dies; work continues, with sporadic interruptions.

1331 Management of construction taken over by the Wool Merchants guild.

1334 Giotto appointed project overseer, designs campanile.

1337 Giotto dies; Andrea Pisano takes leadership role.

1348 The Black Plague; all work ceases.

1366 Vaulting on nave completed; Neri di Fioravante makes model for dome.

1417 Drum for dome completed.

1418 Competition is held to design the dome.

1420 Brunelleschi begins work on the dome.

1436 Dome completed.

1446 Construction of lantern begins; Brunelleschi dies.

1461 Antonio Manetti, a student of Brunelleschi, completes lantern.

1469 Gilt copper ball and cross added by Verrocchio.

1587 Original facade is torn down by Medici court.

1871 Emilio de Fabris wins competition to design new facade.

1887 Facade completed.

WHAT TO LOOK FOR INSIDE THE DUOMO

The interior of the Duomo is a fine example of Florentine Gothic with a beautiful marble floor, but the space feels strangely barren—a result of its great size and the fact that some of the best art has been moved to the nearby **Museo dell'Opera del Duomo**.

Notable among the works that remain are two towering equestrian frescoes of famous mercenaries: Niccolò da Tolentino (1456) by Andrea del Castagno, and Sir John Hawkwood (1436) by Paolo Uccello. There's also fine terra-cotta work by Luca della Robbia. Ghiberti, Brunelleschi's great rival, is responsible for much of the stained glass, as well as a reliquary urn with gorgeous reliefs. A vast fresco of *the Last Judgment*, painted by Vasari and Zuccari, covers the dome's interior. Brunelleschi had wanted mosaics to go there; it's a pity he didn't get his wish.

In the crypt beneath the cathedral, you can explore excavations of a Roman wall and mosaic fragments from the late 6th century; entry is near the first pier on the right. On the way down you pass Brunelleschi's modest tomb.

1. Entrance; stained glass by Ghiberti
2. Fresco of Niccolò da Tolentino by Andrea del Castagno
3. Fresco of John Hawkwood by Paolo Uccello
4. *Dante and the Divine Comedy* by Domenico di Michelino
5. *Lunette: Ascension* by Luca della Robbia
6. Above altar: two angels by Luca della Robbia. Below the altar: reliquary of St. Zenobius by Ghiberti
7. *Lunette: Resurrection* by Luca della Robbia
8. Entrance to dome
9. Bust of Brunelleschi by Buggiano
10. Stairs to crypt
11. Campanile

500 feet

300 feet

MAKING THE CLIMB

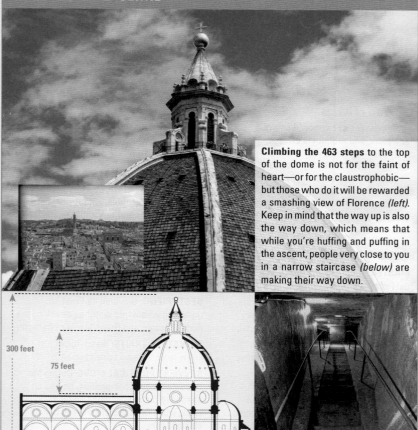

Climbing the 463 steps to the top of the dome is not for the faint of heart—or for the claustrophobic—but those who do it will be rewarded a smashing view of Florence *(left)*. Keep in mind that the way up is also the way down, which means that while you're huffing and puffing in the ascent, people very close to you in a narrow staircase *(below)* are making their way down.

300 feet

75 feet

DUOMO BASICS

- Admission to the church is free, but there's a fee to visit the cupola, and timed-entry reservations are required.

- For an alternative to the dome, consider climbing the less trafficked campanile, which gives you a view from on high of the dome itself.

- Dress code essentials: covered shoulders, no short shorts, and hats off upon entering.

THE CRYPT

The crypt is worth a visit: computer modeling allows visitors to see its ancient Roman fabric and subsequent rebuilding. A transparent plastic model shows exactly what the earlier church looked like.

BRUNELLESCHI vs. GHIBERTI
The Rivalry of Two Renaissance Geniuses

In Renaissance Florence, painters, sculptors, and architects competed for major commissions, with the winner earning the right to undertake a project that might occupy him (and keep him paid) for a decade or more. Stakes were high, and the resulting rivalries fierce—none more so than that between Filippo Brunelleschi and Lorenzo Ghiberti.

The two first clashed in 1401, for the commission to create the bronze doors of the Baptistery. When Ghiberti won, Brunelleschi took it hard, fleeing to Rome, where he would remain for 15 years. Their rematch came in 1418, over the design of the Duomo's cupola, with Brunelleschi triumphant. Thereafter, neither man missed a chance to belittle the other's work.

FILIPPO BRUNELLESCHI (1377–1446)

MASTERPIECE: The dome of Santa Maria del Fiore.

BEST FRIENDS: Donatello, whom he stayed with in Rome after losing the Baptistery doors competition; the Medici family, who rescued him from bankruptcy.

SIGNATURE TRAITS: Paranoid, secretive, bad tempered, practical joker, inept businessman.

SAVVIEST POLITICAL MOVE: Feigned sickness and left for Rome after his dome plans were publicly criticized by Ghiberti, who was second-in-command. The project proved too much for Ghiberti to manage on his own, and Brunelleschi returned triumphant.

MOST EMBARRASSING MOMENT: In 1434, he was imprisoned for two weeks for failure to pay a small guild fee. The humiliation might have been orchestrated by Ghiberti.

OTHER CAREER: Shipbuilder. He built a huge vessel, *Il Badalone*, to transport marble for the dome up the Arno. It sank on its first voyage.

INSPIRED: The dome of St. Peter's in Rome.

LORENZO GHIBERTI (1378–1455)

MASTERPIECE: *The Gates of Paradise*, the ten-paneled east doors of the Baptistery.

BEST FRIEND: Giovanni da Prato, an underling who wrote diatribes attacking the dome's design and Brunelleschi's character.

SIGNATURE TRAITS: Instigator, egoist, know-it-all, shrewd businessman.

SAVVIEST POLITICAL MOVE: During the Baptistery doors competition, he had an open studio and welcomed opinions on his work, while Brunelleschi labored behind closed doors.

OTHER CAREER: Collector of classical artifacts, historian.

INSPIRED: *The Gates of Hell* by Auguste Rodin.

The Gates of Paradise detail

Orsanmichele

CHURCH | This structure has served multiple purposes. Built in the 8th century as an oratory, in 1290, it was turned into an open-air loggia for selling grain. Destroyed by fire in 1304, it was rebuilt as a loggia-market. Between 1367 and 1380, its arcades were closed and two stories were added above. Finally, at century's end, it was turned into a church.

Although the interior contains a beautifully detailed 14th-century Gothic tabernacle by Andrea Orcagna (1308–68), it's the exterior that is most interesting. Niches contain sculptures (all copies) dating from the early 1400s to the early 1600s by Donatello and Verrocchio (1435–88), among others, which were paid for by the guilds. ⊠ *Via dell'Arte della Lana, Duomo* ☎ *055/0649450* ⊕ *www.bargellomusei.beniculturali.it* ⊠ *€8* ⚗ *Reservations recommended.*

Palazzo Davanzati

CASTLE/PALACE | The prestigious Davizzi family owned this 14th-century palace in one of Florence's swankiest medieval neighborhoods (it was sold to the Davanzati in the 15th century). The place is a delight, as you can wander through the surprisingly light-filled courtyard and climb the steep stairs to the piano nobile (there's also an elevator), where the family did most of its living. The beautiful Sala dei Pappagalli (Parrot Room) is adorned with trompe-l'oeil tapestries and gaily painted birds. ⊠ *Piazza Davanzati 13, Piazza della Repubblica* ☎ *055/0649460* ⊕ *www.bargellomusei.beniculturali.it* ⊠ *€6* ⊘ *Closed Mon. and 1st, 3rd, and 5th Sun. of month.*

Palazzo Vecchio (*Old Palace*)

CASTLE/PALACE | **FAMILY** | Presumably designed by Arnolfo di Cambio and begun in 1299, Florence's forbidding, fortress-like city hall was built as a meeting place for the guildsmen governing the city at the time. Although its massive bulk and towering campanile dominate Piazza della Signoria, its interior courtyard is a good deal less severe. Its main attraction, however, is the opulently vast, second-floor Sala dei Cinquecento (Room of the Five Hundred), named for the 500-member Great Council that met here. ⊠ *Piazza della Signoria, Piazza della Signoria* ☎ *055/2768224* ⊕ *www.museicivicifiorentini.comune.fi.it* ⊠ *From €12.50.*

Piazza della Repubblica

PLAZA/SQUARE | The square marks the site of an ancient forum, which was the core of the original Roman settlement and which was replaced in the Middle Ages by the Mercato Vecchio (Old Market). The current piazza, constructed between 1885 and 1895 as a neoclassical showpiece, is lined with cafés that are the perfect spots from which to people-watch. ⊠ *Piazza della Repubblica, Piazza della Repubblica.*

★ Piazza della Signoria

PLAZA/SQUARE | This is by far the most striking square in Florence. It was here, in 1497 and 1498, that the famous "bonfire of the vanities" took place, when the fanatical Dominican friar Savonarola induced his followers to hurl their worldly goods into the flames. The statues in the square and in the 14th-century Loggia dei Lanzi on the south side vary in quality. Cellini's famous bronze *Perseus* holding the severed head of Medusa is certainly the most important. ⊠ *Piazza della Signoria, Piazza della Signoria.*

★ Ponte Vecchio (*Old Bridge*)

BRIDGE | This charmingly simple bridge was built in 1345 to replace an earlier bridge swept away by flood. Its shops first housed butchers, then grocers, blacksmiths, and other merchants. But in 1593, the Medici grand duke Ferdinand I, whose private corridor linking the Medici palace (Palazzo Pitti) with the Medici offices (the Uffizi) crossed the bridge atop the shops, decided that all this plebeian commerce under his feet was unseemly. So he threw out the butchers and blacksmiths and installed 41 goldsmiths and eight jewelers. The bridge has been devoted solely to these two trades ever since. The Corridoio Vasariano (✉ *Piazzale degli Uffizi 6, Piazza della Signoria* ☎ *055/294883*), the private Medici elevated passageway (closed to the general public in 2016 but slated to reopen in May of 2024 so check when you visit), was built by Vasari in 1565. It was most likely designed so that the Medici family wouldn't have to walk amid the commoners. ✉ *Ponte Vecchio, Duomo.*

🍴 Restaurants

Coquinarius

$$ | ITALIAN | This rustically elegant space, which has served many purposes over the past 600 years, offers some of the tastiest food in town at great prices. It's the perfect place to come if you aren't sure what you're hungry for, as it offers a bit of everything, including several fish dishes, among them carpaccio and grilled offerings, and a selection of pasta dishes that make choosing just one very hard, though the ravioli with pecorino and pears is particularly good. **Known for:** many vegetarian options; reasonably priced wine list; inconsistent service. ⑤ *Average main: €22* ✉ *Via delle Oche 11/r, Duomo* ☎ *055/2302153* ⊕ *www. coquinarius.it* ⊙ *Closed Sun.*

★ Gucci Osteria

$$$$ | FUSION | Chef, artist, and visionary Massimo Bottura has joined forces with the creative folks at Gucci to develop a marvelous tasting menu that is both classic and innovative. Though he trained with Ducasse and Adrià, his major influence was his grandmother's cooking. **Known for:** Southern–Italian inspired dishes; an ever-changing menu; outdoor seating in one of Florence's most beautiful squares. ⑤ *Average main: €120* ✉ *Piazza della Signoria 10, Piazza della Signoria* ☎ *055/0621744* ⊕ *www.guccios-teria.com/it/florence.*

★ Rivoire

$$ | ITALIAN | One of the best spots in Florence for people-watching offers stellar service, light snacks, and terrific aperitivi. It's been around since the 1860s, and has been famous for its hot and cold chocolate (with or without cream) for more than a century. **Known for:** delicious (but expensive) hot chocolate; friendly bartenders; the view on the piazza. ⑤ *Average main: €15* ✉ *Piazza della Signoria 5/r, Piazza della Signoria* ☎ *055/214412* ⊕ *rivoire.it/firenze.*

☕ Coffee and Quick Bites

★ 'ino

$ | ITALIAN | Grab a bite and/or a glass of wine after a visit to the nearby Uffizi. Only the very best ingredients go into owner Alessandro Frassica's delectable (if a bit pricey) panini. **Known for:** delicious bread; interesting panini combinations; top-notch ingredients. ⑤ *Average main: €11* ✉ *Via dei Georgofili 3/r–7/r, Piazza della Signoria* ☎ *055/214154* ⊕ *www. inofirenze.com* ⊙ *Closed Mon. and Tues.*

🛏 Hotels

Hermitage

$$$ | HOTEL | Some rooms here have views of the Palazzo Vecchio, and others of the Arno; the rooftop terrace, where you can have breakfast or an aperitivo, is decked with flowers. **Pros:** views; friendly staff; enviable position a stone's throw from the Ponte Vecchio. **Cons:** short flight of stairs to reach elevator; might be time for a refurbishing; street noise sometimes a problem. ⑤ *Rooms from: €249* ✉ *Vicolo Marzio 1, Piazza della Signoria* ☎ *055/287216* ⊕ *www.hermitagehotel. com* ⤴ *28 rooms* ⑩ *Free Breakfast.*

Hotel degli Orafi

$$$$ | HOTEL | A key scene in *A Room with a View* was shot in this pensione, which is today a luxury hotel adorned with chintz and marble. **Pros:** stellar Arno views; rooftop bar; quiet location during the evenings. **Cons:** some street noise in river-facing rooms; on the path of many tour groups during the day; somewhat pricey. ⑤ *Rooms from: €327 ⊠ Lungarno Archibusieri 4, Piazza della Signoria* ☎ *055/26622* ⊕ *www.hoteldegliorafi.it* ↗ *50 rooms* ⫯◯⫯ *Free Breakfast.*

Hotel Helvetia and Bristol
$$$$ | HOTEL | From the cozy yet sophisticated lobby, with its stone columns, to the guest rooms decorated with prints, you might feel as if you're a guest in a manor house. **Pros:** central location; excellent restaurant; old-world charm. **Cons:** rooms facing the street get some noise; breakfast is not always included in the price of a room; books up quickly. ⑤ *Rooms from: €675 ⊠ Via dei Pescioni 2, Piazza della Repubblica* ☎ *055/26651* ⊕ *collezione.starhotels.com* ↗ *89 rooms* ⫯◯⫯ *No Meals.*

Hotel Renaissance
$$ | HOTEL | Nestled in an old building just a stone's throw from the main civic square (Piazza Signoria), this charming little boutique hotel offers peace and elegance. **Pros:** the staff; the sumptuous breakfast; the location. **Cons:** steps up to the elevator; some street noise in some rooms; books up quickly. ⑤ *Rooms from: €190 ⊠ Via della Condotta 4, Piazza della Signoria* ☎ *055/213996* ⊕ *www. hotelrenaissancefirenze.com* ↗ *9 rooms* ⫯◯⫯ *No Meals.*

★ In Piazza della Signoria
$$$$ | B&B/INN | In this home that is part of a 15th-century palazzo, a cozy feeling permeates the charming rooms, all of which are uniquely decorated and lovingly furnished; some have damask curtains, others fanciful frescoes in the bathroom. **Pros:** marvelous staff; tasty breakfast with a view of Piazza della Signoria; some rooms easily accommodate three. **Cons:** short flight of stairs to reach elevator; some of the rooms have steps up into showers and bathtubs; books up quickly during high season. ⑤ *Rooms from: €655 ⊠ Via dei Magazzini 2, Piazza*

della Signoria ☎ *055/2399546* ⊕ *www. boutiquehotelinpiazza.com* ↗ *13 rooms* ⫯◯⫯ *Free Breakfast.*

Palazzo Vecchietti
$$$$ | HOTEL | If you're looking for a swank setting, and the possibility of staying in for a meal (each room has a tiny kitchenette), look no further than this hotel which, while thoroughly modern, dates to the 15th century. **Pros:** great service; central location; public room has a Renaissance fireplace and high ceilings. **Cons:** no restaurant; some street noise a possibility; it's expensive. ⑤ *Rooms from: €1194 ⊠ Via degli Strozzi 4, Duomo* ☎ *055/2302802* ⊕ *www.palazzovecchietti.com* ↗ *12 rooms* ⫯◯⫯ *Free Breakfast.*

Nightlife

Hard Rock Cafe
LIVE MUSIC | Hard Rock packs in young Florentines and travelers eager to sample the music hall chain's take on classic American grub. ⊠ *Via De' Brunelleschi 1, Piazza della Repubblica* ☎ *055/277841* ⊕ *www.hardrock.com.*

Yab
DANCE CLUB | Yab never seems to go out of style, though it increasingly becomes the haunt of Florentine high school and university students intent on dancing and doing vodka shots. ⊠ *Via Sassetti 5/r, Piazza della Repubblica* ☎ *055/215160* ⊕ *www.yab.it.*

⊕ Performing Arts

Orchestra da Camera Fiorentina
MUSIC | This orchestra performs various classical music concerts (many of them free) throughout the year at churches, villas, and museums. Past performances have filled Orsanmichele, the Bargello, and Santo Spirito Church with the orchestra's music. ⊠ *Via Monferrato 2, Piazza della Signoria* ☎ *055/783374* ⊕ *orchestradacamerafiorentina.it.*

Shopping

★ Bernardo

CLOTHING | Come here for men's trousers, cashmere sweaters, and shirts with details like mother-of-pearl buttons. ⊠ *Via Porta Rossa 87/r, Piazza della Repubblica* ☎ *055/283333* ⊕ *www.bernardofirenze.it.*

Diesel

CLOTHING | Trendy Diesel started in Vicenza; its gear is on the "must-have" list of many Italian teens. ⊠ *Via degli Speziali 16/r, Piazza della Signoria* ☎ *055/2399963* ⊕ *shop.diesel.com.*

Fratelli Piccini

JEWELRY & WATCHES | Still in operation after four generations, this Florentine institution sells antique jewelry and makes pieces to order; you can also get old jewelry reset here. ⊠ *Ponte Vecchio 21/23r, Duomo* ☎ *055/294768* ⊕ *www.fratellipiccini.com.*

Gherardi

JEWELRY & WATCHES | Florence's king of coral, Gherardi has the city's largest selection of finely crafted pieces, as well as cultured pearls, jade, and turquoise. ⊠ *Ponte Vecchio 36/r, Piazza della Signoria* ☎ *055/211809* ⊕ *www.gherardigioielli.it.*

Mandragora Art Store

MUSEUM SHOP | This is one of the first attempts in Florence to cash in on the museum-store craze. Look for reproductions of valued works of art and jewelry. ⊠ *Piazza del Duomo 50/r, Duomo* ☎ *055/292559* ⊕ *www.mandragora.it.*

Mercato dei Fiori e Piante (*Flower Market*)

MARKET | Every Thursday morning from September through June the covered loggia in Piazza della Repubblica hosts this lively market—a riot of plants, flowers, and difficult-to-find herbs. ⊠ *Piazza della Repubblica, Piazza della Repubblica.*

Mercato del Porcellino

MARKET | **FAMILY** | If you're looking for cheery, inexpensive trinkets to take home, roam through the stalls under the loggia of the Mercato del Porcellino. ⊠ *Via Por Santa Maria at Via Porta Rossa, Piazza della Repubblica* ☎ *339/3271143 mobile* ⊕ *www.mercatodelporcellino.it.*

Missoni Boutique

CLOTHING | Shop for knitwear at the Florence outpost of the Italian brand known for its bold pieces. ⊠ *Via Porta Rossa 77–79/r, Piazza della Repubblica* ☎ *055/215774* ⊕ *www.missoni.com.*

Oro Due

JEWELRY & WATCHES | Gold jewelry and other beauteous objects are priced according to the level of craftsmanship and the value of gold bullion that day. ⊠ *Via Lambertesca 12/r, Piazza della Signoria* ☎ *055/292143.*

Patrizia Pepe

CLOTHING | The Florentine designer has clothes for those with a tiny streak of rebelliousness. Sizes run small. ⊠ *Piazza San Giovanni 12/r, Duomo* ☎ *055/2645056* ⊕ *www.patriziapepe.com.*

★ Pegna

FOOD | This shop has been selling both Italian and non-Italian food since 1860. If you're tired of mozzarella and feel the need for some cheddar, this is the place to find it. ⊠ *Via dello Studio 8, Duomo* ☎ *055/282701* ⊕ *www.pegna.sangiustosrl.com.*

★ Paolo Penko

JEWELRY & WATCHES | Renaissance goldsmiths provide the inspiration for this dazzling jewelry with a contemporary feel. There is another branch in the San Lorenzo district. ⊠ *Via dell'Oche, 20r, Duomo* ☎ *055/2052577* ⊕ *www.paolopenko.com.*

Quercioli & Lucherini

LINGERIE | This shop has been vending high-quality clothing—the kind that goes next to bare skin—since 1895. Remember that luxury comes at a price. ⊠ *Via Porta Rossa 45/r, Piazza della Repubblica* ☎ *055/292035.*

San Lorenzo

A sculptor, painter, architect, and poet, Florentine native son Michelangelo was a consummate genius, and some of his finest creations remain in his hometown. The Biblioteca Medicea Laurenziana is perhaps his most fanciful work of architecture. A key to understanding Michelangelo's genius can be found in the magnificent Cappelle Medicee, where both his sculptural and architectural prowess can be clearly seen. Planned frescoes were never completed, sadly, for they would have shown in one space the artistic triple threat that he certainly was. The towering yet graceful *David*, perhaps his most famous work, resides in the Galleria dell'Accademia.

Sights

Basilica di San Lorenzo

CHURCH | Filippo Brunelleschi designed this basilica, as well as that of Santo Spirito in the Oltrarno, in the 15th century. He never lived to see either finished. The two interiors are similar in design and effect. San Lorenzo, however, has a grid of dark, inlaid marble lines on the floor, which considerably heightens the dramatic effect. Brunelleschi's Sagrestia Vecchia (Old Sacristy) has stucco decorations by Donatello; it's at the end of the left transept. ⊠ *Piazza San Lorenzo, San Lorenzo* ☎ *055/214042* ⊕ *sanlorenzofirenze.it* ⌦ *€9* ⊘ *Closed Sun.*

Biblioteca Medicea Laurenziana (*Laurentian Library*)

LIBRARY | Michelangelo the architect was every bit as original as Michelangelo the sculptor. He was interested in experimentation, invention, and the expression of a personal vision that was at times highly idiosyncratic. It was never more idiosyncratic than in the Laurentian Library, begun in 1524 and finished in 1568 by Bartolomeo Ammannati. Its famous *vestibolo*, a strangely shaped anteroom, has had scholars scratching their heads for centuries. In a space more than two stories high, why did Michelangelo limit his use of columns and pilasters to the upper two-thirds of the wall? Why didn't he rest them on strong pedestals instead of on huge, decorative curlicue scrolls, which rob them of all visual support? Why did he recess them into the wall, which makes them look weaker still? The architectural elements give the room a soft, rubbery look that is one of the strangest effects ever achieved by 16th-century architecture. ⊠ *Piazza San Lorenzo 9, entrance to left of San Lorenzo, San Lorenzo* ☎ *055/2937911* ⊕ *www.bmlonline.it* ⌦ *Special exhibitions €3* ⊘ *Check ahead on opening days and times as this site has seen temporary closures.*

★ **Cappelle Medicee** (*Medici Chapels*)
CHURCH | This magnificent complex includes the Cappella dei Principi, the Medici chapel and mausoleum begun in 1605 that kept marble workers busy for several hundred years, and the Sagrestia Nuova (New Sacristy), designed by Michelangelo and so called to distinguish it from Brunelleschi's Sagrestia Vecchia (Old Sacristy). Michelangelo received the commission for the New Sacristy in 1520 from Cardinal Giulio de' Medici, who later became Pope Clement VII. The cardinal wanted a new burial chapel for his cousins Giuliano, Duke of Nemours (1478–1534), and Lorenzo, Duke of Urbino (1492–1519). He also wanted to honor his father, also named Giuliano, and his uncle, Lorenzo il Magnifico. The result was a tour de force of architecture and sculpture.

The complex is also home to the Stanza Segreta di Michelangelo (Michelangelo's Secret Room), a small room—covered in exquisite charcoal sketches—where the artist was thought to have hidden for a few months in 1530, after having angered Pope Clement VII. For preservation reasons, access to this room is very

Florence's Trial by Fire

One of the most striking figures of Renaissance Florence was Girolamo Savonarola, a Dominican friar who, for a moment, captured the spiritual conscience of the city. In 1491 he became prior of the convent of San Marco, where he adopted a life of austerity and delivered sermons condemning Florence's excesses and the immorality of his fellow clergy. Following the death of Lorenzo de' Medici in 1492, Savonarola was instrumental in the re-formation of the republic of Florence, ruled by a representative council with Christ enthroned as monarch. In one of his most memorable acts he urged Florentines to toss worldly possessions—from sumptuous dresses to Botticelli paintings—onto a "bonfire of the vanities" in Piazza della Signoria. Savonarola's antagonism toward church hierarchy led to his undoing: he was excommunicated in 1497, and the following year was hanged and burned on charges of heresy. Today, at the Museo di San Marco, you can visit Savonarola's cell.

limited, and the requisite reservations (⊕ *www.b-ticket.com/b-Ticket/uffizi*) tend to sell out very quickly months in advance, so plan well ahead if you want to visit the site. ✉ *Piazza di Madonna degli Aldobrandini 6, San Lorenzo* ☎ *055/294883 reservations* ⊕ *www.bargellomusei.beniculturali.it* ✆ *€9* ⊙ *Closed Tues.*

★ **Galleria dell'Accademia** (*Accademia Gallery*)

ART MUSEUM | FAMILY | The collection of Florentine paintings, dating from the 13th to the 18th century, is largely unremarkable, but the sculptures by Michelangelo are worth the price of admission. The unfinished *Slaves*, fighting their way out of their marble prisons, were meant for the tomb of Michelangelo's overly demanding patron Pope Julius II. But the focal point is the original *David*, commissioned in 1501 by the Opera del Duomo (Cathedral Works Committee), which gave the 26-year-old sculptor a leftover block of marble that had been ruined 40 years earlier by two other sculptors. ✉ *Via Ricasoli 58/60, San Marco* ☎ *055/294883 reservations, 055/0987100 gallery* ⊕ *www.galleriaaccademiafirenze.*

it ✆ *€16* ⊙ *Closed Mon.* ⚐ *€4 advanced booking fee.*

★ **Mercato Centrale**

MARKET | FAMILY | Some of the food at this huge, two-story market hall is remarkably exotic. The ground floor contains meat and cheese stalls, as well as some very good bars that have panini. The upstairs food hall is eerily reminiscent of food halls everywhere, but the quality of the food served more than makes up for this. The downstairs market is closed on Sunday; the upstairs food hall is always open. ✉ *Piazza del Mercato Centrale, San Lorenzo* ☎ *055/2399798* ⊕ *www.mercatocentrale.it/firenze.*

Museo di Casa Martelli

HISTORIC HOME | The wealthy Martelli family, long associated with the all-powerful Medici, lived, from the 16th century, in this palace on a quiet street near the Basilica of San Lorenzo. The last Martelli died in 1986, and, in October 2009, the *casa-museo* (house-museum) opened to the public. It's the only nonreconstructed example of such a house in all of Florence, and for that reason alone it's worth a visit. The family collected art, and while most of the stuff is B-list, a few gems by Beccafumi, Salvatore Rosa, and Piero di Cosimo adorn the walls. ✉ *Via Zanetti 8, San Lorenzo* ☏ *055/0649420* ⊕ *www. bargellomusei.beniculturali.it* 🎫 *Free* ⊘ *Closed Sun., Mon., Tues. morning, Wed.–Fri., and Sat. afternoon.*

Museo di San Marco

ART MUSEUM | A former Dominican convent adjacent to the church of San Marco houses this museum, which contains many stunning works by Fra Angelico (circa 1400–55), the Dominican friar famous for his piety as well as for his painting. When the friars' cells were restructured between 1439 and 1444, he decorated many of them with frescoes meant to spur religious contemplation. His unostentatious and direct paintings exalt the simple beauties of the contemplative life. Don't miss the famous *Annunciation,* on the upper floor, and the works in the gallery off the cloister as you enter. Here you can see his beautiful *Last Judgment*; as usual, the tortures of the damned are far more inventive and interesting than the pleasures of the redeemed. ✉ *Piazza San Marco 3, San Lorenzo* ☏ *055/0882000* ⊕ *museitoscana.cultura.gov.it* 🎫 *€8* ⊘ *Closed Sun. and Mon.*

Palazzo Medici-Riccardi

CASTLE/PALACE | The main attraction of this palace, begun in 1444 by Michelozzo for Cosimo de' Medici, is the interior chapel, the Cappella dei Magi, on the piano nobile (main floor). Painted on its walls is Benozzo Gozzoli's famous *Procession of the Magi,* finished in 1460 and celebrating both the birth of Christ and the greatness of the Medici family. The building also hosts rotating exhibits. ✉ *Via Cavour 3, San Lorenzo* ☏ *055/2760552* ⊕ *www. palazzomediciriccardi.it* 🎫 *Museum only €10* ⊘ *Closed Wed.*

Santissima Annunziata

CHURCH | Dating from the mid-13th century, this church was restructured in 1447 by Michelozzo, who gave it an uncommon (and lovely) entrance cloister with frescoes by Andrea del Sarto

(1486–1530), Pontormo (1494–1556), and Rosso Fiorentino (1494–1540). Another fresco of note is the very fine *Holy Trinity with St. Jerome* in the second chapel on the left. Done by Andrea del Castagno (circa 1421–57), it shows a wiry and emaciated St. Jerome with Paula and Eustochium, two of his closest followers. ✉ *Piazza di Santissima Annunziata, San Lorenzo* ☏ *055/266181* 🎫 *Free.*

Spedale degli Innocenti

ART MUSEUM | **FAMILY** | The edifice built by Brunelleschi in 1419 to serve as an orphanage takes the historical prize as the very first Renaissance building. Brunelleschi designed its portico with his usual rigor, constructing it from the two shapes he considered mathematically (and therefore philosophically and aesthetically) perfect: the square and the circle. Below the level of the arches, the portico encloses a row of perfect cubes; above the level of the arches, the portico encloses a row of intersecting hemispheres. The entire geometric scheme is articulated with Corinthian columns, capitals, and arches borrowed directly from antiquity.

At the time he designed the portico, Brunelleschi was also designing the interior of San Lorenzo, using the same basic ideas. But because the portico was finished before San Lorenzo, the Spedale degli Innocenti can claim the honor of ushering in Renaissance architecture. The 10 ceramic medallions depicting swaddled infants that decorate the portico are by Andrea della Robbia (1435–1525/28), done in about 1487.

Within the building is the Museo degli Innocenti. Although most of the objects are minor works by major artists, they're still worth a look. Of note is Domenico Ghirlandaio's (1449–94) *Adorazione dei Magi* (*Adoration of the Magi*), executed in 1488. The museum also hosts temporary exhibits primarily focused on contemporary art. ✉ *Piazza di Santissima Annunziata 13, San Lorenzo* ☏ *055/2037122* ⊕ *www. museodeglinnocenti.it* 🎫 *From €9.*

San Lorenzo

Sights ▼
1 Basilica di San Lorenzo **D7**
2 Biblioteca Medicea
  Laurenziana **D8**
3 Cappelle Medicee **D7**
4 Galleria dell'Accademia **H5**
5 Mercato Centrale **D6**
6 Museo di Casa Martelli **D8**
7 Museo di San Marco **H4**
8 Palazzo Medici-Riccardi **E7**
9 Santissima Annunziata **I6**
10 Spedale degli Innocenti **I6**

Restaurants ▼
1 La Mescita **H7**
2 Trattoria Mario **D6**
3 Trattoria Sergio Gozzi **D7**

Coffee and Quick Bites ▼
1 Alfio e Beppe **G5**
2 da Nerbone **D6**
3 Shake **G5**

Hotels ▼
1 Antica Dimora Firenze **H3**
2 Antica Dimora Johlea **H2**
3 Firenze Number Nine **C8**
4 Il Guelfo Bianco **F6**

12

Florence SAN LORENZO

Via Duca d'Aosta
Via Bonifacio Lupi
Via Zara
Via Santa Anna
Via San Gallo
Via Cavour
Via La Marmora
Via Gustavo Modena
Via di Camporegio
Via Salvestrina
Via Venezia
Via Pier Antonio
Via G. La Pira
V. Luigi Salvatore Cherubini
Via San Gallo
Via degli Arazzieri
Via Cavour

San Marco 7

Orto Botanico (Giardino Dei Semplici)

Via Cesare Battisti
Via Gino Capponi
Santissima Annunziata 9
Via Laura
Piazza d. Santissima Annunziata
Via della Colonna
10
Via degli Alfani
Via del Servi
Via Ricasoli

SAN GIOVANNI
Via dei Servi
Via M. Bufalini
V. del Castellaccio
Via degli Alfani
Via della Pergola

Santa Maria degli Angeli

Piazza Santa Maria Nuova

0 ———— 300 ft
0 ———— 100 m

KEY
🔵 Sights
🔴 Restaurants
🟠 Quick Bites
🟣 Hotels

🍽 Restaurants

La Mescita

$ | TUSCAN | Come early (or late) to grab a seat at this tiny spot frequented by Florentine university students and businesspeople, who come to enjoy the day's primi (the lasagna is terrific), perhaps followed by the *polpettone* (meat loaf) and tomato sauce. Though seats are cramped, and the wine is no great shakes, the service is friendly, and the food hits the spot. **Known for:** its longevity (it's been around since the 1920s); delicious pastas at rock-bottom prices; local atmosphere. $ *Average main:* €12 ⊠ *Via degli Alfani 70/r, San Lorenzo* ☎ *347/7951604 mobile* ⊕ *vini-la-mescita. business.site* ⊟ *No credit cards* ⊘ *No dinner.*

★ Trattoria Mario

$$ | TUSCAN | Locals flock to this narrow, family-run trattoria to feast on Tuscan favorites served at simple tables under a wooden ceiling dating from 1536. Genuine Florentine hospitality prevails—you'll be seated wherever there's room, which often means with strangers—and, yes, there's a bit of extra oil in most dishes, which imparts calories as well as taste, but aren't you on vacation? **Known for:** grilled meats; roasted potatoes; festive atmosphere. $ *Average main:* €15 ⊠ *Via Rosina 2/r, corner of Piazza del Mercato Centrale, San Lorenzo* ☎ *055/218550* ⊕ *www.trattoriamario.com* ⊘ *Closed Aug. and Sun. No dinner Mon.–Wed. or Sat.*

★ Trattoria Sergio Gozzi

$ | TUSCAN | This restaurant just across from the Basilica of San Lorenzo and run by the Gozzi family since 1915 serves food that's as delicious as it is affordable. The short menu changes daily, though the *lombatina alla griglia* (grilled veal T-bone steak) is almost always available, and meat eaters should not miss it. **Known for:** local favorite; ever-changing menu; terrific pastas. $ *Average main:* €14 ⊠ *Piazza San Lorenzo 8/r, San Lorenzo* ☎ *055/281941* ⊕ *www.facebook. com/TrattoriaGozzi* ⊘ *Closed Sun.*

☕ Coffee and Quick Bites

Alfio e Beppe

$ | ITALIAN | Watch chickens roast over high flames while you decide which of the delightful side dishes you'd like to enjoy as well. Although this place is strictly takeout (there are no tables), it's open on Sunday when many places are not. **Known for:** good ribs; delicious roasted potatoes; roasted chicken to go. $ *Average main:* €9 ⊠ *Via Cavour 118/r, San Marco* ☎ *055/214108* ⊘ *Closed Sat.*

★ da Nerbone

$ | TUSCAN | This *tavola calda* (cafeteria) in the middle of the covered Mercato Centrale has been serving Florentines since 1872. Tasty primi and secondi are always available, as are *bollitos* (boiled beef sandwiches), but the cognoscenti come for the *panino con il lampredotto* (tripe sandwich)—best when it's prepared *bagnato* (with the bread quickly dipped in the tripe cooking liquid) and served slathered with green and/or spicier red sauce. **Known for:** tripe sandwich; frequented by locals (and everyone else); favorite dishes sell out fast. $ *Average main:* €10 ⊠ *Piazza Mercato Centrale, San Lorenzo* ☎ *055/6480251* ⊘ *Closed Sun. No dinner.*

Shake

$ | ITALIAN | Handily located between Piazza San Marco and Piazza San Lorenzo, the first outpost of Shake (there are now four throughout the city) serves up creative juices, tasty baked goods, wonderful salads, and great bowls. It's committed to sustainability and to keeping its carbon footprint small. **Known for:** remarkable way with juices (the De-Tox is especially good); nice, cheerful staff; courtyard seating in a garden. $ *Average main:* €10 ⊠ *Via Cavour 67/69r, San Lorenzo* ☎ *055/0515418* ⊕ *www.shakecafe.it.*

🛏 Hotels

Antica Dimora Firenze

$$ | B&B/INN | Each simply furnished room in this *residenza* (guesthouse) is painted a different pastel color—peach, rose, powder-blue—and double-glazed windows ensure a peaceful night's sleep. **Pros:** ample DVD library; honor bar with Antinori wines; complimentary coffee, tea, and fresh fruit available all day in the sitting room. **Cons:** books up quickly; some might consider it too small; might be too removed for some. $ *Rooms from: €185* ✉ *Via San Gallo 72, San Marco* ☎ *055/4627296* ⊕ *www. antichedimorefiorentine.it* ⤴ *6 rooms* ⦿ *Free Breakfast.*

★ Antica Dimora Johlea

$$$ | B&B/INN | In addition to guest rooms with four-poster beds and sweeping drapes, this 19th-century palazzo has a charming, flower-filled terrace where you can sip a glass of wine while taking in a view of Brunelleschi's cupola. **Pros:** great staff; cheerful rooms; honor bar. **Cons:** staff goes home at 7:30; staircase to roof terrace is narrow; steps to breakfast room. $ *Rooms from: €227* ✉ *Via San Gallo 80, San Marco* ☎ *055/4633292* ⊕ *www.antichedimorefiorentine.it* ⤴ *6 rooms* ⦿ *Free Breakfast.*

Firenze Number Nine

$$$$ | HOTEL | At this elegant hotel, swank reception rooms have comfortable couches and contemporary artwork, and guest rooms feature parquet floors, high ceilings, and furnishings that combine Scandinavian sleekness with the Italian love for fine fabric (think: damask draperies). **Pros:** historic center location; walk-in gym and spa; sumptuous breakfast. **Cons:** some street noise; might be too trendy for some; books up quickly. $ *Rooms from: €614* ✉ *Via del Conti 9, San Lorenzo* ☎ *055/293777* ⊕ *firenzenumbernine. com* ⤴ *45 rooms* ⦿ *Free Breakfast.*

Il Guelfo Bianco

$$$ | HOTEL | The 15th-century building has all modern conveniences, but Renaissance charm still shines in the high-ceiling rooms. **Pros:** great staff; beautiful floors made of either parquet or marble; sumptuous breakfast. **Cons:** rooms facing the street can be noisy; might be too removed for some; not all rooms are well lit. $ *Rooms from: €234* ✉ *Via Cavour 29, San Marco* ☎ *055/288330* ⊕ *ilguelfobianco.it* ⤴ *40 rooms* ⦿ *Free Breakfast.*

🛍 Shopping

★ Baroni Alimentari

FOOD | The cheese selection at Baroni may be the most comprehensive in Florence. It also sells high-quality truffle products, vinegars, and other delicacies, many of which are, or can be, packed for shipping. ✉ *Mercato Central, enter at Via Signa, San Lorenzo* ☎ *055/289576* ⊕ *www.baronialimentari.com.*

Mercato Centrale

MARKET | FAMILY | This huge indoor food market offers a staggering selection of all things edible. Downstairs is full of vendors hawking their wares—meat, fish, fruit, vegetables—upstairs (daily 8 am–midnight) is full of food stalls serving up an array of Italian and international foods. ✉ *Piazza del Mercato Centrale, San Lorenzo* ☎ *055/2399798* ⊕ *www. mercatocentrale.it/firenze.*

Mercato di San Lorenzo

MARKET | FAMILY | The clothing and leather-goods stalls at Mercato di San Lorenzo in the streets next to the San Lorenzo church have bargains for shoppers on a budget. ✉ *Via dell'Ariento, San Lorenzo.*

Santa Maria Novella

Piazza Santa Maria Novella is a gorgeous, pedestrian-only square, with grass (laced with roses) and plenty of places to sit and rest your feet. The streets in and

Meet the Medici

The Medici were the dominant family of Renaissance Florence, wielding political power and financing some of the world's greatest art. You'll see their names at every turn around the city. These are some of the more notable family members.

Cosimo il Vecchio (1389–1464): incredibly wealthy banker to the popes and the first in the family line to act as de facto ruler of Florence. He was a great patron of the arts and architecture; he was the moving force behind the family palace and the Dominican complex of San Marco.

Lorenzo il Magnifico (1449–92): grandson of Cosimo il Vecchio who presided over a Florence largely at peace with its neighbors. A collector of cameos, a writer of sonnets, and a lover of ancient texts, he was the preeminent Renaissance man and, like his grandfather, the de facto ruler of Florence.

Leo X (1475–1521): also known as Giovanni de' Medici, he became the first Medici pope, helping extend the family power base to include Rome and the Papal States. His reign was characterized by a host of problems, the biggest one being a former friar named Martin Luther.

Catherine de' Medici (1519–89): was married by her great uncle Pope Clement VII to Henry of Valois, who later became Henry II of France. Wife of one king and mother of three, she was the first Medici to marry into European royalty. Lorenzo il Magnifico, her great-grandfather, would have been thrilled.

Cosimo I (1537–74): the first grand duke of Tuscany, not to be confused with his ancestor, Cosimo il Vecchio.

---

around the piazza have their share of architectural treasures, including some of Florence's most tasteful palaces. Between Santa Maria Novella and the Arno is Via Tornabuoni, Florence's swankiest shopping street.

◉ Sights

Museo Novecento
ART MUSEUM | It began life as a 13th-century Franciscan hostel offering shelter to tired pilgrims. It later became a convalescent home, and in the late 18th century it was a school for poor girls. Now the former Ospedale di San Paolo houses a museum devoted to Italian art of the 20th century. Admittedly, most of these artists are not exactly household names, but the museum is so beautifully well done that it's worth a visit. The second floor contains works by artists from the second half of the century; start on the third floor and go directly to the collection of Alberto della Ragione, a naval engineer who was determined to be on the cutting edge of art collecting. ⊠ *Piazza Santa Maria Novella 10, Santa Maria Novella* ☎ *055/2768224* ⊕ *www.museonovecento.it* ✆ *€9.50* ⊗ *Closed Thurs.*

★ Museo Salvatore Ferragamo
ART MUSEUM | A shrine to footwear, the shoes in this dramatically displayed collection were designed by Salvatore Ferragamo (1898–1960) beginning in the early 20th century. Born in southern Italy, Ferragamo jump-started his career in Hollywood by creating shoes for the likes of Mary Pickford and Rudolph Valentino. He then returned to Florence and set up shop in the 13th-century Palazzo Spini Ferroni. The collection includes about 16,000 shoes, and those on display are

frequently rotated. Special exhibitions are also mounted here and are well worth visiting—past shows have been devoted to Audrey Hepburn, Greta Garbo, and Marilyn Monroe. ⊠ *Piazza Santa Trinita 5/r, Santa Maria Novella* ☎ *055/3562846* ⊕ *museo.ferragamo.com* 🖾 *€8.*

Museo Stibbert

HISTORY MUSEUM | Frederick Stibbert (1838–1906), born in Florence to an Italian mother and an English father, liked to collect things. Over a lifetime of doing so, he amassed some 50,000 objects. This museum, which was also his home, displays many of them. He had a fascination with medieval armor, as well as costumes, particularly Uzbek costumes, which are exhibited in a room called the Moresque Hall. These are mingled with an extensive collection of swords and guns. ⊠ *Via Federico Stibbert 26, Santa Maria Novella* ☎ *055/475520* ⊕ *www. museostibbert.it* 🖾 *€10* ⊗ *Closed Thurs.*

Palazzo Strozzi

CASTLE/PALACE | The Strozzi family built this imposing palazzo in an attempt to outshine the nearby Palazzo Medici. The exterior is simple, severe, and massive: it's a testament to the wealth of a patrician, 15th-century Florentine family. The interior courtyard is another matter altogether. It is here that the classical vocabulary—columns, capitals, pilasters, arches, and cornices—is given uninhibited and powerful expression. Inside, find rotating exhibits with a focus on contemporary art. ⊠ *Piazza degli Strozzi, Piazza della Repubblica* ☎ *055/2645155* ⊕ *www.palazzostrozzi.org* 🖾 *Courtyard free; exhibits €15.*

Santa Maria Novella

CHURCH | The facade of this church looks distinctly clumsy by later Renaissance standards, and with good reason: it is an architectural hybrid. The lower half was completed mostly in the 14th century and about 100 years later (around 1456), architect Leon Battista Alberti was called in to complete the job, adding architectural motifs in an entirely different style.

Interior highlights include the 14th-century, stained-glass-rose window depicting the *Coronation of the Virgin* (above the central entrance); the Cappella Filippo Strozzi (to the right of the altar) containing late-15th-century frescoes and stained glass by Filippino Lippi; Masaccio's *Trinity* (on the left-hand wall, almost halfway down the nave) painted around 1426–27; the *cappella maggiore* (the area around the high altar) displaying frescoes by Ghirlandaio; and the Cappella Gondi (to the left of the altar) with Filippo Brunelleschi's famous wooden crucifix, carved around 1410 and said to have so stunned the great Donatello when he first saw it that he dropped a basket of eggs. ⊠ *Piazza Santa Maria Novella 18, Santa Maria Novella* ☎ *055/9067593* ⊕ *www.smn.it/en* 🖾 *€7.50* ⊗ *Closed Sun. morning.*

Santa Trinita

CHURCH | Started in the 11th century by Vallombrosian monks and originally Romanesque in style, this church underwent a Gothic remodeling during the 14th century. (Remains of the Romanesque construction are visible on the interior front wall.) The major works are the fresco cycle and altarpiece in the Cappella Sassetti, the second to the high altar's right, painted by Ghirlandaio between 1480 and 1485. His work here possesses graceful decorative appeal and proudly depicts his native city, as most of the cityscapes show 15th-century Florence in all its glory. The wall frescoes illustrate scenes from the life of St. Francis, and the altarpiece, depicting the *Adoration of the Shepherds,* veritably glows. ⊠ *Piazza Santa Trinita, Santa Maria Novella* ☎ *055/216912* ⊗ *Closed noon–4 pm.*

Santa Maria Novella

12

Sights ▼

1	Museo Novecento	D5
2	Museo Salvatore Ferragamo	F8
3	Museo Stibbert	G1
4	Palazzo Strozzi	F7
5	Santa Maria Novella	E4
6	Santa Trinita	F8

Restaurants ▼

1	Buca Lapi	F5
2	Cantinetta Antinori	F6
3	La Sostanza	C5
4	La Spada	E6
5	Mangiafoco Osteria Tartuferia	G8
6	Obicà	F6
7	Osteria Belle Donne	E5
8	Procacci	F6
9	Vincanto	E4

Hotels ▼

1	Gallery Hotel Art	G9
2	Hotel L'Orologio	E5
3	Nuova Italia	F2
4	The Place Firenze	E5

Map labels:

Via Guelfa, Via Nazionale, Via Panicale, Via Taddea, Via Chiara, Via G. B. Zannoni, V. San Orsola, Via San Gallo, Via Guelfa, Via dell'Ariento, Piazza del Mercato, Via Rosina, Borgo la Noce, Via della Stufa, Via de' Ginori, Via Cavour, SAN GIOVANNI, Via Faenza, Piazza Madonna Aldobrandini, Piazza San Lorenzo, San Lorenzo, Via Ricasoli, Via dei Pucci, Borgo San Lorenzo, Via Martelli, Via d. Bitti, Via Ricasoli, Via de' Servi, V. dell'Alloro, Via F. Zannetti, Via dei Cerretani, Piazza del Duomo, Duomo, Via del Pecori, Via dei Pescioni, Via del Vecchietti, Via del Tosinghi, V. Brunelleschi, Via Roma, Via dell'Oche, Via Catalucci, Via S. Elisabetta, d. Studio, Via, Piazza Strozzi, Via del Strozzi, Piazza della Repubblica, Via d. Speziali, Via del Corso, V. Monalda, V. d. Anselmi, V. Calimala, V. del Cerchia, Via Dante Alighieri, V. Pellicceria, V. d. Orsanmichele, V. d. Tavolini, V. del Magazzini, P'za d. Davanzati, Via dei Lamberti, Rossa, Via della Condotta, Via Calimaruzza, Piazza della Signoria, Piazza San Firenze, Via dei Leoni, Fiordali, Via delle Terme, V. Vacchereccia, V. del Gondi, Borgo Santi Apostoli, V. Por Santa, Ch. d. Baroncelli, Via d. Ninna, Via Lambertesca, Galleria degli Uffizi, Via de' Neri, Via Vinegia, Lungarno Acciaioli, Piazza degli Uffizi

🍴 Restaurants

Buca Lapi

$$$$ | ITALIAN | The Antinori family started selling wine from their palace's basement in the 15th century, and, 600 years later, this *buca* (hole) is a lively, subterranean spot filled with Florentine aristocrats chowing down on what might be the best—and the most expensive—*bistecca alla fiorentina* (flavorful, lightly seasoned beef) in town. The classic Tuscan menu has the usual suspects: *crostini di cavolo nero* (black cabbage on toasted garlic bread), along with *ribollita* (vegetable, bean, and bread soup) and *pappa al pomodoro* (tomato and bread soup). **Known for:** gargantuan bistecca; adherence to Tuscan classics; pet-friendly. ⑤ *Average main: €40* ✉ *Via del Trebbio 1r, Santa Maria Novella* ☎ *055/213768* ⊕ *www.bucalapi.com/en* ⊗ *Closed Sun. No lunch.*

Cantinetta Antinori

$$$ | TUSCAN | After a morning of shopping on Via Tornabuoni, stop for lunch in this 15th-century palazzo, a place to see and be seen as well as to dine. The panache of the clientele is matched by that of the food, which is served with olive oil and vegetables from the family farm. **Known for:** chic clientele; most ingredients come from the family farm; outdoor seating in a 15th-century courtyard. ⑤ *Average main: €31* ✉ *Piazza Antinori 3, Santa Maria Novella* ☎ *055/292234* ⊕ *cantinetta-antinori.com* ⊗ *Closed Sun.*

★ La Sostanza

$$ | TUSCAN | Since opening its doors in 1869, this trattoria has been serving top-notch, unpretentious food to Florentines who like their bistecca very large and, of course, very rare, as that's the only way to eat it. The *tartino di carciofi* (artichoke tart) and the *pollo al burro* (chicken with butter) are signature dishes. **Known for:** Tuscan classics; delicious desserts (especially the semifreddo); no-frills, simple decor and communal tables. ⑤ *Average*

main: *€20* ✉ *Via del Porcellana 25/r, Lungarno North* ☎ *055/212691* ⊕ *www.facebook.com/trattoriasostanzailtroia* ⊗ *Closed Sun.*

La Spada

$ | ITALIAN | FAMILY | Near Santa Maria Novella is La Spada. Walk in and inhale the fragrant aromas of meats cooking in the wood-burning oven. **Known for:** grilled meats and aromatic pastas; adherence to Tuscan cuisine; eat in or order takeout. ⑤ *Average main: €11* ✉ *Via della Spada 62/r, Santa Maria Novella* ☎ *055/218757* ⊕ *www.ristorantelaspada.it.*

★ Mangiafoco Osteria Tartuferia

$$$ | TUSCAN | On a romantic medieval side street in the heart of the centro storico, this small restaurant has two menus—one with Tuscan classics that reflect both the whims of the chef and what's in season, and the other that's focused on truffles, either white or black, again based on the season. On the first menu, look for creative salads and pasta, meat, and *taglieri* (mixed meat and cheese plates) that are often served with jams made from Chianti, vin santo, or balsamic vinegar. **Known for:** phenomenal wines by the glass or the bottle; house-made breads and desserts; truffle-focused menu. ⑤ *Average main: €29* ✉ *Borgo Santi Apostoli 26/r, Santa Maria Novella* ☎ *055/2658170* ⊕ *www.mangiafoco.com* ⊗ *Closed Wed.*

Obicà

$$ | ITALIAN | With restaurants worldwide, Obicà, where mozarella takes center stage, has a strong following. This sleek eatery on Florence's swankiest street gets the cheese and its culinary cousin burrata (a fresh cheese filled with cream) from southern Italy and then makes it the centerpiece for various salads and pastas. **Known for:** mozzarella-laden menu; satisfying pizza and desserts; outdoor seating in nice weather. ⑤ *Average main: €18* ✉ *Via Tornabuoni 16, Santa Maria Novella* ☎ *055/2773526* ⊕ *www.obica.com/restaurants/florence.*

Osteria Belle Donne

$$ | TUSCAN | Down the street from the church of Santa Maria Novella, this gaily decorated spot, festooned with plants and portraits of Marilyn Monroe and Audrey Hepburn, has an ever-changing menu and stellar service. The list of Tuscan standards is shaken up with alternatives such as stracciatella with shrimp and cherry tomatoes and truffles, when in season. **Known for:** seasonal ingredients; many dishes not typical of Tuscany; lively atmosphere. $ *Average main: €20* ✉ *Via delle Belle Donne 16/r, Santa Maria Novella* ☎ *055/2382609* ⊕ *www.belledonneosteria.it.*

★ Procacci

$$ | ITALIAN | At this classy Florentine institution dating from 1885, try one of the truffle panini and swish it down with a glass of prosecco. **Known for:** pane tartufato; excellent wines by the glass; serene (but tiny) space. $ *Average main: €15* ✉ *Via Tornabuoni 64/r, Santa Maria Novella* ☎ *055/211656* ⊕ *procacci1885.it.*

Vincanto

$$ | ITALIAN | It opens at 11 am and closes at midnight: this is a rarity in Florentine dining. They do a little bit of everything here, including fine pastas, salads, pizzas, and even an American-style breakfast. **Known for:** a wide-ranging menu; kitchen stays open; outside terrace with views of a beautiful square. $ *Average main: €24* ✉ *Piazza Santa Maria Novella 23/r, Santa Maria Novella* ☎ *055/2741555* ⊕ *www.ristorantevincanto.com.*

🛏 Hotels

Gallery Hotel Art

$$$$ | HOTEL | High design resides at this art showcase near the Ponte Vecchio, where sleek, uncluttered rooms are dressed mostly in neutrals but have luxe touches such as leather headboards and kimono robes. **Pros:** trendy atmosphere; artistic touches; the in-house Fusion Bar serves delightful cocktails. **Cons:** some street noise; books up quickly; might be too trendy for some. $ *Rooms from: €550* ✉ *Vicolo dell'Oro 5, Santa Maria Novella* ☎ *055/27263* ⊕ *www.lungarnocollection.com/gallery-hotel-art* 🛏 *74 rooms* ⊙*| No Meals.*

Hotel L'Orologio

$$$$ | HOTEL | The owner of this understatedly elegant hotel has a real passion for watches, which is why he chose to name his hotel after them (and why you will see them throughout the property)—and the location can't be beat, as it abuts the increasingly beautiful Piazza Santa Maria Novella. **Pros:** location; great staff; stunning breakfast room. **Cons:** some folks think it's too close to the train station; gets the occasional tour group; holds conferences from time to time. $ *Rooms from: €371* ✉ *Piazza Santa Maria Novella 24, Santa Maria Novella* ☎ *055/277380* ⊕ *www.hotelorologioflorence.com* 🛏 *55 rooms* ⊙*| Free Breakfast.*

Nuova Italia

$$ | HOTEL | FAMILY | The genial Viti family oversees this property with clean and simple rooms near the train station and well within walking distance of the sights. **Pros:** reasonable rates; close to everything; great for those on a budget. **Cons:** no elevator; the neighborhood is highly trafficked; some street noise. $ *Rooms from: €147* ✉ *Via Faenza 26, Santa Maria Novella* ☎ *055/287508* ⊕ *www.hotel-nuovaitalia.com* ⊙ *Closed Dec. 20–Dec. 27* 🛏 *20 rooms* ⊙*| Free Breakfast.*

★ The Place Firenze

$$$$ | HOTEL | Hard to spot from the street, this sumptuous place provides all the comforts of a luxe home away from home—expect soothing earth tones in the guest rooms, free minibars, crisp linens, and room service offering organic dishes. **Pros:** private, intimate feel; stellar staff; small dogs allowed. **Cons:** breakfast at a shared table; books up quickly; might be too trendy for some. $ *Rooms from: €765* ✉ *Piazza Santa Maria Novella*

7, Santa Maria Novella ☎ 055/2645181 ⊕ www.theplacefirenze.com ⤴ 20 rooms ❑ Free Breakfast.

Performing Arts

Maggio Musicale Fiorentino

MUSIC | The landmark Parco della Musica (Music Park) complex, designed by Paolo Desideri and associates, is the home of the Maggio Musicale Fiorentino. You can purchase tickets for its symphony performances and operas directly at the box office, by phone or online. ⊠ Piazza Vittorio Gui 1, Santa Maria Novella ☎ 055/2779309 ⊕ www.maggiofiorentino.it.

Tuscany Hall

CONCERTS | This large exhibition space, formerly Teatro Saschall, hosts a variety of events throughout the year, including concerts by visiting rock stars, performances by lesser-known bands from across Europe, and a large art market. ⊠ Lungarno Aldo Moro 3, Lungarno North ☎ 055/6504112 ⊕ www.tuscanyhall.it.

Shopping

★ Alberto Cozzi

STATIONERY | You'll find an extensive line of Florentine papers and paper products in this shop, where artisans also rebind and restore books. ⊠ Via del Parione 35/r, Santa Maria Novella ☎ 055/294968 ⊕ www.legatoriacozzifirenze.it.

★ Angela Caputi

JEWELRY & WATCHES | Angela Caputi wows Florentine cognoscenti with her highly creative, often outsize, acrylic jewelry. A small but equally creative collection of women's clothing made of fine fabrics is also on offer. ⊠ Borgo Santi Apostoli 44/46, Santa Maria Novella ☎ 055/292993 ⊕ www.angelacaputi.com.

Antica Officina del Farmacista Dr. Vranjes

FRAGRANCES | Dr. Vranjes elevates aromatherapy to an art form with scents for the body and home. ⊠ Via della Vigna Nuova 30/r, Santa Maria Novella ☎ 055/0945851 ⊕ www.drvranjes.it.

Bottega Giotti

LEATHER GOODS | You'll find multiple lines of leather bags, wallets, and other accessories here. ⊠ Piazza Ognissanti 3–4/r, Lungarno North ☎ 055/294265 ⊕ www.bottegagiotti.com.

Brandimarte

JEWELRY & WATCHES | Most people want to buy gold (for which Florence is justly famous) when they visit. That said, Brandimarte, which has specialized in exquisitely crafted silver jewelry, decorative objects, and housewares since 1955, is well worth a visit. ⊠ Via del Moro 92/r, Santa Maria Novella ☎ 349/4220269 mobile ⊕ www.brandimarte.com.

Cellerini

LEATHER GOODS | In a city where it seems just about everybody carries an expensive leather bag, Cellerini is an institution. ⊠ Via del Sole 9/r, Santa Maria Novella ☎ 055/282533 ⊕ www.cellerini.it.

Emilio Pucci

CLOTHING | The aristocratic Marchese di Barsento, Emilio Pucci, became an international name in the late 1950s when the stretch ski clothes he designed for himself caught on with the dolce vita ("sweet life") crowd—his pseudopsychedelic prints and "palazzo pajamas" became all the rage. ⊠ Via Tornabuoni 20–22/r, Santa Maria Novella ☎ 055/2658082 ⊕ www.pucci.com.

Ferragamo

SHOES | Set in a 13th-century palazzo, this classy institution displays designer clothing and accessories, though elegant footwear still underlies the Ferragamo success. ⊠ Via Tornabuoni 14/r, Santa Maria Novella ☎ 055/292123 ⊕ store.ferragamo.com.

★ Loretta Caponi

CLOTHING | Synonymous with Florentine embroidery, this shop sells luxury lace, linens, and lingerie that have earned the eponymous signora worldwide renown. There's also beautiful (and expensive) clothing for children. ⊠ *Via delle Belle Donne 28/r, Santa Maria Novella* ☎ *055/213668* ⊕ *www.lorettacaponi.it/en.*

★ **Officina Profumo Farmaceutica di Santa Maria Novella**
FRAGRANCES | The essence of a Florentine holiday is captured in perfumes, candles, and sachets at this cathedral-like emporium of herbal cosmetics and soaps that are made following centuries-old recipes created by friars. See a wire cutter used to make soap in the 19th century, a library of elixirs, and temporary exhibits that will make you feel like you're in a museum rather than the original shop of a brand that's now global. ⊠ *Via della Scala 16, Santa Maria Novella* ☎ *055/216276* ⊕ *eu.smnovella.com.*

Pineider
STATIONERY | Although it has shops throughout the world, Pineider started out in Florence in 1774 and still does all its printing here. Stationery and business cards are the mainstay, but the stores also sell colorful pens and fine-leather bags and desk accessories. ⊠ *Lungarno degli Acciaiuoli 72–76/r, Santa Maria Novella* ☎ *055/284655* ⊕ *www.pineider.com.*

Principe
DEPARTMENT STORE | This Florentine institution sells casual clothes for men, women, and children at far-from-casual prices. It also has a great housewares department. ⊠ *Via del Sole 2, Santa Maria Novella* ☎ *055/292764* ⊕ *www.principedifirenze.com.*

Valli
FABRICS | Gifted seamstresses (and seamsters) should look no further than this place, which sells sumptuous silks, beaded fabrics, lace, wool, and tweeds by the meter. ⊠ *Via della Vigna Nuova 81/r, Santa Maria Novella* ☎ *055/282485* ⊕ *www.vallitessuti.com.*

Santa Croce

The Santa Croce quarter, on the southeast fringe of the historic center, was built up in the Middle Ages outside the second set of medieval city walls. The centerpiece of the neighborhood was (and is) the basilica of Santa Croce, which could hold great numbers of worshippers; the vast piazza could accommodate any overflow and also served as a fairground and, allegedly since the middle of the 16th century, as a playing field for no-holds-barred soccer games. A center of leatherworking since the Middle Ages, the neighborhood is still packed with leatherworkers and leather shops.

◉ Sights

Casa Buonarroti
ART MUSEUM | If you really enjoy walking in the footsteps of the great genius, you may want to complete the picture by visiting the Buonarroti family home. Michelangelo lived here from 1516 to 1525, and later gave it to his nephew, whose son, Michelangelo il Giovane (Michelangelo the Younger), turned it into a gallery dedicated to his great-uncle. The artist's descendants filled it with art treasures, some by Michelangelo himself. Two early marble works—the *Madonna of the Stairs* and *Battle of the Centaurs*—demonstrate his genius. ⊠ *Via Ghibellina 70, Santa Croce* ☎ *055/241752* ⊕ *www.casabuonarroti.it* ⬚ *€8* ⊙ *Closed Tues.*

★ **Piazza Santa Croce**
PLAZA/SQUARE | FAMILY | Originally outside the city's 12th-century walls, this piazza grew with the Franciscans, who used it for public preaching. During the Renaissance, it hosted *giostre* (jousts), including one sponsored by Lorenzo de' Medici. Lined with many palazzi dating from the 15th and 16th centuries, the square remains one of Florence's loveliest and is a great place to people-watch. ⊠ *Piazza Santa Croce, Santa Croce.*

Sights ▾

1 Casa Buonarroti **F7**
2 Piazza Santa Croce **E8**
3 Santa Croce **F8**
4 Sinagoga **H5**

Restaurants ▾

1 Caffè Italiano **D7**
2 Cibrèo Ristorante **H6**
3 Cibrèo Trattoria **H6**
4 Enoteca Pinchiorri **F7**
5 La Giostra **E5**
6 Ruth's **H5**

Coffee and Quick Bites ▾

1 da Rocco **I7**
2 Perché No! **A6**

Hotels ▾

1 Borgo Pinti **F4**
2 The Four Seasons **H1**
3 Hotel Regency **J2**
4 Monna Lisa **F4**

KEY

1 Sights
1 Restaurants
1 Quick Bites
1 Hotels

0   300 ft
0   100 m

★ Santa Croce

CHURCH | This Gothic church, whose facade dates from the 19th century, contains the skeletons of many Renaissance celebrities, including Michelangelo (1475–1564), Galileo Galilei (1564–1642), Niccolò Machiavelli (1469–1527), and Lorenzo Ghiberti (1378–1455). In addition, the collection of art here is by far the most important of any church in Florence.

The most famous works are the Giotto frescoes in the two chapels immediately to the right of the high altar. They illustrate scenes from the lives of St. John the Evangelist and St. John the Baptist (in the right-hand chapel), as well as those from the life of St. Francis (in the left-hand chapel). Among the church's other highlights are Donatello's *Annunciation*; 14th-century frescoes by Taddeo Gaddi (circa 1300–66) illustrating scenes from the life of the Virgin Mary; and Donatello's *Crucifix*, criticized by Brunelleschi for making Christ look like a peasant. ⊠ *Piazza Santa Croce 16, Santa Croce* ☎ *055/2466105* ⊕ *www.santacroce-opera.it* 🎫 *Church and museum €8.*

Sinagoga

SYNAGOGUE | Jews were well settled in Florence by the end of the 14th century. By 1574, however, they were required to live within the large "ghetto" at the north side of today's Piazza della Repubblica, by decree of Cosimo I. Construction of the modern Moorish-style synagogue began in 1874 as a bequest of David Levi, who wished to endow a synagogue "worthy of the city." Falcini, Micheli, and Treves designed the building on a domed Greek cross plan with galleries in the transept and a roofline bearing three distinctive copper cupolas visible from all over Florence. The exterior has alternating bands of tan travertine and pink granite, reflecting an Islamic style repeated in Giovanni Panti's ornate interior. ⊠ *Via Farini 6, Santa Croce* ☎ *055/245252* ⊕ *www.firenzebraica.it/sinagoga* 🎫 *Synagogue and museum €6.50 (reservations €1)* ⊘ *Closed Sat., Sun., and Jewish holidays.*

🍴 Restaurants

Caffè Italiano

$$ | **PIZZA** | **FAMILY** | This small pizzeria is favored by locals. Make a reservation or come early to grab one of the few tables in front or round the back, and don't mind the fact that service here is intentionally rushed: turning tables is paramount. **Known for:** pizza offerings; limited seating; local favorite. $ *Average main: €16* ⊠ *Via Isole delle Stinche 11/r, Santa Croce* ☎ *055/289080* ⊕ *caffeitaliano.it.*

★ Cibrèo Ristorante

$$$$ | **TUSCAN** | This upscale trattoria serves sumptuous options like the creamy crostini *di fegatini* (a savory chicken-liver spread) and melt-in-your-mouth desserts. Many Florentines hail this as the city's best restaurant, and justifiably so—late chef–owner Fabio Picchi (who left behind his Florence culinary legacy in 2022) knew Tuscan food better than anyone, and it shows. **Known for:** authentic Tuscan food, at the original Cibrèo outpost; seasonal menu; multilingual staff. $ *Average main: €40* ⊠ *Via A. del Verrocchio 8/r, Santa Croce* ☎ *055/2341100* ⊕ *www.cibreo.com* ⊘ *No lunch Mon.–Thurs.*

Cibrèo Trattoria

$$ | **TUSCAN** | This intimate trattoria, known to locals as Cibreino, shares its name and its kitchen with the famed Florentine restaurant but has a shorter, less-expensive menu. Save room for dessert, as the pastry chef has a deft hand with chocolate tarts. **Known for:** excellent meal at a moderate price; clever riffs on classic dishes; desserts to save room for. $ *Average main: €18* ⊠ *Via dei Macci 122/r, Santa Croce* ☎ *055/2341100* ⊕ *www.cibreo.com.*

Enoteca Pinchiorri

$$$$ | **ITALIAN** | A sumptuous Renaissance palace with high, frescoed ceilings and bouquets in silver vases provides the backdrop for this restaurant, one of the most expensive in Italy. Some consider it one of the best, and others consider it inauthentic, as the cuisine extends far beyond Italian. **Known for:** creative food; wine cellar; exorbitantly high prices. ⑤ *Average main: €90* ⊠ *Via Ghibellina 87, Santa Croce* ☎ *055/242777* ⊕ *www. enotecapinchiorri.it* ☾ *Closed Sun., Mon., and Aug. No lunch* 🕍 *Jacket required, no shorts, or short-sleeved shirts.*

★ La Giostra

$$$ | **ITALIAN** | Passing by this restaurant at night, you may think there's a club beyond its doors, given the crowd gathering outside. Frequented by celebrities, its name means "carousel," and it was created by the late Prince Dimitri Kunz d'Asburgo Lorena and is now expertly run by Soldano, one of his twin sons. **Known for:** sublime desserts; lively atmosphere; vegetarian and vegan options. ⑤ *Average main: €30* ⊠ *Borgo Pinti 12/r, Santa Croce* ☎ *055/241341* ⊕ *ristorantelagiostra.com* ☾ *No lunch weekends.*

Ruth's

$$ | **KOSHER** | The only kosher–vegetarian restaurant in Tuscany is Ruth's, adjacent to Florence's synagogue. On the menu are inexpensive vegetarian and Mediterranean dishes, and there's also a large selection of kosher wines. **Known for:** harissa; nice wine list; friendly staff. ⑤ *Average main: €20* ⊠ *Via Farini 2/a, Santa Croce* ☎ *055/2480888* ⊕ *www. kosheruth.com* ☾ *No dinner Fri. No lunch Sat.*

☕ Coffee and Quick Bites

da Rocco

$ | **TUSCAN** | **FAMILY** | At one of Florence's biggest markets, you can grab lunch to go, or you can cram into one of the booths and pour from the straw-cloaked flask (wine here is *da consumo*, which means they charge you for how much you drink). Food is abundant and Tuscan, service is fast, and locals pack in. **Known for:** tasty food at rock-bottom prices; ever-changing menu; takeout. ⑤ *Average*

main: €8 ⊠ *Mercato Sant'Ambrogio, Piazza Ghiberti, Santa Croce* ☎ *339/8384555 mobile* ⊕ *www.daroccotrattoria.com* ☾ *Closed Sun. No dinner.*

★ Perché No!

$ | **ICE CREAM** | **FAMILY** | What many consider the best gelateria in the centro storico embodies the "practice makes perfect" adage. It's been making ice cream since 1939. **Known for:** gelati made daily; one of the oldest gelaterias in the city; unusual flavors and vegan options. ⑤ *Average main: €3* ⊠ *Via dei Tavolini 19r, Duomo* ☎ *055/2398969* ⊕ *www.facebook.com/ GelateriaPercheNo.*

Hotels

Borgo Pinti

$ | **B&B/INN** | **FAMILY** | Nuns of the Oblates of the Assumption run this convent holiday house, where some of the simple but spotlessly clean rooms have views of the Duomo's cupola, and others look out onto a garden where you are welcome to relax. **Pros:** great location and (mostly) quiet rooms; Mass held daily; a soothing, somewhat untended garden. **Cons:** some have observed that there's hall noise; rooms facing the street can be noisy; rooms are basic. ⑤ *Rooms from: €90* ⊠ *Borgo Pinti 15, Santa Croce* ☎ *055/2346291* ⊕ *www.oblate.it* ⤴ *40 rooms* ⑩ *Free Breakfast.*

The Four Seasons

$$$$ | **HOTEL** | This 15th-century palazzo is perhaps the city's most luxurious hotel, where many guest rooms have original 17th-century frescoes, and an 11-acre garden is dotted with centuries-old trees. **Pros:** pool; state-of-the-art spa; Michelin-starred Il Palagio restaurant. **Cons:** ultra-pricey; splashing children in the pool can be a nuisance for some; small rooms. ⑤ *Rooms from: €2,200* ⊠ *Borgo Pinti 99, Santa Croce* ☎ *055/26261* ⊕ *www.fourseasons.com/florence* ⤴ *117 rooms* ⑩ *No Meals.*

Hotel Regency

$$$$ | **HOTEL** | Though it's just 10 minutes from the Accademia and Michelangelo's *David,* this hotel—in a 19th-century mansion adorned with rich fabrics and period-appropriate furnishings—is a true retreat from the city's noise and crowds. **Pros:** faces one of the few green spaces in central Florence; quiet residential setting; lovely, on-site Relais le Jardin restaurant. **Cons:** somewhat removed from the city center; rooms facing the park can be noisy; books up quickly. ⑤ *Rooms from: €454* ✉ *Piazza d'Azeglio 3, Santa Croce* ☎ *055/245247* ⊕ *www. regency-hotel.com* ⊗ *Closed Jan.–Mar.* ↰ *31 rooms* ¡○¡ *Free Breakfast.*

★ Monna Lisa

$$$ | **HOTEL** | Although some rooms are small, all are tastefully decorated and housed in a 15th-century palazzo that retains its original staircase and some of its wood-coffered ceilings. **Pros:** lavish buffet breakfast; cheerful, multilingual staff; pretty garden. **Cons:** rooms in annex are less charming than those in palazzo; street noise in some rooms; thin walls have been noted. ⑤ *Rooms from: €293* ✉ *Borgo Pinti 27, Santa Croce* ☎ *055/2479751* ⊕ *www.monnalisa.it* ↰ *48 rooms* ¡○¡ *Free Breakfast.*

Nightlife

Caffè Sant'Ambrogio

BARS | Come here when it's summer for outdoor seating with a view of an 11th-century church (Sant'Ambrogio) directly across the street; the crowd gathers until past 2 am. Come here at any time of the year for perfectly mixed drinks and a lively atmosphere filled with (mostly) locals. ✉ *Piazza Sant'Ambrogio 7–8/r, Santa Croce* ☎ *055/2477277* ⊕ *www.caffesantambrogio.it.*

Jazz Club

LIVE MUSIC | Enjoy live music in this small basement club. ✉ *Via Nuova de' Caccini*

3, at Borgo Pinti, Santa Croce ⊕ *www. facebook.com/jazzclubfirenze.it.*

Rex

BARS | A trendy, artsy clientele frequents this bar at aperitivo time. By 10 pm, the place is packed with mostly young folks sipping cocktails. ✉ *Via Fiesolana 23–25/r, Santa Croce* ☎ *055/2480331* ⊕ *www. rexfirenze.com.*

Shopping

★ Mercato di Sant'Ambrogio

MARKET | **FAMILY** | It's possible to strike gold at this lively market, where clothing stalls abut those with fruits and vegetables. ✉ *Piazza Ghiberti, off Via dei Macci, Santa Croce* ☎ *055/2480778* ⊕ *mercatosantambrogio.it.*

Oreria

JEWELRY & WATCHES | The two women who run Oreria create divine designs using silver and semiprecious stones. ✉ *Borgo Pinti 87/a, Santa Croce* ☎ *055/244708* ⊕ *www.oreria.net.*

★ Scuola del Cuoio

LEATHER GOODS | Leatherworkers ply their trade at Scuola del Cuoio (Leather School), a consortium in the former dormitory of the convent of Santa Croce. High-quality, fairly priced jackets, belts, and purses are sold here. ✉ *Piazza Santa Croce 16, Santa Croce* ☎ *055/244533* ⊕ *www.scuoladelcuoio.com.*

The Oltrarno

A walk through the Oltrarno (literally "the other side of the Arno") takes in two very different aspects of Florence: the splendor of the Medici, manifest in the riches of the mammoth Palazzo Pitti and the gracious Giardino di Boboli; and the charm of the Oltrarno, a gentrified former working-class neighborhood with artisans' and antiques shops.

Continued on page 575

WHO'S WHO IN RENAISSANCE ART

Michelangelo. Leonardo da Vinci. Raphael. This heady triumvirate of the Italian Renaissance is synonymous with artistic genius. Yet they are only three of the remarkable cast of characters whose work defines the Renaissance, that extraordinary flourishing of art and culture in Italy, especially in Florence, as the Middle Ages drew to a close. The artists were visionaries, who redefined painting, sculpture, architecture, and even what it means to be an artist.

THE PIONEER. In the mid-14th century, a few artists began to move away from the flat, two-dimensional painting of the Middle Ages. Giotto, who painted seemingly three-dimensional figures who show emotion, had a major impact on the artists of the next century.

THE GROUNDBREAKERS. Brunelleschi and Botticelli took center stage in the 15th century. Ghiberti, Masaccio, Donatello, Uccello, Fra Angelico, and Filippo Lippi were other major players. Part of the Renaissance (or "re-birth") was a renewed interest in classical sources—the texts, monuments, and sculpture of Ancient Greece and Rome. Perspective (the illusion of three-dimensional space) in painting was another development during this era, known as the Early Renaissance. Suddenly the art appearing on the walls looked real, or more realistic than it used to.

Roman ruins were not the only thing to inspire these artists. There was an incredible exchange of ideas going on. In Santa Maria del Carmine, Filippo Lippi was inspired by the work of Masaccio, who in turn was a friend of Brunelleschi. Young artists also learned from the masters via the apprentice system. Ghiberti's workshop (*bottega* in Italian) included, at one time or another, Donatello, Masaccio, and Uccello. Botticelli was apprenticed to Filippo Lippi.

THE BIG THREE. The mathematical rationality and precision of 15th-century art gave way to what is known as the High Renaissance. Leonardo, Michelangelo, and Raphael were much more concerned with portraying the body in all its glory and with achieving harmony and grandeur in their work. Oil paint, used infrequently up until this time, became more widely employed. As a result, Leonardo's colors are deeper, more sensual, more alive. For one brief period, all three were in Florence at the same time. Michelangelo and Leonardo surely knew one another, as they were simultaneously working on frescoes (never completed) inside Palazzo Vecchio.

When Michelangelo went to Rome in 1508, it started an artistic exodus from which Florence never fully recovered.

A RENAISSANCE TIMELINE

IN THE WORLD

Black Death in Europe kills one third of the population, 1347-50.

Joan of Arc burned at the stake, 1431.

IN FLORENCE

Founding of the Medici bank, 1397.

Medici family made official papal bankers.

1434, Cosimo il Vecchio becomes de facto ruler of Florence. The Medici family will dominate the city until 1494.

Dante, a native of Florence, writes *The Divine Comedy*, 1302-21.

1300

1400

IN ART

EARLY RENAISSANCE

Masaccio and Masolino fresco Santa Maria del Carmine, 1424-28.

GIOTTO (ca. 1267-1337)

BRUNELLESCHI (1377-1446)

Giotto frescoes in Santa Croce, 1320-25.

LORENZO GHIBERTI (ca. 1381-1455)

DONATELLO (ca. 1386-1466)

PAOLO UCCELLO (1397-1475)

FRA ANGELICO (ca. 1400-1455)

1334, 67-year-old Giotto is appointed chief architect of Santa Maria del Fiore, Florence's Duomo *(below)*. He begins to work on the Campanile, which will be completed in 1359, after his death.

MASACCIO (1401-1428)

FILIPPO LIPPI (ca. 1406-1469)

Donatello sculpts his bronze *David*, ca. 1440.

Fra Angelico frescoes friars' cells in San Marco, ca. 1438-45.

Uccello's *Sir John Hawkwood*, ca. 1436.

Ghiberti wins the competition for the Baptistery doors *(above)* in Florence, 1401.

Brunelleschi wins the competition for the Duomo's cupola, 1418.

Gutenberg Bible is printed, 1455.

Columbus discovers America, 1492.

Martin Luther posts his 95 theses on the door at Wittenberg, kicking off the Protestant Reformation, 1517.

Constantinople falls to the Turks, 1453.

Machiavelli's *Prince* appears, 1513.

Copernicus proves that the earth is not the center of the universe, 1530-43.

Lorenzo "il Magnifico" *(right)*, the Medici patron of the arts, rules in Florence, 1449-92.

Two Medici popes Leo X (1513-21) and Clement VII (1523-34) in Rome.

Catherine de'Medici becomes Queen of France, 1547.

1450   **1500**   **1550**

HIGH RENAISSANCE   MANNERISM

Fra Filippo Lippi's *Madonna and Child,* ca. 1452.

1508, Raphael begins work on the chambers in the Vatican, Rome.

Giorgio Vasari publishes his first edition of *Lives of the Artists*, 1550.

1504, Michelangelo's *David* is put on display in Piazza della Signoria, where it remains until 1873.

Michelangelo begins to fresco the Sistine Chapel ceiling, 1508.

Botticelli paints the *Birth of Venus,* ca. 1482.

BOTTICELLI (ca. 1444-1510)

LEONARDO DA VINCI (1452-1519)

RAPHAEL (1483-1520)

MICHELANGELO (1475-1564)

Leonardo paints *The Last Supper (below)* in Milan, 1495-98.

Giotto's *Nativity*

Donatello's *St. John the Baptist*

Ghiberti's *Gates of Paradise*

GIOTTO (CA. 1267-1337)
Painter/architect from a small town north of Florence.

He unequivocally set Italian painting on the course that led to the triumphs of the Renaissance masters. Unlike the rather flat, two-dimensional forms found in then prevailing Byzantine art, Giotto's figures have a fresh, life-like quality. The people in his paintings have bulk, and they show emotion, which you can see on their faces and in their gestures. This was something new in the late Middle Ages. Without Giotto, there wouldn't have been a Raphael.

In Florence: **Santa Croce; Uffizi; Campanile; Santa Maria Novella**
Elsewhere in Italy: **Scrovegni Chapel, Padua; Vatican Museums, Rome**

FILIPPO BRUNELLESCHI (1377-1446)
Architect/engineer from Florence.

If Brunelleschi had beaten Ghiberti in the Baptistery doors competition in Florence, the city's Duomo most likely would not have the striking appearance and authority that it has today. After his loss, he sulked off to Rome, where he studied the ancient Roman structures first-hand. Brunelleschi figured out how to vault the Duomo's dome, a structure unprecedented in its colossal size and great height. His Ospedale degli Innocenti employs classical elements in the creation of a stunning, new architectural statement; it is the first truly Renaissance structure.

In Florence: **Duomo; Ospedale degli Innocenti; San Lorenzo; Santo Spirito; Baptistery Doors Competition Entry, Bargello; Santa Croce**

LORENZO GHIBERTI (CA. 1381-1455)
Sculptor from Florence.

Ghiberti won a competition—besting his chief rival, Brunelleschi—to cast the gilded bronze North Doors of the Baptistery in Florence. These doors, and the East Doors that he subsequently executed, took up the next 50 years of his life. He created intricately worked figures that are more true-to-life than any since antiquity, and he was one of the first Renaissance sculptors to work in bronze. Ghiberti taught the next generation of artists; Donatello, Uccello, and Masaccio all passed through his studio.

In Florence: **Door Copies, Baptistery; Original Doors, Museo dell'Opera del Duomo; Baptistry Door Competition Entry, Bargello; Orsanmichele**

DONATELLO (CA. 1386-1466)
Sculptor from Florence.

Donatello was an innovator who, like his good friend Brunelleschi, spent most of his long life in Florence. Consumed with the science of optics, he used light and shadow to create the effects of nearness and distance. He made an essentially flat slab look like a three-dimensional scene. His bronze sculpture of *David* is probably the first free-standing male nude since antiquity. Not only technically brilliant, his work is also emotionally resonant; few sculptors are as expressive.

In Florence: **David, Bargello; St. Mark, Orsanmichele; Palazzo Vecchio; Museo dell'Opera del Duomo; San Lorenzo; Santa Croce**
Elsewhere in Italy: **Padua; Prato; Venice**

Fra Angelico's *Déposition de Croix*   Masaccio's *Trinity*   Filippo Lippi's *Madonna and Child with Two Angels*

PAOLO UCCELLO (1397-1475)
Painter from Florence.
Renaissance chronicler Vasari once observed that had Uccello not been so obsessed with the mathematical problems posed by perspective, he would have been a very good painter. The struggle to master single-point perspective and to render motion in two dimensions is nowhere more apparent than in his battle scenes. His first major commission in Florence was the gargantuan fresco of the English mercenary Sir John Hawkwood (the Italians called him Giovanni Acuto) in Florence's Duomo.

In Florence: **Sir John Hawkwood, Duomo; Battle of San Romano, Uffizi; Santa Maria Novella**

Elsewhere in Italy: **Urbino, Prato**

FRA ANGELICO (CA. 1400-1455)
Painter from a small town north of Florence.
A Dominican friar, who eventually made his way to the convent of San Marco, Fra Angelico and his assistants painted frescoes for aid in prayer and meditation. He was known for his piety; Vasari wrote that Fra Angelico could never paint a crucifix without a tear running down his face. Perhaps no other painter so successfully translated the mysteries of faith and the sacred into painting. And yet his figures emote, his command of perspective is superb, and his use of color startles even today.

In Florence: **Museo di San Marco; Uffizi**

Elsewhere in Italy: **Vatican Museums, Rome; Fiesole; Cortona; Perugia; Orvieto**

MASACCIO (1401-1428)
Painter from San Giovanni Valdarno, southeast of Florence.
Masaccio and Masolino, a frequent collaborator, worked most famously together at Santa Maria del Carmine. Their frescoes of the life of St. Peter use light to mold figures in the painting by imitating the way light falls on figures in real life. Masaccio also pioneered the use of single-point perspective, masterfully rendered in his His friend Brunelleschi probably introduced him to the technique, yet another step forward in rendering things the way the eye sees them. Masaccio died young and under mysterious circumstances.

In Florence: **Santa Maria del Carmine; Trinity, Santa Maria Novella**

FILIPPO LIPPI (CA. 1406-1469)
Painter from Prato.
At a young age, Filippo Lippi entered the friary of Santa Maria del Carmine, where he was highly influenced by Masaccio and Masolino's frescoes. His religious vows appear to have made less of an impact; his affair with a young nun produced a son, Filippino (Little Philip, who later apprenticed with Botticelli), and a daughter. His religious paintings often have a playful, humorous note; some of his angels are downright impish and look directly out at the viewer. Lippi links the earlier painters of the 15th century with those who follow; Botticelli apprenticed with him.

In Florence: **Uffizi; Palazzo Medici Riccardi; San Lorenzo; Palazzo Pitti**

Elsewhere in Italy: **Prato**

Botticelli's *Primavera*

Leonardo's *Portrait of a Young Woman*

Raphael's *Madonna on the Meadow*

BOTTICELLI (CA. 1444-1510)

Painter from Florence.

Botticelli's work is characterized by stunning, elongated blondes, cherubic angels (something he undoubtedly learned from his time with Filippo Lippi), and tender Christs. Though he did many religious paintings, he also painted monumental, nonreligious panels—his *Birth of Venus* and *Primavera* being the two most famous of these. A brief sojourn took him to Rome, where he and a number of other artists frescoed the Sistine Chapel walls.

In Florence:
Birth of Venus, Primavera, Uffizi; Palazzo Pitti

Elsewhere in Italy:
Vatican Museums, Rome

LEONARDO DA VINCI (1452-1519)

Painter/sculptor/engineer from Anchiano, a small town outside Vinci.

Leonardo never lingered long in any place; his restless nature and his international reputation led to commissions throughout Italy, and took him to Milan, Vigevano, Pavia, Rome, and, ultimately, France. Though he is most famous for his mysterious *Mona Lisa* (at the Louvre in Paris), he painted other penetrating, psychological portraits in addition to his scientific experiments: his design for a flying machine (never built) predates Kitty Hawk by nearly 500 years. The greatest collection of Leonardo's work in Italy can be seen on one wall in the Uffizi.

In Florence: **Adoration of the Magi, Uffizi**
Elsewhere in Italy: **Last Supper, Santa Maria delle Grazie, Milan**

RAPHAEL (1483-1520)

Painter/architect from Urbino.

Raphael spent only four highly productive years of his short life in Florence, where he turned out made-to-order panel paintings of the *Madonna and Child* for a hungry public; he also executed a number of portraits of Florentine aristocrats. Perhaps no other artist had such a fine command of line and color, and could render it, seemingly effortlessly, in paint. His painting acquired new authority after he came up against Michelangelo toiling away on the Sistine ceiling. Raphael worked nearly next door in the Vatican, where his figures take on an epic, Michelangelesque scale.

In Florence: **Uffizi; Palazzo Pitti**
Elsewhere in Italy: **Vatican Museums, Rome**

MICHELANGELO (1475-1564)

Painter/sculptor/architect from Caprese.

Although Florentine and proud of it (he famously signed his St. Peter's *Pietà* to avoid confusion about where he was from), he spent most of his 89 years outside his native city. He painted and sculpted the male body on an epic scale and glorified it while doing so. Though he complained throughout the proceedings that he was really a sculptor, Michelangelo's Sistine Chapel ceiling is arguably the greatest fresco cycle ever painted (and the massive figures owe no small debt to Giotto).

In Florence: **David, Galleria dell'Accademia; Uffizi; Casa Buonarroti; Bargello**
Elsewhere in Italy: **St. Peter's Basilica, Vatican Museums, and Piazza del Campidoglio in Rome**

◎ Sights

Giardino Bardini

GARDEN | FAMILY | Garden lovers, those who crave a view, and those who enjoy a nice hike should visit this lovely villa, whose history spans centuries. It had a walled garden as early as the 14th century; its "Grand Stairs"—a zigzag ascent well worth scaling—have been around since the 16th. In spring, the garden is filled with irises, roses, and heirloom flowers and its magnificent wisteria pergola is in bloom. It also has a Japanese garden and statuary. ⊠ *Costa San Giorgio 2, San Niccolò* ☎ *055/2638599* ⊕ *www.villabardini.it* ⊒ *€6 garden only, €10 garden and exhibits* ۞ *Closed the first and last Mon. of the month.*

★ Giardino di Boboli (*Boboli Gardens*)

GARDEN | FAMILY | The main entrance to these gardens is from the right side of the courtyard of Palazzo Pitti. The landscaping began to take shape in 1549, when the Pitti family sold the palazzo to Eleanor of Toledo, wife of the Medici grand duke Cosimo I. Stone paths lead to vine-covered pergolas and grand staircases, and a walk here also affords excellent views. ⊠ *Piazza de' Pitti, Palazzo Pitti* ☎ *055/294883* ⊕ *www.uffizi.it/giardino-boboli* ⊒ *€6* ۞ *Closed 1st and last Mon. of month.*

Museo Bardini

ART MUSEUM | The 19th-century collector and antiquarian Stefano Bardini turned his palace into his own private museum. Upon his death, the collection was turned over to the state and includes an interesting assortment of Etruscan pieces, sculpture, paintings, and furniture that dates mostly from the Renaissance and Baroque eras. ⊠ *Via dei Renai 37, Oltrarno* ☎ *055/2342427* ⊕ *cultura.comune.fi.it/musei* ⊒ *€7* ۞ *Closed Tues.–Thurs.*

★ Palazzo Pitti

ART MUSEUM | This is one of Florence's largest architectural set pieces. The original palazzo, built for the Pitti family around 1460, consisted of the main entrance and the sections extending as far as three windows on either side. In 1549, the property was sold to the Medici, who commissioned Bartolomeo Ammannati to make substantial additions.

Today, the palace houses several museums. The Museo degli Argenti contains Medici treasures; the Galleria del Costume showcases 300 years of fashion; the Galleria d'Arte Moderna has mostly Tuscan 19th- and 20th-century paintings; and the Galleria Palatina, where paintings from the 15th to the 17th century are displayed in rooms that remain much as the Lorena, the rulers who took over from the Medici in 1737, left them. ⊠ *Piazza Pitti, Palazzo Pitti* ☎ *055/294883* ⊕ *www.uffizi.it/palazzo-pitti* ⊒ *From €10* ۞ *Closed Mon.*

★ Piazzale Michelangelo

PLAZA/SQUARE | FAMILY | From this lookout you have a marvelous view of Florence and the hills around it, rivaling the vista from the Forte di Belvedere. A copy of Michelangelo's *David* overlooks outdoor cafés packed with tourists during the day and evening. In May, the Giardino dell'Iris (Iris Garden) off the piazza is abloom with more than 2,500 varieties of the flower. The Giardino delle Rose (Rose Garden) on the terraces below the piazza is also in full bloom in May and June. ⊠ *Piazzale Michelangelo, San Niccolò.*

San Miniato al Monte

CHURCH | This abbey, like the Baptistery a fine example of Romanesque architecture, is one of the oldest churches in Florence, dating from the 11th century. A 12th-century mosaic topped by a gilt bronze eagle, emblem of San Miniato's sponsors, the Calimala (cloth merchants' guild), crowns the green-and-white marble facade. Inside are a 13th-century inlaid-marble floor and apse mosaic. Artist Spinello Aretino (1350–1410) covered the walls of the Sagrestia with frescoes of scenes from the life of St. Benedict. ⊠ *Via delle Porte Sante 34, San Niccolò*

Sights ▼

1 Giardino Bardini **G4**
2 Giardino di Boboli....... **C5**
3 Museo Bardini **G4**
4 Palazzo Pitti **D3**
5 Piazzale
   Michelangelo **J5**

6 San Miniato al
  Monte.................... **J7**
7 Santa Felicita............ **E2**
8 Santa Maria del
  Carmine.................. **B2**
9 Santo Spirito **C2**

Restaurants ▼

1 Alla Vecchia
  Bettola **A2**
2 Fuori Porta................ **I4**
3 Il Santo Bevitore **C1**
4 La Casalinga............. **C3**

5 Osteria Antica Mescita
  San Niccolò **I4**
6 Zeb **I4**

The Oltrarno

KEY
- **1** Sights
- **1** Restaurants
- **1** Quick Bites
- **1** Hotels

Coffee and Quick Bites ▼
1 Ditta Artigianale......... **D2**
2 Gelateria la Carraia..... **C1**

Hotels ▼
1 Hotel La Scaletta **E2**
2 Hotel Lungarno.......... **E2**
3 Hotel Silla................ **H4**

☎ *055/2342731* ⊕ *sanminiatoalmonte.it* ⊗ *Closed daily 1–3 pm.*

Santa Felicita

CHURCH | This late-Baroque church (its facade was remodeled between 1736 and 1739) contains the Mannerist Jacopo Pontormo's *Deposition,* the centerpiece of the Cappella Capponi (executed 1525–28) and a masterpiece of 16th-century Florentine art. The granite column in the piazza was erected in 1381 and marks a Christian cemetery. ⊠ *Piazza Santa Felicita 3, Palazzo Pitti* ☎ *055/213018* ⊗ *Closed Sun.*

Santa Maria del Carmine

CHURCH | The Cappella Brancacci, at the end of the right transept of this church, contains a masterpiece of Renaissance painting: a fresco cycle that changed the course of Western art. It is the work of Masaccio (1401–1428) and Masolino (1383–circa 1447), who began it around 1424, and Filippino Lippi (1457–1504), who finished it some 50 years later.

It was, however, Masaccio's work that opened a new frontier for painting, as he was among the first artists to employ single-point perspective. His style predominates in the *Tribute Money,* on the upper-left wall; *St. Peter Baptizing,* on the upper altar wall; the *Distribution of Goods,* on the lower altar wall; and the *Expulsion of Adam and Eve,* on the chapel's upper-left entrance pier. The figures of Adam and Eve possess a startling presence thanks to the dramatic way in which their bodies seem to reflect light. In their faces, you also see terrible shame and suffering depicted with a humanity rarely achieved in art. ⊠ *Piazza del Carmine, Santo Spirito* ☎ *055/2768224 reservations* ⊕ *bigliettimusei.comune.fi.it* ⊠ *€11* ⊗ *Closed Tues.–Thurs.* ⊜ *Reservations to visit the Cappella Brancacci are required.*

Santo Spirito

CHURCH | It was here that Filippo Brunelleschi solved two major problems of interior Renaissance church design:

how to build a cross-shape interior using architectural elements borrowed from antiquity (a religious taboo at the time) and how to incorporate the order and regularity that Renaissance scientists (among them Brunelleschi himself) were at the time discovering in the natural world.

His resolution of the first problem was brilliantly simple: while ancient Greek temples were walled buildings surrounded by classical colonnades, Brunelleschi's churches were classical arcades surrounded by walled buildings. His solution to the second problem was mathematically precise: he made it so that the church's components were proportionally related. That is, the transepts and nave have the same width; the side aisles are half as wide as the nave; the chapels off the side aisles are half as deep as the side aisles; the chancel and transepts are one-eighth the depth of the nave; and so on, with dizzying exactitude. ⊠ *Piazza Santo Spirito 30, Oltrarno* ☎ *055/210030* ⊕ *www.basilicasantospirito.it* ⊠ *Church free; tour €2* ⊗ *Closed Wed.*

🍴 Restaurants

Alla Vecchia Bettola

$$ | **TUSCAN** | The name doesn't exactly mean "old dive," but it comes pretty close. The recipes here come from "wise grandmothers" and celebrate Tuscan food in its glorious simplicity—prosciutto is sliced to order, grilled meats are tender, service is friendly, and the wine list is well-priced and good. **Known for:** grilled meats; firmly Tuscan menu; just outside the centro storico but worth the taxi ride. ⑤ *Average main: €16* ⊠ *Viale Vasco Pratolini 3/5/7, Oltrarno* ☎ *055/224158* ⊗ *Closed Sun. and Mon.*

★ Fuori Porta

$ | **WINE BAR** | This wine bar on the way up the hill to Piazzale Michelangelo serves cured meats and cheeses, pastas, salads, and daily specials. Crostini and crostoni—grilled bread topped with a mélange of cheeses and meats—are the house specialty, but the *verdure sott'olio* (vegetables in oil) are divine, too. **Known for:** lengthy wine list; crostini and crostoni; changing daily specials. $ *Average main: €14* ⊠ *Via Monte alle Croci 10, San Niccolò* ☎ *055/2342483* ⊕ *www. fuoriporta.it.*

★ Il Santo Bevitore

$$ | TUSCAN | Florentines and other lovers of good food flock to "The Holy Drinker" for Tuscan-inspired dishes—perhaps the exceptional verdure sott'olio or the *terrina di fegatini* (a creamy chicken-liver spread) to start, followed by one of the divine pastas. Unpretentious white walls, dark wood furniture, and paper place mats provide the simple decor. **Known for:** Tuscan dishes with flair; Norcini (cured meats) menu; friendly waitstaff. $ *Average main: €19* ⊠ *Via Santo Spirito 64/r–66/r, Santo Spirito* ☎ *055/211264* ⊕ *www.ilsantobevitore.com.*

★ La Casalinga

$ | TUSCAN | *Casalinga* means "housewife," and this place, which has been around since 1963, has the nostalgic charm of a mid-century kitchen with Tuscan comfort food to match. If you eat ribollita anywhere in Florence, eat it here—it couldn't be more authentic. **Known for:** ribollita; black pepper beef stew; often packed. $ *Average main: €14* ⊠ *Via Michelozzi 9/r, Santo Spirito* ☎ *055/218624* ⊕ *trattorialacasalinga.it* ⊘ *Closed Sun. and two wks in Dec. and Jan.*

Osteria Antica Mescita San Niccolò

$ | TUSCAN | Always crowded—but always good and inexpensive—this osteria is next to San Niccolò church, and, if you sit in the lower part, you'll be in what was once a chapel dating from the 11th century. The subtle but dramatic background nicely complements the food, which is simple Tuscan at its best. **Known for:** delicious soup; grilled meats; outdoor seating in a small, lovely square.

$ *Average main: €12* ⊠ *Via San Niccolò 60/r, San Niccolò* ☎ *055/2342836* ⊕ *osteriasanniccolo.webnode.it.*

Zeb

$$ | TUSCAN | "Zeb" stands for *zuppa e bollito* (soup and boiled things), but you can't go wrong with anything at this small *alimentari* (delicatessen). It's homestyle Tuscan cuisine at its very best, served in unpretentious, intimate surroundings (there's room for only about 20 diners). **Known for:** fantastic soup; terrific pasta; lovely wine list. $ *Average main: €18* ⊠ *Via San Miniato 2, Oltrarno* ☎ *055/2342864* ⊕ *www.zebgastronomia. com* ⊘ *Closed Wed. No dinner Sun. or on Mon. and Tues. from Nov. to Mar.*

☕ Coffee and Quick Bites

Ditta Artigianale

$ | CAFÉ | Founded in 2013 as a micro coffee roaster on Via de' Neri, Ditta Artigianale now has four spots throughout Florence. Follow a side street off the Palazzo Pitti to take a coffee break with a classic espresso, drip coffee, or the inventive Coffemisu (espresso, cookies, cocoa, and mascarpone cream) in a space that's more like an airy mid-century modern living room, than a coffee shop. **Known for:** fair trade coffee; extensive brunch menu; lively atmosphere, popular with expats. $ *Average main: €10* ⊠ *Via dello Sprone 5/r, Oltrarno* ☎ *055/0457163* ⊕ *www.dittaartigianale.com.*

Gelateria la Carraia

$ | ICE CREAM | FAMILY | At the foot of Ponte Carraia, two bridges down from the Ponte Vecchio, find standard gelato flavors or creative options such as *limone con biscotti* (lemon sorbet with cookies). **Known for:** super-creamy gelato; generous €2 cones; every flavor is worth a taste. $ *Average main: €3* ⊠ *Piazza Nazario Sauro 2, Santo Spirito* ☎ *055/280695* ⊕ *www.gelaterialacarraia.it/en.*

Hotels

Hotel La Scaletta

$$$ | HOTEL | In addition to a tremendous view of the Boboli Gardens, this cozy pensione near the Ponte Vecchio and Palazzo Pitti has simply furnished but large rooms and a sunny breakfast room. **Pros:** in-house restaurant with stunning views; wonderful, multilingual staff; in a lively neighborhood. **Cons:** small elevator, many steps; books up quickly; neighborhood can be noisy. $ *Rooms from: €277* ✉ *Via Guicciardini 13, Palazzo Pitti* ☎ *055/283028* ⊕ *www.hotellascaletta.it* ⋠ *36 rooms* ⦿| *No Meals.*

Hotel Lungarno

$$$$ | HOTEL | Private terraces with views of the Arno and the Palazzo Vecchio are among the draws in many of this hotel's accommodations. **Pros:** upscale without being stuffy; lovely Arno views; Borgo San Jacopo, the hotel restaurant. **Cons:** rooms without Arno views feel less special; street noise happens; walls can be thin. $ *Rooms from: €765* ✉ *Borgo San Jacopo 14, Oltrarno* ☎ *055/27261* ⊕ *www.lungarnocollection.com* ⋠ *63 rooms* ⦿| *No Meals.*

Hotel Silla

$$ | HOTEL | Rooms in this 15th-century palazzo, entered via a courtyard with potted plants and sculpture-filled niches, are simply furnished; some have Arno views, others have stuccoed ceilings. **Pros:** in the middle of everything except the crowds; cordial, friendly staff; great breakfast. **Cons:** street noise; small rooms; some rooms could use an update. $ *Rooms from: €181* ✉ *Via de' Renai 5, San Niccolò* ☎ *055/2342888* ⊕ *www.hotelsilla.it* ⋠ *36 rooms* ⦿| *Free Breakfast.*

Shopping

★ Giulio Giannini e Figlio

STATIONERY | One of Florence's oldest paper-goods stores is *the* place to buy marbleized stock, which comes in many formats, from flat sheets to paper-covered boxes or even pencils. ✉ *Piazza Pitti 37/r, Oltrarno* ☎ *055/212621* ⊕ *www. giuliogiannini.com.*

★ Il Torchio

STATIONERY | Photograph albums, frames, diaries, and other objects dressed in handmade paper are high quality, and the prices lower than usual. ✉ *Via dei Bardi 17, San Niccolò* ☎ *055/2342862* ⊕ *www. legatoriailtorchio.com.*

★ Madova

HATS & GLOVES | Complete your winter wardrobe with a pair of high-quality leather gloves, available in a rainbow of colors and a choice of linings (silk, cashmere, and unlined), from Madova. It's been in business for more than 100 years. ✉ *Via Guicciardini 1/r, Palazzo Pitti* ☎ *055/2396526* ⊕ *www.madova.it.*

Pitti Mosaici

HOUSEWARES | Stones are worked into exquisite tables, pictures, and jewelry at Pitti Mosaici, which continues the *pietre dure* (mosaic) tradition that was all the rage of 16th-century Florence. ✉ *Piazza dei Pitti 23/r, Palazzo Pitti* ☎ *055/282127* ⊕ *www.pittimosaici.com.*

Santo Spirito Markets

MARKET | FAMILY | The second Sunday of every month brings the Oltrarno Arts and Crafts Market in Piazza Santo Spirito with clothing, antiques, and homewares. On the third Sunday of the month, vendors at the La Fierucola in the piazza sell such delectables as honeys, jams, spice mixes, and fresh vegetables. ✉ *Piazza Santo Spirito, Santo Spirito* ⊕ *www.lafierucola. org.*

Side Trip from Florence

Fiesole

10 km (6 miles) north of Florence.

A half-day excursion to Fiesole, in the hills above Florence, gives you a pleasant respite from museums and a wonderful view of the city. From here the view of the Duomo gives you a new appreciation for what the Renaissance accomplished. Fiesole began life as an ancient Etruscan and later Roman village that held some power until it succumbed to barbarian invasions. Eventually it gave up its independence in exchange for Florence's protection. The medieval cathedral, ancient Roman amphitheater, and lovely old villas behind garden walls are clustered on a series of hilltops. A walk around Fiesole can take from one to two or three hours, depending on how far you stroll from the main piazza.

GETTING HERE AND AROUND

The trip from Florence by car takes 20–30 minutes. Drive to Piazza Liberta and cross the Ponte Rosso heading in the direction of the SS65/SR65. Turn right on to Via Salviati and continue on to Via Roccettini. Make a left turn to Via Vecchia Fiesolana which will take you directly to the center of town. There are several possible routes for the two-hour walk from central Florence to Fiesole. One route begins in a residential area of Florence called Salviatino (Via Barbacane, near Piazza Edison, on the No. 7 bus route), and after a short time, offers peeks over garden walls of beautiful villas, as well as the view over your shoulder at the panorama of Florence in the valley. Buses also run to Fiesole from the center of Florence; check Autolinee Toscane for timetables (*www.at-bus.it*).

VISITOR INFORMATION
CONTACT Fiesole Tourism Office. ✉ *Via Portigiani 3, Fiesole* ☎ *055/5961311.*

◉ Sights

Anfiteatro Romano (*Roman Amphitheater*)
RUINS | The beautifully preserved, 2,000-seat Anfiteatro Romano, near the Duomo, dates from the 1st century BC and is still used for summer concerts. To the right of the amphitheater are the remains of the Terme Romani (Roman Baths), where you can see the gymnasium, hot and cold baths, and rectangular chamber where the water was heated. Admission here also gets you access to an archaeological museum and the Bandini Museum, which showcases sacred art. ✉ *Via Portigiani 1, Fiesole* ☎ *055/5961293* ⊕ *www.museidifiesole.it* ⊠ *€12, includes access to archaeological park and museum and Bandini Museum* ☉ *Check website for seasonal closure days.*

Badia Fiesolana
CHURCH | From the church of San Domenico it's a five-minute walk northwest to Fiesole's original cathedral. Dating from the 11th century, it was first the home of the Camaldolese monks. Thanks to Cosimo il Vecchio de' Medici, the complex was substantially restructured. The facade, never completed owing to Cosimo's death, contains elements of its original Romanesque decoration. ✉ *Via della Badia dei Roccettini 9, Fiesole* ☎ *055/4685399* ⊕ *www.eui.eu* ☉ *Closed weekends.*

Duomo
CHURCH | A stark medieval interior yields many masterpieces. In the raised presbytery, the Cappella Salutati was frescoed by 15th-century artist Cosimo Rosselli, but it was his contemporary, sculptor Mino da Fiesole (1430–84), who put the town on the artistic map. The Madonna on the altarpiece and the tomb of Bishop Salutati are fine examples of the artist's work. ✉ *Piazza Mino da Fiesole, Fiesole* ☎ *055/599566.*

San Domenico

CHURCH | If you really want to stretch your legs, walk 4 km (2½ miles) toward the center of Florence along Via Vecchia Fiesolana, a narrow lane in use since Etruscan times, to the church of San Domenico. Sheltered in the church is the *Madonna and Child with Saints* by Fra Angelico, who was a Dominican friar here before he moved to Florence. ⊠ *Piazza San Domenico, off Via Giuseppe Mantellini, Fiesole* ☎ *055/59230* ⊘ *Closed Sun.*

San Francesco

CHURCH | This lovely hilltop church has a good view of Florence and the plain below from its terrace and benches. Off the little cloister is a small, eclectic museum containing, among other things, two Egyptian mummies. Halfway up the hill you'll see sloping steps to the right; they lead to a fragrant wooded park with trails that loop out and back to the church. ⊠ *Via San Francesco 13, Fiesole* ☎ *055/59175* 🖭 *Free.*

 Restaurants

La Reggia degli Etruschi

$$$ | **ITALIAN** | Atop a steep hill, en route to the church of San Francesco, this lovely little eatery is certainly worth the trek. Indulge in inventive reworkings of Tuscan classics, like the *mezzaluna di pera a pecorino* (little half-moon pasta stuffed with pear and pecorino) served with Roquefort and poppy seeds. **Known for:** out-of-the-way location; good wine list and friendly service; small terrace with outdoor seating. ⑤ *Average main: €25* ⊠ *Via San Francesco 18, Fiesole* ☎ *333/3556126 mobile* ⊕ *www.lareggia-deglietruschi.com.*

 Hotels

Villa San Michele

$$$$ | **HOTEL** | In the hills of Fiesole, a cypress-lined driveway provides an elegant preamble to this incredibly gorgeous (and very expensive) hotel, which is housed in a 16th-century building that was originally a Franciscan convent designed by Santi di Tito. **Pros:** exceptional convent conversion; stunning views; shuttle bus makes frequent forays to and from Florence. **Cons:** money must be no object; some rooms are small; you must either depend on the shuttle bus or have a car. ⑤ *Rooms from: €1726* ⊠ *Via Doccia 4, Fiesole* ☎ *055/5678200* ⊕ *www.belmond.com/hotels* ⊘ *Closed Nov.–May* ⇄ *45 rooms* ⦿ *Free Breakfast.*

Chapter 13

TUSCANY

Updated by
Elizabeth Shemaria
and Elisa Scarton

👁 **Sights**
★★★★★

🍴 **Restaurants**
★★★★★

🛏 **Hotels**
★★★★☆

🛍 **Shopping**
★★★☆☆

🍸 **Nightlife**
★★★☆☆

WELCOME TO TUSCANY

TOP REASONS TO GO

★ **Piazza del Campo, Siena:** Sip a cappuccino or enjoy some gelato as you take in the spectacle in and of this shell-shape piazza.

★ **Piero della Francesca's True Cross frescoes, Arezzo:** If your Holy Grail is great Renaissance art, seek out these 12 enigmatic scenes in Arezzo's Basilica di San Francesco.

★ **San Gimignano:** Grab a spot at sunset on the steps of the Collegiata as flocks of swallows swoop in and out of the famous medieval towers.

★ **Wine tasting in Chianti:** Sample the fruits of the region's gorgeous vineyards, either at the wineries themselves or in the wine bars found in the towns.

★ **Leaning Tower of Pisa:** It may be touristy, but it's still a whole lot of fun to climb to the top and admire the view.

1 Lucca. See 16th-century ramparts.

2 Pisa. Its bell tower is known the world over.

3 Chianti. A picturesque wine region.

4 Volterra. Breathtaking hilltop views.

5 San Gimignano. Lovely hill town.

6 Colle di Val d'Elsa. Laid-back hill town.

7 Siena. An enchanting medieval city.

8 Arezzo. Visit for the sublime frescoes.

9 Cortona. Sits above the flat Valdichiana.

10 Montepulciano. Its higher altitude means cooler summers.

11 Pienza. An ideal city planned by Pope Pius II.

12 Montalcino. Famed for its robust red wine.

13 Abbazia di Sant'Antimo. A Romanesque abbey.

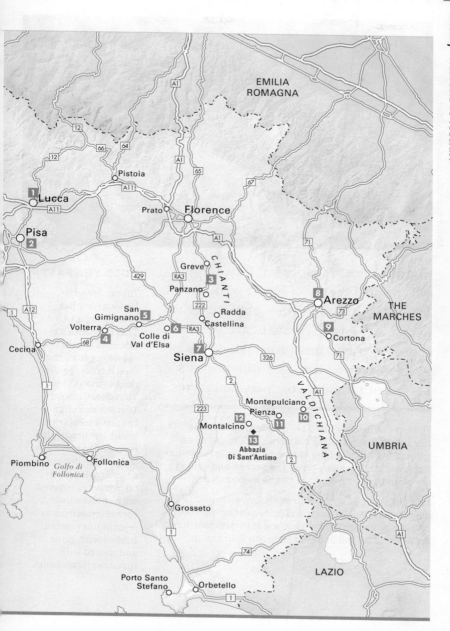

EATING AND DRINKING WELL IN TUSCANY

Affettati misti (Italian cured meat platter)

The influence of the ancient Etruscans—who favored the use of fresh herbs—is still felt in Tuscan cuisine three millennia later. Simple and earthy, Tuscan food celebrates the seasons with fresh vegetable dishes, wonderful bread-based soups, and meats perfumed with sage, rosemary, and thyme.

Throughout Tuscany there are excellent upscale restaurants that serve elaborate dishes, but to get a real taste of the flavors of the region, head for the family-run trattorias found in every town. The service and setting are often basic, but the food can be memorable.

Few places serve lighter fare at midday, so expect substantial meals at lunch and dinner, especially in out-of-the-way towns. Dining hours are fairly standard: lunch between 12:30 and 2, dinner between 7:30 and 10.

HOLD THE SALT

Tuscan bread is famous for what it's missing: salt. That's because it's intended to pick up seasoning from the food it accompanies, not be eaten alone. That doesn't mean Tuscans don't like to start a meal with bread, but usually it's prepared in some way. It can be grilled and drizzled with olive oil (*fettunta*), covered with chicken liver spread (*crostino con fegatini*), or toasted, rubbed with garlic, and topped with tomatoes (*bruschetta*).

AFFETTATI MISTI

The name, roughly translated, means "mixed cold cuts," and it's something Tuscans do exceptionally well. A platter of cured meats, served as an antipasto, is sure to include *prosciutto crudo* (cured pork, cut paper-thin) and *salame* (dry sausage, prepared in dozens of ways—some spicy, some sweet). The most distinctly Tuscan affetati are made from *cinta senese* (a once nearly extinct pig found only in the heart of the region) and *cinghiale* (wild boar, which roam all over Italy). You can eat these delicious slices unadorned or layered on a piece of bread.

PASTA

Restaurants throughout Tuscany serve dishes similar to those in Florence, but they also have their own local specialties. Many recipes are from the *nonna* (grandmother) of the restaurant's owner, handed down over time but never written down.

Look in particular for pasta creations made with *pici* (a long, thick, hand-rolled spaghetti). Pappardelle (a long, ribbonlike pasta noodle) is frequently paired with sauces made with game, such as *lepre* (hare) or cinghiale. In the northwest, a specialty of Lucca is *tordelli di carne al ragù* (meat-stuffed pasta with a meat sauce).

Wines from Tuscany

Ribbonlike pasta with mushrooms

MEAT

Bistecca alla fiorentina (a thick T-bone steak, grilled rare) is the classic meat dish of Tuscany, but there are other specialties as well. Many menus will include *tagliata di manzo* (thinly sliced, roasted beef, drizzled with olive oil), *arista di maiale* (roast pork with sage and rosemary), and *salsiccia e fagioli* (pork sausage and beans). In the southern part of the region, don't be surprised to find *piccione* (pigeon), which can be roasted, stuffed, or baked.

WINE

Grape cultivation here also dates from Etruscan times, and vineyards are abundant, particularly in Chianti. The resulting medium-body red wine is a staple on most tables; however, you can select from a multitude of other varieties, including such reds as Brunello di Montalcino and Vino Nobile di Montepulciano and such whites as vermentino and vernaccia.

Super Tuscans (a fanciful name given to a group of wines by American journalists) now command attention as some of the best produced in Italy; they have great depth and complexity. The dessert wine vin santo is made throughout the region and is often sipped with biscotti (twice-baked almond cookies), perfect for dunking.

Midway down the Italian peninsula, Tuscany (Toscana in Italian) is distinguished by rolling hills, snowcapped mountains, cypress trees, and miles of coastline on the Tyrrhenian Sea—which all adds up to gorgeous views at practically every turn.

The beauty of the landscape proves a perfect foil for the region's abundance of superlative art and architecture. It also produces some of Italy's finest wines and olive oils. The combination of unforgettable art, sumptuous landscapes, and eminently drinkable wines that pair beautifully with its simple food makes a trip to Tuscany something beyond special.

Many of Tuscany's cities and towns have retained the same fundamental character over the past 500 years. Civic rivalries that led to bloody battles centuries ago have given way to soccer rivalries. Renaissance pomp lives on in the celebration of local feast days and centuries-old traditions such as the Palio in Siena and the Giostra del Saracino (Joust of the Saracen) in Arezzo. Often, present-day Tuscans look as though they might have served as models for paintings produced hundreds of years ago. In many ways, the Renaissance lives on in Tuscany.

MAJOR REGIONS

Hill towns southwest of Florence. The search for the best tiny hill town always leads to San Gimignano, known as the "medieval Manhattan" for its 13th-century stone towers.

Southern Tuscany. Among the highlights of Tuscany's southern reaches are the wine-producing centers of Montalcino and Montepulciano.

Northwest Tuscany. Head here to climb the Leaning Tower of Pisa and stroll medieval walls in Lucca, the birthplace of composer Giacomo Puccini.

Planning

Getting Here and Around

BUS
Buses are a reliable but time-consuming means of getting around the region because they tend to stop in every town. Trains are a better option in virtually every respect when you're headed to Pisa, Lucca, Arezzo, and other cities with good rail service. But for most smaller towns, buses are the only option. Be aware that making arrangements for bus travel, particularly for a non–Italian speaker, can be a test of patience.

CAR
Driving is the only way (other than hiking or biking) to reach many of Tuscany's small towns and vineyards. The cities west of Florence are easily accessed by the A11, which leads to Lucca and then to the sea. The A1 takes you south from Florence to Arezzo and Chiusi (where you turn off for Montepulciano). Florence and Siena are connected by a *superstrada* and also the scenic Via Cassia (SR2) and

even more panoramic Strada Chiantigiana (SR222), both of which thread through Chianti, skirting rolling hills and vineyards. The hill towns north and west of Siena lie along superstradas and winding local roads—all are well marked, but you should still arm yourself with a good map.

TRAIN

Trains on Italy's main north–south rail line stop in Florence as well as Prato, Arezzo, and Chiusi. Another major line connects Florence with Pisa, and the coastal line between Rome and Genoa passes through Pisa as well. There's regular, frequent hourly service from Florence to Lucca, and several trips a day between Florence and Siena. Siena's train station is 2 km (1 mile) north of the *centro storico* (historic center), but cabs and city buses are readily available, as is a very handy funicular.

For other parts of Tuscany—Chianti, Montalcino, and Montepulciano, for example—you're better off traveling by bus or by car. Train stations, when they exist, are far from the historic centers (usually in the valleys below hill towns), and service is infrequent.

CONTACT Trenitalia. ☎ *892021 toll-free in Italy* ⊕ *www.trenitalia.com.*

Making the Most of Your Time

Tuscany isn't the place for a jam-packed itinerary. One of the greatest pleasures here is indulging in rustic hedonism, marked by long lunches and showstopping sunsets. Whether by car, by bike, or on foot, you'll want to get out into the glorious landscape, but it's smart to keep your plans modest. Set a church or a hill town or an out-of-the-way restaurant as your destination, knowing that half the pleasure is in getting there—admiring as you go the stately palaces, the tidy geometry of row upon row of grapevines, and the fields vibrant with red poppies, sunflowers, and yellow broom.

You'll need to devise a strategy for seeing the sights. Take Siena: this beautiful, art-filled town simply can't be missed; it's compact enough that you can see the major sights on a day trip, and that's exactly what most people do. Spend the night, though, and you'll get to see the town breathe a sigh and relax on the day-trippers' departure. In Pisa, the famous tower and the rest of the Camposanto are not only worth seeing but a must-see, a highlight of any trip to Italy. But nearby Lucca must not be overlooked either. In fact, this walled town has greater charms than Pisa does, making it a better choice for an overnight, so you should come up with a plan that takes in both places.

Restaurants

A meal in Tuscany traditionally consists of five courses, and every menu you encounter will be organized along this plan of antipasto, primo, secondo, contorno, and dolce. The crucial rule of restaurant dining is that you should order at least two courses. Otherwise, you'll likely end up with a lonely piece of meat and no sides.

Hotels

A visit to the Tuscan countryside is a trip into absolute beauty. There are plenty of good hotels in the larger towns, but the classic experience is to stay in one of the rural accommodations—often converted private homes, sometimes working farms or vineyards (known as *agriturismi*).

Although it's tempting to think you can stumble upon a little out-of-the-way hotel at the end of the day, you're better off not testing your luck. Make reservations before you go. If you don't have a reservation, you may be able to get help finding a room from the local tourist office.

⇨ *Hotel and restaurant reviews have been shortened. For full information, visit Fodors.com. Prices in the hotel reviews are the lowest cost of a standard double room in high season. Prices in the dining reviews are the average cost of a main course at dinner, or, if dinner is not served, at lunch.*

What It Costs in Euros			
$	$$	$$$	$$$$
RESTAURANTS			
under €15	€15–€24	€25–€35	over €35
HOTELS			
under €125	€125–€200	€201–€300	over €300

Visitor Information

Many towns in Tuscany have tourist information offices, which can be useful resources for trip-planning advice (and sometimes maps). Such offices are typically open from 8:30 to 1 and 3:30 to 6 or 7; those in smaller towns are usually closed Saturday afternoon and Sunday, and often shut down entirely from early November through Easter.

The tourist information office in Greve is an excellent source for general information about the Chianti wine region and its hilltop towns. In Siena, the centrally located tourist office in Piazza del Campo has information about Siena and its province. Both offices can help you book hotel rooms. Offices in smaller towns can also be a good place to check if you need last-minute accommodations.

Lucca

90 km (56 miles) west of Florence.

Ramparts built in the 16th and 17th centuries enclose a charming fortress town filled with churches (99 of them), terra-cotta–roofed buildings, and narrow cobblestone streets, along which locals maneuver bikes to do their daily shopping. Here Caesar, Pompey, and Crassus agreed to rule Rome as a triumvirate in 56 BC; Lucca was later the first Tuscan town to accept Christianity. The town still has a mind of its own, and when most of Tuscany was voting communist as a matter of course, Lucca's citizens rarely followed suit. The famous composer Giacomo Puccini (1858–1924) was born here; he is celebrated during the summer Opera Theater and Music Festival of Lucca. The ramparts circling the centro storico are the perfect place to stroll, bicycle, or just admire the view.

GETTING HERE AND AROUND
You can reach Lucca easily by train from Florence; the centro storico is a short walk from the station. If you're driving, take the A11/E76.

VISITOR INFORMATION
CONTACT Lucca Tourism Office. ⊠ *Porta San Donato vecchia, Piazzale Verdi, Lucca* ☎ *0583/583150* ⊕ *www.turismo.lucca.it.*

 Sights

Traffic (including motorbikes) is restricted in the walled historic center of Lucca. Walking is the best, most enjoyable way to get around. Or you can rent a bicycle; getting around on bike is easy, as the center is quite flat.

Duomo
CHURCH | The blind arches on the cathedral's facade are a fine example of the rigorously ordered Pisan Romanesque style, in this case happily enlivened by an extremely varied collection of small, carved columns.

Take a closer look at the decoration of the facade and that of the portico below; they make this one of the most entertaining church exteriors in Tuscany.

The Gothic interior contains a moving Byzantine crucifix—called the Volto Santo, or Holy Face—brought here, according to legend, in the 8th century (though it probably dates from between the 11th and early 13th century). The masterpiece of the Sienese sculptor Jacopo della Quercia (circa 1371–1438) is the marble *Tomb of Ilaria del Carretto* (1407–08). ⊠ *Piazza San Martino 8, Lucca* ☎ *0583/490530* ⊕ *www.museocatte-dralelucca.it* ⊠ *€3.*

Museo Nazionale di Villa Guinigi

ART MUSEUM | Although this museum presents a noteworthy overview of Lucca's artistic traditions up through the 17th century, you might find few other visitors exploring its extensive collections of local Etruscan, Roman, Romanesque, and Renaissance art. It's all housed in the 15th-century former villa of the Guinigi family, on the eastern end of the historic center. ⊠ *Via della Quarquonia 4, Lucca* ☎ *0583/496033* ⊕ *www.luccamuseina-zionali.it* ⊠ *€4* ☉ *Closed Mon. and 2nd, 4th, and 5th Sun. of month.*

★ Passeggiata delle Mura

CITY PARK | FAMILY | On nice days, the citizens of Lucca cycle, jog, stroll, or kick a soccer ball in this green, beautiful, and very large circular park. It's neither inside nor outside the city but rather right atop and around the ring of ramparts that defines Lucca. Sunlight streams through two rows of tall plane trees to dapple the *passeggiata delle mura* (walk on the walls), which is 4 km (2½ miles) long. Ten bulwarks are topped with lawns, many with picnic tables and some with play equipment for children. Be aware at all times of where the edge is—there are no railings, and the drop to the ground outside the city is a precipitous 40 feet. ⊠ *Lucca* ☎ *0583/583150* ⊕ *www.turismo. lucca.it.*

Piazza dell'Anfiteatro

PLAZA/SQUARE | FAMILY | Here's where the ancient Roman amphitheater once stood. Some of the medieval buildings built over the amphitheater retain its original oval shape and brick arches. ⊠ *Piazza dell'An-fiteatro, Lucca.*

San Frediano

CHURCH | A 14th-century mosaic deco-rates the facade of this church just steps from the anfiteatro. Inside are works by Jacopo della Quercia and Matteo Civitali (1436–1501), as well as the lace-clad mummy of St. Zita (circa 1218–78), the patron saint of household servants. ⊠ *Pi-azza San Frediano, Lucca* ☎ *349/8440290* ⊕ *www.sanfredianolucca.com* ⊠ *€3.*

San Michele in Foro

CHURCH | The facade here is even more fanciful than that of the Duomo. Its upper levels have nothing but air behind them (after the front of the church was built, there were no funds to raise the nave), and the winged archangel Michael, who stands at the very top, seems precarious-ly poised for flight. The facade, heavily restored in the 19th century, displays busts of such Italian patriots as Garibaldi and Cavour. Check out the superb Filip-pino Lippi (1457/58–1504) panel painting of Saints Jerome, Sebastian, Rocco, and Helen in the right transept. ⊠ *Piazza San Michele, Lucca* ☎ *0583/53576* ⊕ *www. luccatranoi.it.*

Torre Guinigi

NOTABLE BUILDING | FAMILY | The tower of the medieval Palazzo Guinigi contains one of the city's most curious sights: a grove of ilex trees has grown at the top of the tower, and their roots have pushed their way into the room below. From the top you have a magnificent view of the city and the surrounding countryside. (Only the tower is open to the public, not the palazzo.) ⊠ *Via Sant'Andrea 45, Lucca* ☎ *0583/48090* ⊕ *cultura.comune.lucca.it* ⊠ *From €5.*

Lucca

KEY
- Sights
- Restaurants
- Quick Bites
- Hotels

Sights ▶

1 Duomo	E3
2 Museo Nazionale di Villa Guinigi	G1
3 Passeggiata delle Mura	G3
4 Piazza dell'Anfiteatro	E1
5 San Frediano	D1
6 San Michele in Foro	D2
7 Torre Guinigi	E2

Restaurants ▶

1 Buca di Sant'Antonio	C2
2 Il Giglio	D3

Coffee and Quick Bites ▶

1 Blend	D2

Hotels ▶

1 Alla Corte degli Angeli	D1
2 Hotel Ilaria	F2
3 Hotel La Luna	D1
4 Hotel Palazzo Alexander	B1

200 yards
200 meters

🍴 Restaurants

★ Buca di Sant'Antonio
$$ | TUSCAN | The staying power of Buca di Sant'Antonio—it's been around since 1782—is the result of superlative Tuscan food brought to the table by waitstaff who don't miss a beat. The menu includes the simple but blissful *tortelli lucchesi al sugo* (meat-stuffed pasta with a tomato-and-meat sauce), as well as more daring dishes such as roast *capretto* (kid goat) with herbs. **Known for:** superlative pastas; excellent sommelier; classy, family-run ambience. ⑤ *Average main: €20 ⊠ Via della Cervia 3, Lucca ☎ 0583/55881 ⊕ www.bucadisantantonio.com ⊗ Closed Mon., 1 wk in Jan., and 1 wk in July. No dinner Sun.*

★ Il Giglio
$$$ | TUSCAN | Divine, cutting-edge food and Tuscan classics are served in this one-room space, where in winter there's a roaring fireplace, and in warmer months there's outdoor seating on a pretty little piazza. If mushrooms are in season, try the *tacchoni con funghi,* a homemade pasta with mushrooms and a native herb called *nepitella.* **Known for:** creative menu with seasonal ingredients; fine service; the wine list, especially its selection of local wines. ⑤ *Average main: €35 ⊠ Piazza del Giglio 2, Lucca ☎ 0583/494508 ⊕ www.ristorantegiglio.com ⊗ Closed Tues. and Wed. and 15 days in Nov.*

☕ Coffee and Quick Bites

Blend
$ | ITALIAN | If you're looking for a lovely spot to recharge, stop by this place (just around the corner from the Duomo), and have a fantastic sandwich, or a glass of wine, or a tasty salad, a coffee, or dessert. It's open from late morning to late in the evening. **Known for:** good salads; near the Duomo; open late. ⑤ *Average main: €7 ⊠ Piazza S. Giusto 8, Duomo ☎ 0583/050442.*

🛏 Hotels

Alla Corte degli Angeli
$$$ | B&B/INN | This charming hotel with a friendly staff is right off the main shopping drag, Via Fillungo. **Pros:** many rooms are connecting, making them good for families; great location; fantastic on-site restaurant. **Cons:** some rooms have tubs but no showers; not all rooms are created equal; books up quickly. ⑤ *Rooms from: €227 ⊠ Via degli Angeli 23, Lucca ☎ 0583/469204 ⊕ www.allacortedegliangeli.it ⇲ 21 rooms ⦿ Free Breakfast.*

Hotel Ilaria
$$$ | HOTEL | The former stables of the Villa Bottini have been transformed into a modern hotel with stylish rooms done in a warm wood veneer with blue-and-white fittings. **Pros:** modern; free bicycles; multilingual; pleasant staff. **Cons:** though in the city center, it's a little removed from main attractions; some find it overpriced; books up quickly. ⑤ *Rooms from: €205 ⊠ Via del Fosso 26, Lucca ☎ 0583/47615 ⊕ www.hotelilaria.com ⇲ 44 rooms ⦿ Free Breakfast.*

Hotel La Luna
$$ | B&B/INN | On a quiet, airy courtyard close to the Piazza del Mercato, this hotel, run by the Barbieri family for more than four decades, occupies two renovated wings of an old building. **Pros:** professional staff; the annex has wheelchair-accessible rooms; central location. **Cons:** some rooms feel dated; street noise can be a bit of a problem; may be too central for some. ⑤ *Rooms from: €200 ⊠ Corte Compagni 12, at Via Fillungo, Lucca ☎ 0583/493634 ⊕ www.hotellaluna.it ⇲ 29 rooms ⦿ Free Breakfast.*

Hotel Palazzo Alexander
$$ | HOTEL | This hotel, in a building dating from the 12th century, has public rooms with timbered ceilings, warm yellow walls, and brocaded chairs and guest rooms with high ceilings and still more of that glorious damask. **Pros:** intimate feel; gracious staff; a short walk from San

Michele in Foro. **Cons:** some complain of too-thin walls; books up quickly; might be too quiet for some. ⑤ *Rooms from: €200* ✉ *Via S. Giustina 48, Lucca* ☎ *0583/583571* ⊕ *www.hotelpalazzoalexander.it* ⤳ *13 rooms* ❚◉❚ *Free Breakfast.*

⬤ Shopping

Lucca's justly famed olive oils are available throughout the city (and exported around the world).

★ Antica Bottega di Prospero

FOOD | Stop by this shop for top-quality local food products, including farro, dried porcini mushrooms, olive oil, and wine. ✉ *Via San Lucia 13, Lucca* ☎ *0583/494875* ⊕ *bottegadiprospero1790.com.*

★ Caniparoli

CHOCOLATE | **FAMILY** | If you love sweets then you'll be pleased with the selection of artisanal chocolates, marzipan delights, and gorgeous cakes. Creations become even more fanciful during Christmas and Easter. ✉ *Via San Paolino 44, Lucca* ☎ *0583/53456* ⊕ *caniparolicioccolateria.it.*

★ Enoteca Vanni

WINE/SPIRITS | A huge selection of wines, as well as an ancient cellar, make this place worth a stop. For the cost of the wine only, tastings can be organized through the shopkeepers and are held in the cellar or outside in a lovely little piazza. All of this can be paired with *affettati misti* (sliced cured meats) and cheeses of the highest caliber. ✉ *Piazza San Salvatore 7, Lucca* ☎ *0583/491902* ⊕ *www.enotecavanni.com.*

★ Pasticceria Taddeucci

FOOD | **FAMILY** | A particularly delicious version of *buccellato*—the sweet, anise-flavored bread with raisins that is a Luccan specialty—is baked at Pasticceria Taddeucci. ✉ *Piazza San Michele 34, Lucca* ☎ *0583/494933* ⊕ *www.buccellatotaddeucci.com.*

⬤ Activities

A good way to spend the afternoon is to go biking around the large path atop the city's ramparts. There are two good spots right next to each other where you can rent bikes. The prices are about the same (about €16 per day and €4 per hour for city bikes) and they are centrally located, just beside the town wall.

Poli Antonio Biciclette

BIKING | **FAMILY** | This is one of the best options for bicycle rentals on the east side of town. ✉ *Piazza Santa Maria 42, Lucca East* ☎ *0583/493787* ⊕ *www.biciclettepoli.com.*

Pisa

19 km (11 miles) southwest of Lucca.

If you can get beyond the kitsch of the stalls hawking cheap souvenirs around the Leaning Tower, you'll find that Pisa has much to offer. Its treasures aren't as abundant as those of Florence, to which it is inevitably compared, but the cathedral-baptistery-tower complex of Piazza del Duomo, known collectively as the Campo dei Miracoli (Field of Miracles), is among the most dramatic settings in Italy.

Pisa may have been inhabited as early as the Bronze Age. It was certainly populated by the Etruscans and, in turn, became part of the Roman Empire. In the early Middle Ages this city on the Arno River flourished as an economic powerhouse—along with Amalfi, Genoa, and Venice, it was one of the four maritime republics. The city's economic and political power ebbed in the early 15th century as it fell under Florence's domination, though it enjoyed a brief resurgence under Cosimo I de' Medici in the mid-16th century. Pisa sustained heavy damage during World War II, but the Duomo and the Leaning Tower were spared, along with some other grand Romanesque structures.

"Campo Santo" translates literally to "holy field" because it's supposedly built around a shipload of sacred soil from Golgotha, the site where Jesus was crucified.

GETTING HERE AND AROUND

Pisa is an easy hour's train ride from Florence. By car it's a straight shot on the Firenze–Pisa–Livorno ("Fi-Pi-Li") autostrada. The Pisa–Lucca train runs frequently and takes about 30 minutes.

VISITOR INFORMATION

CONTACT Pisa Tourism Office. ⊠ *Piazza XX Settembre, Pisa* ☎ *050/550100* ⊕ *www. turismo.pisa.it.*

Sights

Pisa, like many Italian cities, is best explored on foot, and most of what you'll want to see is within walking distance. The views along the Arno River are particularly grand and shouldn't be missed—there's a feeling of spaciousness that isn't found along the Arno in Florence.

As you set out, note that there are various combination-ticket options for sights on the Piazza del Duomo.

Battistero

NOTABLE BUILDING | This lovely Gothic baptistery, which faces the Duomo's facade, is best known for the pulpit carved by Nicola Pisano (circa 1220–84; father of Giovanni Pisano) in 1260. Every half hour, an employee will dramatically close the doors, then intone, thereby demonstrating how remarkable the acoustics are in the place. ⊠ *Piazza del Duomo, Pisa* ☎ *050/835011* ⊕ *www.opapisa.it* ✉ *From €7, discounts available if bought in combination with tickets for other monuments* ⊙ *Closed Oct. 2–Dec. 1 and May 6–31.*

Camposanto

CEMETERY | According to legend, the cemetery—a walled structure on the western side of the Piazza dei Miracoli—is filled with earth that returning Crusaders brought back from the Holy Land. Contained within are numerous frescoes, notably *The Drunkenness of Noah,* by Renaissance artist Benozzo Gozzoli (1422–97), and the disturbing *Triumph of Death* (14th century; artist uncertain), whose subject matter shows what was

on people's minds in a century that saw the ravages of the Black Death. ⊠ *Piazza del Duomo, Pisa* ☎ *050/835011* ⊕ *www. opapisa.it* ✆ *From €7.*

Duomo

CHURCH | Pisa's cathedral brilliantly utilizes the horizontal marble-stripe motif (borrowed from Moorish architecture) that became common on Tuscan cathedrals. It is famous for the Romanesque panels on the transept door facing the tower that depict scenes from the life of Christ. The beautifully carved 14th-century pulpit is by Giovanni Pisano. ⊠ *Piazza del Duomo, Pisa* ☎ *050/835011* ⊕ *www.opapisa.it* ✆ *From €7.*

★ Leaning Tower (Torre Pendente)

NOTABLE BUILDING | **FAMILY** | Legend holds that Galileo conducted an experiment on the nature of gravity by dropping metal balls from the top of the 187-foot-high Leaning Tower of Pisa (whether it's true is a matter of debate). Work on this tower, built as a campanile for the Duomo, started in 1173. The lopsided settling began when construction reached the third story. The architects attempted to compensate by making the remaining floors slightly taller on the leaning side, but the extra weight made the problem worse. By the late 20th century, many feared the tower would simply topple over. The structure has since been firmly anchored to the earth and restored to its original tilt of 300 years ago.

Reservations, which are essential, can be made online or by calling the Museo dell'Opera del Duomo. It's also possible to arrive at the ticket office and book for the same day. Note, though, that children under eight aren't allowed to climb. ⊠ *Piazza del Duomo, Pisa* ☎ *050/835011* ⊕ *www.opapisa.it* ✆ *From €20.*

Museo Nazionale di San Matteo

ART MUSEUM | On the north bank of the Arno, this museum contains some beautiful examples of local Romanesque and Gothic art. Despite the fact that it has stunning works by Donatello and Benozzo Gozzoli (among others), here you'll find very few other visitors. ⊠ *Piazza Matteo in Soarta 1, Pisa* ☎ *050/541865* ⊕ *www.museitoscana.cultura.gov.it* ✆ *€6* ⊗ *Closed Mon.*

Piazza dei Cavalieri

PLAZA/SQUARE | The piazza, with its fine Renaissance Palazzo dei Cavalieri, Palazzo dell'Orologio, and Chiesa di Santo Stefano dei Cavalieri, was laid out by Giorgio Vasari in about 1560. The square was the seat of the Ordine dei Cavalieri di Santo Stefano (Order of the Knights of St. Stephen), a military and religious institution meant to defend the coast from possible invasion by the Turks.

Also in this square is the prestigious Scuola Normale Superiore, founded by Napoléon in 1810 on the French model. Here graduate students pursue doctorates in literature, philosophy, mathematics, and science. In front of the school is a large statue of Ferdinando I de' Medici dating from 1596. On the extreme left is the tower where the hapless Ugolino della Gherardesca (died 1289) was imprisoned with his two sons and two grandsons—legend holds that he ate them. Dante immortalized him in Canto XXXIII of his *Inferno.* Duck into the Church of Santo Stefano (if you're lucky enough to find it open) and check out Bronzino's splendid *Nativity of Christ* (1564–65). ⊠ *Piazza dei Cavalieri, Pisa* ⊕ *www.turismo.pisa.it.*

Santa Maria della Spina

CHURCH | Originally an oratory dating from the 13th century, this delicate, tiny church is a fine example of Tuscan Gothic architecture. It has been restored several times, including in 1996–98, after having been damaged by a flood. The results of a recent face-lift are grand. ⊠ *Lungarno Gambacorti, Pisa* ☎ *055/3215446* ⊕ *www.turismo.pisa.it* ✆ *Free.*

Restaurants

Al Madina

$ | MIDDLE EASTERN | Pisa is an incredibly multicultural city, as evidenced by restaurants like this one, which serves the best Middle Eastern food in town. The tables are a little close together, but the atmosphere is lively, and you'll find all the classics—from falafel to hummus—as well as a delicious dessert of ricotta mousse with homemade quince jam. **Known for:** fresh, plentiful salads and sides; shish kebab; dips and pita bread. ⑤ *Average main: €12* ⊠ *Via San Martino 41/45, Pisa* ⊕ *www.ristorantealmadina.it* ⊗ *Closed Mon.*

Osteria dei Cavalieri

$$ | ITALIAN | This charming, white-walled restaurant, a few steps from Piazza dei Cavalieri, serves up exquisitely grilled fish dishes, pleases vegetarians, and prepares tagliata for meat lovers. Three set menus, from the sea, garden, and earth, are available, or you can order à la carte. **Known for:** location in the centro storico; classic Tuscan dishes; catch-of-the-day fish-tasting menu. ⑤ *Average main: €16* ⊠ *Via San Frediano 16, Pisa* ☎ *050/580858* ⊕ *www.osteriacavalieri. pisa.it* ⊗ *Closed Sun., 2 wks in Aug., and Dec. 29–Jan. 7. No lunch Wed.*

★ V. Beny

$$$ | TUSCAN | Apricot walls hung with etchings of Pisa make this small, single-room restaurant warmly romantic. Husband and wife Damiano and Sandra Lazzerini have been running the place for two decades, and it shows in their obvious enthusiasm while talking about the menu (fish is a focus) and daily specials, which often astound. **Known for:** superb fish dishes; gracious service; terrific wine list. ⑤ *Average main: €27* ⊠ *Piazza Chiara Gambacorti 22, Pisa* ☎ *050/25067* ⊕ *beny.eatbu.com* ⊗ *Closed Sun. and 2 wks in mid-Aug. No lunch Sat.*

★ Vineria di Piazza

$$ | ITALIAN | It's set in a lively, historic market square and frequented by locals. The menu adheres to Tuscan tradition, often including high-quality bistecca alla fiorentina, but also indulges in some flights of fantasy, as evidenced by a whimsical dessert that riffs on a liquid Livornese classic. **Known for:** inventive pasta dishes; baccalà (salt cod) served in inventive ways; charming, energetic staff. ⑤ *Average main: €20* ⊠ *Piazza delle Vettovaglie 13, Pisa* ☎ *050/5207846* ⊕ *www. facebook.com/vineriadipiazzavettovaglie.*

Hotels

Royal Victoria

$ | HOTEL | In a pleasant palazzo facing the Arno, a 10-minute walk from the Campo dei Miracoli, this hotel has room styles that range from the 1800s, complete with frescoes, to the 1920s; the most charming are in the old tower. **Pros:** friendly staff; lovely views of the Arno from many rooms; old-world charm. **Cons:** accommodations vary significantly in size; rooms a little worn; not all rooms have views of the Arno. ⑤ *Rooms from: €95* ⊠ *Lungarno Pacinotti 12, Pisa* ☎ *050/940111* ⊕ *www.royalvictoria.it* ⇨ *38 rooms* ��ⓄⱵ *Free Breakfast.*

⊗ Performing Arts

Fondazione Teatro di Pisa

THEATER | Pisa has a lively performing-arts scene, most of which happens at the 19th-century Teatro Verdi. Music and dance performances are presented from September through May. Contact Fondazione Teatro di Pisa for schedules and information. ⊠ *Via Palestro 40, Lungarni, Pisa* ☎ *050/941111* ⊕ *www.facebook. com/teatroverdipisa.*

Chianti

This is the heartland: both sides of the Strada Chiantigiana (SR222) are embraced by glorious panoramic views of vineyards, olive groves, and castle towers. Traveling south from Florence, you first reach the aptly named one-street town of Strada in Chianti. Farther south, the number of vineyards on either side of the road dramatically increases—as do the signs inviting you in for a free tasting. Beyond Strada lies Greve in Chianti, completely surrounded by wineries and filled with wineshops. There's art to be had as well: Passignano, west of Greve, has an abbey that shelters a 15th-century *Last Supper* by Domenico and Davide Ghirlandaio. Farther still, along the Strada Chiantigiana, are Panzano and Castellina in Chianti, both hill towns. It's from near Panzano and Castellina that branch roads head to the other main towns of eastern Chianti: Radda in Chianti, Gaiole in Chianti, and Castelnuovo Berardenga.

The Strada Chiantigiana gets crowded during the high season, but no one is in a hurry. The slow pace gives you time to soak up the beautiful scenery.

Greve in Chianti

40 km (25 miles) north of Siena, 28 km (17½ miles) south of Florence.

If there is a capital of Chianti, it is Greve, a friendly market town with no shortage of cafés, enoteche, and crafts shops lining its streets.

GETTING HERE AND AROUND

Driving from Florence or Siena, Greve is easily reached via the Strada Chiantigiana (SR222). Autolinee Toscane buses travel frequently between Florence and Greve. The bus system also connects Siena and Greve, but a direct trip is virtually impossible. There is no train service to Greve.

VISITOR INFORMATION

CONTACT Greve in Chianti Tourism Office. ⊠ *Piazza Matteotti 10, Greve in Chianti* ☎ *055/8546299* ⊕ *www.visitchianti.net.*

Sights

Montefioralle

TOWN | A tiny hilltop hamlet, about 2 km (1 mile) west of Greve in Chianti, Montefioralle is the ancestral home of Amerigo Vespucci (1454–1512), the mapmaker, navigator, and explorer who named America. (His cousin-in-law, Simonetta, may have been the inspiration for Sandro Botticelli's *Birth of Venus,* painted sometime in the 1480s.) ⊠ *Greve in Chianti.*

Piazza Matteotti

PLAZA/SQUARE | FAMILY | Greve's gently sloping and asymmetrical central piazza is surrounded by an attractive arcade with shops of all kinds. In the center stands a statue of the discoverer of New York harbor, Giovanni da Verrazzano (circa 1480–1527). Check out the lively market held here on Saturday morning. ⊠ *Piazza Matteotti, Greve in Chianti.*

Restaurants

Enoteca Fuoripiazza

$$ | TUSCAN | Detour off Greve's flower-strewn main square for food that relies heavily on local ingredients (like cheese and salami produced nearby). The lengthy wine list provides a bewildering array of choices to pair with affettati misti or one of the primi (first courses)—the *pici* (a thick, hand-rolled spaghetti) are deftly prepared here. **Known for:** alfresco dining; local cheese and salami; attentively prepared food. ⑤ *Average main: €18* ⊠ *Via I Maggio 2, Greve in Chianti* ☎ *055/8546313* ⊕ *www.enotecaristorantefuoripiazza.it* ⊘ *Closed Mon. No dinner Sun.*

★ Falorni

$ | **ITALIAN** | This institution—it's been around since 1806—began life as a butcher shop and, indeed, it still is, but it also has a little restaurant that serves great *taglieri* (plates of mixed cured pork products, usually, though cheese does prominently figure as well). Soups, lasagne, various tartares, and sandwiches are also on hand; the quality of the products is exceptional. **Known for:** cured meats using centuries' old recipes; great wines by the glass; outdoor seating. $ *Average main: €13* ✉ *Piazza G. Matteotti 66, Greve in Chianti* ☎ *055/853029* ⊕ *www. falorni.it.*

★ Ristoro di Lamole

$$ | **TUSCAN** | Up a winding road lined with olive trees and vineyards, this place is worth the effort it takes to find. The view from the outdoor terrace is divine, as is the simple, exquisitely prepared Tuscan cuisine—start with the bruschetta drizzled with olive oil or the sublime *verdure sott'olio* (marinated vegetables) before moving on to any of the fine secondi. **Known for:** coniglio (rabbit) is a specialty; sweeping view from the terrace; your hosts Paolo and Filippo. $ *Average main: €20* ✉ *Via di Lamole 6, Località Lamole, Greve in Chianti* ☎ *055/8547050* ⊕ *www. ristorodilamole.it* ⊗ *Closed Dec.–Feb.*

🛏 Hotels

Albergo del Chianti

$$ | **B&B/INN** | **FAMILY** | Simple but pleasantly decorated bedrooms with plain modern cabinets and wardrobes and wrought-iron beds have views of the town square or out over the tile rooftops toward the surrounding hills. **Pros:** central location; best value in Greve; swimming pool. **Cons:** rooms facing the piazza can be noisy; hotel could use an overall update; remote: a car is a necessity. $ *Rooms from: €165* ✉ *Piazza Matteotti 86, Greve in Chianti* ☎ *055/853763* ⊕ *www.albergodelchianti. it* ⊗ *Closed Jan.–early Mar.* ⇥ *16 rooms* ⍾ *No Meals.*

Castello Vicchiomaggio

$$$ | **B&B/INN** | **FAMILY** | Stay in a fortified castle, which was built more than a millennium ago, was rebuilt during the Renaissance, and is now a charming inn and a prestigious wine estate where you can taste local vintages. **Pros:** spacious rooms; spectacular views; very helpful staff. **Cons:** some rooms lack air-conditioning; might be too remote for some; you need a car to get around. $ *Rooms from: €221* ✉ *Via Vicchiomaggio 4, Località Vicchiomaggio, Greve in Chianti* ☎ *055/854079* ⊕ *www.vicchiomaggio. it* ⊗ *Closed Dec.–mid-Mar.* ⇥ *15 rooms* ⍾ *Free Breakfast.*

★ Villa Bordoni

$$$ | **B&B/INN** | Scottish expats David and Catherine Gardner transformed a ramshackle, 16th-century villa into a stunning retreat where no two rooms are alike—all have stenciled walls; some have four-poster beds, others small mezzanines. **Pros:** splendidly isolated in the hills above Greve; beautiful decor; wonderful hosts. **Cons:** on a long and bumpy dirt road; need a car to get around; books up quickly. $ *Rooms from: €225* ✉ *Via San Cresci 31/32, Greve in Chianti* ☎ *055/8546230* ⊕ *www.villabordoni.com* ⊗ *Closed Dec.– mid-Mar.* ⇥ *12 rooms* ⍾ *Free Breakfast.*

★ Villa Il Poggiale

$$$ | **B&B/INN** | **FAMILY** | Renaissance gardens, beautiful rooms with high ceilings and elegant furnishings, a panoramic pool, and expert staff are just a few of the things that make a stay at this 16th-century villa memorable. **Pros:** beautiful gardens and panoramic setting; elegant historical building; exceptionally professional staff. **Cons:** private transportation necessary; some rooms face a country road and may be noisy during the day; it may be too isolated for some. $ *Rooms from: €213* ✉ *Via Empolese 69, San Casciano Val di Pesa* ✛ *20 km (12 miles) northwest of Greve* ☎ *055/828311* ⊕ *www.villailpoggiale.it* ⊗ *Closed Jan.* ⇥ *26 rooms* ⍾ *Free Breakfast.*

Panzano

7 km (4½ miles) south of Greve, 36 km (22 miles) south of Florence.

The magnificent views of the valleys of the Pesa and Greve rivers easily make Panzano one of the prettiest stops in Chianti. The triangular Piazza Bucciarelli is the heart of the new town. A short stroll along Via Giovanni da Verrazzano brings you up to the old town, Panzano Alto, which is still partly surrounded by medieval walls. The town's 13th-century castle is now almost completely absorbed by later buildings (its central tower is now a private home).

GETTING HERE AND AROUND

From Florence or Siena, Panzano is easily reached by car along the Strada Chiantigiana (SR222). Autolinee Toscane buses travel frequently between Florence and Panzano and less often from Siena. There is no train service to Panzano.

Sights

Pieve di San Leolino

CHURCH | Ancient even by Chianti standards, this hilltop church probably dates from the 10th century, but it was completely rebuilt in the Romanesque style sometime in the 13th century. It has a 14th-century cloister worth seeing. The 16th-century terra-cotta tabernacles are attributed to Giovanni della Robbia, and there's also a remarkable triptych (attributed to the Master of Panzano) that was executed sometime in the mid-14th century. Open days and hours are unpredictable; check with the tourist office in Greve in Chianti for the latest information. ⊠ *Località San Leolino, Panzano* ✛ *3 km (2 miles) south of Panzano* ☎ *055/852003* ⊕ *www.sanleolino.org* ▨ *Free.*

Restaurants

★ Officina della Bistecca

$$$$ | **ITALIAN** | **FAMILY** | Local butcher and restaurateur, Dario Cecchini, has extended his empire of meat to include this space above his butcher's shop. In addition to two tasting menus—one heavily meat-laden, the other with none—you'll find a stellar version of *giardiniera sott'olio* (pickled and preserved vegetables), and exceptional bread (the product of much experimentation). **Known for:** convivial atmosphere; performing waitstaff; enormously popular, especially in summer. ⑤ *Average main: €50* ⊠ *Via XX Luglio 11, Panzano* ☎ *055/852020* ⊕ *www.dariocecchini.com/officina.*

★ Solociccia

$$$$ | **TUSCAN** | **FAMILY** | As at his other eateries, Dario Cecchini, Panzano's local merchant of meat, offers two set menus for lunch—one where beef products dominate every course and the other vegetarian. The *musetto al limone e brodo vero* (an interesting salame served with stunning beef broth) might kick off the proceedings, and on the table you'll find *pinzimonio*, a dish of raw sliced vegetables (carrot, fennel, onions) to be dipped into terrific olive oil and sprinkled with Dario's special house-made herbed salt. **Known for:** choice of two set menus; great service; party atmosphere. ⑤ *Average main: €40* ⊠ *Via XX Luglio 11, Panzano* ☎ *055/852020* ⊕ *www.dariocecchini.com/solociccia* ⊘ *No dinner.*

Hotels

★ Villa Le Barone

$$$ | **B&B/INN** | Once the home of the Viviani della Robbia family, this 16th-century villa in a grove of ancient cypress trees retains many aspects of a private country dwelling, including homey guest quarters. **Pros:** beautiful location; wonderful restaurant; great base for exploring the region. **Cons:** some rooms are a bit small; 15-minute walk to nearest town; a car is a must. $ *Rooms from: €272* ✉ *Via San Leolino 19, Panzano* ☎ *055/852621* ⊕ *villalebarone.com* ⊘ *Closed Nov.–early Apr.* ⊸ *28 rooms* ⦿ *Free Breakfast.*

Radda in Chianti

26 km (15 miles) southeast of Panzano, 55 km (34 miles) south of Florence.

Radda in Chianti sits on a ridge stretching between the Val di Pesa and Val d'Arbia. It is easily reached by following the SR429 from Castellina. It's another one of those tiny villages with steep streets for strolling; follow the signs that point you toward the *camminamento medioevale,* a covered 14th-century walkway that circles part of the city inside the walls.

GETTING HERE AND AROUND
Radda can be reached by car from either Siena or Florence along the SR222 (Strada Chiantigiana), and from the A1 autostrada. A few buses each day travel from Siena to Radda on Autolinee Toscane. There is no direct bus from Florence or train service convenient to Radda.

VISITOR INFORMATION
CONTACT Radda in Chianti Tourism Office.
✉ *Piazza del Castello 6, Radda in Chianti* ☎ *0577/738494* ⊕ *www.chianti.com.*

⊙ Sights

★ **Badia a Coltibuono** (*Abbey of the Good Harvest*)
WINERY | This Romanesque abbey has been owned by internationally acclaimed cookbook author Lorenza de' Medici's family for more than a century and a half (the family isn't related to the Florentine Medici). Wine has been produced here since the abbey was founded by Vallombrosan monks in the 11th century. Today, the family continues the tradition, making wines, cold-pressed olive oil, and various flavored vinegars. Don't miss the jasmine-draped courtyard and the inner cloister with its antique well.

✉ *Località Badia a Coltibuono, Gaiole in Chianti* ✛ *4 km (2½ miles) north of Gaiole* ☎ *0577/74481 tours* ⊕ *www.coltibuono. com* ⊠ *Tour and tasting from €27* ⚲ *Reservations essential.*

★ **Castello di Brolio**
CASTLE/PALACE | If you have time for only one castle in Tuscany, this should be it. At the end of the 12th century, when Florence conquered southern Chianti, Brolio became Florence's southernmost outpost, and it was often said, "When Brolio growls, all Siena trembles." It was built about AD 1000 and owned by the monks of the Badia Fiorentina. The "new" owners, the Ricasoli family, have been in possession since 1141. Bettino Ricasoli (1809–80), the so-called Iron Baron, was one of the founders of modern Italy and is said to have invented the original formula for Chianti wine; you can also visit the on-site Barone Ricasoli winery for a guided cellar tour and wine tasting.

Brolio, one of Chianti's best-known labels, is still justifiably famous. The grounds are worth visiting, and some of the guided tours do provide a glimpse of the castle's interior. The entrance fee includes a wine tasting in the enoteca. A small museum, where the Ricasoli Collection is housed in a 12th-century tower, displays objects that relate the long history of the family and the origins of Chianti wine. There are various options for an overnight here. ✉ *Località Madonna a Brolio, Gaiole in Chianti* ✛ *2 km (1 mile) southeast of Gaiole* ☎ *0577/730280* ⊕ *www.ricasoli.com* ⊠ *Gardens €7; tour and tasting from €35* ⊘ *Gardens closed mid-Dec.–late Mar.* ⚲ *Reservations essential for wine tours.*

Palazzo del Podestà
GOVERNMENT BUILDING | Radda's town hall (aka Palazzo Comunale), in the middle of town, was built in the second half of the 14th century and has always served the same function. The 51 coats of arms (the largest is the Medici's) embedded in

the facade represent the past governors of the town, but unless you have official business, the building is closed to the public. ⊠ *Piazza Ferrucci 1, Radda in Chianti* ⊑ *Free.*

Restaurants

Osteria Le Panzanelle

$ | TUSCAN | Silvia Bonechi's experience in the kitchen—with the help of a few precious recipes handed down from her grandmother—is one of the reasons for the success of this small restaurant in the tiny hamlet of Lucarelli; the other is the front-room hospitality of Nada Michelassi. These two *panzanelle* (women from Panzano) serve a short menu of tasty and authentic dishes at what the locals refer to as *il prezzo giusto* (the right price). **Known for:** fine home cooking; good wine list; unpretentious atmosphere. ⑤ *Average main: €14* ⊠ *Località Lucarelli 29, Radda in Chianti* ✛ *8 km (5 miles) northwest of Radda on road to Panzano* ☎ *0577/733511* ⊕ *www.lepanzanelle.it* ◷ *Closed Mon. and Jan. and Feb.*

Hotels

La Bottega di Giovannino

$ | B&B/INN | This is a fantastic place for the budget-conscious traveler, as rooms are immaculate and most have a stunning view of the surrounding hills. **Pros:** great location in the center of town; close to restaurants and shops; super value. **Cons:** some rooms are small; books up quickly; basic decor. ⑤ *Rooms from: €85* ⊠ *Via Roma 6–8, Radda in Chianti* ☎ *057/735601* ⊕ *www.labottegadigiovannino.it* ◷ *Closed mid-Dec.–Mar.* ⇗ *9 rooms* ⦿ *No Meals.*

Palazzo San Niccolò

$$ | HOTEL | The wood-beam ceilings, terra-cotta floors, and some of the original frescoes of a 19th-century town palace remain, but the marble bathrooms have all been updated, some with whirlpool tubs. **Pros:** central location; friendly staff; pool (though a car is necessary to get there). **Cons:** some rooms face a main street; room sizes vary; street noise in some rooms. ⑤ *Rooms from: €140* ⊠ *Via Roma 16, Radda in Chianti* ☎ *0577/735666* ⊕ *www.hotelsanniccolo.com* ◷ *Closed Nov.–Mar.* ⇗ *18 rooms* ⦿ *No Meals.*

★ Relais Fattoria Vignale

$$$ | B&B/INN | A refined and comfortable country house offers numerous sitting rooms with terra-cotta floors and attractive stonework, as well as wood-beamed guest rooms filled with simple wooden furnishings and handwoven rugs. **Pros:** intimate public spaces; excellent restaurant; nice grounds and pool. **Cons:** single rooms are small; annex across a busy road; a car is necessary. ⑤ *Rooms from: €240* ⊠ *Via Pianigiani 9, Radda in Chianti* ☎ *0577/738300* ⊕ *www.vignale.it* ◷ *Closed Nov.–late Mar.* ⇗ *41 rooms* ⦿ *Free Breakfast.*

Castellina in Chianti

13 km (8 miles) south of Panzano, 59 km (35 miles) south of Florence, 22 km (14 miles) north of Siena.

Castellina in Chianti—or simply Castellina—is on a ridge above three valleys: the Val di Pesa, Val d'Arbia, and Val d'Elsa. No matter what direction you turn, the panorama is bucolic. The strong 15th-century medieval walls and fortified town gate give a hint of the history of this village, which was an outpost during the continuing wars between Florence and Siena. In the main square, the Piazza del Comune, there's a 15th-century palace and a 15th-century fort constructed around a 13th-century tower. It now serves as the town hall.

GETTING HERE AND AROUND

As with all the towns along the Strada Chiantigiana (SR222), Castellina is an easy drive from either Siena or Florence.

From Siena, Castellina is also well served by Autolinee Toscane. There's no direct bus from Florence. The closest train station is at Castellina Scalo, some 15 km (9 miles) away.

VISITOR INFORMATION

CONTACT Castellina in Chianti Tourism Office. ⊠ *Via Ferruccio 40, Castellina in Chianti* ☏ *0577/741392* ⊕ *www.visitchianti.net.*

 Restaurants

Albergaccio di Castellina

$$$ | TUSCAN | The fact that the dining room can seat only about 35 guests makes a meal here an intimate experience, and the ever-changing menu mixes traditional and creative dishes. In late September and October, *zuppa di funghi e castagne* (mushroom and chestnut soup) is a treat; grilled meats and seafood are on offer throughout the year. **Known for:** creative menu; superb wine list; marvelous waitstaff. ⑤ *Average main: €28* ⊠ *Via Fiorentina 63, Castellina in Chianti* ☏ *0577/741042* ⊕ *www.ristorantealbergaccio.com* ⊘ *Closed Sun.*

Ristorante Le Tre Porte

$$$ | TUSCAN | Grilled meat dishes are the specialty at this popular restaurant, with a bistecca alla fiorentina (served very rare, as always) taking pride of place; paired with grilled fresh porcini mushrooms when in season (spring and fall), it's a heady dish. The panoramic terrace is a good choice for dining in summer; inside, the upper floor offers an unmistakable Tuscan setting, while the downstairs is more modern and intimate. **Known for:** views from the terrace; their way with mushrooms; fine wine list with lots of local bottles. ⑤ *Average main: €26* ⊠ *Via Trento e Trieste 4, Castellina in Chianti* ☏ *0577/741163* ⊕ *www.treporte.com* ⊘ *Closed Mon.*

Sotto Le Volte

$$ | TUSCAN | As the name suggests, you'll find this small restaurant under the arches of Castellina's medieval walkway, and the eatery's vaulted ceilings make for a particularly romantic setting. The menu is short and eminently Tuscan, with typical soups and pasta dishes; the *costolette di agnello alle erbe* (herbed lamb chops) are especially tasty. **Known for:** unique setting; flair for Tuscan classics; attentive waitstaff. ⑤ *Average main: €20* ⊠ *Via delle Volte 14–16, Castellina in Chianti* ☏ *0577/741299* ⊕ *www.sottolevolteristorante.it* ⊘ *Closed Wed. and Jan.–Mar.*

 Hotels

★ Palazzo Squarcialupi

$$ | B&B/INN | In this lovely 15th-century palace, spacious rooms have high ceilings, tile floors, and 18th-century furnishings, and many have views of the valley below. **Pros:** great location in town center; elegant public spaces; nice spa, pool, and grounds. **Cons:** on a street with no car access; across from a busy restaurant; rooms facing the street can experience some noise. ⑤ *Rooms from: €175* ⊠ *Via Ferruccio 22, Castellina in Chianti* ☏ *0577/741186* ⊕ *www.squarcialupirelaxinchianti.com* ⊘ *Closed Nov.–Mar.* ↴ *17 rooms* ⏐⊘⏐ *Free Breakfast.*

Volterra

30 km (18 miles) southwest of San Gimignano.

As you approach the town through bleak, rugged terrain, you can see that not all Tuscan hill towns rise above rolling green fields. Volterra stands mightily over Le Balze, a stunning series of gullied hills and valleys formed by erosion that has slowly eaten away at the foundation of the town—now considerably smaller than it was during its Etruscan glory days some 2,000 years ago.

Volterra

KEY
- **1** Sights
- **1** Restaurants
- **1** Hotels

0 100 yards
0 100 meters

GETTING HERE AND AROUND

By car, the best route from San Gimigna-no follows the SP1 south to Castel San Gimignano and then the SS68 west to Volterra. Coming from the west, take the SS1, a coastal road to Cecina, then follow the SS68 east to Volterra. Either way, there's a long, winding climb at the end of your trip. Traveling to Volterra by bus or train is complicated; avoid it if possible, especially if you have lots of luggage. From Florence or Siena the journey by public transit is best made by bus and involves a change in Colle di Val d'Elsa. From Rome or Pisa, it is best to take the train to Cecina and transfer to the Volterra-Saline station. The latter is 10 km (6 miles) from town.

VISITOR INFORMATION

CONTACT Volterra Tourism Office. ✉ *Piazza dei Priori 20, Volterra* ☎ *0588/87257* ⊕ *volterratur.it.*

👁 Sights

Duomo

CHURCH | Behind the textbook 13th-century Pisan–Romanesque facade is proof that Volterra counted for something during the Renaissance, when many important Tuscan artists came to decorate the church. Three-dimensional stucco portraits of local saints are on the gold, red, and blue ceiling (1580) designed by Francesco Capriani, including St. Linus, the successor to St. Peter as pope and claimed by the Volterrans to have been born here.

The highlight of the Duomo is the brightly painted, 13th-century, wooden, life-size *Deposition* in the chapel of the same name. The unusual Cappella dell'Addolorata (Chapel of the Grieved) has two terra-cotta Nativity scenes; the depiction of the arrival of the Magi has a background fresco by Benozzo Gozzoli. ✉ *Piazza San Giovanni, Volterra* ☎ *0588/286300* ⊕ *www.animadivolterra.it/il-duomo* ⬜ €7, includes baptistry ⊗ Closed Jan. 7–Mar. and Mon.–Thurs. Nov. 3–Dec. 24.

★ Museo Etrusco Guarnacci

HISTORY MUSEUM | An extraordinary collection of Etruscan relics is made all the more interesting by clear explanations in English. The bulk of the collection is comprised of roughly 700 carved funerary urns. The oldest, dating from the 7th century BC, were made from tufa (volcanic rock). A handful are made of terra-cotta, but most—dating from the 3rd to 1st century BC—are done in alabaster. The urns are grouped by subject, and, taken together, they form a fascinating testimony about Etruscan life and death. ✉ *Via Don Minzoni 15, Volterra* ☎ *0588/86347* ⊕ *www.comune.volterra.pi.it/turismo* ⬜ €10.

Pinacoteca

ART MUSEUM | One of Volterra's best-looking Renaissance buildings contains an impressive collection of Tuscan paintings arranged chronologically on two floors. Head straight for Room 12, with Luca Signorelli's (circa 1445–1523) *Madonna and Child with Saints* and Rosso Fiorentino's later *Deposition*. Though painted just 30 years apart, they illustrate the shift in style from the early 16th-century Renaissance ideals to full-blown Mannerism: the balance of Signorelli's composition becomes purposefully skewed in Fiorentino's painting, where the colors go from vivid but realistic to emotively bright. Other important paintings in the small museum include Ghirlandaio's *Apotheosis of Christ with Saints* and a polyptych of the *Madonna and Saints* by Taddeo di Bartolo, which once hung in the Palazzo dei Priori. ✉ *Via dei Sarti 1, Volterra* ☎ *0588/87580* ⊕ *www.comune.volterra.pi.it/turismo* ⬜ €10.

Porta all'Arco Etrusco

RUINS | Even if a good portion of the arch was rebuilt by the Romans, three dark, weather-beaten, 4th-century-BC heads (thought to represent Etruscan gods) still face outward to greet those who enter here. A plaque on the outer wall recalls the efforts of the locals who saved the arch from destruction by filling it with stones during the German withdrawal at the end of World War II. ✉ *Via Porta all'Arco, Volterra* ☎ *0588/86099* ⊕ *volterratur.it* ⬜ *Free.*

Teatro Romano

RUINS | Just outside the walls, past Porta Fiorentina, are the ruins of the 1st-century-BC Roman theater, one of the best-preserved in Italy, with adjacent remains of the Roman *terme* (baths). You can enjoy an excellent bird's-eye view of the theater from Via Lungo le Mura. ✉ *Viale Francesco Ferrucci, Volterra* ☎ *0588/86099* ⊕ *volterratur.it* ⬜ €10.

Restaurants

Il Sacco Fiorentino

$$ | TUSCAN | This lovely trattoria has been around for a long time, and with good reason—the Tuscan classics rely heavily on the local cheese (pecorino) and local meats (especially wild boar, among others), and the wine list is long and very well-priced. The white walls, tile floors, and red tablecloths create an understated tone that is unremarkable, but once the food starts arriving, it's easy to forgive the lack of decoration. **Known for:** convenient location near Duomo and Piazza dei Priori; gentle prices; excellent wine list. $ *Average main: €16* ✉ *Via Giusto Turazza 13, Volterra* ☎ *0588/88537* ⊕ *il-sacco-fiorentino.business.site* ⊗ Closed Wed.

Trattoria Da Badò

$ | TUSCAN | Family-run Da Badò—with Lucia in the kitchen and her sons, Giacomo and Michele, waiting tables—is the best place in town to eat traditional food elbow-to-elbow with locals; Lucia likes to concentrate on just a few dishes, so it won't take long to decide between the standards, all prepared with a sure hand. Consider the *zuppa alla volterrana* (a soup made with vegetables and bread), *pappardelle alla lepre* (wide fettuccine with rabbit sauce), or a stew of either rabbit or wild boar—for dessert, a slice of homemade almond tart is a must. **Known for:** excellent traditional dishes; small menu; local favorite. $ *Average main:* €14 ⊠ *Borgo San Lazzaro 9, Volterra* ☎ *0588/80402* ◎ *Closed Wed.*

Hotels

Albergo Etruria

$ | HOTEL | The rooms are modest, and there's no elevator, but the central location, the ample buffet breakfast, and the reasonable rates make this a good choice. **Pros:** great central location; friendly staff; tranquil garden with rooftop views. **Cons:** some rooms can be noisy during the day; books up quickly as it's good value; no elevator. $ *Rooms from: €103* ⊠ *Via Matteotti 32, Volterra* ☎ *0588/87377* ⊕ *albergoetruria. it* ◎ *Closed early Dec.–early Feb.* ⇔ *15 rooms* ⦿ *Free Breakfast.*

Hotel San Lino

$ | HOTEL | Within the town's medieval walls, this convent-turned-hotel has wood-beam ceilings, graceful archways, and terra-cotta floors, with nice contemporary furnishings and ironwork in the rooms. **Pros:** steps from center of town; friendly and helpful staff; convenient parking. **Cons:** rooms facing the street can be noisy; books up quickly; though in the center, somewhat removed from things. $ *Rooms from: €115* ⊠ *Via San Lino 26, Volterra* ☎ *0588/85250* ⊕ *www.*

hotelsanlino.net ◎ *Closed early Nov.–late Mar.* ⇔ *43 rooms* ⦿ *Free Breakfast.*

San Gimignano

14 km (9 miles) northwest of Colle di Val d'Elsa, 38 km (24 miles) northwest of Siena, 54 km (34 miles) southwest of Florence.

When you're on a hilltop surrounded by soaring medieval towers silhouetted against the sky, it's difficult not to fall under the spell of San Gimignano. Its tall walls and narrow streets are typical of Tuscan hill towns, but it's the medieval "skyscrapers" that set the town apart from its neighbors. Today 14 towers remain, but at the height of the Guelph–Ghibelline conflict there was a forest of more than 70, and it was possible to cross the town by rooftop rather than by road.

Today San Gimignano isn't much more than a gentrified walled city, touristy but still very much worth exploring because, despite the profusion of cheesy souvenir shops lining the main drag, there's some serious Renaissance art to be seen here.

GETTING HERE AND AROUND

You can reach San Gimignano by car from the Florence–Siena superstrada. Exit at Poggibonsi Nord and follow signs for San Gimignano. Although it involves changing buses in Poggibonsi, getting to San Gimignano by bus from Florence is a relatively straightforward affair. There's also direct bus service from Siena to San Gimignano several times daily. All the buses are operated by Autolinee Toscane. You cannot reach San Gimignano by train.

VISITOR INFORMATION

CONTACT San Gimignano Tourism Office. ⊠ *Piazza Duomo 1, San Gimignano* ☎ *0577/940008* ⊕ *www.sangimignano. com.*

San Gimignano

KEY

1 Sights
1 Restaurants
1 Hotels

0   100 yards
0   100 meters

◉ Sights

★ Collegiata

CHURCH | The town's main church is not officially a duomo (cathedral), because San Gimignano has no bishop. But behind the simple facade of the Romanesque Collegiata lies a treasure trove of fine frescoes, covering nearly every wall. Bartolo di Fredi's 14th-century fresco cycle of Old Testament scenes extends along one wall. Their distinctly medieval feel, with misshapen bodies, buckets of spurting blood, and lack of perspective, contrasts with the much more reserved scenes from the Life of Christ (attributed to 14th-century artist Lippo Memmi) painted on the opposite wall just 14 years later. ⊠ *Piazza Pecori 1–2, entrance on left side of church, San Gimignano* ☏ *0577/286300* ⊕ *www.duomosangimignano.it* ☞ *€5.*

Museo Civico

CASTLE/PALACE | The impressive civic museum occupies what was the "new" Palazzo del Popolo; the Torre Grossa is adjacent. Dante visited San Gimignano for only one day as a Guelph ambassador from Florence to ask the locals to join the Florentines in supporting the pope—just long enough to get the main council chamber named after him.

Upstairs, paintings by famous Renaissance artists Pinturicchio (*Madonna Enthroned*) and Benozzo Gozzoli (*Madonna and Child*), and two large *tondi* (circular paintings) by Filippino Lippi (circa 1457–1504) attest to the importance and wealth of San Gimignano. ⊠ *Piazza Duomo 2, San Gimignano* ☏ *0577/286300* ⊕ *www.sangimignanomusei.it* ☞ *€9 cumulative ticket, €13 San Gimignano Pass (museums and duomo).*

Sant'Agostino

CHURCH | Make a beeline for Benozzo Gozzoli's superlative 15th-century fresco cycle depicting scenes from the life of St. Augustine. The saint's work was essential to the early development of church doctrine. Benozzo's 17 scenes on the choir wall depict Augustine as a man who traveled and taught extensively in the 4th and 5th centuries. The 15th-century altarpiece by Piero del Pollaiolo (1443–96) depicts *The Coronation of the Virgin* and the various protectors of the city. ✉ *Piazza Sant'Agostino 10, San Gimignano* ☎ *0577/904313* ⊕ *conventosantagostino. it* 🖘 *Free.*

 Restaurants

★ Cum Quibus

$$$ | **ITALIAN** | This is, without a doubt, one of the region's most creative restaurants—an intimate place with a menu that's Tuscan but not (its signature egg yolk starter is done with élan). Not a step is missed, and although it's possible to order à la carte, the tasting menu is also a good way to go. **Known for:** courtyard dining in nice weather; incorporation of non-Tuscan ingredients into Tuscan food; amazing wine list with prices to suit all budgets. ⑤ *Average main: €25* ✉ *Via San Martino 17, San Gimignano* ☎ *0577/943199* ⊕ *en.mktn.it/cumquibus* ☉ *Closed Wed. and Thurs. and Jan. and Feb.*

Enoteca Gustavo

$ | **WINE BAR** | There's no shortage of places to try Vernaccia di San Gimignano, the justifiably famous white wine with which San Gimignano is often singularly associated. At this wine bar, you can buy a glass of Vernaccia di San Gimignano and sit down with a cheese plate or one of the fine crostini. **Known for:** quality products; fine list of wines by the glass; friendly staff. ⑤ *Average main: €15* ✉ *Via San Matteo 7, San Gimignano* ☎ *0577/940057* ⊕ *www.facebook.com/ enotecagustavo.*

Osteria del Carcere

$ | **ITALIAN** | Although it calls itself an *osteria* (tavern), this place much more resembles a wine bar, with a bill of fare that includes several different types of pâtés and a short list of seasonal soups and salads. The sampler of goat cheeses, which can be paired with local wines, should not be missed. **Known for:** excellent chef–proprietor; inventive dishes; housed in a former jail. ⑤ *Average main: €15* ✉ *Via del Castello 13, San Gimignano* ☎ *0577/941905* ☉ *Closed Wed. and early Jan.–Mar. No lunch Thurs.*

 Hotels

★ Hotel La Collegiata

$$$ | **HOTEL** | After serving as a Franciscan convent and then the residence of the noble Strozzi family, the Collegiata has been converted into a fine hotel, with no expense spared in the process. **Pros:** gorgeous views from terrace; elegant rooms in main building; wonderful staff. **Cons:** long walk into town; service can be impersonal; some rooms are dimly lit. ⑤ *Rooms from: €250* ✉ *Località Strada 27, San Gimignano* ✛ *1 km (½ mile) north of San Gimignano town center* ☎ *0577/943201* ⊕ *www.lacollegiatahotel. com* ☉ *Closed Nov.–Mar.* ⤴ *20 rooms* ⍟ *Free Breakfast.*

Hotel Pescille

$$ | **HOTEL** | A rambling farmhouse has been transformed into a handsome hotel with understated contemporary furniture in the bedrooms and country-classic motifs in the bar. **Pros:** splendid views; quiet atmosphere; 10-minute walk to town. **Cons:** furnishings a bit austere; there's an elevator for luggage but not for guests; a vehicle is a must. ⑤ *Rooms from: €172* ✉ *Località Pescille, San Gimignano* ✛ *4 km (2½ miles) south of San Gimignano* ☎ *0577/940186* ⊕ *www. pescille.it* ☉ *Closed mid-Oct.–mid-Apr.* ⤴ *38 rooms* ⍟ *Free Breakfast.*

Tuscany   COLLE DI VAL D'ELSA

Torraccia di Chiusi

$$ | B&B/INN | FAMILY | A perfect retreat for families, this tranquil hilltop *agriturismo* (farm stay) offers simple, comfortably decorated accommodations on extensive grounds 5 km (3 miles) from the hubbub of San Gimignano. **Pros:** great walking possibilities; family-run hospitality; delightful countryside view. **Cons:** 30 minutes from the nearest town on a winding gravel road; need a car to get here; might be too remote for some. ⑤ *Rooms from: €190* ✉ *Località Montauto 16, San Gimignano* ☎ *0577/941972* ⊕ *www.torracciadi-chiusi.it* ⇌ *11 rooms* ⓘⓞⓘ *Free Breakfast.*

Colle di Val d'Elsa

12 km (7 miles) west of Monteriggioni, 25 km (16 miles) northwest of Siena, 51 km (32 miles) south of Florence.

Most people pass through on their way to and from popular tourist destinations Volterra and San Gimignano—a shame, since Colle di Val d'Elsa has a lot to offer. It's another town on the Via Francigena that benefited from trade along the pilgrimage route to Rome. Colle got an extra boost in the late 16th century when it was given a bishopric, probably related to an increase in trade when nearby San Gimignano was cut off from the well-traveled road. The town is arranged on two levels, and from the 12th century onward the flat lower portion was given over to a flourishing papermaking industry; today the area is mostly modern, and efforts have shifted toward the production of fine glass and crystal.

GETTING HERE AND AROUND

You can reach Colle di Val d'Elsa by car on either the SR2 from Siena or the Florence–Siena superstrada. Bus service to and from Siena and Florence is frequent.

VISITOR INFORMATION

CONTACT Colle di Val d'Elsa Tourism Office. ✉ *Via del Castello 33, Colle di Val d'Elsa* ☎ *0577/922791* ⊕ *www.visitcolledivaldelsa.com.*

Sights

Make your way from the newer lower town (Colle Bassa) to the prettier, upper part of town (Colle Alta). The best views of the valley are to be had from Viale della Rimembranza, the road that loops around the western end of town, past the church of San Francesco. The early-16th-century Porta Nuova was inserted into the preexisting medieval walls, just as several handsome Renaissance palazzi were placed into the medieval neighborhood to create what is now called the Borgo.

Chiesa di Santa Caterina

CHURCH | Visit this 15th-century church to view the excellent stained-glass window in the apse, executed by Sebastiano Mainardi (circa 1460–1513), as well as a haunting *Pietà* created by local artist Zacchia Zacchi (1473–1544). ✉ *Via Campana 35, Colle di Val d'Elsa* ☎ *0577/922791* ⊕ *www.visitcolledivaldelsa.com* ⓔ *Free.*

Duomo

CHURCH | Several reconstructions have left little to admire of the once-Romanesque Duomo. Inside is the Cappella del Santo Chiodo (Chapel of the Holy Nail), built in the 15th century to hold a nail allegedly from the cross upon which Christ was crucified. (Perhaps it inspired the locals to go into the nail-making business, which became another of the town's flourishing industries.) ✉ *Piazza del Duomo, Colle di Val d'Elsa* ☎ *0577/920389* ⊕ *www.visitcolledivaldelsa.com* ⓔ *Free.*

Museo San Pietro

ART MUSEUM | The museum of sacred art displays religious relics as well as triptychs from the Sienese and Florentine schools dating from the 14th and 15th centuries. It also contains the

Hill Towns West of Siena

town's tribute to Arnolfo di Cambio, with photos of the buildings he designed for other towns. Down Via del Castello, at Number 63, is the house-tower where Arnolfo was born in 1245. (It's not open to the public.) ⊠ *Via Gracco del Secco 102, Colle di Val d'Elsa* ☎ *0577/286300* ⊕ *www.museisenesi.org* ☒ *€6* ⊙ *Closed mid-Jan.–Feb., and weekdays Mar. and Nov.–late Dec.*

🍽 Restaurants

★ Ristorante Arnolfo

$$$$ | MODERN ITALIAN | Food lovers should not miss Arnolfo, one of Tuscany's most highly regarded restaurants, where chef Gaetano Trovato sets high standards of creativity in dishes that daringly ride the line between innovation and tradition, almost always with spectacular results. The menu changes frequently, but you

are always sure to find fish and lots of fresh vegetables in the summer. **Known for:** tasting menus; imaginative dishes; superb wine list. ⑤ *Average main: €200* ⊠ *Viale della Rimembranza 24, Colle di Val d'Elsa* ☎ *0577/920549* ⊕ *www. arnolfo.com* ⊙ *Closed Tues. and Wed., and mid-Feb.–early Mar., 10 days in early Apr., and mid-Nov.–early Dec.*

🛏 Hotels

Palazzo San Lorenzo Hotel & Spa

$$ | HOTEL | A 17th-century palace in the historic center of Colle has rooms that exude warmth and comfort, with light-color wooden floors, soothingly tinted fabrics, and large windows. **Pros:** central location; lovely spa area; extremely well maintained. **Cons:** caters to business groups; some of the public spaces feel rather sterile; a car is a necessity. $ *Rooms from: €158* ✉ *Via Gracco del Secco 113, Colle di Val d'Elsa* ☏ *0577/923675* ⊕ *www.palazzosanlorenzo.it* ⤴ *48 rooms* ⦿ *Free Breakfast.*

Siena

76 km (47 miles) south of Florence, 27 km (16 miles) southeast of Colle di Val d'Elsa.

With its narrow streets and steep alleys, a Gothic Duomo, a bounty of early Renaissance art, and the glorious Palazzo Pubblico overlooking its magnificent Campo, Siena is often described as Italy's best-preserved medieval city. It is also remarkably modern: many shops sell clothes by up-and-coming designers. Make a point of catching the *passeggiata* (evening stroll), when locals throng the Via di Città, Banchi di Sopra, and Banchi di Sotto, the city's three main streets.

Victory over Florence in 1260 at Montaperti marked the beginning of Siena's golden age. Even though Florentines avenged the loss 29 years later, Siena continued to prosper. During the following decades Siena erected its greatest buildings (including the Duomo); established a model city government presided over by the Council of Nine; and became a great art, textile, and trade center. All of these achievements came together in the decoration of the Sala della Pace in Palazzo Pubblico. It makes you wonder what greatness the city might have gone on to achieve had its fortunes been different, but in 1348 the Black Death decimated the population, brought an end to the Council of Nine, and left Siena economically vulnerable. Siena succumbed to Florentine rule in the mid-16th century, when a yearlong siege virtually eliminated the native population. Ironically, it was precisely this decline that, along with Sienese pride, prevented further development, to which we owe the city's marvelous medieval condition today.

But although much looks as it did in the early 14th century, Siena is no museum. Walk through the streets and you can see that the medieval contrade—17 neighborhoods into which the city has been historically divided—are a vibrant part of modern life. You may see symbols of the *contrada* emblazoned on banners and engraved on building walls: Tartuca (turtle), Oca (goose), Istrice (porcupine), Torre (tower)—among others. The Sienese still strongly identify themselves with the contrada where they were born and raised; loyalty and rivalry run deep. At no time is this more visible than during the centuries-old Palio, a twice-yearly horse race held in the Piazza del Campo, but you need not visit then to come to know the rich culture of Siena, evident at every step.

GETTING HERE AND AROUND

From Florence, the quickest way to Siena is via the Florence–Siena superstrada. Otherwise, take the Via Cassia (SR2) for a scenic route. Coming from Rome, leave the A1 at Valdichiana, and follow the Siena–Bettole superstrada. Autolinee Toscane provides frequent bus service between Florence and Siena. Because buses are direct and speedy, they are preferable to the train, which sometimes involves a change in Empoli.

If you come by car, you're better off leaving it in one of the parking lots around the perimeter of town. Driving is difficult or impossible in most parts of the city center. Practically unchanged since medieval times, Siena is laid out in a "Y" over the slopes of several hills, dividing the city into *terzi* (thirds).

TIMING

It's a joy to walk in Siena—hills notwithstanding—as it's a rare opportunity to stroll through a medieval city rather than just a town. (There is quite a lot to explore, in contrast to tiny hill towns that can be crossed in minutes.) The walk can be done in as little as a day, with minimal stops at the sights. But stay longer and take time to tour the churches and museums, and to enjoy the streetscapes themselves. Many of the sites have reduced hours Sunday afternoon and Monday.

VISITOR INFORMATION

CONTACT Siena Tourism Office. ✉ *Il Campo 1, Siena* ☎ *0577/292222* ⊕ *www. terresiena.it.*

Sights

Battistero

RELIGIOUS BUILDING | The Duomo's 14th-century Gothic Baptistery was built to prop up the apse of the cathedral. There are frescoes throughout, but the highlight is a large bronze 15th-century baptismal font designed by Jacopo della Quercia. It's adorned with bas-reliefs by various artists, including two by Renaissance masters: the *Baptism of Christ* by Lorenzo Ghiberti (1378–1455) and the *Feast of Herod* by Donatello. ✉ *Piazza San Giovanni, Città* ☎ *0577/286300* ⊕ *operaduomo.siena.it* 🎫 *€14–€16 combined ticket includes the Duomo, Cripta, and Museo dell'Opera.*

★ Cripta

CEMETERY | Routine excavation work revealed this crypt, which had been hidden for centuries under the grand *pavimento* (floor) of the Duomo and was opened to the public in 2003. In the late 13th century, an unknown master executed the crypt's breathtaking frescoes, which have sustained remarkably little damage and have retained their original colors. The *Deposition/Lamentation* proves that the Sienese school could paint emotion just as well as the Florentine school—and that it did so some 20 years before Giotto. ✉ *Scale di San Giovanni, Città* ⚜ *Down steps to right side of cathedral* ☎ *0577/286300* ⊕ *operaduomo.siena.it* 🎫 *€13–€15 combined ticket includes the Duomo, Battistero, and Museo dell'Opera.*

★ Duomo

CHURCH | Siena's cathedral, completed in two brief phases at the end of the 13th and 14th centuries, is beyond question one of the finest Gothic churches in Italy. The multicolored marble and painted decoration are typical of the Italian approach to Gothic architecture, and the amazingly detailed facade has few rivals. Highlights of the Duomo's striking interior include dark-green-and-white striping; a coffered and gilded dome; a stained-glass window that's the oldest (circa 1288) example of such work in Italy; a carousel pulpit carved around 1265; and magnificent Renaissance frescoes in the Biblioteca Piccolomini.

The Duomo is most famous, though, for its inlaid-marble floors, which took almost 200 years to complete. More than 40 artists contributed to the magnificent work, made up of 56 separate compositions depicting biblical scenes, allegories, religious symbols, and civic emblems. The floors are covered for most of the year but are unveiled from the end of June until the end of July and from mid-August until mid-October. ✉ *Piazza del Duomo, Città* ☎ *0577/286300* ⊕ *operaduomo.siena.it* 🎫 *€13–€15 combined ticket includes Cripta, Battistero, and Museo dell'Opera; €20 including roofs and all museums.*

★ Museo dell'Opera

ART MUSEUM | Part of the unfinished nave of what was to have been a new cathedral, the museum contains the Duomo's treasury and some of the original decoration from its facade and interior. The first room on the ground floor displays weather-beaten 13th-century sculptures by Giovanni Pisano that were brought inside for protection and replaced by copies, as was a tondo of the *Madonna and Child* (now attributed to Donatello) that once hung on the door to the south transept. The masterpiece is unquestionably Duccio's *Maestà,* one side with 26 panels depicting episodes from the Passion, the other side with a

Madonna and Child Enthroned. The second floor is divided between the treasury, with a crucifix by Giovanni Pisano, and *La Sala della Madonna degli Occhi Grossi* (the Room of the Madonna with the Big Eyes), named after the 13th-century painting. There is a fine view from the tower inside the museum. ⊠ *Piazza del Duomo 8, Città* ☎ *0577/286300* ⊕ *operaduomo.siena.it* 🖾 *€13–€15 combined ticket includes the Duomo, Cripta, and Battistero.*

Palazzo Pubblico
GOVERNMENT BUILDING | The Gothic Palazzo Pubblico, the focal point of the Piazza del Campo, has served as Siena's town hall since the 1300s. It now also contains the Museo Civico, with walls covered in early Renaissance frescoes. The nine governors of Siena once met in the Sala della Pace, famous for Ambrogio Lorenzetti's frescoes called *Allegories of Good and Bad Government,* painted in the late 1330s to demonstrate the dangers of tyranny. The good government side depicts utopia, showing first the virtuous ruling council surrounded by angels and then scenes of a perfectly running city and countryside. Conversely, the bad government fresco tells a tale straight out of Dante. The evil ruler and his advisers have horns and fondle strange animals, and the town scene depicts the seven mortal sins in action.

The Torre del Mangia, the palazzo's famous bell tower, is named after one of its first bell ringers, Giovanni di Duccio (called Mangiaguadagni, or earnings eater). The climb up to the top is long and steep, but the view makes it worth every step. ⊠ *Piazza del Campo 1, Città* ☎ *0577/292232* ⊕ *www.comune.siena.it* 🖾 *Museum €6, museum and tower €15.*

★ Piazza del Campo
PLAZA/SQUARE | The fan-shaped Piazza del Campo, known simply as Il Campo (The Field), is one of the finest squares in Italy. Constructed toward the end of the 12th century on a market area unclaimed by any contrada, it's still the heart of town. Its brickwork is patterned in nine different sections—representing each member of the medieval Council of Nine.

At the top of the Campo is a copy of the early 15th-century Fonte Gaia by Siena's greatest sculptor, Jacopo della Quercia. The 13 sculpted reliefs of biblical events and virtues that line the fountain are 19th-century copies; the originals are in the museum complex of Santa Maria della Scala. On Palio horse-race days (July 2 and August 16), the Campo and all its surrounding buildings are packed with cheering, frenzied locals and tourists craning their necks to take it all in. ⊠ *Piazza del Campo, Città.*

Pinacoteca Nazionale
ART MUSEUM | The superb collection of five centuries of local painting in Siena's national picture gallery can easily convince you that the Renaissance was by no means just a Florentine thing. Accordingly, the most interesting section of the collection, chronologically arranged, has several important firsts. Room 1 contains a painting of the *Stories of the True Cross* (1215) by the so-called Master of Tressa, the earliest identified work by a painter of the Sienese school, and is followed in Room 2 by late-13th-century artist Guido da Siena's *Stories from the Life of Christ,* one of the first paintings ever made on canvas (earlier painters used wood panels).

Rooms 3 and 4 are dedicated to Duccio, a student of Cimabue (circa 1240–1302) and considered to be the last of the proto-Renaissance painters. Ambrogio Lorenzetti's landscapes in Room 8 are among the first truly secular paintings in Western art. Among later works in the rooms on the floor above, keep an eye out for the preparatory sketches used by Domenico Beccafumi (1486–1551) for the 35 etched marble panels he made for the floor of the Duomo. ⊠ *Via San Pietro 29, Città* ☎ *0577/281161* ⊕ *www.*

Siena

KEY

- 1 Sights
- 1 Restaurants
- 1 Hotels

0   200 yd

0   200 meters

pinacotecanazionalesiena.it 🖥 €6
🕐 *Closed Sun. and Mon. after 1:30.*

San Domenico

CHURCH | Although the Duomo is celebrated as a triumph of 13th-century Gothic architecture, this church, built at about the same time, turned out to be an oversize, hulking brick box that never merited a finishing coat in marble, let alone a graceful facade. Named for the founder of the Dominican order, the church is now more closely associated with St. Catherine of Siena. Just to the right of the entrance is the chapel in which she received the stigmata. On the wall is the only known contemporary portrait of the saint, made in the late 14th century by Andrea Vanni (circa 1332–1414). Farther down is the famous Cappella delle Santa Testa, the church's official shrine.

On either side of the chapel are well-known frescoes by Sodoma (aka Giovanni Antonio Bazzi, 1477–1549) of *St. Catherine in Ecstasy.* Don't miss the view of the Duomo and town center from the apse-side terrace. ⊠ *Piazza San Domenico, Camollia* 🕾 *0577/286848* ⊕ *www. basilicacateriniana.it* 🖥 *Free.*

★ Santa Maria della Scala

ART MUSEUM | For more than 1,000 years, this complex across from the Duomo was home to Siena's hospital, but it now serves as a museum. Restored 15th-century frescoes in the Sala del Pellegrinaio tell the history of the hospital, which was created to give refuge to passing pilgrims and others in need and to distribute charity to the poor. Incorporated into the complex is the church of the Santissima Annunziata, with a celebrated *Risen Christ* by Vecchietta (also known as Lorenzo di Pietro, circa 1412–80). Down in the dark, Cappella di Santa Caterina della Notte is where St. Catherine went to pray at night. Displays in the subterranean archaeological museum are clearly marked and serve as a good introduction to the history of regional excavations. Don't miss della Quercia's

stunning original sculpted reliefs from the Fonte Gaia. ⊠ *Piazza del Duomo 2, Città* 🕾 *0577/292615* ⊕ *www.santamariadellascala.com* 🖥 €9 🕐 *Closed Tues. Nov.–mid-Mar.*

🍽 Restaurants

Osteria Il Grattacielo

$$ | TUSCAN | If you're wiped out from too much sightseeing, consider a meal at this hole-in-the-wall restaurant where locals congregate for a simple lunch. There's a collection of verdure sott'olio, a wide selection of affettati misti, and various types of frittatas—all of which can be washed down with the cheap, yet eminently drinkable, house wines. **Known for:** simple, good-value food; earthy ambience; outdoor seating in summer. ⑤ *Average main: €20* ⊠ *Via Pontani 8, Camollia* 🕾 *331/7422835* ⊕ *sites.google. com/view/ilgrattacielo1840* 🕐 *No dinner Sun.*

Antica Trattoria Papei

$$ | TUSCAN | This place, which has been in the Papei family for three generations, attracts both locals and visitors with basic but fine Sienese specialties and reasonable prices. Tucked away behind the Palazzo Pubblico in a square that serves as a parking lot for most of the day, the restaurant's location isn't great, but the food is; thanks to portable heaters, there is outdoor seating all year-round. **Known for:** great place to sample local specialties; lively atmosphere; outdoor seating. ⑤ *Average main: €15* ⊠ *Piazza del Mercato 6, Città* 🕾 *0577/280894* ⊕ *anticatrattoriapapei.com.*

🛏 Hotels

★ Grand Hotel Continental

$$$$ | HOTEL | Pope Alexander VII of the famed Sienese Chigi family gave this palace to his niece as a wedding present in 1600, and, through the centuries, it has been a private home as well as a grand hotel—one that exudes elegance from its stately pillared entrance to its crisp-linen sheets. **Pros:** luxurious accommodations; great location on the main drag; first-rate concierge. **Cons:** sometimes stuffy atmosphere; lots of noise if your room is street-side; breakfast costs extra. ⑤ *Rooms from: €365* ✉ *Banchi di Sopra 85, Camollia* ☎ *0577/56011* ⊕ *collezione.starhotels.com* ⇨ *51 rooms* ⦿︎ *No Meals.*

Hotel Santa Caterina

$ | B&B/INN | The atmosphere here is welcoming, hospitable, and enthusiastic, and the staff goes out of their way to ensure a fine stay; rooms in the back look out onto the lush grounds or the countryside in the distance. **Pros:** friendly staff; a short walk to center of town; breakfast in the garden. **Cons:** on a busy intersection; outside city walls; 15-minute (easy) walk into the historic center. ⑤ *Rooms from: €103* ✉ *Via Piccolomini 7, San Martino* ☎ *0577/221105* ⊕ *www.hotelsantacaterinasiena.com* ⇨ *22 rooms* ⦿︎ *No Meals.*

Palazzo Ravizza

$ | HOTEL | Exuding the charm of a bygone era, this palazzo has guest rooms featuring high ceilings and antique furnishings, as well as bathrooms decorated with hand-painted tiles. **Pros:** 10-minute walk to the center of town; pleasant garden with a view beyond the city walls; professional staff. **Cons:** not all rooms have views; some rooms are a little cramped; somewhat removed from the center of things. ⑤ *Rooms from: €104* ✉ *Pian dei Mantellini 34, Città* ☎ *0577/280462* ⊕ *palazzoravizza.it* ⇨ *41 rooms* ⦿︎ *Free Breakfast.*

Arezzo

63 km (39 miles) northeast of Siena, 81 km (50 miles) southeast of Florence.

Arezzo is best known for the magnificent Piero della Francesca frescoes in the church of San Francesco. It's also the birthplace of the poet Petrarch (1304–74), the Renaissance artist and art historian

Giorgio Vasari, and Guido d'Arezzo (aka Guido Monaco), the inventor of contemporary musical notation. Arezzo dates from pre-Etruscan times, when around 1000 BC the first settlers erected a cluster of huts. Arezzo thrived as an Etruscan capital from the 7th to the 4th century BC, and was one of the most important cities in the Etruscans' anti-Roman 12-city federation, resisting Rome's rule to the last.

The city eventually fell and in turn flourished under the Romans. In 1248 Guglielmino degli Ubertini, a member of the powerful Ghibelline family, was elected bishop of Arezzo. This sent the city headlong into the enduring conflict between the Ghibellines (pro-emperor) and the Guelphs (pro-pope). In 1289 Florentine Guelphs defeated Arezzo in a famous battle at Campaldino. Among the Florentine soldiers was Dante Alighieri (1265–1321), who often referred to Arezzo in his *Divine Comedy.* Guelph–Ghibelline wars continued to plague Arezzo until the end of the 14th century, when Arezzo lost its independence to Florence.

GETTING HERE AND AROUND

Arezzo is easily reached by car from the A1, the main highway running between Florence and Rome. Direct trains connect Arezzo with Rome (2½ hours) and Florence (1 hour). Direct bus service is available from Florence but not from Rome.

VISITOR INFORMATION

CONTACT Arezzo Tourism Office. ✉ *Via Giorgio Vasari, 13, Arezzo* ☎ *0575/377468* ⊕ *www.discoverarezzo.com.*

Sights

★ Basilica di San Francesco

CHURCH | The famous Piero della Francesca frescoes depicting *The Legend of the True Cross* (1452–66) were executed on the three walls of the Capella Bacci, the apse of this 14th-century church. What Sir Kenneth Clark called "the most perfect morning light in all Renaissance painting" may be seen in the lowest section of the right wall, where the troops of Emperor Maxentius flee before the sign of the cross. Reservations are required and can be made online. ⊠ *Piazza San Francesco 2, Arezzo* ☎ *0575/1696258* ⊕ *www.discoverarezzo.com* ⊠ *€9* ⊘ *Closed Wed. and Sun. morning.*

Duomo

CHURCH | Arezzo's medieval cathedral at the top of the hill contains a fresco of a tender *Maria Maddalena* by Piero della Francesca (1420–92); look for it in the north aisle next to the large marble tomb near the organ. Construction of the Duomo began in 1278 but twice came to a halt, and the church wasn't completed until 1510. The ceiling decorations and the stained-glass windows date from the 16th century. The facade, designed by Arezzo's Dante Viviani, was added later (1901–14). ⊠ *Piazza del Duomo 1, Arezzo* ☎ *0575/377468* ⊕ *www. discoverarezzo.com.*

Museo Archeologico

HISTORY MUSEUM | **FAMILY** | The Archaeological Museum in the Convento di San Bernardo, just outside the Anfiteatro Romano, exhibits a fine collection of Etruscan bronzes. The ticket allows admission to the Anfiteatro Romano. ⊠ *Via Margaritone 10, Arezzo* ☎ *0575/1696258* ⊕ *www.discoverarezzo.com* ⊠ *€9, combined ticket with Anfiteatro Romano.*

Piazza Grande

PLAZA/SQUARE | **FAMILY** | With its irregular shape and sloping brick pavement, framed by buildings of assorted centuries, Arezzo's central piazza echoes Siena's Piazza del Campo. Though not quite so magnificent, it's lively enough during the outdoor antiques fair the first weekend of the month and when the Giostra del Saracino (Saracen Joust), featuring medieval costumes and competition, is held here on the third Saturday of June and on the first Sunday of September. ⊠ *Piazza Grande, Arezzo* ☎ *0575/377468* ⊕ *www.discoverarezzo.com.*

Santa Maria della Pieve (*Church of Saint Mary of the Parish*)

CHURCH | The curving, tiered apse on Piazza Grande belongs to a church that was originally an early Christian structure—itself constructed over the remains of a Roman temple. The church was rebuilt in Romanesque style in the 12th century. The splendid facade dates from the early 13th century but includes granite Roman columns. A magnificent polyptych, depicting the Madonna and Child with four saints, by Pietro Lorenzetti (circa 1290–1348), embellishes the high altar. ⊠ *Corso Italia 7, Arezzo* ☎ *0575/377468* ⊕ *www.discoverarezzo.com.*

🍴 Restaurants

Il Grottino

$ | **ITALIAN** | **FAMILY** | It's small, but the very cheery staff is only too happy to provide you with wonderful plates of typical Tuscan food. The kitchen stays open a little bit later than most, which makes this a perfect stop after seeing some of the amazing art that Arezzo has to offer. **Known for:** delicious soups; surprisingly well-composed mixed salads; inventive desserts. $ *Average main: €14* ⊠ *Via della Madonna del Prato 1, Arezzo* ☎ *0575/302537* ⊕ *www.facebook.com/ilgrottinoarezzo.*

La Torre di Gnicche

$ | **WINE BAR** | Wine lovers shouldn't miss this wine bar and eatery, which is just off Piazza Grande and has more than 700 labels on its list. Seasonal traditional dishes, such as *acquacotta del casentino* (porcini mushroom soup) or *baccalà in umido* (salt-cod stew), are served in the simply decorated, vaulted dining room. **Known for:** the extensive wine list, with many choices by the glass; an ever-changing menu; rustic setting. $ *Average main: €12* ⊠ *Piaggia San Martino 8, Arezzo* ☎ *0575/352035* ⊕ *www. latorredignicche.it* ⊘ *Closed Wed. and Jan.*

🛏 Hotels

★ Castello di Gargonza

$$ | HOTEL | FAMILY | Enchantment reigns at this tiny 13th-century countryside hamlet, part of the fiefdom of the aristocratic Florentine Guicciardini family and reinvented by the modern Count Roberto Guicciardini. **Pros:** romantic, one-of-a-kind accommodation in a medieval castle; peaceful, isolated setting; on-site restaurant. **Cons:** standard rooms are extremely basic; a little out of the way for exploring the region; private transportation is a necessity. ⑤ *Rooms from: €180* ⊠ *SR73, Località Gargonza, Monte San Savino* ✛ *32 km (19 miles) southwest of Arezzo* ☎ *0575/847021* ⊕ *gargonza.it* ⊘ *Closed 2nd week of Jan.–Mar.* ➟ *47 rooms* ❍❘ *Free Breakfast.*

★ Il Borro

$$$$ | HOTEL | The location has been described as "heaven on earth," and a stay at this elegant Ferragamo estate—situated near a medieval village and with accommodations that include a 10-bedroom villa (rented out as a single unit) that was once a luxurious hunting lodge—is sure to bring similar descriptions to mind. **Pros:** exceptional service; great location for exploring eastern Tuscany; unique setting and atmosphere. **Cons:** off the beaten track, making private transport a must; not all suites have country views; very expensive. ⑤ *Rooms from: €590* ⊠ *Località Il Borro 1* ✛ *Outside village of San Giustino Valdarno, 20 km (12 miles) northwest of Arezzo* ☎ *055/977053* ⊕ *www.ilborro.it* ⊘ *Closed Dec.–Mar.* ➟ *61 rooms* ❍❘ *Free Breakfast.*

Shopping

Ever since Etruscan goldsmiths set up their shops here more than 2,000 years ago, Arezzo has been famous for its jewelry. Today the town lays claim to being one of the world's capitals of jewelry design and manufacture, and you can find an impressive display of big-time baubles in the town center's shops.

Arezzo is also famous, at least in Italy, for its antiques dealers. The first weekend of every month, between 8:30 and 5:30, a popular and colorful flea market selling antiques and not-so-antique items takes place in the town's main square, Piazza Grande, and in the streets and parks nearby.

Cortona

29 km (18 miles) south of Arezzo, 79 km (44 miles) east of Siena, 117 km (73 miles) southeast of Florence.

Brought into the limelight by Frances Mayes's book *Under the Tuscan Sun* and a subsequent movie, Cortona is no longer the destination of just a few specialist art historians and those seeking reprieve from busier tourist venues. The main street, Via Nazionale, is now lined with souvenir shops and fills with crowds during summer. Although the main sights of Cortona make braving the bustling center worthwhile, much of the town's charm lies in its maze of quiet backstreets. It's here that you will see laundry hanging from windows, find children playing, and catch the smell of simmering pasta sauce. Wander off the beaten track and you won't be disappointed.

GETTING HERE AND AROUND

Cortona is easily reached by car from the A1 autostrada: take the Valdichiana exit toward Perugia, then follow signs for Cortona. Regular bus service, provided by Autolinee Toscane, is available between Arezzo and Cortona (one hour). Train service to Cortona is made inconvenient by the location of the train station, in the valley 3 km (2 miles) steeply below the town itself. From there, you have to rely on bus or taxi service to get up to Cortona.

VISITOR INFORMATION
CONTACT Cortona Tourism Office. ✉ *Piazza Signorelli 9, Cortona* ☎ *0575/637274* ⊕ *www.comunedicortona.it.*

◉ Sights

Museo Diocesano
ART MUSEUM | Housed in part of the original cathedral structure, this nine-room museum has an impressive number of large, splendid paintings by native son Luca Signorelli (1445–1523), as well as a delightful *Annunciation* by Fra Angelico (1387/1400–55). The church was built between 1498 and 1505 and restructured by Giorgio Vasari in 1543. Frescoes depicting sacrifices from the Old Testament by Doceno (1508–56), based on designs by Vasari, line the walls. ✉ *Piazza Duomo 1, Cortona* ☎ *0575/286300* ⊕ *www.cortonatuseibellezza.it* 💶 *€9* ⊘ *Closed Mon.–Thurs. Nov.–Mar.*

Santa Maria al Calcinaio
CHURCH | Legend has it that an image of the Madonna appeared on a wall of a medieval *calcinaio* (lime pit used for curing leather), the site on which the church was then built between 1485 and 1513. The linear gray-and-white interior recalls Florence's Duomo. Sienese architect Francesco di Giorgio (1439–1502) most likely designed the sanctuary: the church is a terrific example of Renaissance architectural principles. ✉ *Località Il Calcinaio 227, Cortona* ⊕ *3 km (2 miles) southeast of Cortona's center* ☎ *0575/62537* ⊕ *www.calcinaio.it.*

Sights ▼

1 Museo
Diocesano .. **A3**

2 Santa Maria al
Calcinaio.... **C5**

Restaurants ▼

1 Osteria del
Teatro **B3**

Hotels ▼

1 Il
Falconiere... **B1**

🍴 Restaurants

Osteria del Teatro

$$ | **TUSCAN** | Photographs from theatrical productions spanning many years line the walls of this tavern off Cortona's large Piazza del Teatro. The food is simply delicious—try the *filetto al lardo di colonnata e prugne* (beef cooked with bacon and prunes); service is warm and friendly. **Known for:** food that's in season; lively atmosphere; pretty dining room. ⓢ *Average main: €20* ✉ *Via Maffei 2, Cortona* ☎ *0575/630556* ⊕ *www.osteria-del-teatro.com* 🕓 *Closed Wed. and 2 wks in Nov.*

🛏 Hotels

★ Il Falconiere

$$$$ | **B&B/INN** | Options at this sumptuous lodging include rooms and suites in an 18th-century villa, or, for more seclusion, private suites and villas at the far end of the property. **Pros:** attractive setting in the valley beneath Cortona; excellent service; elegant, but relaxed. **Cons:** a car is a must; some find rooms in main villa a little noisy; might be too isolated for some. ⓢ *Rooms from: €576* ✉ *Località San Martino 370, Cortona* ✚ *3 km (2 miles) north of Cortona* ☎ *0575/612679* ⊕ *www.ilfalconiere.it* 🕓 *Closed Nov.–Jan.* 🛏 *33 rooms* 🍽 *Free Breakfast.*

Montepulciano

610 km (6 miles) northeast of Chianciano Terme, 65 km (40 miles) southeast of Siena, 114 km (70 miles) southeast of Florence.

Perched on a hilltop, Montepulciano is made up of a pyramid of redbrick buildings set within a circle of cypress trees. At an altitude of almost 2,000 feet, it is cool in summer and chilled in winter by biting winds sweeping down its spiraling streets. The town has an unusually harmonious look, the result of the work of three architects: Antonio da Sangallo "il Vecchio" (circa 1455–1534), Vignola (1507–73), and Michelozzo (1396–1472). The group endowed it with fine palaces and churches in an attempt to impose Renaissance architectural ideals on an ancient Tuscan hill town.

GETTING HERE AND AROUND

From Rome or Florence, take the Chiusi–Chianciano exit from the A1 (Autostrada del Sole). From Siena, take the SR2 south to San Quirico and then the SP146 to Montepulciano. Autolinee Toscane offers bus service from Siena to Montepulciano several times a day. Montepulciano's train station is in Montepulciano Stazione, 10 km (6 miles) away.

VISITOR INFORMATION

CONTACT Montepulciano Tourism Office.
⊠ *Piazza Don Minzoni 1, Montepulciano* ☎ *0578/757341* ⊕ *www.prolocomontepulciano.it.*

 Sights

Duomo

CHURCH | The unfinished facade of Montepulciano's cathedral doesn't measure up to the beauty of its neighboring palaces. On the inside, however, its Renaissance roots shine through. The high altar has a splendid triptych painted in 1401 by Taddeo di Bartolo (circa 1362–1422), and you can see fragments of the tomb of Bartolomeo Aragazzi, secretary to Pope Martin V, that was sculpted by Michelozzo between 1427 and 1436. ⊠ *Piazza Grande, Montepulciano* ☎ *0578/71951.*

Piazza Grande

PLAZA/SQUARE | Filled with handsome buildings, this large square on the heights of the old historic town is Montepulciano's pièce de résistance. ⊠ *Piazza Grande, Montepulciano.*

★ San Biagio

CHURCH | Designed by Antonio da Sangallo il Vecchio, and considered his masterpiece, this church sits on the hillside below the town walls and is a model of High Renaissance architectural perfection. Inside is a painting of the Madonna that, according to legend, was the only thing remaining in an abandoned church that two young girls entered on April 23, 1518. The girls saw the eyes of the Madonna moving, and that same afternoon so did a farmer and a cow, who knelt down in front of the painting. In 1963, the image was proclaimed the *Madonna del Buon Viaggio* (Madonna of the Good Journey), the protector of tourists in Italy. ⊠ *Via di San Biagio, Montepulciano* ☎ *0578/286300* ⊕ *www. tempiosanbiagio.it* 🎟 *€4.50.*

🍴 Restaurants

Le Logge del Vignola

$$ | ITALIAN | In this small and cozy dining room, owner and sommelier Massimo Stella, his daughter Virginia, and chef Carlo Gutierrez bring fine dining flair to traditional Tuscan dishes like handmade pici pasta with black garlic and potato gnocchi. The wine list, which has many options by the glass, focuses on regional favorites. **Known for:** attentive service; well-curated wine list; elegant desserts. ⑤ *Average main: €20* ⊠ *Via delle Erbe 6, Montepulciano* ☎ *0578/717290* ⊕ *www. leloggedelvignola.com* ⊗ *Closed Tues. No lunch Wed.*

Val d'Orcia and the Crete

★ Osteria del Conte

$ | **ITALIAN** | As high in Montepulciano as you can get, just behind the Duomo, this small and intimate restaurant is expertly run by the mother-and-son team of Lorena and Paolo Brachi. Passionate about the food they prepare, both have a flair for the region's traditional dishes—the *pici all'aglione* (pasta with garlic sauce) and the *filetto ai funghi porcini* (steak with porcini mushrooms) are mouthwateringly good. **Known for:** fine home cooking; good local wines; attentive service. *$ Average main: €13* ⊠ *Via di San Donato 19, Montepulciano* ☎ *0578/756062* ⊕ *www.osteriadelconte.it* ☉ *Closed Mon. No dinner Sun.*

🛏 Hotels

La Terrazza

$ | **B&B/INN** | **FAMILY** | On a quiet street in the upper part of town, these unpretentious lodgings are given sparkle by the welcoming and friendly service of the owners, Roberto and Vittoria Giardinelli. **Pros:** family-friendly atmosphere; quiet central location; great value for money. **Cons:** no air-conditioning; no night porter; books up quickly. *$ Rooms from: €95* ⊠ *Via del Piè al Sasso 16, Montepulciano* ☎ *0578/757440* ⊕ *www.laterrazzadi-montepulciano.it* ⇥ *14 rooms* ⊙ *Free Breakfast.*

Pienza

12 km (7 miles) west of Montepulciano, 52 km (31 miles) southeast of Siena, 120 km (72 miles) southeast of Florence.

Pienza owes its appearance to Pope Pius II (1405–64), who had grand plans to transform his hometown of Corsignano—its former name—into a compact model Renaissance town. The man entrusted with the transformation was Bernardo Rossellino (1409–64), a protégé of the great Renaissance architectural theorist Leon Battista Alberti (1404–72). His mandate was to create a cathedral, a papal palace, and a town hall that adhered to the vainglorious pope's principles. Gothic and Renaissance styles were fused, and the buildings were decorated with Sienese paintings. The net result was a project that expressed Renaissance ideals of art, architecture, and civilized good living in a single scheme: it stands as an exquisite example of the architectural canons that Alberti formulated in the early Renaissance and that were utilized by later architects, including Michelangelo, in designing many of Italy's finest buildings and piazzas. Today the cool nobility of Pienza's center seems almost surreal in this otherwise unpretentious village, renowned for its smooth sheep's-milk pecorino cheese.

GETTING HERE AND AROUND

From Siena, drive south along the SR2 to San Quirico d'Orcia and then take the SP146. The trip should take just over an hour. Autolinee Toscane buses travel from Siena to Pienza with a change in Buonconvento. There is no train service to Pienza.

VISITOR INFORMATION

CONTACT Pienza Tourism Office. ⊠ *Corso il Rossellino, Pienza* ☎ *0578/749905* ⊕ *stradedisiena.it.*

Sights

Duomo

CHURCH | This 15th-century cathedral was built by the architect Bernardo Rossellino (1409–64) under the influence of Leon Battista Alberti. The travertine facade is divided into three parts, with Renaissance arches under the pope's coat of arms encircled by a wreath of fruit. Inside, the cathedral is simple but richly decorated with Sienese paintings. The building's perfection didn't last long—the first cracks appeared immediately after it was completed, and its foundations have shifted slightly ever since as rain erodes the hillside behind. You can see this effect if you look closely at the base of the first pier as you enter the church and compare it with the last. ⊠ *Piazza Pio II, Pienza* ☎ *0578/286300* ⊕ *www.pienzacittadiluce.it.*

Museo Diocesano

ART MUSEUM | This museum, which sits to the left of Pienza's Duomo, is small but has a few interesting papal treasures and rich Flemish tapestries. The most precious piece is a rare mantle that belonged to Pope Pius II: it's woven in gold and embellished with pearls and embroidered religious scenes. ⊠ *Corso Il Rossellino 30, Pienza* ☎ *0578/749905* ⊕ *www.pienzacittadiluce.it* ⊠ *From €5* ⊘ *Closed Tues.*

Palazzo Piccolomini

CASTLE/PALACE | In 1459, Pius II commissioned Bernardo Rossellino to design the perfect palazzo for his papal court. The architect took Florence's Palazzo Rucellai by Alberti as a model and designed this 100-room palace. Three sides of the building fit perfectly into the urban plan around it, while the fourth, looking over the valley, has a lovely loggia uniting it with the gardens in back. Guided tours departing every 30 minutes take you to the papal apartments, including a beautiful library, the Sala delle Armi (with an impressive weapons collection), and the

Climb to the top of La Fortezza for the views and then slake your thirst in the on-site enoteca.

music room, with its extravagant wooden ceiling forming four letter Ps, for Pope, Pius, Piccolomini, and Pienza. The last tour departs 30 minutes before closing. ⊠ *Piazza Pio II, Pienza* ☎ *0577/286300* ⊕ *www.palazzopiccolominipienza.it* ⏰ *€8 or €12 including Museo Diocesano, Duomo, and its crypt* ⊘ *Closed Tues., early Jan.–mid-Feb., and mid-Nov.–late Nov.*

🍴 Restaurants

★ Osteria Sette di Vino

$ | TUSCAN | Tasty dishes based on the region's cheeses are the specialty at this simple osteria on a quiet, pleasant, central square. Try versions of pici or the starter of radicchio baked quickly to brown the edges. **Known for:** pecorino tasting menu; bean soup; awesome vegetable options. ⑤ *Average main: €7* ⊠ *Piazza di Spagna 1, Pienza* ☎ *0578/749092* ⊘ *Closed Wed., July 1–15, and Nov.*

Montalcino

19 km (12 miles) northeast of Bagno Vignoni, 41 km (25½ miles) south of Siena, 109 km (68 miles) south of Florence.

Tiny Montalcino, with its commanding view from high on a hill, can claim an Etruscan past. It saw a fair number of travelers, as it was directly on the road from Siena to Rome. During the early Middle Ages it enjoyed a brief period of autonomy before falling under the orbit of Siena in 1201. Now Montalcino's greatest claim to fame is that it produces Brunello di Montalcino, one of Italy's most esteemed reds. Driving to the town, you pass through the brunello vineyards. You can sample the excellent but expensive red in wine cellars in town or visit a nearby winery, such as Fattoria dei Barbi, for a guided tour and tasting; you must call ahead for reservations.

GETTING HERE AND AROUND

By car, follow the SR2 south from Siena, then follow the SP45 to Montalcino. Autolinee Toscane buses travel between Siena and Montalcino daily with a change in Buonconvento. There is no train service available.

VISITOR INFORMATION

CONTACT Montalcino Tourism Office. ⊠ *Via Ricasoli 31, Montalcino* ☎ *0577/846014* ⊕ *visitvaldorcia.it.*

Sights

★ La Fortezza

CASTLE/PALACE | FAMILY | Providing refuge for the last remnants of the Sienese army during the Florentine conquest of 1555, the battlements of this 14th-century fortress are still in excellent condition. Climb the narrow, spiral steps for the 360-degree view of most of southern Tuscany. An on-site enoteca serves delicious snacks that pair beautifully with the local wines. ⊠ *Piazzale Fortezza, Montalcino* ☎ *0577/849221 enoteca* ⊕ *www. enotecalafortezza.com* ☎ *Fortress free, walls €4, tastings from €25* ☉ *Closed Mon. Nov.–Mar.*

Museo Civico e Diocesano d'Arte Sacra

ART MUSEUM | This fine museum is in a building that belonged to Augustinian friars in the 13th-century. The ticket booth is in the glorious refurbished cloister, and the sacred art collection, gathered from churches throughout the region, is displayed on two floors in former monastic quarters. Although the art here might be called B-list, a fine altarpiece by Bartolo di Fredi (circa 1330–1410), the *Coronation of the Virgin*, makes dazzling use of gold. In addition, there's a striking 12th-century crucifix that originally adorned the high altar of the church of Sant'Antimo. Also on hand are many wood sculptures, a typical medium in these parts during the Renaissance. ⊠ *Via Ricasoli 31, Montalcino* ☎ *0577/286300* ⊕ *www.museisenesi.*

org ☎ *€10* ☉ *Closed Mon.–Thurs. Nov. 1–Dec. 24 and Jan. 10–Mar. 31.*

🍴 Restaurants

★ Enoteca Osteria Osticcio

$$$ | WINE BAR | This beautifully remodeled restaurant and wineshop serves a light menu that pairs nicely with the lovely wines here, the main draw. Upon entering, you descend a staircase to a tasting room filled with rustic wooden tables. **Known for:** amazing wine list; gorgeous view of nearby hills; tasty food. $ *Average main: €27* ⊠ *Via Matteotti 23, Montalcino* ☎ *0577/1393288* ⊕ *osticcio.it* ☉ *Closed 2 wks in Nov.*

Il Grappolo Blu

$$ | ITALIAN | Any one of this restaurant's *piatti tipici* (typical plates) is worth trying, though the local specialty, pici all'aglione (thick, long noodles served with sautéed cherry tomatoes and many cloves of garlic), is done particularly well. The chef also has a deft touch with vegetables; if there's fennel on the menu, make sure to order it. **Known for:** great quality and price; kind, caring staff; convivial atmosphere. $ *Average main: €15* ⊠ *Scale di Via Moglio 1, Montalcino* ☎ *0577/847150* ⊕ *www.grappoloblu.it.*

Taverna dei Barbi

$ | TUSCAN | This rustic taverna with a large stone fireplace is amid vineyards that produce excellent Brunello—as well as its younger cousin, Rosso di Montalcino—a few minutes south of Montalcino, in the direction of Sant'Antimo. Many of the ingredients used in soup, gnocchi, bruschetta, and other traditional specialties are grown on the estate farm. **Known for:** heavenly aromas coming from grilled meat on a spit; fantastic wines; superb staff. $ *Average main: €12* ⊠ *Podere Podernuovo 170, Montalcino* ☎ *0577/847143* ⊕ *www.fattoriadeibarbi.it* ☉ *Closed Sat. and Sun.*

Hotels

★ Rosewood Castiglion del Bosco

$$$$ | RESORT | This estate, one of the largest still in private hands in Tuscany, was purchased at the beginning of this century and meticulously converted into a second-to-none resort that incorporates a medieval *borgo* (village) and surrounding farmhouses and has luxurious suites, as well as opulent three- to five-bedroom villas, each with its own pool. **Pros:** exclusive and tranquil location; breathtaking scenery; acclaimed golf course. **Cons:** well off the beaten track, nearest town is 12 km (7½ miles) away; private transportation required; truly exorbitant prices. ⑤ *Rooms from: €1,107* ⊠ *Località Castiglion del Bosco, Montalcino* ☎ *0577/1913001* ⊕ *www.castigliondelbosco.com* ⌛ *53 units* ⦿⦿ *No Meals.*

Abbazia di Sant'Antimo

10 km (6 miles) south of Montalcino, 51 km (32 miles) south of Siena, 19 km (74 miles) south of Florence.

It's well worth your while to go out of your way to visit this 12th-century Romanesque abbey, as it's a gem of pale stone in the silvery green of an olive grove.

GETTING HERE AND AROUND

The Abbazia di Sant'Antimo, nestled below the town of Castelnuovo dell'Abate, is a 15-minute drive from Montalcino. Autolinee Toscane bus service is extremely limited, and the abbey cannot be reached by train.

Sights

★ Abbazia di Sant'Antimo

CHURCH | The exterior and interior sculpture of this Romanesque abbey, dating from the 12th century, is outstanding, particularly the nave capitals, a combination of French, Lombard, and even Spanish influences. The sacristy (seldom open) forms part of the primitive Carolingian church (founded in AD 781), its entrance flanked by 9th-century pilasters. The small vaulted crypt dates from the same period. ⊠ *Localita' S. Antimo 222, Castelnuovo dell'Abate* ☎ *0577/286300* ⊕ *www.antimo.it* ⦿ *Closed for mass on Sun. and religious holidays until 11 am.*

Chapter 14

UMBRIA AND THE MARCHES

14

Updated by
Liz Humphreys

⊙ **Sights**
★★★★☆

🍴 **Restaurants**
★★★★☆

🛏 **Hotels**
★★★★☆

🛍 **Shopping**
★★☆☆☆

🍸 **Nightlife**
★★☆☆☆

WELCOME TO UMBRIA AND THE MARCHES

TOP REASONS TO GO

★ **Palazzo Ducale, Urbino:** A visit here reveals more about the ideals of the Renaissance than a shelf of history books could.

★ **Assisi, shrine to St. Francis:** Recharge your soul in this rose-color hill town with a visit to the gentle saint's majestic basilica, adorned with great frescoes.

★ **Spoleto, Umbria's musical mecca:** Crowds descend and prices ascend here during summer's Festival dei Due Mondi, but Spoleto's hushed charm enchants year-round.

★ **Tantalizing truffles:** Are Umbria's celebrated "black diamonds" coveted for their pungent flavor, their rarity, or their power in the realm of romance?

★ **Orvieto's Duomo:** Arresting visions of heaven and hell on the facade and brilliant frescoes within make this Gothic cathedral a dazzler.

1 Perugia. Umbria's largest town, filled with university students.

2 Assisi. The fascinating city of St. Francis.

3 Gubbio. A medieval mountainous town in north Umbria.

4 Deruta. A 14th-century town famous for its ceramics.

5 Spello. A pretty hilltop town known for its cuisine.

6 Montefalco. A wine town nicknamed "balcony over Umbria."

7 Spoleto. Come to see the Piazza del Duomo.

8 The Valnerina. Valley of the River Nera.

9 Todi. Considered Umbria's prettiest hill town.

10 Orvieto. Carved out of volcanic rock and known for its cathedral.

11 Urbino. See the Palazzo Ducale here.

12 Loreto. Home to the House of the Virgin Mary.

13 Ascoli Piceno. A major producer of fruit and olives in the region.

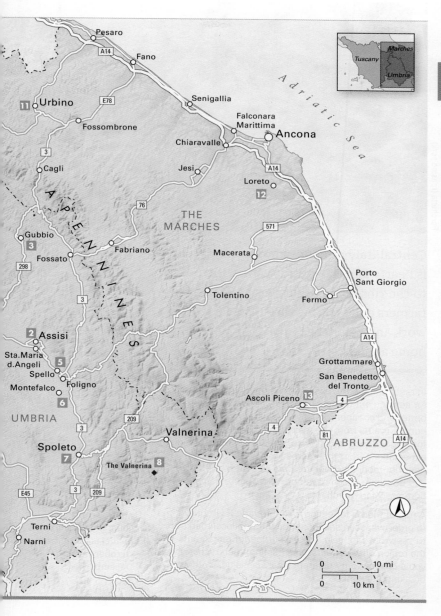

EATING AND DRINKING WELL IN UMBRIA AND THE MARCHES

Porchetta (roasted pork)

Central Italy is mountainous, and its food is hearty and straightforward, with a stick-to-the-ribs quality that sees hardworking farmers and artisans through a long day's work and helps them make the steep climb home at night.

In restaurants here, as in much of Italy, you're rewarded for seeking out the local cuisines, and you'll often find better and cheaper food if you're willing to stray a few hundred yards from the main sights. Spoleto is noted for its good food and service, probably a result of high expectations from the international arts crowd. For gourmet food, however, it's hard to beat Montefalco and Bevagna, which have both excellent restaurants and first-rate wine merchants.

A rule of thumb for eating well throughout Umbria is to order what's in season; stroll through local markets to see what's for sale. Also, a number of restaurants in the region offer *degustazione* (tasting) menus that give you a chance to try different local specialties without breaking the bank.

TASTY TRUFFLES

More truffles are found in Umbria than anywhere else in Italy. Spoleto and Norcia are prime territory for the *tartufo nero* (reddish-black interior and fine white veins), prized for its extravagant flavor and intense aroma.

The mild summer truffle, *scorzone estivo* (black outside and beige inside), is in season from May through December. The *scorzone autunnale* (burnt brown color and visible veins inside) is found from October through December.

OLIVE OIL

Nearly everywhere you look in Umbria, olive trees grace the hillsides. The soil of the Apennines allows the olives to ripen slowly, guaranteeing low acidity, a cardinal virtue of fine oil. Look for restaurants that proudly display their own oil, often a sign that they care about their food.

Umbria's finest oil is found in Trevi, where the local product is intensely green and fruity. You can sample it in the town's wine bars, which often offer olive-oil tastings.

Green and black olives

PORK PRODUCTS

Much of traditional Umbrian cuisine revolves around pork. It can be cooked in wood-fired stoves, sometimes basted with a rich sauce made from innards and red wine. The roasted pork known as *porchetta* is grilled on a spit and flavored with fennel and herbs, leaving a crisp outer sheen.

In Norcia, the art of pork processing has been handed down through generations, so much so that charcuterie producers throughout Italy are often known as *norcini*. Don't miss *prosciutto di Norcia*, which is aged for two years.

LENTILS AND SOUPS

Throughout Umbria, look for *imbrecciata*, a soup of beans and grains,

Salad with spelt

delicately flavored with local herbs. The town of Castelluccio di Norcia is particularly known for its lentils and its *farro* (a grain used by the Romans, similar to wheat), as well as for the variety of beans used in its soups. Other ingredients that find their way into thick Umbrian soups are wild beets, sorrel, mushrooms, spelt, chickpeas, and the elusive, fragrant saffron, grown in nearby Cascia.

WINE

Sagrantino grapes are the star in Umbria's most notable red wines. For centuries they've been used in Sagrantino *passito*, a semisweet wine made by leaving the grapes to dry for a period after picking to intensify their sugar content. In recent decades, Montefalco Sagrantino *secco* (dry) has occupied the front stage. Both passito and secco have a deep, ruby-red color, with a full body and rich flavor.

The abundance of *enotecas* (wineshops and wine bars) has made it easier to arrange tastings. Many establishments also let you sample different olive oils on toasted bread, known as bruschetta. Some wine information centers, such as La Strada del Sagrantino in the town of Montefalco, will help set up appointments for tastings.

Birthplace of saints and home to some of the country's greatest artistic treasures, central Italy is a collection of misty green valleys and picture-perfect hill towns laden with centuries of history.

Umbria and the Marches are the Italian countryside as you've imagined it: verdant farmland, steep hillsides topped with medieval fortresses, and winding country roads. Orvieto's cathedral and Assisi's basilica are two of the most important sights in Italy, while Perugia, Todi, Gubbio, and Spoleto are rich in art and architecture.

East of Umbria, the Marches (Le Marche to Italians) stretch between the Apennines and the Adriatic Sea. It's a region of great turreted castles on high peaks defending passes and roads—a testament to the centuries of battle that have taken place here. Rising majestically in Urbino is a splendid palace, while the town of Ascoli Piceno can lay claim to one of the most beautiful squares in Italy.

MAJOR REGIONS

Northern Umbria. Umbria's largest town, Perugia, is home to some of Perugino's great frescoes. Assisi, the city of St. Francis, is a major pilgrimage site that retains its medieval hill-town character. The quiet towns lying around Perugia include Deruta, which produces exceptional ceramics.

Southern Umbria. A massive castle towers over Spoleto, which is home to the Piazza del Duomo and Filippo Lippi frescoes in its cathedral. Of central Italy's many hill towns, none has a more impressive setting than Orvieto, perched on a plateau 1,000 feet above the surrounding valley. East of Umbria, the steep, twisting roads of this region lead to well-preserved

medieval towns before settling down to the sandy beaches of the Adriatic.

Planning

Getting Here and Around

BUS

Perugia's bus station is in Piazza Partigiani, which you can reach by taking the escalators from the town center.

Local bus services between all the major and minor towns of Umbria are good. Some of the routes in rural areas are designed to serve as many places as possible and are, therefore, quite roundabout and slow. Schedules change often, so consult with local tourist offices before setting out.

CONTACTS Busitalia. ☎ 075/9637001 ⊕ www.fsbusitalia.it. **Flixbus.** ☎ 029/4759208 ⊕ www.flixbus.com. **Sulga.** ☎ 075/5009641 ⊕ www.sulga.it.

CAR

The steep hills and deep valleys that make Umbria and the Marches so idyllic also make for challenging driving. Fortunately, the area has an excellent, modern road network, but be prepared for tortuous roads if your explorations take you off the beaten track.

On the western edge of the region is the Umbrian section of the Autostrada del Sole (A1), Italy's principal north–south highway. It links Florence and Rome with Orvieto and passes near Todi and Terni. The SS3 intersects with the A1 and leads on to Assisi and Urbino. The Adriatica superhighway (A14) runs north–south along the coast, linking the Marches to Bologna and Venice.

Central Umbria is served by a major highway, the RA6, which passes along the shore of Lake Trasimeno and ends in Perugia. Assisi is served by the modern highway S75; the S75 connects to the S3 and S3bis, which cover the heart of the region. Major inland routes connect coastal A14 to large towns in the Marches, but inland secondary roads in mountain areas can be winding and narrow.

TRAIN

Several direct daily trains run by the Italian state railway, Trenitalia, link Florence and Rome with Perugia and Assisi, and local service to the same area is available from Terontola (on the Rome–Florence line) and from Foligno (on the Rome–Ancona line).

Intercity trains between Rome and Florence make stops in Orvieto. The main Rome–Ancona line passes through Narni, Terni, Spoleto, and Foligno.

Making the Most of Your Time

Umbria is a nicely compact collection of character-rich hill towns; you can settle in one, then explore the others, as well as the countryside and forest in between, on day trips.

Perugia, Umbria's largest and liveliest city, is a logical choice for your base, particularly if you're arriving from the north. If you want something a little quieter, virtually any other town in the region will suit your purposes; even Assisi, which overflows with bus tours during the day, is delightfully quiet in the evening and early morning. Spoleto and Orvieto are

the most developed towns to the south, but they're still of modest proportions. Charming Montefalco is a required stop for wine lovers.

If you have the time to venture farther afield, consider trips to Gubbio, northeast of Perugia, and Urbino, in the Marches. Both are worth the time it takes to reach them, and both make for pleasant overnight stays. In southern Umbria, Valnerina and the Piano Grande are out-of-the-way spots with the region's best hiking.

Festivals

If you want to attend an event, make arrangements in advance. During festival time, hotel rooms and restaurant tables are at a premium. A similar caveat applies for Assisi during religious festivals at Christmas, Easter, the feast of St. Francis (October 4), and Calendimaggio (May 1), when pilgrims arrive en masse.

★ Eurochocolate Festival

FESTIVALS | FAMILY | If you've got a sweet tooth and are visiting in fall, book early and head to Perugia for Europe's largest chocolate festival, held for 10 days in mid- to late October. ⊠ *Piazza Moncada, Perugia* ☎ *075/5003848* ⊕ *www.euro-chocolate.com.*

★ Festival dei Due Mondi

FESTIVALS | The annual event, held in late June and early July, is one of the most important cultural happenings in Europe, attracting big names in all branches of the arts, particularly music, opera, and theater. ⊠ *Via Vaita Sant'Andrea, 10, Spoleto* ☎ *0743/776444* ⊕ *www.festivald-ispoleto.com.*

★ Umbria Jazz Festival

FESTIVALS | One of the world's biggest jazz festivals attracts big names and big crowds to Perugia for 10 days in July and to Orvieto for five days in December or January. ⊠ *Piazza Danti, 28, Perugia* ☎ *075/5732432* ⊕ *www.umbriajazz.it.*

Hotels

Virtually every older town, no matter how small, has some kind of hotel. A trend, particularly around Gubbio, Orvieto, and Todi, is to convert old villas, farms, and monasteries into first-class hotels. The natural splendor of the countryside more than compensates for the distance from town—provided you have a car. Hotels in town tend to be simpler than their country cousins, with a few notable exceptions in Spoleto, Gubbio, and Perugia.

Restaurants

As befits a landlocked territory, the cuisine of Umbria is firmly based on local produce. Consequently, most restaurants in the region offer menus that are strictly seasonal, though locals have ensured that the food most associated with Umbria—*tartufi*, or truffles—is available year-round thanks to their mastery of freezing, drying, and preserving techniques.

Truffles are added to a variety of dishes, especially local pastas *stringozzi* (also written *strengozzi* or *strangozzi*) and *ombrichelli*. Lamb, pork, and boar are the most common meats consumed in Umbria, and lentils grown around Castelluccio are highly prized.

Seafood from the Adriatic predominates in the coastal Marches region, often made into *brodetto,* a savory fish soup. Inland, Ascoli Piceno is renowned for its stuffed green olives.

⇨ *Hotel and restaurant reviews have been shortened. For full information, visit Fodors.com. Prices in the hotel reviews are the lowest cost of a standard double room in high season. Prices in the dining reviews are the average cost of a main course at dinner, or, if dinner is not served, at lunch.*

What It Costs in Euros

	$	$$	$$$	$$$$
RESTAURANTS				
	under €15	€15–€24	€25–€35	over €35
HOTELS				
	under €125	€125–€200	€201–€300	over €300

Visitor Information

CONTACT Umbria Regional Tourism Office. ⊠ *Via Mario Angeloni 61, Perugia* ☎ *075/5681260* ⊕ *www.umbriatourism.it.*

Perugia

157 km (98 miles) southeast of Florence, 65 km (40 miles) east of Montepulciano.

Perugia is a majestic, handsome, wealthy city, and with its trendy boutiques, refined cafés, and grandiose architecture, it doesn't try to hide its affluence. A student population of around 30,000 means that the city, with a permanent population of about 165,000, is abuzz with activity throughout the year. Umbria Jazz, one of the region's most important music festivals, attracts music lovers from around the world every July, and Eurochocolate, the international chocolate festival, is an irresistible draw each October for anyone with a sweet tooth.

GETTING HERE AND AROUND
The best approach to the city is by train. The area around the station doesn't attest to the rest of Perugia's elegance, but buses running from the station to Piazza d'Italia, the heart of the old town, are frequent. If you're in a hurry, take the *minimetro,* a one-line subway, to Stazione della Cupa.

If you're driving to Perugia and your hotel doesn't have parking facilities, leave your car in one of the lots close to the center.

Electronic displays indicate the location of lots and the number of available spaces. If you park in the Piazza Partigiani, take the escalators that pass through the fascinating subterranean excavations of the city's Roman foundations and lead to the town center.

👁 Sights

Collegio del Cambio (*Bankers' Guild Hall*)
HISTORIC SIGHT | These elaborate rooms, on the ground floor of the Palazzo dei Priori, served as the meeting hall and chapel of the guild of bankers and money changers. Most of the frescoes were completed by the most important Perugian painter of the Renaissance, Pietro Vannucci, better known as Perugino. He included a remarkably honest self-portrait on one of the pilasters. The iconography includes common religious themes, such

as the Nativity and the Transfiguration seen on the end walls. Booking a time for your visit in advance online or by phone is recommended. ✉ *Corso Vannucci 25, Perugia* ☎ *075/9372110* ⊕ *www.collegiodelcambio.it* 🎟 *€6* 🕐 *Closed Sun. and Mon. afternoon.*

Corso Vannucci
STREET | A string of elegantly connected palazzi expresses the artistic nature of this city center, the heart of which is concentrated along Corso Vannucci. Stately and broad, this pedestrian-only street runs from Piazza Italia to Piazza IV Novembre. Along the way, the entrances to many of Perugia's side streets might tempt you to wander off and explore. But don't stray too far as evening falls, when Corso Vannucci fills with Perugians out for their evening *passeggiata*, a pleasant predinner stroll that may include a pause

Umbria Through the Ages

The earliest inhabitants of Umbria, the Umbri, were thought by the Romans to be the most ancient inhabitants of Italy. Little is known about them: with the coming of Etruscan culture, the tribe fled into the mountains in the eastern portion of the region. The Etruscans, who founded some of the great cities of Umbria, were in turn supplanted by the Romans. Unlike Tuscany and other regions of central Italy, Umbria had few powerful medieval families to exert control over the cities in the Middle Ages—its proximity to Rome ensured that it would always be more or less under papal domination.

In the center of the country, Umbria has, for much of its history, been a battlefield where armies from north and south clashed. Hannibal destroyed a Roman army on the shores of Lake Trasimeno, and the bloody course of the interminable Guelph–Ghibelline conflict of the Middle Ages

was played out here. Dante considered Umbria the most violent place in Italy. Trophies of war still decorate the Palazzo dei Priori in Perugia, and the little town of Gubbio continues a warlike rivalry begun in the Middle Ages—every year it challenges the Tuscan town of Sansepolcro to a crossbow tournament. Today the bowmen shoot at targets, but neither side has forgotten that 500 years ago they were shooting at each other.

In spite of—or perhaps because of—this bloodshed, Umbria has produced more than its share of Christian saints. The most famous is St. Francis, the decidedly pacifist saint whose life shaped the Church of his time. His great shrine at Assisi is visited by hundreds of thousands of pilgrims each year. St. Clare, his devoted follower, was Umbria-born, as were St. Benedict, St. Rita of Cascia, and the patron saint of lovers, St. Valentine.

for an aperitif at one of the many bars that line the street. ⊠ *Perugia.*

Duomo

CHURCH | Severe yet mystical, the Cathedral of San Lorenzo is most famous for being the home of the wedding ring of the Virgin Mary, stolen by the Perugians in 1488 from the nearby town of Chiusi. The ring, kept high up in a red-curtained vault in the chapel immediately to the left of the entrance, is stored under lock and key—15 locks, to be precise—most of the year. It's shown to the public on July 30 (the day it was brought to Perugia) and the second-to-last Sunday in January (Mary's wedding anniversary). The cathedral itself dates from the Middle Ages, and has many additions from the 15th and 16th centuries. ⊠ *Piazza*

IV Novembre, Perugia 🕾 *075/5723832* ⊕ *www.cattedrale.perugia.it* 🕾 *Cathedral audio guide €3, museum €8, Underground Perugia tour €10, Cloister Pass (museum and Underground Perugia) €15* ☉ *Closed during religious services.*

★ Galleria Nazionale dell'Umbria

ART MUSEUM | The region's most comprehensive art gallery is housed on the fourth floor of the Palazzo dei Priori. The collection includes work by native artists—most notably Pintoricchio (1454–1513) and Perugino (circa 1450–1523). In addition to paintings, the gallery has frescoes, sculptures, and some superb examples of crucifixes from the 13th and 14th centuries. ⊠ *Corso Vannucci 19, Piazza IV Novembre, Perugia* 🕾 *075/5721009* *gallerianazionaledellumbria.it* €10 ⊘ *Closed Mon. Nov.–mid-Mar. and Mon. morning mid-Mar.–Oct.*

Museo Archeologico Nazionale

HISTORY MUSEUM | An excellent collection of Etruscan artifacts from throughout the region sheds light on Perugia as a flourishing city long before it fell under Roman domination in 310 BC. Little else remains of Perugia's mysterious ancestors, although the Arco di Augusto, in Piazza Fortebraccio, the northern entrance to the city, is of Etruscan origin. ⊠ *Piazza G. Bruno 10, Perugia* 🕾 *075/5727141* ⊕ *www.musei.umbria.beniculturali.it* €5 ⊘ *Closed Mon. and 3rd Sun. of the month.*

Palazzo dei Priori (*Palace of the Priors*)

GOVERNMENT BUILDING | A series of elegant, connected buildings serves as Perugia's city hall and houses three museums. The buildings string along Corso Vannucci and wrap around the Piazza IV Novembre, where the original entrance is located. The steps here lead to the *Sala dei Notari* (Notaries' Hall). Other entrances lead to the Galleria Nazionale dell'Umbria, the Collegio del Cambio, and the Collegio della Mercanzia.

The Sala dei Notari, which dates from the 13th century and was the original meeting place of the town merchants, had become the seat of the notaries by the second half of the 15th century. Wooden beams and an array of interesting frescoes attributed to Maestro di Farneto embellish the room. ⊠ *Piazza IV Novembre 25, Perugia* Free.

Rocca Paolina

HISTORIC SIGHT | A labyrinth of little streets, alleys, and arches, this underground city was originally part of a fortress built at the behest of Pope Paul III between 1540 and 1543 to confirm papal dominion over the city. Parts of it were destroyed after the end of papal rule, but much still remains. Begin your visit by taking the escalators that descend through the subterranean ruins from Piazza Italia down to Via Masi. In summer, this is the coolest place in the city. ⊠ *Piazza Italia, Perugia* Free.

🍴 Restaurants

Antica Trattoria San Lorenzo Simone Ciccotti

$$$ | **UMBRIAN** | Both the food and the service are outstanding at this popular small, brick-vaulted eatery next to the Duomo. Particular attention is paid to adapting traditional Umbrian cuisine to the modern palate, and there's also a nice variety of seafood dishes on the menu, both à la carte and in good-value tasting menus—the *pacchero* (pasta with smoked eggplant, cod, and scampi) is a real treat. **Known for:** impeccable service; modernized versions of local recipes; fish and truffle tasting menus. $ *Average main: €28* ⊠ *Piazza Danti 19/a, Perugia* 🕾 *075/5721956* ⊕ *anticatrattoriasanlorenzo.com* ⊘ *Closed Wed. and Sun.*

★ Civico 25

$$ | **UMBRIAN** | You won't see many tourists inside this lively bistro-style eatery tucked into an alleyway of Perugia. But you will find tasty Umbrian cuisine, such as Chianina beef tartare and strangozzi pasta, spruced up with an innovative flair and served with a fine choice of wines, including many made by natural producers. **Known for:** local dishes with a gourmet twist; extensive wine selection; friendly service. $ *Average main: €17* ⊠ *Via della Viola 25, Perugia* 🕾 *075/5716376* ⊕ *civico25.com* ⊘ *Closed Sun. No lunch.*

Dal Mi' Cocco

$$ | **UMBRIAN** | Favored by Perugia's university students, this casual spot with vaulted ceilings is fun, crowded, and inexpensive. Fixed-price meals change with the season and include starters, pasta, a main meat course, and dessert; each day of the week brings some new creation *dal cocco* (from the

Perugia

Sights ▼

1 Collegio del Cambio **B2**
2 Corso Vannucci **C2**
3 Duomo **C2**
4 Galleria Nazionale
  dell'Umbria **B2**
5 Museo Archeologico
  Nazionale **C4**
6 Palazzo dei Priori **B2**
7 Rocca Paolina **B4**

Restaurants ▼

1 Antica Trattoria
  San Lorenzo
  Simone Ciccotti **C2**
2 Civico 25 .... **C2**
3 Dal Mi' Cocco **B1**
4 Osteria a Priori **B2**
5 Ristorante
  La Taverna **B3**

Hotels ▼

1 Hotel Castello
  di Reschio **B1**
2 Le Tre Vaselle
  Resort & Spa **D5**
3 Locanda della Posta.... **B3**
4 Posta Donini 1579—
  UNA Esperienze **D5**
5 Sina Brufani **B3**

"coconut," or head) of the chef. **Known for:** authentically casual feel; honest prices; abundant portions. ⑤ *Average main: €18* ✉ *Corso Garibaldi 12, Perugia* ☎ *075/5732511* ⊕ *www.facebook.com/ristorantedalmicocco* ⊘ *Closed Mon. and late July–mid-Aug.*

★ Osteria a Priori

$ | MODERN ITALIAN | This charming wine-and-olive-oil shop with a restaurant (featuring vaulted ceilings and exposed brick) tucked into the back offers up small plates using ingredients with a "zero-kilometer" philosophy: everything comes from local and artisanal Umbrian producers. Regional cheeses, homemade pastas, and slow-cooked meats steal the show, and, as might be expected, the selection of wine is top-notch. **Known for:** all Umbrian products; knowledgeable servers; local, nontouristy atmosphere. ⑤ *Average main: €14* ✉ *Via dei Priori 39, Perugia* ☎ *075/5727098* ⊕ *osteriaapriori.it* ⊘ *Closed Sun.*

Ristorante La Taverna

$$$ | UMBRIAN | Medieval steps lead to a rustic two-story space where wine bottles and artful clutter decorate the walls. The regional menu features lots of delicious homemade pastas and grilled meats prepared by chef Claudio and served up in substantial portions, plus generous shavings of truffle in season. **Known for:** Umbrian specialties; swift and efficient service; welcoming ambience. ⑤ *Average main: €25* ✉ *Via delle Streghe 8, off Corso Vannucci, Perugia* ☎ *075/5732536* ⊕ *www.ristorantelataverna.com.*

Hotels

★ Hotel Castello di Reschio

$$$$ | RESORT | Dating from 1050, this imposing castle-turned-hotel includes two restaurants, tennis courts, an equestrian center, a spa inspired by Roman baths, and exquisite guest rooms featuring beamed ceilings and bespoke furniture designed by the hotel's owners. **Pros:** excellent food options; situated amid gorgeous landscapes; truly a destination in itself. **Cons:** service is stand-offish at times; room decor feels a bit cluttered; incredibly expensive. ⑤ *Rooms from: €1,645* ✉ *34 km (21 miles) SE of Perugia, Tabaccaia di Reschio, Lisciano Niccone* ☎ *075/844362* ⊕ *www.reschio.com* ⊘ *Closed Jan.–mid-Mar.* ⌑ *36 rooms* ❄️ *Free Breakfast.*

Le Tre Vaselle Resort & Spa

$$ | HOTEL | FAMILY | Rooms spread throughout four stone buildings are spacious and graced with floors of typical, red-clay, Tuscan tiles; olive groves surround the outdoor pool, and the indoor spa specializes in wine treatments. **Pros:** perfect for visiting the Torgiano wine area and Deruta; friendly staff; nice pool. **Cons:** somewhat far from Perugia; amid an uninspiring village; service occasionally falters. ⑤ *Rooms from: €199* ✉ *Via Garibaldi 48, Torgiano* ☎ *075/9880447* ⊕ *www.3vaselle.it* ⌑ *52 rooms* ❄️ *Free Breakfast.*

★ Locanda della Posta

$$$ | HOTEL | This friendly, centrally located, converted 18th-century palazzo off the bustling pedestrian-only Corso Vannucci features spacious rooms soothingly decorated in muted colors; some include original frescoes and beamed ceilings. **Pros:** some fine views; central location; exudes good taste and refinement. **Cons:** some street noise; no real lobby; no gym or spa. ⑤ *Rooms from: €201* ✉ *Corso Vannucci 97, Perugia* ☎ *075/5728925* ⊕ *www.locandadellapostahotel.it* ⌑ *17 rooms* ❄️ *Free Breakfast.*

★ Posta Donini 1579 – UNA Esperienze

$$ | HOTEL | FAMILY | Beguilingly comfortable guest rooms set on lovely grounds—where gardeners go quietly about their business—along with a small but charming spa and a well-regarded restaurant make this historical hotel south of Perugia worth a stay. **Pros:** plush atmosphere; a quiet and private getaway;

great restaurant. **Cons:** outside Perugia; uninteresting village; parking area can get full. $ *Rooms from: €143* ✉ *Via Deruta 43, San Martino in Campo* ⊹ *15 km (9 miles) south of Perugia* ☎ *075/609132* ⊕ *www.postadonini.it* ⤴ *48 rooms* ❍ *Free Breakfast.*

Sina Brufani

$$$ | HOTEL | Though a tad old-fashioned, this elegant, centrally located hotel dating from 1884 with a magnificent spa is the most upscale accommodation in town. **Pros:** wonderful location; unique spa area; excellent views from many rooms. **Cons:** could use a refresh; in-house restaurant not up to par; service can be hit-or-miss. $ *Rooms from: €236* ✉ *Piazza Italia 12, Perugia* ☎ *075/5732541* ⊕ *www.sinahotels.com* ⤴ *94 rooms* ❍ *Free Breakfast.*

🍸 Nightlife

With its large student population, the city has plenty to offer in the way of bars and clubs. The best ones are around the city center, off Corso Vannucci.

Bottega del Vino

WINE BAR | This cozy wine bar offers a large selection of *vino* from around Italy as well as light meals; you can't go wrong with the *antipasti* (appetizers), cheese platter, or bruschetta. A live jazz band plays on Wednesday night. ✉ *Via del Sole 1, Perugia* ☎ *075/5716181* ⊕ *www. facebook.com/labottegadelvinopg.*

⭐ Living Café

BARS | Get the best views in town from the large terrace of this café–bar, attached to Ristorante del Sole. It's the most scenic spot in town for aperitivo; happy hour starts daily at 7 pm. ✉ *Via della Rupe 1, Perugia* ☎ *075/5735031* ⊕ *www.ristorantesole.com.*

Marla

COCKTAIL BARS | This eclectic cocktail bar–art gallery showcases DJs and live music, including funk bands on Wednesday evenings. ✉ *Via Bartolo 9/11, Perugia*

☎ *0320/9728186* ⊕ *www.facebook.com/ marla.perugia.*

🛍 Shopping

Stroll down any of Perugia's main streets, including Corso Vannucci, Via dei Priori, Via Oberdan, and Via Sant'Ercolano, and you'll see many well-known designer boutiques and specialty shops.

The most typical thing to buy is chocolate, which you can find almost anywhere. The best-known confections made by Perugina (now owned by Nestlé) are the chocolate-and-hazelnut-filled nibbles called Baci (literally, "kisses"). They're wrapped in silver foil that includes a sliver of paper, like the fortune in a fortune cookie, with multilingual romantic sentiments or sayings.

⭐ Chocostore by Eurochocolate

CHOCOLATE | FAMILY | The official store of the Eurochocolate festival sells bars, truffles, dipped fruits, and more chocolate goodies year-round. There's also a second store at Corso Vannucci 2, as well as a location devoted to Perugina products at Piazza IV Novembre 26/28. ✉ *Piazza IV Novembre 7, Perugia* ☎ *075/5732885* ⊕ *chocostore.eurochocolate.com.*

Perugina

CHOCOLATE | FAMILY | At Baci Perugina's original home, you'll find these iconic chocolates in all shapes and sizes, along with chocolate bars and candies. ✉ *Corso Vannucci 101, Perugia* ☎ *075/5736677* ⊕ *www.sweetcityperugia.it.*

Assisi

28 km (17 miles) southeast of Perugia.

The small town of Assisi is one of the Christian world's most important pilgrimage sites and home of the Basilica di San Francesco—built to honor St. Francis (1182–1226) and erected swiftly after his death. The peace and serenity of the town are a welcome respite from the hustle and bustle of Italy's major cities.

GETTING HERE AND AROUND

Assisi lies on the Terontola–Foligno rail line, with almost hourly connections to Perugia and direct trains to Rome and Florence several times a day. The Stazione Centrale is 4 km (2½ miles) from town, with a bus service about every half hour.

Assisi is easily reached from the A1/E35 autostrada (Rome–Florence) and the SS75 highway. The walled town is closed to traffic, so cars must be left in the parking lots at Porta San Pietro, near Porta Nuova, or beneath Piazza Matteotti. Pay your parking fee at the *cassa* (ticket booth) before you return to your car to get a ticket to insert in the machine that will allow you to exit. It's a short but sometimes steep walk into the center of town; frequent minibuses (buy tickets from a newsstand or tobacco shop near where you park your car) make the rounds for weary pilgrims.

Sights

Assisi is pristinely medieval in architecture and appearance, owing in large part to relative neglect from the 16th century until 1926, when the celebration of the 700th anniversary of St. Francis's death brought more than 2 million visitors. Since then, pilgrims have flocked here in droves, and today several million arrive each year to pay homage. The hill on which Assisi sits rises dramatically from the flat plain, and the town is dominated by a medieval castle at the very top.

★ Basilica di San Francesco

CHURCH | The basilica isn't one church but two: the Gothic church on the upper level, and the Romanesque church on the lower level. Work on this two-tiered monolith was begun in 1228. Both churches are magnificently decorated artistic treasure houses, covered floor to ceiling with some of Europe's finest

frescoes: the Lower Basilica is dim and full of candlelight shadows, while the Upper Basilica is bright and airy.

In the Upper Church, the magnificent frescoes from 13th-century Italian painter Giotto, painted when he was only in his twenties, show that he was a pivotal artist in the development of Western painting. The Lower Church features frescoes by celebrated Sienese painters Simone Martini and Pietro Lorenzetti, as well as by Giotto (or his assistants). ⊠ *Piazza di San Francesco, Assisi* ☎ *075/8190084* ⊕ *www.sanfrancescoassisi.org* ⊠ *Free.*

Basilica di Santa Chiara

CHURCH | The lovely, wide piazza in front of this church is reason enough to visit. The red-and-white-striped facade frames the piazza's panoramic view over the Umbrian plains. Santa Chiara is dedicated to St. Clare, one of the earliest and most fervent of St. Francis's followers and the founder of the order of the Poor Ladies—or Poor Clares—which was based on the Franciscan monastic order. The church contains Clare's body, and in the Cappella del Crocifisso (on the right) is the cross that spoke to St. Francis. A heavily veiled nun of the Poor Clares order is usually stationed before the cross in adoration of the image. ⊠ *Piazza Santa Chiara, Assisi* ☎ *075/812216* ⊕ *www.assisisantachiara. it* ⊠ *Free.*

Cattedrale di San Rufino

CHURCH | St. Francis and St. Clare were among those baptized in Assisi's Cattedrale, which was the principal church in town until the 12th century. The baptismal font has since been redecorated, but it's possible to see the crypt of St. Rufino, the bishop who brought Christianity to Assisi and was martyred on August 11, 238 AD (or 236 AD by some accounts), as well as climb to the bell tower. Admission to the crypt includes the small Museo della Cattedrale, with its detached frescoes and artifacts. ⊠ *Piazza San Rufino, Assisi* ☎ *075/812712* ⊕ *www. assisimuseodiocesano.it* ⊠ *Church free,*

Assisi

Basilica di San Francesco
see feature in this chapter

Rocca Maggiore

Anfiteatro Romano

San Pietro

TO SANTA MARIA DEGLI ANGELI AND TRAIN STATION

TO SAN DAMIANO

0   200 yards
0   200 meters

KEY
- 1 Sights
- 1 Restaurants
- 1 Hotels
- ⌐⌐⌐ Steps

Sights ▶
1 Basilica di San Francesco........**A1**
2 Basilica di Santa Chiara............**F2**
3 Cattedrale di San Rufino..........**F2**
4 Eremo delle Carceri.....**H2**
5 Santa Maria Sopra Minerva................**E2**

Restaurants ▶
1 Buca di San Francesco.........**D2**
2 Osteria Piazzetta dell'Erba.............**E2**
3 Ristorante Bar San Francesco.........**A3**
4 Trattoria Pallotta Assisi **E2**

Hotels ▶
1 Borgo Castello Panicaglia **G1**
2 Castello di Petrata.......**C1**
3 Hotel Umbra **E2**
4 Nun Assisi Relais & Spa Museum **G1**

crypt and museum €3.50, bell tower and museum €4, bell tower €1.50 ☾ *Bell tower and museum closed Wed.*

Eremo delle Carceri

RELIGIOUS BUILDING | About 4 km (2½ miles) east of Assisi is a monastery set in a dense wood against Monte Subasio: the Hermitage of Prisons. This was the place where St. Francis and his followers went to "imprison" themselves in prayer. The only site in Assisi that remains essentially unchanged since St. Francis's time, the church and monastery are the kinds of tranquil places that St. Francis would have appreciated. The walk out from town is very pleasant, and many trails lead from here across the wooded hillside of Monte Subasio. ✉ *Via Eremo delle Carceri 38, Assisi* ✛ *4 km (2½ miles) east of Assisi* ☎ *075/812301* ⊕ *www.santuarioeremodellecarceri.org* 🎟 *Donations accepted.*

Santa Maria Sopra Minerva

CHURCH | Dating from the time of the Emperor Augustus (27 BC–AD 14), this structure was originally dedicated to the Roman goddess of wisdom, and in later times it was used as a monastery and prison before being converted into a church in the 16th century. The expectations raised by the perfect classical facade are not met by the interior, which was subjected to a thorough Baroque transformation in the 17th century. ✉ *Piazza del Comune 14, Assisi* ☎ *075/812361* 🎟 *Free.*

🍴 Restaurants

Buca di San Francesco

$ | **UMBRIAN** | In summer, dine in a cool green garden; in winter, under the low brick arches of the cozy cellars. The unique settings and the first-rate (though straightforward) fare make this central restaurant one of Assisi's busiest; try the namesake homemade spaghetti *alla buca,* served with a roasted mushroom sauce. **Known for:** cozy

atmosphere; historical surroundings; warm and welcoming service. ⑤ *Average main: €14* ✉ *Via Eugenio Brizi 1, Assisi* ☎ *075/812204* ☾ *Closed Mon. and 10 days in late July.*

★ Osteria Piazzetta dell'Erba

$$ | **UMBRIAN** | Hip service and sophisticated presentations attract locals, who enjoy Italian cuisine with unusual twists (think porcini mushroom risotto with blue cheese and blueberries), a nice selection of salads—unusual for an Umbrian restaurant—plus sushi options and intriguing desserts. The enthusiastic young team keep things running smoothly and the energy high. **Known for:** friendly staff; inventive dishes; intimate ambience. ⑤ *Average main: €21* ✉ *Via San Gabriele dell'Addolorata 15/b, Assisi* ☎ *075/815352* ⊕ *www.osteriapiazzetta-dellerba.it* ☾ *Closed Mon. and a few wks in Jan. or Feb.*

Ristorante Bar San Francesco

$$ | **UMBRIAN** | An excellent view of the Basilica di San Francesco from the covered terrace is just one reason to patronize this traditional restaurant, where Umbrian dishes are made with aromatic locally grown herbs. Menus change seasonally and include a fine selection of pastas and mains; appetizers and desserts are also especially good. **Known for:** prime Assisi location; tasty seasonal dishes; pleasant staff. ⑤ *Average main: €23* ✉ *Via di San Francesco 52, Assisi* ☎ *075/812329* ⊕ *www.ristorante-sanfrancesco.com.*

Trattoria Pallotta Assisi

$$ | **UMBRIAN** | At this homey, family-run trattoria with a crackling fireplace and stone walls, the women do the cooking and the men serve the food; try the *strangozzi alla pallotta* (thick spaghetti with a pesto of olives and mushrooms). Connected to the restaurant is an inn whose eight rooms have firm beds and some views across the rooftops of town. **Known for:** traditional local dishes; delicious meat plates, including pigeon and rabbit; fast and courteous service. $ *Average main: €20* ✉ *Vicolo della Volta Pinta 3, Assisi* ☎ *075/8155273* ⊕ *www. trattoriapallotta.it* ⊘ *Closed Tues.*

Hotels

Advance reservations are essential at Assisi's hotels between Easter and October and over Christmas. Latecomers are often forced to stay in the modern town of Santa Maria degli Angeli, 8 km (5 miles) away. As a last-minute option, you can always inquire at restaurants to see if they're renting out rooms.

Until the early 1980s, pilgrim hostels outnumbered ordinary hotels in Assisi, and they present an intriguing and economical alternative to conventional lodgings. They're usually called *conventi* or *ostelli* ("convents" or "hostels") because they're run by convents, churches, or other Catholic organizations. Rooms are spartan but peaceful.

★ Borgo Castello Panicaglia
$$$ | HOTEL | FAMILY | This small, rustic-chic hotel between Assisi and Gubbio, dating from 1266 but thoroughly modernized inside, is a relaxing base for exploring the pretty Umbrian countryside. **Pros:** modern amenities in a historical building; extremely family-friendly atmosphere; tasty and inventive meals. **Cons:** need a car to get around the area; no spa; location is quite rural. $ *Rooms from: €223* ✉ *Località Panicaglia, Nocera* ✛ *24 km (15 miles) northeast of Assisi* ☎ *0742/81663* ⊕ *www.borgocastello-panicaglia.com* ⇄ *17 rooms* ❏ *Free Breakfast.*

★ Castello di Petrata
$$ | HOTEL | Wooden beams and sections of exposed medieval stonework add a lot of character to this 14th-century fortress,

while creature comforts make each individually decorated room a delightful retreat. **Pros:** great views of town and country; medieval character; peaceful pool. **Cons:** slightly isolated; far from Assisi town center; limited choices in restaurant. $ *Rooms from: €142* ✉ *Via Petrata 25, Località Petrata, Assisi* ☎ *075/815451* ⊕ *castellopetrata.it* ⊘ *Closed Sun.–Thurs. Jan. and Feb.* ⇄ *20 rooms* ❏ *Free Breakfast.*

Hotel Umbra
$ | HOTEL | Rooms on the upper floors of this charming 16th-century town house near Piazza del Comune look out over the Assisi rooftops to the valley below, as does the sunny, vine-covered terrace. **Pros:** very central; pleasant small garden; excellent valley views from some rooms. **Cons:** difficult parking; some small rooms; uninspiring breakfasts. $ *Rooms from: €115* ✉ *Via degli Archi 6, Assisi* ☎ *075/812240* ⊕ *www.hotelumbra.it* ⊘ *Closed Nov.–late Mar.* ⇄ *24 rooms* ❏ *Free Breakfast.*

★ Nun Assisi Relais & Spa Museum
$$$$ | HOTEL | Within walking distance of Assisi's restaurants and shops, this monastery built in 1275 has been converted into a thoroughly contemporary, high-end place to stay with a fabulous spa carved out of 2,000-year-old Roman baths. **Pros:** fantastic blend of the historical and modern; excellent restaurant; wonderful place to relax. **Cons:** on the expensive side; on-site parking costs extra; split-level rooms with stairs difficult for those with mobility issues. $ *Rooms from: €697* ✉ *Via Eremo delle Carceri 1A, Assisi* ☎ *075/8155150* ⊕ *www.nunassisi.com* ⇄ *18 rooms* ❏ *Free Breakfast.*

Continued on page 650

ASSISI'S BASILICA DI SAN FRANCESCO

The legacy of St. Francis, founder of the Franciscan monastic order, pervades Assisi. Each year the town hosts several million pilgrims, but the steady flow of visitors does nothing to diminish the singular beauty of one of Italy's most important religious centers. The pilgrims' ultimate destination is the massive Basilica di San Francesco, which sits halfway up Assisi's hill, supported by graceful arches.

The basilica is not one church but two. The Romanesque Lower Church came first; construction began in 1228, just two years after St. Francis's death, and was completed within a few years. The low ceilings and candlelit interior make an appropriately solemn setting for St. Francis's tomb, found in the crypt below the main altar. The Gothic Upper Church, built only half a century later, sits on top of the lower one, and is strikingly different, with soaring arches and tall stained-glass windows (the first in Italy). Inside, both churches are covered floor to ceiling with some of Europe's finest frescoes: the Lower Church is dim and full of candlelit shadows, and the Upper Church is bright and airy.

VISITING THE BASILICA

THE LOWER CHURCH

The most evocative way to experience the basilica is to begin with the dark Lower Church. As you enter, give your eyes a moment to adjust. Keep in mind that the artists at work here were conscious of the shadowy environment—they knew this was how their frescoes would be seen.

In the first chapel to the left, a superb fresco cycle by Simone Martini depicts scenes from the life of St. Martin. As you approach the main altar, the vaulting above you is decorated with the *Three Virtues of St. Francis* (poverty, chastity, and obedience) and *St. Francis's Triumph*, frescoes attributed to Giotto's followers. In the transept to your left, Pietro Lorenzetti's *Madonna and Child with St. Francis and St. John* sparkles when the sun hits it. Notice Mary's thumb; legend has it Jesus is asking which saint to bless, and Mary is pointing to Francis. Across the way in

the right transept, Cimabue's *Madonna Enthroned Among Angels and St. Francis* is a famous portrait of the saint. Surrounding the portrait are painted scenes from the childhood of Christ, done by the assistants of Giotto. Nearby is a painting of the crucifixion attributed to Giotto himself.

You reach the crypt via stairs midway along the nave—on the crypt's altar, a stone coffin holds the saint's body. Steps up from the transepts lead to the cloister, where there's a gift shop, and the treasury, which contains holy objects.

THE UPPER CHURCH

The St. Francis fresco cycle is the highlight of the Upper Church. *(See facing page.)* Also worth special note is the 16th-century choir, with its remarkably delicate inlaid wood. When a 1997 earthquake rocked the basilica, the St. Francis cycle sustained little damage, but portions of the ceiling above the entrance and altar collapsed, reducing their frescoes (attributed to Cimabue and Giotto) to rubble. The painstaking restoration of the Upper Church took two years. ⚠ The dress code is strictly enforced—no bare shoulders or bare knees.

FRANCIS, ITALY'S PATRON SAINT

St. Francis was born in Assisi in 1181, the son of a noblewoman and a well-to-do merchant. His troubled youth included a year in prison. He planned a military career, but after a long illness Francis heard the voice of God, renounced his father's wealth, and began a life of austerity. His mystical embrace of poverty, asceticism, and the beauty of man and nature struck a responsive chord in the medieval mind; he quickly attracted a vast number of followers. Francis was the first saint to receive the stigmata (wounds in his hands, feet, and side corresponding to those of Christ on the cross). He died on October 4, 1226, in the Porziuncola, the secluded chapel in the woods where he had first preached the virtue of poverty to his disciples. St. Francis was declared patron saint of Italy in 1939, and today the Franciscans make up the largest of the Catholic orders.

THE UPPER CHURCH'S ST. FRANCIS FRESCO CYCLE

The 28 frescoes in the Upper Church depicting the life of St. Francis are the most admired works in the entire basilica. They're also the subject of one of art history's biggest controversies. For centuries they thought to be by Giotto (1267–1337), the great early Renaissance innovator, but inconsistencies in style, both within this series and in comparison to later Giotto works, have thrown their origin into question. Some scholars now say Giotto was the brains behind the cycle, but that assistants helped with the execution; others claim he couldn't have been involved at all.

Two things are certain. First, the style is revolutionary— which argues for Giotto's involvement. The tangible weight of the figures, the emotion they show, and the use of perspective all look familiar to modern eyes, but in the art of the time there was nothing like it. Second, these images have played a major part in shaping how the world sees St. Francis. In that respect, who painted them hardly matters.

Starting in the transept, the frescoes circle the church, showing events in the saint's life (and afterlife). Some of the best are grouped near the church's entrance—look for the nativity at Greccio, the miracle of the spring, the death of the knight at Celano, and, most famously, the sermon to the birds.

The St. Francis fresco cycle

1. Homage of a simple man	10. Chasing devils from Arezzo	20. *Death of St. Francis*
2. Giving cloak to a poor man	11. Before the sultan	21. Apparition before Bishop Guido and Fra Agostino
3. Dream of the palace	12. *Ecstasy of St. Francis*	22. Verification of the stigmata
4. Hearing the voice of God	13. Nativity at Greccio	23. *Mourning of St. Clare*
5. Rejection of worldly goods	14. Miracle of the spring	24. Canonization
6. Dream of Innocent III	15. Sermon to the birds	25. Apparition before Gregory IX
7. Confirmation of the rules	16. Death of knight at Celano	26. Healing of a devotee
8. Vision of flaming chariot	17. Preaching to Honorius III	27. Confession of a woman
9. Vision of celestial thrones	18. Apparition at Arles	28. Repentant heretic freed
	19. Receiving the stigmata	

Gubbio

39 km (24 miles) northeast of Perugia, 92 km (57 miles) east of Arezzo.

There's something otherworldly about this jewel of a medieval town, tucked away on the slopes of Monte Ingino. Even in the height of summer, the so-called Città del Silenzio (City of Silence) stays comparatively cool, and its dramatically steep streets remain relatively serene. At Christmas, kitsch is king. From December 7 to January 10, colored lights are strung down the mountainside in a shape resembling an evergreen, creating the world's largest Christmas tree.

Parking in the central Piazza dei Quaranta Martiri—named for 40 hostages murdered by the Nazis in 1944—is easy and secure. It's wise to leave your car there and explore the narrow streets on foot.

GETTING HERE AND AROUND

If you're driving from Perugia, take the SS318, which rises steeply up toward the Gubbio hills. The trip will take you 40 to 50 minutes. The closest train station is Fossato di Vico, about 20 km (12 miles) from Gubbio. Daily buses connect the train station with the city, a 30-minute trip. There are also many buses a day that leave from Perugia's Piazza Partigiani, the main Perugia bus terminal.

VISITOR INFORMATION

CONTACT Gubbio Tourism Office. ✉ *Via Repubblica 15, Gubbio* ☎ *075/9220693* ⊕ *www.ilikegubbio.com.*

 Sights

Basilica di Sant'Ubaldo

CHURCH | Gubbio's famous *ceri*—three 16-foot-tall pillars crowned with statues of Saints Ubaldo, George, and Anthony—are housed in this basilica atop Monte Ingino. The pillars are transported to the Palazzo dei Consoli on the first Sunday of May, in preparation for the Festa dei Ceri, one of central Italy's most spectacular festivals. ✉ *Via Monte Ingino 5, Gubbio* ☎ *075/9273872* ⊕ *diocesigubbio. it* 🖃 *Free.*

Duomo di Gubbio

CHURCH | Set on a narrow street on the highest tier of the town, the Duomo dates from the 13th century, with some Baroque additions—in particular, a lavishly decorated bishop's chapel. ✉ *Via Ducale, Gubbio* ☎ *075/922138* ⊕ *diocesigubbio.it* 🖃 *Free.*

Funivia Colle Eletto

TRANSPORTATION | FAMILY | For a bracing ride to the top of Monte Ingino (where you can see the Basilica di Sant'Ubaldo), hop on the funicular that climbs the hillside just outside the city walls at the eastern end of town. It's more like an oversize metal birdcage than a cable car, and it's definitely not for those who suffer from vertigo. Operating hours vary considerably from month to month; check the funicular's website. ✉ *Via San Girolamo, Gubbio* ☎ *075/9273881* ⊕ *www.funiviagubbio.it* 🖃 *€7 round-trip* 🕙 *Closed Wed. Nov.–Mar.*

Palazzo dei Consoli

HISTORY MUSEUM | Gubbio's striking Piazza Grande is dominated by this medieval palazzo, attributed to a local architect known as Gattapone, who is still much admired by today's residents (though some scholars have suggested that the palazzo was in fact the work of another architect, Angelo da Orvieto). In the Middle Ages, the Parliament of Gubbio assembled in the palace, which has become a symbol of the town and now houses a museum with a collection famous chiefly for the Tavole Eugubine—seven bronze tablets that are written in the ancient Umbrian language, employing Etruscan and Latin characters, and that provide the best key to understanding this obscure tongue.

Also in the museum is a fascinating miscellany of rare coins and earthenware pots. A lofty loggia provides exhilarating views over Gubbio's roofscape and beyond. For a few days at the beginning of May, the palace also displays the famous ceri, the ceremonial wooden pillars at the center of Gubbio's annual festivities. ⊠ *Piazza Grande, Gubbio* ☎ *075/9274298* ⊕ *www.palazzodeiconsoli.it* ⊠ *€7.*

Palazzo Ducale

CASTLE/PALACE | This scaled-down copy of the Palazzo Ducale in Urbino (Gubbio was once the possession of that city's ruling family, the Montefeltro) contains a small museum and a courtyard. Some of the public rooms offer magnificent views. ⊠ *Via Federico da Montefeltro 2, Gubbio* ☎ *075/9275872* ⊕ *www.facebook.com/PalazzoDucaleGubbio* ⊠ *€5* ⊙ *Closed Mon.*

🍴 Restaurants

Ristorante Grotta dell'Angelo

$$ | UMBRIAN | In summer, the handful of outdoor tables are in high demand at this rustic trattoria, which is situated in a hotel of the same name at the lower part of the old town near the main square. The menu features simple local specialties, including *capocollo* (a type of salami), *stringozzi* (Umbrian wheat pasta), and lasagna *tartufata* (with truffles). **Known for:** reasonable prices; good antipasti and grilled meats; homey atmosphere. ⑤ *Average main: €15* ⊠ *Via Gioia 47, Gubbio* ☎ *075/9271747* ⊕ *www.grottadellangelo.it* ⊙ *Closed Tues. and Jan. 7–Feb. 7.*

★ Taverna del Lupo

$$ | UMBRIAN | One of the city's most famous taverns has a menu that includes such indulgences as lasagna made in the Gubbian fashion, with ham and truffles, and the *suprema di faraono* (guinea fowl in a delicately spiced sauce); save room for the excellent desserts. The restaurant also has two fine wine cellars and an extensive wine list. **Known for:** wide menu choice; alluring presentation; good wine list. ⑤ *Average main: €23* ⊠ *Via Ansidei 21, Gubbio* ☎ *075/9274368* ⊕ *www.tavernadellupo.it.*

🛏 Hotels

★ Castello di Petroia

$ | HOTEL | This atmospheric, 12th-century castle 15 km (9 miles) from Gubbio has spacious, antiques-filled, individually decorated rooms—some with decorated or beamed ceilings and stained glass, many with whirlpool tubs—as well as excellent in-house breakfasts and dinners. **Pros:** charming atmosphere; lovely breakfast buffet with handmade cakes and jams; seasonal outdoor swimming pool. **Cons:** decor is on the simple side; beds could be comfier; temperature can be difficult to regulate in guest rooms. ⑤ *Rooms from: €120* ⊠ *Località Petroia, Gubbio* ☎ *075/920287* ⊕ *www.petroia.it* ⊙ *Closed early Jan.–late Mar.* ⬅ *16 rooms* ⦿ *Free Breakfast.*

Hotel Bosone Palace

$ | HOTEL | A former palace is now home to an elegant, if faded, hotel, where elaborate frescoes grace the ceilings of the two enormous suites and delightful breakfast room. **Pros:** friendly welcome; excellent location; low rates. **Cons:** needs a refresh; rooms and bathrooms on the small side; can hear church bells ringing during the night. ⑤ *Rooms from: €92* ⊠ *Via XX Settembre 22, Gubbio* ☎ *075/9220688* ⊕ *www.hotelbosone.com* ⬅ *30 rooms* ⦿ *No Meals.*

★ Vocabolo Moscatelli

$$$$ | HOTEL | Set inside a 12th-century monastery, this romantic boutique hotel is surrounded by greenery and filled with art. **Pros:** gorgeous outdoor pool; breakfast offered all day; supremely comfortable beds. **Cons:** no spa; only kids aged 14 and up allowed; a fair distance from restaurants and sights. ⑤ *Rooms*

*from: €492 ⊠ 44 km (27 miles) w of
Gubbio, Via del Refari 2, Umbertide
☎ 075/5455815 ⊕ www.vocabolo-
moscatelli.com ۞ Closed Jan.–late Mar.
↩ 12 rooms |◎| Free Breakfast.*

Deruta

*19 km (11 miles) southeast of Perugia, 60
km (37 miles) southwest of Gubbio.*

This 14th-century hill town is most
famous for its ceramics. A drive through
the countryside to visit the workshops is
a good way to spend a morning, but be
sure to stop in the medieval town itself.

GETTING HERE AND AROUND
From Perugia, follow the directions for
Rome and the E45 highway; Deruta has
its own exits. There are also buses from
Perugia that take about 30 minutes to
reach Deruta.

VISITOR INFORMATION
CONTACT Deruta Tourism Office.
⊠ *Via Biordo Michelotti 27, Deruta*
☎ *075/9728612* ⊕ *visitderuta.com.*

Sights

Museo Regionale della Ceramica (*Regional
Ceramics Museum*)
HISTORY MUSEUM | It's only fitting that
Deruta is home to an impressive
ceramics museum, which is housed in
the 14th-century former convent of San
Francesco. The most notable pieces are
Renaissance vessels made using the
lustro technique, which originated in Arab
and Middle Eastern cultures some 500
years before coming into use in Italy in
the late 1400s and which incorporates
crushed precious materials such as
gold or silver to create a rich, lustrous
finish. ⊠ *Largo San Francesco, Piazza
del Consoli 12, Deruta* ☎ *075/9711000*
⊕ *www.museoceramicadideruta.it* 🏷 *€7,
includes Pinacoteca Comunale* ۞ *Closed
Tues.–Wed. Nov.–Mar. and Tues. Apr.,
May, and Oct.*

Pinacoteca Comunale
ART MUSEUM | The 14th-century Palazzo
dei Consoli houses Deruta's Municipal
Picture Gallery. The rich collection displayed over two floors includes frescoes
and paintings by the Renaissance artists
Perugino and L'Alunno, among other
works from local churches. Upstairs,
the Pascoli Collection features 17th- and
18th-century canvases, donated by a
descendant of the prominent art collector
and writer Lione Pascoli. Artists represented include Giovanni Battista Gaulli,
Sebastiano Conca, and Francesco Tre-
visani. Note that outside of the summer
months, the museum is only open on
Sunday. ⊠ *Piazza dei Consoli 12, Deruta*
☎ *075/9711000* 🏷 *€7, includes Museo
Regionale Della Ceramica* ۞ *Closed Tues.
June–Sept. and Mon.–Sat. Nov.–May and
Oct.*

Shopping

Deruta is home to dozens of ceramics shops that offer a range of items,
including extra pieces commissioned by
well-known British and North American
tableware manufacturers. A drive along
Via Tiberina Nord takes you past one shop
after another. If you ask, most owners
will take you to see where they actually
throw, bake, and paint their wares.

Spello

*30 km (19 miles) southeast of Perugia, 12
km (7 miles) southeast of Assisi, 33 km
(21 miles) north of Spoleto.*

With well-appointed hotels, this hilltop
town at the edge of Monte Subasio, just
a short drive or train ride from Perugia
or Assisi, makes an excellent base for
exploring the region. Spello's art scene
includes first-rate frescoes by Pinturicchio and Perugino, and contemporary artists can be observed at work in studios
around town. If antiquity is your passion,
the town also has some intriguing

Roman ruins. And the warm, rosy-beige tones of the local *pietra rossa* stone on the buildings brighten even cloudy days.

GETTING HERE AND AROUND

Spello is an easy half-hour drive from Perugia. From the E45 highway, take the exit toward Assisi and Foligno. Merge onto the SS75 and take the Spello exit. There are also regular trains on the Perugia–Assisi line. Spello is 1 km (½ mile) from the train station, and it's a short, steep walk up to Porta Consolare.

From Porta Consolare, continue up the steep main street, which begins as Via Consolare and changes names several times as it crosses the little town. It also follows the original Roman road, so, as it curves around, you'll see winding medieval alleyways to the right and more uniform, Roman-era blocks to the left.

 ## Sights

Santa Maria Maggiore

CHURCH | The two great Umbrian artists Pinturicchio and Perugino hold sway in this 16th-century basilica. Pinturicchio's vivid frescoes in the Cappella Baglioni (1501) are striking for their rich colors, finely dressed figures, and complex symbolism. Among his finest works are the *Nativity, Christ Among the Doctors* and the *Annunciation* (look for Pinturicchio's self-portrait in the Virgin's room). Two pillars on either side of the apse are decorated with frescoes by Perugino (circa 1450–1523). ⊠ *Piazza Matteotti 18, Spello* ☎ *0742/301792* ⊕ *smariamaggiore.com* 🗲 *€3 for Cappella Baglioni* ☾ *Closed Sun. morning and Mon.*

 ## Hotels

Hotel Palazzo Bocci

$ | HOTEL | Lovely sitting areas, a reading room, bucolic ceiling and wall frescoes, and a garden terrace all add quiet, elegant charm to this slightly faded 14th-century property, where you could settle in for a week and take a cooking course or have the staff book you a bicycle or a horseback excursion. **Pros:** central location; splendid views of the valley from public areas and some rooms; abundant breakfasts. **Cons:** noisy in summer months; not all rooms have views; needs a spruce-up. $ *Rooms from: €115* ⊠ *Via Cavour 17, Spello* ☎ *0742/301021* ⊕ *www.palazzobocci.com* 🗲 *23 rooms* ☉❶ *Free Breakfast.*

La Bastiglia

$$ | HOTEL | Polished wooden planks and handwoven rugs have replaced the rustic flooring of a former grain mill, and comfortable sitting rooms and cozy bedrooms are filled with a mix of antique and modern pieces. **Pros:** friendly staff; leisure and wellness facilities; fine views from top-floor rooms, some with terraces. **Cons:** some shared balconies; no elevator and plenty of steps, so pack light; can use an overall refresh. $ *Rooms from: €126* ⊠ *Via Salnitraria 15, Spello* ☎ *0742/651277* ⊕ *labastiglia.com* ☉ *Closed 3 wks in Jan.* 🗲 *34 rooms* ❶ *Free Breakfast.*

Montefalco

18 km (11 miles) south of Spello, 34 km (21 miles) south of Assisi, 48 km (30 miles) southeast of Perugia.

Nicknamed the "balcony over Umbria" for its high vantage point over the valley that runs from Perugia to Spoleto, Montefalco began as an important Roman settlement along the Via Flaminia. The town owes its current name ("Falcon's Mount") to Emperor Frederick II (1194–1250). Obviously a greater fan of falconry than Roman architecture, he destroyed the ancient town, which was known as Coccorone, in 1249, and built in its place what would later become Montefalco. Aside from a few fragments incorporated in a private house just off Borgo Garibaldi, no traces remain of the old Roman center.

The Sagrantino Story

Sagrantino grapes have been used to produce red wine for centuries. The wine began centuries ago as Sagrantino *passito*, a semisweet version in which the grapes are left to dry for a period after picking to intensify the sugar content. One theory traces the origin of Sagrantino back to ancient Rome in the works of Pliny the Elder, the author of the *Natural History*, who referred to the Itriola grape that some researchers think may be Sagrantino. Others believe that, in medieval times, Franciscan friars returned from Asia Minor with the grape. ("Sagrantino" perhaps derives from *sacramenti*, the religious ceremony in which the wine was used.)

The passito is still produced today and is preferred by some. But the big change in Sagrantino wine production came in the past decades, when Montefalco Sagrantino *secco* (dry) came onto the market. Both passito and secco have a deep ruby-red color that tends toward garnet highlights, with a full body and rich flavor.

For the dry wines, producers not to be missed are Paolo Bea, Terre di Capitani, Antonelli, Perticaia, and Arnaldo Caprai. Try those labels for the passito as well, in addition to Ruggeri and Scacciadiavoli. Paolo Bea's biodynamic wines are robust and long-lasting. Terre di Capitani is complex and has vegetable and mineral tones that join tastes of wild berries, cherries, and chocolate—this winemaker pampers his grapes and it shows. Antonelli is elegant, refined, and rich. Perticaia has a full, rounded taste. Caprai is bold and rich in taste. The Ruggeri passito is one of the best, so don't be put off by its homespun label.

At La Strada del Sagrantino in Montefalco's main square, you can pick up a map of the wine route, set up appointments, and book accommodations. Some wineries are small and not equipped to receive visitors. Visit the local *enoteche* (wineshops) and ask the sommeliers to guide you to the smaller producers.

However, Montefalco has more than its fair share of interesting art and architecture and is well worth the drive up the hill. It's also a good place to stop for a meal, as is nearby Bevagna. You need go no farther than the main squares to find a restaurant or bar with a hot meal, and most establishments—both simple and sophisticated—offer a splendid combination of history and small-town hospitality.

GETTING HERE AND AROUND

If you're driving from Perugia, take the E45 toward Rome. Take the Foligno exit, then merge onto the SP445 and follow it into Montefalco. The drive takes around 50 minutes. The nearest train station is in Foligno, about 7 km (4½ miles) away.

From there you can take a taxi or a bus into Montefalco.

VISITOR INFORMATION

CONTACT La Strada del Sagrantino.
✉ *Piazza del Comune 17, Montefalco*
☎ *0742/378490* ⊕ *www.stradadelsagran-tino.it.*

Restaurants

★ Enoteca L'Alchimista

$$ | UMBRIAN | "The Alchemist" is an apt name, as the chef's transformations are magical, and everything can be paired with wines from the restaurant's extensive selection. Though pasta, veggie, and meat dishes change seasonally, the homemade gnocchi in Sagrantino wine sauce, always

Southern Umbria

on offer, wins raves from guests, plus all the delicious desserts are made on the premises. **Known for:** extensive wine list; congenial setting and atmosphere; refined but relaxed dining. $ *Average main: €18* ✉ *Piazza del Comune 14, Montefalco* ☎ *0742/378558* ⊕ *www.ristorantealchimista.it* 🕒 *Closed Tues.*

🛏 Hotels

★ Palazzo Bontadosi Hotel & Spa

$$ | **HOTEL** | This charming boutique hotel, set in an 18th-century palace overlooking the main square, has spacious, individually decorated rooms, where original frescoes and beamed ceilings contrast with modern furnishings and some bathrooms have deep soaking tubs. **Pros:** sophisticated, design-focused vibe; spa in medieval cellars has a private Turkish bath and soaking pool; friendly service.

Cons: rooms facing the square can be noisy; no gym; small breakfast selection. $ *Rooms from: €152* ✉ *Piazza del Comune 19, Montefalco* ☎ *0742/379357* ⊕ *hotelbontadosi.it* 🛏 *12 rooms* ❖ *Free Breakfast.*

Villa Pambuffetti

$$ | **HOTEL** | If you want to be pampered in the refined atmosphere of a private villa, this is the spot, with the warmth of a fireplace in the winter, a pool to cool you down in summer, and cozy reading nooks and guest rooms year-round. **Pros:** peaceful gardens; cooking courses offered; excellent dining room. **Cons:** outside the town center; grounds could be better kept; dated feel. $ *Rooms from: €160* ✉ *Viale della Vittoria 20, Montefalco* ☎ *0742/379417* ⊕ *www.villapambuffetti.it* 🛏 *15 rooms* ❖ *Free Breakfast.*

Spoleto

24 km (15 miles) southeast of Montefalco, 46 km (29 miles) south of Assisi, 63 km (39 miles) southeast of Perugia, 80 km (50 miles) east of Orvieto.

For most of the year, Spoleto is one more in a pleasant succession of sleepy hill towns, resting regally atop a mountain. But for more than two weeks every summer the town shifts into high gear for a turn in the international spotlight during the Festival dei Due Mondi (Festival of Two Worlds), an extravaganza of theater, opera, music, painting, and sculpture.

As the world's top artists vie for honors, throngs of art aficionados vie for hotel rooms. If you plan to spend the night in Spoleto during the festival, make sure you have confirmed reservations, or you may find yourself scrambling at sunset.

GETTING HERE AND AROUND

Spoleto is an hour's drive from Perugia. From the E45 highway, take the exit toward Assisi and Foligno, then merge onto the SS75 until you reach the Foligno Est exit. Merge onto the SS3, which leads to Spoleto. Parking options inside the city walls include Piazza Campello (just below the Rocca) on the southeast end, Via del Trivio to the north, and Piazza San Domenico on the west end. You can also park at Piazza della Vittoria farther north, just outside the walls, or at one of several well-marked lots near the train station.

There are regular trains on the Perugia–Foligno line. If you arrive by train, you can walk 1 km (½ mile) from the station to the entrance to the lower town, but it's a 15-minute uphill walk to the center, so you may want to take a local bus or a taxi. Regular bus connections are every 15–30 minutes.

VISITOR INFORMATION

Consider purchasing the Spoleto Card (€12), which provides entry to several museums—the Casa Romano, La Rocca Albornoz, and the Teatro Romano among them—as well as access to guided tours. It's sold online (⊕ *www.spoletocard.it*), at the included sights, and at some hotels.

CONTACT Spoleto Tourism Office. ⊠ *Largo Ferrer 6, off Corso Mazzini, Spoleto* ☎ *0743/218620* ⊕ *www.comune.spoleto.pg.it.*

Sights

The walled city is set on a slanting hillside, with the most interesting sections clustered toward the upper portion. Like most other towns with narrow, winding streets, Spoleto is best explored on foot. Bear in mind that much of the city is on a steep slope, so there are lots of stairs and steep inclines. The well-worn stones can be slippery even when dry; wear rubber-sole shoes for good traction.

Casa Romana (*Roman House*)
RUINS | FAMILY | Spoleto became a Roman colony in the 3rd century BC, but the best excavated remains date from the 1st century AD. Well preserved among them is the Casa Romana. According to an inscription, it belonged to Vespasia Polla, the mother of Emperor Vespasian (one of the builders of the Colosseum and perhaps better known by the Romans for taxing them to install public toilets, later called "Vespasians"). The rooms, arranged around a large central atrium built over an *impluvium* (rain cistern), are decorated with black-and-white geometric mosaics. ⊠ *Palazzo del Municipio, Via di Visiale 9, Spoleto* ☎ *0743/40255* ⊡ *€3; included with Spoleto Card* ⊗ *Closed Tues.*

★ **Duomo di Spoleto** (*Spoleto Cathedral*)
CHURCH | One of the finest cathedrals in the region is lit by eight rose windows that are especially dazzling in the late afternoon sun. Above the church's

entrance is Bernini's bust of Pope Urban VIII (1568–1644), who had the church redecorated in 17th-century Baroque; fortunately he didn't touch the 15th-century frescoes painted in the apse by Fra Filippo Lippi (circa 1406–69) between 1466 and 1469. These immaculately restored masterpieces—the *Annunciation, Nativity,* and *Dormition*—tell the story of the life of the Virgin. The *Coronation of the Virgin,* adorning the half dome, is the literal and figurative high point. Portraits of Lippi and his assistants are on the right side of the central panel. ⊠ *Piazza del Duomo 2, Spoleto* ☎ *0577/286300* ⊕ *www.duomospoleto.it* ◪ *Cathedral is free, €5 for audio guide, €9 for a tour (Apr.–Oct.) including the upper part of the Cathedral, Bell Tower, Sala della Grande Bellezza, Diocesan Museum, and Church of Sant'Eufemia.*

La Rocca Albornoz

CASTLE/PALACE | FAMILY | Built in the mid-14th century for Cardinal Egidio Albornoz, this massive fortress served as a seat for the local pontifical governors, a tangible sign of the restoration of the Church's power in the area when the pope was ruling from Avignon. Several popes spent time here, and, in 1499, one of them, Alexander VI, sent his capable teenage daughter, Lucrezia Borgia (1480–1519), to serve as governor for three months. The Gubbio-born architect Gattapone (14th century) used the ruins of a Roman acropolis as a foundation and incorporated materials from many Roman-era sites, including the Teatro Romano.

La Rocca's plan is long and rectangular, with six towers and two grand courtyards, an upper loggia, and grand interior reception rooms. In the largest tower, Torre Maestà, you can visit an apartment with some interesting frescoes. ⊠ *Piazza Campello, Spoleto* ☎ *0743/224952* ◪ *€8.50, including the Museo Nazionale del Ducato; free with Spoleto Card.*

★ Palazzo Collicola Arti Visive

ART MUSEUM | Spoleto's compact but delightful modern art museum, housed in an 18th-century palace, features a fine collection of works from Italian contemporary artists, including renowned Spoleto sculptor Leoncillo and Umbria-based American sculptor Barbara Pepper. International artists such as Alexander Calder and Richard Serra are also represented, and an entire room is devoted to a large-scale wall drawing by Sol Lewitt. The Appartamento Nobile is a reproduction of an 18th-century nobleman's house, and the Pictures Gallery has paintings from the 16th to 19th centuries. ⊠ *Piazza Collicola 1, Spoleto* ☎ *0743/46434* ⊕ *www.palazzocollicola.it* ◪ *€9; included with Spoleto Card* ☽ *Closed Tues. and Wed.*

★ Ponte delle Torri (*Bridge of the Towers*)

BRIDGE | Standing massive and graceful through the deep gorge that separates Spoleto from Monteluco, this 14th-century bridge is one of Umbria's most photographed monuments, and justifiably so. Built over the foundations of a Roman-era aqueduct, it soars 262 feet above the forested gorge—higher than the dome of St. Peter's in Rome. A must-see sight, the bridge offers spectacular views of Monteluco, and is particularly impressive on a starry night. ⊠ *Via del Ponte, Spoleto* ◪ *Free.*

Teatro Romano

RUINS | FAMILY | The Romans who colonized the city in 241 BC constructed this small theater in the 1st century AD; for centuries afterward it was used as a quarry for building materials. The most intact portion is the hallway that passes under the *cavea* (stands). The rest was heavily restored in the early 1950s and serves as a venue for Spoleto's Festival dei Due Mondi. The theater was the site of a gruesome episode in Spoleto's history: during the medieval struggle between Guelph (papal) and Ghibelline (imperial) forces, Spoleto took the side of the Holy Roman Emperor. Afterward,

KEY

① Sights

① Restaurants

① Hotels

Spoleto

0   100 yards

0   100 meters

400 Guelph supporters were massacred in the theater, their bodies burned in an enormous pyre. In the end, the Guelphs were triumphant, and Spoleto was incorporated into the states of the Church in 1354. ⊠ *Piazza della Libertà, Spoleto* ☎ *0743/223277* ⌑ *€5, free with Spoleto Card* ⊘ *Closed Mon.–Wed.*

🍴 Restaurants

Il Tartufo

$$ | **UMBRIAN** | As the name indicates, dishes prepared with truffles are the specialty here—don't miss the risotto al tartufo. Incorporating the ruins of a Roman villa, the surroundings are rustic on the ground floor and more modern upstairs; in summer, tables appear outdoors, and the traditional fare is spiced up to appeal to the cosmopolitan crowd attending (or performing in) the Festival dei Due Mondi. **Known for:**

recipes incorporating truffles; charming staff; abundant portions, well presented. ⑤ *Average main: €20* ⊠ *Piazza Garibaldi 24, Spoleto* ☎ *0743/40236* ⊕ *www.ristoranteil-tartufo.it* ⊘ *Closed Mon. and early Jan.– early Feb. No dinner Sun.*

Il Tempio del Gusto

$$ | **UMBRIAN** | In charming shabby-chic environs, this welcoming eatery near the Arco di Druso (ancient Roman arch) serves up Italian with a subtle twist. Along with an extensive selection of thoughtfully chosen Umbrian wines, you'll find lots of veggie options, mounds of truffles in season, and, to finish things off, a superlative version of Spoleto sponge cake. **Known for:** flavorful Umbrian cuisine; friendly atmosphere; quaint setting. ⑤ *Average main: €18* ⊠ *Via Arco di Druso 11, Spoleto* ☎ *0743/47121* ⊕ *www. iltempiodelgusto.com* ⊘ *Closed Thurs.*

★ Ristorante Apollinare

$$ | UMBRIAN | Low wooden ceilings and flickering candlelight make this monastery from the 10th and 11th centuries Spoleto's most romantic spot; in warm weather, you can dine under a canopy on the piazza. The kitchen serves sophisticated, innovative variations on local dishes, including long, slender strengozzi pasta with such toppings as cherry tomatoes, mint, and a touch of red pepper or (in season) porcini mushrooms or truffles. **Known for:** modern versions of traditional Umbrian dishes; intimate and elegant setting; impeccable service. $ *Average main: €22* ⊠ *Via Sant'Agata 14, Spoleto* ☎ *0743/223256* ⊕ *www.ristoranteapollinare.it* ⊗ *Closed Tues.*

Ristorante Il Panciolle

$ | UMBRIAN | A small garden filled with lemon trees in the heart of Spoleto's medieval quarter provides one of the most appealing settings you could wish for. Dishes, which change throughout the year, might include pastas served with asparagus or mushrooms, as well as grilled meats; more expensive dishes prepared with fresh truffles are also available in season. **Known for:** authentic local cuisine; affable staff; panoramic terrace. $ *Average main: €14* ⊠ *Via del Duomo 3/5, Spoleto* ☎ *0743/45677* ⊕ *www.ilpanciolle.it* ⊗ *Closed Wed. Sept.–Mar.*

 Hotels

★ Hotel San Luca

$ | HOTEL | Hand-painted friezes decorate the walls of the spacious guest rooms, and elegant comfort is the grace note throughout—you can sip afternoon tea in oversize armchairs by the fireplace or take a walk in the sweet-smelling rose garden. **Pros:** very helpful staff; spacious rooms; close to escalators for exploring city. **Cons:** outside the town center; restaurant only open for groups; can feel soulless in winter. $ *Rooms from: €104* ⊠ *Via Interna delle Mura 21, Spoleto*

☎ *0743/223399* ⊕ *www.hotelsanluca.com* ↝ *35 rooms* ⫶◯⫶ *Free Breakfast.*

★ Palazzo Leti Residenza d'Epoca

$$ | HOTEL | Fabulously landscaped gardens, complete with fountains and sculptures, along with panoramic views provide a grand entrance to this late-13th-century residence turned charming hotel high up in Spoleto's old town. **Pros:** feels like a private hideaway; unbeatable views; friendly owners happy to help. **Cons:** reaching on-site parking can be tricky; often booked far in advance; few amenities (no restaurant, gym, or spa). $ *Rooms from: €130* ⊠ *Via degli Eremiti 10, Spoleto* ☎ *0743/224930* ⊕ *www.palazzoleti.com* ↝ *12 rooms* ⫶◯⫶ *Free Breakfast.*

The Valnerina

The Valnerina is 27 km (17 miles) southeast of Spoleto.

The Valnerina (the valley of the River Nera, to the southeast of Spoleto) is the most beautiful of central Italy's many well-kept secrets. The twisting roads that serve the rugged landscape are poor, but the drive is well worth the effort for its forgotten medieval villages and dramatic mountain scenery.

GETTING HERE AND AROUND

You can head into the area from Terni on the S209, or on the SP395 bis north of Spoleto, which links the Via Flaminia (SS3) with the middle reaches of the Nera Valley through a tunnel.

 Sights

Cascata delle Marmore

WATERFALL | FAMILY | The road east of Terni (SS3 Valnerina) leads 10 km (6 miles) to the Cascata delle Marmore (Waterfalls of Marmore), which, at 541 feet, are the highest in Europe. A canal was dug by the Romans in the 3rd century BC to prevent flooding in the nearby agricultural

Hiking the Umbrian Hills

Magnificent scenery makes the heart of Italy excellent walking, hiking, and mountaineering country. In Umbria, the area around Spoleto is particularly good; several pleasant, easy, and well-signed trails begin at the far end of the Ponte alle Torri bridge over Monteluco. From Cannara, an easy half-hour walk leads to the fields of Pian d'Arca, the site of St. Francis's sermon to the birds.

For slightly more arduous walks, follow the saint's path uphill from Assisi to the Eremo delle Carceri, and then continue along the trails that crisscross Monte Subasio. At 4,250 feet, the treeless summit affords views of Assisi, Perugia, far-off Gubbio, and the distant mountain ranges of Abruzzo. For even more challenging hiking, the northern reaches of the Valnerina are exceptional; the mountains around Norcia should not be missed.

Throughout Umbria and the Marches, most recognized trails are marked with the distinctive red-and-white blazes of the Club Alpino Italiano. Tourist offices are a good source for walking and climbing itineraries to suit all ages and levels of ability, and bookstores, *tabacchi* (tobacconists), and *edicole* (newsstands) often have maps and guides that detail the best area routes. Wear comfortable walking shoes or hiking boots, depending on your route, and bring plenty of water.

plains. Nowadays, the waters are often diverted to provide hydroelectric power for Terni, reducing the roaring falls to an unimpressive trickle, so check with the information office at the falls (there's a timetable on its website) or with Terni's tourist office before heading here. On summer evenings, when the falls are in full spate, the cascading water is floodlit to striking effect. The falls are usually at their most energetic at midday and at around 4 pm. This is a good place for hiking, except in December and January, when most trails may be closed. ⊠ *SP79, Terni ✛ 10 km (6 miles) east of Terni* ☎ *0744/67561* ⊕ *www.cascatadellemarmore.info* 🎫 *€12.*

Norcia

TOWN | The birthplace of St. Benedict, Norcia is best known for its Umbrian pork and truffles, which you can sample at shops throughout town. Norcia exports truffles to France and hosts a truffle festival, Nero Norcia, every February. Though the town itself is still under reconstruction following a devastating 2016 earthquake, the surrounding mountains provide spectacular hiking. ⊠ *42 km (25 miles) east of Spoleto, 67 km (42 miles) northeast of Terni.*

★ Piano Grande

VIEWPOINT | A spectacular mountain plain 25 km (15 miles) to the northeast of the valley, Piano Grande is a hang glider's paradise and a wonderful place for a picnic or to fly a kite. It's also nationally famous for the quality of the lentils grown here, which are a traditional part of every Italian New Year's feast. ⊠ *Piano Grande, Teramo* 🎫 *Free.*

Hotels

★ Palazzo Seneca

$$ | HOTEL | The Bianconi family oversees this elegant hotel, which is housed in a 16th-century palace—just around the corner from Norcia's main square—and features stone floors, vaulted ceilings, and a Michelin-star restaurant. **Pros:** fabulous restaurant (book well in advance); lots of style and charm; central location. **Cons:** no parking at the hotel; breakfast not up to par; no gym. $ Rooms from: €198 ⊠ Via Cesare Battisti 12, Norcia ☎ 0743/817434 ⊕ www.palazzoseneca. com ⊙ Closed Jan.–Feb. ⟿ 24 rooms ⦿ Free Breakfast.

Todi

34 km (22 miles) south of Perugia, 34 km (22 miles) northeast of Orvieto, 46 km (29 miles) northwest of Spoleto.

As you stand on Piazza del Popolo, looking out onto the Tiber Valley below, it's easy to see why Todi is often described as Umbria's prettiest hill town. Legend has it that the town was founded by the Umbri, who followed an eagle who had stolen a tablecloth. They liked this lofty perch so much that they settled here for good. The eagle is now perched on the insignia of the medieval palaces in the main piazza.

GETTING HERE AND AROUND
Todi is best reached by car, as the town's two train stations are way down the hill and connected to the center by infrequent bus service. From Perugia, follow the E45 toward Rome. Take the Todi/Orvieto exit, then follow the SS79 bis into Todi. The drive takes around 40 minutes.

VISITOR INFORMATION
CONTACT Todi Tourism Office. ⊠ Piazza del Popolo 29–30, Todi ☎ 075/8956227 ⊕ www.comune.todi.pg.it.

Sights

Duomo di Todi (Todi Cathedral)
CHURCH | One end of the Piazza del Popolo is dominated by this 12th-century Romanesque-Gothic masterpiece, built over the site of a Roman temple. The simple facade is enlivened by a finely carved rose window. Look up at that window as you step inside and you'll notice its peculiarity: each "petal" of the rose has a cherub's face in the stained glass. Also take a close look at the capitals of the double columns with pilasters: perched between the acanthus leaves are charming medieval sculptures of saints—Peter with his keys, George and the dragon, and so on. You can see the rich brown tones of the wooden choir near the altar, but unless you have binoculars or request special permission in advance, you can't get close enough to see all the exquisite detail in this Renaissance masterpiece of woodworking (1521–30). The severe, solid mass of the Duomo is mirrored by the Palazzo dei Priori (1595–97) across the way. ⊠ Piazza del Popolo 1, Todi ☎ 335/5420520 ⊕ www.chiesaditodi.it ⛪ Free.

Piazza del Popolo
PLAZA/SQUARE | Built above the Roman Forum, Piazza del Popolo is Todi's high point, a model of spatial harmony with stunning views of the surrounding countryside. In the best medieval tradition, the square was conceived to house both the temporal and the spiritual centers of power. ⊠ Piazza del Popolo, Todi ⛪ Free.

⦿ Restaurants

★ Pane & Vino
$$ | ITALIAN | This charmingly rustic restaurant in Todi's historic center specializes in "dishes of the past" made from local ingredients. Choose from a fine selection of meat and cheese antipasti, house-made pastas and soups, and hearty meat dishes—accompanied by truffles in season—along with tempting daily specials, served with well-priced wines from a comprehensive list. **Known for:** focus on organic products from small producers; fabulous selection of wines from across Italy; friendly, knowledgeable service. $ Average main: €20 ⊠ Via Augusto Ciuffelli 33, Todi ☎ 075/8945448 ⊕ panevinotodi.com ⊙ Closed Wed.

Ristorante Umbria

$$ | **UMBRIAN** | Todi's most popular restaurant for more than four decades is reliable for its sturdy country food and the wonderful view from its terrace; because it has only 16 tables outside, make sure you reserve ahead. In winter, try lentil soup, risotto with saffron and porcini mushrooms, or wild boar with polenta; steaks, accompanied by a rich dark-brown wine sauce, are good any time of year. **Known for:** traditional Umbrian dishes; terrific vista from terrace; friendly atmosphere. $ *Average main: €20* ✉ *Via San Bonaventura 13, Todi* ☎ *075/8942737* ⊕ *www.ristoranteumbria.it* ⊗ *Closed Tues. and 3–4 wks in Jan. and Feb.*

 Hotels

★ Relais Todini

$$$ | **HOTEL** | Inside a 14th-century manor house 9 km (6 miles) southeast of Todi, this elegant hotel sits adjacent to working vineyards (don't forget to sample the Todini wines) and features such welcome amenities as a spa, outdoor pool, and gym. **Pros:** quiet location; lots of relaxing public spaces, including a spa; walking paths around the grounds. **Cons:** spa feels a bit small; priced on the high side; reception not staffed 24/7. $ *Rooms from: €260* ✉ *Frazione Collevalenza, Todi* ☎ *075/887521* ⊕ *www.relaistodini.com* ⊗ *Closed weekdays Nov.–Mar.* ⇨ *12 rooms* ❍❙ *Free Breakfast.*

Residenza D'Epoca San Lorenzo Tre

$ | **HOTEL** | Magnificent valley views are paired with 19th-century charm at this property filled with paintings, antique furnishings, and period knickknacks. **Pros:** old-world atmosphere; excellent central location; spectacular views. **Cons:** few modern amenities; long flight of steps to enter; small basic bathrooms. $ *Rooms from: €115* ✉ *Via San Lorenzo 3, Todi* ☎ *075/8944555* ⊕ *www.sanlorenzo3.it* ⊗ *Closed Nov.–Mar.* ⇨ *6 rooms* ❍❙ *Free Breakfast.*

Orvieto

30 km (19 miles) southwest of Todi, 78 km (48 miles) southwest of Perugia, 81 km (51 miles) west of Spoleto.

Carved from an enormous plateau of volcanic rock high above a green valley, Orvieto has natural defenses that made the high walls seen in many Umbrian towns unnecessary. The Etruscans were the first to settle here, digging a honeycombed network of more than 1,200 wells and storage caves out of the soft stone.

The Romans attacked, sacked, and destroyed the city in 283 BC. Since then, it has grown up out of the rock into an enchanting maze of alleys and squares. Orvieto was solidly Guelph in the Middle Ages, and, for several hundred years, popes sought refuge in the city, at times needing protection from their enemies, at times seeking respite from the summer heat in Rome.

When painting his frescoes inside the Duomo, Luca Signorelli asked that part of his contract be paid in Orvietan wine, and he was neither the first nor the last to appreciate the region's popular white. In past times, the caves carved underneath the town were used to ferment the Trebbiano grapes used in making Orvieto Classico. Although local wine production has moved out to more traditional vineyards, you can still while away the afternoon with tastings at any number of shops in town.

GETTING HERE AND AROUND

Orvieto is well connected by train to Rome, Florence, and Perugia. It's also adjacent to the A1 autostrada that runs between Florence and Rome. Parking areas in the upper town tend to be crowded. A better idea is to follow the signs for the Campo Della Fiera parking lot, then take the escalators or elevator that carry people up the hill.

VISITOR INFORMATION

The Carta Orvieto Unica (single ticket) is expensive but a great deal if you want to visit everything. For €25 you get admission to nine museums and monuments, including the three major sights in town—Cappella di San Brizio (at the Duomo), Museo Etrusco Claudio Faina, and Orvieto Underground—along with entry to the Torre del Moro, with views of Orvieto, plus a bus and funicular pass. You can buy the card online or at any of the included museums.

CONTACT Orvieto Tourism Office. ⊠ *Piazza del Duomo 24, Orvieto* ☎ *0763/341772* ⊕ *liveorvieto.com.*

 Sights

⭐ **Duomo di Orvieto** (*Orvieto Cathedral*)
CHURCH | Orvieto's stunning cathedral was built to commemorate the Miracle at Bolsena. In 1263, a young priest who questioned the miracle of transubstantiation (in which the Communion bread and wine become the flesh and blood of Christ) was saying Mass at nearby Lago di Bolsena. A wafer he had just blessed suddenly started to drip blood, staining the linen covering the altar. Thirty years later, construction began on a duomo in Orvieto to celebrate the miracle and house the stained altar cloth.

The cathedral's interior is rather vast and empty; the major works are in the transepts. To the left is the Cappella del Corporale, where the square linen cloth (*corporale*) is kept in a golden reliquary that's modeled on the cathedral and inlaid with enamel scenes of the miracle. In the right transept is the Cappella di San Brizio, which holds one of Italy's greatest fresco cycles, notable for its influence on Michelangelo's *Last Judgment*, as well as for the extraordinary beauty of the figuration. In these works, a few by Fra Angelico and most by Luca Signorelli, the damned fall to hell, demons breathe fire and blood, and Christians are martyred.

The Museo dell'Opera dell Duomo next to the cathedral is worth a short visit to see its small collection of historical paintings and sculptures, along with the Museo Emilio Greco, which houses 32 bronze sculptures from its namesake sculptor, who created the cathedral's bronze doors. ⊠ *Piazza del Duomo, Orvieto* ☎ *0763/342477* ⊕ *www.duomodiorvieto.it* 🎫 *€5, including Cappella di San Brizio, Museo dell'Opera dell Duomo, and Museo Emilio Greco; included with Carta Unica.*

Museo Etrusco Claudio Faina

HISTORY MUSEUM | This superb private collection, beautifully arranged and presented, goes far beyond the usual smattering of local remains displayed at many museums. The collection is particularly rich in Greek- and Etruscan-era pottery, from large Attic amphorae (6th–4th century BC) to Attic black- and red-figure pieces to Etruscan *bucchero* (dark-reddish clay) vases. Other interesting items include a 6th-century sarcophagus and a substantial display of Roman-era coins. ⊠ *Piazza del Duomo 29, Orvieto* ☎ *0763/341216* ⊕ *museofaina.it* 🎫 *€6* 🕑 *Closed Tues.*

Orvieto Underground

RUINS | **FAMILY** | More than just about any other town, Orvieto has grown from its own foundations. The Etruscans, the Romans, and those who followed dug into the tufa (the same soft volcanic rock from which catacombs were made) to create more than 1,000 separate cisterns, caves, passages, storage areas, and production areas for wine and olive oil. Much of the tufa removed was used as building blocks for the city that exists today, and some was partly ground into *pozzolana*, which was made into mortar. You can see the labyrinth of dugout chambers beneath the city on the Orvieto Underground tour, which runs daily at 11, 12:15, 4, and 5:15 (reservations recommended), departing from Piazza del Duomo 23. ⊠ *Piazza del Duomo 23, Orvieto* ☎ *0763/344891* ⊕ *www.*

orvietounderground.it *Tours €8; included with Carta Unica* ⚷ *Reservations recommended 1 day prior in summer.*

Pozzo della Cava

RUINS | If you're short on time but want a quick look at the cisterns and caves beneath the city, head for the Pozzo della Cava, an Etruscan well for spring water. On a walk through nine excavated caves you can see the fascinating ruins of medieval houses and unearthed archaeological artifacts. ⊠ *Via della Cava 28, Orvieto* ☎ *0763/342373* ⊕ *www.pozzodellacava.it* *€4; included with Carta Unica* ۞ *Closed mid- to late Jan.*

⎊ Restaurants

Le Grotte del Funaro

$$ | **UMBRIAN** | Dine inside tufa caves under central Orvieto, where the two windows afford splendid views of the hilly countryside. The traditional Umbrian food is reliably good, with simple grilled meats and vegetables and pizzas—oddly, though, the food is outclassed by an extensive wine list, with top local and Italian labels and quite a few rare vintages. **Known for:** unusual setting; crusty pizzas; good choice of wines. ⑤ *Average main: €17* ⊠ *Via Ripa Serancia 41, Orvieto* ☎ *0763/343276* ⊕ *www.grottedelfunaro. com* ۞ *Closed Mon. and 10 days in July.*

Ristorante Maurizio

$$ | **UMBRIAN** | Off a busy pedestrian street near the Duomo, this welcoming, family-owned restaurant has an ultra contemporary look but is actually housed in a 14th-century medieval building with arched ceilings. The Martinelli family's own products, including balsamic vinegar, olive oil, and pasta, are used in their robustly flavored dishes, and you can also sample their well-regarded Montefalco wines. **Known for:** complimentary balsamic vinegar tasting to start; traditional Umbrian dishes; local wines. ⑤ *Average main: €17* ⊠ *Via del Duomo 78, Orvieto* ☎ *0763/343212* ⊕ *www.ristorante-maurizio.com.*

Trattoria La Grotta

$ | **UMBRIAN** | The vaulted, plant-filled dining area—where white walls are adorned with paintings, antique vases, and other knickknacks—makes a congenial setting for this small, rustic-style trattoria, which is lauded for its homemade pasta, perhaps with an artichoke, duck, or wild-boar sauce. Roast lamb, veal, and pork are all also good, and the desserts are supplied by Orvieto's most eminent *pasticceria* (pastry shop). **Known for:** tasty homemade pastas; fresh, local ingredients; warm and welcoming service. ⑤ *Average main: €14* ⊠ *Via Luca Signorelli 5, Orvieto* ☎ *0763/341348* ⊕ *www.trattorialagrottaorvieto.com* ۞ *Closed Tues.*

🛏 Hotels

Eremito

$$$ | **GUESTHOUSE** | For a more spiritual slant to your vacation, spend a night or two at this "modern monastery," where you'll sleep in a cell, eat vegetarian food by candlelight, practice yoga, and relax in a whirlpool tub. **Pros:** truly getting away from it all; chance to meet other travelers; lovely scenery. **Cons:** on the pricey side; need a car to get there; very simple accommodations (and no Wi-Fi). ⑤ *Rooms from: €270* ⊠ *Località Tarina 2, Parrano* ✛ *28 km (17 miles) north of Orvieto* ☎ *0763/891010* ⊕ *www.eremito. com* ⟿ *14 rooms* ⎟⦿⎟ *All-Inclusive.*

Hotel Palazzo Piccolomini

$$ | **HOTEL** | This 16th-century family palazzo has been beautifully restored, with inviting public spaces and handsome guest quarters where contemporary surroundings are accented by old beams, vaulted ceilings, and other distinctive touches. **Pros:** private parking; efficient staff; good location. **Cons:** underwhelming breakfasts; four-star category not completely justified; some rooms and bathrooms are small. ⑤ *Rooms from: €150* ⊠ *Piazza Ranieri 36, Orvieto* ☎ *0763/341743* ⊕ *www.*

The Marches

---

palazzopiccolomini.it ⊘ *Closed Jan. and Feb.* ⊷ *32 rooms* ⏁ *Free Breakfast.*

★ Locanda Palazzone

$$$ | HOTEL | Spending the night in this 13th-century building just 5 km (3 miles) northwest of Orvieto is like staying in a sophisticated country home, albeit one with vineyard views, a private chef, and two-level rooms with modern furnishings. **Pros:** tranquil surroundings; extremely friendly owners and staff; tasty meals served nightly. **Cons:** can hear noise from other guest rooms; Wi-Fi can be iffy; split-level rooms can be difficult for those with mobility issues or young children. ⑤ *Rooms from: €273* ⊠ *Località Rocca Ripesena 68, Orvieto* ☎ *0763/393614* ⊕ *www.locandapalazzone.it* ⊘ *Closed Jan.–mid-Mar.* ⊷ *7 rooms* ⏁ *Free Breakfast.*

Urbino

230 km (143 miles) east of Florence, 116 km (72 miles) northeast of Perugia, 75 km (47 miles) north of Gubbio.

Majestic Urbino, atop a steep hill with a skyline of towers and domes, is something of a surprise to come upon. Though quite remote, it was once a center of learning and culture almost without rival in western Europe. The town looks much as it did in the glory days of the 15th century: a cluster of warm brick and pale stone buildings, all topped with russet-color tile roofs. The focal point is the immense and beautiful Palazzo Ducale.

The city is also home to the small but prestigious Università di Urbino—one of the oldest in the world—so its streets are usually filled with students, and it has the usual college town array of bookshops, bars, and coffeehouses. In summer, the Italian student population is replaced by foreigners who come to study Italian language and arts at several prestigious, private, fine-arts academies.

Urbino's fame rests on the reputation of three of its native sons: Duke Federico da Montefeltro (1422–82), the enlightened warrior–patron who built the Palazzo Ducale; Raffaello Sanzio (1483–1520), or Raphael, one of the most influential painters in history and an embodiment of the spirit of the Renaissance; and the architect Donato Bramante (1444–1514), who translated the philosophy of the Renaissance into buildings of grace and beauty. Unfortunately there's little work by either Bramante or Raphael in the city, but the duke's influence can still be felt strongly.

GETTING HERE AND AROUND

Take the SS3 bis from Perugia, and follow the directions for Gubbio and Cesena. Exit at Umbertide and take the SS219, then the SS452, and at Calmazzo, the SS73 bis to Urbino.

VISITOR INFORMATION

CONTACT Urbino Tourism Office. ⊠ *Via Puccinotti 35, Urbino* ☎ *0722/2613* ⊕ *letsmarche.it.*

Sights

Casa Natale di Raffaello (*House of Raphael*)

HISTORIC HOME | This is the house in which the painter was born and where he took his first steps in painting, under the direction of his artist father. There's some debate about the fresco of the Madonna here; some say it's by Raphael, whereas others attribute it to the father—with Raphael's mother and the young painter himself standing in as models for the Madonna and Child. ⊠ *Via Raffaello 57, Urbino* ☎ *0722/320105* ⊕ *www.casaraffaello.com* ⊠ *€4.*

★ **Palazzo Ducale di Urbino** (*Ducal Palace*)

ART MUSEUM | The Palazzo Ducale holds a place of honor in the city. If the Renaissance was, ideally, a celebration of the nobility of man and his works, of the light and purity of the soul, then there's no place in Italy, the birthplace of the Renaissance, where these tenets are better illustrated. From the moment you enter the peaceful courtyard, you know you're in a place of grace and beauty, and the harmony of the building indeed reflects the high ideals of the time.

The palace houses the Galleria Nazionale delle Marche (National Museum of the Marches), with a superb collection of paintings, sculpture, and other objets d'art. Some pieces originally belonged to the Montefeltro family; others were brought here from churches and palaces throughout the region. Masterpieces include Paolo Uccello's *Profanation of the Host,* Titian's *Resurrection* and *Last Supper,* and Piero della Francesca's *Madonna of Senigallia.* But the gallery's highlight is Piero's enigmatic work long known as *The Flagellation of Christ.* Much has been written about this painting, and although few experts agree on its meaning, most agree that this is one of the painter's masterpieces. ⊠ *Piazza Rinascimento 13, Urbino* ☎ *0639/967996 ticket office* ⊕ *gndm.it* ⊠ *€10, free 1st Sun. of month* ☉ *Closed Mon.*

Restaurants

La Fornarina

$$ | **ITALIAN** | Locals often crowd this small, two-room trattoria near the Piazza della Repubblica. The specialty is meaty country fare, such as *coniglio* (rabbit) and *vitello alle noci* (veal cooked with walnuts) or *ai porcini* (with mushrooms); there's also a good selection of pasta dishes. **Known for:** excellent starters; welcoming atmosphere; hospitable staff. ⑤ *Average main: €18* ⊠ *Via Mazzini 14, Urbino* ☎ *0722/320007.*

★ Osteria Angolo Divino

$$$ | **ITALIAN** | Chef Tiziano Rossetti helms this long-standing restaurant in the center of Urbino, where tradition still reigns supreme. Elegant versions of regional dishes feature lots of local ingredients, including truffles, forest mushrooms, game, and pork, along with a wine list focused on small producers from the Marche. **Known for:** calm and pleasant ambience; quality cuisine with experimental elements; traditional osteria-style decor. ⑤ *Average main: €26* ⊠ *Via S. Andrea 14, Urbino* ☎ *0722/327559* ⊕ *www.tizianorossetti.com/osterialangolodivino* ⊗ *No lunch Tues.–Thurs.*

 Hotels

★ Palazzo Giusti Suites and Spa

$$ | **HOTEL** | This hotel in a renovated, 14th-century, historic center palace is an appealing mix of antiquity and modernity, including an expansive spa with a sauna and Turkish bath; a swimming pool that features a glass bottom so you can see the Roman ruins beneath it; and magnificent guest rooms with frescoed walls, vaulted ceilings, and charming decorative fireplaces. **Pros:** ultra-relaxing spa area; convenient location; beautiful historical setting. **Cons:** can be confusing to reach the hotel due to pedestrian streets; no gym; no restaurant. ⑤ *Rooms from: €173* ⊠ *Via Vittorio Veneto 37, Urbino* ☎ *0722/078023* ⊕ *www.palazzogiustiurbino.com* ⟿ *5 rooms* ⊗ *No Meals.*

Loreto

150 km (93 miles) northeast of Perugia, 121 km (75 miles) southeast of Urbino.

There's a strong Renaissance feel to this hilltop town, which is home to one of the most important religious sites in Europe, the Santuario della Santa Casa (House of the Virgin Mary). Bramante and Sansovino gave the church its Renaissance look, although many other artists helped create its special atmosphere.

Today, the town revolves around the religious calendar. If you can be here on December 10, you will witness the Feast of the Translation of the Holy House, when huge bonfires are lighted to celebrate the miraculous arrival, in 1295, of the house in Nazareth where the Virgin Mary was living at the time of the Annunciation.

GETTING HERE AND AROUND

If you're driving from Perugia, take the SS318 and then the SS76 highway to Fabriano and then on to Chiaravalle, where it merges with the A14 autostrada. The drive takes around two hours. Trains also go to Loreto, but the station is about 1½ km (1 mile) outside the town center. Regular buses leave from the station to the center.

VISITOR INFORMATION

CONTACT Loreto Tourism Office. ⊠ *Via Solari 3, Loreto* ☎ *071/970276* ⊕ *letsmarche.it.*

 Sights

★ Basilica della Santa Casa

CHURCH | Loreto is famous for one of the best-loved shrines in the world: the Santuario della Santa Casa (House of the Virgin Mary), within the Basilica della Santa Casa. Legend has it that angels moved the house from Nazareth, where the Virgin Mary was living at the time of the Annunciation, to this hilltop in 1295. The reason for this sudden and divinely inspired move was that Nazareth had fallen into the hands of Muslim invaders, who the angelic hosts viewed as unsuitable keepers of this important shrine.

The house itself consists of three rough stone walls contained within an elaborate marble tabernacle. Built around this centerpiece is the giant Basilica of the Holy House, which dominates the town. Millions of pilgrims come to the site every year (particularly at Easter and on the December 10 Feast of the Translation of the Holy House), and the little town of Loreto can become uncomfortably crowded.

Many great Italian architects—including Bramante, Antonio da Sangallo the Younger (1483–1546), Giuliano da Sangallo (circa 1445–1516), and Sansovino (1467–1529)—contributed to the design of the basilica. It was begun in the Gothic style in 1468 and continued in Renaissance style through the late Renaissance. ⊠ *Piazza della Madonna 1, Loreto* ☎ *071/9747213* ⊕ *www.santuarioloreto. va* ⬛ *Free.*

Ascoli Piceno

156 km (97 miles) southeast of Perugia, 88 km (55 miles) south of Loreto.

Ascoli Piceno sits in a valley ringed by steep hills and cut by the Tronto River. In Roman times, it was one of central Italy's best-known market towns. Today, with around 45,000 residents, it's a major fruit and olive producer, making it one of the most important towns in the region.

Despite growth during the Middle Ages and at other times, the streets in the town center continue to reflect the grid pattern of the ancient Roman city. You'll even find the word *rua,* from the Latin *ruga,* used for "street" instead of the Italian *via.* Now largely closed to traffic, the city center is great to explore on foot.

GETTING HERE AND AROUND
From Perugia, take the SS75 to Foligno, then merge onto the SS3 to Norcia. From here, take the SS4 to Ascoli Piceno. There are also trains, but the journey would be quite long, taking you from Perugia to Ancona, 105 km (65 miles) to the north, before changing for Ascoli Piceno.

VISITOR INFORMATION
CONTACT Ascoli Piceno Tourism Office.
⊠ *Piazza Aringo 7, Ascoli Piceno* ☎ *0736/298916* ⊕ *www.visitascoli.it.*

Sights

Piazza del Popolo
PLAZA/SQUARE | The heart of the town is the majestic Piazza del Popolo, dominated by the Gothic church of San Francesco and the Palazzo del Popolo, a 13th-century town hall that contains a graceful Renaissance courtyard. The square functions as the living room of the entire city and at dusk each evening is packed with people strolling and exchanging news and gossip—the sweetly antiquated ritual called a passeggiata—performed all over the country. ⊠ *Piazza del Popolo, Ascoli Piceno* ⬛ *Free.*

Hotels

★ Hotel Palazzo dei Mercanti
$ | **HOTEL** | This tastefully renovated convent right nearby Ascoli Piceno's historic center includes everything you need for a pleasant stay—a well-regarded restaurant, a relaxing spa, and modern guest rooms that have comfy beds and bathrooms with showers. **Pros:** elegant guest rooms; delicious breakfast buffet; prime central location. **Cons:** some rooms on the small side; restaurant can be noisy; rooms can seem too dark. ⑤ *Rooms from: €117* ⊠ *Corso Trento e Trieste 35, Ascoli Piceno* ☎ *0736/256044* ⊕ *www. palazzodeimercanti.it* ⇥ *25 rooms* ꀍ *Free Breakfast.*

Chapter 15

NAPLES AND CAMPANIA

15

Updated by
Nick Bruno

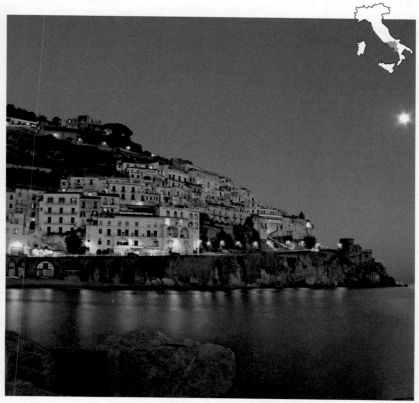

👁 **Sights**
★★★★★

🍴 **Restaurants**
★★★★★

🛏 **Hotels**
★★★★☆

🛍 **Shopping**
★★★★☆

🍸 **Nightlife**
★★★★☆

WELCOME TO NAPLES AND CAMPANIA

TOP REASONS TO GO

★ **Naples, Italy's most operatic city:** Walk through the energy, chaos, and beauty that is Spaccanapoli, the city's historic artery, and you'll create an unforgettable memory.

★ **Pompeii:** The excavated ruins of Pompeii offer a unique, occasionally spooky glimpse into everyday life—and sudden death—in Roman times.

★ **"The Living Room of the World":** Pose oh-so-casually with the beautiful people on La Piazzetta, the central crossroads of the island of Capri—a stage-set square that always seems ready for a gala performance.

★ **Ravello:** High above the famously blue Bay of Salerno, this Amalfi Coast charmer is a contender for the title of "most beautiful village in the world."

★ **Positano, a world made of stairs:** Built like a vertical amphitheater, Positano's only job is to look enchanting on the Amalfi Coast—and it does that very well.

1 Naples. Italy's third-largest city is lush, chaotic, friendly, amusing, confounding, and very beautiful.

2 Herculaneum. The famous archaeological site was once a wealthy seaside resort.

3 Pompeii. The most famous dig of all—the one that arguably kick-started archaeological studies—is Pompeii.

4 Vesuvius. Dominating the skyline southeast of Naples is the destructive Vesuvius caldera.

5 Oplontis (Torre Annunziata). Fascinating lesser-known ruins.

6 Ischia. More than twice the size of Capri, lesser-known Ischia has volcanic-sand beaches, thermal hot-spring spas, and fewer day-trippers.

7 Procida. Sun, cliffs, and sea combine to create the distinctive atmosphere so memorably immortalized in the film *Il Postino.*

8 Capri. The rocky island mixes natural beauty and dolce vita glamour.

9 Sorrento. Perched over the Bay of Naples with an incomparable view of Mt. Vesuvius, this Belle Époque resort town is sheer delight.

10 Positano. The ultimate pastel-brushed, tumbling-to-the-seaside village moves between sophisticated-luxe, beachcomber casual, and selfie-reverential posing.

11 Conca dei Marini. Put on the map by 1960s jet-setters, this tiny but exceedingly picturesque harbor hideaway rubs shoulders with the luminous Emerald Grotto.

12 Amalfi. This buzzy resort is threaded with beguiling, rambling passages, testimony to its Norman and Arab-Sicilian past. The glory of the city's days as a medieval maritime republic is most evident in its fantastic cathedral.

13 Ravello. Just beyond the Valley of the Dragon lies Ravello, perched "closer to the sky than the sea" atop Monte Cereto and set over the breathtaking Bay of Salerno. Ravello is one of Italy's most beautiful towns.

14 Paestum. With its Greek temples and Roman ruins in flowery meadows, this vision of a lost city makes a rousing finale to any Grand Tour.

EATING AND DRINKING WELL IN NAPLES AND CAMPANIA

Cappuccinos at a coffee bar

Think of Neapolitan food and you conjure up images of pasta, pizza, and tomatoes. The stereotype barely scratches the surface of what's available in Naples—to say nothing of the rest of Campania, where the cuisine reflects an enormously diverse landscape.

The region is known for its enclaves of gastronomy, notable among them the tip of the Sorrentine Peninsula. You may well come across *cucina povera*, a cuisine inspired by Campania's *contadino* (peasant) roots, with all the ingredients sourced from a nearby garden. Expect to see roadside stalls selling stellar local produce, including *annurca* apples (near Benevento), giant lemons (Amalfi Coast), roasted chestnuts (especially near Avellino), and watermelons (the plains around Salerno). Try to get to one of the local *sagre*, village feasts celebrating a *prodotto tipico* (local specialty), which could be anything from snails to wild boar to cherries to (commonly) wine.

A TIPPING TIP

Neapolitans are easily recognized in bars elsewhere in Italy by the tip they leave on the counter when ordering. This habit does not necessarily ensure better service in bars in Naples, notorious for their fairly offhand staff, but you do blend in better with the locals.

In restaurants, a service charge is often included (alternatively, 5%–10% is reasonable). In pizzerias, tips are given less often unless you've splurged on side dishes or sweets, or have had particularly good service.

PIZZA

Naples is the undisputed homeland of pizza, and you'll usually encounter it here in two classic forms: *margherita* and *marinara*. Given the larger-than-your-plate portions of standard pizzas, some choose to ask for a *mignon* (kids' portion), or even to share, divided between two plates. Take-away outlets in most town centers sell pizza by the slice, along with the usual range of fried *arancini* (rice balls) and *crocchè di patate* (potato fritters).

Margherita pizza

COFFEE

Given the same basic ingredients—coffee grounds, water, a machine—what makes *caffè* taste so much better in Naples than elsewhere remains a mystery. If you find the end product too strong, ask to have it with a dash of milk (caffè *macchiato*) or a little diluted (caffè *lungo*). Many bars serve with sugar already added, so if you want it without, request *senza zucchero* or *amaro*.

BUFFALO

Long feted for the melt-in-your-mouth mozzarella cheese made from its milk, the water buffalo is also the source of other culinary delights. Throughout the region, look for buffalo ricotta and mascarpone, as well as buffalo *provola* and *scamorza*, which may be

Buffalo mozzarella

lightly smoked (resulting in a golden crust). Caserta has more mature *nero di bufala* (aged like sheep's cheese), while around Salerno you'll find smoked *caciocavallo* cheese as well as *carne di bufala* (buffalo meat).

THE ORAL TRADITION

Locals in Campania like to bypass the restaurant menu and ask what the staff recommend. Take this approach and you'll often wind up with a daily special or the house specialty. Although you're unlikely to get multilingual staff outside the larger hotels and main tourist areas, the person you talk to will spare no effort to get the message across.

WINE

Wine in Campania has an ancient pedigree. Some say fancifully that Campania's undisputed king of reds, the *aglianico*, got its name from the word "Hellenic"; and *fiano*, the primary white grape, closely resembles the Roman variety *apianus*. Horace, the Latin poet, extolled the virtues of drinking wine from Campania. A century later, Pliny the Elder was harsher in his judgment.

In recent decades, though, Campania has gained respect for its boutique reds. Due to the rugged landscape, small farms, and limited mechanization, prices can be relatively high, but the quality is high as well.

A region of evocative names—Capri, Sorrento, Pompeii, Positano, Amalfi—Campania conjures up visions of cliff-shaded, sapphire-hue coves, sun-dappled waters, and mighty ruins. More travelers visit this corner than any other in southern Italy, and it's no wonder.

Home to Vesuvius, the area's unique geology is responsible for Campania's photogenic landscape. A spectacular coastline stretches out along a deep blue sea, punctuated by rocky islands.

Through the ages, the area's temperate climate, warm sea, fertile soil, and natural beauty have attracted Greek colonists, then Roman emperors—who called the region "Campania Felix," or "the happy land"—and later Saracen raiders and Spanish invaders. The result has been a rich and varied history, reflected in everything from architecture to mythology. The highlights span millennia: the near-intact Roman towns of Pompeii and Herculaneum, the Greek temples in Paestum, the Norman and Baroque churches in Naples, the white-dome fisherman's houses of Positano, the dolce vita resorts of Capri. Campania piles them all onto one mammoth must-see sandwich.

The region's complex identity is most intensely felt in its major metropolis, Naples. Few who visit remain ambivalent. You needn't participate in the mad whirl of the city, however. The best pastime in Campania is simply finding a spot with a stunning view and indulging in *il dolce far niente* ("the sweetness of doing nothing").

MAJOR REGIONS

Herculaneum and Pompeii. Volcanic ash and mud preserved the Roman towns of Herculaneum and Pompeii almost exactly as they were on the day Vesuvius erupted in AD 79, leaving them not just archaeological ruins but museums of daily life in the ancient world. The two cities and the volcano that buried them can be visited from either Naples or Sorrento, thanks to the Circumvesuviana, the suburban railroad that provides fast, frequent, and economical service.

Capri, Ischia, and Procida. Capri may get star billing among the islands that line the Bay of Naples, but Ischia and Procida also have their own lower-key appeal. Once entirely dependent on its thermal springs, Ischia is now the archaeological front-runner in the bay, thanks to the noted museum in Lacco Ameno. Procida has opened up to tourism and in 2022 was celebrated for sparking rejuvenation through culture as *Capitale Italiana della Cultura*, helping expand access to its chief natural asset, the unspoiled isle of Vivara.

The Sorrentine Peninsula. As the hub for a whole banquet of must-see sites—Pompeii and Naples to the north, Capri to the west, and the Amalfi Coast to the south—the beautiful, Belle Époque resort town of Sorrento is unequaled.

The rest of the peninsula, with plains and limestone outcroppings, watchtowers and Roman ruins, groves and beaches, monasteries and villages, winding paths leading to isolated coves, and panoramic views of the bays of both Naples and Salerno, remains relatively undiscovered.

The Amalfi Coast. One of the most gorgeous places on Earth is the corner of the Campania region called the Amalfi Coast. The justly famed jewels along the water are Positano, Amalfi, and Ravello. Considering the natural splendor of this region, it's no surprise that it has some of the most beautiful beaches in the world. White, sunbaked villages rise above cliffs hollowed out with grottoes and crystal lagoons lapped by emerald green water. Larger beaches, like those in Positano and Amalfi, are easily accessible, but the magic often lies in finding hidden coves and scenic spots, such as the picture-perfect Marina di Praia.

Planning

Getting Here and Around

BOAT

Several companies offer a variety of fast craft and passenger and car ferries connecting the islands of Capri, Ischia, and Procida with Naples and Pozzuoli year-round. Hydrofoils and other fast craft leave from Naples's Molo Beverello, adjacent to Piazza Municipio, with some departures in high season also from Mergellina, about 1½ km (1 mile) west of Piazza Municipio. Slower car ferries leave from the berths at Calata Porta di Massa, a 10-minute walk, or three-minute shuttle bus ride, east of Molo Beverello.

Information on departures is published every day in the local paper, *Il Mattino*. Alternatively, ask at the tourist office or at the port, check websites, or contact these companies directly. Always double-check schedules in stormy weather.

CONTACTS Caremar. ☎ *081/18966690* ⊕ *www.caremar.it.* **Navigazione Libera del Golfo.** ☎ *081/5520763* ⊕ *www.navlib.it.* **SNAV.** ☎ *081/4285555* ⊕ *www.snav.it.*

BUS

Within Campania there's an extensive network of local buses, although finding information about it can be trying.

CONTACT SITA Buses. ☎ *342/6256442* mobile ⊕ *www.sitasudtrasporti.it.*

CAR

You can get along fine without a car in Campania, and there are plenty of reasons not to have one. Much of Naples is pedestrianized, meaning motorized arteries are often bottlenecked; you can't bring a car to Capri (except in winter, when everything's closed); and parking in the towns of the Amalfi Coast is hard to come by and expensive.

Italy's main north–south route, the A1 (aka the Autostrada del Sole), connects Rome with Naples and Campania. In good traffic the drive to Naples from Rome takes a little more than two hours. The A3 autostrada, a somewhat perilous continuation of the A1, runs south from Naples through Campania and into Calabria. Herculaneum (Ercolano) and Pompeii (Pompei) both have marked exits off the A3. For Vesuvius, take the Portici Ercolano exit. For the Sorrento Peninsula and the Amalfi Coast, exit at Castellammare di Stabia. To get to Paestum, take the A3 to the Battipaglia exit, and follow the road to Capaccio Scalo–Paestum. Roads on the Sorrento Peninsula and Amalfi Coast are narrow and twisting, but they have outstanding views.

If you come to Naples by car, find a garage, agree on the rate, and leave it there for the duration of your stay. (If you park on the street, you run the risk of theft.)

15

Naples and Campania PLANNING

GARAGE CONTACT Petraglia. ⊠ *Via Ferraris 42, Piazza Garibaldi* ☎ *081/3602840* ⊕ *garagepetraglia.it* Ⓜ *Garibaldi.*

TAXI

You may be able to hail a taxi if you see one driving, but your best bet is to call Radio Taxi or ask someone at your hotel to book one. Taxi ranks can be found outside the central Piazza Garibaldi train station and the port (Molo Beverello), as well as throughout the city. Watch out for overcharging at three locations: the airport, the railway station, and the hydrofoil marina. The official fixed rate (be sure to ask for *tariffa predeterminata*!) from the airport to the central station is €18, which covers three people, two large pieces of luggage, and two small pieces. City Airport Taxis offers a private service.

Ask for *il tariffario*, the tariff information sheet of the Comune di Napoli with common fixed-rate journeys when taking a taxi, as drivers may invent an exorbitant price, even hiding the tariff sheet—trips around the city should cost €8–€10. You can of course request that the meter is switched on; this often results in your paying less. Taxis charge approximately €3.50 initially (more on Sunday, holidays, and after 10 pm), then €0.05 per 48 meters (or 8 seconds of idling). A copy of the tariff sheet can be downloaded at ⊕ *www.comune.napoli. it/taxi.* This being Naples, the situation is farcical and confused as the sheet has not been updated in years, hence drivers tend to ignore it, so prepare to haggle! Other options besides Radio Taxi include Consorttaxi (☎ *081/2222*), La Partenope (☎ *081/0101*), and La 570 (☎ *081/5707070*). In summer, many cabs in Naples have no air-conditioning, so you might bake if caught in a traffic jam.

CONTACTS City Airport Taxis. ⊠ *Naples* ⊕ *www.city-airport-taxis.com.* **Taxi Napoli.** ⊠ *Naples* ☎ *081/8888* ⊕ *www.taxinapoli. it.*

TRAIN

There are up to five trains every hour between Rome and Naples. Both the Alta Velocità Frecciarossa and Italo trains (the fastest types of train service) make the trip in a little more than an hour, with the Intercity taking two. All trains to Naples stop at the refurbished but forever scuzzy Stazione Centrale.

The frequent (though run-down) suburban Circumvesuviana runs from Naples's Porta Nolana and stops at Stazione Centrale before continuing to Herculaneum, Pompeii, and Sorrento. Travel time between Naples and Sorrento on the Circumvesuviana line is about 75 minutes.

For ticketing purposes, the region is divided into travel zones by distance from Naples. If you're traveling from Naples to anywhere else in Campania, be sure to ask for a *biglietto integrato*. It's slightly more expensive than the direct ticket (about €1 more), but there will be no need to buy a separate ticket for your subway, tram, or bus ride to the train station as the biglietto integrato covers the whole journey. An integrato ticket to Herculaneum costs €2.90, to Pompeii €3.80, and to Sorrento €5.30. Tap and Go Ticketless now allows you to use your bank card for your journeys.

CONTACTS Circumvesuviana. ☎ *800/211388 toll-free* ⊕ *www.eavsrl. it.* **Trenitalia and Italo.** ⊠ *Piazza Garibaldi* ☎ *892021 Trenitalia (in Italy, fee), 892020 Italo (in Italy, fee)* ⊕ *www.trenitalia.com, www.italotreno.it.*

Making the Most of Your Time

In Campania there are three primary travel experiences: Naples, with its restless exuberance; the resorts (Capri, Sorrento, the Amalfi Coast), dedicated to leisure and indulgence; and the archaeological sites (Pompeii, Herculaneum, Paestum), where the ancient world is frozen in time. Each is wonderful in its own way. If you have a week, you can get a good taste of all three. With less time, you're better off choosing between them rather than stretching yourself thin.

Pompeii, being a day trip, is the simplest to plan for. To get a feel for Naples, you should give it a couple of days at a minimum. The train station makes a harsh first impression (an overhaul has softened the blow), but the city grows on you as you take in the sights and interact with the locals.

That said, many people bypass Naples and head right for the resorts. These places are all about relaxing—you'll miss the point if you're in a rush. Although Sorrento isn't as spectacular as Positano or Capri, it makes a good base because of its central location.

DISCOUNTS AND DEALS
Government-run sites are free on the first Sunday of each month—good for those on a budget, but less so for avoiding crowds. The **Campania ArteCard** with app entitles users to free or discounted admission to about four dozen museums and monuments in Naples and beyond. These are the main passes: Naples, three days (€21), has three sights included and up to 50% off the rest, plus transportation; Campania region, three days (€32), including Pompeii and other Bay of Naples sights and Ravello and Paestum with two sights included and others up to 50% off, plus transportation; Campania region, seven days (€34), with five sights included and many others up to 50% off, but no transportation. For longer stays the new 365 Gold Pass allows two entries to principle attractions and up to 50% off entry to others over an entire year (€43). Other benefits (which vary depending on the pass) include discounts on audio guides, theater tickets,

city tours, and other activities. Visitors aged 18–25 receive generous discounts (10 free admissions) with the three-day Napoli Young card (€12) and 365 Gold Pass Young (€33) for entry to the Arte-Card circuit sights over a year.

Confusingly, in 2019 the e-commerce-driven **Naples Pass** (app only) was introduced in conjunction with ArteCard. It includes some free sights, tours, and added discounts. Transport passes and the Alibus airport shuttle bus can be added. The cheapest three-day option Naples Pass is €37 while the seven-day Whole Campania is €88. For more information, visit ⊕ www.campaniartecard. it and ⊕ www.naplespass.eu, or the tourist office in the Piazza Garibaldi station, which distributes a helpful booklet about the various passes.

Restaurants

As the birthplace of pizza, Naples prides itself on its vast selection of pizzerias, among the most famous of which are Da Michele (where Julia Roberts filmed her pizza scene in *Eat Pray Love*) or Sorbillo. Many Neapolitans make lunch their big meal of the day and then have a pizza for supper.

Dining on the Amalfi Coast, Capri, Ischia, and Procida revolves largely around seafood. Dishes are prepared using the short, rolled handmade *scialatielli* or large *paccheri* pasta and adorned with local *vongole* (clams) or *cozze* (mussels) and other shellfish. Octopus, squid, and the fresh fish of the season are always on the menu for the second course. Cetara has been famous for its *alici* (anchovies) since Roman times, and even produces alici bread. Eateries range from beach-side trattorias to beacons of fine dining with stupendous views.

Hotels

Most parts of Campania have accommodations in all price categories, but they tend to fill up in high season, so reserve well in advance. In summer, on the coast and the islands, hotels that serve meals often require you to take half board.

⇨ *Hotel and restaurant reviews have been shortened. For full information, visit Fodors.com. Prices in the hotel reviews are the lowest cost of a standard double room in high season. Prices in the dining reviews are the average cost of a main course at dinner, or, if dinner is not served, at lunch.*

What It Costs in Euros			
$	$$	$$$	$$$$
RESTAURANTS			
under €15	€15–€24	€25–€35	over €35
HOTELS			
under €125	€125–€200	€201–€300	over €300

Tours

City Sightseeing
BUS TOURS | FAMILY | Close to the port, beside the main entrance to Castel Nuovo, is the terminal for double-decker buses belonging to City Sightseeing. For €25 you can take two different excursions, giving you reasonable coverage of the downtown sights and outlying attractions like the Museo di Capodimonte; tickets are valid for 24 hours, and you can join the tour at any stop. City Sightseeing also offers a shuttle service to Pompeii. ⊠ *Piazza Municipio, Naples* ☎ *081/5517279, 335/7803812 mobile/ WhatsApp* ⊕ *www.city-sightseeing.it/ naples.*

Lino Tour
GUIDED TOURS | Lino Tour offers tailor-made tours of the attractions in and around Naples. ⊠ *Naples* ☎ *081/8772244* ⊕ *www.linotourcarservice.com.*

Naples

Located under the shadow of Vesuvius, Naples is the most vibrant city in Italy—a steaming, bubbling, reverberating minestrone in which each block is a small village and everything seems to be a backdrop for an opera not yet composed.

It's said that northern Italians vacation here to remind themselves of the time when Italy was *molto italiana—really* Italian. In this respect, Naples (Napoli in Italian) doesn't disappoint: Neapolitan rainbows of laundry wave in the wind over alleyways, mothers caress children, men break out into impromptu arias at sidewalk cafés, and street scenes offer an intricate theater of human exchanges.

Everywhere contrasting elements of faded gilt and romance, grandeur and squalor form a pageant of pure *Napoletanità*, a distillation of *Italianità*—Italy at its most Italian.

As the historic capital of the region known as Campania, Naples has been perpetually and tumultuously in a state of flux. Neapolitans are instinctively the most hospitable of people, and they've often paid a price for being so, having unwittingly extended a warm welcome to wave after wave of invaders. Lombards, Goths, Normans, Swabians, Spanish viceroys and kings, and Napoleonic generals arrived in turn; most of them proved to be greedy and self-serving. Still, if these foreign rulers bled the populace dry with taxes, they left the impoverished city with a rich architectural inheritance.

GETTING HERE AND AROUND

Public transportation in Naples is decent, and includes two subway lines, three funiculars, and a multitude of buses. Tickets cost €1.20 per journey (€1.40 on Metro Linea 2), but a Ticket Integrato Campania costs €1.70 and is valid for 90 minutes on all transport for as far as Pozzuoli to the west and Portici to the east; €5.10 buys a *biglietto giornaliero* (all-day ticket).

Now with a couple of art-decorated stations (Toledo and Università) voted among Europe's most attractive, Naples's Metropolitana provides fairly frequent service and can be the fastest way to get across the traffic-clogged city. Linea 1, Metropolitana Collinare, links the hill area of the Vomero and beyond with the National Archaeological Museum and Piazza Municipio near the port, as well as Stazione Centrale. The older Linea 2 stretches from the train station to Pozzuoli. Trains on both lines run 5:45 am–11 pm. To check journey costs and download the app visit ⊕ *www. unicocampania.it.*

Bus service is viable, especially with the introduction of larger buses on the regular R1, R2, R3, and R4 routes. Electronic signs display wait times at many stops. Three tram routes now thread through the streets with new tram rolling stock introduced in 2020, but the service is unreliable and regularly suspended.

VISITOR INFORMATION

Many tourist offices in Naples have closed in recent years (government cuts) and those open have sporadic hours. The official, most reliable is the old AACST office now run by Campania Turismo in Piazza del Gesù. Pick up a free map and info about possible savings through the Campania ArteCard.

CONTACTS AACST Info Turismo. ⊠ *Piazza del Gesù Nuovo 7, Centro Storico* ☎ *081/5512701* ⊕ *www.visitnaples.eu/ en.*

Centro Storico

To experience the true essence of Naples, you need to explore the Centro Storico, an unforgettable neighborhood that is the heart of old Naples. This is the Naples of peeling building facades and hanging laundry, with small alleyways fragrant with fresh flowers laid at the many shrines to the Blessed Virgin. Here the cheapest pizzerias in town feed the locals like kings, and the raucous street carnival of Neapolitan daily life is punctuated with oases of spiritual calm. All the contradictions of Naples—splendor and squalor, palace and slum, triumph and tragedy—meet here and sing a full-throated chorale.

◉ Sights

Duomo di Napoli

CHURCH | Although this cathedral was established in the 1200s, the current building was erected a century later and has since undergone radical changes— especially during the Baroque period. Inside, the 350-year-old wooden ceiling is supported by 110 ancient columns salvaged from pagan buildings. The 4th-century church of Santa Restituta, incorporated into the cathedral, was redecorated in the late 1600s in the Baroque style, though the mosaics in the Battistero (Baptistery) are claimed to be the oldest in the Western world.

In the Cappella del Tesoro di San Gennaro, multicolor marbles and frescoes honor St. Januarius, the miracle-working patron saint of Naples. Three times a year his dried blood is believed to liquefy during rites in his honor. The most spectacular painting is Ribera's *San Gennaro in the Furnace* (1647), depicting the saint emerging unscathed from the furnace. The Museo del Tesoro di San Gennaro houses a rich collection of treasures associated with the saint. ⊠ *Via Duomo 149, Centro Storico* ☎ *081/449097*

Campania Through the Ages

Ancient history. Lying on Mediterranean trade routes plied by several pre-Hellenic civilizations, Campania was settled by the ancient Greeks from approximately 800 BC onward. Here myth and legend blend with historical fact. The town of Herculaneum is said—rather improbably—to have been established by Hercules himself; and Naples in ancient times was called Parthenope, the name attributed to one of the sirens who preyed on hapless sailors in antiquity.

Thanks to archaeological research, some of the layers of myth have been stripped away to reveal a pattern of occupation and settlement well before Rome became established. Greek civilization flourished for hundreds of years all along this coastline, but there was nothing in the way of centralized government until centuries later when the Roman Republic, uniting all Italy for the first time, absorbed the Greek colonies with little opposition. Generally, the peace of Campania was undisturbed during these centuries of Roman rule.

Foreign influences. Naples and Campania, like Italy in general, decayed along with the Roman Empire and was thereafter squabbled over by Europe's foreign dynasties. Naples regained some importance under the rule of the Angevins in the latter part of the 13th century and continued its progress in the 1440s under Aragonese rule. The nobles who served under the Spanish viceroys in the 16th and 17th centuries enjoyed their pleasures, even as Spain milked the area for taxes.

After a short Austrian occupation, Naples became the capital of the Kingdom of the Two Sicilies, which the Bourbon kings established in 1738. Their rule was generally benevolent as far as Campania was concerned, and their support of papal authority in Rome was important in the development of the country as a whole. Their rule was important artistically, too, contributing to the architecture of the region, and attracting great musicians, artists, and writers who were drawn by the easy life at court. Finally, Giuseppe Garibaldi launched his famous expedition, and in 1860 Naples was united with the rest of Italy.

Modern times. Things were relatively tranquil through the years that followed—with visitors thronging to Capri, Sorrento, Amalfi, and, of course, Naples—until World War II. Allied bombings did considerable damage in and around Naples. At the fall of the fascist government, the sorely tried Neapolitans rose up against Nazi occupation troops and in four days of street fighting drove them out of the city. A monument was raised to the *scugnizzo* (the typical Neapolitan street urchin), celebrating the youngsters who participated in the battle. With the end of the war, artists, tourists, writers, and other lovers of beauty returned to the Campania region.

As time passed, some parts of Campania gained increased attention from visitors, while others lost their cachet. Years of misgovernment have left their mark, yet the region's cultural and natural heritage is finally being revalued as local authorities and inhabitants recognize the importance of the area's largest industry—tourism.

Duomo, 081/294980 Tesoro di San
Gennaro ⊕ tesorosangennaro.it 🖃 Tesoro
di San Gennaro with audio guide €12,
guided visits €20 Ⓜ Duomo, Cavour.

Gesù Nuovo

CHURCH | A stunning architectural contrast
to the plain Romanesque frontage of
other nearby churches, the strikingly
austere, recently restored (2023) stone
facade of this elaborate Baroque church
dates to the late 16th century. Originally a
palace, the building was seized by Pedro
of Toledo in 1547 and sold to the Jesuits
with the condition that the facade remain
intact. Behind the entrance is Francesco
Solimena's action-packed *Heliodorus'
Eviction from the Temple.* You can find
the work of familiar Baroque sculptors
(Naccherino, Finelli) and painters inside.
The gracious *Visitation* above the altar in
the second chapel on the right is by Massimo Stanzione, who also contributed the
fine frescoes in the main nave: they're
in the presbytery (behind and around the
main altar). ⊠ Piazza Gesù Nuovo, Centro
Storico 🕾 081/5578111 Ⓜ Dante.

★ LAPIS Museum

RUINS | **FAMILY** | The beautifully restored
17th-century Basilica di Pietrasanta, a
Cosimo Fanzago Baroque masterpiece
built on the site of the Roman Temple
of Diana, hosts regular multimedia
exhibitions, but the star attraction here
is the underground visit to a section of
Naples's oldest aqueduct. Four tours a
day descend 40 meters (131 feet) below
the busy Via dei Tribunali to large lavishly illuminated cisterns hewed from excavated tuff two millennia ago, still filled with
running water (thanks to a collaboration
with the city's waterworks). ⊠ Piazzetta Pietrasanta 17/18, Centro Storico
🕾 081/19230565 ⊕ www.lapismuseum.
com 🖃 €10 ⚠ Reservations essential on
weekends Ⓜ Dante.

The Madonna and Pistol

PUBLIC ART | This piece is by controversial
street artist Banksy. Located on a wall in
front of the grand facade of the chiesa

dei Girolamini, the church where the
17th-century philosopher Giambattista
Vico is buried, the stencilled *La Madonna
con la Pistola* sits behind a protective
glass screen and attracts a regular trickle
of devotees. ⊠ Piazza Girolamini, Centro
Storico Ⓜ Cavour.

Madre (*Museum of Contemporary Art
Donnaregina*)

ART GALLERY | With 86,111 square feet of
exhibition space, a host of young and
helpful attendants, and occasional late-
night events, the Madre is one of the
most visited museums in Naples. Most
of the artworks on the first floor were
installed in situ by their creators, but the
second-floor gallery exhibits works by
international and Italian contemporary
artists. The museum also hosts temporary shows by major international artists.
⊠ Via Settembrini 79, San Lorenzo,
Centro Storico 🕾 081/19528498 ⊕ www.
madrenapoli.it/en 🖃 €8 ☉ Closed Tues.
Ⓜ Cavour.

★ Museo Cappella Sansevero
(*Sansevero Chapel Museum*)

NOTABLE BUILDING | The dazzling funer-
ary chapel of the Sangro di Sansevero
princes combines noble swagger,
overwhelming color, and a touch of the
macabre—which expresses Naples
perfectly. The chapel was begun in 1590
by Prince Giovan Francesco di Sangro to
fulfill a vow to the Virgin if he were cured
of a dire illness. The seventh Sangro
di Sansevero prince, Raimondo, had
the building modified in the mid-18th
century and is generally credited for its
current Baroque styling, the noteworthy
elements of which include the splendid
marble-inlay floor and statuary, including
Giuseppe Sanmartino's spine-chillingly
lifelike *Cristo Velato* (Veiled Christ). ⊠ Via
Francesco de Sanctis 19, off Vicolo
Domenico Maggiore, Centro Storico
🕾 081/5524936 ⊕ www.museosanseve-
ro.it 🖃 €10 ☉ Closed Tues. Ⓜ Dante.

Centro Storico

KEY

- ⓜ → Line 1 Metropolitana Collinare
- ⓜ → Line 2 Metropolitana FS
- ❶ Sights
- ❶ Restaurants
- ❶ Quick Bites
- ❶ Hotels

Napoli Sotterranea (*Underground Naples*)
HISTORIC SIGHT | **FAMILY** | Fascinating
90-minute tours of a portion of Naples's
fabled underground city provide an initiation into the complex history of the city
center. Efforts to dramatize the experience—amphoras lowered on ropes to
draw water from cisterns, candles given
to navigate narrow passages, objects
shifted to reveal secret passages—combine with enthusiastic English-speaking
guides to make this particularly exciting
for older children. Be prepared on the
underground tour to go up and down
many steps and crouch in very narrow
corridors. ⊠ *Piazza San Gaetano 68,
along Via dei Tribunali, Centro Storico*
☎ *081/296944* ⊕ *www.napolisotterranea.
org* 🎫 *€10* Ⓜ *Dante, Cavour.*

★ **Pio Monte della Misericordia**
RELIGIOUS BUILDING | One of the Centro
Storico's defining sites, this octagonal
church was built around the corner from
the Duomo for a charitable institution
seven noblemen founded in 1601. The
institution's aim was to carry out acts of
Christian charity like feeding the hungry,
clothing the poor, nursing the sick,
sheltering pilgrims, visiting prisoners,
and burying the indigent dead—acts
immortalized in the history of art by
Caravaggio's famous altarpiece depicting the *Sette Opere della Misericordia*
(*Seven Acts of Mercy*). Pride of place is
given to the great Caravaggio above the
altar. ⊠ *Via Tribunali 253, Centro Storico*
☎ *081/446973* ⊕ *piomontedellamiseri-
cordia.it* 🎫 *€10* ⊘ *Closed Sun. afternoon*
Ⓜ *Cavour, Duomo.*

★ **San Lorenzo Maggiore**
RELIGIOUS BUILDING | The church of San
Lorenzo features a very unmedieval
facade of 18th-century splendor. Due to
the effects and threats of earthquakes,
the church was reinforced and reshaped
along Baroque lines in the 17th and 18th
centuries. Begun by Robert d'Anjou in
1270 on the site of a previous 6th-century
church, the church has a single, barnlike

nave that reflects the Franciscans' desire
for simple spaces. Also found here is the
church's most important monument: the
tomb of Catherine of Austria (circa 1323),
by Tino da Camaino. ⊠ *Via dei Tribunali
316, Centro Storico* ☎ *081/2110860*
⊕ *www.laneapolissotterrata.it* 🎫 *Excavations and museum €9* Ⓜ *Cavour, Dante.*

★ **Santa Chiara**
RELIGIOUS BUILDING | Offering a stark
contrast to the opulence of the nearby
Gesù Nuovo, Santa Chiara is the leading
Angevin Gothic monument in Naples.
The fashionable house of worship for the
14th-century nobility, the church of St.
Clare was intended to be a great dynastic
monument by Robert d'Anjou. Built in
a Provençal Gothic style between 1310
and 1328 (probably by Gagliardo Primario)
and dedicated in 1340, the church had
its aspect radically altered in the Baroque
period. A six-day fire started by Allied
bombs on August 4, 1943, put an end to
all that, as well as to what might have
been left of the important cycle of frescoes by Giotto and his Neapolitan workshop. Around the left side of the church
is the Chiostro delle Clarisse, the most
famous cloister in Naples. ⊠ *Piazza Gesù
Nuovo, Centro Storico* ☎ *081/5516673*
⊕ *www.monasterodisantachiara.it* 🎫 *Museum and cloister €6* ⊘ *Cloister closed
Sun. afternoon* Ⓜ *Dante, Università.*

🍽 Restaurants

★ **Di Matteo**
$ | **PIZZA** | **FAMILY** | Every pizzeria along
Via dei Tribunali is worth the long wait—
and trust us, all the good ones will be
jam-packed—but just one can claim to
have served a U.S. president: Bill Clinton
enjoyed a Margherita here when the
G8 was held in Naples in 1994. Today
the superlative *pizzaioli* (pizza makers)
turn out a wide array of pizzas, all to the
utmost perfection. **Known for:** functional
decor and pizzaioli working at front; funny
pics of Clinton and the "Pizzaiolo del
Presidente" Ernesto Cacialli in 1994; top

value, including filling pizza fritta (fried). ⑤ *Average main: €8* ✉ *Via Tribunali 94, Centro Storico* ☎ *081/455262* ⊕ *www. pizzeriadimatteo.com* Ⓜ *Cavour, Dante.*

Gino Sorbillo

$ | PIZZA | FAMILY | There are a few restaurants called Sorbillo along Via dei Tribunali, but this one is world-renowned. Order the same thing the locals do, namely a basic Neapolitan pizza (try the unique pizza al pesto or the stunningly simple marinara, with just San Marzano tomatoes, wild garlic, and oregano) that's cooked to perfection by the third generation of pie makers who run the place. **Known for:** the crowd waiting outside; leave your name at the door and listen to be called; head honcho Gino is a celebrity and pizza ambassador. ⑤ *Average main: €10* ✉ *Via Tribunali 32, Centro Storico* ☎ *081/446643* ⊕ *www.sorbillo.it* ☉ *Closed Sun.* Ⓜ *Dante.*

L'Etto

$$ | SOUTHERN ITALIAN | This innovative eatery offers a menu of fixed-price bowls such as the *squisita* (exquisite) with rice, octopus, hummus, and fennel or the *vivace* (lively) with seared tuna fillet, chopped hazelnuts, and three types of rice. The open kitchen looks over a large, high, communal table with stools, and outdoor seating overlooks the bustling Piazza Bellini. **Known for:** healthy Mediterranean (including vegan and vegetarian) dishes; communal interior eating area; outdoor plaza seating. ⑤ *Average main: €15* ✉ *Via Santa Maria di Costantinopoli 102, Centro Storico* ☎ *081/3145078* ⊕ *www.ettoexperience.it* Ⓜ *Dante, Museo.*

Palazzo Petrucci Pizzeria

$ | PIZZA | FAMILY | Here you can dine under vaulted ceilings in the former stables of a 17th-century mansion, eat outdoors overlooking the grand Piazza San Domenico Maggiore, or feast from a table on the roof terrace, facing the *giuglia* (obelisk) di San Domenico. Options include *pizze* or *pizze fritte*—with classic or unusual toppings—as well as robust salads and antipasti. **Known for:** grandest palazzo venue for a pizza feast; atmospheric views and sounds over the piazza; craft beer, pizze fritte, and vegan options. ⑤ *Average main: €12* ✉ *Piazza San Domenico Maggiore 5–7, Centro Storico* ☎ *081/5512460* ⊕ *palazzopetrucci.it* ☉ *Closed 2 wks in Aug.* Ⓜ *Dante.*

Coffee and Quick Bites

★ Scaturchio

$ | CAFÉ | Established in 1905, this Neapolitan institution on Spaccanapoli is a buzzy place to sample some of the finest pastries in town—plus it also makes classic savory dishes, ice cream, and mighty decent coffee. **Known for:** sumptuous babà, sfogliatelle, and pastiera; Ministeriale liquor-filled chocolates; zucchine a scapece, arancini, and other savory bites. ⑤ *Average main: €6* ✉ *Piazza San Domenico Maggiore 19, Centro Storico* ☎ *081/5516944* ⊕ *www.scaturchio.it* Ⓜ *Dante.*

🛏 Hotels

Costantinopoli 104

$$$ | HOTEL | An oasis of what Italians call *stile liberty* (Art Nouveau style), with impressive stained-glass fittings and striking artwork, this serene, elegant hotel is well placed for touring the Centro Storico and visiting the Museo Archeologico Nazionale. **Pros:** pool (a rarity in Neapolitan hotels) and garden; pleasant service; tranquil oasis in the heart of the city. **Cons:** rooms are getting dated; can be difficult to find; some rooms suffer from nightlife disturbance from Piazza Bellini. ⑤ *Rooms from: €270* ✉ *Via Costantinopoli 104, Centro Storico* ☎ *081/5571035* ⊕ *www.costantinopoli104.it* ⌑ *19 rooms* ❍ *Free Breakfast* Ⓜ *Museo.*

★ Hotel Palazzo Decumani

$$ | HOTEL | This contemporary upscale hotel near the Centro Storico's major sights occupies an early-20th-century

palazzo, but you won't find heavy, ornate furnishings—the emphasis is on light and space, both in short supply in old Naples. **Pros:** guests-only lounge-bar; large rooms and bathrooms; service on par with fancier hotels. **Cons:** patchy Internet; unkempt neighborhood; disappointing breakfast. $ Rooms from: €200 ⊠ Piazzetta Giustino Fortunato 8, Centro Storico ☎ 081/4201379 ⊕ www.palazzodecumani.com ⇋ 28 rooms ⎜⍥⎜ Free Breakfast Ⓜ Duomo.

🛍 Shopping

Ferrigno
CRAFTS | Shops selling Nativity scenes cluster along the Via San Gregorio Armeno off Spaccanapoli, and they're all worth a glance. The most famous is Ferrigno. Although Maestro Giuseppe Ferrigno died in 2008, the family business continues, still faithfully using 18th-century techniques. ⊠ Via San Gregorio Armeno 8, Centro Storico ☎ 081/5523148 ⊕ www.arteferrigno.it Ⓜ Cavour, Duomo.

Ospedale delle Bambole
ART GALLERY | FAMILY | In the courtyard of the 16th-century Palazzo Marigliano is this world-famous hospital for dolls, which has a small museum dedicated to its poignant mission. In business since 1850, it's a wonderful place to take kids (and their injured toys). ⊠ Via San Biagio dei Librai 39, Centro Storico ☎ 081/18639797 ⊕ ospedaledellebambole.com ⊙ Closed Sun. afternoon Ⓜ Duomo.

Museo Archeologico Nazionale

It's only fitting that the Museo Archeologico Nazionale—the single most important and remarkable museum of Greco-Roman antiquities in the world (in spite of itself, some observers say)—sits in the upper *decumanus,* or neighborhood, of ancient Neapolis, the district colonized by the ancient Greeks and Romans. Happily, it's almost always open (its core collection, that is).

👁 Sights

★ **Museo Archeologico Nazionale** (*National Museum of Archaeology*)
HISTORY MUSEUM | Also known as MANN, this legendary museum has experienced something of a rebirth in recent years. Its unrivaled collections include world-renowned archaeological finds that put most other museums to shame, from some of the best mosaics and paintings from Pompeii and Herculaneum to the legendary Farnese collection of ancient sculpture. The core masterpiece collection is almost always open to visitors, while seasonal exhibitions feature intriguing cultural events, collaborations, and contemporary artists. Some of the newer rooms, covering archaeological discoveries in the Greco-Roman settlements and necropolises in and around Naples, have helpful informational panels in English. ⊠ Piazza Museo 19, Centro Storico ⊕ mann-napoli.it ⎘ €22 valid for two consecutive days ⊙ Closed Tues. Ⓜ Museo.

Toledo

Naples's setting on what is possibly the most captivating bay in the world has long been a boon for its inhabitants—the expansive harbor has always brought great mercantile wealth to the city—and, intermittently, a curse. Throughout history, a who's who of Greek, Roman, Norman, Spanish, and French despots has quarreled over this gateway to Campania. Each set of conquerors recognized that the area around the city harbor—today occupied by the Molo Beverello hydrofoil terminal and the 1928 Stazione Marittima—functioned as a veritable welcome mat to the metropolis and consequently should be a fitting showcase of regal authority. This had become imperative because of explosive population growth, which, by the mid-16th century, had made Naples the second-largest city in Europe, after Paris. With the mass migration of the rural population to the city, Naples had grown into a capricious, unplanned, disorderly, and untrammeled capital. Thus, the central aim of the ruling dynasties became the creation of a *Napoli nobilissima*—a "most noble" Naples.

◉ Sights

★ Castel Nuovo

CASTLE/PALACE | Known to locals as Maschio Angioino, in reference to its Angevin builders, this imposing castle is now used more for marital than fro military purposes—a portion of it serves as a government registry office. A white four-tiered triumphal entrance arch, ordered by Alfonso of Aragon after he entered the city in 1443 to seize power from the increasingly beleaguered Angevin Giovanna II, upstages the building's looming Angevin stonework. Across the courtyard within the castle is the Sala Grande, also known as the Sala dei Baroni, which has a stunning vaulted ceiling 92 feet high.

■ **TIP→ You must book and pay for entry in advance on the castle's website, but guided tours (in English and Italian), which provide greater access to the castle's rooms, are available only once inside the castle.** ⊠ *Piazza Municipio, Toledo* ☎ *081/7957722* ⊕ *castelnuovo.comune.napoli.it* ◱ *€6, tours €10* ⊙ *Closed Sun.* Ⓜ *Municipio.*

Galleria Umberto I

NOTABLE BUILDING | The galleria was erected during the "cleanup" of Naples following the devastating cholera epidemic of 1884. With facades on Via Toledo—the most animated street in Naples at the time—the Liberty-style arcade with curvy glass and wrought-iron dome and vaulted wings, built between 1887 and 1890 according to a design by

Emanuele Rocco, had a prestigious and important location. ⊠ *Entrances on Via San Carlo, Via Toledo, Via Santa Brigida, and Via Verdi, Toledo* Ⓜ *Toledo.*

Gallerie d'Italia – Palazzo Banco di Napoli

ART GALLERY | Once the headquarters of the Banco di Napoli, this vast 20th-century building houses a small museum that's worth seeking out for its outstanding collection of 17th- and 18th-century paintings. Relocated from the nearby 17th-century Palazzo Zevallos Stigliano in 2022, the star attraction is Caravaggio's last work, *The Martyrdom of Saint Ursula*. The saint here is, for dramatic effect, deprived of her usual retinue of a thousand followers. On the left, with a face of pure spite, is the king of the Huns, who has just shot Ursula with an arrow after his proposal of marriage has been rejected. Free lunchtime concerts are sometimes held in the atrium of the palazzo. ⊠ *Via Toledo 177, Toledo* ☎ *800/167619* ⊕ *gallerieditalia.com* ◱ *€7* ⊙ *Closed Mon.* Ⓜ *Toledo.*

★ Palazzo Reale

CASTLE/PALACE | **FAMILY** | Created to express Bourbon power and values, the Palazzo Reale (circa 1600) was originally commissioned by the Spanish viceroys as a residence for King Philip III, should he chance to visit Naples. He died in 1621 before ever doing so. The palace was subsequently renovated by successive rulers—including one dim-witted king who liked to fire his hunting rifles at the birds in his tapestries—and is filled with lavish, 18th century–style salons.

To the right after climbing the monumental Scalone d'Onore (Staircase) is the Court Theater, built for Charles III and his private opera company. Highlights beyond include the Throne Room, with its ponderous titular object dating to sometime after 1850; the Ambassadors' Room, with choice Gobelin tapestries and a ceiling painted by Belisario Corenzio (1610–20) that honors Spanish military victories; Room IX, which was bedroom to Charles's queen, Maria Cristina; the Great Captain's Room, with ceiling frescoes by Battistello Caracciolo (1610–16) and a jolly wall-mounted series by Federico Zuccari depicting 12 proverbs; Room XIII, a writing room with some furnishings by Adam Weisweiler, cabinetmaker to Marie Antoinette; and the huge Room XXII featuring Sèvres porcelain.

The heavily gilt Palatine Chapel has a multicolor marble intarsia altar, as well as a Nativity scene with some pieces sculpted by Giuseppe Sammartino. Another wing holds the Biblioteca Nazionale Vittorio Emanuele III. Starting out from Farnese bits and pieces, it was enriched with the papyri from Herculaneum found in 1752. There's also a terrace that looks onto Castel Nuovo. In the Bourbon stables, the Galleria del Tempo (open afternoons and evenings only) offers a multimedia trip through the history of Naples. The Museo Caruso (open mornings only) in the monumental Sala Dorica is dedicated to the great Neapolitan tenor Enrico Caruso. ⊠ *Piazza Plebiscito, Toledo* ☎ *081/400547 ticket office, 848/800288* ⊕ *palazzorealedinapoli.org* ⤴ *Palazzo and galleria €10; gardens €2 (unguided) or €5 (guided)* ⊙ *Closed Wed.* Ⓜ *Toledo, Municipio.*

Piazza del Plebiscito

PLAZA/SQUARE | In 1994, after a period of having been used as a parking lot, this square was restored to create one of Napoli Nobilissima's most majestic spaces, with a Doric semicircle of columns resembling St. Peter's Square in Rome. The piazza was erected in the early 1800s under the Napoleonic regime, and after the regime fell, Ferdinand, the new King of the Two Sicilies, ordered the addition of the Church of San Francesco di Paola. On the left as you approach the church is a statue of Ferdinand and on the right one of his father, Charles III, both of them clad in Roman togas. Around dusk, floodlights come on, creating a magical effect. A delightful sea

breeze airs the square, and most days one corner becomes an improvised soccer stadium where local youths emulate their heroes. ⊠ *Piazza del Plebiscito, Toledo* Ⓜ *Toledo, Municipio.*

★ Sant'Anna dei Lombardi

CHURCH | This church, simple and rather anonymous from the outside, houses some of the most important ensembles of Renaissance sculpture in southern Italy. Begun with the adjacent convent of the Olivetani and its four cloisters in 1411, it was given a Baroque makeover in the mid-17th century by Gennaro Sacco.

To the left of the Ligorio Altar is the Mastrogiudice Chapel, whose altar contains *Scenes from the Life of Jesus* (1489) by Benedetto da Maiano, a great name in Tuscan sculpture. On the other side of the entrance is the Piccolomini Chapel, with a *Crucifixion* by Giulio Mazzoni (circa 1550), a refined marble altar (circa 1475), and a funerary monument to Maria d'Aragona by another prominent Florentine sculptor, Antonello Rossellino (circa 1475). ⊠ *Piazza Monteoliveto 15, Toledo* ☎ *081/4420039* ⊕ *www.santannadeilombardi.com* ⤴ *Side chapels, oratory, and sacristy €6; Abbots' Crypt €2* ⊙ *Side chapels, oratory, and sacristy closed Sun. morning* Ⓜ *Dante.*

Teatro San Carlo and Memus Museum

PERFORMANCE VENUE | Of Italy's opera houses, La Scala in Milan is the most famous, but San Carlo is perhaps the most beautiful, and Naples is, after all, the most operatic of cities. The neoclassical structure, designed by Antonio Niccolini, was built in a mere nine months after an 1816 fire destroyed the original. Many operas, including Donizetti's *Lucia di Lammermoor* and Rossini's *La Donna del Lago*, were composed for the house. Its nearly 200 boxes are arranged on six levels, and its 12,000-square-foot stage permits large-scale productions.

If you're not attending an opera, you can still experience the splendid theater on

688

Sights ▼

1 Castel Nuovo **C5**
2 Galleria Umberto I ... **B5**
3 Gallerie d'Italia – Palazzo Banco di Napoli **B4**
4 Palazzo Reale **B6**
5 Piazza del Plebiscito ... **B6**
6 Sant'Anna dei Lombardi.... **B1**
7 Teatro San Carlo and Memus Museum **B5**
8 Via Toledo.. **B2**

Restaurants ▼

1 A' Cucina Ra Casa Mia.... **A5**
2 A Pignata ... **A2**
3 Trattoria San Ferdinando . **A5**

Hotels ▼

1 Palazzo Turchini **C3**
2 Renaissance Naples Hotel Mediterraneo **B3**

KEY

- ⎓Ⓜ⎓ Line 1 Metropolitana Collinare
- ⎓Ⓜ⎓ Line 2 Metropolitana FS
- ❶ Sights
- ❶ Restaurants
- ❶ Hotels

Toledo and the Port

a 30-minute guided tour and a visit to Memus (Museo Memoria e Musica). The theatrically lit museum and archive have props, costumes, stage sets, multimedia displays, and documents galore. ✉ *Via San Carlo 98/F, Toledo* ☎ *081/7972331 ticket office, 081/7972412 tours, 081/7972449 Memus* ⊕ *www.teatrosancarlo.it* 🎫 *Tours €9* Ⓜ *Municipio.*

Via Toledo

HISTORIC DISTRICT | Sooner or later you'll wind up at one of the busiest commercial arteries, also known as Via Roma, which is thankfully closed to through traffic—at least along the stretch leading from the Palazzo Reale. Don't avoid dipping into this parade of shops and coffee bars where plump pastries are temptingly arranged. ✉ *Via Toledo, Toledo* Ⓜ *Toledo.*

🍴 Restaurants

A' Cucina Ra Casa Mia

$ | SOUTHERN ITALIAN | Just off bustling Via Toledo on the basalti flagstones of a narrow Quartieri Spagnoli street, this small trattoria does superb-value, classic Neapolitan dishes. Take a seat at one of the small tables with checkered tablecloths and ask the amiable staff about the day's freshest seafood, meat, and vegetable dishes while taking in the atmospheric surroundings. **Known for:** homey place popular with locals; fresh seafood pasta dishes; veggie and gluten-free options. ⑤ *Average main: €13* ✉ *Via Carlo De Cesare 14, Toledo* ☎ *081/4976297* ⊕ *www.acucinaracasamia.it* 🕐 *Closed Tues.*

A Pignata

$ | SOUTHERN ITALIAN | A hidden gem in the Quartieri Spagnoli, A Pignata is a favorite with locals for its typical Neapolitan cooking. Each antipasto of land and sea is a meal in itself, but save space for the grilled calamari or *involtini di cotica di maiale*, rolled pork rind stuffed with garlic, parsley, pine nuts, and sultanas. **Known for:** sumptuous

local dishes; relaxed atmosphere; a favorite with locals. ⑤ *Average main: €13* ✉ *Vico Lungo del Gelso 110/112, Toledo* ☎ *081/413526* ⊕ *www.trattoriapignata.it* 🕐 *Closed Mon.* Ⓜ *Toledo.*

★ Trattoria San Ferdinando

$$ | SOUTHERN ITALIAN | FAMILY | This family-run trattoria exudes a calm, relaxed atmosphere, offering traditional Neapolitan dishes without fuss or ostentation. Try the excellent fish or the pasta dishes, which are cooked with a light, modern touch, especially those with *verdure* (fresh leafy vegetables) or with *patate con la provola* (potatoes and smoked mozzarella). **Known for:** excellent, fresh seafood specialties; popular with locals in the evening, so reserve ahead; near Teatro San Carlo. ⑤ *Average main: €17* ✉ *Via Nardones 117, Toledo* ☎ *081/421964* ⊕ *www.trattoriasanferdinando.com* 🕐 *Closed Sun. and last 3 wks of Aug. No dinner Sat. and Mon.* Ⓜ *Toledo, Municipio.*

🛏 Hotels

Palazzo Turchini

$$ | HOTEL | Just a few minutes' walk from the Castel Nuovo, Palazzo Turchini is one of the city center's more attractive smaller hotels. **Pros:** close to port and Metro stop; more intimate than neighboring business hotels; rooftop terrace. **Cons:** close to a busy traffic hub; rooms a tad businesslike; rooms on the small and stuffy side. ⑤ *Rooms from: €194* ✉ *Via Medina 21, Toledo* ☎ *081/5510606* ⊕ *www.palazzoturchini.it* 🛏 *27 rooms* 🍽 *Free Breakfast* Ⓜ *Municipio.*

Renaissance Naples Hotel Mediterraneo

$$$$ | HOTEL | Within walking distance of both the Teatro San Carlo and the Centro Storico, this efficient, Marriott-affiliated business hotel has a lobby and guest rooms that are bright and airy. **Pros:** convenient to the port; pleasant rooftop breakfast terrace; good for those who want a modern hotel. **Cons:** in a busy part of town; inflated prices; not for those who want historic atmosphere. $ *Rooms from: €373* ✉ *Via Nuova Ponte di Tappia 25, Toledo* ☎ *081/7970001* ⊕ *www.marriott.com* ⛵ *189 rooms* ⦿ *Free Breakfast* Ⓜ *Toledo, Municipio.*

🎩 Shopping

Ascione

JEWELRY & WATCHES | A family firm established in 1855 and known for its traditionally made coral jewelry and artwork, Ascione has a showroom/gallery on the second floor of a shabby wing of the Galleria Umberto. Don't miss the 30-minute guided tour (€5, book ahead), which explains the company's rich history and takes in displays that include Egypt's King Farouk's elaborate wedding gift to his bride, Farida, as well as what many consider to be the most beautiful cameo in existence. ✉ *Piazzetta Matilde Serao 19, Piazza Municipio* ☎ *081/421111* ⊕ *www.ascione.it* Ⓜ *Municipio.*

Chiaia, Santa Lucia, and Nearby

The Lungomare is the city's grandest stretch of waterfront. In the 19th century, Naples's waterfront harbored the picturesque quarter that was called Santa Lucia, a district dear to artists and musicians and known for its fishermen's cottages. The fishermen were swept away when an enormous landfill project extended the land out to what is now Via Nazario Sauro and Via Partenope, the address for some of Naples's finest hotels. Huge stretches of the waterfront are blessedly traffic-free, only enhancing their distinctly Neapolitan charm. The area also boasts the chic Chiaia neighborhood surrounding Piazza dei Martiri and the gilded 19th-century Villa Pignatelli.

👁 Sights

Castel dell'Ovo (Castle of the Egg)

CASTLE/PALACE | FAMILY | This 12th-century castle, the oldest in Naples, was built atop the ruins of an ancient Roman villa on a thin promontory that dangles over the Porto Santa Lucia. Legend has it that the poet Virgil hid inside the villa an egg that had protective powers as long as it remained intact. The belief was taken so seriously that to quell the people's panic after Naples suffered an earthquake, an invasion, and a plague in quick succession, its monarch felt compelled to produce an intact egg, solemnly declaring it to be the original.

Today, the castle shares its views with some of the city's top hotels, and its gigantic rooms, rock tunnels, and belvederes over the bay are among the city's most striking sights. ■TIP→ **Note that Castel dell'Ovo is closed for renovation work. Although it's scheduled to reopen in 2025, check on its status before visiting.** ✉ *Santa Lucia waterfront, Via Eldorado 3, off Via Partenope, Santa Lucia* ☎ *081/7956180* ⊕ *www.comune.napoli.it/casteldellovo* 🎟 *Free* Ⓜ *Municipio.*

★ Lungomare (Seafront)

PROMENADE | The first thing Mayor Luigi de Magistris did after his 2011 election was to banish traffic from the city's seafront. Strolling, skating, or biking along Via Caracciolo and Via Partenope with Capri, Vesuvius, and the Castel dell'Ovo in your sights is a favorite Neapolitan pastime. ✉ *Via Caracciolo, Chiaia* Ⓜ *Mergellina, Municipio.*

🍴 Restaurants

★ Amici Miei

$$$ | SOUTHERN ITALIAN | Favored by meat eaters who can't abide another bite of bream, this cozy, dimly lit dining den is known for dishes such as tender carpaccio with fresh artichoke hearts.

There are also excellent house-made pasta selections, including orecchiette with chickpeas or *pappardelle al sugo di agnello* (pasta with lamb sauce), but the highlights are the extravagant grilled meat plates. **Known for:** a choice of quality meat dishes; held in high esteem locally; warm, friendly service befitting the name. $ *Average main: €25* ✉ *Via Monte di Dio 78, Chiaia* ☎ *081/7646063* ⊕ *www. ristoranteamicimiei.com* ⊗ *Closed Mon. and late July–early Sept. No dinner Sun.* Ⓜ *Chiaia.*

Da Dora

$$$ | SEAFOOD | Despite its location on an unpromising-looking *vicolo* (alley) off the Riviera di Chiaia, this small restaurant has achieved cult status for its seafood platters. It's remarkable what owner–chef Renato can produce in his tiny kitchen—start with linguine *alla Dora*, laden with local seafood and fresh tomatoes, and perhaps follow up with grilled *pezzogna* (blue-spotted bream). **Known for:** freshest seafood, both raw and cooked; simple, attractive nautical-theme decor; good quality but slow service when busy. $ *Average main: €26* ✉ *Via Ferdinando Palasciano 30, Chiaia* ☎ *081/680519* ⊗ *Closed Mon.* Ⓜ *San Pasquale.*

'O Tabaccaro

$ | SEAFOOD | If you're trying to keep to a budget but want to enjoy a seafood feast alongside the yachts of the Borgo Marinaro harbor, head to this former tobacco store, now a family-run trattoria. While your eyes feast on all the pretty boats, the Lungomare hotels, the Castel dell'Ovo, and Vesuvius, you can savor classic Neapolitan seafood spaghetti or an *impepata di cozze* (mussels with pepper and garlic, available May–Aug.). **Known for:** relatively inexpensive fare; harborside dining; family service. $ *Average main: €14* ✉ *Via Luculliana 28, Santa Lucia* ☎ *081/7646352* ⊕ *www.facebook. com/brunaruoppolo.1990* Ⓜ *Municipio.*

★ Pescheria Mattiucci

$$ | SOUTHERN ITALIAN | This fourth-generation fish shop is also a trendy, if rough-and-ready, spot to enjoy a super-fresh seafood meal—including superb Neapolitan sushi—and cold wine while sitting on a buoy stool. **Known for:** pescheria counter displaying today's catch; intimate and small place, so get here early or call ahead; fish lunches. $ *Average main: €22* ✉ *Vico Belledonne a Chiaia 27, Chiaia* ☎ *081/2512215* ⊕ *www.pescheriamatti-ucci.com* ⊗ *Closed Mon. No dinner Sun.* Ⓜ *San Pasquale.*

★ Umberto

$$ | SOUTHERN ITALIAN | Run by the Di Porzio family since 1916, Umberto is one of the city's classic restaurants, combining the poshness of its neighborhood, Chiaia, and the friendliness found in other parts of Naples. Try the *paccheri d'o treddeta* ("three-finger" pasta with octopus, tomato, olives, and capers), which bears the nickname of the original Umberto, who happened to be short a few digits. **Known for:** authentic Pizza DOC (smaller, with chunky cornicione rim); charming hosts; classic Neapolitan meat sauce alla Genovese. $ *Average main: €18* ✉ *Via Alabardieri 30–31, Chiaia* ☎ *081/418555* ⊕ *www.umberto.it* ⊗ *No lunch Mon.* Ⓜ *Chiaia.*

☕ Coffee and Quick Bites

Gran Caffè Cimmino

$ | CAFÉ | Connoisseurs often say the most refined pastries in town can be found at Gran Caffè Cimmino. Many of the city's lawyers congregate here, to celebrate or commiserate with crisp, light cannoli; airy lemon eclairs; choux paste in the form of a mushroom laced with chocolate whipped cream; and delightful wild-strawberry tartlets. **Known for:** Neapolitan breakfast favorite; babà (rum-soaked sponge cake) to die for; terrace for watching Chiaia's finest. $ *Average main: €4* ✉ *Via G. Filangieri 12/13, Chiaia*

Chiaia, Santa Lucia, and Nearby

KEY

Line 1
Metropolitana
Collinare

Line 2
Metropolitana
FS

Sights

Restaurants

Quick Bites

Hotels

Golfo di Napoli

0   1/4 mi

0   1/4 km

✆ 081/418303 ⊕ www.facebook.com/cimminofilangieri Ⓜ Chiaia.

Moccia Paneficio

$ | NEAPOLITAN | Established in 1936, this *quartiere* Chiaia favorite is the locals' choice for classic Neapolitan pastries like babà (rum-soaked sponge cake), *torta caprese* (chocolate-and-nut cake), *pastiera* (tart), and *sfogliatelle* (shell-shaped pastry), freshly baked bread and panini for picnics and buffet/pastry trays for parties. **Known for:** zeppola di San Giuseppe (cream-filled pastry); pizzette and other savory snacks; taralli (crackers) and other crunchy goodies. ⑤ *Average main:* €5 ✉ *Via Pasquale di Chiaia 21, Chiaia* ✆ 081/402131 ⊕ www.mocciapanificio.com Ⓜ *Piazza Amedeo.*

Hotels

Chiaja Hotel de Charme

$$ | HOTEL | This 18th-century palazzo has a great location, and its apartments, all on the first floor, have plenty of atmosphere. **Pros:** good location near Piazza del Plebiscito and the Palazzo Reale; on a bustling pedestrian-only street; some antiques in guest rooms. **Cons:** no views in a town with some great ones; even with air-conditioning some rooms get hot in summer; entrance up a flight of stairs. ⑤ *Rooms from:* €171 ✉ *Via Chiaia 216, Chiaia* ✆ 081/415555 ⊕ www.hotelchiaia.it ⤳ 33 *rooms* ⦿ *Free Breakfast* Ⓜ *Chiaia.*

★ Grand Hotel Parker's

$$$$ | HOTEL | A little up the hill from Chiaia, with fine views of the bay and distant Capri, this landmark hotel first opened in 1870 and continues to offer a supreme dose of elegance. **Pros:** excellent restaurant; fabulous views; historical hotel. **Cons:** a very long walk or taxi ride from city center and seafront; not much going on in immediate neighborhood; terrace sometimes closed when hosting weddings. ⑤ *Rooms from:* €397 ✉ *Corso Vittorio Emanuele 135, Chiaia*

✆ 081/7612474 ⊕ www.grandhotelparkers.it ⤳ 67 *rooms* ⦿ *Free Breakfast* Ⓜ *Piazza Amedeo.*

★ Grand Hotel Vesuvio

$$$$ | HOTEL | You'd never guess from the blandly modern exterior that this is the oldest of the city's great seafront hotels—the place where Enrico Caruso died, where Oscar Wilde dallied with lover Lord Alfred Douglas, and where Bill Clinton charmed the waitresses—but, fortunately, the spacious, soothing interior compensates for what's lacking on the outside. **Pros:** luxurious atmosphere; historical setting and traditionally furnished rooms; directly opposite Borgo Marinaro. **Cons:** spa and pool cost extra; some rooms are small; public spaces and some rooms need updating. ⑤ *Rooms from:* €495 ✉ *Via Partenope 45, Santa Lucia* ✆ 081/7640044 ⊕ www.vesuvio.it ⤳ 160 *rooms* ⦿ *Free Breakfast* Ⓜ *Municipio.*

Grand Hotel Santa Lucia

$$$ | HOTEL | Neapolitan Lungomare enchantment can be yours if you stay at this luxurious, quietly understated hotel, which overlooks the port immortalized in the song "Santa Lucia." Hundreds of boats bob in the water, seafood restaurants line the harbor, and the medieval Castel dell'Ovo presides over it all. **Pros:** great views from most rooms; proximity to the port is convenient for trips to the islands; fab pastries and baked goods. **Cons:** rooms can be small; extra charges at breakfast; not near a metro stop. ⑤ *Rooms from:* €290 ✉ *Via Partenope 46, Santa Lucia* ✆ 081/7640666 ⊕ www.santalucia.it ⤳ 85 *rooms* ⦿ *Free Breakfast* Ⓜ *Municipio.*

★ Il Transatlantico Napoli

$$ | B&B/INN | Enjoying perhaps the most enchanting setting in all of Naples, this modestly priced hotel tops many a traveler's dream list of places to stay. **Pros:** fabulous views; great location at a reasonable price; boat hire available. **Cons:** basic, somewhat dated rooms; no elevator; sometimes loud music in the

Borgo. **$** *Rooms from: €195* ⊠ *Via Luc-ulliana 15, Santa Lucia* ☎ *081/7648842* ⊕ *www.transatlanticonapoli.com* ⟲ *8 rooms* �‖ *No Meals* Ⓜ *Municipio.*

★ Palazzo Alabardieri

$$$ | **HOTEL** | Just off the chic Piazza dei Martiri, this intimate hotel pairs modern facilities with a traditional feel. **Pros:** impressive public salons; central location close to fancy shops and restaurants; polite, pleasant, and professional staff. **Cons:** no sea view; cell reception, Wi-Fi, and air-conditioning are patchy; small rooms. **$** *Rooms from: €259* ⊠ *Via Alab-ardieri 38, Chiaia* ☎ *081/415278* ⊕ *www. palazzoalabardieri.it* ⟲ *33 rooms* �‖ *Free Breakfast* Ⓜ *Chiaia.*

Pinto-Storey Hotel

$ | **HOTEL** | Named for its founders—an Englishman who fell in love with Naples and a certain Signora Pinto—this hotel overflows with warmth and late-19th-century (but fully renovated) charm. **Pros:** location in the upscale Chiaia shopping quarter; steps away from Metro stop; traditional Anglophile atmosphere. **Cons:** not close to major sights; little in the way of views; not easy to park nearby. **$** *Rooms from: €98* ⊠ *Via G. Martucci 72, Chiaia* ☎ *081/681260* ⊕ *www.pintostorey.it* ⟲ *6 rooms* �‖ *No Meals* Ⓜ *Piazza Amedeo.*

★ Weekend a Napoli

$$ | **B&B/INN** | Patrizia and Paolo run this homey upscale B&B in a handsome stile-liberty (Italian Art Nouveau) palazzo on the well-to-do Vomero hill. **Pros:** residential Vomero atmosphere; home baking and cozy lounge; passionate, knowledgeable hosts. **Cons:** basic rooms lack light and are noisy; some rooms have steps to mezzanine beds; away from the downtown sights. **$** *Rooms from: €158* ⊠ *Via Enrico Alvino 157, Vomero* ☎ *081/5781010* ⊕ *weekendan-apoli.com* ⊗ *Closed Jan.* ⟲ *6 rooms* �‖ *Free Breakfast* Ⓜ *Quattro Giornate.*

Nightlife

★ Enoteca Belledonne

WINE BAR | Between 8 and 9 in the evening, it seems as though the whole upscale Chiaia neighborhood has descended into this tiny space for an aperitivo. The small tables and low stools can be awkward, but the cozy atmosphere, friendly staff, and the pleasure of being surrounded by glass-front cabinets full of wine bottles with beautiful labels more than makes up for it. Excellent local wines are available by the glass at great prices. ⊠ *Vico Belledonne a Chiaia 18, Chiaia* ☎ *081/403162* ⊕ *www.enoteca-belledonne.eu* Ⓜ *San Pasquale.*

Shopping

Marinella

ACCESSORIES | Count the British royal family among the customers of this shop, which has been selling traditional made-to-measure ties for more than 100 years. It also sells scarves and other small accessories for both men and women. ⊠ *Via Riviera di Chiaia 287, Chi-aia* ☎ *081/2451182* ⊕ *www.emarinella.eu* Ⓜ *Chiaia, San Pasquale.*

Tramontano

LEATHER GOODS | Since 1865, this place has been crafting fine leather luggage, bags, belts, and wallets. ⊠ *Via Chiaia 143, Chiaia* ☎ *081/414837* ⊕ *www. tramontano.it* Ⓜ *Chiaia.*

Piazza Garibaldi

The first place many see in Naples thanks to the city's main train station, there is not a lot to hold your attention here. Recently completely rebuilt, it now features a swanky new underground shopping mall based around the train station, but is still a gathering point for street sellers and hawkers and is best avoided at night. The surrounding area has some notable churches as well as the famed Porta Capuana, one of the historic gates to the city walls.

Restaurants

Da Michele

$ | PIZZA | FAMILY | You may recognize Da Michele from the movie *Eat, Pray, Love,* but for more than 140 years before Julia Roberts arrived, this place was a culinary reference point. Despite offering only four types of pizza—marinara (tomato, garlic, and oregano), Margherita (tomato, mozzarella, and basil), *cosacca* (tomato, pecorino, and basil), and *marita* (half marinara, half Margherita)—plus a small selection of drinks, it still manages to draw long lines. **Known for:** pizza purists' favorite; stripped-down choice of pizzas; long lines outside the humble, historic flagship location. ⑤ *Average main: €6* ✉ *Via Sersale 1/3, off Corso Umberto, between Piazza Garibaldi and Piazza Nicola Amore, Piazza Garibaldi* ☎ *081/5539204* ⊕ *www.damichele.net* ☾ *Closed 2 wks in Aug.* Ⓜ *Garibaldi, Duomo.*

Mimì alla Ferrovia

$$ | NEAPOLITAN | Patrons of this local institution have included the filmmaker Federico Fellini and that truly Neapolitan comic genius and self-styled aristocrat Totò. It's in a fairly seedy area, but it's worth taking a taxi (especially at night) to get here and sample updated versions of such classics as grilled octopus or *tubettoni* (short, tubular pasta shapes) with sausage-meat, mushrooms, and provola cheese. **Known for:** crammed with photos of Italian VIPs; classic Neapolitan dishes with modern touches; a merry crowd of diners. ⑤ *Average main: €19* ✉ *Via A. D'Aragona 19/21, Piazza Garibaldi* ☎ *081/5538525* ⊕ *www.mimiallaferrovia. it* ☾ *Closed Sun. and last wk in Aug.* Ⓜ *Garibaldi.*

Capodimonte and Vomero

The Parco di Capodimonte is the crowning point of the vast mountainous plain that slopes down through the city to the waterfront. With views over the entire city and bay, the park was first founded in the 18th century as a hunting preserve by Charles of Bourbon. Before long he commissioned a spectacular Palazzo Reale for the park. Today this palace is the Museo di Capodimonte, which contains among its treasures the city's greatest collection of Old Master paintings.

To the west is the largely residential Vomero. From the balcony belvedere of the Museo di San Martino, a rich spread of southern Italian amplitude fills the eye: hillsides dripping with luxuriant greenery interspersed with streets short and narrow, countless church spires, and far below, the reason it all works, the intensely blue Bay of Naples. To tie together the lower parts with Vomero, everyone uses the *funicolare*—the funicular system that runs up and down the hill.

◉ Sights

Castel Sant'Elmo

CASTLE/PALACE | Perched on the Vomero, this massive castle is almost the size of a small town. Built by the Angevins in the 14th century to dominate the port and the old city, it was remodeled by the Spanish in 1537. The parapets, configured in the form of a six-pointed star, provide fabulous views. Once a major military outpost, the castle these days hosts occasional cultural events. Within the castle, the Museo del Novecento traces Naples's 20th-century artistic output. ✉ *Largo San Martino, Vomero* ☎ *081/5587708* ⊕ *www.beniculturali.it* ☐ *€5* Ⓜ *Vanvitelli.*

★ Certosa e Museo di San Martino

RELIGIOUS BUILDING | Atop a rocky promontory with a fabulous view of the entire city, this monastery seems more like a palace. Indeed, the *certosa*, or charter house, started in 1325, was so sumptuous that by the 18th century Ferdinand IV threatened to halt the religious order's government subsidy. Highlights include the Cappella del Tesoro, with Luca Giordano's ceiling fresco of Judith holding aloft Holofernes's head and Jusepe de Ribera's masterful *Pietà;* the Quarto del Priore (Prior's Quarters), an extravaganza of salons filled with frescoes and paintings; and the Sezione Presepiale, the world's greatest collection of Christmas cribs. ⊠ *Piazzale San Martino 8, Vomero* ☎ *081/2294503* ⊕ *www.beniculturali.it* 🎫 *€6* ⊗ *Closed Wed.* Ⓜ *Vanvitelli.*

★ Museo di Capodimonte

ART MUSEUM | The grandiose, 18th-century, neoclassical, Bourbon royal palace houses fine and decorative art in 124 rooms. The main galleries on the first floor are devoted to the Farnese collection, as well as work from the 13th to the 18th century, including many pieces by Dutch masters, as well as an El Greco and 12 Titian paintings. On the second floor look for stunning paintings by Simone Martini (circa 1284–1344) and Caravaggio (1573–1610). ⊠ *Via Miano 2, Capodimonte* ☎ *081/7499111* ⊕ *capodimonte.cultura.gov.it* 🎫 *€15* ⊗ *Closed Wed.* Ⓜ *Museo then Bus C63, 168, 178, 204, or 3M.*

Nightlife

Fonoteca

BARS | By day, this is the city's best independent record store. By night, it's *the* place to hear eclectic tunes and mingle in Vomero. It serves decent bar snacks, pasta dishes, cakes, and drinks. ⊠ *Via Morghen 31, Vomero* ☎ *081/5560338* ⊕ *www.fonoteca.net* Ⓜ *Vanvitelli.*

Herculaneum

10 km (6 miles) southeast of Naples.

A visit to the archaeological site of Herculaneum neatly counterbalances the hustle of its larger neighbor, Pompeii. Although close to the heart of busy Ercolano—indeed, in places right under the town—the ancient site seems worlds apart.

GETTING HERE AND AROUND

To get to Herculaneum by car, take the A3 Naples–Salerno autostrada and exit at Ercolano. Follow signs for the "Scavi" (excavations). The Circumvesuviana railway connects Herculaneum to Naples, Portici, Torre del Greco, Torre Annunziata, Pompeii, and Sorrento.

Sights

★ Herculaneum Ruins

ARCHAEOLOGICAL SITE | Lying more than 50 feet below the present-day town of Ercolano, the ruins of Herculaneum are set among the acres of greenhouses that make this area an important European flower-growing center. In AD 79, the gigantic eruption of Vesuvius, which also destroyed Pompeii, buried the town under a tide of volcanic mud. Excavation first began in 1738 under King Charles of Bourbon. Today less than half of Herculaneum has been excavated. Nevertheless, what has been found is generally better preserved than Pompeii. In some cases, you can even see the original wooden beams, doors, and staircases. At the entrance, pick up a free map showing the gridlike layout of the dig. Splurge on an audio guide app via ⊕ *www.ercolano. tours* (€10): the standard audio guide (€8 for one, €13 for two) may be available for those without a smartphone. You can also join a group with a local guide (around €15 per person). Most of the houses are open, and a representative cross section of domestic, commercial, and civic buildings can be seen. ⊠ *Corso*

Planning for Your Day in Pompeii

Getting There

The archaeological site of Pompeii has its own stop (Pompei–Villa dei Misteri) on the Circumvesuviana line to Sorrento, close to the main entrance at the Porta Marina, which is the best place from which to start a tour. If, like many visitors every year, you get the wrong train from Naples (stopping at the other "Pompei" station), all is not lost. There's another entrance to the excavations at the far end of the site, just a seven-minute walk to the Amphitheater.

Admission

Single tickets for the vast main sight plus suburban villas cost €22 and are valid for one full day. The site is open April–October, daily 9–7 (last admission at 5:30); and November–March, daily 9–5 (last admission at 3:30). For more information call ☎ 081/8575347 or visit ⊕ www.pompeiisites.org.

What to Bring

The only restaurant inside the site is both overpriced and busy, so bring along water and snacks. There are some shady, underused picnic tables outside the Porta di Nola, to the northeast of the site. Luggage is not allowed in the site.

Timing

Visiting Pompeii does have its frustrating aspects: many buildings are blocked off by locked gates, and enormous group tours tend to clog up more popular attractions. But the site is so big that it's easy to lose yourself. To really see the site, you'll need four or five hours, a bit less if you hire a guide.

To get the most out of Pompeii, rent an audio guide and opt for one of the three itineraries (two hours, four hours, or six hours). If hiring a guide, make sure the guide is registered for an English tour and standing inside the gate; agree beforehand on the length of the tour and the price, and prepare yourself for sound bites of English mixed with dollops of hearsay. For a higher-quality (and more expensive) full-day tour, try Context Travel (⊕ www.contexttravel.com).

Resina 6, Ercolano ☎ 081/7777008 ⊕ ercolano.beniculturali.it ⌨ €13; €5 supplement for Teatro Antico ⏱ Closed Wed.

Museo Archeologico Virtuale (MAV)

HISTORY MUSEUM | FAMILY | With dazzling "virtual" versions of Herculaneum's streets and squares and a multidimensional simulation of Vesuvius erupting, Herculaneum's 1st-century-meets-the-21st-century museum is a must for kids and adults alike. After stopping at the ticket office, you descend, as in an excavation, to a floor below. You'll experience Herculaneum's Villa dei Papiri before and (even more dramatically) during the eruption, courtesy of special effects: enter "the burning cloud" of AD 79; then emerge, virtually speaking, inside Pompeii's House of the Faun, which can be seen both as it is and as it was for two centuries BC. The next re-creation is again Villa dei Papiri. Then comes a stellar pre- and postflooding view of Baia's Nymphaeum, the now-displaced statues arrayed as they were in the days of Emperor Claudius, who commissioned them.

Visitors here are invited to take a front-row seat for "Day and Night in the Forum of Pompeii," with soldiers, litter-bearing slaves, and toga-clad figures moving spectrally to complete the spell; or to make a vicarious visit to the Lupanari brothels, their various pleasures illustrated in graphic virtual frescoes along the walls. A wooden model of Herculaneum's theater, its virtual re-creation, reminds us that it was here that a local farmer, while digging a well, first came across what proved to be not merely a single building but a whole town. Equally fascinating are the virtual baths. There's also a 3D film of Vesuvius erupting, replete with a fatalistic narrative and cataclysmic special effects: the words of Pliny the Younger provide a timeless commentary while the floor vibrates under your feet. ⊠ *Via IV Novembre 44, Ercolano* ☎ *081/7776843* ⊕ *www. museomav.it* ⊠ *€11* ⊙ *Closed Mon.*

Pompeii

22 km (14 miles) southeast of Naples, 17 km (10½ miles) southeast of Herculaneum.

Mention Pompeii and most travelers think of ancient Roman villas, prancing bronze fauns, plaster casts of writhing Vesuvius victims, and the fabled days of the emperors.

GETTING HERE AND AROUND

To get to Pompeii by car, take the A3 Napoli–Salerno highway to the Pompei exit and follow signs for the nearby "Scavi." There are numerous guarded parking lots near the Porta Marina, Piazza Essedra, and Anfiteatro entrances, where you can leave your vehicle for a fee.

Pompeii has two central Circumvesuviana railway stations served by two separate train lines. The Naples–Sorrento train stops at "Pompei Scavi–Villa dei Misteri," 100 yards from the Porta Marina ticket office of the archaeological site, while the Naples–Poggiomarino train stops at Pompei Santuario, more convenient for the Santuario della Madonna del Rosario and the hotels and restaurants in the

modern town center. A third Ferrovie della Statale (FS) train station south of the town center is only convenient if arriving from Salerno or Rome.

◉ Sights

★ Pompeii

ARCHAEOLOGICAL SITE | Petrified memorial to Vesuvius's eruption in 79 AD, Pompeii is the largest, most accessible, and most famous excavation anywhere. Ancient Pompeii had a population of 10,000–20,000 and covered about 170 acres on the seaward end of the Sarno Plain. Today it attracts more than 2 million visitors every year, but if you come in the quieter late afternoon, you can truly fall under the site's spell. Highlights include the Foro (Forum), which served as Pompeii's cultural, political, commercial, and religious hub; homes that were captured in various states by the eruption of Vesuvius, including the Casa del Poeta Tragico (House of the Tragic Poet), a typical middle-class residence with a floor mosaic of a chained dog, and the Casa dei Vettii (House of the Vettii), the best example of a wealthy merchant's home; the Villa dei Misteri (Villa of the Mysteries), a palatial abode with many fresco-adorned rooms; and the Anfiteatro (Amphitheater), built around 70 BC. Consider renting an audio guide and opt for one of the three itineraries (two hours, four hours, or six hours) available at Porta Marina. If hiring a guide, agree beforehand on the length of the tour and the price. Advance tickets can be purchased online at ⊕ *www.ticketone.it/en/artist/scavi-pompei* (there's a link on the official Pompeii website). ⊠ *Pompei* ☎ *081/8575347* ⊕ *www.pompeiisites.org* ⊠ *€18 (Pompeii Express ticket) for the main ancient site; €22 (Pompeii+ ticket) includes the Ville Suburbane: Villa dei Misteri etc; €26 ("3 Days" ticket) also includes Oplontis, Villa Arianna, Villa San Marco, Museo Libero D'Orsi plus shuttle bus.*

Vesuvius

8 km (5 miles) northeast of Herculane-um, 16 km (10 miles) east of Naples.

Vesuvius may have lost its plume of smoke for now, but it has lost none of its fascination—especially for those who live in the towns around the cone.

GETTING HERE AND AROUND

To arrive by car, take the A3 Napoli–Saler-no autostrada to the Torre del Greco exit and follow Via E. De Nicola from the tollbooth and then signs for the Parco Nazionale del Vesuvio.

Vesuvio Express operates a shuttle-bus service (€10) departing every 40 minutes from Ercolano Circumvesuviana station. The vehicles thread their way rapidly up back roads, reaching the top in 20 minutes. Allow at least three hours for the journey, including a 30-minute walk to the crater on a soft cinder track.

BUS CONTACT Vesuvio Express. ⊠ *Piazzale Stazione Circumvesuviano 7, Ercolano* ☎ *081/7393666* ⊕ *vesuvioexpress.info.*

◉ Sights

Vesuvius

VOLCANO | Although Vesuvius's destructive powers are on hold, the threat of an eruption remains ever present. Seen from the other side of the Bay of Naples, Vesuvius appears to have two peaks: on the northern side is the steep face of Monte Somma, possibly part of the original crater wall in AD 79; to the south is the present-day cone of Vesuvius, which has actually formed within the ancient crater. The AD 79 cone would have been considerably higher, perhaps peaking at around 9,000 feet. The upper slopes bear the visible scars left by 19th- and 20th-century eruptions, the most striking being the lava flow from 1944 lying to

the left (north side) of the approach road from Ercolano on the way up.

As you tour the cities that felt the volcano's wrath, you may be overwhelmed by the urge to explore Vesuvius itself, and it's well worth the trip. The view when the air is clear is magnificent, with the curve of the coast and the tiny white houses among the orange and lemon blossoms. When the summit becomes lost in mist, though, you'll be lucky to see your hand in front of your face. If you notice the summit clearing—it tends to be clearer in the afternoon—head for it. If possible, see Vesuvius after you've toured the ruins of buried Herculaneum to appreciate the magnitude of the volcano's power. Admission to the crater includes a compulsory guide, usually a young geologist who speaks a smattering of English. At the bottom you'll be offered a stout walking stick (a small tip is appreciated when you return it). The climb can be tiring if you're not used to steep hikes. Because of the volcanic stone, you should wear athletic or sturdy shoes, not sandals.

Entry requires a timed ticket and must be purchased in advance at ⊕ *vesuvi-opark.vivaticket.it* unless you buy entry as a package from Vesuvio Express. ☎ *081/7775720, 081/8653911* ⊕ *www. parconazionaledelvesuvio.it* ▱ *€12.*

Oplontis (Torre Annunziata)

20 km (12 miles) southeast of Naples, 5 km (3 miles) west of Pompeii.

Surrounded by the fairly drab 1960s urban landscape of Torre Annunziata, Oplontis justifies its reputation as one of the more mysterious archaeological sites to be unearthed in the 20th century. The villa complex has been imaginatively ascribed—from a mere inscription on an

Continued on page 708

ANCIENT POMPEII
TOMB OF A CIVILIZATION

The site of Pompeii, petrified memorial to Vesuvius's eruption in AD 79, is the largest, most accessible, and probably most famous of excavations anywhere.

A busy commercial center with a population of 10,000–20,000, ancient Pompeii covered about 170 acres on the seaward end of the fertile Sarno Plain. Today Pompeii is choked with both the dust of 25 centuries and more than 3 million visitors every year; only by escaping the hordes and lingering along its silent streets can you truly fall under the site's spell.

On a quiet backstreet, all you need is a little imagination to picture life in this ancient town. Come in the late afternoon when the site is nearly deserted and you will understand the true pleasure of visiting Pompei.

Top: Plaster cast of human remains, Pompeii.
Bottom: Standing columns, House of the Faun

A FUNNY THING HAPPENS ON THE WAY TO THE FORUM

as you walk through Pompeii. Covered with dust and decay as it is, the city seems to come alive. Perhaps it's the familiar signs of life observed along the ancient streets: bakeries with large ovens just like those for making pizzas, *thermopolia* (snack bars) tracks of cart wheels cut into the road surface, graffiti etched onto the plastered surfaces of street walls. But a glance up at Vesuvius, still brooding over the scene like an enormous headstone, reminds you that these folks—whether imagined in your head or actually wearing a mantle of

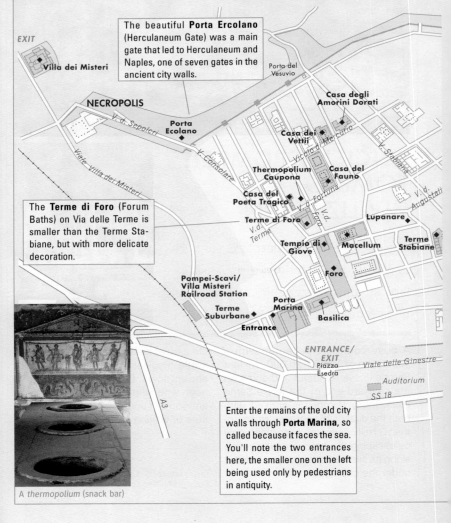

The beautiful **Porta Ercolano** (Herculaneum Gate) was a main gate that led to Herculaneum and Naples, one of seven gates in the ancient city walls.

The **Terme di Foro** (Forum Baths) on Via delle Terme is smaller than the Terme Stabiane, but with more delicate decoration.

Enter the remains of the old city walls through **Porta Marina**, so called because it faces the sea. You'll note the two entrances here, the smaller one on the left being used only by pedestrians in antiquity.

EXIT

Villa dei Misteri

Porta del Vesuvio

NECROPOLIS

V. d. Sepolcri

Porta Ecolano

Viale Villa dei Misteri

V. Consolare

Vicolo di Mercurio

Casa degli Amorini Dorati

Casa dei Vettii

V. Stabiana

Thermopolium Caupona

Casa del Fauno

Casa del Poeta Tragico

V. d. Fortuna

V. d. Augustali

Terme di Foro

V. d. Fora

V. d. Terme

Lupanare

Tempio di Giove

Macellum

Terme Stabiane

Pompei-Scavi/ Villa Misteri Railroad Station

Foro

Terme Suburbane

Porta Marina

Entrance

Basilica

ENTRANCE/ EXIT
Piazza Esedra

Viale delle Ginestre

Auditorium

SS 18

A3

A *thermopolium* (snack bar)

lava dust—have not taken a breath for centuries. The town was laid out in a grid pattern, with two main intersecting streets. The wealthiest took a whole block for themselves; or built a house and rented out the front rooms,

Pompeii's cemetery, or Necropolis

facing the street, as shops. There were good numbers of *tabernae* (taverns) and thermopolia on almost every corner, and frequent shows at the amphitheater.

The **Orto dei Fuggiaschi** (Garden of the Fugitives) contains poignant plaster casts of those overwhelmed by the eruption in AD 79 and left *in situ*. Many of the victims were claimed a day

after the initial eruption not by the rain of lapilli and ash but by the first surge—— a dense cloud of vapor, ash, and other solids that swept down the slopes of the volcano like a boiling avalanche at 40–50 miles per hour.

Togas, the required Roman attire, were washed and wool was dyed at a *fullonica* (fullery). Urine was used to bleach and clean garments in large stone vats and basins, that you can see all over Pompeii.

PUBLIC LIFE IN ANCIENT POMPEII

Forum

THE CITY CENTER

As you enter the ruins at Porta Marina, make your way uphill to the **Foro** (Forum), which served as Pompeii's commercial, cultural, political, and religious center. You can still see some of the two stories of colonnades that used to line the square. Like the ancient Greek *agora* in Athens, the Forum was a busy shopping area, complete with public officials to apply proper standards of weights and measures. Fronted by an elegant three-column portico on the eastern side of the forum is the **Macellum**, the covered meat and fish market dating to the 2nd century BC; here vendors sold goods from their reserved spots in the central market. It was also in the Forum that elections were held, politicians let rhetoric fly, speeches and official announcements were made, and worshippers crowded around the **Tempio di Giove** (Temple of Jupiter), at the northern end of the forum.

Basilica

On the southwestern corner is the **Basilica**, the city's law court and the economic center. These rectangular aisled halls were the model for early Christian churches, which had a nave (central aisle) and two side aisles separated by rows of columns. Standing in the Basilica, you can recognize the continuity between Roman and Christian architecture.

THE GAMES

The **Anfiteatro** (Amphitheater) was the ultimate in entertainment for Pompeians and offered a gamut of experiences, but essentially this was for gladiators rather than wild animals. By Roman standards, Pompeii's amphitheater was quite small (seating 20,000). Built in about 70 BC,

Amphitheater

making it the oldest extant permanent amphitheater in the Roman world, it was oval and divided into three seating areas. There were two main entrances—at the north and south ends—and a narrow passage on the west called the Porta Libitinensis, through which the dead were probably dragged out. A wall painting found in a house near the theater (now in the Naples Museum) depicts the riot in the amphitheater in AD 59 when several citizens from the nearby town of Nocera were killed. After Nocerian appeals to Nero, shows were suspended for three years.

BATHS AND BROTHELS

In its day, Pompeii was celebrated as the Côte d'Azur of the ancient Roman empire. Evidence of a Sybaritic bent is everywhere—in the town's grandest villas, in its baths and rich decorations, and murals revealing a worship of hedonism. Satyrs, bacchantes, hermaphrodites, and acrobatic couples are pictured.

The first buildings to the left past the ticket turnstiles are the **Terme Suburbane** (Suburban Baths), built—by all accounts without permission—right up against the city walls. The baths have eyebrow-raising frescoes in the *apodyterium* (changing room) that strongly suggest that more than just bathing and massaging went on here. On the walls of **Lupanari** (brothels) are scenes of erotic games in which clients could engage. The **Terme Stabiane** (Stabian Baths) had underground furnaces, the heat from which circulated beneath the floor, rose through flues in the walls, and escaped through chimneys. The sequence of the rooms is standard: changing room (apoditerium), tepid (tepidarium), hot (calidarium), and cold (frigidarium). A vigorous massage with oil was followed by rest and conversation.

Fresco of Pyramus and Thisbe in the House of Loreius Tiburtinus

Thanks to those deep layers of pyroclastic deposits from Vesuvius that protected the site from natural wear and tear over the centuries, graffiti found in Pompeii provide unique insights into the sort of things that the locals found important 2,000 years ago. A good many were personal and lend a human dimension to the disaster that not even the sights can equal.

At the baths: **"What is the use of having a Venus if she's made of marble?"**

At the entrance to the front lavatory at a private house: **"May I always and everywhere be as potent with women as I was here."**

On the Viale ai Teatri: **"A copper pot went missing from my shop. Anyone who returns it to me will be given 65 bronze coins."**

In the Basilica: **"A small problem gets larger if you ignore it."**

PRIVATE LIFE IN ANCIENT POMPEII

The facades of houses in Pompeii were relatively plain and seldom hinted at the care and attention lavished on the private rooms within. When visitors arrived they passed the shops and entered an atrium, from which the occupants received air, sunlight, and rainwater, the latter caught by the *impluvium*, a rectangular-shaped receptacle under the sloped roof. In the back was a receiving room, the *tablinum*, and behind was another open area, the peristyle. Life revolved around this uncovered inner courtyard, with rows of columns and perhaps a garden with a fountain. The atrium was surrounded by *cubicula* (bedrooms) and the *triclinium* (dining area). Interior floors and walls were covered with colorful marble tiles, mosaics, and frescoes.

Mosaic, Casa del Poeta Tragico

Several homes were captured in various states by the eruption of Vesuvius, each representing a different slice of Pompeiian life. The **Casa del Fauno** (House of the Faun) displayed wonderful mosaics, now at the Museo Archeologico Nazionale in Naples. The **Casa del Poeta Tragico** (House of the Tragic Poet) is a typical middle-class house. On the floor is a mosaic of a chained dog and the inscription *cave canem* ("Beware of the dog"). The **Casa degli Amorini Dorati** (House of the Gilded Cupids) is an elegant, well-preserved home with original decorations. Many paintings and mosaics were executed at **Casa del Menandro** (House of Menander), a patrician's villa named for a fresco of the Greek playwright. Two blocks beyond the Stabian Baths you'll notice on the left the current digs at the **Casa dei Casti Amanti** (House of the Chaste Lovers). A team of plasterers and painters were at work here when Vesuvius erupted, redecorating one of the rooms and patching up the cracks in the bread oven near the entrance—possibly caused by tremors a matter of days before.

Small Garden
Triclinium   Owner's Quarters
Kitchen   Servant's Quarters
Secondary Atrium
Entrance
Garden
Atrium
Impluvium
Peristyle

CASA DEI VETTII

The House of the Vettii (reopened in January 2023 after two decades of restoration) is the best example of a house owned by wealthy *mercatores* (merchants). It contains vivid murals—a magnificent *pinacoteca* (picture gallery) within the very heart of Pompeii. The scenes here—except for those in the two wings off the atrium—were all painted after the earthquake of AD 62. Once inside, look at the delicate frieze around the wall of the triclinium (on the right of the peristyle garden as you enter from the atrium), depicting cupids engaged in various activities, such as selling oils and perfumes, working as goldsmiths and metalworkers, acting as wine merchants, or performing in chariot races. Another of the main attractions in the Casa dei Vettii is the small cubicle beyond the kitchen area (to the right of the atrium) with its faded erotic frescoes now protected by Perspex screens.

UNLOCKING THE VILLA DEI MISTERI

Villa dei Misteri

There is no more astounding, magnificently memorable evidence of Pompeii's devotion to the pleasures of the flesh than the frescoes on view at the **Villa dei Misteri** (Villa of the Mysteries), a palatial abode 400 yards outside the city gates, northwest of Porta Ercolano. Unearthed in 1909, this villa had many beautiful rooms painted with frescoes; the finest are in the *triclinium*. Painted in the most glowing Pompeiian reds and ochers, the panels may relate the saga of a young bride (Ariadne) and her initiation into the mysteries of the cult of Dionysus, who was a god imported to Italy from Greece and then given the Latin name of Bacchus. The god of wine and debauchery also represented the triumph of the irrational—of all those mysterious forces that no official state religion could fully suppress.

> **Pompeii's best frescoes, painted in glowing reds and oranges, retain an amazing vibrancy.**

The Villa of the Mysteries frescoes were painted circa 50 BC, most art historians believe, and represent the peak of the Second Style of Pompeiian wall painting. The triclinium frescoes are thought to have been painted by a local artist, although the theme may well have been copied from an earlier cycle of paintings from the Hellenistic period. In all there are 10 scenes, depicting children and matrons, musicians and satyrs, phalluses and gods. There are no inscriptions (such as are found on Greek vases), and after 2,000 years historians remain puzzled by many aspects of the triclinium cycle. Scholars endlessly debate the meaning of these frescoes, but anyone can tell they are among the most beautiful paintings left to us by antiquity. In several ways, the eruption of Vesuvius was a blessing in disguise, for without it, these masterworks of art would have perished long ago.

amphora—to Nero's second wife, Poppaea Sabina. Her family was well known among the landed gentry of neighboring Pompeii, although, after a kick in the stomach from her emperor husband, she died some 15 years before the villa was overwhelmed by the eruption of 79.

GETTING HERE AND AROUND

By car, take the A3 Napoli–Salerno autostrada to the Torre Annunziata exit. Follow Via Veneto west, then turn left onto Via Sepolcri for the excavations. By train, take the Circumvesuviana railway to Torre Annunziata, the town's modern name (€3 from Naples).

Sights

Oplontis

ARCHAEOLOGICAL SITE | For those overwhelmed by the throngs at Pompeii, a visit to the site of Oplontis offers a chance for contemplation and intellectual stimulation. What has been excavated so far of the Villa of the Empress Poppaea covers more than 75,000 square feet, and because the site is bound by a road to the west and a canal to the south, its full extent may never be known.

Complete with porticoes, a large peristyle, a pool, baths, and extensive gardens, the villa is thought by some to have been a school for young philosophers and orators. You have to visit to appreciate the full range of Roman wall paintings; one highlight is found in Room 5, a sitting room that overlooked the sea. ⊠ *Via Sepolcri 1, Torre Annunziata* ☎ *081/8575347* ⊕ *www.pompeiisites.org* 🎫 *€8* 🕙 *Closed Tues.*

Ischia

45 mins by hydrofoil, 90 mins by car ferry from Naples, 60 mins by ferry from Pozzuoli.

Although Capri leaves you breathless with its charm and beauty, Ischia (pronounced "EES-kee-ah") takes time to cast its spell. In fact, an overnight stay is not long enough; you have to look harder here for the signs of antiquity, the traffic can be reminiscent of Naples, and the island displays all the hallmarks of rapid, uncontrolled urbanization. Ischia does have many jewels, though. There are the wine-growing villages beneath the lush volcanic slopes of Monte Epomeo, and unlike Capri, the island enjoys a life of its own that survives when the tourists head home.

GETTING HERE AND AROUND

Ischia is well connected with the mainland in all seasons. The last boats leave for Naples and Pozzuoli at about 8 pm (though in the very high season there is a midnight sailing), and you should allow plenty of time for getting to the port and buying a ticket. Ischia has three ports—Ischia Porto, Casamicciola, and Forio (hydrofoils only)—so you should choose your ferry or hydrofoil according to your destination. Non-Italians can bring cars to the island relatively freely. Up-to-date schedules are published at ⊕ *www. traghetti-ischia.info.*

Ischia's bus network reaches all the major sites and beaches on one of its 18 lines. The principal lines are CD and CS, circling the island in clockwise and counterclockwise directions—in the summer months runs continue until after midnight. The main bus terminus is in Ischia Porto at the start of Via Cosca, where buses run by the company EAV radiate out around the island. There are also convenient *fermate* (stops) at the two main beaches—Citara and Maronti—with timetables displayed at the terminus. Tickets cost €1.50 per ride, €1.80 for 100 minutes. A one-day pass is €4.50, a seven-day pass €14.50. Note that conditions can get hot and crowded at peak beach-visiting times.

VISITOR INFORMATION

CONTACT Infopoint Ischia. ✉ *Via Iasolino 7, Ischia* ☎ *081/984163* ⊕ *www.agenziaturismocampania.it.*

◉ Sights

Forio

TOWN | FAMILY | The far-western and southern coasts of Ischia are more rugged and attractive than other areas. Forio, at the extreme west, has a waterfront church, Chiesa del Soccorso, and is a good spot for lunch or dinner. ■**TIP**→ **Head to the whitewashed Soccorso church to watch a gorgeous sunset—perhaps the best spot on the island to do so.** ✉ *Forio.*

Giardini Poseidon Terme

HOT SPRING | FAMILY | The largest spa on the island has the added boon of a natural sauna hollowed out of the rocks. Here you can sit like a Roman senator on stone chairs recessed in the rock and let the hot water cascade over you. With countless thermally regulated pools, promenades, and steam pools, plus lots of kitschy toga-clad statues of the Caesars, Poseidon exerts a special pull on tourists, many of them grandparents shepherding grandchildren. On certain days, the place is overrun with people, so be prepared for crowds and wailing babies. ✉ *Baia di Citara, Via Giovanni Mazzella, Forio* ☎ *081/9087111* ⊕ *www.giardiniposeidonterme.com* 💶 *€40 low season, €42 high season* ⊗ *Closed Nov.–late Apr.*

Ischia Ponte

NEIGHBORHOOD | FAMILY | Most of the hotels are along the beach in the part of town called Ischia Ponte, which gets its name from the *ponte* (bridge) built by Alfonso of Aragon in 1438 to link the picturesque castle on a small islet offshore with the town and port. For a while the castle was the home of Vittoria Colonna, poetess, granddaughter of Renaissance Duke Federico da Montefeltro (1422–82), and platonic soulmate of Michelangelo, with whom she carried on a lengthy correspondence. You'll find a typical resort atmosphere in this area: countless cafés, shops, and restaurants, and a 1-km (½-mile) fine-sand beach. ✉ *Ischia Ponte.*

Ischia Porto

TOWN | FAMILY | This is the island's largest town and the usual point of debarkation. It's no workaday port, however, but rather a lively resort with plenty of hotels, restaurants, the island's best shopping area, and low, flat-roof houses on terraced hillsides overlooking the water. Its narrow streets and villas and gardens are framed by pines. ✉ *Ischia Porto.*

Monte Epomeo

VOLCANO | The inland town of Fontana is the base for excursions to the top of this long-dormant volcano that dominates the island landscape. You can reach its 2,589-foot peak in less than 1½ hours of relatively easy walking. ✉ *Ischia.*

★ Sant'Angelo

TOWN | FAMILY | On the southern coast, this is a charming village with a narrow path leading to its promontory; the road doesn't reach all the way into town, so it's free of traffic. It's a five-minute boat ride from the beach of Maronti, at the foot of cliffs. ✉ *Sant'Angelo.*

🍴 Restaurants

Da Cocò

$$ | SOUTHERN ITALIAN | This inviting restaurant with a terrace is on the causeway that links the Aragonese castle to the rest of Ischia. It's renowned for its fresh seafood, which is highly prized by the Ischitani: shoreline classics dominate, including the antipasto *polipo con patate* (octopus with potatoes) and primo summer favorite spaghetti *allo scoglio* (mixed seafood). **Known for:** magical setting near the castello; deliciously light lemon and almond cake; good spot to just sit with an aperitivo and nibbles. $ *Average main: €21* ✉ *Via Aragonese 1, Ischia Ponte* ☎ *081/981823* ⊕ *www.facebook.com/ ristorantecoco* ⊘ *Closed Jan. and Feb.*

O' Padrone Dò Mare

$$ | **SOUTHERN ITALIAN** | In a gorgeous seaside location just off the pedestrian stretch, this is the ideal place to enjoy fresh seafood—the name, "owner of the sea," says it all. For more than 75 years, the island institution has welcomed locals and visitors to its terrace. **Known for:** cracking harbor views; spot-on fritto misto di mare seafood medley; local institution. $ *Average main: €16* ✉ *Corso A. Rizzoli 6, Lacco Ameno* ☎ *081/900244* ⊘ *Closed Nov.–Mar.*

★ Umberto a Mare

$$$ | **SOUTHERN ITALIAN** | This iconic eatery has occupied the space below the Santuario del Soccorso since 1936, when the original Umberto began to grill the local catch on the seafront. The setting is divine, with a terrace overlooking the Bay of Citara and the green tuff *scogli degli innamorati* (lovers' rocks). **Known for:** breathtaking sunset sea views; changing displays of artworks; decades-long reputation for exquisite seafood. $ *Average main: €30* ✉ *Via Soccorso 8, Forio* ☎ *081/997171* ⊕ *www.umbertoamare.it* ⊘ *Closed Nov.–Mar.*

☕ Coffee and Quick Bites

Ice da Luciano

$ | **ICE CREAM** | A stop here for some gelato or granita is a must upon arriving in Ischia Ponte. **Known for:** the best ice cream on the island; inexpensive prices; large selection. $ *Average main: €3* ✉ *Via Luigi Mazzella 140, Ischia Ponte* ☎ *081/0123228* ⊕ *www.facebook.com/icedaluciano.*

Hotels

★ Albergo Il Monastero

$$ | **HOTEL** | The Castello Aragonese, on its own island, is the unrivaled location for this unique hotel with a peaceful ambience and simple but comfortable rooms overlooking the Mediterranean. **Pros:** stunning views and peaceful garden; situated inside the castle; great restaurant on terrace. **Cons:** a long way from the entrance to your room; perhaps too far from the town's action; some may not like the understated decor. $ *Rooms from: €190* ✉ *Castello Aragonese 3, Ischia Ponte* ☎ *081/992435* ⊕ *www. ilmonasteroischia.com* ⊘ *Closed Nov.– late Apr.* ⤳ *20 rooms* ⏐⊙⏐ *Free Breakfast.*

Albergo L'Approdo

$$ | **HOTEL** | A short walk from Casamicciola's port, spas, and town center, this small hotel has a fine array of facilities and guest rooms with private terraces. **Pros:** wonderful elevated views; pool perched above bay; great beauty treatments. **Cons:** the beach is across a busy road; showers are tiny and decor dated; not quite in the town. $ *Rooms from: €149* ✉ *Via Eddomade 29, Casamicciola Terme* ☎ *081/3330190* ⊕ *www.albergolapprodo.it* ⤳ *38 rooms* ⏐⊙⏐ *Free Breakfast.*

★ Mezzatorre Hotel & Thermal Spa

$$$$ | **HOTEL** | Far from the madding, sunburned crowds—in a sleekly renovated former fortress on Punta Cornacchia above the Bay of San Montano—this luxurious getaway (part of the chic Pellicano Hotels Group) tempts its privileged guests to stay put and *relax*, with a glamorous heated pool overlooking a storybook cove, fine restaurants, spa treatments, and hundreds of pretty pine and pomegranate trees. **Pros:** tranquil retreat with wonderful views; fab restaurants and spa; private bay. **Cons:** very isolated; pricey; far from the action. $ *Rooms from: €722* ✉ *Via Mezzatorre 23, Forio* ☎ *081/986111* ⊕ *www.mezzatorre.com* ⊘ *Closed Nov.– Apr.* ⤳ *48 rooms* ⏐⊙⏐ *Free Breakfast.*

Procida

35 mins by hydrofoil, 1 hr by car ferry from Naples.

Lying barely 3 km (2 miles) from the mainland and 10 km (6 miles) from the nearest port (Pozzuoli), Procida is an island of enormous contrasts. It's the most densely populated island in Europe—just more than 10,000 people crammed into less than 2 square miles—and yet there are oases like Marina Corricella and Vivara, which seem to have been bypassed by modern civilization. The inhabitants of the island—the Procidani—have an almost symbiotic relationship with the Mediterranean: many join the merchant navy, others either fish or ferry vacationers around local waters. And yet land traffic here can be more intense than on any other island in the Bay of Naples.

GETTING HERE AND AROUND

Procida's ferry timetable caters to the many daily commuters who live on the island and work in Naples or Pozzuoli. The most frequent—and cheapest—connections are from the Port of Pozzuoli. After stopping at Procida's main port, Marina Grande (also called Sancio Cattolico), many ferries and hydrofoils continue on to Ischia, for which Procida is considered a halfway house.

🍴 Restaurants

La Conchiglia

$$ | **SOUTHERN ITALIAN** | A meal at this restaurant, on the beach about a half-mile east of Corricella, encapsulates Procida's seaside simplicity. Lapping waves and views of the marina and Capri form the backdrop for the fresh seafood and vegetable creations. **Known for:** beachside views and breezes through open windows; freshest ingredients; boat trips and bathing nearby. $ *Average main: €18* ⊠ *Via Pizzaco 10, Procida* ☎ *081/8967602*

⊕ *www.laconchigliaristorante.com*
⊘ *Closed mid-Nov.–Mar.*

☕ Coffee and Quick Bites

Bar Dal Cavaliere

$ | **CAFÉ** | This busy café-bar has outside seating on the *basalti* flagstones with views of the port, so you can watch the boats coming in and out while munching on a sfogliatella, panino, or *semifreddo* (a frozen dessert similar to ice cream). **Known for:** pastries sold by weight—great for groups; near the ferry port; stuzzichini snacks with beers and aperitivi. $ *Average main: €5* ⊠ *Via Roma 42, Marina Grande, Procida* ☎ *081/8101074.*

Capri

50 mins by hydrofoil, 50–85 mins by car ferry from Naples.

Gorgeous grottoes, soaring conical peaks, caverns great and small, plus villas of the emperors and thousands of legends brush Capri with an air of whispered mystery. Emperor Augustus was the first to tout the island's pleasures by nicknaming it Apragopolis (City of Sweet Idleness), and Capri has drawn escapists of all kinds ever since. Ancient Greek and Roman goddesses were moved aside by the likes of Jacqueline Onassis, Elizabeth Taylor, and Brigitte Bardot, who made the island into a paparazzo's playground in the 1960s. Today, new generations of glitterati continue to answer the island's call.

Life on Capri gravitates around the two centers of Capri Town (on the saddle between Monte Tiberio and Monte Solaro) and Anacapri, higher up (902 feet). The main road connecting Capri Town with the upper town of Anacapri is well plied by buses. On arriving at the main harbor, the Marina Grande, everyone heads for the famous funicular, which ascends (and descends) several

Capri

1000 yards
1000 meters

TO
NAPLES AND SORRENTO

P. del Capo

Villa Jovis
Villa Lysis
Monte Tiberio

Via Tiberio

P. della Chiavica

Arco Naturale

Grotta di Matermania

Villa Malaparte

P. Massullo

Moneta

Via Mater Mania

Matermania

Monte Tuoro

Capri Town

Via Pizzolungo

Porto de Tragara
Monacone

Punta Tragara

I Faraglioni

Via Tragara

La Piazzetta
La Fontelina
P. di Tragara

Certosa di San Giacomo

Faraglioni de Fuori

Strada S Francesco Stairway

Saluto
Stefano

Museo Caprense Ignazio Cerio

Marina Grande

Giardini di Augusto

Funicolare

Via Krupp

Marina Piccola

P. Mulo

S. Constanzo

Bagni di Tiberio

Phoenician Stairway

Monte Cappello

Monte S. Maria

Santa Maria a Cetrella

P. di Terita

P. Trasete

Villa San Michele

Segovia Cable Car

Monte Solaro

P. Ventroso

Casa Rossa

Piazza Vittoria

Caprile

San Michele

Anacapri

Villa di Damecuta

Pagliaro

Philosophical Park

P. del Tuono

Grotta Azzurra

P. dell' Arcera

Cala del Rio

Materita

P. Capocchia

P. Campetello

Lido del Faro

P. del Pino

P. Carena

times an hour. Once you're lofted up to Anacapri by bus, you can reach the island heights by taking the spectacular chairlift that ascends to the top of Monte Solaro (1,932 feet) from Anacapri's town center. Within Capri Town and Anacapri foot power is the preferred mode of transportation, as much for convenience as for the sheer delight of walking along these gorgeous streets and roads.

GETTING HERE AND AROUND

Capri is well connected with the mainland in all seasons, though there are more sailings April–October. Hydrofoils, Sea Cats, and similar vessels leave from Molo Beverello (below Piazza Municipio) in Naples, while far less frequent car ferries leave from Calata Porta di Massa, 1,000 yards to the east. There's also service to and from Sorrento's Marina Piccola. Much of Capri is pedestrianized, and a car is a great hindrance, not a help.

Several ferry and hydrofoil companies ply the waters of the Bay of Naples, making frequent trips to Capri. Schedules change from season to season; the tourist office's website (⊕ *www.capritourism. com*) gives updated departure times. However, you can't return to Naples after the last sailing (11 pm in high season, often 8 pm or even earlier in low season). There's little to be gained—sometimes nothing—from buying a round-trip ticket, which will just tie you down to the return schedule of one line. However, book in advance in spring and summer for a Sunday return to the mainland.

VISITOR INFORMATION

CONTACT Azienda Autonoma di Cura, Soggiorno e Turismo. ⊠ *Piazza Umberto I, Capri* ☏ *081/8370686* ⊕ *www.capritourism.com.*

Sights

★ Anacapri

TOWN | A tortuous road leads up to Anacapri, the island's "second city," about 3 km (2 miles) from Capri Town.

Crowds are thick down Via Capodimonte leading to Villa San Michele and around Piazza Vittoria, the square where you catch the chairlift to the top of Monte Solaro. Via Finestrale leads to the noted Le Boffe quarter, centered on the Piazza Diaz. Elsewhere, Anacapri is quietly appealing. It's a good starting point for walks, such as the 80-minute round-trip journey to the Migliara Belvedere, on the island's southern coast. ⊠ *Anacapri.*

Capri Town

TOWN | On arrival at the port, pick up the excellent map of the island at the tourist office. You may have to wait for the funicular railway (€2.20 one-way) to Capri Town, some 450 feet above the harbor. So this might be the time to splurge on an open-top taxi—it could save you an hour in line and a sweaty ride packed into a tiny, swaying bus. From the upper station, walk out into Piazza Umberto I, better known as the Piazzetta, the island's social hub. ⊠ *Capri.*

Certosa di San Giacomo

HISTORIC SIGHT | An eerie atmosphere hangs around neglected corners of this once grand, palatial complex between the Castiglione and Tuoro hills, founded between 1371 and 1374. After the monastery was sacked by the pirates Dragut and Barbarossa in the 16th century, it was restored and rebuilt—thanks in part to heavy taxes exacted from the populace. The Quarto del Priore hosts occasional art exhibitions, but the showstopper here is the Museo Diefenbach, with restored canvases by German painter K.W. Diefenbach, who visited Capri in 1899 and stayed until his death in 1913. ⊠ *Via Certosa, Capri Town* ☏ *081/8376218* ⊕ *www.beniculturali. it/luogo/certosa-di-san-giacomo* ⊿ *€6* ⊙ *Closed Mon.*

★ Giardini di Augusto

(*Gardens of Augustus*)

GARDEN | From the terraces of this beautiful public garden, you can see the village of Marina Piccola below—restaurants, cabanas, and swimming platforms huddle among the shoals—and admire the steep, winding Via Krupp, actually a staircase cut into the rock. Friedrich Krupp, the German arms manufacturer, loved Capri and became one of the island's most generous benefactors. After being closed for nine years due to the danger of rockfalls, the path down to Marina Piccola finally reopened in June 2023. ⊠ *Via Matteotti, beyond monastery of San Giacomo, Capri Town* ☎ *353/4523908 mobile* ⊕ *www.capriculturaeturismo.it* 🎫 *€1.50.*

Grotta Azzurra

CAVE | Only when the Grotta Azzurra was "discovered" in 1826, by the Polish poet August Kopisch and Swiss artist Ernest Fries, did Capri become a tourist destination. The watery cave's blue beauty became a symbol of the return to nature. In reality, the grotto had long been a local landmark. During the Roman era it had been the elegant, mosaic-decorated nymphaeum of the adjoining villa of Gradola. The water's extraordinary sapphire color is caused by a hidden opening in the rock that refracts the light. Locals say the afternoon light is best from April to June, and the morning in July and August. The Blue Grotto can be reached from Marina Grande or from the small embarkation point below Anacapri on the northwest side of the island, accessible by bus from Anacapri. You board one boat to get to the grotto, then transfer to a smaller boat that takes you inside. ⊠ *Anacapri* 🎫 *From €21 from Marina Grande via various companies, then €18 by rowboat with Coop. Battellieri* ⊗ *Closed if the sea is even minimally rough.*

★ I Faraglioni

NATURE SIGHT | Few landscapes set more artists dreaming than that of the famous Faraglioni—three enigmatic, pale-ocher limestone colossi that loom out of the sea just off the Punta Tragara on the southern coast of Capri. Soaring almost 350 feet above the water, the Faraglioni have become a beloved symbol of Capri.

The first rock is called Faraglione di Terra, since it's attached to the land; at its base is the famous restaurant and bathing lido Da Luigi. The second is called Faraglione di Mezzo, or Stella, and little boats can often be seen going through its picturesque tunnel. The rock farthest out to sea is Faraglione di Scopolo and is inhabited by a wall lizard species with a striking blue belly. ⊠ *End of Via Tragara, Capri.*

★ Marina Piccola

BEACH | **FAMILY** | Marina Piccola is a delightfully picturesque inlet that provides the Capresi and other sun worshippers with their best access to beaches and safe swimming. The entire cove is lined with *stabilimenti*—elegant bathing lidos where the striped cabanas are often air-conditioned. The most famous of these lidos (there's a fee to use the facilities) is La Canzone del Mare. Its seaside restaurant offers a dreamy view of the Faraglioni and a luncheon here, although pricey, can serve as an indelible Capri moment. Jutting out into the bay at the center of the marina is the Scoglio delle Sirene, or Sirens' Rock—a small natural promontory—which the ancients believed to be the haunt of the Sirens, the mythical temptresses whose song seduced Odysseus in Homer's *Odyssey*. ⊠ *Via Marina Piccola, Capri.*

★ Monte Solaro

VIEWPOINT | An impressive limestone formation and the highest point on Capri (1,932 feet), Monte Solaro affords gasp-inducing views toward the bays of both Naples and Salerno. A serene 13-minute chairlift ride will take you right to the top (refreshments available at the bar), where you can launch out on a number of scenic trails on the western side of the island. Picnickers should note that even in summer it can get windy at this height, and there are few trees to provide shade or refuge. ⊠ *Piazza Vittoria, Anacapri* ☎ *081/8371438* ⊕ *www.capriseggiovia.it* 🎫 *€11 one-way, €14 return* ⊗ *Chairlift closed in adverse weather.*

★ Villa Jovis

RUINS | In Roman times, Capri was the site of 12 spacious villas, but Villa Jovis is both the best preserved and the largest. Named in honor of the ancient Roman god Jupiter, or Jove, the villa of the emperor Tiberius is riveted to the towering Rocca di Capri like an eagle's nest overlooking the strait separating Capri from Punta Campanella. The Salto di Tiberio (Tiberius's Leap) is where ancients believed Tiberius had enemies (among them his discarded lovers and even unfortunate cooks) hurled over the precipice into the sea some 1,000 feet below. ⊠ *Via A. Maiuri, Capri* ☎ *081/8374549* ⊕ *www.coopculture.it/it/prodotti/biglietto-con-audioguida-villa-jovis* 🎫 *€6, with audio guide* ⊙ *Closed Mon. and Jan. and Feb.*

★ Villa San Michele

HISTORIC HOME | From Anacapri's Piazza Vittoria, picturesque Via Capodimonte leads to Villa San Michele, the charming former home of Swedish doctor and philanthropist Axel Munthe (1857–1949). At the ancient entranceway to Anacapri at the top of the Scala Fenicia, the villa is set around Roman-style courtyards and marble walkways. Rooms display the doctor's varied collections, which range from bric-a-brac to antiquities. A spectacular pergola path overlooking the entire Bay of Naples leads from the villa to the famous Sphinx Parapet, where an ancient Egyptian sphinx looks out toward Sorrento. ⊠ *Viale Axel Munthe 34, Anacapri* ☎ *081/8371401* ⊕ *www.villasanmichele.eu* 🎫 *€10.*

⏰ Restaurants

Al Grottino

$$ | **SOUTHERN ITALIAN** | In a 14th-century building close to the Piazzetta, this small, friendly, family-run restaurant has arched ceilings, autographed photos of famous patrons, and lots of atmosphere. Specialties include scialatielli *ai fiori di zucchine e gamberetti* (with zucchini

flowers and shrimp) and *cocotte* (house-made pasta with mussels, clams, and shrimp), but the owner delights in taking his guests through the menu of regional dishes. **Known for:** good value for Capri; Caprese specialties with the freshest ingredients; gluten-free options. ⑤ *Average main: €21* ⊠ *Via Longano 27, Capri* ☎ *081/8370584* ⊕ *www.ristorantealgrottino.net* ⊙ *Closed Nov.–late Mar.*

Aurora

$$$ | **SOUTHERN ITALIAN** | Often frequented by celebrities, whose photographs adorn the walls inside and out, the island's oldest restaurant offers courtesy and *simpatia* (irrespective of your star status), a sleekly minimalist interior, and tables outside along a chic thoroughfare. The cognoscenti start by sharing a pizza *all'Acqua*—thin-crust, with mozzarella and a sprinkling of *peperoncino* (chili)—but the genuine *gnocchetti al pesto con fagiolini croccanti e pinoli* (dumplings with pesto, beans, and pine nuts) and house-made sweets are good, too. **Known for:** historic jet-set hangout; Papà Gennaro's unusually light pizza all'Acqua; incredible wine cellar and choice. ⑤ *Average main: €28* ⊠ *Via Fuorlovado 18/22, Capri Town* ☎ *081/8370181* ⊕ *www.auroracapri.com* ⊙ *Closed Nov.–Easter.*

Barbarossa

$$ | **SOUTHERN ITALIAN** | Take the staircase behind Piazza Vittoria's bus stop to the covered terrace of this ristorante–pizzeria with panoramic views of the Barbarossa castle and the sea. The no-frills ambience belies the quality of the à la carte *cucina*: besides *pizze* they specialize in local dishes—including risotto *con gamberi a limone* (shrimp with lemon). **Known for:** authentic (certified) Vera Pizza Napoletana; lively function room during events; chef's semifreddi and other dessert specials. ⑤ *Average main: €18* ⊠ *Piazza della Vittoria 1, Anacapri* ☎ *081/8371483* ⊕ *www.ristorantebarbarossa.com.*

★ Da Gelsomina

$$ | SOUTHERN ITALIAN | Amid its own terraced vineyards with inspiring views to the island of Ischia and beyond, this is much more than just a well-reputed restaurant. The owner's mother was a friend of Axel Munthe, and he encouraged her to open a food kiosk, which evolved into Da Gelsomina; today the specialties include *pollo a mattone* (chicken grilled under bricks) and locally caught rabbit. **Known for:** opened in the 1960s with family links to Axel Munthe; chicken grilled under bricks; fresh produce and wine from their verdant gardens. ⑤ *Average main: €22* ✉ *Via Migliara 72, Anacapri* ☎ *081/8371499* ⊕ *www.dagelsomina. com* ⓧ *Closed Nov.–Mar.*

★ Il Solitario

$$ | NEAPOLITAN | FAMILY | Tucked away from Via G. Orlandi, there's always a warm, relaxed family welcome and deliciously simple Caprese food here. Do book a spot in the gorgeously gnarled, vine-dappled garden setting. **Known for:** sumptuous ravioli; cheery dining room and leafy pergola; grilled fish and meat. ⑤ *Average main: €18* ✉ *Via Giuseppe Orlandi 96, Anacapri* ☎ *081/8371382* ⊕ *www.ilsolitarioanacapri.com* ⓧ *No dinner Sun.*

La Canzone del Mare

$$$ | SOUTHERN ITALIAN | Although it's not primarily a restaurant, a luncheon dominated by fresh seafood and vegetables in the covered pavilion of this legendary bathing lido of the Marina Piccola is Capri at its most picture-perfect. With two seawater pools, a rocky beach, and I Faraglioni in the distance, it was the erstwhile haunt of Gracie Fields, Emilio Pucci, Noël Coward, and any number of 1950s and '60s glitterati. **Known for:** open terrace overlooking Marina Piccola; sunset wine and peaches served with stuzzichini (appetizers); famous dolce vita–era haunt—popular and pricey. ⑤ *Average main: €35* ✉ *Via Marina Piccola 93, Marina Piccola* ☎ *081/8370104* ⊕ *www.*

lacanzonedelmare.com ⓧ *No dinner. Closed Oct.–late Apr.*

★ La Capannina

$$$ | SOUTHERN ITALIAN | Near the busy piazzetta and long one of Capri's most celebrity-haunted restaurants, La Capannina has a discreet flower-decked veranda that's ideal for dining by candlelight. Specialties change daily depending on the season, but the menu always includes ravioli capresi, linguine *con lo scorfano* (with scorpion fish), and an exquisite "Pezzogna" (sea bream cooked whole and topped with a layer of potatoes). **Known for:** walls strewn with photos of celebrity clientele; wine bar next door; family-run since 1931. ⑤ *Average main: €27* ✉ *Via Le Botteghe 12b, Capri Town* ☎ *081/8370732* ⊕ *www.capannin-acapri.com* ⓧ *Closed Nov.–mid-Mar.*

La Fontelina

$$$ | SOUTHERN ITALIAN | Given its position right on the water's edge, seafood is almost de rigueur here, but also expect fabulous fresh vegetable creations like *polpette di melanzane* (eggplant fritters), and then dip into the vegetable buffet. La Fontelina also functions as a lido, with steps and ladders into fathoms-deep blue water, and this location—accessible on foot from Punta Tragara or by boat from Marina Piccola (10 minutes; €30 up to four passengers)—makes it a good place to spend a delightfully comatose day. **Known for:** lunch stop for beach-club bathers; shuttle boat from Marina Piccola; chef Mario's daily seafood specials. ⑤ *Average main: €29* ✉ *Via Faraglioni 2, Località Faraglioni, Capri* ☎ *081/8370845* ⊕ *www.fontelina-capri.com* ⓧ *Closed mid-Oct.–Easter. No dinner.*

Le Grottelle

$$$ | SOUTHERN ITALIAN | This extremely informal trattoria enjoys a distinctive setting up against limestone rocks not far from the Arco Naturale, with the kitchen in a cave at the back. Whether you stumble over it (and are lucky enough to get a table) or intentionally head for it after

an island hike, Le Grottelle will prove memorable, thanks to the ambience, the views of Li Galli islands, and a menu that includes ravioli and local rabbit but is best known for seafood dishes such as fusilli *con gamberi e zucchine* (with shrimp and zucchini). **Known for:** breathtaking cliff-clinging location; seafood dishes; cool grotto interiors. ⓢ *Average main: €26* ⊠ *Via Arco Naturale 13, Capri* ☎ *081/8375719* ⓢ *Closed Nov.–mid-Mar.*

Coffee and Quick Bites

★ Buonocore

$ | **ITALIAN** | **FAMILY** | Follow your nose to this legendary, sweet-smelling Caprese fave for breakfast, beach picnics, and on-the-hoof snacks. Buonocore lures you down its steps on a Capri Town lane with all manner of pizze, panini, gelati, and paste, including their speciality almond and lemon Caprilú biscotti. **Known for:** tempting smells of freshly made cones and pastries; small pizze to take away; very popular so may have to fare la coda. ⓢ *Average main: €9* ⊠ *Via Vittorio Emanuele 35, Capri Town* ☎ *081/8377826* ⊕ *www.facebook.com/capri.gelateriabuonocore.*

🛏 Hotels

Caesar Augustus

$$$$ | **HOTEL** | A favorite of the Hollywood set, this landmark villa hotel is a Caprese paradise thanks to its breathtaking perch atop a cliff; its grand gardens, terraces, and pool; and its charming, casual-chic rooms with their plump chairs and fragrant bouquets. **Pros:** serene terrace views; summer concerts on-site; infinity pool. **Cons:** a bit far from the action for some; no kids under 14 allowed; pricey. ⓢ *Rooms from: €850* ⊠ *Via G. Orlandi 4, Anacapri* ☎ *081/8373395* ⊕ *www.caesar-augustus.com* ⓢ *Closed Nov.–mid-Apr.* ⇸ *55 rooms* ⦿ *Free Breakfast.*

★ Capri Palace Jumeirah

$$$$ | **RESORT** | This Anacapri icon with unique design, spa, exquisite food, and luxurious retreat atmosphere throughout has amassed a noted art collection and even launched a fashion and home line and hosted A-list cultural events. **Pros:** noted art collection; stunning (and sometimes surprising) design; award-winning spa and dining. **Cons:** all that glam comes at a price; some may find the quiet Anacapri location removed from the action (and water); service can be slow. ⓢ *Rooms from: €980* ⊠ *Via Capodimonte 14, Anacapri* ☎ *081/9780111* ⊕ *www.capripalace.com* ⓢ *Closed mid-Oct.–mid-Apr.* ⇸ *67 rooms* ⦿ *Free Breakfast.*

★ Capri Tiberio Palace

$$$$ | **HOTEL** | Offering guests comfort, style, luxury, and sigh-inducing views since the 19th century, this hotel is a short walk from the piazzetta—near the action, but not quite in the thick of it. **Pros:** friendly staff; pure luxury; fabulous design. **Cons:** no port-to-door guest shuttle; the pool is too close to the restaurant; tiny gym. ⓢ *Rooms from: €1525* ⊠ *Via Croce 11–15, Capri Town* ☎ *081/9787111* ⊕ *www.capritiberiopalace.com* ⓢ *Closed Nov.–mid-Apr.* ⇸ *54 rooms* ⦿ *Free Breakfast.*

★ J.K. Place Capri

$$$$ | **HOTEL** | Occupying an 1876 villa above Marina Grande harbor, this glamorous hotel makes other Capri accommodations seem dull. **Pros:** exquisite pool; pleasant walk to the magical Tiberio beach; free shuttle to town. **Cons:** expensive; only for high rollers; pool visible from main road. ⓢ *Rooms from: €1273* ⊠ *Via Provinciale Marina Grande 225, Marina Grande* ☎ *081/8384001* ⊕ *www.jkcapri.com* ⓢ *Closed mid-Oct.–mid-Apr.* ⇸ *22 rooms* ⦿ *Free Breakfast.*

La Tosca

$$ | **HOTEL** | Up a tiny side street above the Certosa, this simple, quiet hotel offers unassuming vibes, terrace views, and reasonable rates. **Pros:** simple, unadorned

charm; pleasant, helpful owner; quiet spot near Capri Town. **Cons:** not all rooms have good views; books up early; rooms might seem to lack panache. ⑤ *Rooms from: €199* ✉ *Via Birago 5, Capri Town* ☎ *081/8370989* ⊕ *www.latoscahotel.com* ⊘ *Closed Nov.–Feb.* ⇆ *11 rooms* ⑩ *Free Breakfast.*

★ Punta Tragara

$$$$ | HOTEL | Designed by Le Corbusier, this former private villa became a satellite headquarters for America's central command during WWII and hosted Churchill and Eisenhower; today, it's one of Capri's most beautiful hotels, with a breathtaking location on Punta Tragara; public areas adorned with baronial fireplaces, gilded antiques, and travertine marble; and guest rooms that are simultaneously sumptuous and cozy-casual. **Pros:** decadent and luxurious; wonderful views of the famed Faraglioni rocks; two gorgeous pools. **Cons:** a 15-minute walk from the center; some find the style dated (others find it a plus); small gym. ⑤ *Rooms from: €1200* ✉ *Via Tragara 57, Capri* ☎ *081/8370844* ⊕ *www.hoteltragara.com* ⊘ *Closed mid-Oct.–mid-Apr.* ⇆ *43 rooms* ⑩ *Free Breakfast.*

Quisisana

$$$$ | HOTEL | Some say Capri has three villages: Capri Town, Anacapri, and this landmark hotel, which looms large in island mythology, attracts utterly devoted guests, and has an enormous lobby and theater-cum-convention center that are 1930s jewels designed by noted modernist Gio Ponti. **Pros:** luxe atmosphere on a large scale; stumbling distance from La Piazzetta; top spa facilities. **Cons:** patchy service; convention-size and far from cozy; not quite as ritzy as in bygone days. ⑤ *Rooms from: €950* ✉ *Via Camerelle 2, Capri Town* ☎ *081/8370788* ⊕ *www.quisisana.com* ⊘ *Closed late Oct.–Apr.* ⇆ *140 rooms* ⑩ *Free Breakfast.*

Villa Sarah

$$$ | HOTEL | This yellow, two-story, Mediterranean-style hostelry—complete with Capri's signature round windows and a setting amid lovely gardens in a pleasant residential district—has lots of Caprese spirit and simple but homey and brightly accented rooms that will make you feel like a guest in a private villa. **Pros:** friendly and helpful staff; lush gardens; unfussy decor. **Cons:** a long and steep climb from the Piazzetta; many rooms tiny; small pool. ⑤ *Rooms from: €225* ✉ *Via Tiberio 3/a, Capri Town* ☎ *081/8377817* ⊕ *www.villasarah.it* ⊘ *Closed Nov.–Mar.* ⇆ *20 rooms* ⑩ *Free Breakfast.*

Sorrento

50 km (31 miles) south of Naples.

Winding along a cliff above a small beach and two harbors, the town is split in two by a narrow ravine formed by a former mountain stream. To the east, dozens of hotels line busy Via Correale along the cliff—many have "grand" included in their names, and some indeed are. To the west, however, is the historic sector, which still enchants. It's a relatively flat area, with winding, stone-paved lanes bordered by balconied buildings, some joined by medieval stone arches. The bustling, coach- and car-traffic-fringed central piazza is named after the poet Torquato Tasso, born here in 1544. Away from the vehicles this part of town is a delightful place to walk through. Craftspeople are often at work in their stalls and shops and are happy to let you watch; in fact, that's the point. Music spots and bars cluster in the side streets near Piazza Tasso.

GETTING HERE AND AROUND

From downtown Naples, take a Circumvesuviana train from Stazione Centrale (Piazza Garibaldi) or a hydrofoil from Molo Beverello. If you're coming directly from the airport in Naples, pick up a direct bus to Sorrento. By car, take the A3 Naples–Salerno autostrada, exiting at

Sorrento and Amalfi Coast

Castellammare, and then following signs for Penisola Sorrentina, then for Sorrento.

VISITOR INFORMATION

CONTACT Ufficio Campania Turismo. ✉ *Via L. De Maio 35, Sorrento* ☎ *081/8074033* ⊕ *www.facebook.com/aziendaautono-madisoggiornodisorrentoesantagnello.*

◉ Sights

★ Chiesa e Chiostro di San Francesco

CHURCH | Near the Villa Comunale gardens and sharing its view over the Bay of Naples, the church and convent is celebrated for its 12th-century cloister. Filled with greenery and flowers, the Moorish-style cloister has interlaced pointed arches of tufa rock, alternating with octagonal columns, supporting smaller arches. The combination makes a suitably evocative setting for summer concerts and theatrical presentations. The interior's 17th-century decoration includes an altarpiece by a student of Francesco Solimena, depicting St. Francis receiving the stigmata. Above the cloisters **Galleria Raffaele Celentano** exhibits the candid black-and-white photographs of Italian life by a contemporary local photographer. There's an adjoining panoramic terrace ripe for sunset views and a joyous installation featuring an arbor rope swing, a cut-up Fiat 500 and washing line of photos and clothes. ✉ *Piazza S. Francesco, Sorrento* ☎ *081/8781269* 🎟 *cloisters free; gallery €5.*

Marina Grande

MARINA/PIER | Close to the historic quarter (but not that close—many locals prefer to use the town bus to shuttle up and down the steep hill), the port, or *borgo*, of the Marina Grande is Sorrento's fishing harbor. In recent years it has become unashamedly touristy, with outdoor restaurants and cafés encroaching on what little remains of the original harbor. The marina still remains a magical location for an evening out on the waterfront. Don't confuse this harbor with Marina Piccola, at the base of the cliff, below Piazza Tasso and the Hotel Excelsior Vittoria; that's the area where ferries and hydrofoils dock. ⊠ *Via del Mare, Sorrento.*

Museo Correale di Terranova

ART MUSEUM | In an 18th-century villa with a lovely garden, on land given to the patrician Correale family by Queen Joan of Anjou in 1428, this museum is a highlight of Sorrento. It has an eclectic private collection amassed by the count of Terranova and his brother—one of the finest devoted to Neapolitan paintings, decorative arts, and porcelains. Magnificent 18th- and 19th-century inlaid tables by Giuseppe Gargiulo, Capodimonte porcelains, and Rococo portrait miniatures are reminders of the age when pleasure and delight were everything in wealthy circles. Also on view are regional Greek and Roman archaeological finds, Old Master paintings, and 17th-century majolicas—even the poet Tasso's death mask. ⊠ *Via Correale 50, Sorrento* ☎ *081/8781846* ⊕ *www.museocorreale. it* ☎ *€15; included in the €31 Sorrento Musei ticket* ⊗ *Closed Mon.*

Sedile Dominova

NOTABLE BUILDING | Enchanting showpiece of the Largo Dominova—the little square that is the heart of Sorrento's historic quarter—the Sedile Dominova is a picturesque open loggia with expansive arches, balustrades, and a green-and-yellow-tile cupola, originally constructed in the 16th century. The open-air structure is frescoed with 18th-century trompe-l'oeil columns and the family coats of arms, which once belonged to the *sedile* (seat), the town council where nobles met to discuss civic problems as early as the Angevin period. Today, Sorrentines still

like to congregate around the umbrella-topped tables near the tiny square. ⊠ *Largo Dominova, at Via S. Cesareo and Via P.R. Giuliani, Sorrento* ☎ *Free.*

★ Villa Comunale

VIEWPOINT | The largest public park in Sorrento sits on a cliff top overlooking the entire Bay of Naples. It offers benches, flowers, palms, and people-watching, plus a seamless vista that stretches from Capri to Vesuvius. From here steps lead down to Sorrento's main harbor, the Marina Piccola. ⊠ *Adjoining church of San Francesco, Sorrento.*

🍴 Restaurants

Da Emilia

\$\$ | SOUTHERN ITALIAN | Near the steps of the Marina Grande, this reliable choice for seafood (established in 1947) might not be Sorrento's most visually prepossessing place, but its homespun, family feel—complete with wooden tables and checked tablecloths—is a refreshing change from the town's (occasionally pretentious) elegance. **Known for:** tasty and fresh seafood combos like mussels with Sorrentine lemons; harbor terrace above the rocks; competed in Italian TV show 4 Ristoranti. ⑤ *Average main: €22* ⊠ *Via Marina Grande 62, Sorrento* ☎ *081/8072720* ⊕ *www.daemilia.it* ⊗ *Closed Nov.–Feb.*

★ Don Alfonso 1890

\$\$\$\$ | SOUTHERN ITALIAN | A gastronomic giant and pioneer in upscale farm-to-table cuisine (it even grows its own produce on a small farm nearby), Don Alfonso is considered one of Italy's best restaurants. It's a family affair, with mamma (Livia) handling the dining room, papà (former chef Alfonso Iaccarino) tending to the organic plot, one son working as the current chef (preparing classic dishes alongside edgier creations), and the other serving as maître d'. **Known for:** stellar tasting menus; slow-food pioneer; Punta Campanella local garden produce.

$ *Average main: €40* ⊠ *Corso Sant'Agata 13, Sant'Agata sui Due Golfi* ⊹ *SITA Bus to via Nastro Verde or taxi from Sorrento* ☎ *081/8780026* ⊕ *www.donalfonso.com* ⊘ *Closed Nov.–Apr. No lunch weekdays. No dinner Mon. and Tues.*

★ Ristorante Bagni Delfino
$$$ | SOUTHERN ITALIAN | At this informal, waterside restaurant and snack bar, you won't see many locals—they're unlikely to be impressed by the four-language menus—but the seafood platters are fresh and flavorful, and you can eat alfresco in the sunshine or inside a glass-enclosed dining area with a nautical motif. You can even go for a swim. **Known for:** bountiful portions; sunny terrace beside a sunbathing/swimming jetty; great views of the Marina Grande and beyond. $ *Average main: €25* ⊠ *Via Marina Grande 216, Sorrento* ☎ *081/8782038* ⊕ *www.ristoranteildelfinosorrento.com* ⊘ *Closed Nov.–Mar.*

★ Ristorante Museo Caruso
$$$$ | SOUTHERN ITALIAN | Sorrentine favorites, including *acquerello* (fresh fish appetizer) and ravioli with crab and zucchini sauce, are tweaked creatively here. The staff is warm and helpful, the singer on the sound system is the long-departed "fourth tenor" himself, and the operatic memorabilia (including posters and old photos of Caruso) and subtle lighting add to the atmosphere. **Known for:** Caruso memorabilia aplenty; Torna a Surriento and the Neapolitan songbook; tasting menus and a few à la carte choices. $ *Average main: €40* ⊠ *Via S. Antonino 12, Sorrento* ☎ *081/8073156* ⊕ *www.ristorantemuseocaruso.com.*

Ristorante 'o Parrucchiano La Favorita
$$ | SOUTHERN ITALIAN | Opened in 1868 by an ex-priest ('o parrucchiano means "the priest" in the local dialect), this restaurant serves classic Sorrentine cuisine in a 19th-century setting that's enchanting, although it can feel overly touristy: a sprawling, multilevel greenhouse packed with tables and chairs amid fruit trees and enough tropical foliage to fill a Victorian conservatory. **Known for:** fecund greenhouse and terrace foliage and fruit; signature cannelloni created in 1870; gorgeous setting but may disappoint foodwise. $ *Average main: €22* ⊠ *Corso Italia 71, Sorrento* ☎ *081/8781321* ⊕ *www.parrucchiano.com* ⊘ *Closed Jan.*

☕ Coffee and Quick Bites

★ A'Marenna
$ | ITALIAN | FAMILY | Run with enthusiasm and love by two young Sorrentine women, this small rustic-styled bakery and bistro makes generously filled panini using fresh ingredients on ciabatta and *panuozzo* pizza-dough bread. It's also a fab spot to linger with some local wine and a cheese platter. **Known for:** friendly service; local wines; vegan and veggie options. $ *Average main: €8* ⊠ *Via Tasso 23, Sorrento* ☎ *081/18495183* ⊕ *www.facebook.com/amarennasorrento.*

🛏 Hotels

★ Bellevue Syrene
$$$$ | HOTEL | This luxurious retreat, magnificently set on a bluff high over the Bay of Naples, is one of Italy's most legendary hotels, complete with Art Deco touches throughout; lounges and salons decorated with avant-garde artwork and trompe-l'oeil frescoes; and guest rooms that range from sleekly modern to sumptuously fanciful. **Pros:** impeccable design elements; elegant common areas; incredible views. **Cons:** minimum 3-night stay high season; pricey parking; small pool. $ *Rooms from: €736* ⊠ *Piazza della Vittoria 5, Sorrento* ☎ *081/8781024* ⊕ *www.bellevue.it* ⊘ *Closed Jan.–Mar.* ⇥ *49 rooms* ⦿ *Free Breakfast.*

★ Excelsior Vittoria
$$$$ | HOTEL | Overlooking the Bay of Naples, this luxurious Belle Époque dream has been in the same family since 1834, which means that public spaces are virtual museums—with

elegant Victorian love seats and *stile liberty* (Art Nouveau) ornamentation—and guest rooms are spacious, with soigné furnishings and balconies and terraces that overlook gardens or the bay. **Pros:** beyond the protected gates, you're in the heart of town; gardens buffer city noise; grand spaces and handsome furnishings. **Cons:** not all rooms have sea views; some rooms are comparatively small; dated gym. $ *Rooms from: €1024 ⊠ Piazza Tasso 34, Sorrento ☎ 081/8777111 ⊕ www.exvitt.it ⊗ Closed Jan.–Mar. ⟿ 83 rooms* ⦿l *Free Breakfast.*

La Favorita

$$$$ | **HOTEL** | The lobby might be a glamorous white-on-white extravaganza of Caprese columns, tufted sofas, shimmering crystal chandeliers, silver ecclesiastical objects, and gilded Baroque mirrors, but the charming staff ensure the vibe is elegantly casual, the guest rooms are well equipped and spacious, and the rooftop pool area has magnificent bay and Vesuvius vistas. **Pros:** central location; beautiful terrace; idyllic garden. **Cons:** no views to speak of from guest rooms; lack of decent air-conditioning and room thermostat control; rooms near the bar noisy after midnight. $ *Rooms from: €633 ⊠ Via T. Tasso 61, Sorrento ☎ 081/8782031 ⊕ www.hotellafavorita.com ⊗ Closed Jan.–Mar. ⟿ 85 rooms* ⦿l *Free Breakfast.*

Positano

14 km (9 miles) east of Sorrento, 57 km (34 miles) south of Naples.

When John Steinbeck visited Positano in 1953, he wrote that it was difficult to consider tourism an industry because "there are not enough [tourists]." Alas, there are more than enough now, and the town's vertical landscape with pastel-hue houses, drapes of bright pink bougainvillea, and sapphire-blue sea make it easy to understand why.

The most photographed fishing village in the world, this fabled locale is home to some 4,000 Positanesi, who are joined daily by hordes arriving from Capri, Sorrento, and Amalfi. The town clings to the Monti Lattari with arcaded, cubist buildings, set in tiers up the mountainside, in shades of rose, peach, purple, and ivory.

GETTING HERE AND AROUND

SITA buses leave from the Circumvesuviana train station in Sorrento. Buses also run from Naples and, in summer, Rome. There is a ferry from Sorrento in the summer months.

A word of advice: wear comfortable walking shoes and be sure your back and legs are strong enough to negotiate those picturesque but daunting and ladderlike *scalinatelle*. In the center of town, where no buses can go, you're on your own from Piazza dei Mulini. To begin your explorations, make a left turn onto the boutique-flanked Via dei Mulini and head down to the Palazzo Murat, Santa Maria Assunta, and the beach—one of the most charming walks of the coast.

VISITOR INFORMATION

CONTACT Ufficio del Turismo Luca Vespoli. ⊠ *Via Regina Giovanna 13, Positano ☎ 331/2085821 mobile ⊕ www.facebook.com/prolocopositano.*

Sights

★ MAR – Museo Archeologico Romano

ARCHAEOLOGICAL SITE | Painstaking excavations begun in 2003 below the oratory of Santa Maria Assunta are now open to the public and showcase tantalizing traces of Positano's vast Roman settlement buried by the AD 79 eruption. Through volcanic debris some 30 feet below the *piazzetta* is a cool subterranean world with different captivating chambers and crypts. The new entrance leads to the most recently discovered Roman villa excavations, which sit below the Cripta Superiore with its spine-tingling funereal seating, reserved for Positano's most

Marina Grande Beach in Positano is a nice, long stretch of sand that attracts a cosmopolitan crowd.

upstanding 18th-century citizens. Among the Roman artifacts are vibrant frescoes, ornate stucco reliefs, and intricate bronzes. Another entrance nearby leads to the Cripta Inferiore, with two naves, marble columns, and later additions. ⊠ *Piazza Flavio Gioia 7, Positano* ☎ *331/2085821 WhatsApp* ⊕ *marpositano.it* ▱ *€15.*

Palazzo Murat

NOTABLE BUILDING | Past a bevy of resort boutiques, head to Via dei Mulini to view the prettiest garden in Positano: the 18th-century courtyard of the Palazzo Murat, named for Joachim Murat, who sensibly chose the palazzo as his summer residence. This was where Murat, designated by his brother-in-law Napoleon as king of Naples in 1808, came to forget the demands of power and lead a simpler life. He built this grand abode (now a hotel) near the church of Santa Maria Assunta, just steps from the main beach. ⊠ *Via dei Mulini 23, Positano* ☎ *089/875177* ⊕ *www.palazzomurat.it.*

Santa Maria Assunta

CHURCH | The Chiesa Madre, or parish church of Santa Maria Assunta, lies just south of the Palazzo Murat, its green-and-yellow majolica dome topped by a perky cupola. Built on the site of the former Benedictine abbey of St. Vito, the 13th-century Romanesque structure was almost completely rebuilt in 1700. At the altar is a Byzantine 13th-century painting on wood of Madonna with Child, known popularly as the Black Virgin. A replica is carried to the beach every August 15 to celebrate the Feast of the Assumption. Embedded over the doorway of the church's bell tower is a medieval bas-relief of fish, a fox, and a pistrice (the mythical half-dragon, half-dog sea monster). This is one of the few relics of the medieval abbey of Saint Vito. ⊠ *Piazza Flavio Gioia, Positano* ☎ *089/875480* ⊕ *www.chiesapositano.it.*

Spiaggia Grande

BEACH | FAMILY | The walkway from
the Piazza Flavio Gioia leads down to
Spiaggia Grande, Positano's main beach,
bordered by an esplanade and some of
the town's busiest restaurants. Surrounded by the spectacular amphitheater of
houses and villas that leapfrog up the
hillsides of Monte Comune and Monte
Sant'Angelo, this remains one of the
most picturesque beaches in the world.
Amenities: food and drink; lifeguards;
showers; toilets; water sports. **Best for:**
swimming. ⊠ *Spiaggia Grande, Positano.*

★ Via Positanesi d'America

PROMENADE | FAMILY | Just before the
ferry ticket booths to the right of Spiaggia
Grande, a tiny road that is the loveliest
seaside walkway on the entire coast
rises up and borders the cliffs leading
to Fornillo Beach. The road is named for
the town's large number of 19th-century
emigrants to the United States—Positano
virtually survived during World War II
thanks to the money and packages their
descendants sent back home. Halfway
up the path lies the Torre Trasìta (Trasìta
Tower), the most distinctive of Positano's
three coastline defense towers. Now a
residence occasionally available for summer rental, the tower was used to spot
pirate raids. As you continue along the Via
Positanesi d'America, you'll pass a tiny
inlet and an emerald cove before Fornillo
Beach comes into view. ⊠ *Via Positanesi
d'America, Positano.*

 Restaurants

★ Da Vincenzo

$$$ | SOUTHERN ITALIAN | Established in
1958, this buzzy family-run place pairs
generations of tradition and genuine love
of hospitality with ever-evolving innovation, reflected in the exceptional takes on
classic Neapolitan dishes and the stylish,
up-to-date yet rustic decor. Expect
warm banter with busy staff, who greet
passersby while introducing a menu
with both sea and robust land mainstays

such as grilled octopus, linguine with
anchovies, lamb chops with braised artichokes, and eggplant Parmesan. **Known
for:** charming hosts, from the owner to
the young waitstaff; entertaining outside
terrace on street; sumptuous dolci,
including cheesecake. $ *Average main:
€27* ⊠ *Via Pasitea 172/178, Positano*
☎ *089/875128* ⊕ *www.davincenzo.it*
⊘ *Closed Nov.–Mar. No lunch Tues.*

Il Ritrovo

$$$ | SOUTHERN ITALIAN | FAMILY | In the tiny
town square of Montepertuso, 1,500
feet up the mountainside from Positano
(call for the free shuttle service to and
from), the Ritrovo has been noted for its
cucina for more than 20 years. The menu
showcases food from both the sea and
the hills: try the scialatielli *ai frutti di mare*
accompanied by well-grilled vegetables;
the house specialty *zuppa saracena,* a
paella-like affair brimming with assorted seafood; and the lemon tiramisu,
perhaps paired with one of 80 different
kinds of a homemade liqueur, including
carob and chamomile options. **Known for:**
airy, tranquil mountainside location; local
spigola (sea bass) grilled or poached;
amiable padrone Salvatò, who also runs
a cooking school. $ *Average main: €30*
⊠ *Via Montepertuso 77, Montepertuso*
☎ *089/812005* ⊕ *www.ilritrovo.com*
⊘ *Closed mid-Jan.–mid-Feb.*

Lo Guarracino

$$$ | SOUTHERN ITALIAN | This partly
arbor-covered restaurant is a romantic
place to enjoy *scialatielli di mare* (seafood
pasta) above the waves, with a terrace
vista that takes in the cliffs, the sea,
the Li Galli islands, Spiaggia del Fornillo,
and Torre Clavel. **Known for:** seafood and
wood-fired pizza; family-made liquori
digestivi including a wild-herb number
(agrumi); romantic Robinson Crusoe–
esque terrace. $ *Average main: €26*
⊠ *Via Positanesi d'America 12, Positano*
☎ *089/875794* ⊕ *www.loguarracinoposi-
tano.it* ⊘ *Closed Jan.–Mar.*

Next2

$$$$ | **SOUTHERN ITALIAN** | Wrought-iron gates open from scenic Via Pasitea into Next2's *bianco e nero*–chic courtyard, replete with a cocktail bar and a whiff of edgy, youthful swagger. You can watch the talented *squadra* at work in the open kitchen crafting elegant, subtly flavored creations such as the grilled octopus antipasto, the seared tuna *secondo*, and—for those with bigger, bolder appetites and wallets—the *pescato del giorno* (catch of the day baked in a charcoal oven, served with vegetables). **Known for:** exquisite-looking small-portioned dishes; delectable dessert pairings such as pear and walnut ice cream; cocktails with novel, fresh infusions. $ *Average main: €36* ⊠ *Via Pasitea 242, Positano* ☎ *089/8123516* ⊕ *next2.it* ☾ *No lunch.*

☕ Coffee and Quick Bites

Paradise Lounge Bar

$ | **SANDWICHES** | **FAMILY** | With an outdoor terrace overlooking the Spiaggia Grande, this is an ideal stop for a coffee, a sandwich, or an ice cream. By night, the latest music pumps from the stereo and the clamor of sporting events blares from the large-screen TVs, as movers, groovers, and soccer fans from around the globe sip cocktails after a hard day on the beach. **Known for:** fab gelato artigianale; warm counter service; pastries, pizza, and panini. $ *Average main: €5* ⊠ *Via del Saracino 32, Positano* ☎ *089/811915* ⊕ *www.bucapositano.it/en/bar-paradise* ☾ *Closed Mon.*

🛏 Hotels

Hotel Eden Roc

$$$$ | **HOTEL** | The closest hotel to the Sponda bus stop, this luxury property (perfect for either couples or families) has spectacular views and service and spacious, pastel-hue guest rooms—all with terraces overlooking the town and some with whirlpool tubs. **Pros:** friendly and engaging staff; magical views; good on-site amenities (gym, steam bath, wellness center, rooftop pool). **Cons:** on the main road (take care as you exit the hotel); a bit of a climb from the town center; some rooms are dated. $ *Rooms from: €1150* ⊠ *Via G. Marconi 110, Positano* ☎ *089/875844* ⊕ *www.edenroc.it* ☾ *Closed Nov.–mid-Mar.* ⇨ *25 rooms* ❖❙ *Free Breakfast.*

Hotel L'Ancora

$$$$ | **HOTEL** | Set back a little from the main road and a short walk up from the main beach, this hotel has commanding views and bright coved-ceilinged guest rooms decorated with local artwork and boldly patterned mosaic tile. **Pros:** bright and sunny; many rooms have balconies or terraces and sea views; not far from the Sponda bus stop. **Cons:** a slight climb from the main drag; no on-site pool; no in-room soundproofing. $ *Rooms from: €550* ⊠ *Via Cristoforo Colombo 36, Positano* ☎ *089/875318* ⊕ *www.hotelancorapositano.com* ☾ *Closed Nov.–Mar.* ⇨ *18 rooms* ❖❙ *Free Breakfast.*

★ La Fenice

$$$ | **HOTEL** | This tiny, unpretentious hotel on the outskirts of Positano beckons with bougainvillea-laden views, castaway cottages, terraces growing produce, and a turquoise seawater pool—all perched over a private beach where a boat can whisk you away to Capri. **Pros:** small private beach with kayaks; famiglia Mandara's home-grown small-holding produce; secluded pool with bar service. **Cons:** a 10-minute walk to town; roadside rooms are small and noisy; lots of steps. $ *Rooms from: €260* ⊠ *Via G. Marconi 4, Positano* ☎ *089/875513* ⊕ *www.lafenicepositano.com* ☾ *Sometimes closed Dec.–Feb.* ⇨ *14 rooms* ❖❙ *Free Breakfast.*

★ Le Sirenuse

$$$$ | **HOTEL** | As legendary as its namesake sirens, this 18th-century palazzo has long set the standard for luxury in Italian hotels: it opened in 1951 with just 12 rooms (John Steinbeck stayed here while writing "Positano" for *Harper's Bazaar* in 1953) and now sprawls over eight floors, where extravagantly stylish guest rooms are accented with antiques and fine linens. **Pros:** unrivaled views, including from poolside terrace; many rooms have whirlpool tubs; gorgeous artworks around every corner. **Cons:** a bit of a climb from the town center; lower-priced rooms are small; can be noisy. $ *Rooms from: €2428* ⊠ *Via Cristoforo Colombo 30, Positano* 🕾 *089/875066* ⊕ *www. sirenuse.it* ⊘ *Closed Nov.–Mar.* 🥢 *58 rooms* �🍽️ *Free Breakfast.*

Palazzo Murat

$$$$ | HOTEL | A central-yet-secreted location, an infinity pool below the cupola of Santa Maria Assunta, and a magical bougainvillea-draped patio garden are among the things that make the Murat much coveted by hotel bucket-listers. **Pros:** once a regal residence; stunning garden and surroundings; shops and passeggiata on the doorstep. **Cons:** only five rooms have seaside views; staff can be snooty; not all balconies secluded. $ *Rooms from: €900* ⊠ *Via dei Mulini 23, Positano* 🕾 *089/875177* ⊕ *www.palazzomurat.it* ⊘ *Closed Nov.–Mar.* 🥢 *31 rooms* �🍽️ *Free Breakfast.*

Nightlife

L'Alternativa

GATHERING PLACE | The Tiffany-blue hut by the ferry ticket office at the far end of Spiaggia Grande is a refreshingly no-frills spot for a granita or snack by day or late-night cocktail or bottle of Peroni beer. Expect a friendly and unpretentious crowd, where local fishermen mix with young visitors who congregate in and around the harbor seats into the evening enjoying the reasonable (shock!)-for-Positano prices. ⊠ *Molo Spiaggia Grande, Positano.*

La Zagara

COCKTAIL BARS | Come evening, things heat up at this bar and *pasticceria* (pastry shop) where a local pianist tickles the ivories and summer sees DJ jams on the leafy terrace. ⊠ *Via dei Mulini 8, Positano* 🕾 *089/875964* ⊕ *www.lazagara.com.*

Conca dei Marini

13 km (8 miles) east of Positano, 29 km (18 miles) east of Sorrento.

A longtime favorite of the off-duty rich and famous, Conca dei Marini (the name means "seafarers' basin") hides many of its charms, as any sublime hideaway should. On a curve in the road sits the village's most noteworthy attraction, the Emerald Grotto.

Sights

Grotta dello Smeraldo (*Emerald Grotto*)

BODY OF WATER | FAMILY | The tacky road sign, squadron of tour buses, Dean Martin–style boatmen, and free-form serenading (Andrea is the king of the grotto crooners) scream tourist trap, but there is, nevertheless, a compelling, eerie *bellezza* in the rock formations and luminous waters here. The karstic cave was originally part of the shore, but the lowest end sank into the sea. Intense greenish light filters into the water from an arch below sea level and is reflected off the cavern walls. You visit the Grotta dello Smeraldo, which is filled with huge stalactites and stalagmites, on a large rowboat. Don't let the boatman's constant spiel detract from the experience—just tune out and enjoy the sparkles, shapes, and brilliant colors. The light at the grotto is best from noon to 3 pm. You can take an elevator from the coast road down to the grotto, or in the summer you can drive to Amalfi and arrive by boat (€25 including admission fee). Companies in Positano, Amalfi, and elsewhere along the coast provide passage to the grotto, but consider one of the longer boat trips that also explore Punta Campanella, Li Galli, and the more secluded spots along the coast. ⊠ *Via Smeraldo, west of Capo di Conca, Conca dei Marini* ☎ *089/831535* 🖃 *€10* ⊙ *Closed in adverse weather conditions.*

📷 Hotels

★ Monastero Santa Rosa Hotel & Spa

$$$$ | HOTEL | One of Italy's most exclusive retreats—in a 17th-century monastery on dramatic coastal cliffs—this boutique hotel has just 20 rooms, all with vaulted ceilings, Italian antiques, modern amenities, sumptuous bathrooms, and dazzling views framed by Mediterranean gardens. **Pros:** excellent service; meticulously restored property with spa; gorgeous gardens and infinity pool. **Cons:** out of reach for many budgets; some rooms could be more spacious; a bit remote. ⑤ *Rooms from: €1210* ⊠ *Via Roma 2, Conca dei Marini* ☎ *089/8321199* ⊕ *www.monasterosantarosa.com* ⊙ *Closed Nov.–mid-Apr.* ➡ *20 rooms* ❑ *Free Breakfast.*

Amalfi

18 km (11 miles) east of Positano, 35 km (22 miles) east of Sorrento.

At first glance, it's hard to imagine that this resort destination was one of the world's great naval powers and a sturdy rival of Genoa and Pisa for control of the Mediterranean in the 11th and 12th centuries. Once the seat of the Amalfi Maritime Republic, the town is set in a verdant valley of the Lattari Mountains, with cream-color and pastel-hue buildings tightly packing a gorge on the Bay of Salerno. The harbor, which once launched the greatest fleet in Italy, now bobs with ferries and blue-and-white fishing boats. The main street, lined with shops and pasticcerie, has replaced a raging mountain torrent, and terraced hills flaunt the green and gold of lemon groves. Bearing testimony to its great trade with

Tunis, Tripoli, and Algiers, Amalfi remains honeycombed with Arab-Sicilian cloisters and covered passages. In a way Amalfi has become great again, showing off its medieval glory days with sea pageants, convents-turned-hotels, ancient paper mills, covered streets, and its glimmering cathedral.

GETTING HERE AND AROUND

From April to October the optimal way to get to Amalfi is by ferry from Salerno or Naples (sometimes via Sorrento). Sita Sud buses run from Naples and Sorrento throughout the year. By car, take the Statale 163 (Amalfitana) from outside Sorrento or Salerno, or take the Angri exit on the A3 autostrada and cross the mountainous Valico di Chiunsi.

VISITOR INFORMATION

CONTACT Info Point. (*Amalfi Tourist Office*) ⊠ *Arsenale della Repubblica e Molo Pennello, Piazza Flavio Gioia e Largo Cesareo Console, Amalfi* ☎ *089/8736222* ⊕ *www.amalfitouristoffice.it.*

Sights

Arsenale di Amalfi

HISTORIC SIGHT | Get a feel of the architecture and naval might of the *repubblica marinara* (maritime republic) of Amalfi at this fascinating museum within the impressive Arsenale shipyard, which was first documented in 1059. As well as a cultural and performance space, the Arsenal contains the Museo della Bussola e del Ducato Marinaro, which largely focuses on the golden age of the Amalfi Republic between 839 and 1139, displaying artifacts such as money, manuscripts, navigational and other nautical instruments, costumes, art, and religious objects. ⊠ *Largo Cesario Console 3, Amalfi* ☎ *089/8736204* ⊕ *arsenalediamalfi.it* 🖃 *Free* ⊙ *Closed Mon. Nov.–Mar.*

★ Duomo di Sant'Andrea

CHURCH | Complicated, grand, delicate, and dominating, the 9th-century Amalfi cathedral has been remodeled over the years with Romanesque, Byzantine, Gothic, and Baroque elements but retains a predominantly Arab-Norman style. Built around 1266 as a burial ground for Amalfi's elite, the cloister, the first stop on a tour of the cathedral, is one of southern Italy's architectural treasures. Its flower-and-palm-filled quadrangle has a series of exceptionally delicate intertwining arches on slender double columns. The chapel at the back of the cloister leads into the 9th-century basilica, now a museum housing sarcophagi, sculpture, Neapolitan goldsmiths' artwork, and other treasures from the cathedral complex. Steps from the basilica lead down into the Cripta di Sant'Andrea (Crypt of St. Andrew). The cathedral above was built in the 13th century to house the saint's bones, which came from Constantinople. Following the one-way traffic up to the cathedral, you can admire the elaborate polychrome marbles and painted, coffered ceilings from its 18th-century restoration. ⊠ *Piazza Duomo, Amalfi* ☎ *089/871324* ⊕ *museodiocesanoamalfi. it* ▣ *€4* ☉ *Generally closed early Jan. and Feb. except for daily services.*

★ **Museo della Carta** (*Paper Museum*) **HISTORY MUSEUM | FAMILY** | Uphill from town, the Valle dei Mulini (Valley of the Mills) was for centuries Amalfi's center for papermaking, an ancient trade learned from the Arabs, who learned it from the Chinese. Beginning in the 12th century, former flour mills were converted to produce paper made from cotton and linen. The paper industry was a success, and by 1811 more than a dozen mills here, with more along the coast, were humming. Natural waterpower ensured that the handmade paper was cost-effective. Yet, by the late 1800s the industry had moved to Naples and other more geographically accessible areas. Flooding in 1954 closed most of the mills for good, and many have been converted into private housing. The Museo della Carta (Museum of Paper) opened in 1971 in a 15th-century mill. Paper samples, tools of the trade, old machinery, and the audio-visual presentation are all enlightening. You can also participate in a paper-making laboratory. ⊠ *Via delle Cartiere 23, Amalfi* ☎ *089/8304561* ⊕ *www.museodellacarta.it* ▣ *€5, includes guided tour; €7 with paper-making experience* ☉ *Closed Feb. and Mon. Nov.–Jan.*

🍴 Restaurants

La Caravella
$$$$ | **SOUTHERN ITALIAN** | Opened in 1959 and southern Italy's first restaurant to earn a Michelin star (in 1966), this atmospheric place—graced with frescoes, marble floors, vibrant ceramics, and fresh flowers—once had a gilded guest list that included Andy Warhol and Federico Fellini. The menu maintains dishes favored 50 years ago (picture slices of fish grilled in lemon leaves marinated with an almond and wild fennel sauce); there's also a tasting menu, but don't miss the antipasti. **Known for:** the Mezzogiorno's original fine-dining eatery; cheerful "art gallery" dining room; seafood scialatielli (pasta with seafood) and soufflé al limone. ⑤ *Average main: €80* ⊠ *Via Matteo Camera 12, near Arsenale, Amalfi* ☎ *089/871029* ⊕ *www.ristorantelacaravella.it* ☉ *Closed Tues. and Nov. and Jan.*

☕ Coffee and Quick Bites

Andrea Pansa
$ | **CAFÉ** | Amalfi's historic pasticceria is famed for its candied fruits and assortment of tempting Neapolitan pastries. If you have no time to linger and indulge at their piazza tables, order at the bar for a cheaper stand-up coffee and *sflogliatella* (shell-shaped pastry) fix. **Known for:** historic facade and interiors on Piazza Duomo; delizia di limone cake; excellent but pricey. ⑤ *Average main: €6* ⊠ *Piazza Duomo 40, Amalfi* ☎ *089/871065* ⊕ *www.pasticceriapansa.it.*

🛏 Hotels

Albergo Sant'Andrea

$$$ | HOTEL | Just across from the magnificent steps leading to Amalfi's cathedral, this tiny, family-run *pensione* has a cute "Room with a View" lobby that's as big as a Victorian closet and guest rooms (most overlooking the Duomo) that range from cozy to vast. **Pros:** great location on the main square; divine Duomo views; old-school family-run pensione (with half-board available). **Cons:** steep flight of steps to entrance; simple, dated decor; on the piazza, so expect noise. ⑤ *Rooms from: €300* ✉ *Salita Costanza D'Avalos 1, Amalfi* ☎ *089/871145* ⊕ *www.albergo-santandrea.it* ⊘ *Closed Feb. and Mar.* 🛏 *8 rooms* 🍽 *Free Breakfast.*

★ Anantara Hotel Convento di Amalfi

$$$$ | RESORT | This fabled medieval monastery was lauded by such guests as Longfellow and Wagner, and after a luxurious overhaul by the esteemed Anantara hotel group, it still retains its historic charm and features, including a celebrated Arab-Sicilian cloister and Baroque church. **Pros:** a slice of paradise; impeccable service; sublime terrace and garden walkways. **Cons:** food pricey and inconsistent; 15-minute walk to town; noise from occasional wedding and events. ⑤ *Rooms from: €1800* ✉ *Via Annunziatella 46, Amalfi* ☎ *089/8736711* ⊕ *www.anantara.com/en/convento-di-amalfi* ⊘ *Closed Jan.–mid-Mar.* 🛏 *52 rooms* 🍽 *Free Breakfast.*

🛍 Shopping

Leading off from Piazza Duomo is the main street of Amalfi, Via Lorenzo d'Amalfi, which is lined with some of the loveliest shops on the coast. While it can be crowded during the day, be sure to take a stroll along here in the evening.

Ravello

5 km (3 miles) northeast of Amalfi, 40 km (25 miles) northeast of Sorrento.

Positano may focus on pleasure, and Amalfi on history, but cool, serene Ravello revels in refinement. Thrust over the S163 and the Bay of Salerno on a mountain buttress, below forests of chestnut and ash, above terraced lemon groves and vineyards, it early on beckoned the affluent with its island-in-the-sky views and secluded defensive positioning. Gardens out of the *Arabian Nights*, pastel palazzi, tucked-away piazzas with medieval fountains, architecture ranging from Romano-Byzantine to Norman-Saracen, and those sweeping blue-water, blue-sky vistas have inspired a panoply of large personalities. Today, many visitors flock here to discover this paradisiacal place, some to enjoy the town's celebrated two-month-long summer music festival (the Ravello Festival ⊕ *www.ravellofestival.com*), others just to stroll through the hillside streets to gape at the bluer-than-blue panoramas of sea and sky.

GETTING HERE AND AROUND

Buses from Amalfi make the 20-minute trip along white-knuckle roads. From Naples, take the A3 Naples–Salerno autostrada; then exit at Angri and follow signs for Ravello. The journey takes about 75 minutes. Save yourself the trouble of driving by hiring a car and driver.

VISITOR INFORMATION

CONTACT Infopoint. ✉ *Piazza Fontana Moresca 10, Ravello* ☎ *089/857096.*

👁 Sights

Auditorium Oscar Niemeyer

ARTS CENTER | Crowning Via della Repubblica and the hillside, which overlooks the spectacular Bay of Salerno, Auditorium Niemeyer is a startling piece of modernist architecture. Designed with a dramatically curved, all-white roof by

Ravello's History

The town itself was founded in the 9th century, under Amalfi's rule. Residents prosperous from cotton tussled with the superpower republic and elected their own doge in the 11th century; Amalfitani dubbed them *ribelli* (rebels). In the 12th century, with the aid of the Norman King Roger, Ravello even succeeded in resisting Pisa's army for a couple of years, though the powerful Pisans returned to wreak destruction along the coast. Even so, Ravello's skilled seafaring trade with merchants and Moors from Sicily and points east led to a burgeoning wealth, which peaked in the 13th century, when there were 13 churches, four cloisters, and dozens of sumptuous villas. Neapolitan princes built palaces and life was privileged.

Ravello's bright light eventually diminished, first through Pisa's maritime rise in the 14th century, then through rivalry between its warring families in the 15th century. When plague cast its shadow in the 17th century, the population plummeted from upward of 30,000 to perhaps a couple of thousand souls, where it remains today. When Ravello was incorporated into the diocese of Amalfi in 1804, a kind of stillness settled in. Despite the decline of its power and populace, Ravello's cultural heritage and special loveliness continued to blossom. Gardens flowered and music flowed in the ruined villas, and artists, sophisticates, and their lovers filled the crumbling palazzi. Grieg, Wagner, D. H. Lawrence, Chanel, Garbo and her companion, conductor Leopold Stokowski, and then, slowly, tourists followed in their footsteps.

the Brazilian architect Oscar Niemeyer (designer of Brasília), it was conceived as an alternative indoor venue for concerts, including those of the famed summer Ravello Festival and is now also used as a cinema. The subject of much controversy since its first conception back in 2000, it raised the wrath of some locals who denounced such an ambitious modernist building in medieval Ravello. They need not have worried. The result, inaugurated in 2010, is a design masterpiece—a huge, overhanging canopied roof suspended over a 400-seat concert area, with a giant eye-shape window allowing spectators to contemplate the extraordinary bay vista during performances. ✉ *Via della Repubblica 12, Ravello* ☎ *089/857096.*

★ Duomo

CHURCH | Ravello's first bishop, Orso Papiciò, founded this cathedral, dedicated to San Pantaleone, in 1086. Rebuilt in the 12th and 17th centuries, it retains traces of medieval frescoes in the transept, an original mullioned window, a marble portal, and a three-story 13th-century bell tower playfully interwoven with mullioned windows and arches. The 12th-century bronze door has 54 embossed panels depicting Christ's life, and saints, prophets, plants, and animals, all narrating biblical lore. Ancient columns divide the nave's three aisles, and treasures include sarcophagi from Roman times and paintings by the southern Renaissance artist Andrea da Salerno. Most impressive are the two medieval pulpits: the earlier one is inset with a mosaic scene of Jonah and the whale, while the more famous one opposite boasts exquisite mosaic work and six twisting columns sitting on lion pedestals. In the crypt is the **Museo del Duomo**, which displays 13th-century treasures from the reign of Frederick II of Sicily. ⊠ *Piazza del Duomo, Ravello* ☎ *089/858311* ⚁ *€3.*

Giardini del Vescovo (*Monsignore*)
GARDEN | A onetime bishop's residence that dates from at least the 12th century, the Villa Episcopio (formerly Villa di Sangro) today hosts concerts and exhibitions and has an open-air theater in its splendid gardens—the same gardens where André Gide found inspiration for his novel *The Immoralist,* where Italy's King Vittorio Emanuele III abdicated in favor of his son in 1944, and where Jackie Kennedy enjoyed breaks from her obligations as First Lady during a much publicized 1962 visit. Wheelchair access is via a new ramp on via San Giovanni del Toro. ⊠ *Via Richard Wagner/Via dei Episcopio, Ravello* ⚁ *Free.*

Mamma Agata
COOKING CLASSES | Learn about Costiera Amalfitana cooking traditions with Mamma Agata, known for a popular cookbook, moreish meatballs and eggplant parmigiana, and for hosting Astaire, Bogart, Burton and Taylor, and Jackie Kennedy; while cheerful daughter Chiara has swapped spoons with Michael Jordan, Pierce Brosnan, and Woody Harrelsen among others. The family will walk you through the preparation of its many generation-spanning recipes. A morning session is followed by lunch and an introduction to the family's organic lemons, zucchini, tomatoes, and abundant produce grown in their wonderful garden and sent around the world. Classes must be arranged in advance (they are not offered on Wednesdays). ⊠ *Piazza San Cosma 9, Ravello* ☎ *089/857845* ⊕ *www. mammaagata.com* ⚁ *Cooking class and lunch from €350* ⊗ *Closed Wed., weekends, Dec.–Mar., Easter and Aug.10–25.*

★ **Museo del Corallo** (*Coral Museum*)
ART MUSEUM | To the left of the Duomo, the entrance to this private museum is through the tempting shop CAMO, and both are the creation of master-craftsman-in-residence Giorgio Filocamo. The museum celebrates the venerable tradition of Italian workmanship in coral, harvested in bygone centuries from the gulfs of Salerno and Naples and crafted into jewelry, cameos, and figurines. The fascinating collection, not confined solely to coral work, includes a painting of Sisto IV from the 14th century. Look also in particular for a carved Christ from the 17th century, for which the J. Paul Getty Museum offered $525,000 in 1987 (the offer was refused), and a tobacco box covered in cameos, one of only two in the world. There is also a statue of the Madonna dating to 1532. Giorgio has crafted coral for Pope John Paul II, the Clintons, and Princess Caroline, as well as numerous Hollywood stars. ⊠ *Piazza Duomo 9, Ravello* ☎ *089/857461* ⊕ *www.museodel-corallo.com* ⚁ *Free* ⊗ *Closed Fri.–Sun.*

★ **Villa Cimbrone**
GARDEN | To the south of Ravello's main square, a somewhat hilly 15-minute walk along Via San Francesco brings you to Ravello's showstopper, the Villa Cimbrone, whose dazzling gardens perch 1,500 feet above the sea. This medieval-style fantasy was created in 1905 by England's Lord Grimthorpe and made world-famous in the 1930s when Greta Garbo found sanctuary from the press here. The Gothic *castello-palazzo* sits amid idyllic gardens that are divided by the grand Avenue of Immensity pathway, leading in turn to the literal high point of any trip to the Amalfi Coast—the Belvedere of Infinity. This grand stone parapet, adorned with stone busts, overlooks the entire Bay of Salerno and frames a panorama that the late writer Gore Vidal, a longtime Ravello resident, described as the most beautiful in the world. The villa itself is now a five-star hotel. ⊠ *Via Santa Chiara 26, Ravello* ☎ *089/857459* ⊕ *www. villacimbrone.it* ⚁ *€10.*

★ Villa Rufolo

GARDEN | Directly off Ravello's main piazza is the Villa Rufolo, home to some of the most spectacular gardens in Italy, framing a stunning vista of the Bay of Salerno, often called the "bluest view in the world." If one believes the master storyteller Boccaccio, the villa was built in the 13th century by Landolfo Rufolo, whose immense fortune stemmed from trade with the Moors and the Saracens. Norman and Arab architecture mingle in a welter of color-filled gardens so lush the composer Richard Wagner used them as inspiration for Klingsor's Garden, the home of the Flower Maidens, in his opera *Parsifal*. Beyond the Arab-Sicilian cloister and the Norman tower lie the two terrace gardens. The lower one, the "Wagner Terrace," is often the site of Ravello Festival concerts. Highlights of the house are its Moorish cloister—an Arabic-Sicilian delight with interlacing lancet arcs and polychromatic palmette decoration—and the 14th-century Torre Maggiore, or Klingsor's Tower. ⊠ *Piazza del Duomo, Ravello* ☎ *089/857621* ⊕ *www.villarufolo.it* 🎫 *€8, extra charge for concerts.*

Restaurants

Vittoria

$$ | **PIZZA** | **FAMILY** | Just south of the Duomo, this airy, unfussy place with coved stone ceilings is a good bet for an informal bite. The *pizza al forno di legna* with fresh toppings is the star attraction: locals praise it, and even Gore Vidal allegedly approved. **Known for:** extensive menu; very popular with locals and tourists; Campanian classics, including seafood frittura and eggplant parmigiana. ⑤ *Average main: €23* ⊠ *Via dei Rufolo 3, Ravello* ☎ *089/857947* ⊕ *www.ristorantepizzeriavittoria.it.*

Hotels

Belmond Hotel Caruso

$$$$ | **HOTEL** | In a grand palazzo on the highest point of Ravello, with some buildings dating from the 16th century and with a Bay of Salerno panorama that's incomparable and timeless, this member of the exclusive Belmond hotel brand has been a slice of hospitality paradise since the 19th century; today it shimmers with modern luxuries amid its frescoes, Norman arches, and beautifully terraced garden. **Pros:** infinity pool; spacious suites with terraces; complimentary boat and shuttle services. **Cons:** way out of most visitors' price range; service can be inconsistent; overrated restaurant. ⑤ *Rooms from: €1880* ⊠ *Piazza San Giovanni del Toro 2, Ravello* ☎ *089/858801* ⊕ *www.hotelcaruso.com* ⊙ *Closed Nov.–mid-Apr.* ⌁ *50 rooms* ⑩ *Free Breakfast.*

Hotel Parsifal

$$ | **HOTEL** | In 1288, this diminutive property overlooking the coastline housed an order of Augustinian friars; today the intact cloister hosts travelers intent on enjoying themselves under the coved ceilings of the former *eremitani scalzi* (shaved hermit) cells. **Pros:** staying in a former Ravello convent; charming manager and his family dote on Americans; open year-round. **Cons:** some may not like the '70s vibe; tiny rooms; can be chilly in colder months. ⑤ *Rooms from: €200* ⊠ *Viale Gioacchino d'Anna 5, Ravello* ☎ *089/857144* ⊕ *www.hotelparsifal.com* ⌁ *17 rooms* ⑩ *Free Breakfast.*

Hotel Rufolo

$$$$ | **HOTEL** | The quarters might be snug and simply furnished, but many have balconies with gorgeous sea and sky vistas framed by the palm trees of the Villa Rufolo, just below the hotel. **Pros:** parking included in room rates; beautiful views over Villa Rufolo; great pool and spa services. **Cons:** car park clutters the entrance; dated decor; overpriced: paying for the location. ⑤ *Rooms from: €310* ⊠ *Via*

San Francesco 1, Ravello ☎ 089/857133 ⊕ www.hotelrufolo.it ۞ Closed Jan.–Mar. ⚓ 34 rooms �‖‖ Free Breakfast.

Hotel Villa Cimbrone

$$$$ | HOTEL | Suspended over the azure sea and set amid legendary rose-filled gardens, this Gothic-style castle was once home to Lord Grimthorpe and a hideaway for Greta Garbo; since the 1990s, it's been an exclusive if pricey visitors haven, with guest rooms ranging from palatial to cozy. **Pros:** gorgeous pool and views; surrounded by beautiful gardens; top-rated restaurant. **Cons:** a longish hike from town center (porters can help with luggage); daily arrival of respectful day-trippers; special place comes at a price. ⑤ *Rooms from:* €990 ✉ Via Santa Chiara 26, Ravello ☎ 089/857459 ⊕ www.villacimbrone.com ۞ Closed Nov.–mid-Apr. ⚓ 19 rooms �‖‖ Free Breakfast.

Villa Amore

$$$ | HOTEL | A 10-minute walk from the Piazza Duomo, this secluded hotel with a garden is family-run and shares the same exhilarating view of the Bay of Salerno as Ravello's most expensive hotels. **Pros:** wonderful views; inexpensive alternative to its illustrious neighbors; good-value restaurant. **Cons:** away from the main drag; some rooms are very cramped and without views; long flight of steps to reach entrance. ⑤ *Rooms from:* €280 ✉ Via dei Fusco 5, Ravello ☎ 089/857135 ⊕ www.villaamore.it ۞ Closed Nov.–Mar. ⚓ 12 rooms �‖‖ Free Breakfast.

Paestum

99 km (62 miles) southeast of Naples.

For history buffs, a visit to Campania is not complete without seeing the ancient ruins of Paestum. A visit to the ruins to stroll past the incredibly well-preserved temples and see the top-notch collection at the Museo Nazionale is a great day trip from the Amalfi Coast or Naples.

GETTING HERE AND AROUND

By car, take the A3 autostrada south from Salerno, take the Battipaglia exit to SS18. Exit at Capaccio Scala. You can also take a CRAL Busitalia or SCAT bus (departs hourly) or an FS train from Salerno. The archaeological site is a 10-minute walk from the station.

VISITOR INFORMATION

CONTACT Infopoint Paestum. (*Paestum Tourist Office*) ✉ Via Magna Grecia 887, Paestum ☎ 0828/811016.

◉ Sights

★ Paestum Archaeological Park

ARCHAEOLOGICAL SITE | One of Italy's most majestic sights lies on the edge of a flat coastal plain: the remarkably preserved Greek temples of Paestum. This is the site of the ancient city of Poseidonia, founded by Greek colonists probably in the 6th century BC. When the Romans took it over in 273 BC, they Latinized the name to Paestum and changed the layout of the settlement, adding an amphitheater and a forum. Much of the archaeological material found on the site is displayed in the Museo Nazionale within the park, and several rooms are devoted to the unique tomb paintings—rare examples of Greek and pre-Roman pictorial art—discovered in the area.

At the northern end of the site opposite the ticket barrier is the Tempio di Cerere (Temple of Ceres). Built in about 500 BC, it is thought to have been originally dedicated to the goddess Athena. Follow the road south past the Foro Romano (Roman Forum) to the Tempio di Nettuno (Temple of Poseidon), a showstopping Doric edifice with 36 fluted columns and an entablature (the area above the capitals) that rivals those of the finest temples in Greece. Beyond is the so-called Basilica, which dates from the early 6th century BC. The name is an 18th-century misnomer, though, since it was, in fact, a temple devoted to Hera, the wife of

Zeus. Try to see the temples in the early morning or late afternoon when the stone takes on a golden hue. ⊠ *Via Magna Grecia, Paestum* ☎ *0828/811023 ticket office* ⊕ *www.museopaestum.beniculturali.it* ⊠ *Site and museum: Mar.–Nov. €15, Dec.–Feb. €10.*

★ **Tenuta Vannulo—Buffalo Farm and Shop**
FARM/RANCH | **FAMILY** | Foodies, families, and the curious flock to this novel farm attraction that celebrates humane animal husbandry, organic mozzarella di bufala, and other wonderful products. A tour of the ranch run by the Palmieri family—headed by the serene octogenerian Antonio—brings you nose to glistening snout with probably the most pampered buffalo in the world. Some 600 of them wallow in pools, get a mechanical massage, and flap their ears to classical music. The shop/restaurant is the place to taste and take away cheese, ice cream, yogurt, chocolate, and leather products. ⊠ *Contrada Vannulo, Via Galileo Galilei 101, Capaccio, Paestum* ☎ *0828/727894* ⊕ *www.vannulo.it* ⊠ *€5 guided group tours; book in advance.*

Hotels

Azienda Agrituristica Seliano
$$ | **B&B/INN** | At this working farm about 3 km (2 miles) from Paestum's Greek temples, befriend the resident dogs so they will accompany you on country walks or bike rides, and opt for half board to enjoy home-produced mozzarella and rich buffalo stew. **Pros:** a great taste of a working farm; a banquet every evening; cooking classes. **Cons:** confusing to find; not for non–dog fans; rustic, dated decor. ⑤ *Rooms from: €140* ⊠ *Via Seliano, Paestum* ✛ *About 1 km (½ mile) down dirt track west off main road from Capaccio Scalo to Paestum* ☎ *0828/723634* ⊕ *www.agriturismoseliano.it* ۞ *Closed Nov.–Mar.* ➡ *14 rooms* ۞ *Free Breakfast.*

Chapter 16

PUGLIA, BASILICATA, AND CALABRIA

16

Updated by
Nick Bruno

👁 **Sights**
★★★☆☆

🍴 **Restaurants**
★★★★★

🛏 **Hotels**
★★★☆☆

🛍 **Shopping**
★★☆☆☆

🍸 **Nightlife**
★☆☆☆☆

WELCOME TO PUGLIA, BASILICATA, AND CALABRIA

TOP REASONS TO GO

★ **A wander through Sassi:** The Basilicata town of Matera is endowed with one of the most unusual landscapes in Europe—a complex network of ancient cave dwellings partially hewn from rock, some of which now house chic bars and restaurants.

★ **A trip to peasant-food heaven:** Dine on Puglia's famous puree of fava beans with chicory and olive oil in a humble country restaurant.

★ **Lecce and its Baroque splendors:** The beautiful, friendly city of Lecce might be known for its peculiar brand of fanciful Baroque architecture, but it's not yet famous enough to have lost its Pugliese charm.

★ **The trulli of the Valle d'Itria:** Strange conical houses—many of them still in use—dot the rolling countryside of Puglia, centering around Alberobello, a town still composed almost entirely of these *trulli*. They must be seen to be believed.

1 Bari. An atmospheric *centro storico* is a highlight of this busy Adriatic port.

2 Trani. Don't miss this harbor town's stunning cathedral.

3 Polignano a Mare. Steep cliffs draw thrill-seekers and those looking to relax overlooking gorgeous inlets.

4 Castel del Monte. This town's octagonal, eponymous fortress is mysterious.

5 Mattinata. The Gulf of Manfredonia beaches here will dazzle you.

6 Vieste. The spectacular Gargano Promontory is the site of this resort town.

7 Alberobello. It's hard not to be enchanted by Alberobello's fairy-tale stone trulli.

8 Ostuni. The so-called Città Bianca (White City) is perched above azure waters.

9 Ceglie Messapica. The heart of this town is beguilingly medieval.

10 Martina Franca. Lose yourself in a maze of alleys and piazzas.

11 Taranto. An engaging archaeological museum is the main draw of this port town with a naval base.

12 Lecce. Here, it's all about Baroque beauty and lively locals.

13 Otranto. Look out over the sea from Otranto's medieval fortress.

14 Gallipoli. This fishing town is famed for its island *borgo antico*.

15 Matera. The so-called City of Sassi is filled with the intriguing cave dwellings.

16 Maratea. The mountains here seem to fall into the sea.

17 Diamante. This Calabrese resort is lively.

18 Castrovillari. For hiking, this gateway to mountainous Pollino National Park is a great hub.

19 Cosenza. Come to explore attractive medieval sights.

20 Camigliatello. The mountainous Sila National Park surrounds this town.

21 Crotone. The Treasure of Hera is among Crotone's draws.

22 Tropea. Gorgeous beaches will beckon you to Tropea.

23 Reggio Calabria. This busy port city plays footsie with Sicily.

ADRIATIC SEA

0   30 mi

0   30 km

Peschici
Vieste
GARGANO PROMONTORY
Mattinata
Manfredonia
San Severo
Foggia
Barletta
Trani
Canosa
Bari
Castel del Monte
Polignano a Mare
Monopoli
Fasano
Ostuni
PUGLIA
Alberobello
Altamura
Brindisi
Martina Franca
Ceglie Messapica
CAMPANIA
Potenza
Matera
Lecce
Salerno
BASILICATA
Taranto
Manduria
Otranto
Aliano
Bernalda
LUCANO
Gallipoli
SALEN...
Gagliano
Golfo di Taranto
Maratea
Castrovillari
Diamante
TYRRHENIAN SEA
Cosenza
Camigliatello
Paola
CALABRIA
Crotone
Catanzaro
Vibo Valentia
IONIAN SEA
Tropea
AEOLIAN ISLANDS
Salina
Lipari
Vulcano
Rosarno
Palmi
Siderno
Locri
Messina
Reggio Calabria
SICILY
Cape Spartivento

A14
16
89
A14
16
89
A16
A14
96
16
A14
172
E847
598
106
653
A3
18
A3
106
19
20
107
21
111
106
106
106
379
7
613
174
275
611
274

EATING AND DRINKING WELL IN PUGLIA, BASILICATA, AND CALABRIA

Meat and cheese products flavored with chili peppers

The Mediterranean diet was born in the south of Italy. The cuisine here is based on seasonal local produce, so don't expect to find, say, grapes in May or watermelon in November, although the mild climate and fertile soil, linked to modern farming methods, mean that most vegetable products have a long growing season.

Traditional cuisine reflects its peasant origins, with hearty homemade pasta, thick bean soups, and grilled meat and fish. The emphasis, though, is on vegetables, with zucchini, eggplant, beans, sweet peppers, and at least a dozen varieties of tomatoes transformed into imaginative dishes. Naturally, the local olive oil is never lacking on the table. Dribbled over soup or a thick chunk of bread, it can transform the plainest dish into a gourmet treat. One defining principle of Italian cooking is to use excellent ingredients in simple preparations. That philosophy reaches its purest expression here.

FABULOUS FAVA

Puré di fave e cicorielle, a puree of fava beans topped with sautéed chicory, is unique to Puglia and Basilicata. The simple recipe has been prepared here for centuries and continues to be a staple of the local diet. The dried favas are soaked overnight, cooked with potatoes, seasoned with salt and olive oil, and served warm with wild green chicory, often with a sprinkling of ground *peperoncino* (chili pepper). Mix it together before eating, and wash it down with a glass of *primitivo* or *aglianico*.

MEAT

In addition to its excellent beef, Basilicata is known for its *salsicce lucane* (sausages), seasoned with salt, cayenne pepper, and fennel seeds. Enormous grills are a feature of many of the region's restaurants, infusing the dining area with the aroma of freshly cooked meat. Adventurous eaters in Puglia should look for *turcinieddhri* (a blend of lamb's innards) and *pezzetti di cavallo* (braised horse meat).

PASTA

Puglia is the home of orecchiette with *cime di rapa* (broccoli rabe) and olive oil, a melodious dish that's wondrous in its simplicity. Try also cavatelli and *strascinati* (rectangles of pasta with one rough side and one smooth side).

PEPPERS

Calabria is known for its use of little hot peppers that can range from a mild sprinkling in tomato sauce to the tongue-scorching *'nduja* (spicy pork salami) paste. Local cured meats like *soppressata* (dried spicy salami) and *salsiccia piccante* (hot sausage), often sold by street vendors on a roll with peppers, onions, french fries, and mayonnaise, are all spiced with peperoncini.

Orecchiette pasta

Baked fish with potatoes

SEAFOOD

Fish can be grilled (*alla griglia*), baked (*al forno*), roasted (*arrosto*), or steamed (*in umido*). Among the highlights are delicate *orata* (sea bream), branzino (sea bass), *gamberi rossi* (sweet red shrimp), and calamari. Puglia is the home of *cozze pelose* (hairy-shelled mussels), and Calabria's version of sushi is freshly caught *ricci di mare* (sea urchins), considered a delicacy—and an aphrodisiac!

WINES

Puglia produces around 17% of Italy's wine, more than the output of Australia. In the past, most of it was *vino sfuso* (jug wine), but over the past 20 years, producers have been concentrating on quality—with impressive results. The ancient *primitivo* grape (an ancestor of California's zinfandel) yields strong, heady wines like Primitivo di Manduria. The *negroamaro* grape is transformed into palatable *rosati* (rosés), as well as the robust Salice Salentino. Pair a dessert with the sweet red Aleatico di Puglia or Moscato di Trani.

In Basilicata, producers use the aglianico grape to outstanding effect in the prestigious Aglianico del Vulture. In Calabria, they've worked wonders with *gaglioppo*.

Venture off the traffic-filled highways and explore the countryside of Italy's boot, made up of three separate regions—Puglia, Basilicata, and Calabria—each one with its own character. This is Italy's deep south, where whitewashed buildings stand silently over three turquoise seas, castles guard medieval alleyways, and grandmothers dry their handmade orecchiette in the afternoon heat.

At every turn, these three regions boast dramatic scenery. Geographical divides have preserved an astonishing cultural and linguistic diversity that's unequaled elsewhere on the Italian mainland. Southern Italians are extremely proud of their hometowns and will gladly direct you to some forgotten local chapel in an olive grove, an unmarked monument, or an obscure work of art.

One of southern Italy's most popular vacation destinations is the Gargano Promontory, where safe sandy shores and secluded coves are nestled between whitewashed coastal towns and craggy limestone cliffs. You'll also find many beautiful stretches of sandy beaches along the coast of the Salento Peninsula and the Mediterranean shoreline of Calabria and Basilicata.

MAJOR REGIONS

Bari and the Adriatic Coast. The busy port of Bari offers architectural nuggets in its labyrinthine old quarter. In nearby Trani a distinctive Apulian-Romanesque church stands by the sea, while Polignano a Mare has cliff-top medieval charm above sparkling waters. For a unique excursion, head to Castel del Monte, home to an enigmatic 13th-century octagonal castle.

The Gargano Promontory. Amid the Foresta Umbra's landscape of craggy limestone, pine trees, and scrubby Mediterranean *macchia* (underbrush) are the beguiling coastal resorts of Vieste and Mattinata.

The Trulli District. The inland area southeast of Bari has a mostly flat, rock-strewn terrain that's been given over to olive cultivation. The area is also interspersed with idiosyncratic limestone habitations called *trulli*. The center of the Trulli District is Alberobello in the enchanting Valle d'Itria. Amid this fairy-tale-like landscape are the dazzling whitewashed hilltop market towns of Martina Franca, Ceglie Messapica, and Ostuni.

The Salento Penninsula. South of the Trulli District the monotony of endless olive trees is redeemed by an alluring coastline of dramatic sandstone cliffs and intimate fishing towns such as Otranto and Gallipoli. Taranto has a captivating archaeological museum amid its rusty, industrial surroundings, while Lecce is an oasis of grace and sophistication, with swirling Baroque architecture and a lively cultural scene.

Basilicata. Occupying the instep and part of the heel of Italy's boot, this and the neighboring Calabria region formed part of Magna Graecia, southern Italy's Greek colonies. Today, Basilicata attracts travelers in search of bucolic settings, great food, and archaeological treasures. The village of Aliano was made famous by writer Carlo Levi (1902–75). Matera, a recently rejuvenated city with Baroque splendor, is built on the side of a ravine honeycombed with Sassi that have been transformed into swanky homes, restaurants, and hotels. On a spectacularly mountainous section of the Tyrrhenian coast is the gorgeous resort Maratea.

Calabria. Italy's southernmost mainland region has fantastic beaches in lively resort communities such as Tropea and Diamante. Castrovillari, Cosenza, and Camigliatello are great rustic bases for exploring the Sila Mountains and Pollino National Park. Crotone was a major ancient cultural center, and, toward Sicily, the busy port of Reggio Calabria is home to two arresting ancient Greek statues, the *Bronzi di Riace*.

Planning

Getting Around

BUS
There is direct, if not always frequent, service between most destinations within Calabria, Puglia, and Basilicata. In many cases, bus service is the backup when problems with train service arise. Matera is linked with Bari by frequent Ferrovie Appulo Lucane trains and buses

and with Taranto by SITA bus. In Calabria the Romano bus company runs a regular service between various towns. Ferrovie della Calabria operates many of the local routes.

CONTACTS Bus Romano. ☎ *0962/21709* ⊕ *www.autolineeromano.com.* **Ferrovie della Calabria.** ☎ *0961/896306 Catanzaro Stazione* ⊕ *www.ferroviedellacalabria. it.* **SITA.** ☎ *0835/385007 Matera office, 080/5790111 Puglia regional office, Bari, 0971/506811 Basilicata regional office, Potenza* ⊕ *www.sitasudtrasporti.it.*

CAR
Although roads are generally good in the south, and major cities are linked by fast autostradas, driving here is a major test of navigation skills. Driving into the center of many cities and towns can be particularly complicated, owing to mazes of one-way streets, pedestrianized zones, and limited parking facilities. The good news is that you can bypass many communities via ring roads. Also, if you're staying at an in-town hotel, check with the staff about parking: the more upscale properties often have garage facilities or valet services for guests.

If you're squeamish about getting lost, don't drive at night in the countryside—roads can be confusing without the visual aid of landmarks, and GPS is far from infallible. Also, Bari, Brindisi, and Reggio Calabria are notorious for car thefts and break-ins. In these cities, don't leave valuables in the car, and find a guarded parking space if possible.

The toll-free A3 autostrada (Napoli–Reggio Calabria) links Naples to the south, with major exits at Sicignano (for the interior of Basilicata and Matera), Cosenza (the Sila Massif and Crotone), and Pizzo (for Tropea). Parts of the A3 in northern Calabria cross uplands more than 3,000 feet high, and snow chains may be required during winter months. In the summer and during holiday weekends this is the main north–south route for

16

Puglia, Basilicata, and Calabria PLANNING

Italy's sun seekers, so factor in plenty of time for delays and avoid peak travel times.

Take the SS18 for coastal destinations on the Tyrrhenian side and the E90 for the Ionian, alongside various state roads that crisscross toward the Adriatic. Given speed detectors and driver-tracking technology, it's best to stick to speed limits and be careful not to enter ZTL (*zona a traffico limitato*) restricted traffic areas (cameras are set up in towns such as Matera and Altamura): you'll be spared an unwelcome ticket when you get home.

TRAIN

Trenitalia runs to Calabria, either following the Ionian Coast as far as Reggio Calabria or swerving inland to Cosenza and the Tyrrhenian Coast. Italo runs high-speed services along the coasts to Bari and Reggio Calabria.

CONTACTS Ferrovie Appulo Lucane. ☎ *080/5725421 Bari Centrale, 800/050500 toll-free* ⊕ *www.ferrovieappulolucane.it.* **Ferrovie Sud-Est.** ☎ *800/079090 toll-free* ⊕ *www.fseonline.it.* **Italo.** ☎ *892020* ⊕ *www.italotreno.it/en.* **Trenitalia.** ☎ *892021 in Italy, 06/5210550 outside Italy* ⊕ *www.trenitalia.com.*

Making the Most of Your Time

If your priority is relaxing on the beach, plan on a few days at a seaside resort in one of the Gargano Promontory's fishing villages, such as Peschici, Rodi Garganico, and Vieste, and perhaps a further stay at one of the Calabrian coastal resorts, such as Diamante or Tropea, or Maratea in Basilicata.

Otherwise, choose a base like Polignano a Mare or Trani, especially if you land or dock in Bari. Take day trips out to the Valle d'Itria, or to the remarkable octagonal Castel del Monte. Then head

east along the Adriatic route (SS16), stopping to see the idyllic hilltop Ostuni before continuing on to Lecce, where you'll want to spend at least two to three nights exploring the city's Baroque wonders and taking a day trip down to Otranto and Gallipoli.

Next, take regional roads and the Via Appia (SS7) to reach Matera, whose Sassi cave dwellings are a southern Italian highlight; allow at least two nights here. Then it's back out to the SS106 to Calabria, along the coast dotted with ancient Greek settlements, as far as Tropea. At this point, cut inland on the SS107 across the Sila Massif, stopping at the hill resort of Camigliatello or carrying on to the more vibrant lowland Cosenza. Reggio Calabria is worthwhile just to see the celebrated Riace bronzes.

Restaurants

Italy's southern region is home to numerous restaurants that feature home cooking or Slow Food–inspired menus, which boils down to everything is made with the freshest ingredients. Meals are meant to be enjoyed at leisure, however, and service is not swift. Whether you decide to dine in a well-known restaurant or at a humble country trattoria, plan to give some thought to your menu choices (it's expected) and ask questions (also expected).

Hotels

Hotels in the region range from grand upscale establishments to small and stylish bijou inns to family-run rural *agriturismi* (country hostelries, often part of farms) that compensate for a lack of amenities with their famous southern hospitality. *Fattorie* and *masserie* (small farms and grander farm estates) offering accommodations are listed at local tourist offices.

In beach areas such as the Gargano Promontory and Salento, campgrounds and bungalow lodgings are ubiquitous and popular with families and budget travelers. Note that many seaside hotels open up just for the summer season, when they often require several-day stays with full or half board. And do remember that in a region like this—blazingly hot in summer and chilly in winter—air-conditioning and central heating can be important.

⇨ *Hotel and restaurant reviews have been shortened. For full information, visit Fodors.com. Prices in the hotel reviews are the lowest cost of a standard double room in high season. Prices in the dining reviews are the average cost of a main course at dinner, or, if dinner is not served, at lunch.*

What It Costs in Euros

	$	$$	$$$	$$$$
RESTAURANTS				
	under €15	€15–€24	€25–€35	over €35
HOTELS				
	under €125	€125–€200	€201–€300	over €300

Bari

260 km (162 miles) southeast of Naples, 450 km (281 miles) southeast of Rome.

The biggest city in the region, Bari is a major port and a transit point for travelers catching ferries across the Adriatic to Greece, Croatia, and Albania. It's also a cosmopolitan city with one of the most interesting historic centers in the region. In recent years, it has become a major center of pilgrimage for Russian Orthodox visitors, due to its connection with St. Nicholas, the patron saint of Russia, as well as of Bari. The old quarter of the city, around the basilica and the

harbor castle, is a lively maze of white-washed alleyways buzzing with bars, cafés, restaurants, and crafts shops. Most of the modern town is set out in a logical 19th-century grid, following the designs of Joachim Murat (1767–1815), Napoléon's brother-in-law and King of the Two Sicilies. The heart is **Piazza della Libertà,** where old and young gather in the evenings to stroll up and down and see and be seen.

GETTING HERE AND AROUND

By car, take the Bari-Nord exit from the A14 autostrada. Bari's train station is a hub for Puglia-bound trains. Alitalia and Ryanair fly to Bari Airport from Rome and Milan. Bari, Brindisi, and Milan are also connected by easyJet.

VISITOR INFORMATION

CONTACT Infopoint Turistico Bari. ✉ *Piazza del Ferrarese 29, Bari* ☎ *080/5242244* ⊕ *www.viaggiareinpuglia.it.*

Sights

★ **Bari Vecchia and Via Sparano**
HISTORIC DISTRICT | FAMILY | By day, you can lose yourself in the maze of white alleyways in Bari Vecchia, the Old Town stretching along the harbor, now humming with restaurants, cafés, and crafts shops. Residents tend to leave their doors wide open, so you can catch a glimpse into the daily routine of southern Italy: matrons hand-rolling orecchiette, their grandchildren home from school for the midday meal, and workers busy patching up centuries-old arches and doorways. Back in the new town, join the evening passeggiata on pedestrian-only Via Sparano, then, when night falls, saunter out among the outdoor bars and restaurants in Piazza Mercantile, past Piazza Ferrarese at the end of Corso Vittorio Emanuele. ✉ *Via Sparano, Bari.*

★ **Basilica di San Nicola**
CHURCH | The 11th-century Basilica di San Nicola, overlooking the sea in the *città vecchia* (old city), houses the bones of

Puglia, Past and Present

Puglia has long been inhabited and invaded. On sea voyages to their colonies and trading posts in the west, the ancient Greeks invariably headed for Puglia first—it was the shortest crossing—before filtering southward into Sicily and westward to the Tyrrhenian Coast. In turn, the Romans—often bound in the opposite direction—were quick to recognize the strategic importance of the peninsula. Later centuries would see a procession of other empires raiding or colonizing Puglia: Byzantines, Saracens, Normans, Swabians, Turks, and Spaniards all swept through, each group leaving their mark. Romanesque churches and the powerful castles built by 13th-century Holy Roman Emperor Frederick II (who also served as king of Sicily and Jerusalem) are among the most impressive buildings in the region. Frederick II, dubbed "Stupor Mundi" (Wonder of the World) for his wide-ranging interests in literature, science, mathematics,

and nature, was one of the foremost personalities of the Middle Ages.

The region experienced a huge economic revival after decades of neglect following World War II. Since then, EU funding, state incentive programs, and irrigation subsidies have helped Puglia to become Italy's top regional producer of wine, with the remainder of land devoted to olives, citrus, and vegetables. The main ports of Bari, Brindisi, and Taranto are thriving economic centers, though there remain serious problems of unemployment and poverty. However, the much-publicized arrival of thousands of asylum seekers from Eastern Europe and beyond has not significantly destabilized these cities (as had been feared), and economic and political refugees have dispersed throughout Italy. Today, despite several years of region-wide *recessione*, an air of prosperity still wafts through the smarter streets of Lecce, Trani, and smaller towns like Otranto and Peschici.

St. Nicholas, the inspiration for Santa Claus. His relics were stolen from Myra, in present-day Turkey, by a band of sailors from Bari and are now buried in the crypt. Because St. Nicholas is also the patron saint of Russia, the church draws both Roman Catholic and Russian Orthodox pilgrims; souvenir shops in the area display miniatures of the Western saint and his Eastern counterpart side by side. ⊠ *Largo Abate Elia 13, Piazza San Nicola, Bari* ☎ *080/5737111* ⊕ *www.basilicasannicola.it.*

Castello Svevo

CASTLE/PALACE | Looming over the cathedral is the symbol of Bari: huge Castello Svevo, which houses a number

of archaeological and art collections within its evocative courtyards, towers, and rooms. The current building dates from the time of Holy Roman Emperor Frederick II (1194–1250), who rebuilt an existing Norman-Byzantine castle to his own exacting specifications. Designed more for power than beauty, it looks out beyond the cathedral to the small Porto Vecchio (Old Port). Inside are displays that include plaster-cast reproductions of the city's sculptural riches, Byzantine archaeological finds, photo collections from Bari's past, and historic ceramics and other precious objects. ⊠ *Piazza Federico II di Svevia, Bari* ☎ *080/8869304* ⊕ *www.musei.puglia.beniculturali.it* ⊡ *€10 during exhibitions* ⊙ *Closed Mon.*

Cattedrale di San Sabino

CHURCH | Bari's 12th-century cathedral is the seat of the local bishop and was the scene of many significant political marriages between important families in the Middle Ages. The cathedral is dedicated to San Sabino, a 6th-century bishop who apparently lived to be 105. The architecture reflects the Romanesque style favored by the Normans of that period. ⊠ *Piazza dell'Odegitria, Bari* ☎ *080/5210605* ⊕ *www.arcidiocesibaribitonto.it/luoghi-di-culto/cattedrale.*

Restaurants

Ristorante al Pescatore

$$$ | **SEAFOOD** | In the lively heart of the old town, opposite the castle, stands one of Bari's best seafood restaurants. The interior is rather sparse, with white-washed walls and a vaulted ceiling, and the dining room can be crowded and noisy, but during the summer you can sit on the quieter outdoor veranda. **Known for:** seafood antipasto (crudo misto); lively atmosphere with tables packed together; ricci di mare—a taste of the Puglian sea. ⑤ *Average main: €27* ⊠ *Piazza Federico II di Svevia 6/8, Bari* ☎ *080/5237039* ⊕ *www.alpescatorebari.com* ⊘ *Closed Tues.*

Ristorante Opera

$$ | **SOUTHERN ITALIAN** | Don't be put off by its nondescript modernist street location, as Opera delivers a well-crafted menu of superb-value seafood dishes, from sushi-style antipasti to beautifully prepared fillets of sea bream. The always innovative food is served on arty tableware in the smart yet welcoming contemporary space or on the street-side terrace outside. **Known for:** loved by locals and families; freshest seafood with a twist; innovative vegetarian options. ⑤ *Average main: €19* ⊠ *Via Nicolo' Piccinni 151, Bari* ☎ *340/1774153 mobile* ⊕ *www.instagram.com/ristoranteoperabari* ⊘ *Closed Mon. No dinner Sun.*

Coffee and Quick Bites

★ Caffè Vergnano 1882 Amendola

$ | **SOUTHERN ITALIAN** | Grand stone rooms and a pretty terrazza sprouting olive trees make this a flexible and fab venue to breakfast, brunch, and lunch—and to socialize with evening drinks. As well as a constant stream of excellent coffee, they do a selection of pastries, great-value daily specials (pasta for just €6.50), and various snacks. **Known for:** historic stone building and courtyard seating; daily pasta, grilled meat, and veggie dishes; evening buffet and DJ sets. ⑤ *Average main: €8* ⊠ *Via Amendola 128/b, Bari* ☎ *080/5586586* ⊕ *www.facebook.com/caffevergnanobari.*

🛌 Hotels

Dilman Luxury Stay

$$$ | **B&B/INN** | Contemporary minimalism, a soothing color palate, and cool design, including travertine-lined spa-like bathrooms and mood lighting, make this central boutique B&B a reliably serene and clean choice. **Pros:** well-maintained rooms; warm and knowledgeable staff; Jacuzzi and saunas in the chicest suites. **Cons:** decor and breakfast choice may be too sparse for some; costly parking at nearby garage; reception not always manned. ⑤ *Rooms from: €250* ⊠ *Via Calefati 14, Bari* ☎ *080/5940165* ⊕ *www.dilman.it* ⇱ *5 rooms* ⊙❘ *Free Breakfast.*

Dimora Fantasia Charme B&B

$$ | **B&B/INN** | Handily placed nearish the train station on a residential street, this small, homey and well-run B&B has five immaculate contemporary rooms and suites in restful hues, some with large shower enclosures and balconies. **Pros:** welcoming, helpful, flexible owner; garage for parking opposite; in-room breakfast or "box" brekkie for early risers. **Cons:** bit of a schlep to the main sights; nondescript Bari street; some may find the decor sterile. ⑤ *Rooms from: €150* ⊠ *Via Michele de Napoli 4,*

Puglia

ADRIATIC SEA

30 miles

50 km

Isole Tremiti
I Cameroni
Isole S. Domino

TO TERMOLI

Peschici
Rodi Garganico
San Giovanni Rotondo
Vieste
Mattinata
Foresta Umbra
GARGANO PROMONTORY
Monte Sant'Angelo
Manfredonia
L'Annunziata
Golfo di Manfredonia
Zapponeta

San Severo
Lucera
Foggia
PUGLIA
Cerignola
Melfi
S. Angelo dei Lombardi
CAMPANIA

Molfetta
Trani
Barletta
Andria
Corato
Castel del Monte
Spinazzola
Gravina in Puglia
Altamura
Santeramo in Colle
Bari
Polignano a Mare
Grotte di Castellana
TRULLI DISTRICT
Alberobello
Locorotondo
Gioia del Colle
Fasano
Ostuni
PUGLIA
Ceglie Messapica
Martina Franca
Grottaglie
Massafra
Taranto
Mare Piccolo
Mare Grande
Via Appia
Brindisi
Via Appia
Mesagne
Francavilla Fontana
Manduria
Campi
Lecce
SALENTO
Nardò
Gallipoli
Maglie
Otranto
Santa Cesarea Terme
Castro
Leuca
Golfo di Taranto

Matera
BASILICATA
Potenza
Via Appia
LUCANO
Castellaneta Marina
Lido di Metaponto
Scanzano

Auletta
Eboli
Battipaglia
Salerno
Golfo di Salerno
TO NAPLES

Via Appia
Scansano

Bari ☎ *339/4517227 mobile* ⊕ *www. dimorafantasia.it* ⊷ *5 rooms* ⦿ *Free Breakfast.*

Trani

43 km (27 miles) northwest of Bari.

Trani has a harbor filled with fishing boats and a quaint old town with cobblestone streets, gleaming medieval churches, and palazzi built from local limestone. The town is also justly famous for its sweet dessert wine, Moscato di Trani. It's smaller than the other ports along this coast.

GETTING HERE AND AROUND
By car, take the Trani exit from the A14 autostrada. Frequent trains run from Bari.

VISITOR INFORMATION
CONTACT Info Point Trani. ⊠ *Palazzo Palmieri, Piazza Trieste 10, Trani* ☎ *375/5575405 mobile and WhatsApp messaging* ⊕ *www.prolocotrani.it.*

 Sights

Castello Svevo
CASTLE/PALACE | One of Frederick II's most imposing fortresses, the quadrangular Trani Castle guarded the Adriatic sea route throughout the Middle Ages. It was the scene of several royal weddings of the Swabian and Anjou houses, as well as the place of imprisonment for life of Siffridina, Countess of Caserta, who had supported the losing Swabian dynasty against Charles I of Anjou. In the early 20th century it became a state prison and remained so until 1974. The ground floor contains a museum telling the story of the castle alongside archaeological finds, sculpture, and a wealth of ceramics. ⊠ *Piazza Re Manfredi 14, Trani* ☎ *0883/506603* ⊠ *€8* ⊗ *Closed Mon. and Tues., and Sun. in Nov.*

★ Cattedrale
CHURCH | The stunning pinkish-white 11th-century cathedral, considered one of the finest in Puglia, is built on a spit of land jutting into the sea. Dedicated to St. Nicholas the Pilgrim, it was a favorite place of prayer for crusaders embarking for war in the Holy Land. Its lofty bell tower can be visited, and guided tours arranged by request at the nearby Museo Diocesano and via the website calendar slots; the views are worth the climb. ⊠ *Piazza Duomo, Trani* ☎ *0883/500293* ⊕ *www.cattedraletrani.it* ⊠ *Free, bell tower €5.*

Polo Museale Trani
SPECIALTY MUSEUM | Four floors of the handsome 18th-century Palazzo Lodispoto, near the Duomo, contain two very different collections: the Museo Diocesano showcases Trani's wealth of religious artifacts, while the Museo della Macchina per Scrivere follows the evolution of the typewriter. Among the highlights in the former are fragments from the 6th-century basilica, medieval and Baroque architectural elements, and funereal treasures commissioned by Charles I of Anjou on the death of his son Philip. The latter collection has 400 examples of typewriters from around the world, including some iconic Olivetti models as well as those used to type Braille, Arabic, and Japanese. A reasonably priced café serves drinks and pastries. ⊠ *Palazzo Lodispoto, Piazza Duomo 8/9, Trani* ☎ *0883/582470* ⊕ *www.fondazioneseca. it* ⊠ *Free* ⊗ *Closed Mon.*

 Hotels

★ Palazzo Filisio
$$ | HOTEL | Superbly positioned in front of the Duomo on a quiet seaside piazza, this small, handsome, beautifully maintained hotel has guest rooms with contemporary wooden furniture, white and azure fabrics, and marbled bathrooms. **Pros:** right next to the cathedral; superb

breakfast and restaurant; most rooms have sea views. **Cons:** no parking outside hotel; often occupied by wedding parties; books up in high season. $ *Rooms from: €130 ⊠ Via M. Reginaldo Giuseppe Maria Addazi 2, Trani ☎ 0883/500931 ⊕ www.palazzofilisio.it ⊘ Restaurant closed Mon.* ⤴ *14 rooms* ⦿ *Free Breakfast.*

Polignano a Mare

35 km (22 miles) southeast of Bari, 14 km (9 miles) north of Castellana.

This well-preserved, whitewashed old town, perched on limestone cliffs overlooking the Adriatic, makes an atmospheric base for exploring the surrounding area. Film crews and adrenaline junkies come to experience the town's spectacular cliff-diving championships, which usually take place in June. In recent years a social media buzz has led to an influx of day-trip crowds in the summer months.

GETTING HERE AND AROUND
From Bari, take the Polignano exit from the SS16. Frequent trains run from Bari.

VISITOR INFORMATION
CONTACT Prololo Turismo F.F. Favale.
⊠ *Via Dante Alighieri, Polignano a Mare* ☎ *080/4252336* ⊕ *www.prolocopolignanoamare.com.*

 Restaurants

Antica Trattoria Comes Dal 1926
$$ | **SOUTHERN ITALIAN** | **FAMILY** | Run by genial Giuseppe, this family-run trattoria serves classic seafood dishes in a relaxed, modern dining room. Freshly netted catches are heaped on hearty plates, like *insalata di mare* (seafood salad), seafood cavatelli pasta, and grilled *gamberoni* (prawns). **Known for:** superb Pugliese seafood antipasti; big helpings, big value; cold cuts, cheeses, and Angus steaks. $ *Average main: €19 ⊠ Via Pompeo Sarnelli 14, Polignano a Mare ☎ 080/4248888* ⊘ *Closed Wed. No lunch Sun.*

 Hotels

Borgobianco Resort & Spa
$$$$ | **RESORT** | **FAMILY** | Housed in a handsome masseria farmhouse building, this countryside resort provides a tranquil base for relaxing by the pool, eating alfresco in courtyards and terraces, and spa pampering. **Pros:** cool, white-washed luxury in tranquil location; shuttle bus to town; gorgeous pool, spa, and outdoor spaces. **Cons:** town not in easy walking distance; service can be patchy; decor could be a tad soulless for some. $ *Rooms from: €351 ⊠ Contrada Casello Cavuzzi, Polignano a Mare ☎ 080/2049060 ⊕ borgobianco.it* ⤴ *48 rooms* ⦿ *Free Breakfast.*

Hotel Covo dei Saraceni
$$$ | **HOTEL** | It would be difficult to find a more romantic location than that occupied by this hotel, dramatically perched on the rocks above the narrow cove of Polignano. **Pros:** magnificent sea views; suites with spacious terraces; spa center in the hotel. **Cons:** popular for wedding receptions (can be busy); some rooms noisy and have views of parking lot; some rooms and bathrooms small with odd layouts. $ *Rooms from: €220 ⊠ Via Conversano 1, Polignano a Mare ☎ 080/4241177 ⊕ www.covodeisaraceni.com* ⤴ *32 rooms* ⦿ *Free Breakfast.*

Castel del Monte

56 km (35 miles) southwest of Bari.

The isolated Norman Castel del Monte dominates the surrounding countryside from the top of a 1,778-foot-high hill. The nearest town is Andria, 17 km (10½ miles) away, largely modern and congested—avoid traffic by taking the ring road around it.

GETTING HERE AND AROUND
Take the Andria-Barletta exit from the A14 autostrada, then follow the SS170dir to Castel del Monte. From April through

The imposing Castel del Monte is a 13th-century structure built by Emperor Frederick II on land he inherited from his mother, Constance of Sicily.

October (and weekends November–March) there's a daily minibus service from Piazza Bersaglieri d'Italia in Andria.

VISITOR INFORMATION

CONTACT Castel del Monte Tourism Office. ⊠ *Via Vespucci 114, Andria* ☎ *0883/592283* ⊕ *www.proloco.andria. ba.it.*

 Sights

Castel del Monte

CASTLE/PALACE | Crowning an isolated hill 1,778 feet above sea level in the heart of the Alta Murgia National Park, this enigmatic octagonal fortress, built by Frederick II in the first half of the 13th century, has puzzled historians and researchers for centuries. Rooms are arranged in a seemingly illogical sequence through eight towers around a central courtyard. Recent interpretations suggest it was an elaborate cultural center conceived by Frederick to study various scientific disciplines of the Western and the Arabic worlds. Umberto Eco used it as his

inspiration for riddles in *The Name of the Rose.* To avoid disappointment: it's an impressive if largely empty building, and can be tricky to get to and pricey to visit when adding parking, guided tours, etc. ⊠ *On signposted minor road, 17 km (10½ miles) south of Andria, Andria* ☎ *327/9805551 mobile* ⊕ *aditusculture. com* ⊠ *€10; guided tour €7; €5 parking and €2 return shuttle bus from lot.*

Mattinata

138 km (86 miles) northwest of Bari.

The town of Mattinata is a good center for hikes in the Foresta Umbra and for visiting the Santuario di San Michele. It also has attractive stretches of sandy beach.

GETTING HERE AND AROUND

From Foggia (the chief city in Puglia's northernmost province), take the winding SS89. Regular buses leave from Foggia's train station.

VISITOR INFORMATION

CONTACT Info Point Mattinata. ✉ *Largo Agnuli, Mattinata* ☎ *0884/597291 municipal office* ⊕ *www.facebook.com/ infopointmattinata.*

Sights

Foresta Umbra

NATURE PRESERVE | In the middle of the Gargano Promontory is the majestic Foresta Umbra (Shady Forest), a dense growth of beech, maple, pine, and oak generally found in more northerly climates, thriving here because of the altitude, which reaches 3,200 feet above sea level. Between the trees in this national park are occasional dramatic vistas opening out over the Golfo di Manfredonia. There are nature trails and picnic areas easily reached from Vieste, Peschici, and Mattinata. ✉ *Visitor center, Laghetto Umbra, SP52bis, Monte Sant'Angelo* ☎ *0884/568911 national park* ⊕ *www.doveandiamosulgargano.it/en/ visit-umbra-forest* ۞ *Visitor center closed Oct.–Easter.*

Santuario di San Michele

RELIGIOUS BUILDING | Pilgrims have flocked to the mountain community of Monte Sant'Angelo for nearly 1,500 years— among them St. Francis of Assisi and crusaders setting off for the Holy Land from the then-flourishing port of Manfredonia. Monte Sant'Angelo is centered on the Santuario di San Michele, built over the grotto where the archangel Michael is believed to have appeared before shepherds in the year 490. Walk down a long series of steps to get to the grotto itself; on its walls you can see the hand tracings left by pilgrims. The Sanctuary was declared a UNESCO World Heritage site in 2011. To learn more about the history and myth surrounding the site visit the adjoining Musei TECUM. ✉ *Via Reale Basilica 127, Monte Sant'Angelo* ☎ *0884/561150* ⊕ *www.santuariosanmichele.it* 🎟 *Musei TECUM €5.*

Restaurants

Trattoria dalla Nonna

$$$ | **SEAFOOD** | **FAMILY** | Waves lap at the shore just inches from your table at this elegant but unpretentious trattoria, which often has a cozy fireplace ablaze in winter. You must follow a narrow twisting lane to get here, but it's worth the effort for specialties like the raw seafood antipasto, which features shellfish you might not find anywhere else. **Known for:** unique cozze pelose mussels; fabulous sea views; also run a B&B. ⑤ *Average main: €26* ✉ *Contrada Funni al Lido, Località Funni, Mattinata* ✛ *Off the main road (watch for signs)* ☎ *0884/559205* ⊕ *www.facebook.com/trattoria.dallanonna* ۞ *Closed Tues., Nov., and Jan.*

🛏 Hotels

Baia delle Zagare

$$$$ | **HOTEL** | Overlooking one of the Gargano Peninsula's loveliest bays, this secluded cluster of whitewashed buildings houses simply furnished modern rooms, some of which have balconies. **Pros:** incredible views and location; fab pool and gardens; access to wonderful beach. **Cons:** impossible to get to without a car; rooms may be a tad sparse for some; lots of steps. ⑤ *Rooms from: €305* ✉ *Litoranea Mattinata–Vieste, 17 km (10 miles) northeast of Mattinata, Mattinata* ☎ *0884/550155* ⊕ *www.hotelbaiadellezagare.it* ۞ *Closed Nov.–mid-May* ➹ *143 rooms* ⦿ *Free Breakfast.*

Vieste

93 km (58 miles) northeast of Foggia, 179 km (111 miles) northwest of Bari.

This large whitewashed town jutting off the tip of the spur of Italy's boot is an attractive place to wander around. Although curvy mountain roads render it slightly less accessible from autostradas and main rail stations than, say,

Mattinata, it is, nevertheless, a good base for exploring Gargano. The resort attracts legions of tourists in summer, some bound for the Isole Tremiti, a tiny archipelago connected to Vieste by regular ferries.

GETTING HERE AND AROUND
If you're driving from Foggia, take the winding SS89. Regular buses leave from Foggia's train station.

VISITOR INFORMATION
CONTACT IAT Vieste Tourism Office.
⊠ *Piazza John Fitzgerald Kennedy, Vieste* ☎ *0884/708806* ⊕ *www.viaggiarein-puglia.it.*

Sights

Castello Svevo
CASTLE/PALACE | Originally built by Frederick II, this impressive structure was enlarged by the Spanish to defend against attacks from the Turks, and it has remained a military base ever since. It is only open to the public for guided visits and temporary exhibitions and events; call ahead for the latest information. ⊠ *Via Duomo, Vieste* ☎ *0884/708806* ⊕ *www.viaggiareinpuglia.it.*

Museo Civico Archeologico Michele Petrone
HISTORY MUSEUM | Opened in 2019 and housed in the Beata Vergine degli Angeli convent, next to the church of SS. Sacramento, there's a small municipal museum with Greco-Roman artifacts excavated in the area here, plus temporary art shows (Warhol and Banksy in recent years). Multimedia displays bring to life handsome amphorae, Roman bathhouse bronze statuary, and finds from the necropolis at nearby Villa di Santa Maria di Merino. ⊠ *Lungomare A. Vespucci, Vieste* ☎ *0884/712223* ⊕ *www.facebook. com/poloculturalevieste* 🎟 *€10 including art show* ⊗ *Closed weekends.*

Restaurants

★ Al Dragone
$$$ | **SOUTHERN ITALIAN** | Dine on exquisite Gargano fare at this atmospheric eatery set in a natural grotto just next to the cathedral in the heart of the old center. The menu is dominated by locally caught fish, and although dishes draw on traditional recipes, you can expect the occasional innovation. **Known for:** small plates of beautifully crafted seafood; gorgeous setting; impressive wine cellar and cigar selection. ⑤ *Average main: €26* ⊠ *Via Duomo 8, Vieste* ☎ *0884/701212* ⊕ *www.aldragone.it* ⊗ *Closed Tues. and mid-Oct.–Mar.*

🛏 Hotels

Navicri
$$ | **B&B/INN** | **FAMILY** | Run by the friendly *famiglia* De Mauro, this modern B&B ticks all the boxes for those seeking great value in a tranquil, scenic setting near the beach. **Pros:** fab rooftop pool and Jacuzzi; great breakfast spread, including homemade jams; immaculate rooms. **Cons:** having to walk to town and beach might not appeal to some; one triple doesn't have a balcony; minimum night stays in high season. ⑤ *Rooms from: €127* ⊠ *Via Saragat, Vieste* ☎ *0884/705022* ⊕ *www. bbnavicri.it* ⇝ *6 rooms* ◎ *Free Breakfast.*

Alberobello

59 km (37 miles) southeast of Bari, 45 km (28 miles) north of Taranto.

With more than 1,000 trulli along its steep, narrow streets, Alberobello has been designated a UNESCO World Heritage site. It is one of the more popular and well-established destinations in Puglia and has some excellent restaurants (and some less-than-excellent trinket shops).

GETTING HERE AND AROUND

By car, take the Monopoli exit from the SS16, follow the SP237 to Putignano, then SS172 to Alberobello. Trains and buses run half-hourly from Bari to Putignano, where you then take a bus. The total journey takes around two hours. There's an infrequent but quicker (70 minutes) direct bus from Largo Sorrentino.

VISITOR INFORMATION

CONTACT Alberobello Tourism Office.
✉ *Via Monte Nero 1, Alberobello* ☎ *379/2987173 mobile* ⊕ *www.prolocoalberobello.it.*

Sights

Alberobello–Martina Franca Road

SCENIC DRIVE | The trulli in Alberobello itself are impressive, but the most scenic concentration of these unique conical structures is along a 15-km (9-mile) stretch of the SS172 (Alberobello–Martina Franca) through the tranquil Valle d'Itria. Stop to visit some of the area's vineyards and oil mills—many of which have a welcoming open-door policy—surrounded by vast groves of ancient gnarled olive trees. ✉ *Alberobello.*

Trullo Sovrano

MUSEUM VILLAGE | FAMILY | Although this 18th-century house, Alberobello's largest trullo, originally belonged to a wealthy family, it has been furnished in a traditional style, providing insight into what everyday life was like in these unique beehive constructions. Guided tours are included with admission; there's an information center and shop, and gastronomic events are held in the garden. Check out the classic film *Casanova '70*, starring Marcello Mastroianni and Moira Orfei, which was partly filmed in and around the trullo. ✉ *Piazza Sacramento 10, Alberobello* ✛ *Follow Corso Vittorio Emanuele up past the obelisk and basilica* ☎ *080/4326030* ⊕ *www.trullosovrano. eu* 🎫 *€2.*

Restaurants

Il Poeta Contadino

$$$ | SOUTHERN ITALIAN | There are actually two eateries here, but superior is the well-regarded Poeta Contadino, which specializes in regional cooking with a creative twist and offers a refined dining experience amid candlelight that casts shadows on ancient stone walls. If you're on a budget, though, the more affordable Osteria del Poeta also serves bite-size traditional dishes. **Known for:** exquisite seafood and meat dishes; stunning vaulted ceiling; extensive wine list. ⑤ *Average main: €28* ✉ *Via Indipendenza 21–27, Alberobello* ☎ *080/4321917* ⊕ *www. ilpoetacontadino.it* 🕐 *Closed Mon.*

L'Aratro

$$ | SOUTHERN ITALIAN | Welcoming and rustic, this eatery is set inside adjoining trulli, complete with dark-wood beams, whitewashed walls, and a patio for summer dining. It's a certified Slow Food restaurant, so local ingredients figure prominently in the traditional, often seasonal dishes. **Known for:** diligent use of local produce; classic regional fare; gorgeous trulli venue. ⑤ *Average main: €24* ✉ *Via Monte San Michele 25–29, Alberobello* ☎ *080/4322789* ⊕ *www.ristorantearatro.it.*

☕ Coffee and Quick Bites

Principotto

$ | SOUTHERN ITALIAN | FAMILY | For a great-value on-the-hoof snack, pop into this tiny, popular place for filled *panzerotti* (deep-fried pockets), *friselle* (crunchy durum-wheat bread), and *schiacciatella Romana* (pizza-like flatbread). Check the board for daily specials, including meaty ragù sauces and seafood like *polpi* (octopus) to fill your freshly fried pockets. **Known for:** buzzy place with crowds spilling out; cime di rapa and other Pugliese produce; bar next door for a vino accompaniment. ⑤ *Average main: €6* ✉ *Via Bissolati 16, Alberobello* ☎ *347/4529922 mobile*

⊕ *www.facebook.com/principotto*
☾ *Closed Thurs.*

 Hotels

★ Le Alcove

$$$ | HOTEL | This cluster of trulli has been transformed into luxury suites with original architectural features, modern comforts, and tasteful flourishes that make everything seem straight out of a lifestyle-magazine spread. **Pros:** centrally located near the Trullo Sovrano; quaint, unusual accommodations; heated floors. **Cons:** rooms and bathrooms are rather small; three rooms aren't in the main building; some rooms have a narrow, awkward metal staircase to upper areas. ⑤ *Rooms from: €251* ⊠ *Piazza Ferdinando IV 7, Alberobello* ☎ *080/4323754* ⊕ *www.lealcove.it* ⇥ *9 rooms* ⚭ *Free Breakfast.*

Ostuni

50 km (30 miles) west of Brindisi, 85 km (53 miles) southeast of Bari.

This sun-bleached medieval town lies on three hills not far from the coast. From a distance, Ostuni is a jumble of blazing white houses and churches spilling over a hilltop and overlooking the sea. Don't be surprised if you hear a lot of English and German spoken in the cobbled streets. The Città Bianca (White City), as it is called, has cast its spell on a large number of British and German nationals, who have bought second homes here. That doesn't mean that the town has lost its local flavor; fairs, religious festivals, and colorful traditional events are held as always with the same enthusiasm and fervor.

GETTING HERE AND AROUND

By car, take the Ostuni exit from the SS16. Trenitalia runs frequent trains from Bari. The station, however, is 5 km (3 miles) from the town—there is almost hourly local bus service.

VISITOR INFORMATION
CONTACT Info-Point Ostuni. ⊠ *Piazza della Liberta 69, Ostuni* ☎ *0831/1982471* ⊕ *www.facebook.com/infopointostuni.*

 Sights

Ostuni Old Town

HISTORIC DISTRICT | Known as the Città Bianca for its dazzling white buildings and cobbled streets, Ostuni commands stupendous views out over the coast and the surrounding plain. Its unpolluted sea and clean beaches have earned it international Blue Flag recognition since 2008. The surrounding countryside contains a number of interesting 17th- and 18th-century masserie, many of which have been converted into agriturismi. ⊠ *Old Town, Ostuni* ⊕ *www.viaggiareinpuglia.it.*

Piazza Libertà

PLAZA/SQUARE | The city's main square divides the new town to the west and the old town to the east. The triangular piazza contains the town symbol: the towering Guglia di Sant'Oronzo (Spire of St. Oronzo), named after the patron of Ostuni, in whose honor an elaborate festival is held every year in late August. ⊠ *Piazza Libertà, Ostuni* ⊕ *www.viaggiareinpuglia.it.*

 Beaches

★ Torre Guaceto

BEACH | The transparent water and chalky sand of this marine reserve extend 19 km (12 miles) along the coast and 6 km (4 miles) inland, where the wetlands are a haven for wildlife. Those seeking a spectacular walk in an unspoiled expanse head to the Spiaggia delle Conchiglie, which consists of tiny white shells. Note: it's protected and off-limits to bathers. A shuttle bus operates from the main car park. **Amenities:** food and drink; lifeguards; parking (fee); toilets. **Best for:** snorkeling; sunrise; sunset; swimming; walking. ⊠ *Riserva Naturale di Torre Gauceto, Ostuni* ☎ *0831/989976 for info* *and guided visits* ⊕ *www.riservaditorre-guaceto.it.*

 Restaurants

Osteria del Tempo Perso

$$ | SOUTHERN ITALIAN | On an old-town side street, this laid-back restaurant occupies two caves, where ancient rough-hewn stone walls contrast with elegant table settings. The service is friendly, and local seasonal dishes include antipasti mainstays like eggplant Parmesan or salumi di Martina Franca, as well as both meat and fish *secondi*. **Known for:** house-made pasta with classic Pugliese sauces; excellent changing menu; local meat, including donkey. ⑤ *Average main: €23* ⊠ *Via G. Tanzarella Vitale 47, Ostuni* ☎ *0831/304819* ⊕ *www.osteriadeltemporperso.com* ☉ *Closed Mon. Sept.–June.*

 Hotels

Hotel Relais Sant'Eligio

$$ | HOTEL | Nestled in a valley just below Ostuni and surrounded by venerable olive trees, this stylish adaptation of a 16th-century posthouse—with characteristic stone archways and roughcasted walls—has whitewashed, simply furnished guest rooms whose beds have wrought-iron headboards. **Pros:** pleasant, modern environment with touches of old-world charm; free parking at hotel; fab views. **Cons:** outside the city walls and short walk uphill to the old center of Ostuni; limited breakfast choice; rather dated and small rooms and bathrooms. ⑤ *Rooms from: €145* ⊠ *Via Giosuè Pinto 50, Ostuni* ☎ *0831/1985171* ⊕ *www.santeligiorelais.it* ⇱ *22 rooms* ⍾ *Free Breakfast.*

La Terra Hotel

$$ | B&B/INN | It doesn't get more historic than this 14th-century noble residence, where spacious, tastefully decorated rooms and a cocktail-perfect, colonnaded rooftop loggia offer character and comfort aplenty. **Pros:** inside the walls of the old city, near all sights; great seafood restaurant; some rooms have superb views. **Cons:** parking outside town (with shuttle service); street can be noisy in high season; standard rooms look a bit tired. ⑤ *Rooms from: €193* ⊠ *Via Gaspare Petrarolo 16, near the Concattedrale di Santa Maria Assunta, Ostuni* ☎ *0831/336651* ⊕ *www.laterrahotel.it* ⇱ *17 rooms* ⍾ *Free Breakfast.*

Ceglie Messapica

11 km (7 miles) southwest of Ostuni, 18 km (11 miles) southeast of Martina Franca.

With its 14th-century Piazza Vecchia, tattered Baroque balconies, and lordly medieval castles, the little whitewashed town of Ceglie Messapica is the epitome of everyone's notion of the sleepy southern Italian town. Situated at the center of the triangle formed by Taranto, Brindisi, and Fasano, this town was once the military capital of the region and often defended itself against invasions from the Taranto city-state, which wanted to clear a route to the Adriatic. Nowadays, Ceglie Messapica is a gourmet destination with a surprising number of excellent restaurants.

GETTING HERE AND AROUND

By car, take the Ostuni exit from the SS16, and follow the SP22 to Ceglie Messapica. Ferrovie del Sud-Est runs frequent bus and train connections from Bari.

VISITOR INFORMATION

CONTACT Info-Point Ceglie Messapica. ⊠ *Via G. Elia 18, Ceglie Messapica* ☎ *0831/371003* ⊕ *www.ceglieturismo.it.*

 Restaurants

⭐ **Cibus**

$$ | SOUTHERN ITALIAN | Amid the stone vaults and vine-leafy, light-dappled courtyard of this highly acclaimed old-town

osteria turned Slow Food destination, the freshest Pugliese meat and produce are transformed into exquisite tapas-like dishes. Be sure to ask the amiable owner to show you his wine cellar and equally impressive cheese larder, where he personally controls the maturing process. **Known for:** gorgeous setting; friendly service and Slow Food ethos; noteworthy wine and cheese. $ *Average main: €18* ⊠ *Via Chianche di Scarano, Ceglie Messapica* ☎ *0831/388980* ⊕ *www.ristorantecibus.it* ⊘ *Closed Mon. and Tues. No dinner Sun.*

Martina Franca

29 km (18 miles) southwest of Ostuni, 36 km (22 miles) north of Taranto.

Martina Franca is a beguiling town with a dazzling mixture of medieval and Baroque architecture in the light-color local limestone. Developed as a military stronghold in the 14th century, all that remains of the defensive walls are the four gates that divide the old part from the modern suburbs. Lose yourself in the maze of twisting white alleyways, where erstwhile palaces jostle with ancient churches and narrow stairways leading up to humbler abodes. No longer a little-known backwater, the centro storico can be crowded with sightseers on the weekends. The positive side is that this has led to the emergence of top-quality restaurants, and you'll be spoiled for choice. Each July into early August, the town hosts the Valle d'Itria music festival, which showcases classical music and opera.

GETTING HERE AND AROUND
By car, take the Fasano exit from the SS16, then follow the SS172. The Ferrovie Sud-Est runs frequent trains and buses from Bari and Taranto.

VISITOR INFORMATION
CONTACT Martina Franca Tourism Office. ⊠ *Via Dottor Adolfo Ancona 5, Martina Franca* ☎ *366/1266045 mobile* ⊕ *www.facebook.com/prolocomartina.*

Sights

Basilica di San Martino
CHURCH | A splendid example of southern Italian Baroque architecture, the basilica contains rows of lavishly decorated altars in polychrome marbles, as well as treasures like the silver statues of the two patron saints, San Martino and Santa Comasia. To the right of the gorgeous main altar (1773) by Neapolitan master Sanmartino (of San Severo, Naples fame), note the illuminated niche with the vibrant sculpture of the Madonna Pastorella as a shepherd girl in a gown of cloth-of-gold, defending Christ's flock from demons. ⊠ *Via Vittorio Emanuele 30, Martina Franca* ☎ *080/4302664* ⊕ *www.muba-sanmartino.it* 🎫 *€3 museum; €2 for guided tour* ⊘ *Museum closed Mon.*

Restaurants

★ Garibaldi Bistrot
$$ | **MODERN ITALIAN** | **FAMILY** | The location—right on the piazza by the Duomo, with tables outside and a cool white-washed dining room inside—is what initially draws people to this restaurant. But it's the tasty Pugliese produce used in simple salads, antipasti, pasta dishes, and classic seafood or meat mains that keeps people coming back. **Known for:** heaping salads and bountiful bruschetta; stunning spot on the piazza; great value and warm service. $ *Average main: €18* ⊠ *Piazza Plebiscito 13, Martina Franca* ☎ *080/4837987* ⊕ *www.facebook.com/garibaldibistrot.*

Taranto

100 km (62 miles) southeast of Bari, 40 km (25 miles) south of Martina Franca.

Taranto (stress the first syllable) was an important port even in Greek times, and it's still Italy's largest naval base. It lies toward the back of the instep of the boot on the broad Mare Grande bay, which is connected to a small internal Mare Piccolo basin by two narrow channels. The old town is a collection of palazzi (in varying states of decay) along narrow cobblestone streets on an island between the two bodies of water, linked by causeways to the modern city, which stretches inward along the mainland.

GETTING HERE AND AROUND
By car, the A14 autostrada takes you almost directly to Taranto. Trenitalia runs frequent trains from Bari and Brindisi.

VISITOR INFORMATION
CONTACT Infopoint Taranto. ⊠ *Galleria Comunale di Taranto, Piazza Castello, Taranto* ☎ *334/2844098 mobile.*

Sights

Castel Sant'Angelo
CASTLE/PALACE | The monumental Castel Sant'Angelo, more commonly referred to as the Castello Aragonese, guards the drawbridge leading from the island center of Taranto to the newer city on the mainland. The castle is occupied by the Italian navy, but it's open to the public, and navy personnel conduct regular, free guided tours. The castle, built in its present form by King Ferdinand of Aragon, King of Naples, in the 15th century, contains ruins of older Greek, Byzantine, and Norman constructions as well as the Renaissance Chapel of San Leonardo. ⊠ *Piazza Castello 4, Taranto* ☎ *099/7753438* ⊕ *www.castelloaragonesetaranto.com* ⊠ *Free.*

Cattedrale di Di San Cataldo
CHURCH | Originally dedicated to Santa Maria Maddalena before San Cataldo (St. Cathal of Munster) got the Papal nod, Puglia's oldest Duomo has 5th-century origins and been rebuilt several times—its present shape layered on top of an 11th-century Byzantine layout. Striking features include the ornate Baroque facade (1713) by the Leccese Mauro Manieri, geometric motifs in the nave and transept, 16 ancient marble columns with ornate capitals, and a recently rebuilt campanile and 1657 cupola. ⊠ *Piazza Duomo, Taranto* ☎ *099/4608268* ⊕ *www.cattedraletaranto.com.*

★ MArTA – Museo Archeologico Nazionale Taranto
SPECIALTY MUSEUM | Taranto's outstanding National Archaeological Museum (MArTA) occupies the historic premises of the ex-monastery of San Pasquale. The museum dates from 1887, and its collection of Greek and Roman antiquities is considered to be one of the most important in Italy. Admire the rich cache of tomb goods, including magnificent gold jewelry, objects in ivory and bone, and rare colored glass. A display of Jewish, Christian, and Muslim funeral epitaphs, dating from the 4th century, demonstrate the peaceful coexistence of the three religions in this multicultural Mediterranean hub from the Byzantine era to the Middle Ages. ⊠ *Via Cavour 10, Taranto* ☎ *099/4532112* ⊕ *aditusculture.com* ⊠ *€10.*

San Domenico Maggiore
CHURCH | Taranto's most important monument is the ancient church and monastery of San Domenico in the heart of the centro storico. Situated on the narrow strip of land that divides Taranto's two bays, Mare Piccolo and Mare Grande, the present, rather neglected church rises over the ancient Greek acropolis of Taranto where the city is considered to

have originated. The statue of Our Lady of Sorrows, much venerated by the local people, stands in the last chapel on the left. Pop into the beautiful 13th-century cloister for a moment's respite from sightseeing. ⊠ *Via Duomo 33, Taranto* ☎ *099/4713511* 🖬 *Free* ⊙ *Erratic hrs; cloister closed Sun.*

🍴 Restaurants

Al Gatto Rosso

$$$ | **SOUTHERN ITALIAN** | Set in a handsome Stile Liberty palazzo, with outdoor seating and a smart, minimalist dining room, the well-regarded "Red Cat" has been serving elegant seafood since 1952. The third-generation owner and head chef Agostino Bartoli is renowned for his innovative dishes using the freshest fish and seasonal vegetables. **Known for:** raw seafood antipasti; delicious gelato and semifreddo desserts; near MArTA. ⑤ *Average main: €27* ⊠ *Via Cavour 2, Taranto* ☎ *340/5337800 mobile* ⊕ *www. ristorantegattorosso.com* ⊙ *Closed Mon.*

🛏 Hotels

Hotel L'Arcangelo

$ | **HOTEL** | Set in a handsome 17th-century palazzo on slightly scruffy but charming Piazza Fontana, this self-styled "boutique hotel" has limestone walls, coved ceilings and warm off-white hues throughout, with many guest rooms having sea or church views and terraces. **Pros:** central piazza location near San Nicola church; gorgeous roof terrace; fish restaurants nearby. **Cons:** some corners dated; area undergoing renovation works; noise from piazza. ⑤ *Rooms from: €105* ⊠ *Piazza Fontana, angolo via Garibaldi 3, Taranto* ☎ *099/4715940* ⊕ *www.hotelarcangelotaranto.it* ⌐ *11 rooms* ⦿ *Free Breakfast.*

Lecce

40 km (25 miles) southeast of Brindisi, 87 km (54 miles) east of Taranto.

Lecce is the crown jewel of the Mezzogiorno. The city is called "the Florence of the south," but that term doesn't do justice to Lecce's uniqueness in the Italian landscape. Although its pretty boutiques, lively bars, laid-back student cafés, and evening passeggiata draw comparisons to the cultural capitals of the north, Lecce's impossibly intricate Baroque architecture and its hyperanimated crowds are distinctively southern. Summer is a great time to visit, when courtyards and piazzas host dramatic productions or performances. Baroque music concerts are often held in Lecce's beautiful churches and cultural spaces.

GETTING HERE AND AROUND

By car from Bari, take the main coast road via Brindisi and continue along the SS613 to Lecce. Frequent trains run along the coast from Bari and beyond. The closest airport is in Brindisi.

VISITOR INFORMATION

CONTACT Infopoint Castello. ⊠ *Castello Carlo V, Via XXV Luglio, Lecce* ☎ *0832/246517* ⊕ *www.facebook.com/ castellocarlov.*

Sights

★ Duomo

CHURCH | Dominating a vast square concealed by a maze of alleyways, Lecce's magnificent cathedral of Santa Maria Assunta never fails to take visitors by surprise. The goal when building the 17th-century structure was to stun the faithful with a vision of opulence and power. Constructed in rosy local stone, the church is flanked by the ornate Bishops' Palace (1694), the seminary, whose first-floor Museum of Sacred Art (MuDAS) displays papier-mâché sculptures alongside brooding

Caravaggio-esque paintings. Adding to this melodious architectural scene is the visitable 236-foot-high *campanile* (bell tower), which dominates the centro storico skyline. ⊠ *Piazza Duomo, off Corso Vittorio Emanuele II, Lecce* ☎ *0832/308557* ⊕ *www.cattedraledilecce.it* ⊠ *Duomo and campanile €12; LeccEcclesiae ticket museum and religious sites €11; ticket "completo" including campanile €21.*

Fondazione Biscozzi Rimbaud

ART GALLERY | Contemporary and modern art enthusiasts should seek out this 2018-established collection lovingly amassed since the late '60s by a wealthy Pugliese couple. Among the 200-plus works, striking geometric and abstract paintings and sculpture from 1950–80 predominate. The permanent exhibits are a wonderful introduction to masters of *modernismo italiano* and less well-known Pugliese artists from Burri to Zorio. ⊠ *Piazzetta Baglivi 4, Lecce* ☎ *0832/1994743* ⊕ *www.fondazionebiscozzirimbaud.it* ⊠ *€8* ⊙ *Closed Mon.*

Museo Faggiano

HISTORY MUSEUM | FAMILY | Wannabe restauranteur Luciano Faggiano excavated fascinating discoveries when he bought this building and investigated the blocked toilet back in the year 2000. After initially finding a false floor that led to a Messapian tomb, more digging with the help of family and friends unearthed incredible artifacts including Roman devotional bottles, ancient vases, a ring with Christian symbols, and dusty frescoes. With encouragement and help from the Lecce government and university, an atmospheric homespun museum was born that allows visitors to explore the layers of history beneath the site's seemingly mundane masonry and toilet cisterns. ⊠ *Via Ascanio Grandi 56, Lecce* ☎ *0832/300528* ⊕ *www.museofaggiano. it* ⊠ *€5.*

Piazza Sant'Oronzo

PLAZA/SQUARE | This is the buzzing hub of Lecce's social life in the heart of the maze of pedestrianized alleyways lined with cafés, little restaurants, and crafts shops. Named after Oronzo, the city's patron saint, who crowns a Roman column that once marked the end of the Via Appia Antica, the piazza is also occupied by another city symbol, the somewhat odd-looking 17th-century Sedile, formerly the town hall but now an art and exhibition center. ⊠ *Piazza Sant'Oronzo, Lecce.*

Santa Croce

CHURCH | Although Lecce was founded before the time of the ancient Greeks, it's often associated with the term *Barocco leccese*, the result of a citywide impulse in the 17th century to redo the town in an exuberant fashion. But this was Baroque with a difference: generally, such architecture is heavy and monumental, but here it took on a lighter, more fanciful air, and the church of Santa Croce is a fine example, along with the adjoining Palazzo della Prefettura. The facade is a riot of sculptures of saints, angels, leaves, vines, and columns—all in glowing local honey-color stone, creating an overall lighthearted effect. ⊠ *Via Umberto I 3, Lecce* ☎ *0832/241957* ⊕ *www.chieselecce.it/en/santa-croce* ⊠ *Church €6; LeccEcclesiae ticket €9.*

🍴 Restaurants

Alle Due Corti

$$ | SOUTHERN ITALIAN | FAMILY | Renowned local culinary experts run this cove-ceilinged trattoria, where traditional Salentine cuisine is treated with both respect and originality. The white-walled interior is stark, but there's plenty of character in the simple, tasty fare and the gregarious chatter of local families. **Known for:** cookery courses; small plates of hearty Pugliese food; Anthony Bourdain dined here for his Parts Unknown

series. $ *Average main: €17* ✉ *Corte dei Giugni 1, corner of Via Prato 42, Lecce* ☎ *0832/242223* ⊕ *www.alleduecorti.com* ⊘ *Closed Sun.*

Le Zie Trattoria Casereccia
$$ | SOUTHERN ITALIAN | FAMILY | Local families favor this tiny old-fashioned trattoria, where no-frills charm is matched by wholesome, unfussy food. *Cucina casereccia* (home-cooked) specialties include *polpo in teglia* (stewed octopus), *baccalà al forno* (baked salt cod), and the ubiquitous rustic *purè di fave e cicoria* (bean puree with wild chicory). **Known for:** warm hospitality; genuine local color and cuisine; best to book ahead. $ *Average main: €16* ✉ *Via Costadura 19, Lecce* ☎ *0832/245178* ⊘ *Closed Mon. No dinner Sun.*

☕ Coffee and Quick Bites

Caffè Alvino
$ | SOUTHERN ITALIAN | This historic caffè-gelateria is in the heart of Lecce, with handsome interiors and seating out on Piazza Sant'Oronzo. From early morning to late at night this is a buzzy place where Leccesi come to meet and refuel on classic Salentino pastries like *pasticciotti* (ricotta- or egg-filled pastry) and zeppole. **Known for:** arguably the best pastries in town; great coffee and gelato; centrally located. $ *Average main: €7* ✉ *Piazza Sant'Oronzo 30, Lecce* ☎ *0832/246748* ⊕ *www.facebook.com/alvino.catamo.*

🛏 Hotels

★ 8piuhotel
$ | HOTEL | FAMILY | Its design is more "international style" than "rustic Pugliese," but this hotel offers superb value, combining contemporary creature comforts with fancy tech. **Pros:** fitness center and guest cycles; abundant breakfast; on-site restaurant, Negroamaro. **Cons:** lack of local character might not appeal to some; a bit out of town; tech overload. $ *Rooms from: €114* ✉ *Viale del Risorgimento, Lecce* ☎ *0832/306686* ⊕ *www.8piuhotel.com* ⬿ *83 rooms* ⭐ *Free Breakfast.*

Patria Palace
$$$$ | HOTEL | Lecce's grandest hotel—impeccable from top to bottom, with vaulted ceilings, frescoes, and antique furnishings—also happens to have a stellar location in front of the monumental Santa Croce Basilica, the crown jewel of Lecce Baroque. **Pros:** many sumptuous, high-ceilinged rooms; fabulous roof terrace; valet parking for guests. **Cons:** a few rooms overlook noisy backstreets; some rooms outdated and less grand; style of the lobby doesn't match that of the handsome facade. $ *Rooms from: €330* ✉ *Piazzetta Riccardi 13, Lecce* ☎ *0832/245111* ⊕ *www.patriapalace.com* ⬿ *67 rooms* ⭐ *Free Breakfast.*

Risorgimento Resort Lecce
$$$ | HOTEL | Although this hotel has been a centro storico landmark since 1880, it feels unmistakably 21st century, with modern decor and vibrant color schemes. **Pros:** highly professional staff; fab location; wellness spa. **Cons:** smart, international-style hotel without much local atmosphere; may be noisy in rooms at the front; tiny gym. $ *Rooms from: €207* ✉ *Via Augustus Imperatore 19, Lecce* ☎ *0832/246311* ⊕ *www.risorgimentoresort.it* ⬿ *47 rooms* ⭐ *Free Breakfast.*

Otranto

36 km (22 miles) southeast of Lecce, 188 km (117 miles) southeast of Bari.

In one of the first great Gothic novels, Horace Walpole's *The Castle of Otranto*, published in 1764, the English writer immortalized this city and its mysterious medieval fortress, and indeed Otranto (stress the first syllable) has had more than its share of dark thrills. As the easternmost point in Italy—and, therefore, closest to the Balkan Peninsula—it's often borne the brunt of foreign invasions, including the massacre of 800 citizens by the Moors in 1480 because they refused to give up their faith. From here, you can see across the sea to Albania on a clear day. If you are a fan of the Neolithic, you will be interested in the Grotta dei Cervi, a few miles down the coast. The walls of the cave are covered with hundreds of prehistoric images, painted with red ocher and black bat guano.

GETTING HERE AND AROUND

By car from Lecce, take the southbound SS16 and exit at Maglie. To follow the coast, take the SS53 from Lecce, then follow the SS611 south. There's regular train service from Lecce on Ferrovie del Sud-Est.

VISITOR INFORMATION

CONTACT Pro Loco Otranto Tourism Office. ⌧ *Via Lopez 2, Otranto* ☎ *0836/806585* ⊕ *www.prolocotranto.it.*

Sights

Castello Aragonese

CASTLE/PALACE | The massive Aragonese Castle is considered a masterpiece of 16th-century military architecture. Rebuilt by the Spanish viceroy Don Pedro di Toledo in 1535 after it was badly damaged in the siege of Otranto (1480), when invading Ottoman armies destroyed the city, its impressive walls and bastions dominate the port and seashore. Escape the heat with a walk around its cool interiors and more fascinating cellars (underground tours available for extra €4) that snake around its recently landscaped moats. Various art and photographic exhibitions are held here in the summer, although it lacks engaging interpretation materials. ⌧ *Piazza Castello, Otranto* ☎ *0836/801436, 0836/210094* ⊕ *www.comune.otranto.le.it* ⌧ *€12 during exhibitions.*

Cattedrale

CHURCH | By far the best sight in Otranto is the cathedral, Santa Maria Annunziata, consecrated in 1088. Its highlight

is a 12th-century Pantaleone mosaic: covering the entire length of the nave, the sanctuary, and the apse, it depicts scenes from the Old Testament and traditional medieval chivalric tales and animals set alongside a Tree of Life. The walls behind the main altar are lined with glass cases containing the skulls and tibias of the 800 martyrs of Otranto, slain by the Ottomans after the seige of 1480 for not renouncing their faith. ⌧ *Piazza Basilica, Otranto* ☎ *0836/802720* ⊕ *www.comune. otranto.le.it.*

Hotels

Corte di Nettuno

$$ | **HOTEL** | Handily moored near the marina and the castello, this hotel has a nautical theme with wrought-iron gates in the shape of waves, a statue of the sea god Neptune at the entrance, the owner's maritime antiques throughout, and guest rooms accented by shades of blue. **Pros:** good location near the marina and sights; quirky decor full of artsy surprises; decent food. **Cons:** some people may find the sea theme overly eccentric; clinical feel in some dated and gloomy rooms; lackadaisical service in low season. ⑤ *Rooms from: €180* ⌧ *Via Madonna del Passo, Otranto* ☎ *0832/351321* ⊕ *www. cdshotels.it* ⊙ *Closed Nov.–Mar.* ⤳ *28 rooms* ⦿ *Free Breakfast.*

Masseria Montelauro

$$$$ | **B&B/INN** | **FAMILY** | Beautifully restored, with high-style interiors, this 19th-century former masseria is an oasis of comfort just a short drive from lovely Otranto. **Pros:** interesting building; lovely grounds and pool; friendly, helpful service. **Cons:** a car is absolutely necessary; food is pricey; some rooms rather stuffy. ⑤ *Rooms from: €330* ⌧ *SP358, Località Montelauro, Otranto* ☎ *0836/806203* ⊕ *www.masseriamontelauro.it* ⊙ *Closed Nov.–Apr.* ⤳ *29 rooms* ⦿ *Free Breakfast.*

Gallipoli

37 km (23 miles) south of Lecce, 190 km (118 miles) southeast of Bari.

The fishing port of Gallipoli, on the eastern tip of the Golfo di Taranto, is divided between a new town, on the mainland, and the beautiful fortified *borgo antico* (old town) across a 17th-century bridge, crowded onto its own small island in the gulf. The Greeks called it Kallipolis ("the fair city"), the Romans Anxa. Like the infamous Turkish town of the same name on the Dardanelles, the Italian Gallipoli occupies a strategic location and thus was repeatedly attacked through the centuries—by the Normans in 1071, the Venetians in 1484, and the British in 1809. Today life in Gallipoli revolves around fishing. Boats in primary colors breeze in and out of the bay during the day, and Gallipoli's fish market, below the bridge, throbs with activity all morning.

GETTING HERE AND AROUND

From Lecce, take the SS101. From Taranto, follow the coastal SS174. Frequent trains run from Lecce.

VISITOR INFORMATION

CONTACT Pro Loco Gallipoli Tourism Office. ✉ *Via Kennedy, Gallipoli* ☎ *0833/264283* ⊕ *www.prolocogallipoli.it.*

Sights

Castello Aragonese

CASTLE/PALACE | The massive bulk of Gallipoli's castle guards the entrance to the island of the borgo antico, which is linked to the new town by a bridge. Rising out of the sea, the present fortress, dating from the 17th to 18th century, is built on the foundations of an earlier Byzantine citadel. It has four towers, plus a separate fifth known as the Rivellino, where open-air shows are held in summer. A visit allows grandstand sea views, but there's little to see inside between exhibitions. ✉ *Rampa Castello, Gallipoli*

☎ *0833/262775* ⊕ *www.facebook.com/castellogallipoli* 🎟 *€5.*

Duomo

CHURCH | In the center of the borgo antico, Gallipoli's Duomo is a notable Baroque cathedral from the late 17th century, dedicated to Sant'Agata, patron saint of the city. Built in local limestone, the ornate facade is matched by an equally elaborate interior with columns and altars in fine polychrome marble and paintings by leading local Gallipoli and Neapolitan maestros of the time. Particularly interesting are the stone carvings that depict episodes from the city's history. ✉ *Via Duomo 1, Gallipoli* ☎ *0833/261987* ⊕ *www.cattedralegallipoli.it.*

La Purità

CHURCH | A fine example of Gallipoli Baroque, the 17th-century Church of Santa Maria della Purità stands at the end of the borgo antico overlooking famed Purità Beach. It contains an eye-popping wealth of art and decoration, including the painting at the high altar by Luca Giordano, intricately carved wooden choir stalls, and a 19th-century majolica pavement. ✉ *Riviera Nazario Sauro, Gallipoli* ☎ *0833/261699.*

Beaches

★ Beaches of Gallipoli

BEACH | **FAMILY** | Ample swimming and clean, fine-grained sand make Gallipoli's beaches a good choice for families. The 5-km (3-mile) strand reaches from Punta Pizzo to Lido San Giovanni and is divided among a series of bathing establishments, all of which provide sun beds, umbrellas, showers, changing facilities, and snack bars. Parco Gondar hosts a fun fair and music events. Water-sports equipment can be bought or rented at the waterfront shops in town. **Amenities:** food and drink; lifeguards; parking (fee); showers; toilets; water sports. **Best for:** partiers; snorkeling; sunset; swimming; walking; windsurfing. ✉ *Gallipoli* ⊕ *www.prolocogallipoli.it.*

Restaurants

La Vinaigrette

$$ | SEAFOOD | Within shell-like earshot of the sea, this professionally run trattoria with sleek white interiors and a panoramic terrace serves some of the finest seafood in the Salento. Expect classic Pugliese salty preparations like *crudi, grigliate,* and *fritture* (raw, grilled, and fried) beautifully cooked and elegantly presented. **Known for:** well-considered wine list; pick from the freshest catch on display; sea views and sushi-like crudi like tuna tartare. $ *Average main: €22* ⊠ *Riviera Armando Diaz 75, Gallipoli* ☎ *0833/264501* ⊕ *www.lavinaigrette.it.*

Hotels

★ Relais Corte Palmieri

$$ | HOTEL | Set in an aristocratic 18th-century house in the center of the borgo antico and near Purità Beach, the Relais Corte Palmieri has been tastefully renovated to meet modern standards while preserving its frescoes, mosaics, antique doors, and other historical features. **Pros:** individually decorated rooms; roof garden with spectacular views; on-site spa. **Cons:** difficult to reach; parking is mighty tricky in narrow alleys; noisy rooms streetside and near breakfast room. $ *Rooms from: €140* ⊠ *Corte Palmieri 3, Gallipoli* ☎ *0833/265318* ⊕ *www.relaiscortepalmieri.it* ☉ *Closed late Oct.–late Mar. or early Apr.* ➥ *20 rooms* ⦿ *Free Breakfast.*

Matera

62 km (39 miles) south of Bari.

This town of unique Sassi (cave dwellings) is one of southern Italy's most intriguing places. The so-called New Town is full of elegant Baroque churches, palazzi, and broad piazzas, which are filled to bursting during the evening passeggiata. It's perched on the verge of a steep gully crowded with ancient rock churches, some of which you can tour, and other Sassi converted into modern-day homes as well as hotels and restaurants. This is a particularly good time to visit: Matera's designation as the European Capital of Culture for 2019 reenergized the community with investment, cultural initiatives, and plenty of buzz.

GETTING HERE AND AROUND

From Bari, take the SS96 to Altamura, then the SS99 to Matera. One or two trains per hour (Ferrovie Appulo Lucane) leave Bari Centrale for Matera.

VISITOR INFORMATION

CONTACT Proloco Matera Città dei Sassi (Tourism Office). ⊠ *Via Ridola 60, Matera* ☎ *328/9333548 mobile* ⊕ *www.materawelcome.it.*

Sights

★ Duomo

CHURCH | Matera's splendidly restored cathedral, dedicated to the Madonna della Bruna and Sant'Eustachio, was built in the late 13th century and occupies a prominent position between the two Sassi. Lavishly decorated, it has a typical Puglian Romanesque flavor; inside, there's a recovered fresco, probably painted in the 14th century, showing scenes from the Last Judgment. On the Duomo's facade the figures of Sts. Peter and Paul stand on either side of a sculpture of Matera's patron, the Madonna della Bruna. ⊠ *Piazza Duomo, Matera* ☎ *0835/332012* 🎟 *€3.50.*

Museo Nazione di Matera (MNM) – Domenico Ridola Archaeological Museum

HISTORY MUSEUM | Named after local 19th-century medical doctor Domenico Ridola, who investigated archaeological sites in the surrounding area, this seat of the MNM highlights his excavations of the remains of Paleolithic and Neolithic settlements, as well as a richly endowed 4th-century-BC tomb. Ridola's finds are on view in the museum, which is housed in the former monastery of Santa Chiara.

The collection includes an extensive selection of prehistoric and classical artifacts, notably Bronze Age implements and beautifully decorated red-figure pottery from Magna Graecia. ⊠ *Via Ridola 24* ☏ *0835/310058* ⊕ *www.museonazionaledimatera.it* 🎟 *€10; cumulative 2-day museum ticket €15* ⊘ *Closed Mon.*

Museo Nazione di Matera (MNM) – Museo Nazionale d'Arte Medievale e Moderna della Basilicata

ART MUSEUM | Housed within the handsome 17th-century Palazzo Lanfranchi, this part of the MNM is divided into three contrasting thematic sections: Sacred Art, Collectibles, and Contemporary Art. You may want to skim through the many restored artifacts from Basilicata's churches and the 300-plus works of the Neapolitan school: the main attraction are the paintings of Carlo Levi and his must-stop-to-absorb humanist masterpiece *Lucania '61*. ⊠ *Piazza G. Pascoli 1, Matera* ☏ *0835/310058* ⊕ *www.museonazionaledimatera.it* 🎟 *€10; cumulative 2-day museum ticket €15* ⊘ *Closed Tues.*

MUSMA (Museo della Scultura Contemporanea)

ART GALLERY | Amid otherworldly cave interiors, medieval courtyards, frescoed corners, and the grand spaces of 17th-century Palazzo Pomarici, this museum charts the evolution of Italian sculpture from the early 1800s to the present. Innovative curation, atmospheric lighting, and eerie acoustics make for a one-of-a-kind gallery experience. ⊠ *Palazzo Pomarici, Via San Giacomo, Matera* ☏ *366/9357768* ⊕ *www.musma.it* 🎟 *€7.*

San Giovanni Battista

CHURCH | Considered a jewel of medieval architecture, the 13th-century Romanesque church of San Giovanni Battista was restored to its pre-Baroque simplicity in 1926. The elaborately carved portal is a riot of entwining stone vines, flowers, leaves, human figures, and allegorical creatures. Inside, the three naves are flanked by columns crowned with capitals, each one decorated with symbolic animal forms and other images—no two are alike. ⊠ *Via San Biagio, Matera* ☏ *0835/334182.*

★ Sassi di Matera

HISTORIC DISTRICT | Matera's Sassi are piled chaotically atop one another down the sides of a steep ravine. Some date from Paleolithic times, when they were truly just caves. Over time, they were transformed into enclosed houses. In the 1960s, most inhabitants moved into ugly apartment blocks. The 1993 designation as a UNESCO World Heritage site, however, resulted in a cleanup and gentrification, with hotels, bars, and restaurants taking over many structures. From the upper town, the Strada Panoramica walk offers stellar views of the two areas known as Sasso Caveoso and Sasso Barisano. ⊠ *Sasso Caveoso, Matera* ⊕ *www.materawelcome.it.*

★ Storica Casa Grotta di Vico Solitario

MUSEUM VILLAGE | Head to this house-museum in the Sasso Caveoso district for moving insights into what peasant life was like in a limestone cave dwelling. The cramped quarters are filled with traditional utensils and furniture, the belongings of its last inhabitants, who left in 1956 as part of a forced relocation of some 15,000 Sassi residents to apartment blocks. With its rainwater cistern, hand loom, storage niches, and tiny kitchen area and other living spaces (for both the family and their animals), the cave also demonstrates the ingenuity that made living here possible. ⊠ *Vicinato di vico Solitario 11, Matera* ☏ *0835/310118* ⊕ *www.casagrotta.it* 🎟 *€5.*

🍴 Restaurants

Il Terrazzino

$$ | **SOUTHERN ITALIAN** | The dining area is carved out of a cliff, and the terrace overlooks the famous Sassi ravine. From both you can enjoy such rustic specialties as

foglie d'ulivo (stuffed olive leaves), *zuppa di grano e ceci* (cheese and chickpea soup), and *pignata* (lamb stew with seasonal vegetables). **Known for:** stupendous views; classic Basilicata meat dishes and fresh pasta; interesting interiors (including a spectacular three-level wine cellar). $ *Average main: €17* ⊠ *Vico S. Giuseppe 7, Matera* ☎ *0835/332503* ⊕ *www.ilterrazzino.it* ☉ *Closed Tues.*

★ **Vitantonio Lombardo**

$$$$ | **MODERN ITALIAN** | An open kitchen and contemporary table lamps heighten the culinary theater of Matera's fanciest restaurant, set in a cool, minimalist Rione Sassi grotto. The chef's innovative five-course tasting menus feature vibrant seasonal creations served on artsy ceramics and in wooden bowls. **Known for:** glass-screened wine cellar; imaginative, changing tasting menu; exquisite bread and olive oil. $ *Average main: €140* ⊠ *Via Madonna delle Virtù 13/14, Matera* ☎ *0835/335475* ⊕ *www.vlristorante.it* ☉ *Closed Tues. No lunch Wed.–Fri.*

☕ Coffee and Quick Bites

I Vizi degli Angeli – Laboratorio di Gelateria Artigianale

$ | **SOUTHERN ITALIAN** | **FAMILY** | As befitting the "artisan gelato laboratory" moniker, this whitewashed parlor with vibrant colors has an array of vegan-friendly and alchemical ice-cream combos. Among the more unusual "angels" vices' flavors served in *coppe* (tubs) and freshly made *coni* (cones) are pineapple and ginger, lavender and licorice. **Known for:** refreshing granita di melone; fruity smoothies; icy frappè and caffè shakerato. $ *Average main: €4* ⊠ *Via Domenico Ridola 36, Matera* ☎ *0835/310637* ⊕ *www. ivizidegliangeli.it.*

Hotels

★ **Locanda di San Martino**

$$ | **HOTEL** | Situated at the bottom of the Sassi ravine on Via Fiorentini (limited car access), the Locanda is a more upscale cave-dwelling hotel, with all modern comforts, including an elevator to whisk you up the cliff to your room. **Pros:** convenient location if you come by car; comfortable rooms; on-site ancient Roman–style spa. **Cons:** rooms reached via outdoor walkway; limited parking nearby; spa may be a tad intimate for some. $ *Rooms from: €155* ⊠ *Via Fiorentini 71, Matera* ☎ *0835/256600* ⊕ *www.locandadisanmartino.it* ⤴ *40 rooms* ⦿| *Free Breakfast.*

★ **Palazzo Margherita**

$$$$ | **HOTEL** | On the main square in the town of Francis Ford Coppola's ancestors, a large palazzo has been transformed (by French designer Jacques Grange) into Basilicata's top lodging, complete with hidden gardens, spacious porticoes, frescoed ceilings, and Moroccan-tile floors. **Pros:** professional, courteous staff; a garden pool; spacious rooms with lots of high-tech gadgetry. **Cons:** film-star prices; private transport needed; not much to do in Bernalda. $ *Rooms from: €1040* ⊠ *Corso Umberto 64, Matera* ⤴ *A 40-min drive south of Matera: take the SS7 out of Matera heading for Potenza and then join the SS407 for Metaponto and Taranto. Look for the turnoff to Bernalda after 25 km (16 miles)* ☎ *0835/549060* ⊕ *www.thefamilycoppolahideaways.com/en/palazzo-margherita* ⤴ *9 rooms* ⦿| *Free Breakfast.*

Sant'Angelo Resort

$$$ | **HOTEL** | Authentic rough-hewn walls and arches contrast with chic furnishings and modern amenities at this Sassi hotel, created by interior designer Stefano Tardito and situated across a piazza from the Church of San Pietro Caveoso. **Pros:** unrivaled views; atmospheric rooms with minimalist design; stylish cave-dwelling

experience. **Cons:** no elevator and many steps to climb; can feel stuffy and humid at times; lack of natural light. ⑤ *Rooms from: €257* ⊠ *Piazza San Pietro Caveoso, Matera* ☎ *0835/314010* ⊕ *www.santangeloresort.it* ⟿ *21 rooms* ⍾⍾ *Free Breakfast.*

Maratea

217 km (135 miles) south of Naples.

The high, twisty road into the Maratea region affords breathtaking glimpses of the turquoise sea and a gigantic statue of Cristo Redentore (reminiscent of the one in Rio de Janeiro) atop a hill. Steep crags separate the area into villages that include Maratea Porto, Marina di Maratea, Fiumicello, and Cersuta. The main inland town of Maratea proper is a tumble of cobblestone streets, where the ruins of a much older settlement (Maratea Antica) can be seen. Between the rocky headlands, there's no shortage of secluded beaches, which can get crowded in August. A summer minibus service connects all the different points once or twice an hour.

GETTING HERE AND AROUND
By car, take the Lagonegro exit from the A3 autostrada and continue along the SS585. Intercity, regional, and seasonal high-speed Frecciarossa trains from Reggio Calabria and Naples stop at Maratea. In the summer months there's a bus linking the train station to the upper town 4 km (2½ miles) away.

VISITOR INFORMATION
CONTACT Pro Loco di Maratea La Perla.
⊠ *Via Santavenere 144, Maratea* ☎ *0973/876026* ⊕ *marateaproloco.it.*

Beaches

Cala Jannita
BEACH | FAMILY | Maratea's dramatic rock topography is best experienced from this fab little bay and its Spiaggia Nera (Black Beach) with sparkling limpid waters and striking dark, volcanic pebbles. Bring sandals or shoes as it's a tricky approach. **Amenities:** food and drink; lifeguards; parking (fee); showers; toilets. **Best for:** swimming. ■**TIP**➡ **For a kayak adventure around Maratea's beaches and sea caves visit** ⊕ ***www.flymaratea.it*, which also offers guided treks for all abilities.** ⊠ *Maratea* ☎ *375/7723896 mobile.*

Restaurants

Da Cesare
$$ | SOUTHERN ITALIAN | With an open kitchen and a veranda—so you can keep an eye on both the chef and the azure waters of the Golfo di Policastro—there's always something to see at this family-run seafood restaurant. Even better: it serves some of the freshest catches in town, with specialties like linguine *con nero di seppia* (with cuttlefish ink sauce), grilled squid, and *grigliata mista* (mixed grilled fish and seafood). **Known for:** seafood dishes aplenty; open veranda with views; prominent position on coastal road. ⑤ *Average main: €22* ⊠ *Via Nazionale Cersuta 52, Maratea* ✛ *On the SS18 (main coast road) in village of Cersuta, about 5 km (3 miles) north of Maratea, 3 km (2 miles) south of Acquafredda* ☎ *0973/871840* ⊘ *Closed Thurs. Nov.–Mar.*

Hotels

Villa Cheta
$$ | HOTEL | FAMILY | This Stile Liberty villa in the seaside village of Acquafredda has original features and period pieces, a tranquil garden, a pool where you can idle the days away, and a flowery terrace for sunset dining. **Pros:** surrounded by Mediterranean greenery; beautiful coast and mountain views; lovely Art Nouveau building. **Cons:** hotel is quite remote, so shops and the town require a car; popular in high season; steps to entrance and Porticello beach. ⑤ *Rooms from: €190*

✉ *Via Timpone 46, Località Acquafredda, Maratea* ☎ *0973/878134* ⊕ *www.villacheta.it* ◷ *Closed Oct.–Apr.* ⇌ *22 rooms* ○ *Free Breakfast.*

Diamante

51 km (32 miles) south of Maratea, 225 km (140 miles) south of Naples.

A lively and attractive little resort on Calabria's north Tyrrhenian Coast, Diamante styles itself as "the town of murals and *peperoncini* (hot chili peppers)." The pedestrianized seafront promenade is the town hub, lined with small shops, ice cream parlors, and bars. Flanking the broad palm-lined promenade are sparkling beaches and interesting archaeological remains in the nearby Cirella district. September's annual Peperoncino Festival brings spicy cultural and gastronomic events.

GETTING HERE AND AROUND

Driving from Maratea, take the SS18; from Cosenza, take the SS107 to Paola, then the SS18. Regional trains leave from Naples a few times a day, with regular service from Paola and Cosenza.

VISITOR INFORMATION

CONTACT Proloco Diamante & Cirella.
✉ *Via Gullo 1, Diamante* ☎ *0985/81130* ⊕ *www.prolocodiamante.it.*

Restaurants

A' Cucchiarella

$$ | SEAFOOD | FAMILY | One of Diamante's most popular restaurants, in the old town center just off the seafront promenade, has atmospheric stone interiors. In the summer, sidewalk tables are the perfect relaxed place to watch the evening *passeggiata* while savoring inventive fish dishes. **Known for:** exceptional seafood with arty presentation; good vegetarian options; handsome stone-walled dining rooms and a terrace. ⑤ *Average main: €19* ✉ *Via Cavour 6, Diamante* ☎ *0985/877287* ◷ *Closed Mon.–Thurs. Oct.–Mar.*

Hotels

Grand Hotel San Michele

$$$ | HOTEL | Set in a Belle Époque–style villa surrounded by gardens, atop a cliff near the village of Cetraro, the San Michele offers Mediterranean charm and old-style elegance. **Pros:** beautiful setting; 9-hole golf course; pool and private beaches. **Cons:** some garden levels accessed by steps; breakfast lacks variety; isolated, if you lack your own transport. ⑤ *Rooms from: €250* ✉ *Località Bosco 8/9, Cetraro* ✛ *20 km (12 miles) south of Diamante on the SS18* ☎ *0982/91012* ⊕ *www.sanmichele.it* ◷ *Closed Nov.–Easter* ⇌ *65 rooms* ○ *Free Breakfast.*

Castrovillari

68 km (43 miles) northeast of Diamante, 75 km (48 miles) northwest of Cosenza.

Stress the first "i" when you pronounce the name of this provincial Calabrian city, nestled in the deep valley beneath 7,375-foot Mt. Pollino. The town is notable as a venue for summer's Calabria-wide Peperoncino Jazz Festival (⊕ *www.facebook.com/peperoncinojazzfestival*). Its synagogue, which you can visit, dates from the early Middle Ages; its San Giuliano church from the 16th century.

GETTING HERE AND AROUND

By car, take the A3 autostrada and exit at Frascineto-Castrovillari. Ferrovie della Calabria runs around four buses per day from Cosenza.

Sights

Parco Nazionale del Pollino

NATIONAL PARK | FAMILY | Italy's largest national park straddles Calabria and Basilicata, rises to over 7,000 feet at Serra Dolcedorme, and offers many opportunities for outdoors enthusiasts. Its ancient wooded valleys are home to

Europe's oldest tree, a 1,230-year-old Hel-dreich's pine. There are five summits all over 6,562 feet, the highest point being Serra Dolcedorme at 7,438 feet above sea level, the highest point of the Southern Apennines. It's the only peak from where it's possible to see three seas: the Ionian, the Tyrrhenian, and the Adriatic. Hiking trails dot the landscape with excursions for most abilities—and there are popular picnicking viewpoints, often near *rifugi* (rustic hostels that tend to offer food). ✉ *Via Cairoli 80, Castrovillari* ☎ *334/1005054 Club Alpino Italiano–Sezione di Castrovillari, 0973/669311 Ente Parco Nazionale del Pollino* ⊕ *parconazionalepollino.it; www.caicastrovillari.it.*

🍴 Restaurants

⭐ La Locanda di Alia

$$$ | MODERN ITALIAN | International food magazines have lauded this restaurant, where the wine cellar is well stocked and renowned chef-owner Gaetano Alia incorporates local produce and imaginative twists into the Calabrese dishes on the changing menu. La Locanda also has guest rooms in its adjoining Alia Jazz Hotel, which is surrounded by a lush garden and has a swimming pool. **Known for:** award-winning but unpretentious cuisine; candele pasta with spicy Calabrese 'nduja sauce; gorgeous setting with a leafy terrace. ⑤ *Average main: €26* ✉ *Via Ietticelli 55, Castrovillari* ✛ *Off the main street in Castrovillari (look for signs)* ☎ *0981/46370* ⊕ *www.facebook.com/locandadialia* ⊙ *No dinner Sun.*

Cosenza

75 km (48 miles) southeast of Diamante, 185 km (115 miles) northeast of Reggio Calabria.

A construction boom in the 1950s and '60s encased Cosenza's medieval city—which winds up the hillsides between the Busento and Crati rivers. Respite

from the sprawling, traffic-clogged modern town can be found on pedestrianized Corso Mazzini, where you can dine, shop and *passeggiare* amid the sculptures of the MAB open-air museum. Highlights include Dalí's *St. George and the Dragon* and haunting works by De Chirico. South of the Busento, the steep, stair-filled centro storico truly hails from another age: wrought-iron balconies overlook narrow alleyways lined with old-fashioned storefronts and bars. The palazzi that line the route to the 12th-century Duomo, a UNESCO World Heritage monument, once housed nobility but today serve as studio spaces for many artists and artisans. The medieval castle, open to the public, crowns Pancrazio Hill, where the views of the town and the surrounding countryside are magnificent.

Cosenza is also the gateway to the cool and silent forests of the Sila mountains, hilltop villages and nearby university town Rende (only 13 km [8 miles] away), and the Pollino National Park area (less than 80 km [50 miles]).

GETTING HERE AND AROUND

By car, take the Cosenza exit from the A3 autostrada. By train, change at Paola or Napoli on the main Rome–Reggio Calabria line. Regional trains run from Naples. Ferrovie della Calabria runs buses from Spezzano della Sila, Castrovillari, and Camigliatello.

VISITOR INFORMATION

CONTACT Cosenza Tourist Office. ✉ *Piazza XI Settembre, Cosenza* ☎ *328/1754422 mobile, 0984/813015* ⊕ *www.cosenzaturismo.com.*

Sights

Castello Svevo

CASTLE/PALACE | Castello Normanno Svevo crowns Pancrazio Hill above the old city, and the uphill walk rewards with wonderful views across to the Sila Mountains. Its origins are lost to memory: the locals' fort was built upon by the Byzantines and the Saracens. Before being enlarged by the Normans, it was the residence of the Arab caliph Saati Cayti. What is known is that the castle takes its name from the great Swabian emperor Frederick II (1194–1250), who added two octagonal towers. Angevin, Aragonese, and Bourbon dynasties made additions. Although extensively restored and open to the public, with audio guide/tablet tours and occasional cultural events amid its sparse spaces, the castle shows the ravages of successive earthquakes and a lightning strike that ignited gunpowder once stored within. ⊠ *Via del Castello, Colle Pancrazio, Cosenza* ☎ *0984/1811234* ⊕ *www.castellocosenza.it* 🎫 *€5* 🕐 *Closed Mon.*

Duomo

CHURCH | Cosenza's original Duomo, probably built in the middle of the 11th century, was destroyed by an earthquake in 1184. A new cathedral was consecrated in the presence of Emperor Frederick II in 1222. After many Baroque additions, later alterations have restored some of the Provençal Gothic style. Inside, on the left of the main altar, you'll see the lovely monument to Isabella of Aragon, who died after falling from her horse en route to France in 1271. ⊠ *Piazza del Duomo 1, Cosenza* ☎ *0984/77864* ⊕ *www.cattedraledicosenza.it* 🕐 *Closed daily 12:30 pm–4 pm.*

Museo Diocesano di Cosenza

HISTORY MUSEUM | Situated between the archbishop's palace and the Duomo, the museum contains paintings, silverware, vestments, and other precious objects collected by the archbishops of Cosenza over centuries. Look for the filigreed silver cup known as "the Pope," the 15th-century "Torquemada" chalice, and paintings by Luca Giordano, Andrea Vaccaro, and Giuseppe Pascaletti. The heart of the museum contains La Stauroteca, emblem of Cosenza and the city's greatest treasure: a unique reliquary cross dating back to the 13th century. ⊠ *Piazza Aulo Giano Parrasio 16, Cosenza* ☎ *0984/687750* ⊕ *www.museodiocesanocosenza.it* 🎫 *Free* 🕐 *Closed after 1:30 and Sun. (except by appointment).*

🍴 Restaurants

★ Hippocampus

$$$ | SEAFOOD | Renowned for its simply crafted dishes made with the freshest seasonal catch, Cosenza's best seafood restaurant has (appropriately enough) a minimalist, blue-and-white, nautical-theme interior. Guided by a waiter, you might start with a selection of antipasti to share, followed by a classic pasta *allo scoglio* (spaghetti with mixed seafood) and a main *fritto misto di mare* (medley of fried seafood). **Known for:** exceptional, superfresh seafood; a chef happy to create vegetarian dishes; unfussy, welcoming vibe. ⑤ *Average main: €26* ⊠ *Via Piave 33, Cosenza* ☎ *0984/22103* 🕐 *Closed Mon. No dinner Sun. No lunch Tues.–Fri.*

🛏 Hotels

Royal Hotel

$ | HOTEL | Like most hotels in Cosenza, the Royal caters mainly to a business clientele, yet it's nevertheless a good choice for a stopover: what it lacks in local flavor, it makes up for with functional whitewashed decor, spacious bathrooms, and reasonable room rates. **Pros:** close to pedestrian-only shopping area; free parking; good customer service. **Cons:** 20-minute walk from centro storico; beige '70s time-capsule decor in parts; can be busy during events. ⑤ *Rooms from: €90* ⊠ *Via delle Medaglie d'Oro 1, Cosenza* ☎ *0984/412165* ⊕ *www.hotelroyalcosenza.it* 🛏 *34 rooms* 🍴 *Free Breakfast.*

Take a break from sightseeing and enjoy the great outdoors in La Fossiata nature preserve.

Camigliatello

30 km (19 miles) east of Cosenza.

Lined with chalets, Camigliatello is one of the Sila Massif's major resort towns. Most of the Sila isn't mountainous at all; rather, it's an extensive, sparsely populated plateau with areas of thick forest. There was, at one point, considerable deforestation, but in 1968 the area received a special designation as the Parco Nazionale della Sila, and strict rules have limited the felling of timber, which has allowed the forests to regenerate. There are well-marked trails through pine and beech woods and ample opportunities for horseback riding. Autumn sees droves of locals hunting mushrooms and gathering chestnuts; winter brings crowds to nearby ski slopes.

GETTING HERE AND AROUND

By car, take the Cosenza Nord exit from the A3 autostrada, then follow the SS107, or if you are following the SS106 along the Ionian Coast, branch off at Sibari and follow the signs.

VISITOR INFORMATION

CONTACT Proloco Camigliatello Tourism Office. ✉ *Via Roma 147, Camigliatello* ☎ *0984/452850* ⊕ *www.prolococamigliatello.it.*

Sights

★ **Parco Nazionale della Sila—La Fossiata**
NATIONAL PARK | Calabria's granite plateau of Sila National Park is a wonderful place for lovers of the wild outdoors. Rising to nearly 7,000 feet at its highest peak, Botte Donato, the park was inaugurated in 2002, with forests, valleys, and rivers home to 175 species of vertebrates, including the park's now protected symbol, *il lupo*, the wolf. The forestry commission office in nearby Cupone can provide tourist information, maps, and assistance, such as arranging guides. ✉ *Via Nazionale, Lorica di San Giovanni in Fiore, Camigliatello* ☎ *0984/537109*

Forestry Commission Office ⊕ www.
parcosila.it ⊗ Office closed weekends.

Hotels

Tasso

$ | **HOTEL** | **FAMILY** | On the edge of
Camigliatello, less than 1 km (½ mile)
from the ski slopes, this hotel is in a
peaceful, picturesque location. **Pros:**
beautiful surroundings; lively evening
and family entertainment; conveniently
located near the ski area. **Cons:** nondescript architecture and out-of-date decor;
scant breakfast choice lacking Calabrese
products; dated bathrooms. ⑤ *Rooms
from: €90* ⊠ *Via Torquato Tasso, Spezzano
della Sila, Camigliatello* ☎ *0984/578113*
⊕ *www.hoteltasso.it* ⟿ *82 rooms*
⏍ *Free Breakfast.*

Crotone

*105 km (65 miles) east of Cosenza, 150
km (94 miles) northeast of Locri.*

One of the most important Magna Graecia colonies in Italy, Crotone was a major
cultural center in the 5th century BC,
when it was the home of thinkers like
philosopher and mathematician Pythag-
oras. Sadly, modern development has
eclipsed much of its former beauty, but it
preserves something of an old-town feel,
with its imposing 16th-century castle
and an archaeological museum of some
importance. Its coastal waters, stretching
to Capo Rizzuto, make up Italy's largest
protected marine area; and the island
castle Le Castella, 15 km (9 miles) from
Crotone, is a vision out of a fairy tale.

GETTING HERE AND AROUND

By car, take the Cosenza Nord exit from
the A3 autostrada, then follow the SS107.
There are regular trains from Sibari.

**CONTACT Proloco Crotone Tourism
Office.** ⊠ *Via Molo Sanità 2, Crotone*
☎ *329/8154963 mobile* ⊕ *www.facebook.
com/prolococrotone.*

Sights

Museo Archeologico Nazionale

HISTORY MUSEUM | Constructed to house
the treasures found at the Sanctuary of
Hera Lacinia, as well as many antiquities
recovered from the surrounding seabed,
the museum is situated in the heart
of the old city of Crotone, close to the
seafront castle. The most precious part of
the collection is the so-called Treasure of
Hera, with the goddess's finely wrought
gold diadem and belt pendant. You can
also see the rare 5th-century-BC bronze
askos (container for oil) in the form of a
mermaid, illegally exported to the United
States and subsequently recovered by the
Italian government from the Getty Museum in California. ⊠ *Via Risorgimento 121,
Crotone* ☎ *0962/23082* ⊕ *musei.calabria.
beniculturali.it* ⊡ *€4* ⊗ *Closed Mon.*

★ Museo e Parco Archeologico Nazionale di Capo Colonna

RUINS | Il Santuario di Hera Lacinia
(Sanctuary of Hera Lacinia) was once one
of the most important shrines of Magna
Graecia. Only one column remains standing, but the site (known as Capo Colonna
because of that single pillar) occupies a
stunning position on a promontory 11 km
(7 miles) south of the town of Crotone.
The ruins are part of a vast park, which
also contains a well-appointed museum
documenting finds from prehistory to the
Roman era. The sanctuary itself, which
dates from the 7th century BC, is fenced
off for safety reasons, but a walkway
allows viewing. ⊠ *Via Michele Di Donato,
Capo Colonna, Crotone* ☎ *0962/934814*
⊕ *musei.calabria.beniculturali.it* ⊡ *Free*
⊗ *Closed Mon.*

Beaches

★ Capo Rizzuto—Spiagge Rosse

BEACH | FAMILY | If practicalities and time allow, make the short trip toward Capo Rizzuto just down the coast for some of the most fabulous bathing and snorkeling in the region. Among its bays and protected marine reserve waters is Spiagge Rosse, whose orange-red sand beach and crystalline waters make it the most alluring on this stretch of coast. **Amenities:** food and drink; lifeguards; parking (no fee); showers; toilets. **Best for:** snorkeling; swimming. ☒ *Contrada Fratte, Capo Rizzuto, Crotone* ☎ *0962/1916760* ⊕ *www.villaggiospiaggerosse.it.*

🛏 Hotels

Hotel Helios

$$ | HOTEL | On the coastal road between Crotone and Capo Colonna, a little out of town and just 8 km (5 miles) from the Sanctuary of Hera Lacinia, the '70s-style Helios has crystal clear shores nearby and a fab pool, terrace, restaurant, and snack bar—all on-site. **Pros:** elevated sea views; efficient, courteous staff; on bus route into town and open year-round. **Cons:** uninspiring architecture; lacks room soundproofing; rooms need a refresh. ⑤ *Rooms from: €132* ☒ *Viale Magna Grecia at Via Makalla 2, Crotone* ☎ *0962/901291* ⊕ *www.helioshotels.it* ⇗ *42 rooms* ⦿⎮ *Free Breakfast.*

Tropea

120 km (75 miles) southwest of Cosenza, 107 km (66 miles) north of Reggio Calabria.

Ringed by cliffs and wonderful sandy beaches, the Tropea promontory is still just beginning to be discovered by foreign tourists. The main town of Tropea, its old palazzi built in simple golden stone, easily wins the contest for prettiest town on Calabria's Tyrrhenian Coast. On a clear day the seaward views from the waterfront promenade take in Stromboli's cone and at least four of the other Aeolian Islands; you can visit them by motorboat, departing daily in summer. Accommodations are good, and beach addicts won't be disappointed by the choice of magnificent sandy bays within easy reach. The beach beside Santa Maria dell'Isola is said to be one of the Mediterranean's most beautiful, but there are other fine beaches south at Capo Vaticano and north at Briatico.

GETTING HERE AND AROUND

By car, exit the A3 autostrada at Pizzo and follow the southbound SP6/SS522. Frequent trains depart daily from Lamezia Terme.

VISITOR INFORMATION

CONTACT Proloco Tropea Tourism Office. ☒ *Piazza Ercole 19–23, Tropea* ☎ *0963/61475* ⊕ *www.prolocotropea.eu.*

Sights

Cattedrale

CHURCH | In Tropea's beguiling warren of lanes, seek out the old Norman cathedral, whose main altar contains the locally revered icon of the Madonna di Romania, protectress of the city. Also of interest are the imposing 14th-century "Black Crucifix," in one of the side chapels, and the adjoining Museo Diocesano, which contains an archaeological section and a collection of sacred art, including a life-size statue of Santa Domenica in solid silver, dating from 1738. ■**TIP→ November through March, the cathedral is open for church services only, but if you're quiet and respectful, you can probably sneak a peek.** ☒ *Largo Duomo, Tropea* ☎ *0963/61034* 🎫 *Cathedral free, Museo Diocesano €5* ⊗ *Closed Nov.–Mar., except for services.*

★ Santa Maria dell'Isola

VIEWPOINT | The sanctuary of Santa Maria dell'Isola is the symbol of Tropea, and it is easy to see why. Perched high on a rocky promontory and accessible only by a winding flight of stone steps cut into the cliffside, it dominates the sea view from Piazza Ercole, the main town square. Believed to date from the 4th century AD, it has been rebuilt many times and took its present form in the 18th century, after it was damaged by an earthquake. The inside of the church is unadorned, but visitors can climb up to the roof to admire the splendid view or wander through the pleasant garden set on the rocks behind the building. The beach below the rock is considered to be among the most beautiful in Italy. ✉ *Largo Marina dell'Isola, Tropea* ☎ *377/306 5825 mobile* ⊕ *www.facebook.com/san-tuariosantamariadellisola* ☜ *Church free, garden €3.*

🏖 Beaches

★ Marasusa
BEACH | FAMILY | The most famous of Calabria's beaches is backed by sheer cliffs topped by Tropea's stacked buildings—seemingly growing out of the rock. Beyond this popular vacation destination stretch sits the gleaming island promontory sanctuary of Santa Maria dell'Isola. For bathers, snorkelers, and frolickers the light-hued sand is quite fine underfoot and the greenish-blue waters are wonderful. Adding to the drama is the smoking cone of island volcano Stromboli on the western horizon. **Amenities:** lifeguards; parking (no fee); showers; toilets. **Best for:** snorkeling; surfing; swimming; windsurfing. ✉ *Via Lungomare, Tropea.*

🍴 Restaurants

Osteria Antico Androne
$$ | SOUTHERN ITALIAN | With intimate tables around the interior courtyard and mezzanine of the 18th-century Palazzo Teotino, this osteria is a truly atmospheric place to dine. The menu is a mix of traditional local dishes and classic southern

Italian pasta combinations—with subtle Tropeana twists here and there. **Known for:** grilled and fried seafood; Calabrese fileja pasta with Tropea onions; meat and vegetarian options. ⑤ *Average main: €20* ✉ *Via Boiano 6, Tropea* ☎ *349/2887969 mobile* ⊙ *Closed Mon.*

Pimm's
$$ | SOUTHERN ITALIAN | Since the 1960s, this basement restaurant in the historic center has offered Tropea's top seafood dining experience, with such specialties as pasta with monkfish and almond pesto, smoked swordfish and prawns on red Tropea onions, and gnocchi filled with tiny clams and creamed pistachio nuts. The splendid sea views from the rear windows (ask for the *tavolo in nicchia panoramica*) are a surprising—and substantial—reason to head here. **Known for:** excellent fresh seafood; perched high above the beach; book a window table for the azure views. ⑤ *Average main: €23* ✉ *Largo Migliarese 2, at the foot of Corso Vittorio Emanuele, Tropea* ☎ *0963/666105* ⊕ *www.facebook.com/ristorantepimms.*

🛏 Hotels

★ Hotel Rocca della Sena
$$$$ | HOTEL | Overlooking Tropea's golden sands and azure waters, this intimate, self-styled boutique hotel—with modern, quirky, equatorial-themed rooms—is a reliable option. **Pros:** tranquil location on Tropea's periphery; fab sea views; a terrace with a large whirlpool bath. **Cons:** standard rooms on the cramped and gloomy side; lack of bar menu options; some may find the LED mood lighting and furnishings tacky. ⑤ *Rooms from: €317* ✉ *Via Paolo Orsi, Tropea* ☎ *0963/62374* ⊕ *www.hotelroccadel-lasena.it* ⊙ *Closed Nov.–early Apr.* ⇨ *12 rooms* ⎮⊙⎮ *Free Breakfast.*

Reggio Calabria

115 km (71 miles) south of Tropea, 499 km (311 miles) south of Naples.

This raw city is one of Italy's busiest ports, where you can find not only container ships and cranes but also the wonderful Lungomare Falcomatà, a promenade made for lazy passeggiatas. Hydrofoils for Sicily depart from here; vehicle-carrying ferries depart from Villa San Giovanni, 13 km (8 miles) north.

Reggio Calabria is also a great base for visiting *borghi* (historic villages) like the beautiful town of Stilo, which is known for being the birthplace and home of the philosopher Tommaso Campanella (1568–1639), whose magnum opus was the socialistic *La Città del Sole* (*The City of the Sun*, 1602). Stilo is 138 km (86 miles) northeast of Reggio Calabria along the Ionian coastal road, SS106. Regular trains run from Lamezia Terme.

GETTING HERE AND AROUND

The A3 autostrada runs directly to Reggio Calabria. A dozen direct trains depart from Naples and Rome daily. There are daily flights from all over Italy and seasonal services from around Europe.

VISITOR INFORMATION

CONTACT I.A.T. Reggio Calabria Tourism Office. ⊠ *329 Corso Garibaldi, Reggio Calabria* ☎ *0965/89212* ⊕ *turismo.reggiocal.it.*

Sights

Lungomare Falcomatà

PROMENADE | FAMILY | Reggio's panoramic palm tree–lined promenade, with views across the Straits of Messina towards Sicily and Etna (on nice days), is named after the former mayor who helped the city's 1990s "Reggio Spring" rebirth. Join the joggers, teens, and families along the 1.6-km (1-mile) route taking in the sea air, handsome Stile Liberty architecture, and Arena dello Stretto,

an open-air Greek-style theater, which hosts summer events, performances, and concerts. ⊠ *Lungomare Falcomatà, Reggio Calabria.*

★ Museo Nazionale della Magna Grecia

HISTORY MUSEUM | Reggio Calabria is home to one of southern Italy's most important archaeological museums. Its prize exhibit, of course, is the two ancient Greek statues known as the Bronzi di Riace, which were discovered by an amateur deep-sea diver off Calabria's Ionian Coast in 1972. After a lengthy but necessary conservation effort, these 5th-century-BC statues of two Greek warriors, thought to be the work of either Pheidias or Polykleitos, now take pride of place in their special temperature-controlled room, complete with earthquake-resistant bases. ⊠ *Piazza de Nava 26, Reggio Calabria* ☎ *0965/613988* ⊕ *www.museoarcheologicoreggiocalabria.it* ⊠ *€8* ⊙ *Closed Mon.*

Hotels

★ Hotel Medinblu

$$ | HOTEL | The sleek, contemporary guest rooms at this hotel in an imaginatively renovated 1915 palazzo are warmed up a bit by fabrics with bold prints; fabulous public areas include a spacious, chic roof terrace and cocktail bar that serve aperitivi. **Pros:** central location; warm, professional customer service; rooftop breakfast and seasonal evening concerts. **Cons:** hotel's garage a short walk away; traffic noise in some rooms; some may find decor lacks character. ⑤ *Rooms from: €130* ⊠ *Via Demetrio Tripepi 98, Reggio Calabria* ☎ *0965/312982* ⊕ *www.hotelmedinblu.com* ⇌ *33 rooms* ⍟ *Free Breakfast.*

Chapter 17

SICILY

Updated by
Nick Bruno
and Laura Itzkowitz

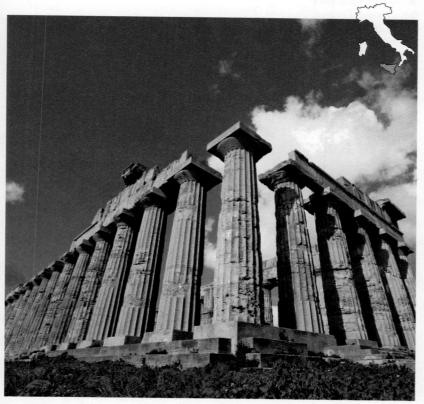

⊙ **Sights**
★★★★☆

🍴 **Restaurants**
★★★★★

🛏 **Hotels**
★★★★☆

👜 **Shopping**
★★☆☆☆

🍸 **Nightlife**
★★☆☆☆

WELCOME TO SICILY

TOP REASONS TO GO

★ **Taormina, Sicily's most beautiful resort:** The view of the sea and Mount Etna from its jagged cactus-covered cliffs is as close to perfection as a panorama can get.

★ **A walk on Siracusa's Ortigia Island:** Classical ruins rub elbows with Baroque palaces and fish markets in Sicily's most striking port city, where the Duomo is literally built atop an ancient Greek temple.

★ **Palermo's palaces, churches, and crypts:** Virtually every great European empire ruled Sicily's strategically positioned capital at some point, and it shows most of all in the diverse architecture, from Roman to Byzantine to Arab-Norman.

★ **Valley of the Temples, Agrigento:** This stunning set of ruins is proudly perched above the sea in a grove full of almond trees; not even in Athens will you find Greek temples this finely preserved.

1 Palermo.

2 Monreale.

3 Segesta.

4 Erice.

5 Trapani.

6 Marsala.

7 Selinunte.

8 Agrigento.

9 Enna.

10 Piazza Armerina.

11 Caltagirone.

12 Ragusa.

13 Modica.

14 Scicli.

15 Noto.

16 Siracusa.

17 Catania.

18 Acireale.

19 Mount Etna.

20 Taormina.

21 Castelmola.

22 Messina.

23 Lipari.

24 Salina.

25 Panarea.

26 Stromboli.

27 Filicudi.

28 Cefalù.

EATING AND DRINKING WELL IN SICILY

Street vegetable market

Sicilian cuisine is one of the oldest in existence, with records of cooking competitions dating to 600 BC. Food in Sicily today reflects the island's unique cultural mix, imaginatively combining fish, fruits, vegetables, and nuts with Italian pastas and Arab and North African elements—couscous is a staple in Palermo.

It's hard to eat badly here. From the lowliest of trattorias to the most highfalutin *ristorante*, you'll find classic dishes that have long been staples of the family dinner table—basically pasta and seafood. In more formal restaurants, you'll find greater attention to detail and a more sophisticated atmosphere, while less pretentious trattorias tend to be family-run affairs, occasionally without so much as a menu to guide you. There's also a new wave of creative restaurants that have come up with interesting versions of old standbys, using local and often organic ingredients and changing menus with the season. No matter where you choose to eat in the most gregarious of regions in the most convivial of countries, you can expect a lively dining experience.

SICILIAN MARKETS

Sicily's natural fecundity is evident wherever you look, from the prickly pears sprouting on roadsides, to the slopes of vineyards and citrus groves covering the interior, to the ranks of fishing boats moored in every harbor. You can come face-to-face with this bounty in the clamorous street markets of Palermo and Catania where you'll encounter teetering piles of olives and oranges, enticing displays of cheeses and meats, and vegetables of every description.

WINES

The earthy *nero d'avola* grape bolsters many of Sicily's traditionally sunny, expansive reds, and it's often softened with fruity, bright *frappato* to make Sicily's only DOCG wine, Cerasuolo di Vittoria. Red wines from around Mount Etna that use the grapes *nerello mascalese* and *nerello cappuccio* have also gained renown. Sicily produces crisp white varieties, too, such as *carricante, catarratto bianco, inzolia,* and *grillo.* When it comes to sweet accompaniments, the small island of Pantelleria produces the smooth *passito* dessert wine, made from *zibibbo* grapes, while the Aeolian Islands are known for Malvasia delle Lipari.

DELICIOUS FISH

Pasta *con le sarde*, with fresh sardines, olive oil, raisins, pine nuts, and wild fennel gets a different treatment at every restaurant. Grilled *tonno* (tuna) and *orata* (dorado) are coastal staples, while delicate *ricci* (sea urchins) are a specialty. King, however, is *pesce spada* (swordfish), best enjoyed *marinato* (marinated), *affumicato* (smoked), or as the traditional *involtini di pesce spada* (roulades).

LOCAL SPECIALTIES

In Catania, you'll be offered *caserecci alla Norma* (a short pasta with a sauce

Arancini (deep-fried rice balls)

Sardines

of tomato, eggplant, salted ricotta, and basil). The *mandorla* (bitter almond), the pride of Agrigento and Noto, plays into everything from risotto *alle mandorle* (with almonds, butter, Grana cheese, and parsley) to almond granita—a must in summer. Pistachios produced around Bronte, on the lower slopes of Etna, go into pasta sauces as well as ice cream and granita, while salted capers from the Aeolian Islands and Pantelleria add zest to salads and fish sauces.

SNACKS

Two favorite Sicilian snacks are *arancini* ("little oranges," or deep-fried rice croquettes with a cheese or meat filling) and *panelle* (seasoned chickpea flour boiled to a paste, cooled, sliced, and fried). Also look for special foods associated with festivals, such as the ominously named *ossa dei morti* ("bones of the dead," or hard almond cookies). But the most eye-catching of all are the *frutta martorana*: sweet fruit-shaped marzipan confections sold in *pasticcerie* (pastry shops). The Baroque town of Modica is famous for its chocolate, produced using an Aztec recipe brought to Sicily by Spanish conquistadores.

The island of Sicily has an abundance of history, its legacy tangible in magnificent Greek temples, prehistoric cave-towns, extravagant Roman mosaics, flamboyant Baroque palaces, and Arab-Norman cathedrals bejeweled with Byzantine mosaics. Add the spectacular sights of Mount Etna and Stromboli—two of Europe's most active volcanoes—and Sicily's unique cuisine—mingling Arab, Roman and Greek, Spanish and French—and you understand why visitors continue to be drawn here.

Sicily has beckoned seafaring wanderers since the trials of Odysseus were first sung in Homer's *Odyssey*—an epic that is sometimes called the world's first travel guide. Strategically poised between Europe and Africa, this mystical land of three corners and a fiery volcano once hosted two of the most enlightened capitals of the West: Siracusa and Palermo. And it has been a melting pot of every great civilization on the Mediterranean—Greek and Roman, then Arab and Norman, and finally French, Spanish, and Italian. Invaders through the ages weren't just attracted by its strategic location, however; they recognized a paradise in Sicily's deep blue skies and temperate climate, in its lush vegetation and rich marine life—all of which prevail to this day.

In modern times, the traditional graciousness and nobility of the Sicilian people have survived alongside the destructive influences of the Mafia under Sicily's semiautonomous government. The island has more recently emerged as something of an international travel hot spot, drawing increasing numbers of visitors. Brits and Germans flock in ever-growing numbers to Agrigento and Siracusa, and in high season Chinese and American tour groups seem to outnumber the locals in Taormina and the Baroque hill towns. And yet, in Sicily's windswept heartland, vineyards, olive groves, and lovingly kept dirt roads leading to family farmhouses still tie Sicilians to the land and to tradition, forming a happy connectedness that can't be defined by economic measures.

MAJOR REGIONS

Palermo and Nearby. In the west, Palermo's crumbling splendor creates an almost irresistible pull toward the Sicilian capital, and nearby Monreale's cathedral glitters fine mosaics. The coastal town of Marsala offers tantalizing historical artifacts, while the cobblestone streets of hilltop Erice retain a strong medieval complexion. The crowning glory are the Greek temples at Agrigento and the cliffside temples at Selinunte.

Siracusa and the South. The marvelous ruins of Siracusa await, combined with the seaside allure of the tiny island of Ortigia. Sicily's pretty interior has grand architecture and unspoiled vistas—in particular, the Baroque towns of Ragusa, Modica, Noto, Scicli, and Caltagirone.

Messina. On Sicily's northeastern corner, lively and chaotic Messina commands an unparalleled position across from Calabria. Halfway down the coast, Catania has a gritty, vivacious charm and is a good base for exploring lofty Mount Etna. The sparkling seaside of Taormina and festive carnival floats of Acireale can all be explored nearby.

Aeolian Islands. Off Sicily's northeast coast lies an archipelago of seven spectacular islands of volcanic origin. The Aeolian Islands (Isole Eolie), also known as the Lipari Islands (Isole Lipari), tempt with superb snorkeling and challenging treks. Lipari is the largest of them and provides the widest range of lodging. Most exclusive are Vulcano and Panarea: the former is noted for black-sand beaches, as well as for the acrid smell of sulfur, whereas the latter is considered the prettiest of the islands. Stromboli island has constant, spectacular eruptions, while Salina is the greenest. The farthest are Filicudi and Alicudi, where electricity was introduced only in the 1980s.

Tyrrhenian Coast. Sicily's northern shore is mostly a succession of small holiday towns, but the biggest attraction is the old town of Cefalù, with one of the island's most remarkable cathedrals.

Planning

When to Go

Sicily's high season (mid-June through mid-September) is hot, often humid, expensive, and busy. During the peak season from late July to late August, beaches are crowded, and hotels and restaurants are often booked up, so advance reservations are necessary—often several weeks or even months for hotels and a day or two for restaurants.

April–May and mid-September–October are the ideal months for more temperate weather, more elbow room on the beaches, and more capacity and availability at hotels and restaurants. Keep in mind that the Mediterranean takes a long time to warm up, and a long time to cool down, so if beaches and swimming are a priority, autumn is better than spring. The Easter period (lasting a few days around Good Friday) can be very busy, and some resort destinations may close in late October.

The winter months of November through March see many places outside the cities closed, if only for a few weeks, while tourist facilities at most of Sicily's beach resorts and on all the offshore islands shut down for the entire period. Flights, accommodation rates, and car rentals are at their lowest at this time of year, but bear in mind that November and December can see a lot of rain while January and February are the coldest months.

Getting Here and Around

AIR

There are frequent internal flights from Milan, Rome, and other regional airports to Sicily's two major airports, Palermo's Falcone Borsellino Airport (PMO) and Catania's Fontanarossa Airport (CTA) as well as to Trapani-Birgi's Vincenzo Florio Airport.

CONTACTS Aeroporto Vincenzo Florio Trapani Birgi. ✉ *Contrada Birgi Nivaloro, Trapani* 🕿 *0923/610111* ⊕ *www.airgest. it.* **Catania-Fontanarossa Airport.** ✉ *Via Fontanarossa, Catania* 🕿 *095/7239111* ⊕ *www.aeroporto.catania.it/en.* **Palermo Airport.** ✉ *Punta Raisi, Cinisi, Palermo* 🕿 *800/541880* ⊕ *www.aeroportodipalermo.it.*

BUS

Air-conditioned buses connect major and minor cities in Sicily and are often faster and more convenient than local trains. Various companies serve different routes. SAIS runs frequently between Palermo and Catania, Messina, and other cities, in each case arriving at and departing from near the train stations. Giuntabus operates a direct service from Catania Airport to the port of Milazzo, ideal for anyone heading for the Aeolian Islands.

CONTACTS Cuffaro. 🕿 *091/6161510* ⊕ *www.cuffaro.info.* **Giuntabus.** 🕿 *090/673782* ⊕ *www.giuntabus.com.* **Interbus/Etna Trasporti/Segesta/Sicilbus/ AST.** 🕿 *0935/565111* ⊕ *www.interbus.it.* **SAIS.** 🕿 *091/2776999* ⊕ *www.saisautolinee.it.*

CAR

Driving is the ideal way to explore Sicily. Modern highways circle and bisect the island, making all main cities easily reachable. Along the north coast, the A20 autostrada (also known as E90) connects Messina, Cefalù, and Palermo while along the eastern coast, Messina, Taormina, Catania, and Siracusa are linked by the A18/E45, which is being extended (slowly) as far as Gela. At the time of writing the Modica-Gela stretch was yet to be completed. Running through the interior, from Catania to west of Cefalù, is the A19, a beautiful and rarely busy route; threading west from Palermo, the A29/E933 runs to Trapani, with a leg stretching down to Mazara del Vallo. In general, the south side of the island is less well served, though stretches of the SS115 west of Agrigento are relatively fast and traffic-free. The A18 between Messina and Catania and the A20 autostradas are subject to tolls. You'll likely hear stories about the dangers of driving in Sicily. In the big cities—especially Palermo, Catania, and Messina—streets can be a honking mess, with lane markings and stop signs taken as mere suggestions; you can avoid the chaos by driving through at off-peak times or on weekends. However, once outside the urban areas and resort towns, most of the highways and regional state roads are a driving enthusiast's dream—they're winding, sparsely populated, and reasonably well maintained, with striking new views around many bends. The worst roads are in the remote center, around Vallelunga Pratameno, which are subject to landslides. Obviously, don't leave valuables in your car, and make sure baggage is stowed out of sight, if possible.

TRAIN

There are direct express trains from Rome to Palermo, Catania, and Siracusa. The Rome–Palermo and Rome–Siracusa trips take at least 11 hours. After Naples, the run is mostly along the coast, so try to book a window seat on the right if you're not on an overnight train. At Villa San Giovanni, in Calabria, the train is separated and loaded onto a ferryboat to cross the strait to Messina—a favorite for kids.

There are no high-speed lines within Sicily, but main lines connect Messina, Taormina, Siracusa, Catania, and Palermo. The Messina–Palermo run, along the northern coast, and Messina–Taormina, along the eastern coast, are especially scenic. Secondary lines are generally very slow and may be unreliable. For schedules, check the website of the Italian state railway, Trenitalia.

CONTACT Trenitalia. ☎ *892021 in Italy, 06/5210550 outside Italy* ⊕ *www.trenitalia.com.*

Restaurants

As befits a major city, Palermo has a huge selection of interesting and varied restaurants, while Catania is best known for its high-quality seafood. In the tourist-heavy coastal towns, dining can be hit or miss, while inland there has been a mini-explosion of new-wave gourmet restaurants in the Baroque towns of Ragusa, Modica, and Noto, as well as some intriguing options popping up on Mount Etna.

In the west of the island, expect to find a Sicilian variant of North African couscous on the menus, often made with seafood and well worth sampling. In the countryside, *agriturismi* (farm bed-and-breakfasts), country hotels, and wineries are your best bets for a good meal.

Hotels

Luxurious grand hotels tend to be confined to the major cities and resorts of Palermo, Catania, Taormina, and Siracusa. More recently there has been a Renaissance of extremely chic, charming, exquisitely designed, and often very expensive boutique and rural hotels in the southeast towns of Modica, Ragusa, and Noto and surrounding countryside, on Mount Etna, and in the Aeolian Islands. B&Bs exist everywhere, with the greatest choice in Palermo, Catania, and Taormina, including both period and more modern designer places. Beach resorts tend to have a range of options, while rural lodgings range from sophisticated wine estates to agriturismi (farm-stays), some quite basic, others extremely comfortable, and usually offering half-board plans that can make for some of Sicily's most memorable meals. There are also excellent-quality villas available to rent—a perfect option for large groups and families.

⇨ *Hotel and restaurant reviews have been shortened. For full information, visit Fodors.com. Prices in the hotel reviews are the lowest cost of a standard double room in high season. Prices in the dining reviews are the average cost of a main course at dinner, or, if dinner is not served, at lunch.*

What It Costs in Euros

	$	$$	$$$	$$$$
RESTAURANTS				
	under €15	€15–€24	€25–€35	over €35
HOTELS				
	under €125	€125–€200	€201–€300	over €300

Palermo

Once the intellectual capital of southern Europe, Palermo has always been at the crossroads of civilization. Favorably located on a crescent bay at the foot of Monte Pellegrino, it has attracted almost every culture touching the Mediterranean world. To Palermo's credit, it's absorbed these diverse cultures into a unique personality that's at once Arab and Christian, Byzantine and Roman, Norman and Italian. The city's heritage encompasses all of Sicily's varied ages, but its distinctive aspect is its Arab-Norman identity, an improbable marriage that, mixed in with Byzantine and Jewish elements, resulted in resplendent works of art. These are most notable in its churches, from small jewels such as San Giovanni degli Eremiti to larger-scale works such as the cathedral. No less noteworthy than the architecture is Palermo's chaotic vitality, on display at some of Italy's most vibrant outdoor markets, public squares, street bazaars, and food vendors, and, above all, in its grand, discordant symphony of motorists, motorcyclists, and pedestrians that triumphantly climaxes in the new town center each evening with Italy's most spectacular passeggiata.

Sicily's capital is a multilayered, vigorous metropolis with a strong historical profile; approach it with an open mind. You're likely to encounter some frustrating instances of inefficiency and, depending on the season, stifling heat. If you have a car, park it in a garage as soon as you can, and don't take it out until you're ready to depart.

Palermo is easily explored on foot, but you may choose to spend a morning taking a bus tour to help you get oriented. The Quattro Canti, or Four Corners, is the hub that separates the four sections of the old city: La Kalsa (the old Arab section) to the southeast, Albergheria to the southwest, Capo to the northwest, and Vucciria to the northeast. Each of these is a tumult of activity during the day, though at night the narrow alleys empty out and are best avoided in favor of the more animated avenues of the new city north of Teatro Massimo. Sights to see by day are scattered along three major streets: Corso Vittorio Emanuele, Via Maqueda, and Via Roma.

GETTING HERE AND AROUND

Palermo is home to one of Sicily's two major international airports, Aeroporto di Falcone Borsellino at Punta Raisi, 30 km (18 miles) west of town, and as such is a main gateway for those arriving in Sicily by plane. Along with international flights, there are regular connections from and to other Italian cities such as Milan, Rome, and Naples, as well as to Sicily's far-flung isles of Pantelleria and Lampedusa.

Trains run from the station below Palermo's airport to the city center every half hour or so, with tickets dispensed from machines. Don't forget to validate your ticket before travel by punching it at one of the station's machines. Prestia e Comandè buses run every 30 minutes to Piazza Ruggero Settimo in the city center. It is essential to book in advance, via the app or website or in person, because unless there are advance bookings, buses do not run. A taxi from Palermo's airport to the center should cost €50, while shared taxis cost €10 per person, with drop-offs at a range of points within the city (though you may have to wait for the minimum of five passengers before setting off). Journey time by taxi or bus between Palermo airport and city center is 30 minutes to one hour, depending on traffic; by train, it's around one hour, with stops within walking distance of Palazzo Reale and Via della Libertà before reaching the main station.

You'll find you can walk to most spots within central Palermo, though it's worth taking advantage of city bus services, run by AMAT, for longer stretches—for example, between the main train station and Piazza Castelnuovo (Bus 101); between the main train station and Piazza dell'Indipendenza, for the Palazzo Reale (Bus 109); and out to Monreale (Bus 389 from Piazza dell'Indipendenza) and Mondello (Bus 806 from the Politeama or Viale della Libertà).

Bus tickets can be purchased from kiosks and shops showing the AMAT sticker and cost €1.40 for any journeys made within 90 minutes (timed from when you punch your ticket in the machine onboard the bus) with a €0.40 supplement if you purchase on board; €3.50 for tickets lasting an entire day; €6 for tickets lasting two days; €8 for three days; and €16.50 for a week.

CONTACT AMAT. ⊠ Palermo ☎ 091/350111 ⊕ www.amat.pa.it.

CONTACT Palermo Tourism Office. ⊠ *Via Principe di Belmonte 92, Palermo* ☎ *091/585172* ⊕ *turismo.cittametropolitana.pa.it.*

Sights

Catacombe dei Cappuccini

CEMETERY | The spookiest sight in all of Sicily, this 16th-century catacomb houses more than 8,000 corpses of men, women, and young children—some in tombs but many mummified and preserved—hanging in rows on the walls, divided by social caste, age, or gender. Most wear signs indicating their names and the years they lived, and many are Capuchin friars, who were founders and proprietors of this bizarre establishment from 1599 to 1911. The site is still managed by the nearby Capuchin church, but was closed to new corpses when an adjacent cemetery was opened, making the catacombs redundant. Though memorable, this is not a spot for the faint of heart; children might be frightened or disturbed. ⊠ *Piazza Cappuccini 1, off Via Cappuccini, Near Palazzo Reale* ☎ *091/6527389* ⊕ *www.catacombepalermo.it* ⊠ *€5.*

Cattedrale

CHURCH | This church is a lesson in Palermitano eclecticism—originally Norman (1182), then Catalan Gothic (14th to 15th century), then fitted out with a Baroque and neoclassical interior (18th century). Its turrets, towers, dome, and arches come together in the kind of meeting of diverse elements that King Roger II (1095–1154), whose tomb is inside along with that of Frederick II, fostered during his reign. The exterior is more intriguing than the interior, but the back of the apse is gracefully decorated with interlacing Arab arches inlaid with limestone and black volcanic tufa. It's possible to visit the cathedral's roof for some fabulous city views. ⊠ *Corso Vittorio Emanuele, Capo* ☎ *329/3977513 mobile* ⊕ *www.cattedrale.palermo.it* ⊠ *Free; €15 treasury,*

crypt, apses, royal tombs, and roof visit; *€6 treasury, crypt, apses and tombs.*

Chiesa del Gesù

CHURCH | It is more than worth the short detour from the lively Ballarò Market to step into the serene Baroque perfection of Chiesa del Gesù (Church of St. Mary of Gesù). The ornate church was built by the Jesuits not long after their arrival in Palermo in the late 16th century, and was constructed at the site of their religious seat in the city, so the chuch is also sometimes known as Casa Professa (mother house). The interior is almost completely covered with intricate marble bas-reliefs and elaborate black, tangerine, and cream stone work. The splendid church was severely damaged in World War II, but careful restoration has returned it to its shiny, swirling glory. ⊠ *Piazza Casa Professa 21, Albergheria* ☎ *377/3397612 mobile (Whatsapp text messages only)* ⊕ *www.casaprofessa.it* ⊠ *Free (contributions requested)* ⊗ *Museum closed Sun. and during festivals.*

Galleria Regionale della Sicilia – Palazzo Abatellis

ART MUSEUM | Housed in this late-15th-century Catalan Gothic palace with Renaissance elements is the Galleria Regionale. Among its treasures are the *Annunciation* (1474), a painting by Sicily's prominent Renaissance master Antonello da Messina (1430–79), and an arresting fresco spanning two floors (and visible from both the ground floor and a first-floor gallery) by an unknown 15th-century painter, titled *The Triumph of Death*, a macabre depiction of the plague years. ⊠ *Via Alloro 4, Kalsa* ☎ *331/6581788 mobile* ⊕ *www.facebook.com/abatellis* ⊠ *€8; free 1st Sun. of month* ⊗ *Closed Mon.*

★ La Martorana

(*Santa Maria dell'Ammiraglio*)
CHURCH | One piazza over from the dancing nymphs of Fontana Pretoria, this church, with its elegant Norman campanile, was erected in 1143 but had

Palermo

KEY

- Sights
- Restaurants
- Quick Bites
- Hotels

Sights ▶

1	Catacombe dei Cappuccini	A2
2	Cattedrale	D2
3	Chiesa del Gesù	E2
4	Galleria Regionale della Sicilia - Palazzo Abatellis	G2
5	La Martorana	E2
6	Museo Archeologico Regionale Salinas	E1
7	Museo Internazionale delle Marionette Antonio Pasqualino	G1
8	Palazzo Butera	G1
9	Palazzo Reale	C3
10	Piazza Pretoria	E2
11	Quattro Canti	E2
12	San Cataldo	E2
13	San Giovanni degli Eremiti	C3
14	Santa Caterina	E2
15	Teatro Massimo	D1

Restaurants ▶

1	Casa del Brodo	F2
2	Comparucci	D1
3	MadoniEAT	G2
4	MEC Restaurant	D2

Coffee and Quick Bites ▶

1	Antica Focacceria San Francesco	F2
2	Cappadonia	D2
3	Pani Cà Meusa	F1

Hotels ▶

1	Grand Hotel Piazza Borsa	F2
2	Le Terrazze	D2
3	Massimo Piazza Hotel	E1
4	Palazzo Pantaleo	E1
5	Villa Igiea	F1

300 yards

300 meters

its interior altered considerably during the Baroque period. High along the western wall, however, is some of the oldest and best-preserved mosaic artwork of the Norman period. Near the entrance is an interesting mosaic of King Roger II being crowned by Christ. In it Roger is dressed in a bejeweled Byzantine stole, reflecting the Norman court's penchant for all things Byzantine. Archangels along the ceiling wear the same stole wrapped around their shoulders and arms. The much plainer San Cataldo is next door. ⊠ *Piazza Bellini 3, Quattro Canti* ☎ *345/8288231 mobile* ⊕ *turismo. comune.palermo.it* ✉ *€2.*

Museo Archeologico Regionale Salinas (*Salinas Regional Museum of Archaeology*)

HISTORY MUSEUM | This archaeology museum is the oldest public museum in Sicily, with a small but excellent collection, including a marvelously reconstructed Doric frieze from the Greek temple at Selinunte, which reveals the high level of artistic culture attained by the Greeks in Sicily some 2,500 years ago. There are also lion's head water spouts from 480 BC, as well as other excavated pieces from around Sicily, including Taormina and Agrigento, which make up part of an informative exhibition on the broader history of the island. After admiring the artifacts, wander through the two plant-filled courtyards, and be sure to check the website for special culture nights, when the museum is open late to host musical performances. ⊠ *Piazza Olivella 24, Via Roma, Olivella* ☎ *091/6116807* ⊕ *turismo.comune.palermo.it* ✉ *€7, free 1st Sun. of month* ⊗ *Closed Mon.*

Museo Internazionale delle Marionette Antonio Pasqualino

SPECIALTY MUSEUM | FAMILY | This collection of more than 4,000 masterpieces showcasing the traditional Opera dei Pupi (puppet show), both Sicilian and otherwise, will delight visitors of all ages with their glittering armor and fierce expressions. The free audio guide to the colorful displays is only available in Italian, but the well-designed exhibits include video clips of the puppets in action, which requires no translation. There are also regular live performances in the museum's theater (Monday 11 am and Tuesday–Saturday 5 pm), which center on the chivalric legends of troubadours of bygone times. The museum can be hard to find: look for the small alley just off Piazzetta Antonio Pasqualino 5. ⊠ *Piazzetta Antonio Pasqualino 5, near Via Butera, Kalsa* ☎ *091/328060* ⊕ *www.museodelle-marionette.it/en* ✉ *€5.*

★ Palazzo Butera

ART MUSEUM | Dating from the 18th century but closed for most of the last four decades, the Palazzo Butera has been transformed by its gallerista owners, Massimo and Francesca Valsecchi, into one of Sicily's (and Italy's) most imaginative museum collections. Its labyrinthine rooms now display a heady mixture of old and new art. The collection's strength lies in its bold juxtapositions, with works by an international roster of experimental modern artists of the likes of Gilbert and George, and David Tremlett, exhibited alongside classical landscapes and graceful Sicilian furniture from the 19th century. Painted ceilings remain from the palace's Baroque beginnings, some of them artfully peeled back to reveal the wooden construction behind them. Diverse temporary exhibitions displayed on the ground floor add to the mix. There's a lot to take in, but if you need a break from all the hectic creativity, head for the terrace, accessed from the second floor, which provides benches and a walk around one of the two courtyards as well as views over the harbor. You can get even better views from the viewing platform reached from the roof, while further up, steps lead to a lofty view of the harbor, Monte Pellegrino, and, inland, the whole of the Conca d'Oro bowl in which the city sits. ⊠ *Via Butera 18, Kalsa*

☎ 091/7521754 ⊕ www.palazzobutera.it
✉ €9 ⊙ Closed Mon.

★ **Palazzo Reale** (Royal Palace)
CASTLE/PALACE | This historic palace, also
called Palazzo dei Normanni (Norman
Palace), was the seat of Sicily's semiautonomous rulers for centuries; the building
is a fascinating mesh of 10th-century
Norman and 17th-century Spanish structures. Because it now houses the Sicilian
Parliament, parts of the palace are closed
to the public from Tuesday to Thursday
when the regional assembly is in session, but the must-see Cappella Palatina
(Palatine Chapel) remains open. Built
in 1132, it's a dazzling example of the
harmony of artistic elements produced
under the Normans. Upstairs are the
royal apartments, including the Sala di Re
Ruggero (King Roger's Hall), decorated
with ornate medieval mosaics of hunting
scenes. From Friday to Monday, the Sala
is included with entry to the palace or
chapel. ⊠ Piazza del Parlamento, Near
Palazzo Reale ☎ 091/7055611 ⊕ www.
federicosecondo.org ✉ €19 Fri.–Mon.;
€15.50 Tues.–Thurs. ⊙ Royal Apartments
closed Tues.–Thurs.

Piazza Pretoria
FOUNTAIN | The square's centerpiece, a
lavishly decorated fountain with 500 separate pieces of sculpture and an abundance of nude figures, so shocked some
Palermitans when it was unveiled in 1575
that it got the nickname "Fountain of
Shame." It's even more of a sight when
illuminated at night. ⊠ Piazza Pretoria,
Quattro Canti.

Quattro Canti
STREET | The Four Corners is the decorat-
ed intersection of two main thoroughfares: Corso Vittorio Emanuele and Via
Maqueda. Four rather exhaust-blackened
Baroque palaces from Spanish rule meet
at concave corners, each with its own
fountain and representations of a Spanish
ruler, patron saint, and one of the four
seasons. ⊠ Corso Vittorio Emanuele and
Via Maqueda, Quattro Canti.

San Cataldo
CHURCH | Three striking Saracenic scarlet
domes mark this church, built in 1154
during the Norman occupation of
Palermo. The church now belongs to the
Knights of the Holy Sepulchre and has a
spare but intense stone interior. ⊠ Piazza
Bellini 3, Kalsa ☎ 091/7829684 ⊕ turis-
mo.comune.palermo.it ✉ €2.50.

San Giovanni degli Eremiti
CHURCH | Distinguished by its five red-
dish-orange domes and stripped-clean
stone interior, this 12th-century church
was built by the Normans on the site of
an earlier mosque—one of 200 that once
stood in Palermo. The emirs ruled Palermo for nearly two centuries and brought
to it their passion for lush gardens and
fountains. One is reminded of this while
sitting in San Giovanni's delightful cloister
of twin half columns, surrounded by palm
trees, jasmine, oleander, and citrus trees.
⊠ Via dei Benedettini 14–20, Near Palazzo
Reale ☎ 091/6515019 ⊕ turismo.comune.
palermo.it ✉ €7.

Santa Caterina
CHURCH | The walls of this splendid
Baroque church (1596) in Piazza Bellini
are covered with extremely impressive
decorative 17th-century inlays of precious
marble. There are marvelous views from
the terrace, and a bakery selling delicacies made using the nuns' recipes. ⊠ Piazza Bellini, Quattro Canti ☎ 091/2713837
⊕ www.monasterosantacaterina.com
✉ €3; €10 combined ticket, includes
church, monastery, and rooftop.

Teatro Massimo
PERFORMANCE VENUE | Construction of
this formidable neoclassical theater, the
largest in Italy, was started in 1875 by
Giovanni Battista Basile and completed
by his son Ernesto in 1897. A recon-
struction project started in 1974 ran into
severe delays, and the facility remained
closed until just before its centenary, in
1997. Its interior is as glorious as ever,
but the exterior remains more famous
thanks to The Godfather Part III, which

ended with a famous shooting scene on the theater's steps. Visits, by 30-minute guided tour only, are available in five languages, including English, while a tour of the current production's *palconscenico* (stage-set) is also available daily at changing times (call to check). ⊠ *Piazza Verdi 9, at top of Via Maqueda, Olivella* ☎ *091/6053267 tours, 091/6053580 ticket office* ⊕ *www.teatromassimo.it* 🎫 *€12 tour; €5 stage visit.*

🍴 Restaurants

Casa del Brodo

$$ | SICILIAN | On the edge of the Vucciria, this is one of Palermo's oldest restaurants, dating back to 1890, and still dear to the hearts of locals for its wintertime namesake dish, tortellini *in brodo* (in beef broth), the specialty of the house. There's an extensive antipasto buffet, and you can't go wrong with the *fritella di fave, piselli,* and *carciofi e ricotta* (fried fava beans, peas, artichokes, and ricotta). **Known for:** large selection of antipasti; tortellini in brodo; good choice of traditional offal dishes. 💲 *Average main: €16* ⊠ *Corso Vittorio Emanuele 175, Vucciria* ☎ *091/321655* ⊕ *www.casadelbrodo. it* 🕐 *Closed Tues. Oct.–May, and Sun. June–Sept.*

Comparucci

$ | PIZZA | FAMILY | One of Palermo's best modern pizzerias serves delicious Neapolitan pies from a big oven in the open kitchen—the genius is in the crust, which is seared in a matter of seconds. The owners make their money on a quick turnover (so don't expect a long, leisurely meal), but the pizza is delicious and the place often serves until midnight—later than almost any other restaurant in the neighborhood. **Known for:** pizza, pizza, and more pizza; outdoor seating in summer; late-night dining. 💲 *Average main: €10* ⊠ *Via Messina 36/e, Libertà* ☎ *091/6090467* 🕐 *No lunch* 🍴 *Take-away available.*

★ MadoniEAT

$ | SICILIAN | Only the finest agricultural produce of the nearby Madonie mountains goes into the simple but fabulous dishes served in this informal eatery attached to the Palazzo Butera art gallery. The frequently changing menu—dependent on the season and what's available from their suppliers—might include chicken breasts in orange sauce and almonds; vegetarian meatballs with ricotta cheese; or sausages braised in red wine with kale. **Known for:** seasonal, fresh, and locally produced ingredients; convenient for lunch after a visit to Palazzo Butera; gourmet sandwiches. 💲 *Average main: €13* ⊠ *Palazzo Butera, Via Butera 20, Kalsa* ☎ *091/7521749* ⊕ *www.madonieat.com* 🕐 *Closed Mon. and 2 wks in Jan. No dinner Sun.–Tues.*

★ MEC Restaurant

$$$ | SICILIAN | Here's a novelty for Palermo in the form of a superb modern restaurant located in a museum dedicated to Steve Jobs and Apple products, a surprisingly successful combination; you not only have the ability to revisit ancient IT devices and learn about the history of the tech company, but the food is pretty excellent. Each of the dishes is a revelation, from the pumpkin with miso and fermented black garlic to the ravioli with stewed veal cheek and pigeon with red-wine scented quince. **Known for:** restaurant and museum in one gorgeous historic building; innovative modern dishes; attentive service. 💲 *Average main: €34* ⊠ *Via Vittorio Emanuele 452, Quattro Canti* ☎ *091/9891901* ⊕ *www.mecrestaurant.it* 🕐 *Closed Sun. No lunch.*

☕ Coffee and Quick Bites

Antica Focacceria San Francesco

$ | SICILIAN | Turn-of-the-20th-century wooden cabinets, marble-top tables, and cast-iron ovens characterize this neighborhood bakery, celebrated for its Sicilian snacks and inexpensive meals. The big pot on the counter holds the delicious regional specialty *pani cà meusa* (boiled calf's spleen with caciocavallo cheese and salt), but the squeamish can opt for chickpea fritters or an enormous arancina (stuffed, fried rice ball). **Known for:** Sicilian street food; historic atmosphere; meat and pasta specialties. ⑤ *Average main: €13* ⊠ *Via A. Paternostro 58, Kalsa* ☎ *091/320264* ⊕ *www.anticafocacceria. it.*

★ Cappadonia

$ | ICE CREAM | FAMILY | After experiencing the cozy but basic trattorias located down Palermo's twisting alleyways, take a sweet break at this modern gelateria along the main drag, which serves exceptional gourmet ice cream. The flavors change with the seasons, but don't miss the tangerine sorbet that bursts with sweet citrus tang or the classic zabaglione custard. **Known for:** delicious ice cream; seasonal flavors; central location. ⑤ *Average main: €3* ⊠ *Via Vittorio Emanuele 401, Capo* ☎ *392/5689784 mobile* ⊕ *cappadonia.it* ⊘ *Closed Nov.–Feb.*

Pani Cà Meusa

$ | SANDWICHES | A civic institution facing Palermo's old fishing port, this standing-room-only joint has been serving its titular calf's spleen sandwich for more than 70 years. The original owner's grandsons still produce this local specialty sprinkled with a bit of salt and some lemon and served with or without cheese to a buzzing crowd of Palermo's well-weathered elders. **Known for:** calf's spleen sandwich that might be the best in town; a bit of Sicilian history; no seating. ⑤ *Average main: €3* ⊠ *Via Cala 62, Porta Carbone, Kalsa* ☎ *091/323433* ⊕ *www.facebook.com/panicameusaportacarbone* ⊘ *Closed Sun.*

Hotels

Grand Hotel Piazza Borsa

$$ | HOTEL | Cleverly converted from three historic buildings—a bank, a palazzo, and a monastery—this hotel with modern,

unadorned rooms is ideally located just off the central axis of Corso Vittorio Emanuele. **Pros:** quiet but central location; beguiling architecture and courtyard; wellness center with fitness equipment, rare for Sicily hotels. **Cons:** somewhat indifferent staff; some noise issues in rooms; some corners feel a bit sterile. ⑤ *Rooms from: €150* ⊠ *Via dei Cartari 18, Kalsa* ☎ *091/320075* ⊕ *piazzaborsa.it* ⌖ *127 rooms* ⑩ *Free Breakfast.*

★ Le Terrazze

$$ | B&B/INN | Although just steps from the bustling Cattedrale area, complete calm envelops this small, beautifully restored B&B, named for its five lush roof terraces, all with sublime views. **Pros:** convenient location; in summer, breakfast is served on the glorious rooftop; period-style rooms. **Cons:** parking can be difficult; books up quickly; Wi-Fi sometimes patchy. ⑤ *Rooms from: €130* ⊠ *Via Pietro Novelli 14, Albergheria* ☎ *091/6520866, 320/4328567 mobile* ⊕ *www.leterrazzebb.it* ⊟ *No credit cards* ⌖ *2 rooms* ⑩ *Free Breakfast.*

Massimo Plaza Hotel

$$ | HOTEL | Small and select, this hotel enjoys one of Palermo's best locations—opposite the Teatro Massimo, on the border of the old and new towns—and has guest rooms that are spacious, comfortably furnished, and well insulated from the noise on pedestrianized Via Maqueda. **Pros:** central location; low-season bargains; tasty breakfast made to order. **Cons:** 21 steps (no elevator) up to the rooms; in pedestrian zone, so vehicles have to keep their distance; cheaper rooms have no views. ⑤ *Rooms from: €179* ⊠ *Via Maqueda 437, Olivella* ☎ *091/325657* ⊕ *www.massimoplazahotel.com* ⌖ *11 rooms* ⑩ *Free Breakfast.*

★ Palazzo Pantaleo

$$ | B&B/INN | Accessed from a quiet courtyard situated between Palermo's two great theaters, with large, airy rooms and a charming host, this top-floor apartment is part of a beautifully renovated palazzo dating from the mid-19th century. **Pros:** free private parking; pleasant and welcoming host; very close to airport bus stop. **Cons:** often booked up; occasional noise intrusion from other guests; a little hard to find. ⑤ *Rooms from: €130* ✉ *Via Ruggero Settimo 74, Libertà* ☎ *335/7006091 mobile* ⊕ *www.palazzopantaleo.it* ⤴ *7 rooms* ❖❖ *Free Breakfast.*

★ Villa Igiea

$$$$ | **HOTEL** | Following a magnificent renovation by the Rocco Forte group, this Art Nouveau fantasy created by architect Ernesto Basile for the Florio family at the turn of the 20th century has been restored to its original glamour and glory. **Pros:** secluded setting; historic building with lots of atmosphere; free shuttle to city center in the summer. **Cons:** price range out of reach for most; no amenities in the nearby area; a bit far from Palermo attractions. ⑤ *Rooms from: €1360* ✉ *Salita Belmonte 43, Acquasanta* ☎ *091/6312111* ⊕ *www.roccofortehotels.com* ⊙ *Closed early Nov.–mid-Mar.* ⤴ *100 rooms* ❖❖ *Free Breakfast.*

ⓨ Nightlife

BARS AND CAFÉS
★ Bocum Fuoco

COCKTAIL BARS | This multilevel cocktail bar between the Vucciria market and the marina is serious about mixology and has created a dedicated oasis in the city's trendiest area. Linger over complex cocktails while lounging on vintage chairs under sparkling chandeliers, all while rubbing elbows with Palermo's cool crowd as records spin on the audiophile turntable in the corner. A short menu of pasta, meat, and seafood dishes is also available. ✉ *Via dei Cassari 6, Vucciria* ☎ *091/332009* ⊕ *www.bocum.it.*

🎭 Performing Arts

CONCERTS AND OPERA
★ Teatro Massimo

CONCERTS | As the biggest theater in Italy, Teatro Massimo is truly larger than life. Concerts and operas are presented throughout the year, though in summer concerts are usually held outdoors. An opera at the Massimo is an unforgettable Sicilian experience. ✉ *Piazza Verdi, at top of Via Maqueda, Olivella* ☎ *091/6053580 tickets, 091/8486000 call center, 091/6053267 tours* ⊕ *www.teatromassimo.it* ✉ *Performances from €20, tours €12.*

🛍 Shopping

Ballarò Market

MARKET | Wind your way through the Albergheria district and this historic market, where the Saracens did their shopping in the 11th century—joined by the Normans in the 12th. The market's name is said to come from nearby Monreale, named Bahlara when Arab traders resided there, and it remains faithful to their original commerce of fruit, vegetables, and grain. These days the stalls are dotted with bars and outdoor restaurants where you can sample the produce, but the market has lost none of its authenticity—just keep a close eye on your belongings in the crowd. And go early: the action dies out by 4 pm most days. Take a wander around the district to view the wonderful "Postcards of Ballarò" project murals (documented in a 2018 Netflix film), including Fulvio di Piazza's *Turbo Ballarò*, a vibrant whirlpool of fish alluding to the market. ✉ *Ballarò Market, Albergheria* ✛ *Between La Martorana and Quattro Canti.*

Pasticceria Alba

FOOD | One of the most famous sweets shops in Italy, this is the place to find pastry favorites like cannoli and cassata siciliana, as well as excellent gelato in summer. There is also an on-site restaurant pizzeria. ⊠ *Piazza Don Bosco 7/c, Libertà* ⊹ *Off Via della Libertà near La Favorita Park* ☎ *091/309016* ⊕ *www. baralbadonbosco.it.*

Vucciria Market

MARKET | A ghost of its former self, Vucciria—whose name translates to "voices" or "hubbub"—was once the most vibrant market in Palermo, memorably captured in Renato Guttuso's canvas of the same name (now exhibited in Palazzo Steri). It is now reduced to barely more than a single street and piazza. It takes on more of a street food/block party atmosphere at night, when no-name bars open to sell cheap cocktails to the crowds gathering around the smoking grills that are wheeled outside after dark. ⊠ *Vucciria Market, Vucciria.*

Monreale

10 km (6 miles) southwest of Palermo.

Only a short drive or bus ride from Palermo, the sleepy town of Monreale is well worth the effort of a visit just to see the spectacular gold mosaics inside its Duomo. Try to arrive early in the morning or later in the afternoon to avoid the tour bus hordes.

GETTING HERE AND AROUND

You can reach Monreale on frequent AMAT buses that depart from Palermo's Piazza Indipendenza or on AST buses from Piazza Giulio Cesare, outside the central station. From Palermo, drivers can follow Corso Calatafimi west, though the going can be slow. Park in the car park a little way outside Monreale's center.

 Sights

Cloister

RELIGIOUS BUILDING | The lovely cloister of the abbey adjacent to the Duomo was built at the same time as the church but enlarged in the 14th century. The beautiful enclosure is surrounded by 216 intricately carved double columns, every other one decorated in a unique glass mosaic pattern. Afterward, don't forget to walk behind the cloister to the belvedere, with stunning panoramic views over the Conca d'Oro (Golden Conch) valley toward Palermo. ⊠ *Piazza del Duomo, Monreale* ⊕ *www.coopculture.it* ⊠ *€7; €13 with Duomo.*

★ Duomo

CHURCH | Monreale's splendid cathedral is lavishly executed with mosaics depicting events from the Old and New Testaments. It's a glorious fusion of Eastern and Western influences, widely regarded as the finest example of Norman architecture in Sicily. William II (1154–89) built the church complex with a cloister and palace between 1174 and 1185, employing Byzantine craftsmen. The major attraction is the 68,220 square feet of glittering gold mosaics decorating the cathedral interior. The painted wooden ceiling dates from 1816–37. The roof commands a great view (a reward for climbing 172 stairs). Bonnano Pisano's bronze doors, completed in 1186, depict 42 biblical scenes and are considered among the most important of medieval artifacts. Barisano da Trani's 42 panels on the north door, dating from 1179, present saints and evangelists. ⊠ *Piazza del Duomo, Monreale* ⊕ *www.coopculture.it* ⊠ *€6; €13 including cloister.*

 Restaurants

La Botte 1962

$$ | SICILIAN | It's worth the short drive or inexpensive taxi ride from Monreale to reach this restaurant, which is famous for well-prepared local specialties (just keep in mind it has limited open hours, so call before you come). Seafood dishes might include *bavette don Carmelo,* a pasta dish with sauce of swordfish, squid, shrimp, and pine nuts, while other favorites include *tagliatelle al ragout di cinghiale* (pasta ribbons with wild boar sauce) and grilled beef fillet. **Known for:**

sophisticated cooking and local wines; good-value set menus; hazelnut semi-freddo with hot chocolate dessert. $ Average main: €18 ⊠ Contrada Lenzitti 20, SS186 Km 10, Monreale ☎ 091/414051, 338/4383962 mobile ⊕ www.maurizio-cascino.it ⊗ Closed Mon., Tues., and Aug. No lunch Fri. and Sat. Sept–June. No dinner Sun.

Segesta

85 km (53 miles) southwest of Palermo.

Segesta is the site of one of Sicily's most impressive temples, constructed on the side of a barren windswept hill overlooking a valley of giant fennel. Virtually intact today, the temple is considered by some to be finer in its proportions and setting than any other Doric temple left standing.

GETTING HERE AND AROUND

At least four Tarantola e Cuffaro buses travel from Trapani to Segesta every day but Sunday. About as many trains from Palermo and Trapani stop at the Segesta–Tempio station, a 20-minute uphill walk from Segesta. The site is easily reached via the A29 autostrada.

BUS CONTACT Tarantola e Cuffaro.
☎ 0924/31020 ⊕ www.tarantolacuffaro.it.

 Sights

★ Parco Archeologico di Segesta
(*Doric Temple*)

RUINS | Segesta's imposing temple was actually started in the 5th century BC by the Elymians, who may have been refugees from Troy—or at least non-Greeks, since it seems they often sided with Carthage. In any case, the style of the temple is in many ways Greek, but it was never finished; the walls and roof never materialized, and the columns were never fluted.

Wear comfortable shoes, as you need to park your car in the lot at the bottom of

the hill and walk about five minutes up to the temple. If you're up for a longer hike, a little more than 1 km (½ mile) away near the top of the hill are the remains of a fine theater with impressive views, especially at sunset, of the plains and the Bay of Castellammare (there's also a shuttle bus to the theater for €2.50 that leaves every 15–30 minutes). Concerts and plays are staged here in summer. ⊠ Contrada Barbaro, SR22, Calatafimi-Segesta ☎ 0924/952356 ⊕ www.parcodisegesta.com ☞ €10.

Erice

38 km (24 miles) south of San Vito Lo Capo, 15 km (9 miles) northeast of Trapani.

Perched 2,450 feet above sea level, Erice is an enchanting medieval mountaintop aerie of palaces, fountains, and cobblestone streets. Shaped like an equilateral triangle, the town was the ancient landmark Eryx, dedicated to Aphrodite (Venus). When the Normans arrived, they built a castle on Monte San Giuliano, where today there's a lovely public park with benches and belvederes offering striking views of Trapani, the Egadi Islands offshore, and, on a very clear day, Cape Bon and the Tunisian coast. Because of Erice's elevation, clouds conceal much of the view for most of winter. Sturdy shoes (for the cobblestones) and something warm to wear are recommended.

GETTING HERE AND AROUND

Make your approach via Trapani, which is on the A29 autostrada and well connected by bus and train with Marsala and Palermo. In late March to early January, a *funivia* (suspended cable car) runs from the outskirts of Trapani to Erice (Monday 2–8, Tuesday–Thursday 8:30–8, Friday and weekends 9:30–8:30; extended hours from late June to mid-September; see ⊕ www.funiviaerice.it for seasonal

details). Going by car or bus from Trapani takes around 40 minutes. By car, take the route via Valderice, not the "direct route," to avoid an extremely winding and steep country road. Buses depart from the terminal on Trapani's Piazza Malta.

 Restaurants

Monte San Giuliano

$$ | SICILIAN | At this traditional restaurant located on a side street near the main piazza, you can sit on a tree-lined patio overlooking the sea or in the white-walled dining room and munch on free panelle (chickpea fritters) while waiting for your main dish, which will be served tableside, spooned from the cooking pots to your plate by the friendly staff. The fresh pastas and couscous are exemplary, there are a few seafood mains (sea bass and baccalà often) and a glut of meat (lamb, pork, and veal). **Known for:** great pasta and couscous; charming setting; extensive and interesting wine list. ⑤ *Average main: €16* ⊠ *Vicolo San Rocco 7, Erice* ☎ *0923/869595* ⊕ *www. montesangiuliano.it* ⊗ *Closed Mon., 6 wks in Jan. and Feb., and 4 wks in Nov. and Dec.*

☕ Coffee and Quick Bites

★ La Tonda Fritta

$ | SICILIAN | Arancine—fried rice balls—are ubiquitous all over Sicily, but rarely do you find them prepared while you wait or offered in such a range as in this little snack shop near Porta Trapani. The menu lists more than 35 varieties, which include swordfish, smoked salmon, and curry fillings, as well as vegetarian and vegan options. **Known for:** more than 35 types of arancine; great snacks on the go; fast service. ⑤ *Average main: €4* ⊠ *Via Vittorio Emanuele 100, Erice* ☎ *328/1378708 mobile* ⊕ *www.facebook. com/latondafritta* ⊗ *Closed Nov.–Feb.*

Pasticceria Grammatico

$ | BAKERY | Fans of Sicilian sweets and pastries make a beeline for this place run by Maria Grammatico, who gained international fame with *Bitter Almonds*, her life story of growing up in a convent orphanage, cowritten with Mary Taylor Simeti. Her almond-paste creations are works of art, molded into striking shapes, including dolls and animals. **Known for:** delicious pastries, sweets and biscuits; uniquely shaped desserts; nice views. ⑤ *Average main: €5* ⊠ *Via Vittorio Emanuele 14, Erice* ☎ *0923/869390* ⊕ *www. mariagrammatico.it* ⊗ *Closed Wed.*

🛏 Hotels

Moderno

$ | HOTEL | This delightful hotel has a creaky old feel to it, but that's part of the charm—the lobby area, scattered with books, magazines, and tchotchkes, calls to mind an elderly relative's living room; but the rooms themselves are simple, light, and comfortable. **Pros:** central location; great rooftop terrace; well-regarded restaurant. **Cons:** very modest rooms; street-facing rooms can be noisy; old-fashioned feel not for everyone. ⑤ *Rooms from: €90* ⊠ *Via Vittorio Emanuele 67, Erice* ☎ *0923/869300* ⊕ *www. hotelmodernoerice.it* ⇄ *40 rooms* ⦿| *Free Breakfast.*

🛍 Shopping

Ceramica Ericina

CERAMICS | Among Italians, Erice is known for the quality and delicate floral designs of its majolica ceramics, well represented in this ceramics store off Piazza San Domenico, one of the best in town. ⊠ *Via Gian Filippa Guarnotti 20, Erice* ☎ *334/2303855 mobile* ⊕ *www. facebook.com/CeramicaEricina.*

Trapani

11 km (7 miles) southwest of Erice, 30 km (19 miles) northwest of Segesta, 75 km (47 miles) southwest of Palermo.

The provincial capital of Trapani (both province and city share the same name) was originally founded by the ancient Elymians, who claimed descent from the Trojans, as a port for Eryx (Erice). Its Greek name, Drepanon, meaning "sickle," refers to the long, curving limb of land trailing into the sea on which the city is built. Much of its later wealth was founded on the salt pans lying to the south that are still active today.

Although the outskirts of town are uninspiring, Trapani's old town has a busy, buzzy feel to it, especially in the evenings when families crowd the main, pedestrianized Corso Vittorio Emanuele and bars and restaurants spill onto the street. Via Garibaldi, linking the old and new districts, is also a busy shopping and promenading thoroughfare. North of the hydrofoil port, the old Jewish quarter is a warren of somewhat down-at-heel alleys centered on the 16th-century Palazzo della Giudecca on Via della Giudecca.

Linked to Palermo and Mazara del Vallo by autostrada A20, the town has its own airport and is also an important nexus for trips to Erice, Mozia, San Vito Lo Capo, and the Egadi Islands.

GETTING HERE AND AROUND

Trapani's airport is located in Birgi, 15 km (9 miles) to the south. The town is linked to Palermo by the A29 autostrada and by infrequent slow trains. Most using public transport travel on the much faster bus services, which all terminate at Piazza Malta, though fast buses from the airport, Palermo, Palermo airport, and Agrigento also make a stop at the ferry and hydrofoil port.

With much of the old town closed to traffic and available parking spots hard to find,

drivers should take advantage of the large and inexpensive car park on Piazza Vittorio Emanuele, at the bottom of Via Garibaldi. The old town is easy to negotiate on foot, though visitors to the Museo Pepoli and Santuario Annunziata should either drive or make use of the frequent city bus services.

Tickets to the Egadi islands can be picked up from the ticket offices at the port or from the Egatour agency, which also offers island tours, tickets for Pantelleria, and bus tickets.

AIRPORT CONTACT Trapani–Birgi Airport. ⊠ *Trapani* ☎ *0923/610111* ⊕ *www.airgest. it.*

◉ Sights

Museo Regionale Pepoli

ART MUSEUM | Trapani's foremost museum collection is located in a former Carmelite monastery that was attached to the important religious site of Santuario dell'Annunziata. The art sections take in some excellent examples of medieval and Renaissance art, including statuary by Antonello Gagini and a painting by Titian. Among the archaeological exhibits is a selection of low-key finds from Mozia and Selinunte. There's also a guillotine from 1800, and a good collection of memorabilia from Garibaldi's Sicilian campaign against the Bourbons in 1860.

The usual entrance to the museum is in the Villa Pepoli public garden; when this is closed enter from Via Madonna, behind the garden. ⊠ *Via Conte Agostino Pepoli 180, Trapani* ☎ *0923/553269* ⊕ *www2. regione.sicilia.it/beniculturali/museopepoli/museopepoli.html* 🎟 *€7* ⊗ *Closed Mon.*

Restaurants

Ai Lumi

$$ | SICILIAN | This popular restaurant on the pedestrianized Corso Vittorio Emanuele occupies some former stables, though the modern art on the walls and its candlelit tables evoke far more romantic

associations. Dishes are predominantly local and sea-based, like a delicious fish couscous, *ghiotta di pesce misto* (mixed seafood in a rich sauce of tomatoes, olives, and capers), and swordfish *involtini* (roulades) served with orange. **Known for:** quirky interiors; delicious local dishes; laid-back vibe. ⑤ *Average main: €16* ✉ *Corso Vittorio Emanuele 75, Trapani* ☎ *0923/872418* ⊕ *www.ailumi.it.*

☕ Coffee and Quick Bites

★ Meno Tredici

$ | ICE CREAM | FAMILY | There's a regular trickle of locals to this gelateria conveniently located opposite the hydrofoil port. Most opt for the local favorite: ice cream in a brioche with a couple of wafer biscuits poking out. **Known for:** tangy ice creams; thirst-quenching granitas; tasty desserts. ⑤ *Average main: €3* ✉ *Via Staiti 61, Trapani* ☎ *0923/1781797* ⊕ *www. gelateriamenotredici.it.*

🛏 Hotels

Room of Andrea

$$ | HOTEL | A 19th-century palazzo is now home to this hotel opposite a public garden in central Trapani, which provides pampering accommodation in swish surroundings. **Pros:** small rooftop pool; characterful surroundings and decor; good location. **Cons:** most rooms lack much of a view; no hotel parking; some rooms cramped. ⑤ *Rooms from: €160* ✉ *Viale Regina Margherita 31, Trapani* ☎ *0923/365728* ⊕ *www.roomofandrea.it* ⬆ *45 rooms* ⑩ *Free Breakfast.*

Marsala

30 km (19 miles) south of Trapani.

Marsala is readily associated with its world-famous, richly colored eponymous fortified wine, and your main reason for stopping may be to visit some of the many wineries in the area and sample the product. But this quiet seaside town, together with the nearby island of Mozia, was also once the main Carthaginian base in Sicily: it was from here that Carthage fought for supremacy over the island against Greece and Rome, leaving behind intriguing archaeological sites. In 1773, a British merchant named John Woodhouse happened upon the town and discovered that the wine here was as good as the port long imported by the British from Portugal. Two other wine merchants, Whitaker and Ingram, rushed in, and by 1800 Marsala was exporting wine all over the British Empire.

Later in the 18th century, Marsala played a significant role in the Risorgimento, the movement for Italian liberty. It was here that the swashbuckling national hero Giuseppe Garibaldi landed in 1860 with his thousand Redshirts to begin the campaign to oust the Bourbons from southern Italy.

GETTING HERE AND AROUND

Buses and trains from Palermo, Trapani, and Castelvetrano stop in Marsala. Drivers can take the coastal SS115.

VISITOR INFORMATION

CONTACT Marsala Tourism Office. ✉ *Via XI Maggio 100, Marsala* ☎ *0923/714097* ⊕ *www.turismocomunemarsala.com.*

👁 Sights

★ Donnafugata Winery

WINERY | A respected Sicilian wine producer, the 160-year-old Donnafugata Winery is open for tastings and tours of its *cantina* (wine cellar); reservations are required and can be made online or by phone. It's an interesting look at the wine-making process in Sicily, and it ends with a sampling of several whites and reds, an optional food pairing, and a chance to buy a bottle. Don't miss the delicious, full-bodied red Mille e Una Notte, and the famous Ben Ryè Passito di Pantelleria, a sweet dessert wine made from dried grapes.

✉ *Via Sebastiano Lipari 18, Marsala*
☎ *0923/724245* ⊕ *www.donnafugata.it*
🍽 *Tastings from €30* ⊗ *Closed Sun.*

★ Marsala Salt Pans

SCENIC DRIVE | Driving along the flat and winding coast road north of Marsala, you'll soon come across the extraordinary series of salt pans glistening in the shallows of Sicily's largest lagoon, the Stagnone di Marsala. The shallow depth of the lagoon, ranging from 2 to 6 feet, has made it perfect for the production of salt, and it has been put to this purpose since Phoenician times. The sheer flatness of the scene is varied only by the conical heaps of salt and a scattering of the disused windmills once used to supply power. The scene is still and quiet most of the time, but you'll sometimes see pockets of activity, with full wheelbarrows of salt being hauled to the conveyor belts that create the mounds. The stacks of earthenware tiles you'll see everywhere are used to weigh down the salt to prevent it being from blown away by gusts of wind. It's an extremely photogenic tableau, with the light changing through the day and Mozia and the Egadi archipelago looming through the haze.

The narrow coastal road is one-way for much of its length, and the cycle track running alongside it enables the area to be comfortably toured on two wheels. ✉ *Marsala.*

Museo Archeologico Baglio Anselmi

HISTORY MUSEUM | A sense of Marsala's past as a Carthaginian stronghold is captured by the well-preserved Punic warship displayed in this museum, along with some of the amphorae and other artifacts recovered from the wreck. The vessel, which was probably sunk during the great sea battle that ended the First Punic War in 241 BC, was dredged up from the mud near the Egadi Islands in the 1970s. There's also a good display of maritime and archaeological finds, as well as some Roman ruins with mosaics just beyond the museum's

doors. ✉ *Lungomare Boeo 30, Marsala*
☎ *0923/952535* ⊕ *www.turismocomune-marsala.com/museo-archeologico-lilibeo*
🍽 *€4* ⊗ *Closed Mon.*

Selunte

35 km (22 miles) southeast of Mazara del Vallo, 114 km (71 miles) southwest of Palermo.

Numerous ruined Greek temples perch on a high, undulating plateau overlooking the Mediterranean at Selinunte (or Selinus). The town is named after a local variety of wild celery (*Apium graveolens* or *petroselinum*) that in spring grows in profusion among the ruined columns and overturned capitals. Although the nearest village of Marinella di Selinunte is a rather unremarkable seaside resort, there are some very nice places to stay just inland as well as some good beaches, including Porto Palo and the wild dunes of the Foce del Belice nature reserve. Although many travelers treat Selinunte as a quick stop between the temples of Segesta and Agrigento, the area makes a very pleasant holiday base.

GETTING HERE AND AROUND

Selinunte is a half-hour drive from Mazara del Vallo, and an 85-minute drive from Agrigento, which means it can be easily visited via car as a day trip from any of the towns south along the coast. Getting here by public transport is trickier. There are four buses daily to Selinunte from the town of Castelvetrano, 11 km (7 miles) north, which is itself accessible from Palermo by bus and train.

Sights

★ Greek Temple Ruins

RUINS | Selinunte was one of the most important colonies of ancient Greece, recently discovered to have been home to the largest industrial quarter found in any ancient European city. Founded in the 7th century BC, the city became the rich and prosperous rival of Segesta, making its money on trade and manufacturing ceramics. When in 409 BC Segesta turned to the Carthaginians for help in vanquishing their rival, the Carthaginians sent an army to destroy Selinunte. The temples were demolished, the city was razed, and 16,000 of Selinunte's inhabitants were slaughtered. Archaeologists recently discovered pots with the remains of food inside, proof that some were in the middle of eating when the attackers arrived. The remains of Selinunte are in many ways unchanged from the day of its sacking—burn marks still scar the Greek columns, and much of the site still lies in rubble at its exact position of collapse. The original complex held seven temples scattered over two sites separated by a harbor. Of the seven, only one—reconstructed in 1958—is whole. ■TIP→ **This is a large archaeological site, so you might make use of the private navetta (shuttle) to save a bit of walking. Alternatively, if you have a car, you can visit the first temples close to the ticket office on foot and then drive westward to the farther site. Be prepared to show your ticket at various stages.** ☒ *SS115, Marinella Selinunte* ✛ *13 km (8 miles) southeast of Castelvetrano* ☏ *0924/923970* ⊕ *parchiarcheologici.regione.sicilia.it/selinunte-cave-cusa-pantelleria* ☒ *€10.*

🍽 Restaurants

Da Vittorio
$$ | SEAFOOD | Located right on the beach at Porto Palo, Da Vittorio is something of a local legend, highly regarded and much loved by everyone from wine and olive oil makers to celebrating families. The focus is on fresh fish and seafood, with pasta for the first course, and grilled fish for a second, all enhanced with traditional Sicilian flavors such as capers, almonds, and wild fennel. **Known for:** creative seafood on the beach; neighborhood institution since the 1960s; open all year

long. ⑤ *Average main: €17* ☒ *Via Friuli Venezia Giulia 9, Marinella Selinunte* ☏ *0925/78381* ⊕ *www.ristorantevittorio.it* ⊘ *Closed mid-Dec.–mid-Jan.*

Agrigento

8 km (5 miles) northeast of Porto Empedocle, 128 km (80 miles) south of Palermo.

Agrigento owes its fame almost exclusively to its stunning ancient Greek temples—though it was also the birthplace of playwright Luigi Pirandello (1867–1936) and the setting for the Montelusa scenes of Andrea Camilleri's Inspector Montalbano books. For fans of the books in particular, the old town is an evocative place for a wander, culminating in a visit to nuns for an almond pastry and the fascinating Museo di Santo Spirito. There is much to fascinate and intrigue in the area around Agrigento, too, both in the rural hinterland and along the coast south to Licata, scene of the Allied landings of 1943.

GETTING HERE AND AROUND
If you're driving, take the A19 autostrada to Caltanissetta, then follow the SS640 to Agrigento. Motorists can also access the town easily via the coastal SS115 and, from Palermo, by the SS189. Buses and trains run from Enna, Palermo, and Catania; both bus and train stations are centrally located.

VISITOR INFORMATION
CONTACT Agrigento Tourism Office. ☒ *Via Empedocle 73, Agrigento* ☏ *0922/20391* ⊕ *www.visitsicily.info.*

◉ Sights

Monastero di Santo Spirito
RELIGIOUS BUILDING | First built in 1299, these cloisters and courtyard, up the hill above the Valle dei Templi near the modern city, are open to the public. However, most visitors stop by the adjacent abbey

for a treat and tour of the church, so be sure to ring the doorbell and try the chewy almond cookies. On special occasions, there may be *kus-kus dolce*—a sweet dessert dish made from pistachio nuts, almonds, and chocolate—that the Cistercian nuns learned from Tunisian servants back in the 13th century. ⊠ *Cortile Santo Spirito 9, off Via Porcello, Agrigento* ☎ *0922/1552737* ⊕ *monasterosspirito.wixsite.com/agrigento.*

★ Valle dei Templi

RUINS | Along with the Acropolis in Athens, the monuments in the Valley of the Temples are considered to be the finest Greek ruins in the world. Built to celebrate the Greek victory over Carthage, the entire valley is awash with ancient grandeur. Of particular note are the eight pillars of the Tempio di Ercole (Temple of Hercules) that make up Agrigento's oldest temple complex, dating from the 6th century BC; the almost uncannily intact Tempio della Concordia (Temple of Concord); and, at the top of the hill, the most graceful temple of all, the Tempio di Giunone (Temple of Juno). ⊠ *Zona Archeologica, Via dei Templi, Agrigento* ☎ *0922/1839996* ⊕ *www.parcovalledeitempli.it* 🎟 *€12, €16.80 with museum (free 1st Sun. of month).*

🍴 Restaurants

★ Il Re di Girgenti

$$ | **SICILIAN** | You might not expect to find an ultramodern—even hip—place to dine within a few minutes' drive of Agrigento's ancient temples, yet Il Re di Girgenti offers up pleasing versions of Sicilian classics in a trendy, country-chic atmosphere (think moody lighting and funky geometric tile floors mixed with walls lined with old-fashioned crockery and cookware) popular with young locals. The thoughtful wine list offers good prices on both local wines and those from throughout Sicily. **Known for:** Sicilian dishes with a twist; contemporary setting with lovely views; delightful wine selections.

Ⓢ*Average main: €21* ⊠ *Via Panoramica dei Templi 51, Agrigento* ☎ *0922/401388* ⊕ *www.ilredigirgenti.it* ⊘ *Closed Tues.*

Trattoria dei Templi

$$ | **SICILIAN** | Along a road on the way up to Agrigento proper from the temple area, this vaulted family-run restaurant serves up tasty traditional food, namely daily house-made pasta specials and plenty of fresh fish dishes, all prepared with Sicilian flair. Your best bet is to ask the advice of brothers Giuseppe and Simone, the owners and chief orchestrators in the restaurant, who can also help select a Sicilian wine to pair with your meal. **Known for:** exceptional antipasti, like carpaccio of cernia (grouper); fresh fish; good choice of local wines. Ⓢ*Average main: €15* ⊠ *Via Panoramica dei Templi 15, Agrigento* ☎ *0922/403110* ⊕ *www.facebook.com/trattoriadeitempli* ⊘ *Closed Sun.*

Hotels

Foresteria Baglio della Luna

$$$ | **HOTEL** | In the valley below the temples, fiery sunsets and moonlight cast a glow over the ancient 12th-century watchtower at the center of this farmhouse-hotel complex, which is composed of stone buildings surrounding a peaceful geranium- and ivy-filled courtyard and the garden beyond. **Pros:** quiet setting; pretty gardens; top-notch restaurant. **Cons:** hotel a little dark inside; no pool; location a bit remote. Ⓢ*Rooms from: €240* ⊠ *Via Serafino Amabile Guastella 1, Contrada Maddalusa, Agrigento* ☎ *0922/511061* ⊕ *www.bagliodellaluna.com* ⊘ *Closed Dec.–Feb.* 🛏 *23 rooms* 🍴*Free Breakfast.*

★ Villa Athena

$$$$ | **HOTEL** | The 18th-century Villa Athena, updated into a sleek, luxurious place to stay, complete with gorgeous manicured gardens and swimming pool, holds a privileged position directly overlooking the Temple of Concordia, a

10-minute walk away—an amazing sight both during the day and when it's lit up at night. **Pros:** unbeatable location for the Valle dei Templi, with phenomenal temple views; good restaurant and spa; plenty of free parking. **Cons:** lobby on the small side; expensive compared to other area options; lack of information on local attractions. $ *Rooms from: €400* ✉ *Via Passeggiata Archeologica 33, Agrigento* ☎ *0922/596288* ⊕ *www.hotelvillaathena. it* ⟿ *27 rooms* ⦿ *Free Breakfast.*

Enna

33 km (21 miles) northwest of Piazza Armerina.

Deep in Sicily's interior, the fortress city of Enna (altitude 2,844 feet) commands exceptional views of the surrounding rolling plains, and, in the distance, Mount Etna. It's the highest provincial capital in Italy and, thanks to its central location, is nicknamed the "Navel of Sicily." Virtually unknown by tourists and relatively untouched by industrialization, this lively town charms and prospers in a distinctly old-fashioned Sicilian way. Its surrounding towns and areas are also well worth exploring and will take you even further off the beaten track.

Due to its historic lack of tourists, the most appealing lodgings are outside town. Those short on time will discover that Enna makes a good stopover for a touch of sightseeing with lunch, as it is right along the autostrada about halfway between Palermo and Catania.

GETTING HERE AND AROUND

Just off the A19 autostrada, Enna is easily accessible by car. With the train station 5 km (3 miles) below the upper town, the most practical public transportation is by the efficient bus service from Palermo or Catania.

Sights

Castello di Lombardia

CASTLE/PALACE | Enna's narrow, winding streets are dominated at one end by the impressive cliff-hanging Castello di Lombardia, rebuilt by Frederick II to create an expansive summer residence on the foundations of an ancient Sicani fort raised more than 2,000 years ago. While there is little to see inside the castle, climb up the tower for great views from the dead center of the island—on a very clear day, you can see to all three coasts. Immediately to the south you see Lake Pergusa (dry, in late summer), now almost swallowed by Enna's sprawling suburbs and the racetrack around its perimeter. According to Greek mythology, this was where Persephone was abducted by Hades. While a prisoner in his underworld realm she ate six pomegranate seeds, and was therefore doomed to spend half of each year there. For the ancients, she emerged at springtime, triggering a display of wildflowers that can still be admired all over Sicily. ✉ *Piazza di Castello di Lombardia, Enna* ☎ *0935/24911* ⊕ *www.icastelli.it/it/sicilia/ enna/enna/castello-di-lombardia-a-en- na* 🎫 *€4 combined ticket with Torre di Federico II.*

Piazza Vittorio Emanuele

PLAZA/SQUARE | In town, head straight for Via Roma, which leads to Piazza Vittorio Emanuele—the center of Enna's shopping scene and evening passeggiata. The attached Piazza Crispi, dominated by what used to be the grand old Hotel Belvedere, affords breathtaking panoramas of the hillside and smoking Etna looming in the distance. The bronze fountain in the middle of the piazza is a reproduction of Gian Lorenzo Bernini's famous 17th-century sculpture *The Rape of Persephone,* a depiction of Hades abducting Persephone. ✉ *Piazza Vittorio Emanuele, Enna.*

Rocca di Cerere (*Rock of Demeter*)
VIEWPOINT | The Greek cult of Demeter, goddess of the harvest—known as Ceres to the Romans—was said to have centered on Enna, where its adherents built a temple atop the Rocca di Cerere, protruding out on one end of town next to the Castello di Lombardia. The spot enjoys spectacular views of the expansive countryside and windswept Sicilian interior. ✉ *Enna* ☎ *0935/504717* ⊕ *www. roccadiceleregeopark.it.*

Torre di Federico II
VIEWPOINT | This mysterious octagonal tower stands above the lower part of town and has been celebrated for millennia as marking the exact geometric center of the island—thus the tower's (and the city's) nickname, Umbilicus Siciliae (Navel of Sicily). Climb the 97 steps of the spiral staircase for views over the city and beyond. ✉ *Enna* ☎ *329/8965116 mobile* ⊕ *www.pro-loco-enna-proserpina. it/torre-di-federico* 🎟 *€4, combined ticket with Castello di Lombardia.*

 Restaurants

Centrale
$$ | **SICILIAN** | Housed in an old palazzo, this casual place has served meals since 1889 and famously keeps a medieval specialty, *controfiletto all'Ennese* (a veal fillet with onions, artichokes, guanciale, and white wine), on the menu, in addition to a range of slightly more modern seasonal dishes. Choose from a decent selection of Sicilian wines to accompany your meal while you take in the large mirrored wall and local pottery. **Known for:** antipasti buffet; classic Sicilian dishes and local wines; atmospheric outdoor terrace in summer. 💲 *Average main: €19* ✉ *Piazza VI Dicembre 9, Enna* ☎ *0935/500963* ⊕ *www.ristorantecentrale.net* ⊘ *No lunch Sat. Sept.–Mar.*

Piazza Armerina

30 km (18 miles) northwest of Caltagirone.

Crowned by a mighty cathedral, the medieval hill town of Piazza Armerina is a magnificent sight from afar. Up close, the historic center's crumbling yellow-stone architecture with Sicily's trademark bulbous balconies creates quite an effect despite a feeling of dilapidation and abandonment (most locals have moved to the modern suburbs). It is a place to visit rather than stay, with the most appealing lodging options in the surrounding countryside.

Piazza Armerina is most famous for the ancient Roman mosaics down the road at Villa Romana del Casale, but lovers of ancient history may be even more entranced by the huge and rarely visited Greek town of Morgantina and the incredible finds from the site, which once graced the galleries of the Getty museum in Malibu, California.

GETTING HERE AND AROUND
Piazza Armerina is linked to Catania, Enna, and Palermo by regular buses, with less frequent buses also connecting to Caltagirone. There's no train station.

TOURS
Serena Raffiotta
PRIVATE GUIDES | A freelance archeologist and researcher, Serena is the perfect guide to Morgantina and Aidone as well as the Villa Romana del Casale. She has also helped identify objects illegally excavated from Sicily's archeological sights, including a blue-painted curl of terra-cotta that was on display at the Getty Museum in Malibu. She identified it as belonging to the head of a god from Morgantina; it was repatriated to Italy in 2016 and is now displayed in the village of Aidone. ✉ *Piazza Armerina* ☎ *329/1561022 mobile* ⊕ *www.facebook.com/morgantinavilladelcasale* 🎟 *Half-day tour €150; full-day tour €250.*

VISITOR INFORMATION
CONTACT Piazza Armerina Tourism Office.
☒ Via Monsignore Sturzo 3, Piazza Arme-
rina ☎ 338/8524872 mobile.

 Sights

★ Villa Romana del Casale (*Imperial Roman Villa*)
HISTORIC HOME | The exceptionally well-preserved Imperial Roman Villa is thought to have been a hunting lodge of the emperor Maximian (3rd–4th century AD) and offers some of the best mosaics of the Roman world, artfully covering more than 12,000 square feet. The excavations were not begun until 1950, and most of the wall decorations and vaulting have been lost, but the shelter over the site hints at the layout of the original building. The peristyle leads to the main villa, where in the Salone del Circo you look down on mosaics illustrating scenes from the Circus Maximus in Rome. ☒ SP15, Contrada Casale, 4 km (2½ miles) southwest of Piazza Armerina, Piazza Armerina ☎ 0935/680036 ticket office, 0935/687667 office ⊕ www.villaromanadelcasale.it ☒ €12 (free 1st Sun. of month).

🍴 Restaurants

★ Al Fogher
$$ | MODERN ITALIAN | This culinary beacon in Sicily's interior features ambitious— and successful—dishes with the creative flair of chef Angelo Treno, whose unforgettable pastas topped with truffles or caviar, for example, offer a decidedly different expression of traditional regional ingredients. The unassuming and elegant dining room is inside an old railway house and is the perfect place to enjoy a bottle from the 500-label wine list; in cold weather, you can cozy up to a fireplace, but the terrace is the place to be in summer. **Known for:** sophisticated preparations; local ingredients; well-thought-out wine list. $ Average main:

€21 ☒ Contrada Bellia, Piazza Armerina ✠ Near SS117 bis, Aidone exit, about 1 km (½ mile) north of Piazza Cascino ☎ 0935/684123 ⊕ www.facebook.com/ristorantealfogher ⊘ Closed Mon. No dinner Sun.

Caltagirone

72 km (41 miles) northeast of Licata.

Built over three hills, Caltagirone's functional modern periphery gives way to an imposing, if slightly run-down, Baroque town center. The town is one of the main centers of Sicily's ceramics industry, evidenced by churches and palazzi featuring majolica decorations on their balustrades, domes, windowsills, and facades. The best-known sight is the monumental Scala Santa Maria del Monte.

GETTING HERE AND AROUND
Driving is the best way to get to Caltagirone. Regular buses from Catania stop in the lower town, which is a pleasant stroll from the center. Connections by bus with other towns in Sicily are infrequent, and train connections are even worse.

VISITOR INFORMATION
CONTACT Caltagirone Tourism Office.
☒ Via Volta Libertini 3, Caltagirone ☎ 0933/53809 ⊕ www.cittadicaltagirone.it.

 Sights

Museo della Ceramica
SPECIALTY MUSEUM | Caltagirone was declared a UNESCO World Heritage site for its ceramics as well as for its numerous Baroque churches. Although the museum offers little information in English about the beautiful items displayed in its many glass cases, you can still see one of Sicily's most extensive ceramics collections, ranging from Neolithic finds to red-figure pottery from 5th-century-BC Athens and 18th-century terra-cotta Nativity figures. ☒ Via Roma,

inside Giardini Pubblici, Caltagirone
☎ *0933/58418* ⊕ *parchiarcheologici.*
regione.sicilia.it/catania-valle-aci/biglietti/
museo-della-ceramica-caltagirone 🎟 *€5.*

★ Scala Santa Maria del Monte

VIEWPOINT | While you can see examples
of Caltagirone's long ceramic tradition
throughout the city, the most impressive display can be found in the 142
individually decorated tiled steps of this
monumental staircase leading up to the
neglected Santa Maria del Monte church.
On July 24 (the feast of San Giacomo,
the city's patron saint) and again on
August 15 (the feast of the Assumption),
the stairs are illuminated with candles
that form a tapestry design. Months of
work go into preparing the 4,000 *coppi,*
or cylinders of colored paper, that hold
oil lamps—then, at 9:30 pm on the
nights of July 24, July 25, August 14,
and August 15, a squad of hundreds of
youngsters (tourists are welcome to
participate) spring into action to light the
lamps, so that the staircase flares up all
at once. ✉ *Begins at Piazza Municipio,
Caltagirone.*

Ragusa

21 km (13 miles) northwest of Modica.

Ragusa, a modern city with a beautiful
historic core, is known for some great
local red wines and wonderful cheese—a
creamy, doughy, flavorful version of
caciocavallo, made by hand every step
of the way. It also has some wonderful
Baroque buildings with fabulous vantage
points throughout its narrow, twisty, and
steep old town.

GETTING HERE AND AROUND

Trains and buses leave from Siracusa four
or five times daily.

VISITOR INFORMATION

CONTACT Ragusa Tourism Office. ✉ *Piazza
della Repubblica, Ragusa* ☎ *0932/684780*
⊕ *www.visitragusa.it.*

Sights

Basilica di San Giorgio

CHURCH | Designed by Rosario Gagliardi
in 1738, the Duomo is a fine example
of the Sicilian Baroque. ✉ *Salita Duomo
15, Ragusa* ☎ *0932/220085* ⊕ *www.
duomosangiorgioragusa.it.*

Giardino Ibleo

GARDEN | Set on the edge of the old
town, Giardino Ibleo is a tranquil public
garden lined with palm trees and dotted
with fountains and churches along stone
paths. The ambling walkways skirt the
cliffside and offer dramatic views of the
valley below. ✉ *Via Giardino, Ragusa*
☎ *0932/652374.*

Ragusa Ibla

HISTORIC DISTRICT | The lovely historic
center of Ragusa, known as Ibla, was
completely rebuilt after the devastat-
ing earthquake of 1693. Its tumble of
buildings are perched on a hilltop and
suspended between a deep ravine and a
sloping valley. The tiny squares and narrow lanes make for pleasant meandering,
but expect plenty of stairs. ✉ *Ragusa.*

🍴 Restaurants

Duomo

$$$$ | **SICILIAN** | In an understated palazzo
on a cobblestone street near the Duomo,
star chef Ciccio Sultano prepares imaginative and beautifully plated splurge-wor-
thy dinners and a four-course set lunch
menu (a terrific value) that include
unforgettable variations on classic Sicilian
cuisine. Although dishes can be ordered
à la carte, tasting menus convey a fuller
sense of the chef's signature style,
which uses the finest ingredients from
around the island in subtly extravagant
combinations. **Known for:** being one of
Sicily's most renowned restaurants;
imaginative wine pairings; intriguing
range of set menus. ⑤ *Average main:
€45* ✉ *Via Capitano Bocchieri 31, Ragusa*
☎ *0932/651265* ⊕ *www.cicciosultano.it*

Closed early Jan.–mid-Mar. and Sun. No lunch Mon., except in Aug.

Locanda Gulfi

$$ | SICILIAN | On the grounds of the expansive Gulfi winery, which produces well-regarded organic wines, you'll find a unique place for a sophisticated lunch or dinner, with sweeping views of the Chiaramonte hills and vineyards (about a half-hour drive north of Ragusa). The chef skillfully uses local ingredients to prepare Sicilian dishes with a twist in the modern dining room which features handblown chandeliers and a design-focused black-and-red color scheme; in warmer months, enjoy your meal on the lovely terrace. **Known for:** seasonal, local Sicilian dishes; renowned Gulfi wine; vineyard views and an inn to stay the night. ⑤ *Average main: €18* ✉ *Contrada Patria, Chiaramonte Gulfi* ☎ *0932/928081 reservations, 0932/921654 winery* ⊕ *www.locandagulfi.it.*

 Hotels

★ Eremo della Giubiliana

$$ | B&B/INN | Set in the countryside, a 20-minute drive from Ragusa, this charming family-run monastery-turned-hotel features friendly service and a relaxed but luxurious vibe, with unique rooms in former monks' chambers that vary in size and lay-out but are all quiet and well-appointed. **Pros:** peaceful atmosphere; rooms filled with character; top-notch service. **Cons:** grounds, while lovely, could use better upkeep; restaurant food could be better; no other nearby eateries due to remote location. ⑤ *Rooms from: €145* ✉ *Contrada Giubiliana, Marina di Ragusa* ☎ *0932/669119* ⊕ *www.eremodellagiubiliana.it* ⏎ *24 rooms* ⦿ *Free Breakfast.*

★ Locanda Don Serafino

$$ | HOTEL | This small boutique hotel offers contemporary rooms and excellent service inside a historic manor house in the heart of Ragusa Ibla—one of the rooms has a bathroom inside a natural cave. **Pros:** modern design in a historic setting; incredibly attentive staff; valet parking service. **Cons:** bathrooms can be small or quirky; some rooms are a few doors down from the main building; steep stairs limit the accessibility of some rooms. ⑤ *Rooms from: €158* ✉ *Via XI Febbraio 15, Ragusa* ☎ *0932/220065 hotel, 0932/248778 restaurant* ⊕ *www.locandadonserafino.it* ⦿ *Closed early Feb.–early Mar.* ⏎ *11 rooms* ⦿ *Free Breakfast.*

Modica

37 km (23 miles) west of Noto.

Modica and Ragusa are the two chief cities in Sicily's smallest province (also called Ragusa), and the centers of a region dominated by the limestone hills of the Monti Iblei. The dry, rocky, and gentle countryside filled with canyons and grassy knolls is a unique landscape for Sicily. In Modica, the main artery—Corso Umberto I—is lined with shops and restaurants and is in the valley at the bottom of the town (called Modica Bassa), while the old town of Modica Alta is built atop a ridge. That's part of this UNESCO-listed area's charm; it's a joy to wander its steep 14th-century lanes traversed by endless staircases and lined with Baroque architecture. Modica is also famed for its chocolate—don't miss trying it at one of the many stores on Corso Umberto I.

GETTING HERE AND AROUND

Trains leave from Siracusa six times a day, while buses from Catania, Siracusa, Ragusa, and Noto also stop in Modica on a regular basis.

VISITOR INFORMATION

CONTACT Modica Tourism Office. ✉ *Corso Umberto I 141, Modica* ☎ *346/6558227 mobile* ⊕ *comunemodica.rg.it/site/ufficio-turistico/.*

⊙ Sights

Cattedrale di San Pietro

CHURCH | Statues of the apostles line the staircase of Modica's cathedral, which was originally constructed in the 14th century, then rebuilt in an impressive Baroque style following its destruction in the 1693 earthquake. ⊠ *Corso Umberto I 120, Modica* ☎ *0932/941074* ⊕ *www. scoprimodica.it/cosa-vedere/le-chiese/ san-pietro* ⊠ *Free.*

★ Chiesa di San Giorgio

CHURCH | This lovely Baroque church in Modica Alta, dating from after the 1693 earthquake, is reached by climbing 250 steps that crisscross in a monumental staircase leading up to the main doors. It's worth the effort for the amazing views over the old town. ⊠ *Corso San Giorgio, Modica* ☎ *0932/941279* ⊕ *www. scoprimodica.it/cosa-vedere/le-chiese/ san-giorgio* ⊠ *Free.*

Museo del Cioccolato di Modica

SPECIALTY MUSEUM | There is an abundance of choice when it comes to indulgent desserts in Sicily, but the chocolate of Modica—cooked at a low temperature and possessed of a distinctive granular texture—is prized above all others. It feels only natural, then, to find a museum in the center of the old town dedicated to the local sweet. The small exhibits (with English translations) follow the history of chocolate in general, before describing the way cacao beans first arrived in Modica and how they were traditionally processed by being ground on a board made of volcanic stone. There is also an eccentric collection of sculptures and celebrity portraits made entirely of chocolate. ⊠ *Corso Umberto I 149, 1st fl., behind Museo Civico, Modica* ☎ *347/4612771 mobile* ⊕ *www.facebook. com/museocioccolatomodica* ⊠ *€3* ⊙ *Closed Mon.*

🍽 Restaurants

★ Accursio Ristorante

$$$$ | SICILIAN | This intimate Michelin-starred restaurant is a fantastic option if you are staying in Modica overnight. Forget the usual starchy tablecloths and formal service, this place is all about the food, with the chef cooking his own personal takes on classic Sicilian dishes, including options like *trucioli* pasta with cheese fondue, lemon, capers, and coffee; grilled lettuce with pork cheek, caviar, and walnuts; and cannoli with ricotta cheese and cotton candy for dessert. **Known for:** relaxed atmosphere; equally extensive and more affordable lunch menu; Michelin-starred food at reasonable prices. ⑤ *Average main: €45* ⊠ *Via Grimaldi 41, Modica* ☎ *0932/941689* ⊕ *www.accursioristorante.it* ⊙ *Closed Mon. No dinner Sun. No lunch Tues.*

☕ Coffee and Quick Bites

Pasticceria Di Lorenzo

$ | BAKERY | FAMILY | Wood-lined and unadorned, this family-run pastry shop is one of the best places to try Modica's signature crescent-shape cookies, the *'mpanatigghi*. These soft cookies are filled with a mixture of chocolate, almonds, and veal, a combination that works surprisingly well. **Known for:** chocolate squares that resemble the city's cobblestones; specialty cookies; family-run. ⑤ *Average main: €5* ⊠ *Corso Umberto I 225, Modica* ☎ *0932/945324* ⊕ *www.pasticceriad-ilorenzo.it* ⊙ *Closed Wed.*

🛍 Shopping

★ Antica Dolceria Bonajuto

CHOCOLATE | Bonajuto is the oldest chocolate producer in town, dating from 1880. This busy shop on Modica Bassa's main street lets you sample many varieties of their delightful product before you buy, and also makes renowned cannoli and candied orange peel. Don't miss the wonderfully tongue-in-cheek video showing an American paratrooper during World War II, caught in a tree. He tries to bribe a little girl to get help with a Hershey bar, but she is unimpressed and wanders away eating Bonajuto chocolate. ✉ *Corso Umberto I 159, Modica* ☎ *0932/941225* ⊕ *www.bonajuto.it.*

Scicli

44 km (27 miles) west of Noto.

Overshadowed by its larger neighbors, Modica and Ragusa, Scicli is a Baroque beauty in its own right and one of the eight villages designated by UNESCO in the Val di Noto. In recent years, it has entered Italian popular culture as the filming location of the hugely popular *Montalbano* series, but its decorated stone palaces and unique Madonna delle Milizie (Virgin Mary of Militias) will delight visitors whether or not they know the Sicilian detective show.

GETTING HERE AND AROUND
Buses from Siracusa, Ragusa (by way of Modica), and Noto stop in Scicli on a regular basis.

Sights

Chiesa di San Bartolomeo
CHURCH | The fabulously voluptuous facade makes a stunning contrast with the limestone cliffs soaring above. An enchanting fusion of the Baroque and rococo lies behind the lace grate doors of this church on the edge of the town's historic center. Inside the single-nave church is a wooden nativity scene that dates back to the 16th century. ✉ *Via S. Bartolomeo, Scicli* ☎ *0932/931251* ⊕ *www.ilovescicli.it* ✆ *Free.*

Chiesa di Sant'Ignazio
CHURCH | Founded in the 17th century as a Jesuit church, this was rebuilt following the 1693 earthquake. Housing the remains of Scicli's patron saint

Guglielmo the hermit, a side chapel also hosts the life-size papier-mâché statue of the Madonna *su cavallo* (on a horse), the Madonna delle Milizie. This is paraded through the streets on the last Saturday in May to celebrate her feast day. ✉ *Piazza Italia, Scicli* ☎ *0932/931278* ⊕ *www.ilovescicli.it.*

Noto

38 km (23 miles) southwest of Siracusa.

If Siracusa's Baroque beauties whet your appetite for that over-the-top style, head to Noto, a UNESCO World Heritage site. Lying about 40 minutes away on the A18, the compact and easy-to-navigate city is doable as a day trip—though staying overnight lets you see the lovely buildings glow in the setting sun after the tourist hordes have departed. Noto's remarkable architectural integrity is due to the fact that the original town—known as Noto Antica and located 14 km (8 miles) away from the current town—was decimated by an earthquake in 1693. When it came to rebuilding, the present site was selected. It lies on a steep slope, with the palaces of the aristocrats concentrated in the lower town, with simpler housing for more ordinary folk, set on a grid plan in the upper town. The two sections are a short, steep walk from one another. A prime example of design from the island's Baroque heyday, it presents a pleasing ensemble of honey-color buildings, strikingly uniform in style but never dull. Simply walking Corso Vittorio Emanuele, the pedestrianized main street, qualifies as an aesthetic experience.

GETTING HERE AND AROUND
Trains leave from Siracusa at least eight times daily (fewer trains on Sunday); there are also four trains a day from Ragusa, though the station is a bit outside of town. Buses depart numerous times a day from Siracusa, Catania, and Ragusa.

VISITOR INFORMATION

CONTACT Noto Tourism Office. ⊠ *Corso Vittorio Emanuele 135, Noto* ☏ *339/4816218 mobile* ⊕ *www.notoinforma.it.*

Sights

★ Cattedrale di San Nicolò

CHURCH | Noto's domed cathedral (divine in more ways than one) is an undisputed highlight of the extraordinary Baroque architecture for which the town is world-famous. Climb the monumental staircase to get a glimpse of the interior—restored over a 10-year period after the dome collapsed in 1996—which is simple compared to the magnificent exterior, but still worth a look. ⊠ *Corso Vittorio Emanuele, Noto* ☏ *0931/835286* ⊕ *www.diocesinoto.it.*

Palazzo Nicolaci di Villadorata

CASTLE/PALACE | Set on a steep hill above the main Corso, the mythical monsters supporting the palace's magnificent balconies are one of the most iconic—and photographed—sights in Sicily. For a rare insight into the lifestyle of social climbers in the 18th century you can take a tour of the interior to see some of 90 rooms belonging to the noble Nicolaci family, the highlight being the splendid frescoed ballroom. ⊠ *Via Corrado Nicolaci, Noto* ☏ *338/7427022 mobile* ⊠ *€4.*

🍴 Restaurants

Anche gli Angeli

$$$ | **ITALIAN** | Part concept store, part bar, and part fine gourmet dining experience, this unique eatery is built into a grotto underneath the Chiesa di San Carlo and specializes in deceptively simple grilled dishes and contemporary cocktails. There's live music on the weekends, but it's quite laid-back and unobtrusive. **Known for:** beautiful design under historic arched ceiling; excellent burrata-filled ravioli; high-end takes on local meat dishes. ⑤ *Average main: €25* ⊠ *Via Arnaldo*

da Brescia 2, Noto ☏ 0931/576023 ⊕ www.anchegliangeli.it.

★ Ristorante Crocifisso

$$$ | **SICILIAN** | Considered by many as one of Noto's best restaurants, getting to Crocifisso is a bit of a hike as it's in the upper town. Most walking routes involve long flights of steps, although you could also take a car or taxi up around the edge of town. **Known for:** new takes on classic Sicilian dishes; the a la carte menu requires a minimum of two courses per person; fantastic wine selection with a focus on Sicilian and natural wines. ⑤ *Average main: €80* ⊠ *Via Principe Umberto 48, Noto* ☏ *0931/968608* ⊕ *www.ristorantecrocifisso.it* ⊗ *Closed mid-Jan.–late Feb. and Wed. No lunch Tues. and Thurs.*

★ Ristorante Manna

$$$ | **SICILIAN** | The plain exterior here gives no hint of the sleek, cool design inside this welcoming restaurant just off of Noto's main street where all of the dishes—from fresh pastas to creative seafood and exceptional daily specials— shine a light on local premium ingredients. Although the small outdoor patio allows for great people-watching, it's inside that the restaurant really shines; the chic multilevel dining area highlights modern art, a stylish complement to the restaurant's thoroughly modern food. **Known for:** modern, creative Sicilian cuisine; delightful staff; cool, contemporary setting. ⑤ *Average main: €25* ⊠ *Via Rocco Pirri 19, Noto* ☏ *0931/836051* ⊕ *www. mannanoto.it* ⊗ *Closed Nov., Jan.–Mar., and Tues. No lunch weekdays.*

☕ Coffee and Quick Bites

Caffè Sicilia

$ | **BAKERY** | When you need a break from the architectural eye candy, indulge in an edible sweet (and a restorative coffee or granita) at this wondrous cake shop. Their cannoli, biscotti, and gelato are particularly highly rated and considered some of the best in the country. **Known for:**

perfect almond granita; delicious cannoli; house-made ice cream. $ *Average main:* €5 ✉ *Corso Vittorio Emanuele 125, Noto* ☎ *0931/835013* ⊕ *www.caffesicilia.it* ⊘ *Closed Nov. and mid-Jan.–late Mar.*

🛏 Hotels

Gagliardi Boutique Hotel

$$$ | HOTEL | For an unbeatable location only a block from the main pedestrian street, visitors to Noto can't do better than this hotel with an industrial vibe and spacious minimalist rooms accented with chandeliers—all inside a former 18th-century palace. **Pros:** extremely central location; friendly service; large rooms and good public spaces. **Cons:** only one room has a bathtub; tricky parking—ask ahead; short on amenities (no restaurant, spa, or pool). $ *Rooms from: €238* ✉ *Via Silvio Spaventa 41, Noto* ☎ *0931/839730* ⊕ *www.gagliardihotel.com* ⌁ *11 rooms* ⫟◯⫠ *Free Breakfast.*

Siracusa

28 km (17 miles) northeast of Noto.

Siracusa, known to English speakers as Syracuse, is a wonder to behold. One of the great ancient capitals of Western civilization, the city was founded in 734 BC by Greek colonists from Corinth and soon grew to rival—and even surpass—Athens in splendor and power. It became the largest, wealthiest city-state in the west and a bulwark of Greek civilization. Although Siracusa lived under tyranny, rulers such as Dionysius filled their courts with Greeks of the highest cultural stature—among them the playwrights Aeschylus and Euripides and the philosopher Plato. The Athenians, who didn't welcome Siracusa's rise, set out to conquer Sicily, but the natives outsmarted them in what was one of the greatest military campaigns in ancient history (413 BC). The city continued to prosper until it was conquered two centuries later by the Romans.

Present-day Siracusa still has some of the finest examples of Baroque art and architecture; dramatic Greek and Roman ruins; and a Duomo that's the stuff of legend—a microcosm of the city's entire history in one building. The modern city also has a wonderful, lively Baroque old town worthy of extensive exploration, as well as pleasant piazzas, outdoor cafés and bars, and a wide assortment of excellent seafood. There are essentially two areas to explore in Siracusa: the Parco Archeologico (Archaeological Zone) on the mainland, and the island of Ortigia, the ancient city first inhabited by the Greeks, which juts out into the Ionian Sea and is connected to the mainland by two small bridges. Ortigia has become increasingly popular with tourists, and although it's filled with lots of modern boutiques (and tourist shops), it still retains its charm despite the crowds.

GETTING HERE AND AROUND
On the main train line from Messina and Catania, Siracusa is also linked to Catania and the nearby Val di Noto by frequent buses.

Although Ortigia is a compact area and a pleasure to amble around without getting unduly tired, mainland Siracusa is a grid of wide modern avenues. At the northern end of Corso Gelone, above Viale Paolo Orsi, the orderly grid gives way to the ancient quarter of Neapolis, where the sprawling Parco Archeologico is accessible from Viale Teracati (an extension of Corso Gelone). East of Viale Teracati, about a 10-minute walk from the Parco Archeologico, the district of Tyche holds the archaeological museum and the church and catacombs of San Giovanni, both off Viale Teocrito (drive or take a taxi or city bus from Ortigia). Coming from the train station, it's a 15-minute trudge to Ortigia along Via Francesco Crispi and Corso Umberto. If you're not up for that, take a taxi. Siracusa's bus system is terribly unreliable and best avoided.

At the Parco Archeologico della Neapolis, walk inside the Ear of Dionysius (the Greek god of wine, fertility, and religious ecstasy), which was used as a prison in ancient Greek times.

VISITOR INFORMATION

CONTACT Siracusa Tourism Office. ✉ *Via Roma 31, Ortigia* ☎ *800/055500* ⊕ *www. siracusaturismo.net.*

Archaeological Zone

Sights

Catacomba di San Giovanni

RUINS | Not far from the Archaeological Park, off Viale Teocrito, the catacombs below the church of San Giovanni are one of the earliest known Christian sites in the city. Inside the crypt of San Marciano is an altar where St. Paul preached on his way through Sicily to Rome. The frescoes in this small chapel are mostly bright and fresh, though some dating from the 4th century AD show their age. To visit the catacombs, you must take a 45-minute guided tour (included with the admission price), which leaves about every half hour and is conducted in Italian and English. ✉ *Piazza San Giovanni, Tyche* ☎ *0931/64694* ⊕ *www.kairos-web.com* 🎫 *€10* ⊙ *Closed Mon. and Jan.*

Museo Archeologico Regionale Paolo Orsi

HISTORY MUSEUM | The impressive collection of Siracusa's splendid archaeological museum is organized by region and time period around a central atrium and ranges from Neolithic pottery to fine Greek statues and vases. Compare the Landolina Venus—a headless goddess of love who rises out of the sea in measured modesty (a 1st-century-AD Roman copy of the Greek original)—with the much earlier (300 BC) elegant Greek statue of Hercules in Section C. Of a completely different style is a marvelous fanged Gorgon, its tongue sticking out, that once adorned the cornice of the Temple of Athena to ward off evildoers. ✉ *Viale Teocrito 66, Tyche* ☎ *0931/489514* ⊕ *www.aditusculture.com* 🎫 *€10; combined ticket with Parco Archeologico della Neapolis €19* ⊙ *Closed Mon.*

★ Parco Archeologico della Neapolis

RUINS | Siracusa is most famous for its dramatic set of Greek and Roman ruins, which are considered to be some of the best archaeological sites in all of Italy and should be combined with a stop at the Museo Archeologico. If the park is closed, go up Viale G. Rizzo from Viale Teracati to the belvedere overlooking the ruins, which are floodlit at night. The Teatro Greco is the chief monument in the Archaeological Park. Indeed it's one of Sicily's greatest classical sites and the most complete Greek theater surviving from antiquity. Climb to the top of the seating area (which could accommodate 15,000) for a fine view: all the seats converge upon a single point—the stage—which has the natural scenery and the sky as its backdrop. ⊠ *Viale Teocrito, entrance on Via Agnello, Archaeological Zone* ☎ *0931/489511* ⊕ *www.aditusculture.com* ⊠ *€13.50, combined ticket with Museo Archeologico €19.*

☕ Coffee and Quick Bites

Leonardi

$ | **BAKERY** | For some great Sicilian cakes and ice cream on your way to the Archaeological Park, visit this bar-cum-*pasticceria*. It's popular with locals, especially on Sunday mornings, when they come for a late breakfast and take away golden trays of exquisite pastries for lunch, so you may have to line up for your cakes.
Known for: great coffee and cakes; a favorite of locals; handy location near the Archaeological Park. **$** *Average main: €3* ⊠ *Viale Teocrito 123, Tyche* ☎ *0931/61411* ⊕ *pasticcerialeonardi.com.*

Hotels

Grand Hotel Villa Politi

$$ | **HOTEL** | Winston Churchill, European royalty, and other VIPs have frequented the grand 18th-century Villa Politi, and although it's now a little faded, it retains a sense of charm and elegance with rococo furnishings alongside modern luxuries like comfy beds. **Pros:** excellent service; free parking in the hotel lot; expansive outdoor pool and nearby private beach. **Cons:** a fair distance from the sights of Ortigia; not many restaurants in the neighborhood; not as sparkling and fresh as in the past. **$** *Rooms from: €132* ⊠ *Via M. Politi 2, Archaeological Zone* ☎ *0931/412121* ⊕ *www.villapoliti.com* ⊷ *100 rooms* ⦿ *Free Breakfast.*

🎟 Performing Arts

Teatro Greco (*Greek Theater*)

THEATER | From early May to mid-July, Siracusa's ancient Teatro Greco stages performances of classical tragedy and comedy. Tickets begin from €28. The ticket office is at ⊠ *Corso Matteotti 29,* in Ortigia. ⊠ *Via del Teatro Greco, Archaeological Zone* ☎ *0931/487248 ticket office* ⊕ *www.indafondazione.org.*

Ortigia
⊙ Sights

Castello Maniace

CASTLE/PALACE | The southern tip of Ortigia island is occupied by this castle built by Frederick II (1194–1250), from which there are fine sea views (until recently, it was an army barracks). The grounds (with bar) are open to the public and have become a popular spot for picnics and lunch breaks. Highlights of the castle are the vaulted main hall and the cannon emplacements in the basement—at their most evocative on stormy days when you can hear the waves crashing against the walls. Contemporary art shows, usually featuring sculpture, are staged in the cathedral-like interiors and even in the surrounding waters. ⊠ *Via del Castello Maniace 51, Ortigia* ☎ *0931/4508211* ⊕ *www.aditusculture.com* ⊠ *€5; €9 with exhibition.*

Siracusa with Ortigia Island

KEY

- **1** *Sights*
- **1** *Restaurants*
- **1** *Quick Bites*
- **1** *Hotels*

Piazza Sant Lucia

Via Trapani

Via T. Cadorna

Riviera Dionisib il Grande

Via Agatocle

Viale A. Diaz

Porto Piccolo

V. Reg. Margherita

Corso Umberto Primo

Via Malta

Lungomare di Levante E. Vittorini

Via Vittoria Veneto

IONIAN SEA

Via Triente

Via Trento

V. De Benedictis

Piazza Pancali

Via del Mille

Via XX Settembre

Via Spirito

Via Resalibera

Via Mirabella

Via V. Veneto

Via Cavour

Via Diane

Ortigia Island

Via Maestranza

Via Roma

Palazzo Beneventano del Bosco

Foro Vittorio Emanuele Secondo

Piazza del Duomo

Santa Lucia alla Badia

Via Capodieci

Via Nizza

Porto Grande

Via Maniace

Ortigia

Via Alfeo

IONIAN SEA

0   3/4 mile

0   1 km

★ Duomo di Siracusa

RELIGIOUS BUILDING | Siracusa's Duomo is an archive of more than 2,000 years of island history, and has creatively incorporated ruins through the many time periods it has survived, starting with the bottommost, where excavations have unearthed remnants of Sicily's distant past, when the Siculi inhabitants worshipped their deities here. During the 5th century BC (the same time Agrigento's Temple of Concord was built), the Greeks erected a temple to Athena over it, and in the 7th century, Siracusa's first Christian cathedral was built on top of the Greek structure. The massive columns of the original Greek temple were incorporated into the present structure and are clearly visible, embedded in the exterior wall along Via Minerva. The Greek columns were also used to dramatic advantage inside, where on one side they form chapels connected by elegant wrought-iron gates. The Baroque facade, added in the 18th century, displays a harmonious rhythm of concaves and convexes. In front, the sun-kissed stone piazza is encircled by pink and white oleanders and elegant buildings ornamented with filigree grillwork, and is typically filled with frolicking children and street musicians. Check with the tourist office for guided tours of its underground tunnels, which are located to the right when you stand facing the cathedral. ☒ *Piazza del Duomo, Ortigia* ☎ *0931/65328* ⊕ *arcidiocesi.siracusa.it/chiesa-cattedrale* 🎫 *€2.*

Fonte Aretusa

FOUNTAIN | A freshwater spring, the Fountain of Arethusa, sits next to the sea, studded with Egyptian papyrus that's reportedly natural. This anomaly is explained by a Greek legend that tells how the nymph Arethusa was changed into a fountain by the goddess Artemis (Diana) when she tried to escape the advances of the river god Alpheus. She fled from Greece, into the sea, with Alpheus in close pursuit, and emerged in Sicily at this spring. It's said if you throw a cup into the Alpheus River in Greece, it will emerge here at this fountain, which is home to a few tired ducks and some faded carp—but no cups. If you want to stand right by the fountain, you need to gain admission through the aquarium; otherwise look down on it from Largo Aretusa. ☒ *Largo Aretusa, Ortigia* ✛ *Off promenade along harbor* ☎ *0931/65861* ⊕ *www.fontearetusasiracusa.it* 🎫 *€5* ⊗ *Closed Tues.*

Galleria Regionale di Palazzo Bellomo

ART MUSEUM | Palazzo Bellomo looks unlike any other palace in Ortigia, a formidable 13th-century building, whose austere minimalist facade (with scarcely a window) could almost seem contemporary but dates from a time when Sicily was part of the Holy Roman Empire. Conflicts between Emperor Frederick II and the Pope were rife—the Pope was encouraging the mercantile cities Venice and Genoa to make war on Sicily, promising Siracusa as prize. That defense was paramount is not surprising. The Gothic upper floor was added, along with the courtyard—a perfect Shakespearean film set—in the 15th century. Highlight of the collection is an Annunciation by Antonello da Messina, painted for a church in Palazzolo Acreide, with the Hyblaean mountains visible through the windows behind the angel and the Madonna. Early Christian sculpture and a fine collection of altarpieces and icons are fascinating evidence of the enduring Byzantine and Gothic influence in Sicily. While the rest of Italy was swept by the Renaissance, Siracusa's artists were still painting heavily stylized Byzantine or Gothic works. ☒ *Via Capodieci 14, Ortigia* ☎ *0931/69511* ⊕ *aditusculture.com* 🎫 *€9* ⊗ *Closed Mon.*

Museo del Papiro

SPECIALTY MUSEUM | Housed in the 16th-century former convent of Sant'Agostino, the small but intriguing Papyrus Museum uses informative exhibits and videos to demonstrate how papyri are prepared from reeds and then painted—an ancient tradition in the city. Siracusa, it seems, has the only climate outside the Nile Valley in which the papyrus plant—from which the word "paper" comes—thrives. ⊠ *Via Nizza 14, Ortigia* ☏ *0931/22100* ⊕ *www.museodelpapiro. it* 🎫 *€5* ⊗ *Often closed for conferences and sporadic hours, so call ahead.*

Piazza Archimede

PLAZA/SQUARE | The center of this piazza has a Baroque fountain, the Fontana di Diana, festooned with fainting sea nymphs and dancing jets of water. Look for the Chiaramonte-style **Palazzo Montalto,** an arched-window gem just off the piazza on Via Montalto. ⊠ *Piazza Archimede, Ortigia.*

Tempio di Apollo

RUINS | Scattered through the piazza just across the bridge to Ortigia are the ruins of a temple dedicated to Apollo, which dates back to the 6th century BC. A model of this is in the Museo Archeologico. In fact, little of this noble Doric temple remains except for some crumbled walls and shattered columns; the window in the south wall belongs to a Norman church that was built much later on the same spot. ⊠ *Largo XXV Luglio, Ortigia* 🎫 *Free.*

Restaurants

Bianco Pepe

$$ | **PIZZA** | With tables on one of Ortigia's most picturesque piazzas—right below the rose-window of the roofless church of San Giovannino—the pizza chef here creates magnificent light crisp, blistered pizzas made of a tasty dough slow-risen for 48 hours. There's a dazzling and inspired choice, but the best pizzas are those with gourmet toppings—San Daniele prosciutto, buffalo mozzarella, burrata, chopped cherry tomatoes, homemade pesto, and even raw prawns, smoked tuna, and thyme-infused octopus—added as soon as the pizza base leaves the oven. **Known for:** inventive, original, and delicious gourmet pizza; romantic but casual outdoor dining on a beautiful piazza; pizza with burrata, cherry tomatoes, and homemade pesto. ⑤ *Average main: €15* ⊠ *Piazza del Precursore 7–9, Ortigia* ☏ *0931/1852406* ⊕ *www.facebook.com/ biancopepe.pepe* ⊗ *No lunch.*

★ Don Camillo

$$$ | **SICILIAN** | A gracious series of delicately arched rooms at this beloved local eatery are lined with wine bottles and sepia-tone images of the old town. À la carte preparations bring together fresh seafood and inspired creativity: sample, for instance, the sublime spaghetti *delle Sirene* (with sea urchin and shrimp in butter) or cod with saffron from the Iblean hills with a courgette puree. If you want, you can put yourself in the hands of the chef and opt for one of the exquisite tasting menus, which start at €80 excluding wine. **Known for:** fish, meat, and vegetarian tasting menus; helpful service; fantastic wine list. ⑤ *Average main: €25* ⊠ *Via Maestranza 96, Ortigia* ☏ *0931/67133* ⊕ *www.ristorantedon- camillosiracusa.it* ⊗ *Closed Sun., 2 wks in Jan., and 2 wks in July.*

Osteria Sveva

$$ | **SICILIAN** | At this slow-food tavern, conveniently located right behind the Castello Maniace, you can sit back and enjoy both surf and turf dishes in the vaulted interior or—even better—on the outdoor terrace. One major plus is that you can order half portions of several pasta dishes or opt for a secondo, like the unusual *pesce in crosta di patate* (grilled fish in a potato crust)—all served on hand-painted ceramic ware. **Known for:** authentic Sicilian dishes; good-value meals; charming setting on a square. ⑤ *Average main: €17* ⊠ *Piazza Federico di Svevia 1, Ortigia* ☏ *0931/24663* ⊗ *Closed Jan., Nov., and Wed. mid-Sept.–June. No lunch June–Sept.*

Hotels

★ Algilà Ortigia Charme Hotel

$$$ | **HOTEL** | It's hard to say what's more charming about this boutique hotel: its location overlooking the sea on the edge of the old town, or its delightful interiors, including guest rooms done up in country-chic style, with a mix of modern amenities (Bulgari toiletries, free minibar) and antique touches (wood-beamed ceilings, hand-painted tiles in the bathroom). **Pros:** wonderfully central location; prime water views; eager-to-please service with valet parking (fee). **Cons:** no spa, pool, or gym; lots of stairs could be an issue for some; not all rooms have sea views. ⑤ *Rooms from: €222* ✉ *Via Vittorio Veneto 93, Ortigia* ☎ *0931/465186* ⊕ *www. algila.it* ↪ *54 rooms* |◎| *Free Breakfast.*

★ Domus Mariae

$$ | **HOTEL** | On Ortigia's eastern shore, this hotel, in an unusual twist, is owned by Ursuline nuns, who help to make the mood placid and peaceful, but the elegant accommodations are far from monastic. **Pros:** decent breakfast; gorgeous sea views and rooftop terrace; enthusiastic staff. **Cons:** stairs to climb; not much street parking near the hotel; not all rooms spacious or with sea views. ⑤ *Rooms from: €175* ✉ *Via Vittorio Veneto 76, Ortigia* ☎ *0931/60087* ⊕ *www. domusmariaebenessere.com* ↪ *12 rooms* |◎| *Free Breakfast.*

Grand Hotel Ortigia

$$$ | **HOTEL** | An elegant though somewhat old-fashioned design of inlaid wood furniture and stained-glass windows prevails in the guest rooms at this venerable institution, which has enjoyed a prime position on the Porto Grande at the base of Ortigia since 1890. **Pros:** wonderful seafront views from the restaurant; private parking (a rarity on Ortigia); convenient location. **Cons:** back rooms have no view; small bathrooms; very pricey bar. ⑤ *Rooms from: €270* ✉ *Viale Mazzini 12, Ortigia*

☎ *0931/464611* ⊕ *www.grandhotelortigia. it* ↪ *57 rooms* |◎| *Free Breakfast.*

 Shopping

★ Ortigia Street Market

MARKET | This historic food market is still the daily shopping center for residents of Ortigia and mainland Siracusa. Seafood stalls display the catch of the day, ranging from local clams that you'll find in most restaurants to sea urchins that normally only appear on the more expensive menus. Even in the colder months, the vegetable and fruit stalls are still vibrant and inviting. One thing to look out for is the local Pachino tomato. It has protected status and can be found fresh, dried, or reduced to a gloriously intense thick paste called *strattu*, dried in the sun, which adds fantastic deep flavors to soups and pasta sauces. Intertwined within the stalls are several local bars where you can rest and take in the hustle and bustle of local Italian food culture. The market is open every day except for Sunday, from 7 am to 1:45 pm. ✉ *Vicolo Bagnara, Ortigia.*

Catania

210 km (130 miles) southeast of Palermo, 60 km (37 miles) north of Siracusa.

The chief wonder of Catania, Sicily's second city, is that it's there at all. Nearly every century has seen its share of tragedy for the Catanesi: a Greek tyrant that cast the population out, another who sold the majority of the citizens into slavery, Carthaginians who drove the successive occupants away once again. Each time, the city was rebuilt, only to meet more destruction. The plague hit hard in the Middle Ages, severely decimating the population. Mount Etna erupted in 1669, with a mile-wide stream of lava covering part of the city, and just 25 years after that, a disastrous earthquake forced Catania to begin again.

Today Catania is in the midst of yet another resurrection—this time from crime, filth, and urban decay. Although the city remains loud and full of traffic, signs of gentrification are everywhere. The elimination of vehicles from the Piazza del Duomo and the main artery of Via Etnea, and the cleaning of many of the historic buildings have added to its newfound charm. Home to what is arguably Sicily's best university, Catania is full of youthful exuberance, which comes through in its designer bistros, the chic osterias that serve wine, and the trendy boutiques that have cropped up all over town. Even more impressive is the vibrant cultural life.

GETTING HERE AND AROUND

Catania is well connected by bus and train with Messina, Taormina, Siracusa, Enna, and Palermo. The airport of Fontanarossa serves as a transportation hub for the eastern side of the island. From here you can get buses to most major destinations without going into the city center. The Alibus runs a loop from the airport through the city center (🚌 €4; approximately every 25 mins).

Within the city, use the AMTS bus service (🚌 €1 ⊕ www.amts.ct.it), which also connects to outlying areas such as Aci Castello. The website can be difficult to use, but the AMT Catania app offers useful route suggestions, online ticket purchasing, and timetables—and it's available in English. Catania also has an underground Metro line (🚌 €1 ⊕ www.circumetnea.it), but with only 10 stations centered on the downtown area, it's often easier to just walk.

VISITOR INFORMATION

CONTACT Catania Tourism Office. ⊠ Via Vittorio Emanuele II 172, Catania ☎ 095/7425573 ⊕ www.comune.catania.it/la-citta/turismo.

Sights

Amenano River

NATURE SIGHT | This underground river flows beneath much of Catania. You can glimpse it at the Fontana dell'Amenano, but the best place to experience the river is at the bar-restaurant A Putia dell'Ostello. Here you can sit at an underground table as swirls of water rush by. If you're not planning to stay for a drink, someone from the bar will sell you a €1 ticket to walk into the cavelike seating area. Aside from the underground river, the bar area aboveground is a lively, fun spot to hang out on a Monday evening when many other places are closed. ⊠ Piazza Currò 6, Catania ☎ 095/7233010 ⊕ www.agorahostel.com.

Cattedrale di Sant'Agata (Duomo)

CHURCH | Giovanni Vaccarini designed the contrasting black lava and white limestone facade of city's cathedral, which dominates the Piazza del Duomo and which houses the tomb of composer Vincenzo Bellini. Also of note are the three apses of lava that survive from the original Norman structure and a fresco from 1675 in the sacristy that portrays Catania's submission to Etna's eruption. Guided tours of the cathedral, which is dedicated to Catania's protector, are available in English if reserved in advance. The cathedral's treasures are on view in the Museo Diocesano Catania (⊕ www.museodiocesanocatania.com), and underneath the cathedral are the ruins of Greco-Roman baths. ⊠ Piazza del Duomo, bottom end of Via Etnea, Catania ☎ 095/320044, 339/4859942 mobile, for tours ⊕ www.cattedrale-catania.it 🏛 Museum €7, sacristy €3, baths €5; combined ticket €10.

Centro Storico

HISTORIC DISTRICT | Black lava stone from Etna, combined with largely Baroque architecture, give Catania's historic center a very distinctive feel. After Catania's destruction by lava and earthquake at the end of the 17th century, the city was rebuilt and its informal mascot "U Liotru" (an elephant carved out of lava balancing an Egyptian obelisk) was placed outside the cathedral as a kind of talisman. This square also marks the entrance to Catania's famous *pescheria* (fish market) and is one of the few points in the city where you can see the Amenano River aboveground. Another point of interest is Via Garibaldi, which runs from Piazza del Duomo up toward the impressively huge Porta Garibaldi, a black-and-white triumphal arch built in 1768 to commemorate the marriage of Ferdinando I. Also of note in the center are Castello Ursino, which is now a museum, the Greco-Roman theater off Via Vittorio Emanuele II, and the Roman amphitheater in Piazza Stesicoro. ⊠ *Catania.*

Via Etnea

STREET | With the ever-looming volcano perfectly framed at the end of the road, this main street is lined with cafés and stores selling high-street jewelry, clothing, and shoes. At sunset, it plays host to one of Sicily's most enthusiastic passeggiatas, in which Catanesi of all ages take part. From 2022 the central stretch became a pedestrianised zone, limiting all vehicle traffic. ⊠ *Via Etnea, Catania.*

🍴 Restaurants

★ Km.0

$$ | SICILIAN | For the best of what's locally in season, look to chef Marco Cannizzaro and his 25-seat fine-dining restaurant. Harvested from Etna to the Ionian Sea, the primary ingredients of the area simply shine in his hands: *Nerello mascelese* grapes show up as rich sauces, wild greens harvested from the slopes of Etna make their way into risottos or stuffed into tender calamari meatballs, and donkey, an economical protein staple of the area, is transformed into flavorful and refined tartare. **Known for:** Robiola cheese–stuffed smoked onion with strawberry; fine dining with

a neighborhood feel; four-, five-, or seven-course tasting menus. ⑤ *Average main: €22* ⊠ *Via Antonino Longo 26, Catania* ☏ *347/7327788 mobile* ⊕ *www.km0ristorante.com* ⊗ *Closed Wed. Closed Sun. in summer.*

Oasi Frutti di Mare da Nitto

$$ | SEAFOOD | Located in the Ognina port, the little Nitto empire has exploded: what began as a mobile market in the 1960s (from the back of a Piaggio Ape) is now a standing fresh fish market and series of restaurants. Locals line up outside the little market to get their daily catch, while next door the fast-casual restaurant serves some of the best-prepared seafood in the area, including squid ink pastas, skewers of grilled fish, and raw seafood platters. **Known for:** vivacious atmosphere; tuna agrodolce, a sweet-and-sour tuna side-dish studded with pine nuts and raisins; fresh-off-the-boat seafood. ⑤ *Average main: €20* ⊠ *Piazza Mancini Battaglia 6, Catania* ☏ *095/491165* ⊕ *www.nittopescheria.it.*

☕ Coffee and Quick Bites

Caffè del Duomo

$ | CAFÉ | Dive right into the hustle and bustle of Catania at Caffè del Duomo, which has handmade cookies and cakes and a great local atmosphere. The piazza-front location is the main draw, but the fantastic cannoli are another reason to stop for coffee and watch the world go by. **Known for:** great spot for people-watching; handmade treats; typical Sicilian breakfast. ⑤ *Average main: €5* ⊠ *Piazza Duomo 11–13, Catania* ☏ *095/7150556* ⊕ *www.caffedelduomo-catania.com.*

★ Scirocco Sicilian Fish Lab

$ | SEAFOOD | In the heart of the fish market, you'll find the best fritto misto (fried seafood mix) in the area. Walk up to the little counter on the stone balcony overlooking the action and place your order for a paper cone of fried seafood made with the lightest and crispiest batter. **Known for:** unique seafood sandwiches called tramezzini; superfresh seafood; fast service. $ *Average main: €7* ✉ *Piazza Alonzo di Benedetto 7, Catania* ☎ *095/8361194* ⊕ *www.sciroccolab.com.*

Hotels

⭐ Palazzo Marletta

$$$ | HOTEL | Baroque architecture punctuates the city, and one of the best ways to see it up close is with a stay at Palazzo Marletta, a private palace turned plush hotel. **Pros:** copious breakfast; prime location just off the Duomo; arrangement with a local car valet service for parking. **Cons:** some of the bathrooms have little privacy; can be difficult to navigate the historic district if arriving by car; modern rooms lack some of the charm of historic ones. $ *Rooms from: €295* ✉ *Via Erasmo Merletta 7, Catania* ☎ *380/2160253 mobile* ⊕ *www.palazzomarletta.it* ⇄ *7 rooms* ◯ *Free Breakfast.*

Una Hotel Palace

$$$ | HOTEL | For great views of Etna, this centrally located hotel overlooking Catania's main shopping street has a rooftop terrace where you can enjoy breakfast or take in the scenery during happy hour over a cocktail and antipasti buffet. **Pros:** amazing rooftop views; extremely central location; eager-to-please staff. **Cons:** bit of a generic feel; some noisy rooms; fee for parking. $ *Rooms from: €229* ✉ *Via Etnea 218, Catania* ☎ *095/2505111* ⊕ *www.gruppouna.it* ⇄ *94 rooms* ◯ *Free Breakfast.*

Acireale

6 km (4 miles) north of Aci Trezza, 16 km (10 miles) north of Catania.

Acireale sits amid a clutter of rocky pinnacles and lush lemon groves. The craggy coast is known as the Riviera dei Ciclopi, after the legend narrated in the *Odyssey* in which the blinded Cyclops, Polyphemus, hurled boulders at the retreating Ulysses, thus creating spires of rock, or *faraglioni* (pillars of rock rising dramatically out of the sea). Tourism has barely taken off here, so it's a good destination if you feel like putting some distance between yourself and the busloads of tourists in Taormina, or if seeking an easy day trip from Catania. And though the beaches are rocky, there's good swimming here, too.

GETTING HERE AND AROUND

Buses arrive frequently from Taormina and Catania. Acireale is on the main coastal train route, though the station is a long walk south of the center. Local buses pass every 20 minutes or so.

VISITOR INFORMATION

CONTACT Acireale Tourism Office. ✉ *Via Oreste Scionti 15, Acireale* ☎ *095/895249* ⊕ *www.visitsicily.info/en/acireale.*

Sights

Belvedere di Santa Caterina

VIEWPOINT | Lord Byron (1788–1824) visited the Belvedere di Santa Caterina to look out over the Ionian Sea during his Italian wanderings. Today, the viewing point is south of the old town, near the Terme di Acireale, off SS114, and is a tranquil spot for photos or quiet reflection on one of the several benches positioned toward the water. ✉ *Off SS114, Acireale.*

Duomo

CHURCH | With its cupola and twin turrets, Acireale's Duomo is an extravagant Baroque construction dating from the 17th century. In the chapel to the right of the altar, look for the 17th-century silver statue of Santa Venera (patron saint of Acireale) by Mario D'Angelo, and the early-18th-century frescoes by Antonio Filocamo. Climb up to the belvedere for stunning views. ✉ *Piazza del Duomo, Acireale* ☎ *095/601102* ⊕ *www.diocesiacireale.it* ⇄ *Tower access €2.50.*

Santa Maria La Scala

TOWN | A half-hour walk (or a very twisty drive) from Acireale's center, this picturesque harbor, with lava stone steps leading to the water, is filled with fishermen unloading brightly colored boats. Inexpensive lunches are served in the many restaurants along the harbor; your fresh fish dish is priced by weight. ⊠ *Santa Maria La Scala, Acireale* ⊕ *www. visitsicily.info/en/santa-maria-la-scala.*

🍴 Restaurants

★ La Grotta

$$$ | SEAFOOD | With its dining room set in a cave above the harbor of Santa Maria La Scala, this rustic trattoria specializes in seafood. Try the *insalata di mare* (a selection of delicately boiled fish served with lemon and olive oil), pasta with clams or cuttlefish ink, or fish grilled over charcoal. **Known for:** the catch of the day; superfresh seafood; unique cave setting. ⑤ *Average main: €27* ⊠ *Via Scalo Grande 46, Acireale* ☎ *095/7648153* ⊕ *www.facebook. com/77saro* ☉ *Closed Tues. and late Oct.*

☕ Coffee and Quick Bites

Gran Caffè Eldorado

$ | CAFÉ | Delicious ice creams and *granita di mandorla* (almond granita) make Eldorado a must-visit when in Acireale. Just steps from the cathedral, it makes for a nice *pausa caffè* during a day of sightseeing. **Known for:** great ice creams; wonderful desserts; friendly staff. ⑤ *Average main: €3* ⊠ *Corso Umberto 3, Acireale* ☎ *347/9717926 mobile.*

Mount Etna

30 km (19 miles) northwest of Acireale, 35 km (22 miles) north of Catania, 64 km (40 miles) southwest of Taormina.

The first time you see Mount Etna, whether it's trailing clouds of smoke or emitting fiery streaks of lava, is certain to be unforgettable. The best-known symbol of Sicily and one of the world's major active volcanoes, Etna is the largest and highest volcano in Europe—the cone of the crater rises 11,014 feet above sea level. Etna is so important to locals that she's often affectionately called Mamma Etna. Although you'll get wonderful vantage points of Etna from Taormina, Castelmola, and Catania in particular, it also makes a rewarding day or overnight trip to see the mountain up close, with a hike or climb; you can find routes suitable for every fitness level. It's also become a popular destination for wine lovers thanks to the many boutique wineries on its slopes; most accept visitors with an appointment.

GETTING HERE AND AROUND

Reaching the lower slopes of Mount Etna is easy, either by car or by bus from Catania. Getting to the more interesting, higher levels requires taking one of the stout four-wheel-drive minibuses that leave from Piano Provenzana on the north side and from Rifugio Sapienza on the south side. A cable car, called the Funivia dell'Etna, from Rifugio Sapienza takes you part of the way.

CABLE CAR Funivia dell'Etna. ⊠ *Piazzale Funivia, Etna Sud* ☎ *095/914141* ⊕ *www. funiviaetna.com.*

TOURS

★ Etna Experience

ADVENTURE TOURS | Your answer to all things outdoors in the area, Etna Experience offers sailing tours between Catania and Aci Trezza, full-day hikes to volcanic caves and the Alcantara gorges, half-day sunset hikes, wine tasting jaunts and the signature Mount Etna Summit tour, which includes high-level trekking up to 10,800 feet to get you as close to the crater as humanly possible. ☎ *349/3053021 mobile* ⊕ *www.etnaexperience.com* ⊠ *From €44.*

Eastern Sicily,
the Tyrrhenian Coast,
and the Aeolian Islands

AEOLIAN ISLANDS

TO NAPLES
TO NAPLES
TO TROPEA

Stromboli

Panarea

Alicudi **Filicudi** **Salina**

Lipari

TYRRHENIAN SEA

Vulcano

Golfo di Milazzo

Milazzo A20 **Villa San Giovanni** A3

113 **Messina**

Capo D'orlando 113 A20 Patti 113

St Agata di Militello 116 185 A18 114 **Reggio Calabria**

Cefalù *TYRRHENIAN COAST* 106

Caldura A20 113 A20

Pizzo Carbonara

117 Randazzo **Castelmola**

120 120 Linguaglossa **Taormina**

Nicosia Bronte **Mount Etna** Giardini-Naxos

121 Milo Riposto

A19 Adrano Zafferara Etnea Giarre

192 Biancavilla Trecastagni Barone di Villagrande

Enna Nicolosi Santa Maria La Scala

Caltanissetta Paterno **Acireale**

288 **Catania** Aci Castello

Villa Romana del Casale Aci Trezza

Piazza Armerina 417 *Golfo di Catania*

626 191 Casale 117b 385 Agnone

Mazzarino Palagonia

194 Lentini **Augusta** *IONIAN SEA*

Caltagirone 124

115 Vizzini Euryalus

Gela 194 Palazzolo Acreide **Siracusa with Ortigia Island** see detail map

115 Vittoria 124 A18 115

Golfo di Gela Comiso **Ragusa** **Noto** Avola

Modica *Golfo di Noto*

Scicli

Pachino

TO MALTA

MEDITERRANEAN SEA *Capo Passero*

0 — 20 mi
0 — 20 km

KEY

Ferry lines

Ski Area

Etna Wine School

FOOD AND DRINK TOURS | For a comprehensive overview of the wine world on Mount Etna, look to Benjamin North Spencer, an American-born wine expert, Etna resident, and author of *The New Wines of Mount Etna*. He and his team offer half-day and full-day courses suitable for professionals and casual enthusiasts alike. You'll visit a vineyard, taste wines based on Carricante and Nerello Mascalese grapes, eat local delicacies, and learn about Etna wine-making traditions at the source. ☎ *347/3348782 mobile ⊕ www.etnawineschool.com ✉ ½-day tours €140 ☞ Transportation is optional: not included.*

Gruppo Guide Alpine Etna Sud

ADVENTURE TOURS | Led by highly qualified alpine guides, excursions leave from the Rifugio Sapienza, near the cable car station. The price includes the ascent by cable car followed by a trip by Jeep to 2,900 meters (9,514 feet), from where you continue on foot to the Summit Craters, at 3,340 meters (10,958 feet), then down back along slopes of volcanic ash to the cable car station for the descent. Sunset trips, easier excursions for families with children, and two- and five-day treks can also be organized. Their website is in English, and English-speaking guides are available. ⊠ *Piazza Vittorio Emanuele 43, Catania* ☎ *095/7914755 ⊕ www.etnaguide.eu ✉ €120.*

VISITOR INFORMATION

CONTACT Nicolosi Tourism Office. (*Porta dell'Etna*) ⊠ *Piazza Vittorio Emanuele, Nicolosi* ☎ *095/914488 ⊕ www.nicolosietna.it.*

Sights

★ Barone di Villagrande

WINERY | At the oldest winery on Etna, the expansive terrace shaded by oak trees looks out over vineyards and down to the sea. The staff offers friendly and informative tours (with excellent English) followed by a tasting of five wines with food pairings or a more formal lunch. Reservations are required. There are also four charming guest rooms overlooking the vineyards for overnight stays. ⊠ *Via del Bosco 25, Milo* ☎ *095/7082175 ⊕ www.villagrande.it ✉ €40 tour and tasting.*

Circumetnea

TRAIN/TRAIN STATION | Instead of climbing up Mount Etna, you can circle it on this private railroad, which runs between Catania and Riposto, with a change at Randazzo. By following the base of the volcano, the Circumetnea stretches out a 31-km (19-mile) journey along the coastal road to 114 km (71 miles). The line was first constructed between 1889 and 1895 and remains small, slow, and single-track, but it has some dramatic vistas of the volcano and goes through lava fields. The one-way trip takes about 3½ hours, with departures every 90 minutes or so. After you've made the trip, you can get back to where you started from on the much quicker, but less scenic, conventional rail service between Riposto and Catania. ⊠ *Via Caronda 352* ☎ *095/541111 ⊕ www.circumetnea.it ✉ €6.80 one-way ☉ Closed Sun.*

★ Mount Etna

VOLCANO | Affectionally called Idda (or "she" in Sicilian dialect), Etna is basically always active, and occasionally there are airspace closures due to the spewing ash. But for the locals who live in her shadow, Etna is not some ever-present doomsday reminder. She's a living part of the dynamic landscape, loved and revered.

In 387 BC, Plato sailed in just to catch a glimpse of it; in the 9th century AD, the first granita of all time was shaved off its snowy slopes; in 1669, it erupted continuously for four months and lava flows reached Catania; and in the 21st century, the volcano still grabs headlines on an annual basis. Significantly notable eruptions have occurred in the modern era, such as in 1971 (when lava buried the Etna Observatory), in 1981 (when the village of Randazzo narrowly missed destruction), in 2001 (when there was a large flank eruption), in 2002 (when a column of ash spewed that could be seen from space), and in 2008 (when the eruption lasted 417 days and triggered some 200 earthquakes). In February and March 2021, she erupted 11 times in a matter of three weeks, scattering wind-blown ash throughout the towns below, including Catania. Traveling to the prox-imity of the crater depends on Mount Etna's temperament, but you can walk up and down the enormous lava dunes and wander over its moonlike surface of dead craters. The rings of vegetation change markedly as you rise, with vineyards and pine trees gradually giving way to birch forests and growths of broom and lichen. ⊠ *Parco dell'Etna* ☎ *095/821111* ⊕ *www. parcoetna.it.*

🍴 Restaurants

★ Cave Ox

$ | **ITALIAN** | This casual osteria is frequent-ed by local winemakers who come for pizza dinners and rustic daily lunch specials, but most visitors are smitten with the small but amazing cellar focused on Etna natural wines. Everything's fresh, simple, and delicious—and made to pair with one of the delightful wines suggest-ed by owner and wine enthusiast Sandro. **Known for:** superlative selection of natural wines from Etna; filling lunches and pizza dinners; local winemaker crowd. $ *Aver-age main: €13* ⊠ *Via Nazionale Solicchiata 159* ☎ *0942/986171* ⊕ *www.caveox.it* ⊙ *Closed Tues.*

★ Shalai

$$$ | **MODERN ITALIAN** | You might not expect to find a thoroughly contempo-rary restaurant on the slopes of Mount Etna, but Shalai, in the boutique hotel of the same name, is truly a modern oasis, where young chef Giovanni San-toro prepares updated and beautifully

presented versions of Sicilian classics. For the full Michelin-starred experience, choose from the six-course meat or fish tasting menus; to finish, the decon-structed cannoli are a true delight. **Known for:** innovative modern Sicilian dishes; delicious tasting menus; excellent wine list. $ *Average main: €27* ⊠ *Via Marconi 25, Linguaglossa* ☎ *095/643128* ⊕ *www. shalai.it* ⊙ *No lunch weekdays.*

Hotels

★ Monaci delle Terre Nere

$$$$ | **HOTEL** | This cozy boutique hotel in the foothills of Mount Etna features spacious rustic-chic rooms on a working organic farm with vineyards, along with an elegant Slow Food–inspired restau-rant. **Pros:** eco-conscious atmosphere and policies; delicious food and wine; pool with countryside views. **Cons:** accommo-dations may be a little quirky for some; no televisions in bedrooms; bathrooms can be quite minimalist. $ *Rooms from: €780* ⊠ *Via Monaci, Zafferana Etnea* ☎ *095/7083638* ⊕ *www.monacidelleter-renere.it* ⊙ *Closed Jan.–mid-Mar.* ⤴ *27 rooms* ⏏ *Free Breakfast.*

Taormina

35 km (22 miles) north of Riposto, 54 km (34 miles) northeast of Catania.

The view of the sea and Mount Etna from Taormina's jagged, cactus-covered cliffs is as close to perfection as a pano-rama can get—especially on clear days, when the snowcapped volcano's white puffs of smoke rise against the blue sky. Even when overrun with tourists, its natural beauty is hard to dispute. Writers have extolled Taormina's charms almost since it was founded in the 6th centu-ry BC by Greeks from nearby Naxos; Goethe and D.H. Lawrence were among its well-known enthusiasts. The town's boutique-lined main streets lose their charm pretty quickly, but the many hiking paths that wind through the beautiful hills surrounding Taormina promise a timeless alternative. A trip up to stunning Castelmola (whether on foot or by car) should also be on your itinerary. It should be noted that in general, Taormina becomes a ghost town in January and February, with almost every hotel and restaurant closed.

GETTING HERE AND AROUND

Buses from Messina or Catania arrive near the center of Taormina, while trains from these towns pull in at the station at the bottom of the hill. Local buses bring you the rest of the way. A cable car takes passengers up the hill from a parking lot about 2 km (1 mile) north of the train station.

VISITOR INFORMATION

CONTACT Taormina Tourism Office.
⊠ *Palazzo Corvaja, Piazza Santa Caterina, Taormina* ☎ *0942/23243* ⊕ *www. comune.taormina.me.it.*

 Sights

Castello Saraceno

VIEWPOINT | An unrelenting 20-minute walk up the Via Crucis footpath takes you to the church of the Madonna della Rocca, hollowed out of the limestone rock. Above it towers the 1,000-year-old stone walls of Castello Saraceno, which is built on the site of earlier Greek and Roman fortifications. Although the gate to the castle has been locked for decades, it's worth the climb just for the panoramic views. ⊠ *Monte Tauro, Taormina.*

Funivia

OTHER ATTRACTION | Taormina Mare and the Bay of Mazzarò are accessible by a funivia, or suspended cable car, that glides past incredible views on its way down to the beach at Mazzarò. It departs every 15 minutes, until 8 pm. In June, July, and August, the normal hours are extended until 1:30 am. ⊠ *Via L. Pirandello, downhill from town center toward bus station, Taormina* ☎ *0942/23906* ⊕ *www.*

taorminaservizipubblici.it ⊠ *€6 one-way, €10 day ticket.*

Palazzo Corvaja

NOTABLE BUILDING | Many of Taormina's 14th- and 15th-century palaces have been carefully preserved. Especially beautiful is the Palazzo Corvaja, with characteristic black-lava and white-limestone inlays and the the seat of the first Sicilian parliament in 1411. Today it houses the tourist office and the bequest of a local antique dealer's historic art, local crafts, and everyday objects in the Museo di Arte e Tradizioni Popolari. ⊠ *Largo Santa Caterina, Taormina* ☎ *0942/620198* ⊠ *€3* ⊗ *Museum closed Mon.*

★ Teatro Greco

RUINS | The Greeks put a premium on finding impressive locations to stage their dramas, such as Taormina's hillside Teatro Greco. Beyond the columns, you can see the town's rooftops spilling down the hillside, the arc of the coastline, and Mount Etna in the distance. The theater was built during the 3rd century BC and rebuilt by the Romans during the 2nd century AD. Its acoustics are exceptional: even today a stage whisper can be heard in the last rows. In summer, many music and dance performances are held in the Teatro Greco after sunset, when the marvelous vistas of the sparkling Ionian Sea are shrouded in darkness, but the glow of Sicily's most famous volcano can sometimes be seen in the distance. ⊠ *Via Teatro Greco, Taormina* ☎ *0942/23220* ⊕ *www.aditusculture.com* ⊠ *€12.*

★ Villa Comunale

GARDEN | Stroll down Via Bagnoli Croce from the main Corso Umberto to the Villa Comunale to enjoy the stunning views from the seaside city's best terrace walkways. Also known as the Parco Duca di Cesarò, the lovely public gardens were designed by Florence Trevelyan Cacciola, a Scottish lady "invited" to leave England following a romantic liaison with the future Edward VII (1841–1910). Arriving in Taormina in 1889, she married a local professor and devoted herself to the gardens, filling them with native Mediterranean and exotic plants, ornamental pavilions, and fountains. ⊠ *Via Bagnoli Croce, Taormina.*

Beaches

Mazzarò

BEACH | Below the main city of Taormina is Mazzarò, where summertime beachgoers jostle for space on a pebble beach against the scenic backdrop of the aptly named Isola Bella. The first section of beach is reserved for expensive resorts but the far end, next to Isola Bella, has a large free area. The tiny "beautiful island" of Isola Bella was once a private residence but is now a nature preserve reached by walking along a narrow rocky path and visited for a small fee of €4. **Amenities:** none. **Best for:** walking. ⊠ *Taormina Mare, Taormina* ⊕ *www. parconaxostaormina.com* ⨳ *€4 for Isola Bella.*

🍴 Restaurants

L'Arco dei Cappuccini

$$$ | **SEAFOOD** | Just off Via Costantino Patricio, by the far side of the Cappuccini arch, lies this diminutive restaurant. Outdoor seating and an upstairs kitchen help make room for a few extra tables—a necessity, as locals are well aware that neither the price nor the quality is equaled elsewhere in town. **Known for:** fine dining; authentic local cooking; a great wine list. ⑤ *Average main: €25* ⊠ *Via Cappuccini 7, off Via Costantino Patricio, Taormina* ☎ *0942/480750* ⊕ *www.arcodeicappuccini.com* ⊘ *Closed Feb.*

⭐ Trattoria Il Barcaiolo

$$$ | **SEAFOOD** | Just behind the public beach in Mazzarò Bay, this intimate little terrace restaurant is shrouded by an enormous old grapevine and looks out onto postcard-perfect views of paradise.

Since 1981, the family-owned trattoria has been serving pristine seafood to discerning locals and in-the-know tourists. **Known for:** extensive wine list; swordfish carpaccio with citrus and capers; cassata and cannoli for dessert. ⑤ *Average main: €30* ⊠ *Via Castelluccio 43, Taormina* ☎ *379/2089564 mobile* ⊕ *www.barcaiolo.altervista.org* ⊘ *Closed Tues. Nov.–Easter.*

☕ Coffee and Quick Bites

Pasticceria Etna

$ | **BAKERY** | Fans of marzipan will delight at the range of almond sweets on offer here in the shape of the ubiquitous *fico d'India* (prickly pear) and other fruit. A block of almond paste makes a good souvenir—you can bring it home to make an almond latte or granita. **Known for:** almond sweets; fresh cannoli; house-made granita. ⑤ *Average main: €3* ⊠ *Corso Umberto I 112, Taormina* ☎ *0942/24735* ⊕ *www. pasticceriaetna.com.*

🛏️ Hotels

⭐ Belmond Grand Hotel Timeo

$$$$ | **HOTEL** | On a princely perch overlooking the town, the Greek theater, and the bay, this truly grand hotel, Taormina's oldest, wears a graceful patina that suggests la dolce vita, with a splash of Baroque and a dash of Mediterranean design in the lobby, which has tile- and brickwork walls and vaulted ceilings. **Pros:** feeling of indulgence; amazing location with fantastic views; exemplary service. **Cons:** very expensive; lower category rooms only have partial views; spa is on the small side. ⑤ *Rooms from: €1500* ⊠ *Via Teatro Greco 59, Taormina* ☎ *0942/6270200* ⊕ *www.belmond.com/ grand-hotel-timeo-taormina* ⊘ *Closed Jan.–mid-Mar.* ⟿ *70 rooms* ❖ *Free Breakfast.*

⭐ Belmond Villa Sant'Andrea

$$$$ | **HOTEL** | **FAMILY** | In a prime location on its own private beach at Taormina

Mare, this elegant hotel in a late-1800s villa offers phenomenal views of the water, attentive service, and luxurious and comfortable guest rooms. **Pros:** glorious private beach; flawless service; free shuttle service to Taormina town. **Cons:** limited on-site parking; spa is small; pricey food and drinks. $ *Rooms from: €1220* ✉ *Via Nazionale 137, Taormina* ☎ *0942/6271200* ⊕ *www.belmond.com/villa-sant-andrea-taormina-mare* ⊘ *Closed Nov.–mid-Apr.* ⤴ *70 rooms* ❍ *Free Breakfast.*

Hotel Villa Paradiso

$$$ | HOTEL | On the edge of the town's historic center, overlooking lovely public gardens and facing the sea, this under-the-radar family-run hotel was renovated in 2021 and 2023, but still maintains its antique furnishings, paintings, and Persian rugs, as well as its delightful service, good rooftop restaurant, and Etna views from many guest rooms. **Pros:** fab, bountiful table-service breakfast; shuttle bus to beach; great rooftop views. **Cons:** not all rooms have views; limited free parking spaces (paid parking nearby); beach club fee is extra. $ *Rooms from: €262* ✉ *Via Roma 2, Taormina* ☎ *0942/23921* ⊕ *www.hotelvillaparadisotaormina.com* ⤴ *37 rooms* ❍ *Free Breakfast.*

San Domenico Palace, A Four Seasons Hotel

$$$$ | HOTEL | The sweeping views of the castle, the sea, and Mount Etna from this converted 14th-century Dominican monastery will linger in your mind, along with the equally memorable levels of luxury and wonderful food in the hotel's highly lauded restaurant, Principe Cerami. **Pros:** strong sense of history and grandeur; gorgeous infinity pool with amazing views; gorgeous grounds. **Cons:** very expensive parking and bar; events can be noisy; beach access through partner affiliates. $ *Rooms from: €2500* ✉ *Piazza San Domenico 5, Taormina* ☎ *0942/613111* ⊕ *www.fourseasons.com/taormina*

⊘ *Closed early Jan.–mid-Mar.* ⤴ *111 rooms* ❍ *Free Breakfast.*

Castelmola

5 km (3 miles) west of Taormina.

Although many believe that Taormina has the most spectacular views, tiny Castelmola—floating 1,800 feet above sea level—takes the word "scenic" to a whole new level. Along the cobblestone streets within the ancient walls, 360-degree panoramas of mountain, sea, and sky are so ubiquitous that you almost get used to them (but not quite). Collect yourself with a sip of the sweet almond wine (best served cold) made in local bars, or with lunch at one of the humble pizzerias or panino shops.

A 10-minute drive on a winding but well-paved road leads from Taormina to Castelmola; you must park in one of the public lots below the village and walk up to the center, only a few minutes away. On a nice day, hikers are in for a treat if they make the trip from Taormina on foot instead. It's a serious uphill climb, but the 1½-km (¾-mile) path offers breathtaking views, which compensate for the somewhat poor maintenance of the path itself. You'll begin at Porta Catania in Taormina, with a walk along Via Apollo Arcageta past the Chiesa di San Francesco di Paola on the left. The Strada Comunale della Chiusa then leads past Piazza Andromaco, revealing good views of the jagged promontory of Cocolonazzo di Mola to the north. Allow around an hour for the ascent, a half hour for the descent. There's another, slightly longer (2-km [1-mile]) path that heads up from Porta Messina past the Roman aqueduct, Convento dei Cappuccini, and the northeastern side of Monte Tauro. You could take one up and the other down. In any case, avoid the midday sun, wear comfortable shoes, and carry plenty of water with you.

GETTING HERE AND AROUND
Regular buses bound for Castelmola leave from Taormina's bus station on Via Pirandello.

 Sights

★ Castello di Mola

RUINS | In all of Sicily there may be no spot more scenic than atop this crumbling hilltop fortification reached by a set of steep staircases rising out of the town center. From here you can gaze upon two coastlines, smoking Mount Etna, and the town spilling down the mountainside. Mention of its foundations go back to the 4th-century Hellenistic Siceliote inhabitants, it was remodeled by 9th-century Byzantines and then the Normans, but all that stands today are the remains of the 16th-century castle walls. Come during daylight hours to take full advantage of the vista. ⊠ *Castello Normanno, Castelmola* ⊕ *www.comune.castelmola.me.it.*

🍴 Restaurants

Il Vicolo

$$ | SICILIAN | Located on a side street, this trattoria is one of the simpler dining choices in town, and also one of the better ones—what it lacks in views it makes up for with a pleasant rustic ambience plus a great selection of handmade pasta and, in the evening, *forno a legna* (from a wood-fired oven). In winter, pizzas are served weekends only. **Known for:** cozy, homey environs; pasta and pizza; signature totano (flying squid) ragù. ⑤ *Average main: €15* ⊠ *Via Papa Pio IX 26, Castelmola* ☎ *0942/28481* ⊕ *www.facebook.com/ilvicolo.difalcone* ☉ *Closed Tues. Sept.–June and 2 wks late Jan.–early Feb.*

 Hotels

Villa Sonia

$$ | HOTEL | Many guest rooms at this well-situated hotel have private terraces with gorgeous Instagrammable views of Etna without the crowds (or high prices) of nearby Taormina. **Pros:** bus stop to Taormina outside door; on-site sauna and pool; friendly service. **Cons:** some rooms are quite small; not much to do in the evening; lots of steps to get here. ⑤ *Rooms from: €188* ⊠ *Via Porta Mola 9, Castelmola* ☎ *0942/28082* ⊕ *www.hotelvillasonia.com* ☉ *Closed Nov.–mid-Mar* ⤴ *44 rooms* ⍾ *Free Breakfast.*

Messina

42 km (26 miles) north of Savoca, 94 km (59 miles) northeast of Catania, 237 km (149 miles) east of Palermo.

Messina's ancient history recounts a series of disasters, but the city once vied with Palermo in a bid to become the island's capital, developing a fine university, a bustling commercial center, and a thriving cultural environment. At 5:20 am on December 28, 1908, Messina was reduced from a flourishing metropolis of 120,000 to a heap of rubble, shaken to pieces by an earthquake that turned into a tidal wave; 80,000 people died as a result, and the city was almost completely leveled. As you approach by ferry, you won't notice any outward indication of the disaster, just the modern countenance of a 3,000-year-old city. The somewhat flat look is a precaution of seismic planning: tall buildings are not permitted.

GETTING HERE AND AROUND
Frequent hydrofoils and ferries carry passengers, cars, and trains across the Strait of Messina from Villa San Giovanni, from just below the train station. There are also regular hydrofoil departures for

foot passengers from Reggio Calabria. Cruise ships also stop in Messina's port. There is at least one hydrofoil departure daily for the Aeolian Islands.

From within Sicily, Messina is easily reachable by car, as it sits just off the E45 autostrada from Catania and the E90 autostrada from Palermo. There are regular train and bus services from both cities as well.

VISITOR INFORMATION

CONTACT Messina Tourism Office. ⊠ *Via dei Mille 270, Messina* ☎ *090/2935292* ⊕ *turismoecultura.cittametropolitana. me.it.*

◉ Sights

★ Duomo

CHURCH | The reconstruction of Messina's Norman and Romanesque cathedral, originally built by the Norman king Roger II and consecrated in 1197, has retained much of the original plan—including a handsome crown of Norman battlements, an enormous apse, and a splendid wood-beamed ceiling. The adjoining bell tower contains one of the largest and most complex mechanical clocks in the world: constructed in 1933, it has a host of gilded automatons (a roaring lion and crowing rooster among them) that spring into action every day at the stroke of noon, lasting for 12 minutes.

Don't miss the chance to climb the bell tower itself. As you head up the internal stairs, you'll see the system of levers and counterweights that operates the movements of the gilded bronze statues that parade through the open facade high over the Duomo's square. At the top, an open-air terrace offers 360-degree views of Messina and the Strait. ⊠ *Piazza del Duomo 29, Messina* ☎ *090/774895* ⊕ *www.messinarte.it* ☑ *Clock tower €5.*

⑪ Restaurants

★ A Cucchiara

$$ | MODERN ITALIAN | Light and elegance permeates this stone-walled restaurant, where the open kitchen provides theater and owner Peppe Giamboi takes the stage as a gustatory storyteller, roaming from table to table. The menu is constantly changing, but you'll find excellent work with vegetables (a rarity in Sicily) and really lovely preparations of local cod. **Known for:** elegant food in a relaxed, welcoming atmosphere; locally, sustainably sourced seafood; robust wine program. ⑤ *Average main: €23* ⊠ *Strada San Giacomo 19, Messina* ☎ *090/711023* ⊕ *www.ristoranti.messina.it* ⊙ *Closed Sun. No lunch Sat.*

Lipari

2 hours, 10 minutes from Milazzo by ferry, 1 hour by hydrofoil.

The largest and most developed of the Aeolians, Lipari welcomes you with distinctive pastel-color houses. Fields of spiky agaves dot the northernmost tip of the island, Acquacalda, indented with disused pumice and obsidian quarries. In the west is San Calogero, where you can explore hot springs and mud baths. From the red-lava base of the island rises a plateau crowned with a 16th-century castle and a 17th-century cathedral.

GETTING HERE AND AROUND

Ferries and hydrofoils from Milazzo via Vulcano stop here, and there are also connections with the other Aeolian islands. There's also a more limited hydrofoil service from Messina via Reggio di Calabria, a daily hydrofoil from Palermo in summer, and ferries year round from Naples. On the island, if you plan to explore extensively, you should rent a car or a scooter. Lipari is the largest of the Aeolians and navigating it can be difficult without your own mode of transport.

◉ Sights

★ Museo Archeologico Regionale Eoliano Luigi Bernabò Brea

HISTORY MUSEUM | This vast, multi-building museum named after its founder is terrific, with an intelligently arranged collection of prehistoric finds—some dating as far back as 4000 BC—from various sites in the archipelago, as well as Greek and Roman artifacts, including an outstanding collection of Greek theatrical masks, and even interesting information on volcanoes. Basic descriptions about the exhibits are provided in English and Italian, though more comprehensive information is in Italian only. That said, there is so much to see, the museum is worth at least a few hours of your time. ✉ Via Castello 2, Lipari ☎ 090/9880174 ⊕ www.aditusculture.com ⊠ €7 ☉ Closed Sun. afternoon.

★ Vulcano

ISLAND | True to its name, the island of Vulcano has a profusion of fumaroles sending up jets of hot vapor, and although the volcano itself is dormant, emissions have recently reached dangerous levels, occasionally resulting in parts of the island being evacuated. When it is safe, visitors can come to soak in the strong-smelling sulfur springs or to sunbathe and walk on some of the archipelago's best beaches, though the volcanic black sand can be off-putting at first glance. Volcanic conditions permitting, you can climb the volcano and walk right around the crater. Advenzu offer a number of guided trekking tours around Vulcano, as well as kayaking, sailing, tandem paragliding, snorkeling, and other activities. ☎ 389/1447708 mobile ⊕ www.advenzu.com ⊠ from €55 for an Advenzu 2½-hr guided trek of the Gran Cratere della Fossa.

⏀ Restaurants

★ Osteria San Bartolo

$$ | ITALIAN | Chef Danilo Conti started with a passion for wine and subsequently grew deeper respect for the soil of his home territory. The dishes at his osteria just steps from the port in Lipari are clean and balanced—the opposite of fussy—but primarily celebrate the fishing and agricultural traditions of the island; think lime-scented carpaccio of swordfish and pasta with anchovies, wild fennel, and orange zest. **Known for:** natural wine (chef owns a wineshop a few doors down); stuffed calamari; showcasing the best of both sea and land. ⑤ Average main: €20 ✉ Via Francesco Crispi 109, Lipari ☎ 090/8961317 ⊕ www.sanbartolovineriaedispensa.com ☉ Closed Wed.

⏢ Hotels

Hotel Villa Enrica

$$ | HOTEL | This hotel's hillside position gives it one of the best views on the island, looking south over Marina Lunga and the castle, and it seems like nearly every part of the hotel (from rooms to common areas) takes advantage of that vista. **Pros:** cliffside infinity pool with snack bar for light lunches; heated hydromassage pool; shuttle service to beach. **Cons:** cramped shower enclosures; service can be slow; often hosts events, so can get crowded with nonguests. ⑤ Rooms from: €130 ✉ Strada Serra Pirrera 11, Lipari ☎ 090/9880826 ⊕ www.hotelvillaenricalipari.com ☉ Closed mid-Oct.–Easter ⇋ 20 rooms ⏥ Free Breakfast.

Les Sables Noirs

$$$ | HOTEL | Named for the black sands of the beach it sits in front of, this luxury hotel is superbly sited on the beautiful Porto di Ponente and its cool modern furnishings and inviting pool and spa induce a sybaritic mood. **Pros:** stunning beachfront location; delicious breakfasts; quick five-minute walk to town. **Cons:** no on-site

restaurant; five-night minimum stay in August; the spa is not included in the price. ⑤ *Rooms from: €280* ✉ *Porto di Ponente, Vulcano* ☎ *335/1552650 mobile* ⊕ *www.lessablesnoirs.it* ⊘ *Closed mid-Oct.–Apr.* ⥲ *53 rooms* ⦿ *Free Breakfast.*

Salina

50 minutes from Lipari by ferry, 20 minutes by hydrofoil.

The second largest of the Aeolians, Salina is also the most fertile, which accounts for its excellent Malvasia wine. Salina is the archipelago's lushest and highest island, too: Mount Fossa delle Felci rises to more than 3,000 feet and offers a challenging two-hour hike to the summit, and the vineyards and fishing villages along its slopes add to the allure. Pollara, in the west of the island, has capitalized on its fame as one of the locations in the 1990s cult movie *Il Postino* (*The Postman*) and is an ideal location for sunset watching and an evening passeggiata on well-maintained paths along the volcanic terrain.

GETTING HERE AND AROUND

Ferries and hydrofoils arrive here from Milazzo via Vulcano and Lipari, connecting on to the other islands of the archipelago. There's also a more limited hydrofoil service from Messina via Reggio di Calabria, a daily hydrofoil from Palermo in summer, and ferries year-round from Naples. Note that there are two ports on Salina: Santa Marina Salina and Rinella. Not all ferries and hydrofoils arrive at both ports, so double-check your tickets and timetables. Once on the island, you can get around by taxi, or rent a car or a scooter. The island's bus service, C.I.T.I.S., runs reliably and (usually) on time between the island's towns. Tickets cost €2–€3 depending on distance.

TOURS

Sogno Eoliano

BOAT TOURS | Though the island's verdant hills beckon, Salina is best experienced by water. Native son Samuele, with a sparkling smile and easy charm, navigates the sea on his 21-foot boat, taking guests on excursions ranging from a two-hour aperitivo sunset cruise to Pollara Bay to full-day trips to neighboring islands. He grew up on the sea (and fishes during the off-season), so he knows these waters intimately and that comes through in his tours, which are all customizable according to your specific interests. ✉ *Salina* ☎ *331/9928032 mobile* ⊕ *www.sognoeoliano.it* ⬛ *From €200 for the Sunset Cruise (up to 8 people).*

🍽 Restaurants

★ **Da Alfredo**

$$ | SICILIAN | Starting in 1968, the mini-empire of owner Alfredo Olivieri was built one granita and one *pane cunzato* at a time, and no summer on Salina is complete without a stop at his little shop off the Marina Garibaldi piazza in Lingua. You'll find all the classic granita flavors (almond, coffee, lemon, pistachio), but it's the seasonal fruits that shine here: mulberry, fig, wild blackberries, watermelon, and cantaloupe. **Known for:** joyous atmosphere; seasonally focused granita; charismatic owner. ⑤ *Average main: €15* ✉ *Via Marina Garibaldi, Santa Marina, Salina* ☎ *090/9843980* ⊕ *www.facebook.com/daalfredosalina* ⊘ *Closed Nov.–Easter.*

🛏 Hotels

★ **Principe di Salina**

$$$ | HOTEL | Awash in white with vibrant pops of color, this family-run boutique property that hugs the Malfa hillside defines barefoot chic. **Pros:** house-made breads and pastries; gorgeous private terraces; excellent wine and cocktail list. **Cons:** not directly on the sea; restaurant has limited places for external guests; no kids under age 10. ⑤ *Rooms from: €279* ✉ *SP 182 3, Malfa, Salina* ☎ *090/9844415* ⊕ *www.principedisalina.it* ⊘ *Closed mid-Oct.–late Mar.* ⥲ *12 rooms* ⦿ *Free Breakfast.*

Panarea

2 hours from Lipari by ferry, 25–50 minutes by hydrofoil; 30 minutes from Salina by hydrofoil.

Panarea is the second smallest of the islands but has some of the most dramatic scenery, including wild caves carved out of rock and dazzling flora. The exceptionally clear water and the richness of life on the seafloor make Panarea especially suitable for underwater exploration. The outlying rocks and islets make a gorgeous sight, and you can enjoy the panorama on an easy excursion to the small Bronze Age village at Capo Milazzese.

GETTING HERE AND AROUND

Ferries and hydrofoils arrive here from Milazzo, Lipari, Salina, and Stromboli. There is a less frequent hydrofoil service from Messina via Reggio di Calabria, and in summer a daily connection with Palermo. There are also weekly ferries to and from Naples. For a super-splurge, you can book a helicopter flight with Air Panarea (⊕ *www.airpanarea.com*) from the airports of Palermo, Catania, Naples, Lamezia Terme, and Reggio Calabria. Prices on request. Once on the island, you'll need to rely on walking, Vespas, or electric golf carts to get around—cars are banned.

Hotels

Hotel Raya

\$\$\$\$ | HOTEL | Although some visitors say it's resting on past laurels, Raya is perfectly in keeping with the elite style of Panarea—discreet and expensive, with a pool and terrace that enjoy views over the sea toward Stromboli. **Pros:** great views of Stromboli; hippie-chic ambience; lovely pool area. **Cons:** snooty staff; uphill trudge to rooms; in need of renovations. ⑤ *Rooms from: €500* ✉ *Via San Pietro, San Pietro, Panarea* ☎ *090/983013* ⊕ *www.hotelraya.it*

⊘ *Closed mid-Oct.–mid-Apr.* ⇆ *34 rooms* ✝Ⓞ *Free Breakfast* ☞ *No young children allowed.*

Stromboli

3 hours, 45 minutes from Lipari by ferry, 65–90 minutes by hydrofoil; 80 minutes from Salina by hydrofoil; 9 hours from Naples by ferry, 5 hours by hydrofoil.

This northernmost of the Aeolians consists entirely of the cone of an active volcano. The view from the sea—especially at night, as an endless stream of glowing red-hot lava flows into the water—is unforgettable. Stromboli is in a constant state of activity, with minor explosions happening every 20 minutes or so. In periods of high activity, eruptions can be seen from the other islands. The volcano is closely monitored, and the main danger would be from an underwater landslide that could trigger a tsunami. Access to the volcano is permitted only with an official guide. The main town has a small selection of reasonably priced hotels and restaurants, a choice of lively clubs and cafés, and plenty of trekking outfits. In addition to the island tour, excursions might include boat trips around the sea stack of Strombolicchio, which is all that remains of the original volcano that gave rise to Stromboli. At night, boats offer trips to see the Sciara del Fuoco, the lava channel that rises out of the blue waters.

GETTING HERE AND AROUND

Ferries and hydrofoils arrive here from Milazzo via Vulcano, Lipari, Salina, and Panarea. There's also a more limited hydrofoil service from Messina via Reggio di Calabria, one hydrofoil daily from Palermo in summer, and ferries year-round from Naples. Once on the island, you'll need to navigate by foot, or you can book one of the golf cart taxis located near the port.

TOURS

★ MagmaTrek

ADVENTURE TOURS | You can freely hike the volcano up to 954 feet, but for anything beyond that safe limit you'll need an authorized guide (who can take you up to 1,312 feet). MagmaTrek offers five-hour hikes that get you as close as humanly possible to the volcanic activity as you ascend approximately 8 km (5 miles) up the flanks of Stromboli. The guides are true experts and in constant radio contact with the volcano monitoring station. They provide the mandatory helmets, but you should be sure to pack sturdy walking shoes. ✉ *Via Vittorio Emanuele, Stromboli* ☎ *090/9865768* ⊕ *www.magmatrek.it* 🎫 *From €25* ⊙ *No excursions Nov.–mid-Mar.*

Filicudi

30–60 minutes from Salina and Lipari by hydrofoil; 2 hours from Cefalù and Palermo, 2 hours from Milazzo, and 10 hours from Naples by ferry.

Just a dot in the sea, Filicudi is famous for its unusual volcanic rock formations, the enchanting Grotta del Bue Marino (Grotto of the Sea Ox), and the crumbled remains of a prehistoric village at Capo Graziano. The island, which is spectacular for walking and hiking, is still a truly undiscovered, restful haven, and has a handful of hotels and *pensioni* as well as some more informal rooms with families who put up guests. Car ferries are available only in summer.

GETTING HERE AND AROUND

Ferries and hydrofoils arrive throughout the year from Milazzo, Salina, and Lipari, and also in summer from Palermo and Naples. Once you've arrived, you can rent a car or a scooter at the port. You can also find the minibus taxi of D&G Servizio Navetta (☎ *347/7575916 mobile*) usually waiting at the port.

 ## Hotels

La Canna

$$ | HOTEL | Set above the tiny port and commanding fabulous views of sea and sky from its flower-filled terrace, this friendly hotel offers small but adequate guest rooms, kept clean and tidy by the family-friendly staff. **Pros:** relaxing pool and lounge area; family-friendly atmosphere; great views. **Cons:** an uphill climb from the port; half board required in peak season; no Wi-Fi in guest rooms. ⑤ *Rooms from: €160* ✉ *Via Rosa 43* ☎ *090/9889956* ⊕ *www.lacannahotel.it* ⊙ *Closed mid-Oct.–mid-Apr.* ⇌ *14 rooms* ⑩ *No Meals.*

Cefalù

69 km (42 miles) east of Palermo.

The jewel of the Tyrrhenian Coast is no doubt Cefalù, a classically appealing old Sicilian town built on a spur jutting out into the sea.

The city's medieval origins have left behind many interesting historical sites to explore. The Palazzo Maria in Piazza Duomo and the Osteria Magno in Corso Ruggero are palaces that date back to the 13th century. They were both owned by the Ventimiglia family, an influential aristocratic family that dominated and owned most of the agricultural wealth of this part of the island in the Middle Ages.

Another piece of history here is the medieval washhouse. Carved out of rustic lava stone and used until the early 20th century, the ancient bathhouse is home to a series of basins fed by the waters of the Cefalino River, which flow out from 22 iron lion-shape mouths. Here, you can get a sense of how life was in Sicily in the Middle Ages.

Cefalù's historical heritage continues with remnants of the Baroque period from the 18th century, which gave birth to the elaborate decorations and style that are quite unique to Sicily. There are the ornate facades of the church of the Monte della Pietà, which dates from 1716, and the stunning Church of Purgatory (1668). The town's historical center is dotted with endless portholes, squares, facades, and architectural details.

GETTING HERE AND AROUND

Trains and buses run between Palermo and Messina, and stop at the station about a 10-minute walk from town. Drivers can take the A20 autostrada, though the traffic going in and out of Cefalù can be heavy in summer and the 50-minute train ride from Palermo may be the better option.

VISITOR INFORMATION

CONTACT Cefalù Tourism Office. ⊠ Corso Ruggeri 77, Cefalù ☎ 0921/421050 ⊕ www.visitcefalu.com.

Sights

Duomo

CHURCH | Cefalù is dominated by a massive headland—la rocca—and a 12th-century Romanesque Duomo, which is one of the finest Norman cathedrals in Italy. Roger II began the church in 1131 as an offering of thanks for having been saved here from a shipwreck. Its mosaics rival those of Monreale. (Whereas Monreale's Byzantine Christ figure is an austere and powerful image, emphasizing Christ's divinity, the Cefalù Christ is softer, more compassionate, and more human.) At the Duomo you must be respectfully attired—no shorts or beachwear permitted. Three themed tours explore the Duomo complex, taking in the museum, cloisters, roof and towers (from €10). ⊠ Piazza del Duomo, Cefalù ☎ 0921/926366 ⊕ duomocefalu.it/en ☑ "Green" Museum and Cloister tour €10 ۞ Cloister closed weekends.

Restaurants

Al Porticciolo

$$ | SICILIAN | Nicola Mendolia's seaside restaurant is comfortable, casual, and faithfully focused on food—primarily pizza, but with an extensive selection of seafood, pasta, and meat, too. Dark, heavy wooden tables create a comfortable environment filled with a mix of jovial locals and businesspeople, though the most memorable option is to dine on the spacious terrace. **Known for:** high-quality pizza; local seafood; lovely terrace overlooking the water. ⑤ Average main: €20 ⊠ Via Carlo Ortolani di Bordonaro 66, Cefalù ☎ 0921/921981 ⊕ www.alporticciol000ristorante.com ۞ Closed Dec.–Mar.

Hotels

Kalura

$$$ | HOTEL | FAMILY | This modern hotel is on a small promontory in Caldura, 2 km (1 mile) east of Cefalù, a few minutes away by taxi or a 30-minute walk, and offers mostly bright rooms with some eccentric decorative touches, many with balconies overlooking the sea. **Pros:** beautiful sea views; good swimming; family-friendly environment. **Cons:** outside town; food underwhelming; dated decor. ⑤ Rooms from: €290 ⊠ Via Cavallaro 13, Cefalù ☎ 0921/421354 ⊕ www.hotelkalura.com ۞ Closed mid-Nov.–mid-Mar. ⟲ 84 rooms ۞ Free Breakfast.

Chapter 18

SARDINIA

Updated by
Robert Andrews

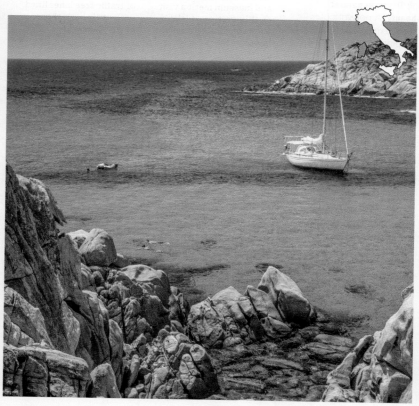

◉ Sights	🍴 Restaurants	🏨 Hotels	👜 Shopping	🍸 Nightlife
★★★☆☆	★★★★☆	★★★★☆	★★☆☆☆	★☆☆☆☆

WELCOME TO SARDINIA

TOP REASONS TO GO

★ **Relax on idyllic beaches:** Covering more than 1,900 km (1,200 miles) of coastline, Sardinia's beaches beckon with their turquoise waters, white sand, and rippled dunes.

★ **Discover natural beauty:** A network of trails explores Sardinia's resplendent mountains, deep gorges, lush forests, and cascading waterfalls.

★ **Explore charming towns and villages:** From coastal towns to rural villages, the island is dotted with a variety of settlements that take pride in their history and tradition. Each has its own culture, cuisine, and unique way of life.

★ **Dive or snorkel the outer reefs:** Crystalline waters, warm weather, and outer reefs make Sardinia a paradise for underwater adventurers. Sunken ships and marine reserves provide the ideal place to discover marine life.

★ **Savor Sardinian delicacies:** From pasta and prosciutto to lamb and cheese, the island's cuisine is sure to satisfy any appetite.

1 Cagliari. Sardinia's capital is a hive of cultural attractions, dining hot spots, and glamorous shops.

2 Pula. Just south of Cagliari, Pula is home to resorts, beaches, and a major archaeological site.

3 Sant'Antioco. A significant archaeological site and museum merit a visit on this west-coast island, once a major Carthaginian base.

4 San Pietro. This offshore isle makes a perfect bolt-hole, with its lively port and undeveloped beaches.

5 Costa Verde. A high, cliffy coastline and alluring beaches are the main attractions on Sardinia's "Green Coast."

6 Barumini. The island's ancient and enigmatic nuraghic culture are showcased at Su Nuraxi, just outside Barumini.

7 Oristano. Little visited by tourists, this provincial center makes an appealing base for the nearby Sinis Peninsula.

8 Tharros. Explore Carthaginian and Roman ruins at this site near the town of Oristano.

9 Nuoro. The largest inland town is a must-see for anyone interested in Sardinia's traditional culture.

10 Fonni. Near the island's highest peaks, Fonni makes an ideal hiking base.

11 Alghero. Alghero's historic center is a warren of traffic-free lanes lined with lively bars, shops, and restaurants.

12 Sassari. Sardinia's second city has an atmospheric old quarter.

13 Castelsardo. This former north coast stronghold is renowned for its basketware.

14 Santa Teresa Gallura. On the island's northern tip, this resort is surrounded by excellent beaches.

15 La Maddalena. Garibaldi's former home is a highlight of any tour of this archipelago.

16 Porto Cervo. Day-trippers are drawn to this jet-setter enclave on the famed Costa Smeralda.

17 Olbia. Sardinia's northern gateway is a short drive from some of Italy's most exclusive hotels and beaches.

FRANCE

Santa Teresa
Gallura
Palau
La Maddalena
Porto Cervo
Bassacutena
Arzachena
Golfo Aranci
Olbia
Golfo di Olbia
Telti
Monti
Padru

Punta
Caprara

Isola
Asinara

Stintino
Porto Torres
Castelsardo
Sedini
Chiaramonti
Oschiri
Ozieri
Budduso
Siniscola

Golfo
dell'Asinara

Tempio
Pausania

Sorso
Sassari

Villanova
Monteleone
Alghero

Bultei
Bitti
Sas Linnas
Siccas
Orosei

Padria

Nuoro
Monte
Ortobene
Dorgali
Cala
Gonone

Bosa
Tresnuraghes
Macomer
Orotelli
Golfo di
Orosei

Abbasanta
Fonni

Cabras
Tharros
Oristano
Asuni
Laconi
Nurallao
Tortoli
Bari
Sardo

Golfo di
Oristano

MEDITERRANEAN
SEA

Marrubiu
Uras
Su Nuraxi
Barumini

Porto Palma

Guspini
Furtei

Piscinas
Samassi

Buggerru
Villasor
Monastir
Dolianova
Muravera

Iglesias
Decimomannu

Portoscuso
Carloforte
Isola
San Pietro
Carbonia
Cagliari
Villasimius

Golfo di
Cagliari

Sant'Antioco
Giba
Sarroch
Pula

Isola
Sant'antioco
Chia

Golfo di
Palmas
Capo Teulada
Capo Spartivento

TYRRHENIAN SEA

COSTA SMERALDA

COSTA VERDE

0   10 mi

0   10 km

EATING AND DRINKING WELL IN SARDINIA

Traditional Sardinian ravioli

Wining and dining in Sardinia is not just a richly delicious experience, it's also a way to have a close-up encounter with the history, geography, and cultural traditions of the island. Sardinian food has its own culinary identity, a complex and eclectic mix that makes for mouthwatering and often revelatory dishes.

Sardinia's proximity to North Africa and its long Spanish occupation mean that elements of both cultures can be found in the island's kitchens, including couscous and paella. There are also strong regional variations within Sardinia itself, as well as a traditional division between the land-based fare of the interior and the fresh seafood on the coasts. Wherever you go here, you'll find a strong emphasis on seasonal ingredients and ancient cooking techniques.

BREADS, CHEESES, AND SWEET SPECIALTIES

Sardinia has a strong tradition of bread making and is famous for crispy paperthin *pane carasau* flatbread (*carta di musica* in Italian).

Ever wondered about all those sheep roaming the rugged slopes of the interior? They're there to produce the raw materials for Italy's original and best pecorino. It's ubiquitous in Sardinia, and comes in various strengths and consistencies.

Sardinian desserts include *sospiri* (morsels of almond dough stuffed with citrus-infused almond paste), *torrone di mandorle* (almond nougat), and *seadas* (cheese-filled pastries topped with honey, also called *sebadas*). The *candelaus*, a fruit-and-almond dessert, and sweet ricotta-stuffed *pardula* cakes are popular in Cagliari. Unmissable is *amaro di corbezzolo*, made by bees that suck nectar from a plant known as *arbutus*, the tree strawberry.

MEAT

The most popular meat dishes are veal, roast *agnello* (lamb), and *porcheddu* (spit-roasted suckling pig). *Cavallo*, or *carne equino* (horse meat), is also commonly found on restaurant menus, particularly in Sassari, where it's generally served in the form of a *bistecca* (thin steak). Donkey (*asino*) and wild boar (*cinghiale*) are other Sardinian specialties. Sometimes cinghiale is roasted on a spit or prepared using the ancient Sardinian technique of *incarralzadu*, for which it's placed in a large hole lined with fragrant myrtle leaves. Another option is *zuppa cuata*, a hearty soup that's made from beef broth, bread, and aged pecorino cheese.

SEAFOOD

Whole fish are best eaten roasted or grilled, though you may also find them sautéed in pasta or incorporated into *copaxa de peix*, a fish soup from

Almond nougat

Roast lamb

Alghero. The most famous Alghero dish is lobster, known as *langouste* or *aragosta*. Lobster doesn't appear on restaurant menus in winter—fortunately, the very time when *riccio di mare* (sea urchin), another local specialty, is best enjoyed. Winter is also the best season for *bottarga*, the dried, cured roe of gray mullet or tuna.

STARTERS

Opt for antipasti *di mare* or *di terra* to kick off your meal. Traditional pastas include *malloreddus* (small shells), *culurgiones* (ravioli), and *maccarones de busa* (thick pasta twists). Homemade pastas might be topped with a wild-boar sauce; *fregola*, a semolina pasta, is often served with *arselle* (clams).

WINE

Among the whites, the dry *torbato* of the Alghero Coast and the slightly sparkling *vermentino* from Gallura are standouts. The Oristano region produces the dry, sherrylike *vernaccia* (unrelated to the Tuscan variety), Bosa produces amber-tone *malvasia*, and Barbagia is one of the best sources of *cannonau*, a red wine with an ancient pedigree. The traditional liqueur *mirto*, which makes a fine after-dinner drink, is made from native wild myrtle berries.

The second-largest island in the Mediterranean, Sardinia remains unique and enigmatic with its rugged coastline and white-sand beaches, dramatic granite cliffs, and mountainous inland tracts. Glamorous resorts lie within a short distance of quiet, medieval villages, and ruined castles and ancient churches testify to an eventful history.

But although conquerors from all directions—Phoenicians, Carthaginians, Romans, Catalans, Pisans, Genoans, Piedmontese—have left their traces, no outside culture has had a dominant impact. Pockets of foreign influence persist along the coasts, but inland, a proud Sardinian culture flourishes.

As a travel destination, Sardinia's identity is split: the island has some of Europe's most expensive resorts, but it's also home to pristine terrain untouched by commercial development. Fine sand and clean waters draw summer sun worshippers to beaches that rank among the Mediterranean's best. Most famous are those along the Costa Smeralda (Emerald Coast), where the ultrarich have anchored their yachts since the 1960s.

Apart from the glamorous shores and upscale locales found in the east, much of Sardinia's coast is rugged and unreachable, a jagged series of wildly beautiful inlets accessible only by sea. Inland, Sardinia remains shepherd's country, silent and stark.

MAJOR REGIONS

Cagliari and the Southern Coast. Sardinia's capital and largest city, Cagliari (pronounced *cahl*-yah-ree) contains the island's principal art and archaeology museums as well as an intact old citadel with lofty views of the sea, lagoons, and mountains. To the southwest is Pula, an inland resort within easy reach of good beaches and the excavations at Nora.

Su Nuraxi to the Costa Smeralda. Inland and north of Cagliari, explore the apogee of the island's prehistoric Nuraghic civilization at Su Nuraxi, just outside the village of Barumini. Northwest of here, Oristano makes an ideal stopover for exploring the ruins at Tharros. In the mountainous interior, Nuoro has a first-rate ethnographic museum highlighting Sardinia's traditional culture. The rugged granite landscape of Sardinia's northeast is probably best known for the Costa Smeralda, a short strip of elite hotels and beaches.

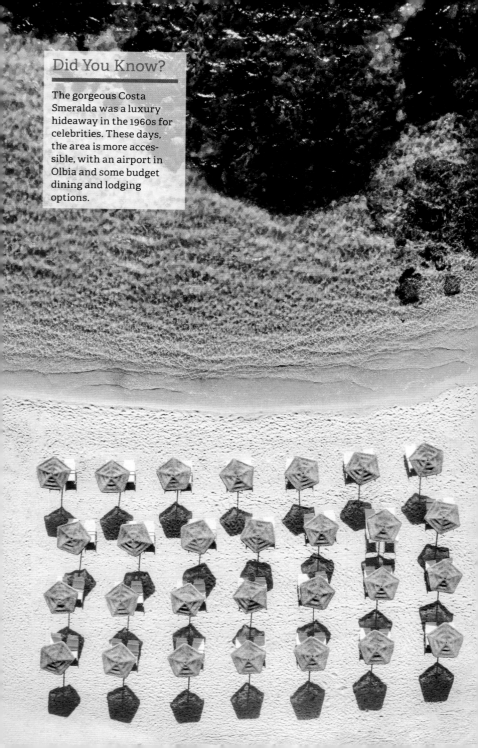

Planning

Getting Here and Around

AIR

Flying is by far the fastest and easiest way to get to the island. Sardinia's major airport, Aeroporto di Elmas, is in Cagliari, with smaller ones at Alghero (Aeroporto Fertilia) and Olbia (Aeroporto Costa Smeralda).

CONTACTS Aeroporto di Alghero. ✉ *Regione Nuraghe Biancu, 9½ km (6 miles) north of Alghero* ☎ *079/935011* ⊕ *www. aeroportodialghero.it.* **Aeroporto di Cagliari.** ✉ *Via dei Trasvolatori, 8 km (5 miles) northwest of city center, Elmas* ☎ *070/211211* ⊕ *www.sogaer.it.* **Aeroporto di Olbia Costa Smeralda.** ✉ *Strada Statale Orientale Sarda, 4 km (2½ miles) southeast of city center, Olbia* ☎ *0789/563444* ⊕ *www.geasar.it.*

BUS

Cagliari is linked with the other towns of Sardinia by a network of buses. All major cities and most local destinations are served by ARST. City buses in Cagliari, Oristano, Olbia, Alghero, and Sassari operate on the same system as those on the mainland: either buy your ticket first, at a tobacco shop, ticket booth, or machine, and punch it in the machine on the bus, or buy onboard incurring a supplementary charge.

CONTACT ARST. ☎ *351/8374226 mobile* ⊕ *www.arst.sardegna.it.*

CAR

Sardinia is about 270 km (167 miles) long from north to south, which takes three to four hours to drive on main roads; it's roughly 120 km (75 miles) across, but there are no fast east–west routes. Most of the ferries that connect the island with the mainland transport cars.

Roads are generally in good condition, with clear signposting. Superstrada double-lane routes are well developed and toll-free. Expect winding inland mountain and coastal roads with hairpin turns. Most gas stations are closed in the afternoon, at night, and on Sunday, though at those times you can still use cards to automatically gas up. Try to avoid driving at night, when mountain roads are particularly hazardous and roadside facilities are infrequent, especially in the east. Be alert for sheep on rural routes. Fog and snow may be issues in winter.

FERRIES

Large modern ferries operated by Grimaldi Lines, Tirrenia Lines, Moby Lines, and Grandi Navi Veloci, connect mainland Italy (Genoa, Livorno, Piombino, Civitavecchia, and Naples) and Sicily (Palermo) with Sardinian ports at Porto Torres, Olbia, Arbatax, and Cagliari. Crossing time is 8–12 hours; the longer crossings are usually overnight. Moby Lines operates much smaller ferries year round between Santa Teresa di Gallura and Bonifacio, Corsica, taking less than an hour. These ferries are a popular mode of transport, however, and should be booked ahead in July and August.

CONTACTS Grandi Navi Veloci. ☎ *010/2094591* ⊕ *www.gnv.it.* **Grimaldi Lines.** ☎ *081/496444* ⊕ *www.grimaldi-lines.com.* **Moby Lines.** ⊕ *www. mobylines.com.* **Tirrenia.** ☎ *0781/965020* ⊕ *www.tirrenia-traghetti.it.*

TRAIN

Trenitalia, or Ferrovie dello Stato (FS), is the national railway of Italy. You can plan itineraries, purchase tickets, and look for special deals online. The Stazione Centrale in Cagliari is next to the bus station on Piazza Matteotti. There are fairly good connections between Olbia, Cagliari, Sassari, and Oristano. Service on the few other local lines is infrequent and slow. The fastest train between Olbia and Cagliari takes 3½ hours. Local trains run by ARST connect Sassari with Alghero (around 40 minutes).

If you can stand a little agitation and are a fan of slow travel, consider taking a trip on the rickety old narrow-gauge railroad operated by Trenino Verde della Sardegna through the island's interior. The service, which started as a public transport utility in 1893, now only operates limited routes once or twice weekly throughout the year in the form of tourist excursions that take in some of Sardinia's most panoramic landscapes. The main Trenino Verde routes currently run from the village of Mandas (linked to Cagliari by local trains) to Laconi via Serri, Isili, and Nurallao; from Arbatax, a small port on the island's east coast, to the mountain village of Lanusei; and from the inland town of Tempio Pausania, in the northeast of the island, to the village of Luras. Check on the latest routes and itineraries. Journeys take between 40 minutes and 2¾ hours, and may include guided tours of some of the places en route plus lunch stops.

CONTACTS Trenitalia. ☎ 892021, 06/3000 ⊕ www.trenitalia.com. **Trenino Verde della Sardegna.** ⊕ www.treninoverde.com.

When to Go

The best time to visit Sardinia is Easter through September. European vacationers flock to the island for sunshine in July and August. Expect to pay the highest rates during these two peak summer months, when roads, tourist sites, and beaches are most crowded. Nature is at its most exuberant during the spring, while from September to October, when accommodations start to shut down for the year, you'll find end-of-season deals and fewer tourists. During the winter months, the smaller resorts can resemble ghost towns—with closed restaurants, hotels, and shops.

Restaurants

The full range of eateries can be found in every Sardinian town, from pizzerias to gourmet restaurants, and you'll be especially spoiled for choice in the island's capital, Cagliari, and the resort of Alghero, where good-value fixed-price menus are common. Seafood is ubiquitous, though the most authentic Sard cuisine is based on land products, such as lamb, boar, and suckling pig, not to mention mushrooms, artichokes, and other seasonal produce. Note that, as in other parts of Italy, fish dishes are often priced according to weight (usually by the *etto*, or 100 grams). Many places close in winter; in summer, book ahead to be sure of a table.

Hotels

In Sardinia, there are numerous luxury resorts with stunning beachfront vistas, bed-and-breakfast inns in medieval villages, private villas tucked away on lush hills, modern hotels in the trendy capital, and farmhouses on tranquil mountainsides. During summer months, the most popular destination on the island is the Costa Smeralda in the east. High demand during July and August raises nightly rates to an astronomical range, above €2,000 for the most deluxe accommodations. Find more reasonable hotel rates in other parts of the island, which are equally breathtaking and less crowded. Plan dates well in advance, as many hotels close at the end of September until the following April or May.

⇨ *Hotel and restaurant reviews have been shortened. For full information, visit Fodors.com. Prices in the hotel reviews are the lowest cost of a standard double room in high season. Prices in the dining reviews are the average cost of a main course at dinner, or, if dinner is not served, at lunch.*

What It Costs in Euros			
$	**$$**	**$$$**	**$$$$**
RESTAURANTS			
under €15	€15–€24	€25–€35	over €35
HOTELS			
under €125	€125–€200	€201–€300	over €300

Tours

Visos Viaggi
PRIVATE GUIDES | This travel agent and tour operator specializes in individual tours and villa and hotel accommodations. ✉ *Via Puccini 41, Cagliari* ☎ *070/658772* ⊕ *www.visosviaggi.com.*

Cagliari

268 km (166 miles) south of Olbia.

Known in the local dialect as Casteddu, the island's capital has a warren of pedestrianized streets at its heart and a range of impressive Italianate architecture, from modern to medieval. The city comprises around 170,000 people and has a busy commercial port and waterfront with broad avenues and arched arcades, while the old hilltop citadel (called, simply, Castello) makes a good starting point to a visit, not least for the Museo Archeologico located here. The imposing Bastione di Saint Remy and Mercato di San Benedetto (one of the best fish markets in Italy) are both must-sees.

GETTING HERE AND AROUND
The easiest way to arrive in Cagliari is by plane or boat. From the airport, it's easy to get into the city center by train. You can also rent a car at the airport; booking before arrival is highly recommended. If you arrive by boat, travel from Palermo (Sicily), Civitavecchia (Rome), or Naples. The port is near the city center.

Piazza Matteotti is the terminal for long-distance buses and Cagliari's city buses, which are operated by Consorzio Trasporti e Mobilità (CTM). Buy city bus tickets (€1.30 for a ticket valid for 90 minutes, or €3.30 for an all-day ticket) at the kiosk or machine here before boarding. From nearby Via Roma or Piazza Yenne, you can pick up the circular Bus 7, useful for reaching the old quarter in the upper town. If you don't mind the steep walk, you could get there on foot (about 10 minutes from Piazza Yenne), but you can't drive there—only residents' cars are allowed. Most of Cagliari's restaurants and bars are located in the Marina area, near the port, which is only accessible on foot.

CONTACT Consorzio Trasporti e Mobilità. ✉ *Cagliari* ☎ *800/078870, 070/20911.*

VISITOR INFORMATION
CONTACTS Cagliari Tourism Office. ✉ *Palazzo Civico, Piazza Matteotti, Cagliari* ☎ *338/6498498 mobile, 070/6777397* ⊕ *cagliariturismo.comune.cagliari.it.* **Infopoint Aeroporto Elmas.** ✉ *Arrivals hall, Cagliari airport, Via dei Trasvolatori, Elmas* ☎ *070/21121281* ⊕ *www.sardegnaturismo.it.*

Sights

Anfiteatro Romano
RUINS | This substantial amphitheater arena dating from the 2nd century AD attests to the importance of this area to the Romans. You can view it from a raised walkway but not (at least for the time being) enter the seating area or the underground passages. ■**TIP→ If you don't want to enter the site, good views can be had from Viale Sant'Ignazio.** ✉ *Viale Sant'Ignazio da Laconi, Cagliari* ☎ *070/6777900* ⊕ *www.beniculturali-cagliari.it* 🎟 *€3.*

Castello
VIEWPOINT | Perched over the vast expanse of Cagliari and its port, this hillside quarter has narrow streets that

Cagliari and the Southern Coast

hold ancient monuments and piazzas amid apartments with wash hung out to dry on elaborate wrought-iron balconies. The most impressive entrance is through the commanding late-19th-century archway of the Bastione di St. Remy on Piazza Costituzione. Entering this way means climbing numerous steps; if this is a problem, walk up Viale Regina Elena to find an elevator. At the top is an impressive panorama of the cityscape and the Gulf of Cagliari. From Piazza Palazzo, holding Cagliari's cathedral, it's a level walk to Piazza Indipendenza and the Museo Archeologico. ⊠ *Cagliari.*

Duomo
CHURCH | The Cattedrale di Santa Maria, also known as the Duomo, was begun in the 12th century, but major renovation in the 17th century and reconstruction during the mid-1930s have left little of the original medieval church. The tiers of columns on the facade resemble those of medieval Romanesque Pisan churches, but only sections of the central portal, the bell tower, and the two side entrances are from the 13th century. Look for one of the most memorable features inside—the oversize marble pulpit sculpted in the 1300s and divided in half to fit into the church nave; it now lies on either side of the main entrance. ⊠ *Piazza Palazzo, Cagliari* ☎ *070/663837* ⊕ *www. duomodicagliari.it* ⊙ *Closed 1 pm–4 pm Mon.–Sat. and 1 pm–4:30 pm Sun.*

★ Museo Archeologico
HISTORY MUSEUM | Built within the walls of the Pisan castle erected in the early 1300s, Cagliari's archaeological museum is the world's foremost authority on Sardinia's ancient Nuraghic civilization, named after the curious stone towers,

or nuraghi, that are unique to the island. Archaeologists date most of these enigmatic structures to about 1300–1200 BC, the same time the ancient Israelites were establishing themselves in Canaan. Among the highlights on display are *bronzetti* (bronze statuettes) from nuraghic towers and tombs, displayed in the basement, and the much-celebrated Giganti di Mont'e Prama, giant nuraghic stone statues representing warriors and boxers, unearthed in the 1970s and only recently restored and displayed to the public, on the top floor.

The same entry ticket also allows you to visit the Spazio di San Pancrazio, a new exhibition space located within the thick city walls opposite the museum, showing a motley collection of lapidary monuments and majolica and azulejos tiles. ⊠ *Cittadella dei Musei, Piazza Arsenale, Cagliari* ☎ *070/655911* ⊕ *museinazionalicagliari.cultura.gov.it* ⊠ *€9* ☉ *Closed Tues. Nov.–Feb.*

Orto Botanico

GARDEN | FAMILY | Located just below Cagliari's amphitheater, the city's Botanical Garden offers a welcome refuge from the summer's heat, and a shady spot for a pause from sightseeing. The 12-acre site is managed by Cagliari university and includes plants from all over the Mediterranean as well as Africa and further afield, plus herbariums, ponds, and a scattering of Roman remains, notably cisterns, tanks, and a well. As the only green space in the city center, it's ideal for kids to let off steam, and perfect for a picnic. Guided tours are also available (book ahead). ⊠ *Viale Sant'Ignazio da Laconi 11, Cagliari* ☎ *070/6753512* ⊕ *sites.unica.it/hbk* ⊠ *€4* ☉ *Closed Mon.*

Torre dell'Elefante

HISTORIC SIGHT | Part of Cagliari's imposing Pisan defenses, this medieval fortified tower was built in 1307 by Giovanni Capula as one of the main entrances to the Castello quarter. It is named after the small carving of an elephant visible

on one wall. The side facing the old citadel was left entirely open, allowing you to view the series of wooden stairs and landings inside without climbing a step. If you are tempted to climb to the top, you'll be rewarded by a fabulous panorama of the city and its surrounding lagoons. Visits are only possible on guided tours, scheduled at 15 minutes past the hour; under-12s are not permitted for safety reasons. The structure is the twin of Torre San Pancrazio, located near the archaeological museum and currently closed for renovation work. ⊠ *Via Santa Croce, Cagliari* ☎ *070/6777900* ⊕ *www.beniculturalicagliari.it* ⊠ *€3.*

🏖 Beaches

★ Poetto Beach

BEACH | FAMILY | Only 5 km (3 miles) southeast of the city center, Poetto Beach is one of the most enticing spots to relax in summer for both locals and tourists. Its clean, shallow, turquoise waters stretch for some 8 km (5 miles), and the beach is lined with cafés, restaurants, snack bars, and parks. Beach chairs and umbrellas are available for rent for around €15. Away from the sea, you can explore the nearby Molentargius lagoon, and admire the pink flamingos that nest in the marshy reeds there. ■TIP→ **Poetto is easy to reach on the frequent public transport services: take Bus PF, PQ, or, in summer, Poetto Express, from Piazza Matteotti. Amenities:** food and drink; lifeguards; parking (fee in summer); showers; toilets; water sports. **Best for:** swimming; walking; windsurfing. ⊠ *Cagliari* ✈ *By car, take Viale Diaz from Cagliari to Viale Poetto.*

🍴 Restaurants

★ Dal Corsaro

$$$$ | ITALIAN | This elegant but simply furnished Michelin-starred restaurant near the port offers modern and creative Italian haute cuisine on two wide-ranging

tasting menus (€120 and €155 per person), consisting of a series of dishes that are only revealed when presented to your table (any food allergies can be communicated beforehand). Dal Corsaro shares its kitchen and chef, Stefano Deidda, with the adjacent Fork, a modern bistro where you may find such mouthwatering concoctions as battered salt-cod with a dusting of smoked pepperoni, and steak tartare with a Parmesan sauce, while desserts might include a thyme-based panna cotta infused with white peach and topped with white chocolate. **Known for:** adventurous and sophisticated cuisine; surprise dishes on fixed-price menus; subdued, sober atmosphere (in Dal Corsaro). ⑤ *Average main: €120* ✉ *Viale Regina Margherita 28, Cagliari* ☏ *070/664318* ⊕ *www.stefanodeidda.it* ⊗ *Fork closed Mon. and Tues. and 2 wks in Jan. Dal Corsaro closed for lunch.*

Sa Ide e S'Ollia

$$ | ITALIAN | Take a tour of contemporary Sardinian gastronomy in this trendsetting place that has become a huge hit with the *cagliaritani.* You can choose between eating à la carte or the small dishes offered on the tasting menus (€27, €32, and €37, including desserts and drinks), which might include such bold pairings as tagliatelle with pesto, hazelnut, cherry, and fresh orange, beef strips with berries and myrtle liqueur, and sea bream fillet with cherry, thyme, and orange oil. **Known for:** innovative food pairings; enthusiastic service; good-value set menus. ⑤ *Average main: €17* ✉ *Corso Vittorio Emanuele II 370, Cagliari* ☏ *327/9649391 mobile* ⊕ *www.facebook.com/saideesollia* ⊗ *June–Oct. no lunch weekends, no dinner Tues.; Nov.–May no lunch Sat., no dinner Sun. and Tues.*

Su Cumbidu

$$ | ITALIAN | A meal at this restaurant in Cagliari's lively Marina quarter, near the port, makes for a quick and affordable introduction to Sardinia's rural cuisine. Dishes can be ordered as part of a fixed-price meal or separately, and portions are large, so go easy on antipasti to leave room for main courses of lamb, sausage, and the famous Sardinian *maialetto* (roast suckling pig, aka *porcheddu*). **Known for:** traditional meat-based dishes; casual, friendly atmosphere; range of set-price menus. ⑤ *Average main: €15* ✉ *Via Napoli 13, Cagliari* ☏ *070/670712* ⊕ *www. facebook.com/sucumbiduterra.*

☕ Coffee and Quick Bites

Antico Caffè

$$ | ITALIAN | The gilded Antico Caffè once served as an intellectual haunt for famous writers like D.H. Lawrence and Grazia Deledda, who won the Nobel Prize in Literature in 1926.With its street-front terrace and polished-wood interior, it has anchored the base of the Bastione di St. Remy since 1855, serving as a social center from breakfast time until well after midnight; the menu features local fish and meat specialties. **Known for:** traditional ambience; swift lunches; late closing. ⑤ *Average main: €20* ✉ *Piazza Costituzione 10/11, Cagliari* ☏ *070/658206* ⊕ *www.anticocaffe1855.it.*

Caffè Svizzero

$ | ITALIAN | Entering this antique, vaulted bar a stone's throw from the port is like stepping back into the 19th century. Order a steaming cappuccino, a glass of the local vermentino wine, or a freshly squeezed fruit juice, and nibble on a panino, a pizzetta, or a pastry. **Known for:** historic interior; great pastries; courteous staff. ⑤ *Average main: €5* ✉ *Largo Carlo Felice 6–8, Cagliari* ☏ *070/664578* ⊗ *Closed Tues.*

Hotels

Hotel AeR BJ Vittoria

$$ | B&B/INN | The airy white rooms, period-style furnishings, and ceramic flooring make this third-floor pension directly opposite the port cozy and characterful. **Pros:** clean rooms; central location near port; family atmosphere. **Cons:** breakfast is not served in the hotel; no parking; shabby entrance. ⑤ *Rooms from: €130* ⊠ *Via Roma 75, Cagliari* ☎ *349/4473556 mobile, 070/667970* ⊕ *www.hotelbjvittoria.it* ↝ *14 rooms* ¶◎¶ *Free Breakfast.*

Hotel Regina Margherita

$$ | **HOTEL** | Close to the port and the main downtown sights, this large, modern hotel attracts both vacationers and businesspeople with a quiet, friendly ambience and spacious, sober rooms. **Pros:** central location; higher rooms have harbor views; free parking. **Cons:** lacks local character; few leisure facilities; breakfast sometimes disappoints. ⑤ *Rooms from: €145* ⊠ *Viale Regina Margherita 44, Cagliari* ☎ *070/670342* ⊕ *www.hotelreginamargherita.com* ↝ *100 rooms* ¶◎¶ *Free Breakfast.*

Il Gallo Bianco

$ | **B&B/INN** | A broad sun terrace and white, plant-filled decor make this sleek boutique hotel a good choice, as do the spacious and surprisingly quiet—given the busy location—guest rooms, all of which have modern bathrooms and some of which have private balconies. **Pros:** sun terrace; central location near the train and bus stations; friendly staff. **Cons:** no parking; neighborhood is traffic-heavy and run-down; breakfast is a bit basic. ⑤ *Rooms from: €123* ⊠ *Via Roma 237, Cagliari* ☎ *334/9533149 mobile* ⊕ *www.gallobiancocagliari.it* ↝ *16 rooms* ¶◎¶ *Free Breakfast.*

La Ghirlanda

$ | **B&B/INN** | At this quiet haven in the heart of the Marina quarter, the spacious, high-ceilinged rooms are decorated with taste and restraint with period furnishings redolent of the 19th century, making you feel as if you're a guest at a palazzo. **Pros:** elegant rooms; reasonable rates; convenient location near the port and bus and train stations. **Cons:** no views from the rooms; no parking; scarce breakfast.

⑤ *Rooms from: €120* ⊠ *Via Lodovico Baylle 7, Cagliari* ☎ *351/5364248 mobile* ⊕ *www.bnblaghirlanda.com* ↝ *3 rooms* ¶◎¶ *Free Breakfast.*

★ T Hotel

$$ | **HOTEL** | In the vicinity of Parco di Monte Claro, about a 15-minute taxi or bus ride from Cagliari's center, this trendy hotel offers contemporary styling and upscale guest rooms in a 15-floor circular tower with sweeping city views. **Pros:** great views from most rooms; free parking; outstanding service. **Cons:** 2 km (1¼ miles) from port; spa facilities can get busy; constant bustle in public areas. ⑤ *Rooms from: €135* ⊠ *Via Dei Giudicati 66, Cagliari* ☎ *070/47400* ⊕ *www.thotel.it* ↝ *207 rooms* ¶◎¶ *Free Breakfast.*

ⓨ Nightlife

Al Merlo Parlante

PUB | This backstreet *birroteca* ("beer bar") has been dispensing distinguished brews for the last 40 years, and is a favorite haunt of students and beer aficionados of all ages. Local Sardinian craft beers and lagers and ales from around the world feature on its extensive and changing menu, many of them hand-pulled. The list of panini is almost equally long and equally impressive, and nachos are also served. ⊠ *Via Portoscalas 69, Cagliari* ☎ *351/6638849 mobile* ⊕ *www.facebook.com/al.merlo.parlante.*

Caffè Libarium Nostrum

WINE BAR | A dim bohemian haunt full of wooden beams and brick-lined nooks and crannies, Libarium Nostrum is one of Cagliari's coolest café-bars. It's an occasional venue for live music and DJs, but the real draw is the outdoor terrace high atop medieval ramparts, the perfect spot for enjoying cocktails and sunset views. Food is available, from panini and other snacks to meat and fish dishes, and it stays open late. ⊠ *Via Santa Croce 33/35, Cagliari* ☎ *346/5220212 moblie.*

🎭 Performing Arts

The Teatro Lirico stages concerts with local and well-known European artists throughout the year. See ⊕ *www.teatroliricodicagliari.it* or contact the tourist office for information.

🛍 Shopping

Cagliari's best shopping street—full of boutiques and specialty shops for clothes, shoes, bags, and jewelry—is **Via Manno,** just up from the port off Piazza Yenne. Via Manno climbs to Piazza Costituzione, from where **Via Garibaldi** trails back downhill, where you'll find an equally good range of slightly cheaper stores.

Galinanoa

CRAFTS | This smart store in the Marina neighborhood holds a cornucopia of original and eye-catching artifacts inspired by traditional Sardinian arts and crafts, but with an original modern slant. Particularly appealing are the vividly colored ceramics, woven and wooden goods, elegant handbags, and highly stylized sheep and bulls sculptures. Ask about shipping items home. ⊠ *Via Baylle 71, Cagliari* 📞 *070/7563543* ⊕ *www.facebook.com/galinanoa.*

Sapori di Sardegna

SPECIALTY STORE | Drop into this shop for Sardinian food products, including local wines, artisanal biscuits, pecorino cheeses, carasau flatbread, honey, and olives. There's a great range of items, and the English-speaking staff are always willing to help you out. If you want to sample some of the foodstuffs first, try the branches nearby at Pipette (⊠ *Via dei Mille 8)* and Sabores (⊠ *Via Baylle 6)*, where snacks and full meals are served. ⊠ *Vico dei Mille 1, Cagliari* 📞 *070/6848747* ⊕ *www.saborescagliari.com.*

🏃 Activities

WINDSURFING
Windsurfing Club Cagliari

WINDSURFING | **FAMILY** | Sardinia has some of Europe's best windsurfing spots. This outfit located in Cagliari's beach resort of Poetto provides advice, lessons, and courses for everyone from beginners to experts. ⊠ *Viale Marina Piccola, Cagliari* 📞 *070/372694* ⊕ *www.windsurfingclub.it.*

Pula

29 km (18 miles) southwest of Cagliari, 314 km (195 miles) southwest of Olbia.

Resort villages sprawl along the coast southwest of the capital, which has its share of fine scenery and good beaches. On the marshy shoreline between Cagliari's Aeroporto di Elmas and Pula, huge flocks of flamingos are a common sight. Beaches and lodging catering to summer crowds are concentrated 4 km (2½ miles) south of Pula, a little more than 1½ km (1 mile) south of Nora, in a conglomeration that makes up Santa Margherita di Pula. At Chia, 19 km (12 miles) southwest of Pula, is one of Sardinia's most magnificent coastal stretches, with white-sand beaches, turquoise waters, placid coves, and powdery dunes.

GETTING HERE AND AROUND
From Cagliari, drive approximately 40 km (25 miles) on the SS195. Follow directions for Pula/Chia. From Olbia, take SS131 toward Cagliari-Sassari; then, follow SS554 toward Pula/Chia. The journey is approximately 300 km (190 miles).

Sights

★ Nora

MUSEUM VILLAGE | The narrow promontory outside Pula was the site of a Phoenician, Carthaginian, and then, later, Roman settlement that was first inhabited some 2,800 years ago. Nora was a prime location as a stronghold and an important trading town; Phoenician settlers scouted for good harbors, cliffs to shelter their craft from the wind, and an elevation from which they could defend themselves. An old Roman paved road passes the temple ruins, which include baths, a Roman theater, and an amphitheater now used for summer music festivals. ⊠ *3 km (2 miles) south of Pula, Pula* ☎ *329/6715230 mobile* ⊕ *www. fondazionepulacultura.it* ⊠ *€8.*

Sant'Efisio

CHURCH | The simple 11th-century church at the base of the Nora promontory is key to one of the island's most colorful annual events. Don't be put off by the inappropriate modern frontage added to the building in 2021—the interior retains its ancient character. A four-day procession during the Festa di Sant'Efisio accompanies a statue of the martyred St. Efisius all the way from Cagliari to here and back again. The event culminates in a huge parade of costumed Sardinians and decorated *traccas* (ox-drawn carriages) along Cagliari's main avenue. Try to catch this if you're in southern Sardinia from May 1 to May 4. ⊠ *Nora Beach, Pula* ⊹ *3 km (2 miles) south of Pula* ☎ *347/1436054 mobile* ⊕ *www.facebook.com/confraternitadisantefisio.pula* ☉ *Closed weekdays and Sat. morning.*

🏖 Beaches

★ Chia Beach

BEACH | FAMILY | Although there is a perfectly serviceable sandy beach right outside the archaeological site of Nora, infinitely more enticing is the series of long expanses of sand 18 km (11 miles) farther south toward the cape of Capo Spartivento, Sardinia's southernmost tip. **Amenities:** food and drink; lifeguards; parking (fee in summer); toilets. **Best for:** swimming. ⊠ *Santa Margherita di Pula* ⊹ *By car, head south down the SS195 past Santa Margherita di Pula.*

🍽 Restaurants

Su Furriadroxu

$$ | SOUTHERN ITALIAN | Amid the lime and lemon trees in this courtyard trattoria in the center of Pula, you'll find down-home Sard cooking at its most authentic, with the accent firmly on meat dishes. The menu (in the local Campidanese dialect, with Italian and English translations) lists a selection of meaty fare, with pride of place going to the most famous of island dishes, *porceddu* (roast suckling pig), which you'll find displayed sizzling on a spit to satisfy the most purist of local gourmands. **Known for:** authentic Campidanese cooking; traditional outdoor setting; carnivorous feast. ⑤ *Average main: €16* ⊠ *Via XXIV Maggio 11, Pula* ☎ *070/9246148* ⊕ *www.sufurriadroxu.it* ☉ *Closed Nov.; Wed. June–Sept.; and Tues. and Wed. Oct.–May. No lunch Mon.–Sat. No dinner Sun.*

🛏 Hotels

★ Conrad Chia Laguna Sardinia

$$$$ | RESORT | Now relaunched under Hilton's Conrad banner, the Chia Laguna hotel still has its captivating position overlooking Monte Cogoni beach and the sleek expanse of Chia lagoon, and its five-star facilities are geared to maximizing guests' enjoyment of these natural advantages. **Pros:** first-class facilities; choice of fine restaurants; proximity to some of Sardinia's best beaches. **Cons:** remote location; extravagant room rates and extras; music can be intrusive in the evening. ⑤ *Rooms from: €619* ⊠ *Via dei Fenicotteri 52, Chia* ☎ *070/92393000* ⊕ *www.chialagunaresort. com* ☉ *Closed mid-Oct.–early Apr.* ⊅ *107 rooms* ⫶⊘⫶ *Free Breakfast.*

Costa dei Fiori

$$$$ | **HOTEL** | **FAMILY** | Worry and stress seem to melt away upon arriving at this beach hideaway, where modern guest rooms with stone floors, big windows, and rural Sardinian touches are surrounded by peaceful gardens planted with pines and palms. **Pros:** great leisure facilities; lovely grounds; good low-season rates. **Cons:** poor road access; you need a car; the beach may disappoint. $ *Rooms from: €311* ✉ *SS195 Km 33, Santa Margherita di Pula* ☎ *070/9245333* ⊕ *www.costadeifiori.it* ⊘ *Closed late Oct.–Apr.* ⌁ *82 rooms* ⦚ *Free Breakfast.*

★ Faro Capo-Spartivento

$$$$ | **HOTEL** | Atop a cliff at the end of a rocky track on Sardinia's southernmost tip, a working lighthouse dating from 1856 contains this unusual hotel—a self-described "door suspended between the sky and the sea"—where it's easy to switch off and tune out amid luxurious surroundings. **Pros:** select and secluded; excellent restaurant; unique character and setting. **Cons:** remote and isolated location; restaurant service can be slow; extravagant rates. $ *Rooms from: €810* ✉ *Viale Spartivento* ✛ *5 km (3 miles) southwest of Chia* ☎ *393/8276800 mobile* ⊕ *www.farocapospartivento.com* ⌁ *10 rooms* ⦚ *Free Breakfast.*

Is Molas Resort

$$$ | **HOTEL** | **FAMILY** | If you love golf and stargazing, then the place to stay in southern Sardinia is this peaceful hotel, with 72 Mediterranean-style rooms and a 27-hole golf complex. **Pros:** immediate access to golf course; freshwater pool; tranquil setting with rural views. **Cons:** lacks charm; isolated location; service occasionally lacking. $ *Rooms from: €299* ✉ *SS195, Località Is Molas, Pula* ☎ *070/9241006* ⊕ *www.ismolas.it* ⊘ *Closed Nov.–May* ⌁ *72 rooms* ⦚ *Free Breakfast.*

Sant'Antioco

75 km (47 miles) west of Pula, 100 km (62 miles) west of Cagliari.

Off Sardinia's southwest coast is the sleepy island of Sant'Antioco, whose good beaches have made it a popular holiday spot. Outside the peak summer months, though, the most hectic activity seems to be the silent repairing of nets by local fishermen who have already pulled in their daily catch. The island has been connected to the mainland since Carthaginian times by a causeway that's still standing (the modern causeway that you cross runs parallel), and Sant'Antioco town (the island and its main town share the same name) has a fascinating collection of archaeological remains from this period.

GETTING HERE AND AROUND

Sant'Antioco is about 90 minutes from Cagliari by bus or car. Drive on the SS130 as far as Iglesias, then the SS126 in the direction of Carbonia and Sant'Antioco.

Sights

Calasetta

TOWN | On the island of Sant'Antioco, off the southwestern coast of Sardinia, the fishing village and port of Calasetta draws visitors year-round for its beautiful beaches and fresh-seafood dishes. The pristine beaches of Spiaggia Grande and Le Saline, alternating with rocky areas, dunes, and local vegetation, form a rugged paradise. Founded by Ligurian settlers who worked as coral and tuna fishermen, Calasetta is connected daily by ferry boats with the smaller island of San Pietro, which also keeps intact its Ligurian cultural history and dialect. ✉ *10 km (6 miles) northwest of Sant'Antioco town, Sant'Antioco.*

Carbonia

TOWN | If you like to seek out the esoteric, explore the rugged inland hills and town of Carbonia, less than 30 minutes' drive from Sant'Antioco and about an hour by car or train from Cagliari. Built in 1938 by Mussolini to serve as an administrative center of a once-booming coal-mining area, its time-frozen architecture—ordered rows of workers' houses around a core of monumental public buildings on the broad Piazza Roma—has been called an urban UFO set down in the Sardinian landscape. ⊠ *Piazza Roma 1, Carbonia* ☎ *0781/6941 tourist office* ⊕ *www. carboniaturismo.it.*

Iglesias

TOWN | Perched at about 600 feet in the southwest hills of the island, this authentic Sardinian town 35 km (22 miles) north of Sant'Antioco has two notable medieval churches: the Cattedrale di Santa Chiara and Madonna delle Grazie. The town is famous for its theatrical, Spanish-inflected Easter festivities. A short drive away, on the Costa Verde, you can enjoy unspoiled, uncrowded beaches, including the beautiful Masua cove at Porto Cauli beach. ⊠ *Piazza Municipio, Iglesias* ☎ *0781/274507 tourist office* ⊕ *www. iglesiasturismo.it.*

Monte Sirai

ARCHAEOLOGICAL SITE | Just outside Carbonia and strategically positioned atop a plateau that provides views inland and far out to sea, the remains of one of Sardinia's most important Carthaginian military strongholds were discovered by chance in 1962. The walls of Mt. Sirai were erected around 375 BC, and they continued to function as impregnable fortress barriers until the Roman conquest in 238 BC. For the full picture, try to combine your visit with a look at Carbonia's archaeological museum on Via Campania. ⊠ *Off SS126, Km 17, Località Sirai ✛ 1 km (½ mile) north of Carbonia, direction Sant'Antioco* ☎ *345/7559751 archaeological site (mobile), 345/8886058 museum (mobile)* ⊕ *www.carboniamusei.it* ⊠ *Site €6, museum €6, or €10 for both* ⊙ *Closed Mon., also Tues. Oct.–Mar.*

Zona Archeologica

RUINS | The chief point of interest in Sant'Antioco island's eponymous main town is the Archaeological Zone at the top of the old section, which has terrific views of the Sardinian mainland. Here you can see a *tophet*—a Punic sanctuary, necropolis, and burial site—which is scattered with urns that contained the cremated remains of stillborn children. Below the site is Sant'Antioco's excellent archaeological museum that showcases artifacts from the tophet as well as from the Neolithic, Byzantine, and Roman eras. You can also visit a nearby ethnographic collection and a Piedmontese fort. Various combined tickets are available. ⊠ *Via Sabatino Moscati, Sant'Antioco* ☎ *0781/82105, 389/7962114 mobile* ⊕ *www.mabsantantioco.it* ⊠ *Archaeological zone €4, museum €6, combined tickets for both €7, ethnographic collection €3, Piedmontese fort €2.50.*

San Pietro

5 km (3 miles) northwest of Sant'Antioco.

A ferry at the small northern port of Calasetta connects Sant'Antioco with Carloforte, the main town on the smaller island of San Pietro. This classic little Italian port and its surrounding coastline are a favorite of wealthy Cagliaritans, many of whom have built weekend cottages here. The best views are from Capo Sandalo, on San Pietro's rugged western coast, but head to the island's southern tip for the beaches. Accommodation is especially scarce during the annual music festival (⊕ *www.carlofortefestival.com*) that takes place in late July and early August. During daylight hours the ferry departs approximately hourly in summer and every 90 minutes in winter—the trip takes 30 minutes.

GETTING HERE AND AROUND

Car ferries operated by Delcomar connect San Pietro with Calasetta on Sant'Antioco, or Portoscuso near Iglesias on the Sardinian mainland. Round-trip tickets are €10–€15 per person, €20–€25 for a car.

CONTACT Delcomar. ☎ *800/195344* ⊕ *www.delcomar.it.*

Hotels

Hotel Hieracon

$ | **HOTEL** | This hotel on Carloforte's harborfront combines its elegant, historic flavor with modern whitewashed accommodation. **Pros:** helpful English-speaking staff; characterful historic ambience; good location. **Cons:** cheaper rooms are cramped; few sea-facing rooms; not up to its four-star grading. ⑤ *Rooms from: €103* ⊠ *Corso Cavour 62, Carloforte* ☎ *0781/854028, 393/7953214 mobile* ⊕ *www.hotelhieracon.com* ⊘ *Closed early Oct.–late Apr.* ⇋ *23 rooms* ¶◎¶ *Free Breakfast.*

Costa Verde

80 km (50 miles) northwest of Cagliari.

If you've come to Sardinia in search of untrammeled wilderness and sweeping sands as far as the eye can see, this semideserted coast will fit the bill. Hidden away in the forgotten southwest corner of the island, the Costa Verde, or Green Coast, is a succession of cliffs and beaches, many of them accessible only by bumpy, unpaved tracks. The effort is worth it. The dune-backed sands shelter rare grasses and birdlife, and the area offers magnificent swimming along stretches of beach that seem endless.

GETTING HERE AND AROUND

The best way to access the Green Coast is by car, though roads can be dangerously steep and winding. Take precautions and drive during daytime, also because

roads and exits are poorly lit. Roads designated "SS" are developed freeways with fast-flowing traffic.

You can approach one of the most evocative stretches of the coast, Piscinas, either from the town of Guspini, on the straggling S126, or from a turnoff a couple of miles farther south, which leads through the abandoned mining town of Ingurtosu. It's a strange, ghostly cluster of chimneys and workers' dwellings, forlorn amid the encroaching scrubland. Drive down the dirt track another 10 km (6 miles) or so, through woods of juniper, to reach the sea.

Beaches

Piscinas

BEACH | **FAMILY** | Sea and nature are the big draws of Sardinia's Costa Verde, where you'll find such wild and unpopulated beaches as Piscinas, at the southern end of the coast and reached via a rough mountain road that passes deserted mines and herds of goats. **Amenities:** none. **Best for:** solitude; sunset; swimming; walking. ⊠ *Via Bau, Arbus.*

Torre dei Corsari

BEACH | **FAMILY** | At the northern end of the Costa Verde, Torre dei Corsari is a long and wide stretch of quartz sand, easily accessible and with plenty of facilities including bars, restaurants, and sun beds to rent. **Amenities**: food and drink; parking (fee in summer); toilets. **Best for:** sunset; swimming. ⊠ *Viale della Torre, Arbus.*

Hotels

Hotel Le Dune

$$$$ | **HOTEL** | A remote Green Coast oasis on lovely Piscinas Beach—between Capo Pecora and Capo Frasca—this luxury hotel occupies a former warehouse, built in the late 1800s to house minerals excavated from surrounding hills. **Pros:** beachfront property; breathtaking setting;

yoga sessions available. **Cons:** remote location; somewhat basic, overpriced rooms; small gym. $ *Rooms from: €328* ✉ *Via Bau 1, Piscinas di Ingurtosu, Arbus* ☎ *070/7058030* ⊕ *www.ledunepiscinas. com* ☾ *Closed Oct.–late Apr.* ⟿ *20 rooms* ❄ *Free Breakfast.*

Barumini

65 km (40 miles) north of Cagliari.

Take a detour along good roads into Sardinia's interior to visit the extraordinary stone village-fortress of Su Nuraxi, just outside the quiet village of Barumini.

GETTING HERE AND AROUND
The best way to reach Su Nuraxi is by car. From the capital, follow SS131 to SS197. Direct buses to the site are few and far between.

 Sights

⭐ **Su Nuraxi**
RUINS | FAMILY | The most extensive of the island's 7,000 discovered nuraghi, Su Nuraxi is on the UNESCO World Heritage list. Concentric rings of thick stone walls conceal dark chambers and narrow passages in a central beehive-shape tower. In the ruins of the surrounding village there are benches, ovens, wells, and other Bronze Age remnants. Tours start every 30 minutes and last about 50 minutes. The same ticket includes entry to a museum and exhibition center in Barumini. ■**TIP→ If you're driving from SS131, don't be misled to other, lesser nuraghi—follow the signs all the way to Barumini.** ✉ *Viale Su Nuraxi, Barumini* ⚓ *SP5 Barumini–Tuili, 1 km (½ mile) west of Barumini* ☎ *070/9368128* ⊕ *www. fondazionebarumini.it* 🎫 *€15.*

Oristano

60 km (37 miles) northwest of Barumini, 93 km (58 miles) northwest of Cagliari.

The elegant and compact old quarter of this provincial center off the tourist track exudes a distinct serenity. Oristano's evening passeggiata teems with vivacious children and has a relaxed friendliness about it.

GETTING HERE AND AROUND
Oristano is easily accessible and well connected to other major areas of Sardinia by car, train, or bus. Trains and buses between Cagliari, Sassari, Olbia, and Nuoro stop here several times per day. The central bus station is in the city center, the train station on the outskirts, a short bus or taxi ride away. By car, turn off the SS131 highway for Oristano. The part-pedestrianized old center is easily negotiable on foot.

VISITOR INFORMATION
CONTACT Oristano Tourist Office. ✉ *Piazza Eleonora 19, Oristano* ☎ *0783/308691* ⊕ *www.gooristano.com.*

 Sights

Cabras
BEACH | FAMILY | Extensive marshlands and shallow lagoons teeming with eels, crayfish, and wildlife surround this calm and compact 11th-century town. Make a stop at the archaeological museum here for its awe-inspiring nuraghic statues, then drive north and west into the Sinis Peninsula to access the pristine beaches of Is Arutas, Maimoni, and Mari Ermi, characterized by fine white quartzified sand grains. ✉ *SP3 off SP1, 10 km (6 miles) northwest of Oristano, Cabras.*

 Restaurants

Cocco e Dessi
$$ | ITALIAN | The building dates from 1925 but the interior shows a diversity of styles, with the main dining area (one of

five) inside a glass gazebo. Dishes featuring fresh catches of the day, vegetables, and herb-infused sauces are complemented by pizzas and pastas—just save room for a dessert of orange-flavored crème caramel topped with walnuts and chocolate or pastry with Chantilly cream and berries. **Known for:** quirky decor; convivial setting; great pizzas. ⑤ *Average main: €19 ⊠ Via Tirso 31, Oristano* ☎ *0783/252648* ⊕ *www.coccoedessi.it.*

Ristorante Craf da Banana

$$ | ITALIAN | The brick walls, dim lighting, and arched ceilings here make you feel as if you've stepped into a wine cellar. Aged photographs of Oristano's Sa Sartiglia jousting festival and specialty dishes from Oristano and Montiferru do a good job capturing local flavor. **Known for:** traditional Sardinian dishes; historical setting; cozy, romantic atmosphere. ⑤ *Average main: €18 ⊠ Via de Castro 34, Oristano* ☎ *0783/70669* ⊕ *www.ristorantecrafdabanana.com* ⊘ *No lunch Sun. June–Sept. No dinner Sun. Oct.–May.*

Trattoria Gino

$$ | SOUTHERN ITALIAN | Light-color walls lined with bottles of wine and two simple rows of tables deck out the single room of Trattoria Gino, beloved by locals, especially at lunch, and run by the same family for nearly a century. Although the lobster is a memorable splurge, consider trying any of the antipasto selections or spaghetti *ai ricci* (with sea urchins). **Known for:** honest, local cooking; reasonable prices; cordial, attentive service. ⑤ *Average main: €15 ⊠ Via Tirso 13, Oristano* ☎ *0783/71428* ⊘ *Closed Sun. and late Aug.–mid-Sept.*

 Hotels

Mariano IV Palace Hotel

$ | HOTEL | This central downtown hotel has a reassuringly old-fashioned style, with its grand, columned exterior and elegant neoclassical lobby hung with chandeliers. **Pros:** convenient location; good restaurant; low online rates. **Cons:** dated feel; caters mostly to business travelers; no parking for cars. ⑤ *Rooms from: €90 ⊠ Piazza Mariano 50, Oristano* ☎ *0783/360101* ⊕ *www.hotelmarianoiv.com* ⇆ *80 rooms* †⊙† *Free Breakfast.*

Residenza d'Epoca Regina d'Arborea

$$ | HOTEL | One floor of a 19th-century palazzo, next to the town hall on Oristano's traffic-free main square, has been tastefully converted into a small but stylish guest house, with rich furnishings, chandeliers, antique murals, and domed ceilings. **Pros:** period character; central location; helpful hosts. **Cons:** few facilities; no car access possible; not suitable for children. ⑤ *Rooms from: €144 ⊠ Piazza Eleonora d'Arborea 4, Oristano* ☎ *0783/302101* ⊕ *www.reginadarborea.it* ⊘ *Closed 10 days in Dec.* ⇆ *6 rooms* †⊙† *Free Breakfast.*

 Activities

BIKING
Bike Or

BIKING | Oristano and the flat terrain surrounding it is ideal for cycling, in particular the Sinis peninsula to the north and west, which ranks as Sardinia's most rewarding area for exploring on two wheels. Bike Or has a range of bikes to rent that can be delivered to and collected from a location of your choosing, and also arranges guided cycling excursions. ⊠ *Viale Repubblica 54, Oristano* ☎ *349/3967335 museum* ⊕ *www.bikeor.it.*

Tharros

16 km (10 miles) west of Oristano, 52 km (32 miles) northwest of Barumini.

Spread across a thin tongue of land that dangles off the Sinis Peninsula, the archaeological site of Tharros ranks as one of Sardinia's most important Phoenician, Carthaginian, and Roman settlements. It's not hard to understand why this evocative site was selected by the ancients, given its sweeping views across the Gulf of Oristano, its defensibility, and the shelter it provides vessels. Founded around 800 BC, the city was finally abandoned in the 11th century AD, in favor of Oristano.

GETTING HERE AND AROUND
Whether you're heading to Tharros from the north or south, follow the SS131 to Oristano. Drive through Oristano toward Cabras, branching off on SP6 for San Giovanni di Sinis and Tharros. There's frequent bus service from Oristano.

◉ Sights

Museo Civico di Cabras
HISTORY MUSEUM | This lagoon-side archaeological museum displays many of the better-preserved urns and other artifacts recovered from nearby excavation sites, including Tharros. It is also the main home of the Giganti di Mont'e Prama—unique nuraghic stone statues recovered from the Sinis Peninsula in the 1970s but only recently viewable in their restored state. The visit takes about an hour. Buy a combination ticket to see the Museo Civico and the ruins at Tharros. ⊠ *Via Tharros 121, off SP6, 10 km (6 miles) northwest of Oristano, Cabras* ☎ *0783/290636* ⊕ *www.museocabras.it* ✉ *€9; €13 combined ticket, includes Tharros* ⊗ *Closed Mon. Nov.–Mar.*

Tharros
RUINS | FAMILY | The spectacular site of the Carthaginian and Roman city of Tharros was, like Nora to the south, chosen because it commanded the best views of the gulf and could provide an easy escape route if inland tribes threatened. The Phoenician-Punic city planning here includes sophisticated water channeling and masonry foundations. Two reconstructed Corinthian columns stand as testament to the site's Roman history, and there are baths visible and mosaic fragments from the Roman city. ⊠ *Off SP6, 16 km*

En Route ◉

On the way to the archaeological ruins in Tharros you pass the ghost town of **San Salvatore**, revived briefly in the 1960s as a locale for spaghetti Westerns and since abandoned, except for a few days every summer, when it is the focus of a religious festival. The saloon from the movie set still stands. Among the dunes past San Salvatore are large huts formerly used by fishermen and now much in demand as vacation homes. The 5th-century church of **San Giovanni di Sinis**, on the Sinis Peninsula, is claimed to be the oldest Christian church in Sardinia.

(10 miles) west of Oristano, 113 km (70 miles) northwest of Cagliari, San Giovanni di Sinis ☎ *0783/370019* ⊕ *www.tharros.sardegna.it* ✉ *€9; €13 combined ticket, includes Museo Civico di Cabras; tower €4* ⊗ *Closed Mon. Nov.–Mar.*

Nuoro

107 km (67 miles) northeast of Tharros, 181 km (113 miles) north of Cagliari.

The strongly traditional but somewhat nondescript provincial capital of Nuoro stands on the edge of the Gennargentu massif, home to the island's highest peaks (6,000 feet). Apart from a brace of engaging museums, a lively restaurant scene and a well-attended evening *passeggiata* along the part-pedestrianized main street of the old town, not much happens here; you can do some shopping amid strolling locals, or try the local Barbagia sausage, which is great.
■ **TIP→ Entry to Nuoro's museums is free on the first Sunday of the month.**

GETTING HERE AND AROUND

From Cagliari, the drive to Nuoro takes about two hours. Take the SS131 toward Sassari/Oristano/Nuoro, then continue on SS131 DCN toward Nuoro/Olbia. After 55 km (34 miles), turn off, following signs for Nuoro Centro until you reach Nuoro.

◉ Sights

Monte Ortobene

MOUNTAIN | About 7 km (4 miles) northeast of Nuoro is Monte Ortobene, a granite peak at 2,900 feet offering lofty views over the gulch below. Here you can also see up close the imposing bronze statue of the Rendentore, or Christ the Redeemer, overlooking the valley. Pilgrimages and Masses take place in summer here. Picnic tables make this a favorite spot for an alfresco lunch throughout the year. The mountain is easily reachable from Nuoro by bus or car via SP45. ⊠ *Nuoro* ⊕ *www.comune.nuoro.it.*

Museo Deleddiano

HISTORIC HOME | Nuoro is the literary capital of Sardinia and was the home of the island's most celebrated writer, the Nobel Prize–winner Grazia Deledda (1871–1936), who was born and grew up in this dwelling in the old center. The restored building is now a museum dedicated to the novelist, elegantly furnished in the style of the late 19th century and permitting a fascinating insight into how people lived in that period. The kitchen and garden are especially interesting, and letters and photographs relating to Deledda are displayed on the top floor. ⊠ *Via Grazia Deledda 42, Nuoro* ☎ *0784/242900* ⊕ *www.isresardegna.it* 🎟 *€5, or €8 with the Ethnographic Museum.*

★ Museo Etnografico Sardo

HISTORY MUSEUM | Also known as the Museo del Costume, this ethnographic collection is a must for anyone interested in the cultural context of Sardinia's customs and traditions. Among the 8,000 items in the museum's collection, you can view domestic and agricultural implements, splendid jewelry, traditional musical instruments, and dozens of local costumes. Audio guides are available, and guided tours can be booked. The nearby park on Sant'Onofrio Hill affords magnificent views over Nuoro and the surrounding country. ⊠ *Via A. Mereu 56, Nuoro* ☎ *0784/257035* ⊕ *www.isresardegna.it* 🎟 *€5, or €8 with the Museo Deleddiano.*

🍴 Restaurants

★ Il Portico

$$ | ITALIAN | Brotherly love (and ownership) and quality seafood are among the things that make this old-town restaurant so exceptional. Modern artwork, stone pillars, and arched ceilings help to provide a fitting setting for the predominantly traditional cuisine livened up with modern elements. **Known for:** innovative takes on traditional cuisine; locals' choice; welcoming atmosphere. ⑤ *Average main: €16* ⊠ *Via Mons. Bua 13, Nuoro* ☎ *0784/232909* ⊕ *www. ilporticonuoro.it* ⊗ *Closed Mon., 2 wks in July and Aug., and 2 wks in Jan. and Feb. No dinner Sun.*

Il Rifugio

$$ | SOUTHERN ITALIAN | FAMILY | At this family-run local spot, the rustic dining area—with terra-cotta floors, brick pillars, and a wood-burning stove—is packed nearly every night. The service, presentation, and wine list are as exceptional as the food: only the freshest local meats and cheeses are served, and all the dishes are made from scratch, including the pizza (available evenings only), the pasta, and the semifreddo ice cream drizzled with honey. **Known for:** lively and convivial air; unpretentious but expertly prepared local dishes; amiable staff. ⑤ *Average main: €19* ⊠ *Via A. Mereu 28/36, Nuoro* ☎ *0784/232355* ⊕ *www.trattoriarifugio. com* ⊗ *Closed Wed. No dinner Tues.*

Hotels

★ Casa Solotti

$ | B&B/INN | You don't have to venture far out of Nuoro to appreciate its magnificent mountainous setting, and mountain views don't get much grander than from this excellent lodging immersed in the oak forests of Monte Ortobene. **Pros:** beautiful mountain views; warm and friendly hospitality; terrific breakfasts. **Cons:** remote rural location; not ideal for anyone with impaired mobility; few facilities. ⑤ *Rooms from: €70* ✉ *Località Monte Ortobene, Nuoro* ☎ *0784/33954, 328/6028975 mobile* ⊕ *www.casasolotti. it* ⊘ *Closed mid-Nov.–late Dec. and late Jan.–late Mar.* ⊷ *6 rooms* ⊚ *Free Breakfast.*

Euro Hotel

$ | HOTEL | This simple block-style hotel—more or less standard for provincial Nuoro—is ideal for a stopover; rooms are spacious and clean, with parquet flooring and modern amenities, breakfasts are abundant, and the staff are friendly and professional. **Pros:** enthusiastic staff; ample parking; near train station. **Cons:** old-fashioned character; some facilities need updating; a longish walk from the old town. ⑤ *Rooms from: €103* ✉ *Via Trieste 62, Nuoro* ☎ *0784/34071* ⊕ *www. eurohotelnuoro.it* ⊷ *54 rooms* ⊚ *Free Breakfast.*

Su Gologone Experience Hotel

$$$$ | HOTEL | Just southeast of Nuoro, in the foothills of the Supramonte range, Su Gologone combines luxury with rural flavor in guest rooms that feel like country retreats (exposed beams, wooden chests, traditional Sardinian fabrics) and a rustic restaurant that pairs local cannon-au reds with such Sardinian specialties as *maccarones de busa* (thick home-made pasta twists), *culurgiones* (ravioli), suckling pig, and, for dessert, *sebadas* (fried-dough pockets stuffed with cheese and lemon peel). **Pros:** locally influenced restaurant; great opportunities for hiking in the Supramonte Valley; museumlike decor. **Cons:** used by groups and wedding parties; many stairs to negotiate; remote location. ⑤ *Rooms from: €418* ✉ *Località Su Gologone* ☎ *0784/287512* ⊕ *www. sugologone.it* ⊘ *Closed early Nov.–early Apr.* ⊷ *68 rooms* ⊚ *Free Breakfast.*

⬤ Shopping

Latteria Zia Marianna 1936

FOOD | Named after the nonna of the current generation that runs this specialty food shop dating from 1936, this place on the main axis of Nuoro's old town offers an enticing array of jams, wines, pastas, cheeses, hams, and bread—in short all the great food and drink that this part of the island is famous for. You can sample the various wares, too, in the adjacent bar/restaurant. ✉ *Corso Garibaldi 174–176, Nuoro* ☎ *0784/1823005* ⊕ *www. facebook.com/latteriaziamarianna1936.*

Fonni

30 km (19 miles) south of Nuoro, 137 km (85 miles) south of Olbia.

In the heart of the Barbagia region, Fonni is the highest town on the island. This mountainous district, including Monte Spada and the Bruncu Spina refuge on the Gennargentu massif, is Sardinia's most primitive. Life in some villages seems not to have changed much since the Middle Ages.

GETTING HERE AND AROUND

To reach Fonni, the highest town in Sardinia, drive or take a bus from Nuoro. There is no train service.

From Nuoro, take SS389 from the junction of Mamoiada, or take SS128 to the town of Gavoi. From Cagliari, follow SS131, exiting toward the village of Ottana. Continue on SS128, turning at Fonni. From Sassari, follow SS131 south, turning east onto SS129 at Macomer. Continue on SS128, following signs for Fonni.

Hotels

Hotel Sa Orte

$ | HOTEL | Close to the highest peaks of the Gennargentu range in the center of Sardinia, this hotel, a palazzo in the center of Fonni, provides a warm welcome at any time of the year. **Pros:** generous breakfasts; affable staff; convenient for mountain excursions. **Cons:** some rooms are small and dark; restaurant food is patchy; no views. ⑤ *Rooms from: €100* ⊠ *Via Roma 14, Fonni* ☎ *0784/58020* ⊕ *www.facebook.com/hotelsaorte* ⋥ *26 rooms* ❮❍❯ *Free Breakfast.*

Shopping

Special candies made from honey and nougat are sold in hilltop Tonara, 15 km (9 miles) southwest of Fonni.

In the mountain village of Aritzo, about 45 km (28 miles) south of Fonni, high up in the Barbagia, look for handcrafted wooden utensils and furniture.

Alghero

137 km (85 miles) southwest of Olbia.

A tourist-friendly town of about 45,000 inhabitants, with a distinctly Spanish flavor, Alghero is also known as "Barcelonetta" (Little Barcelona) for its strong Catalan ties. Rich wrought-iron scrollwork decorates balconies and screened windows, street names appear in the Catalan-tinged local dialect as well as Italian, and Spanish motifs can be seen in stone portals and bell towers.

Besides its historic architectural gems, the fortified town is well worth a visit to simply stroll along its narrow cobblestone lanes, admire the sea views from its mighty city walls, and browse its pretty boutiques. To dip into the local culture, pick up from the tourist office or one of the participating attractions an "Alghero Ticket," allowing free entry into all the principal sights (€25, or €50 for a family ticket).

GETTING HERE AND AROUND

Alghero Airport is 15 km (9 miles) from the city center, which you can reach by car, taxi, or public transport. Regional buses and local trains connect the town with Sassari, and there are buses to local villages. The closest passenger port to Alghero is Porto Torres, approximately 40 km (25 miles) away, with links to Genoa, Civitavecchia (Rome), Corsica, and France.

VISITOR INFORMATION

CONTACT Alghero Tourism Office. ⊠ *Via Cagliari 2, in the public gardens, Alghero* ☎ *079/979054* ⊕ *www.algheroturismo. eu.*

Sights

Capo Caccia

NATURE SIGHT | Head 25 km (16 miles) west of Alghero for the spectacular heights of the imposing limestone headland of Capo Caccia. The rugged promontory, blanketed by thick maquis, forms part of the Porto Conte nature reserve and is home to deep caves such as the Grotta di Nettuno. Close by are the beaches of Porto Ferro, Cala Viola, and, on the beautiful Porto Conte inlet, Cala Dragunara. ⊠ *West of Alghero, Alghero* ☎ *079/945005* ⊕ *www.algheroparks.it* ⊠ *Free.*

★ Grotta di Nettuno (*Neptune's Cave*)

CAVE | FAMILY | At the base of a sheer cliff, the pounding sea has carved an entrance to a vast fantastic cavern filled with stunning water pools, stalactites, and stalagmites. The dramatic cave and coves, discovered by fishermen in the 18th century, are popular tourist attractions for their sheer natural beauty. You must visit with a guide; tours start on the hour. It's possible to reach the caves by boat or by land. Between April and November, boat trips depart regularly from the port of Alghero for €17 round-trip (admission to the grotto is extra). To reach the grotto by land, you can descend the 654 dizzying steps of Escala del Cabirol ("Goat Steps"), which are cut into the steep cliff here. ■TIP➔ **By public bus from Alghero's Via Catalogna, the trip to the top of the stairway takes about 50 minutes. Allow 15 minutes for the descent by foot.** Visitors arriving by land must book beforehand by telephone or online at ⊕ *www.algheroexperience.it.* ✉ *Off SP55, 13 km (8 miles) west of Alghero, Alghero* ☎ *345/7418361 grotto (mobile), 079/946540 office* ⊕ *www.grottadinettuno.it* 🎫 *€14* ⊙ *Closed in rough seas.*

Museo del Corallo

SPECIALTY MUSEUM | The coast around Alghero is one of the Mediterranean's most abundant sources of red coral, the subject of this entertaining and informative museum housed in a Liberty-era villa near Piazza Sulis. Old photographs and films show the process of harvesting the substance, and there are impressive displays of coral jewelry and ornaments. ✉ *Via Venti Settembre 8, Alghero* ☎ *079/4134690* ⊕ *www.museialghero. it* 🎫 *€5* ⊙ *Closed mornings Mon. and Wed., afternoons Tues. and Thurs.*

San Francesco

RELIGIOUS BUILDING | Alghero's cathedral on Via Manno hosts most of the town's official religious functions, but this 15th–16th-century church built in the Catalan-Gothic style is closest to the hearts of the *algheresi* and is the one place where you might come across the local dialect, used in some of the masses here. The simple interior holds a particularly emaciated-looking wooden Christ, while the crypt and cloister have an atmospheric charm, but the highlight of a visit is to climb the hexagonal bell tower—not too arduous—for some great views of the Old Town (open Tuesday morning, Friday, and Saturday). Evening concerts are held here in the summer months. ✉ *Via Carlo Alberto 46, Alghero* ☎ *351/6428081 mobile* ⊕ *www.complessosanfrancescoalghero.com* 🎫 *€6, €3 church and*

cloister only ⊙ *Closed Mon. morning, Thurs. afternoon, and Sun.*

🏖 Beaches

Le Bombarde and Lazzaretto Beaches

BEACH | FAMILY | A couple of kilometers north of Alghero's old town, backed by pine woods, Maria Pia beach offers a convenient though unspectacular spot for an afternoon of bathing and sunbathing, but if you don't mind going farther afield, head for the altogether superior beaches of Le Bombarde and Lazzaretto, on adjacent inlets 10 km (6 miles) west of town. Sheltered from the wind and equipped with bars and facilities for renting pedalos and canoes, the beaches are similar in style—both curves of soft sand studded with a few rocks, and both packed in August. ■TIP➔ **The beaches are easy to reach on the frequent tourist bus service, Il Trottolo (May–September). Amenities:** food and drink; lifeguards; parking (fee in summer); showers; toilets; water sports. **Best for:** snorkeling; swimming; windsurfing. ✉ *Alghero* ✛ *By car, take Via Garibaldi and then SS127bis north and west along the coast toward Fertilia.*

🍴 Restaurants

★ Al Vecchio Mulino

$$ | SOUTHERN ITALIAN | Slightly off the tourist track but well known to locals, this grotto-like former mill has two long rooms with low, vaulted ceilings and a brisk but cheerful atmosphere. There's a good balance between meat and seafood dishes, the menu taking in everything from *malloreddus alla sarda* (local pasta with sausage-meat sauce) and *fritto misto di mare* (fried squid, prawns, and fresh fish) to crusty pizzas. **Known for:** reliable cuisine reasonably priced; locals' choice; crusty pizzas. $ *Average main: €18* ✉ *Via Don Deroma 3, Alghero* ☎ *079/977254* ⊕ *www.facebook.com/alvecchiomulinoalghero* ⊙ *Closed Tues., 2 wks in late Jan., and Nov. No lunch.*

Il Pavone

$$$ | ITALIAN | Fresh flowers on white linen tablecloths add color to the bright glass-enclosed dining area of this delightful eatery on busy Piazza Sulis; gold-framed paintings and oversize wine bottles capped in wax add Italian charm—as does the seasonally changing menu of pasta and seafood dishes such as tagliolini pasta with mullet roe, artichokes, and pecorino cheese, or potato-stuffed *culurgiones* (a ravioli-like pasta) topped with sheep's cheese, dried tomatoes, and wild rocket. Many opt for the three- or four-course prix-fixe menus (€40, €50, and €60), which include a traditional dessert. **Known for:** delicious mains and desserts; impressive wine list; attentive and knowledgeable service. $ *Average main: €25* ⊠ *Piazza Sulis 3, Alghero* ☎ *079/979584* ⊕ *www. ilpavone-ristorante.com* ⊗ *Closed Wed. and 10 days in Dec. No dinner Sun. late Nov.–Easter.*

La Lepanto

$$ | SEAFOOD | A covered veranda by the seafront marks out Alghero's top seafood restaurant, an expansive and sunny room complete with crustacean-filled aquarium. Summer sees crowds of both locals and tourists, many of whom come for the specialty *aragosta* (lobster) cooked different ways, including with linguine or *alla Lepanto* (with tomato, onions, and orange). **Known for:** superior seafood in all its forms; bright interior with covered veranda seating; central location. $ *Average main: €20* ⊠ *Via Carlo Alberto 135, Alghero* ☎ *079/979116* ⊕ *www.lalepanto. com* ⊗ *Closed Feb. and Tues.*

Mabrouk

$$$$ | SEAFOOD | There's always a lively crowd at this backstreet trattoria, where diners pack into three rooms to enjoy the same multicourse set menu. If this seems limiting, think again—you'll be presented with a range of fresh, delicious, seasonally appropriate dishes (perhaps prawns, squid, swordfish, or sea bass) in abundant portions. **Known for:** prix-fixe menus with unlimited drinks; fresh seafood; vivacious atmosphere. $ *Average main: €55* ⊠ *Via Santa Barbara 4, Alghero* ☎ *079/970000* ⊕ *www. facebook.com/mabroukalghero* ⊗ *Closed Mon. and mid-Oct.–mid-Mar., and restricted opening in winter. No lunch Tues.–Sat.*

☕ Coffee and Quick Bites

Bar Pasticceria Ciro

$ | ITALIAN | For a delicious cannolo, fruit tart, or *bignè* (cream puff), local cognoscenti make a beeline for this classic bar and pastry shop, where the sweet delights displayed are made with the lightest pastry and the freshest fillings. Good coffees, ice creams, and sandwiches are also available, and there are tables inside and out back. **Known for:** light pastries; old-fashioned style; cordial service. $ *Average main: €5* ⊠ *Via Sassari 35/b, Alghero* ☎ *079/979960* ⊗ *Closed Mon.*

Cafè Latino

$ | ITALIAN | In prime position on Alghero's broad city walls, with views down to the yachting marina and across to Capo Caccia, this makes a wonderful place to pause by day or night with a spritz or fruit juice. The menu has a number of food items, too. **Known for:** superb views over the port; good selection of snacks and cocktails; friendly service. $ *Average main: €10* ⊠ *Bastioni Magellano 10, Alghero* ☎ *079/6766044* ⊕ *www.cafelatino.it* ⊗ *Closed Jan.–mid-Feb. and Tues. mid-Feb.–June and Sept.–Dec.*

🛏 Hotels

Hotel San Francesco

$ | B&B/INN | The only hotel located in Alghero's central Catalan quarter occupies an ex-convent once attached to the church of San Francesco. **Pros:** historic ambience; central location; breakfast in the cloister. **Cons:** no frills or extras; not a good choice for kids; no parking nearby.

⑤ *Rooms from: €108* ✉ *Via Machin 2, Alghero* ☎ *079/980330* ⊕ *www.sanfrancescohotel.com* ⊘ *Closed Nov.–Mar.* ⇝ *20 rooms* ⦿ *Free Breakfast.*

★ Villa Las Tronas Hotel & Spa

$$$$ | **HOTEL** | A stunning mansion dating from the 1880s has been transformed into this elegant secluded hotel that blends gold tapestries, crystal chandeliers, marble floors, canopy-draped beds, vaulted ceilings, and other Belle Époque treasures with modern amenities such as a luxury spa with a gym and an illuminated pool. **Pros:** promontory setting with regal sea views; incredible service; luxury spa. **Cons:** usually a two-night minimum stay in July and August; no meat dishes served at dinner; very expensive. ⑤ *Rooms from: €475* ✉ *Lungomare Valencia 1, Alghero* ☎ *079/981818* ⊕ *www.hotelvillalastronas.it* ⇝ *24 rooms* ⦿ *Free Breakfast.*

Sassari

34 km (21 miles) northeast of Alghero, 212 km (132 miles) north of Cagliari.

With a population of about 130,000, Sassari, the island's second-largest city, is an important university town and administrative center, notable for its history of intellectualism and bohemian student culture. Look for downtown vendors of *fainè*, a pizzalike chickpea-flour pancake glistening with olive oil, which is a Genoese and Sassarese specialty. The mazelike old town is blissfully isolated from the chaotic traffic swirling through the newer neighborhoods—Sassari is the hub of several highways and secondary roads leading to various coastal resorts, among them Stintino and Castelsardo.

GETTING HERE AND AROUND

Sassari can be reached by plane, ferry, train, bus, or car. The nearest airport is Alghero-Fertilia, about 30 km (19 miles) from Sassari. Inexpensive buses can get you to the center of Sassari. The closest port is Porto Torres, about 20 km (12½ miles) away, connected by ferry to Spain, France, Corsica, Genoa, and Civitavecchia (Rome). Frequent bus and train services operate between Sassari and Cagliari, Olbia, and Alghero.

VISITOR INFORMATION

CONTACT Sassari. ✉ *Via Sebastiano Satta 13, Sassari* ☎ *079/2008072* ⊕ *turismosassari.it.*

Sights

Duomo

CHURCH | The highly ornate stone Duomo is Sassari's must-see sight. The cathedral, dedicated to St. Nicolas (of Santa Claus inspiration), took more than half a millennium to build: the foundations were laid in the 12th century, and the Spanish colonial–style facade was completed in the 18th. Of particular interest in the plainer interior are the ribbed Gothic vaults, the 14th-century painting of the Madonna del Bosco on the high altar, and the early-19th-century tomb of Placido Benedetto di Savoia, the uncle of united Italy's first king. Look out, too, for the *candelieri* displayed in the lateral chapels here—10-foot-tall wooden candlesticks which, festooned with ribbons and flowers, are carried through the streets of Sassari every August 14th by members of the local guilds in one of the city's major festivals. ✉ *Piazza Duomo 3, Sassari* ☎ *079/232574* ⊟ *Free.*

🍴 Restaurants

L'Assassino

$$ | **SOUTHERN ITALIAN** | Get a true taste of regional cuisine at this family-run trattoria in the Old Town. The menu is not for the squeamish or for vegetarians: horse, donkey, and—one of the standouts— roasted suckling pig feature prominently, as do typical Sassarese dishes such as *trippa alla parmigiana* (tripe with Parmesan), *lumaconi in rosso* (snails in a rich tomato sauce), and *cordula con piselli* (sheep's intestines with peas). **Known for:** authentic local dishes; superb roasted suckling pig; pleasant courtyard seating in summer. $ *Average main: €18* ⊠ *Via Pettenadu 19, Sassari* ☎ *079/233463* ⊕ *www.trattoriatipica.sassari.it* ⊘ *Closed late Dec.–late Jan.*

Castelsardo

32 km (20 miles) northeast of Sassari.

The seaside citadel of Castelsardo is surmounted by an impressive fortress, which now contains a museum highlighting the basketware for which the town is famous. Wandering the upper town's maze of steep alleys is a delight, as is browsing the numerous shops in the lower town. Good souvenirs include not only woven baskets but also rugs and wrought-iron items. On the road into Castelsardo from the east, note the **Roccia dell'Elefante** (Elephant Rock), which was hollowed out by primitive man to be used as a burial chamber. The local name for this type of structure is *domus de janas* (literally, "fairy house").

GETTING HERE AND AROUND
Castelsardo is a 40-minute drive from Sassari on SS200. Frequent ARST buses also connect the two towns. Cars cannot enter Castelsardo's historic center, though you can drive part of the way up from Piazza La Pianedda. Parking is extremely limited, however, and if you're fit enough to tackle the steep streets you're best off leaving your car in the lower town and walking up.

VISITOR INFORMATION
CONTACT Castelsardo Tourism Office.
⊠ *Piazza Maestro di Castelsardo, Castelsardo* ☎ *079/6762792* ⊕ *www.comune.castelsardo.ss.it.*

◉ Sights

★ Museo dell'Intreccio Mediterraneo
CASTLE/PALACE | Castelsardo is best known in Sardinia for its intricate and colorful basketwork, numerous examples of which can be seen in the stores lining the main road and on the walls of the old center. The Museo dell'Intreccio Mediterraneo, located in the formidable 13th-century castle that dominates the town, puts it all into context, displaying a diverse range of woven baskets, culinary equipment, fishing equipment, and even an example of *fassonis*, the reed-constructed fishing boats once used around Oristano. The well-preserved castle was the Sardinian base of the powerful Doria family in the Middle Ages and has replicas of armor, catapults, and other medieval weaponry on the walls; try to time your visit to be here at sunset for the unforgettable views. The castle stays open till midnight and beyond in July and August. Your entry ticket includes admission to a museum dedicated to Castelsardo and its Genoan origins, housed nearby in an old Franciscan convent and mainly consisting of panels and videos—from here, too, there are awesome panoramic views of the coast. ⊠ *Via Marconi, Castelsardo* ☎ *079/6014769* ⊕ *www.mimcastelsardo.it* 🎫 *€5.*

Santa Teresa Gallura

70 km (43 miles) northeast of Castelsardo, 65 km (41 miles) northwest of Olbia.

At the northern tip of Sardinia, Santa Teresa Gallura retains the relaxed, carefree air of a former fishing village. Nearby beaches rival those farther down the coast yet somehow aren't as crowded with tourists.

GETTING HERE AND AROUND
Ferry crossings from Bonifacio in Corsica operated by Moby Lines run up to four times per day. The trip lasts about 50 minutes.

By car, you can drive from Olbia following the SS125 in the direction of Arzachena-Palau. At the fork in Palau, turn left to Santa Teresa Gallura. Continue for 25 km (16 miles). From Cagliari, follow SS131 to Sassari. Before the city center, exit at Sassari Latte Dolce, heading in the direction of Platamona/Castelsardo, which leads to the scenic coastal road Porto Torres–Santa Teresa.

From Alghero, follow SS291 until Sassari. Continue toward Porto Torres until you reach the northern part of the island.

There are frequent bus connections with Olbia, but there is no train station in Santa Teresa Gallura. The nearest main-line train station is in Olbia.

FERRY CONTACT Moby Lines. ⊠ *Santa Teresa Gallura* ☎ *0789/751449* ⊕ *www. mobylines.com.*

VISITOR INFORMATION
CONTACT Santa Teresa Gallura Tourist Office. ⊠ *Piazza Vittorio Emanuele 24, Santa Teresa Gallura* ☎ *0789/740986* ⊕ *www.santateresagalluraturismo.com.*

 ## Hotels

★ Hotel Canne al Vento
$ | B&B/INN | Family-run Canne al Vento has been a quiet, cheerful haven in town since the late 1950s. **Pros:** abundant and memorable breakfasts; personal, friendly service; convenient parking. **Cons:** on a main road; rooms overlooking bar can be noisy; no elevator for upper-floor rooms. ⑤ *Rooms from: €105* ⊠ *Via Nazionale 23, Santa Teresa Gallura* ☎ *0789/754219, 366/4215601 mobile* ⊕ *hotelcannealvento.com* ⊗ *Closed Jan.* ⌒ *22 rooms* ⦿ *Free Breakfast.*

Hotel Corallaro
$$$ | HOTEL | FAMILY | A brief walk from the town center, this hotel occupies a panoramic spot right by the splendid Rena Bianca beach and has functional rooms—most of them spacious, a few of them with balconies and sea views. **Pros:** welcoming

management and staff; steps away from the beach; airy rooms with plenty of storage space. **Cons:** rooms with sea views and balconies fill up early; steep uphill walk to town center; attracts groups. ⑤ *Rooms from: €246* ⊠ *Spiaggia Rena Bianca, Santa Teresa Gallura* ☎ *0789/755475* ⊕ *www. hotelcorallaro.it* ⊗ *Closed mid-Oct.–early May* ⌒ *83 rooms* ⦿ *Free Breakfast.*

La Maddalena

45 km (20 miles) northwest of Olbia, 68 km (42 miles) northeast of Castelsardo.

From the port of Palau you can visit the archipelago of La Maddalena, seven granite islands embellished with aromatic scrub and wind-bent pines. The most significant of the handful of sites to see here is Giuseppe Garibaldi's home and tomb. Explore the lively port (also called La Maddalena), then head to one of several picture-postcard coves, the perfect spot for a picnic and a swim in the crystal clear waters.

GETTING HERE AND AROUND
The only way to get to this small island is by boat or ferry. From Olbia, take a bus or drive to Palau, then catch the ferry to La Maddalena. During the day, car ferries make the 3-km (2-mile) trip two to four times an hour. The town center is right in front of the dock. Local buses are available for accessing the beaches, although the island is best explored by scooter or bike.

VISITOR INFORMATION
CONTACT La Maddalena Tourist Office. ⊠ *Via Venti Settembre 20, La Maddalena* ☎ *0789/736321* ⊕ *www.comunelamaddalena.it.*

 ## Sights

★ Compendio Garibaldino
HISTORIC HOME | FAMILY | Pilgrims from around the world converge on the Compendio Garibaldino, a complex on the island of Caprera that contains not

only the restored home of Giuseppe Garibaldi (1807–82) but also his tomb. The national hero and military leader who laid the groundwork for the unification of Italy in 1861 lived a simple life as a farmer on Caprera, the island that he eventually owned. Exhibits include a collection of weaponry, numerous items of furniture belonging to the family, Garibaldi's famous red shirt, and the poncho he wore during his South American campaigns. The grounds contain the hero's tomb alongside those of his family, all surrounded by the olive grove that he planted. There are explanatory panels in Italian and English, and visitors can also download an app providing more comprehensive information. A combined ticket takes in the Memoriale Giuseppe Garibaldi, 4 km (2½ miles) away—a multimedia museum, housed within a stern fortress dating from 1895, that chronicles the swashbuckling career of the Italian hero.

To visit the Compendio and Memoriale, take the ferry from Palau to Isola Maddalena, from where a causeway bridge crosses to Caprera. Note that visits to the Compendio Garibaldino must always be booked ahead for a specific time slot. A tour of the house and grounds should take less than an hour. ■ TIP→ **Caprera island is now a nature reserve, its woods and Mediterranean scrub crisscrossed by a network of waymarked trails that offer great opportunities for scenic walks and picnics.** ✉ *7 km (4½ miles) east of Isola Maddalena, Caprera, La Maddalena* ☎ *0789/727162 for information, 335/7505401 for booking visits (mobile)* ⊕ *www.garibaldicaprera.beniculturali. it* ✎ *€8; €12 combined ticket includes Memoriale Giuseppe Garibaldi* ⊘ *Usually closed Sun. except for 1st Sun. of month when entry is free (check first)* ⌕ *Book ahead for Compendio Garibaldino.*

Porto Cervo

35 km (22 miles) southeast of La Maddalena, 30 km (19 miles) north of Olbia.

Sardinia's northeastern coast is fringed with low cliffs, inlets, and small bays. This has become an upscale vacationland, with glossy resorts such as Baia Sardinia and Porto Rotondo just outside the confines of the famed Costa Smeralda. Some of Italy's most expensive hotels are here, and magnificent yachts anchor in the waters of Porto Cervo. Golf courses, yacht clubs, and numerous alfresco restaurants and bars cater to those who want to see and be seen.

GETTING HERE AND AROUND
Porto Cervo is accessible by boat, car, taxi, and bus. Buses run regularly from Olbia and Palau.

Whichever airport or port of entry into Sardinia you choose, head to Olbia. By car, follow SS125 north toward Arzachena and Costa Smeralda. After 10 km (6 miles), turn right onto SP73 toward Porto Rotondo/Porto Cervo. Continue on SP94 and turn onto SP59 to Porto Cervo. The trip takes about 30 minutes.

🏖 Beaches

The beaches around the Costa Smeralda are some of the most exclusive in Europe, and they don't disappoint—with fine golden sand sheltered by red cliffs and fronting azure waters. Many can only be reached by boat, and there are regular launches from Porto Cervo. Rentals of sun beds and towels are as expensive as you'd expect.

Spiaggia del Principe
BEACH | FAMILY | Among the less developed of the Costa Smeralda's five-star beaches, the Spiaggia del Principe is tucked well away from the crowds, mainly because it is not so readily accessible as some of the others. The rewards, however, are all the greater. Edged by jagged, gold-tinted rocks, the beach has fine white sand and

water ranging from emerald to a Caribbean shade of turquoise. Access from the car park is tricky—a 10-minute walk along a rough path (stout sneakers needed)—but a tuk-tuk service is sometimes on hand for a small charge. **Amenities:** food and drink; parking (fee in summer); toilets. **Best for:** swimming; walking. ⊠ *Porto Cervo* ✛ *3 km (2 miles) east of Cala di Volpe on Via Romazzino and Via delle Mimose.*

Restaurants

I Frati Rossi

$$$ | **ITALIAN** | In the hills above Porto Cervo, this soothing hideaway—where a sheltered terrace looks out onto a verdant garden—is a great place to take a break from the coast's glossy trappings. Recommended antipasti include *sa cannacca* (dried sausage with pecorino cheese) and octopus salad with potatoes; *ravioli di cernia e carciofi* (homemade ravioli with grouper fish, artichokes, and truffle) is a great pasta choice; and the grilled fish is an excellent main. **Known for:** secluded dining; tasty seafood dishes; terrace seating with garden views. ⑤ *Average main: €35* ⊠ *Via Paolino Azara, Pantogia, off SP59, Pantogia* ☎ *0789/94395* ⊕ *www.fratirossi.it* ⊘ *Closed Nov.–early Jan. No lunch Mon.*

Hotels

★ **Cala di Volpe**

$$$$ | **RESORT** | Long a magnet for the beautiful people, this hyperglamorous Marriott Luxury Collection hotel was designed by Jacques Couëlle to resemble an ancient Sardinian fishing village, complete with its own covered bridge; the exterior is complemented by a rustic-elegant interior with beamed ceilings, terra-cotta floors, Sardinian arts and crafts, and porticoes overlooking the Cala di Volpe Bay. **Pros:** stunning architecture and grounds; luxurious ambience; professional staff. **Cons:** some rooms disappoint; astronomical rates

for room, additional amenities, drinks, and meals; car necessary. ⑤ *Rooms from: €3067* ⊠ *Cala di Volpe, Porto Cervo* ☎ *0789/976111, 800/4484066 toll-free* ⊕ *www.caladivolpe.com* ⊘ *Closed mid-Oct.–late Apr.* ↬ *121 rooms* ❀❀❀ *Free Breakfast.*

★ **Petra Segreta Resort and Spa**

$$$$ | **HOTEL** | Sea and mountain views, top-quality cuisine, and chic and spacious guest rooms are the main draws at this romantic boutique hotel outside the picturesque village of San Pantaleo. **Pros:** tranquil mountainside setting with spectacular views; blend of traditional surroundings and modern amenities; two good restaurants. **Cons:** two-night minimum stay applies on specific dates; remote and isolated; not suitable for families. ⑤ *Rooms from: €554* ⊠ *Via Buddeu, San Pantaleo, Olbia* ☎ *0789/1876441* ⊕ *www.petrasegretaresort.com* ⊘ *Closed Nov.–Mar.* ↬ *27 rooms* ❀❀❀ *Free Breakfast.*

Activities

BOATING AND SAILING
Yacht Club Costa Smeralda

SAILING | The Aga Khan IV founded this yacht club with some local associates in 1967 in order to promote nautical activities. The club provides use of its pool, restaurant, bar, and guest rooms to those with memberships at associated yacht clubs. Watch for regattas from June to September, and check out the YCCS Sailing School, which organizes courses on dinghies and cabin cruisers. ⊠ *Via della Marina, Porto Cervo* ☎ *0789/902200* ⊕ *www.yccs.it.*

GOLF
Pevero Golf Course

GOLF | Designed by Robert Trent Jones Sr. and opened in 1972, Pevero is a world-class course with some of Europe's most beautiful fairways. Stretching nearly 6½ km (4 miles) between the Gulf of Pevero and Cala di Volpe (Bay of Foxes), it provides challenging playing conditions that incorporate 70 bunkers, several rock formations, and vegetation. The dress code is formal on the course and in the upscale clubhouse. Note that the course and clubhouse are closed on Monday and Tuesday between November and February. ⊠ *Località Cala di Volpe 20, Porto Cervo* 🕾 *0789/976400* ⊕ *www.peverogolfclub.com* 🖃 *€110–€170, depending on season and course; €45–€60 for club car* 🏌 *18 holes, 6700 yards, par 72.*

Olbia

30 km (19 miles) south of Porto Cervo.

Amid the resorts of Sardinia's northeastern coast, Olbia, a town of about 61,000, is a lively little seaport and port of call for mainland ferries at the head of a long, wide bay.

GETTING HERE AND AROUND

The main airport, Olbia–Costa Smeralda, is only 1½ km (1 mile) from the town center. Inexpensive city buses and taxis are available outside the terminal. Trains operate between Olbia and Cagliari and take about four hours.

The Olbia–Isola Bianca harbor provides daily connections with the Italian mainland, less than 300 km (186 miles) away. Regular ferries arrive from Genoa, Civitavecchia (Rome), and Livorno. Most ferries take 8–12 hours.

VISITOR INFORMATION

CONTACT Olbia. ⊠ *Municipio, Piazza Terranova Pausania 1, at Corso Umberto I, Olbia* 🕾 *334/9809802 mobile, 0789/52206* ⊕ *www.helloolbia.com.*

 ## Sights

Basilica San Simplicio

CHURCH | Olbia's little basilica, a short walk from the main Corso Umberto I, is the city's unmissable sight. The simple granite structure dates from the 11th century, part of the great Pisan church-building program, using pillars and columns recycled from Roman buildings.

The basilica has a bare, somewhat somber interior; its three naves are separated by a series of Romanesque arches, and fragments of frescoes are visible behind the altar. ◼**TIP→ Recent renovations of the monument have unearthed the remains of a Greek and Roman necropolis, which is now open to the public (the entrance is in the car park beneath the piazza).** ⊠ *Piazza San Simplicio, Olbia* 🕾 *0789/396241* ⊕ *www.museumtempioampurias.it/basilica-di-san-simplicio.*

 ## Restaurants

Il Gambero

$$ | SOUTHERN ITALIAN | This backstreet trattoria has a strong rustic flavor, its two rooms adorned with brass cooking pots, colorful embroideries, old photographs, and agricultural knickknacks. The menu, too, has a local focus and might include roast pecorino with honey, and *bottarga* (mullet roe) with fennel and orange. **Known for:** simple, rustic decor; fresh, local meat and seafood dishes; informal but discreet service. 💲 *Average main: €19* ⊠ *Via Lamarmora 6, Olbia* 🕾 *0789/23874* ⊕ *www.facebook.com/ilgamberotrattoria* 🕙 *Closed Mon. and Nov.*

 ## Hotels

La Locanda del Conte Mameli

$$ | HOTEL | Housed in a remodeled palazzo built at the end of the 19th century for the count after which it is named, this small and select hotel occupies a quiet location on a traffic-free backstreet just a few steps from Corso Umberto. **Pros:** small hotel with personal service; antique furnishings; central but quiet location. **Cons:** tricky to access by car; some rooms are slightly cramped and gloomy; no parking. 💲 *Rooms from: €179* ⊠ *Via delle Terme 8, Olbia* 🕾 *0789/23008* ⊕ *www.lalocandadelcontemameli.com* 🛏 *11 rooms* ⫙🍴 *Free Breakfast.*

Index

Photo Credits

Front Cover: Alexandru Albu/Getty Images [Descr.: Beautiful view of Manarola, Cinque Terre.] **Back cover, from left to right:** Fabiomax/ iStockphoto. Shaiith/iStockphoto. Aleh Varanishcha/iStockphoto. **Spine:** ChiccoDodiFC/iStockphoto. **Interior, from left to right:** Freesurf69/ Dreamstime (1). Shaiith/Dreamstime (2-3). Sanga Park/iStockphoto (5). **Chapter 1: Experience Italy:** Minnystock/Dreamstime (8-9). Mapics/ Dreamstime (10-11). Carso80/Shutterstock (11). Pcruciatti/Shutterstock (11). Vladimir Korostyshevskiy/Shutterstock (12). Kimberly A F/shutterstock (12). Renata Sedmakova/Shutterstock (12). Chen Min Chun/shutterstock (12). Janoka82/iStockphoto (13). Jaroslaw Pawlak/Shutterstock (13). Mi.Ti./ Shutterstock (14). Inguaribile Vlaggiatore/Shutterstock (14). Alessandro Cristiano/Shutterstock (14). Parilov/Shutterstock (14). Cheryl Ramalho/ iStockphoto (15). Alexirina27000/Dreamstime (16). Siempreverde22/Dreamstime (16). Gaspar Janos/Shutterstock (16). Andrei Molchan/Shutterstock (16). Bucha Natallia/Shutterstock (17). Anibal Trejo/Shutterstock (17). Marianceccarelli/iStockphoto (18). Cge2010/Shutterstock (18). Cge2010/ Shutterstock (18). Stefano Garau/Shutterstock (18). Omas_Photo/Shutterstock (19). Kavalenkava/Shutterstock (26). StevanZZ/Shutterstock (27). Vololibero/Shutterstock (28). Marcin Krzyzak/Shutterstock (28). Tour Liguria by Volver (28). Poludziber/Shutterstock (28). Franco Cappellari/ Pugliapromozione (29). Fokke baarssen/Shutterstock (29). Roman Babakin/Shutterstock (29). Lucamato/iStockphoto (29). Daniela marchi/Castiglion del Bosco (30). Alessandro Moggi (31). Phant/Shutterstock (32). Boris Stroujko/Shutterstock (32). R.nagy/Shutterstock (32). Nattee Chalermtiragool/ Shutterstock (33). Luxerendering/Shutterstock (33). Mazerath/Shutterstock (34). Giannis Papanikos/Shutterstock (35). Taste Bologna (36). Montese Cooking Experiences (36). Monni & Pirisi/Tasting Sardinia (36). Joaquin Corbalan P/Shutterstock (37). Dr. Ronald Pitcock/Cook with us in Rome (37). AndrewSoundarajan/iStockphoto (38). AndreaAstes/iStockphoto (38). Robert Zehetmayer/Dreamstime (38). LizCoughlan/Shutterstock (38). Venezia Palazzo Ducale (39). **Chapter 3: Rome:** AngeloCampus (69). EricaDuecy (72). AngeloCampus (73). Lisay/iStockphoto (73). Gush Photography/ Shutterstock (94-95). TTaylor/Wikimedia Commons (94). RPBaiao/Shutterstock (96). Imaengine/Dreamstime (98-99). Imaengine/Dreamstime (100-101). **Chapter 4: Side Trips from Rome:** Marco Rubino/Shutterstock (159). Ragemax/Shutterstock (180). **Chapter 5: Venice:** Paul D'Innocenzo (183). Paul D'Innocenzo (186). Jess_h/Shutterstock (187). Iz89/Shutterstock (187). Mapics/Dreamstime (195). Felix Lipov/Shutterstock (196). Ratnakorn Piyasirisorost/GettyImages (197). Npershaj/Dreamstime (197). Serenarossi/Shutterstock (198). Maremagnum/GettyImages (199). Givaga/ Shutterstock (199). Miragik/Dreamstime (200). FooTToo/Shutterstock (201). Ekaterinabelova/Dreamstime (201). Minnystock/Dreamstime (243). **Chapter 6: The Veneto and Friuli–Venezia Giulia:** Gistel Cezary Wojtkowski/iStockphoto (251). Giovanni1232/iStockphoto (254). From_my_ point_of_view/iStockphoto (255). ChiccoDodiFC/iStockphoto (255). **Chapter 7: The Dolomites:** Angelani/fototeca Trentino (299). Tati Liberta/ Shutterstock (302). Davide Bianco Photo/Shutterstock (303). CuboImages srl/Alamy (303). Elena Brunelli/Shutterstock (326). Pridalo/Shutterstock (332). **Chapter 8: Milan, Lombardy, and the Lakes:** Boris Stroujko/Shutterstock (343). OlgaBombologna/Shutterstock (346). Nagy Julia/ Shutterstock (347). Valerio Pardi (347). Alexandre Rotenberg/Shutterstock (380). Gambarini Gianandrea/Shutterstock (383). **Chapter 9: Piedmont and the Valle d'Aosta:** RostislavGlinskyPhotography (407). S74/Shutterstock (410). Alessandro Cristiano/Shutterstock. (411). B Work et Art/ Shutterstock (411). Mlkhail Varentsov/Shutterstock (431). **Chapter 10: The Italian Riviera:** Silvano audisio/Shutterstock (437). Zagorulko Inka/ Shutterstock (440). Alessio Orru/Shutterstock (441). Maxsala/Dreamstime (441). Gaspar Janos/Shutterstock (447). Whatafoto/Shutterstock (448). F11photo/Shutterstock (448). Elephotos/Shutterstock (448). Nightcap/Shutterstock (448). Xsaga Park/iStockphoto (449). Aliaksandr Antanovich/ Shutterstock (449). Viviane Teles (449). Valeria Cantone/Shutterstock (480). **Chapter 11: Emilia–Romagna:** Cristiano Palazzini/Shutterstock (483). Fabiomax/iStockphoto (486). Dietmarrauscher/Dreamstime (487). Alemasche72/Dreamstime (487). EStock/Shutterstock (499). Piccerella/ iStockphoto (500). Alessia Pierdomenico/Shutterstock (500). Consorzio del Prosciutto di Parma (500). Udo Schröter/Flickr (500). Grischa Georgiew/ iStockphoto (500). Consorzio del Formaggio (501). Consorzio del Formaggio (501). M Laky/Shutterstock (501). Roberto A Sanchez/iStockphoto (501). Consorzio del Formaggio (501). AGF Srl/Alamy (502). Verysmallplanet/Shutterstock (502). EStock/Shutterstock (503). Foodlove/Shutterstock (503). Giorgio Morara/Shutterstock (503). Archivio Fotografico Di Bologna Turismo (503). Claudio Baldini/Shutterstock (503). **Chapter 12: Florence:** Alysta/ Shutterstock (525). Thekovtun/Shutterstock (528). George M. Groutas/Flickr (529). Lesya Dolyuk/Shutterstock (529). George Diamonds/Shutterstock (540-541). Sailko/WikimediaCommons (542). Sailko/WikimediaCommons (542). Skovalsky/Shutterstock (543). Alberto Valenzuela/Shutterstock (543). Rough Guides/Alamy (543). Mary Evans Picture Library/Alamy (544). Library of Congress Prints and Photographs Division (544). Kritskaya/Shutterstock (544). Fae/WikimediaCommons (569). Gustav Schauer/WikimediaCommons (569). Marzolino/Shutterstock (569). Romas_Photo/Shutterstock (570). Steve Allen/Shutterstock (570). Allen Lugmayer/Shutterstock (571). Giannit/Dreamstime (571). MisterStock/Shutterstock (571). Yuri Turkov/ Shutterstock (571). Web Gallery of Art/Wikimedia Commons (572). Virtusincertus/Flickr (572). Cysun/Shutterstock (572). Jean louis mazieres/Flickr (573). Bill Perry/Shutterstock (573). Deb Nystrom/Flickr (573). Sailko/WikimediaCommons (574) Oursana/WikimediaCommons (574). Dguendel/ WikimediaCommons (574). **Chapter 13: Tuscany:** Christopher Salerno/Shutterstock (583). Kuvona/Dreamstime (586). Kwasny221/iStockphoto (587). Frantic00/Shutterstock (587). Kiev.Victor/Shutterstock (595). Simona Bottone/Shutterstock (626). **Chapter 14: Umbria and the Marches:** Sergey Dzyuba/Shutterstock (629). Vividaphoto/Dreamstime (632). 5 second Studio/Shutterstock (633). Bonchan/Shutterstock (633). StevanZZ/Shutterstock (647). Santiago Urquijo/GettyImages (648). Threerivers11/Dreamstime (648). Frans Vandewalle/Flickr (649). Petrusbarbygere/Wikimedia Commons (649). Eloquence/WikimediaCommons (649). Petrusbarbygere/WikimediaCommons (649). Petrusbarbygere/Wikimedia Commons (649). **Chapter 15: Naples and Campania:** Stephen Miller1 (669). Look Die Bildagentur der Fotografen GmbH/Alamy (672). Bon Appetit/Alamy (673). CuboImages srl/ Alamy (673). Wjarek/Shutterstock (701). Pablo Debat/Shutterstock (701). Kated/Shutterstock (702). Erica Ruth Neubauer/Alamy (703). Balounm/ Shutterstock (703). Leonid Andronov/Shutterstock (704). Dennis Degnan/GettyImages (704). Maurizio De Mattei/Shutterstock (704). Leonid Andronov/ Shutterstock (705). Smartshots International/GettyImages (706). Alfiya Safuanova/Shutterstock (707). Laszlo Konya/dreamstime (723). **Chapter 16: Puglia, Basilicata, and Calabria:** Josefskacel/Dreamstime (735). Jcartwright01/Dreamstime (738). Kato/Dreamstime (739). Claudia Longo/ Shutterstock (739). Fabio Dell/Shutterstock (749). Marco Fine/Shutterstock (770). **Chapter 17: Sicily:** Peeter Viisimaa/iStockphoto (775). Pramen/ Shutterstock (778). Gyro/iStockphoto (779). ChiccoDodiFC FotoOk.it/iStockphoto (779). Vvoe/shutterstock (810). **Chapter 18: Sardinia:** Eva Bocek/ Shutterstock (833). Marmo81/Shutterstock (836). Marmo81/Shutterstock (837). Oxana Denezhkina/Shutterstock (837). Travelwild/Shutterstock (839).

About Our Writers: All photos are courtesy of the writers except for the following: Nick Bruno, courtesy of Graeme Ogston; Elizabeth Shemaria, courtesy of Ian Tuttle.* *Every effort has been made to trace the copyright holders, and we apologize in advance for any accidental errors. We would be happy to apply the corrections in the following edition of this publication.*

Fodor's ESSENTIAL ITALY 2025

Publisher: Stephen Horowitz, *General Manager*

Editorial: Douglas Stallings, *Editorial Director;* Jill Fergus, Amanda Sadlowski, *Senior Editors;* Brian Eschrich, Alexis Kelly, *Editors;* Angelique Kennedy-Chavannes, Yoojin Shin, *Associate Editors*

Design: Tina Malaney, *Director of Design and Production;* Jessica Gonzalez, *Senior Designer;* Jaimee Shaye, *Graphic Design Associate*

Production: Jennifer DePrima, *Editorial Production Manager;* Elyse Rozelle, *Senior Production Editor;* Monica White, *Production Editor*

Maps: Rebecca Baer, *Map Director;* David Lindroth, Mark Stroud (Moon Street Cartography), *Cartographers*

Photography: Viviane Teles, *Director of Photography;* Namrata Aggarwal, Neha Gupta, Payal Gupta, Ashok Kumar, *Photo Editors;* Jade Rodgers, Shanelle Jacobs, *Photo Production Interns*

Business and Operations: Chuck Hoover, *Chief Marketing Officer;* Robert Ames, *Group General Manager*

Public Relations and Marketing: Joe Ewaskiw, *Senior Director of Communications and Public Relations*

Fodors.com: Jeremy Tarr, *Editorial Director;* Rachael Levitt, *Managing Editor*

Technology: Jon Atkinson, *Executive Director of Technology;* Rudresh Teotia, *Associate Director of Technology;* Alison Lieu, *Project Manager*

Writers: Robert Andrews, Nick Bruno, Erica Firpo, Liz Humphreys, Laura Itzkowitz, Natalie Kennedy, Elisa Scarton, Elizabeth Shemaria, Erla Zwingle

Editor: Jill Fergus

Production Editor: Elyse Rozelle

7th Edition

ISBN 978-1-64097-742-6

ISSN 2476-0692

SPECIAL SALES

This book is available at special discounts for bulk purchases for sales promotions or premiums. For more information, e-mail SpecialMarkets@fodors.com.

About Our Writers

Born of Sicilian stock, **Robert Andrews** has been living and working in various parts of Italy for most of his adult life. He has written articles and guidebooks on this multifaceted peninsula, and provides travel consultancy services as well as leading individual and small-group tours in Sicily and Sardinia. For this edition, Robert updated the Sardinia and the Naples and Campania chapters.

Nick Bruno is an Italy specialist and frequent Fodor's contributor. As well as authoring and updating books and features, he makes radio packages for the BBC. A lifelong interest in history and Italian language has led to a project researching his paternal Italian family during the Il Ventennio Fascista period. Nick updated the Experience; Travel Smart; Venice, Veneto and Friuli-Venezia Giulia; Puglia, Basilicata, and Calabria; Naples and Campania; and Emilia-Romagna chapters. Follow him on Instagram and Twitter @nickjgbruno and at ⊕ barbruno.com.

Erica Firpo, an experienced travel and lifestyle journalist and podcaster based in Rome, contributes to AFAR, Washington Post, Insider, Conde Nast Traveler, Travel + Leisure, BBC Travel, The Guardian, Fathom, and more. She updated Rome.

Liz Humphreys is a transplant to Europe from New York City, where she edited for media companies including Condé Nast and Time Inc. Since then she's written for publications including Condé Nast Traveler, Michelin Green Guides, and Forbes Travel Guide. Liz has an advanced certificate in wine studies from WSET (Wine & Spirit Education Trust), which comes in handy when exploring her beloved Italian wine regions. Liz updated the Dolomites; Piedmont and the Valle D'Aosta; Umbria and the Marches; Tuscany, and Venice chapters. Follow her online @winederlust_wanderings.

Laura Itzkowitz is a freelance writer and editor based in Rome with an MFA in creative writing and a passion for covering travel, arts and culture, lifestyle, design, food, and wine. Her writing has appeared in Travel + Leisure, Architectural Digest, Vogue, GQ, Departure, AFAR, and others. Laura updated the Rome and Naples and Campania chapters. Follow her on Instagram and Twitter @lauraitzkowitz.

Originally from California, **Natalie Kennedy** moved to Rome planning to stay for only a year, but has now called the Eternal City home for nearly a decade and runs a popular blog about Roman life (⊕ www.anamericaninrome.com). For this edition she updated Rome and Side Trips from Rome.

Elisa Scarton worked as an English teacher in Southern Tuscany in the early 2000s. Over the past two decades, she has written extensively about her adoptive home. She updated Tuscany.

About Our Writers

 Elizabeth Shemaria is an Italy-based journalist and third-generation Northern Californian who has trekked solo in Himalaya, interviewed artists in military-ruled Burma, and once rode an overnight train across Egypt on her birthday. She has contributed to more than a dozen travel and news publications including Fodor's guidebooks, *AFAR*, *BBC Travel*, and *Roads & Kingdoms*. Spontaneous dance parties are essential to her creative process. For this edition, Liz updated the Milan, Lombardy, and the Lakes; Tuscany; Italian Riviera; and Florence chapters. Follow her on Instagram @lizshemaria.

 Erla Zwingle has been a contributor to National Geographic since 1982 and wrote their guidebook to Venice, as well as writing for other publications including Smithsonian and Esquire. She lives in Venice and writes a blog called "Venice: I am not making this up." She updated Venice.